SUBARU

SUBARU 1985-96 REPAIR MANUAL

CHILTON'S

Senior Vice President	Ronald A. Hoxter
Publisher & Editor-In-Chief	Kerry A. Freeman, S.A.E.
Executive Editors	Dean F. Morgantini, S.A.E., W. Calvin Settle, Jr., S.A.E.
Managing Editor	Nick D'Andrea
Senior Editors	Jacques Gordon, Michael L. Grady, Ben Greisler, S.A.E., Debra McCall, Kevin M. G. Maher, Richard J. Rivele, S.A.E., Richard T. Smith, Jim Taylor, Ron Webb
Project Managers	Martin J. Gunther, Will Kessler, A.S.E., Richard Schwartz
Production Manager	Andrea Steiger
Product Systems Manager	Robert Maxey
Director of Manufacturing	Mike D'Imperio
Editor	Gordon L. Tobias, S.A.E.

CHILTON BOOK COMPANY

ONE OF THE **DIVERSIFIED PUBLISHING COMPANIES,**
A PART OF **CAPITAL CITIES/ABC, INC.**

Manufactured in USA
© 1996 Chilton Book Company
Chilton Way, Radnor, PA 19089
ISBN 0-8019-8797-0
Library of Congress Catalog Card No. 96-85130
2345678901 6543210987

Contents

Contents

SAFETY NOTICE

Proper service and repair procedures are vital to the safe, reliable operation of all motor vehicles, as well as the personal safety of those performing repairs. This manual outlines procedures for servicing and repairing vehicles using safe, effective methods. The procedures contain many NOTES, CAUTIONS and WARNINGS which should be followed along with standard procedures to eliminate the possibility of personal injury or improper service which could damage the vehicle or compromise its safety.

It is important to note that the repair procedures and techniques, tools and parts for servicing motor vehicles, as well as the skill and experience of the individual performing the work vary widely. It is not possible to anticipate all of the conceivable ways or conditions under which vehicles may be serviced, or to provide cautions as to all of the possible hazards that may result. Standard and accepted safety precautions and equipment should be used when handling toxic or flammable fluids, and safety goggles or other protection should be used during cutting, grinding, chiseling, prying, or any other process that can cause material removal or projectiles.

Some procedures require the use of tools specially designed for a specific purpose. Before substituting another tool or procedure, you must be completely satisfied that neither your personal safety, nor the performance of the vehicle will be endangered.

Although information in this manual is based on industry sources and is complete as possible at the time of publication, the possibility exists that some car manufacturers made later changes which could not be included here. While striving for total accuracy, Chilton Book Company cannot assume responsibility for any errors, changes or omissions that may occur in the compilation of this data.

PART NUMBERS

Part numbers listed in this reference are not recommendation by Chilton for any product by brand name. They are references that can be used with interchange manuals and aftermarket supplier catalogs to locate each brand supplier's discrete part number.

SPECIAL TOOLS

Special tools are recommended by the vehicle manufacturer to perform their specific job. Use has been kept to a minimum, but where absolutely necessary, they are referred to in the text by the part number of the tool manufacturer. These tools can be purchased, under the appropriate part number, from your local dealer or regional distributor, or an equivalent tool can be purchased locally from a tool supplier or parts outlet. Before substituting any tool for the one recommended, read the SAFETY NOTICE at the top of this page.

ACKNOWLEDGMENTS

The Chilton Book Company expresses appreciation to Subaru of America, Inc., Cherry Hill, NJ, for their generous assistance.

1

GENERAL INFORMATION AND MAINTENANCE

HOW TO USE THIS BOOK

Chilton's Total Car Care manual for 1985-96 Subaru cars is intended to help you learn more about the inner workings of your vehicle while saving you money on its upkeep and operation.

The beginning of the book will likely be referred to the most, since that is where you will find information for maintenance and tune-up. The other sections deal with the more complex systems of your vehicle. Operating systems from engine through brakes are covered to the extent that the average do-it-yourselfer becomes mechanically involved. This book will not explain such things as rebuilding a differential for the simple reason that the expertise required and the investment in special tools make this task uneconomical. It will, however, give you detailed instructions to help you change your own brake pads and shoes, replace spark plugs, and perform many more jobs that can save you money, give you personal satisfaction and help you avoid expensive problems.

A secondary purpose of this book is a reference for owners who want to understand their vehicle and/or their mechanics better. In this case, no tools at all are required.

Where to Begin

Before removing any bolts, read through the entire procedure. This will give you the overall view of what tools and supplies will be required. There is nothing more frustrating than having to walk to the bus stop on Monday morning because you were short one bolt on Sunday afternoon. So read ahead and plan ahead. Each operation should be approached logically and all procedures thoroughly understood before attempting any work.

All sections contain adjustments, maintenance, removal and installation procedures, and in some cases, repair or overhaul procedures. When repair is not considered practical, we tell you how to remove the part and then how to install the new or rebuilt replacement. In this way, you at least save the labor costs. Backyard repair of some components is just not practical.

Avoiding Trouble

Many procedures in this book require you to "label and disconnect . . . " a group of lines, hoses or wires. Don't be lulled into thinking you can remember where everything goes — you won't. If you hook up vacuum or fuel lines incorrectly, the vehicle will run poorly, if at all. If you hook up electrical wiring incorrectly, you may instantly learn a very expensive lesson.

You don't need to know the official or engineering name for each hose or line. A piece of masking tape on the hose and a piece on its fitting will allow you to assign your own label such as the letter A or a short name. As long as you remember your own code, the lines can be reconnected by matching similar letters or names. Do remember that tape will dissolve in gasoline or other fluids; if a component is to be washed or cleaned, use another method of identification. A permanent felt-tipped marker can be very handy for marking metal parts. Remove any tape or paper labels after assembly.

Maintenance or Repair?

It's necessary to mention the difference between maintenance and repair. Maintenance includes routine inspections, adjustments, and replacement of parts which show signs of normal wear. Maintenance compensates for wear or deterioration. Repair implies that something has broken or is not working. A need for repair is often caused by lack of maintenance. Example: draining and refilling the automatic transmission fluid is maintenance recommended by the manufacturer at specific mileage intervals. Failure to do this can ruin the transmission/transaxle, requiring very expensive repairs. While no maintenance program can prevent items from breaking or wearing out, a general rule can be stated: MAINTENANCE IS CHEAPER THAN REPAIR.

Two basic mechanic's rules should be mentioned here. First, whenever the left side of the vehicle or engine is referred to, it is meant to specify the driver's side. Conversely, the right side of the vehicle means the passenger's side. Second, most screws and bolts are removed by turning counterclockwise, and tightened by turning clockwise.

Safety is always the most important rule. Constantly be aware of the dangers involved in working on an automobile and take the proper precautions. See the information in this section regarding SERVICING YOUR VEHICLE SAFELY and the SAFETY NOTICE on the acknowledgment page.

Avoiding the Most Common Mistakes

Pay attention to the instructions provided. There are 3 common mistakes in mechanical work:

1. Incorrect order of assembly, disassembly or adjustment. When taking something apart or putting it together, performing steps in the wrong order usually just costs you extra time; however, it CAN break something. Read the entire procedure before beginning disassembly. Perform everything in the order in which the instructions say you should, even if you can't immediately see a reason for it. When you're taking apart something that is very intricate, you might want to draw a picture of how it looks when assembled at one point in order to make sure you get everything back in its proper position. We will supply exploded views whenever possible. When making adjustments, perform them in the proper order; often, one adjustment affects another, and you cannot expect even satisfactory results unless each adjustment is made only when it cannot be changed by any other.

2. Overtorquing (or undertorquing). While it is more common for overtorquing to cause damage, undertorquing may allow a fastener to vibrate loose causing serious damage. Especially when dealing with aluminum parts, pay attention to torque specifications and utilize a torque wrench in assembly. If a torque figure is not available, remember that if you are using the right tool to perform the job, you will probably not have to strain yourself to get a fastener tight enough. The pitch of most threads is so slight that the tension you put on the wrench will be multiplied many times in actual force on what you are tightening. A good example of how critical torque is can be seen in the case of spark plug installation, especially

where you are putting the plug into an aluminum cylinder head. Too little torque can fail to crush the gasket, causing leakage of combustion gases and consequent overheating of the plug and engine parts. Too much torque can damage the threads or distort the plug, changing the spark gap.

There are many commercial products available for ensuring that fasteners won't come loose, even if they are not torqued just right (a very common brand is Loctite®). If you're worried about getting something together tight enough to hold, but loose enough to avoid mechanical damage during assembly, one of these products might offer substantial insurance. Before choosing a threadlocking compound, read the label on the package and make sure the product is compatible with the materials, fluids, etc. involved.

3. Crossthreading. This occurs when a part such as a bolt is screwed into a nut or casting at the wrong angle and forced. Crossthreading is more likely to occur if access is difficult. It helps to clean and lubricate fasteners, then to start threading with the part to be installed positioned straight in. Then, start the bolt, spark plug, etc. with your fingers. If you encounter resistance, unscrew the part and start over again at a different angle until it can be inserted and turned several times without much effort. Keep in mind that many parts, especially spark plugs, have tapered threads, so that gentle turning will automatically bring the part you're threading to the proper angle, but only if you don't force it or resist a change in angle. Don't put a wrench on the part until it's been tightened a couple of turns by hand. If you suddenly encounter resistance, and the part has not seated fully, don't force it. Pull it back out to make sure it's clean and threading properly.

Always take your time and be patient; once you have some experience, working on your vehicle may well become an enjoyable hobby.

TOOLS AND EQUIPMENT

▶ **See Figures 1, 2, 3, 4, 5, 6, 7, 8, 9, 10, 11, 12, 13 and 14**

Naturally, without the proper tools and equipment it is impossible to properly service your vehicle. It would also be virtually impossible to catalog every tool that you would need to perform all of the operations in this book. Of course, It would be unwise for the amateur to rush out and buy an expensive set of tools on the theory that he/she may need one or more of them at some time.

The best approach is to proceed slowly, gathering a good quality set of those tools that are used most frequently. Don't be misled by the low cost of bargain tools. It is far better to spend a little more for better quality. Forged wrenches, 6 or 12-point sockets and fine tooth ratchets are by far preferable to their less expensive counterparts. As any good mechanic can tell you, there are few worse experiences than trying to work on a vehicle with bad tools. Your monetary savings will be far outweighed by frustration and mangled knuckles.

Begin accumulating those tools that are used most frequently: those associated with routine maintenance and tune-

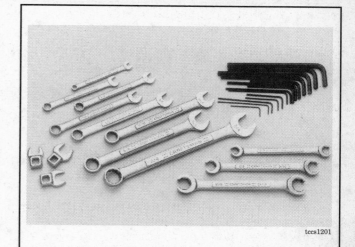

tccs1201

Fig. 2 In addition to ratchets, a good set of wrenches and hex keys will be necessary

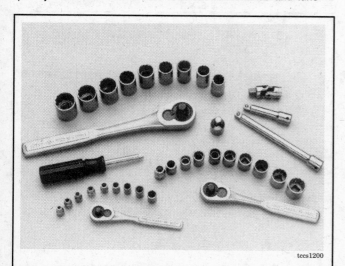

tccs1200

Fig. 1 All but the most basic procedures will require an assortment of ratchets and sockets

tccs1202

Fig. 3 A hydraulic floor jack and a set of jackstands are essential for lifting and supporting the vehicle

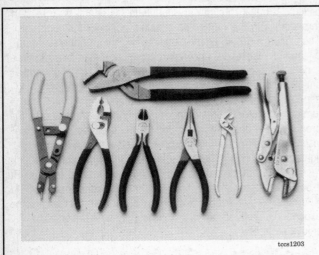

Fig. 4 An assortment of pliers, grippers and cutters will be handy for old rusted parts and stripped bolt heads

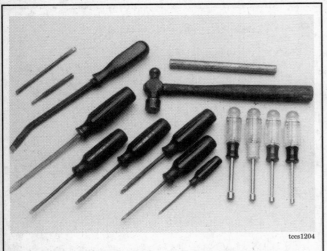

Fig. 5 Various drivers, chisels and prybars are great tools to have in your toolbox

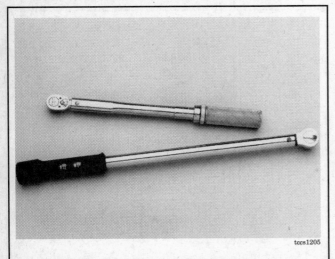

Fig. 6 Many repairs will require the use of a torque wrench to assure the components are properly fastened

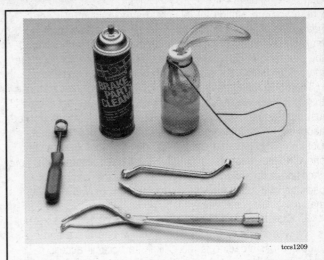

Fig. 7 Although not always necessary, using specialized brake tools will save time

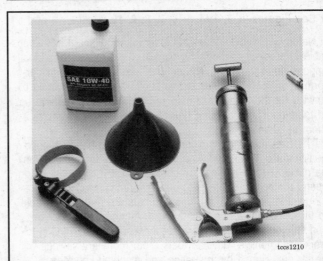

Fig. 8 A few inexpensive lubrication tools will make maintenance easier

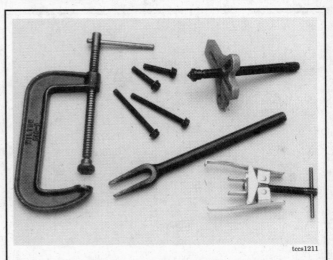

Fig. 9 Various pullers, clamps and separator tools are needed for many larger, more complicated repairs

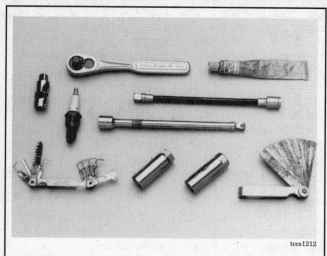

Fig. 10 A variety of tools and gauges should be used for spark plug gapping and installation

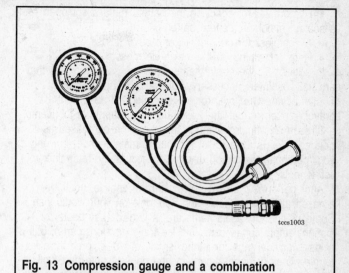

Fig. 13 Compression gauge and a combination vacuum/fuel pressure test gauge

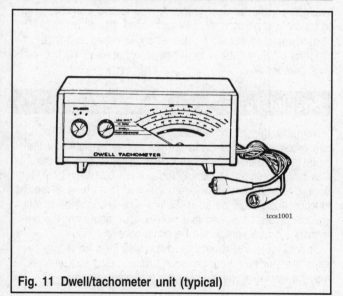

Fig. 11 Dwell/tachometer unit (typical)

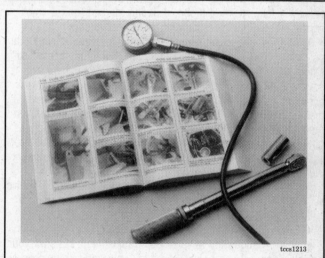

Fig. 14 Proper information is vital, so always have a Chilton Total Car Care manual handy

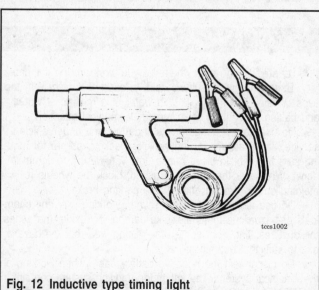

Fig. 12 Inductive type timing light

up. In addition to the normal assortment of screwdrivers and pliers, you should have the following tools:

• Wrenches/sockets and combination open end/box end wrenches in sizes from 1/8-3/4 in. or 3mm-19mm (depending on whether your vehicle uses standard or metric fasteners) and a 13/16 in. or 5/8 in. spark plug socket (depending on plug type).

➥If possible, buy various length socket drive extensions. Universal-joint and wobble extensions can be extremely useful, but be careful when using them, as they can change the amount of torque applied to the socket.

• Jackstands for support.
• Oil filter wrench.
• Spout or funnel for pouring fluids.
• Grease gun for chassis lubrication (unless your vehicle is not equipped with any grease fittings — for details, please refer to information on Fluids and Lubricants found later in this section).

- Hydrometer for checking the battery (unless equipped with a sealed, maintenance-free battery).
  - A container for draining oil and other fluids.
  - Rags for wiping up the inevitable mess.

In addition to the above items there are several others that are not absolutely necessary, but handy to have around. These include Oil Dry® (or an equivalent oil absorbent gravel — such as cat litter) and the usual supply of lubricants, antifreeze and fluids, although these can be purchased as needed. This is a basic list for routine maintenance, but only your personal needs and desire can accurately determine your list of tools.

After performing a few projects on the vehicle, you'll be amazed at the other tools and non-tools on your workbench. Some useful household items are: a large turkey baster or siphon, empty coffee cans and ice trays (to store parts), ball of twine, electrical tape for wiring, small rolls of colored tape for tagging lines or hoses, markers and pens, a note pad, golf tees (for plugging vacuum lines), metal coat hangers or a roll of mechanics's wire (to hold things out of the way), dental pick or similar long, pointed probe, a strong magnet, and a small mirror (to see into recesses and under manifolds).

A more advanced set of tools, suitable for tune-up work, can be drawn up easily. While the tools are slightly more sophisticated, they need not be outrageously expensive. There are several inexpensive tach/dwell meters on the market that are every bit as good for the average mechanic as a professional model. Just be sure that it goes to a least 1200-1500 rpm on the tach scale and that it works on 4, 6 and 8-cylinder engines. (If you have one or more vehicles with a diesel engine, a special tachometer is required since diesels don't use spark plug ignition systems). The key to these purchases is to make them with an eye towards adaptability and wide range. A basic list of tune-up tools could include:

- Tach/dwell meter.
- Spark plug wrench and gapping tool.
- Feeler gauges for valve or point adjustment. (Even if your vehicle does not use points or require valve adjustments, a feeler gauge is helpful for many repair/overhaul procedures).

A tachometer/dwell meter will ensure accurate tune-up work on vehicles without electronic ignition. The choice of a timing light should be made carefully. A light which works on the DC current supplied by the vehicle's battery is the best choice; it should have a xenon tube for brightness. On any vehicle with an electronic ignition system, a timing light with an inductive pickup that clamps around the No. 1 spark plug cable is preferred.

In addition to these basic tools, there are several other tools and gauges you may find useful. These include:

- Compression gauge. The screw-in type is slower to use, but eliminates the possibility of a faulty reading due to escaping pressure.
- Manifold vacuum gauge.
- 12V test light.
- A combination volt/ohmmeter
- Induction Ammeter. This is used for determining whether or not there is current in a wire. These are handy for use if a wire is broken somewhere in a wiring harness.

As a final note, you will probably find a torque wrench necessary for all but the most basic work. The beam type models are perfectly adequate, although the newer click types (breakaway) are easier to use. The click type torque wrenches tend to be more expensive. Also keep in mind that all types of torque wrenches should be periodically checked and/or re-calibrated. You will have to decide for yourself which better fits your purpose.

Special Tools

Normally, the use of special factory tools is avoided for repair procedures, since these are not readily available for the do-it-yourself mechanic. When it is possible to perform the job with more commonly available tools, it will be pointed out, but occasionally, a special tool was designed to perform a specific function and should be used. Before substituting another tool, you should be convinced that neither your safety nor the performance of the vehicle will be compromised.

Special tools can usually be purchased from an automotive parts store or from your dealer. In some cases special tools may be available directly from the tool manufacturer.

SERVICING YOUR VEHICLE SAFELY

▶ **See Figures 15, 16, 17 and 18**

It is virtually impossible to anticipate all of the hazards involved with automotive maintenance and service, but care and common sense will prevent most accidents.

The rules of safety for mechanics range from "don't smoke around gasoline," to "use the proper tool for the job." The trick to avoiding injuries is to develop safe work habits and to take every possible precaution.

Do's

- Do keep a fire extinguisher and first aid kit handy.
- Do wear safety glasses or goggles when cutting, drilling, grinding or prying, even if you have 20-20 vision. If you wear glasses for the sake of vision, wear safety goggles over your regular glasses.

- Do shield your eyes whenever you work around the battery. Batteries contain sulfuric acid. In case of contact with the eyes or skin, flush the area with water or a mixture of water and baking soda, then seek immediate medical attention.
- Do use safety stands (jackstands) for any undervehicle service. Jacks are for raising vehicles; jackstands are for making sure the vehicle stays raised until you want it to come down. Whenever the vehicle is raised, block the wheels remaining on the ground and set the parking brake.
- Do use adequate ventilation when working with any chemicals or hazardous materials. Like carbon monoxide, the asbestos dust resulting from some brake lining wear can be hazardous in sufficient quantities.
- Do disconnect the negative battery cable when working on the electrical system. The secondary ignition system contains EXTREMELY HIGH VOLTAGE. In some cases it can even exceed 50,000 volts.

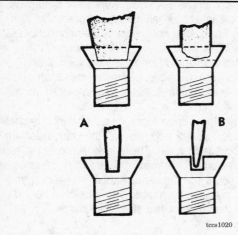

tccs1020

Fig. 15 Screwdrivers should be kept in good condition to prevent injury or damage which could result if the blade slips from the screw

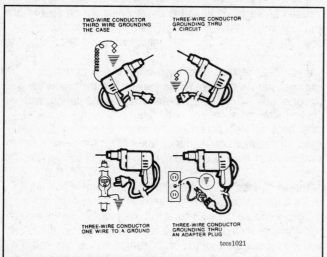

tccs1021

Fig. 16 Power tools should always be properly grounded

tccs1022

Fig. 17 Using the correct size wrench will help prevent the possibility of rounding off a nut

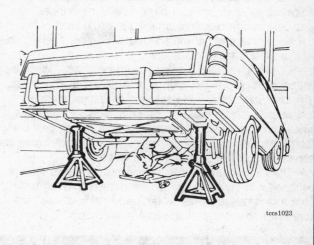

tccs1023

Fig. 18 NEVER work under a vehicle unless it is supported using safety stands (jackstands)

• Do follow manufacturer's directions whenever working with potentially hazardous materials. Most chemicals and fluids are poisonous if taken internally.

• Do properly maintain your tools. Loose hammerheads, mushroomed punches and chisels, frayed or poorly grounded electrical cords, excessively worn screwdrivers, spread wrenches (open end), cracked sockets, slipping ratchets, or faulty droplight sockets can cause accidents.

• Likewise, keep your tools clean; a greasy wrench can slip off a bolt head, ruining the bolt and often harming your knuckles in the process.

• Do use the proper size and type of tool for the job at hand. Do select a wrench or socket that fits the nut or bolt. The wrench or socket should sit straight, not cocked.

• Do, when possible, pull on a wrench handle rather than push on it, and adjust your stance to prevent a fall.

• Do be sure that adjustable wrenches are tightly closed on the nut or bolt and pulled so that the force is on the side of the fixed jaw.

• Do strike squarely with a hammer; avoid glancing blows.

• Do set the parking brake and block the drive wheels if the work requires a running engine.

Don'ts

• Don't run the engine in a garage or anywhere else without proper ventilation — EVER! Carbon monoxide is poisonous; it takes a long time to leave the human body and you can build up a deadly supply of it in your system by simply breathing in a little every day. You may not realize you are slowly poisoning yourself. Always use power vents, windows, fans and/or open the garage door.

• Don't work around moving parts while wearing loose clothing. Short sleeves are much safer than long, loose sleeves. Hard-toed shoes with neoprene soles protect your toes and give a better grip on slippery surfaces. Jewelry such as watches, fancy belt buckles, beads or body adornment of any kind is not safe working around a vehicle. Long hair should be tied back under a hat or cap.

• Don't use pockets for toolboxes. A fall or bump can drive a screwdriver deep into your body. Even a rag hanging from your back pocket can wrap around a spinning shaft or fan.

• Don't smoke when working around gasoline, cleaning solvent or other flammable material.

• Don't smoke when working around the battery. When the battery is being charged, it gives off explosive hydrogen gas.

• Don't use gasoline to wash your hands; there are excellent soaps available. Gasoline contains dangerous additives which can enter the body through a cut or through your pores. Gasoline also removes all the natural oils from the skin so that bone dry hands will suck up oil and grease.

• Don't service the air conditioning system unless you are equipped with the necessary tools and training. When liquid or compressed gas refrigerant is released to atmospheric pressure it will absorb heat from whatever it contacts. This will chill or freeze anything it touches. Although refrigerant is normally non-toxic, R-12 becomes a deadly poisonous gas in the presence of an open flame. One good whiff of the vapors from burning refrigerant can be fatal.

• Don't use screwdrivers for anything other than driving screws! A screwdriver used as an prying tool can snap when you least expect it, causing injuries. At the very least, you'll ruin a good screwdriver.

• Don't use a bumper or emergency jack (that little ratchet, scissors, or pantograph jack supplied with the vehicle) for anything other than changing a flat! These jacks are only intended for emergency use out on the road; they are NOT designed as a maintenance tool. If you are serious about maintaining your vehicle yourself, invest in a hydraulic floor jack of at least a 1½ ton capacity, and at least two sturdy jackstands.

FASTENERS, MEASUREMENTS AND CONVERSIONS

Bolts, Nuts and Other Threaded Retainers

▶ See Figures 19, 20, 21 and 22

Although there are a great variety of fasteners found in the modern car or truck, the most commonly used retainer is the threaded fastener (nuts, bolts, screws, studs, etc). Most threaded retainers may be reused, provided that they are not damaged in use or during the repair. Some retainers (such as stretch bolts or torque prevailing nuts) are designed to deform when tightened or in use and should not be reinstalled.

Whenever possible, we will note any special retainers which should be replaced during a procedure. But you should always inspect the condition of a retainer when it is removed and replace any that show signs of damage. Check all threads for rust or corrosion which can increase the torque necessary to achieve the desired clamp load for which that fastener was originally selected. Additionally, be sure that the driver surface of the fastener has not been compromised by rounding or other damage. In some cases a driver surface may become only partially rounded, allowing the driver to catch in only one direction. In many of these occurrences, a fastener may be installed and tightened, but the driver would not be able to grip and loosen the fastener again. (This could lead to frustration down the line should that component ever need to be disassembled again).

If you must replace a fastener, whether due to design or damage, you must ALWAYS be sure to use the proper replacement. In all cases, a retainer of the same design, material and strength should be used. Markings on the heads of most bolts will help determine the proper strength of the fastener. The same material, thread and pitch must be selected to assure proper installation and safe operation of the vehicle afterwards.

Thread gauges are available to help measure a bolt or stud's thread. Most automotive and hardware stores keep gauges available to help you select the proper size. In a pinch, you can use another nut or bolt for a thread gauge. If the bolt you are replacing is not too badly damaged, you can select a match by finding another bolt which will thread in its place. If you find a nut which threads properly onto the damaged bolt, then use that nut to help select the replacement bolt. If however, the bolt you are replacing is so badly damaged (broken

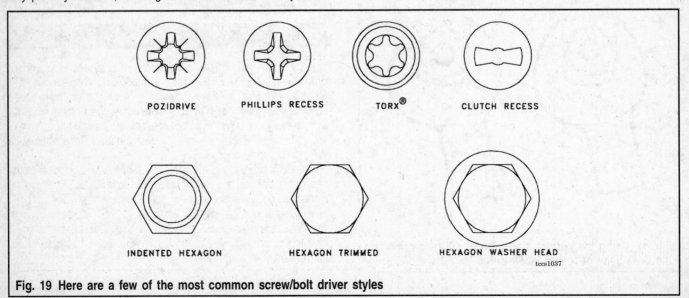

POZIDRIVE   PHILLIPS RECESS   TORX®   CLUTCH RECESS

INDENTED HEXAGON   HEXAGON TRIMMED   HEXAGON WASHER HEAD

tccs1037

Fig. 19 Here are a few of the most common screw/bolt driver styles

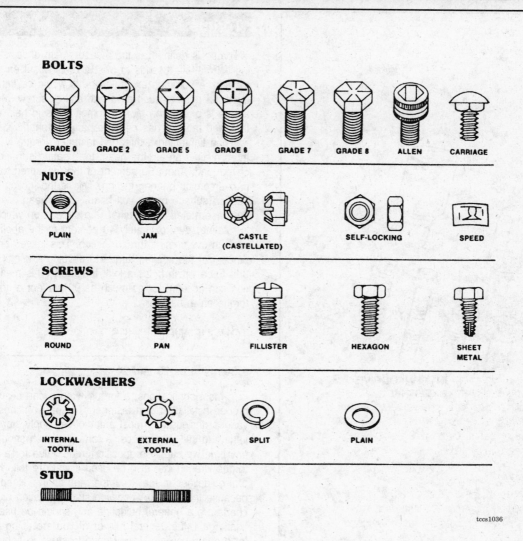

BOLTS

GRADE 0 GRADE 2 GRADE 5 GRADE 6 GRADE 7 GRADE 8 ALLEN CARRIAGE

NUTS

PLAIN JAM CASTLE (CASTELLATED) SELF-LOCKING SPEED

SCREWS

ROUND PAN FILLISTER HEXAGON SHEET METAL

LOCKWASHERS

INTERNAL TOOTH EXTERNAL TOOTH SPLIT PLAIN

STUD

tccs1036

Fig. 20 There are many different types of threaded retainers found on vehicles

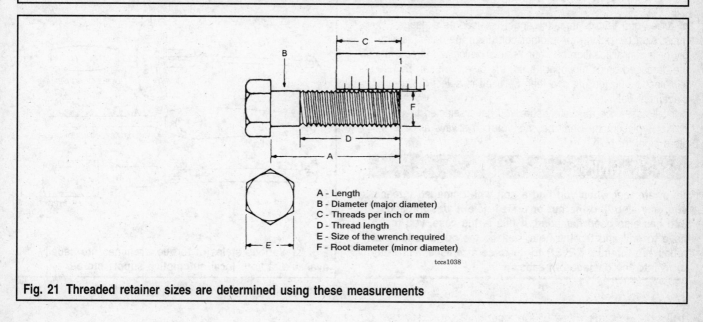

A - Length
B - Diameter (major diameter)
C - Threads per inch or mm
D - Thread length
E - Size of the wrench required
F - Root diameter (minor diameter)

tccs1038

Fig. 21 Threaded retainer sizes are determined using these measurements

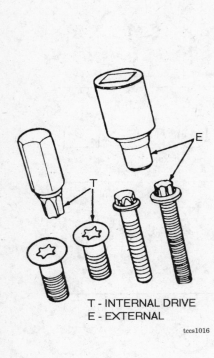

T - INTERNAL DRIVE
E - EXTERNAL

tccs1016

Fig. 22 Special fasteners such as these Torx® head bolts are used by manufacturers to discourage people from working on vehicles without the proper tools

or drilled out) that its threads cannot be used as a gauge, you might start by looking for another bolt (from the same assembly or a similar location on your vehicle) which will thread into the damaged bolt's mounting. If so, the other bolt can be used to select a nut; the nut can then be used to select the replacement bolt.

In all cases, be absolutely sure you have selected the proper replacement. Don't be shy, you can always ask the store clerk for help.

✲✲WARNING

Be aware that when you find a bolt with damaged threads, you may also find the nut or drilled hole it was threaded into has also been damaged. If this is the case, you may have to drill and tap the hole, replace the nut or otherwise repair the threads. NEVER try to force a replacement bolt to fit into the damaged threads.

Torque

Torque is defined as the measurement of resistance to turning or rotating. It tends to twist a body about an axis of rotation. A common example of this would be tightening a threaded retainer such as a nut, bolt or screw. Measuring torque is one of the most common ways to help assure that a threaded retainer has been properly fastened.

When tightening a threaded fastener, torque is applied in three distinct areas, the head, the bearing surface and the clamp load. About 50 percent of the measured torque is used in overcoming bearing friction. This is the friction between the bearing surface of the bolt head, screw head or nut face and the base material or washer (the surface on which the fastener is rotating). Approximately 40 percent of the applied torque is used in overcoming thread friction. This leaves only about 10 percent of the applied torque to develop a useful clamp load (the force which holds a joint together). This means that friction can account for as much as 90 percent of the applied torque on a fastener.

TORQUE WRENCHES

▶ **See Figures 23 and 24**

In most applications, a torque wrench can be used to assure proper installation of a fastener. Torque wrenches come in various designs and most automotive supply stores will carry a variety to suit your needs. A torque wrench should be used any time we supply a specific torque value for a fastener. A torque wrench can also be used if you are following the general guidelines in the accompanying charts. Keep in mind that because there is no worldwide standardization of fasteners, the charts are a general guideline and should be used with caution. Again, the general rule of "if you are using the right tool for the job, you should not have to strain to tighten a fastener" applies here.

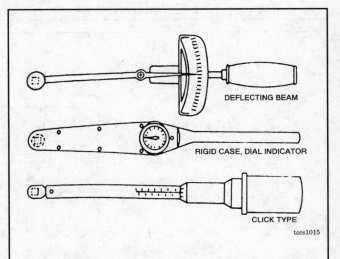

DEFLECTING BEAM

RIGID CASE, DIAL INDICATOR

CLICK TYPE

tccs1015

Fig. 23 Various styles of torque wrenches are usually available at your local automotive supply store

Standard Torque Specifications and Fastener Markings

In the absence of specific torques, the following chart can be used as a guide to the maximum safe torque of a particular size/grade of fastener.

- There is no torque difference for fine or coarse threads.
- Torque values are based on clean, dry threads. Reduce the value by 10% if threads are oiled prior to assembly.
- The torque required for aluminum components or fasteners is considerably less.

U.S. Bolts

SAE Grade Number	1 or 2			5			6 or 7		
Number of lines always 2 less than the grade number.									
Bolt Size (Inches)—(Thread)	**Maximum Torque**			**Maximum Torque**			**Maximum Torque**		
	Ft./Lbs.	Kgm	Nm	Ft./Lbs.	Kgm	Nm	Ft./Lbs.	Kgm	Nm
¼ — 20	5	0.7	6.8	8	1.1	10.8	10	1.4	13.5
— 28	6	0.8	8.1	10	1.4	13.6			
5/16 — 18	11	1.5	14.9	17	2.3	23.0	19	2.6	25.8
— 24	13	1.8	17.6	19	2.6	25.7			
3/8 — 16	18	2.5	24.4	31	4.3	42.0	34	4.7	46.0
— 24	20	2.75	27.1	35	4.8	47.5			
7/16 — 14	28	3.8	37.0	49	6.8	66.4	55	7.6	74.5
— 20	30	4.2	40.7	55	7.6	74.5			
½ — 13	39	5.4	52.8	75	10.4	101.7	85	11.75	115.2
— 20	41	5.7	55.6	85	11.7	115.2			
9/16 — 12	51	7.0	69.2	110	15.2	149.1	120	16.6	162.7
— 18	55	7.6	74.5	120	16.6	162.7			
5/8 — 11	83	11.5	112.5	150	20.7	203.3	167	23.0	226.5
— 18	95	13.1	128.8	170	23.5	230.5			
¾ — 10	105	14.5	142.3	270	37.3	366.0	280	38.7	379.6
— 16	115	15.9	155.9	295	40.8	400.0			
7/8 — 9	160	22.1	216.9	395	54.6	535.5	440	60.9	596.5
— 14	175	24.2	237.2	435	60.1	589.7			
1 — 8	236	32.5	318.6	590	81.6	799.9	660	91.3	894.8
— 14	250	34.6	338.9	660	91.3	849.8			

Metric Bolts

Relative Strength Marking	4.6, 4.8			8.8		
Bolt Markings						
Bolt Size Thread Size x Pitch (mm)	**Maximum Torque**			**Maximum Torque**		
	Ft./Lbs.	Kgm	Nm	Ft./Lbs.	Kgm	Nm
6 x 1.0	2–3	.2–.4	3–4	3–6	4–.8	5–8
8 x 1.25	6–8	.8–1	8–12	9–14	1.2–1.9	13–19
10 x 1.25	12–17	1.5–2.3	16–23	20–29	2.7–4.0	27–39
12 x 1.25	21–32	2.9–4.4	29–43	35–53	4.8–7.3	47–72
14 x 1.5	35–52	4.8–7.1	48–70	57–85	7.8–11.7	77–110
16 x 1.5	51–77	7.0–10.6	67–100	90–120	12.4–16.5	130–160
18 x 1.5	74–110	10.2–15.1	100–150	130–170	17.9–23.4	180–230
20 x 1.5	110–140	15.1–19.3	150–190	190–240	26.2–46.9	160–320
22 x 1.5	150–190	22.0–26.2	200–260	250–320	34.5–44.1	340–430
24 x 1.5	190–240	26.2–46.9	260–320	310–410	42.7–56.5	420–550

tccs1098

Fig. 24 Standard and metric bolt torque specifications based on bolt strengths — WARNING: use only as a guide

Beam Type
▶ **See Figure 25**

The beam type torque wrench is one of the most popular types. It consists of a pointer attached to the head that runs the length of the flexible beam (shaft) to a scale located near the handle. As the wrench is pulled, the beam bends and the pointer indicates the torque using the scale.

Click (Breakaway) Type
▶ **See Figure 26**

Another popular design of torque wrench is the click type. To use the click type wrench you pre-adjust it to a torque setting. Once the torque is reached, the wrench has a reflex signalling feature that causes a momentary breakaway of the torque wrench body, sending an impulse to the operator's hand.

Pivot Head Type
▶ **See Figures 26 and 27**

Some torque wrenches (usually of the click type) may be equipped with a pivot head which can allow it to be used in areas of limited access. BUT, it must be used properly. To hold a pivot head wrench, grasp the handle lightly, and as you pull on the handle, it should be floated on the pivot point. If the handle comes in contact with the yoke extension during the process of pulling, there is a very good chance the torque readings will be inaccurate because this could alter the wrench loading point. The design of the handle is usually such as to make it inconvenient to deliberately misuse the wrench.

➡ **It should be mentioned that the use of any U-joint, wobble or extension will have an effect on the torque readings, no matter what type of wrench you are using. For the most accurate readings, install the socket directly on the wrench driver. If necessary, straight extensions (which hold a socket directly under the wrench driver) will have the least effect on the torque reading. Avoid any extension that alters the length of the wrench from the handle to the head/driving point (such as a crow's foot). U-joint or Wobble extensions can greatly affect the readings; avoid their use at all times.**

Rigid Case (Direct Reading)
▶ **See Figure 28**

A rigid case or direct reading torque wrench is equipped with a dial indicator to show torque values. One advantage of these wrenches is that they can be held at any position on the wrench without affecting accuracy. These wrenches are often preferred because they tend to be compact, easy to read and have a great degree of accuracy.

TORQUE ANGLE METERS

▶ **See Figure 29**

Because the frictional characteristics of each fastener or threaded hole will vary, clamp loads which are based strictly

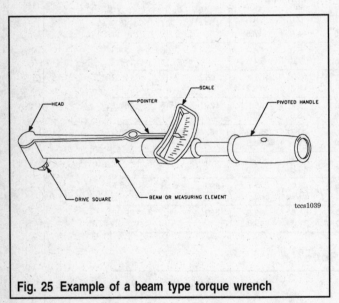

Fig. 25 Example of a beam type torque wrench

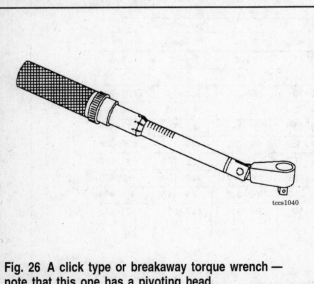

Fig. 26 A click type or breakaway torque wrench — note that this one has a pivoting head

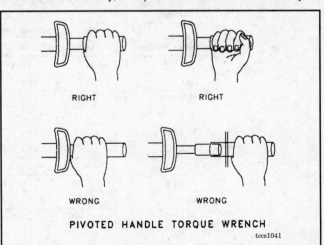

Fig. 27 Torque wrenches with pivoting heads must be grasped and used properly to prevent an incorrect reading

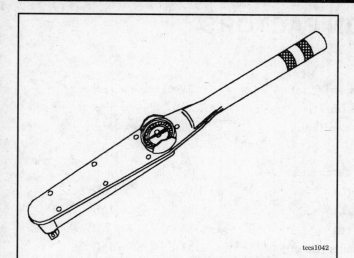

tccs1042

Fig. 28 The rigid case (direct reading) torque wrench uses a dial indicator to show torque

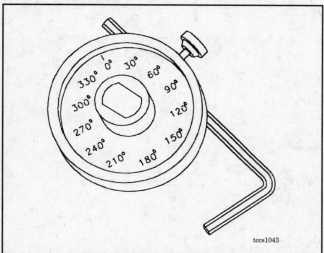

tccs1043

Fig. 29 Some specifications require the use of a torque angle meter (mechanical protractor)

on torque will vary as well. In most applications, this variance is not significant enough to cause worry. But, in certain applications, a manufacturer's engineers may determine that more precise clamp loads are necessary (such is the case with many aluminum cylinder heads). In these cases, a torque angle method of installation would be specified. When installing fasteners which are torque angle tightened, a predetermined seating torque and standard torque wrench are usually used first to remove any compliance from the joint. The fastener is then tightened the specified additional portion of a turn measured in degrees. A torque angle gauge (mechanical protractor) is used for these applications.

Standard and Metric Measurements

Throughout this manual, specifications are given to help you determine the condition of various components on your vehicle, or to assist you in their installation. Some of the most common measurements include length (in. or cm/mm), torque (ft. lbs., inch lbs. or Nm) and pressure (psi, in. Hg, kPa or mm Hg). In most cases, we strive to provide the proper measurement as determined by the manufacturer's engineers.

Though, in some cases, that value may not be conveniently measured with what is available in your toolbox. Luckily, many of the measuring devices which are available today will have two scales so the Standard or Metric measurements may easily be taken. If any of the various measuring tools which are available to you do not contain the same scale as listed in the specifications, use the accompanying conversion factors to determine the proper value.

The conversion factor chart is used by taking the given specification and multiplying it by the necessary conversion factor. For instance, looking at the first line, if you have a measurement in inches such as "free-play should be 2 in." but your ruler reads only in millimeters, multiply 2 in. by the conversion factor of 25.4 to get the metric equivalent of 50.8mm. Likewise, if the specification was given only in a Metric measurement, for example in Newton Meters (Nm), then look at the center column first. If the measurement is 100 Nm, multiply it by the conversion factor of 0.738 to get 73.8 ft. lbs.

CONVERSION FACTORS

LENGTH–DISTANCE

Inches (in.)	x 25.4	= Millimeters (mm)	x .0394	= Inches
Feet (ft.)	x .305	= Meters (m)	x 3.281	= Feet
Miles	x 1.609	= Kilometers (km)	x .0621	= Miles

VOLUME

Cubic Inches (in3)	x 16.387	= Cubic Centimeters	x .061	= in3
IMP Pints (IMP pt.)	x .568	= Liters (L)	x 1.76	= IMP pt.
IMP Quarts (IMP qt.)	x 1.137	= Liters (L)	x .88	= IMP qt.
IMP Gallons (IMP gal.)	x 4.546	= Liters (L)	x .22	= IMP gal.
IMP Quarts (IMP qt.)	x 1.201	= US Quarts (US qt.)	x .833	= IMP qt.
IMP Gallons (IMP gal.)	x 1.201	= US Gallons (US gal.)	x .833	= IMP gal.
Fl. Ounces	x 29.573	= Milliliters	x .034	= Ounces
US Pints (US pt.)	x .473	= Liters (L)	x 2.113	= Pints
US Quarts (US qt.)	x .946	= Liters (L)	x 1.057	= Quarts
US Gallons (US gal.)	x 3.785	= Liters (L)	x .264	= Gallons

MASS–WEIGHT

Ounces (oz.)	x 28.35	= Grams (g)	x .035	= Ounces
Pounds (lb.)	x .454	= Kilograms (kg)	x 2.205	= Pounds

PRESSURE

Pounds Per Sq. In. (psi)	x 6.895	= Kilopascals (kPa)	x .145	= psi
Inches of Mercury (Hg)	x .4912	= psi	x 2.036	= Hg
Inches of Mercury (Hg)	x 3.377	= Kilopascals (kPa)	x .2961	= Hg
Inches of Water (H_2O)	x .07355	= Inches of Mercury	x 13.783	= H_2O
Inches of Water (H_2O)	x .03613	= psi	x 27.684	= H_2O
Inches of Water (H_2O)	x .248	= Kilopascals (kPa)	x 4.026	= H_2O

TORQUE

Pounds–Force Inches (in–lb)	x .113	= Newton Meters (N·m)	x 8.85	= in–lb
Pounds–Force Feet (ft–lb)	x 1.356	= Newton Meters (N·m)	x .738	= ft–lb

VELOCITY

Miles Per Hour (MPH)	x 1.609	= Kilometers Per Hour (KPH)	x .621	= MPH

POWER

Horsepower (Hp)	x .745	= Kilowatts	x 1.34	= Horsepower

FUEL CONSUMPTION*

Miles Per Gallon IMP (MPG)	x .354	= Kilometers Per Liter (Km/L)
Kilometers Per Liter (Km/L)	x 2.352	= IMP MPG
Miles Per Gallon US (MPG)	x .425	= Kilometers Per Liter (Km/L)
Kilometers Per Liter (Km/L)	x 2.352	= US MPG

*It is common to covert from miles per gallon (mpg) to liters/100 kilometers (1/100 km), where mpg (IMP) x 1/100 km = 282 and mpg (US) x 1/100 km = 235.

TEMPERATURE

Degree Fahrenheit (°F)	= (°C x 1.8) + 32
Degree Celsius (°C)	= (°F – 32) x .56

tccs1044

HISTORY

Subaru vehicles are built by Fuji Heavy Industries of Japan. The first Subaru automobile, a minicar, was introduced in 1958. The little car was highly successful in Japan because of its low price and operating cost.

In 1968 the Subaru 360 was introduced into the United States, but the car proved to be too small and was replaced by the larger FF-1 series.

The FF-1, or Star as it was known, was a 1.1 liter engine car. Models included a two-door and four-door sedan, and a station wagon. All models, as they do today, featured a horizontally opposed (flat) water cooled engine, and independent suspension at all four wheels.

Engine size has increased over the years, from 1100cc to 3300cc. A four wheel drive unit, a five speed manual transaxle, and an automatic transaxle were all introduced in 1975. The four wheel drive, which engages the rear wheels when required, first appeared in station wagon models.

From the one model of the late 60's, to the restyled models of the 90's, Subaru (which is the Japanese name for the six star constellation we call Pleiades) has increased its sales in the U.S. market until it is now ranked in the Top Ten of all imported cars.

SERIAL NUMBER IDENTIFICATION

Vehicle

♦ **See Figures 30, 31, 32, 33, 34 and 35**

Model Year Chart	
Code	Year
F	1985
G	1986
H	1987
J	1988
K	1989
L	1990
M	1991
N	1992
P	1993
R	1994
NA	1995
T	1996

87971c00

The Vehicle Identification Number (VIN) is stamped on a tab at the top left-side of the dashboard, visible through the windshield. There is also a vehicle identification plate in the engine compartment on the bulkhead.

In addition to the VIN information in the engine compartment, there is also an identification plate attached to the driver side door jam. This plate contains the VIN as well as production date, vehicle weight and tire data.

The serial number consists of a series of model identification numbers followed by a six-digit production number.

Engine

♦ **See Figures 36 and 37**

The engine number is stamped on a plate attached to the front, right-hand side of the crankcase, near the distributor. The serial number consists of an engine code number which is followed by a six-digit production number.

Transaxle

♦ **See Figures 38, 39, 40, 41, 42 and 43**

The transaxle number label is attached to the upper surface of the main case on manual transaxles and to the converter housing on automatic transaxles.

Drive Axle

The drive axle identification number is stamped on a tag, located on the rear of the differential. The information includes a part number and gear ratio information.

Transfer Case

The transfer case for All Wheel Drive (AWD) equipped models does not have an externally visible serial number stamped on the case.

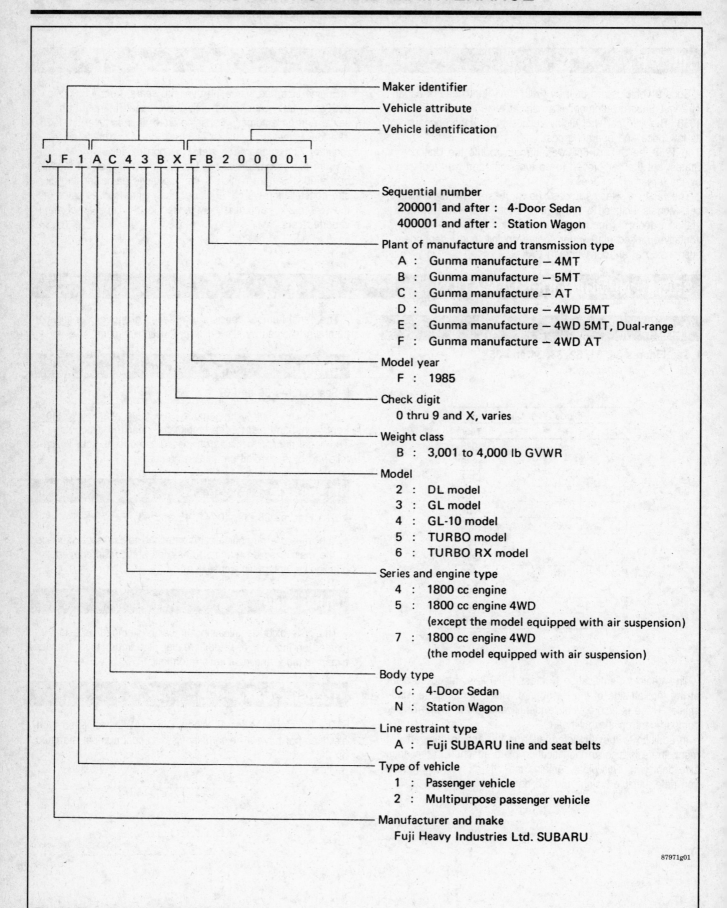

J F 1 A C 4 3 B X F B 2 0 0 0 0 1

Maker identifier

Vehicle attribute

Vehicle identification

Sequential number
200001 and after : 4-Door Sedan
400001 and after : Station Wagon

Plant of manufacture and transmission type
A : Gunma manufacture — 4MT
B : Gunma manufacture — 5MT
C : Gunma manufacture — AT
D : Gunma manufacture — 4WD 5MT
E : Gunma manufacture — 4WD 5MT, Dual-range
F : Gunma manufacture — 4WD AT

Model year
F : 1985

Check digit
0 thru 9 and X, varies

Weight class
B : 3,001 to 4,000 lb GVWR

Model
2 : DL model
3 : GL model
4 : GL-10 model
5 : TURBO model
6 : TURBO RX model

Series and engine type
4 : 1800 cc engine
5 : 1800 cc engine 4WD
(except the model equipped with air suspension)
7 : 1800 cc engine 4WD
(the model equipped with air suspension)

Body type
C : 4-Door Sedan
N : Station Wagon

Line restraint type
A : Fuji SUBARU line and seat belts

Type of vehicle
1 : Passenger vehicle
2 : Multipurpose passenger vehicle

Manufacturer and make
Fuji Heavy Industries Ltd. SUBARU

87971g01

Fig. 30 Explanation of 1985-89 VINs

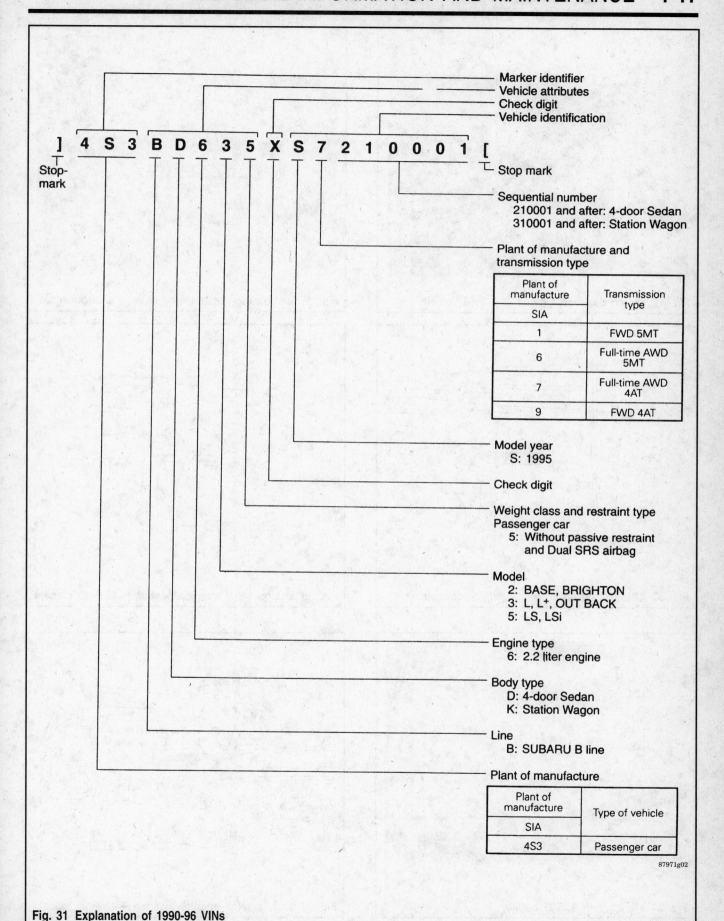

Fig. 31 Explanation of 1990-96 VINs

Fig. 32 VIN on dashboard panel of a 1985 vehicle

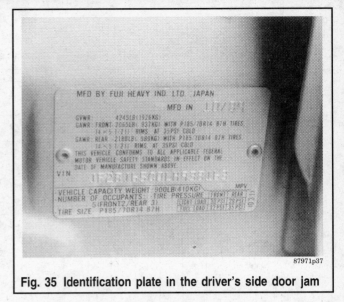

Fig. 35 Identification plate in the driver's side door jam

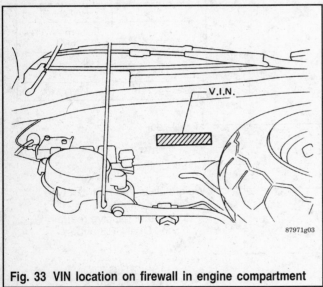

Fig. 33 VIN location on firewall in engine compartment

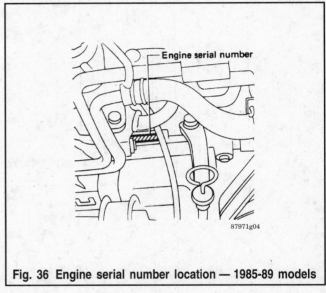

Fig. 36 Engine serial number location — 1985-89 models

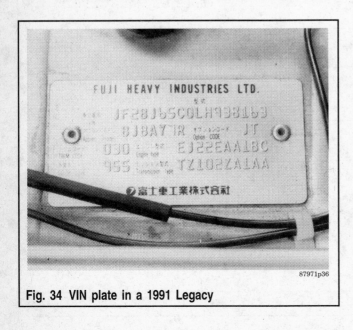

Fig. 34 VIN plate in a 1991 Legacy

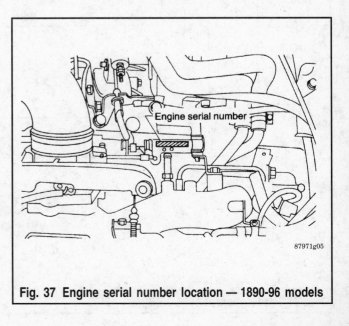

Fig. 37 Engine serial number location — 1890-96 models

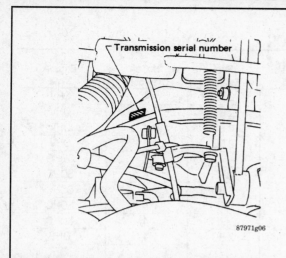

Fig. 38 Manual transaxle serial number location — 1985-89 models

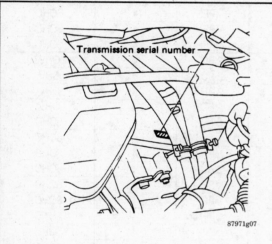

Fig. 39 Automatic transaxle serial number location — 1985-89 models

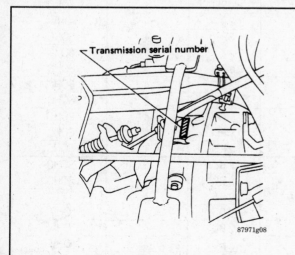

Fig. 40 Transaxle serial number location on models with AWD — 1985-89 models

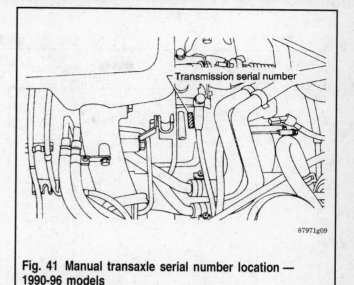

Fig. 41 Manual transaxle serial number location — 1990-96 models

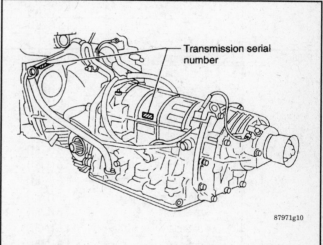

Fig. 42 Automatic transaxle serial number location — 1990-96 models

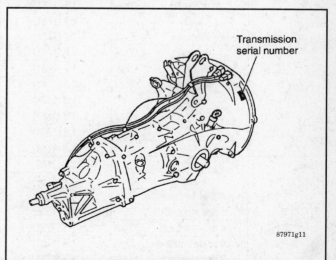

Fig. 43 Transaxle serial number location on models with AWD — 1990-96 models

ENGINE IDENTIFICATION

Year	Model		Engine Displacement Liters (cc)	Engine Series (ID/VIN)	Fuel System	No. of Cylinders	Engine Type
1985	4 dr Hatchback	①	1.6 (1595)	2	2 BC	4	OHV
	4 dr Hatchback	②	1.6 (1595)	3	2 BC	4	OHV
	4 dr Hatchback	①	1.8 (1781)	4	2 BC	4	OHV
	4 dr Hatchback	②	1.8 (1781)	5	2 BC	4	OHV
	4 dr Sedan	① ③	1.8 (1781)	4	⑥	4	SOHC
	4 dr Sedan	① ④	1.8 (1781)	4	MPFI	4	SOHC
	4 dr Sedan	② ③	1.8 (1781)	5	2 BC	4	SOHC
	4 dr Sedan	② ④	1.8 (1781)	5	MPFI	4	SOHC
	4 dr Sedan	④	1.8 (1781)	7	MPFI	4	SOHC
	Brat		1.8 (1781)	5	2 BC	4	OHV
	Wagon	① ③	1.8 (1781)	4	⑥	4	SOHC
	Wagon	① ④	1.8 (1781)	4	MPFI	4	SOHC
	Wagon	② ③	1.8 (1781)	5	2 BC	4	SOHC
	Wagon	② ④	1.8 (1781)	5	MPFI	4	SOHC
	Wagon	④	1.8 (1781)	7	MPFI	4	SOHC
	XT	①	1.8 (1781)	4	MPFI	4	SOHC
	XT	②	1.8 (1781)	7	MPFI	4	SOHC
1986	4 dr Hatchback	①	1.6 (1595)	2	2 BC	4	OHV
	4 dr Hatchback	②	1.6 (1595)	3	2 BC	4	OHV
	4 dr Hatchback	①	1.8 (1781)	4	2 BC	4	OHV
	4 dr Hatchback	②	1.8 (1781)	5	2 BC	4	OHV
	2 dr Hatchback	① ③	1.8 (1781)	5	SPFI	4	SOHC
	2 dr Hatchback	① ③	1.8 (1781)	4	⑥	4	SOHC
	2 dr Hatchback	① ④	1.8 (1781)	4	MPFI	4	SOHC
	2 dr Hatchback	② ③	1.8 (1781)	5	2 BC	4	SOHC
	2 dr Hatchback	② ④	1.8 (1781)	5	MPFI	4	SOHC
	2 dr Hatchback	④	1.8 (1781)	7	MPFI	4	SOHC
	4 dr Sedan	① ③	1.8 (1781)	5	SPFI	4	SOHC
	4 dr Sedan	① ③	1.8 (1781)	4	⑥	4	SOHC
	4 dr Sedan	① ④	1.8 (1781)	4	MPFI	4	SOHC
	4 dr Sedan	② ③	1.8 (1781)	5	2 BC	4	SOHC
	4 dr Sedan	② ④	1.8 (1781)	5	MPFI	4	SOHC
	4 dr Sedan	⑤	1.8 (1781)	7	MPFI	4	SOHC
	Brat		1.8 (1781)	5	2 BC	4	OHV
	Wagon	① ③	1.8 (1781)	5	SPFI	4	SOHC
	Wagon	① ③	1.8 (1781)	4	⑥	4	SOHC
	Wagon	① ④	1.8 (1781)	4	MPFI	4	SOHC
	Wagon	② ③	1.8 (1781)	5	2 BC	4	SOHC
	Wagon	② ④	1.8 (1781)	5	MPFI	4	SOHC
	Wagon	④	1.8 (1781)	7	MPFI	4	SOHC
	XT	①	1.8 (1781)	4	MPFI	4	SOHC
	XT	②	1.8 (1781)	7	MPFI	4	SOHC
1987	Justy	①	1.2 (1189)	7	2 BC	3	SOHC
	Justy	②	1.2 (1189)	8	2 BC	3	SOHC
	4 dr Hatchback	①	1.6 (1595)	2	2 BC	4	OHV
	4 dr Hatchback	②	1.6 (1595)	3	2 BC	4	OHV
	4 dr Hatchback	①	1.8 (1781)	4	2 BC	4	OHV
	4 dr Hatchback	②	1.8 (1781)	5	2 BC	4	OHV
	2 dr Hatchback	① ③	1.8 (1781)	4	SPFI	4	SOHC
	2 dr Hatchback	① ④	1.8 (1781)	4	MPFI	4	SOHC

87971c01

ENGINE IDENTIFICATION

Year	Model		Engine Displacement Liters (cc)	Engine Series (ID/VIN)	Fuel System	No. of Cylinders	Engine Type
1987	2 dr Hatchback	② ③	1.8 (1781)	5	2 BC	4	SOHC
	2 dr Hatchback	② ④	1.8 (1781)	5	MPFI	4	SOHC
	2 dr Hatchback	④	1.8 (1781)	7	MPFI	4	SOHC
	4 dr Sedan	① ③	1.8 (1781)	4	SPFI	4	SOHC
	4 dr Sedan	① ④	1.8 (1781)	4	MPFI	4	SOHC
	4 dr Sedan	② ③	1.8 (1781)	5	2 BC	4	SOHC
	4 dr Sedan	② ④	1.8 (1781)	5	MPFI	4	SOHC
	4 dr Sedan	④	1.8 (1781)	7	MPFI	4	SOHC
	Wagon	① ③	1.8 (1781)	4	SPFI	4	SOHC
	Wagon	① ④	1.8 (1781)	4	MPFI	4	SOHC
	Wagon	② ③	1.8 (1781)	5	2 BC	4	SOHC
	Wagon	② ④	1.8 (1781)	5	MPFI	4	SOHC
	Wagon	④	1.8 (1781)	7	MPFI	4	SOHC
	XT	①	1.8 (1781)	4	MPFI	4	SOHC
	XT	②	1.8 (1781)	7	MPFI	4	SOHC
1988	Justy	①	1.2 (1189)	7	2 BC	3	SOHC
	Justy	②	1.2 (1189)	8	2 BC	3	SOHC
	4 dr Hatchback	①	1.6 (1595)	2	2 BC	4	OHV
	4 dr Hatchback	②	1.6 (1595)	3	2 BC	4	OHV
	4 dr Hatchback	①	1.8 (1781)	4	2 BC	4	OHV
	4 dr Hatchback	②	1.8 (1781)	5	2 BC	4	OHV
	2 dr Hatchback	① ③	1.8 (1781)	4	SPFI	4	SOHC
	2 dr Hatchback	① ④	1.8 (1781)	4	MPFI	4	SOHC
	2 dr Hatchback	② ③	1.8 (1781)	5	SPFI	4	SOHC
	2 dr Hatchback	② ④	1.8 (1781)	5	MPFI	4	SOHC
	2 dr Hatchback	④	1.8 (1781)	7	MPFI	4	SOHC
	4 dr Sedan	① ③	1.8 (1781)	4	SPFI	4	SOHC
	4 dr Sedan	① ④	1.8 (1781)	4	MPFI	4	SOHC
	4 dr Sedan	② ③	1.8 (1781)	5	SPFI	4	SOHC
	4 dr Sedan	② ④	1.8 (1781)	5	MPFI	4	SOHC
	4 dr Sedan	④	1.8 (1781)	7	MPFI	4	SOHC
	Wagon	① ③	1.8 (1781)	4	SPFI	4	SOHC
	Wagon	① ④	1.8 (1781)	4	MPFI	4	SOHC
	Wagon	② ③	1.8 (1781)	5	SPFI	4	SOHC
	Wagon	② ④	1.8 (1781)	5	MPFI	4	SOHC
	Wagon	④	1.8 (1781)	7	MPFI	4	SOHC
	XT	①	1.8 (1781)	4	MPFI	4	SOHC
	XT	②	1.8 (1781)	7	MPFI	4	SOHC
	XT6	①	2.7 (2672)	8	MPFI	6	SOHC
	XT6	②	2.7 (2672)	9	MPFI	6	SOHC
1989	Justy	①	1.2 (1189)	7	2 BC	3	SOHC
	Justy	②	1.2 (1189)	8	2 BC	3	SOHC
	4 dr Hatchback	①	1.6 (1595)	2	2 BC	4	OHV
	4 dr Hatchback	②	1.6 (1595)	3	2 BC	4	OHV
	4 dr Hatchback	①	1.8 (1781)	4	2 BC	4	OHV
	4 dr Hatchback	②	1.8 (1781)	5	2 BC	4	OHV
	2 dr Hatchback	① ③	1.8 (1781)	4	SPFI	4	SOHC
	2 dr Hatchback	① ④	1.8 (1781)	4	MPFI	4	SOHC
	2 dr Hatchback	② ③	1.8 (1781)	5	SPFI	4	SOHC
	2 dr Hatchback	② ④	1.8 (1781)	5	MPFI	4	SOHC

87971c02

ENGINE IDENTIFICATION

Year	Model		Engine Displacement Liters (cc)	Engine Series (ID/VIN)	Fuel System	No. of Cylinders	Engine Type
1989	2 dr Hatchback	④	1.8 (1781)	7	MPFI	4	SOHC
	4 dr Sedan	① ③	1.8 (1781)	4	SPFI	4	SOHC
	4 dr Sedan	① ④	1.8 (1781)	4	MPFI	4	SOHC
	4 dr Sedan	② ③	1.8 (1781)	5	SPFI	4	SOHC
	4 dr Sedan	② ④	1.8 (1781)	5	MPFI	4	SOHC
	4 dr Sedan	④	1.8 (1781)	7	MPFI	4	SOHC
	Wagon	① ③	1.8 (1781)	4	MPFI	4	SOHC
	Wagon	① ④	1.8 (1781)	4	MPFI	4	SOHC
	Wagon	② ③	1.8 (1781)	5	SPFI	4	SOHC
	Wagon	② ④	1.8 (1781)	5	MPFI	4	SOHC
	Wagon	④	1.8 (1781)	7	MPFI	4	SOHC
	XT	①	1.8 (1781)	4	MPFI	4	SOHC
	XT	②	1.8 (1781)	7	MPFI	4	SOHC
	XT6	①	2.7 (2672)	8	MPFI	6	SOHC
	XT6	②	2.7 (2672)	9	MPFI	6	SOHC
1990	Justy	①	1.2 (1189)	7	2BC	3	SOHC
	Justy	①	1.2 (1189)	7	MPFI	3	SOHC
	Justy	②	1.2 (1189)	8	MPFI	3	SOHC
	Loyale	①	1.8 (1781)	4	SPFI	4	SOHC
	Loyale	②	1.8 (1781)	5	SPFI	4	SOHC
	Loyale	②	1.8 (1781)	7	MPFI	4	SOHC
	XT	①	1.8 (1781)	4	MPFI	4	SOHC
	XT	②	1.8 (1781)	7	MPFI	4	SOHC
	Legacy		2.2 (2212)	6	MPFI	4	SOHC
	XT6	①	2.7 (2672)	8	MPFI	6	SOHC
	XT6	②	2.7 (2672)	9	MPFI	6	SOHC
1991	Justy	①	1.2 (1189)	7	2BC	3	SOHC
	Justy	①	1.2 (1189)	7	MPFI	3	SOHC
	Justy	②	1.2 (1189)	8	MPFI	3	SOHC
	Loyale	①	1.8 (1781)	4	SPFI	4	SOHC
	Loyale	②	1.8 (1781)	5	SPFI	4	SOHC
	XT	①	1.8 (1781)	4	MPFI	4	SOHC
	XT	②	1.8 (1781)	7	MPFI	4	SOHC
	Legacy		2.2 (2212)	6	MPFI	4	SOHC
	XT6	①	2.7 (2672)	8	MPFI	6	SOHC
	XT6	②	2.7 (2672)	9	MPFI	6	SOHC
1992	Justy	①	1.2 (1189)	7	2BC	3	SOHC
	Justy	①	1.2 (1189)	7	MPFI	3	SOHC
	Justy	②	1.2 (1189)	8	MPFI	3	SOHC
	Loyale	①	1.8 (1781)	4	SPFI	4	SOHC
	Loyale	②	1.8 (1781)	5	SPFI	4	SOHC
	Legacy		2.2 (2212)	6	MPFI	4	SOHC
	SVX		3.3 (3318)	3	MPFI	6	DOHC
1993	Justy	①	1.2 (1189)	7	MPFI	3	SOHC
	Justy	②	1.2 (1189)	8	MPFI	3	SOHC
	Loyale	①	1.8 (1781)	4	SPFI	4	SOHC
	Loyale	②	1.8 (1781)	5	SPFI	4	SOHC
	Impreza		1.8 (1829)	2	MPFI	4	SOHC
	Legacy		2.2 (2212)	6	MPFI	4	SOHC
	SVX		3.3 (3318)	3	MPFI	6	DOHC

ENGINE IDENTIFICATION

Year	Model		Engine Displacement Liters (cc)	Engine Series (ID/VIN)	Fuel System	No. of Cylinders	Engine Type
1994	Justy	①	1.2 (1189)	7	MPFI	3	SOHC
	Justy	②	1.2 (1189)	8	MPFI	3	SOHC
	Loyale	①	1.8 (1781)	4	SPFI	4	SOHC
	Loyale	②	1.8 (1781)	5	SPFI	4	SOHC
	Impreza		1.8 (1820)	2	MPFI	4	SOHC
	Legacy		2.2 (2212)	6	MPFI	4	SOHC
	SVX		3.3 (3318)	3	MPFI	6	DOHC
1995	Impreza		1.8 (1820)	2	MPFI	4	SOHC
	Impreza		2.2 (2212)	6	MPFI	4	SOHC
	Legacy		2.2 (2212)	6	MPFI	4	SOHC
	SVX		3.3 (3318)	3	MPFI	6	DOHC
1996	Impreza	①	1.8 (1820)	1	MPFI	4	SOHC
	Impreza	②	1.8 (1820)	2	MPFI	4	SOHC
	Impreza		2.2 (2212)	4	MPFI	4	SOHC
	Legacy	①	2.2 (2212)	3	MPFI	4	SOHC
	Legacy	②	2.2 (2212)	4	MPFI	4	SOHC
	Legacy		2.5 (2457)	6	MPFI	4	DOHC
	SVX		3.3 (3318)	8	MPFI	6	DOHC

BC - Barrel carburetor
DOHC - Double overhead camshaft
MPFI - Multi-Point Fuel Injection NOTE:
This is Subaru terminology for Multi-port Fuel Injection

OHV - Overhead Valve
SOHC - Single overhead camshaft
SPFI - Single-Point Fuel Injection NOTE:
This is Subaru terminology for Throttle-body Fuel Injection

① 2WD
② 4WD
③ Non-Turbo

④ Turbo with air suspension
⑤ DL and GL: 2 BC
GL10 = SPFI

87971c04

ROUTINE MAINTENANCE AND TUNE-UP

Proper maintenance and tune-up is the key to long and trouble-free vehicle life, and the work can yield its own rewards. Studies have shown that a properly tuned and maintained vehicle can achieve better gas mileage than an out-of-tune vehicle. As a conscientious owner and driver, set aside a Saturday morning, say once a month, to check or replace items which could cause major problems later. Keep your own personal log to jot down which services you performed, how much the parts cost you, the date, and the exact odometer reading at the time. Keep all receipts for such items as engine oil and filters, so that they may be referred to in case of related problems or to determine operating expenses. As a do-it-yourselfer, these receipts are the only proof you have that the required maintenance was performed. In the event of a warranty problem, these receipts will be invaluable.

The literature provided with your vehicle when it was originally delivered includes the factory recommended maintenance schedule. If you no longer have this literature, replacement copies are usually available from the dealer. A maintenance schedule is provided later in this section, in case you do not have the factory literature.

Air Cleaner

The air cleaner element used on all vehicles is an oil-impregnated, disposable type. No attempt should be made to clean it. The air cleaner should be replaced at 30,000 mile (48,300 km) intervals.

MAINTENANCE ITEMS - 2.2L ENGINE SHOWN

1. Oil fill cap
2. Oil dipstick
3. Power-steering fluid reservoir
4. Brake fluid reservoir
5. Windshield washer reservoir

6. Coolant overflow reservoir
7. Radiator cap
8. Battery
9. Air filter assembly
10. Spark plugs

11. Fuel filter
12. Accessory belt cover
13. Fuse box
14. Upper radiator hose
15. Warning label

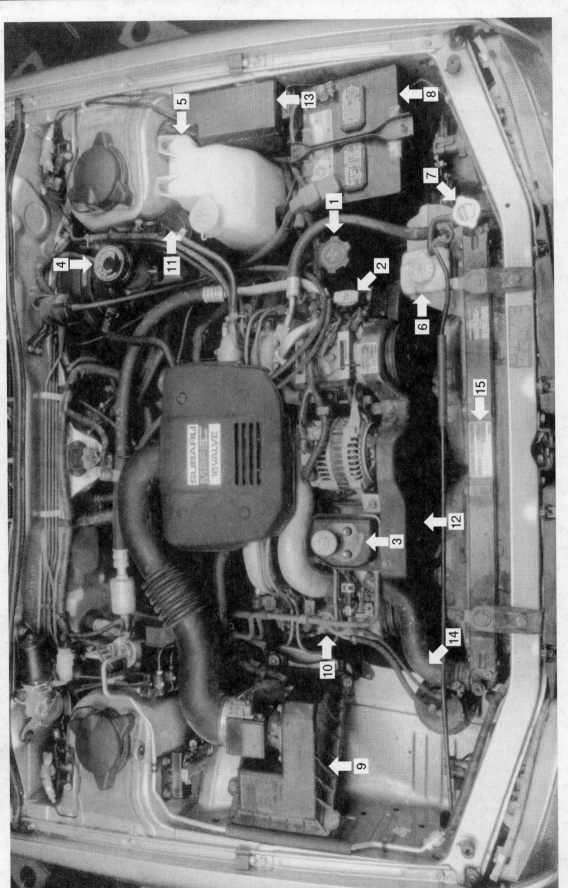

87971pt6

REMOVAL & INSTALLATION

Carbureted Engines
▶ **See Figures 44 and 45**

1. Remove the wingnut on the top of the air cleaner housing. Set it aside carefully, as on some models the emission control system hoses are fastened to it.
2. Lift out the old air filter element and discard it.
3. Clean the air filter base with a rag.

To install:

4. Place the new element in the air cleaner assembly and install the cover.
5. Tighten the wingnut securely.

➡**When checking the air cleaner, it is also a good idea to look at the PCV air filter. The filter is located on the rim of the air filter housing. If it is dirty, replace it.**

Fuel Injected Engines
▶ **See Figures 46, 47, 48, 49, 50 and 51**

1. Loosen the clamps or remove the retaining bolts, depending on model, which secure the cover to the rest of the air cleaner assembly. Lift the cover off and set it aside carefully, as on some models the emission control system hoses are fastened to it.
2. Lift out the old air filter element and discard it.
3. Clean the air filter base with a rag.

To install:

4. Place the new air filter element in the base and install the cover over the filter. Make sure the cover aligns properly with the base.
5. Attach the clamps or install the retaining bolts, depending on model, around the cover to complete the procedure.

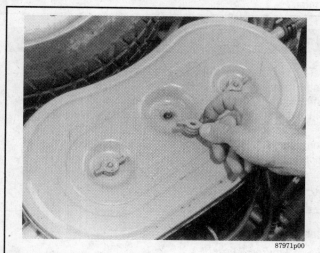

87971p00

Fig. 44 Remove the wingnuts from the top of the air cleaner housing

87971p38

Fig. 46 Unfasten the air cleaner cover retainer screws — 1991 Legacy

87971p01

Fig. 45 Lift the filter element out of the filter housing

87971p39

Fig. 47 An appropriate sized socket can also be used to remove the retainer screws

Fig. 48 Lift the air filter element out of the cleaner assembly

Fig. 51 Lift the top of the air cleaner and remove the filter

Fig. 49 Unfasten the airflow sensor harness will provide needed room

Fuel Filter

The fuel filter should be replaced and all fuel system hoses and connection should be inspected at 12,000 mile (19,000 km) interval for carburetor equipped models, and 30,000 mile (48,300 km) intervals for fuel injected models. When the vehicle is operated in extremely cold or hot conditions, contamination of the filter may occur and the filter should be replaced more often.

REMOVAL & INSTALLATION

Carbureted Engines
▶ **See Figures 52 and 53**

➡Before removing the fuel lines, use hose pliers or equivalent, to pinch off the fuel lines on both sides of the fuel filter.

Fig. 50 Unsnap the clips that fasten the air cleaner assembly — 1996 Legacy

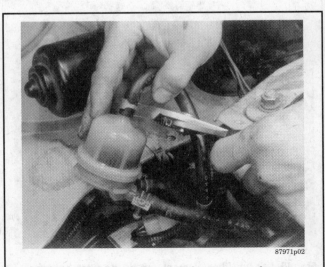

Fig. 52 Use pliers to squeeze and remove spring-type hose clamps

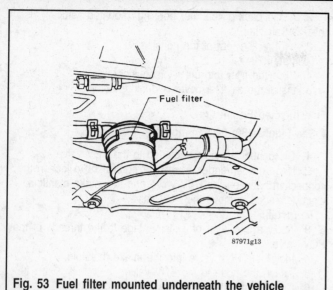

Fig. 53 Fuel filter mounted underneath the vehicle

On carbureted models, the fuel filter is located in the engine compartment, close to the passenger side of the firewall or under the vehicle beneath the driver's seat.

1. Disconnect the negative battery cable.
2. If the fuel filter is located in the engine compartment;
   a. Snap the filter out of its mounting bracket.
   b. Loosen, but **DO NOT** remove, the two hose clamp retainers, located at either end of the filter.
   c. Remove the hoses from the filter necks.
   d. Discard the old filter.
3. If the filter is located under the vehicle;
   a. Raise and support the vehicle safely on jackstands.
   b. Locate the fuel filter on a bracket under the center of the vehicle.
   c. Place a pan under the filter, to catch any excess spilled fuel.
   d. Disconnect the fuel pump electrical connector. Unfasten the hose clamps at both ends of the filter and slide the hoses off the filter.
   e. As required, remove the bolts from the fuel pump bracket and pull the filter off the bracket to remove. Once removed, discard the filter.

✳✳CAUTION

When removing the old filter, be careful not to allow any fuel to drop onto hot engine components.

To install:
4. Check the hoses for cracks and wear, and replace if needed.
5. Install the new filter into the mounting bracket.
6. Connect the hoses on the filter necks and tighten the hose clamps securely.
7. Connect the negative battery cable.
8. Lower the vehicle if raised.
9. Start the vehicle and check for leaks.

Fuel Injected Models
▶ See Figures 54, 55 and 56

1. Locate the fuel filter in the engine compartment on the left inside fender.
2. Reduce the fuel pressure as follows:
   a. Disconnect the electrical wiring connector from the fuel pump.
   b. Crank the engine for five seconds or more. If the engine starts, let the engine run until it stops.
   c. Turn the ignition switch **OFF** and reconnect the electrical wiring connector to the fuel pump.
3. Disconnect the negative battery cable.
4. Loosen the hose clamp screws and slide the hoses off the filter. Remove the filter from the bracket.

To install:
5. Inspect the hoses for wear or cracks, and replace if needed.
6. Install the new filter into the bracket and tighten the hose clamp screws.

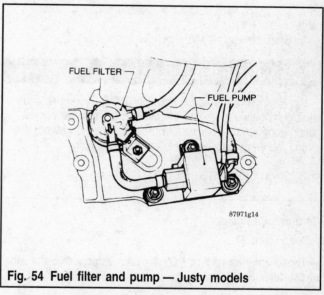

Fig. 54 Fuel filter and pump — Justy models

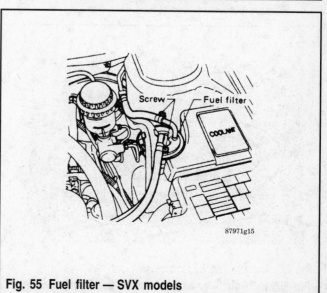

Fig. 55 Fuel filter — SVX models

Fig. 56 Loosen the hose clamps securing the fuel lines to the filter

7. Lower the vehicle and connect the negative battery cable.
8. Start the engine and check for leaks.

PCV Valve/Filter

The Positive Crankcase Ventilation (PCV) System recirculates crankcase vapors into the intake stream to be burned during combustion. This system prevents pollution by not allowing the crankcase vapors to escape the engine.

REMOVAL & INSTALLATION

Carbureted Engines
▶ See Figure 57

➥These engines have a PCV air filter attached to the side of the filter housing.

1. Remove the cover over the air filter element.

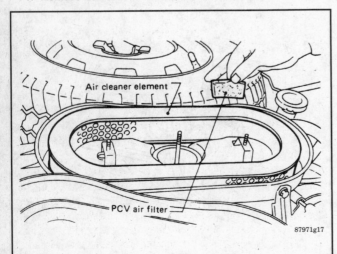

Fig. 57 PCV air filter at the back of the filter housing — carbureted engines

2. At the back of the filter housing, mounted vertically, is the PCV air filter.
3. Lift the filter out of the housing.
To install:
4. Slide the filter into the filter housing.
5. Install the air filter cover and wingnuts.

Fuel Injected Engines
▶ See Figures 58, 59, 60 and 61

1. Disconnect the hose attached to the PCV valve.
2. Use an open-ended wrench or equivalent to loosen the connection between the PCV valve and the intake manifold. Once loosened, remove the PCV valve.
To install:
3. Apply a thin layer of Teflon® tape to the threads of the PCV valve.
4. Install the PCV valve into the intake manifold.
5. Attach the hose to the PCV valve.
6. Start the engine and check for leaks around the connections.

SERVICING

1. Check the PCV ventilation hoses for clogging and leaks. The hoses may be cleaned with compressed air.
2. Check the oil filler cap to insure that the gasket is not damaged and the cap fits firmly on the filler cap end.
3. Disconnect the hose from the PCV valve.
4. Start the engine and place your finger over the top of the PCV valve. Lightly increase the throttle.
5. The valve and system are operating properly when a vacuum is felt. If no vacuum is felt, replace the PCV valve and check the hoses for obstructions.
6. The PCV valve can be checked while off the vehicle by shaking. If a distinct rattling is noticed, the PCV valve is functioning properly.

Evaporative Emission Canister

The evaporative emission canister is part of a system that prevents fuel vapors contained in the fuel tank and carburetor bowl from being discharged into the air. The gas fumes are absorbed by activated charcoal located in the canister.

REMOVAL & INSTALLATION

1. Mark or tag each hose prior to removal.
2. Loosen the hose clamp securing the hose to the canister.
3. After the clamp is loosened, slide the hose off. Continue the process until all the hose are disconnected.
4. Slide the evaporative canister out of the mounting bracket securing it in the engine compartment.
To install:
5. Slide the canister into the mounting bracket.
6. Slide each hose on to the respective end on the canister.
7. Tighten each hose clamp.

Fig. 58 PCV valve attached to the intake manifold — fuel injected models

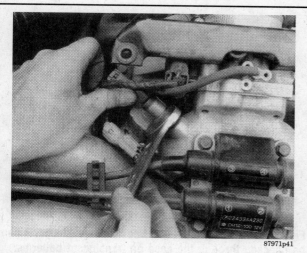

Fig. 59 Disconnect the hose, then use a wrench to loosen the PCV valve at the intake manifold

Fig. 60 Remove the PCV valve from the manifold — 1991 Legacy shown

Fig. 61 Apply Teflon® tape to the PCV valve threads before installing

8. Start the vehicle and check for leaks.

SERVICING

▶ See Figure 62

1. Inspect the canister for holes or damage caused by debris.
2. Inspect the hoses to the canister for holes, cracks or other damage.
3. Disconnect the vacuum hose from the canister. Blow air through the hose to ensure that air does not leak.
4. Disconnect the purge hose from the canister. Blow air through the hose to ensure that air does not leak.

✷✷CAUTION

Do not suck on the hose as this will cause fuel vapors to enter your mouth.

5. Disconnect the evaporation hose from the fuel tank side. Blow air through the hose to ensure that air flows.
6. Replace the canister and/or hoses if damaged.

Battery

GENERAL MAINTENANCE

All batteries, regardless of type, should be carefully secured by a battery hold-down device. If this is not done, the battery terminals or casing may crack from stress applied to the battery during vehicle operation. A battery which is not secured may allow acid to leak out, making it discharge faster; such leaking corrosive acid can also eat away components under the hood. A battery that is not sealed must be checked periodically for electrolyte level. You cannot add water to a sealed maintenance-free battery (though not all maintenance-free batteries are sealed), but a sealed battery must also be checked for proper electrolyte level as indicated by the color of the built-in hydrometer "eye."

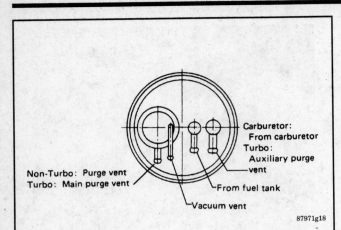

Fig. 62 Hose connections for evaporative emission canister

Keep the top of the battery clean, as a film of dirt can completely discharge a battery that is not used for long periods. A solution of baking soda and water may be used for cleaning, but be careful to flush this off with clear water. DO NOT let any of the solution into the filler holes. Baking soda neutralizes battery acid and will de-activate a battery cell.

❊❊CAUTION

Always use caution when working on or near the battery. Never allow a tool to bridge the gap between the negative and positive battery terminals. Also, be careful not to allow a tool to provide a ground between the positive cable/terminal and any metal component on the vehicle. Either of these conditions will cause a short circuit leading to sparks and possible personal injury.

Batteries in vehicles which are not operated on a regular basis can fall victim to parasitic loads (small current drains which are constantly drawing current from the battery). Normal parasitic loads may drain a battery on a vehicle that is in storage and not used for 6-8 weeks. Vehicles that have additional accessories such as a cellular phone, an alarm system or other devices that increase parasitic load may discharge a battery sooner. If the vehicle is to be stored for 6-8 weeks in a secure area and the alarm system, if present, is not necessary, the negative battery cable should be disconnected at the onset of storage to protect the battery charge.

Remember that constantly discharging and recharging will shorten battery life. Take care not to allow a battery to be needlessly discharged.

BATTERY FLUID

▶ **See Figures 63, 64 and 65**

❊❊CAUTION

Battery electrolyte contains sulfuric acid. If you should splash any on your skin or in your eyes, flush the affected area with plenty of clear water. If it lands in your eyes, get medical help immediately.

The fluid (sulfuric acid solution) contained in the battery cells will tell you many things about the condition of the battery. Because the cell plates must be kept submerged below the fluid level in order to operate, maintaining the fluid level is extremely important. And, because the specific gravity of the acid is an indication of electrical charge, testing the fluid can be an aid in determining if the battery must be replaced. A battery in a vehicle with a properly operating charging system

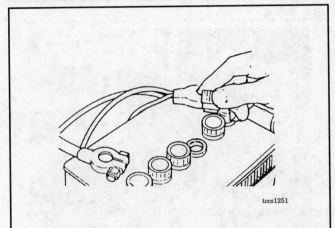

Fig. 63 On non-maintenance free batteries, the level can be checked through the case on translucent batteries; the cell caps must be removed on other models

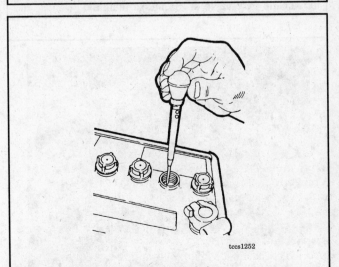

Fig. 64 Check the specific gravity of the battery's electrolyte with a hydrometer

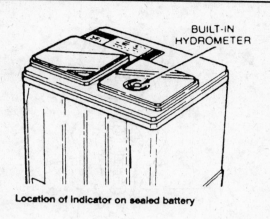

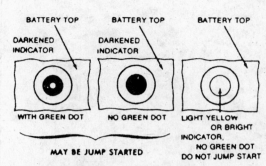

Fig. 65 A typical sealed (maintenance-free) battery with a built-in hydrometer — NOTE that the hydrometer eye may vary between battery manufacturers; always refer to the battery's label

should require little maintenance, but careful, periodic inspection should reveal problems before they leave you stranded.

Fluid Level

Check the battery electrolyte level at least once a month, or more often in hot weather or during periods of extended vehicle operation. On non-sealed batteries, the level can be checked either through the case on translucent batteries or by removing the cell caps on opaque-cased types. The electrolyte level in each cell should be kept filled to the split ring inside each cell, or the line marked on the outside of the case.

If the level is low, add only distilled water through the opening until the level is correct. Each cell is separate from the others, so each must be checked and filled individually. Distilled water should be used, because the chemicals and minerals found in most drinking water are harmful to the battery and could significantly shorten its life.

If water is added in freezing weather, the vehicle should be driven several miles to allow the water to mix with the electrolyte. Otherwise, the battery could freeze.

Although some maintenance-free batteries have removable cell caps for access to the electrolyte, the electrolyte condition and level on all sealed maintenance-free batteries must be checked using the built-in hydrometer "eye." The exact type of eye varies between battery manufacturers, but most apply a sticker to the battery itself explaining the possible readings. When in doubt, refer to the battery manufacturer's instructions to interpret battery condition using the built-in hydrometer.

➡ **Although the readings from built-in hydrometers found in sealed batteries may vary, a green eye usually indicates a properly charged battery with sufficient fluid level. A dark eye is normally an indicator of a battery with sufficient fluid, but one which may be low in charge. And a light or yellow eye is usually an indication that electrolyte supply has dropped below the necessary level for battery (and hydrometer) operation. In this last case, sealed batteries with an insufficient electrolyte level must usually be discarded.**

Specific Gravity

As stated earlier, the specific gravity of a battery's electrolyte level can be used as an indication of battery charge. At least once a year, check the specific gravity of the battery. It should be between 1.20 and 1.26 on the gravity scale. Most auto supply stores carry a variety of inexpensive battery testing hydrometers. These can be used on any non-sealed battery to test the specific gravity in each cell.

The battery testing hydrometer has a squeeze bulb at one end and a nozzle at the other. Battery electrolyte is sucked into the hydrometer until the float is lifted from its seat. The specific gravity is then read by noting the position of the float. If gravity is low in one or more cells, the battery should be slowly charged and checked again to see if the gravity has come up. Generally, if after charging, the specific gravity between any two cells varies more than 50 points (0.50), the battery should be replaced as it can no longer produce sufficient voltage to guarantee proper operation.

On sealed batteries, the built-in hydrometer is the only way of checking specific gravity. Again, check with your battery's manufacturer for proper interpretation of its built-in hydrometer readings.

CABLES

▶ **See Figures 66, 67, 68, 69, 70 and 71**

Once a year (or as necessary), the battery terminals and the cable clamps should be cleaned. Loosen the clamps and remove the cables, negative cable first. On batteries with posts on top, the use of a puller specially made for this purpose is recommended. These are inexpensive and available in most auto parts stores. Side terminal battery cables are secured with a small bolt.

Clean the cable clamps and the battery terminal with a wire brush, until all corrosion, grease, etc., is removed and the metal is shiny. It is especially important to clean the inside of the clamp (an old knife is useful here) thoroughly, since a small deposit of foreign material or oxidation there will prevent a sound electrical connection and inhibit either starting or

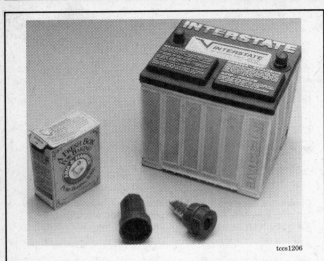

Fig. 66 Maintenance is performed with household items and with special tools like this post cleaner

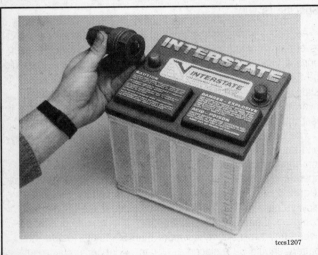

Fig. 67 The underside of this special battery tool has a wire brush to clean post terminals

Fig. 68 Place the tool over the terminals and twist to clean the post

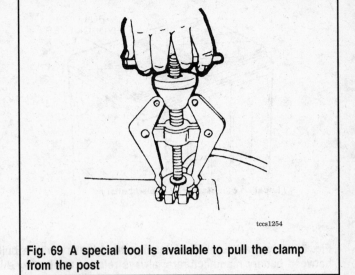

Fig. 69 A special tool is available to pull the clamp from the post

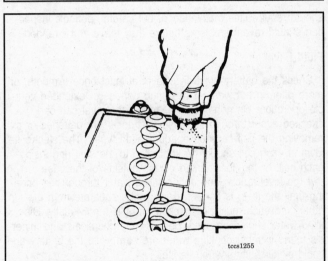

Fig. 70 Clean the battery terminals until the metal is shiny

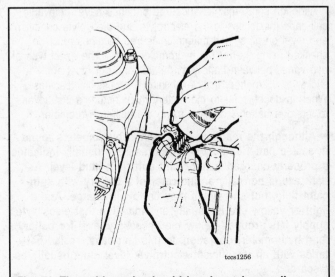

Fig. 71 The cable ends should be cleaned as well

charging. Special tools are available for cleaning these parts, one type for conventional top post batteries and another type for side terminal batteries.

Before installing the cables, loosen the battery hold-down clamp or strap, remove the battery and check the battery tray. Clear it of any debris, and check it for soundness (the battery tray can be cleaned with a baking soda and water solution). Rust should be wire brushed away, and the metal given a couple coats of anti-rust paint. Install the battery and tighten the hold-down clamp or strap securely. Do not overtighten, as this can crack the battery case.

After the clamps and terminals are clean, reinstall the cables, negative cable last; DO NOT hammer the clamps onto post batteries. Tighten the clamps securely, but do not distort them. Give the clamps and terminals a thin external coating of grease after installation, to retard corrosion.

Check the cables at the same time that the terminals are cleaned. If the cable insulation is cracked or broken, or if the ends are frayed, the cable should be replaced with a new cable of the same length and gauge.

CHARGING

✳✳CAUTION

The chemical reaction which takes place in all batteries generates explosive hydrogen gas. A spark can cause the battery to explode and splash acid. To avoid serious personal injury, be sure there is proper ventilation and take appropriate fire safety precautions when connecting, disconnecting, or charging a battery and when using jumper cables.

A battery should be charged at a slow rate to keep the plates inside from getting too hot. However, if some maintenance-free batteries are allowed to discharge until they are almost "dead," they may have to be charged at a high rate to bring them back to "life." Always follow the charger manufacturer's instructions on charging the battery.

REPLACEMENT

When it becomes necessary to replace the battery, select one with a rating equal to or greater than the battery originally installed. Deterioration and just plain aging of the battery cables, starter motor, and associated wires makes the battery's job harder in successive years. The slow increase in electrical resistance over time makes it prudent to install a new battery with a greater capacity than the old.

Belts

INSPECTION

▶ **See Figures 72, 73, 74, 75 and 76**

Belts should be inspected at 30,000 mile (48,300 km) intervals and replaced at 60,000 mile (96,500 km) intervals or at the first sign of deterioration.

Inspect belts for signs of glazing or cracking. A glazed belt will be perfectly smooth from slippage, while a good belt will have a slight texture of fabric visible. Cracks usually start at the inner edge of the belt and run outward. All worn or damaged drive belts should be replaced immediately. It is best to replace all drive belts at one time, as a preventive maintenance measure, during this service operation.

Proper drive belt tension adjustment is important, inadequate tension will result in slippage and wear, while excessive ten-

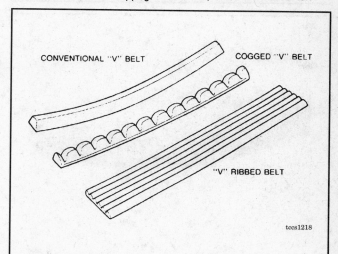

Fig. 72 There are typically 3 types of accessory drive belts found on vehicles today

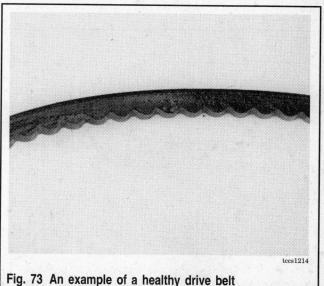

Fig. 73 An example of a healthy drive belt

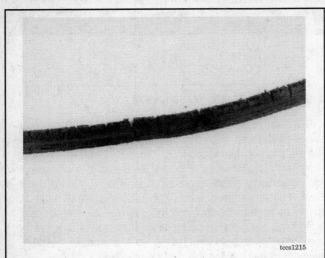

Fig. 74 Deep cracks in this belt will cause flex, building up heat that will eventually lead to belt failure

Fig. 75 The cover of this belt is worn, exposing the critical reinforcing cords to excessive wear

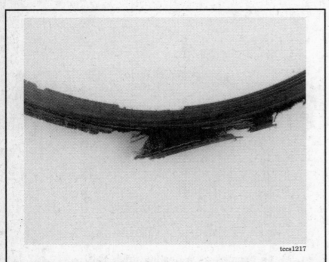

Fig. 76 Installing too wide a belt can result in serious belt wear and/or breakage

sion will damage the water pump and alternator bearings and cause the belt to fray and crack.

TENSION ADJUSTMENT

▶ See Figures 77 and 78

Front Side Belt

EXCEPT LEGACY AND SVX

▶ See Figures 79 and 80

1. Loosen the alternator mounting bolts.
2. Move the alternator to increase the tension, or decrease to reduce the belt tension.
3. Tighten the alternator mounting bolts.

LEGACY AND SVX

▶ See Figures 81, 82, 83, 84 and 85

1. Remove the drive belt cover over the belt by removing the retaining bolts at both ends of the bracket.

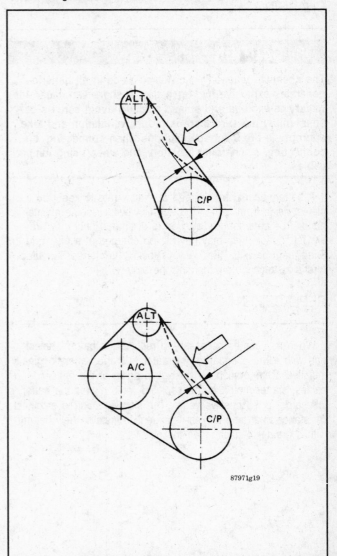

Fig. 77 Check the accessory belt tension by pressing and measuring the amount of deflection

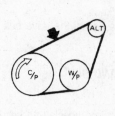
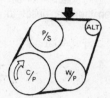
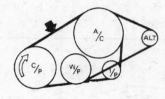
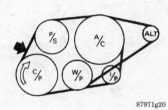

Fig. 78 Check the belt tension on 1.8L and 2.7L engines at the appropriate arrowed area, based on the number of pulleys

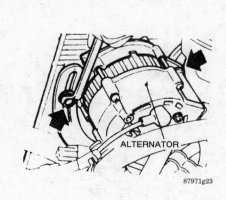

Fig. 79 Loosen the retaining and bracket bolt, and move the alternator to adjust the belt tension — 1.2L, 1.8L and 2.7L engines

Fig. 80 Use a suitable prytool to tension the belt while tightening the bolt — 1.6L engine shown

Fig. 81 Loosen and remove the belt cover retainer bolts — 2.2L, 2.5L and 3.3L engines

Fig. 82 Lift the belt cover off and place aside

Fig. 83 Loosen the belt adjuster bolt

Fig. 84 Loosen the adjuster bolt's lower clamp retainer bolt

Fig. 85 Remove the belts from the pulleys

2. Loosen the locknut and adjust the slider bolt to obtain the correct belt tension.

3. Tighten the locknut.

4. When complete, install the drive belt cover.

Rear Side Belt

EXCEPT LEGACY AND SVX

▶ **See Figure 86**

1. Loosen the bolt and special nut securing the idler pulley.

2. Tighten or loosen the idler pulley to obtain the correct belt tension.

3. Tighten the bolt and special nut.

LEGACY AND SVX

▶ **See Figure 87**

1. Loosen both the lockbolt and locknut on the slider bracket.

2. Adjust the slider pulley forward or backwards to obtain the correct belt tension.

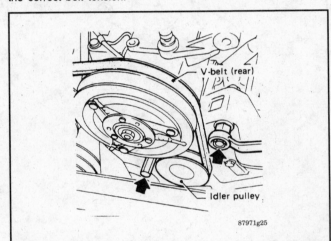

Fig. 86 Loosen the lockbolt below the belt and next to the pulley, then adjust the idler pulley to correct the belt tension

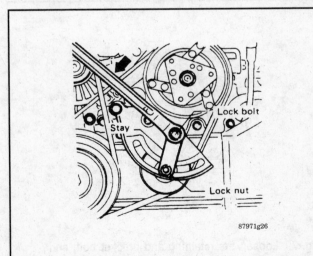

Fig. 87 Loosen the locknut and lockbolt, and rotate the pulley to adjust the belt tension

3. Tighten the lockbolt.

Timing Belt

The cogged timing belt at the front of all Subaru engines is a combination of woven fabric and rubber. Although this type of belt offers many advantages over the traditional timing chain, including extended service intervals and a smoother more quiet running engines, this type of belt should be inspected on a regular basis, and changed according to the manufacturer change interval.

➡The recommended timing belt change interval for all engines covered by this manual is 60,000 miles (96,000 km).

INSPECTION

◆ **See Figures 88, 89, 90, 91, 92 and 93**

1. Remove both left and right side timing belt covers by unfastening the retaining bolts.
2. Disconnect the high tension wire from the coil.
3. Have an assistant crank the engine at least four rotations while you inspect the timing belt. Inspect the back surface of the timing belt for cracks or damage. Inspect the inside of the belt for cracks, missing teeth or other signs of damage.
4. Measure the timing belt width. If the width is less than 1.06 in. (27mm), inspect the idler, tension, water pump and cam pulley for proper alignment.
5. If during inspection, the timing belt shows any sign of wear or damage, replace the belt immediately. Refer to the procedure in Section 3 for more details.

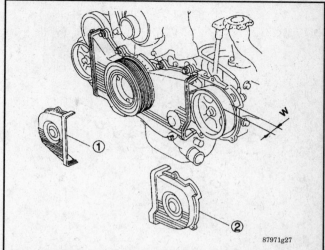

Fig. 89 Remove the timing belt covers (1 and 2), and measure the timing belt width (W)

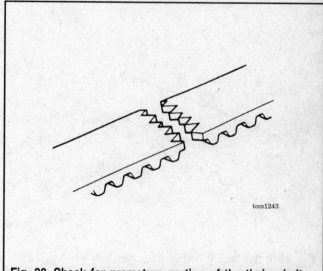

Fig. 90 Check for premature parting of the timing belt

Fig. 88 Do not bend, twist or turn a timing belt inside out. Never expose a timing belt to oil, water or steam

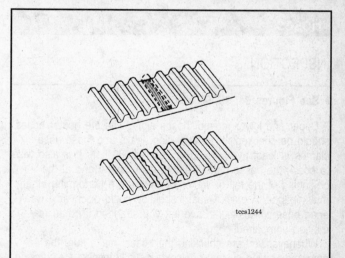

Fig. 91 Check the teeth of the timing belt for cracks or damage

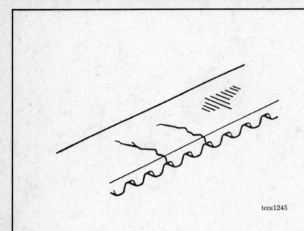

Fig. 92 Check the belt face for noticeable cracks or wear

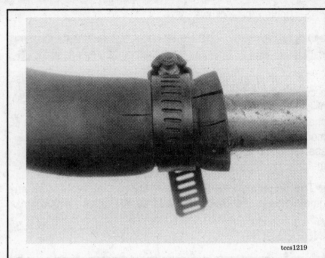

Fig. 94 The cracks developing along this hose are a result of age-related hardening

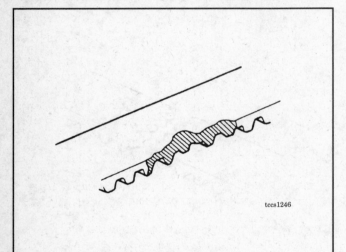

Fig. 93 If the timing belt is damaged only on one side, a pulley may be the culprit

Fig. 95 A hose clamp that is too tight can cause older hoses to separate and tear on either side of the clamp

Hoses

INSPECTION

▶ See Figures 94, 95, 96 and 97

Upper and lower radiator hoses along with the heater hoses should be checked for deterioration, leaks and loose hose clamps at least every 15,000 miles (24,000 km). It is also wise to check the hoses periodically in early spring and at the beginning of the fall or winter when you are performing other maintenance. A quick visual inspection could discover a weakened hose which might have left you stranded if it had remained unrepaired.

Whenever you are checking the hoses, make sure the engine and cooling system are cold. Visually inspect for cracking, rotting or collapsed hoses, and replace as necessary. Run your hand along the length of the hose. If a weak or swollen

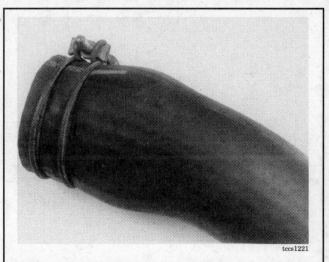

Fig. 96 A soft spongy hose (identifiable by the swollen section) will eventually burst and should be replaced

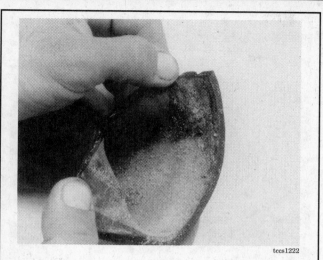

tccs1222

Fig. 97 Hoses are likely to deteriorate from the inside if the cooling system is not periodically flushed

spot is noted when squeezing the hose wall, the hose should be replaced.

REMOVAL & INSTALLATION

▶ See Figure 98

1. Remove the radiator pressure cap, or cap from the expansion tank.

❊❊CAUTION

Never remove the pressure cap while the engine is running, or personal injury from scalding hot coolant or steam may result. If possible, wait until the engine has cooled to remove the pressure cap. If this is not possible, wrap a thick cloth around the pressure cap and turn it

87971p25

Fig. 98 Use a screwdriver to loosen the clamp around the hose

slowly to the stop. Step back while the pressure is released from the cooling system. When you are sure all the pressure has been released, use the cloth to turn and remove the cap.

2. Position a clean container under the radiator and/or engine draincock or plug, then open the drain and allow the cooling system to drain to an appropriate level. For some upper hoses, only a little coolant must be drained. To remove hoses positioned lower on the engine, such as a lower radiator hose, the entire cooling system must be emptied.

❊❊CAUTION

When draining coolant, keep in mind that cats and dogs are attracted to ethylene glycol antifreeze, and could drink any that is left in an uncovered container or in puddles on the ground. This will prove fatal in sufficient quantity. Always drain coolant into a suitable container. Coolant may be reused unless it is contaminated or several years old.

3. Loosen the hose clamps at each end of the hose requiring replacement. Clamps are usually either of the spring tension type (which require pliers to squeeze the tabs and loosen) or of the screw tension type (which require screw or hex drivers to loosen). Pull the clamps back on the hose away from the connection.

4. Twist, pull and slide the hose off the fitting, taking care not to damage the neck of the component from which the hose is being removed.

➡If the hose is stuck at the connection, do not try to insert a screwdriver or other sharp tool under the hose end in an effort to free it, as the connection and/or hose may become damaged. Heater connections especially may be easily damaged by such a procedure. If the hose is to be replaced, use a single-edged razor blade to make a slice along the portion of the hose which is stuck on the connection, perpendicular to the end of the hose. Do not cut deep so as to prevent damaging the connection. The hose can then be peeled from the connection and discarded.

5. Clean both hose mounting connections. Inspect the condition of the hose clamps and replace them, if necessary.

To install:

6. Dip the ends of the new hose into clean engine coolant to ease installation.

7. Slide the clamps over the replacement hose, then slide the hose ends over the connections into position.

8. Position and secure the clamps at least 1/4 in. (6.35mm) from the ends of the hose. Make sure they are located beyond the raised bead of the connector.

9. Close the radiator or engine drains and properly refill the cooling system with the clean drained engine coolant or a suitable mixture of ethylene glycol coolant and water.

10. If available, install a pressure tester and check for leaks. If a pressure tester is not available, run the engine until normal

operating temperature is reached (allowing the system to naturally pressurize), then check for leaks.

✳✳CAUTION

If you are checking for leaks with the system at normal operating temperature, BE EXTREMELY CAREFUL not to touch any moving or hot engine parts. Once temperature has been reached, shut the engine OFF, and check for leaks around the hose fittings and connections which were removed earlier.

CV-Boots

INSPECTION

▶ **See Figures 99 and 100**

The CV (Constant Velocity) boots should be checked for damage each time the oil is changed and any other time the vehicle is raised for service. These boots keep water, grime, dirt and other damaging matter from entering the CV-joints. Any of these could cause early CV-joint failure which can be expensive to repair. Heavy grease thrown around the inside of the front wheel(s) and on the brake caliper/drum can be an indication of a torn boot. Thoroughly check the boots for missing clamps and tears. If the boot is damaged, it should be replaced immediately. Please refer to Section 7 for procedures.

Spark Plugs

▶ **See Figure 101**

A typical spark plug consists of a metal shell surrounding a ceramic insulator. A metal electrode extends downward through the center of the insulator and protrudes a small distance. Located at the end of the plug and attached to the side of the outer metal shell is the side electrode. The side electrode bends in at a 90° angle so that its tip is just past and parallel

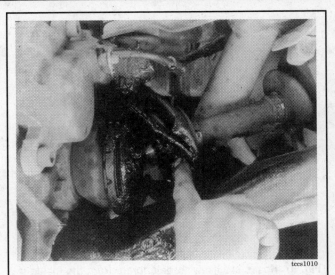

tccs1010

Fig. 100 A torn boot should be replaced immediately

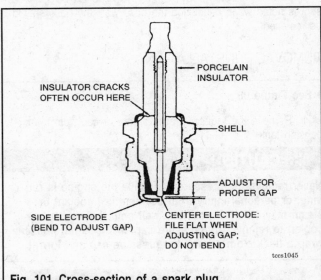

tccs1045

Fig. 101 Cross-section of a spark plug

to the tip of the center electrode. The distance between these two electrodes (measured in thousandths of an inch or hundredths of a millimeter) is called the spark plug gap.

A typical spark plug consists of a metal shell surrounding a ceramic insulator. A metal electrode extends downward through the center of the insulator and protrudes a small distance. Located at the end of the plug and attached to the side of the outer metal shell is the side electrode. The side electrode bends in at a 90° angle so that its tip is just past and parallel to the tip of the center electrode. The distance between these two electrodes (measured in thousandths of an inch or hundredths of a millimeter) is called the spark plug gap.

The spark plug does not produce a spark but instead provides a gap across which the current can arc. The coil produces anywhere from 20,000 to 50,000 volts (depending on the type and application) which travels through the wires to the spark plugs. The current passes along the center electrode and jumps the gap to the side electrode, and in doing so, ignites the air/fuel mixture in the combustion chamber.

tccs1011

Fig. 99 CV-boots must be inspected periodically for damage

SPARK PLUG HEAT RANGE

◗ **See Figure 102**

Spark plug heat range is the ability of the plug to dissipate heat. The longer the insulator (or the farther it extends into the engine), the hotter the plug will operate; the shorter the insulator (the closer the electrode is to the block's cooling passages) the cooler it will operate. A plug that absorbs little heat and remains too cool will quickly accumulate deposits of oil and carbon since it is not hot enough to burn them off. This leads to plug fouling and consequently to misfiring. A plug that absorbs too much heat will have no deposits but, due to the excessive heat, the electrodes will burn away quickly and might possibly lead to preignition or other ignition problems. Preignition takes place when plug tips get so hot that they glow sufficiently to ignite the air/fuel mixture before the actual spark occurs. This early ignition will usually cause a pinging during low speeds and heavy loads.

The general rule of thumb for choosing the correct heat range when picking a spark plug is: if most of your driving is long distance, high speed travel, use a colder plug; if most of your driving is stop and go, use a hotter plug. Original equipment plugs are generally a good compromise between the 2 styles and most people never have the need to change their plugs from the factory-recommended heat range.

REMOVAL & INSTALLATION

◗ **See Figures 103 and 104**

➡ **Remove the spark plugs and wires one at a time to avoid confusion and miswiring during installation.**

1. Disconnect the negative battery cable, and if the vehicle has been run recently, allow the engine to thoroughly cool.
2. If removing the spark plugs on 3.3L engines, remove the ignition coil over the spark plug. Refer to the procedure in Section 2.
3. Carefully twist the spark plug wire boot to loosen it, then pull upward and remove the boot from the plug. Be sure to

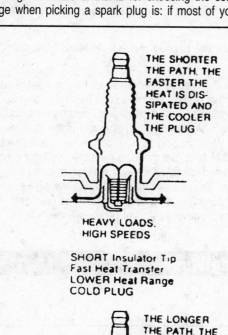

THE SHORTER THE PATH, THE FASTER THE HEAT IS DISSIPATED AND THE COOLER THE PLUG

HEAVY LOADS. HIGH SPEEDS

SHORT Insulator Tip
Fast Heat Transfer
LOWER Heat Range
COLD PLUG

THE LONGER THE PATH, THE SLOWER THE HEAT IS DISSIPATED AND THE HOTTER THE PLUG

SHORT TRIP
STOP-AND-GO

LONG Insulator Tip
Slow Heat Transfer
HIGHER Heat Range
HOT PLUG

tccs1046

Fig. 102 Spark plug heat range

87971p49

Fig. 103 Unfasten the spark plug wire to access the spark plug

87971p50

Fig. 104 Use the correct sized spark plug socket to loosen and remove the spark plug

pull on the boot and not on the wire, otherwise the connector located inside the boot may become separated.

4. Using compressed air, blow any water or debris from the spark plug well to assure that no harmful contaminants are allowed to enter the combustion chamber when the spark plug is removed. If compressed air is not available, use a rag or a brush to clean the area.

→Remove the spark plugs when the engine is cold, if possible, to prevent damage to the threads. If removal of the plugs is difficult, apply a few drops of penetrating oil or silicone spray to the area around the base of the plug, and allow it a few minutes to work.

5. Using a spark plug socket that is equipped with a rubber insert to properly hold the plug, turn the spark plug counter-clockwise to loosen and remove the spark plug from the bore.

❈❈WARNING

Be sure not to use a flexible extension on the socket. Use of a flexible extension may allow a shear force to be applied to the plug. A shear force could break the plug off in the cylinder head, leading to costly and frustrating repairs.

To install:

6. Inspect the spark plug boot for tears or damage. If a damaged boot is found, the spark plug wire must be replaced.

7. Using a wire feeler gauge, check and adjust the spark plug gap. When using a gauge, the proper size should pass between the electrodes with a slight drag. The next larger size should not be able to pass while the next smaller size should pass freely.

8. Carefully thread the plug into the bore by hand. If resistance is felt before the plug is almost completely threaded, back the plug out and begin threading again. In small to reach areas, an old spark plug wire and boot could be used as a threading tool. The boot will hold the plug while you twist the end of the wire and the wire is supple enough to twist before it would allow the plug to crossthread.

❈❈WARNING

Do not use the spark plug socket to thread the plugs. Always carefully thread the plug by hand or using an old plug wire to prevent the possibility of cross-threading and damaging the cylinder head bore.

9. Carefully tighten the spark plug. If the plug you are installing is equipped with a crush washer, seat the plug, then tighten about ¼ turn to crush the washer. If you are installing a tapered seat plug, tighten the plug to specifications provided by the vehicle or plug manufacturer.

10. Apply a small amount of silicone dielectric compound to the end of the spark plug lead or inside the spark plug boot to prevent sticking, then install the boot to the spark plug and push until it clicks into place. The click may be felt or heard, then gently pull back on the boot to assure proper contact.

INSPECTION & GAPPING

▶ See Figures 105, 106, 107, 108, 109, 110, 111, 112, 113, 114 and 115

Check the plugs for deposits and wear. If they are not going to be replaced, clean the plugs thoroughly. Remember that any kind of deposit will decrease the efficiency of the plug. Plugs can be cleaned on a spark plug cleaning machine, which can sometimes be found in service stations, or you can do an acceptable job of cleaning with a stiff brush. If the plugs are cleaned, the electrodes must be filed flat. Use an ignition points file, not an emery board or the like, which will leave deposits. The electrodes must be filed perfectly flat with sharp edges; rounded edges reduce the spark plug voltage by as much as 50%.

Check spark plug gap before installation. The ground electrode (the L-shaped one connected to the body of the plug) must be parallel to the center electrode and the specified size wire gauge (please refer to the Tune-Up Specifications chart for details) must pass between the electrodes with a slight drag.

→NEVER adjust the gap on a used platinum type spark plug.

Always check the gap on new plugs as they are not always set correctly at the factory. Do not use a flat feeler gauge when measuring the gap on a used plug, because the reading may be inaccurate. A wire type gapping tool is the best way to check the gap. Wire gapping tools usually have a bending tool attached. Use that to adjust the side electrode until the proper distance is obtained. Absolutely never attempt to bend the center electrode. Also, be careful not to bend the side electrode too far or too often as it may weaken and break off within the engine, requiring removal of the cylinder head to retrieve it.

Spark Plug Wires

TESTING

▶ See Figures 116 and 117

At every tune-up/inspection, visually check the spark plug cables for burns cuts, or breaks in the insulation. Check the boots and the nipples on the distributor cap and coil. Replace any damaged wiring.

Every 30,000 miles (48,000 km) or 60 months, the resistance of the wires should be checked with an ohmmeter. Wires with excessive resistance will cause misfiring, and may make the engine difficult to start in damp weather.

To check resistance, remove the distributor cap, leaving the wires attached. Connect one lead of an ohmmeter to an electrode within the cap. Connect the other lead to the corresponding spark plug terminal (remove it from the plug for this test). Replace any wire which shows excessive resistance.

GAP BRIDGED

IDENTIFIED BY DEPOSIT BUILD-UP CLOSING GAP BETWEEN ELECTRODES.

CAUSED BY OIL OR CARBON FOULING. REPLACE PLUG, OR, IF DEPOSITS ARE NOT EXCESSIVE THE PLUG CAN BE CLEANED.

OIL FOULED

IDENTIFIED BY WET BLACK DEPOSITS ON THE INSULATOR SHELL BORE ELECTRODES.

CAUSED BY EXCESSIVE OIL ENTERING COMBUSTION CHAMBER THROUGH WORN RINGS AND PISTONS, EXCESSIVE CLEARANCE BETWEEN VALVE GUIDES AND STEMS, OR WORN OR LOOSE BEARINGS. CORRECT OIL PROBLEM. REPLACE THE PLUG.

CARBON FOULED

IDENTIFIED BY BLACK, DRY FLUFFY CARBON DEPOSITS ON INSULATOR TIPS, EXPOSED SHELL SURFACES AND ELECTRODES.

CAUSED BY TOO COLD A PLUG, WEAK IGNITION, DIRTY AIR CLEANER, DEFECTIVE FUEL PUMP, TOO RICH A FUEL MIXTURE, IMPROPERLY OPERATING HEAT RISER OR EXCESSIVE IDLING. CAN BE CLEANED.

NORMAL

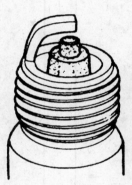

IDENTIFIED BY LIGHT TAN OR GRAY DEPOSITS ON THE FIRING TIP.

PRE-IGNITION

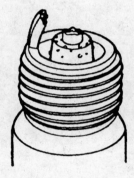

IDENTIFIED BY MELTED ELECTRODES AND POSSIBLY BLISTERED INSULATOR. METALIC DEPOSITS ON INSULATOR INDICATE ENGINE DAMAGE.

CAUSED BY WRONG TYPE OF FUEL, INCORRECT IGNITION TIMING OR ADVANCE, TOO HOT A PLUG, BURNT VALVES OR ENGINE OVERHEATING. REPLACE THE PLUG.

OVERHEATING

IDENTIFIED BY A WHITE OR LIGHT GRAY INSULATOR WITH SMALL BLACK OR GRAY BROWN SPOTS AND WITH BLUISH-BURNT APPEARANCE OF ELECTRODES.

CAUSED BY ENGINE OVERHEATING, WRONG TYPE OF FUEL, LOOSE SPARK PLUGS, TOO HOT A PLUG, LOW FUEL PUMP PRESSURE OR INCORRECT IGNITION TIMING. REPLACE THE PLUG.

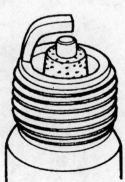

FUSED SPOT DEPOSIT

IDENTIFIED BY MELTED OR SPOTTY DEPOSITS RESEMBLING BUBBLES OR BLISTERS.

CAUSED BY SUDDEN ACCELERATION. CAN BE CLEANED IF NOT EXCESSIVE, OTHERWISE REPLACE PLUG.

tccs2002

Fig. 105 Inspect the spark plug to determine engine running conditions

Fig. 106 A normally worn spark plug should have light tan or gray deposits on the firing tip

Fig. 107 A carbon fouled plug, identified by soft, sooty, black deposits, may indicate an improperly tuned vehicle. Check the air cleaner, ignition components and engine control system

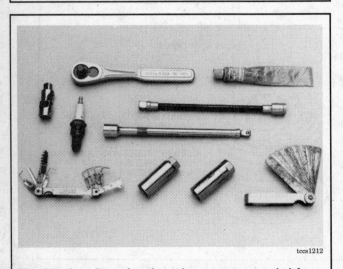

Fig. 108 A variety of tools and gauges are needed for spark plug service

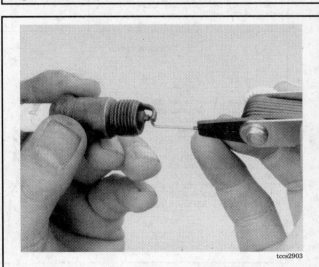

Fig. 109 Checking the spark plug gap with a feeler gauge

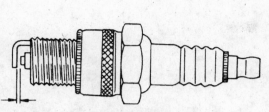

1.0 — 1.1 mm (0.039 — 0.043 in)

Spark plug thread
Dia. = 14 mm (0.55 in)
Pitch = 1.25 mm (0.0492 in)

87971g28

Fig. 110 Correct spark plug gap

tccs2138

Fig. 112 An oil fouled spark plug indicates an engine with worn piston rings and/or bad valve seals, allowing excessive oil to enter the chamber

tccs2137

Fig. 111 A physically damaged spark plug may be evidence of severe detonation in that cylinder. Watch that cylinder carefully between services, as a continued detonation will not only damage the plug, but could also damage the engine

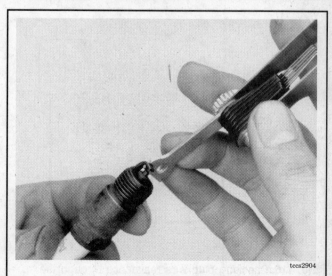

tccs2904

Fig. 113 Adjusting the spark plug gap

Fig. 114 This spark plug has been left in the engine too long, as evidenced by the extreme gap. Plugs with such an extreme gap can cause misfiring and stumbling, accompanied by a noticeable lack of power

Fig. 115 A bridged or almost bridged spark plug, identified by a build-up between the electrodes, caused by excessive carbon or oil build-up on the plug

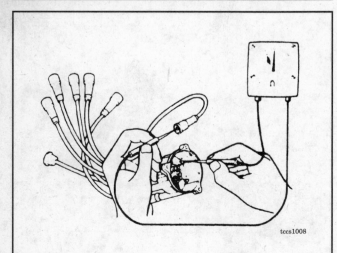

Fig. 116 Checking plug wire resistance through the distributor cap with an ohmmeter

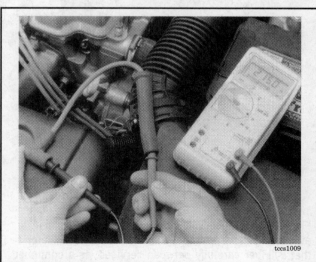

Fig. 117 Checking individual plug wire resistance with a digital ohmmeter

It should be remembered that resistance is also a function of length; the longer the wire the greater the resistance. The following is a guide to the resistance of spark plug wires:

- Up to 15 in. (381mm): 3000-10,000 ohms
- 15-25 in. (381-635mm): 4000-15,000 ohms
- 25-35 in. (635-889mm): 6000-20,000 ohms
- Over 35 in. (889mm): 6000-25,000 ohms

If the spark plug wires are found to be defective, replace the wires one at a time. Install the boot firmly over the spark plug. Route the wire over the same path as the original. Insert the nipple firmly into the tower on the cap or the coil.

➡**A little smear of dielectric grease inside the boots of the spark plug wires will prevent corrosion, and aid in boot removal the next time the plugs are serviced.**

REMOVAL & INSTALLATION

▶ **See Figure 118**

1. Label each spark plug wire before removing. If you are removing more than one wire at a time, mark both the plug wire and the corresponding location on the distributor cap, or ignition coil pack.
2. Remove the plug wire from the end of the spark plug by grasping the wire by the rubber boot. If the boot sticks to the plug, remove it by twisting back and forth, then pulling up on the boot. DO NOT pull the wire itself or you will damage the core.
3. Remove the plug wire from the distributor cap or ignition coil pack, by grasping the wire by the rubber boot and pulling upward. If the boot sticks, twist back and forth on the boot, then pull up on the boot. DO NOT pull the wire itself or you will damage the core.

To install:

4. Insert the smaller end of the plug wire into the distributor cap until tight.
5. Insert the other end of the spark plug wire on to the correct spark plug, by twisting the plug wire down on the spark plug.
6. Continue until all wires are installed.

Distributor Cap and Rotor

REMOVAL & INSTALLATION

1. Disconnect the negative battery cable.
2. Identify and tag each spark plug wire, then make a corresponding identification mark on the distributor cap.
3. Remove each spark plug wire from the distributor cap, one at a time.
4. Remove the distributor cap by unfastening the two spring clips securing the cap to the distributor body.
5. Detach the rotor cap from the assembly by pulling the cap straight up and off.

To install:

6. Position the rotor on to the distributor shaft, making sure the tab on the distributor aligns correctly with the tab on the rotor. Once aligned, push the rotor down until secured in position.
7. Place the distributor cap on to the distributor, making sure the tab on the distributor aligns with the tab on the cap. When in place, secure the cap by depressing the spring clips into place.
8. Install each spark plug wire to the correct position on the distributor cap as outlined in the spark plug wire procedure in this section

INSPECTION

▶ **See Figure 119**

1. Check the outside and inside of the distributor cap for signs of cracks, damage, burns or dirt, and replace if needed.
2. Inspect the electrodes inside the cap and replace if the contacts are either burnt or excessively rusted.
3. Inspect the center carbon contact point. Make sure the contact spring can move freely, and the amount of carbon protruding out of the cap is at least 0.87 in. (2.2mm).

Fig. 118 Twist off the plug wire from the distributor cap or coil pack — 2.2L engine shown

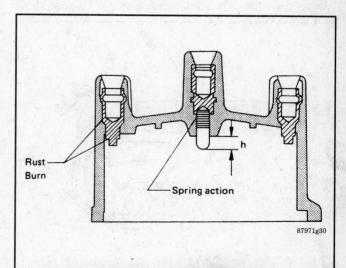

Fig. 119 The carbon contact length should be at least 0.087 in. (2.2mm) for proper distributor cap operation

Ignition Timing

GENERAL INFORMATION

▶ See Figure 120

Ignition timing is the measurement, in degrees of crankshaft rotation, of the point at which the spark plugs fire in the cylinders. It is measured in degrees before or after Top Dead Center (TDC) of the compression stroke.

Because it takes a fraction of a second for the spark plug to ignite the mixture in the cylinder, the spark plug must fire a little before the piston reaches TDC. Otherwise, the mixture will not be completely ignited as the piston passes TDC and the full power of the explosion will not be used by the engine.

The timing measurement is given in degrees of crankshaft rotation before the piston reaches TDC (BTDC). If the setting for the ignition timing is 8° BTDC, the spark plug must fire 8° before each piston reaches TDC. This only holds true, however, when the engine is at idle speed.

As the engine speed increases, the pistons go faster. The spark plugs have to ignite the fuel even sooner if it is to be completely ignited when the piston reaches TDC. To do this, the distributor has two means to advance the timing of the spark as the engine speed increases: a set of centrifugal weights within the distributor, and a vacuum diaphragm, mounted on the side of the distributor.

If the ignition is set too far advanced (BTDC), the ignition and expansion of the fuel in the cylinder will occur too soon and tend to force the piston down while it is still traveling up. This causes engine ping. If the ignition spark is set too far retarded, after TDC (ATDC), the piston will have already passed TDC and started on its way down when the fuel is ignited. This will cause the piston to be forced down for only a portion of its travel. This results in poor engine performance and lack of power.

Timing marks consist of a scale of degrees on the flywheel and a pointer on the flywheel cover hole. The scale corresponds to the position of the flywheel and a pointer on the flywheel cover hole. The pointer corresponds to the position of the piston in the number 1 cylinder. A stroboscopic (dynamic) timing light is used, which is hooked into the circuit of the No. 1 cylinder spark plug. Every time the spark plug fires, the timing light flashes. By aiming the timing light at the timing marks, the exact position of the piston within the cylinder can be read, since the stroboscopic flash makes the mark appear to be standing still. Proper timing is indicated when the pointer is aligned with the correct number on the scale.

There are three basic types of timing light available. The first is a simple neon bulb with two wire connections (one for the spark plug and one for the plug wire, connecting the light in series). This type of light is quite dim, and must be held closely to the marks to be seen, but it is inexpensive. The second type of light operates from the car battery. Two alligator clips connect to the battery terminals, while a third wire connects to the spark plug with an adapter. This type of light is more expensive, but the xenon bulb provides a nice bright flash which can even be seen in sunlight. The third type replaces the battery source with 110 volt house current. Some timing lights have other functions built into them, such as dwell meters, tachometers, or remote starting switches. These are convenient, in that they reduce the tangle of wires under the hood, but may duplicate the functions of tools you already have.

If your Subaru has electronic ignition, you should use a timing light with an inductive pickup. This pickup simply clamps onto the No. 1 plug wire, eliminating the adapter. It is not susceptible to crossfiring or false triggering, which may occur with a conventional light, due to the greater voltages produced by electronic ignition.

TIMING MARK LOCATIONS

▶ See Figures 121, 122, 123, 124, 125 and 126

The ignition timing marks on the 1.2L engine, are located at the front of the engine, on the crankshaft pulley. On 1.6L and 1.8L engines except XT models, the ignition timing marks are located on the edge of the flywheel, at the rear of the engine. The marks mounted on the flywheel are visible through a port in the flywheel housing located just behind the oil dipstick

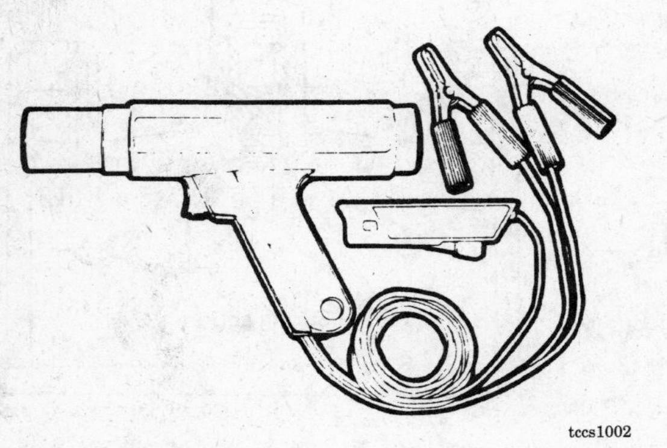

tccs1002

Fig. 120 An example of an inductive timing light

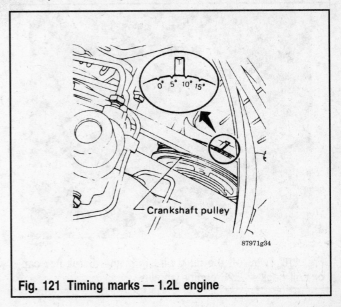

Crankshaft pulley

87971g34

Fig. 121 Timing marks — 1.2L engine

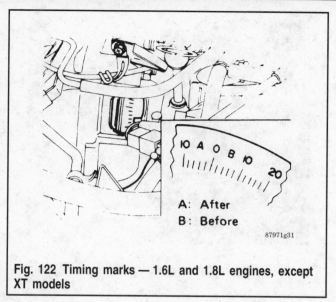

Fig. 122 Timing marks — 1.6L and 1.8L engines, except XT models

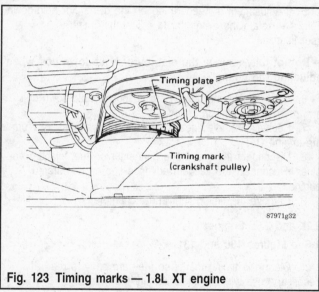

Fig. 123 Timing marks — 1.8L XT engine

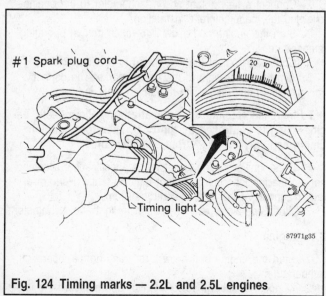

Fig. 124 Timing marks — 2.2L and 2.5L engines

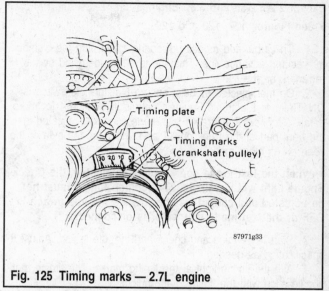

Fig. 125 Timing marks — 2.7L engine

Fig. 126 Timing marks on a transaxle bell housing — 1.6L engine

tube. A plastic cover protects the port through which the fly-wheel-mounted marks are visible.

The ignition timing marks on XT models (1.8L and 2.7L engines), are located on the right front side of the engine, near the crankshaft pulley.

On 2.2L and 2.5L engine, the ignition timing marks are located on the front of the engine, near the crankshaft pulley.

The 3.3L engine has no timing marks because timing on the 3.3L engine is determined by the fuel injection system control unit and cannot be adjusted without the use of a Subaru Select Monitor test tool.

ADJUSTMENT

➡An inductive timing light is highly recommended, as it is not susceptible to cross-firing or false triggering.

Except 2.2L, 2.5L and 3.3L Engines

▶ **See Figures 127, 128 and 129**

1. On carbureted models, disconnect and plug the distributor vacuum advance line. This line is easily identified by the red mark on the line.

2. On fuel injected models, ensure that the idle switch is **ON**. Refer to Electronic Engine Controls in Section 4 for more details. Connect the (green) test mode connector, located in the front part of the trunk on XT and under the left side of the dash on all other models.

➡ **When the test mode connector is connected, the Check Engine light will illuminate. The ignition timing must not be adjusted and cannot be check while the idle switch is OFF or the test mode connector is disconnected.**

3. Start the engine and check and the idle speed. Adjust to specification as needed.

4. Aim the timing light at the timing marks. The timing mark should align with the timing mark indicator.

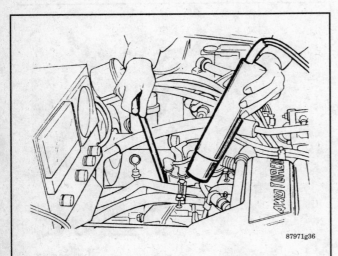

Fig. 127 Loosen the distributor hold-down bolt and rotate the distributor until the timing marks are aligned

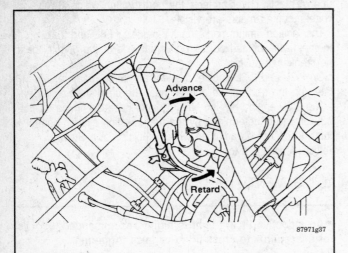

Fig. 128 Rotate the distributor clockwise to advance the timing, or counterclockwise to retard it

Fig. 129 Timing light pointed at the bell housing timing marks

5. If adjustment is needed, loosen the distributor hold-down bolt, then rotate the distributor to adjust the timing to specification.

➡ **Do not fully remove the distributor hold-down bolt when adjusting the timing.**

6. After adjustment, tighten the distributor hold-down bolt and recheck the ignition timing.

7. Recheck the idle speed and correct as necessary. Turn the engine **OFF**.

8. Disconnect the test mode connector on fuel injected engines. Reconnect the vacuum advance line on carbureted engines.

9. Remove the timing light and tachometer.

2.2L and 2.5L Engines

▶ **See Figures 130 and 131**

1. Clean the timing marks so they are easy to read. If necessary, use white paint to identify the marks.

2. Connect a timing light and a tachometer to the engine following the manufacturer's instruction.

3. Start the engine and allow it to reach normal operating temperature.

4. Check and adjust the idle speed to specification.

5. Aim the timing light at the timing marks. The correct timing mark should align with the timing mark indicator.

➡ **To increase stability on automatic transaxle models, engine idling is controlled by the ECU. Therefore, ignition timing can vary up to 8° from specification.**

6. If the ignition timing is not within specification, a component in the ignition control system may be faulty. Perform a fault diagnosis of the ignition control system.

7. When complete, remove the timing light and tachometer.

3.3L Engine

1. Start the engine and allow it to reach normal operating temperature.

2. Connect a Subaru Select Monitor and measure the ignition timing (function mode 07).

Fig. 130 Timing marks on lower portion of the engine block — 2.2L and 2.5L engines

Fig. 131 With the engine running, point the timing light at the marks

3. If the ignition timing is not correct, a component in the ignition control system may be faulty. Perform a fault diagnosis of the ignition control system.

4. When complete, disconnect the monitor and turn the engine **OFF**.

Valve Lash

Valve lash determines how far the valves enter the cylinder and how long they stay open and closed.

If the valve clearance is too large, part of the lift of the camshaft will be used in removing the excessive clearance. Consequently, the valve will not be opening as far or for as long as it should. This condition has two effects: the valve train components will emit a tapping sound as they take up the excessive clearance and the engine will perform poorly because the valves are not open fully to allow the proper amount of gases to flow into and out of the engine.

If the valve clearance is too small, the intake valves and the exhaust valves will open too far, stay open too long and will

not fully seat on the cylinder head when they close. When a valve seats itself on the cylinder head, it does two things: it seals the combustion chamber so that none of the gases in the cylinder escape, and it cools itself by transferring some of the heat it absorbs from the combustion in the cylinder to the cylinder head and into the cooling system. If the valve clearance is too small, the engine will run poorly because of the gases escaping from the combustion chamber. It may also run too lean. The valves will also become overheated and will warp, since they cannot transfer heat unless they are touching the valve seat in the cylinder head.

✳✳WARNING

While all valve adjustments must be made as accurately as possible, it is better to have the valve adjustment slightly loose than slightly tight, as a burned valve may result from overly tight adjustments.

ADJUSTMENT

▶ See Figures 132, 133, 134, 135 and 136

➡ The only engines which require valve lash adjustment are the 1.2L, 1.6L and 1.8L engines. The remaining engines are equipped with hydraulic lifter assemblies which adjust automatically.

The valve lash should be checked and adjusted every 15,000 miles (24,000 km). It is not necessary to adjust the valve lash on hydraulic lifter equipped vehicles.

➡ Before adjusting the valve clearance, check the cylinder head torque.

1. With the engine cold, rotate the engine so that the No. 1 piston is at Top Dead Center (TDC) of its compression stroke. The No. 1 piston is at top dead center when the distributor rotor is pointing to the No. 1 terminal (as though the distributor cap were in place) and the 0 mark on the flywheel or front pulley is opposite the pointer on the housing or front cover.

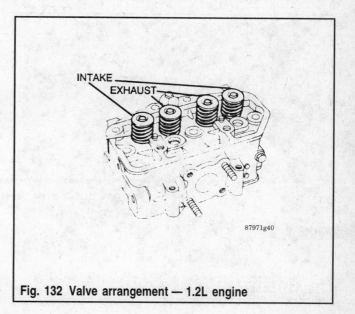

Fig. 132 Valve arrangement — 1.2L engine

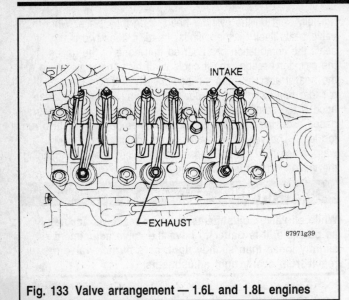

Fig. 133 Valve arrangement — 1.6L and 1.8L engines

Fig. 134 Remove the valve cover — 1.6L engine shown

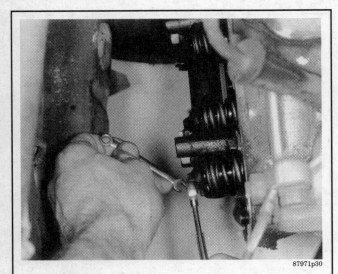

Fig. 135 Loosen the adjuster locknut

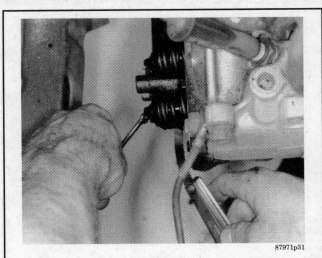

Fig. 136 Use a feeler gauge and wrench to adjust the gap if needed

2. Check the clearance of both the intake and exhaust valves of the No. 1 cylinder by inserting a feeler gauge between each valve stem and rocker arm.

3. If the clearance is not within specifications, loosen the locknut with the proper size wrench and turn the adjusting stud either in or out until the valve clearance is correct.

➡Proper valve clearance is obtained when the feeler gauge slides between the valve stem and the rocker arm with a minimum amount of resistance.

4. Tighten the locknut and recheck the valve stem-to-rocker clearance.

5. The rest of the valves are adjusted in the same way. Bring each piston to TDC of its compression stroke, then check and adjust the valves for that cylinder. The proper valve adjustment sequence is 1-3-2-4 for the 1.6L and 1.8L engines; 1-3-2 for the 1.2L engine.

6. Rotate the crankshaft at least two revolutions, then recheck the valve clearance.

7. Tighten the rocker arm locknuts to 12-17 ft. lbs. (17-23 Nm) for the 1.2L engine, and 10-13 ft. lbs. (14-18 Nm) for the 1.6L and 1.8L engines.

8. Install the valve covers using new gaskets. Tighten the retaining nuts to 5-6 ft. lbs. (6-7 Nm) on the 1.2L engine and 2-3 ft. lbs. (3-4 Nm) on the 1.6L and 1.8L engines.

Idle Speed and Mixture

ADJUSTMENT

Manual Carburetor
▶ See Figure 137

➡Inspection of engine idle speed should be carried out after checking the ignition timing and intake and exhaust valve clearances (except hydraulic lifter equipped models).

1. Position gear selector lever in the **N** position on vehicles equipped with manual transaxles, and in the **P** position on

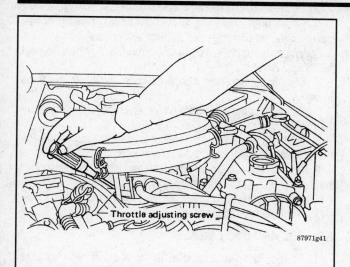

Fig. 137 Adjust the idle by rotating the throttle adjusting screw

vehicles equipped with automatic transaxles. Connect a tachometer in accordance with the manufacturer's instructions.

2. Start the engine and allow it to reach normal operating temperature.

3. Disconnect and plug the air suction hose on the air cleaner and the purge hose leading to the purge canister.

4. Check and adjust the engine to the proper idle speed by turning the throttle adjusting screw.

5. Remove the tachometer.

Electronic Feedback Carburetor (EFC)

WITHOUT AIR CONDITIONING

▶ See Figure 138

➡Before checking or adjusting the idle speed, check the ignition timing and adjust, if necessary.

1. Position gear selector lever in the **N** position on vehicles equipped with manual transaxles, and in the **P** position on vehicles equipped with automatic transaxles.

2. Connect the Test Mode connector and the Read Memory connector located under the left side of the dash.

3. Start the engine and allow it to reach normal operating temperature. Then, run engine at 2500 rpm for 1 minute.

4. Disconnect and plug the purge hose at the intake manifold,

5. To adjust the Idle-up system OFF, turn all accessories **OFF** and adjust idle to specification by rotating the throttle adjusting screw.

6. To adjust the Idle-up system ON, turn the headlights **ON** and adjust the idle by rotating the idle-up adjusting screw.

7. Turn the headlights **OFF**.

WITH AIR CONDITIONING

▶ See Figure 139

➡Before checking or adjusting the idle speed, check the ignition timing and adjust, if necessary.

1. Position gear selector lever in the **N** position on vehicles equipped with manual transaxles, and in the **P** position on vehicles equipped with automatic transaxles.

2. Fasten the Test Mode connector and the Read Memory connector located under the left side of the dash.

3. Start the engine and allow it to reach normal operating temperature. Then, run engine at 2500 rpm for 1 minute.

4. Disconnect and plug the purge hose at the intake manifold,

5. To adjust the Idle-up system OFF, turn all accessories and A/C **OFF** and adjust idle to specification by rotating the throttle adjusting screw.

6. To adjust the Idle-up system ON, turn the A/C **ON** and adjust the idle by rotating the fast-idle adjusting screw.

7. Turn the headlights **ON** and turn the A/C **OFF** and check the idling speed. If adjustment is needed, loosen the locknut and rotate the idle-up adjusting screw.

8. When complete. disconnect the test mode and read memory connectors. Remove the tachometer.

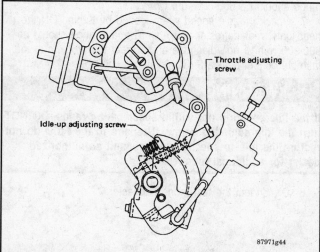

Fig. 138 Location of throttle adjusting and idle-up adjusting screw

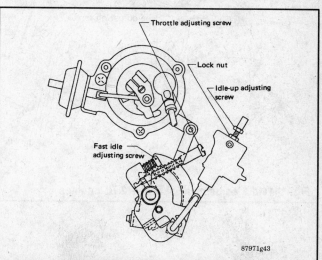

Fig. 139 Location of fast-idle, throttle adjusting and idle-up adjusting screws

Fuel Injection

1.6L, 1.8L AND 2.7L ENGINES

▶ See Figures 140 and 141

1. Position gear selector lever in the **N** position on vehicles equipped with manual transaxles, and in the **P** position on vehicles equipped with automatic transaxles.

2. Connect a tachometer according to the manufacturer's instructions. Start the engine and allow it to reach normal operating temperature.

3. Check and adjust the ignition timing to specification.

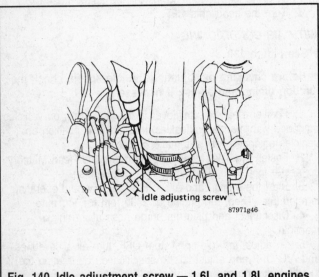

Fig. 140 Idle adjustment screw — 1.6L and 1.8L engines

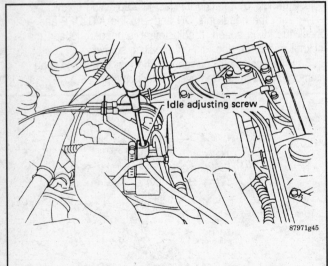

Fig. 141 Idle adjustment screw — 2.7L engines

4. Check and make sure all vacuum hoses, blow-by hoses, rocker cover, oil filler cap and oil filter are secure.

5. Increase engine speed to 2500 rpm for 1 minute to heat the oxygen sensor.

6. Disconnect and plug the purge hose leading to the throttle body.

7. Disconnect the air control valve electrical connector from the throttle body.

8. Inspect the auxiliary air control valve attached to the intake manifold, and make sure it is closed.

9. Access the idle adjusting screw located at the side of the throttle body and rotate to adjust the idle.

10. When complete, connect all hoses plugged earlier.

11. Remove the tachometer.

2.2L, 2.5L AND 3.3L ENGINES

1. Position gear selector lever in the **N** position on vehicles equipped with manual transaxles, and in the **P** position on vehicles equipped with automatic transaxles.

2. Check and make sure the ignition timing is correct, the spark plugs are gapped correctly and in good condition, and the air filter is clean.

3. Inspect all vacuum hoses for any leaks, and repair if needed.

4. Check and make sure the CHECK ENGINE light does not illuminate.

5. Connect the Subaru select monitor to the harness located under the left side of the dash. When connected use mode F04 for this procedure.

❋❋WARNING

When connecting the Subaru select monitor, make sure the ignition is OFF, or damage could occur to the monitor and or ignition components.

➡On 1995-96 models, an OBD-II scan tool can be used in place of the Subaru select monitor. Refer to the instruction manual for the proper operation procedures.

6. With all accessories **OFF**, check the idle speed. The idle range should be 600-800 rpm.

7. Check the idle speed when loaded by turning **ON** the headlights, rear defroster and A/C. The idle range should be 800-900 rpm. If not, diagnose and correct the problem in the fast idle control device (FICD) system.

❋❋WARNING

If the idle speed is not within specification range, DO NOT turn the idle adjusting screw. If repairs to the FICD do not restore the idle to specification, consult an authorized dealer for additional repairs.

8. Disconnect the test mode connector.

GASOLINE ENGINE TUNE-UP SPECIFICATIONS

Year	Model	Engine ID/VIN	Engine Displacement Liters (cc)	Spark Plugs Gap (in.)	Ignition Timing (deg.) MT	AT	Fuel Pump (psi)	Idle Speed (rpm) MT	AT	Valve Clearance In.	Ex.
1985	Brat	5	1.8 (1781)	0.039–0.043	8B	8B	2.6–3.3	800	800	.009–.011	.013–.015
	2DR	2	1.6 (1595)	0.039–0.043	8B	—	1.4–2.1	650	—	.009–.011	.013–.015
	2DR GL	4②	1.8 (1781)	0.039–0.043	8B	8B	2.6–3.3	700	800	.009–.011	.013–.015
	4DR DL④	4②	1.8 (1781)	0.039–0.043	6B	—	2.6–3.3	650	—	Hyd.	Hyd.
	4DR/Wagon	4②	1.8 (1781)	0.039–0.043	8B	8B	2.6–3.3	700	700	Hyd.	Hyd.
	4DR/Wagon GL-10	4②	1.8 (1781)	0.039–0.043	6B	6B	61–71	700	800	Hyd.	Hyd.
	4DR/Wagon Turbo	4②	1.8 (1781)	0.039–0.043	25B	25B	61–71	700	800	Hyd.	Hyd.
	XT	4②	1.8 (1781)	0.039–0.043	6B	6B	61–71	700	800	Hyd.	Hyd.
	XT Turbo	4②	1.8 (1781)	0.039–0.043	25B	25B	61–71	700	800	Hyd.	Hyd.
1986	Brat	5	1.8 (1781)	0.039–0.043	8B	—	2.6–3.3	700	—	.009–.011	.013–.015
	2DR	2	1.6 (1595)	0.039–0.043	8B	—	1.4–2.1	650	—	.009–.011	.013–.015
	2DR GL	2	1.6 (1595)	0.039–0.043	8B	—	1.4–2.1	700	—	.009–.011	.013–.015
	2DR GL	4②	1.8 (1781)	0.039–0.043	8B	8B	2.6–3.3	700	800	.009–.011	.013–.015
	3DR/4DR/Wagon	4②	1.8 (1781)	0.039–0.043	8B	8B	2.6–3.3	700	800	Hyd.	Hyd.
	3DR/4DR/Wagon⑤	4②	1.8 (1781)	0.039–0.043	—	20B	28–43	—	700	Hyd.	Hyd.
	4DR/Wagon Turbo	4②	1.8 (1781)	0.039–0.043	25B	25B	61–71	700	800	Hyd.	Hyd.
	XT	4②	1.8 (1781)	0.039–0.043	6B	6B	61–71	700	800	Hyd.	Hyd.
	XT Turbo	4②	1.8 (1781)	0.039–0.043	25B	25B	61–71	700	800	Hyd.	Hyd.
1987	Brat	5	1.8 (1781)	0.039–0.043	8B	—	2.6–3.3	700	—	.009–.011	.013–.015
	2DR	2	1.6 (1595)	0.039–0.043	8B	—	1.4–2.1	650	—	.009–.011	.013–.015
	2DR GL	2	1.6 (1595)	0.039–0.043	8B	—	1.4–2.1	700	—	.009–.011	.013–.015
	2DR GL	4②	1.8 (1781)	0.039–0.043	8B	8B	2.6–3.3	700	800	.009–.011	.013–.015
	3DR/4DR/Wagon	4②	1.8 (1781)	0.039–0.043	8B	8B	2.6–3.3	700	800	Hyd.	Hyd.
	3DR/4DR/Wagon⑤	4②	1.8 (1781)	0.039–0.043	20B	20B	28–43	700	700	Hyd.	Hyd.
	3DR/4DR Wagon Turbo	4②	1.8 (1781)	0.039–0.043	20B	20B	61–71	700	800	Hyd.	Hyd.
	XT	4②	1.8 (1781)	0.039–0.043	20B	20B	61–71	700	800	Hyd.	Hyd.
	XT Turbo	4②	1.8 (1781)	0.039–0.043	20B	20B	61–71	700	800	Hyd.	Hyd.
	Justy	7⑧	1.2 (1189)	0.039–0.043	5B	—	1.3–2.0	800	—	.006	.010
1988	2DR GL	4②	1.8 (1781)	0.039–0.043	8B	8B	2.6–3.3	700	800	.009–.011	.013–.015
	3DR/4DR/Wagon⑤	4②	1.8 (1781)	0.039–0.043	20B	20B	28–43	700	700	Hyd.	Hyd.
	3DR/4DR Wagon Turbo	4②	1.8 (1781)	0.039–0.043	20B	20B	61–71	700	800	Hyd.	Hyd.
	XT	4②	1.8 (1781)	0.039–0.043	20B	20B	61–71	700	800	Hyd.	Hyd.
	XT-6	4②	2.7 (2672)	0.039–0.043	20B	20B	61–71	700	800	Hyd.	Hyd.
	Justy	7⑧	1.2 (1189)	0.039–0.043	5B	—	1.3–2.0	800	—	.006	.010
1989	2DR GL	4②	1.8 (1781)	0.039–0.043	8B	8B	2.6–3.3	700	800	.009–.011	.013–.015
	3DR/4DR/Wagon⑤	4②	1.8 (1781)	0.039–0.043	20B	20B	28–43	700	700	Hyd.	Hyd.
	3DR/4DR Wagon Turbo	4②	1.8 (1781)	0.039–0.043	20B	20B	61–71	700	800	Hyd.	Hyd.
	XT	4②	1.8 (1781)	0.039–0.043	20B	20B	61–71	700	800	Hyd.	Hyd.
	XT-6	4②	2.7 (2672)	0.039–0.043	20B	20B	61–71	750	750	Hyd.	Hyd.
	Justy	7⑧	1.2 (1189)	0.039–0.043	5B	5B	1.3–2.0	800	800	.006	.010
1990	XT	4②	1.8 (1781)	0.039–0.043	20B	20B	61–71	700	800	Hyd.	Hyd.
	XT-6	4②	2.7 (2672)	0.039–0.043	20B	20B	61–71	750	750	Hyd.	Hyd.
	Justy	7⑧	1.2 (1189)	0.039–0.043	5B	5B	1.3–2.0	800	800	.006	.010

87971c15

GASOLINE ENGINE TUNE-UP SPECIFICATIONS

Year	Model	Engine ID/VIN	Engine Displacement Liters (cc)	Spark Plugs Gap (in.)	Ignition Timing (deg.) MT	Ignition Timing (deg.) AT	Fuel Pump (psi)	Idle Speed (rpm) MT	Idle Speed (rpm) AT	Valve Clearance In.	Valve Clearance Ex.
1990	Justy GL	7 ⑧	1.2 (1189)	0.039–0.043	5B	5B	43	700	700	.006	.010
	Loyale	4 ②	1.8 (1781)	0.039–0.043	20B	20B	28–43	700	700	Hyd.	Hyd.
	Loyale Turbo	4 ②	1.8 (1781)	0.039–0.043	20B	20B	61–71	700	800	Hyd.	Hyd.
	Legacy	6	2.2 (2212)	0.039–0.043	20B	20B	36	700	700	Hyd.	Hyd.
1991	XT	4 ②	1.8 (1781)	0.039–0.043	20B	20B	61–71	700	800	Hyd.	Hyd.
	XT-6	4 ②	2.7 (2672)	0.039–0.043	20B	20B	61–71	750	750	Hyd.	Hyd.
	Justy	7 ⑧	1.2 (1189)	0.039–0.043	5B	5B	1.3–2.0	800	800	.006	.010
	Justy GL	7 ⑧	1.2 (1189)	0.039–0.043	5B	5B	43	700	700	.006	.010
	Loyale	4 ②	1.8 (1781)	0.039–0.043	20B	20B	28–43	700	700	Hyd.	Hyd.
	Legacy	6	2.2 (2212)	0.039–0.043	20B	20B	36	700	700	Hyd.	Hyd.
	Legacy Turbo	6	2.2 (2212)	0.039–0.043	15B	15B	36	700	700	Hyd.	Hyd.
1992	Justy	7 ⑧	1.2 (1189)	0.039–0.043	5B	5B	1.3–2.0	800	800	.006	.010
	Justy GL	7 ⑧	1.2 (1189)	0.039–0.043	5B	5B	43	700	700	.006	.010
	Loyale	4 ②	1.8 (1781)	0.039–0.043	20B	20B	28–43	700	700	Hyd.	Hyd.
	Legacy	6	2.2 (2212)	0.039–0.043	20B	20B	36	700	700	Hyd.	Hyd.
	Legacy Turbo	6	2.2 (2212)	0.039–0.043	15B	15B	36	700	700	Hyd.	Hyd.
	SVX	3	3.3 (3318)	0.039–0.043	—	20B	43	—	610	Hyd.	Hyd.
1993	Justy	7	1.2 (1189)	0.039-0.043	5B	5B	1.3-2.0	800	800	.006	.010
	Justy	7 ⑧	1.2 (1189)	0.039-0.043	5B	5B	43	700	700	.006	.010
	Impreza	2	1.8 (1820)	0.039-0.043	20B	20B	36	700	700	Hyd.	Hyd.
	Loyale	4 ②	1.8 (1781)	0.039-0.043	20B	20B	28–43	700	700	Hyd.	Hyd.
	Legacy	6	2.2 (2212)	0.039-0.043	20B	20B	36	700	700	Hyd.	Hyd.
	Legacy Turbo	6	2.2 (2212)	0.039-0.043	15B	15B	36	700	700	Hyd.	Hyd.
	SVX	3	3.3 (3318)	0.039-0.043	-	20B	43	-	610	Hyd.	Hyd.
1994	Justy	7 ⑧	1.2 (1189)	0.039-0.043	5B	5B	43	700	700	.006	.010
	Impreza	2	1.8 (1820)	0.039-0.043	20B	20B	36	700	700	Hyd.	Hyd.
	Loyale	4 ②	1.8 (1781)	0.039-0.043	20B	20B	28–43	700	700	Hyd.	Hyd.
	Legacy	6	2.2 (2212)	0.039-0.043	20B	20B	36	700	700	Hyd.	Hyd.
	Legacy Turbo	6	2.2 (2212)	0.039-0.043	15B	15B	36	700	700	Hyd.	Hyd.
	SVX	3	3.3 (3318)	0.039-0.043	-	20B	43	-	610	Hyd.	Hyd.
1995	Impreza	2	1.8 (1820)	0.039-0.043	20B	20B	36	700	700	Hyd.	Hyd.
	Impreza	6	2.2 (2212)	0.039-0.043	20B	20B	36	700	700	In.	Hyd.
	Legacy	6	2.2 (2212)	0.039-0.043	14B	20B	36	700	700	Hyd.	Hyd.
	SVX	3	3.3 (3318)	0.039-0.043	-	20B	43	-	610	Hyd.	Hyd.
1996	Impreza	1 ⑥	1.8 (1820)	0.039-0.043	20B	20B	36	700	700	Hyd.	Hyd.
	Impreza	4	2.2 (2212)	0.039-0.043	14B	20B	36	700	700	Hyd.	Hyd.
	Legacy	3 ⑦	2.2 (2212)	0.039-0.043	14B	20B	36	700	700	Hyd.	Hyd.
	Legacy	6	2.5 (2457)	0.039-0.043	15B	15B	36	700	700	Hyd.	Hyd.
	SVX	8	3.3 (3318)	0.039-0.043	-	20B	43	-	610	Hyd.	Hyd.

NOTE: The underhood specifications sticker often reflects tune-up specification changes during production. Sticker figures must be used if they disagree with those in this chart.

① Idle Speed in Neutral (M/T) or Park (A/T) with accessories OFF
② Code 5: with 4WD
　Code 7: with pneumatic suspension
　Code 9: with pneumatic suspension
③ B = Before top dead center

④ 4-speed
⑤ SPFI - Single-Point Fuel Injection
⑥ Code 2: with 4WD
⑦ Code 4: With 4WD
⑧ Code 8: with 4WD

87971c16

Air Conditioning

➡Be sure to consult the laws in your area before servicing the air conditioning system. In most areas, it is illegal to perform repairs involving refrigerant unless the work is done by a certified technician. Also, it is quite likely that you will not be able to purchase refrigerant without proof of certification.

SAFETY PRECAUTIONS

◆ See Figure 142

There are two major hazards associated with air conditioning systems and they both relate to the refrigerant gas. First, the refrigerant gas (R-12 or R-134a) is an extremely cold substance. When exposed to air, it will instantly freeze any surface it comes in contact with, including your eyes. The other hazard relates to fire (if your vehicle is equipped with R-12. Although normally non-toxic, the R-12 gas becomes highly poisonous in the presence of an open flame. One good whiff of the vapor formed by burning R-12 can be fatal. Keep all forms of fire (including cigarettes) well clear of the air conditioning system.

Because of the inherent dangers involved with working on air conditioning systems, these safety precautions must be strictly followed.

• Avoid contact with a charged refrigeration system, even when working on another part of the air conditioning system or vehicle. If a heavy tool comes into contact with a section of tubing or a heat exchanger, it can easily cause the relatively soft material to rupture.

• When it is necessary to apply force to a fitting which contains refrigerant, as when checking that all system couplings are securely tightened, use a wrench on both parts of the fitting involved, if possible. This will avoid putting torque on refrigerant tubing. (It is also advisable to use tube or line wrenches when tightening these flare nut fittings.)

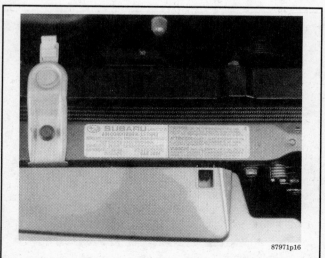

Fig. 142 Read all A/C labels. They provide important information including refrigerant type — Legacy shown

➡R-12 refrigerant is a chlorofluorocarbon which, when released into the atmosphere, can contribute to the depletion of the ozone layer in the upper atmosphere. Ozone filters out harmful radiation from the sun.

• Do not attempt to discharge the system without the proper tools. Precise control is possible only when using the service gauges and a proper A/C refrigerant recovery station. Wear protective gloves when connecting or disconnecting service gauge hoses.

• Discharge the system only in a well ventilated area, as high concentrations of the gas which might accidentally escape can exclude oxygen and act as an anesthetic. When leak testing or soldering, this is particularly important, as toxic gas is formed when R-12 contacts any flame.

• Never start a system without first verifying that both service valves are properly installed, and that all fittings throughout the system are snugly connected.

• Avoid applying heat to any refrigerant line or storage vessel. Charging may be aided by using water heated to less than 125°F (50°C) to warm the refrigerant container. Never allow a refrigerant storage container to sit out in the sun, or near any other source of heat, such as a radiator or heater.

• Always wear goggles to protect your eyes when working on a system. If refrigerant contacts the eyes, it is advisable in all cases to consult a physician immediately.

• Frostbite from liquid refrigerant should be treated by first gradually warming the area with cool water, and then gently applying petroleum jelly. A physician should be consulted.

• Always keep refrigerant drum fittings capped when not in use. If the container is equipped with a safety cap to protect the valve, make sure the cap is in place when the can is not being used. Avoid sudden shock to the drum, which might occur from dropping it, or from banging a heavy tool against it. Never carry a drum in the passenger compartment of a vehicle.

• Always completely discharge the system into a suitable recovery unit before painting the vehicle (if the paint is to be baked on), or before welding anywhere near refrigerant lines.

• When servicing the system, minimize the time that any refrigerant line or fitting is open to the air in order to prevent moisture or dirt from entering the system. Contaminants such as moisture or dirt can damage internal system components. Always replace O-rings on lines or fittings which are disconnected. Prior to installation coat, but do not soak, replacement O-rings with suitable compressor oil.

GENERAL SERVICING PROCEDURES

➡It is recommended, and possibly required by law, that a qualified technician perform the following services.

✳✳WARNING

Some of the vehicles covered by this manual may be equipped with R-134a refrigerant systems, rather than R-12. Be ABSOLUTELY SURE what type of system you are working on before attempting to add refrigerant. Use of the wrong refrigerant or oil will cause damage to the system.

The most important aspect of air conditioning service is the maintenance of a pure and adequate charge of refrigerant in the system. A refrigeration system cannot function properly if a significant percentage of the charge is lost. Leaks are common because the severe vibration encountered underhood in an automobile can easily cause a sufficient cracking or loosening of the air conditioning fittings; allowing, the extreme operating pressures of the system to force refrigerant out.

The problem can be understood by considering what happens to the system as it is operated with a continuous leak. Because the expansion valve regulates the flow of refrigerant to the evaporator, the level of refrigerant there is fairly constant. The receiver/drier stores any excess refrigerant, and so a loss will first appear there as a reduction in the level of liquid. As this level nears the bottom of the vessel, some refrigerant vapor bubbles will begin to appear in the stream of liquid supplied to the expansion valve. This vapor decreases the capacity of the expansion valve very little as the valve opens to compensate for its presence. As the quantity of liquid in the condenser decreases, the operating pressure will drop there and throughout the high side of the system. As the refrigerant continues to be expelled, the pressure available to force the liquid through the expansion valve will continue to decrease, and, eventually, the valve's orifice will prove to be too much of a restriction for adequate flow even with the needle fully withdrawn.

At this point, low side pressure will start to drop, and a severe reduction in cooling capacity, marked by freeze-up of the evaporator coil, will result. Eventually, the operating pressure of the evaporator will be lower than the pressure of the atmosphere surrounding it, and air will be drawn into the system wherever there are leaks in the low side.

Because all atmospheric air contains at least some moisture, water will enter the system mixing with the refrigerant and oil. Trace amounts of moisture will cause sludging of the oil, and corrosion of the system. Saturation and clogging of the filter/drier, and freezing of the expansion valve orifice will eventually result. As air fills the system to a greater and greater extent, it will interfere more and more with the normal flows of refrigerant and heat.

From this description, it should be obvious that much of the repairman's focus in on detecting leaks, repairing them, and then restoring the purity and quantity of the refrigerant charge. A list of general rules should be followed in addition to all safety precautions:

- Keep all tools as clean and dry as possible.
- Thoroughly purge the service gauges/hoses of air and moisture before connecting them to the system. Keep them capped when not in use.
- Thoroughly clean any refrigerant fitting before disconnecting it, in order to minimize the entrance of dirt into the system.
- Plan any operation that requires opening the system beforehand, in order to minimize the length of time it will be exposed to open air. Cap or seal the open ends to minimize the entrance of foreign material.
- When adding oil, pour it through an extremely clean and dry tube or funnel. Keep the oil capped whenever possible. Do not use oil that has not been kept tightly sealed.
- Purchase refrigerant intended for use only in automatic air conditioning systems.

- Completely evacuate any system that has been opened for service, or that has leaked sufficiently to draw in moisture and air. This requires evacuating air and moisture with a good vacuum pump for at least one hour. If a system has been open for a considerable length of time it may be advisable to evacuate the system for up to 12 hours (overnight).
- Use a wrench on both halves of a fitting that is to be disconnected, so as to avoid placing torque on any of the refrigerant lines.
- When overhauling a compressor, pour some of the oil into a clean glass and inspect it. If there is evidence of dirt, metal particles, or both, flush all refrigerant components with clean refrigerant before evacuating and recharging the system. In addition, if metal particles are present, the compressor should be replaced.
- Schrader valves may leak only when under full operating pressure. Therefore, if leakage is suspected but cannot be located, operate the system with a full charge of refrigerant and look for leaks from all Schrader valves. Replace any faulty valves.

Additional Preventive Maintenance

USING THE SYSTEM

The easiest and most important preventive maintenance for your A/C system is to be sure that it is used on a regular basis. Running the system for five minutes each month (no matter what the season) will help assure that the seals and all internal components remain lubricated.

ANTIFREEZE

▶ See Figure 143

In order to prevent heater core freeze-up during A/C operation, it is necessary to maintain a proper antifreeze protection. Use a hand-held antifreeze tester (hydrometer) to periodically check the condition of the antifreeze in your engine's cooling system.

➡**Antifreeze should not be used longer than the manufacturer specifies.**

tccs1233

Fig. 143 An antifreeze tester can be used to determine the freezing and boiling level of the coolant

RADIATOR CAP

For efficient operation of an air conditioned vehicle's cooling system, the radiator cap should have a holding pressure which meets manufacturer's specifications. A cap which fails to hold these pressures should be replaced.

CONDENSER

Any obstruction of or damage to the condenser configuration will restrict the air flow which is essential to its efficient operation. It is therefore a good rule to keep this unit clean and in proper physical shape.

➡ **Bug screens which are mounted in front of the condenser (unless they are original equipment) are regarded as obstructions.**

CONDENSATION DRAIN TUBE

This single molded drain tube expels the condensation, which accumulates on the bottom of the evaporator housing, into the engine compartment. If this tube is obstructed, the air conditioning performance can be restricted and condensation buildup can spill over onto the vehicle's floor.

SYSTEM INSPECTION

➡ **R-12 refrigerant is a chlorofluorocarbon which, when released into the atmosphere, can contribute to the depletion of the ozone layer in the upper atmosphere. Ozone filters out harmful radiation from the sun.**

The easiest and often most important check for the air conditioning system consists of a visual inspection of the system components. Visually inspect the air conditioning system for refrigerant leaks, damaged compressor clutch, compressor drive belt tension and condition, plugged evaporator drain tube, blocked condenser fins, disconnected or broken wires, blown fuses, corroded connections and poor insulation.

A refrigerant leak will usually appear as an oily residue at the leakage point in the system. The oily residue soon picks up dust or dirt particles from the surrounding air and appears greasy. Through time, this will build up and appear to be a heavy dirt impregnated grease. Most leaks are caused by damaged or missing O-ring seals at the component connections, damaged charging valve cores or missing service gauge port caps.

For a thorough visual and operational inspection, check the following:

1. Check the surface of the radiator and condenser for dirt, leaves or other material which might block air flow.

2. Check for kinks in hoses and lines. Check the system for leaks.

3. Make sure the drive belt is under the proper tension. When the air conditioning is operating, make sure the drive belt is free of noise or slippage.

4. Make sure the blower motor operates at all appropriate positions, then check for distribution of the air from all outlets with the blower on **HIGH**.

➡ **Keep in mind that under conditions of high humidity, air discharged from the A/C vents may not feel as cold as expected, even if the system is working properly. This is** because the vaporized moisture in humid air retains heat more effectively than does dry air, making the humid air more difficult to cool.

5. Make sure the air passage selection lever is operating correctly. Start the engine and warm it to normal operating temperature, then make sure the hot/cold selection lever is operating correctly.

DISCHARGING, EVACUATING AND CHARGING

Discharging, evacuating and charging the air conditioning system must be performed by a properly trained and certified mechanic in a facility equipped with refrigerant recovery/recycling equipment that meets SAE standards for the type of system to be serviced.

If you don't have access to the necessary equipment, we recommend that you take your vehicle to a reputable service station to have the work done. If you still wish to perform repairs on the vehicle, have them discharge the system, then take your vehicle home and perform the necessary work. When you are finished, return the vehicle to the station for evacuation and charging. Just be sure to cap ALL A/C system fittings immediately after opening them and keep them protected until the system is recharged.

Windshield Wipers

ELEMENT (REFILL) CARE AND REPLACEMENT

◆ **See Figures 144, 145, 146, 147, 148, 149, 150, 151, 152, 153, 154 and 155**

For maximum effectiveness and longest element life, the windshield and wiper blades should be kept clean. Dirt, tree sap, road tar and so on will cause streaking, smearing and blade deterioration if left on the glass. It is advisable to wash the windshield carefully with a commercial glass cleaner at least once a month. Wipe off the rubber blades with the wet rag afterwards. Do not attempt to move wipers across the windshield by hand; damage to the motor and drive mechanism will result.

To inspect and/or replace the wiper blade elements, place the wiper switch in the **LOW** speed position and the ignition switch in the **ACC** position. When the wiper blades are approximately vertical on the windshield, turn the ignition switch to **OFF**.

Examine the wiper blade elements. If they are found to be cracked, broken or torn, they should be replaced immediately. Replacement intervals will vary with usage, although ozone deterioration usually limits element life to about one year. If the wiper pattern is smeared or streaked, or if the blade chatters across the glass, the elements should be replaced. It is easiest and most sensible to replace the elements in pairs.

If your vehicle is equipped with aftermarket blades, there are several different types of refills and your vehicle might have any kind. Aftermarket blades and arms rarely use the exact same type blade or refill as the original equipment. Here are some typical aftermarket blades; not all may be available for your vehicle:

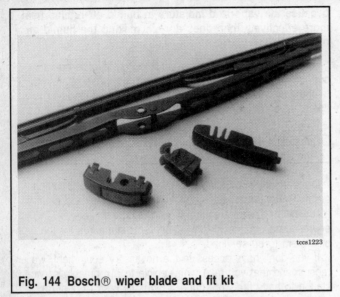

Fig. 144 Bosch® wiper blade and fit kit

Fig. 147 Trico® wiper blade and fit kit

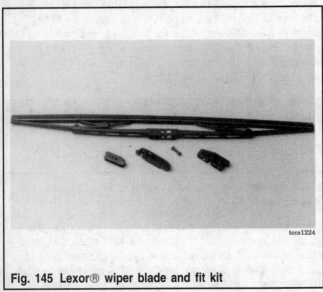

Fig. 145 Lexor® wiper blade and fit kit

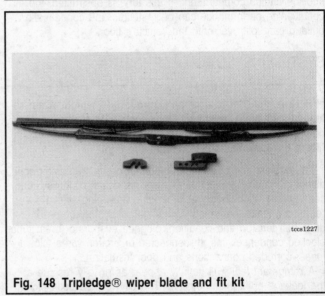

Fig. 148 Tripledge® wiper blade and fit kit

Fig. 146 Pylon® wiper blade and adaptor

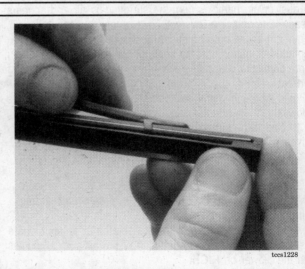

Fig. 149 To remove and install a Lexor® wiper blade refill, slip out the old insert and slide in a new one

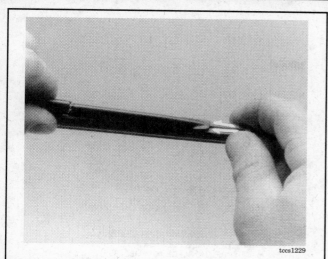

Fig. 150 On Pylon® inserts, the clip at the end has to be removed prior to sliding the insert off

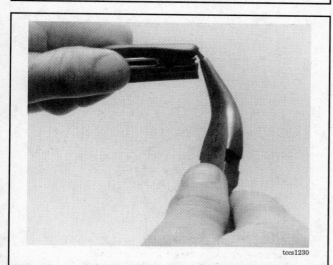

Fig. 151 On Trico® wiper blades, the tab at the end of the blade must be turned up . . .

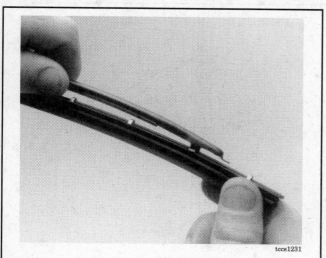

Fig. 152 . . . then the insert can be removed. After installing the replacement insert, bend the tab back

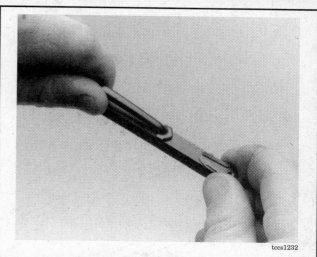

Fig. 153 The Tripledge® wiper blade insert is removed and installed using a securing clip

The Anco® type uses a release button that is pushed down to allow the refill to slide out of the yoke jaws. The new refill slides back into the frame and locks in place.

Some Trico® refills are removed by locating where the metal backing strip or the refill is wider. Insert a small screwdriver blade between the frame and metal backing strip. Press down to release the refill from the retaining tab.

Other types of Trico® refills have two metal tabs which are unlocked by squeezing them together. The rubber filler can then be withdrawn from the frame jaws. A new refill is installed by inserting the refill into the front frame jaws and sliding it rearward to engage the remaining frame jaws. There are usually four jaws; be certain when installing that the refill is engaged in all of them. At the end of its travel, the tabs will lock into place on the front jaws of the wiper blade frame.

Another type of refill is made from polycarbonate. The refill has a simple locking device at one end which flexes downward out of the groove into which the jaws of the holder fit, allowing easy release. By sliding the new refill through all the jaws and pushing through the slight resistance when it reaches the end of its travel, the refill will lock into position.

To replace the Tridon® refill, it is necessary to remove the wiper blade. This refill has a plastic backing strip with a notch about 1 in. (25mm) from the end. Hold the blade (frame) on a hard surface so that the frame is tightly bowed. Grip the tip of the backing strip and pull up while twisting counterclockwise. The backing strip will snap out of the retaining tab. Do this for the remaining tabs until the refill is free of the blade. The length of these refills is molded into the end and they should be replaced with identical types.

Regardless of the type of refill used, be sure to follow the part manufacturer's instructions closely. Make sure that all of the frame jaws are engaged as the refill is pushed into place and locked. If the metal blade holder and frame are allowed to touch the glass during wiper operation, the glass will be scratched.

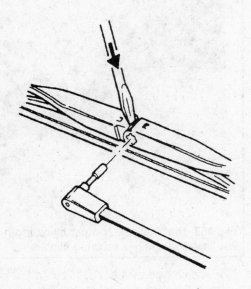

VIEW A

BLADE REPLACEMENT

1. CYCLE ARM AND BLADE ASSEMBLY TO UP POSITION-ON THE WINDSHIELD WHERE REMOVAL OF BLADE ASSEMBLY CAN BE PERFORMED WITHOUT DIFFICULTY. TURN IGNITION KEY OFF AT DESIRED POSITION.

2. TO REMOVE BLADE ASSEMBLY, INSERT SCREWDRIVER IN SLOT, PUSH DOWN ON SPRING LOCK AND PULL BLADE ASSEMBLY FROM PIN (VIEW A)

3. TO INSTALL, PUSH THE BLADE ASSEMBLY ON THE PIN SO THAT THE SPRING LOCK ENGAGES THE PIN (VIEW A). BE SURE THE BLADE ASSEMBLY IS SECURELY ATTACHED TO PIN

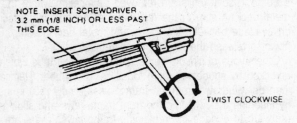

NOTE INSERT SCREWDRIVER 3 2 mm (1/8 INCH) OR LESS PAST THIS EDGE

TWIST CLOCKWISE

ELEMENT REPLACEMENT

1. INSERT SCREWDRIVER BETWEEN THE EDGE OF THE SUPER STRUCTURE AND THE BLADE BACKING DRIP (VIEW B) TWIST SCREWDRIVER SLOWLY UNTIL ELEMENT CLEARS ONE SIDE OF THE SUPER STRUCTURE CLAW

2. SLIDE THE ELEMENT INTO THE SUPER STRUCTURE CLAWS

VIEW B

4. INSERT ELEMENT INTO ONE SIDE OF THE END CLAWS (VIEW D) AND WITH A ROCKING MOTION PUSH ELEMENT UPWARD UNTIL IT SNAPS IN (VIEW E)

VIEW D

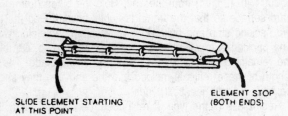

SLIDE ELEMENT STARTING AT THIS POINT

ELEMENT STOP (BOTH ENDS)

3. SLIDE THE ELEMENT INTO THE SUPER STRUCTURE CLAWS, STARTING WITH SECOND SET FROM EITHER END (VIEW C) AND CONTINUE TO SLIDE THE BLADE ELEMENT INTO ALL THE SUPER STRUCTURE CLAWS TO THE ELEMENT STOP (VIEW C)

VIEW C

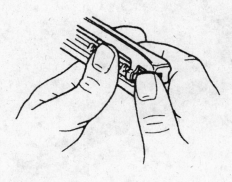

VIEW E

tccs1236

Fig. 154 Trico® wiper blade insert (element) replacement

BLADE REPLACEMENT

1. Cycle arm and blade assembly to a position on the windshield where removal of blade assembly can be performed without difficulty. Turn ignition key off at desired position.
2. To remove blade assembly from wiper arm, pull up on spring lock and pull blade assembly from pin (View A). Be sure spring lock is not pulled excessively or it will become distorted.
3. To install, push the blade assembly onto the pin so that the spring lock engages the pin (View A). Be sure the blade assembly is securely attached to pin.

ELEMENT REPLACEMENT

1. In the plastic backing strip which is part of the rubber blade assembly, there is an 11.11mm (7/16 inch) long notch located approximately one inch from either end. Locate either notch.
2. Place the frame of the wiper blade assembly on a firm surface with either notched end of the backing strip visible.
3. Grasp the frame portion of the wiper blade assembly and push down until the blade assembly is tightly bowed.
4. With the blade assembly in the bowed position, grasp the tip of the backing strip firmly, pulling up and twisting C.C.W. at the same time. The backing strip will then snap out of the retaining tab on the end of the frame.
5. Lift the wiper blade assembly from the surface and slide the backing strip down the frame until the notch lines up with the next retaining tab, twist slightly, and the backing strip will snap out. Continue this operation with the remaining tabs until the blade element is completely detached from the frame.
6. To install blade element, reverse the above procedure, making sure all six (6) tabs are locked to the backing strip before installing blade to wiper arm.

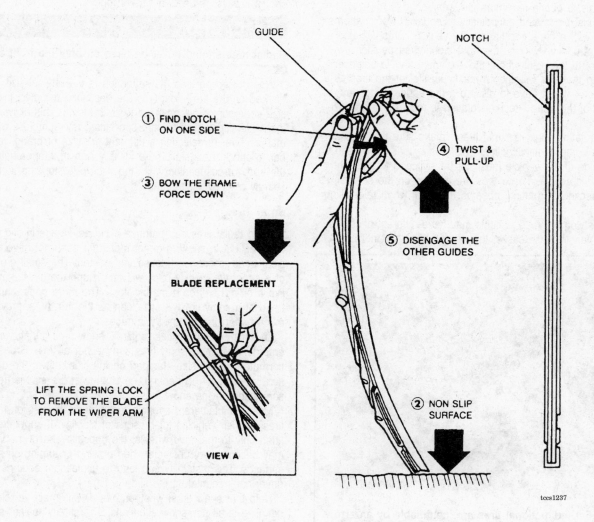

GUIDE

NOTCH

① FIND NOTCH ON ONE SIDE

④ TWIST & PULL-UP

③ BOW THE FRAME FORCE DOWN

⑤ DISENGAGE THE OTHER GUIDES

BLADE REPLACEMENT

LIFT THE SPRING LOCK TO REMOVE THE BLADE FROM THE WIPER ARM

② NON SLIP SURFACE

VIEW A

tccs1237

Fig. 155 Tridon® wiper blade insert (element) replacement

Tires and Wheels

Common sense and good driving habits will afford maximum tire life. Fast starts, sudden stops and hard cornering are hard on tires and will shorten their useful life span. Make sure that you don't overload the vehicle or run with incorrect pressure in the tires. Both of these practices will increase tread wear.

Inspect your tires frequently. Be especially careful to watch for bubbles in the tread or sidewall, deep cuts or underinflation. Replace any tires with bubbles in the sidewall. If cuts are so deep that they penetrate to the cords, discard the tire. Any cut in the sidewall of a radial tire renders it unsafe. Also look for uneven tread wear patterns that may indicate the front end is out of alignment or that the tires are out of balance.

TIRE ROTATION

▶ See Figures 156 and 157

Tire rotation is recommended every 6,000 miles (9,600 km) or so, and a tire pressure check should be performed at regular intervals to obtain maximum tire wear.

Tires must be rotated periodically to equalize wear patterns that vary with a tire's position on the vehicle. Tires will also wear in an uneven way as the front steering/suspension system wears to the point where the alignment should be reset.

Rotating the tires will ensure maximum life for the tires as a set, so you will not have to discard a tire early due to wear on only part of the tread. Regular rotation is required to equalize wear.

When rotating "unidirectional tires," make sure that they always roll in the same direction. This means that a tire used on the left side of the vehicle must not be switched to the right side and vice-versa. These tires are marked on the sidewall as to the direction of rotation; observe the mark when reinstalling the tire(s).

Some styled or "mag" wheels may have different offsets front to rear. In these cases, the rear wheels must not be used up front and vice-versa. Furthermore, if these wheels are equipped with unidirectional tires, they cannot be rotated unless the tire is remounted for the proper direction of rotation.

➥The compact or space-saver spare is strictly for emergency use. It must never be included in the tire rotation or placed on the vehicle for everyday use.

TIRE DESIGN

▶ See Figure 158

For maximum satisfaction, tires should be used in sets of four. Mixing of different types (radial, bias-belted, fiberglass belted) must be avoided. In most cases, the vehicle manufacturer has designated a type of tire on which the vehicle will perform best. Your first choice when replacing tires should be to use the same type of tire that the manufacturer recommends.

When radial tires are used, tire sizes and wheel diameters should be selected to maintain ground clearance and tire load capacity equivalent to the original specified tire. Radial tires should always be used in sets of four.

✳✳CAUTION

Radial tires should never be used on only the front axle.

When selecting tires, pay attention to the original size as marked on the tire. Most tires are described using an industry size code sometimes referred to as P-Metric. This allows the exact identification of the tire specifications, regardless of the manufacturer. If selecting a different tire size or brand, remember to check the installed tire for any sign of interference with the body or suspension while the vehicle is stopping, turning sharply or heavily loaded.

Snow Tires

Good radial tires can produce a big advantage in slippery weather, but in snow, a street radial tire does not have sufficient tread to provide traction and control. The small grooves of a street tire quickly pack with snow and the tire behaves like a billiard ball on a marble floor. The more open, chunky tread of a snow tire will self-clean as the tire turns, providing much better grip on snowy surfaces.

To satisfy municipalities requiring snow tires during weather emergencies, most snow tires carry either an M + S designation after the tire size stamped on the sidewall, or the designation "all-season." In general, no change in tire size is necessary when buying snow tires.

Most manufacturers strongly recommend the use of 4 snow tires on their vehicles for reasons of stability. If snow tires are fitted only to the drive wheels, the opposite end of the vehicle may become very unstable when braking or turning on slippery surfaces. This instability can lead to unpleasant endings if the driver can't counteract the slide in time.

Note that snow tires, whether 2 or 4, will affect vehicle handling in all non-snow situations. The stiffer, heavier snow tires will noticeably change the turning and braking characteris-

tccs1234

Fig. 156 Unidirectional tires are identifiable by an arrow or the word "rotation"

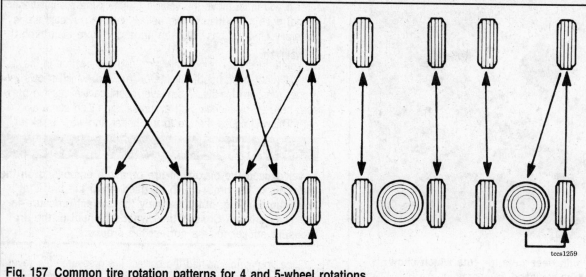

Fig. 157 Common tire rotation patterns for 4 and 5-wheel rotations

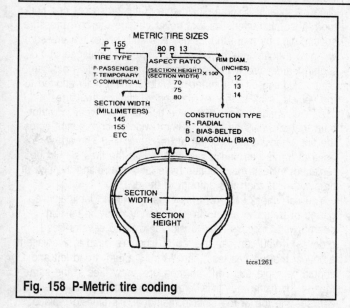

Fig. 158 P-Metric tire coding

tics of the vehicle. Once the snow tires are installed, you must re-learn the behavior of the vehicle and drive accordingly.

➡**Consider buying extra wheels on which to mount the snow tires. Once done, the "snow wheels" can be installed and removed as needed. This eliminates the potential damage to tires or wheels from seasonal removal and installation. Even if your vehicle has styled wheels, see if inexpensive steel wheels are available. Although the look of the vehicle will change, the expensive wheels will be protected from salt, curb hits and pothole damage.**

TIRE STORAGE

If they are mounted on wheels, store the tires at proper inflation pressure. All tires should be kept in a cool, dry place. If they are stored in the garage or basement, do not let them stand on a concrete floor; set them on strips of wood, a mat or a large stack of newspaper. Keeping them away from direct moisture is of paramount importance. Tires should not be stored upright, but in a flat position.

INSPECTION

▶ **See Figures 159, 160, 161, 162, 163, 164, 165 and 166**

The importance of proper tire inflation cannot be overemphasized. A tire employs air as part of its structure. It is designed around the supporting strength of the air at a specified pressure. For this reason, improper inflation drastically reduces the tires's ability to perform as intended. A tire will lose some air in day-to-day use; having to add a few pounds of air periodically is not necessarily a sign of a leaking tire.

Two items should be a permanent fixture in every glove compartment: an accurate tire pressure gauge and a tread depth gauge. Check the tire pressure (including the spare) regularly with a pocket type gauge. Too often, the gauge on the end of the air hose at your corner garage is not accurate because it suffers too much abuse. Always check tire pressure when the tires are cold, as pressure increases with tempera-

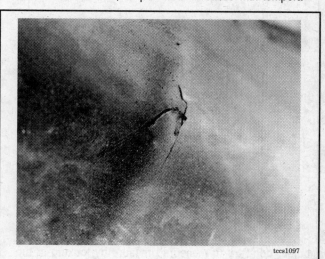

Fig. 159 Tires should be checked frequently for any sign of puncture or damage

Fig. 160 Tires with deep cuts, or cuts which show bulging, should be replaced immediately

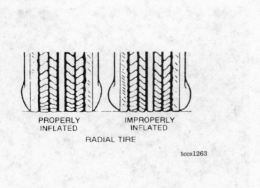

- DRIVE WHEEL HEAVY ACCELERATION
- OVERINFLATION

- HARD CORNERING
- UNDERINFLATION
- LACK OF ROTATION

tccs1262

Fig. 161 Examples of inflation-related tire wear patterns

PROPERLY INFLATED   IMPROPERLY INFLATED

RADIAL TIRE

tccs1263

Fig. 162 Radial tires have a characteristic sidewall bulge; don't try to measure pressure by looking at the tire. Use a quality air pressure gauge

ture. If you must move the vehicle to check the tire inflation, do not drive more than a mile before checking. A cold tire is generally one that has not been driven for more than three hours.

A plate or sticker is normally provided somewhere in the vehicle (door post, hood, tailgate or trunk lid) which shows the proper pressure for the tires. Never counteract excessive pressure build-up by bleeding off air pressure (letting some air out). This will cause the tire to run hotter and wear quicker.

❊❊CAUTION

Never exceed the maximum tire pressure embossed on the tire! This is the pressure to be used when the tire is at maximum loading, but it is rarely the correct pressure for everyday driving. Consult the owner's manual or the tire pressure sticker for the correct tire pressure.

Once you've maintained the correct tire pressures for several weeks, you'll be familiar with the vehicle's braking and handling personality. Slight adjustments in tire pressures can fine-tune these characteristics, but never change the cold pressure specification by more than 2 psi. A slightly softer tire pressure will give a softer ride but also yield lower fuel mileage. A slightly harder tire will give crisper dry road handling but can cause skidding on wet surfaces. Unless you're fully attuned to the vehicle, stick to the recommended inflation pressures.

All tires made since 1968 have built-in tread wear indicator bars that show up as 1/2 in. (13mm) wide smooth bands across the tire when 1/16 in. (1.5mm) of tread remains. The appearance of tread wear indicators means that the tires should be replaced. In fact, many states have laws prohibiting the use of tires with less than this amount of tread.

You can check your own tread depth with an inexpensive gauge or by using a Lincoln head penny. Slip the Lincoln penny (with Lincoln's head upside-down) into several tread grooves. If you can see the top of Lincoln's head in 2 adjacent grooves, the tire has less than 1/16 in. (1.5mm) tread left and should be replaced. You can measure snow tires in the same manner by using the "tails" side of the Lincoln penny. If you can see the top of the Lincoln memorial, it's time to replace the snow tire(s).

CARE OF SPECIAL WHEELS

If you have invested money in magnesium, aluminum alloy or sport wheels, special precautions should be taken to make sure your investment is not wasted and that your special wheels look good for the life of the vehicle.

Special wheels are easily damaged and/or scratched. Occasionally check the rims for cracking, impact damage or air leaks. If any of these are found, replace the wheel. But in order to prevent this type of damage and the costly replacement of a special wheel, observe the following precautions:

• Use extra care not to damage the wheels during removal, installation, balancing, etc. After removal of the wheels from the vehicle, place them on a mat or other protective surface. If they are to be stored for any length of time, support them on strips of wood. Never store tires and wheels upright; the tread may develop flat spots.

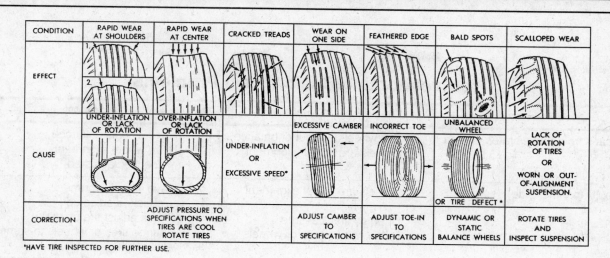

CONDITION	RAPID WEAR AT SHOULDERS	RAPID WEAR AT CENTER	CRACKED TREADS	WEAR ON ONE SIDE	FEATHERED EDGE	BALD SPOTS	SCALLOPED WEAR
EFFECT							
CAUSE	UNDER-INFLATION OR LACK OF ROTATION	OVER-INFLATION OR LACK OF ROTATION	UNDER-INFLATION OR EXCESSIVE SPEED*	EXCESSIVE CAMBER	INCORRECT TOE	UNBALANCED WHEEL OR TIRE DEFECT *	LACK OF ROTATION OF TIRES OR WORN OR OUT-OF-ALIGNMENT SUSPENSION.
CORRECTION	ADJUST PRESSURE TO SPECIFICATIONS WHEN TIRES ARE COOL ROTATE TIRES			ADJUST CAMBER TO SPECIFICATIONS	ADJUST TOE-IN TO SPECIFICATIONS	DYNAMIC OR STATIC BALANCE WHEELS	ROTATE TIRES AND INSPECT SUSPENSION

*HAVE TIRE INSPECTED FOR FURTHER USE.

tccs1267

Fig. 163 Common tire wear patterns and causes

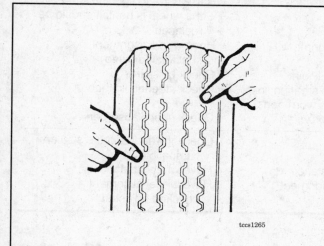

tccs1265

Fig. 164 Tread wear indicators will appear when the tire is worn

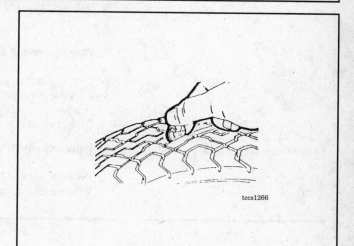

tccs1266

Fig. 166 A penny works well for a quick check of tread depth

• When driving, watch for hazards; it doesn't take much to crack a wheel.

• When washing, use a mild soap or non-abrasive dish detergent (keeping in mind that detergent tends to remove wax). Avoid cleansers with abrasives or the use of hard brushes. There are many cleaners and polishes for special wheels.

• If possible, remove the wheels during the winter. Salt and sand used for snow removal can severely damage the finish of a wheel.

• Make certain the recommended lug nut torque is never exceeded or the wheel may crack. Never use snow chains on special wheels; severe scratching will occur.

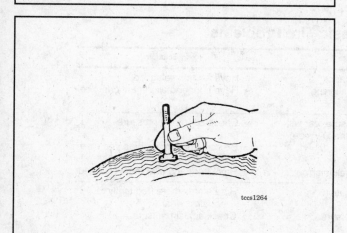

tccs1264

Fig. 165 Accurate tread depth indicators are inexpensive and handy

Troubleshooting Basic Wheel Problems

Problem	Cause	Solution
The car's front end vibrates at high speed	• The wheels are out of balance • Wheels are out of alignment	• Have wheels balanced • Have wheel alignment checked/adjusted
Car pulls to either side	• Wheels are out of alignment • Unequal tire pressure • Different size tires or wheels	• Have wheel alignment checked/adjusted • Check/adjust tire pressure • Change tires or wheels to same size
The car's wheel(s) wobbles	• Loose wheel lug nuts • Wheels out of balance • Damaged wheel • Wheels are out of alignment • Worn or damaged ball joint • Excessive play in the steering linkage (usually due to worn parts) • Defective shock absorber	• Tighten wheel lug nuts • Have tires balanced • Raise car and spin the wheel. If the wheel is bent, it should be replaced • Have wheel alignment checked/adjusted • Check ball joints • Check steering linkage • Check shock absorbers
Tires wear unevenly or prematurely	• Incorrect wheel size • Wheels are out of balance • Wheels are out of alignment	• Check if wheel and tire size are compatible • Have wheels balanced • Have wheel alignment checked/adjusted

87971c09

Troubleshooting Basic Tire Problems

Problem	Cause	Solution
The car's front end vibrates at high speeds and the steering wheel shakes	• Wheels out of balance • Front end needs aligning	• Have wheels balanced • Have front end alignment checked
The car pulls to one side while cruising	• Unequal tire pressure (car will usually pull to the low side) • Mismatched tires • Front end needs aligning	• Check/adjust tire pressure • Be sure tires are of the same type and size • Have front end alignment checked
Abnormal, excessive or uneven tire wear See "How to Read Tire Wear"	• Infrequent tire rotation • Improper tire pressure • Sudden stops/starts or high speed on curves	• Rotate tires more frequently to equalize wear • Check/adjust pressure • Correct driving habits
Tire squeals	• Improper tire pressure • Front end needs aligning	• Check/adjust tire pressure • Have front end alignment checked

87971c10

FLUIDS AND LUBRICANTS

Fluid Disposal

Used fluids such as engine oil, transmission fluid, antifreeze and brake fluid are hazardous wastes and must be disposed of properly. Before draining any fluids, consult with the local authorities; in many areas, waste oil, etc. is being accepted as a part of recycling programs. A number of service stations and auto parts stores are also accepting waste fluids for recycling.

Be sure of the recycling center's policies before draining any fluids, as many will not accept different fluids that have been mixed together.

Recommendations

OIL

▶ **See Figures 167 and 168**

When adding oil to the crankcase or changing the oil and filter, it is important that oil of an equal quality to original equipment be used in your vehicle. The use of inferior oils may void the warranty, damage the engine, or both.

The Society of Automotive Engineers (SAE) grade number indicates the viscosity of the engine oil, and thus its ability to lubricate at a given temperature. The lower the SAE grade number, the lighter the oil. The lower the viscosity, the easier it is to crank the engine in cold weather but the less the oil will lubricate and protect the engine at high temperature. This number is marked on every oil container.

Oil viscosities should be chosen from those oils recommended for the lowest anticipated temperatures during the oil change interval.

Multi-viscosity oils (10W-30, 20W-50, etc.) offer the important advantage of being adaptable to temperature extremes. They

Fig. 168 Look for the API oil identification label when choosing your engine oil

allow easy starting at low temperatures, yet give good protection at high speeds and engine temperatures. This is a decided advantage in changeable climates or in long distance touring.

The American Petroleum Institute (API) designation indicates the classification of engine oil for use under given operating conditions. Only oils designated for use Service **SE** or **SF** or greater should be used. Oils of this type perform a variety of functions inside the engine in addition to the basic function as a lubricant. Through a balanced system of metallic detergents and polymeric dispersants, the oil prevents the formation of high and low temperature deposits, and also keeps sludge and dirt particles in suspension. Acids, particularly sulfuric acid, as well as other by-products of combustion, are neutralized. Both the SAE grade number and the API designation can be found on the oil container.

✻✻WARNING

Non-detergent or straight mineral oils must never be used.

FUEL

Your Subaru is designed to operate on unleaded fuel. The minimum octane rating of the fuels used must be at least 91 RON. All unleaded fuels sold in the U.S. are required to meet this minimum rating.

Use of a fuel too low in octane (a measurement of anti-knock quality) will result in spark knock. Since many factors affect operating efficiency, such as altitude, terrain, air temperature and humidity, knocking may result even though the recommended fuel is being used. If persistent knocking occurs, it may be necessary to switch to a slightly higher grade of gaso-

Oil Viscosity—Temperature Chart

When Outside Temperature is Consistently	Use SAE Viscosity Number
SINGLE GRADE OILS	
– 10°F to 32°F	10W
10°F to 60°F	20W-20
32°F to 90°F	30
Above 60°F	40
MULTIGRADE OILS	
Below 32°F	5W-30*
– 10°F to 90°F	10W-30
Above – 10°F	10W-40
Above 10°F	20W-40
Above 20°F	20W-50

*When sustained high-speed operation is anticipated, use the next higher grade.

87971g50

Fig. 167 Choose your oil based on anticipated driving conditions and temperatures for the next 3 months

line. Continuous or heavy knocking may result in engine damage.

➡Your engine's fuel requirement can change with time, mainly due to carbon buildup, which changes the compression ratio. If your engine pings, knocks, or runs on, switch to a higher grade of fuel, if possible, and check the ignition timing. Sometimes changing brands will cure the problem. If it is necessary to retard timing from specifications, don't change it more than a few degrees. Retarded timing will reduce power output and fuel mileage, and will increase engine temperature.

Engine

OIL LEVEL CHECK

▶ See Figures 169 and 170

The engine oil level should be checked at regular intervals. For example, whenever the car is refueled. Wait a few minutes after the engine is stopped before checking the oil level or an inaccurate reading will result. Also, the vehicle should be parked on a level surface.

✳✳CAUTION

If the low oil pressure warning light comes on while the engine is running, stop the engine immediately and check the oil level.

Remove the dipstick, which is located on the right (passenger) side of the crankcase, and wipe it with a clean cloth. Insert it again and withdraw it. The oil level should be at the F (FULL) upper mark or between the F mark and the lower mark (ADD) on the dipstick. Do not run the engine if the oil level falls below the lower mark.

Add oil as necessary. Use only oil which carries the API designation SF or SG. Always use oil with the proper viscosity rating (SAE number) for your particular driving conditions. Do not overfill. The oil level should never rise above the F mark.

Fig. 170 Add engine oil in small increments

OIL AND FILTER CHANGE

▶ See Figures 171, 172, 173, 174 and 175

The engine oil should be changed every 3000 miles (4,800 km). When the vehicle is operated in severe conditions (dusty conditions, stop-and-go driving or short distance conditions) more frequent changing is recommended.

Use a good quality motor oil of a known brand which meets the API classification SF/SG. The viscosity of the oil to be used should be determined by the driving conditions most frequently encountered.

All Subaru models are equipped with a spin-off oil filter. On all models, except the Justy, the filter is mounted at the left front of the engine (driver's side). On the Justy, the oil filter is mounted on the side of the engine facing the passengers' compartment. It is accessible from either above or below the car's engine compartment.

1. Run the engine until normal operating temperature is reached. This will make the oil flow more freely and it will carry off more contaminants. Stop the engine.

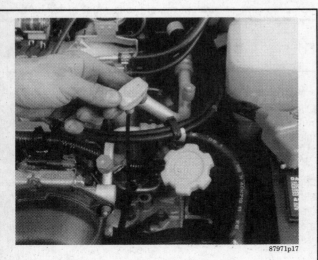

Fig. 169 Remove the dipstick from the tube — 2.5L engine shown

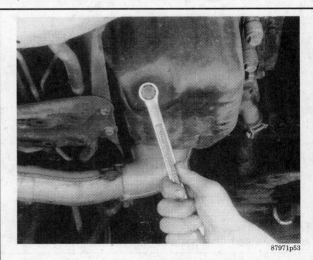

Fig. 171 With a suitable sized drain pan placed beneath the plug, loosen the oil pan drain plug

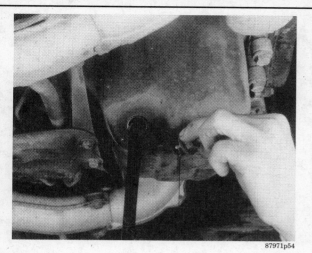

Fig. 172 Remove the drain plug, and allow the oil to drain into the pan beneath

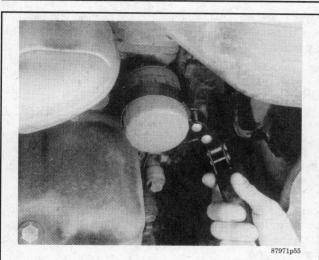

Fig. 173 Use an oil filter wrench to loosen and remove the oil filter — 2.2L engine shown

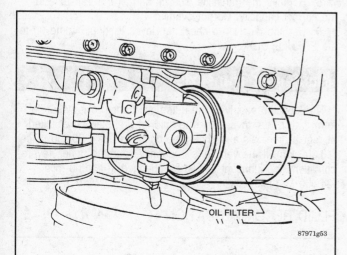

OIL FILTER

Fig. 174 Oil filter mounted at the side of the engine — 1.8L engine shown

Fig. 175 Apply a light coating of engine oil to the rubber gasket before installing the filter

2. Raise and support the vehicle safely on jackstands.

3. Remove the oil filler cap from the oil filler tube which is located on the right side of the engine (except on the 1.6L where it is on the left side).

4. Place a drain pan of adequate capacity below the drain plug which is located either at the front of the pan (Justy), or on the driver's side of the oil pan (all other models). A large, flat pan makes a good container to catch oil.

5. Use a wrench, ratchet and socket of the proper size to loosen the oil pan drain plug. Remove the drain plug while maintaining a slight upward force on it, to keep the oil from running out around it. Allow all of the oil to drain into the container.

6. Remove the container from under the drain hole and wipe any excess oil from around the drain area. Dispose of the old oil properly.

7. Install the drain plug and tighten to 29-33 ft. lbs. (39-44 Nm).

8. Since the oil filter is mounted horizontally, place a pan underneath it to catch the oil that will run out as soon as the filter is loosened.

9. Using a band wrench or other type oil filter wrench and turn the filter counterclockwise to remove it.

10. Wipe off the oil filter case and mounting boss with a clean cloth.

To install:

11. Install a new filter and gasket, after lubricating the gasket with clean engine oil. Hand-tighten the filter after the rubber gasket contacts the mounting boss. See instructions printed on or packed with the filter as tightening recommendations vary.

➡**Do not use the band wrench to tighten the oil filter. Tighten it by hand. Over tightening the filter will cause leaks.**

12. Add clean oil of the proper grade and viscosity through the oil filler tube at the top of the engine. Be sure that the oil level is near the upper F (FULL) mark on the dipstick.

13. Start the engine and allow it to idle until the oil light goes out. Stop the engine, wait a few minutes, and check the oil level. Add oil as necessary, but do not overfill.

14. Remember to replace the oil filler cap. Check for leaks.

Manual Transaxle

In manual transaxle equipped models, the transaxle and drive axle share a common supply of lubricant. On all models, the lubricant level should be checked at regular intervals and changed at 30,000 mile (48,300 km) intervals. When the vehicle is frequently operated under severe conditions, the lubricant should be changed at 15,000 mile (24,000 km) intervals.

FLUID RECOMMENDATIONS

When changing the fluid, use API GL-5 hypoid gear oil in one of the following viscosities:
- SAE 90 — above 30°F (-1°C)
- SAE 85W — below 30°F (-1°C)
- SAE 80W — below 0°F (-18°C)

LEVEL CHECK

▶ See Figures 176 and 177

The level is checked with a dipstick in much the same manner as the engine oil level. The fluid should be checked at the same intervals as the engine oil. The dipstick is located at the right rear of the transaxle housing.

➡**Be careful not to confuse it with the engine oil dipstick, which is located on the same side of the engine.**

Check the transaxle oil level with the car parked on a level surface and the engine stopped. The engine should be stopped for at least three minutes before the transaxle oil level is checked.

Pull the dipstick out and wipe it with a clean cloth. Insert the dipstick again and then remove it. The oil level should be between the upper F (FULL) and lower L (LOW) marks. If it is

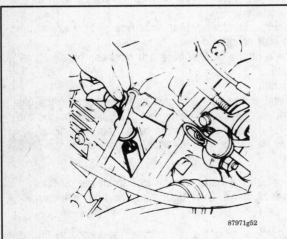

Fig. 176 Manual transaxle dipstick — all models except Justy

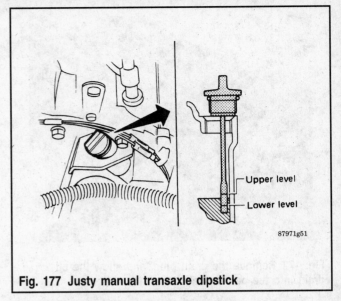

Fig. 177 Justy manual transaxle dipstick

below L, replenish it through the dipstick opening with GL-5 hypoid gear oil, of proper weight. Add a little oil at a time. The distance between the marks on the dipstick is less than a pint. Do not overfill.

DRAIN AND REFILL

1. Raise and support the vehicle safely.
2. Place a container of adequate capacity beneath the drain plug which is located underneath the car, on the bottom of the transaxle housing.
3. Use the proper size wrench or socket and ratchet to loosen the drain plug slowly while maintaining a slight upward pressure. This will keep the oil from leaking out around the plug. The drain plug is located at the bottom center of the transaxle case.
4. Allow all of the lubricant to drain from the transaxle, then install the drain plug and gasket (if so equipped). Tighten the drain plug to 30-35 ft. lbs. (41-47 Nm).
5. Remove the transaxle dipstick and fill the transaxle to the correct capacity. Do not overfill.
6. Use the dipstick to check the level. It should come up to the F (FULL) mark.

Automatic Transaxle

The lubricant supply in the automatic transaxle is separate from that in the drive axle. The fluid level should be checked at regular intervals and should be changed every 30,000 miles (48,300 km). If the vehicle is frequently operated under severe conditions the lubricant should be changed at 15,000 mile (24,000 km) intervals.

FLUID RECOMMENDATION

Dexron® type automatic transmission fluid is recommended by Subaru for use in their automatic transaxles.

LEVEL CHECK

▶ **See Figures 178, 179 and 180**

To check the automatic transmission fluid, drive the car several miles to bring the transaxle up to normal operating temperature. Park the car on a level surface, place the gear selector in **P** position and leave the engine idling.

Open the hood and locate the automatic transaxle dipstick on the left side of the engine, near the fire wall. Remove the dipstick, wipe it with a clean rag and reinsert it all the way. Remove it and note the reading.

➡ **While checking the fluid level, smell the oil on the dipstick. If the fluid has a burnt smell, serious transaxle problems are indicated.**

As long as the reading is between the upper level and lower level marks the fluid level is correct. If the level is at or below the lower mark, additional fluid is necessary. Add automatic transmission fluid with the Dexron® designation only.

Fig. 180 Use a funnel to add fluid through the dipstick tube

Fluid should be added through the neck of the dipstick hole using a funnel. With the engine still idling, add fluid in small quantities at a time and recheck the level after each addition. Stop when the fluid level is close to the upper level mark. Avoid overfilling; do not fill above the upper mark.

DRAIN AND REFILL

▶ **See Figures 181 and 182**

1. Raise and support the vehicle safely on jackstands.
2. Place a container of adequate capacity beneath the drain plug located at the bottom, center of the transaxle case.
3. Remove the drain plug and allow the fluid to drain. The drain plug is located on the bottom left side of the transaxle case.
4. After draining, replace the drain plug and gasket. Tighten the plug to 17-20 ft. lbs. (23-26 Nm). Do not overtighten.
5. Remove the transaxle dipstick and fill the transaxle through the dipstick hole with the proper amount of automatic transmission fluid.

Fig. 178 Remove the dipstick from the tube — Legacy

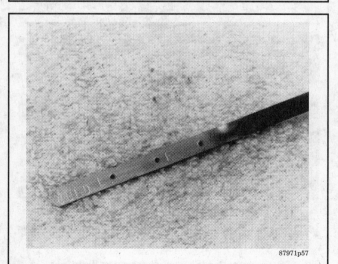

Fig. 179 With the dipstick clean, the upper and lower hash marks are visible

Fig. 181 Loosen the transaxle pan drain plug

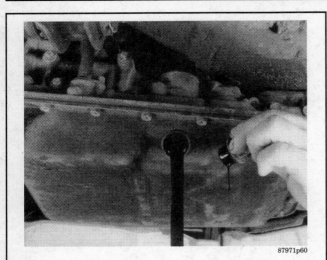
Fig. 182 Remove the drain plug and allow the fluid to drain into the pan beneath

6. Check the fluid level.

PAN AND FILTER SERVICE

▶ See Figures 183, 184, 185, 186, 187, 188, 189, 190, 191 and 192

Normal maintenance does not require removal of the transaxle oil pan, or changing or cleaning of the filter. However, if a leak is detected at the transaxle oil pan gasket, it must be replaced. Some models do not incorporate an oil strainer.

1. Raise and support the vehicle safely on jackstands.
2. Remove the drain plug and drain the transmission fluid into a suitable container.
3. Remove the mounting bolts and lower the oil pan and gasket.
4. If you wish to remove the oil strainer, simply unbolt it from the valve body. It can be cleaned in a nonflammable solvent and dried with compressed air or allowed to air dry.

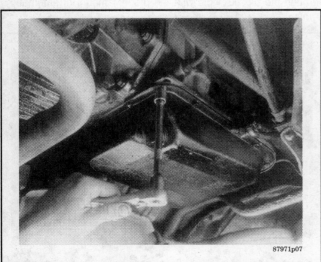
Fig. 183 Loosen the fluid pan retaining bolts — 1.8L engine

Fig. 184 After the fluid has been drained, loosen the pan bolts — Legacy transaxle shown

Fig. 185 Lower the transaxle's fluid pan and . . .

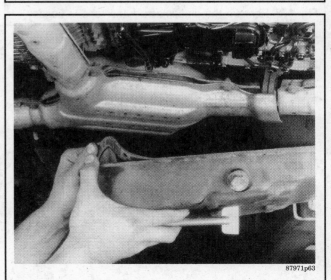
Fig. 186 . . . remove the gasket from the fluid pan

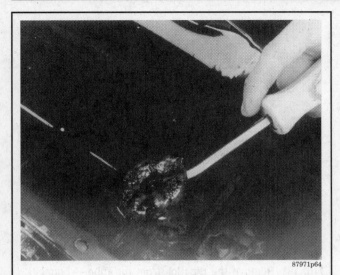

Fig. 187 Remove and clean the magnet inside the pan

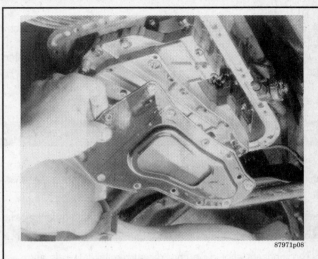

Fig. 190 After the filter has been removed, inspect the screen for debris — 1.8L transaxle shown

Fig. 188 Loosen and remove the filter screen retainer bolts

Fig. 191 Removing the filter screen from a Legacy transaxle

Fig. 189 On some models, a fluid tube must be removed before the filter can be detached

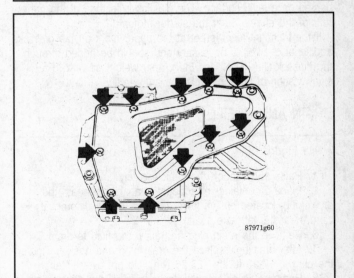

Fig. 192 Automatic transaxle filter and retaining bolts

To install:

5. Install the oil strainer and tighten the bolts to 26-35 inch lbs. (4-5 Nm).

6. Using a new gasket, install the oil pan and bolts. Tighten the bolts to 30-39 inch lbs. (3.5-4.5 Nm).

7. Lower the vehicle and fill the transaxle with fluid. Start the engine and check the transmission fluid level.

Transfer Case

Lubricant to the transfer case is supplied through the transaxle. If the level of fluid in the transaxle is full, so is the transfer case.

Drive Axle (Front)

The lubricant should be checked at regular intervals and changed at 60,000 mile (96,500 km) intervals. When the vehicle is frequently operated under severe conditions, the lubricant should be changed at 30,000 mile (48,300 km) intervals.

➡This section pertains to automatic transaxle-equipped vehicles only.

FLUID RECOMMENDATIONS

Use gear oil with API classification GL-5 for open differentials and GLS for limited slip differential. Viscosity should be:
- SAE 90 — above 30°F (-1°C)
- SAE 85W — above 30°F (-1°C)
- SAE 80W — below 0°F (-18°C)

LEVEL CHECK

▶ See Figures 193, 194, 195 and 196

The lubricant level in the drive axle is checked in the same manner as the engine oil, with the engine off and the vehicle parked on a level surface. The dipstick is located at the right rear of the engine, near the starter motor.

If the lubricant level is not at the upper mark on the dipstick additional gear oil is necessary and should be added through the dipstick filler tube. Use the proper weight oil with API classification of GL-5 or GLS. Do not overfill.

DRAIN AND REFILL

▶ See Figure 197

1. Raise and support the vehicle safely.

2. Place a container of adequate capacity beneath the drain plug, located on the lower left side of the differential case, near the left axle shaft.

3. Remove the drain plug and allow the fluid to drain.

4. After draining, replace the drain plug and gasket. Tighten the plug to 17-20 ft. lbs. (23-26 Nm). Do not overtighten.

5. Remove the differential dipstick and fill the differential to the upper mark on the dipstick.

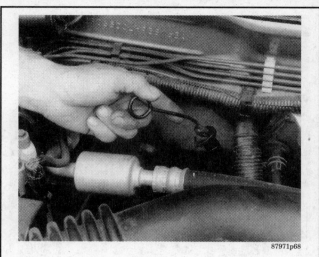

Fig. 193 Remove the dipstick from the tube — Legacy shown

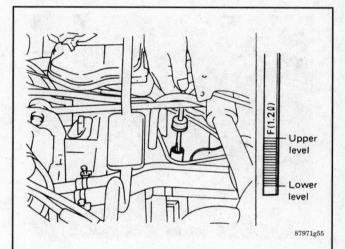

Fig. 194 Front drive axle dipstick and level marks — 1.8L models

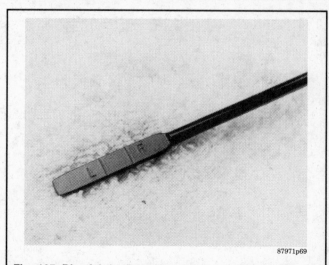

Fig. 195 Dipstick hash marks — Legacy shown, other models similar

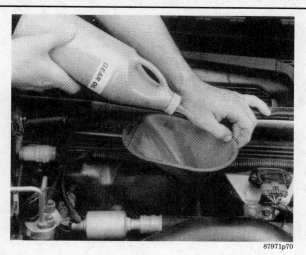

Fig. 196 Use a funnel to add fluid through the dipstick tube

Fig. 197 Front differential case's drain plug — automatic transaxle equipped models only

Rear Drive Axle (4WD)

The lubricant should be checked at regular intervals and changed at 60,000 mile (96,500 km) intervals. When the vehicle is frequently operated under severe conditions, the lubricant should be changed at 30,000 mile (48,300 km) intervals.

FLUID RECOMMENDATIONS

Use gear oil with API classification GL-5 for open differentials and GLS for limited slip differential. Viscosity should be:
- SAE 90 — above 30°F (-1°C)
- SAE 85W — above 30°F (-1°C)
- SAE 80W — below 0°F (-18°C)

LEVEL CHECK

▶ See Figures 198 and 199

Unlike the procedures outlined above, the lubricant level in the rear differential must be checked from underneath the vehicle.

1. Park the car on a level surface, turn **OFF** the engine and engage the parking brake.
2. Crawl under the car from the rear until the differential housing can be reached easily.
3. Remove the filler hole (upper) plug from the back of the differential case.
4. The lubricant should be at the level of the filler hole. If not, add the proper weight gear oil with API classification of GL-5 or GLS.
5. Install the filler plug and tighten to 33 ft. lbs. (44 Nm).

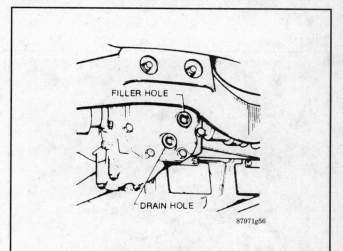

Fig. 198 Rear differential fill and drain plugs — all 4WD models except Justy

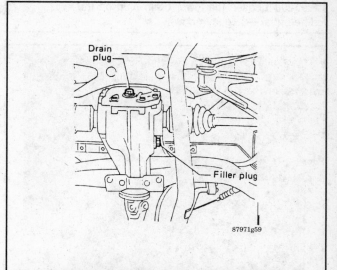

Fig. 199 Justy rear differential fill and drain plugs

DRAIN AND REFILL

▶ **See Figures 200, 201, 202 and 203**

1. Park the car on a level surface, turn off the engine and engage the parking brake.

2. Crawl under the car from the rear until the differential housing can be reached easily.

3. Place a container of adequate capacity beneath the drain plug.

4. Remove the filler hole (upper) plug from the back of the differential case.

5. Remove the drain hole (lower) plug from the back of the differential case and drain all lubricant from the differential.

6. Install the drain hole plug and tighten to 33 ft. lbs. (44 Nm).

7. Fill the differential with the proper grade of lubricant until the level of the lubricant is at the filler hole.

8. Install the filler hole plug and tighten to 33 ft. lbs. (44 Nm).

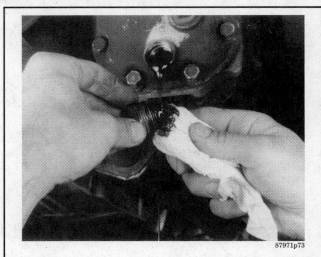

Fig. 202 Clean any metal particles from the magnetic tip of the drain plug

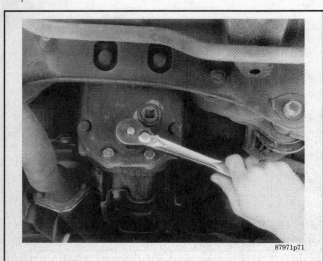

Fig. 200 Loosen the lower drain plug on the differential — Legacy shown

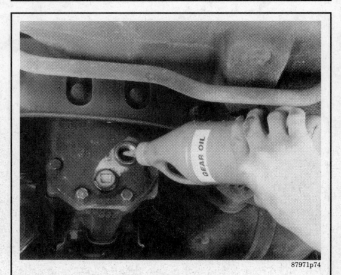

Fig. 203 Add fluid through the upper fill hole

Cooling System

▶ **See Figures 204 and 205**

A complete cooling system check should be performed and the antifreeze replaced at 30,000 mile (48,300 km) intervals.

FLUID RECOMMENDATION

▶ **See Figure 206**

A 50/50 mixture of an anti-corrosive ethylene glycol coolant or other type antifreeze and water is recommended. Since the Subaru crankcase is aluminum, the antifreeze should contain an anti-rust agent.

➡ **Inexpensive antifreeze testers are available to measure the degree of protection provided by the cooling system.**

Fig. 201 With a suitable drain pan placed beneath the differential, remove the plug and allow the fluid to drain

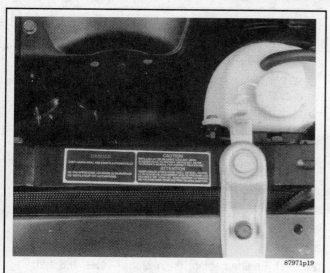

Fig. 204 Read all warning labels on the radiator . . .

Fig. 205 . . . and radiator cap

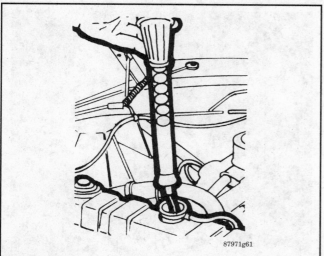

Fig. 206 Testing the coolant concentration with an antifreeze tester

LEVEL CHECK

♦ See Figures 207 and 208

The coolant level should be checked at regular intervals or if the temperature gauge registers HOT (H). The coolant level should not fall below the FULL mark on the side of the reserve tank.

✳✳CAUTION

NEVER remove a radiator cap when the vehicle is hot or has been driven for an extended period of time. The coolant temperature and pressure could cause serious injury.

Fig. 207 Many radiator caps have warnings written on them; read and observe them for safety's sake

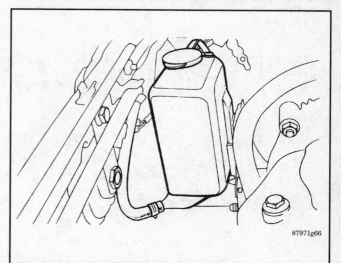

Fig. 208 An example of a coolant reservoir — Justy shown

DRAIN AND REFILL

▶ See Figures 209, 210, 211, 212 and 213

1. Pull out the end of the drain tube to the underside of the body from between the undercover and skirt.

2. Place a container of adequate capacity beneath the drain plug and open the plug.

3. Loosen the radiator cap or overflow tank to drain the coolant.

4. Remove and drain the coolant from the reserve tank, if equipped.

5. On all models except Justy, remove the drain plugs on the side of the engine near the oil filter and drain the coolant from the engine block.

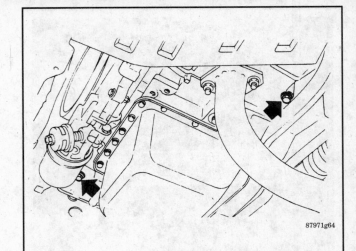

Fig. 211 Engine coolant drain plugs — 1.6L and 1.8L engines

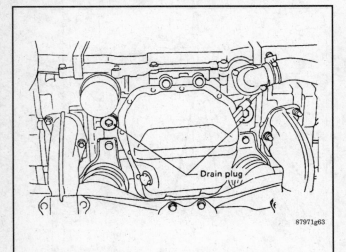

Fig. 209 Loosen the radiator drain plug and tube

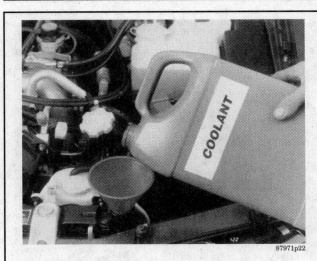

Fig. 212 Fill the radiator with fresh coolant and water — 2.5L engine shown

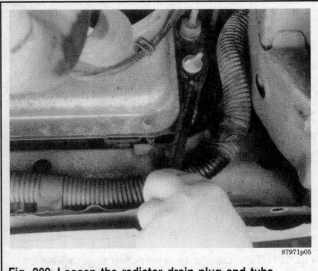
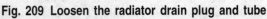

Fig. 210 Engine drain plug — 2.2L, 2.5L and 3.3L engines

Fig. 213 Also add coolant to the reservoir, if equipped

6. Install and securely tighten the engine drain plugs. Tighten the radiator drain plug.

➡Some vehicles are equipped with an air vent plug on the radiator. This plug must be removed while filling the system to allow trapped air to escape the system.

7. Slowly pour a 50/50 mixture of antifreeze and water into the radiator until it is filled. Install the radiator cap.
8. Fill the coolant recovery tank to the FULL mark.
9. Start the engine and allow it to reach operating temperature.
10. Stop the engine and allow it to cool.
11. Open the radiator cap and fill the radiator with antifreeze. Wait until the engine cools further, then fill the recovery tank to the FULL mark.
12. Start the engine and allow it to reach operating temperature. Check the level in the recovery tank and add antifreeze as necessary.

FLUSHING AND CLEANING THE SYSTEM

▶ See Figures 209, 210, 211, 212 and 213

The cooling system should be drained, thoroughly flushed and refilled at least every 30,000 miles (48,300 km). This operation should be done with the engine cold.
1. Pull out the end of the drain tube to the underside of the body from between the undercover and skirt.
2. Place a container of adequate capacity beneath the drain plug and open the plug.
3. Loosen the radiator cap to drain the coolant.
4. Remove and drain the coolant from the reserve tank.
5. On all models except Justy, remove the drain plugs on the side of the engine near the oil filter and drain the coolant from the engine block.
6. Install and securely tighten the engine drain plugs. Tighten the radiator drain plug.
7. Slowly pour water into the radiator until the system is full. Repeat the draining and filling process several times, until the liquid is nearly colorless.

➡Some vehicles are equipped with an air vent plug on the radiator. This plug must be removed while filling the system to allow trapped air to escape the system.

8. After the last draining, slowly pour a 50/50 mixture of antifreeze and water into the radiator until it is filled. Install the radiator cap.
9. Fill the coolant recovery tank to the FULL mark.
10. Start the engine and allow it to reach operating temperature.
11. Stop the engine and allow it to cool.
12. Open the radiator cap and fill the radiator with antifreeze. Wait until the engine cools further, then fill the recovery tank to the FULL mark.
13. Start the engine and allow it to reach operating temperature. Check the level in the recovery tank and add antifreeze as necessary.

Brake Master Cylinder

FLUID RECOMMENDATIONS

Always use a brake fluid which meets DOT-3 or DOT-4 heavy duty specifications.

LEVEL CHECK

▶ See Figures 214, 215 and 216

The brake fluid level should be check at regular intervals. Drain the brake fluid and replace it at 30,000 mile (48,300 km) intervals. When the vehicle is frequently used in humid conditions or mountainous areas, change the brake fluid at 15,000 mile (24,000 km) intervals.

Fig. 214 Brake fluid reservoir — 1985 model shown

Fig. 215 Some brake fluid caps have warnings written on them. Read and observe all warnings

Fig. 216 Slowly add brake fluid to the reservoir, being careful not to overfill

Fig. 217 Power steering fluid reservoir cap with fluid recommendation written on it — Legacy shown

The brake master cylinder reservoir(s) are made of translucent plastic so that the fluid level may be checked without removing the caps. Check the brake fluid level at regular intervals. If the brake system warning light comes on, stop the car and immediately check the brake fluid level.

If the fluid level in either of the master cylinder reservoir(s) falls below the bottom (MIN) line molded on the side of the reservoir, add brake fluid to bring the level up to the top (MAX) line. Clean the top of the reservoir off before removing the cap to prevent dirt from entering the master cylinder. Pour the fluid slowly to prevent air bubbles from forming. Brake fluid is a good paint remover, so don't spill any on the car's paint.

❊❊CAUTION

Do not use a lower grade of brake fluid than specified. Never mix different types of brake fluid. Doing either of the above could cause a brake system failure.

Power Steering Pump

Power steering pump fluid level should be checked at 15,000 mile (24,000 km) intervals.

FLUID RECOMMENDATION

Dexron®II ATF is the recommended fluid for the power steering pump.

LEVEL CHECK

▶ See Figures 217, 218, 219, 220 and 221

1. Drive the vehicle several miles to raise the power steering system up to normal operating temperature.
2. Park the vehicle on a level surface and stop the engine.
3. Remove the level gauge, wipe it clean, then replace it fully.

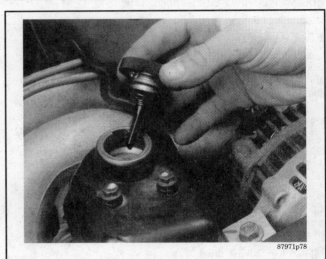

Fig. 218 Remove the cap and clean the dipstick portion . . .

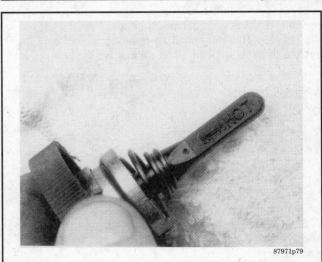

Fig. 219 . . . to reveal the hot level markings on one side . . .

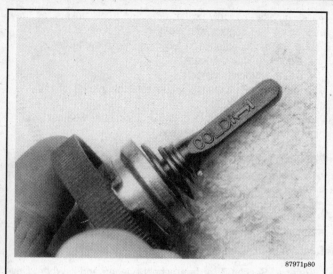

Fig. 220 . . . and the cold level markings on the other

Fig. 221 Use a funnel to add fluid to the reservoir

4. Remove it again and read the level at the HOT side of the gauge. If the fluid reading is at the lower level or below, add the recommended power steering fluid until it reaches the upper mark.

5. When the fluid level has to be checked without warming up the power steering system, read the level at the COLD side of the gauge and add fluid accordingly.

Steering Gear

FLUID RECOMMENDATION

Subaru recommends only genuine Subaru Valiant Grease M2, Part No. 003608001.

LEVEL CHECK

The steering box does not require greasing unless it has been disassembled.

Windshield Washer

FLUID RECOMMENDATION

Use a commercial solvent and water solution, one part solvent to two parts water for summer. Use the solvent undiluted in winter.

LEVEL CHECK

▶ See Figure 222

Check the level of the windshield washer solution in the front and rear container, if equipped with a rear wiper, in the translucent reservoir tank at the same time the oil is being checked.

Chassis Greasing

Under normal conditions regular chassis greasing is unnecessary, because there are no chassis grease fittings used on Subaru models. The only time greasing is required is as part of chassis component repair or replacement, or if component dust boots and seals have become damaged. If its boot or seal is damaged or leaking, the component will have to be removed, repacked with grease, and a new boot or seal installed.

Because there are no recommended chassis greasing intervals, the chassis suspension and drive train components should be inspected regularly. If a visual inspection turns up a damaged component, dust boot, or seal, consult the appropriate Section for the correct repair or replacement procedure.

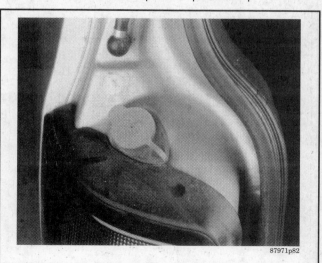

Fig. 222 Rear washer fill location on station wagon models

Pedals and Linkage

The clutch, brake, and accelerator linkages should be lubricated at the recommended intervals found in the owners manual, with multipurpose chassis grease.

1. Working inside the car, apply a small amount of grease to the pedal pivots and linkage.

2. Working under the hood, grease all pivoting and sliding parts of the accelerator and brake linkages.

Body Lubrication

▶ See Figure 223

Body lubrication should be performed at regularly scheduled intervals.

Apply multipurpose chassis grease to the following areas:
• Hood hinges, lock, and striker
• Door hinges, latch, and striker
• Trunk hinges and striker

Use grease sparingly on the door and trunk strikers, as they may come into contact with clothing.

Use powdered graphite to lubricate the following items:
• Door key lock cylinders
• Trunk key lock cylinders

Do not use oil or grease to lubricate the insides of lock cylinders.

Use silicone lubricant to preserve the rubber weather stripping around the doors and trunk.

Wheel Bearings

REMOVAL, PACKING AND INSTALLATION

Rear Wheel Bearings

Refer to Section 7 for front wheel bearing and 4-Wheel Drive wheel bearing service.

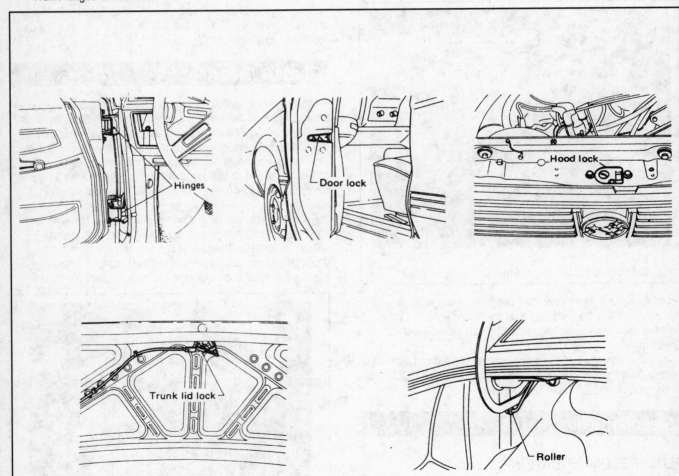

Fig. 223 Body lubrication points

87971g69

DRUM BRAKES

▶ **See Figures 224 and 225**

1. Raise and support the vehicle safely.
2. Remove the rear wheels and tires.
3. Pry the brake drum cap off using a suitable tool.
4. Flatten the lockwasher and loosen the axle nut, then remove the lockwasher, lock plate and brake drum. Remove the brake drum taking care not to drop the outer bearing.
5. Check the condition of the bearing grease. If either the grease appears to be white or if only a small amount of grease remains, remove the bearing from the housing, clean it and pack it with fresh grease.
6. To remove the inner bearing, remove the grease seal using a seal puller or equivalent.
7. Clean the bearings with solvent and let air dry on a shop rag.

➡Do not use compressed air to dry the bearings as damage will result.

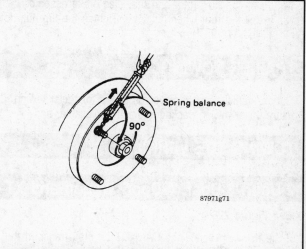

Fig. 225 Measuring the starting force of a rear drum — except Legacy and SVX

8. Place a ball of grease in the palm of your hand and roll the bearing through the grease. Force the grease through the bearing cage into the rollers. Continue to roll the bearing, adding grease to your hand, until the bearing is completely filled with grease.
9. Install the rear bearing and using a soft faced hammer, install the grease seal. Ensure that the seal is fully seated.
10. Install the drum, outer bearing, lock plate, lockwasher and axle nut in this order on to the spindle. Always use a new lockplate and lockwasher.
11. Tighten the locknut to 36 ft. lbs. (49 Nm) and rotate the drum in both directions to seat the bearings.
12. Loosen the locknut ⅛ turn. Tighten the locknut to obtain a starting force of 2-3 lbs. (8-14 N) on all models except Justy; 3-4 lbs. (14-20 N) on Justy. Ensure that there is no free-play in the bearing.
13. Install the brake drum cap, wheel and tire. Tighten lug nuts to 58-72 ft. lbs. (78-98 Nm).
14. Lower the vehicle and test drive.

DISC BRAKES

1. Raise and support the vehicle safely.
2. While holding the rear wheel by hand, try to move it in and out (toward you and away from you) to check bearing free-play.
3. Remove the rear wheel and tire.
4. If bearing free-play exists, attach a dial gauge to the hub and measure the axial free-play.
5. If free-play is greater than 0.0020 in. (0.05mm), disassemble the rear hub and check the bearings.
6. Pry the rotor cap off with a suitable tool.
7. Unlock the axle nut and remove the nut and washer.
8. Remove the rear disc brake assembly from the backing plate and suspend it out of the way using a wire.
9. Remove the disc rotor from the hub, then remove the hub.
10. Inspect the hub bearings for damage and replace the hub assembly as necessary.
11. Install the hub, then, using a new washer and locknut, tighten to 123-152 ft. lbs. (167-206 Nm) and lock into place. Install the rotor cap.

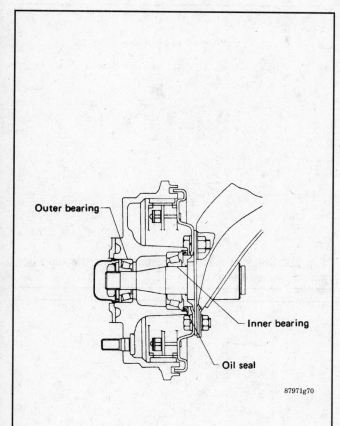

Fig. 224 Rear wheel bearing assembly — except Legacy and SVX models

12. Install the disc rotor and rear disc brake assembly.

13. Install the rear wheel and tire. Tighten the lug nuts to 58-72 ft. lbs. (78-98 Nm).

14. Lower the vehicle and test drive.

TRAILER TOWING

Subaru vehicles are not recommended for trailer towing. Factory trailer towing packages are not available, and aftermarket towing hitches should not be installed on your Subaru.

TOWING THE VEHICLE

2-Door, 3-Door, 4-Door, Wagon and XT

▶ See Figure 226

If the following conditions CANNOT be met, transport the vehicle using a flat-bed truck.

1. On manual transaxle equipped vehicles, turn the differential lock switch to the **OFF** position and make sure that the differential lock indicator light is not illuminated.

2. If the engine cannot be started to switch the differential lock switch, raise the front wheels and move the lock lever on the right side of the transaxle towards the rear.

3. On automatic transaxle equipped vehicles, set the car in front wheel drive mode by inserting a spare fuse in the FWD connector inside the engine compartment.

4. Place the vehicle in Neutral.

5. Check the transaxle oil level and add oil if the level is low.

6. Do not tow the vehicle at more than 30 mph (48 kp/h) or for more than 31 miles (50 km).

Loyale

▶ See Figures 227 and 228

If the following conditions cannot be met, transport the vehicle using a flat-bed truck.

1. On manual transaxle and 3-speed automatic transaxle equipped vehicles, turn the differential lock switch to the **OFF** position and make sure that the differential lock indicator light is not illuminated.

2. On 4-speed automatic transaxle equipped vehicles, set the car in front wheel drive mode by inserting a spare fuse in the FWD connector inside the engine compartment.

3. Disconnect the harness connector for the 4WD solenoid valve (manual transaxle) or the transfer solenoid (automatic transaxle) inside the engine compartment.

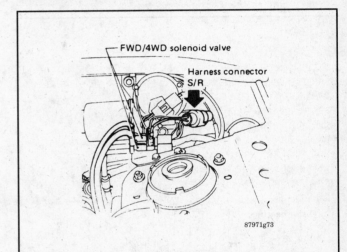

Fig. 227 Unfasten the AWD solenoid valve, if equipped with a manual transaxle

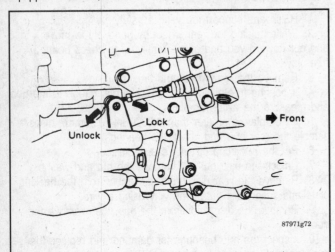

Fig. 226 Differential lock lever — 2-door, 3-door, 4-door, wagon and XT models

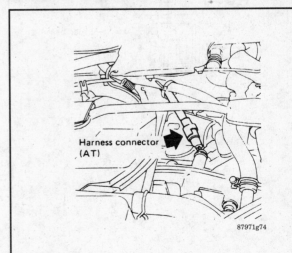

Fig. 228 If equipped with an automatic transaxle, unfasten the transfer solenoid harness

4. Place the vehicle in neutral.

5. Check the transaxle oil level and oil if level is low.

6. Do not tow the vehicle at more than 30 mph (48 kp/h) or for more than 31 miles (50 km).

JUMP STARTING A DEAD BATTERY

▶ See Figure 229

Whenever a vehicle is jump started, precautions must be followed in order to prevent the possibility of personal injury. Remember that batteries contain a small amount of explosive hydrogen gas which is a by-product of battery charging. Sparks should always be avoided when working around batteries, especially when attaching jumper cables. To minimize the possibility of accidental sparks, follow the procedure carefully.

❈❈CAUTION

NEVER hook the batteries up in a series circuit or the entire electrical system will go up in smoke, including the starter!

Vehicles equipped with a diesel engine may utilize two 12 volt batteries. If so, the batteries are connected in a parallel circuit (positive terminal to positive terminal, negative terminal to negative terminal). Hooking the batteries up in parallel circuit increases battery cranking power without increasing total battery voltage output. Output remains at 12 volts. On the other hand, hooking two 12 volt batteries up in a series circuit (positive terminal to negative terminal, positive terminal to negative terminal) increases total battery output to 24 volts (12 volts plus 12 volts).

Legacy and SVX

➡**Do not tow these vehicles with either the front or rear wheels on the ground. Damage to the viscous coupling may result. Transport the vehicle using a flat-bed truck.**

Jump Starting Precautions

• Be sure that both batteries are of the same voltage. Vehicles covered by this manual and most vehicles on the road today utilize a 12 volt charging system.

• Be sure that both batteries are of the same polarity (have the same terminal, in most cases NEGATIVE grounded).

• Be sure that the vehicles are not touching or a short could occur.

• On serviceable batteries, be sure the vent cap holes are not obstructed.

• Do not smoke or allow sparks anywhere near the batteries.

• In cold weather, make sure the battery electrolyte is not frozen. This can occur more readily in a battery that has been in a state of discharge.

• Do not allow electrolyte to contact your skin or clothing.

Jump Starting Procedure

1. Make sure that the voltages of the 2 batteries are the same. Most batteries and charging systems are of the 12 volt variety.

2. Pull the jumping vehicle (with the good battery) into a position so the jumper cables can reach the dead battery and that vehicle's engine. Make sure that the vehicles do NOT touch.

3. Place the transmissions/transaxles of both vehicles in **Neutral** (MT) or **P** (AT), as applicable, then firmly set their parking brakes.

➡**If necessary for safety reasons, the hazard lights on both vehicles may be operated throughout the entire procedure without significantly increasing the difficulty of jumping the dead battery.**

4. Turn all lights and accessories OFF on both vehicles. Make sure the ignition switches on both vehicles are turned to the **OFF** position.

5. Cover the battery cell caps with a rag, but do not cover the terminals.

6. Make sure the terminals on both batteries are clean and free of corrosion or proper electrical connection will be impeded. If necessary, clean the battery terminals before proceeding.

7. Identify the positive (+) and negative (-) terminals on both batteries.

8. Connect the first jumper cable to the positive (+) terminal of the dead battery, then connect the other end of that cable to the positive (+) terminal of the booster (good) battery.

9. Connect one end of the other jumper cable to the negative (-) terminal on the booster battery and the final cable

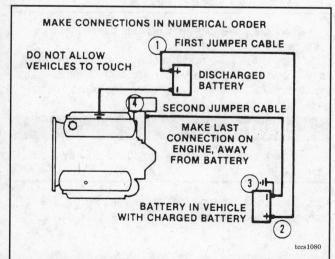

MAKE CONNECTIONS IN NUMERICAL ORDER

① FIRST JUMPER CABLE

DO NOT ALLOW VEHICLES TO TOUCH

DISCHARGED BATTERY

SECOND JUMPER CABLE

MAKE LAST CONNECTION ON ENGINE, AWAY FROM BATTERY

BATTERY IN VEHICLE WITH CHARGED BATTERY

tccs1080

Fig. 229 Connect the jumper cables to the batteries and engine in the order shown

clamp to an engine bolt head, alternator bracket or other solid, metallic point on the engine with the dead battery. Try to pick a ground on the engine that is positioned away from the battery in order to minimize the possibility of the 2 clamps touching should one loosen during the procedure. DO NOT connect this clamp to the negative (-) terminal of the bad battery.

✳✳CAUTION

Be very careful to keep the jumper cables away from moving parts (cooling fan, belts, etc.) on both engines.

10. Check to make sure that the cables are routed away from any moving parts, then start the donor vehicle's engine. Run the engine at moderate speed for several minutes to allow the dead battery a chance to receive some initial charge.

11. With the donor vehicle's engine still running slightly above idle, try to start the vehicle with the dead battery. Crank the engine for no more than 10 seconds at a time and let the starter cool for at least 20 seconds between tries. If the vehicle does not start in 3 tries, it is likely that something else is also wrong or that the battery needs additional time to charge.

12. Once the vehicle is started, allow it to run at idle for a few seconds to make sure that it is operating properly.

13. Turn ON the headlights, heater blower and, if equipped, the rear defroster of both vehicles in order to reduce the severity of voltage spikes and subsequent risk of damage to the vehicles' electrical systems when the cables are disconnected. This step is especially important to any vehicle equipped with computer control modules.

14. Carefully disconnect the cables in the reverse order of connection. Start with the negative cable that is attached to the engine ground, then the negative cable on the donor battery. Disconnect the positive cable from the donor battery and finally, disconnect the positive cable from the formerly dead battery. Be careful when disconnecting the cables from the positive terminals not to allow the alligator clips to touch any metal on either vehicle or a short and sparks will occur.

JACKING

Scissors Type Jack

▶ **See Figures 230 and 231**

All Subaru models come with a scissors type jack for tire changing. The jack on all models is stored in the engine compartment, rather than in the trunk.

Jacking points are located on both sides of the car, just behind the front wheel well and just forward of the rear wheel well. Do not place the jack underneath the floor pan sheet metal or bumpers.

There are certain safety precautions which should be observed when jacking the vehicle:

1. Always jack the car on a level surface.
2. Set the parking brake if the rear wheels are to be raised (parking brake works on the front wheels). This will keep the car from rolling off the jack.
3. If the front wheels are to be raised, block the rear wheels.

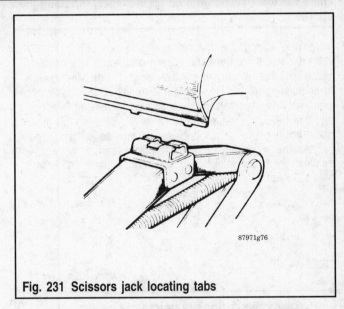

Fig. 231 Scissors jack locating tabs

4. Block the wheel diagonally opposite the one which is being raised.

5. If the car is being raised in order to work underneath it, support it with jackstands. Do not place the jackstands against the sheet metal panels beneath the car. The panels will become distorted.

✳✳CAUTION

Do not work beneath a vehicle supported only by a tire changing jack.

6. Do not use a bumper jack to raise the vehicle. The bumpers are not designed for this purpose.

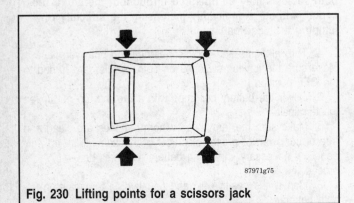

Fig. 230 Lifting points for a scissors jack

Floor Jack

⬧ **See Figures 232, 233 and 234**

When jacking up the front of the car using a floor jack always use the front crossmember as the contact point, never a suspension or steering part and never the engine oil pan. Always block the rear of the back wheels, and always use a block of wood between the saddle of the jack and the crossmember.

When jacking up the rear of the car using a floor jack, place blocks in front of the front wheels and always place the jack in contact with the center of the rear crossmember. On four wheel drive models contact the bottom of the rear differential carrier.

Always jack slowly until the car is high enough to place the safety stands in their proper positions. The safety stands should be placed in the same location points as shown for the scissors type jack. Make sure the stands are set on the flange of the side sill.

Fig. 232 Raising the front of the vehicle at the crossmember with a floor jack

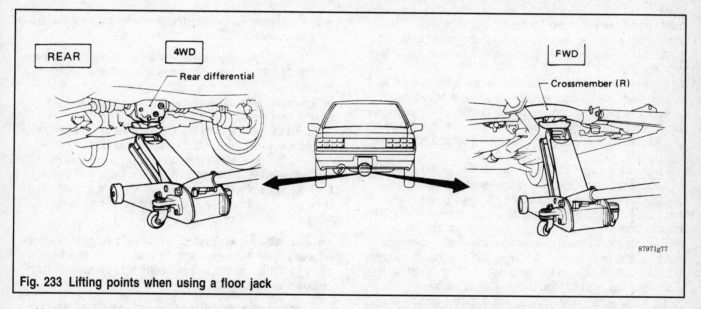
Fig. 233 Lifting points when using a floor jack

• Never work under a vehicle that is supported by a jack alone. Always use jackstands.
• Never use cinder blocks or stacks of wood, even if you are only going to be under the vehicle for a few minutes.
• Drive-on trestles or ramps are also handy and a safe way to both raise and support the vehicle.

Fig. 234 Lifting the rear of an All Wheel Drive (AWD) model by the differential

HOW TO BUY A USED VEHICLE

Many people believe that a two or three year old used car or truck is a better buy than a new vehicle. This may be true as most new vehicles suffer the heaviest depreciation in the first two years and, at three years old, a vehicle is usually not old enough to present a lot of costly repair problems. But keep in mind, when buying a non-warranted automobile, there are no guarantees. Whatever the age of the used vehicle you might want to purchase, this section and a little patience should increase your chances of selecting one that is safe and dependable.

Tips

1. First decide what model you want, and how much you want to spend.

2. Check the used car lots and your local newspaper ads. Privately owned vehicles are usually less expensive, however, you may not get a warranty that, in many cases, comes with a used vehicle purchased from a lot. Of course, some aftermarket warranties may not be worth the extra money, so this is a point you will have to debate and consider based on your priorities.

3. Never shop at night. The glare of the lights make it easy to miss faults on the body caused by accident or rust repair.

4. Try to get the name and phone number of the previous owner. Contact him/her and ask about the vehicle. If the owner of a lot refuses this information, look for a vehicle somewhere else.

A private seller can tell you about the vehicle and maintenance. But remember, there's no law requiring honesty from private citizens selling used vehicles. There is a law that forbids tampering with or turning back the odometer mileage. This includes both the private citizen and the lot owner. The law also requires that the seller or anyone transferring ownership of the vehicle must provide the buyer with a signed statement indicating the mileage on the odometer at the time of transfer.

5. You may wish to contact the National Highway Traffic Safety Administration (NHTSA) to find out if the vehicle has ever been included in a manufacturer's recall. Write down the year, model and serial number before you buy the vehicle, then contact NHTSA (there should be a 1-800 number that your phone company's information line can supply). If the vehicle was listed for a recall, make sure the needed repairs were made.

6. Refer to the Used Vehicle Checklist in this section and check all the items on the vehicle you are considering. Some items are more important than others. Only you know how much money you can afford for repairs, and depending on the price of the vehicle, may consider performing any needed work yourself. Beware, however, of trouble in areas that will affect operation, safety or emission. Problems in the Used Vehicle Checklist break down as follows:

• Numbers 1-8: Two or more problems in these areas indicate a lack of maintenance. You should beware.

• Numbers 9-13: Problems here tend to indicate a lack of proper care, however, these can usually be corrected with a tune-up or relatively simple parts replacement.

• Numbers 14-17: Problems in the engine or transmission can be very expensive. Unless you are looking for a project, walk away from any vehicle with problems in 2 or more of these areas.

7. If you are satisfied with the apparent condition of the vehicle, take it to an independent diagnostic center or mechanic for a complete check. If you have a state inspection program, have it inspected immediately before purchase, or specify on the bill of sale that the sale is conditional on passing state inspection.

8. Road test the vehicle — refer to the Road Test Checklist in this section. If your original evaluation and the road test agree — the rest is up to you.

USED VEHICLE CHECKLIST

▶ See Figure 235

➡The numbers on the illustrations refer to the numbers on this checklist.

1. Mileage: Average mileage is about 12,000-15,000 miles (19,324-24,155 km) per year. More than average mileage may indicate hard usage or could indicate many highway miles (which could be less detrimental than half as many tough around town miles).

2. Paint: Check around the tailpipe, molding and windows for overspray indicating that the vehicle has been repainted.

3. Rust: Check fenders, doors, rocker panels, window moldings, wheel wells, floorboards, under floormats, and in the trunk for signs of rust. Any rust at all will be a problem. There is no way to permanently stop the spread of rust, except to replace the part or panel.

➡If rust repair is suspected, try using a magnet to check for body filler. A magnet should stick to the sheet metal parts of the body, but will not adhere to areas with large amounts of filler.

4. Body appearance: Check the moldings, bumpers, grille, vinyl roof, glass, doors, trunk lid and body panels for general overall condition. Check for misalignment, loose hold-down clips, ripples, scratches in glass, welding in the trunk, severe misalignment of body panels or ripples, any of which may indicate crash work.

5. Leaks: Get down and look under the vehicle. There are no normal leaks, other than water from the air conditioner evaporator.

6. Tires: Check the tire air pressure. One old trick is to pump the tire pressure up to make the vehicle roll easier. Check the tread wear, open the trunk and check the spare too. Uneven wear is a clue that the front end may need an alignment.

7. Shock absorbers: Check the shock absorbers by forcing downward sharply on each corner of the vehicle. Good shocks will not allow the vehicle to bounce more than once after you let go.

8. Interior: Check the entire interior. You're looking for an interior condition that agrees with the overall condition of the vehicle. Reasonable wear is expected, but be suspicious of

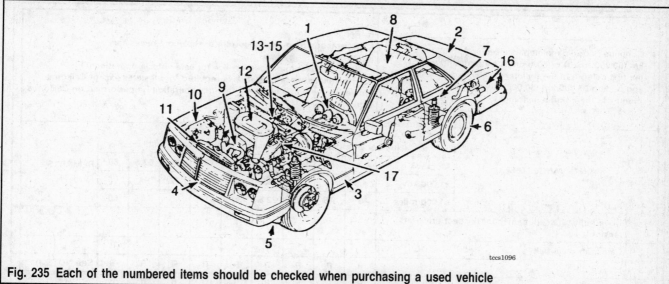

Fig. 235 Each of the numbered items should be checked when purchasing a used vehicle

new seat covers on sagging seats, new pedal pads, and worn armrests. These indicate an attempt to cover up hard use. Pull back the carpets and look for evidence of water leaks or flooding. Look for missing hardware, door handles, control knobs, etc. Check lights and signal operations. Make sure all accessories (air conditioner, heater, radio, etc.) work. Check windshield wiper operation.

9. Belts and Hoses: Open the hood, then check all belts and hoses for wear, cracks or weak spots.

10. Battery: Low electrolyte level, corroded terminals and/or cracked case indicate a lack of maintenance.

11. Radiator: Look for corrosion or rust in the coolant indicating a lack of maintenance.

12. Air filter: A severely dirty air filter would indicate a lack of maintenance.

13. Ignition wires: Check the ignition wires for cracks, burned spots, or wear. Worn wires will have to be replaced.

14. Oil level: If the oil level is low, chances are the engine uses oil or leaks. Beware of water in the oil (there is probably a cracked block or bad head gasket), excessively thick oil (which is often used to quiet a noisy engine), or thin, dirty oil with a distinct gasoline smell (this may indicate internal engine problems).

15. Automatic Transmission: Pull the transmission dipstick out when the engine is running. The level should read FULL, and the fluid should be clear or bright red. Dark brown or black fluid that has distinct burnt odor, indicates a transmission in need of repair or overhaul.

16. Exhaust: Check the color of the exhaust smoke. Blue smoke indicates, among other problems, worn rings. Black smoke can indicate burnt valves or carburetor problems. Check the exhaust system for leaks; it can be expensive to replace.

17. Spark Plugs: Remove one or all of the spark plugs (the most accessible will do, though all are preferable). An engine in good condition will show plugs with a light tan or gray deposit on the firing tip.

ROAD TEST CHECKLIST

1. Engine Performance: The vehicle should be peppy whether cold or warm, with adequate power and good pickup. It should respond smoothly through the gears.

2. Brakes: They should provide quick, firm stops with no noise, pulling or brake fade.

3. Steering: Sure control with no binding harshness, or looseness and no shimmy in the wheel should be expected. Noise or vibration from the steering wheel when turning the vehicle means trouble.

4. Clutch (Manual Transmission/Transaxle): Clutch action should give quick, smooth response with easy shifting. The clutch pedal should have free-play before it disengages the clutch. Start the engine, set the parking brake, put the transmission in first gear and slowly release the clutch pedal. The engine should begin to stall when the pedal is $1/2$-$3/4$ of the way up.

5. Automatic Transmission/Transaxle: The transmission should shift rapidly and smoothly, with no noise, hesitation, or slipping.

6. Differential: No noise or thumps should be present. Differentials have no normal leaks.

7. Driveshaft/Universal Joints: Vibration and noise could mean driveshaft problems. Clicking at low speed or coast conditions means worn U-joints.

8. Suspension: Try hitting bumps at different speeds. A vehicle that bounces excessively has weak shock absorbers or struts. Clunks mean worn bushings or ball joints.

9. Frame/Body: Wet the tires and drive in a straight line. Tracks should show two straight lines, not four. Four tire tracks indicate a frame/body bent by collision damage. If the tires can't be wet for this purpose, have a friend drive along behind you and see if the vehicle appears to be traveling in a straight line.

Continue periodic maintenance beyond 96,000 km (60,000 miles) or 60 months by returning to the first column of the maintenance schedule and adding 96,000 km (60,000 miles) or 60 months to the column headings.

Symbols used:

R: Replace
I: Inspect, and then adjust, correct or replace if necessary.
P: Perform
  (I) or (P): Recommended service for safe vehicle operation
*: This maintenance operation is required for all states except California. However, we do recommend that this operation be performed on California vehicles as well.

MAINTENANCE ITEM	MAINTENANCE INTERVAL (Number of months or km (miles), whichever occurs first)									REMARKS
	Months	3	7.5	15	22.5	30	37.5	45	52.5	60
	x1,000 km	4.8	12	24	36	48	60	72	84	96
	x1,000 miles	3	7.5	15	22.5	30	37.5	45	52.5	60
1 Drive belt(s) [Except camshaft] (Inspect drive belt tension)						I				R	
2 Camshaft drive belt						I*				R	
3 Engine oil		R	R	R	R	R	R	R	R	R	See NOTE 1)
4 Engine oil filter		R	R	R	R	R	R	R	R		
5 Replace engine coolant and inspect cooling system, hoses and connections						P				P	
6 Replace fuel filter and inspect fuel system hoses and connections						(P)				P	See NOTE 2), 6) & 7)
7 Air filter elements						R				R	
8 Spark plug						R				R	
9 Transmission/Differential (Front & Rear) Lubricants (Gear oil)						I					See NOTE 3)
10 Automatic transmission fluid						I					See NOTE 4)
11 Brake fluid						R				R	See NOTE 5)
12 Disc brake pad and disc, Front and rear axle boots and axle shaft joints				I		I		I		I	See NOTE 6)
13 Brake linings and drums (Parking brake)						I				I	See NOTE 6)
14 Inspect brake line and check operation of parking and service brake system			P			P		P		P	See NOTE 6)
15 Clutch and hill-holder system				I		I		I		I	
16 Steering and suspension				I		I		I		I	See NOTE 6)
17 Front and rear wheel bearing lubricant										(I)	

1) When the vehicle is used under severe driving conditions such as those mentioned below**, the engine oil should be changed more often.

2) When the vehicle is used in extremely cold or hot weather areas, contamination of the filter may occur and filter replacement should be performed more often.

3) When the vehicle is frequently operated under severe conditions, replacement should be performed every 48,000 km (30,000 miles).

4) When the vehicle is frequently operated under severe conditions, replacement should be performed every 24,000 km (15,000 miles).

5) When the vehicle is used in high humidity areas or in mountainous areas, change the brake fluid every 24,000 km (15,000 miles) or 15 months, whichever occurs first.

6) When the vehicle is used under severe driving conditions such as those mentioned below*, inspection should be performed every 12,000 km (7,500 miles) or 7.5 months, whichever occurs first.

7) This inspection is not required to maintain emission warranty eligibility and it does not affect the manufacturer's obligations under EPA's in-use compliance program. ** Examples of severe driving conditions:

  (1) Repeated short distance driving. (item 3, 12 and 13 only)
  (2) Driving on rough and/or muddy roads. (Item 12, 13 and 16 only)
  (3) Driving in dusty conditions.
  (4) Driving in extremely cold weather. (Item 3 and 16 only)
  (5) Driving in areas where roads salts or other corrosive materials are used. (Item 6, 12, 13, 14 and 16 only)
  (6) Living in coastal areas. (Item 6, 12, 13, 14 and 16 only)

CAPACITIES

Year	Model	Engine Crankcase	Transaxle Manual 4-Speed	5-Speed 2WD	5-Speed 4WD	Automatic 2WD	Automatic 4WD	Rear Drive Axle	Front Drive Axle	Gasoline Tank (gals.)	Cooling System
1985	Brat	4.2	3.0	—	—	—	6.3–6.8	1.7	1.3	14.5	5.8
	2 Door	4.2⑭	2.6⑯	2.6	—	5.9–6.3	—	1.7	1.3	13.2⑮	5.8⑰
	4 Door	4.2	2.7	2.7	3.5①	6.3–6.8	7.2–7.6	.8	1.3	15.9	5.8
	Wagon	4.2	—	2.7	3.5	6.3–6.8	7.2–7.6①	.8	1.3	15.9	5.8
	XT	4.2	—	2.7	3.5	6.3–6.8	7.2–7.6	.8	1.3	15.9	6.1
1986	Brat	4.2	3.0	—	—	—	—	1.7	1.3	14.5	5.8
	2 Door	4.2⑭	2.6	2.6	3.0	5.9–6.3	—	1.7	1.3	13.2⑮	5.8⑰
	4 Door	4.2	—	2.7②	3.5	6.3–6.8	7.2–7.6	.8	1.3	15.9	5.8
	Wagon	4.2	—	2.7②	3.5	6.3–6.8	7.2–7.6	.8	1.3	15.9	5.8
	3 Door	4.2	—	2.7	3.5	6.3–6.8	7.2–7.6	.8	1.3	15.9	5.8
	XT	4.2	—	2.7	3.5	6.3–6.8	7.2–7.6	.8	1.3	15.9	6.1
1987	Brat	4.2	3.0	—	—	—	—	1.7	1.3	14.5	5.8
	2 Door	4.2⑭	2.7⑯	2.7	—	5.9–6.3	—	1.7	1.3	13.2⑮	5.8⑰
	4 Door	4.2	—	2.7②	3.5	6.3–6.8	7.2–7.6	.8	1.3	15.9	5.8④
	Wagon	4.2	—	2.7②	3.5	6.3–6.8	7.2–7.6	.8	1.3	15.9	5.8④
	3 Door	4.2	—	2.7②	3.5③	6.3–6.8	7.2–7.6	.8	1.3	15.9	5.8
	XT	4.2	—	2.6②	3.5③	9.0	9.0	.8	1.5	15.9	5.8
	Justy	3.0	—	2.1	—	—	—	—	—	9.2	4.5
1988	Brat	4.2	3.0	—	—	—	—	1.7	1.3	14.5	5.8
	2 Door	4.2⑭	2.7⑯	2.7	—	5.9–6.3	—	1.7	1.3	13.2⑮	5.8⑰
	4 Door	4.2	—	2.7	3.5③	6.5–6.7	6.8–7.0⑤	1.7	2.5	15.9	5.8④
	Wagon	4.2	—	2.7	3.5	6.5–6.7	6.8–7.0⑤	1.7	2.5	15.9	5.8④
	3 Door	4.2	—	2.7	3.5③	6.5–6.7	6.8–7.0	1.7	2.5	15.9	5.8

87971c11

CAPACITIES

Year	Model	Engine Crankcase	4-Speed	5-Speed 2WD	5-Speed 4WD	Automatic 2WD	Automatic 4WD	Rear Drive Axle	Front Drive Axle	Gasoline Tank (gals.)	Cooling System
1988	XT	4.2	—	2.7	3.5	9.8	—	.8	1.5	15.9	5.8
	XT-6	5.3	—	—	—	9.8	10.0	.8	1.5	15.9	7.4
	Justy	3.0	—	2.4	3.5	—	—	.8	—	9.2	4.5
1989	Brat	4.2	3.0	—	—	—	—	1.7	1.3	14.5	5.8
	2 Door	4.2⑭	2.7⑯	2.7	—	5.9–6.3	—	1.7	1.3	13.2⑮	5.8⑰
	4 Door	4.2	—	2.7	3.5③	6.5–6.7	6.8–7.0⑤	.8	1.3⑥	15.9	5.8④
	Wagon	4.2	—	2.7	3.5③	6.5–6.7	6.8–7.0⑤	.8	1.3⑥	15.9	5.8④
	XT	4.2	—	2.7	3.5	9.8	—	.8	1.5	15.9	5.8
	XT-6	5.3	—	—	3.7	9.8	10.0	.8	1.5	15.9	7.4
	Justy	3.0	—	2.4	3.5	3.3–3.6	—	.8	—	9.2	4.9⑦
1990	XT	4.2	—	2.7	3.5	9.8	10.0	.8	1.5	15.9	5.8
	XT-6	5.3	—	—	3.7	9.8	10.0	.8	1.5	15.9	7.4
	Loyale 4 Door	4.2	—	2.7	3.5	6.5–6.7	6.9–7.1⑤	.8	1.3⑧	15.9	5.8⑨
	Loyale Wagon	4.2	—	2.7	3.5	6.5–6.7	6.9–7.1⑤	.8	1.3⑧	15.9	5.8⑨
	Loyale 3 Door	4.2	—	2.7	2.7⑩	6.5–6.7	6.5–6.7⑤⑪	.8	1.3⑧	15.9	5.8⑨
	Legacy 4 Door	4.2	—	2.7	3.5	6.5–6.7	6.9–7.1⑤	.8	1.3⑧	15.9	5.8⑨
	Legacy Wagon	4.2	—	2.7	3.5	6.5–6.7	6.9–7.1⑤	.8	1.3⑧	15.9	5.8⑨
	Justy	3.0	—	2.5	3.6	3.5	4.4	.8	—	9.2	4.9⑨
1991	XT	4.2	—	2.7	3.5	9.8	10.0	.8	1.5	15.9	5.8
	XT-6	5.3	—	—	3.7	9.8	10.0	.8	1.5	15.9	7.4
	Loyale 4 Door	4.2	—	2.7	3.5	6.5–6.7	6.9–7.1⑤	.8	1.3⑧	15.9	5.8⑨
	Loyale Wagon	4.2	—	2.7	3.5	6.5–6.7	6.9–7.1⑤	.8	1.3⑧	15.9	5.8⑨
	Legacy 4 Door	4.8	—	3.5	3.7	8.8	8.8⑫	.8	1.5	15.9	6.2⑬
	Legacy Wagon	4.8	—	3.5	3.7	8.8	8.8⑫	.8	1.5	15.9	6.2⑬
	Justy	3.0	—	2.5	3.6	3.5	4.4	.8	—	9.2	4.9⑦
1992	Loyale 4 Door	4.2	—	2.7	3.5	6.0	6.4	.8	1.3	15.9	5.8
	Loyale Wagon	4.2	—	2.7	3.5	6.0	6.4	.8	1.3	15.9	5.8
	Legacy 4 Door	4.8	—	3.5	3.7	8.8	8.8⑫	.8	1.3	15.9	6.2⑬
	Legacy Wagon	4.8	—	3.5	3.7	8.8	8.8⑫	.8	1.3	15.9	6.2⑬
	Justy	3.0	—	2.5	3.6	3.5	4.4	.8	—	9.2	4.9⑦
	SVX	6.3	—	—	—	10.0	10.0	.8	1.3	18.2	7.4

87971c12

CAPACITIES

Year	Model	Engine Crankcase	Transaxle Manual 4-Speed	Transaxle Manual 5-Speed 2WD	Transaxle Manual 5-Speed 4WD	Automatic 2WD	Automatic 4WD	Rear Drive Axle	Front Drive Axle	Gasoline Tank (gals.)	Cooling System
1993	Impreza 4 Door	4.2	—	2.7	3.7	8.4	8.4	.8	1.3	13.2	6.2
	Impreza Wagon	4.2	—	2.7	3.7	8.4	8.4	.8	1.3	13.2	6.2
	Loyale 4 Door	4.2	—	2.7	3.5	6.0	6.4	.8	1.3	15.9	5.8
	Loyale Wagon	4.2	—	2.7	3.5	6.0	6.4	.8	1.3	15.9	5.8
	Legacy 4 Door	4.2	—	3.5	3.7	8.8	8.8	.8	1.3	15.9	[18]
	Legacy Wagon	4.2	—	3.5	3.7	8.8	8.8	.8	1.3	15.9	[18]
	Justy	3.0	—	2.5	3.6	3.5	4.4	.8	—	9.2	4.9 [7]
	SVX	6.3	—	—	—	10.0-10.4	10.0-10.4	.9	1.2-1.4	18.5	7.4
1994	Impreza 4 Door	4.2	—	2.7	3.7	8.4	8.4	.8	1.3	13.2	6.2
	Impreza Wagon	4.2	—	2.7	3.7	8.4	8.4	.8	1.3	13.2	6.2
	Loyale 4 Door	4.2	—	2.7	3.5	6.0	6.4	.8	1.3	15.9	5.8
	Loyale Wagon	4.2	—	2.7	3.5	6.0	6.4	.8	1.3	15.9	5.8
	Legacy 4 Door	4.2	—	3.5	3.7	8.8	8.8	.8	1.3	15.9	[18]
	Legacy Wagon	4.2	—	3.5	3.7	8.8	8.8	.8	1.3	15.9	[18]
	Justy	3.0	—	2.5	3.6	3.5	4.4	.8	—	9.2	4.9 [7]
	SVX	6.3	—	—	—	10.0-10.4	10.0-10.4	.9	1.2-1.4	18.5	7.4
1995	Impreza 2 Door	4.2	—	2.7	3.7	8.4	8.4	.8	1.3	13.2	6.2
	Impreza 4 Door	4.2	—	2.7	3.7	8.4	8.4	.8	1.3	13.2	6.2
	Impreza Wagon	4.2	—	2.7	3.7	8.4	8.4	.8	1.3	13.2	6.2
	Legacy 4 Door	4.2	—	3.5	4.2	8.4	8.4	.8	1.3	15.9	6.4
	Legacy Wagon	4.2	—	3.5	4.2	8.4	8.4	.8	1.3	15.9	6.4
	SVX	6.3	—	—	—	10.0-10.4	10.0-10.4	.9	1.2-1.4	18.5	7.4
1996	Impreza 2 Door	4.2	—	—	4.2	8.4	8.4	.8	1.3	13.2	6.6 [19]
	Impreza 4 Door	4.2	—	—	4.2	8.4	8.4	.8	1.3	13.2	6.6 [19]
	Impreza Wagon	4.2	—	—	4.2	8.4	8.4	.8	1.3	13.2	6.6 [19]
	Legacy 4 Door	4.2 [20]	—	3.5	3.7	8.4	8.4 [22]	.8	1.3	15.9	6.1 [21]
	Legacy Wagon	4.2 [20]	—	—	3.7	8.4	8.4 [22]	.8	1.3	15.9	6.1 [21]
	SVX	6.3	—	—	—	10.0-10.4	10.0-10.4	.9	1.2-1.4	18.5	7.4

[1] Turbo
[2] 3.5 w/Turbo
[3] 3.7 w/Turbo
[4] 6.3 GL10 Turbo
[5] 10.0 w/Turbo
[6] 3.0 GL10 Turbo 2.5 w/4WD
[7] 5.2 W/EVCT
[8] 1.5 w/Turbo
[9] 6.3 w/Turbo
[10] 3.5 w/RS
[11] 6.9-7.1 w/RS
[12] 9.4 w/Turbo
[13] 7.4 w/Turbo
[14] 3.7 w/1.6L engine
[15] 11.9 w/4WD
[16] 3.0 w/4WD
[17] 5.6 w/1.6L
[18] Turbo: 7.4 qts. Non-Turbo: 6.2 qts.
[19] 1.8L shown. 2.2L: 6.1 qts.
[20] 2.2L shown. 2.5L: 4.7 qts.
[21] 2.2L shown. 2.5L: 6.3 qts.
[22] 2.2L shown. 2.5L: 10.0 qts.

87971c13

ENGLISH TO METRIC CONVERSION: MASS (WEIGHT)

Current mass measurement is expressed in pounds and ounces (lbs. & ozs.). The metric unit of mass (or weight) is the kilogram (kg). Even although this table does not show conversion of masses (weights) larger than 15 lbs, it is easy to calculate larger units by following the data immediately below.

To convert ounces (oz.) to grams (g): multiply th number of ozs. by 28
To convert grams (g) to ounces (oz.): multiply the number of grams by .035

To convert pounds (lbs.) to kilograms (kg): multiply the number of lbs. by .45
To convert kilograms (kg) to pounds (lbs.): multiply the number of kilograms by 2.2

lbs	kg	lbs	kg	oz	kg	oz	kg
0.1	0.04	0.9	0.41	0.1	0.003	0.9	0.024
0.2	0.09	1	0.4	0.2	0.005	1	0.03
0.3	0.14	2	0.9	0.3	0.008	2	0.06
0.4	0.18	3	1.4	0.4	0.011	3	0.08
0.5	0.23	4	1.8	0.5	0.014	4	0.11
0.6	0.27	5	2.3	0.6	0.017	5	0.14
0.7	0.32	10	4.5	0.7	0.020	10	0.28
0.8	0.36	15	6.8	0.8	0.023	15	0.42

ENGLISH TO METRIC CONVERSION: TEMPERATURE

To convert Fahrenheit (°F) to Celsius (°C): take number of °F and subtract 32; multiply result by 5; divide result by 9

To convert Celsius (°C) to Fahrenheit (°F): take number of °C and multiply by 9; divide result by 5; add 32 to total

Fahrenheit (F)		Celsius (C)		Fahrenheit (F)		Celsius (C)		Fahrenheit (F)		Celsius (C)	
°F	°C	°C	°F	°F	°C	°C	°F	°F	°C	°C	°F
−40	−40	−38	−36.4	80	26.7	18	64.4	215	101.7	80	176
−35	−37.2	−36	−32.8	85	29.4	20	68	220	104.4	85	185
−30	−34.4	−34	−29.2	90	32.2	22	71.6	225	107.2	90	194
−25	−31.7	−32	−25.6	95	35.0	24	75.2	230	110.0	95	202
−20	−28.9	−30	−22	100	37.8	26	78.8	235	112.8	100	212
−15	−26.1	−28	−18.4	105	40.6	28	82.4	240	115.6	105	221
−10	−23.3	−26	−14.8	110	43.3	30	86	245	118.3	110	230
−5	−20.6	−24	−11.2	115	46.1	32	89.6	250	121.1	115	239
0	−17.8	−22	−7.6	120	48.9	34	93.2	255	123.9	120	248
1	−17.2	−20	−4	125	51.7	36	96.8	260	126.6	125	257
2	−16.7	−18	−0.4	130	54.4	38	100.4	265	129.4	130	266
3	−16.1	−16	3.2	135	57.2	40	104	270	132.2	135	275
4	−15.6	−14	6.8	140	60.0	42	107.6	275	135.0	140	284
5	−15.0	−12	10.4	145	62.8	44	112.2	280	137.8	145	293
10	−12.2	−10	14	150	65.6	46	114.8	285	140.6	150	302
15	−9.4	−8	17.6	155	68.3	48	118.4	290	143.3	155	311
20	−6.7	−6	21.2	160	71.1	50	122	295	146.1	160	320
25	−3.9	−4	24.8	165	73.9	52	125.6	300	148.9	165	329
30	−1.1	−2	28.4	170	76.7	54	129.2	305	151.7	170	338
35	1.7	0	32	175	79.4	56	132.8	310	154.4	175	347
40	4.4	2	35.6	180	82.2	58	136.4	315	157.2	180	356
45	7.2	4	39.2	185	85.0	60	140	320	160.0	185	365
50	10.0	6	42.8	190	87.8	62	143.6	325	162.8	190	374
55	12.8	8	46.4	195	90.6	64	147.2	330	165.6	195	383
60	15.6	10	50	200	93.3	66	150.8	335	168.3	200	392
65	18.3	12	53.6	205	96.1	68	154.4	340	171.1	205	401
70	21.1	14	57.2	210	98.9	70	158	345	173.9	210	410
75	23.9	16	60.8	212	100.0	75	167	350	176.7	215	414

tccs1c01

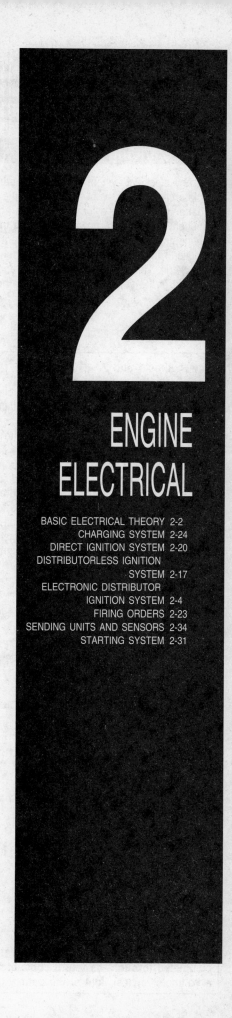

2

ENGINE
ELECTRICAL

BASIC ELECTRICAL THEORY

Understanding Electricity

For any electrical system to operate, there must be a complete circuit. This simply means that the power flow from the battery must make a full circle. When an electrical component is operating, power flows from the battery to the components, passes through the component (load) causing it to function, and returns to the battery through the ground path of the circuit. This ground may be either another wire or a metal part of the vehicle (depending upon how the component is designed).

BASIC CIRCUITS

▶ **See Figures 1 and 2**

Perhaps the easiest way to visualize a circuit is to think of connecting a light bulb (with two wires attached to it) to the battery. If one of the two wires was attached to the negative post (-) of the battery and the other wire to the positive post (+), the circuit would be complete and the light bulb would illuminate. Electricity could follow a path from the battery to the bulb and back to the battery. It's not hard to see that with longer wires on our light bulb, it could be mounted anywhere on the vehicle. Further, one wire could be fitted with a switch so that the light could be turned on and off. Various other items could be added to our primitive circuit to make the light flash, become brighter or dimmer under certain conditions, or advise the user that it's burned out.

Ground

Some automotive components are grounded through their mounting points. The electrical current runs through the chassis of the vehicle and returns to the battery through the ground (-) cable; if you look, you'll see that the battery ground cable connects between the battery and the body of the vehicle.

tccs2003

Fig. 2 Damaged insulation can allow wires to break (causing an open circuit) or touch (causing a short)

Load

Every complete circuit must include a "load" (something to use the electricity coming from the source). If you were to connect a wire between the two terminals of the battery (DON'T do this, but take out word for it) without the light bulb, the battery would attempt to deliver its entire power supply from one pole to another almost instantly. This is a short circuit. The electricity is taking a short cut to get to ground and is not being used by any load in the circuit. This sudden and uncontrolled electrical flow can cause great damage to other components in the circuit and can develop a tremendous amount of heat. A short in an automotive wiring harness can develop sufficient heat to melt the insulation on all the surrounding wires and reduce a multiple wire cable to one sad lump of plastic and copper. Two common causes of shorts are broken insulation (thereby exposing the wire to contact with

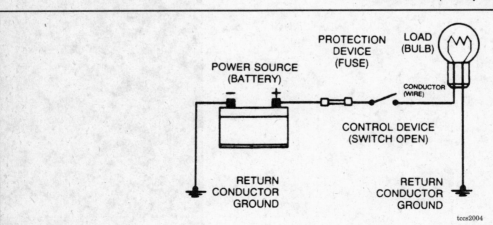

tccs2004

Fig. 1 Here is an example of a simple automotive circuit. When the switch is closed, power from the positive battery terminal flows through the fuse, then the switch and to the load (light bulb), the light illuminates and then, the circuit is completed through the return conductor and the vehicle ground. If the light did not work, the tests could be made with a voltmeter or test light at the battery, fuse, switch or bulb socket

surrounding metal surfaces or other wires) or a failed switch (the pins inside the switch come out of place and touch each other).

Switches and Relays

Some electrical components which require a large amount of current to operate also have a relay in their circuit. Since these circuits carry a large amount of current (amperage or amps), the thickness of the wire in the circuit (wire gauge) is also greater. If this large wire were connected from the load to the control switch on the dash, the switch would have to carry the high amperage load and the dash would be twice as large to accommodate wiring harnesses as thick as your wrist. To prevent these problems, a relay is used. The large wires in the circuit are connected from the battery to one side of the relay and from the opposite side of the relay to the load. The relay is normally open, preventing current from passing through the circuit. An additional, smaller wire is connected from the relay to the control switch for the circuit. When the control switch is turned on, it grounds the smaller wire to the relay and completes its circuit. The main switch inside the relay closes, sending power to the component without routing the main power through the inside of the vehicle. Some common circuits which may use relays are the horn, headlights, starter and rear window defogger systems.

Protective Devices

It is possible for larger surges of current to pass through the electrical system of your vehicle. If this surge of current were to reach the load in the circuit, it could burn it out or severely damage it. To prevent this, fuses, circuit breakers and/or fusible links are connected into the supply wires of the electrical system. These items are nothing more than a built-in weak spot in the system. It's much easier to go to a known location (the fuse box) to see why a circuit is inoperative than to dissect 15 feet of wiring under the dashboard, looking for what happened.

When an electrical current of excessive power passes through the fuse, the fuse blows (the conductor melts) and breaks the circuit, preventing the passage of current and protecting the components.

A circuit breaker is basically a self-repairing fuse. It will open the circuit in the same fashion as a fuse, but when either the short is removed or the surge subsides, the circuit breaker resets itself and does not need replacement.

A fuse link (fusible link or main link) is a wire that acts as a fuse. One of these is normally connected between the starter relay and the main wiring harness under the hood. Since the starter is usually the highest electrical draw on the vehicle, an internal short during starting could direct about 130 amps into the wrong places. Consider the damage potential of introducing this current into a system whose wiring is rated at 15 amps and you'll understand the need for protection. Since this link is very early in the electrical path, it's the first place to look if nothing on the vehicle works, but the battery seems to be charged and is properly connected.

TROUBLESHOOTING

▶ See Figures 3, 4 and 5

Electrical problems generally fall into one of three areas:
• The component that is not functioning is not receiving current.
• The component is receiving power but is not using it or is using it incorrectly (component failure).
• The component is improperly grounded.

The circuit can be can be checked with a test light and a jumper wire. The test light is a device that looks like a pointed screwdriver with a wire on one end and a bulb in its handle. A jumper wire is simply a piece of wire with alligator clips or special terminals on each end. If a component is not working,

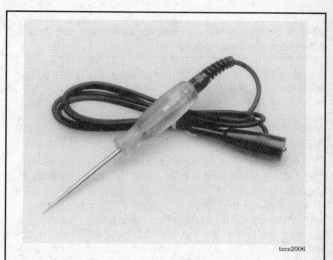

tccs2006

Fig. 3 A 12 volt test light is useful when checking parts of a circuit for power

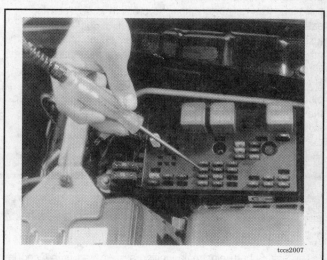

tccs2007

Fig. 4 Here, someone is checking a circuit by making sure there is power to the component's fuse

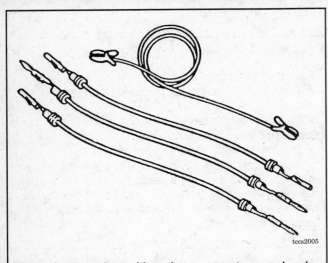

Fig. 5 Jumper wires with various connectors are handy for quick electrical testing

you must follow a systematic plan to determine which of the three causes is the villain.

1. Turn ON the switch that controls the item not working.

➡**Some items only work when the ignition switch is turned ON.**

2. Disconnect the power supply wire from the component.

3. Attach the ground wire of a test light or a voltmeter to a good metal ground.

4. Touch the end probe of the test light (or the positive lead of the voltmeter) to the power wire; if there is current in the wire, the light in the test light will come on (or the voltmeter will indicate the amount of voltage). You have now established that current is getting to the component.

5. Turn the ignition or dash switch **OFF** and reconnect the wire to the component.

If there was no power, then the problem is between the battery and the component. This includes all the switches, fuses, relays and the battery itself. The next place to look is the fuse box; check carefully either by eye or by using the test light across the fuse clips. The easiest way to check is to simply replace the fuse. If the fuse is blown, and upon replacement, immediately blows again, there is a short between the fuse and the component. This is generally (not always) a sign of an internal short in the component. Disconnect the power wire at the component again and replace the fuse; if the fuse holds, the component is the problem.

❋❋WARNING

DO NOT test a component by running a jumper wire from the battery UNLESS you are certain that it operates on 12 volts. Many electronic components are designed to operate with less voltage and connecting them to 12 volts could destroy them. Jumper wires are best used to bypass a portion of the circuit (such as a stretch of wire or a switch) that DOES NOT contain a resistor and is suspected to be bad.

If all the fuses are good and the component is not receiving power, find the switch for the circuit. Bypass the switch with the jumper wire. This is done by connecting one end of the jumper to the power wire coming into the switch and the other end to the wire leaving the switch. If the component comes to life, the switch has failed.

❋❋WARNING

Never substitute the jumper for the component. The circuit needs the electrical load of the component. If you bypass it, you will cause a short circuit.

Checking the ground for any circuit can mean tracing wires to the body, cleaning connections or tightening mounting bolts for the component itself. If the jumper wire can be connected to the case of the component or the ground connector, you can ground the other end to a piece of clean, solid metal on the vehicle. Again, if the component starts working, you've found the problem.

A systematic search through the fuse, connectors, switches and the component itself will almost always yield an answer. Loose and/or corroded connectors, particularly in ground circuits, are becoming a larger problem in modern vehicles. The computers and on-board electronic (solid state) systems are highly sensitive to improper grounds and will change their function drastically if one occurs.

Remember that for any electrical circuit to work, ALL the connections must be clean and tight.

➡**For more information on Understanding and Troubleshooting Electrical Systems, please refer to Section 6 of this manual.**

ELECTRONIC DISTRIBUTOR IGNITION SYSTEM

General Information

▶ **See Figures 6, 7 and 8**

The first Subaru electronic ignition system was introduced in the late 1970's. Since that time, production changes have been made from year to year, but the basic design has remained the same. All 1.2L, 1.6L, 1.8L and 2.7L models are equipped with electronic ignition systems.

The electronic ignition system differs from a points type ignition only in the manner in which the spark is triggered. The secondary side of the ignition system is the same as a points type system.

Located in the distributor, is a four spoke rotor (reluctor) which rests on the distributor shaft where the breaker points are normally found. A pickup coil, consisting of a magnet, coil and wiring, rests on the breaker plate next to the reluctor.

When a reluctor spoke is not aligned with the pickup coil, it generates large lines of flux between itself, the magnet and the pickup coil. This large flux variation results in a high generated voltage in the pickup coil. When a reluctor spoke lines up with the pickup coil, the flux variation is low, thus allowing current to flow to the pickup coil. The ignition primary current

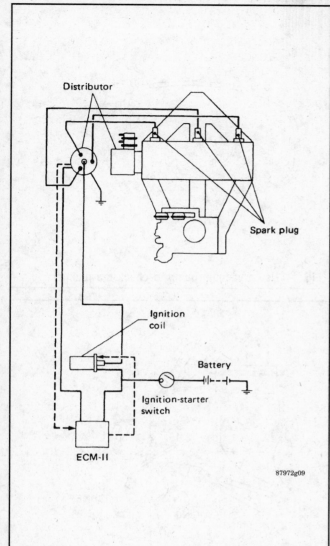

Fig. 6 Schematic of a carbureted 1.2L engine's ignition system

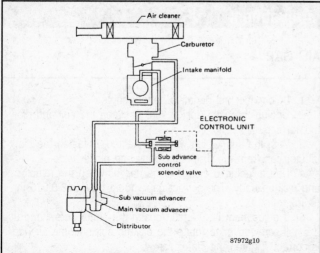

Fig. 7 Schematic of a typical carbureted engine's ignition system

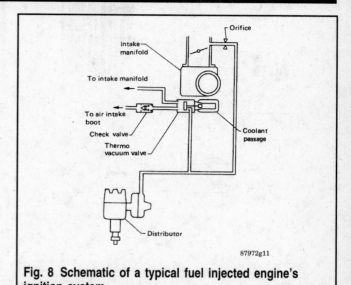

Fig. 8 Schematic of a typical fuel injected engine's ignition system

is then cut off by the electronic unit, allowing the field in the ignition coil to collapse. The collapse of the ignition coil induces a high secondary voltage in the conventional manner. The high voltage then flows through the distributor to the spark plug, as usual.

The systems also use a transistorized ignition unit mounted above the ignition coil.

The 1.2L carbureted and fuel injected engine is equipped with a newly designed electronic advance angle igniter. The igniter has no mechanical frictional parts. It features vibration proofing, a high level of ignition timing accuracy and minimal quality changes with operation.

The ignition system consists of a magnetic pickup, built into the distributor, a control unit, an ignition coil and other related components. The magnetic pickup consists of a reluctor, which rotates in relation to the crankshaft, and a pickup coil. The power transistor, which controls current flow of the coil primary circuit, is housed in the control unit.

The magnetic pickup detects the crankshaft angle and sends a corresponding signal to the operation circuit of the control unit. This determines the optimum length of current flow to the primary circuit of the ignition coil and ignition timing (equivalent to governor advance angle). Current to the primary circuit of the ignition coil is made and broken by the power transistor of the control unit used as a switching control.

Diagnosis and Testing

Fault diagnosis of the electronic ignition system is carried out via the fuel injection control unit. See Electronic Engine Controls in Section 4 for further information.

INSPECTION

Carbon Point
◢ See Figure 9

Measure the length of the carbon point in the distributor cap. Standard length should be 0.49-0.47 in. (10-12mm). If not within specification, replace the carbon point.

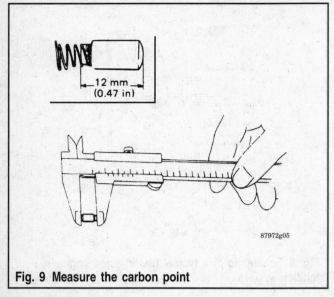

Fig. 9 Measure the carbon point

Distributor Cap and Rotor
▶ **See Figures 10, 11 and 12**

1. Inspect the distributor cap for any breather hole clogging, electrode cracks or damage, center carbon wear or weak spring action. Check the rotor for cracks and damage.

2. Measure the insulation resistance of the cap and rotor. Resistance should be 50,000 ohms or more. If not, replace the cap and rotor.

3. Check that the vacuum canister plunger actuates when vacuum is applied using a hand vacuum pump.

4. Using an ohmmeter, check the signal generator. Connect the ohmmeter leads to the wiring harness. Resistance should be 130-190 ohms. Move a screwdriver close to and away from the coil iron core. The tester needle should deflect. If the signal generator fails any test, replace it.

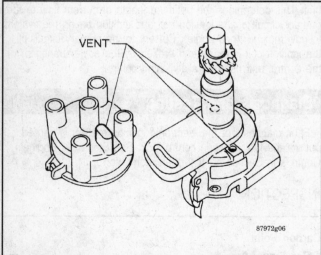

Fig. 10 Inspect the vent holes in the distributor base and cap

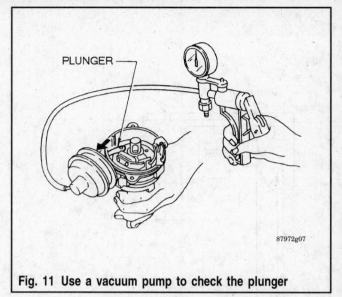

Fig. 11 Use a vacuum pump to check the plunger

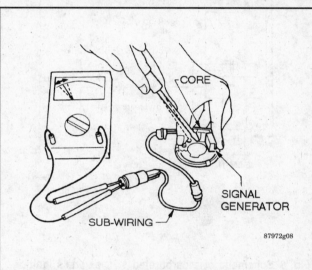

Fig. 12 Measure the signal generator resistance

Adjustment

AIR GAP

1. Disconnect the negative battery cable.
2. Unplug the high tension wire between the coil and distributor cap.
3. With the spark plug wires connected, unfasten the distributor cap from the distributor body and place aside.
4. Use a feeler to measure the gap between the reluctor and pick-up body. The correct gap should be 0.012-0.016 in. (0.3-0.4mm).
5. If adjustment is needed, loosen the stator screw and use a small screwdriver to rotate the pick-up coil until the air gap is correct. Tighten the stator screw.
6. Install the distributor cap and high tension wire. Connect the negative battery cable.

Ignition Coil

TESTING

Primary Coil Resistance

➡Make sure the vehicle ignition is OFF.

1. Remove the ignition coil cover, if equipped.
2. Disconnect the high tension wire from the coil.
3. Use a multimeter or suitable circuit tester and check the primary resistance by connecting the meter ends to the positive and negative ends of the coil.
4. If the resistance is not 0.84-1.02 ohms, replace the coil.
5. When complete, install the high tension wire and ignition coil cover, if equipped.

Secondary Coil Resistance

1. Remove the ignition coil cover, if equipped.
2. Disconnect the high tension wire from the coil.
3. Use a multimeter or suitable circuit tester and check the secondary resistance by connecting the meter ends to the negative end and the high voltage terminal of the coil.
4. If the resistance is not 8.5-1.02 kilo-ohms, replace the coil.
5. When complete, install the high tension wire and ignition coil cover, if equipped.

REMOVAL & INSTALLATION

▶ See Figures 13, 14, 15 and 16

➡The ignition coil is located on the firewall.

1. Disconnect the negative battery cable.
2. Remove the ignition coil cover, if equipped.
3. Disconnect the high tension wire from the coil.
4. Tag, then remove the lead wires attached to the coil.

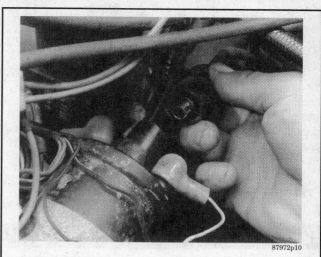

Fig. 14 Remove the high tension wire from the coil — 1.8L engine shown

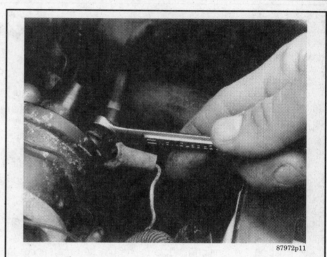

Fig. 15 Remove the wires attached to the coil. Some are secured with nuts, while others slip on

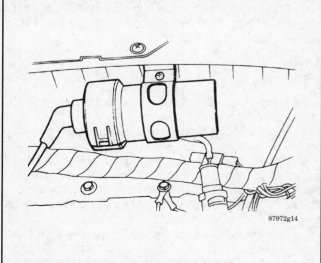

Fig. 13 Ignition coil attached to the firewall

Fig. 16 Remove the bracket retaining bolts and lift the coil assembly out of the engine

5. Remove the coil by either loosening the nut and bolt on the coil bracket, and sliding the coil out, or removing the retaining screws securing the coil and bracket to the firewall.

To install:

6. If the coil and bracket were removed together, then align the holes in the bracket with the holes in the firewall, and secure the coil in place with the retaining screws. If the coil was removed with the bracket in place on the firewall, then slide the coil into the bracket and secure by tightening the nut and bolt on the bracket.

7. Attach the lead wires to the coil.

8. Fasten the high tension wire to the coil.

9. Install the coil cover, if equipped.

10. Connect the negative battery cable.

Ignition Module

REMOVAL & INSTALLATION

▶ See Figure 17

➡The ignition module is located below the steering column inside the vehicle.

1. Disconnect the negative battery cable.

2. Remove the retaining screws securing the interior panel below the steering column. Disconnect any harnesses that may be attached to the panel, and place the panel aside.

3. Remove the retaining bolts securing the ignition module to the bracket.

4. Unfasten the large and small connectors attached to the ignition module.

To install:

5. Fasten the large and small harnesses into the ignition module. Take care to connect the harnesses correctly. Do not force any connect into the module.

6. Position the ignition module to the bracket and secure in place using the retaining bolts.

7. Connect any harnesses removed earlier to the interior panel. Position the panel below the steering column and secure using the retaining screws.

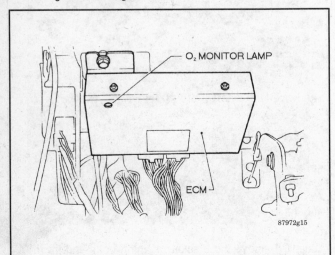

87972g15

Fig. 17 Ignition module mounted below the steering column

8. Connect the negative battery cable.

Distributor

REMOVAL & INSTALLATION

1.2L Engine

ENGINE NOT ROTATED

1. Disconnect the negative battery cable.

2. Unfasten the distributor wire harness.

3. Remove the high tension wire from the coil.

4. If any vacuum lines are attached to the distributor, tag, then disconnect them.

5. Tag then remove each individual spark plug wire at the spark plug.

6. Remove the distributor cap from the distributor body, by loosening the retaining screws.

7. Paint alignment marks on the rotor, distributor body and cylinder head at the base of the distributor.

8. Loosen and remove the retaining bolts which secure the distributor to the cylinder head.

9. Carefully lift the distributor out of the cylinder head. Remove the gasket at the base of the distributor and discard.

To install:

10. Before installing the distributor into the cylinder head, place a new gasket on the base of the distributor.

11. Align the paint marks on the rotor and distributor body.

12. Align the paint marks on the distributor body and cylinder head, then carefully insert the distributor into the hole in the cylinder head.

13. Install the distributor retainer bolts, and tighten.

14. Install any vacuum hoses removed, as well as the wire harness to the distributor.

15. Install the distributor cap on the distributor body and tighten the retaining screws. Connect the plug wires to the correct spark plugs. Attach the high tension wire from the distributor cap to the coil.

16. Connect the negative battery cable.

17. Start the engine and allow it to reach normal operating temperature, then check the ignition timing. Adjust the timing if needed. Refer to the procedure in Section 1.

ENGINE ROTATED

▶ See Figure 18

If the engine has been cranked, disassembled, or the timing otherwise lost, proceed as follows:

1. Remove the plastic dust cover from the timing port on the flywheel housing.

2. Remove the No. 1 spark plug. Use a wrench on the crankshaft pulley bolt (on manual transmission cars place transmission in NEUTRAL) and slowly rotate the engine until the TDC 0 mark on the flywheel aligns with the pointer on the transaxle/transmission. While turning the engine place your finger over the No. 1 spark plug hole, when you feel air escaping past your finger the piston is on the compression stroke and when the marks align the piston is at TDC (top dead center).

3. An alternate method is to remove the bolts that hold the valve cover to expose the valves on No. 1 cylinder. Rotate the

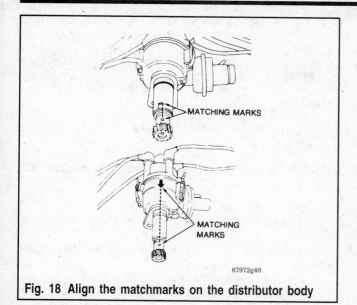

Fig. 18 Align the matchmarks on the distributor body

Fig. 20 Paint alignment marks on the distributor body, rotor and cylinder head

Fig. 21 With the hold-down bolt removed, lift out the distributor

engine so that the valves in No. 1 cylinder are closed and the TDC 0 mark on the flywheel lines up with the pointer.

4. Align the small depression on the distributor drive pinion with the mark on the distributor body. This will align the rotor with the No. 1 spark plug terminal on the distributor cap. Make sure the base gasket is located in the proper position.

5. Align the matchmarks you have made on the distributor body with those on the engine block and install the distributor in the engine. Make sure the drive is engaged.

6. Install the hold-down bolt(s) finger-tight.

7. Connect the negative battery cable.

8. Start the engine and adjust the ignition timing.

1.6L, 1.8L and 2.7L Engines

▶ See Figures 19, 20 and 21

ENGINE NOT ROTATED

1. Disconnect the negative battery cable.
2. Unfasten the distributor wire harness.
3. Remove the high tension wire from the coil.

Fig. 19 Remove the distributor cap — 1.8L engine shown

4. If any vacuum lines are attached to the distributor, tag, then disconnect them.

5. Tag then remove each individual spark plug wire at the spark plug.

6. Remove the distributor cap from the distributor body by loosening the retainer screws or unfastening the two clips.

7. Paint alignment marks on the rotor, distributor body and cylinder head at the base of the distributor.

8. Loosen and remove the retaining bolt , or bolts depending on model which secure the distributor to the cylinder head.

9. Carefully lift the distributor out of the cylinder head. Remove the gasket at the base of the distributor and discard.

To install:

10. Before installing the distributor into the cylinder head, place a new gasket on the base of the distributor.

11. Align the paint marks on the rotor and distributor body.

12. Align the paint marks on the distributor body and cylinder head, then carefully insert the distributor into the hole in the cylinder head.

13. Install the distributor retainer bolts, or bolts depending on model, and tighten.

14. Install any vacuum hoses removed, as well as the wire harness to the distributor.

15. Install the distributor cap on the distributor body and secure Connect the plug wires to the correct spark plugs. Attach the high tension wire from the distributor cap to the coil.

16. Connect the negative battery cable.

17. Start the engine and allow it to reach normal operating temperature, then check the ignition timing. Adjust the timing if needed. Refer to the procedure in Section 1.

ENGINE ROTATED

▶ See Figure 18

If the engine has been cranked, disassembled, or the timing otherwise lost, proceed as follows:

1. Remove the plastic dust cover from the timing port on the flywheel housing.

2. Remove the No. 1 spark plug. Use a wrench on the crankshaft pulley bolt (on manual transmission cars place transmission in NEUTRAL) and slowly rotate the engine until the TDC 0 mark on the flywheel aligns with the pointer. While turning the engine place your finger over the No. 1 spark plug hole, when you feel air escaping past your finger the piston is on the compression stroke and when the marks align the piston is at TDC (top dead center).

3. An alternate method is to remove the bolts that hold the right (passenger's) side valve cover and remove the cover to expose the valves on No. 1 cylinder. Rotate the engine so that the valves in No. 1 cylinder are closed and the TDC 0 mark on the flywheel lines up with the pointer.

4. Align the small depression on the distributor drive pinion with the mark on the distributor body. This will align the rotor with the No. 1 spark plug terminal on the distributor cap. Make sure the O-ring is located in the proper position.

5. Align the matchmarks you have made on the distributor body with those on the engine block and install the distributor in the engine. Make sure the drive is engaged.

6. Install the hold-down bolt(s) finger-tight.

7. Connect the negative battery cable.

8. Start the engine and adjust the ignition timing.

2.2L, 2.5L and 3.3L Engines

The 2.2L, 2.5L and 3.3L engines do not use a distributor.

DISASSEMBLY

1.2L Engines

▶ See Figures 22 and 23

1. Remove the distributor from the engine.

2. Remove the rotor of the distributor body.

3. Remove the rubber packing at the base of the rotor, if equipped.

4. Remove the harness from the holder on the distributor body. Disconnect the ground strap as necessary.

5. On the carbureted model, place two standard screwdrivers under the reluctor and pry upward to remove.

6. On the carbureted model, remove the screws which secure the breaker assembly and remove the assembly. On fuel injected models, remove the screws which secure the generator assembly and remove the assembly including the harness.

➡**Do not disassemble the breaker or generator assemblies.**

Nippondenso Model 100291 Distributor

▶ See Figure 24

➡**This distributor was installed in many 1.6L and 1.8L engines.**

1. Remove the rotor from the distributor.

2. Remove the vacuum controller by removing the snapring and screw.

3. Remove the screw plate which secures the breaker plate in position.

4. Remove the igniter by loosening the screws.

5. Remove the breaker plate.

6. Unfasten the dust cover. Be careful not to break the cover.

7. Remove the governor spring using needle nose pliers. Remove the snapring, then remove the flyweight. Be careful not to deform the governor spring.

8. Remove the cap from the top of the governor shaft and remove the screw. Pull out the governor shaft and signal rotor.

9. Remove the roll pin from the spiral gear using a punch.

10. Slide the governor shaft from the housing.

Hitachi Model D4R84 Distributor

▶ See Figure 25

1. Disconnect the negative battery cable.

2. Remove the distributor from the engine

3. Remove the cap by detaching the spring clip or removing the attaching screws.

4. Remove the rotor and remove the carbon point from the cap.

5. Remove the vacuum controller by removing the screws.

6. Remove the harness by disconnecting the control unit terminals.

7. Pry the reluctor off the shaft using small pry bars.

8. Remove the retaining screws and remove the breaker plate.

9. Remove the screws attaching the control unit to the breaker plate. Remove the control unit.

10. Remove the screws attaching the stator and separate the magnet from the stator.

11. Remove the O-ring and toll pin from the spiral gear. Remove the spiral gear from the distributor shaft.

12. Remove the distributor shaft from the housing.

13. Remove the governor springs from the shaft.

14. Remove the governor weights from the shaft.

Hitachi D4P84 and D6P84 Distributors

➡**These distributors were installed on late model 1.8L fuel injected and all 2.7L fuel injected engines.**

Subaru does not recommend disassembly of the Model D4P84 or D6P84 distributors. If component replacement is necessary, the distributor should be replaced as an assembly.

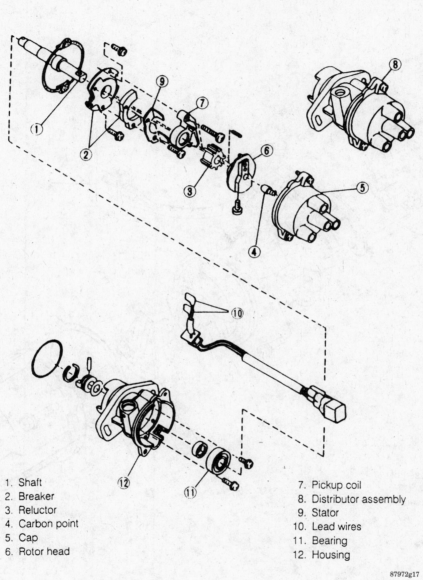

1. Shaft
2. Breaker
3. Reluctor
4. Carbon point
5. Cap
6. Rotor head

7. Pickup coil
8. Distributor assembly
9. Stator
10. Lead wires
11. Bearing
12. Housing

87972g17

Fig. 22 Disassembled 1.2L engine's distributor — carbureted version

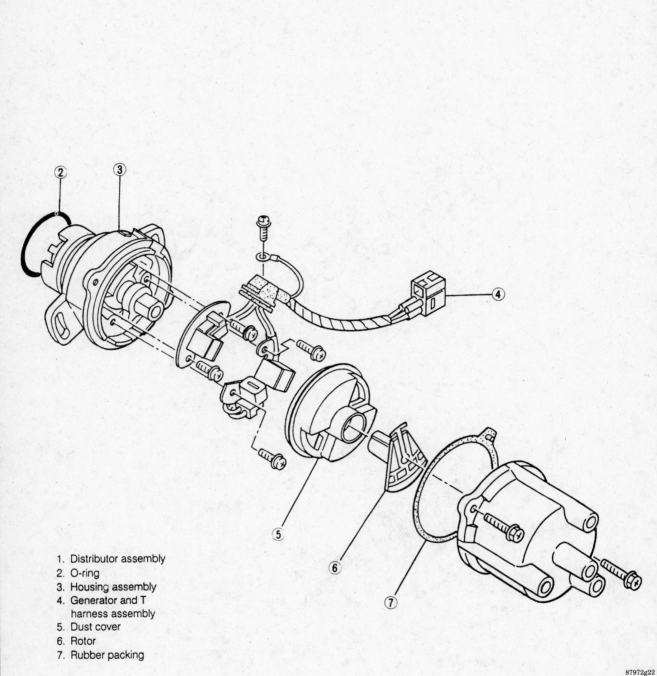

1. Distributor assembly
2. O-ring
3. Housing assembly
4. Generator and T
   harness assembly
5. Dust cover
6. Rotor
7. Rubber packing

87972g22

Fig. 23 Disassembled 1.2L engine's distributor — fuel injected version

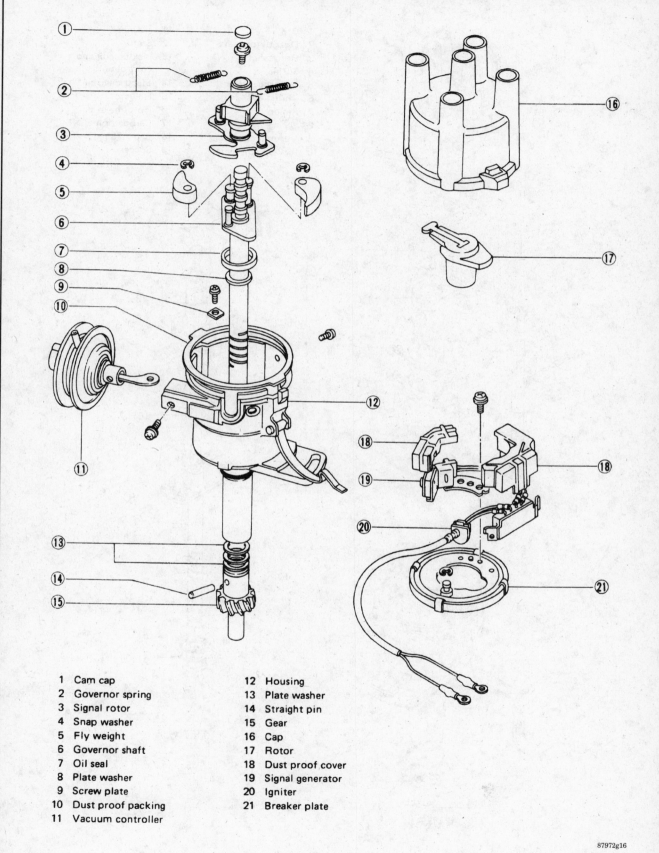

1   Cam cap
2   Governor spring
3   Signal rotor
4   Snap washer
5   Fly weight
6   Governor shaft
7   Oil seal
8   Plate washer
9   Screw plate
10 Dust proof packing
11 Vacuum controller
12 Housing
13 Plate washer
14 Straight pin
15 Gear
16 Cap
17 Rotor
18 Dust proof cover
19 Signal generator
20 Igniter
21 Breaker plate

87972g16

Fig. 24 Disassembled Nippondenso 100291 distributor

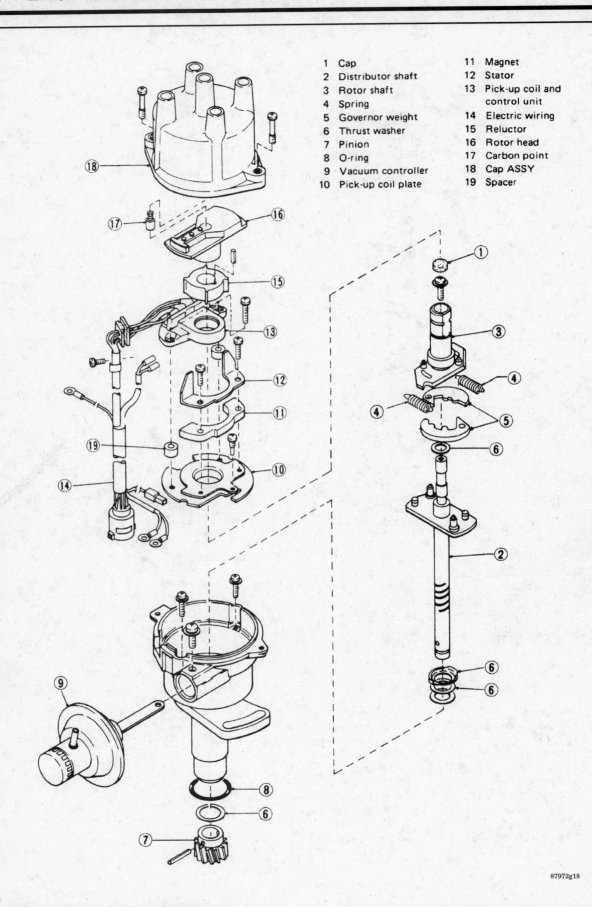

1	Cap	11	Magnet
2	Distributor shaft	12	Stator
3	Rotor shaft	13	Pick-up coil and
4	Spring		control unit
5	Governor weight	14	Electric wiring
6	Thrust washer	15	Reluctor
7	Pinion	16	Rotor head
8	O-ring	17	Carbon point
9	Vacuum controller	18	Cap ASSY
10	Pick-up coil plate	19	Spacer

87972g18

Fig. 25 Disassembled Hitachi D4R84 distributor

INSPECTION

1.2L Engine

1. Check the carbon point for free movement in the cap.
2. Measure the carbon point length with calipers. Minimum length is 0.39 in. (10mm). Replace if not within specification.
3. Check all terminals for corrosion or damage. Clean as necessary.
4. Check the rotor head for deformity or corrosion. Replace as necessary.
5. Check the reluctor for deformity, damage and free play. Replace as necessary.
6. Check the stator for damage or bending. Replace as necessary.
7. Check the breaker plate frictional section for free movement. Lubricate as required.

Nippondenso Model 100291 Distributor
♦ See Figure 26

1. Inspect the distributor base for any clogging of the breather hole.
2. Check all components for signs of cracking, burn marks or other damage.
3. Using a vacuum pump or equivalent, check the canister plunger to make sure it functions with vacuum.
4. Use an ohmmeter to check the signal generator. Connect the meter to the wire harness, and check the resistance. The correct resistance should be 130-190 ohms.

Hitachi Model D4R84 Distributor

1. Replace the reluctor if damaged and the stator if bent or scratched.
2. Replace the breaker plate if it binds or does not move smoothly.
3. With the shaft held stationary, manually turn the reluctor counterclockwise. It is working properly if it returns to the original position when released. If not, replace.
4. Apply a vacuum to the vacuum controller using a hand vacuum pump. If it does not hold vacuum, replace it.

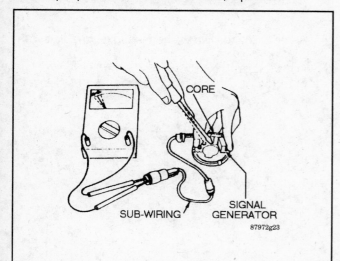

Fig. 26 Use an ohmmeter to test the signal generator

ASSEMBLY

1.2L Engine
♦ See Figures 27, 28 and 29

1. Assembly is the reverse of disassembly. Install the breaker assembly by aligning the mark on the plate with that on the housing.
2. Connect the lead wires to their proper locations.
3. Adjust the air gap between the reluctor and the stator to 0.008-0.016 in. (0.2-0.4mm). Loosen the stator screw to adjust the gap.

Nippondenso Model 100291 Distributor
♦ See Figures 30 and 31

1. Assembly is the reverse of disassembly. Lubricate and install the governor shaft and spiral gear. Select washers that will give a gear-to-housing clearance of 0.0059-0.0197 in. (0.15-0.50mm). Install the roll pin and stake it in place.

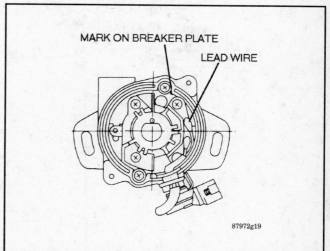

Fig. 27 Proper alignment of breaker plate — carbureted 1.2L engine's distributor

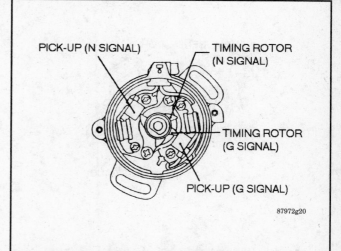

Fig. 28 Proper alignment of generator plate — fuel injected 1.2L engine's distributor

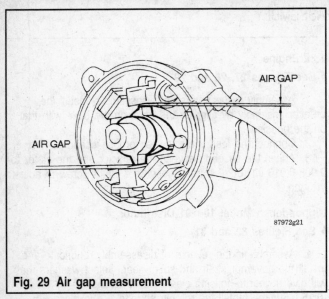

Fig. 29 Air gap measurement

2. Install the signal rotor by aligning the matchmark scribed on the notch with that of the spiral gear.

3. Install the breaker plate, evenly fitting the set springs into the housing.

4. Adjust the air gap between the signal generator and the signal rotor to 0.008-0.016 in. (0.2-0.4mm).

5. Install the vacuum controller, dust cover, rotor and cap.

6. Install the distributor into the engine, start the engine and check the timing.

Hitachi Model D4R84 Distributor
▶ See Figures 32, 33 and 34

1. Assembly is the reverse of disassembly. Apply a coat of grease to the shaft bearing and sliding surface for the breaker plate.

2. Install the governor and weights and springs. Attach the springs to the hook pins.

3. Position the cutout section of the rotor shaft and roll pin holes in line.

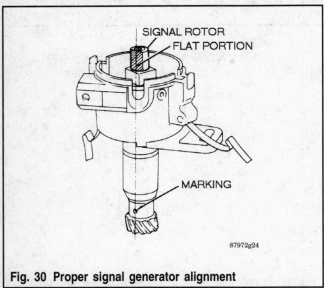

Fig. 30 Proper signal generator alignment

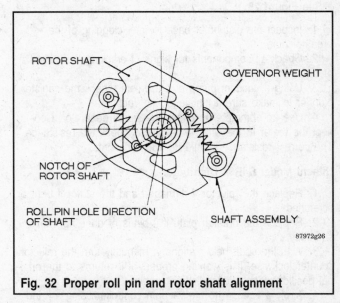

Fig. 32 Proper roll pin and rotor shaft alignment

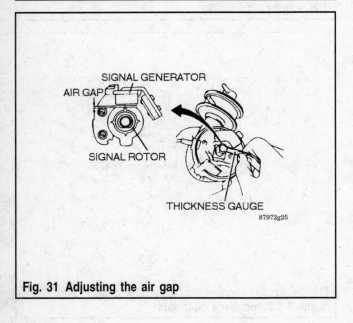

Fig. 31 Adjusting the air gap

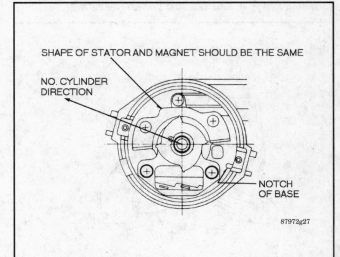

Fig. 33 Alignment of distributor for roll pin installation

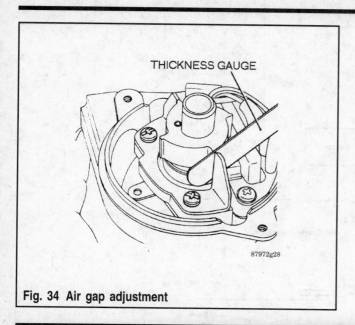

THICKNESS GAUGE

87972g28

Fig. 34 Air gap adjustment

4. Using a new roll pin, install the spiral gear so that its alignment mark is aligned with the mark on the housing when the cutout section of the rotor shaft faces the No. 1 cylinder mark on the cap.

5. Align the breaker plate with the retaining screw hole during installation.

6. Press the roll pin into place in parallel with the cutout section of the reluctor.

7. Connect the harness to the control unit.

8. After properly assembling the parts, measure the air gap between the reluctor and stator with a feeler gauge. The air gap should be 0.012-0.020 in. (0.3-0.5mm). If not within specification, adjust the stator to gain specified clearance.

DISTRIBUTORLESS IGNITION SYSTEM

General Information

▶ See Figure 35

A distributorless ignition system is used on all 2.2L and 2.5L models. The system consists of a cam and crankshaft angle sensor, knock sensor, two ignition coils, an Electronic Control Unit (ECU) and assorted sensors.

The system control features a quick response learning control method that compares data stored in the ECU memory to data received from the sensors. Thus, the ECU constantly provides the optimum ignition timing in relation to output, fuel consumption, exhaust gas and other variables.

The ECU receives signals from the airflow sensor, water temperature sensor, crank angle sensor, cam angle sensor, knock senor and other various indicators to judge the operating condition of the engine. It then selects the optimum ignition timing stored in the memory and immediately transmits a primary current OFF signal to the igniter to control the ignition timing.

The ECU also receives signals emitted from the knock sensor. Ignition timing is controlled so that advanced ignition timing is maintained immediately before engine knock occurs.

Two ignition coils are used, one for the No. 1 and No. 2 cylinders, and one for the No. 3 and No. 4 cylinders. A simultaneous ignition type is employed for each bank of cylinders. This eliminates the distributor and achieves maintenance free operation.

Ignition control under normal conditions is performed by the ECU measuring engine revolutions. Using the data it receives, the ECU decides the ignition timing according to engine operation. Ignition control under starting conditions is set by the ECU at 10° BTDC.

Testing

The majority of the diagnosis and testing of the distributorless ignition system is performed via the self-diagnosis function of the fuel injection control unit. See Electronic Engine Controls in Section 4 for more information.

IGNITION COIL

▶ See Figure 36

Primary Resistance

➡**The coil does not have to be removed from the vehicle to perform this test.**

1. Disconnect the negative battery cable.

2. Tag, then remove each spark plug wire from the ignition coil.

3. Using a multimeter, check the resistance between spark plug wire connections No. 1 and No. 2. Then check the resistance between spark plug connections No. 3 and No. 4. If the resistance between the connections is between 0.59-0.79 ohms, the coil is within specification. If the resistance is below this amount, replace it.

Secondary Resistance

1. Disconnect the negative battery cable, if not already done.

2. Tag then remove each spark plug wire from the ignition coil, if not already done.

3. Using a multimeter, check the resistance between wire harness connections No. 1 and No. 2. Then check the resistance between wire harness connections No. 2 and No. 3. If the resistance between the connections is between 17-24 kiloohms, the coil is within specification. If the resistance is below this amount, replace it.

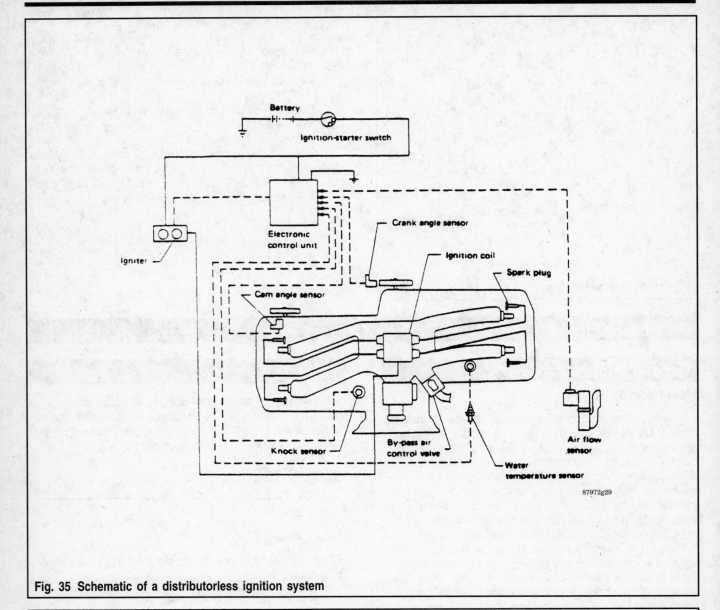

Fig. 35 Schematic of a distributorless ignition system

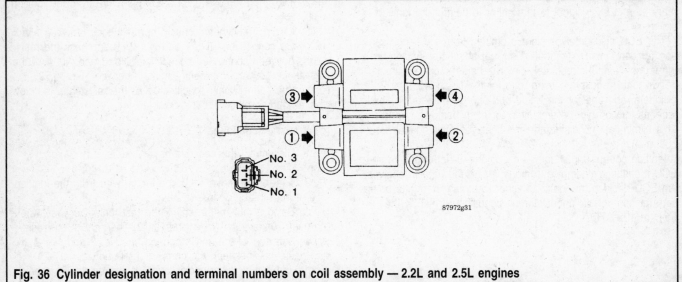

Fig. 36 Cylinder designation and terminal numbers on coil assembly — 2.2L and 2.5L engines

Adjustments

All ignition adjustments are carried out by the ignition control module. In the event the ignition system is not functioning correctly, check for a worn ignition part.

Ignition Coil Pack

REMOVAL & INSTALLATION

1. Disconnect the negative battery cable.
2. Tag, then remove each spark plug wire from the coil assembly.
3. Disconnect the wire harness attached to the coil assembly.

✳✳WARNING

Failure to identify the correct spark plug wire placement could cause serious coil damage during installation.

4. Remove the retaining bolts which secure the coil assembly to the intake manifold, and remove the coil from the engine compartment.

To install:
5. Position the coil on top of the intake manifold, and secure in place with the retaining bolts.
6. Attach the spark plug wires to the coil in the correct order.
7. Fasten the wire harness to the coil.
8. Connect the negative battery cable.

Ignitor Module

REMOVAL & INSTALLATION

▶ **See Figure 37**

The ignitor module can be found attached to a bracket against the firewall in the engine compartment.
1. Disconnect the negative battery cable.
2. Remove the wire harness attached to the ignitor module.
3. Detach the ignitor from the bracket by removing the retaining bolts.
4. After removing the ignitor, check the mounting bracket and clean off any rust or grease on the bracket mounting surface.

To install:
5. Position the ignitor module on the bracket and secure in place with the retaining bolts.
6. Attach the wire harness to the ignitor.
7. Connect the negative battery cable.

Fig. 37 Unfasten the harness from the ignitor assembly

Electronic Control Unit (ECU)

➡The ECU is incorporated into the Engine Control Module (ECM).

REMOVAL & INSTALLATION

The ECM is located on the floor of the passenger side of the vehicle.
1. Disconnect the negative battery cable.
2. Move front passenger floor mat and carpet out of the way to access the protective cover over the ECM.
3. Remove the retaining bolts securing the cover over the ECM. Detach the cover and place aside.
4. Release the lock securing the wiring harness to the ECM module. Slide the harness out of the connector.
5. Remove the retaining nuts securing the ECM to the floor. Lift the ECM out.

To install:
6. Connect the wire harness to the ECM module.
7. Place the ECM in the vehicle and secure in place with the retaining nuts
8. Position the protective cover over the ECM and secure with the protective bolts.
9. Install the interior carpet and floor mat in place.
10. Connect the negative battery cable.

Crankshaft Position Sensor

➡Refer to the appropriate procedure in Section 4 of this manual.

Camshaft Position Sensor

➡Refer to the appropriate procedure in Section 4 of this manual.

DIRECT IGNITION SYSTEM

General Information

▶ **See Figure 38**

A direct ignition system is used on all SVX models. The system consists of crank and camshaft angle sensors, two knock sensors, an igniter, six ignition coils, an electronic control unit (ECU) and assorted sensors.

The ignition coils are directly mounted to the spark plugs of the respective cylinders. This results in a reduced energy loss because no high tension wires are used.

The ignition system is controlled by the Electronic Control Unit (ECU). The ECU determines the ignition timing based on the signal from crank angle sensor 1, and sends the signal to the igniter to spark the cylinder which is judged to be at top dead center of the compression stroke by crank angle sensor 2 and the camshaft angle sensor. When engine speed is low, the ECU fixes the timing at 10° BTDC.

One knock sensor is install on the left cylinder block and another on the right cylinder block, thus ensuring accurate digital engine knock control.

Testing

The majority of the diagnosis and testing of the direct ignition system is performed via the self-diagnosis function of the fuel injection control unit. See Electronic Engine Controls in Section 4 for more information.

SPARK PLUG IGNITION COIL

▶ **See Figure 39**

Each spark plug has a separate ignition coil attached to it.

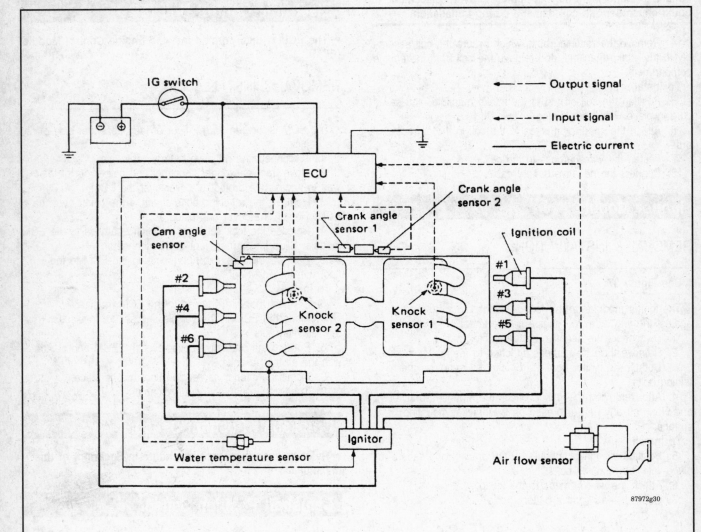

Fig. 38 Direct ignition system — SVX models

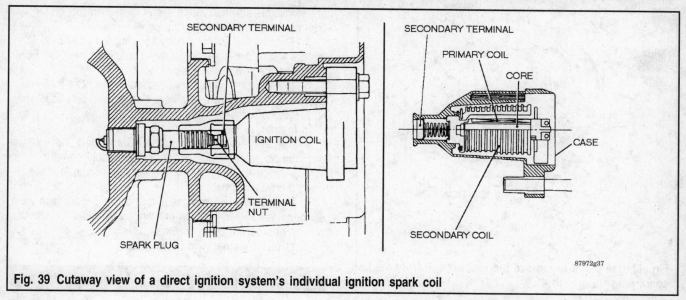

Fig. 39 Cutaway view of a direct ignition system's individual ignition spark coil

Primary Coil

▶ See Figure 40

1. Disconnect the negative battery cable.
2. Remove the coil from the spark plug and engine compartment.
3. Using a multimeter or equivalent, measure the resistance between terminals No. 1 and No. 2 of the coil wire harness. The resistance should be between 0.68-0.83 ohms. If not within this range, replace the coil.

Secondary Coil

▶ See Figure 41

➡This procedure requires the use of a digital ammeter or multimeter. Do not use an analog model.

1. Disconnect the negative battery cable.
2. Remove the coil from the spark plug and engine compartment.

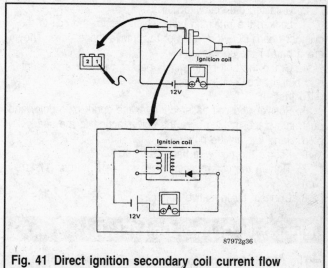

Fig. 41 Direct ignition secondary coil current flow check

3. Using a digital multimeter and a 12 volt power supply, connect the meter in series between the primary and secondary terminals of the coil.
4. Measure the current amount. If the reading is not between 0.29-33 milo-amps, replace the coil.

Spark Plug Ignition Coil

REMOVAL & INSTALLATION

▶ See Figures 39 and 42

Each cylinder has a separate ignition coil attached to the spark plug.

1. Disconnect the negative battery cable.

➡Depending on which coil is being removed, the air cleaner case may have to be removed for increased access space.

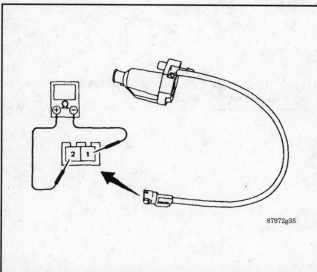

Fig. 40 Direct ignition primary coil resistance check

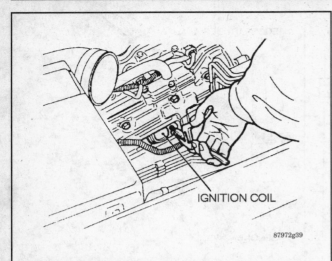

Fig. 42 Use pliers to remove the ignition coil from the spark plug

2. Unfasten the coil wire harness.

3. Loosen the retaining bolts which secure the coil to the cylinder head. DO NOT attempt to remove these bolts. They are a part of the coil assembly.

4. Grasp the bolt head with a pair of pliers or equivalent and pull the coil out.

To install:

5. Position the coil assembly over the spark plug hole, and push into place making sure the coil attached to the spark plug. Hand tighten the bolts.

6. Fasten the coil wire harness.

7. Tighten the coil retaining bolts to 13-15 ft. lbs. (17-20 Nm).

8. Connect the negative battery cable.

Electronic Control Unit (ECU)

➡The ECU is incorporated into the Engine Control Module.

REMOVAL & INSTALLATION

▶ **See Figure 43**

1. Disconnect the negative battery cable.

2. Remove the retaining screws securing trim panel below the steering column in the interior of the vehicle. If there are ant harnesses attached to the inside of the trim panel, tag then disconnect them. Place the panel aside.

3. Remove the retaining bolts securing the ECM module the bracket to the left of the steering column. Lower the ECM to access the harnesses attached to it.

4. Unfasten the harnesses attached to the ECM module. Since this connector are of different sizes, and only fit in one way, they do not need to be marked.

To install:

5. Connect the harnesses to the ECM module. Do not force any connectors into place or the contacts could be bent.

6. Position the ECM to the bracket and secure in place using the retaining bolts.

7. Fasten any wire harnesses to the trim panel which were disconnected earlier. Position the trim panel under the steering column and secure using the retaining screws.

8. Connect the negative battery cable.

Crankshaft Position Sensor

➡Refer to the appropriate procedure in Section 4 of this manual.

Camshaft Position Sensor

➡Refer to the appropriate procedure in Section 4 of this manual.

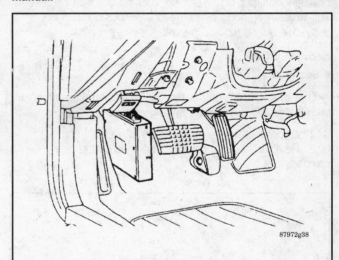

Fig. 43 ECM module removed and lowered to access the attached wiring harnesses

FIRING ORDERS

→To avoid confusion, remove and tag the wires one at a time, for replacement.

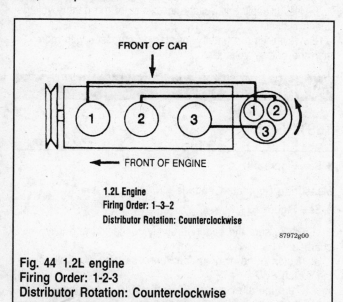

1.2L Engine
Firing Order: 1–3–2
Distributor Rotation: Counterclockwise

87972g00

Fig. 44 1.2L engine
Firing Order: 1-2-3
Distributor Rotation: Counterclockwise

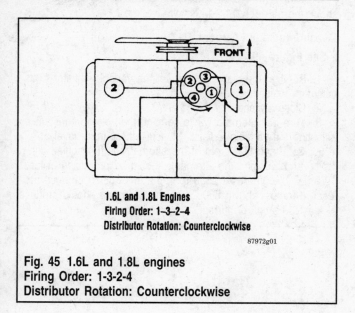

1.6L and 1.8L Engines
Firing Order: 1–3–2–4
Distributor Rotation: Counterclockwise

87972g01

Fig. 45 1.6L and 1.8L engines
Firing Order: 1-3-2-4
Distributor Rotation: Counterclockwise

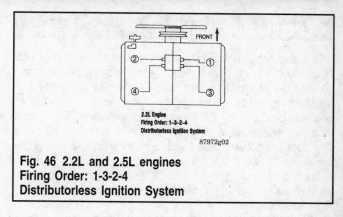

2.2L Engine
Firing Order: 1–3–2–4
Distributorless Ignition System

87972g02

Fig. 46 2.2L and 2.5L engines
Firing Order: 1-3-2-4
Distributorless Ignition System

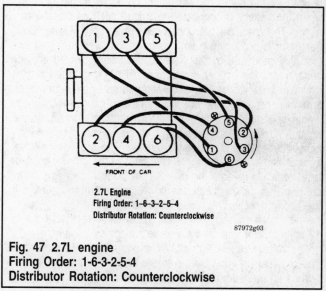

2.7L Engine
Firing Order: 1–6–3–2–5–4
Distributor Rotation: Counterclockwise

87972g03

Fig. 47 2.7L engine
Firing Order: 1-6-3-2-5-4
Distributor Rotation: Counterclockwise

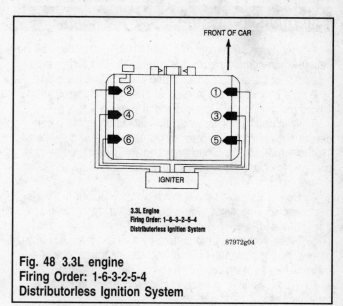

3.3L Engine
Firing Order: 1–6–3–2–5–4
Distributorless Ignition System

87972g04

Fig. 48 3.3L engine
Firing Order: 1-6-3-2-5-4
Distributorless Ignition System

CHARGING SYSTEM

General Information

The automobile charging system provides electrical power for operation of the vehicle's ignition system, starting system and all electrical accessories. The battery serves as an electrical surge or storage tank, storing (in chemical form) the energy originally produced by the engine driven generator. The system also provides a means of regulating output to protect the battery from being overcharged and to avoid excessive voltage to the accessories.

The storage battery is a chemical device incorporating parallel lead plates in a tank containing a sulfuric acid/water solution. Adjacent plates are slightly dissimilar, and the chemical reaction of the two dissimilar plates produces electrical energy when the battery is connected to a load such as the starter motor. The chemical reaction is reversible, so that when the generator is producing a voltage (electrical pressure) greater than that produced by the battery, electricity is forced into the battery, and the battery is returned to its fully charged state.

Newer automobiles use alternating current generators or alternators, because they are more efficient, can be rotated at higher speeds, and have fewer brush problems. In an alternator, the field usually rotates while all the current produced passes only through the stator winding. The brushes bear against continuous slip rings. This causes the current produced to periodically reverse the direction of its flow. Diodes (electrical one way valves) block the flow of current from traveling in the wrong direction. A series of diodes is wired together to permit the alternating flow of the stator to be rectified back to 12 volts DC for use by the vehicle's electrical system.

The voltage regulating function is performed by a regulator. The regulator is often built in to the alternator; this system is termed an integrated or internal regulator.

Alternator Precautions

1. Pay particular attention to the polarity connections of the battery when connecting the battery cables. Make sure that you connect the correct cable to the corresponding terminal.
2. If a jumper battery is used to start the vehicle, refer to the correct method of jump starting in Section 1.
3. When testing or adjusting the alternator, install a condenser between the alternator output terminal and the ground. This is to prevent the diode from becoming damaged by a spark which occurs due to testing equipment with a defective connection.
4. Do not operate the alternator with the output terminals disconnected. The diode would be damaged by the high voltage generated.
5. When recharging the battery by a quick charge or any other charging apparatus, disconnect the alternator output terminal before hooking up the charging leads.
6. When installing a battery, always connect the positive terminal first.
7. Never disconnect the battery while the engine is running.

8. Never electric weld around the car without disconnecting the alternator.
9. Never apply any voltage in excess of the battery voltage during testing.
10. Never jump a battery for starting purposes with more than the battery voltage.

Alternator

TESTING

▶ See Figure 49

Measuring Regulated Voltage

▶ See Figure 49

1. Make sure the battery is firmly connected and fully charged.
2. Refer to the diagram, and open switch SW1 while closing switch SW2.
3. Turn the alternator at 5000 rpm and record the voltage.
4. If the alternator is functioning correctly, the voltage should be between 14.3-14.8 volts.

Measuring Output Current

▶ See Figure 49

1. Refer to the diagram, and set the variable resistor to its minimum resistance.
2. Close switches SW1 and SW2.
3. Turn the alternator while keeping the voltage constant by adjusting the variable resistor. Measure the current level at 1250, 2500 and 5000 rpm. If the alternator is functioning correctly, at 1250 rpm, the alternator should be producing at least 18 amps of current. At 2500 rpm, the unit should produce at least 49 amps, and at 5000 rpm, the alternator should produce at least 58 amps of current.

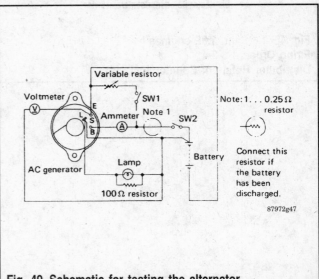

Fig. 49 Schematic for testing the alternator

Alternator Speed at 13.5 Volts

▶ **See Figure 49**

1. Refer to the diagram, and open switch SW1 while closing switch SW2.

2. Slowly raise the alternator speed and record the voltage level.

3. If the alternator is functioning correctly, at 900 rpm, the voltage should be 13.5 volts.

REMOVAL & INSTALLATION

▶ **See Figures 50, 51 and 52**

1. Disconnect the negative battery cable.

2. Label and disconnect the alternator electrical wiring harness and battery cable.

3. Loosen the belt tension bracket adjusting bolt at the top of the alternator. Loosen the lower retaining bolt at the base of

Fig. 50 Unfasten the power wire and indicator light wire from the back of the alternator — 1.8L engine shown

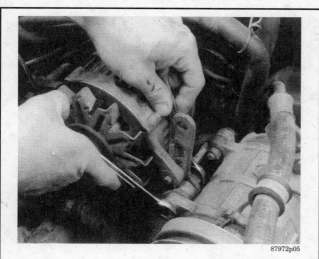

Fig. 51 Remove the adjusting bolt and bracket, as well as the lower retaining nut and bolt

Fig. 52 Lift the alternator out of the engine compartment

the alternator. Push the alternator in and remove the accessory drive belt.

4. Remove the alternator adjusting bolt followed by the lower retaining bolt.

5. Remove the alternator from the engine compartment.

➡Now is a good time to inspect the drive belt for wear, replace if necessary.

To install:

6. Install the alternator on the engine and insert the lower retaining bolt loosely. Attach the bracket and adjusting bolt to the top of the alternator.

7. Install the accessory drive belt and tension. Tighten all bolts securely.

8. Connect the alternator electrical wiring harness and battery cable.

9. Connect the negative battery cable. Start the engine and check the alternator for proper operation.

BRUSH REPLACEMENT

▶ **See Figures 53, 54, 55, 56, 57 and 58**

1. Disconnect the negative battery cable.

2. Remove the alternator from the engine.

3. Remove the through-bolts from the alternator.

4. Detach the front cover with the rotor from the rear cover with the stator by lightly tapping on the front cover with a plastic hammer.

5. Separate the brush assembly from the rear cover by removing the nuts on the rear cover.

6. As required, disconnect the brush and diode assemblies as well as the IC regulator from the stator coil lead wires using a soldering iron.

To install:

7. Inspect the movement of the brush. If the movement is not smooth, check the brush holder and clean it.

8. Check the brush for wear. If worn beyond the wear marks located on the brushes, replace the brush assembly.

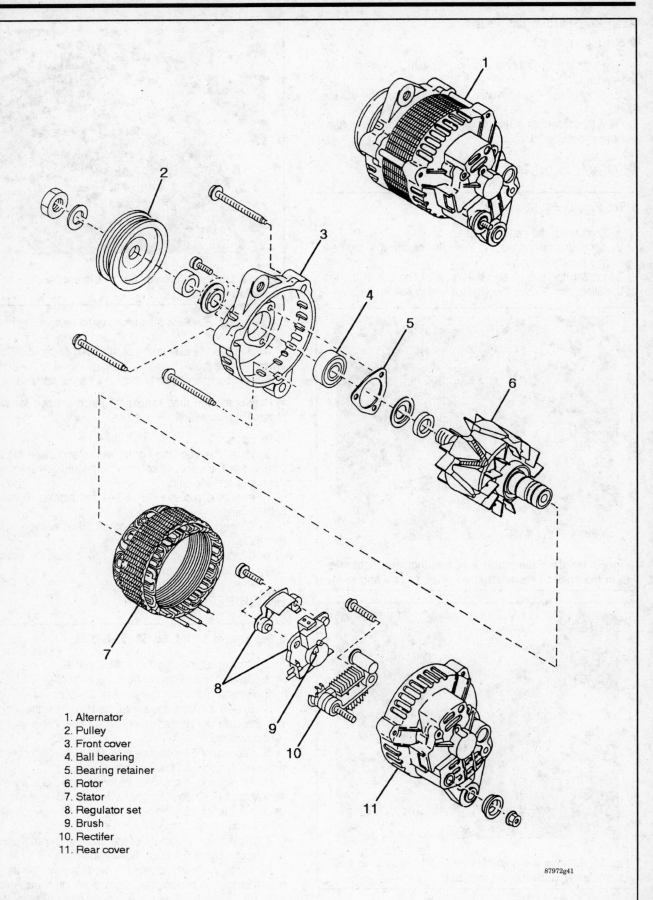

1. Alternator
2. Pulley
3. Front cover
4. Ball bearing
5. Bearing retainer
6. Rotor
7. Stator
8. Regulator set
9. Brush
10. Rectifer
11. Rear cover

87972g41

Fig. 53 Disassembled alternator — 1.2L engine

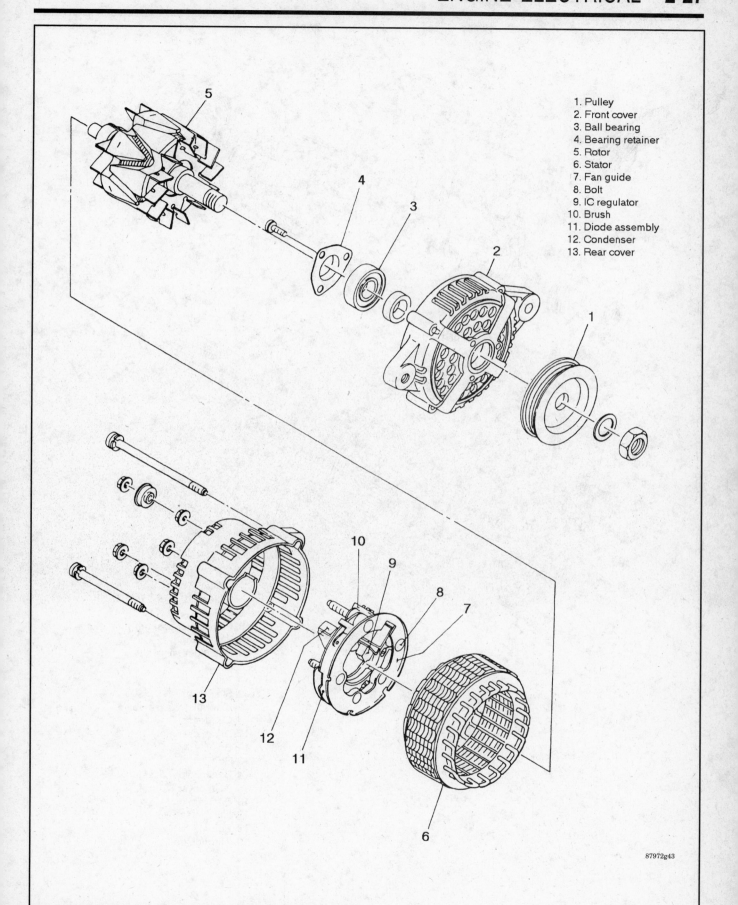

1. Pulley
2. Front cover
3. Ball bearing
4. Bearing retainer
5. Rotor
6. Stator
7. Fan guide
8. Bolt
9. IC regulator
10. Brush
11. Diode assembly
12. Condenser
13. Rear cover

87972g43

Fig. 54 Disassembled alternator — 1.6L and 1.8L engines

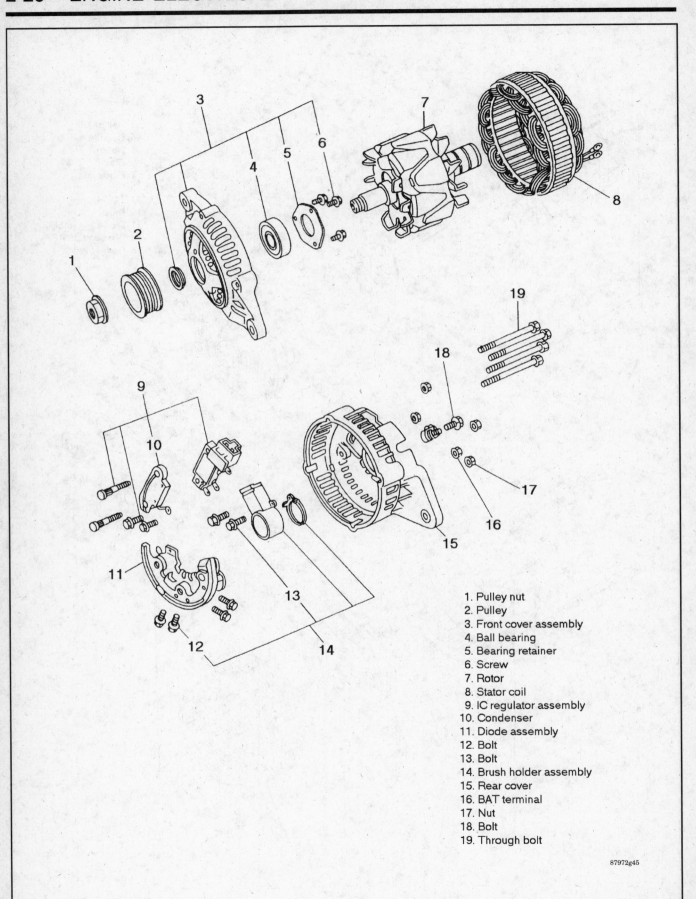

1. Pulley nut
2. Pulley
3. Front cover assembly
4. Ball bearing
5. Bearing retainer
6. Screw
7. Rotor
8. Stator coil
9. IC regulator assembly
10. Condenser
11. Diode assembly
12. Bolt
13. Bolt
14. Brush holder assembly
15. Rear cover
16. BAT terminal
17. Nut
18. Bolt
19. Through bolt

87972g45

Fig. 55 Disassembled alternator — 2.2L and 2.5L engines

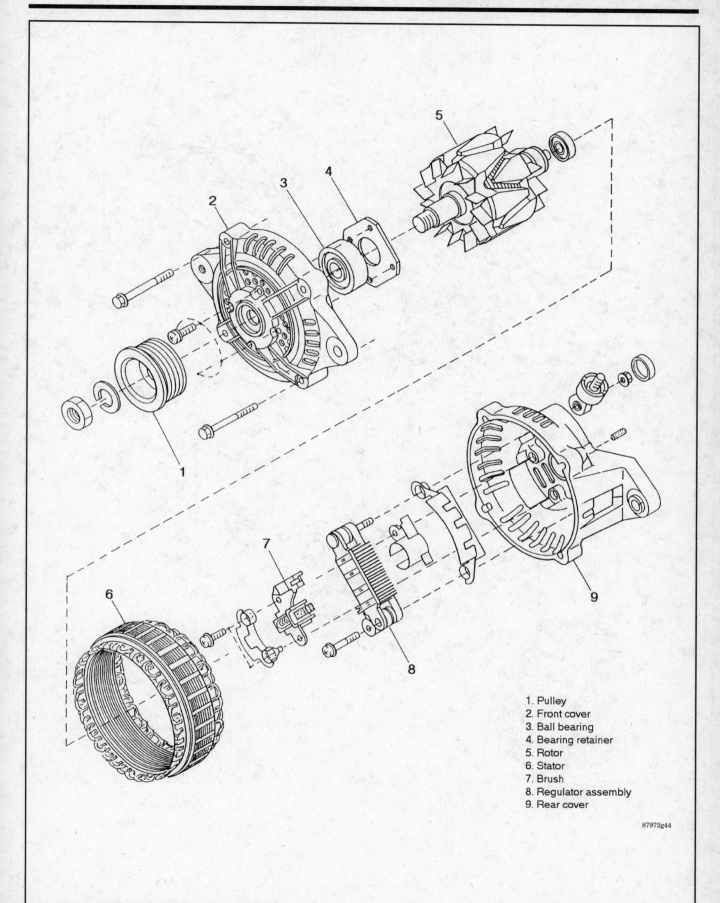

1. Pulley
2. Front cover
3. Ball bearing
4. Bearing retainer
5. Rotor
6. Stator
7. Brush
8. Regulator assembly
9. Rear cover

87972g44

Fig. 56 Disassembled alternator — 2.7L engine

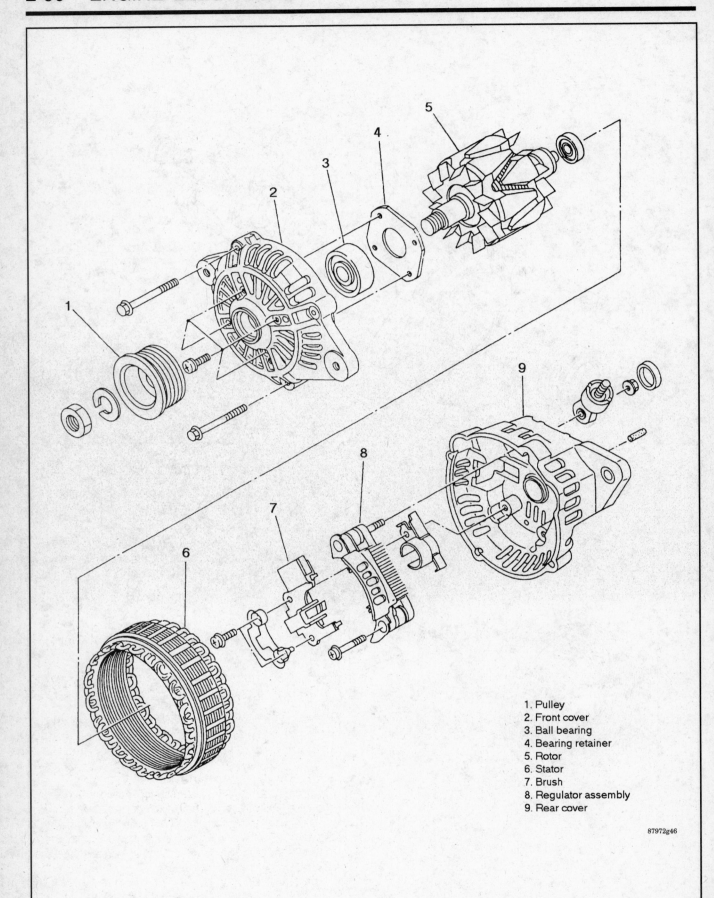

1. Pulley
2. Front cover
3. Ball bearing
4. Bearing retainer
5. Rotor
6. Stator
7. Brush
8. Regulator assembly
9. Rear cover

87972g46

Fig. 57 Disassembled alternator — 3.3L engine

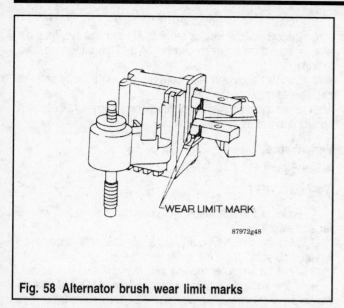

Fig. 58 Alternator brush wear limit marks

WEAR LIMIT MARK

87972g48

9. Install the brush assembly, diode assembly and IC regulator into the rear cover. Solder the wires as required.

➡**Soldering should be done quickly as to not damage the diodes.**

10. Push the brushes into their holders and insert a wire into the back of the alternator to hold the brushes in place. An unfolded paper clip works good.

11. Tighten the diode assembly and brush assembly retaining nuts to 2-3 ft. lbs. (3-4 Nm).

12. Assemble the front and rear case halves. Tighten the through-bolts to 2-4 ft. lbs. (3-5 Nm).

Regulator

The voltage regulator controls the output of the alternator. Without this voltage limiting function of the regulator, the excessive output of the alternator could burn out components of the electrical system. In addition, the regulator compensates for seasonal changes in temperature as it affects voltage output.

All Subaru models have a solid state regulator built into the alternator. The regulator is non-adjustable and is serviced, when necessary, by replacement.

REMOVAL & INSTALLATION

▶ **See Figures 53, 54, 55, 56 and 57**

1. Disconnect the negative battery cable.
2. Remove the alternator from the vehicle.
3. Remove the through-bolts from the alternator.
4. Detach the front cover with the rotor from the rear cover with the stator by lightly tapping on the front cover with a plastic hammer.
5. Separate the voltage regulator assembly from the rear cover by removing the nuts on the rear cover and the retaining bolt securing the regulator to the case.

To install:

6. Install the regulator assembly to the inside of the alternator case and secure with the retainer bolt and nut.
7. Assemble the front and rear case halves. Tighten the through-bolts to 2-4 ft. lbs. (3-5 Nm).

Battery

REMOVAL & INSTALLATION

1. Disconnect the negative battery cable. Then disconnect the positive battery cable.
2. Loosen the battery hold-down clamps and remove.
3. Using a battery strap or lifting tool, carefully remove battery from the vehicle.

➡**Use care in handling the battery, remember, it is filled with a highly corrosive acid. Do not smoke while servicing the battery as the vapors are explosive.**

To install:

4. Clean the battery tray and terminals of all corrosion.
5. Install the battery and tighten the hold-down clamps.
6. Install the battery terminals; positive terminal first followed by the negative.

STARTING SYSTEM

General Information

The magnetic switch starter, used on all engines except the 1.2L and 1.6L, uses a permanent magnetic field system instead of field coils inside the yoke. A spring steel retaining ring is used to retain the magnet, and keep it from springing out when an unexpectedly strong shock is applied to the yoke circumference. When the starter is engaged, current flows through the pull-in and holding coils. This causes the plunger to be pulled in, applying pressure to the shifter lever, which pushes the pinion out. Current flows through the armature and starts it to turn the pinion at a moderate speed, meshing it with the ring gear. When the main switch contacts are closed, full current flows through the armature, fully meshing the pinion with the ring gear, starting the vehicle.

On all engines except the 1.2L and 1.6L, the starter is fitted with a gear reduction mechanism. The gear reduction mechanism may drive the over-running clutch shaft through its own pinion or an idler gear and pinion, depending on the required reduction. The purpose of this system is to increase the torque produced by the starter for its weight.

Starter

TESTING

Switch Assembly
▶ See Figures 59 and 60

1. Connect terminal **S** of starter switch to the positive terminal of the battery using a lead wire or equivalent.

2. Connect the starter body to the negative terminal of the battery.

3. If the switch assembly is working correctly, the pinion should be be forced out. If the starter motor rotates, this is OK. Sometimes current will flow through the pull in coil to the motor and cause this.

4. With the pinion forced outward, measure the pinion gap. It should be between 0.02-0.08 in. (0.5-2.0mm).

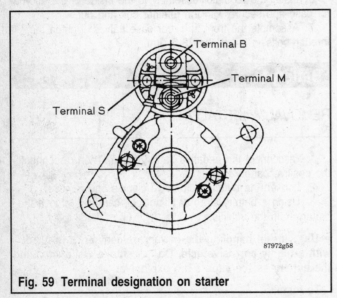

Fig. 59 Terminal designation on starter

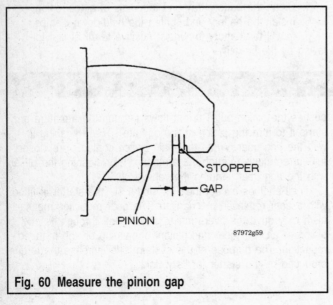

Fig. 60 Measure the pinion gap

5. Unfasten all connections.

6. Disconnect the wire at terminal **M**, and attach a lead wire or equivalent between terminal **M** and the battery positive terminal.

7. Connect a ground lead between the stater body and the negative terminal of the battery.

8. If the switch assembly is functioning correctly, the pinion should return it its original position.

Performance
▶ See Figure 61

NO-LOAD TEST

1. Refer to the illustration and connection ammeter, voltmeter and switch.

2. With the switch ON, adjust the variable resistance to obtain 11.0 volts.

3. Take an ammeter reading and record the starter speed.

4. If the starter is functioning properly, at 11.0 volts, with a maximum of 90 amps, the starter will be rotating at 3000 rpm.

LOAD TEST

1. Refer to the illustration and connection ammeter, voltmeter and switch.

2. Apply braking torque to the starter.

3. Measure the current draw and starter speed at 7.7 volts.

4. If the starter is functioning correctly, at a load of 7.7 volts and 7 ft. lbs. (10 Nm) of torque, the should be a maximum current draw of 300 amps at 1000 rpm.

LOCK TEST

1. Refer to the illustration and connection ammeter, voltmeter and switch.

2. with the starter stalled, or not rotating, measure the torque developed and the current draw when the voltage is adjusted to 4.0 volts.

3. If the starter is functioning properly, at 4.0 volts, the starter will draw a maximum of 980 amps at a torque of 17 ft. lbs. (23 Nm).

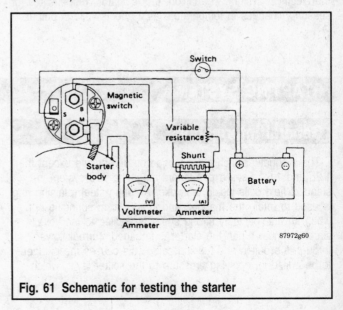

Fig. 61 Schematic for testing the starter

REMOVAL & INSTALLATION

▶ **See Figures 62, 63 and 64**

1. Disconnect the negative battery cable, followed by the positive cable.

2. Label and disconnect the wiring harness attached to the starter. Remove the battery cable attached. All starter control wires are located on top of the transaxle at the rear of the engine.

3. Remove the starter attaching bolts (nuts) and pull the starter away from the engine and out.

To install:

4. Install the starter and tighten the attaching bolts to 34-40 ft. lbs. (46-54 Nm). Tighten the nuts to 22-27 ft. lbs. (30-36 Nm).

5. Connect the wiring harness.

6. Connect the positive battery cable, followed by the negative battery cable.

MAGNETIC SWITCH REPLACEMENT

On all engines except the 1.2L and 1.6L, the magnetic switch is an integral part of the starter housing. The starter must be completely disassembled to gain access to the switch.

1.2L and 1.6L Engines

1. With the starter removed from the vehicle, loosen the magnetic switch nut to remove the connecting wire.

2. Remove the magnetic switch by removing the attaching bolts.

3. Separate the torsion spring from the switch.

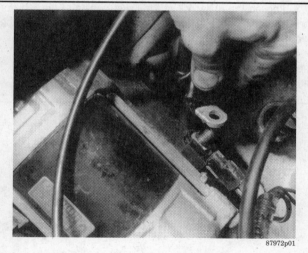

Fig. 62 Unfasten the power wire and signal wire from the starter

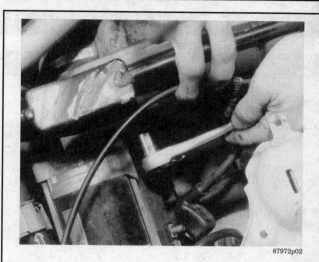

Fig. 63 Remove the retaining bolts from the sides of the starter

Fig. 64 With the bolts removed, lift the starter out

To install:

4. Check conductivity between terminal **S** (the smaller post) and the switch body. If none, replace the switch.

5. Check conductivity between terminal **M** (the large post) and terminal **S**. If none, replace the switch.

6. With the plunger pushed inward, check conductivity between terminals **M** and **B**. If none, replace the switch.

7. Assemble the switch with the torsion spring and install on the starter.

8. Insert and tighten the switch attaching bolts to 5-6 ft. lbs. (6-8 Nm).

9. Install the connecting wire and the nut securely.

10. Install the starter in the vehicle.

SENDING UNITS AND SENSORS

Coolant Temperature Sensor

OPERATION

▶ **See Figures 65 and 66**

The coolant temperature sensor, or Thermometer as it is referred to by Subaru, is installed in either the intake manifold (1.2L engines), the side of the radiator(1.6L, 1.8L and 2.7L), or separate water pipe connecting the cylinder heads (2.2L, 2.5L and 3.3L engine), and monitors the coolant temperature. A signal is sent from the sender to the engine temperature gauge in the combination meter, and also to the ECU where the radiator fan operation signal is generated. In addition to fan operation, the ECM uses coolant temperature to adjust fuel delivery and ignition timing.

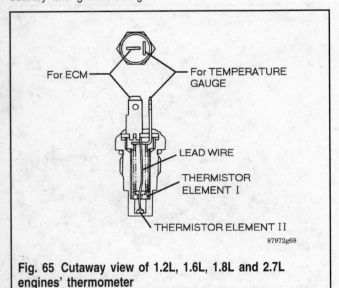

Fig. 65 Cutaway view of 1.2L, 1.6L, 1.8L and 2.7L engines' thermometer

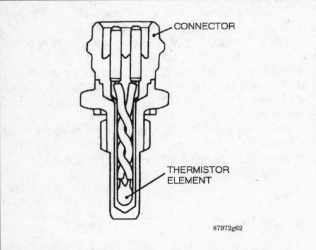

Fig. 66 Cutaway view of 2.2L, 2.5L and 3.3L engines' thermometer

TESTING

▶ **See Figure 67**

1. Refer to the illustration and connect the temperature gauge and sender in series.
2. Make sure that the gauge indicates C when the ignition switch is **OFF**.
3. Start the vehicle and record the resistance with a multimeter or equivalent at the sender.
4. At 122°F (50°C) the correct resistance should be between 133.9-178.9 ohms. At 176°F (80°C) the correct resistance should be between 47.5-56.8 ohms. At 212°F (100°C) the correct resistance should be between 26.2-29.3 ohms. And at 248°F (120°C) the correct resistance should be between 14.9-17.3 ohms.

REMOVAL & INSTALLATION

❄❄CAUTION

Use extreme care if removing a sender from a vehicle which has been driven recently. The coolant could be extremely hot.

1. Disconnect the negative battery cable.
2. Access the thermometer on the intake manifold (1.2L engine), radiator (1.6L, 1.8L, 2.7L engines), or coolant pipe (2.2L, 2.5L and 3.3L engines) and unfasten the wire harness attached.
3. Loosen the draincock at the lower portion of the radiator and drain enough coolant into a suitable container to bring the level below the thermometer.
4. Loosen and remove the thermometer. Inspect the threads of the manifold, radiator or pipe, and use a thread chaser to restore the threads if damaged.

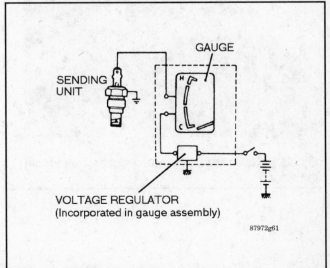

Fig. 67 Schematic of thermometer and gauge

5. If reinstalling the original thermometer, remove sealing gasket and replace with a new one.

To install:

6. Position thermometer, and new sealing gasket into hole in manifold, radiator or coolant pipe, depending on model, and hand-tighten.

7. Using an appropriate socket, tighten the thermometer to 2-3 ft. lbs. (3-4 Nm).

8. Connect the wire harness to the thermometer. Tighten the radiator draincock, if not already done.

9. Connect the negative battery cable.

10. Fill the cooling system with coolant and bleed.

Thermosensor

The 1.2L engine is equipped with a second coolant sensor, referred to by Subaru as a Thermosensor. This sensor works in cooperation with the thermometer to control the radiator fan and delivery coolant information to the ECM.

REMOVAL & INSTALLATION

✳✳CAUTION

Use extreme care if removing a sender from a vehicle which has been driven recently. The coolant could be extremely hot.

The thermosensor is located to the left of the thermometer on the intake manifold.

1. Disconnect the negative battery cable.

2. Access the thermosensor on the intake manifold, and unfasten the wire harness attached.

3. Loosen the draincock at the lower portion of the radiator, and drain enough coolant into a suitable container to bring the level below the thermosensor.

4. Loosen and remove the thermosensor. Inspect the threads of the manifold, and use a thread chaser to restore the threads if damaged.

5. If reinstalling original thermosensor, remove sealing gasket and replace with a new one.

To install:

6. Position thermosensor, and new sealing gasket into hole in manifold, and hand-tighten.

7. Using an appropriate socket, tighten the thermosensor to 2-3 ft. lbs. (3-4 Nm).

8. Connect the wire harness to the thermosensor. Tighten the radiator draincock, if not already done.

9. Connect the negative battery cable.

10. Fill the cooling system with coolant and bleed.

Oil Pressure Sensor

OPERATION

▶ See Figure 68

The oil pressure switch is attached to the crankcase (1.2L engine), oil pump case (1.6L, 1.8L and 2.7L engines) or cylin-

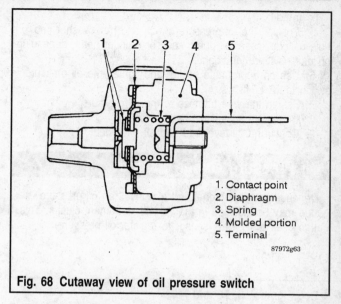

1. Contact point
2. Diaphragm
3. Spring
4. Molded portion
5. Terminal

87972g63

Fig. 68 Cutaway view of oil pressure switch

der block (2.2L, 2.5L and 3.3L engines). It monitors oil pressure and activates the oil pressure indicator light in the combination meter.

The sensor is made up of a diaphragm which is operated by oil pressure. A set of contacts open and close in relation to the diaphragm movement. The entire sensor is encased in phenol resin which is not effected by temperature or oil. The sensor is not serviceable, and must be replaced if found to be defective.

TESTING

1. Remove the oil pressure switch from the engine.

2. Install a T-fitting into the oil pressure switch hole and connect the oil pressure switch to one end, and a suitable oil pressure gauge to the other.

3. Start the vehicle and allow it to reach normal operating temperature. Upon starting the vehicle, the oil pressure light should illuminate. If it does not, check the wiring to the indicator lamp for power.

4. At an oil pressure of 2.1 psi (15 kPa), the oil pressure indicator light should go out. If the light does not go out, replace the oil pressure switch.

REMOVAL & INSTALLATION

1. Disconnect the negative battery cable.

2. Access the oil pressure switch on the crankcase (1.2L engine), oil pump case (1.6L, 1.8L and 2.7L engines) or cylinder head (2.2L, 2.5L and 3.3L engines). Unfasten the wire harness from the switch.

3. Place a suitable drain pan underneath the oil pressure switch to capture any oil which may spill out during the removal and installation of the switch.

4. Use an appropriate wrench or socket to loosen and remove the oil pressure switch. If reinstalling original oil pressure switch, remove and discard washer on switch.

To install:

5. Position the oil pressure switch and new washer into hole on crankcase, oil pump case or cylinder head, depending on models, and hand-tighten.

6. Use an appropriate socket and tighten the oil pressure switch to 12-17 ft. lbs. (17-23 Nm).

7. Fasten the wire harness to the oil pressure switch.

8. Connect the negative battery cable.

9. Check the oil level and add oil if needed.

Oil Pressure Gauge Switch

Depending on the model and trim level, an oil pressure gauge may be installed in the vehicle instrument cluster. This gauge uses a separate sensor to register oil pressure.

OPERATION

▶ **See Figures 69, 70 and 71**

The oil pressure gauge switch monitors the oil pressure at the pump. Depending on the model, it is attached to the oil pump case (1.6L, 1.8L and 2.7L engines) or cylinder head (2.2L, 2.5L and 3.3L engines).

This sensor consists of a moving diaphragm which reacts according to the oil pump pressure, a temperature compensating bimetal, a heat wire and two contacts.

When no oil pressure is presents, the two contact points are open slightly. As oil pressure increases, the point arm begins to contact the bimetal. With the ignition switch **ON**, current flows to the heat wire in the sensor and begins to create heat which bends the bimetal and point arm in the sensor. As the bimetal in the sensor heats and bends, current is created which is transported through the sensor wire to the gauge, where it begins to heat a bimetal in the gauge. The bending bimetal moves the point arm in the gauge. As the oil pressure changes, it creates a different current flow and resulting generated heat to the bimetal in the sensor and gauge.

REMOVAL & INSTALLATION

1. Disconnect the negative battery cable.

2. Access the oil pressure sensor on the oil pump case (1.6L, 1.8L and 2.7L engines) or cylinder head (2.2L, 2.5L and 3.3L engines). Unfasten the wire harness from the switch.

3. Place a suitable drain pan underneath the oil pressure sensor to capture any oil which may spill out during the removal and installation of the switch.

4. Use an appropriate wrench to loosen and remove the oil pressure sensor. If reinstalling original oil pressure sensor, remove and discard washer on sensor.

To install:

5. Position the oil pressure sensor and new washer into hole in oil pump case or cylinder head, depending on models, and hand-tighten.

6. Use an appropriate socket and tighten the pressure sensor to 12-17 ft. lbs. (17-23 Nm).

7. Fasten the wire harness to the oil pressure sensor.

8. Connect the negative battery cable.

9. Check the oil level and add if needed.

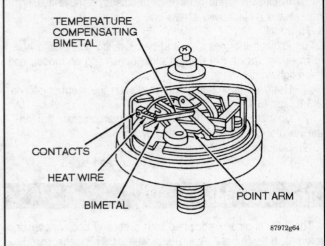

Fig. 69 Cutaway view of oil pressure gauge sensor switch

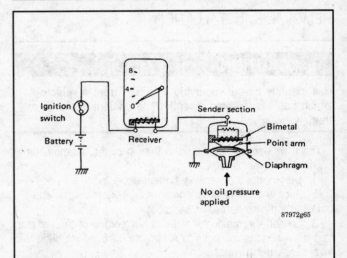

Fig. 70 Schematic of oil pressure gauge and sensor with no oil pressure

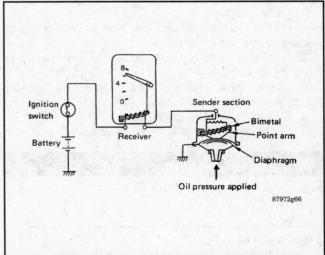

Fig. 71 Schematic of oil pressure gauge and sensor with oil pressure applied

Troubleshooting Basic Starting System Problems

Problem	Cause	Solution
Starter motor rotates engine slowly	• Battery charge low or battery defective	• Charge or replace battery
	• Defective circuit between battery and starter motor	• Clean and tighten, or replace cables
	• Low load current	• Bench-test starter motor. Inspect for worn brushes and weak brush springs.
	• High load current	• Bench-test starter motor. Check engine for friction, drag or coolant in cylinders. Check ring gear-to-pinion gear clearance.
Starter motor will not rotate engine	• Battery charge low or battery defective	• Charge or replace battery
	• Faulty solenoid	• Check solenoid ground. Repair or replace as necessary.
	• Damaged drive pinion gear or ring gear	• Replace damaged gear(s)
	• Starter motor engagement weak	• Bench-test starter motor
	• Starter motor rotates slowly with high load current	• Inspect drive yoke pull-down and point gap, check for worn end bushings, check ring gear clearance
	• Engine seized	• Repair engine
Starter motor drive will not engage (solenoid known to be good)	• Defective contact point assembly	• Repair or replace contact point assembly
	• Inadequate contact point assembly ground	• Repair connection at ground screw
	• Defective hold-in coil	• Replace field winding assembly
Starter motor drive will not disengage	• Starter motor loose on flywheel housing	• Tighten mounting bolts
	• Worn drive end busing	• Replace bushing
	• Damaged ring gear teeth	• Replace ring gear or driveplate
	• Drive yoke return spring broken or missing	• Replace spring
Starter motor drive disengages prematurely	• Weak drive assembly thrust spring	• Replace drive mechanism
	• Hold-in coil defective	• Replace field winding assembly
Low load current	• Worn brushes	• Replace brushes
	• Weak brush springs	• Replace springs

tccs2c01

Troubleshooting Basic Charging System Problems

Problem	Cause	Solution
Noisy alternator	• Loose mountings • Loose drive pulley • Worn bearings • Brush noise • Internal circuits shorted (High pitched whine)	• Tighten mounting bolts • Tighten pulley • Replace alternator • Replace alternator • Replace alternator
Squeal when starting engine or accelerating	• Glazed or loose belt	• Replace or adjust belt
Indicator light remains on or ammeter indicates discharge (engine running)	• Broken belt • Broken or disconnected wires • Internal alternator problems • Defective voltage regulator	• Install belt • Repair or connect wiring • Replace alternator • Replace voltage regulator/alternator
Car light bulbs continually burn out— battery needs water continually	• Alternator/regulator overcharging	• Replace voltage regulator/alternator
Car lights flare on acceleration	• Battery low • Internal alternator/regulator problems	• Charge or replace battery • Replace alternator/regulator
Low voltage output (alternator light flickers continually or ammeter needle wanders)	• Loose or worn belt • Dirty or corroded connections • Internal alternator/regulator problems	• Replace or adjust belt • Clean or replace connections • Replace alternator/regulator

tccs2c02

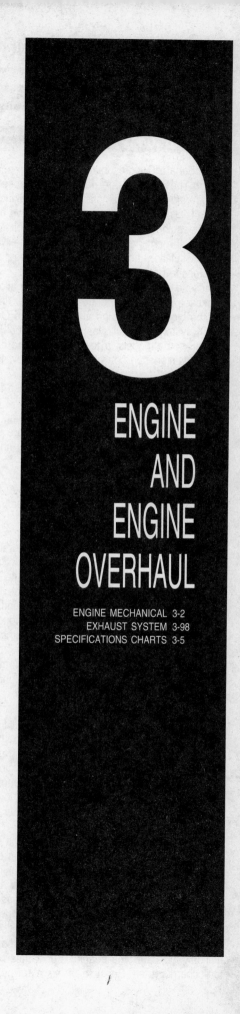

3

ENGINE
AND
ENGINE
OVERHAUL

ENGINE MECHANICAL

Description

The Subaru Quadrozontal four cylinder engine is a unique design. The cylinders are horizontally opposed (flat), giving the engine very compact dimensions, and making it run smoother than an inline four. Unlike other well known flat fours, the Subaru engine is water cooled. Water cooling provides two benefits: the engine is quieter because the water acts as sound insulation, and water cooling makes it easier to provide heat for the passenger compartment.

The engine block is made of aluminum alloy. The split crankcase design incorporates dry cylinder liners that are cast into the block. The engine also adopts the Overhead Camshaft (OHC) system, hydraulic lash adjusters, fuel injection system and, on some models, a turbocharger. The engine offers easier maintenance servicing, reliability, low fuel consumption, low noise and powerful performance.

The pistons are made of aluminum which features a small expansion rate. Its top land is provided with valve relief and its skirt section has an elliptical, tapered design to provide heat and wear resistance. Three piston rings are used for each piston, two compression rings and one oil ring. The cylinder liner is a cast dry type.

The cylinder head is also aluminum alloy, with good cooling and high combustion efficiency which, when combined with the bathtub shaped combustion chambers means better performance.

The camshaft case holds the camshaft, and is an aluminum die casting. The oil relief valve for the hydraulic lash adjuster is built into the cam case. The oil filler duct is mounted on the right-hand camshaft case, and the distributor on the left-hand camshaft case. The valve rockers ride directly on the cam lobes, eliminating the need for pushrods and lifters.

The crankshaft is made from special wrought iron which provides sturdiness. All corners of the journals are processed with "deep roll" treatment.

The horizontally opposed engine configuration provides greater strength against bending and torsional stress while reducing the total length of the crankshaft.

Some engines in the Subaru lineup are fitted with turbochargers. The turbocharger is essentially a tiny, ultra high speed air pump. Its compressor is a tiny pinwheel whose finely machined vanes grab air and accelerate it, and then collect the air in a housing to force it into the engine under as much as 7.0 psi (48.26 kPa) of pressure. The engine, instead of gasping for air (actually drawing it in), as is usually the case, is pressure fed air and fuel in much greater quantities than is normally supplied.

At the other end of a metal shaft lies the turbine which drives the turbocharger. Utilizing expansion of the hot exhaust coming out of the engine, the turbine actually converts some of what would usually be wasted heat into the power which spins the turbocharger and helps the engine to breathe.

A precision, full floating sleeve type bearing supports the shaft in the middle. Engine oil is supplied to this bearing by the engine's oil pump through a special supply tube. This oil not only lubricates the bearing, but carries heat from the turbocharger shaft. Because of this extra heat, and that generated by the increased power, this is the only Subaru engine to have an external oil cooler.

Pressure charging can raise the temperature of compressed fuel/air mixture to the point where detonation can occur in the cylinders. Several modifications keep detonation from occurring. One is the use of a reduced (7.7:1 vs 8.7:1) compression ratio. Another is the addition of a double acting diaphragm on the distributor. When there is positive pressure in the intake manifold, this diaphragm actually retards distributor timing beyond its normal setting. An electronic knock sensor mounted on the cylinder head detects the particular frequency of detonation and may still further retard spark electronically to compensate for unanticipated variations in fuel quality, engine temperature, etc.

In order to protect the engine from excessive stress, which can occur at high rpm where the turbocharger begins to do its maximum work, a waste gate bypasses exhaust gas that would otherwise drive the turbocharger's turbine. Should this device fail, a pressure relief valve in the intake would protect the engine. The waste gate, by forcing more exhaust through the turbine at lower rpms, also helps guarantee good turbocharger performance, and engine torque, over a wide range of rpm.

Engine Overhaul Tips

Most engine overhaul procedures are fairly standard. In addition to specific parts replacement procedures and specifications for your individual engine, this section is also a guide to acceptable rebuilding procedures. Examples of standard rebuilding practice are given and should be used along with specific details concerning your particular engine.

Competent and accurate machine shop services will ensure maximum performance, reliability and engine life. In most instances it is more profitable for the do-it-yourself mechanic to remove, clean and inspect the component, buy the necessary parts and deliver these to a shop for actual machine work.

On the other hand, much of the rebuilding work (crankshaft, block, bearings, piston rods, and other components) is well within the scope of the do-it-yourself mechanic's tools and abilities. You will have to decide for yourself the depth of involvement you desire in an engine repair or rebuild.

TOOLS

The tools required for an engine overhaul or parts replacement will depend on the depth of your involvement. With a few exceptions, they will be the tools found in a mechanic's tool kit (see Section 1 of this manual). More in-depth work will require some or all of the following:
- A dial indicator (reading in thousandths) mounted on a universal base
- Micrometers and telescope gauges
- Jaw and screw-type pullers
- Scraper
- Valve spring compressor
- Ring groove cleaner

- Piston ring expander and compressor
- Ridge reamer
- Cylinder hone or glaze breaker
- Plastigage®
- Engine stand

The use of most of these tools is illustrated in this chapter. Many can be rented for a one-time use from a local parts jobber or tool supply house specializing in automotive work.

Occasionally, the use of special tools is called for. See the information on Special Tools and the Safety Notice in the front of this book before substituting another tool.

INSPECTION TECHNIQUES

Procedures and specifications are given in this chapter for inspecting, cleaning and assessing the wear limits of most major components. Other procedures such as Magnaflux® and Zyglo® can be used to locate material flaws and stress cracks. Magnaflux® is a magnetic process applicable only to ferrous materials. The Zyglo® process coats the material with a fluorescent dye penetrant and can be used on any material.

Checking for suspected surface cracks can be more readily made using spot check dye. The dye is sprayed onto the suspected area, wiped off and the area sprayed with a developer. Cracks will show up brightly.

OVERHAUL TIPS

Aluminum has become extremely popular for use in engines, due to its low weight. Observe the following precautions when handling aluminum parts:

- Never hot tank aluminum parts (the caustic hot tank solution will eat the aluminum.
- Remove all aluminum parts (identification tag, etc.) from engine parts prior to the tanking.
- Always coat threads lightly with engine oil or anti-seize compounds before installation, to prevent seizure.
- Never overtorque bolts or spark plugs especially in aluminum threads.

Stripped threads in any component can be repaired using any of several commercial repair kits (Heli-Coil®, Microdot®, Keenserts®, etc.).

When assembling the engine, any parts that will be exposed to frictional contact must be prelubed to provide lubrication at initial start-up. Any product specifically formulated for this purpose can be used, but engine oil is not recommended as a prelube in most cases.

When semi-permanent (locked, but removable) installation of bolts or nuts is desired, threads should be cleaned and coated with Loctite® or another similar, commercial non-hardening sealant.

REPAIRING DAMAGED THREADS

▶ See Figures 1, 2, 3, 4 and 5

Several methods of repairing damaged threads are available. Heli-Coil® (shown here), Keenserts® and Microdot® are among the most widely used. All involve basically the same principle — drilling out stripped threads, tapping the hole and installing a prewound insert — making welding, plugging and oversize fasteners unnecessary.

Two types of thread repair inserts are usually supplied: a standard type for most inch coarse, inch fine, metric course and metric fine thread sizes and a spark lug type to fit most spark plug port sizes. Consult the individual tool manufacturer's catalog to determine exact applications. Typical thread repair kits will contain a selection of prewound threaded inserts, a tap (corresponding to the outside diameter threads of the insert) and an installation tool. Spark plug inserts usually differ because they require a tap equipped with pilot threads and a

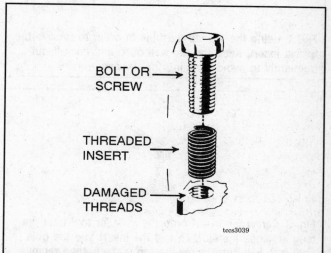

Fig. 1 Damaged bolt hole threads can be replaced with thread repair inserts

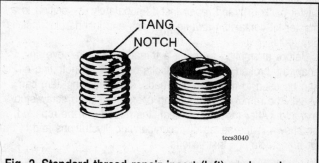

Fig. 2 Standard thread repair insert (left), and spark plug thread insert

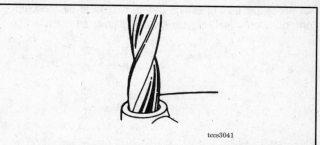

Fig. 3 Drill out the damaged threads with the specified size bit. Be sure to drill completely through the hole or to the bottom of a blind hole

Fig. 4 Using the kit, tap the hole in order to receive the thread insert. Keep the tap well oiled and back it out frequently to avoid clogging the threads

Fig. 5 Screw the insert onto the installer tool until the tang engages the slot. Thread the insert into the hole until it is ¼-½ turn below the top surface, then remove the tool and break off the tang using a punch

combined reamer/tap section. Most manufacturers also supply blister-packed thread repair inserts separately in addition to a master kit containing a variety of taps and inserts plus installation tools.

Before attempting to repair a threaded hole, remove any snapped, broken or damaged bolts or studs. Penetrating oil can be used to free frozen threads. The offending item can usually be removed with locking pliers or using a screw/stud extractor. After the hole is clear, the thread can be repaired, as shown in the series of accompanying illustrations and in the kit manufacturer's instructions.

Compression Testing

A noticeable lack of engine power, excessive oil consumption and/or poor fuel mileage measured over an extended pe-

riod are all indicators of internal wear. Worn piston rings, scored or worn cylinder bores, blown head gaskets, sticking or burnt valves and worn valve seats are all possible culprits here. A check of each cylinder's compression will help you locate the problems.

As mentioned in Tools and Equipment in Section 1, a screw-in type compression gauge is more accurate than the type that you simply hold against the spark plug hole, although it takes slightly longer to use. It's worth it to obtain a more accurate reading. Engine compression is checked in the following manner:

1. Warm up the engine to normal operating temperature.
2. Tag the plug wires and remove all spark plugs.
3. Disconnect the high tension lead from the ignition coil.
4. On carbureted cars, fully open the throttle either by operating the carburetor throttle linkage by hand or by having an assistant floor the accelerator pedal. On fuel injected cars, disconnect the cold start valve and all injector connections.
5. Screw the compression gauge into the No.1 spark plug hole until the fitting is snug.

✳✳WARNING

Be careful not to crossthread the plug hole. On aluminum cylinder heads use extra care, as the threads in these heads are easily ruined.

6. Ask an assistant to depress the accelerator pedal fully on both carbureted and fuel injected cars. Then while you read the compression gauge, ask the assistant to crank the engine two or three times in short bursts using the ignition switch.
7. Read the compression gauge at the end of each series of cranks, and record the highest of these readings. Repeat this procedure for each of the engines cylinders. Compare the highest reading of each cylinder to the other cylinders. The difference between each cylinder should not be more than 12-14 lbs. (5.4-6.3 kg).
8. If a cylinder is usually low, pour a tablespoon of clean engine oil into the cylinder through the spark plug hole and repeat the compression test. If the compression comes up after adding the oil, it appears that the cylinder's piston rings or bore are damaged or worn. If the compression remains low, the valves may not be seating properly, (a valve job is needed), or the head gasket may be blown near that cylinder. If the compression in any two adjacent cylinders is low, and if the addition of oil doesn't help the compression, there is leakage past the head gasket. Oil and coolant water in the combustion chamber can result from this problem. There may be evidence of water droplets on the engine dipstick when a head gasket has blown.

GENERAL ENGINE SPECIFICATIONS

Year	Model	Engine ID/VIN	Engine Displacement Liters (cc)	Fuel System Type	Net Horsepower @ rpm	Net Torque @ rpm (ft. lbs.)	Bore × Stroke (in.)	Com-pression Ratio	Oil Pressure @ rpm
1985	BRAT	5	1.8 (1781)	2 bbl	73 @ 4800	94 @ 2400	3.62 × 2.64	8.7:1	57 @ 2500
	2DR	2	1.6 (1595)	2 bbl	69 @ 4800	86 @ 2400	3.62 × 2.36	9.0:1	57 @ 2500
	2DR GL	4②	1.8 (1781)	2 bbl	73 @ 4800	94 @ 2400	3.62 × 2.64	8.7:1	57 @ 2500
	4DR DL④	4②	1.8 (1781)	2 bbl	82 @ 4800	101 @ 2800	3.62 × 2.64	9.5:1	43 @ 5000
	4DR/Wagon	4②	1.8 (1781)	2 bbl	82 @ 4800	101 @ 2800	3.62 × 2.64	9.0:1	43 @ 5000
	4DR/Wagon GL-10	4②	1.8 (1781)	MPFI	94 @ 5200	101 @ 2800	3.62 × 2.64	9.0:1	43 @ 5000
	4DR/Wagon Turbo	4②	1.8 (1781)	MPFI	111 @ 4800	134 @ 2800	3.62 × 2.64	7.7:1	43 @ 5000
	XT	4②	1.8 (1781)	MPFI	94 @ 5200	101 @ 2800	3.62 × 2.64	9.0:1	43 @ 5000
	XT Turbo	4②	1.8 (1781)	MPFI	111 @ 4800	134 @ 2800	3.62 × 2.64	7.7:1	43 @ 5000
1986	BRAT	5	1.8 (1781)	2 bbl	73 @ 4800	94 @ 2400	3.62 × 2.64	8.7:1	57 @ 2500
	2DR	2	1.6 (1595)	2 bbl	69 @ 4800	86 @ 2400	3.62 × 2.36	9.0:1	57 @ 2500
	2DR GL	4②	1.8 (1781)	2 bbl	73 @ 4800	94 @ 2400	3.62 × 2.64	8.7:1	57 @ 2500
	3DR/4DR/Wagon	4②	1.8 (1781)	2 bbl	82 @ 4800	101 @ 2800	3.62 × 2.64	9.5:1	43 @ 5000
	3DR/4DR/Wagon	4②	1.8 (1781)	SPFI	90 @ 5600	101 @ 2800	3.62 × 2.64	9.5:1	43 @ 5000
	3DR/4DR/Wagon Turbo	4②	1.8 (1781)	MPFI	111 @ 4800	134 @ 2800	3.62 × 2.64	7.7:1	43 @ 5000
	XT	4②	1.8 (1781)	MPFI	94 @ 5200	101 @ 2800	3.62 × 2.64	9.0:1	43 @ 5000
	XT Turbo	4②	1.8 (1781)	MPFI	111 @ 4800	134 @ 2800	3.62 × 2.64	7.7:1	43 @ 5000
1987	BRAT	5	1.8 (1781)	2 bbl	73 @ 4800	94 @ 2400	3.62 × 2.64	8.7:1	57 @ 2500
	2DR	2	1.6 (1595)	2 bbl	69 @ 4800	86 @ 2400	3.62 × 2.36	9.0:1	57 @ 2500
	2DR GL	4②	1.8 (1781)	2 bbl	73 @ 4800	94 @ 2400	3.62 × 2.64	8.7:1	57 @ 2500
	3DR/4DR/Wagon	4②	1.8 (1781)	2 bbl	84 @ 5200	101 @ 3200	3.62 × 2.64	9.5:1	43 @ 5000
	4DR⑤	4②	1.8 (1781)	SPFI	84 @ 5200	101 @ 3200	3.62 × 2.64	9.5:1	43 @ 5000
	3DR/4DR/Wagon	4②	1.8 (1781)	SPFI	90 @ 5200	101 @ 2800	3.62 × 2.64	9.5:1	43 @ 5000
	3DR/4DR/Wagon Turbo	4②	1.8 (1781)	MPFI	115 @ 5200	134 @ 2800	3.62 × 2.64	7.7:1	43 @ 5000
	XT	4②	1.8 (1781)	MPFI	97 @ 5200	103 @ 3200	3.62 × 2.64	9.5:1	43 @ 5000
	XT Turbo	4②	1.8 (1781)	MPFI	115 @ 5200	134 @ 2800	3.62 × 2.64	7.7:1	43 @ 5000
	Justy	7①	1.2 (1189)	2 bbl	66 @ 5200	70 @ 3600	3.07 × 3.27	9.0:1	47 @ 3000
1988	2DR	2	1.6 (1595)	2 bbl	69 @ 4800	86 @ 2400	3.62 × 2.36	9.0:1	57 @ 2500
	4DR⑤	4②	1.8 (1781)	SPFI	84 @ 5200	101 @ 3200	3.62 × 2.64	9.5:1	43 @ 5000
	3DR/4DR/Wagon	4②	1.8 (1781)	SPFI	90 @ 5200	101 @ 2800	3.62 × 2.64	9.5:1	43 @ 5000
	3DR/4DR/Wagon Turbo	4②	1.8 (1781)	MPFI	115 @ 5200	134 @ 2800	3.62 × 2.64	7.7:1	43 @ 5000
	XT	4②	1.8 (1781)	MPFI	97 @ 5200	103 @ 3200	3.62 × 2.64	9.5:1	43 @ 5000
	XT-6	8③	2.7 (2672)	MPFI	145 @ 5200	156 @ 4000	3.62 × 2.64	7.7:1	43 @ 5000
	Justy	7①	1.2 (1189)	2 bbl	66 @ 5200	70 @ 3600	3.07 × 3.27	9.1:1	47 @ 3000
1989	2DR	2	1.6 (1595)	2 bbl	69 @ 4800	86 @ 2400	3.62 × 2.36	9.0:1	57 @ 2500
	4DR⑤	4②	1.8 (1781)	SPFI	84 @ 5200	101 @ 3200	3.62 × 2.64	9.5:1	43 @ 5000
	3DR/4DR/Wagon	4②	1.8 (1781)	SPFI	90 @ 5200	101 @ 2800	3.62 × 2.64	9.5:1	43 @ 5000
	3DR/4DR/Wagon Turbo	4②	1.8 (1781)	MPFI	115 @ 5200	134 @ 2800	3.62 × 2.64	7.7:1	43 @ 5000
	XT	4②	1.8 (1781)	MPFI	97 @ 5200	103 @ 3200	3.62 × 2.64	9.5:1	43 @ 5000
	XT-6	8③	2.7 (2672)	MPFI	145 @ 5200	156 @ 4000	3.62 × 2.64	7.7:1	43 @ 5000
	Justy	7①	1.2 (1189)	2 bbl	66 @ 5200	70 @ 3600	3.07 × 3.27	9.1:1	47 @ 3000

87973c01

GENERAL ENGINE SPECIFICATIONS

Year	Model	Engine ID/VIN	Engine Displacement Liters (cc)	Fuel System Type	Net Horsepower @ rpm	Net Torque @ rpm (ft. lbs.)	Bore x Stroke (in.)	Compression Ratio	Oil Pressure @ rpm
1990	XT	4②	1.8 (1781)	MPFI	97 @ 5200	103 @ 3200	3.62 × 2.64	9.5:1	43 @ 5000
	XT-6	8③	2.7 (2672)	MPFI	145 @ 5200	156 @ 4000	3.62 × 2.64	7.7:1	43 @ 5000
	Justy	7①	1.2 (1189)	2 bbl	66 @ 5200	70 @ 3600	3.07 × 3.27	9.1:1	47 @ 3000
	Justy	7①	1.2 (1189)	MPFI	73 @ 5600	71 @ 3600	3.07 × 3.27	9.1:1	47 @ 3000
	Loyale	4②	1.8 (1781)	SPFI	90 @ 5200	101 @ 2800	3.62 × 2.64	9.5:1	43 @ 5000
	Loyale Turbo	4②	1.8 (1781)	MPFI	115 @ 5200	134 @ 2800	3.62 × 2.64	7.7:1	43 @ 5000
	Legacy	6	2.2 (2212)	MPFI	130 @ 5600	137 @ 2400	3.82 × 2.95	9.5:1	43 @ 5000
1991	XT	4②	1.8 (1781)	MPFI	97 @ 5200	103 @ 3200	3.62 × 2.64	9.5:1	43 @ 5000
	XT-6	8③	2.7 (2672)	MPFI	145 @ 5200	156 @ 4000	3.62 × 2.64	7.7:1	43 @ 5000
	Justy	7①	1.2 (1189)	2 bbl	66 @ 5200	70 @ 3600	3.07 × 3.27	9.1:1	47 @ 3000
	Justy	7①	1.2 (1189)	MPFI	73 @ 5600	71 @ 3600	3.07 × 3.27	9.1:1	47 @ 3000
	Loyale	4②	1.8 (1781)	SPFI	90 @ 5200	101 @ 2800	3.62 × 2.64	9.5:1	43 @ 5000
	Legacy	6	2.2 (2212)	MPFI	130 @ 5600	137 @ 2400	3.82 × 2.95	9.5:1	43 @ 5000
	Legacy Turbo	6	2.2 (2212)	MPFI	160 @ 5600	181 @ 2800	3.82 × 2.95	8.0:1	43 @ 5000
1992	Justy	7①	1.2 (1189)	2 bbl	66 @ 5200	70 @ 3600	3.07 × 3.27	9.1:1	47 @ 3000
	Justy	7①	1.2 (1189)	MPFI	73 @ 5600	71 @ 3600	3.07 × 3.27	9.1:1	47 @ 3000
	Loyale	4②	1.8 (1781)	SPFI	90 @ 5200	101 @ 2800	3.62 × 2.64	9.5:1	43 @ 5000
	Legacy	6	2.2 (2212)	MPFI	130 @ 5600	137 @ 2400	3.82 × 2.95	9.5:1	43 @ 5000
	SVX	3	3.3 (3318)	MPFI	230 @ 5400	228 @ 4400	3.82 × 2.95	10.1:1	43 @ 5000
1993	Justy	7	1.2 (1189)	2 bbl	66 @ 5200	70 @ 3600	3.07 3.27	9.1:1	47@3000
	Justy	7 ①	1.2 (1189)	MPFI	73 @ 5600	71 @ 3600	3.07 3.27	9.1:1	47@3000
	Impreza	2	1.8 (1820)	MPFI	110 @ 5600	110 @ 4400	3.46 X 2.95	9.5:1	43@5000
	Loyale	4 ②	1.8 (1781)	SPFI	90 @ 5200	101 @ 2800	3.62 2.64	9.5:1	43@5000
	Legacy	6	2.2 (2212)	MPFI	130 @ 5400	137 @ 4400	3.82 2.95	9.5:1	43@5000
	Legacy Turbo	6	2.2 (2212)	MPFI	160 @ 5600	181 @ 2800	3.82 2.95	8.0:1	43@5000
	SVX	3	3.3 (3318)	MPFI	230 @ 5400	228 @ 4400	3.82 2.95	10.0:1	43@5000
1994	Justy	7 ①	1.2 (1189)	MPFI	73 @ 5600	71 @ 3600	3.07 X 3.27	9.1:1	47@3000
	Impreza	2	1.8 (1820)	MPFI	110 @ 5600	110 @ 4400	3.46 2.95	9.5:1	43@5000
	Loyale	4 ②	1.8 (1781)	SPFI	90 @ 5200	101 @ 2800	3.62 X 2.64	9.5:1	43@5000
	Legacy	6	2.2 (2212)	MPFI	130 @ 5400	137 @ 4400	3.82 X 2.95	9.5:1	43@5000
	Legacy Turbo	6	2.2 (2212)	MPFI	160 @ 5600	181 @ 2800	3.82 X 2.95	8.0:1	43@5000
	SVX	3	3.3 (3318)	MPFI	230 @ 5400	228 @ 4400	3.82 X 2.95	10.0:1	43@5000
1995	Impreza	2	1.8 (1820)	MPFI	110 @ 5600	110 @ 4400	3.46 X 2.95	9.5:1	43@5000
	Impreza	6	2.2 (2212)	MPFI	135 @ 5400	140 @ 4400	3.82 X 2.95	9.5:1	43@5000
	Legacy	6	2.2 (2212)	MPFI	135 @ 5400	140 @ 4400	3.82 X 2.95	9.5:1	43@5000
	SVX	3	3.3 (3318)	MPFI	230 @ 5400	228 @ 4400	3.82 X 2.95	10.0:1	43@5000
1996	Impreza	1 ⑥	1.8 (1820)	MPFI	110 @ 5600	110 @ 4400	3.46 X 2.95	9.5:1	43@5000
	Impreza	4	2.2 (2212)	MPFI	135 @ 5400	140 @ 4400	3.82 X 2.95	9.5:1	43@5000
	Legacy	3 ⑦	2.2 (2212)	MPFI	135 @ 5400	140 @ 4400	3.82 X 2.95	9.7:1	43@5000
	Legacy	6	2.5 (2457)	MPFI	155 @ 5600	155 @ 2800	3.92 X 3.11	9.7:1	43@5000
	SVX	8	3.3 (3318)	MPFI	230 @ 5400	228 @ 4400	3.82 X 2.95	10.0:1	43@5000

① Code 8: with 4WD
② Code 5: with 4WD
   Code 7: with pneumatic suspension
③ Code 9: with pneumatic suspension
④ 4-speed
⑤ 2WD
⑥ Code 2: with 4WD
⑦ Code 4: with 4WD

87973c02

VALVE SPECIFICATIONS

Year	Engine ID/VIN	Engine Displacement Liters (cc)	Seat Angle (deg.)	Face Angle (deg.)	Spring Test Pressure (lbs. @ in.)	Spring Installed Height (in.)	Stem-to-Guide Clearance (in.)		Stem Diameter (in.)	
							Intake	Exhaust	Intake	Exhaust
1985	2	4-1.6 (1595)	45	45	33–38 ⑤	1.555	0.0014–0.0026	0.0016–0.0028	0.3130–0.3136	0.3128–0.3134
	4/5/7	4-1.8 (1781)	45	45	112–129 ② ③	1.240	0.0014–0.0026	0.0016–0.0028	0.2736–0.2742	0.2734–0.2740
1986	2	4-1.6 (1595)	45	45	33–38 ⑤	1.555	0.0014–0.0026	0.0016–0.0028	0.3130–0.3136	0.3128–0.3134
	4/5/7	4-1.8 (1781)	45	45	100–115	1.240	0.0014–0.0026	0.0016–0.0028	0.2736–0.2742	0.2734–0.2740
1987	7/8	3-1.2 (1189)	45	45	112–129	1.248	0.0008–0.0020	0.0016–0.0028	0.2742–0.2748	0.2734–0.2740
	2	4-1.6 (1595)	45	45	33–38 ⑤	1.555	0.0014–0.0026	0.0016–0.0028	0.3130–0.3136	0.3128–0.3134
	4/5/7	4-1.8 (1781)	45	45	112–129 ③	1.240	0.0014–0.0026	0.0016–0.0028	0.2736–0.2742	0.2734–0.2740
1988	7/8	3-1.2 (1189)	45	45	112–129	1.248	0.0008–0.0020	0.0016–0.0028	0.2742–0.2748	0.2734–0.2740
	2	4-1.6 (1595)	45	45	33–38 ⑤	1.555	0.0014–0.0026	0.0016–0.0028	0.3130–0.3136	0.3128–0.3134
	4/5/7	4-1.8 (1781)	45	45	112–129 ③	1.240	0.0014–0.0026	0.0016–0.0028	0.2736–0.2742	0.2734–0.2740
	8/9	6-2.7 (2672)	45	45	100–115 ③	1.240	0.0014–0.0026	0.0016–0.0028	0.2736–0.2741	0.2734–0.2740
1989	7/8	3-1.2 (1189)	45	45	112–129	1.248	0.0008–0.0020	0.0016–0.0028	0.2742–0.2748	0.2734–0.2740
	2	4-1.6 (1595)	45	45	33–38 ⑤	1.555	0.0014–0.0026	0.0016–0.0028	0.3130–0.3136	0.3128–0.3134
	4/7	4-1.8 (1781)	45	45	112–129 ③	1.240	0.0014–0.0026	0.0016–0.0028	0.2736–0.2742	0.2734–0.2740
	8/9	6-2.7 (2672)	45	45	100–115 ③	1.240	0.0014–0.0026	0.0016–0.0028	0.2736–0.2741	0.2734–0.2740
1990	7/8	3-1.2 (1189)	45	45	112–129	1.248	0.0008–0.0020	0.0016–0.0028	0.2742–0.2748	0.2734–0.2740
	4/7	4-1.8 (1781)	45	45	112–129 ③	1.240	0.0014–0.0026	0.0016–0.0028	0.2736–0.2742	0.2734–0.2740
	6	4-2.2 (2212)	45	45	92–106	1.150	0.0014–0.0024	0.0016–0.0026	0.2343–0.2348	0.2341–0.2346
	8/9	6-2.7 (2672)	45	45	100–115 ③	1.240	0.0014–0.0026	0.0016–0.0028	0.2736–0.2741	0.2734–0.2740
1991	7/8	3-1.2 (1189)	45	45	112–129	1.248	0.0008–0.0020	0.0016–0.0028	0.2742–0.2748	0.2734–0.2740
	4/7	4-1.8 (1781)	45	45	112–129 ③	1.240	0.0014–0.0026	0.0016–0.0028	0.2736–0.2742	0.2734–0.2740
	6	4-2.2 (2212)	45	45	92–106	1.150	0.0014–0.0024	0.0016–0.0026	0.2343–0.2348	0.2341–0.2346
	8/9	6-2.7 (2762)	45	45	100–115 ③	1.240	0.0014–0.0026	0.0016–0.0028	0.2736–0.2741	0.2734–0.2740

87973c03

VALVE SPECIFICATIONS

Year	Engine ID/VIN	Engine Displacement Liters (cc)	Seat Angle (deg.)	Face Angle (deg.)	Spring Test Pressure (lbs. @ in.)	Spring Installed Height (in.)	Stem-to-Guide Clearance (in.)		Stem Diameter (in.)	
							Intake	Exhaust	Intake	Exhaust
1992	7/8	3-1.2 (1189)	45	45	112–129	1.248	0.0008–0.0020	0.0016–0.0028	0.2742–0.2748	0.2734–0.2740
	4/7	4-1.8 (1781)	45	45	112–129 ③	1.240	0.0014–0.0026	0.0016–0.0028	0.2736–0.2742	0.2734–0.2740
	6	4-2.2 (2212)	45	45	92–106	1.150	0.0014–0.0024	0.0016–0.0026	0.2343–0.2348	0.2341–0.2346
	3	6-3.3 (3318)	45	45	70–80 ④	0.831	0.0012–0.0022	0.0016–0.0026	0.2344–0.2350	0.2341–0.2346
1993	7/8	3-1.2 (1189)	45	45	112-129	1.248	0.0008-0.0020	0.0016-0.0028	0.2742-0.2748	0.2734-0.2740
	4/5	4-1.8 (1781)	45	45	112-129 ③	1.240	0.0014-0.0026	0.0016-0.0028	0.2736-0.2742	0.2734-0.2740
	2	4-1.8 (1820)	45	45	43-49@ 1.457	1.150	0.0014-0.0024	0.0016-0.0026	0.2343-0.2348	0.2341-0.2346
	6	4-2.2 (2212)	45	45	43-49@ 1.457	1.150	0.0014-0.0024	0.0016-0.0026	0.2343-0.2348	0.2341-0.2346
	3	6-3.3 (3318)	45	45	70-80 ④	0.831	0.0012-0.0022	0.0016-0.0026	0.2344-0.2350	0.2341-0.2346
1994	7/8	3-1.2 (1189)	45	45	112-129	1.248	0.0008-0.0020	0.0016-0.0028	0.2742-0.2748	0.2734-0.2740
	4/5	4-1.8 (1781)	45	45	112-129 ③	1.240	0.0014-0.0026	0.0016-0.0028	0.2736-0.2742	0.2734-0.2740
	2	4-1.8 (1820)	45	45	43-49@ 1.457	1.150	0.0014-0.0024	0.0016-0.0026	0.2343-0.2348	0.2341-0.2346
	6	4-2.2 (2212)	45	45	43-49@ 1.457	1.150	0.0014-0.0024	0.0016-0.0026	0.2343-0.2348	0.2341-0.2346
	3	6-3.3 (3318)	45	45	70-80 ④	0.831	0.0012-0.0022	0.0016-0.0026	0.2344-0.2350	0.2341-0.2346
1995	2	4-1.8 (1820)	45	45	43-49@ 1.457	1.150	0.0014-0.0024	0.0016-0.0026	0.2343-0.2348	0.2341-0.2346
	6	4-2.2 (2212)	45	45	39-45@ 1.417	1.110	0.0014-0.0024	0.0016-0.0026	0.2343-0.2348	0.2341-0.2346
	3	6-3.3 (3318)	45	45	70-80 ④	0.831	0.0012-0.0022	0.0016-0.0026	0.2344-0.2350	0.2341-0.2346
1996	1/2	4-1.8 (1820)	45	45	43-49@ 1.457	1.150	0.0014-0.0024	0.0016-0.0026	0.2343-0.2348	0.2341-0.2346
	3/4	4-2.2 (2212)	45	45	39-45@ 1.417	1.110	0.0014-0.0024	0.0016-0.0026	0.2343-0.2348	0.2341-0.2346
	6	4-2.5 (2457)	45	45	51-59@ 1.220	0.913	0.0014-0.0024	0.0016-0.0026	0.2343-0.2348	0.2342-0.2348
	8	6-3.3 (3318)	45	45	70-80 ④	0.831	0.0012-0.0022	0.0016-0.0026	0.2344-0.2350	0.2341-0.2346

① XT
② GL with manual transmission: 102-118 lbs.
③ Outer/Inner: 45-52 @ 1.122 in.
④ Outer/Inner: 33-38 @ 0.772 in.
⑤ Outer/Inner: 19-22 @ 1.476 in.

87973c04

CAMSHAFT SPECIFICATIONS

All measurements given in inches.

Year	Engine ID/VIN	Engine Displacement Liters (cc)	Journal Diameter					Elevation		Bearing Clearance	Camshaft End Play
			1	2	3	4	5	In.	Ex.		
1985	2	4-1.6L (1595)	1.0220–1.0226	1.0220–1.0226	1.4157 1.4163	—	—	1.2693–1.2732	1.2693–1.2732	0.0010–0.0023	0.0008–0.0035
	4/5/7	4-1.8L (1781)	1.4946–1.4953	1.9080–1.9087	1.4946–1.4953	1.5340–② 1.5346	—	③ ④	③ ④	0.0008–0.0021	0.0012–0.0102
	4/5/7	4-1.8L (1781) ①	1.4946–1.4953	1.9080–1.9087	1.8883–1.8890	1.5340–② 1.5346	—	1.5650–1.5689	1.5650–1.5689	0.0008–0.0021	0.0012–0.0102
1986	2	4-1.6L (1595)	1.0220–1.0226	1.0220–1.0226	1.4157 1.4163	—	—	1.2693–1.2732	1.2693–1.2732	0.0010–0.0023	0.0008–0.0035
	4/5/7	4-1.8L (1781)	1.4946–1.4953	1.9080–1.9087	1.4946–1.4953	1.5340–② 1.5346	—	④	④	0.0008–0.0021	0.0012–0.0102
	4/5/7	4-1.8L (1781) ①	1.4946–1.4953	1.9080–1.9087	1.8883–1.8890	1.5340–② 1.5346	—	1.5650–1.5689	1.5650–1.5689	0.0008–0.0021	0.0012–0.0102
1987	7/8	3-1.2L (1189)	—	—	—	—	—	1.4520–1.4528	1.4520–1.4528	—	0.0012–0.0150
	2	4-1.6L (1595)	1.0220–1.0226	1.0220–1.0226	1.4157 1.4163	—	—	1.2693–1.2732	1.2693–1.2732	0.0010–0.0023	0.0008–0.0035
	4/5/7	4-1.8L (1781)	1.8883–1.8890	1.9080–1.9087	1.8889–1.8890	1.5340–② 1.5346	—	1.5650–1.5689	1.5650–1.5689	0.0008–0.0021	0.0012–0.0102
	4/5/7	4-1.8L (1781) ①	1.4946–1.4953	1.9080–1.9087	1.8883–1.8890	1.5340–② 1.5346	—	1.5650–1.5689	1.5650–1.5689	0.0008–0.0021	0.0012–0.0102
1988	7/8	3-1.2L (1189)	—	—	—	—	—	1.4520–1.4528	1.4520–1.4528	—	0.0012–0.0150
	2	4-1.6L (1595)	1.0220–1.0226	1.0220–1.0226	1.4157 1.4163	—	—	1.2693–1.2732	1.2693–1.2732	0.0010–0.0023	0.0008–0.0035
	4/7	4-1.8L (1781)	1.8883–1.8890	1.9080–1.9087	1.8889–1.8890	1.5340–② 1.5346	—	1.5650–1.5689	1.5650–1.5689	0.0008–0.0021	0.0012–0.0102
	4/7	4-1.8L (1781) ①	1.4946–1.4953	1.9080–1.9087	1.8883–1.8890	1.5340–② 1.5346	—	1.5650–1.5689	1.5650–1.5689	0.0008–0.0021	0.0012–0.0102
	8/9	6-2.7L (2672)	1.4946–1.4953	1.9080–1.9087	1.8883–1.8890	1.9474–1.8693	1.5340–② 1.5346	1.5606–1.5646	1.5606–1.5646	0.0008–0.0021	0.0012–0.0102

87973c05

CAMSHAFT SPECIFICATIONS

All measurements given in inches.

Year	Engine ID/VIN	Engine Displacement Liters (cc)	Journal Diameter					Elevation		Bearing Clearance	Camshaft End Play
			1	2	3	4	5	In.	Ex.		
1989	7/8	3-1.2L (1189)	—	—	—	—	—	1.4520–1.4528	1.4520–1.4528	—	0.0012–0.0150
	2	4-1.6L (1595)	1.0220–1.0226	1.0220–1.0226	1.4157–1.4163	—	—	1.2693–1.2732	1.2693–1.2732	0.0010–0.0023	0.0008–0.0035
	4/7	4-1.8L (1781)	1.8883–1.8890	1.9080–1.9087	1.8889–1.8890	1.5340–② 1.5346	—	1.5650–1.5689	1.5650–1.5689	0.0008–0.0021	0.0012–0.0102
	4/7	4-1.8L (1781)①	1.4946–1.4953	1.9080–1.9087	1.8883–1.8890	1.5340–② 1.5346	—	1.5650–1.5689	1.5650–1.5689	0.0008–0.0021	0.0012–0.0102
	8/9	6-2.7L (2672)	1.4946–1.4953	1.9080–1.9087	1.8883–1.8890	1.9474–1.8693	1.5340–② 1.5346	1.5606–1.5646	1.5606–1.5646	0.0008–0.0021	0.0012–0.0102
1990	7/8	3-1.2L (1189)	—	—	—	—	—	1.4520–1.4528	1.4520–1.4528	—	0.0012–0.0150
	4/7	4-1.8L (1781)	1.8883–1.8890	1.9080–1.9087	1.8889–1.8890	1.5340–② 1.5346	—	1.5650–1.5689	1.5650–1.5689	0.0008–0.0021	0.0012–0.0102
	4/7	4-1.8L (1781)①	1.4946–1.4953	1.9080–1.9087	1.8883–1.8890	1.5340–② 1.5346	—	1.5650–1.5689	1.5650–1.5689	0.0008–0.0021	0.0012–0.0102
	6	4-2.2L (2212)	1.4963–1.4970	1.4766–1.4774	1.2300–1.2608			1.2752–1.2791	1.2752–1.2791	0.0022–0.0035	0.0012–0.0102
	8/9	6-2.7L (2672)	1.4946–1.4953	1.9080–1.9087	1.8883–1.8890	1.9474–1.8693	1.5340–② 1.5346	1.5606–1.5646	1.5606–1.5646	0.0008–0.0021	0.0012–0.0102
1991	7/8	3-1.2L (1189)	—	—	—	—	—	1.4520–1.4528	1.4520–1.4528	—	0.0012–0.0150
	4/7	4-1.8L (1781)	1.8883–1.8890	1.9080–1.9087	1.8889–1.8890	1.5340–② 1.5346	—	1.5650–1.5689	1.5650–1.5689	0.0008–0.0021	0.0012–0.0102
	4/7	4-1.8L (1781)①	1.4946–1.4953	1.9080–1.9087	1.8883–1.8890	1.5340–② 1.5346	—	1.5650–1.5689	1.5650–1.5689	0.0008–0.0021	0.0012–0.0102
	6	4-2.2L (2212)	1.4963–1.4970	1.4766–1.4774	1.2300–1.2608	—	—	1.2752–1.2791	1.2752–1.2791	0.0022–0.0035	0.0012–0.0102
	8/9	6-2.7L (2672)	1.4946–1.4953	1.9080–1.9087	1.8883–1.8890	1.9474–1.8693	1.5340–② 1.5346	1.5606–1.5646	1.5606–1.5646	0.0008–0.0021	0.0012–0.0102
1992	7/8	3-1.2L (1189)	—	—	—	—	—	1.4520–1.4528	1.4520–1.4528	—	0.0012–0.0150
	4/7	4-1.8L (1781)	1.8883–1.8890	1.9080–1.9087	1.8889–1.8890	1.5340–② 1.5346	—	1.5650–1.5689	1.5650–1.5689	0.0008–0.0021	0.0012–0.0102
	6	4-2.2L (2212)	1.4963–1.4970	1.4766–1.4774	1.2300–1.2608	—	—	1.2752–1.2791	1.2752–1.2791	0.0022–0.0035	0.0012–0.0102
	3	6-3.3L (3318)	1.2577–1.2584	1.1002–1.1009	1.1002–1.1009	1.1002–1.1009	—	1.5374–1.5413	1.5689–1.5728	0.0015–0.0028	⑤

87973c06

CAMSHAFT SPECIFICATIONS
All measurements given in inches.

Year	Engine ID/VIN	Engine Displacement Liters (cc)	Journal Diameter 1	2	3	4	5	Elevation In.	Ex.	Bearing Clearance	Camshaft End Play
1993	7/8	3-1.2L (1189)	—	—	—	—	—	1.4520-1.4528	1.4520-1.4528	—	0.0012-0.0150
	4/5	4-1.8L (1781)	1.8883-1.8890	1.9080-1.9087	1.8889-1.8890	1.5340-1.5346 ②	—	1.5650-1.5689	1.5650-1.5689	0.0008-0.0021	0.0012-0.0102
	2	4-1.8L (1820)	1.2573-1.2579	1.4738-1.4744	1.4935-1.4941	—	—	1.2742-1.2781	1.2742-1.2781	0.0022-0.0035	0.0012-0.0102
	6	4-2.2L (2212)	1.2573-1.2579	1.4738-1.4744	1.4935-1.4941	—	—	⑥	⑦	0.0022-0.0035	0.0012-0.0102
	3	6-3.3L (3318)	1.2577-1.2584	1.1002-1.1009	1.1002-1.1009	1.1002-1.1009	—	1.5374-1.5413	1.5689-1.5728	0.0015-0.0028	⑤
1994	7/8	3-1.2L (1189)	—	—	—	—	—	1.4520-1.4528	1.4520-1.4528	—	0.0012-0.0150
	4/5	4-1.8L (1781)	1.8883-1.8890	1.9080-1.9087	1.8889-1.8890	1.5340-1.5346 ②	—	1.5650-1.5689	1.5650-1.5689	0.0008-0.0021	0.0012-0.0102
	2	4-1.8L (1820)	1.2573-1.2579	1.4738-1.4744	1.4935-1.4941	—	—	1.2742-1.2781	1.2742-1.2781	0.0022-0.0035	0.0012-0.0102
	6	4-2.2L (2212)	1.2573-1.2579	1.4738-1.4744	1.4935-1.4941	—	—	⑥	⑦	0.0022-0.0035	0.0012-0.0102
	3	6-3.3L (3318)	1.2577-1.2584	1.1002-1.1009	1.1002-1.1009	1.1002-1.1009	—	1.5374-1.5413	1.5689-1.5728	0.0015-0.0028	⑤
1995	2	4-1.8L (1820)	1.2573-1.2579	1.4738-1.4744	1.4935-1.4941	—	—	1.2742-1.2781	1.2742-1.2781	0.0022-0.0035	0.0012-0.0102
	6	4-2.2L (2212)	1.2573-1.2579	1.4738-1.4744	1.4935-1.4941	—	—	1.2596-1.2635	1.2844-1.2883	0.0022-0.0035	0.0012-0.0102
	3	6-3.3L (3318)	1.2577-1.2584	1.1002-1.1009	1.1002-1.1009	1.1002-1.1009	—	1.5374-1.5413	1.5689-1.5728	0.0015-0.0028	⑤
1996	1/2	4-1.8L (1820)	1.2573-1.2579	1.4738-1.4744	1.4935-1.4941	—	—	1.2742-1.2781	1.2742-1.2781	0.0022-0.0035	0.0012-0.0102
	3/4	4-2.2L (2212)	1.2573-1.2579	1.4738-1.4744	1.4935-1.4941	—	—	1.2596-1.2635	1.2844-1.2883	0.0022-0.0035	0.0012-0.0102
	6	4-2.5L (2457)	1.2577-1.2584	1.1002-1.1009	1.1002-1.1009	—	—	1.6409-1.6449	1.6528-1.6567	0.0015-0.0028	0.0016-0.0031
	8	6-3.3L (3318)	1.2577-1.2584	1.1002-1.1009	1.1002-1.1009	1.1002-1.1009	—	1.5374-1.5413	1.5689-1.5728	0.0015-0.0028	⑤

① XT
② Distributor journal left-hand camshaft only
③ 1985 DL 4-speed manual transmission 1.5394-1.5433
④ Carbureted and MPFI Turbo 1.5606-1.5646
SPFI and MPFI 1.5650 - 1.5689

⑤ Exhaust 0.0008-0.0031
Intake 0.0012-0.0035
⑥ Non-Turbo: 1.2728-1.2767. Turbo: 1.2711-1.2750
⑦ Non-Turbo: 1.2742-1.2781. Turbo: 1.2711-1.2750

87973c07

CRANKSHAFT AND CONNECTING ROD SPECIFICATIONS

All measurements are given in inches.

Year	Engine ID/VIN	Engine Displacement Liters (cc)	Crankshaft Main Brg. Journal Dia.	Crankshaft Main Brg. Oil Clearance	Crankshaft Shaft End-play	Thrust on No.	Connecting Rod Journal Diameter	Connecting Rod Oil Clearance	Connecting Rod Side Clearance
1985	2	4-1.6 (1595)	2.1636–2.1642	⑥	0.0004–0.0037	2	1.7715–1.7720	0.0008–0.0028	0.0028–0.0130
	4/5/7	4-1.8 (1781)	①	②	0.0004–0.0037	2	1.7715–1.7720	0.0004–0.0021	0.0028–0.0130
1986	2	4-1.6 (1595)	2.1636–2.1642	⑥	0.0004–0.0037	2	1.7715–1.7720	0.0008–0.0028	0.0028–0.0130
	4/5/7	4-1.8 (1781)	①	②	0.0004–0.0037	2	1.7715–1.7720	0.0004–0.0021	0.0028–0.0130
1987	7/8	3-1.2 (1189)	1.6250–1.6290	0.0006–0.0018	0.0031–0.0070	4	0.6531–1.6535	0.0008–0.0021	0.0028–0.0118
	2	4-1.6 (1595)	2.1636–2.1642	⑥	0.0004–0.0037	2	1.7715–1.7720	0.0008–0.0028	0.0028–0.0130
	4/5/7	4-1.8 (1781)	①	②	0.0004–0.0037	2	1.7715–1.7720	0.0004–0.0021	0.0028–0.0130
1988	7/8	3-1.2 (1189)	1.6250–1.6290	0.0006–0.0018	0.0031–0.0070	4	0.6531–1.6535	0.0008–0.0021	0.0028–0.0118
	2	4-1.6 (1595)	2.1636–2.1642	⑥	0.0004–0.0037	2	1.7715–1.7720	0.0008–0.0028	0.0028–0.0130
	4/5/7	4-1.8 (1781)	①	②	0.0004–0.0037	2	1.7715–1.7720	0.0004–0.0021	0.0028–0.0130
	8/9	6-2.7 (2672)	①	②	0.0004–0.0037	3	1.7715–1.6535	0.0004–0.0021	0.0028–0.0118
1989	7/8	3-1.2 (1189)	1.6250–1.6290	0.0006–0.0018	0.0031–0.0070	4	0.6531–1.6535	0.0008–0.0021	0.0028–0.0118
	2	4-1.6 (1595)	2.1636–2.1642	⑥	0.0004–0.0037	2	1.7715–1.7720	0.0008–0.0028	0.0028–0.0130
	4/7	4-1.8 (1781)	①	②	0.0004–0.0037	2	1.7715–1.7720	0.0004–0.0021	0.0028–0.0130
	8/9	6-2.7 (2672)	①	②	0.0004–0.0037	3	1.7715–1.6535	0.0004–0.0021	0.0028–0.0118
1990	7/8	3-1.2 (1189)	1.6250–1.6290	0.0006–0.0018	0.0031–0.0070	4	0.6531–1.6535	0.0008–0.0021	0.0028–0.0118
	4/7	4-1.8 (1781)	①	②	0.0004–0.0037	2	1.7715–1.7720	0.0004–0.0021	0.0028–0.0130
	6	4-2.2 (2212)	2.3616–2.3622	④	0.0012–0.0045	3	2.0466–2.0472	0.0006–③ 0.0017	0.0028–0.0130
	8/9	6-2.7 (2672)	①	②	0.0004–0.0037	3	1.7715–1.6535	0.0004–0.0021	0.0028–0.0118
1991	7/8	3-1.2 (1189)	1.6250–1.6290	0.0006–0.0018	0.0031–0.0070	4	0.6531–1.6535	0.0008–0.0021	0.0028–0.0118
	4/7	4-1.8 (1781)	①	②	0.0004–0.0037	2	1.7715–1.7720	0.0004–0.0021	0.0028–0.0130
	6	4-2.2 (2212)	2.3616–2.3622	④	0.0012–0.0045	3	2.0466–2.0472	0.0006–③ 0.0017	0.0028–0.0130
	8/9	6-2.7 (2672)	①	②	0.0004–0.0037	3	1.7715–1.6535	0.0004–0.0021	0.0028–0.0118

87973c08

CRANKSHAFT AND CONNECTING ROD SPECIFICATIONS
All measurements are given in inches.

Year	Engine ID/VIN	Engine Displacement Liters (cc)	Crankshaft Main Brg. Journal Dia.	Crankshaft Main Brg. Oil Clearance	Crankshaft Shaft End-play	Crankshaft Thrust on No.	Connecting Rod Journal Diameter	Connecting Rod Oil Clearance	Connecting Rod Side Clearance
1992	7/8	3-1.2 (1189)	1.6250-1.6290	0.0006-0.0018	0.0031-0.0070	4	0.6531-1.6535	0.0008-0.0021	0.0028-0.0118
	4/7	4-1.8 (1781)	①	②	0.0004-0.0037	2	1.7715-1.7720	0.0004-0.0021	0.0028-0.0130
	6	4-2.2 (2212)	2.3616-2.3622	④	0.0012-0.0045	3	2.0466-2.0472	0.0006-③ 0.0017	0.0028-0.0130
	3	6-3.3 (3318)	2.3619-2.3625	⑤	0.0012-0.0045	5	2.0466-2.0472	0.0008-0.0018	0.0028-0.0130
1993	7/8	3-1.2 (1189)	1.6250-1.6290	0.0006-0.0018	0.0031-0.0070	4	1.6531-1.6535	0.0008-0.0021	0.0028-0.0118
	4/5	4-1.8 (1781)	①	②	0.0004-0.0037	2	1.7715-1.7720	0.0004-0.0021	0.0028-0.0130
	2	4-1.8 (1820)	2.3616-2.3622	0.0004-0.0012	0.0012-0.0045	3	2.0466-2.0472	0.0006-0.0017	0.0028-0.0130
	6	4-2.2 (2212)	2.3616-2.3622	0.0004-0.0012	0.0012-0.0045	3	2.0466-2.0472	0.0006-③ 0.0017	0.0028-0.0130
	3	6-3.3 (3318)	2.3619-2.3625	⑤	0.0012-0.0045	5	2.0466-2.0472	0.0008-0.0018	0.0028-0.0130
1994	7/8	3-1.2 (1189)	1.6250-1.6290	0.0006-0.0018	0.0031-0.0070	4	1.6531-1.6535	0.0008-0.0021	0.0028-0.0118
	4/5	4-1.8 (1781)	①	②	0.0004-0.0037	2	1.7715-1.7720	0.0004-0.0021	0.0028-0.0130
	2	4-1.8 (1820)	2.3616-2.3622	0.0004-0.0012	0.0012-0.0045	3	2.0466-2.0472	0.0006-0.0017	0.0028-0.0130
	6	4-2.2 (2212)	2.3616-2.3622	0.0004-0.0012	0.0012-0.0045	3	2.0466-2.0472	0.0006-③ 0.0017	0.0028-0.0130
	3	6-3.3 (3318)	2.3619-2.3625	⑤	0.0012-0.0045	5	2.0466-2.0472	0.0008-0.0018	0.0028-0.0130
1995	2	4-1.8 (1820)	2.3616-2.3622	0.0004-0.0012	0.0012-0.0045	3	2.0466-2.0472	0.0006-0.0017	0.0028-0.0130
	6	4-2.2 (2212)	2.3619-2.3625	⑦	0.0012-0.0045	3	2.0466-2.0472	0.0006-0.0018	0.0028-0.0130
	3	6-3.3 (3318)	2.3619-2.3625	⑤	0.0012-0.0045	5	2.0466-2.0472	0.0008-0.0018	0.0028-0.0130
1996	1/2	4-1.8 (1820)	2.3616-2.3622	0.0004-0.0012	0.0012-0.0045	3	2.0466-2.0472	0.0006-0.0017	0.0028-0.0130
	3/4	4-2.2 (2212)	2.3619-2.3625	⑦	0.0012-0.0045	3	2.0466-2.0472	0.0006-0.0018	0.0028-0.0130
	6	4-2.5 (2457)	2.3619-2.3625	⑦	0.0012-0.0045	3	1.8891-1.8898	0.0004-0.0015	0.0028-0.0130
	8	6-3.3 (3318)	2.3619-2.3625	⑤	0.0012-0.0045	5	2.0466-2.0472	0.0008-0.0018	0.0028-0.0130

① Front: 2.1637-2.1642
Center: 2.1635-2.1642
Rear: 2.1636-2.1642
② Front and Rear: 0.0001-0.0014
Center: 0.0003-0.0011

③ Turbo: 0.0010-0.0021
④ No. 1-5: 0.0004-0.0012
⑤ No. 1,3,7: 0.0002-0.0014
No. 2,4,6: 0.0005-0.0015
No. 5: 0.0005-0.0013

⑥ Front and Rear: 0.0004-0.0014
Center: 0.0004-0.0012
⑦ No. 1,5: 0.0001-0.0012
No. 2,3,4: 0.0004-0.0013

87973c09

PISTON AND RING SPECIFICATIONS

All measurements are given in inches.

| Year | Engine ID/VIN | Engine Displacement Liters (cc) | Piston Clearance | Ring Gap | | | Ring Side Clearance | | |
				Top Compression	Bottom Compression	Oil Control	Top Compression	Bottom Compression	Oil Control
1985	2	4-1.6L (1595)	0.0004–0.0016	0.0079–0.0138	0.0079–0.0138	0.0120–0.0350	0.0016–0.0031	0.0012–0.0028	0
	4/5/7	4-1.8L (1781)	0.0004–0.0016	0.0079–0.0138	0.0079–0.0138	0.0120–0.0350	0.0016–0.0031	0.0012–0.0028	0
	4/5/7	4-1.8L (1781) ①	0.0006–0.0014	0.0079–0.0138	0.0079–0.0138	0.0120–0.0350	0.0016–0.0031	0.0012–0.0028	0
1986	2	4-1.6L (1595)	0.0004–0.0016	0.0079–0.0138	0.0079–0.0138	0.0120–0.0350	0.0016–0.0031	0.0012–0.0028	0
	4/5/7	4-1.8L (1781)	0.0004–0.0016	0.0079–0.0138	0.0079–0.0138	0.0120–0.0350	0.0016–0.0031	0.0012–0.0028	0
	4/5/7	4-1.8L (1781) ①	0.0006–0.0014	0.0079–0.0138	0.0079–0.0138	0.0120–0.0350	0.0016–0.0031	0.0012–0.0028	0
1987	7/8	3-1.2L (1189)	0.0015–0.0024	0.0079–0.0138	0.0079–0.0138	0.0120–0.0350	0.0014–0.0030	0.0010–0.0026	0
	2	4-1.6L (1595)	0.0004–0.0016	0.0079–0.0138	0.0079–0.0138	0.0120–0.0350	0.0016–0.0031	0.0012–0.0028	0
	4/5/7	4-1.8L (1781)	0.0004–0.0016	0.0079–0.0138	0.0079–0.0138	0.0120–0.0350	0.0016–0.0031	0.0012–0.0028	0
	4/5/7	4-1.8L (1781) ①	0.0006–0.0014	0.0079–0.0138	0.0079–0.0138	0.0120–0.0350	0.0016–0.0031	0.0012–0.0028	0
1988	7/8	3-1.2L (1189)	0.0015–0.0024	0.0079–0.0138	0.0079–0.0138	0.0120–0.0350	0.0014–0.0030	0.0010–0.0026	0
	2	4-1.6L (1595)	0.0004–0.0016	0.0079–0.0138	0.0079–0.0138	0.0120–0.0350	0.0016–0.0031	0.0012–0.0028	0
	4/5/7	4-1.8L (1781)	0.0004–② 0.0016	0.0079–0.0138	0.0079–0.0138	0.0120–0.0350	0.0016–0.0031	0.0012–0.0028	0
	4/5/7	4-1.8L (1781) ①	0.0006–0.0014	0.0079–0.0138	0.0079–0.0138	0.0120–0.0350	0.0016–0.0031	0.0012–0.0028	0
	8/9	6-2.7L (2672)	0.0006–0.0014	0.0079–0.0138	0.0079–0.0138	0.0120–0.0350	0.0016–0.0031	0.0012–0.0028	0

87973c10

PISTON AND RING SPECIFICATIONS

All measurements are given in inches.

Year	Engine ID/VIN	Engine Displacement Liters (cc)	Piston Clearance	Ring Gap			Ring Side Clearance		
				Top Compression	Bottom Compression	Oil Control	Top Compression	Bottom Compression	Oil Control
1989	7/8	3-1.2L (1189)	0.0015–0.0028	0.0079–0.0138	0.0079–0.0138	0.0120–0.0350	0.0014–0.0030	0.0010–0.0026	0
	2	4-1.6L (1595)	0.0004–0.0016	0.0079–0.0138	0.0079–0.0138	0.0120–0.0350	0.0016–0.0031	0.0012–0.0028	0
	4/7	4-1.8L (1781)	0.0004–② 0.0016	0.0079–0.0138	0.0079–0.0138	0.0120–0.0350	0.0016–0.0031	0.0012–0.0028	0
	4/7	4-1.8L (1781)①	0.0006–0.0014	0.0079–0.0138	0.0079–0.0138	0.0120–0.0350	0.0016–0.0031	0.0012–0.0028	0
	8/9	6-2.7L (2672)	0.0006–0.0014	0.0079–0.0138	0.0079–0.0138	0.0120–0.0350	0.0016–0.0031	0.0012–0.0028	0
1990	7/8	3-1.2L (1189)	0.0015–0.0028	0.0079–0.0138	0.0079–0.0138	0.0120–0.0350	0.0014–0.0030	0.0010–0.0026	0
	4/7	4-1.8L (1781)	0.0006–② 0.0014	0.0079–0.0138	0.0079–0.0138	0.0120–0.0350	0.0016–0.0031	0.0012–0.0028	0
	4/7	4-1.8L (1781)①	0.0006–0.0014	0.0079–0.0138	0.0079–0.0138	0.0120–0.0350	0.0016–0.0031	0.0012–0.0028	0
	6	4-2.2L (2212)	0.0004–0.0012	0.0079–③ 0.0138	0.0146–0.0205	0.0079–0.0276	0.0016–0.0031	0.0012–0.0028	0
	8/9	6-2.7L (2672)	0.0006–0.0014	0.0079–0.0138	0.0079–0.0138	0.0120–0.0350	0.0016–0.0031	0.0012–0.0028	0
1991	7/8	3-1.2L (1189)	0.0015–0.0028	0.0079–0.0138	0.0079–0.0138	0.0120–0.0350	0.0014–0.0030	0.0010–0.0026	0
	4/7	4-1.8L (1781)	0.0006–② 0.0014	0.0079–0.0138	0.0079–0.0138	0.0120–0.0350	0.0016–0.0031	0.0012–0.0028	0
	4/7	4-1.8L (1781)①	0.0006–0.0014	0.0079–0.0138	0.0079–0.0138	0.0120–0.0350	0.0016–0.0031	0.0012–0.0028	0
	6	4-2.2L (2212)	0.0004–0.0012	0.0079–③ 0.0138	0.0146–0.0205	0.0079–0.0276	0.0016–0.0031	0.0012–0.0028	0
	8/9	6-2.7L (2672)	0.0006–0.0014	0.0079–0.0138	0.0079–0.0138	0.0120–0.0350	0.0016–0.0031	0.0012–0.0028	0
1992	7/8	3-1.2L (1189)	0.0015–0.0028	0.0079–0.0138	0.0079–0.0138	0.0120–0.0350	0.0014–0.0030	0.0010–0.0026	0
	4/7	4-1.8L (1781)	0.0006–② 0.0014	0.0079–0.0138	0.0079–0.0138	0.0120–0.0350	0.0016–0.0031	0.0012–0.0028	0
	6	4-2.2L (2212)	0.0004–0.0012	0.0079–③ 0.0138	0.0146–0.0205	0.0079–0.0276	0.0016–0.0031	0.0012–0.0028	0
	3	6-3.3L (3318)	0.0004–0.0012	0.0079–0.0118	0.0146–0.0205	0.0079–0.0236	0.0016–0.0035	0.0012–0.0028	0

87973c11

PISTON AND RING SPECIFICATIONS

All measurements are given in inches.

Year	Engine ID/VIN	Engine Displacement Liters (cc)	Piston Clearance	Ring Gap			Ring Side Clearance		
				Top Compression	Bottom Compression	Oil Control	Top Compression	Bottom Compression	Oil Control
1993	7 / 8	3-1.2L (1189)	0.0015-0.0028	0.0079-0.0138	0.0079-0.0138	0.0120-0.0350	0.0014-0.0030	0.0010-0.0026	0
	4 / 5	4-1.8L (1781)	0.0006-0.0014	0.0079-0.0138	0.0079-0.0138	0.0120-0.0350	0.0016-0.0031	0.0012-0.0028	0
	2	4-1.8L (1820)	0.0004-0.0012	0.0079-0.0138	0.0146-0.0205	0.0079-0.0276	0.0016-0.0031	0.0012-0.0028	0
	6	4-2.2L (2212)	0.0004-0.0012	0.0079- ③ 0.0138	0.0146-0.0205	0.0079-0.0276	0.0016-0.0031	0.0012-0.0028	0
	3	6-3.3L (3318)	0.0004-0.0012	0.0079-0.0118	0.0146-0.0205	0.0079-0.0236	0.0016-0.0035	0.0012-0.0028	0
1994	7 / 8	3-1.2L (1189)	0.0015-0.0028	0.0079-0.0138	0.0079-0.0138	0.0120-0.0350	0.0014-0.0030	0.0010-0.0026	0
	4 / 5	4-1.8L (1781)	0.0006-0.0014	0.0079-0.0138	0.0079-0.0138	0.0120-0.0350	0.0016-0.0031	0.0012-0.0028	0
	2	4-1.8L (1820)	0.0004-0.0012	0.0079-0.0138	0.0146-0.0205	0.0079-0.0276	0.0016-0.0031	0.0012-0.0028	0
	6	4-2.2L (2212)	0.0004-0.0012	0.0079- ③ 0.0138	0.0146-0.0205	0.0079-0.0276	0.0016-0.0031	0.0012-0.0028	0
	3	6-3.3L (3318)	0.0004-0.0012	0.0079-0.0118	0.0146-0.0205	0.0079-0.0236	0.0016-0.0035	0.0012-0.0028	0
1995	2	4-1.8L (1820)	0.0004-0.0012	0.0079-0.0138	0.0146-0.0205	0.0079-0.0276	0.0016-0.0031	0.0012-0.0028	0
	6	4-2.2L (2212)	0.0004-0.0012	0.0079-0.0138	0.0079-0.0197	0.0079-0.0276	0.0016-0.0031	0.0012-0.0028	0
	3	6-3.3L (3318)	0.0004-0.0012	0.0079-0.0118	0.0146-0.0205	0.0079-0.0236	0.0016-0.0035	0.0012-0.0028	0
1996	1 / 2	4-1.8L (1820)	0.0004-0.0012	0.0079-0.0138	0.0146-0.0205	0.0079-0.0276	0.0016-0.0031	0.0012-0.0028	0
	3 / 4	4-2.2L (2212)	0.0004-0.0012	0.0079-0.0138	0.0079-0.0197	0.0079-0.0276	0.0016-0.0031	0.0012-0.0028	0
	6	4-2.5L (2457)	0.0004-0.0012	0.0079-0.0138	0.0146-0.0205	0.0079-0.0236	0.0016-0.0031	0.0012-0.0028	0
	8	6-3.3L (3318)	0.0004-0.0012	0.0079-0.0118	0.0146-0.0205	0.0079-0.0236	0.0016-0.0035	0.0012-0.0028	0

① XT
② Turbo: 0.0004-0.0012
③ Turbo: 0.0079-0.0098

87973c12

TORQUE SPECIFICATIONS

All readings in ft. lbs.

Year	Engine ID/VIN	Engine Displacement Liters (cc)	Cylinder Head Bolts	Main Bearing Bolts	Rod Bearing Bolts	Crankshaft Damper Bolts	Flywheel Bolts	Manifold Intake	Manifold Exhaust	Spark Plugs	Lug Nut
1985	2	1.6L (1595)	②	⑥	29–31	66–79	30–33	13–16	19–22	13–17	58–72
	4/5/7	1.8L (1781)	②	⑥	29–31	66–79	51–55	13–16	19–22	13–17	58–72
1986	2	1.6L (1595)	②	⑥	29–31	66–79	30–33	13–16	19–22	13–17	58–72
	4/5/7	1.8L (1781)	②	⑥	29–31	66–79	51–55	13–16	19–22	13–17	58–72
1987	7/8	1.2L (1189)	①	30–35	29–33	58–72	65–71	14–22	14–22	13–17	58–72
	2	1.6L (1595)	②	⑥	29–31	66–79	30–33	13–16	19–22	13–17	58–72
	4/5/7	1.8L (1781)	②	⑥	29–31	66–79	51–55	13–16	19–22	13–17	58–72
1988	7/8	1.2L (1189)	①	30–35	29–33	58–72	65–71	14–22	14–22	13–17	58–72
	2	1.6L (1595)	②	⑥	29–31	66–79	30–33	13–16	19–22	13–17	58–72
	4/5/7	1.8L (1781)	②	⑥	29–31	66–79	51–55	13–16	19–22	13–17	58–72
	8/9	2.7L (2672)	④	⑥	29–31	66–79	51–55	13–16	19–22	13–17	58–72
1989	7/8	1.2L (1189)	①	30–35	29–33	58–72	65–71	14–22	14–22	13–17	58–72
	2	1.6L (1595)	②	⑥	29–31	66–79	30–33	13–16	19–22	13–17	58–72
	4/7	1.8L (1781)	②	⑥	29–31	66–79	51–55	13–16	19–22	13–17	58–72
	8/9	2.7L (2672)	④	⑥	29–31	66–79	51–55	13–16	19–22	13–17	58–72
1990	7/8	1.2L (1189)	①	30–35	29–33	58–72	65–71	14–22	14–22	13–17	58–72
	4/7	1.8L (1781)	②	⑥	29–31	66–79	51–55	13–16	19–22	13–17	58–72
	6	2.2L (2212)	③	⑥	32–34	69–76	51–55	21–25	19–26	13–17	58–72
	8/9	2.7L (2672)	④	⑥	29–31	66–79	51–55	13–16	19–22	13–17	58–72
1991	7/8	1.2L (1189)	①	30–35	29–33	58–72	65–71	14–22	14–22	13–17	58–72
	4/7	1.8L (1781)	②	⑥	29–31	66–79	51–55	13–16	19–22	13–17	58–72
	6	2.2L (2212)	③	⑥	32–34	69–76	51–55	21–25	19–26	13–17	58–72
	8/9	2.7L (2672)	④	⑥	29–31	66–79	51–55	13–16	19–22	13–17	58–72
1992	7/8	1.2L (1189)	①	30–35	29–33	58–72	65–71	14–22	14–22	13–17	58–72
	4/7	1.8L (1781)	②	⑥	29–31	66–79	51–55	13–16	19–22	13–17	58–72
	6	2.2L (2212)	③	⑥	32–34	69–76	51–55	21–25	19–26	13–17	58–72
	3	3.3L (3318)	⑤	⑥	32–34	108–123	51–55	17–20	22–29	13–17	58–72
1993	7/8	1.2L (1189)	①	30–35	29–33	58–72	65–71	14–22	14–22	13–17	58–72
	4/5	1.8L (1781)	②	⑥	29–31	66–79	51–55	13–16	19–22	13–17	58–72
	2	1.8L (1820)	③	⑦	32–34	69–76	51–55	15–25	18–26	14–22	58–72
	6	2.2L (2212)	③	⑥	32–34	69–76	51–55	21–25	19–26	13–17	58–72
	3	3.3L (3318)	⑤	⑥	32–34	108–123	51–55	17–20	22–29	13–17	58–72
1994	7/8	1.2L (1189)	①	30–35	29–33	58–72	65–71	14–22	14–22	13–17	58–72
	4/5	1.8L (1781)	②	⑥	29–31	66–79	51–55	13–16	19–22	13–17	58–72
	2	1.8L (1820)	③	⑦	32–34	69–76	51–55	15–25	18–26	14–22	58–72
	6	2.2L (2212)	③	⑥	32–34	69–76	51–55	21–25	19–26	13–17	58–72
	3	3.3L (3318)	⑤	⑥	32–34	108–123	51–55	17–20	22–29	13–17	58–72

87973c13

TORQUE SPECIFICATIONS
All readings in ft. lbs.

Year	Engine ID/VIN	Engine Displacement Liters (cc)	Cylinder Head Bolts	Main Bearing Bolts	Rod Bearing Bolts	Crankshaft Damper Bolts	Flywheel Bolts	Manifold		Spark Plugs	Lug Nut
								Intake	Exhaust		
1995	2	1.8L (1820)	③	⑦	32-34	69-76	51-55	15-25	18-26	14-22	58-72
	6	2.2L (2212)	③	⑦	32-34	76-86	51-55	17-20	19-26	13-17	58-72
	3	3.3L (3318)	⑤	⑥	32-34	108-123	51-55	17-20	22-29	13-17	58-72
1996	1 / 2	1.8L (1820)	③	⑦	32-34	69-76	51-55	15-25	18-26	14-22	58-72
	3 / 4	2.2L (2212)	③	⑦	32-34	76-86	51-55	17-20	19-26	13-17	58-72
	6	2.5L (2457)	③	⑦	32-34	91-97	51-55	17-20	19-26	13-17	58-72
	8	3.3L (3318)	⑤	⑥	32-34	108-123	51-55	17-20	25-32	13-17	58-72

① Tighten all bolts in sequence to 29 ft. lbs. (39Nm).
Tighten all bolts in sequence to 54 ft. lbs. (73Nm).
Loosen all bolts 90° or more in the reverse order of the tighening sequence.
Tighten all bolts in sequence to 51–57 ft. lbs. (70–77Nm).

② Tighten all bolts in sequence to 22 ft. lbs. (29Nm).
Tighten all bolts in sequence to 43 ft. lbs. (59Nm).
Tighten all bolts in sequence to 47 ft. lbs. (64Nm).

③ Tighten all bolts in sequence to 22 ft. lbs. (29Nm).
Tighten all bolts in sequence to 51 ft. lbs. (69Nm).
Loosen all bolts by 180°, then loosen an additional 180°.
Tighten bolts 1 and 2 to 25 ft. lbs. (24Nm) for non-turbo engines and 27 ft. lbs. (37Nm) for turbo engines.

Tighten bolts 3, 4, 5 and 6 to 11 ft. lbs. (15Nm) for non-turbo engines and 14 ft. lbs. (20Nm) for turbo engines.
Tighten all bolts in sequence by 80–90°.
Tighten all bolts in sequence an additional 80–90°.

④ Tighten all bolts in sequence to 29 ft. lbs. (39Nm).
Tighten all bolts in sequence to 47 ft. lbs. (64Nm).
Loosen all bolts at least 90° in the reverse order of the tightening sequence.
Tighten all bolts in sequence to 44–50 ft. lbs. (60–68Nm).

⑤ Tighten all bolts in sequence to 22 ft. lbs. (29Nm).
Tighten all bolts in sequence to 51 ft. lbs. (69Nm).
Loosen all bolts by 180°, then loosen an additional 180°.
Tighten all bolts in sequence to 20 ft. lbs. (27Nm).

Tighten bolts 1, 2, 3 and 4 in the sequence shown by 80–90°.
Tighten bolts 5, 6, 7 and 8 in the sequence shown to 33 ft. lbs. (44Nm).
Tighten all bolts in sequence an additional 80–90°.

⑥ Engine is of the split case design and does not use main bearing caps. Tighten the case half bolts as follows: 3–4 ft. lbs. (6mm); 17–20 ft. lbs. (8mm); 29–35 ft. lbs. (10mm).

⑦ Engine is of the split case design and does not use main bearing caps. Tighten the case half bolts as follows: (10mm), 33–37 ft. lbs. (6 and 8mm) bolts 1-7, 14-20 ft. lbs.; bolt 8, 4.7 ft. lbs.

87973c14

Engine

REMOVAL & INSTALLATION

▶ See Figures 6 and 7

※※CAUTION

The EPA warns that prolonged contact with used engine oil may cause a number of skin disorders, including cancer! You should make every effort to minimize your exposure to used engine oil. Protective gloves should be worn when changing the oil. Wash your hands and any other exposed skin areas as soon as possible after exposure to used engine oil. Soap and water, or waterless hand cleaner should be used.

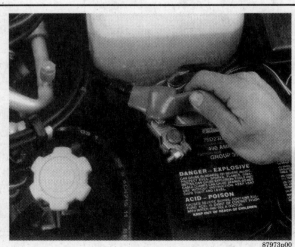

87973p00

Fig. 6 Before beginning any engine removal procedure, disconnect the negative battery cable

Fig. 7 It may look like an impossible job, but with organization and patience, this engine can be removed

1.2L Engine

✳✳CAUTION

When draining the coolant, keep in mind that cats and dogs are attracted to ethylene glycol antifreeze, and could drink any that is left in an uncovered container or in puddles on the ground. Always drain the coolant into a sealable container. Coolant should be reused unless it is contaminated or several years old.

1. Disconnect the negative battery cable.
2. Raise and safely support the vehicle on jackstands.
3. Scribe alignment marks around the hood hinges, then remove the retainer bots and hood.
4. Drain the cooling system into a suitable container.
5. Remove the front bumper bumper and the grille. Refer to Section 10 for removal and installation steps.
6. Tag and disconnect the electrical harnesses and hoses from the radiator, Remove the radiator. Refer to the procedure in this section.
7. Disconnect the hood release cable and remove the radiator upper support member.
8. Tag and disconnect the hoses and cables to the air cleaner, fuel distribution system, heater unit, brake booster, clutch, if equipped with a manual transaxle, accelerator and speedometer cables and wiring to the distributor.
9. Disconnect the pitching stopper from the bracket.
10. Remove the engine splash covers and the exhaust pipes to the manifold.
11. Disconnect the gearshift rod and stay from the transaxle.
12. Remove the transverse link. Using a suitable prytool, remove the halfshafts from the transaxle.
13. Remove the engine/transaxle mounting brackets. Refer to the procedures in this section.
14. Using a suitable engine hoist and a cable, attach the cable to the lifting points on the engine and lift slightly.
15. Remove the center member and crossmember from the vehicle.
16. Lift the engine/transaxle assembly carefully and remove from the vehicle.

17. If necessary, separate the engine from the transaxle, If you intend to work on the engine, secure it to a suitable workstand.

To install:

18. Attach the engine to the transaxle. Attach the engine assembly to the hoist and cable at the appropriate lifting points.
19. Slowly lower the engine/transaxle assembly into the vehicle.
20. With the engine/transaxle assembly slightly raised, install the center member and crossmember to the vehicle. Tighten the bolts to 27-49 ft. lbs. (37-67 Nm).
21. Completely lower the engine/transaxle into place and install the mounting brackets. Tighten the bolts to 13-23 ft. lbs. (18-31 Nm).
22. Install the halfshaft. Refer to the procedure in Section 7. Instal the transverse link.
23. Install the gearshift rod and stay into the transaxle.
24. Install the exhaust pipes to the manifold. Refer to the procedure in this section.
25. Install the engine splash cover securing in place with the retainer screws.
26. Install the pitching stopper.
27. Install all removed hoses.
28. Install the hood release cable.
29. Install the radiator, then connect the coolant hoses and electrical harnesses.
30. Install the grille and bumper. Refer to Section 10 for installation steps.
31. Check to make sure the radiator drain plug is tight, then fill the radiator with coolant.
32. Lower the vehicle.
33. Connect the negative battery cable.
34. Start the vehicle. Adjust the timing, if needed and check for leaks.

1.6L and 1.8L Carbureted Engines

➡**On all models, the engine is removed separately from the transaxle.**

1. Open the hood and scribe alignment marks around the hood hinge. Remove the hinge retainer bolts and hood. Place the hood aside.
2. Disconnect the negative battery terminal from the battery.
3. Remove the ground cable-to-intake manifold bolt and disconnect the cable. It is unnecessary to remove the cable fully: leave it routed along the side of the body.
4. Remove the spare tire from the engine compartment.
5. Remove the emission control hoses from the air cleaner. Remove the air cleaner brackets and the wingnut, then lift the air cleaner assembly off the carburetor.
6. Position a drain pan under the fuel line union. At the union, remove the hose clamp, then pull the hose(s) off. Cap the open hose ends to prevent fuel spillage.
7. Position a drain pan under the engine, remove the drain plug and drain the oil from the crankcase.
8. Drain the engine coolant by performing the following procedures:
   a. Position a clean container, large enough to hold the contents of the cooling system, under the radiator drain plug.

b. Open the draincock on the radiator; turn it so that the slot faces downward.

c. Disconnect both the hoses from the radiator.

d. Disconnect the heater hoses from the pipe on the side of the engine.

e. If equipped with an automatic transaxle, disconnect the oil cooler lines from the radiator.

9. Disconnect the following electrical wiring connectors:
- Alternator
- Oil pressure sender
- Engine cooling fan
- Temperature sender
- Primary distributor lead
- Secondary ignition leads (ignition side)
- Starter wiring harness
- Anti-dieseling solenoid lead
- Automatic choke lead
- EGR vacuum solenoid
- EGR coolant temperature switch

10. If equipped with an automatic transaxle, disconnect the neutral safety switch harness and downshift solenoid harness.

11. Remove the radiator-to-chassis bolts, then remove the ground lead from the upper side of the radiator and remove the radiator.

➡**On 4WD models, remove the engine fan.**

12. Remove the crankshaft damper as follows:

a. Remove the front nut from the damper.

b. Remove the nut on the body bracket and withdraw the damper.

c. Pull the damper rearward, away from the engine lifting hook; be careful not to lose any of the damper parts.

13. Remove the starter-to-engine bolts and wires followed by the starter.

14. Loosen the screw on the carburetor throttle lever. Remove the outer end of the accelerator cable.

15. Tag and remove the vacuum hose and the purge hose from the vapor canister.

16. If equipped with a manual transaxle, remove the clutch return spring and clutch cable from the lever.

17. If equipped with an automatic transaxle, disconnect the vacuum hose from the transaxle.

18. Disconnect the vacuum hose from the brake booster unit (if equipped).

19. On 4WD models, remove the skid plate-to-chassis bolts and the plate.

20. To remove the Y-shaped exhaust pipe, perform the following procedures:

a. Remove the exhaust pipe-to-manifold nuts.

b. Remove the exhaust pipe-to-pre-muffler nuts/bolts.

c. While supporting the exhaust pipe by hand, remove the exhaust pipe-to-transaxle bracket bolts, then lower the exhaust pipe.

21. If equipped with an automatic transaxle, remove the torque converter bolts by performing the following procedures:

a. Remove the timing hole cover from the torque converter housing.

b. Through the timing hole, remove the torque converter-to-drive plate bolts.

➡**Be careful that the bolts DO NOT fall into the torque converter housing.**

22. Connect a chain hoist or equivalent to the engine, with hooks at the front and rear engine hangers. Adjust the hoist so that the weight of the engine is supported, but DO NOT raise the engine.

23. Position a floor jack under the transaxle to support the transaxle weight when the engine is removed.

24. Remove the engine-to-transaxle nuts.

25. Remove the front engine mount-to-crossmember nuts.

26. Using the hoist to raise the engine slightly, about 1 in. (25mm). Keeping it level, move the engine forward, off the transaxle input shaft.

✳✳CAUTION

DO NOT raise the engine more than 1 in. (25mm) prior to removing it from the input shaft or damage may occur to the driveshaft double offset joints. If equipped with a manual transaxle, be sure that the input shaft does not interfere with the clutch spring assembly; if equipped with an automatic transaxle, leave the torque converter on the transaxle input shaft.

27. Hoist the engine carefully until it is completely out of the vehicle, then secure it onto a workstand.

To install:

28. Use new gaskets and observe the following torque specifications. Tighten the transaxle-to-engine bolts to 34-40 ft. lbs. (46-54 Nm), the torque converter-to-drive plate bolts to 17-20 ft. lbs. (23-27 Nm), the engine mount-to-crossmember bolts to 14-24 ft. lbs. (19-33 Nm), the crankshaft damper nut to 7-10 ft. lbs. (9-14 Nm), the exhaust pipe-to-engine bolt to 19-22 ft. lbs. (26-30 Nm), the exhaust pipe-to-pre-muffler nuts to 31-38 ft. lbs. (42-51 Nm) and the radiator-to-chassis bolts to 6-10 ft. lbs. (8-14 Nm). Adjust the clutch and accelerator linkage. Refill the crankcase and cooling system.

➡**Use care not to damage the input shaft splines or the clutch spring when lowering the engine in place.**

29. When installing the crankshaft damper, perform the following adjustments:

a. Tighten the body bracket nut.

b. Turn the front nut until there is no clearance between the front washer and rubber cushion.

c. Insert the bushing and tighten the front nut.

1.8L Fuel Injected and Turbocharged Engines

1. Open the hood and scribe alignment marks around the hood hinge. Remove the hinge retainer bolts and hood. Place the hood aside.

2. Remove the spare tire and tire bracket.

3. If equipped with Turbo or MPFI, perform the following procedures to reduce the fuel pressure:

a. From under the vehicle, disconnect the fuel pump electrical harness connector.

b. Crank the engine for at least 5 seconds. If the engine starts, allow it to run until it stalls.

c. Reconnect the fuel pump connector.

4. Disconnect the negative battery cable.

5. Remove the air cleaner assembly.

6. Tag and disconnect the fuel system hoses and the evaporative emissions system hoses.

7. Tag and disconnect the vacuum hoses for the cruise control, Master-Vac®, air intake shutter and the heater air intake door.

8. Disconnect the electrical wiring from the alternator, EGR, thermoswitch, cooling fan (if electric), A/C condenser and the ignition coil. Unfasten the main engine harness.

9. Tag and disconnect the spark plug wires, the engine ground strap and the fusible link assembly.

10. Disconnect the accelerator linkage. Remove the windshield washer reservoir and position it behind the right strut tower.

11. Remove the power steering pump as follows:
    a. Loosen the alternator pivot and mounting bolts, then remove the drive belt.
    b. Remove the pulley retainer bolts and pulley from the power steering pump.
    c. Remove the power steering pump-to-engine bolts and clamp.
    d. Remove the engine oil filler tube and brace.
    e. Remove the power steering pump and secure it to the bulkhead without disconnecting the pressure lines.

12. Loosen the air intake duct hose clamps and remove the duct. Seal the openings to keep dirt out of the intake passages.

13. Remove the air intake-to-flow meter line and cover the openings.

14. Remove the horizontal damper and clip.

15. Remove the center exhaust section by performing the following procedures:
    a. Disconnect the temperature sensor harness.
    b. Remove the rear cover.
    c. Remove the center exhaust section-to-transaxle bolt.
    d. Remove the hanger bolts, then carefully remove the exhaust pipe (clearance is tight) to avoid damage.
    e. Loosen the attaching bolts, then remove the torque converter/flywheel cover.

16. If equipped, disconnect the turbocharger oil supply and drain lines. Remove the turbo-to-exhaust bolts, the turbo assembly, the lower cover and the gasket.

17. Unfasten the electrical connector from the O_2 sensor. Remove the torque converter/flywheel-to-drive plate bolts.

18. Using a hoist and suitable engine lift, connect the hoist to the crankshaft damper bracket and lifting eye. Support the engine, but do not lift. Remove the upper engine-to-transaxle bolts; leave the starter in place.

19. Drain the engine coolant into a suitable container. Disconnect the upper/lower radiator hoses, oil cooler lines at the radiator, if equipped, ground wire and radiator.

20. Disconnect the oil cooler lines from the engine. Drain the crankcase oil into a suitable container. Disconnect the heater hoses from the side of the engine.

21. Remove the front engine mount, then the lower engine-to-transaxle nuts.

22. Position a floor jack under the transaxle, then raise the engine/transaxle slightly. Pull the engine forward until the transaxle shaft clears the torque converter/clutch, then carefully raise the engine out of the engine compartment.

To install:

23. Carefully install the engine into the engine compartment. Push the engine rearward and engage it with the transaxle. Mark sure the clutch clears the transaxle shaft.

24. Install the front engine mount.

25. Connect the heater hoses to the engine and connect the oil cooler lines.

26. Install the radiator and connect the transaxle oil cooler lines, ground wire and the upper and lower radiator hoses.

27. Install the upper engine-to-transaxle bolts and remove the engine lifting fixture. Tighten the bolts to 34-40 ft. lbs. (44-52 Nm).

28. Install the torque converter-to-driveplate bolts. Tighten the bolts one at a time to 17-20 ft. lbs. (22-26 Nm).

29. Connect the O_2 sensor electrical connector.

30. To install the center section of the exhaust pipe, perform the following procedures:
    a. Install the torque converter cover.
    b. Carefully install the exhaust pipe and install the hangar bolts.
    c. Install the center exhaust section-to-transaxle bolt.
    d. Install the rear cover.
    e. Connect the temperature sensor connector.

31. Install the remaining exhaust components, adhering to the following torque specifications;
    • Turbocharger-to-exhaust system bolts to 31-38 ft. lbs. (42-51 Nm), if equipped
    • Exhaust system-to-transaxle bolt to 18-25 ft. lbs. (24-34 Nm)
    • Exhaust system hanger bolts to 7-13 ft. lbs. (9-18 Nm)
    • Rear exhaust pipe joint nuts to 7-13 ft. lbs. (9-18 Nm)

32. Install the horizontal damper and clip.

33. Install the air intake-to-flow meter line.

34. Install air intake the duct and tighten the air intake duct hose clamps. Install the upper cover.

35. To install the power steering pump, perform the following procedures:
    a. Install the power steering pump on the mounting bracket.
    b. Install the engine oil filler pipe brace.
    c. Install the power steering pump-to-engine bolts and clamp. tighten the bolts to 22-36 ft. lbs. (29-47 Nm).
    d. Install the pulley on the power steering pump. Tighten the retainer bolts to 31-46 ft. lbs. (40-60 Nm).
    e. Install the alternator belt and tension the belt. Tighten the alternator pivot and mounting bolts.

36. Install the windshield washer reservoir.

37. Install and the crankshaft damper by tightening the nuts on the body side of the damper until the clearance is 0.08 in. (2mm). Tighten the locknuts to 6-9 ft. lbs. (8-12 Nm).

38. Connect the spark plug wires, the engine ground strap and the fusible link assembly.

39. Connect the main engine harness. Connect the electrical wiring connectors to the alternator, EGI, thermoswitch, electric fan, A/C condenser and the ignition coil.

40. Connect the vacuum hoses to the cruise control, Master-Vac®, air intake shutter and the heater air intake door.

41. Connect the fuel system hoses and the evaporative emissions system hoses.

42. Adjust the accelerator pedal so there is 0.4-1.2 in. (10-30mm) between the pin and stop. Adjust the cable for an end-play of 0-0.08 in. (0-2mm) on the actuator side.

43. Install the air cleaner assembly.

44. Connect the negative battery cable.

45. Install the spare tire and the spare tire bracket.

46. Refill the crankcase with oil, the radiator with coolant and check the transmission fluid. Start the engine and check for leaks.

2.2L and 2.5L Engines

✳✳CAUTION

Fuel injection systems remain under pressure after the engine has been turned OFF. Properly relieve fuel pressure before disconnecting any fuel lines. Failure to do so may result in fire or personal injury.

1. Relieve the fuel system pressure.
2. Disconnect the battery cables, negative first then positive. Remove the battery from the vehicle.
3. Drain the engine oil and coolant into suitable containers.
4. Disconnect the radiator hoses and fan motor harness, then remove the radiator.
5. If equipped with A/C, discharge the system using an approved recovery/recycling machine. Disconnect and cap the lines from the compressor.
6. Remove the air intake duct.
7. Remove the air cleaner element and upper cover.
8. Remove the evaporator canister and bracket.
9. Unfasten the following electrical connectors:
   - O_2 sensor
   - Engine ground terminal
   - Crank angle sensor connector
   - Cam angle sensor connector
   - Knock sensor connector
   - Alternator connector and terminal
   - A/C compressor connectors, if equipped
   - Accelerator cable
   - Cruise control cable, if equipped
   - Clutch release spring, clutch cable and hill holder cable, if equipped with a manual transaxle
10. Disconnect the following hoses:
    - Brake booster hose
    - Heater inlet and outlet hoses
11. Remove the alternator drive belt.
12. Disconnect the wires from the spark plugs on the left side of the engine.
13. Remove the power steering pump line bracket.
14. Remove the power steering pump, leaving the lines connected and position it aside.
15. Raise and support the engine safely.
16. Remove the exhaust Y-pipe.
17. Remove the lower starter nuts.
18. Remove the lower engine-to-transaxle nuts.
19. Remove the front engine mount-to-crossmember nuts.
20. Lower the vehicle.
21. Remove the starter.
22. If equipped with an automatic transaxle, perform the following:
    a. Remove the torque converter service hole plug.
    b. Rotate the engine engine remove the torque converter-to-drive plate bolts as they become accessible.
23. Remove the pitching stopper.
24. Disconnect the fuel delivery, return and evaporation hoses.

25. Support the engine with a suitable lifting device attached to the engine lifting eyes.
26. Slightly raise the engine.
27. Raise the transaxle with a floor jack.
28. Slowly remove the engine from the vehicle.
To install:
29. Apply a small amount of grease to the splines of the mainshaft.
30. Position the engine in the engine compartment and align it with the transaxle.
31. Install the engine and tighten the upper bolts to 34-40 ft. lbs. (44-54 Nm).
32. Remove the lifting device and floor jack.
33. Install the pitching stopper and tighten the bolts to the following specifications:
    - Body side — 49 ft. lbs. (67 Nm)
    - Bracket side — 40 ft. lbs. (54 Nm)
34. If equipped with an automatic transaxle, perform the following:
    a. Install the torque converter-to-drive plate bolts while rotating the engine, and tighten to 20 ft. lbs. (26 Nm).
    b. Install the service hole cover.
35. Install the evaporator canister and bracket.
36. Install the power steering pump. Tighten the retainer bolts to 22-36 ft. lbs. (29-47 Nm).
37. Install and tension the drive belt.
38. Install the starter. Tighten the bolts to 34-40 ft. lbs. (44-52 Nm).
39. Raise and support the vehicle safely.
40. Install the lower engine-to-transaxle nuts and tighten them to 34-40 ft. lbs. (44-52 Nm).
41. Install the lower engine mounting nuts. Tighten them to 61 ft. lbs. (83 Nm) in the inner most elliptical hole in the front crossmember so the clearance is 0.16-0.24 in. (4-6mm).
42. Install the exhaust Y-pipe with new gaskets and nuts.
43. Connect the following hoses:
    - Brake booster hose
    - Heater inlet and outlet hoses
44. Attach the following connectors:
    - Accelerator cable
    - Cruise control cable, if equipped
    - Clutch release spring, clutch cable, hill holder cable, if equipped with a manual transaxle
45. Fasten the following electrical connectors:
    - Engine harness connectors
    - O_2 sensor
    - Engine ground terminal
    - Crank angle sensor connector
    - Cam angle sensor connector
    - Knock sensor connector
    - Alternator connector and terminal
    - A/C compressor connectors, if equipped
46. Install the air cleaner element and cover.
47. If equipped, connect the A/C lines with new O-rings and tighten the bolts to 23 ft. lbs. (31 Nm).
48. Install the radiator.
49. Install the engine cover.
50. Install the battery.
51. Fill the engine with the recommended oil.
52. Fill and bleed the cooling system.
53. Charge the A/C system using an approved recovery/recycling machine.

54. Adjust the clutch cable.

55. If equipped, check the automatic transaxle fluid level and add Dexron II® if necessary.

56. Start the engine and allow it to reach normal operating temperature. Check for leaks.

2.7L Engine

1. Properly relieve the fuel system pressure.
2. Disconnect the negative battery cable.
3. Matchmark and remove the hood.
4. Raise and support the vehicle safely on jackstands.
5. Discharge the air conditioning system, if equipped using an approved recovery/recycling machine. Drain the engine oil and cooling system into suitable containers.
6. Tag and disconnect the canister hose and the hose bracket.
7. Disconnect and plug the fuel lines.
8. Disconnect the power brake vacuum line booster. If equipped with manual transaxle and 4WD, disconnect the differential lock vacuum hose.
9. Disconnect the engine wiring harnesses, oxygen sensor plug, bypass air valve control harness, ignition coil and the distributor connector to the crank sensor.
10. Unfasten the alternator wires, A/C compressor, engine ground, radiator fan motor and thermo-switch electrical connector.
11. Disconnect the accelerator cable. Disconnect the cruise control cable, if equipped. Disconnect and plug the heater hoses.
12. Disconnect the hill holder cable on the clutch release fork side of the assembly, if equipped with a manual transaxle.
13. Disconnect the front exhaust pipe from the manifold.
14. Lower the vehicle. Disconnect and plug the air conditioning compressor hoses, if equipped.
15. Remove the radiator fan and shroud assembly. If equipped with an automatic transaxle, disconnect and plug the cooler lines. Remove the radiator from the vehicle.
16. Remove the timing hole plug. Remove the bolts that retain the torque converter to the driveplate, if equipped with an automatic transaxle.
17. Disconnect and remove the starter.
18. Remove the buffer rod mounting bolts. Remove the bolts that support the engine mount to the front crossmember. Remove the bolts that hold the lower side of the engine to the transaxle assembly.
19. Install the proper engine lifting equipment using the engine lifting eyes. Properly support the transaxle assembly with a suitable transmission jack.
20. Remove the upper transaxle retainer bolts.
21. Carefully remove the engine from the vehicle. If equipped with manual transaxle, move the engine toward the rear of the vehicle until the mainshaft is withdrawn from the clutch cover.

To install:

22. Install the engine into the engine compartment. If equipped with a manual transaxle, be careful to align the mainshaft. Install the retainer bolts and tighten to 34-40 ft. lbs. (44-52 Nm).

23. On automatic transaxle equipped models, connect the torque converter to the engine flywheel. Tighten the bolts to 17-20 ft. lbs. 22-26 Nm).

24. Tighten the front rubber cushion mounts to 28-50 ft. lbs. (36-65 Nm).

25. Install the buffer rod and tighten the mounting bolt to 14-25 ft. lbs. (18-32 Nm).

26. Install the timing hole plug.

27. Install the radiator, radiator shroud and transaxle fluid cooler lines, if equipped.

28. Install the air conditioner compressor and lines. Install the exhaust system.

29. Install the hill holder, if equipped. Attach all vacuum lines and hoses disconnected earlier. Reconnect all electrical harnesses taking care to clean all connectors and ground locations.

30. Install the fuel lines. Fill the crankcase with oil, the transaxle with fluid and the cooling system with coolant.

31. Connect the negative battery cable.

32. Start the engine and allow it to reach operating temperature. Check for leaks and test drive the vehicle.

3.3L Engine

✳✳CAUTION

Fuel injection systems remain under pressure after the engine has been turned OFF. Properly relieve fuel pressure before disconnecting any fuel lines. Failure to do so may result in fire or personal injury.

1. Raise and support the vehicle safely on jackstands.
2. Scribe alignment marks on the hood hinges, then remove the hinge retainer bolts and hood.
3. Release the fuel system pressure.
4. Disconnect the negative battery cable.
5. Remove the underbody cover and drain the engine coolant.
6. Remove the radiator and all coolant hoses.
7. If equipped with A/C, discharge the air conditioning system using an approved recovery/recycling machine.
8. Disconnect and plug the air conditioning lines.
9. Remove the air cleaner assembly.
10. Disconnect the accelerator cable.
11. Disconnect the cruise control cable.
12. Label and disconnect all wiring harnesses and cables.
13. Tag and remove the evaporation canister, vacuum hoses and bracket.
14. Disconnect the exhaust system from the exhaust manifold.
15. Place a drain pan beneath the power steering lines and disconnect.
16. Disconnect the automatic transaxle cooler lines from the radiator, if equipped.
17. Remove the nuts which secure the lower side of the engine to the transaxle.
18. Remove the starter.
19. Remove the nuts which attach the front cushion rubber to the subframe.
20. If equipped with an automatic transaxle, separate the torque converter from the drive plate by removing the converter retainer bolts.
21. Remove the pitching stopper and bracket.
22. Disconnect the fuel delivery hose, return hose and evaporation hoses.

23. Support the engine with a suitable lifting device and the transaxle with a suitable transmission jack.

24. Remove the bolts which secure the engine to the transaxle.

25. Slowly raise the engine and remove from the vehicle.

To install:

26. Install the engine to the transaxle and tighten the bolts which secure the right upper side of the engine to 37 ft. lbs. (50 Nm).

27. Remove the lifting device and transmission jack.

28. Install the pitching stopper and tighten to 37 ft. lbs. (50 Nm).

29. if equipped with an automatic transaxle, install the torque converter to drive plate bolts and tighten to 19 ft. lbs. (25 Nm).

30. Connect all hoses disconnected earlier.

31. Install the evaporation canister and bracket.

32. Install the radiator and coolant lines.

33. Install the nuts which hold the lower side of the engine to the transaxle. Tighten the bolts to 37 ft. lbs. (50 Nm).

34. Install the starter and wiring. Tighten the bolts to 37 ft. lbs. (50 Nm).

35. Install the nuts which hold the front cushion rubber to the subframe. Tighten to 50 ft. lbs. (84 Nm).

36. Connect the power steering and automatic transaxle cooler lines.

37. Install the exhaust system to the manifold.

38. Install the engine under cover.

39. Connect all electrical harnesses.

40. Connect the accelerator cable.

41. Connect the cruise control cable.

42. Connect the high pressure hoses to the A/C compressor. Tighten to 18 ft. lbs. (24 Nm).

43. Install the air intake system

44. Connect the negative battery cable.

45. Fill the cooling system with coolant.

46. Check the automatic transaxle oil level and add as required.

47. Check the power steering fluid level. Add as necessary and bleed all air from the system.

48. Check the engine oil level.

49. Charge the A/C system using an approved recovery/recycling machine.

50. Start the engine and allow it to reach normal operating temperature. Check for leaks.

Rocker Arm (Valve) Cover

The rocker cover is a light weight and compact aluminum die casting. It adopts a float supporting system with a rubber ring type gasket and an oil seal washer to reduce the noise level.

REMOVAL & INSTALLATION

▶ **See Figures 8, 9, 10, 11, 12, 13, 14 and 15**

1. Disconnect the negative battery cable.

2. Disconnect the breather hose attached to the valve cover, if equipped. Depending on which valve cover is being removed, there may not be an attached hose.

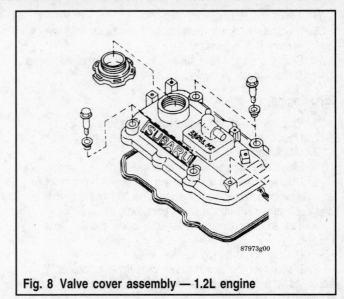

Fig. 8 Valve cover assembly — 1.2L engine

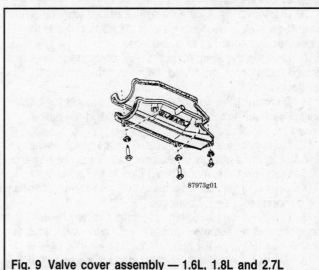

Fig. 9 Valve cover assembly — 1.6L, 1.8L and 2.7L engines

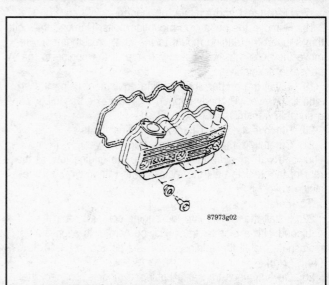

Fig. 10 Valve cover assembly — 2.2L engine

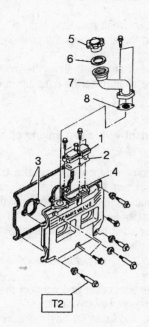

1. Oil separator cover
2. Gasket
3. Rocker cover gasket (LH)
4. Rocker cover (LH)
5. Oil filler cap
6. Gasket
7. Oil filler duct
8. Gasket

Tightening torque: N·m (kg-m, ft-lb)
T1: Refer to [W4E1]☆2.
T2: 5 (0.5, 3.6)
T3: 10 (1.0, 7)

87973gm2

Fig. 11 Valve cover assembly — 2.5L engine

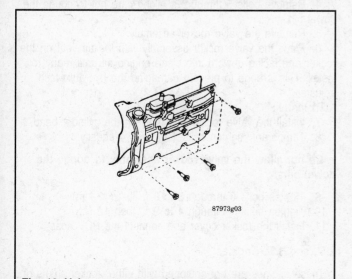

87973g03

Fig. 12 Valve cover assembly — 3.3L engine

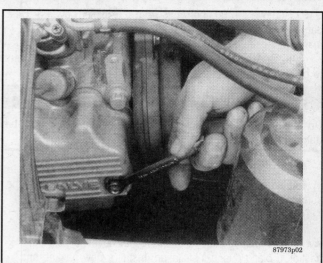

87973p02

Fig. 13 Remove the valve cover retainer bolts — 2.2L engine shown

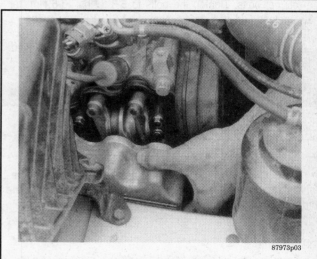

87973p03

Fig. 14 Lift the valve cover off and out of the engine compartment

87973p04

Fig. 15 Remove the valve cover gasket. This one remained stuck to the cylinder head surface

3. Remove the retainer bolts from the rocker cover(s). Depending on engine, there may be as few as two bolts or as many as eight.

4. If needed, using a rubber hammer, tap the rocker covers to break the seal between the gasket and the valve cover.

❊❊WARNING

Do not tap the rocker cover too hard, or the cover may be damaged or distorted.

5. Remove the rocker cover from the cylinder head.

6. Remove the old gasket from the rocker cover. Clean the surface of the cylinder head and the rocker cover.

To install:

7. Spread a thin layer of Permatex® or equivalent adhesive on the mating surface of the rocker cover to hold the gasket in place during installation. Install a new gasket, and press lightly to seat.

8. Position the rocker cover on the cylinder head and install the retainer bolts. Tighten the bolts to 5-6 ft. lbs. (6-8 Nm) for 1.2L engines, 3-4 ft. lbs. (4-5 Nm) for 1.6L, 1.8L, 2.7L and 3.3L engines, or 4 ft. lbs. (5 Nm) for 2.2L and 2.5L engines.

9. Attach the breather hose to the valve cover, if removed.

10. Connect the negative battery cable.

Rocker Shafts

REMOVAL & INSTALLATION

➡The OHC engines DO NOT use a rocker arm shaft. The valve rocker simply floats between the valve stem and the hydraulic lifter, and the center of the valve rocker rides against the camshaft.

1.2L Engine

▶ See Figure 16

1. Disconnect the negative battery cable.
2. Disconnect the PCV hose from the rocker arm cover.

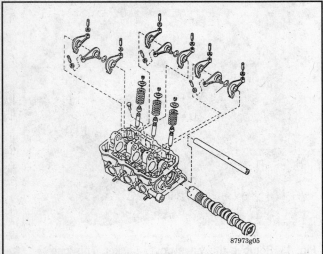

87973g05

Fig. 16 Cylinder head and rocker assembly — 1.2L engine

3. Remove the rocker arm cover mounting bolts and lift off the rocker arm cover.

4. Remove the rocker shaft mounting bolt.

5. Before removing the shaft, note the positions of the rocker arms and spring washers.

6. Remove the rocker arm shaft slowly. Remove each component as it clears the shaft. Line the parts up in order as they are removed.

To install:

➡Coat each component with clean engine oil as it is installed.

7. Install the individual components one at a time while slowly sliding the rocker arm shaft into the shaft carrier. Make sure the hole in the rocker shaft is lined up with the bolt hole in the center of the carrier.

8. Install the rocker shaft bolt. Tighten the bolt to 8-11 ft. lbs. (10-14 Nm).

9. Adjust the valve lash. Refer to the procedure in Section 1.

10. Install the rocker arm cover and connect the PCV hose.

11. Connect the negative battery cable.

12. Start the engine and listen for any rocker noise or leaking.

1.6L, 1.8L and 2.7L Engines

These engines are not equipped with rocker shaft assemblies. Instead, the rocker arm is driven directly by the camshaft.

Refer to the Camshaft removal and installation procedure in this section for details.

2.2L Engine

▶ See Figures 17, 18, 19 and 20

1. Disconnect the PCV hose and remove the rocker cover.
2. Remove the valve rocker assembly by removing bolts 2 through 4 in numerical sequence.
3. Loosen bolt 1, but leave it engaged to retain the valve rocker assembly.
4. Remove bolts 5 through 8, taking care not to gouge the dowel pin.
5. Remove the valve rocker assembly.
6. Place the valve rocker assembly with the air vent on the rocker arm facing upward into clean engine oil until ready to install. This is done to prevent damaging the hydraulic lash adjuster.

To install:

7. Install the valve rocker assembly on the cylinder head.
8. Temporarily tighten bolts 1 through 4 equally.

➡Do not allow the valve rocker assembly to gouge the dowel pins.

9. Tighten bolts 5 through 8 to 9 ft. lbs. (12 Nm).
10. Tighten bolts 1 through 4 to 9 ft. lbs. (12 Nm).
11. Install the rocker cover and connect the PCV hose.

2.5L and 3.3L Engines

These engines are not equipped with either rocker shafts or rocker arms. Instead, the camshaft drives the opening and closing of the individual valves.

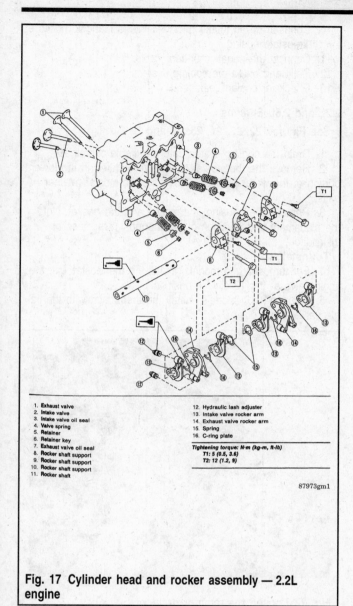

1. Exhaust valve
2. Intake valve
3. Intake valve oil seal
4. Valve spring
5. Retainer
6. Retainer key
7. Exhaust valve oil seal
8. Rocker shaft support
9. Rocker shaft support
10. Rocker shaft support
11. Rocker shaft

12. Hydraulic lash adjuster
13. Intake valve rocker arm
14. Exhaust valve rocker arm
15. Spring
16. C-ring plate

Tightening torque: N·m (kg-m, ft-lb)
T1: 5 (0.5, 3.6)
T2: 12 (1.2, 9)

87973gm1

Fig. 17 Cylinder head and rocker assembly — 2.2L engine

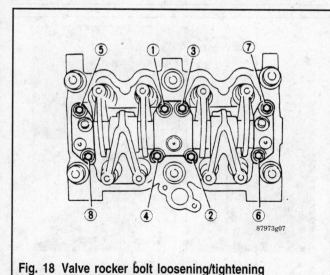

87973g07

Fig. 18 Valve rocker bolt loosening/tightening sequence — 2.2L engine

87973p05

Fig. 19 Loosen and remove the bolts in numerical order

87973p06

Fig. 20 Remove the rocker shaft and components from the engine as an assembly

Thermostat

REMOVAL & INSTALLATION

▶ See Figure 21

❋❋CAUTION

When draining the coolant, keep in mind that cats and dogs are attracted to ethylene glycol antifreeze, and could drink any that is left in an uncovered container or in puddles on the ground. This will prove fatal in sufficient quantity. Always drain the coolant into a sealable container. Coolant should be reused unless it is contaminated or several years old.

1.2L Engine

1. Disconnect the negative battery cable.

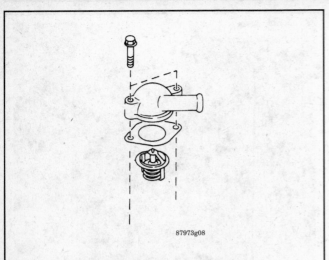

Fig. 21 An example of a Subaru thermostat and housing

2. Drain the cooling system to a level below the thermostat housing.

3. Disconnect the upper coolant hose from the thermostat housing.

4. Remove the thermostat housing retainer bolts and remove the thermostat housing. If the housing is difficult to remove, tap it lightly with a plastic-faced hammer.

5. Remove the thermostat and gasket.

➡Note the placement and direction of the old thermostat, so that the replacement unit is installed in the same way.

6. Clean all gasket material from both mating surfaces.

To install:

7. Install the thermostat into the housing using a new gasket. Install the retainer bolts. Tighten the bolts to 7-9 ft. lbs. (9-12 Nm).

8. Connect the upper radiator hose to the thermostat housing.

9. Refill the cooling system.

10. Connect the negative battery cable.

11. Start the engine and bleed the cooling system.

12. Check for coolant leaks.

1.6L, 1.8L and 2.7L Engines

1. Drain the cooling system into a suitable container to a level below the intake manifold.

2. Disconnect the negative battery cable.

3. Disconnect the air intake duct and intake manifold hoses from the thermostat housing.

4. Loosen the hose clamp, and disconnect the upper radiator hose from the thermostat housing.

5. Remove the thermostat housing mounting bolts, then remove the housing and thermostat. Note the placement and direction of the thermostat for ease of installation.

To install:

6. Clean all gasket surfaces completely.

7. Install the thermostat in the intake manifold.

8. Using a new gasket, install the thermostat housing and tighten the mounting bolts to 7 ft. lbs. (10 Nm).

9. Connect the upper radiator hose.

10. Connect the air intake duct and intake manifold hoses to the thermostat housing.

11. Connect the negative battery cable.

12. Refill and bleed the cooling system.

13. Check for coolant leaks.

2.2L and 2.5L Engines

▶ **See Figures 22, 23, 24, 25, 26 and 27**

1. Drain the cooling system into a suitable container.

2. Remove the thermostat case cover located in the lower portion of the water pump. Remove the thermostat retainer bolts.

3. Remove the housing, thermostat and the gasket. Note the placement and direction of the thermostat for ease of installation.

To install:

4. For turbocharged models, install the thermostat with the jiggle valve at the 12 o'clock position.

5. For non-turbo models, install the thermostat with the jiggle valve facing down.

Fig. 22 Loosen the radiator draincock . . .

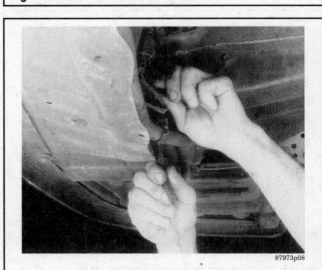

Fig. 23 . . . and drain the coolant into a suitable container

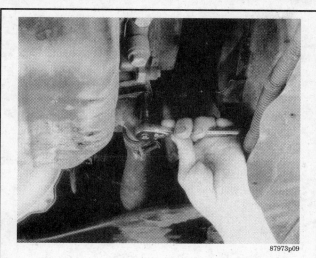

Fig. 24 Loosen and remove the thermostat housing retainer bolts

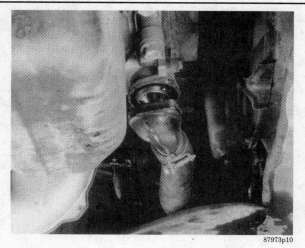

Fig. 25 Detach the housing to reveal the thermostat and gasket

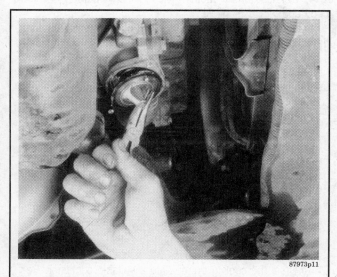

Fig. 26 Remove the thermostat and gasket assembly

Fig. 27 Loosen the bleeder screw on top of the radiator to bleed air from the cooling system

6. Install the housing with a new gasket, and tighten the bolts to 52-61 inch lbs. (6-7 Nm).
7. Fill and bleed the cooling system.
8. Check the system for coolant leaks.

3.3L Engine

1. Disconnect the negative battery cable.
2. Drain the cooling system into a suitable container.
3. Disconnect the radiator hose from the thermostat housing.
4. Remove the thermostat housing mounting bolts.
5. Remove the thermostat housing, thermostat and gasket.
To install:
6. Install the thermostat and housing with a new gasket. Tighten the mounting bolts to 60 inch lbs. (7 Nm).
7. Connect the upper radiator hose.
8. Refill the cooling system.
9. Connect the negative battery cable.
10. Start the vehicle and bleed the system.
11. Check for coolant leaks.

Intake Manifold

REMOVAL & INSTALLATION

❋❋CAUTION

When draining the coolant, keep in mind that cats and dogs are attracted to ethylene glycol antifreeze, and could drink any that is left in an uncovered container or in puddles on the ground. This will prove fatal in sufficient quantity. Always drain the coolant into a sealable container. Coolant should be reused unless it is contaminated or several years old.

1.2L Engine

▶ See Figures 28 and 29

1. Disconnect the negative battery cable.

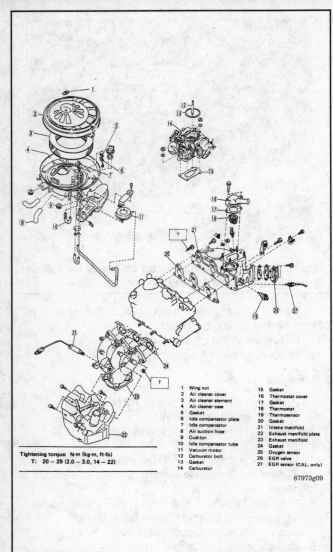

1	Wing nut	15	Gasket
2	Air cleaner cover	16	Thermostat cover
3	Air cleaner element	17	Gasket
4	Air cleaner case	18	Thermostat
5	Gasket	19	Thermosensor
6	Idle compensator plate	20	Gasket
7	Idle compensator	21	Intake manifold
8	Air suction hose	22	Exhaust manifold plate
9	Cushion	23	Exhaust manifold
10	Idle compensator tube	24	Gasket
11	Vacuum motor	25	Oxygen sensor
12	Carburetor bolt	26	EGR valve
13	Gasket	27	EGR sensor (CAL. only)
14	Carburetor		

Tightening torque: N-m (kg-m, ft-lb)
  T: 20 − 29 (2.0 − 3.0, 14 − 22)

87973g09

Fig. 28 Intake and exhaust manifold assembly — 1.2L carbureted engine

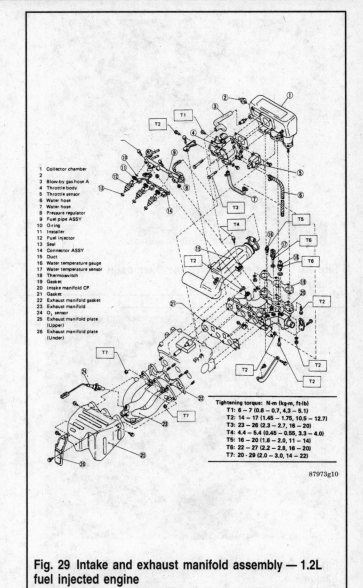

1	Collector chamber
3	Blow-by gas hose A
4	Throttle body
5	Throttle sensor
6	Water hose
7	Water hose
8	Pressure regulator
9	Fuel pipe ASSY
10	O-ring
11	Installer
12	Fuel injector
13	Seal
14	Connector ASSY
15	Duct
16	Water temperature gauge
17	Water temperature sensor
18	Thermoswitch
19	Gasket
20	Intake manifold CP
21	Gasket
22	Exhaust manifold gasket
23	Exhaust manifold
24	O₂ sensor
25	Exhaust manifold plate (Upper)
26	Exhaust manifold plate (Under)

Tightening torque: N-m (kg-m, ft-lb)
T1: 6 − 7 (0.6 − 0.7, 4.3 − 5.1)
T2: 14 − 17 (1.45 − 1.75, 10.5 − 12.7)
T3: 23 − 26 (2.3 − 2.7, 16 − 20)
T4: 4.4 − 5.4 (0.45 − 0.55, 3.3 − 4.0)
T5: 16 − 20 (1.6 − 2.0, 11 − 14)
T6: 22 − 27 (2.2 − 2.8, 16 − 20)
T7: 20 - 29 (2.0 − 3.0, 14 − 22)

87973g10

Fig. 29 Intake and exhaust manifold assembly — 1.2L fuel injected engine

2. Drain the cooling system into a suitable container.

3. Remove the air cleaner assembly.

4. Tag and disconnect the upper radiator hose and heater hose from the intake manifold.

5. Disconnect the electrical harnesses and ground straps from the intake manifold.

6. Disconnect the accelerator linkage from the carburetor or throttle body assembly.

7. Tag and disconnect all the vacuum lines from the intake manifold, carburetor or throttle body.

8. Remove the air suction manifold pipe.

9. Remove the intake manifold mounting bolts.

10. Remove the intake manifold assembly.

11. Remove all gasket material from both mating surfaces.

To install:

12. Position the intake manifold on the engine using a new gasket, and loosely install the intake manifold bolts. With all the bolts installed, tighten them (starting from the center and moving outward) to 14-22 ft. lbs. (20-29 Nm).

13. Install the air suction manifold pipe.

14. Connect all the vacuum lines to the carburetor or throttle body and intake manifold.

15. Connect the accelerator cable to the carburetor or throttle body.

16. Connect the electrical harnesses to the intake manifold.

17. Connect the upper radiator and heater hose to the intake manifold.

18. Install the air cleaner assembly.

19. Refill the cooling system.

20. Connect the negative battery cable.

21. Start the vehicle and check for any sucking noise indicating a leak.

1.6L and 1.8L Engines

▶ **See Figures 30, 31 and 32**

1. Relieve the fuel system pressure.

2. Disconnect the negative battery cable.

3. Disconnect the fuel lines.

4. Drain the cooling system into a suitable container. Remove the radiator hoses.

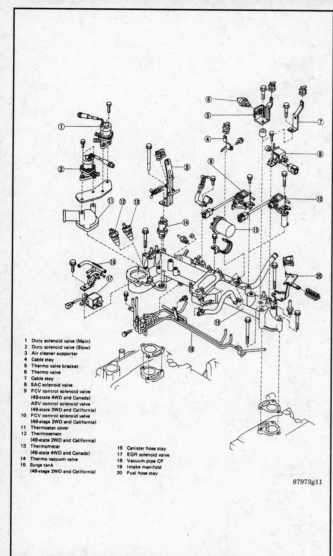

Fig. 30 Intake manifold assembly — 1.6L and 1.8L carburetor engine

1 Duty solenoid valve (Main)
2 Duty solenoid valve (Slow)
3 Air cleaner supporter
4 Cable stay
5 Thermo valve bracket
6 Thermo valve
7 Cable stay
8 SAC solenoid valve
9 FCV control solenoid valve (49-state 4WD and Canada) ASV control solenoid valve (49-state 2WD and California)
10 FCV control solenoid valve (49-stage 2WD and California)
11 Thermostat cover
12 Thermosensor (49-state 2WD and California)
13 Thermometer (49-state 4WD and Canada)
14 Thermo vacuum valve
15 Surge tank (49-stage 2WD and California)
16 Canister hose stay
17 EGR solenoid valve
18 Vacuum pipe CP
19 Intake manifold
20 Fuel hose stay

87973g11

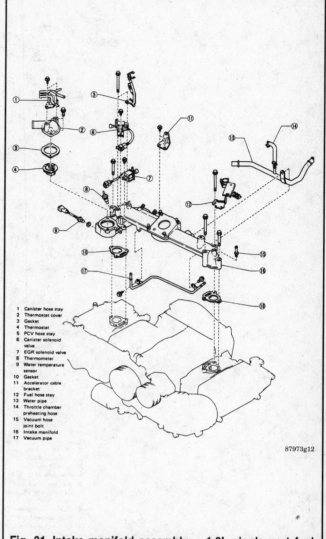

Fig. 31 Intake manifold assembly — 1.8L single port fuel injected engine

1 Canister hose stay
2 Thermostat cover
3 Gasket
4 Thermostat
5 PCV hose stay
6 Canister solenoid valve
7 EGR solenoid valve
8 Thermometer
9 Water temperature sensor
10 Gasket
11 Accelerator cable bracket
12 Fuel hose stay
13 Water pipe
14 Throttle chamber preheating hose
15 Vacuum hose joint bolt
16 Intake manifold
17 Vacuum pipe

87973g12

5. On turbocharged models, remove the air duct with the airflow meter attached. On all other models, remove the air duct.

6. On turbocharged models, remove the turbo cooling hose and turbocharger.

7. Remove the front exhaust pipe from the cylinder head as required.

8. Tag and disconnect the distributor high tension wires, then matchmark and remove the distributor.

9. Label and disconnect all applicable vacuum hoses.

10. Remove the alternator, if needed for additional working space.

11. Remove the silencers and silencer hoses. Remove the air cleaner assembly.

12. Remove the air suction valves and hoses.

13. Remove the EGR cover and EGR pipe.

14. Remove the PCV valve and blow-by hoses.

15. Label and disconnect all applicable electrical harnesses.

16. Disconnect the accelerator cable.

17. Remove the intake manifold bolts and carefully lift the intake manifold off the engine.

18. Clean all gasket material from the mating surfaces.

To install:

19. Use a straightedge feeler gauge to inspect the intake manifold for flatness. Distortion should not exceed 0.020 in. (0.5mm).

20. Install the intake manifold using new gaskets, and secure in place with the mounting bolts. Tighten the bolts to 13-16 ft. lbs. (18-22 Nm).

21. Inspect all electrical connectors for damage and replace as necessary. Attach all electrical connectors.

22. Install the PCV valve and hoses. Install the EGR cover and pipe, and tighten bolts to 23-27 ft. lbs. (31-37 Nm). Install the air suction valve and hoses.

23. Install the silencers and hoses. Install the alternator if removed.

24. Inspect all vacuum lines for damage and replace as necessary. Install all vacuum lines.

25. On turbocharged models, install the turbo cooling hose and turbocharger. Install the front exhaust pipe from the cylinder head if removed.

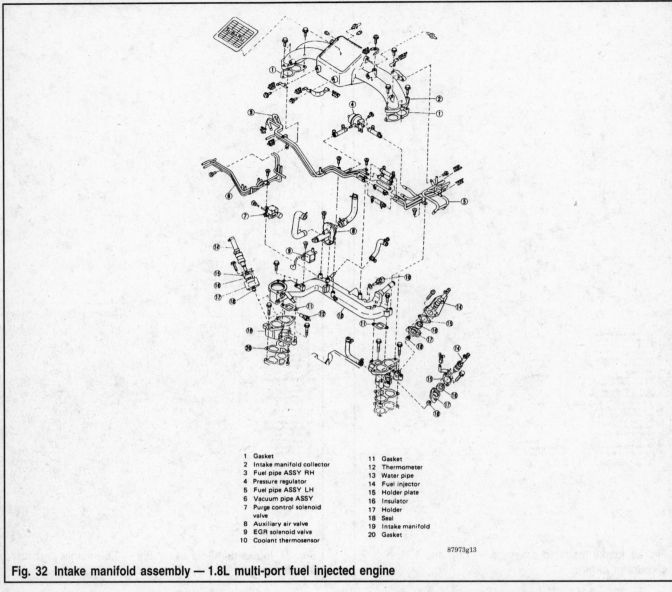

1	Gasket	11	Gasket
2	Intake manifold collector	12	Thermometer
3	Fuel pipe ASSY RH	13	Water pipe
4	Pressure regulator	14	Fuel injector
5	Fuel pipe ASSY LH	15	Holder plate
6	Vacuum pipe ASSY	16	Insulator
7	Purge control solenoid valve	17	Holder
8	Auxiliary air valve	18	Seal
9	EGR solenoid valve	19	Intake manifold
10	Coolant thermosensor	20	Gasket

87973g13

Fig. 32 Intake manifold assembly — 1.8L multi-port fuel injected engine

26. On turbocharged models, install the air duct with the airflow meter. On all other models, install the air duct.

27. Install the distributor, if removed. Connect all distributor high tension wires.

28. Install the radiator hose and fill the cooling system.

29. Connect all fuel lines and install the air cleaner assembly.

30. Connect the negative battery cable, start the engine and allow it to reach operating temperature. Check for leaks. Test drive the vehicle.

2.2L Engines

▶ **See Figures 33, 34, 35 and 36**

1. Release the fuel system pressure.
2. Disconnect the negative battery cable and remove the engine cover.
3. Drain the cooling system into a suitable container.
4. Remove the accessary drive belt(s).
5. Remove power steering pump and or, alternator for added clearance.
6. Label and disconnect all electrical harnesses leading to the intake manifold.
7. Label and disconnect all vacuum hoses leading to the intake manifold. Disconnect the PCV and blow-by hoses.
8. Label and disconnect the ignition high tension wires at the spark plugs and lay them aside.
9. Remove the connector bracket attaching bolt.
10. Remove the crank angle sensor and cam angle sensor.
11. Disconnect the oil pressure switch connector.
12. Remove the knock sensor.
13. Disconnect the air intake duct.

Fig. 34 Loosen and remove the intake manifold retainer bolts — 2.2L engine shown

Fig. 35 Carefully lift off the intake manifold assembly

Fig. 36 Remove and discard the intake manifold gaskets

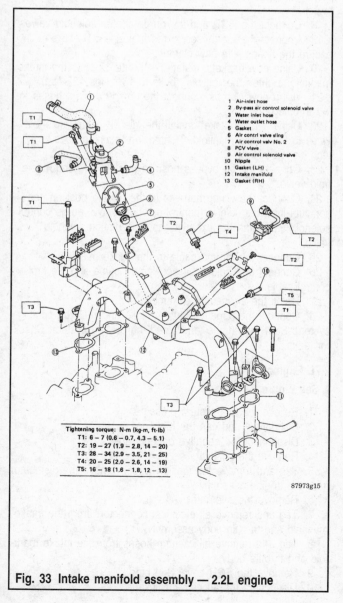

1 Air-inlet hose
2 By-pass air control solenoid valve
3 Water inlet hose
4 Water outlet hose
5 Gasket
6 Air contrl valve sling
7 Air control valv No. 2
8 PCV vlave
9 Air control solenoid valve
10 Nipple
11 Gasket (LH)
12 Intake manifold
13 Gasket (RH)

Tightening torque: N·m (kg-m, ft-lb)
T1: 6 – 7 (0.6 – 0.7, 4.3 – 5.1)
T2: 19 – 27 (1.9 – 2.8, 14 – 20)
T3: 28 – 34 (2.9 – 3.5, 21 – 25)
T4: 20 – 25 (2.0 – 2.6, 14 – 19)
T5: 16 – 18 (1.6 – 1.8, 12 – 13)

Fig. 33 Intake manifold assembly — 2.2L engine

14. On turbocharged models, disconnect the turbo from the intake manifold and remove.

15. Disconnect the fuel supply lines and accelerator linkage.

16. Remove the intake manifold bolts and remove the intake manifold and discard the gaskets.

17. Remove the water pipe.

18. Clean all gasket material from both mating surfaces.

To install:

19. Use a straightedge and a feeler gauge to inspect the intake manifold for flatness. Distortion should not exceed 0.020 in. (0.5mm).

20. Install the intake manifold and secure in place with retainer bolts. Tighten the short bolts to 21-25 ft. lbs. (28-34 Nm); the long bolts to 4-5 ft. lbs. (6-7 Nm).

21. Install the fuel lines and accelerator linkage.

22. Install the turbocharger assembly, if equipped.

23. Install the air intake duct.

24. Install the knock sensor.

25. Connect the oil pressure switch electrical connector.

26. Clean the crank and cam angle sensors with compressed air and install them.

27. Install the connector bracket bolt.

28. Check the ignition high tension wires for damage and install on the spark plugs.

29. Check all vacuum lines for deterioration and replace as necessary. Install the vacuum lines.

30. Check all electrical connectors for damage and replace as necessary. Install the electrical connectors.

31. Install the PCV valve and blow-by hose.

32. Install the power steering pump and alternator if removed.

33. Install the water pipes and fill the cooling system.

34. Install the engine cover.

35. Start the engine and allow it to reach operating temperature. Check for leaks and test drive the vehicle.

2.5L Engine

✲✲CAUTION

Fuel injection systems remain under pressure after the engine has been turned OFF. Properly relieve fuel pressure before disconnecting any fuel lines. Failure to do so may result in fire or personal injury.

1. Disconnect the negative battery cable.

2. Drain the cooling system into a suitable container.

3. Remove the air intake duct, air cleaner upper cover and the air cleaner element.

4. Properly release the fuel pressure.

5. Disconnect the accelerator cable and the cruise control cable, if equipped.

6. Disconnect the ground cable from the intake manifold.

7. Disconnect the wiring harness from the throttle position sensor, fuel injectors, idle air control solenoid valve, purge control solenoid valve, and the exhaust gas recirculation solenoid valve.

8. Disconnect the air bypass hose from the idle air control solenoid valve.

9. Remove the idle air control solenoid valve from the intake manifold.

10. Disconnect the engine coolant hoses from the throttle body.

11. Remove the throttle body from the intake manifold and discard the gasket.

12. Disconnect the fuel hoses from the fuel pipes.

13. Disconnect the EGR and the purge control solenoid valves.

14. Disconnect the wiring harness from the knock sensor, camshaft position sensor, crankshaft position sensor and the oil pressure switch.

15. Remove the intake manifold mounting bolts. Remove the manifold and discard the gaskets.

➡**The intake manifold sits on pins that protrude from the cylinder heads. Be sure the pins remain in the cylinder heads.**

To install:

16. Using new gaskets, install the manifold to the engine. Tighten the mounting bolts to 19 ft. lbs. (26 Nm).

17. Connect the wiring to the knock sensor, camshaft position sensor, crankshaft position sensor and the oil pressure switch.

18. Connect the EGR and the purge control solenoid valves.

19. Connect the fuel hoses to the fuel pipes. Be sure to secure the hoses with new clamps.

20. Using new gaskets, install the throttle body to the intake manifold. Tighten the retaining bolts to 16 ft. lbs. (22 Nm).

21. Using new clamps, connect the engine coolant hoses to the throttle body.

22. Using a new gasket, install the idle air control solenoid valve to the intake manifold. Tighten the retaining bolts to 57 inch lbs. (6.4 Nm).

23. Connect the air bypass hose to the idle air control solenoid valve.

24. Connect the wiring harness to the throttle position sensor, fuel injectors, idle air control solenoid valve, purge control solenoid valve and the exhaust gas recirculation solenoid valve.

25. Connect the ground cable to the intake manifold.

26. Connect and adjust the accelerator cable and the cruise control cable.

27. Install the air cleaner assembly.

28. Connect the negative battery cable and refill the cooling system. Start the engine, and bleed the cooling system. Check for leaks.

2.7L Engine

▶ **See Figure 37**

1. Relieve the fuel system pressure.

2. Disconnect and cap the fuel lines.

3. Disconnect the negative battery cable.

4. Remove the air duct.

5. Tag and remove the ignition wires. remove the distributor from the engine assembly.

6. Remove the alternator.

7. Tag and remove all electrical connectors from the intake manifold and throttle body assembly.

8. Tag and remove all vacuum hoses from the intake manifold and throttle body.

9. Remove the EGR cover and pipe.

10. Disconnect the accelerator linkage.

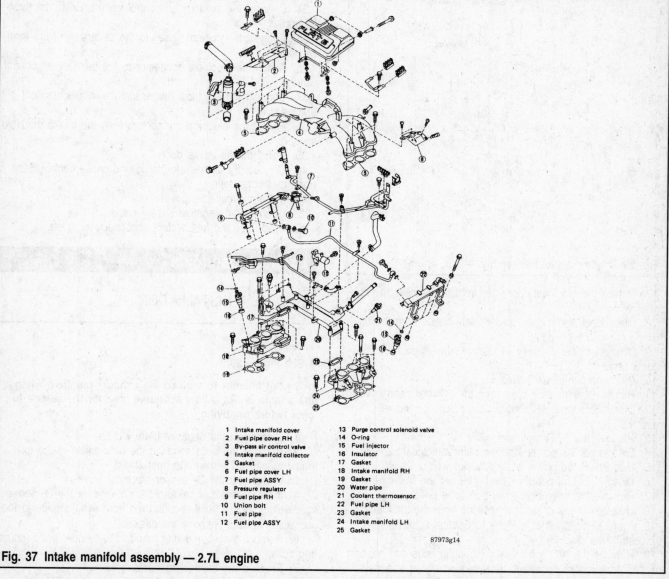

1	Intake manifold cover	13	Purge control solenoid valve
2	Fuel pipe cover RH	14	O-ring
3	By-pass air control valve	15	Fuel injector
4	Intake manifold collector	16	Insulator
5	Gasket	17	Gasket
6	Fuel pipe cover LH	18	Intake manifold RH
7	Fuel pipe ASSY	19	Gasket
8	Pressure regulator	20	Water pipe
9	Fuel pipe RH	21	Coolant thermosensor
10	Union bolt	22	Fuel pipe LH
11	Fuel pipe	23	Gasket
12	Fuel pipe ASSY	24	Intake manifold LH
		25	Gasket

87973g14

Fig. 37 Intake manifold assembly — 2.7L engine

11. Remove the intake manifold mounting bolts, then remove the intake manifold and gaskets.
To install:
12. Clean the gasket mating surfaces thoroughly.
13. Using a straightedge and a feeler gauge, inspect the intake manifold for flatness. Distortion should not exceed 0.020 in. (0.5mm).
14. Install the intake manifold using new gaskets and tighten the mounting bolts to 15 ft. lbs. (20 Nm).
15. Connect the fuel lines.
16. Install the EGR pipe and tighten to 25 ft. lbs. (34 Nm). Install the EGR cover.
17. Connect the vacuum lines to the intake manifold and throttle body.
18. Connect the electrical connectors to the intake manifold and throttle body.
19. Install the alternator.
20. Install the distributor and connect the ignition wires.
21. Install the air duct.
22. Connect the negative battery cable.

23. Start the engine and allow it to reach operating temperature. Check for leaks and test drive the vehicle.

3.3L Engine
▶ See Figure 38

✻✻CAUTION

Fuel injection systems remain under pressure after the engine has been turned OFF. Properly relieve fuel pressure before disconnecting any fuel lines. Failure to do so may result in fire or personal injury.

1. Relieve the fuel system pressure.
2. Disconnect the negative battery cable.
3. Remove the collector cover.
4. Disconnect the accelerator cable and cruise control cable from the throttle lever, if equipped.
5. Remove the air intake ducts.
6. Disconnect the electrical harnesses from the intake manifold sensors and brackets.

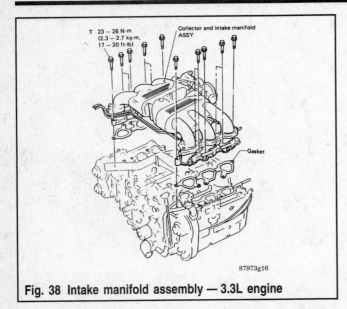

T 23 – 26 N·m
(2.3 – 2.7 kg-m,
17 – 20 ft·lb)

Collector and intake manifold
ASSY

Gasket

87973g16

Fig. 38 Intake manifold assembly — 3.3L engine

7. Detach the electrical connector from the auxiliary air control valve.

8. Disconnect and cap the two coolant hoses from the underside of the throttle body.

9. Disconnect the auxiliary air control valve hose from the throttle body.

10. Disconnect the PCV hose.

11. Remove the blow-by hose from the cylinder head cover.

12. Disconnect the EGR control hoses from the intake manifold.

13. Remove the EGR pipe and cover.

14. Disconnect the power steering pump electrical harness

15. Disconnect the power brake booster vacuum hose.

16. Disconnect and cap the fuel lines from the fuel pipes.

17. Remove the drive belt cover and drive belts.

18. Unfasten the electrical connections from the alternator.

19. Remove the alternator. Refer to Section 2 for removal and installation steps.

20. Remove the A/C compressor mounting bolts and position the A/C compressor aside with the refrigerant lines attached.

21. Remove the intake manifold mounting bolts.

22. Remove the intake manifold.

23. Clean all gasket material from both mating surfaces.

To install:

24. Install the intake manifold using new gaskets. Tighten the intake manifold bolts to 18 ft. lbs. (24 Nm).

25. Install the A/C compressor.

26. Install the alternator and connect the electrical harnesses.

27. Install the drive belts and tension as necessary. Install the drive belt cover.

28. Connect the fuel lines to the fuel pipes.

29. Connect the vacuum line to the power booster.

30. Connect the electrical harnesses to the power steering pump.

31. Install the EGR pipe and cover and connect the EGR control hoses to the intake manifold.

32. Install the blow by hose to the cylinder head cover.

33. Connect the PCV hose.

34. Connect the auxiliary air control valve hose to the throttle body.

35. Connect the coolant hoses to the underside of the throttle body.

36. Attach the electrical connector to the auxiliary air control valve.

37. Connect the electrical harness to the intake manifold bracket.

38. Fasten the electrical connectors from the intake manifold sensors.

39. Install the air intake ducts.

40. Connect the accelerator cable and cruise control cable from the throttle lever.

41. Install the collector cover.

42. Connect the negative battery cable.

43. Pressurize the fuel system and check for leaks.

Exhaust Manifolds

REMOVAL & INSTALLATION

1.2L Engine

▶ **See Figure 39**

➡ **Do not attempt to remove the exhaust manifold when the engine is hot. Allow adequate time for the engine to cool before removing.**

1. Disconnect the negative battery cable.

2. Remove the bolts securing the heat shield to the exhaust manifold. Remove the heat shield.

3. Disconnect the O_2 sensor electrical harness.

4. If the manifold is being replaced, remove the O_2 sensor.

5. Remove the bolts securing the front exhaust pipe to the exhaust manifold. Remove the gasket.

6. Remove the six exhaust manifold-to-cylinder head mounting bolts.

7. Remove the exhaust manifold.

8. Clean all gasket material from both mating surfaces.

To install:

9. Install the exhaust manifold using new gaskets.

10. Install the manifold nuts and tighten to 14-22 ft. lbs. (20-29 Nm). Start tightening in the middle of the manifold and work toward the ends.

11. Using a new gasket connect the front exhaust pipe to the manifold. Install the bolts and tighten to 17-31 ft. lbs. (23-42 Nm).

12. Install the O_2 sensor, if removed, and connect the electrical harness.

➡ **When installing the O_2 sensor, make sure the threads are coated with anti-seize compound before installing.**

13. Install the heat shield and install the mounting bolts. Tighten the bolts to 10-18 ft. lbs. (13-23 Nm).

14. Connect the negative battery cable.

15. Start the engine and check for exhaust leaks.

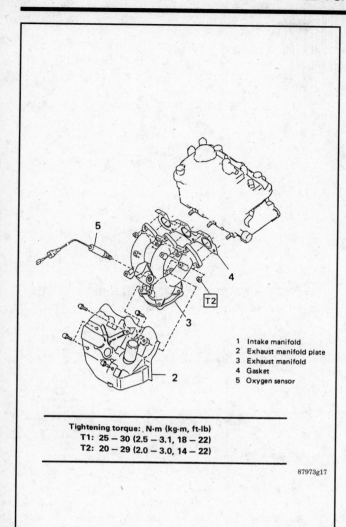

1 Intake manifold
2 Exhaust manifold plate
3 Exhaust manifold
4 Gasket
5 Oxygen sensor

Tightening torque: N·m (kg-m, ft-lb)
T1: 25 — 30 (2.5 — 3.1, 18 — 22)
T2: 20 — 29 (2.0 — 3.0, 14 — 22)

87973g17

Fig. 39 Exhaust manifold assembly — 1.2L engine

1.6L, 1.8L, 2.2L, 2.5L and 2.7L Engines

▶ See Figure 40

✳✳CAUTION

The exhaust pipe may be hot; DO NOT perform any work until the system has completely cooled.

1. Disconnect the negative battery cable.
2. Disconnect the O_2 sensor electrical connector.
3. Remove the front under cover.
4. Remove the bolts securing the exhaust manifold covers and remove the covers.
5. Remove the front pipe-to-center pipe mounting nuts.
6. Remove the nuts that secure the exhaust pipe to the cylinder head and remove the exhaust pipe.
7. Discard the gaskets.
To install:
8. Clean all gasket surfaces completely.

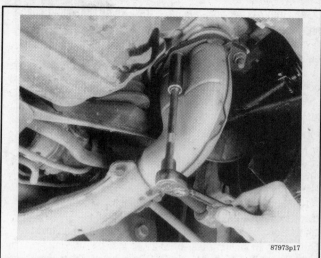

87973p17

Fig. 40 Loosen and remove the exhaust manifold the exhaust-to-exhaust retainer nuts — 2.2L engine shown

9. Install the exhaust pipe to the cylinder head using new gaskets. Tighten the mounting nuts as follows:
    a. Turbocharged engines — 28-33 ft. lbs. (34-44 Nm).
    b. Non-turbocharged engines — 22-30 ft. lbs. (30-40 Nm).
10. Using new gaskets, connect the exhaust pipe to the center pipe. Tighten the mounting nuts as follows:
    a. Turbocharged engines — 19-26 ft. lbs. (25-35 Nm).
    b. Non-turbocharged engines — 9-17 ft. lbs. (13-23 Nm).
11. Install the exhaust manifold covers and cover mounting bolts.
12. Connect the O_2 sensor electrical connector.
13. Install the front under cover.
14. Lower the vehicle.
15. Connect the negative battery cable.
16. Start the engine and check for exhaust leaks.

3.3L Engine

▶ See Figure 41

1. Disconnect the negative battery cable.
2. Disconnect the O_2 sensor electrical harness.
3. Remove the front undercover, if equipped.

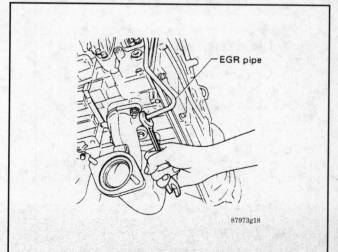

87973g18

Fig. 41 Loosen the EGR pipe attached to the exhaust manifold — 3.3L engine

4. Remove the bolts securing the exhaust manifold covers and remove.

5. Remove the front pipe-to-exhaust manifold mounting nuts.

6. Disconnect the EGR pipe from the exhaust manifold, only if the right side manifold is being removed.

7. Remove the exhaust manifold mounting nuts, then remove the exhaust manifold.

8. Clean all gasket material from both mating surfaces.

To install:

9. Install the exhaust manifold using new gaskets. Install the mounting nuts and tighten the nuts to 25-33 ft. lbs. (32-43 Nm).

10. Connect the EGR pipe to the right manifold, if disconnected.

11. Connect the exhaust pipe to the exhaust manifold and tighten the mounting nuts to 22-29 ft. lbs. (29-38 Nm).

12. Install the exhaust manifold covers and cover mounting bolts. Tighten the bolts to 13-15 ft. lbs. (17-19 Nm).

13. Install the front under cover.

14. Connect the O_2 sensor electrical harness.

15. Lower the vehicle.

16. Connect the negative battery cable.

Turbocharger

REMOVAL & INSTALLATION

1.8L Engine

▶ See Figure 42

❋❋WARNING

Do not allow dirt to enter either the inlet or outlet openings of the turbocharger, or the unit may be damaged at start-up.

1. Loosen the clamps and remove the air intake duct from the airflow meter (throttle body) and the turbocharger assembly.

2. Disconnect the vacuum lines from the waste gate valve controller.

3. Place a suitable drain pan beneath the turbo assembly. Loosen and remove the cooling and oil lines from the turbocharger.

4. Remove the mounting bolts from the turbocharger exhaust outlet. Separate the pipe from the turbocharger.

5. Remove the turbocharger.

6. Remove the sealing gaskets, and clean all gasket mating surfaces.

To install:

7. Using new gaskets, install the turbocharger on the exhaust manifold. Tighten the turbocharger mounting bolts to 18-25 ft. lbs. (25-34 Nm) alternately and evenly.

8. Install the oil and cooling lines. Tighten the oil line banjo bolt to 11-13 ft. lbs. (15-18 Nm) and the cooling line banjo bolt to 16-18 ft. lbs. (21-24 Nm).

9. Connect the vacuum line to the waste gate valve controller.

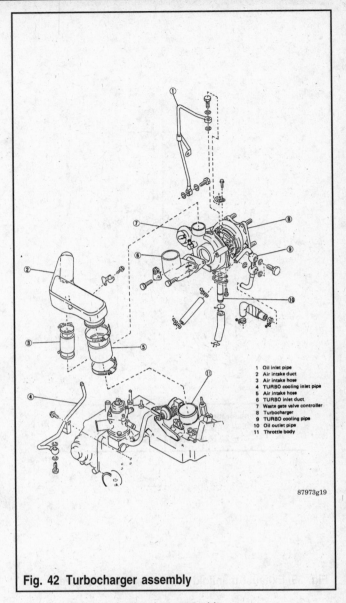

1 Oil inlet pipe
2 Air intake duct
3 Air intake hose
4 TURBO cooling inlet pipe
5 Air intake hose
6 TURBO inlet duct
7 Waste gate valve controller
8 Turbocharger
9 TURBO cooling pipe
10 Oil outlet pipe
11 Throttle body

87973g19

Fig. 42 Turbocharger assembly

10. Install the air intake duct assembly.

❋❋WARNING

Do not run the engine at a high RPM during the first few minutes of operation after servicing. This may damage the turbocharger, as the pressurized oil may not reach the turbocharger immediately.

11. Start the engine and allow it to reach operating temperature. Check for leaks. Test drive the vehicle.

2.2L Engine

▶ See Figure 42

1. Disconnect the negative battery cable.

2. Drain the cooling system into a suitable container.

3. Remove the air cleaner.

4. Disconnect the airflow meter-to-turbocharger inlet clamp, then remove the air intake duct. Cover the airflow meter and turbocharger openings.

5. Loosen the turbocharger-to-air outlet hose clamp and the throttle body inlet to air inlet hose clamp. Remove the turbo-charger-to-throttle body hose. Plug all of the openings.

6. Remove the turbocharger-to-center exhaust pipe nuts and the front exhaust pipe to turbocharger nuts.

7. Disconnect and plug the coolant lines.

8. Remove the oil feed line to turbocharger bolt and disconnect the turbocharger to oil return hose clamp and the return hose.

9. Remove the turbocharger from the exhaust manifold.

➡When removing the turbocharger from the vehicle, disconnect the oil return hose.

To install:

10. Connect the oil return hose and mount the turbocharger to the exhaust manifold using new nuts.

11. Connect the oil return and feed hose to the hose to the turbocharger with new gaskets. Tighten the bolts as follows:
- Union bolts — 17 ft. lbs. (24 Nm)
- Clamp bolt — 48 inch lbs. (5 Nm)

12. Connect the coolant lines.

13. Connect the crossover pipe to the turbocharger with a new gasket and nuts.

14. Connect the throttle body and air inlet hoses to the turbocharger.

15. Connect the airflow meter hose to the turbocharger.

16. Install the air cleaner assembly.

17. Connect the negative battery cable.

18. Fill and bleed the cooling system. Start the engine and check for leaks.

Radiator

REMOVAL & INSTALLATION

✳✳CAUTION

When draining the coolant, keep in mind that cats and dogs are attracted to ethylene glycol antifreeze, and could drink any that is left in an uncovered container or in puddles on the ground. This will prove fatal in sufficient quantity. Always drain the coolant into a sealable container. Coolant should be reused unless it is contaminated or several years old.

1.2L Engine

▶ See Figure 43

1. Disconnect the negative battery cable.
2. Drain the cooling system into a suitable container.
3. Disconnect the upper and lower hoses from the radiator.
4. Disconnect the cooling fan lead wire.
5. Disconnect the oil cooler hose from the pipe at the transaxle, if equipped.
6. Remove the radiator mounting bracket screws.
7. Remove the radiator and the oil cooler hose, if equipped, from the vehicle as a unit.
8. Inspect the rubber cushion on the base of the radiator and replace if worn or cracked.

To install:

9. Install the radiator in the vehicle, making sure the rubber cushions align correctly with the indents in the lower support of the engine compartment.

10. Install the radiator mounting brackets and screws. Tighten the screws to 24-48 inch lbs. (3-5 Nm).

11. Connect the oil cooler hose to the pipe at the transaxle, if equipped.

12. Connect the cooling fan lead wire.

13. Connect the upper and lower radiator hoses.

14. Refill the cooling system.

15. Connect the negative battery cable.

16. Start the vehicle and check for coolant leaks.

1.6L and 1.8L Engines

▶ See Figure 44

1. Drain the cooling system into a suitable container.
2. Disconnect the negative battery cable.
3. Disconnect the upper and lower hoses from the radiator.
4. On automatic transaxle models, disconnect and cap the transaxle oil cooler lines.
5. Disconnect the cooling fan motor electrical connector.
6. Disconnect the thermoswitch electrical connector.
7. Remove the two radiator mounting bolts.
8. Lift the radiator out of the radiator support.

To install:

9. Install the radiator mounting cushions onto the lower radiator pins.

10. Position the radiator in to the vehicle and install the two mounting bolts.

11. Connect the electrical connector to the thermoswitch.

12. Connect the electrical connector to the fan motor.

13. Connect the transaxle oil cooler lines to the radiator, if equipped.

14. Connect the upper and lower radiator hoses.

15. Connect the negative battery cable.

16. Fill and bleed the cooling system.

2.2L and 2.5L Engines

▶ See Figures 45, 46, 47, 48, 49, 50, 51, 52, 53 and 54

1. Disconnect and remove the battery.
2. Drain the coolant from the radiator into a suitable container.
3. Disconnect the upper and lower hoses from the radiator.
4. Remove the drive belt cover.
5. Remove the reservoir tank and overflow hose.
6. Disconnect the fan motor electrical connectors.
7. Remove the upper radiator brackets.
8. Lift the radiator slightly and slide it to the left.
9. If equipped with an automatic transaxle, disconnect the cooling lines from the radiator.
10. Lift the radiator from the engine compartment.

To install:

11. Attach the radiator mounting cushions to the pins on the lower side of the radiator.

12. Fit the pins on the lower portion of the radiator into the holes on the radiator support.

13. If equipped, connect the transaxle cooling lines to the radiator.

14. Install the radiator brackets and tighten the bolts to 9-17 ft. lbs. (12-22 Nm).

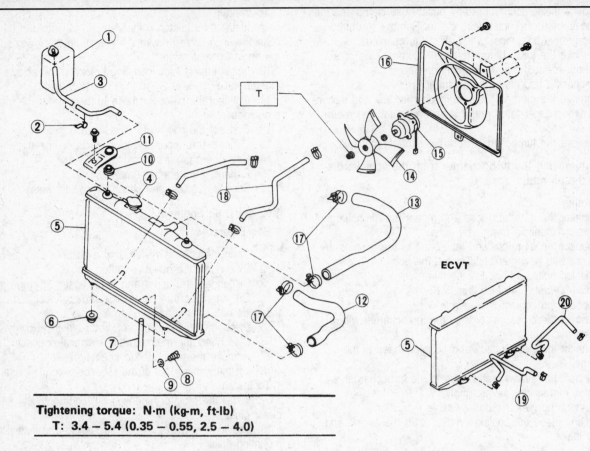

Tightening torque: N·m (kg-m, ft-lb)
T: 3.4 — 5.4 (0.35 — 0.55, 2.5 — 4.0)

1	Reserve tank	8	Drain plug	15	Motor
2	Clamp	9	O-ring	16	Shroud
3	Overflow hose	10	Cushion upper	17	Hose clamp
4	Radiator cap	11	Bracket	18	Oil cooler hose
5	Radiator	12	Radiator outlet hose	19	Oil cooler inlet hose (ECVT)
6	Cushion lower	13	Radiator inlet hose	20	Oil cooler outlet hose (ECVT)
7	Drain hose	14	Fan		

87973g20

Fig. 43 Radiator and cooling fan assembly — 1.2L engine

15. Connect the fan motor electrical connectors.
16. Connect the inlet and outlet hoses to the radiator.
17. Install the reservoir tank and overflow hose.
18. Install the drive belt cover.
19. Fill and bleed the cooling system.
20. Install the battery.

2.7L Engine
▶ **See Figure 55**

1. Drain the cooling system into a suitable container.
2. Disconnect the negative battery cable.
3. Disconnect the upper and lower hoses from the radiator.
4. On automatic transaxle models, disconnect and cap the transaxle oil cooler lines.
5. Disconnect the cooling fan motor electrical connector.
6. Disconnect the thermoswitch electrical connector.
7. Remove the two radiator mounting bolts.
8. Lift the radiator out of the radiator support.
To install:
9. Install the radiator mounting cushions onto the lower radiator pins.

10. Position the radiator in to the vehicle and install the two mounting bolts. Tighten the bolts to 9-17 ft. lbs. (12-22 Nm)
11. Fasten the electrical connector to the thermoswitch.
12. Fasten the electrical connector to the fan motor.
13. If equipped, connect the transaxle oil cooler lines to the radiator.
14. Connect the upper and lower radiator hoses.
15. Connect the negative battery cable.
16. Fill and bleed the cooling system.
17. Start the engine and check for coolant leaks.

3.3L Engine
▶ **See Figure 56**

1. Disconnect the battery cables, negative first and then the positive.
2. Remove the battery from the engine compartment.
3. Drain the cooling system into a suitable container.
4. Disconnect the outlet hose from the water pump.
5. Disconnect the transaxle cooler hose from the pipe, if equipped.
6. Disconnect the cooling fan electrical connectors.

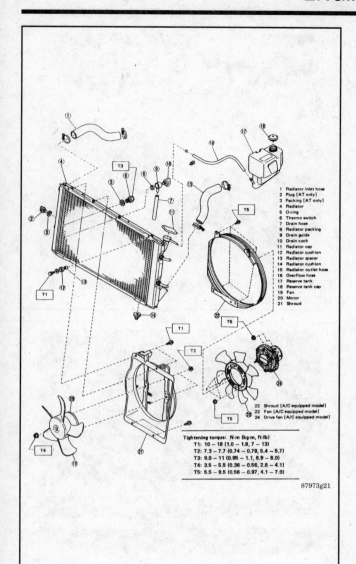

Fig. 44 Radiator and cooling fan assembly — 1.6L and 1.8L engines

Legend:
1 Radiator inlet hose
2 Plug [AT only]
3 Packing [AT only]
4 Radiator
5 O-ring
6 Thermo switch
7 Drain hose
8 Radiator packing
9 Drain guide
10 Drain cock
11 Radiator cap
12 Radiator cushion
13 Radiator spacer
14 Radiator cushion
15 Radiator outlet hose
16 Overflow hose
17 Reserve tank
18 Reserve tank cap
19 Fan
20 Motor
21 Shroud

22 Shroud [A/C equipped model]
23 Fan [A/C equipped model]
24 Drive fan [A/C equipped model]

Tightening torque: N·m (kg-m, ft-lb)
T1: 10 – 18 (1.0 – 1.8, 7 – 13)
T2: 7.3 – 7.7 (0.74 – 0.79, 5.4 – 5.7)
T3: 9.0 – 11 (0.95 – 1.1, 6.9 – 8.0)
T4: 3.5 – 5.5 (0.36 – 0.56, 2.6 – 4.1)
T5: 5.5 – 9.5 (0.56 – 0.97, 4.1 – 7.0)

87973g21

Fig. 45 Loosen and remove the drive belt cover — 2.2L model shown

87973p18

Fig. 46 Remove the radiator retainer bracket bolts . . .

87973p19

Fig. 47 . . . and brackets from the radiator

87973p20

Fig. 48 Loosen the radiator hose clamps, and disconnect the hoses from the radiator assembly

87973p21

Fig. 49 Disconnect the reservoir hose connection from the radiator

Fig. 50 Unfasten the reservoir bracket's upper retainer bolt . . .

Fig. 51 . . . and the lower retainer screw . . .

Fig. 52 . . . then lift the reservoir assembly out of the engine compartment

Fig. 53 With all the installation hardware removed, carefully lift out the radiator

7. Disconnect the coolant overflow hose from the radiator.
8. Remove the drive belt cover.
9. Disconnect the inlet hose from the thermostat housing.
10. Remove the upper radiator mounting brackets.
11. Remove the radiator from the vehicle.
To install:
12. Install the radiator in the vehicle.
13. Install the upper radiator brackets.
14. Connect the inlet hose to the thermostat housing.
15. Install the belt cover.
16. Connect the coolant overflow hose to the radiator.
17. Fasten the electrical connector to the fan motor.
18. Connect the transaxle hose, if equipped.
19. Connect the outlet hose to the water pump.
20. Refill the cooling system.
21. Install the battery and connect the battery cables, positive cable followed by the negative cable.
22. Start the engine and check for leaks.

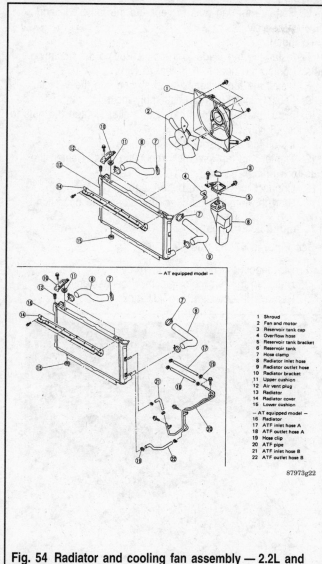

1 Shroud
2 Fan and motor
3 Reservoir tank cap
4 Overflow hose
5 Reservoir tank bracket
6 Reservoir tank
7 Hose clamp
8 Radiator inlet hose
9 Radiator outlet hose
10 Radiator bracket
11 Upper cushion
12 Air vent plug
13 Radiator
14 Radiator cover
15 Lower cushion
— AT equipped model —
16 Radiator
17 ATF inlet hose A
18 ATF outlet hose A
19 Hose clip
20 ATF pipe
21 ATF inlet hose B
22 ATF outlet hose B

87973g22

Fig. 54 Radiator and cooling fan assembly — 2.2L and 2.5L engines

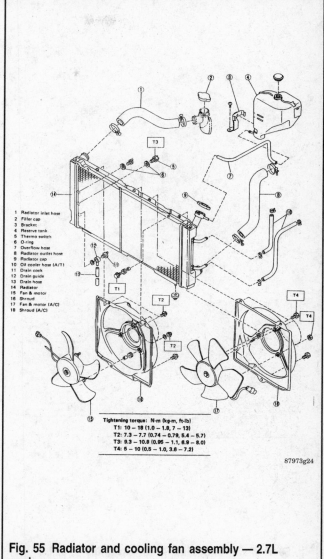

1 Radiator inlet hose
2 Filler cap
3 Bracket
4 Reserve tank
5 Thermo switch
6 O-ring
7 Overflow hose
8 Radiator outlet hose
9 Radiator cap
10 Oil cooler hose (A/T)
11 Drain cock
12 Drain guide
13 Drain hose
14 Radiator
15 Fan & motor
16 Shroud
17 Fan & motor (A/C)
18 Shroud (A/C)

Tightening torque: N·m (kg-m, ft-lb)
T1: 10 – 18 (1.0 – 1.8, 7 – 13)
T2: 7.3 – 7.7 (0.74 – 0.79, 5.4 – 5.7)
T3: 9.3 – 10.8 (0.95 – 1.1, 6.9 – 8.0)
T4: 5 – 10 (0.5 – 1.0, 3.6 – 7.2)

87973g24

Fig. 55 Radiator and cooling fan assembly — 2.7L engine

Engine Fan

REMOVAL & INSTALLATION

1.2L Engine

1. Disconnect the negative battery cable.
2. Tag and disconnect the fan motor lead wire.
3. Remove the cooling fan frame mounting bolts.
4. Remove the cooling fan assembly from the vehicle.
5. Remove the fan motor-to-frame mounting bolts.
6. Remove the fan blade assembly mounting nut, then remove the fan blade from the motor.

To install:

7. Install the fan blade to the motor and secure with the mounting nut. Tighten the mounting nut to 4 ft. lbs. (5 Nm).
8. Install the fan motor to the motor frame and secure with the mounting bolts. Tighten the bolts to 4 ft. lbs. (5 Nm).

9. Install the fan assembly to the radiator and install the 3 fan motor frame-to-radiator support. Tighten the bolts to 4 ft. lbs. (5 Nm).
10. Connect the electrical lead wire to the fan motor.
11. Connect the negative battery cable.
12. Start the engine and check for correct fan operation.

1.6L, 1.8L and 2.7L Engines

WITHOUT A/C

1. Disconnect the negative battery cable.
2. Unfasten the fan motor electrical connector at the motor assembly, then remove the harness from the bracket on the fan frame.
3. Remove the fan motor frame mounting bolts, then remove the frame assembly.
4. Remove the fan motor-to-frame mounting bolts and remove the fan motor.
5. Remove the fan blade mounting nut, then remove the blade from the fan motor.

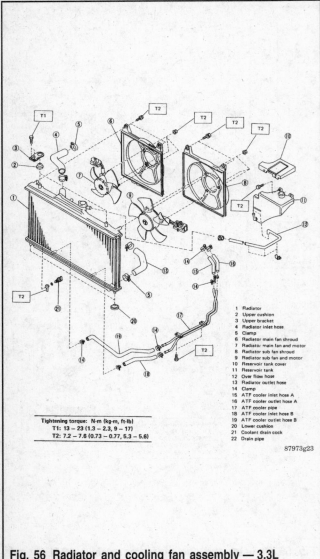

Fig. 56 Radiator and cooling fan assembly — 3.3L engine

1 Radiator
2 Upper cushion
3 Upper bracket
4 Radiator inlet hose
5 Clamp
6 Radiator main fan shroud
7 Radiator main fan and motor
8 Radiator sub fan shroud
9 Radiator sub fan and motor
10 Reservoir tank cover
11 Reservoir tank
12 Over flow hose
13 Radiator outlet hose
14 Clamp
15 ATF cooler inlet hose A
16 ATF cooler outlet hose A
17 ATF cooler pipe
18 ATF cooler inlet hose B
19 ATF cooler outlet hose B
20 Lower cushion
21 Coolant drain cock
22 Drain pipe

Tightening torque: N·m (kg-m, ft-lb)
T1: 13 – 23 (1.3 – 2.3, 9 – 17)
T2: 7.2 – 7.6 (0.73 – 0.77, 5.3 – 5.6)

87973g23

To install:

6. Install the fan blade on the motor and install the mounting nut. Tighten the nut to 3 ft. lbs. (4 Nm).

7. Install the motor onto the frame using the mounting nuts. Tighten the mounting bolts to 6 ft. lbs. (8 Nm).

8. Install the fan assembly into the vehicle with the mounting bolts. Tighten the bolts to 10 ft. lbs. (14 Nm).

9. Fasten the electrical connector to the cooling fan and route the harness through the bracket on the frame.

10. Connect the negative battery cable.

11. Start the engine and check for proper fan operation.

WITH A/C

1. Disconnect the negative battery cable.

2. Loosen, but do not remove the fan clutch mounting nuts.

3. Remove the accessory drive belt.

4. Remove the fan shroud mounting bolts.

5. Remove the fan clutch assembly and shroud by removing the clutch mounting nuts loosened earlier. Remove the fan and shroud together.

6. Remove the fan nuts to separate the fan blade and clutch assembly.

To install:

7. Install the fan blade to the clutch using the mounting nuts. Tighten the nuts to 6 ft. lbs. (8 Nm).

8. Install the fan assembly and shroud into the vehicle.

9. Loosely install the fan assembly mounting nuts.

10. Install the fan shroud mounting bolts. Tighten the nuts to 6 ft. lbs. (8 Nm).

11. Install the accessory drive belt.

12. Tighten the fan assembly mounting nuts. Tighten the nuts to 6 ft. lbs. (8 Nm).

13. Connect the negative battery cable.

14. Start the engine and check for proper fan operation.

2.2L and 2.5L Engines

▶ See Figures 57, 58 and 59

1. Disconnect the negative battery cable.

2. Unfasten the fan motor electrical connector.

3. Remove the coolant reservoir tank.

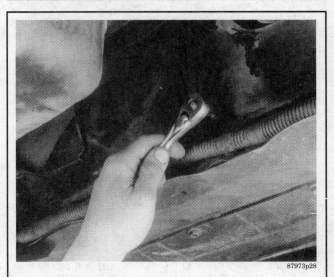

Fig. 57 Disconnect the fan motor harness from the fan cover — 2.2L engine shown

87973p27

Fig. 58 Unfasten the fan cover-to-radiator bolts . . .

87973p28

87973p29

Fig. 59 . . . then lift the fan and cover assembly out of the engine compartment

4. Remove the 4 fan shroud bolts.

5. Remove the fan blade retainer nut, then remove the motor retainer nuts to separate the motor from the shroud.

To install:

6. Install the fan motor in the shroud, and secure in place with the retainer nuts. Tighten the nuts to 2-3 ft. lbs. (3-4 Nm).

7. Install the fan blade to the motor and tighten the retainer nut to 1-2 ft. lbs. (1-3 Nm).

8. Install the fan assembly and tighten the mounting bolts to 2-3 ft. lbs. (3-4 Nm).

9. Install the coolant reservoir tank. Tighten the retainer bolts to 4-7 ft. lbs. (5-9 Nm).

10. Attach the fan motor electrical connector.

11. Connect the negative battery cable.

12. Start the engine and check for proper fan operation.

3.3L Engine

1. Disconnect the negative battery cable.

2. Unfasten the electrical connector from the cooling fan assembly.

3. Remove the upper radiator bracket.

4. Remove the two bolts securing the cooling fan frame to the radiator.

5. Remove the cooling fan assembly.

6. Remove the cooling fan from the frame assembly.

To install:

7. Install the cooling fan assembly on the frame. Tighten the motor retainer nuts to 5-6 ft. lbs. (6-8 Nm).

8. Install the cooling fan assembly into the vehicle.

9. Install the two cooling fan mounting bolts. Tighten the bolts to 5-6 ft. lbs. (6-8 Nm)

10. Install the upper radiator bracket. Tighten the retainer bolts to 9-17 ft. lbs. (12-22 Nm).

11. Connect the electrical harness to the fan motor.

12. Connect the negative battery cable.

13. Start the vehicle and check for proper fan operation.

Water Pump

REMOVAL & INSTALLATION

✳✳CAUTION

When draining the coolant, keep in mind that cats and dogs are attracted to ethylene glycol antifreeze, and could drink any that is left in an uncovered container or in puddles on the ground. This will prove fatal in sufficient quantity. Always drain the coolant into a sealable container. Coolant should be reused unless it is contaminated or several years old.

1.2L Engine

► See Figure 60

1. Disconnect the negative battery cable.

2. Drain the coolant and engine oil into a suitable containers.

3. Remove the dipstick and tube.

4. Remove the alternator. Refer to the procedure in Section 2.

5. Remove the crankshaft pulley.

6. Remove the timing belt cover.

7. Remove the timing belt, tensioner and camshaft sprocket, as described later in this section.

8. Remove the rear timing belt cover.

9. Raise and safely support the vehicle on jackstands.

10. Remove the flywheel housing cover.

11. Remove the oil pan, oil pan plate and oil strainer.

12. Remove the air suction manifold bracket from the air manifold and crankcase cover.

13. Remove the water pump cover retainer bolts from the crankcase cover. Lift the water pump cover off and clean all gasket material from both mating surfaces.

14. Remove the water pump impeller bolt and impeller, as well as the seal.

To install:

15. Install a new water pump seal using seal installer 499795400 or equivalent. Install the water pump impeller and bolt. Tighten the bolt to 7-9 ft. lbs. (9-12 Nm).

16. Install the water pump cover to the crankcase cover. Tighten the retainer bolts to 8-12 ft. lbs. (10-16 Nm)).

17. Install the air suction manifold bracket from the air suction manifold to the crankcase cover.

18. Install the oil strainer, oil pan plate and oil pan. Refer to the procedure in this section.

19. Install the flywheel housing cover.

20. Lower the vehicle.

21. Install the rear timing belt cover.

22. Install the camshaft sprocket, tensioner and timing belt. Refer to the procedures in this section.

23. Install the timing belt cover.

24. Install the crankshaft pulley.

25. Install the alternator.

26. Install the dipstick and tube.

27. Refill the crankcase with clean oil.

28. Refill the cooling system.

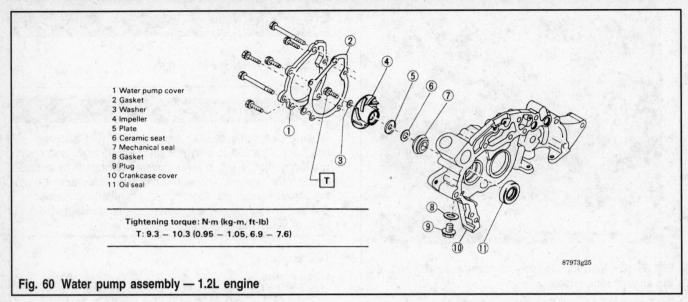

1 Water pump cover
2 Gasket
3 Washer
4 Impeller
5 Plate
6 Ceramic seat
7 Mechanical seal
8 Gasket
9 Plug
10 Crankcase cover
11 Oil seal

Tightening torque: N·m (kg-m, ft-lb)
T: 9.3 — 10.3 (0.95 — 1.05, 6.9 — 7.6)

87973g25

Fig. 60 Water pump assembly — 1.2L engine

29. Connect the negative battery cable.
30. Start the vehicle and check for leaks.

1.6L, 1.8L and 2.7L Engines

▶ See Figure 61

1. Drain the coolant into a suitable container.
2. Disconnect the radiator outlet hose and water bypass hose from the water pump.
3. Loosen the pulley nuts. Loosen the alternator assembly and remove the drive belt.
4. Remove the front belt cover.
5. Unfasten the water pump mounting bolts and remove the water pump.

To install:

6. Clean the gasket material from both mating surfaces. Always use new gaskets during installation.
7. Install the water pump and pump mounting bolts. Tighten the mounting bolts to 7-8 ft. lbs. (9-10 Nm).
8. Install the front belt cover.

9. Install the alternator drive belt and drive belt cover. Adjust the drive belt to the proper tension. Tighten the water pump pulley bolts to 7-8 ft. lbs. (9-10 Nm).
10. Inspect the coolant hoses and replace as necessary. Install the radiator outlet hose and water bypass hose on the water pump.
11. Fill the radiator with coolant. Start the engine and allow it to reach operating temperature. Check for leaks.

2.2L, 2.5L and 3.3L Engines

▶ See Figures 62, 63, 64, 65, 66, 67 and 68

1. Disconnect the negative battery cable.
2. Drain the coolant into a suitable container.
3. Disconnect the radiator outlet hose.
4. Remove the radiator fan motor assembly.
5. Remove the accessory drive belts.
6. Remove the timing belt, tensioner and camshaft angle sensor. Refer to the procedure in this section for removal and installation steps.
7. Remove the left side camshaft pulley(s) and left side rear timing belt cover. Remove the tensioner bracket.

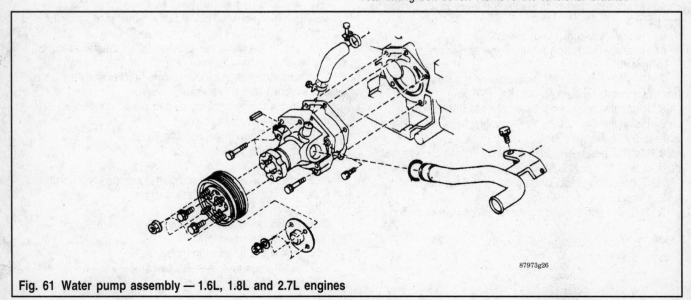

87973g26

Fig. 61 Water pump assembly — 1.6L, 1.8L and 2.7L engines

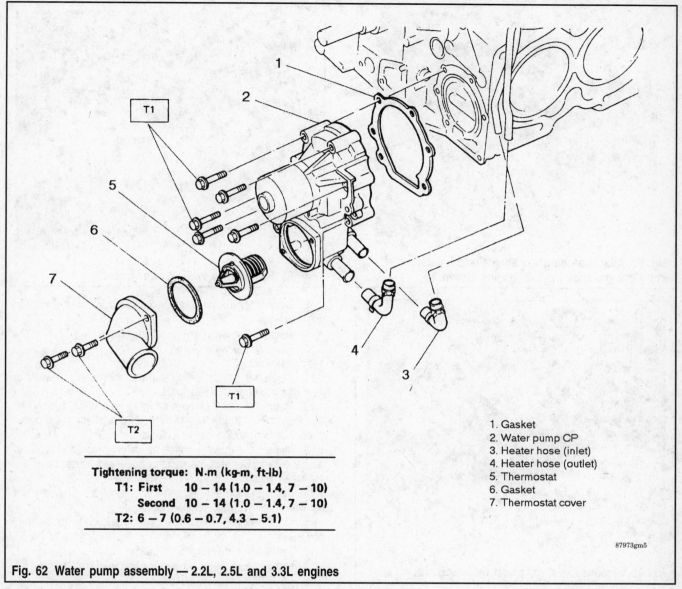

Tightening torque: N·m (kg-m, ft-lb)
T1: First   10 — 14 (1.0 — 1.4, 7 — 10)
    Second 10 — 14 (1.0 — 1.4, 7 — 10)
T2: 6 — 7 (0.6 — 0.7, 4.3 — 5.1)

1. Gasket
2. Water pump CP
3. Heater hose (inlet)
4. Heater hose (outlet)
5. Thermostat
6. Gasket
7. Thermostat cover

87973gm5

Fig. 62 Water pump assembly — 2.2L, 2.5L and 3.3L engines

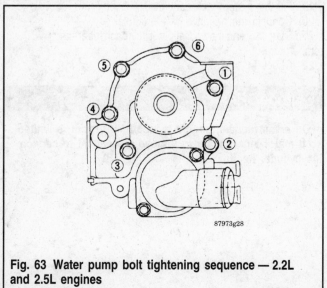

87973g28

Fig. 63 Water pump bolt tightening sequence — 2.2L and 2.5L engines

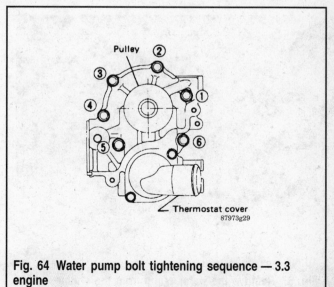

87973g29

Fig. 64 Water pump bolt tightening sequence — 3.3 engine

Fig. 65 After loosening the hose clamps, detach the water pump's hoses — 2.2L engine shown

Fig. 66 Remove the water pump retainer bolts

Fig. 67 Remove the water pump from the engine

Fig. 68 Remove the water pump gasket

8. Disconnect the radiator hose and heater hose from the water pump.

9. Remove the water pump retainer bolts.

10. Remove the water pump.

To install:

11. Clean the gasket mating surfaces thoroughly. Always use new gaskets during installation.

12. Install the water pump and tighten the bolts, in sequence, to 7-10 ft. lbs. (10-14 Nm). After tightening the bolts once, retighten to the same specification again.

13. Inspect the radiator hoses for deterioration and replace as necessary. Connect the radiator hose and heater hose to the water pump.

14. Install the left side rear timing belt cover, left side camshaft pulley(s) and tensioner bracket.

15. Install the camshaft angle sensor, tensioner and timing belt.

16. Install the accessory drive belts.

17. Install the radiator ran motor assembly.

18. Install the radiator outlet hose.

19. Fill the system with coolant.

20. Connect the negative battery cable.

21. Start the engine and allow it to reach operating temperature.

22. Check for leaks.

Cylinder Head

➡On some models, engine compartment room is limited, so it may be necessary to remove the engine to service the cylinder heads.

REMOVAL & INSTALLATION

✳✳CAUTION

When draining the coolant, keep in mind that cats and dogs are attracted to ethylene glycol antifreeze, and could drink any that is left in an uncovered container or in puddles on the ground. This will prove fatal in sufficient quantity. Always drain the coolant into a sealable container. Coolant should be reused unless it is contaminated or several years old.

1.2L Engine

▶ See Figures 69 and 70

1. Disconnect the negative battery cable.
2. Drain the engine oil and coolant into suitable containers.
3. Remove the timing belt cover. Align the timing marks, then remove the timing belt and related components.

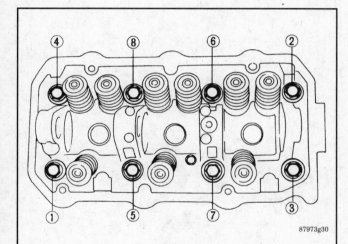

Fig. 69 Cylinder head bolt loosening sequence — 1.2L engine

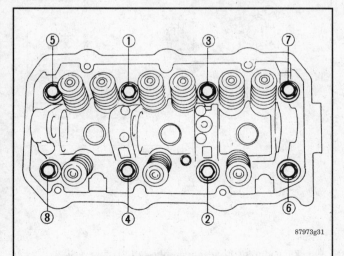

Fig. 70 Cylinder head bolt tightening sequence — 1.2L engine

4. Remove the rocker arm cover.
5. Scribe alignment marks on the distributor and cylinder head; then remove the distributor.
6. Remove the exhaust manifold mounting bolts and separate the manifold from the cylinder head. Refer to the exhaust manifold procedure in this section.
7. Tag and disconnect the electrical harnesses and vacuum hoses attached to the intake manifold.
8. Remove the air suction valve and pipe, if equipped.
9. Remove the intake manifold assembly. Refer to the intake manifold procedure in this section.
10. Loosen the cylinder head mounting bolts in the correct sequence. DO NOT remove any of the bolts until all the bolts have been loosened.
11. Remove the cylinder head bolts.
12. Lift off the cylinder head and gasket from the engine block.
13. Clean all gasket material from both mating surfaces.
To install:
14. Install the cylinder head and gasket on the engine block.
15. Install the cylinder head bolts and tighten in three steps as follows:
    a. Tighten in sequence to 29 ft. lbs. (39 Nm).
    b. Tighten in sequence to 43 ft. lbs. (59 Nm).
    c. Tighten in sequence to 51 ft. lbs. (69 Nm).
16. Install the intake manifold. Refer to the procedure in this section.
17. Install the air suction valve and pipe.
18. Connect the electrical harnesses and vacuum hoses to the intake manifold.
19. Install the exhaust manifold using a new gasket. Refer to the procedure in this section.
20. Align and install the distributor.
21. Install the rocker arm cover.
22. Install the timing belt components and timing belt cover.
23. Connect the negative battery cable.
24. Change the oil filter and fill the engine with clean oil. Fill the cooling system and bleed.
25. Start the vehicle and check for leaks. Adjust the ignition timing, if needed.

1.6L, 1.8L and 2.7L engines

▶ See Figures 71, 72, 73, 74, 75 and 76

1. Disconnect the negative battery cable.
2. Remove the timing belt, belt cover and related components.
3. On turbocharged engines, remove the turbo cooling pipe together with the union screws and gaskets from the cylinder head.
4. Remove the camshaft cases, lash adjusters and related components.
5. On turbocharged engines, remove the EGR pipe.
6. Remove the plug attaching the EGR pipe to the cylinder head.
7. Remove the accessory drive belts, alternator and air conditioner compressor, if equipped. Remove the bolt attaching the alternator bracket to the cylinder head.
8. On vehicles without A/C, remove the bolt securing the adjusting bar to the cylinder.
9. On fuel injected engines, relieve the fuel system pressure.

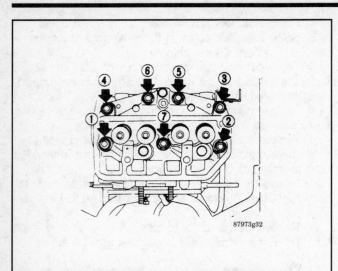

Fig. 71 Cylinder head bolt loosening sequence — 1.6L and 1.8L engines

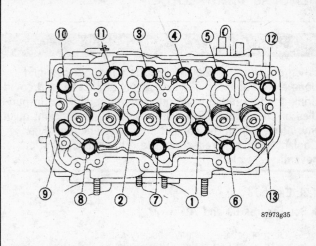

Fig. 74 Cylinder head bolt tightening sequence — 2.7L engine

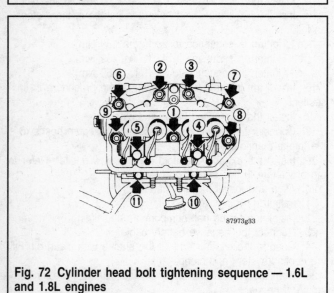

Fig. 72 Cylinder head bolt tightening sequence — 1.6L and 1.8L engines

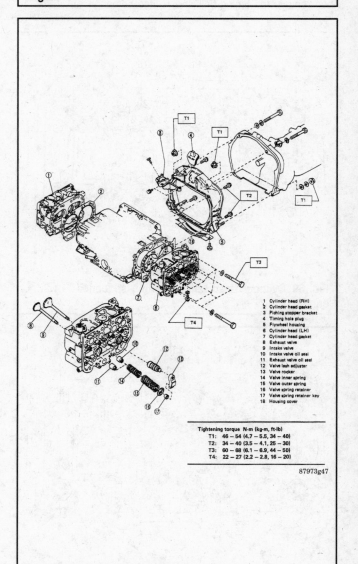

Fig. 75 Cylinder head assembly — 1.6L and 1.8L engines

1 Cylinder head (RH)
2 Cylinder head gasket
3 Piching stopper bracket
4 Timing hole plug
5 Flywheel housing
6 Cylinder head (LH)
7 Cylinder head gasket
8 Exhaust valve
9 Intake valve
10 Intake valve oil seal
11 Exhaust valve oil seal
12 Valve lash adjuster
13 Valve rocker
14 Valve inner spring
15 Valve outer spring
16 Valve spring retainer
17 Valve spring retainer key
18 Housing cover

Tightening torque N·m (kg-m, ft-lb)
T1: 46 — 54 (4.7 — 5.5, 34 — 40)
T2: 34 — 40 (3.5 — 4.1, 25 — 30)
T3: 60 — 68 (6.1 — 6.9, 44 — 50)
T4: 22 — 27 (2.2 — 2.8, 16 — 20)

Fig. 73 Cylinder head bolt loosening sequence — 2.7L engine

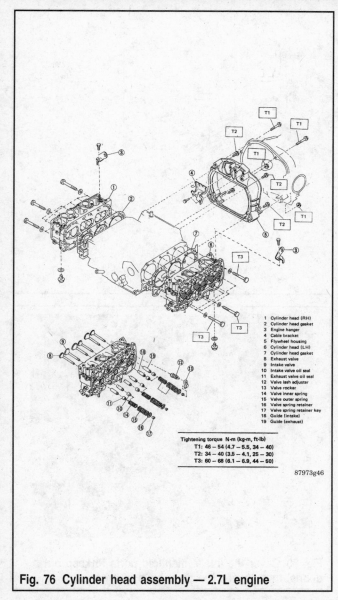

1 Cylinder head (RH)
2 Cylinder head gasket
3 Engine hanger
4 Cable bracket
5 Flywheel housing
6 Cylinder head (LH)
7 Cylinder head gasket
8 Exhaust valve
9 Intake valve
10 Intake valve oil seal
11 Exhaust valve oil seal
12 Valve lash adjuster
13 Valve rocker
14 Valve inner spring
15 Valve outer spring
16 Valve spring retainer
17 Valve spring retainer key
18 Guide (intake)
19 Guide (exhaust)

Tightening torque N·m (kg-m, ft-lb)
T1: 46 — 54 (4.7 — 5.5, 34 — 40)
T2: 34 — 40 (3.5 — 4.1, 25 — 30)
T3: 60 — 68 (6.1 — 6.9, 44 — 50)

87973g46

Fig. 76 Cylinder head assembly — 2.7L engine

10. Remove the bolts attaching the intake manifold to the cylinder head and remove the manifold.

11. Remove the bolt attaching the water bypass pipe bracket to the cylinder head.

12. Remove the spark plugs.

➡**On 2.7L engines, there are two types of cylinder head bolts used. Take note of cylinder head bolt arrangement as the bolts must be placed in their proper locations. Bolts number 1, 2, 9 and 13 measure 4.665 in. (118.5mm). All other bolts measure 5.217 in. (132.5mm).**

13. Loosen the cylinder head bolts in the proper sequence. Remove the cylinder heads from the block.

14. Clean all gasket material from the mating surfaces.

To install:

15. Inspect the cylinder head for warpage. Warpage should not exceed 0.0020 in. (0.05mm).

16. Install the cylinder head using a new gasket.

17. On the 1.6L and 1.8L engines, tighten the cylinder head bolts in three steps as follows:

   a. Tighten all bolts in sequence to 22 ft. lbs. (29 Nm).

   b. Tighten all bolts in sequence to 43 ft. lbs. (59 Nm).

   c. Tighten all bolts in sequence to 47 ft. lbs. (64 Nm).

18. On the 2.7L engine, tighten the cylinder head bolts in four steps as follows:

   a. Tighten all bolts in sequence to 29 ft. lbs. (39 Nm).

   b. Tighten all bolts in sequence to 47 ft. lbs. (64 Nm).

   c. Loosen all bolts at least 90° in the reverse order of the tightening sequence.

   d. Tighten all bolts in sequence to 44-50 ft. lbs. (60-68 Nm).

19. Install the spark plugs. Install the water bypass pipe bracket.

20. Install the intake manifold and tighten the bolts to 13-16 ft. lbs. (18-22 Nm).

21. Install the alternator and bracket, air conditioner compressor, if equipped, and accessory drive belt.

22. On turbocharged engines, install the EGR pipe. Tighten the bolts to 23-27 ft. lbs. (31-37 Nm).

23. Install the camshaft cases, lash adjusters and related components.

24. On turbocharged engines, install the turbo cooling pipe. Tighten the bolts to 16-18 ft. lbs. (21-24 Nm).

25. Install the timing belt, belt cover and related components.

26. Connect the negative battery cable.

27. Adjust the valve lash, as required. Start the engine and allow it to reach operating temperature. Adjust the ignition timing.

28. Check for leaks, then test drive the vehicle.

2.2L Engine

▶ **See Figures 77, 78, 79, 80, 81, 82 and 83**

1. Disconnect the negative battery cable.

2. Remove the drive belt.

3. Remove the power steering pump, alternator and bracket.

4. Remove the valve rocker cover.

5. Tag and disconnect the PCV hose and spark plug wires.

6. Remove the connector bracket attaching bolt.

7. Remove the crank angle and cam angle sensors.

8. Disconnect the oil pressure switch. Remove the knock sensor.

9. Disconnect the blow-by hose.

10. Relieve the fuel system pressure and disconnect the fuel pipes.

11. Remove the intake manifold and gasket. Remove the water pipe.

12. Remove the timing belt, camshaft sprocket and related components.

13. Remove the oil level gauge guide attaching bolt on the left cylinder head.

14. Remove the cylinder head bolts in the proper sequence. Leave bolts 1 and 3 installed loosely to prevent the cylinder head from falling.

15. Separate the cylinder head from the block, Use a plastic-faced hammer, if needed, to separate the head from the cylinder block.

16. Remove bolts 1 and 3. Remove the cylinder head and gasket.

17. Clean all gasket material from both mating surfaces.

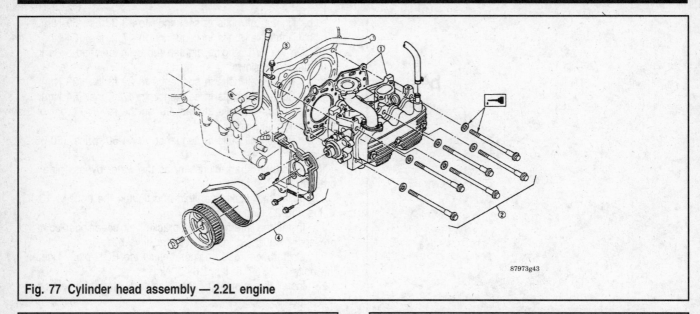

Fig. 77 Cylinder head assembly — 2.2L engine

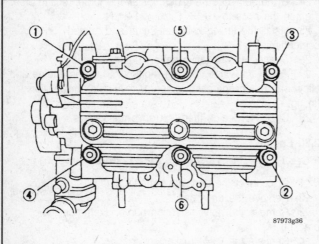
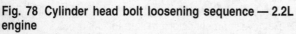

Fig. 78 Cylinder head bolt loosening sequence — 2.2L engine

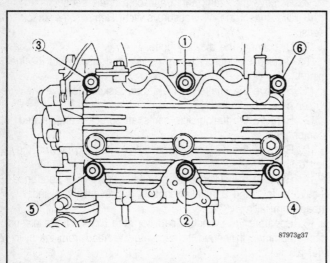

Fig. 79 Cylinder head bolt tightening sequence — 2.2L engine

Fig. 80 Cover the intake manifold ports to keep out debris, then loosen the head bolts in order

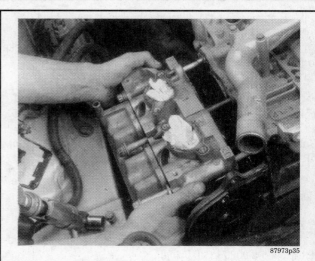

Fig. 81 Carefully remove the cylinder head. Notice how close it is to the side of the engine compartment

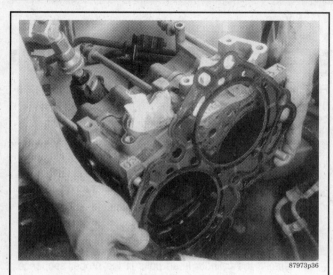

Fig. 82 Remove the cylinder head gasket

Fig. 83 Clean both mating surfaces with a suitable gasket scraper

To install:

18. Inspect the cylinder head for warpage. Warpage should not exceed 0.0020 in. (0.05mm).

19. Install the cylinder head on the block using a new gasket. Secure in place with the mounting bolts. Coat each bolts with clean engine oil, and hand-tighten.

20. Tighten the cylinder head bolts to the following specifications:

    a. Tighten all bolts in sequence to 22 ft. lbs. (29 Nm).

    b. Tighten all bolts in sequence to 51 ft. lbs. (69 Nm).

    c. Loosen all bolts by 180°, then loosen an additional 180°.

    d. Tighten bolts 1 and 2 to 25 ft. lbs. (24 Nm) for non-turbo engines and 27 ft. lbs. (37 Nm) for turbo engines.

    e. Tighten bolts 3, 4, 5 and 6 to 11 ft. lbs. (15 Nm) for non-turbo engines and 14 ft. lbs. (20 Nm) for turbo engines.

    f. Tighten all bolts in sequence 80-90°.

    g. Tighten all bolts in sequence an additional 80-90°.

➡**Do not exceed 180° total tightening.**

21. Install the oil level gauge guide attaching bolt on the left cylinder head.

22. Install the timing belt, camshaft sprocket and related components.

23. Install the water pipe.

24. Install the intake manifold and tighten bolts to 21-25 ft. lbs. (28-34 Nm). Connect the fuel delivery pipes.

25. Connect the blow-by hose. Install the knock sensor.

26. Connect the oil pressure switch connector.

27. Install the crank and cam angle sensors.

28. Install the connector bracket attaching bolt.

29. Connect the spark plug wires. Connect the PCV hose.

30. Install the valve rocker cover and tighten bolts to 4 ft. lbs. (9 Nm).

31. Install the alternator, power steering pump and accessory drive belt.

32. Connect the negative battery cable. Start the engine and allow it to reach operating temperature. Check for leaks.

2.5L Engine

▶ **See Figures 84 and 85**

1. Disconnect the negative battery cable.

2. Remove the V-belt.

3. Remove the power steering pump, alternator and bracket.

4. Remove the valve rocker cover.

5. Remove the connector bracket attaching bolt.

6. Remove the crank angle and cam angle sensors.

7. Remove the coolant filler tank.

8. Relieve the fuel system pressure and disconnect the fuel pipes.

9. Remove the intake manifold and gasket. Remove the water pipe.

10. Remove the timing belt, camshaft sprocket and related components.

11. Remove the oil level gauge guide attaching bolt on the left cylinder head.

12. Remove the cylinder head bolts in the proper sequence. Leave bolts 1 and 3 installed loosely to prevent the cylinder head from falling.

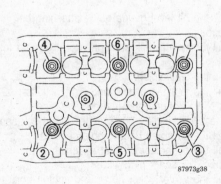

Fig. 84 Cylinder head bolt loosening sequence — 2.5L engine

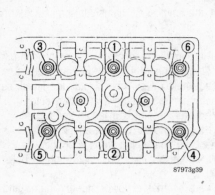

Fig. 85 Cylinder head bolt tightening sequence — 2.5L engine

13. Separate the cylinder head from the block, Use a plastic-faced hammer, if needed.

14. Remove bolts 1 and 3. Remove the cylinder head and gasket.

15. Clean all gasket material from both mating surfaces.

To install:

16. Inspect the cylinder head for warpage. Warpage should not exceed 0.0020 in. (0.05mm).

17. Install the cylinder heads on the block using new gaskets. Secure in place with the mounting bolts. Coat each bolts with clean engine oil, and hand-tighten.

18. Tighten the cylinder head bolts to the following specifications:

   a. Tighten all bolts in sequence to 22 ft. lbs. (29 Nm).

   b. Tighten all bolts in sequence to 51 ft. lbs. (69 Nm).

   c. Loosen all bolts by 180°, then loosen an additional 180°.

   d. Tighten bolts 1 and 2 to 25 ft. lbs. (24 Nm).

   e. Tighten bolts 3, 4, 5 and 6 to 11 ft. lbs. (15 Nm).

   f. Tighten all bolts in sequence by 80-90°.

   g. Tighten all bolts in sequence an additional 80-90°.

➡**Do not exceed 180° total tightening.**

19. Install the oil level gauge guide attaching bolt on the left cylinder head.

20. Install the timing belt, camshaft sprocket and related components.

21. Install the water pipe.

22. Install the intake manifold and tighten bolts to 21-25 ft. lbs. (28-34 Nm). Connect the fuel delivery pipes.

23. Connect the blow-by hose. Install the knock sensor.

24. Install the crank and cam angle sensors.

25. Install the connector bracket attaching bolt.

26. Connect the spark plug wires.

27. Install the valve rocker cover and tighten bolts to 4 ft. lbs. (9 Nm).

28. Install the alternator, power steering pump and accessory drive belt.

29. Connect the negative battery cable. Start the engine and allow it to reach operating temperature. Check for leaks.

3.3L Engine

▶ **See Figures 86, 87 and 88**

❊❊CAUTION

Fuel injection systems remain under pressure after the engine has been turned OFF. Properly relieve fuel pressure before disconnecting any fuel lines. Failure to do so may result in fire or personal injury.

1. Disconnect the negative battery cable.

2. Remove the intake and exhaust manifolds from the cylinder head. Refer to the needed procedures in this section.

3. Remove the timing belt and sprockets.

4. Remove both the camshafts.

5. Remove the oil dipstick and tube.

6. Remove the heater pipe.

7. Remove the cylinder head bolts in the proper sequence. DO NOT fully remove bolt number 5 or 8. One of these bolts

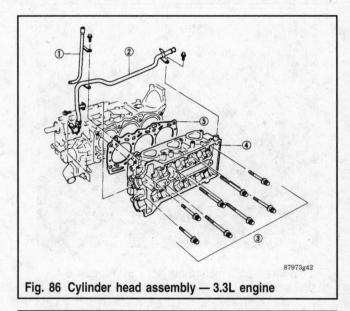

Fig. 86 Cylinder head assembly — 3.3L engine

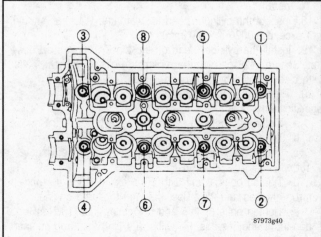

Fig. 87 Cylinder head bolt loosening sequence — 3.3L engine

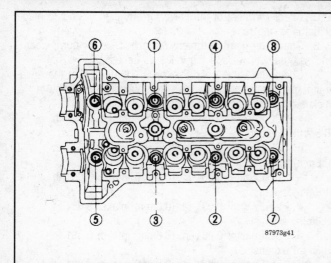

Fig. 88 Cylinder head bolt tightening sequence — 3.3L engine

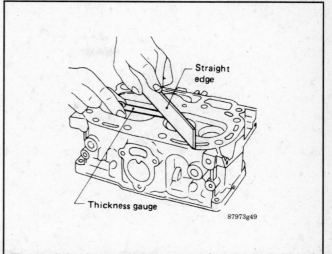

Fig. 89 Using a straightedge to check the cylinder head for signs of warpage

should remain three of four threads into the block to prevent the cylinder head from falling.

8. Free the cylinder head from the block then remove the bolt left loosely in place. If the cylinder head will not come free easily, then tap the side of the head with a plastic-faced hammer.

9. Remove the cylinder head and gasket.

10. Clean all gasket material from both mating surfaces.

To install:

11. Install the cylinder head using a new gasket. Loosely install the cylinder head mounting bolts, coating each with clean engine oil.

12. Tighten the mounting bolts as follows:

    a. Tighten the bolts in sequence to 22 ft. lbs. (29 Nm).

    b. Tighten the bolts in sequence to 51 ft. lbs. (69 Nm).

    c. Back off all the bolts 180°.

    d. Back off all bolts an additional 180°.

    e. Tighten the bolts in sequence to 20 ft. lbs. (27 Nm).

    f. Tighten bolts 1, 2, 3 and 4 an additional 90°.

    g. Tighten bolts 5, 6, 7, and 8 to 33 ft. lbs. (44 Nm).

    h. Tighten all bolts in sequence an additional 90°.

13. Install the camshafts.

14. Install the heater pipe.

15. Install the oil dipstick and tube.

16. Connect the intake and exhaust manifolds to the cylinder head.

17. Install the timing belt and sprockets.

18. Connect the negative battery cable.

CLEANING, INSPECTION AND RESURFACING

▶ **See Figure 89**

Invert the cylinder head and clean the carbon from the valve faces and combustion chambers. Use a permanent felt-tip marker and mark the valves for location.

Use a valve spring compressor and compress the valve springs. Lift out the keepers, release the valve spring compressor and remove the valve, spring and spring retainer. Place all parts removed in order so that they can be reinstalled on the same cylinder.

Remove the valves from the cylinder head. Chip away any remaining carbon from the valve heads, combustion chambers and ports. Use a rotary wire brush on an electric drill. Be sure that the deposits are actually removed, rather than burnished. Clean the valve faces with a wire wheel taking care not to remove the location numbering. Clean the cylinder head and component parts in an engine cleaning solvent.

Check the cylinder head for warpage by placing a straightedge across the gasket surface. Using feeler gauges, determine the clearance at the center of the straightedge. Measure across the diagonals, along the longitudinal centerline and across the cylinder head at several points. Should the warpage exceed 0.0020 in. (0.05mm) the cylinder head must be resurfaced. Be sure to observe the following grinding limits:

- 1.2L Engine: 0.008 in. (0.2mm)
- 1.6L, 1.8L and 2.7L Engines: 0.012 in. (0.3mm)
- 2.2L and 2.5L Engines: 0.004 in. (0.1mm)
- 3.3L Engine: 0.012 in. (0.3mm)

Clean the valve stems with lacquer thinner. Clean the valve guides using solvent and an expanding wire type valve guide cleaning brush. Insert the valve into the guide from which it was removed. With the valve slightly off of the valve seat, rock the valve face and stem back and forth. Excessive wobble means a worn guide, valve stem or both.

Measure the valve stems with a micrometer and compare the reading with the specifications to determine whether valve stem or guide wear is responsible for any excessive clearance. Replace or repair as necessary.

Valves

REMOVAL

▶ **See Figure 90**

1. Remove the valve system and related components.

2. Remove the cylinder head.

3. On all models except 2.5L and 3.3L engines, use a valve spring compressor to compress the valve spring and remove the valve spring key retainer.

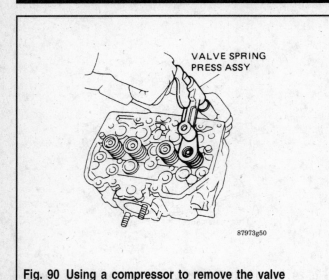

Fig. 90 Using a compressor to remove the valve spring — except 2.5L and 3.3L engines

4. On 2.5L and 3.3L engines, remove the camshafts. Refer to the Camshaft removal and installation procedure in this section for removal steps.

5. Remove each valve spring assembly.

➡**Mark each valve assembly for location, as the valves must be installed on their original seats.**

6. Remove the valve oil seal using suitable pliers.

➡**Take care not to damage the lips of the valve oil seals.**

7. Remove the valves.

INSPECTION

▶ **See Figure 91**

1. Inspect the cylinder head in the valve seat area for signs of damage or cracking.

2. Check the seat of the valve for any sign of poor contact or damage and repair as necessary.

3. Check the head and stem of each valve for burn, wear and deformation; replace the valve as necessary.

4. Check the valve head thickness "H". If smaller than minimum specification, replace the valve. Valve head minimum thickness specifications are as follows:

- 1.2L Engine: 0.020 in. (0.5mm) intake; 0.020 in. (0.5mm) exhaust.
- 1.6L Engine: 0.020 in. (0.5mm) intake; 0.031 in. (0.8mm) exhaust
- 1.8L Engine: 0.031 in. (0.8mm) intake; 0.051 in. (1.3mm) exhaust
- 2.2L Engine: 0.031 in. (0.8mm) intake; 0.031 in. (0.8mm) exhaust
- 2.5L Engine: 0.031 in. (0.8mm) intake; 0.031 in. (0.8mm) exhaust
- 2.7L Engine: 0.031 in. (0.8mm) intake; 0.031 in. (0.8mm) exhaust
- 3.3L Engine: 0.024 in. (0.6mm) intake; 0.031 in. (0.8mm) exhaust

5. Check the valve springs for damage, free-length and tension. Replace the valve spring if not to specification.

REFACING

▶ **See Figure 92**

Using a valve grinder, resurface the valves according to specifications. The valve head thickness should be greater than the minimum specification after refacing. The valve stem top should also be squared and resurfaced, by placing the stem in the V-block of the grinder, and turning it while pressing lightly against the grinding wheel.

Reaming the Valve Seat
▶ **See Figure 93**

Select a reamer of the correct seat angle, slightly larger than the diameter of the valve seat, and assemble it with a pilot of

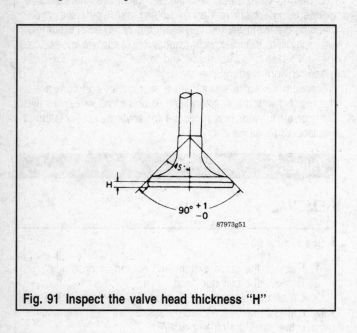

Fig. 91 Inspect the valve head thickness "H"

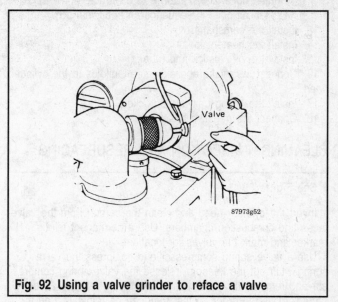

Fig. 92 Using a valve grinder to reface a valve

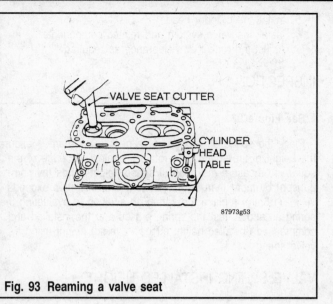

Fig. 93 Reaming a valve seat

the correct size. Install the pilot into the valve guide, and using steady pressure, turn the reamer clockwise.

❋❋WARNING

Do not turn the reamer counterclockwise.

Remove only as much material as necessary to clean the seat. Check the concentricity of the seat. Coat the valve face with Prussian blue dye, install and rotate it on the valve seat. Using the dye marked area as a centering guide, center and narrow the valve seat to specifications with correction cutters.

After making correction cuts, recheck the position of the valve seat on the valve face using Prussian blue dye.

Power Resurfacing

Select a pilot of the correct size, and a coarse stone of the correct seat angle. Lubricate the pilot if necessary, and install the tool in the valve guide. Move the stone on and off the seat at approximately two cycles per second, until all flaws are removed from the seat. Install a fine stone, and finish the seat. Center and narrow the seat using correction stones, as described above.

Valve Seals

Due to the pressure differential that exists at the ends of the intake valve guides (atmospheric pressure above, manifold vacuum below), oil is drawn through the valve guides into the intake port. This has been alleviated somewhat since the addition of positive crankcase ventilation, which lowers the pressure above the guides. To reduce blow-by, Subaru employs valve stem seals which must be pressed (or tapped) into position over the valve stem and guide boss. Recently, Teflon® guide seals have become popular. Consult a parts supplier or machinist concerning availability and suggested usages.

➡When installing seals, ensure that a small amount of oil is able to pass by the seal to lubricate the valve guides. Otherwise, excessive wear may result.

Factory seals should be inspected and replaced if the seal lip is damaged or the spring is out of place. Also, whenever

the seating surfaces of valve and seat are reconditioned or the guide is replaced, the seal should be replaced.

INSTALLATION

1. Lubricate the valve stems, and install the valves in the cylinder head as numbered.
2. Lubricate and position the seals (if used) and the valve springs.
3. Install the spring retainers, compress the springs, and insert the keys.
4. Tap the head of the valve lightly with a wooden hammer to seat the keys.
5. Install the cylinder head.
6. Install the valve system and related components.
7. Adjust the rocker arm clearance as required.

Valve Stem Seals

REPLACEMENT

▶ **See Figures 94 and 95**

Replace the oil seal if the lip is damaged or the spring is out of place. Also replace the oil seal when the surfaces of the valves and valve seats are refaced or the valve guides are replaced.

The following procedure may be performed with the cylinder head on the cylinder block by using a chuck and a compressed air source to fill the cylinder with air. This will hold the valve closed and prevent it from dropping into the cylinder.

1. Remove the cylinder head.
2. Remove the valve and valve spring assembly.
3. Using pliers, remove the valve stem oil seal.
4. Install the new oil seal with an oil seal driver.
5. On the 1.6L engine, install the seal so that it is positioned 0.913 in. (23.2mm) above the spring perch.

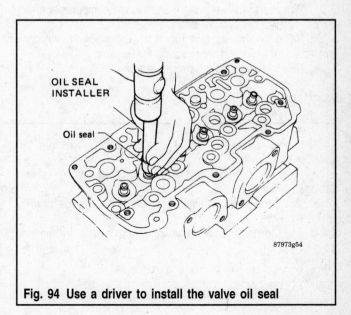

Fig. 94 Use a driver to install the valve oil seal

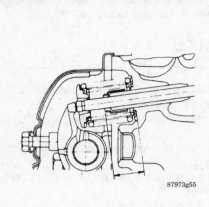

Fig. 95 Proper oil seal installation — 1.6L and 1.8L engines shown

6. On the 1.2L, 1.8L and 2.7L engines, do not confuse the intake and exhaust oil seals. The intake seal measures 0.512 in. (13mm) and the exhaust seal measures 0.425 in. (10.8mm).

7. On the 2.2L, 2.5L and 3.3L engines, do not confuse the intake and exhaust oil seals. The intake seal is black and the exhaust seal is brown.

8. Install the valve and valve spring assembly.

9. Install the cylinder head.

Valve Springs

REMOVAL

▶ See Figure 90

The following procedure may be performed with the cylinder head on the cylinder block by using a chuck and a compressed air source to fill the cylinder with air. This will hold the valve closed and prevent it from dropping into the cylinder.

1. Remove the valve system and related components.

2. Remove the cylinder head.

3. Using a valve spring compressor, compress the valve spring and remove the valve spring key retainer.

4. Remove each valve spring assembly.

INSTALLATION

1. Lubricate the valve stems, and install the valves in the cylinder head as numbered.

2. Lubricate and position the seals (if used) and the valve springs.

3. Install the spring retainers, compress the springs, and insert the keys.

4. Tap the head of the valve lightly with a wooden hammer to seat the keys.

5. Install the cylinder head.

6. Install the valve system and related components.

7. Adjust the rocker arm clearance as required.

INSPECTION

▶ See Figure 96

Place the spring on a flat surface next to a square. Measure the height of the spring, and rotate it against the edge of the square to measure distortion. If spring height varies (by comparison) by more than $1/16$ in. (1.6mm) or if distortion exceeds $1/16$ in. (1.6mm) replace the spring. In addition to evaluating the spring as above, test the spring pressure at the installed and compressed (installed height minus valve lift) height using a valve spring tester.

VALVE SPRING INSTALLED HEIGHT

Measure the distance between the spring pad and the lower edge of the spring retainer, and compare to specifications. If the installed height is incorrect, add shim washers between the spring pad and the spring. Be sure only to use shims designed for this purpose

Valve Seats

The valve seats in your Subaru engine cannot be replaced. The intake and the exhaust valve seats should be inspected for wear and defects. If the valve seat is found to be damaged, the contact surface can be corrected with a valve seat cutter or reamer.

The valve seats should be corrected when the valve guides are replaced. If valve seat wear exceeds specifications, the heads will have to be replaced. Valve seat wear limit is measured in the direction of the valve axis.

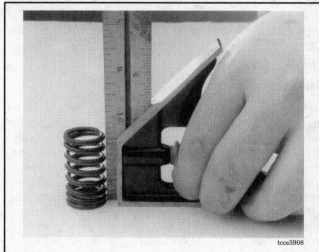

Fig. 96 Check the valve spring for squareness on a flat surface; a carpenter's square can be used

Valve Guides

REMOVAL & INSTALLATION

▶ See Figure 97

Replacing the valve guides involves heating the head to high temperatures and driving the old guide out with the use of special tools. The head may have to be machined for an oversize guide if the bushing bore dimension is over the standard specifications. The new guide is then reamed for the proper valve stem-to-guide clearance. This repair requires a high level of mechanical skill and should only be performed by a reputable machine shop.

Valve guides which are not excessively worn or distorted may, in some cases, be knurled rather than replaced. Knurling is a process in which metal inside the valve guide bore is displaced and raised, thereby reducing clearance. The possibility of knurling rather than replacing the guides should be discussed with a machinist.

1. Remove the cylinder head.
2. Remove the valve springs, keepers, retainers and oil seals.
3. Mount a dial indicator at a 90° angle to the valve stem. With the valve lifted off the seat, wiggle the valve and measure the valve-to-stem clearance.
4. If not within specification, remove the valve and measure the valve stem diameter. If valve stem diameter is not within specification, replace the valve.
5. If the valve stem diameter is within specification, the valve guide is worn and must be replaced.
6. Drive the valve guide out using a valve guide remover.
7. Ream the cylinder head to provide the necessary interference fit for the new valve guide. Check with the manufacturer for specifications.

8. Install the new valve guide using a valve guide installation tool. The valve guide should project as follows:
- 1.2L Engine: 0.807 in. (20.5mm) intake; 0.807 in. (20.5mm) exhaust.
- 1.6L Engine : 0.708 in. (18mm) intake; 0.905 in. (23mm) exhaust.
- 1.8L Engine: 0.709 in. (18mm) intake; 0.709 in. (18mm) exhaust.
- 2.2L Engine: 0.699 in. (17.8mm) intake; 0.699 in. (17.8mm) exhaust.
- 2.5L Engine: 0.699 in. (17.8mm) intake; 0.699 in. (17.8mm) exhaust.
- 2.7L Engine : 0.690 in. (17.5mm) intake; 0.690 in. (17.5mm) exhaust.
- 3.3L Engine: 0.335 in. (8.5mm) intake; 0.335 in. (8.5mm) exhaust.

9. Ream the inside of the valve guide to provide the required oil clearance for the valve.
10. Install the valve, oil seal, spring, retainer and keeper.
11. Reassemble the cylinder head and install.

Hydraulic Lash Adjuster

REMOVAL & INSTALLATION

1.6L Engine
▶ See Figure 98

✳✳CAUTION

The EPA warns that prolonged contact with used engine oil may cause a number of skin disorders, including cancer! You should make every effort to minimize your exposure to used engine oil. Protective gloves should be worn when changing the oil. Wash your hands and any other exposed skin areas as soon as possible after exposure to used engine oil. Soap and water, or waterless hand cleaner should be used.

1. Disconnect the blow-by and PCV hoses.

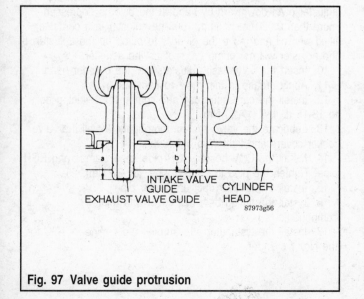

Fig. 97 Valve guide protrusion

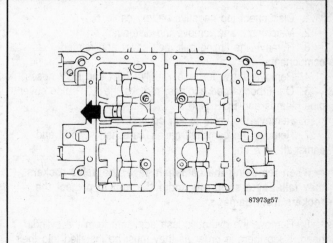

Fig. 98 Removing the hydraulic lash adjuster — 1.6L engine

2. Remove the valve rocker cover.

3. Loosen the valve rocker assembly and remove the pushrod.

4. Raise and support the vehicle safely.

5. Remove the nuts which support the front engine mounting and slightly raise the engine using a floor jack.

6. Remove the drain plug and drain the engine oil into a suitable container.

7. Remove the oil pan.

8. Remove the hydraulic lifter. Use a magnet for removal.

To install:

9. Install the hydraulic lifter.

10. Install the oil pan and tighten the bolts to 3-4 ft. lbs. (4-5 Nm). Install the drain plug.

11. Lower the engine and reconnect the front engine mount.

12. Lower the vehicle.

13. When adjusting the hydraulic lash adjusters, position the engine so that the No. 1 cylinder is at TDC on the compression stroke. Then, adjust the intake and exhaust valves on cylinder No. 1, the exhaust valve on cylinder No. 3 and the intake valve on cylinder No. 4.

14. Adjust the hydraulic lash adjuster as follows:

a. Raise the bend of the lockwasher and loosen the locknut. Turn the valve rocker screw clockwise 4 turns. This will open the valves.

b. Leave the valves open for 15 minutes to bleed down the lash adjusters.

c. Unscrew the valve rocker screw gradually. The rocker arm will stop moving due to the closing of the valve. This is the zero lash point.

d. Unscrew the valve rocker 1½ additional turns.

e. Tighten the locknut and bend the lockwasher.

15. Position the No. 1 cylinder at TDC on the compression stroke to adjust the intake and exhaust valve on cylinder No. 1, exhaust valve on cylinder No. 3, and intake valve on cylinder No. 4.

16. Turn the engine so that the No. 2 cylinder is at TDC on the compression stroke. Then, adjust the remaining valves.

17. Install the valve rocker cover. Connect the blow-by and PCV hoses.

1.8L and 2.7L Engines

▶ **See Figures 99 and 100**

1. Disconnect the negative battery cable.

2. Matchmark and remove the distributor.

3. Remove the timing belt, belt cover and related components.

4. Remove the water pipe, oil filler duct and PCV hoses.

5. On turbocharged engines, remove the EGR pipe cover, pipe clamps and EGR pipe.

6. Remove the valve rocker covers.

7. Remove the camshaft cases, camshaft support and camshaft as a unit.

➡**When removing the camshaft case, the valve rockers may fall. Lay a shop rag under the unit to protect the rockers from damage.**

8. Remove the hydraulic lash adjusters from the cylinder head. Keep them in order as they must be installed into their original positions.

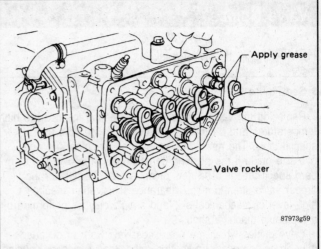

Fig. 99 Hydraulic lash adjuster and rocker arm assembly — 1.8L and 2.7L engines

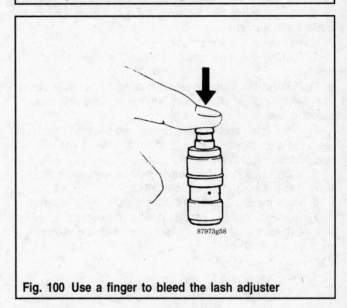

Fig. 100 Use a finger to bleed the lash adjuster

To install:

9. With the adjuster set in a vertical position, push the adjuster pivot downward by hand. If the pivot is depressed more than 0.020 in. (0.5mm), put the adjuster in a container filled with oil and move the plunger to pump up the adjuster. If the adjuster will not pump up, replace the adjuster.

10. Insert the valve lash adjusters into the cylinder head.

11. Apply grease to the valve rockers and install.

12. Install the camshaft case and tighten the retaining bolts to 13-15 ft. lbs. (17-20 Nm).

13. Lubricate the valve system thoroughly. Install the valve rocker covers and tighten to 3-4 ft. lbs. (4-5 Nm).

14. Install the PCV hoses, EGR pipe, pipe clamps and EGR pipe. Tighten the pipe to 23-27 ft. lbs. (31-37 Nm).

15. Install the oil filler duct and water pipe.

16. Install the timing belt, belt cover and related components.

17. Install the distributor after turning the engine to TDC for the No. 1 cylinder.

2.2L Engine

▶ See Figures 101, 102 and 103

1. Disconnect the PCV hose and remove the rocker cover.
2. Remove the valve rocker assembly. Remove bolts 2-4 in numerical sequence. Loosen bolt 1 and leave engaged to support the rocker assembly. Remove bolts 5-8 in numerical sequence.
3. Remove the hydraulic lash adjuster from the tip of the rocker arm. If necessary use pliers, but take care not to scratch the adjuster.

To install:

4. Inspect the adjuster for scratches and replace as necessary. Submerge the lash adjuster in oil and push the check ball in using an appropriately sized rod.
5. With the check ball pushed in, move the plunger up and down at one second intervals until all air bubbles disappear.

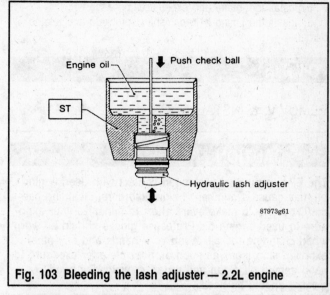

Fig. 103 Bleeding the lash adjuster — 2.2L engine

6. When all air bubbles are removed, remove the rod and quickly push the plunger in to ensure it is locked. If the plunger does not lock properly, replace the adjuster.
7. Install the valve lash adjusters on the rocker arms.
8. Install the valve rocker assembly on the cylinder head. Temporarily tighten the four outer bolts.
9. Tighten the four inner bolts to 9 ft. lbs. (12 Nm). Tighten the four outer bolts to the same specification.
10. Disconnect the PCV hose and remove the rocker cover. Tighten the rocker cover bolts to 4 ft. lbs. (5 Nm).

3.3L Engine

▶ See Figure 104

1. Remove the timing belt, camshaft sprockets and related parts.
2. Remove the intake and exhaust camshafts.
3. Remove the hydraulic lash adjusters from the tops of the valve springs. Keep the adjusters in order as they must be installed to their original positions.
4. Lubricate the lash adjusters and install on the valve springs.

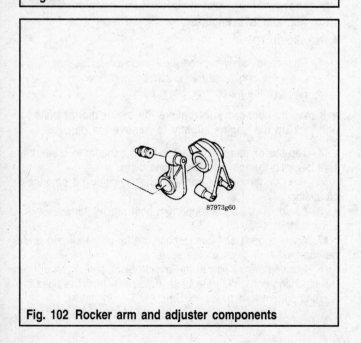

Fig. 101 Adjuster removed from rocker arm — 2.2L engine

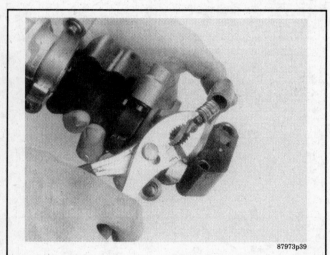

Fig. 102 Rocker arm and adjuster components

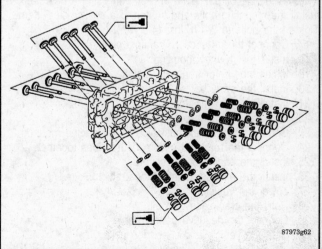

Fig. 104 Valve spring, adjuster and components — 3.3L engine

5. Install the intake and exhaust camshafts.

6. Install the timing belt, camshaft sprockets and related parts.

Oil Pan

REMOVAL & INSTALLATION

✳✳CAUTION

The EPA warns that prolonged contact with used engine oil may cause a number of skin disorders, including cancer! You should make every effort to minimize your exposure to used engine oil. Protective gloves should be worn when changing the oil. Wash your hands and any other exposed skin areas as soon as possible after exposure to used engine oil. Soap and water, or waterless hand cleaner should be used.

1.2L Engine

▶ See Figure 105

1. Disconnect the negative battery cable.
2. Raise and safely support the vehicle on jackstands.
3. Drain the engine oil into a suitable container.
4. Remove the exhaust manifold cover.
5. Remove the engine under cover.
6. Disconnect the front and rear exhaust pipes from one another.
7. Disconnect the rear exhaust pipe from the engine mount.
8. Support the engine with a suitable fixture.
9. Remove the pitching stopper.
10. Remove the sway bar, if equipped.
11. Remove the center transaxle mount.
12. Remove the flywheel housing.
13. Disconnect the air suction manifold pipe.
14. Remove the oil pan mounting bolts, then remove the oil pan and oil pan plate.
15. Clean all gasket material from both mating surfaces.

To install:

16. Install the oil pan plate and oil pan using a new gasket. Install the mounting bolts and tighten in a crisscross pattern. Tighten the bolts to 3-4 ft. lbs. (4-5 Nm).
17. Connect the air suction manifold pipe.
18. Install the flywheel housing.
19. Install the center transaxle mount.
20. Install the sway bar.
21. Install the pitching stopper.
22. Remove the support fixture.
23. Connect the rear exhaust pipe to the engine mount.
24. Connect the rear and front exhaust pipes together.
25. Install the engine under cover.
26. Install the exhaust manifold heat shield.
27. Lower the vehicle.
28. Refill the crankcase with oil.
29. Connect the negative battery cable.
30. Start the vehicle and check for leaks.

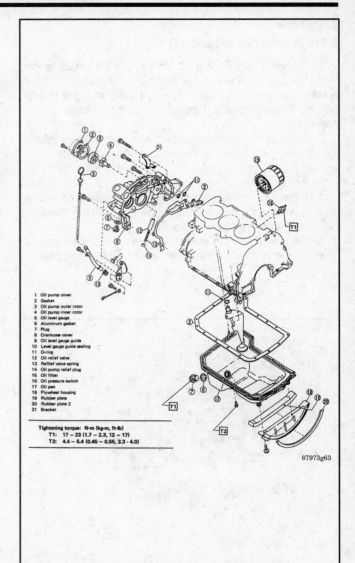

1 Oil pump cover
2 Gasket
3 Oil pump outer rotor
4 Oil pump inner rotor
5 Oil level gauge
6 Aluminum gasket
7 Plug
8 Crankcase cover
9 Oil level gauge guide
10 Level gauge guide sealing
11 O-ring
12 Oil relief valve
13 Relief valve spring
14 Oil pump relief plug
15 Oil filter
16 Oil pressure switch
17 Oil pan
18 Flywheel housing
19 Rubber plate
20 Rubber plate 2
21 Bracket

Tightening torque: N·m (kg-m, ft-lb)
T1: 17 – 23 (1.7 – 2.3, 12 – 17)
T2: 4.4 – 5.4 (0.45 – 0.55, 3.3 - 4.0)

87973g63

Fig. 105 Oil pan and lubrication components — 1.2L engine

1.6L, 1.8L and 2.7L Engines

▶ See Figure 106

1. Raise and safely support the vehicle on jackstands.
2. Drain the engine oil into a suitable container.
3. Remove the oil pan mounting bolts.

➡**It may be necessary to remove the motor mount bolts and jack up the engine slightly to remove the oil pan.**

4. Tap the oil pan with a plastic-faced hammer to break the seal between the pan and the engine block.
5. Remove the oil pan from the engine, guiding it past the oil strainer.
6. Clean all gasket material from both mating surfaces.

To install:

7. Apply a bead of sealer around the lip of the oil pan and set the gasket in place on the sealer.
8. Position the oil pan to the engine block and install all the mounting bolts. With the bolts in place, tighten the bolts in a cross pattern to 4 ft. lbs. (5 Nm).

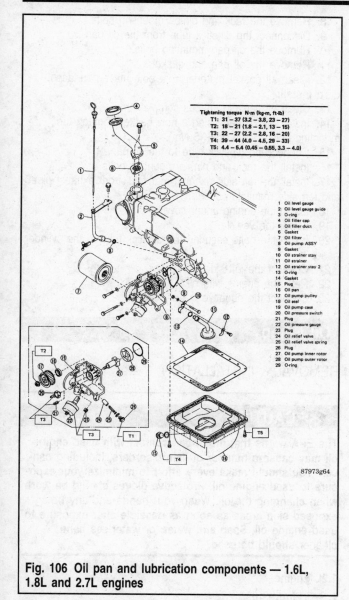

Tightening torque N·m (kg-m, ft-lb)
T1: 31 – 37 (3.2 – 3.8, 23 – 27)
T2: 18 – 21 (1.8 – 2.1, 13 – 15)
T3: 22 – 27 (2.2 – 2.8, 16 – 20)
T4: 39 – 44 (4.0 – 4.5, 29 – 33)
T5: 4.4 – 5.4 (0.45 – 0.55, 3.3 – 4.0)

1. Oil level gauge
2. Oil level gauge guide
3. O-ring
4. Oil filler cap
5. Oil filler duct
6. Gasket
7. Oil filter
8. Oil pump ASSY
9. Gasket
10. Oil strainer stay
11. Oil strainer
12. Oil strainer stay 2
13. O-ring
14. Gasket
15. Plug
16. Oil pan
17. Oil pump pulley
18. Oil seal
19. Oil pump case
20. Oil pressure switch
21. Plug
22. Oil pressure gauge
23. Plug
24. Oil relief valve
25. Oil relief valve spring
26. Plug
27. Oil pump inner rotor
28. Oil pump outer rotor
29. O-ring

87973g64

Fig. 106 Oil pan and lubrication components — 1.6L, 1.8L and 2.7L engines

9. Lower the engine and connect the engine mounts, if removed.
10. Tighten the oil pan drain plug to 18 ft. lbs. (25 Nm).
11. Lower the vehicle.
12. Refill the crankcase with oil.
13. Start the engine and check for leaks.

2.2L and 2.5L Engines

▶ **See Figure 107**

1. Raise and support the vehicle safely on jackstands.
2. Drain the oil from the engine into a suitable container.
3. Install the drain plug with a new gasket and tighten it to 33-36 ft. lbs. (43-47 Nm).
4. Remove the air intake duct.
5. Disconnect the oxygen sensor electrical connector.
6. Remove the pitching stopper.
7. Remove the upper radiator brackets.
8. Remove the exhaust front Y-pipe.
9. Remove the nuts which secure the front engine mounts to the front crossmember.

10. Support the engine with a suitable lifting device.
11. Lift up the engine slightly.
12. Remove the bolts that secure the oil pan.
13. While supporting the oil pan. use a rubber mallet and tap the oil pan to free it from the engine. Be sure to support the oil pan.
14. Clean all gasket material from both mating surfaces.
To install:
15. Apply a continuous bead of sealer to a new oil pan gasket.
16. Install the oil pan assembly. Tighten the bolts to 3-4 ft. lbs. (4-5 Nm).
17. Lower the engine onto the front crossmember.
18. Install the front engine mount nuts and tighten to 61 ft. lbs. (83 Nm).
19. Remove the engine lifting device.
20. Install the front Y-pipe with new gaskets. Tighten the nuts that secure the pipe to the engine to 23 ft. lbs. (30 Nm).
21. Connect the oxygen sensor electrical connector.

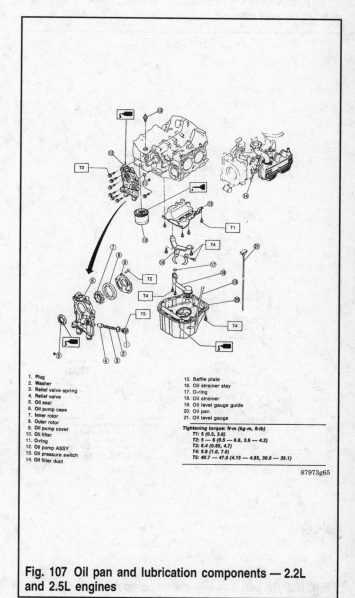

1. Plug
2. Washer
3. Relief valve spring
4. Relief valve
5. Oil seal
6. Oil pump case
7. Inner rotor
8. Outer rotor
9. Oil pump cover
10. Oil filter
11. O-ring
12. Oil pump ASSY
13. Oil pressure switch
14. Oil filler duct
15. Baffle plate
16. Oil strainer stay
17. O-ring
18. Oil strainer
19. Oil level gauge guide
20. Oil pan
21. Oil level gauge

Tightening torque: N·m (kg-m, ft-lb)
T1: 5 (0.5, 3.6)
T2: 5 – 6 (0.5 – 0.6, 3.6 – 4.3)
T3: 6.4 (0.65, 4.7)
T4: 9.8 (1.0, 7.0)
T5: 40.7 – 47.6 (4.15 – 4.85, 30.0 – 35.1)

87973g65

Fig. 107 Oil pan and lubrication components — 2.2L and 2.5L engines

22. Install the pitching stopper and tighten the bolts as follows:

- Front bolt — 40 ft. lbs. (54 Nm)
- Rear bolt — 49 ft. lbs. (67 Nm)

23. Install the upper radiator brackets.
24. Install the air intake duct.
25. Install the wheels.
26. Fill the engine to the proper level with the recommended oil and run the engine. Check for leaks.

3.3L Engine

▶ See Figure 108

1. Disconnect the negative battery cable.
2. Disconnect the left side O$_2$ sensor connector.
3. Remove the bolts securing the dipstick tube to the cylinder head.
4. Raise and safely support the vehicle on jackstands.
5. Drain the engine oil into a suitable container.
6. Remove the engine under covers.
7. Remove the left side exhaust manifold cover, front pipe and left exhaust manifold.

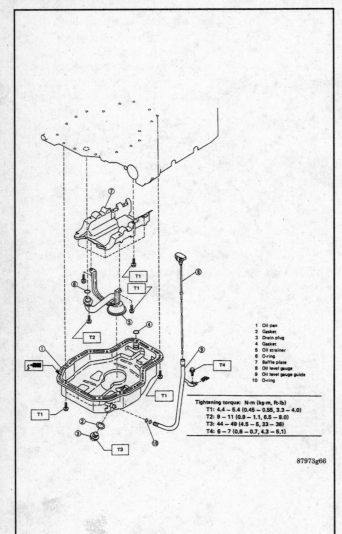

Fig. 108 Oil pan and lubrication components — 3.3L engine

8. Remove the rack and pinion mounting bolts.
9. Disconnect the dipstick tube from the oil pan.
10. Remove the oil pan mounting bolts.
11. Remove the oil pan and gasket.
12. Clean all gasket material from both mating surfaces.

To install:

13. Clean all gasket surfaces completely.
14. Install the oil pan using a new gasket. Tighten the mounting bolts to 4 ft. lbs. (5 Nm).
15. Connect the dipstick tube to the oil pan.
16. Install the rack and pinion mounting bolts.
17. Install the left side exhaust manifold, front exhaust pipe and left side manifold cover.
18. Install the engine under covers.
19. Lower the vehicle.
20. Install the bolts securing the dipstick tube to the cylinder head.
21. Connect the left side O$_2$ sensor.
22. Refill the engine with oil.
23. Connect the negative battery cable.

Oil Pump

REMOVAL & INSTALLATION

❊❊CAUTION

The EPA warns that prolonged contact with used engine oil may cause a number of skin disorders, including cancer! You should make every effort to minimize your exposure to used engine oil. Protective gloves should be worn when changing the oil. Wash your hands and any other exposed skin areas as soon as possible after exposure to used engine oil. Soap and water, or waterless hand cleaner should be used.

1.2L Engine

▶ See Figure 109

The oil pump is an integral part of the crankcase cover, located at the front of the engine.

1. Raise and support the vehicle safely.
2. Drain the engine oil into a suitable container.
3. Remove the oil level gauge, the oil level gauge guide and the level gauge guide seal.
4. Disconnect the electrical harness from the alternator. Remove the alternator-to-engine mounting bolts, drive belt and the alternator from the engine.
5. Remove the crankshaft pulley bolt and the crankshaft pulley.
6. Remove the timing belt cover-to-engine bolts and the cover from the engine.
7. Remove the timing belt tensioner-to-engine bolts, the spring and the tensioner.
8. Using a piece of chalk, mark the rotating direction of the timing belt.
9. Remove the crankshaft drive plate and the timing belt.
10. Remove the camshaft sprocket-to-camshaft bolts and the sprocket from the camshaft.

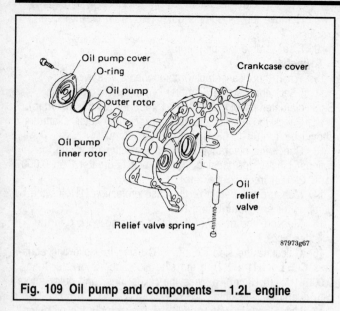

Fig. 109 Oil pump and components — 1.2L engine

11. Remove the inner timing belt cover-to-engine bolts and the cover from the engine.

12. From under the engine, remove the flywheel housing cover-to-engine bolts and the cover from the engine.

13. Remove the oil pan-to-engine bolts and the pan from the engine; discard the gasket. Remove the oil strainer-to-engine bolts and the strainer assembly from the engine.

14. Remove the water pump cover-to-crankcase cover bolts and the water pump cover. Use a screwdriver to lock the balance shaft, then remove the water pump impeller.

15. Remove the crankcase cover-to-engine bolts and the cover from the engine.

16. Remove the oil pump cover-to-crankcase cover bolts, the cover, the outer rotor and the inner rotor with the shaft.

To install:

17. Clean all gasket mating surfaces thoroughly.

18. Inspect the oil pump parts for wear and/or damage; replace the parts if necessary.

19. Pack the oil pump with petroleum jelly and reassemble. By packing the oil pump, a vacuum will be created upon initial fire-up and allow oil pressure to build immediately.

20. Install the crankcase cover and water pump.

21. Install the oil strainer using a new O-ring, and oil pan using a new gasket. Tighten the oil pan bolts to 3-4 ft. lbs. (4-5 Nm).

22. Install the flywheel housing cover.

23. Install the camshaft sprockets, crankshaft sprocket, timing belt and related components.

24. Install the crankshaft pulley and bolt.

25. Install the alternator and connect the electrical connectors.

26. Install the oil level gauge, the oil level gauge guide and the level gauge guide seal.

27. Fill the engine with oil. Connect the negative battery cable.

28. Start the engine and allow it to reach operating temperature. Check for adequate oil pressure. Then, check for leaks.

29. Adjust the ignition timing as required.

1.6L Engine

▶ **See Figure 110**

The oil pump can be removed with the engine in the vehicle. The oil pump is located on the front of the engine, and has the oil filter mounted on it. The pump and filter may be removed as an assembly.

1. Place a drip pan below the oil pump assembly to catch any oil that may spill out during removal and installation.

2. Unfasten the 4 bolts which secure the oil pump to the engine.

3. Remove the pump, complete with the gasket and filter.

4. Remove the filter from the pump and disassemble the pump.

To install:

5. Wash the disassembled oil pump in solvent. Allow the parts to dry completely before assembling.

6. Check the outside diameter of the oil pump rotor shaft. If worn or damaged, replace it.

7. Check the gear and rotor. Drive gear outside diameter should be 1.1693-1.1709 in. (29.70-29.74mm). Rotor outside diameter should be 1.5957-1.5968 in. (40.53-40.56mm). If not within specification, replace as necessary.

8. Check the clearance between the pump drive gear and pump rotor. If clearance is greater than 0.008 in. (0.2mm), replace the drive gear and rotor as an assembly.

9. Check the side clearance between the pump case and pump rotor, and between the pump case and drive gear. If clearance is greater than 0.008 in. (0.2mm), replace the necessary components.

10. Lay a straightedge across the pump case and measure the clearance between the pump case and the rotor. If greater than 0.0098 in. (0.25mm), replace the necessary components.

11. Check the relief valve spring. Free-length should be 1.854 in. (47.1mm).

12. Check the bypass valve and spring in the same manner.

13. Install the oil filter on the pump boss.

14. Using new gaskets and O-rings, fit the pump to the crankcase and carefully engage the pump drive with the slot in the end of the camshaft. Be sure that the pump mounts flush to the block.

15. Secure the pump with the 4 mounting bolts.

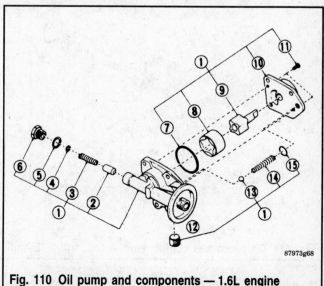

Fig. 110 Oil pump and components — 1.6L engine

16. Check the engine oil level and add oil, as necessary, to replace any that was lost.

1.8L and 2.7L Engines
▶ See Figures 111 and 112

The engine oil pump is located at the front of the engine. The oil filter is attached to the oil pump.

1. Disconnect the negative battery cable.
2. Place an oil pan under the crankcase, remove the drain plug and drain the oil from the crankcase.
3. Remove the left and right front timing belt covers.
4. Loosen the tensioner mounting bolts on the No. 1 cylinder.
5. Turn the tensioner to fully loosen the belt, then tighten the mounting bolts.
6. Using a piece of chalk, mark the rotating direction of the timing belt, then remove the belt from the vehicle.
7. Remove the oil pump-to-engine bolts and the oil pump along with the oil filter from the cylinder block.

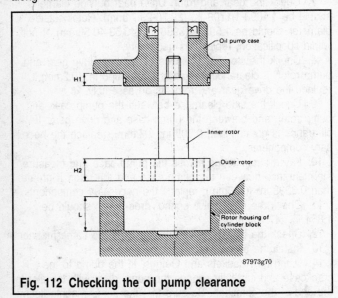

Fig. 112 Checking the oil pump clearance

8. Remove the oil pump's outer rotor from the cylinder block.
9. Disassemble the oil pump.

To install:

10. Wash the disassembled components in solvent.
11. Check the outside diameter of the inner rotor shaft. Shaft diameter should be 1.4035-1.4055 in. (35.65-35.70mm).
12. Check the outside diameter of the outer rotor. Diameter should be 1.9665-1.9685 in. (49.95-50.00mm).
13. Check the clearance between the outer rotor and the cylinder block rotor housing. If clearance is greater than 0.0087 in. (0.22mm), replace the rotor.
14. Measure the height of the case projection **H1** plus the oil pump inner and outer rotors **H2**.
15. Measure the depth of the rotor housing bore **L** in the cylinder block.
16. Calculate the side clearance **C** using the following equation: **C = L - (H1 + H2)**. If the side clearance is greater than 0.00071 in. (0.18mm), replace the pump inner and outer rotors with oversized versions.
17. Using new gaskets and O-rings, assemble the oil pump. Tighten the oil pump pulley to 13-15 ft. lbs. (18-21 Nm). Tighten the by-pass spring plug to 23-27 ft. lbs. (31-37 Nm).
18. Install the oil pump on the cylinder block.
19. Install the timing belt and related components.
20. Fill the engine with oil. Connect the negative battery cable.
21. Start the engine and allow it to reach operating temperature. Check for adequate oil pressure. Check for leaks.
22. Adjust the ignition timing as required.

2.2L Engine
▶ See Figure 113

1. Disconnect the negative battery cable.
2. Drain the engine oil into a suitable container.
3. Drain the coolant into a suitable separate container.
4. Remove the water pump. Refer to the water pump removal and installation procedure in this section for details.
5. Remove the oil pump mounting bolts.

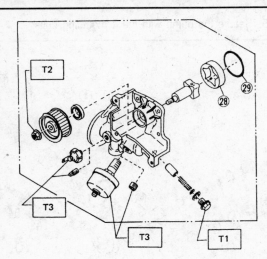

Tightening torque N·m (kg-m, ft-lb)		
T1: 31 — 37	(3.2 — 3.8,	23 — 27)
T2: 18 — 21	(1.8 — 2.1,	13 — 15)
T3: 22 — 27	(2.2 — 2.8,	16 — 20)
T4: 39 — 44	(4.0 — 4.5,	29 — 33)
T5: 4.4 — 5.4	(0.45 — 0.55,	3.3 — 4.0)

87973g69

Fig. 111 Oil pump and components — 1.8L and 2.7L engines

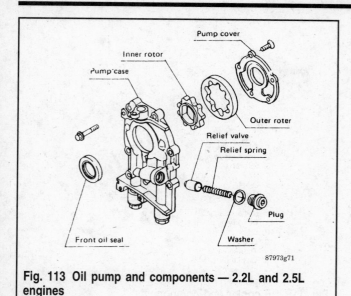

Fig. 113 Oil pump and components — 2.2L and 2.5L engines

6. Carefully pry the oil pump from the engine block.

☀☀WARNING

Use extreme care not to damage the engine block or the oil pump during removal of the pump.

7. Remove the front crankshaft seal.
To install:
8. Measure the tip clearance of the rotors. If clearance is greater than 0.0071 in. (0.18mm), replace the rotors.
9. Measure the clearance between the outer rotor and the cylinder block rotor housing. If clearance exceeds 0.0079 in. (0.20mm), replace the rotor.
10. Measure the side clearance between the oil pump inner rotor and the pump cover. If clearance exceeds 0.0047 in. (0.12mm), replace the rotor or pump body.
11. Install a new front oil seal on the pump cover using a driver.
12. Assemble the oil pump.
13. Install a new front crankshaft seal using installer 499587100 or equivalent.
14. Apply sealant and a new O-ring to the oil pump.
15. Install the oil pump and torque the bolts to 5 ft. lbs. (7 Nm).
16. Install the water pump.
17. Fill the crankcase to the proper level with the recommended oil.
18. Fill and bleed the cooling system.
19. Connect the negative battery cable.
20. Start the engine and check for leaks.

2.5L Engine
▶ See Figure 113

1. Disconnect the negative battery cable.
2. Drain the cooling system into a suitable container.
3. Raise and support the vehicle safely.
4. Drain the engine oil into a separate container.
5. Remove the belt covers, timing belt and related parts.
6. Remove the belt tensioner bracket.
7. Remove the engine coolant pipe.

8. Remove the water pump assembly.
9. Remove the oil pump mounting bolts and pry the pump from the engine block.

➡Use extreme care not to damage the engine block or the oil pump during removal of the pump.

To install:
10. Install a new front seal to the oil pump.
11. Apply a continuous bead sealant to the mating surfaces of the oil pump.
12. Install a new O-ring to the oil pump.
13. Install the oil pump and torque the bolts to 56 inch lbs. (6.4 Nm).
14. Install the water pump.
15. Install the engine coolant pipe.
16. Install the belt tensioner bracket, timing belt and the covers.
17. Fill the engine to the proper level with the recommended oil and coolant.
18. Connect the negative battery cable.
19. Fill and bleed the cooling system.

3.3L Engine
▶ See Figure 114

1. Disconnect the negative battery cable.
2. Raise and safely support the vehicle.
3. Drain the engine oil into a suitable container.
4. Remove the engine under covers.
5. Remove the bolts securing the power steering oil cooler pipe. DO NOT remove the pipe.
6. Remove the cooling fan assemblies.
7. Remove the drive belt cover and drive belt.
8. Remove the crank angle sensors.
9. Remove the crankshaft pulley.
10. Remove the timing belt, tensioners and tensioner brackets.
11. Remove the oil pump mounting bolts.
12. Separate the oil pump from the block by inserting a suitable prying tool between the pump and the block.
13. Remove the oil pump and gasket.
14. Remove the front seal from the oil pump.
To install:
15. Measure the tip clearance of the rotors. If clearance is greater than 0.0071 in. (0.18mm), replace the rotors.
16. Measure the clearance between the outer rotor and the cylinder block rotor housing. If clearance exceeds 0.0079 in. (0.20mm), replace the rotor.
17. Measure the side clearance between the oil pump inner rotor and the pump cover. If clearance exceeds 0.0047 in. (0.12mm), replace the rotor or pump body.
18. Install a new oil seal in the oil pump.
19. Clean all gasket surfaces completely.
20. Install the oil pump using a new gasket. Tighten the mounting bolts to 5 ft. lbs. (7 Nm).
21. Install the timing belt components.
22. Install the crankshaft pulley.
23. Install the crank angle sensors.
24. Install the drive belts and drive belt cover.
25. Install the cooling fan assembly.
26. Install the bolts securing the power steering oil cooler pipe.

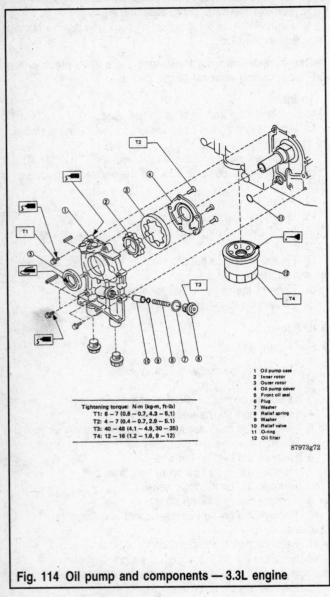

Tightening torque: N·m (kg-m, ft-lb)
T1: 6 − 7 (0.8 − 0.7, 4.3 − 5.1)
T2: 4 − 7 (0.4 − 0.7, 2.9 − 5.1)
T3: 40 − 48 (4.1 − 4.9, 30 − 35)
T4: 12 − 16 (1.2 − 1.6, 9 − 12)

1 Oil pump case
2 Inner rotor
3 Outer rotor
4 Oil pump cover
5 Front oil seal
6 Plug
7 Washer
8 Relief spring
9 Washer
10 Relief valve
11 O-ring
12 Oil filter

87973g72

Fig. 114 Oil pump and components — 3.3L engine

27. Install the engine under covers.
28. Lower the vehicle.
29. Refill the crankcase with oil.
30. Connect the negative battery cable.
31. Start the vehicle and verify no oil leaks.

Oil Cooler

REMOVAL & INSTALLATION

Turbocharged Models
▶ See Figure 115

❊❊CAUTION

The EPA warns that prolonged contact with used engine oil may cause a number of skin disorders, including cancer! You should make every effort to minimize your exposure to used engine oil. Protective gloves should be worn

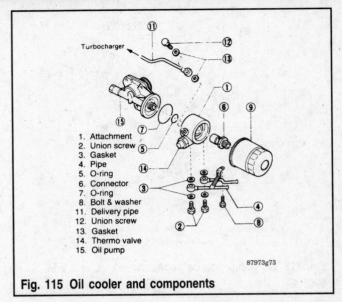

1. Attachment
2. Union screw
3. Gasket
4. Pipe
5. O-ring
6. Connector
7. O-ring
8. Bolt & washer
11. Delivery pipe
12. Union screw
13. Gasket
14. Thermo valve
15. Oil pump

87973g73

Fig. 115 Oil cooler and components

when changing the oil. Wash your hands and any other exposed skin areas as soon as possible after exposure to used engine oil. Soap and water, or waterless hand cleaner should be used.

1. Place a drain pan below the cooler assembly. Remove the two bolts connecting the oil cooler lines to the bottom of the filter housing. Drain oil into the pan.
2. Remove the bolt connecting the bracket for the two oil lines to the block. Pull the oil lines away from the block and drain them into the pan.
3. Remove the three oil cooler mounting bolts and remove the assembly.
   To install:
4. Install the oil cooler and tighten the mounting bolts to 20 ft. lbs. (26 Nm).
5. Install the cooler lines using new seal washers. Tighten the bolts to 25 ft. lbs. (32 Nm).
6. Attach the bracket for the cooler lines.
7. Start the engine and add engine oil. Check for leaks.

Crankshaft Pulley

REMOVAL & INSTALLATION

▶ **See Figures 116, 117 and 118**

1. Disconnect the negative battery cable.
2. Remove the accessory drive belt(s).
3. Using a suitable puller, remove the crankshaft pulley.
4. Install the pulley and tighten the pulley bolt to 69-76 ft. lbs. (93-103 Nm) for 1.6L, 1.8L and 2.7L engines. Tighten the bolt on 1.2L engines to 58-72 ft. lbs. (78-98 Nm). Tighten the bolt on 2.5 engines to 94 ft. lbs. (127 Nm). Tighten the crankshaft pulley bolt on 2.7L and 3.3L engines to 115 ft. lbs. (157 Nm).
5. Install the accessory drive belt and adjust the tension to specification.
6. Connect the negative battery cable.

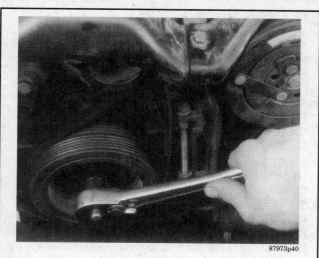

Fig. 116 Loosen the crankshaft pulley retainer bolt — 2.2L engine shown

Fig. 117 Remove the pulley retainer bolt . . .

Fig. 118 . . . then remove the crankshaft pulley

Timing Belt Cover and Seal

REMOVAL & INSTALLATION

1.2L Engine
▶ See Figure 119

1. Disconnect the negative battery cable.
2. Loosen the alternator-to-engine bolts, relax the drive belt tension and remove the drive belt from the front of the engine.
3. Using a socket wrench (through the hole in the right fender) and the Crankshaft Pulley Wrench tool No. 499205500 or equivalent, remove the crankshaft pulley-to-crankshaft bolt and the pulley from the crankshaft.
4. Remove the timing belt cover-to-engine bolts and the cover from the engine.
5. Remove the rubber cover seal. Clean all mating surfaces.

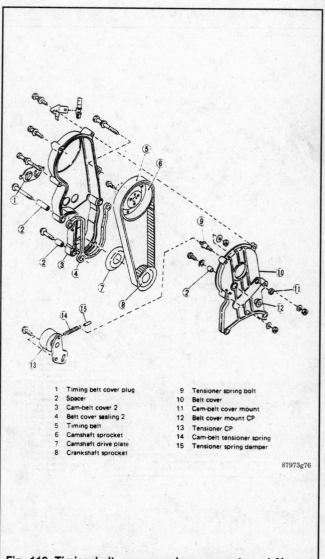

1	Timing belt cover plug	9	Tensioner spring bolt
2	Spacer	10	Belt cover
3	Cam-belt cover 2	11	Cam-belt cover mount
4	Belt cover sealing 2	12	Belt cover mount CP
5	Timing belt	13	Tensioner CP
6	Camshaft sprocket	14	Cam-belt tensioner spring
7	Camshaft drive plate	15	Tensioner spring damper
8	Crankshaft sprocket		

Fig. 119 Timing belt covers and components — 1.2L engine

To install:

6. Install a new timing belt cover seal.

7. Install the timing belt cover and tighten the bolts securely to 8-9 ft. lbs. (10-12 Nm).

8. Install the crankshaft pulley and tighten the bolt to 58-72 ft. lbs. (78-98 Nm).

9. Install the accessory drive belt and tighten to the proper tension.

10. Connect the negative battery cable.

1.8L Engine

▶ See Figure 120

1. Disconnect the negative battery cable.

2. Loosen the water pump pulley mounting bolts.

3. Loosen the alternator mounting bolts and remove the alternator belt.

4. Remove the water pump pulley bolts and remove the water pump pulley.

5. Disconnect the electrical harness from the oil pressure switch.

6. Remove the dipstick tube.

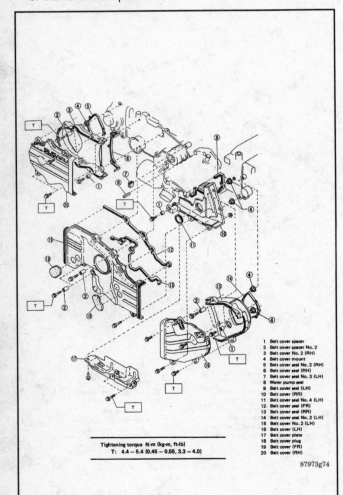

Tightening torque N·m (kg-m, ft-lb)
T: 4.4 — 5.4 (0.45 — 0.55, 3.3 — 4.0)

1 Belt cover spacer
2 Belt cover spacer No. 2
3 Belt cover No. 2 (RH)
4 Belt cover mount
5 Belt cover seal No. 2 (RH)
6 Belt cover seal (RH)
7 Belt cover seal No. 3 (LH)
8 Water pump seal
9 Belt cover seal (LH)
10 Belt cover (RR)
11 Belt cover seal No. 4 (LH)
12 Belt cover seal (FR)
13 Belt cover seal (RR)
14 Belt cover seal No. 2 (LH)
15 Belt cover No. 2 (LH)
16 Belt cover (LH)
17 Belt cover plate
18 Belt cover plug
19 Belt cover (FR)
20 Belt cover (RH)

87973g74

Fig. 120 Timing belt covers and components — 1.8L engine

7. Remove the crankshaft pulley.

8. Remove the timing belt cover plate, if equipped.

9. Remove the timing belt cover bolts on the left, right, and center covers.

10. Remove the timing belt covers.

11. Remove the rubber cover seal. Clean all mating surfaces.

To install:

12. Install a new timing belt cover seal.

13. Install the timing belt covers on the engine using the mounting bolts. Tighten the bolts to 48 inch lbs. (5 Nm).

14. Install the timing belt cover plate, if removed.

15. Install the crankshaft pulley, and tighten the bolt to 69-76 ft. lbs. (93-103 Nm)

16. Install the dipstick tube.

17. Connect the electrical harness to the oil pressure switch.

18. Install the water pump pulley and loosely install the mounting bolts.

19. Install the drive belt and adjust the tension as necessary. Tighten the alternator mounting bolts.

20. Tighten the water pump pulley mounting bolts.

21. Connect the negative battery cable.

2.2L Engine

▶ See Figure 121

1. Disconnect the negative battery cable.

2. Remove the accessory drive belts.

3. Remove the power steering pump, alternator, air conditioner compressor brackets.

4. Secure the crankshaft pulley with tool No. 499977000 or equivalent.

5. Remove the crankshaft pulley bolt and pulley.

6. Remove the timing belt cover mounting bolts.

7. Remove the belt covers.

8. Remove the rubber cover seal. Clean all mating surfaces.

To install:

9. Install a new timing belt cover seal.

10. Install the belt covers and tighten the bolts to 36-48 inch lbs. (4-5 Nm).

11. Install the crankshaft pulley and tighten the bolt to 69-76 ft. lbs. (93-103 Nm).

12. Install the power steering pump, alternator, air conditioner compressor and associated brackets.

13. Install the accessory drive belts.

14. Connect the negative battery cable.

2.5L Engine

1. Disconnect the negative battery cable.

2. Disconnect the radiator electric fan motor wiring connectors.

3. Remove the coolant reservoir tank.

4. Remove the four bolts that secure the radiator shroud and remove the fan assembly.

5. Position the No. 1 piston to TDC of its compression stroke.

6. Remove the drive belt and the A/C compressor drive belt tensioner.

7. Remove the accessory drive belt cover.

8. Secure the crankshaft pulley with tool No. ST499977000 or equivalent.

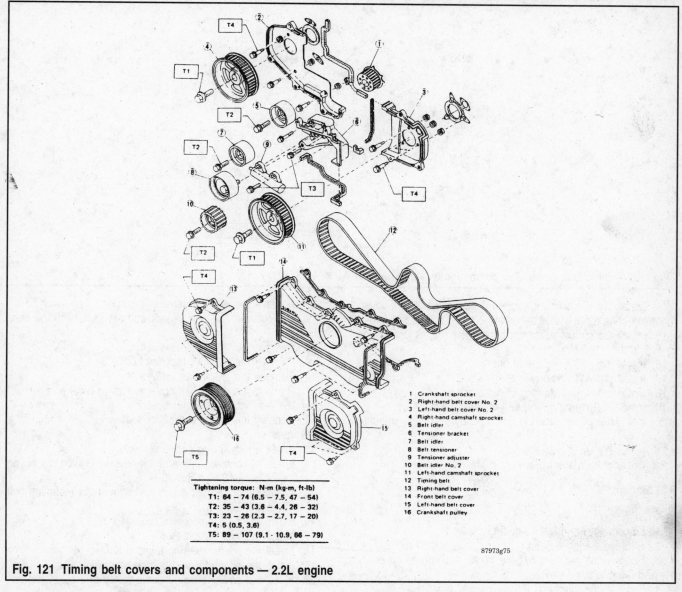

Tightening torque: N·m (kg-m, ft-lb)
T1: 64 — 74 (6.5 — 7.5, 47 — 54)
T2: 35 — 43 (3.6 — 4.4, 26 — 32)
T3: 23 — 26 (2.3 — 2.7, 17 — 20)
T4: 5 (0.5, 3.6)
T5: 89 — 107 (9.1 - 10.9, 66 — 79)

87973g75

1 Crankshaft sprocket
2 Right-hand belt cover No. 2
3 Left-hand belt cover No. 2
4 Right-hand camshaft sprocket
5 Belt idler
6 Tensioner bracket
7 Belt idler
8 Belt tensioner
9 Tensioner adjuster
10 Belt idler No. 2
11 Left-hand camshaft sprocket
12 Timing belt
13 Right-hand belt cover
14 Front belt cover
15 Left-hand belt cover
16 Crankshaft pulley

Fig. 121 Timing belt covers and components — 2.2L engine

9. Remove the crankshaft pulley bolt and pulley.
10. Remove the left timing belt cover mounting bolts and remove the left cover.
11. Remove the right timing belt cover mounting bolts and remove the right cover.
12. Remove the center timing belt cover mounting bolts and remove the center cover.
13. Remove the timing belt cover rubber seal and discard.
To install:
14. Install a new timing belt cover rubber seal.
15. Install the center, right then the left timing belt covers and tighten the bolts to 44 inch lbs. (5 Nm).
16. Install the crankshaft pulley and tighten the bolt to 94 ft. lbs. (127 Nm).
17. Install the A/C compressor drive belt tensioner and install the drive belts.
18. Install the fan shroud and fan motor assembly.
19. Install the accessory drive belt cover.
20. Connect the negative battery cable.

2.7L Engine
▶ See Figure 122

1. Disconnect the negative battery cable.
2. Remove the drive belts.
3. Remove the nut securing the power steering pump pulley and remove the pulley.
4. Remove the alternator and belt cover bracket.
5. Remove the power steering pump bracket.
6. Remove the A/C belt tensioner bracket.
7. Remove the A/C compressor and set aside with the lines attached.
8. Remove the A/C compressor bracket.
9. Remove the crankshaft pulley bolt.
10. Remove the crankshaft pulley.
11. Remove the timing belt cover mounting bolts and remove the left, right and center covers.
12. Remove the timing belt cover seal.
To install:
13. Install a new timing belt cover seal.

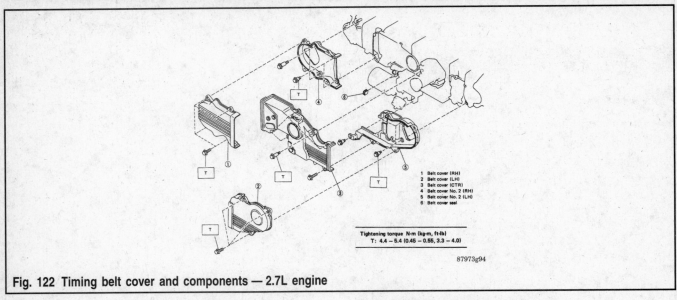

Fig. 122 Timing belt cover and components — 2.7L engine

1 Belt cover (RH)
2 Belt cover (LH)
3 Belt cover (CTR)
4 Belt cover No. 2 (RH)
5 Belt cover No. 2 (LH)
6 Belt cover seal

Tightening torque N·m (kg-m, ft-lb)
T: 4.4 — 5.4 (0.45 — 0.55, 3.3 — 4.0)

87973g94

14. Install the center, right and left covers. Tighten the cover mounting bolts to 48 inch lbs. (5 Nm).

15. Install the crankshaft pulley and tighten the mounting bolt to 115 ft. lbs. (157 Nm).

16. Install the A/C compressor bracket.

17. Install the A/C compressor.

18. Install the power steering pump bracket.

19. Install the alternator and belt cover bracket.

20. Install the power steering pump pulley and pulley mounting nut.

21. Install the drive belts.

22. Connect the negative battery cable.

3.3L Engine

▶ See Figure 123

1. Disconnect the negative battery cable.

2. Remove the drive belts.

3. Remove the nut securing the power steering pump pulley and remove the pulley.

4. Remove the alternator and belt cover bracket.

5. Remove the power steering pump bracket.

6. Remove the A/C belt tensioner bracket.

7. Remove the A/C compressor and set aside with the lines attached.

8. Remove the A/C compressor bracket.

9. Remove the crankshaft pulley bolt.

10. Remove the crankshaft pulley.

11. Remove the timing belt cover mounting bolts and remove the left, right and center covers.

12. Remove the timing belt cover seal.

To install:

13. Install a new timing belt cover seal.

14. Install the center, right and left covers. Tighten the cover mounting bolts to 48 inch lbs. (5 Nm).

15. Install the crankshaft pulley and tighten the mounting bolt to 115 ft. lbs. (157 Nm).

16. Install the A/C compressor bracket.

17. Install the A/C compressor.

18. Install the power steering pump bracket.

19. Install the alternator and belt cover bracket.

20. Install the power steering pump pulley and pulley mounting nut.

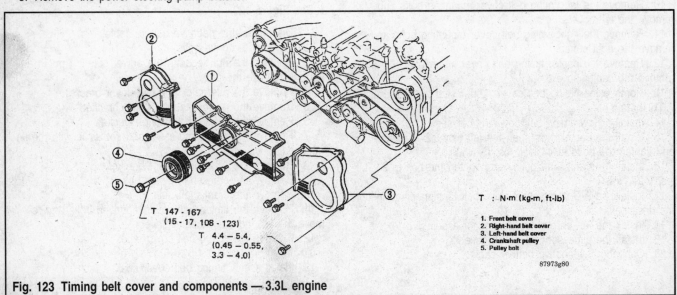

T 147 - 167
(15 - 17, 108 - 123)

T 4.4 - 5.4,
(0.45 - 0.55,
3.3 - 4.0)

T : N·m (kg-m, ft-lb)

1. Front belt cover
2. Right-hand belt cover
3. Left-hand belt cover
4. Crankshaft pulley
5. Pulley bolt

87973g80

Fig. 123 Timing belt cover and components — 3.3L engine

21. Install the drive belts.
22. Connect the negative battery cable.

Timing Gear Cover

REMOVAL & INSTALLATION

1.6L Engine

The timing gears on the 1.6L engine are located at the rear of the engine and are covered by the flywheel housing. In order to remove the flywheel housing the engine must be removed from the vehicle.

1. Remove the engine from the vehicle.
2. Separate the engine from the transaxle. If equipped with an automatic transaxle, remove the torque converter with the transaxle.
3. On manual transaxle equipped vehicles, remove the clutch assembly from the flywheel and the flywheel from the crankshaft. On automatic transaxle equipped vehicles, remove the converter drive plate from the crankshaft.
4. Remove the flywheel housing-to-engine bolts and work the housing from the two aligning dowels.
5. Using a puller, remove the flywheel housing oil seal.

To install:

6. Using a driver, install a new flywheel housing oil seal.
7. Clean the gasket mating surface thoroughly and apply a fresh coat of Three Bond® or equivalent.
8. Install the flywheel housing and tighten the bolts to 14-20 ft. lbs. (19-27 Nm).
9. On manual transaxle equipped vehicles, install the flywheel and tighten the bolts to 30-33 ft. lbs. (41-45 Nm). Install the clutch assembly.
10. On automatic transaxle equipped vehicles, tighten the drive plate to crankshaft bolts to 36-39 ft. lbs. (49-53 Nm).
11. Install the transaxle to the engine and tighten the bolts to 34-40 ft. lbs. (46-54 Nm).
12. Install the engine and transaxle assembly in the vehicle.

OIL SEAL REPLACEMENT

The flywheel housing cover oil seal is pressed in.

1. Remove the engine from the vehicle and separate the engine from the transaxle.
2. Remove the flywheel and clutch assembly from the engine as detailed in Section 7.
3. Remove the flywheel housing from the engine and remove the oil seal from the housing.
4. Install the new oil seal pressing it into place.
5. Reassemble the engine and install it in the reverse order of disassembly and removal.

Timing Belt

PRECAUTIONS

- Do not let oil, grease or coolant contact the belt. Wipe the belt quickly if a spill occurs.
- Do not bend the belt sharply.
- When replacing the belts, be sure to replace both belts as a matched set.

REMOVAL & INSTALLATION

1.2L Engine

▶ See Figures 124 and 125

1. Disconnect the negative battery cable.
2. Remove the accessory drive belt.
3. Loosen the crankshaft pulley bolts but do not remove.

➡**An access hole is provided in the wheelhouse panel to loosen and then remove the crankshaft pulley bolts.**

4. Position the crankshaft with No. 3 cylinder at TDC.
5. Remove the crankshaft bolts and pulley.
6. Remove the front timing belt cover bolts and timing belt cover.
7. Loosen the tensioner bolt and rotate the tensioner in the direction that loosens the belt. With the tensioner fully retracted, tighten the tensioner bolt.
8. Remove the camshaft sprocket mounting bolts. Mark the timing belt, if it is to be used again, with the direction of rotation for reinstallation. Remove the belt from the sprockets.
9. Remove the camshaft sprocket.
10. Slide the crankshaft sprocket off the crankshaft. With the sprocket removed be careful that the key does not fall out of the crankshaft keyway.
11. Remove the tensioner mounting bolts and remove the tensioner and spring from the engine.

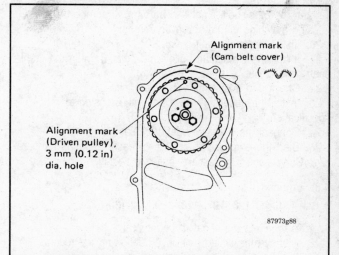

Fig. 124 Camshaft timing belt alignment mark — 1.2L engine

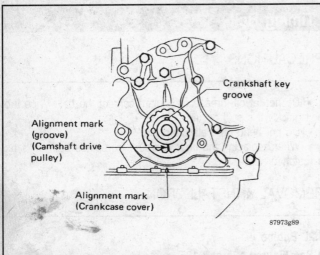

Fig. 125 Crankshaft timing belt alignment mark — 1.2L engine

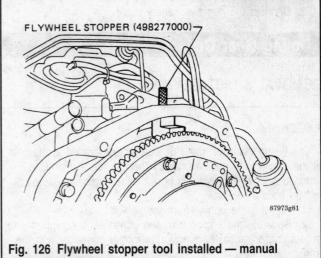

Fig. 126 Flywheel stopper tool installed — manual transaxle equipped models

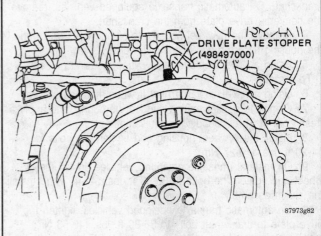

Fig. 127 Driveplate stopper tool installed — automatic transaxle equipped models

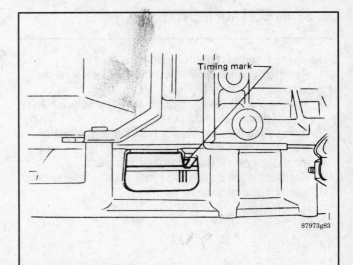

Fig. 128 Aligning the marks on the flywheel with the marks on the flywheel cover

To install:

12. Install the tensioner, spring and mounting bolts. Rotate the tensioner to the fully retracted position and tighten the mounting bolts.

13. Install the key into the crankshaft keyway, if removed. Install the crankshaft sprocket.

14. Install the camshaft pulley with the dowel pin lined up with the hole in the sprocket. Install the three mounting bolts and tighten to 9 ft. lbs. (12 Nm).

15. Align the timing marks as follows:

   a. Align the mark on the crankshaft sprocket with the dot on the crankcase cover below the sprocket. The keyway should be pointing almost straight up.

   b. Align the hole in the camshaft pulley with the notch cut into the top of the rear timing cover.

16. Ensure that each rocker arm can be moved.

17. If the old timing belt is being used install the belt with the direction arrow pointed in the correct direction.

18. Loosen the tensioner mounting bolts ½ turn and allow the tensioner to seat against the belt.

19. Tighten the tensioner bolt below the adjusting wheel first. Tighten the other bolt. Check to be sure all sprocket and housing matching marks are in agreement.

20. Install the timing belt cover.

21. Install the crankshaft pulley and bolts. Tighten the crankshaft bolts to 58-72 ft. lbs. (78-98 Nm).

22. Check and adjust the valve clearance.

23. Install the accessory drive belts and tension to specification.

24. Connect the negative battery cable.

25. Start the engine and allow it to reach operating temperature. Check, and if necessary, adjust the ignition timing.

1.8L Engine

◆ See Figures 126, 127, 128, 129 and 130

1. Disconnect the negative battery cable.

2. Remove the timing belt covers following the recommended procedure.

3. Loosen the tensioner mounting bolts on the number 1 cylinder by 1/2 turn.

Fig. 129 Driver side timing belt (No. 2) and No. 2 tensioner — 1.8L engine

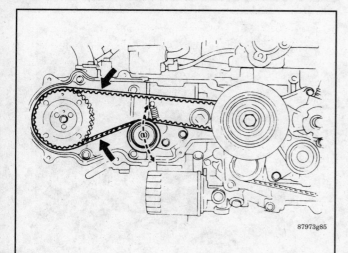

Fig. 130 Passenger side timing belt (No. 1) and No. 1 tensioner

4. Rotate the tensioner to the fully retracted position and tighten the mounting bolts.

5. Mark the direction of the belt and remove the belt from the engine.

6. Loosen the tensioner mounting bolts on the number 2 cylinder by 1/2 turn.

7. Rotate the tensioner using a tensioner wrench, to the fully retracted position and tighten the mounting bolts.

8. Mark the direction of the belt and remove the belt from the engine.

9. Remove the crankshaft pulley.

10. Remove the timing belt after marking the direction of rotation.

11. Remove the outer crankshaft sprocket.

12. Remove the tensioner mounting bolts and remove the tensioners and spring on the number 2 tensioner.

13. Remove the idler pulley mounting bolt and remove the idler.

14. Remove the camshaft sprockets using tool 49920700, or an equivalent camshaft sprocket wrench.

To install:

15. Install the camshaft sprockets using tool 49920700, or an equivalent camshaft sprocket wrench to hold the camshaft in place while tightening the camshaft sprocket bolts to 7 ft. lbs. (10 Nm).

16. To install the tensioners, perform the following:

    a. Attach the tensioner spring to the tensioner, then install the assembly on the cylinder block. Tighten the bolts by hand.

    b. Attach the tensioner spring to the bolt. Tighten the bolt then loosen 1/2 turn.

    c. Push the tensioner into the fully retracted position and tighten the mounting bolts.

17. Install the timing belt idler pulley and tighten the mounting bolt to 32 ft. lbs. (43 Nm).

18. Install the timing belt.

19. Install the crankshaft sprockets.

20. Install the crankshaft pulley and tighten the mounting bolt temporarily.

21. Line up the center of the three lines scribed on the flywheel with the timing mark on the flywheel housing.

22. Align the timing mark on the left side camshaft sprocket with the notch in the belt cover.

23. Attach timing belt No. 2 to the crankshaft sprocket No. 2, oil pump sprocket, belt idler and camshaft sprocket in that order, avoiding downward slackening of the belt.

24. Loosen tensioner No. 2 mounting bolts by 1/2 turn and let the tensioner contact the belt.

25. Push on the belt by hand to ensure smooth tensioner operation.

26. Apply torque to the camshaft sprocket in the counterclockwise direction using a belt tension wrench. While applying the torque tighten the tensioner mounting bolts temporarily.

27. Tighten the slide bolt to 14 ft. lbs. (18 Nm).

28. Tighten the pivot bolt to 14 ft. lbs. (18 Nm).

29. Verify the timing marks are still in alignment.

30. Rotate the crankshaft one full turn and line up the center of the three lines on the flywheel with the housing mark.

31. Align the right side camshaft sprocket timing mark with the notch in the cover.

32. Attach the timing belt to the crankshaft sprocket and camshaft sprocket. Avoid slackening the belt on the upper side.

33. Loosen the tensioner mounting bolts 1/2 turn and allow the tensioner to contact the belt.

34. Push on the belt by hand to ensure smooth tensioner operation.

35. Apply torque to the camshaft sprocket in the counterclockwise direction using a belt tension wrench. While applying the torque tighten the tensioner mounting bolts temporarily.

36. Tighten the slide bolt to 14 ft. lbs. (18 Nm).

37. Tighten the pivot bolt to 14 ft. lbs. (18 Nm).

38. Verify the timing marks are still in alignment.

39. Remove the crankshaft pulley.

40. Install the timing belt covers.

41. Install the crankshaft pulley.

42. Connect the negative battery cable.

2.2L Engine

▶ See Figures 131, 132, 133, 134, 135, 136, 137, 138, 139, 140, 141, 142, 143, 144, 145 and 146

The engine uses a single cam belt drive system with a serpentine type belt. The left side of the engine uses a hydraulic cam belt tensioner which is self-adjusting.

➡It is recommended that the timing belt be replaced every 60,000 miles (96,618 km).

1. Disconnect the negative battery cable.
2. Position the No. 1 piston to TDC of its compression stroke.
3. Remove the engine drive belts.
4. Remove the timing belt covers.
5. Align the camshaft sprockets so each sprocket notch aligns with the cam cover notches. Align the crankshaft sprocket top tooth notch, located at the rear of the tooth, with the notch on the crank angle sensor boss. Mark the three alignment points as well as the direction of cam belt rotation.

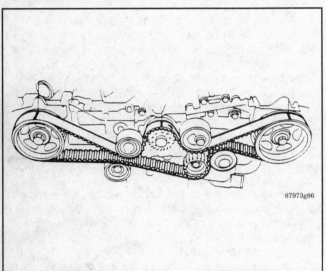

Fig. 131 Timing belt routing — 2.2L engine shown

Fig. 132 Remove the drive belt cover and retainer bolts

Fig. 133 Loosen the drive belt adjuster to remove the drive belt

Fig. 134 Remove the drive belt adjuster assembly, in order to access and remove the timing belt cover

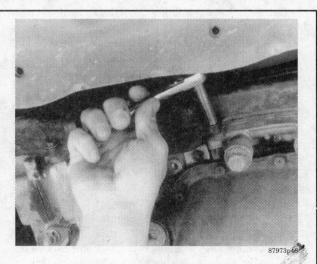

Fig. 135 Loosen the timing belt cover retainer bolts. Do not forget the bottom retainer bolts

Fig. 136 Remove the timing belt covers and seal

Fig. 139 . . . also align the No. 1 camshaft sprocket timing marks

Fig. 138 Align the timing marks on the No. 2 camshaft sprocket . . .

Fig. 140 Loosen and remove the tensioner pulley . . .

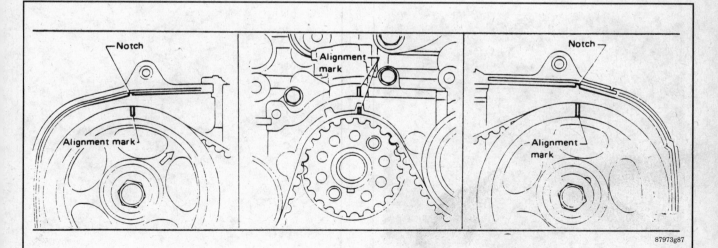

Fig. 137 Aligning the camshaft and crankshaft timing marks

Fig. 141 . . . and remove the timing belt

Fig. 142 Remove the lower timing belt pulleys . . .

Fig. 143 . . . and camshaft sprocket, if needed

Fig. 144 Remove the tensioner retainer bolts . . .

Fig. 145 . . . and remove the tensioner from the engine block

Fig. 146 Compress the tensioner in a vise and lock in place with a pin or Allen wrench

6. Loosen the tensioner adjusting bolts. Remove the bottom three idlers, the cam belt and the cam belt tensioner. The cam sprockets can then be removed with a modified camshaft sprocket wrench tool.

7. Remove the sprockets, if necessary. Note the reference sensor at the rear of the left cam sprocket.

To install:

8. Install the sprockets, if removed and torque the retaining bolts to 47-54 ft. lbs. (64-74 Nm).

9. Install the crankshaft sprocket and the non-adjustable right side idler. Do not install the tensioner idler at this time.

10. Compress the hydraulic tensioner in a vise slowly and temporarily secure the plunger with a pin or suitable Allen wrench. Install the tensioner and the pulley with the adjustable idler pulley. Temporarily tighten the tensioner while the tensioner is pushed to the right.

11. Align the crankshaft sprocket notch on the rear sprocket tooth with the crank angle sensor boss. This places the sprocket notch in the 12 o'clock position.

12. Align the camshaft sprockets with the notches in the cam rear belt cover. This places the sprocket notch in the 12 o'clock position for each camshaft.

13. Install the timing belt with the directional mark and alignment marks properly positioned (if belt was reused).

14. Loosen the tensioner retaining bolts and slide the tensioner to the left. Tighten the mounting bolts.

15. After verifying the timing marks are correct, remove the stopper pin from the tensioner.

16. Verify the correctness of the timing by noting that the notches on the 2 cam pulleys and the notch on the crankshaft pulley all point to the 12 o'clock position when the belt is properly installed.

17. Complete the engine component assembly by installing the cam belt covers, the crankshaft pulley bolt and pulley and the remaining components.

18. Connect the negative battery cable.

2.5L Engine

The engine uses a single cam belt drive system with a serpentine type belt. The left side of the engine uses a hydraulic cam belt tensioner which is self-adjusting.

➡**It is recommended that the timing belt be replaced every 60,000 miles (96,618 km).**

1. Disconnect the negative battery cable.
2. Disconnect the radiator electric fan motor wiring connectors.
3. Remove the coolant reservoir tank.
4. Remove the four bolts that secure the radiator shroud and remove the fan assembly.
5. Position the No. 1 piston to TDC of its compression stroke.
6. Remove the engine drive belts.
7. Remove the A/C compressor drive belt tensioner.
8. Using holding tool ST499977000 or equivalent, remove the bolt that secures the crankshaft sprocket and remove the sprocket.
9. Remove the left, right then the center timing belt covers.
10. Align the camshaft sprockets so each sprocket notch aligns with the rear cover notches. Align the crankshaft sprocket top tooth notch, located at the rear of the tooth with

the notch. The crankshaft notch will be at 12 o'clock and the keyway will be at 6 o'clock.

➡**Mark the sprocket alignment points as well as the direction of cam belt rotation for reinstallation purposes if the belt is to be reused.**

11. Loosen the tensioner adjusting bolts.
12. Remove the lower timing belt idler.
13. Remove the timing belt from the pulleys.

✳✳WARNING

After the timing belt is removed, DO NOT rotate the camshaft sprockets or the crankshaft. Severe internal damage will result from the valve and/or piston contact.

14. Remove the timing belt tensioner and the timing belt tension adjuster.

To install:

➡**Inspect the timing belt and tensioner for wear or damage and replace as necessary.**

15. Inspect the timing belt tensioner as follows:
    a. When compressing the pushrod of the tensioner with a force of 33 lbs. (147 N), the tensioner should not sink.
    b. When compressing the pushrod of the tensioner with a force of 33-110 lbs. (147-490 N), the tensioner should not sink within 8.5 seconds.
    c. Measure the extension of the rod beyond the body of the tensioner for a length of 0.606-0.646 in. (15.4-16.4mm). If not within specifications, replace the tensioner.

➡**Check the idler sprockets for smooth operation. Replace as necessary.**

16. Using a press, compress the tensioner gradually, taking three minutes or more, and insert a 0.059 in. (1.5mm) pin to secure the rod.

17. Install the tensioner and the pulley with the adjustable idler pulley. Temporarily tighten the tensioner while the tensioner is pushed to the right.

18. Align the crankshaft sprocket notch on the rear sprocket tooth with the crank angle sensor boss. This places the sprocket notch in the 12 o'clock position and the and the key way at the 6 o'clock position.

19. Align the camshaft sprockets with the notches in the cam rear belt cover. This places the sprocket notch in the 12 o'clock position for each camshaft.

20. Install the timing belt in a clockwise direction starting at the crankshaft with the directional mark and alignment marks properly positioned (if belt was reused).

21. Install the lower timing belt idler and tighten the mounting bolt to 29 ft. lbs. (39 Nm).

✳✳WARNING

Make sure all the timing marks are properly aligned.

22. Loosen the tensioner retaining bolts and slide the tensioner to the left. Tighten the mounting bolts to 18 ft. lbs. (25 Nm).

23. After verifying the timing marks are correct, remove the stopper pin from the tensioner and recheck the timing marks.

24. Install the center, right and then the center timing belt covers. Torque the bolts to 44 inch lbs. (5 Nm).

25. Install the crankshaft sprocket and tighten the mounting bolt to 94 ft. lbs. (127 Nm) while securing the crankshaft pulley.

26. Install the A/C drive belt tensioner.

27. Install the engine drive belts.

28. Install the fan shroud and motor assembly.

29. Connect the negative battery cable.

2.7L Engine

▶ **See Figures 147, 148, 149 and 150**

1. Disconnect the negative battery cable.

2. Loosen the water pump pulley mounting bolts.

3. Remove the drive belt.

4. Remove the water pump pulley mounting bolts and remove the water pump pulley.

5. Remove the crankshaft pulley.

6. Disconnect the electrical harness to the oil pressure switch.

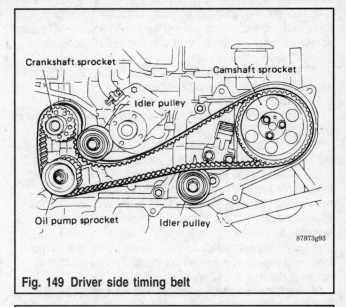

Fig. 149 Driver side timing belt

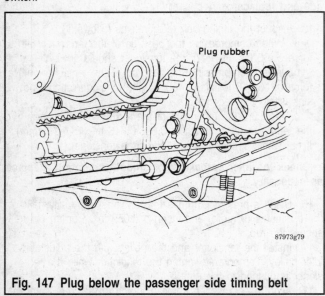

Fig. 147 Plug below the passenger side timing belt

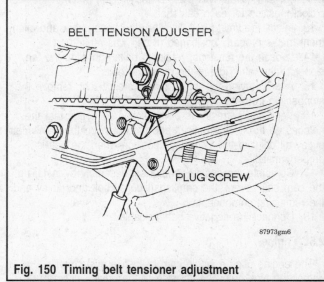

Fig. 150 Timing belt tensioner adjustment

7. Remove the dipstick tube.

8. Remove the three timing belt covers.

9. To remove the right side timing belt use the following procedure:

   a. Loosen the tensioner mounting bolts on the number 1 cylinder about ½ turn.

   b. Rotate the tensioner to remove tension from the belt. With the tensioner fully retracted tighten the mounting bolt.

   c. Mark the direction of rotation on the belt and remove it.

   d. Remove the tensioner mounting bolts and remove the tensioner and spring.

   e. Remove the outer crankshaft sprocket.

   f. Remove the camshaft sprocket mounting bolts and remove the camshaft sprocket.

10. To remove the left side timing belt use the following procedure:

   a. Remove the idler pulley mounting bolt and remove the idler pulley.

   b. Remove the plug rubber.

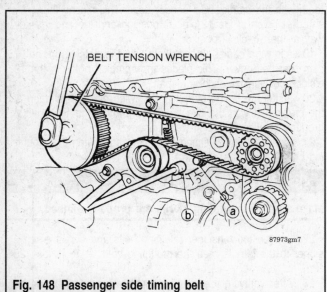

Fig. 148 Passenger side timing belt

c. Remove the plug screw from the lower side of the tension adjuster.

d. Using a flat blade screwdriver, turn the adjuster screw inside the tension adjuster to loosen tension on the belt.

e. Mark the direction of rotation on the belt and remove it.

f. Remove the idler pulley.

g. Remove the inner crankshaft sprocket.

h. Remove the two bolts and remove the belt tension adjuster.

i. Remove the camshaft sprocket mounting bolts and re-move the camshaft sprocket.

To install:

11. To install the left side timing belt proceed as follows:

a. Install the camshaft sprocket and camshaft sprocket mounting. Tighten the mounting bolts to 8 ft. lbs. (12 Nm).

b. De-adjust the tension adjuster fully and install a belt adjuster stopper, 13082AA0000, or the equivalent. Using a syringe fill the adjuster with engine oil until the boot over-flows. Install a new plug screw.

c. Install the belt tension adjuster. Tighten the mounting bolts to 18 ft. lbs. (25 Nm).

d. Install the plug rubber.

e. Install the idler pulley. Tighten the mounting bolt to 32 ft. lbs. (43 Nm).

f. Install the inner crankshaft sprocket.

g. Align the center of the three lines scribed on the fly-wheel with the mark on the flywheel housing. Align the tim-ing mark on the camshaft pulley with the notch in the timing belt rear cover.

h. Install the timing belt in the correct direction of rotation.

i. Install the tensioner and mounting bolt.

j. Remove the belt adjuster stopper and tighten the mounting bolt to 32 ft. lbs. (43 Nm).

12. To install the right side timing belt as follows:

a. Rotate the crankshaft one full turn from the position it was in for installation of the left side belt and line up the timing marks again.

b. Install the camshaft sprocket and camshaft sprocket mounting. Tighten the mounting bolts to 8 ft. lbs. (12 Nm).

c. Align the timing mark on the camshaft pulley with the notch in the timing belt rear cover.

d. Install the tensioner and spring and the mounting bolts. Push the tension down fully and tighten the mounting bolts.

e. Install the outer crankshaft sprocket.

f. Install the timing belt in the correct direction of rotation.

g. Loosen the tensioner mounting bolts on the number 1 cylinder about 1/2 turn and allow the tensioner pulley to contact the belt.

h. Tension the belt with a belt tensioner and tighten the tension mounting bolts to 18 ft. lbs. (25 Nm).

13. Verify all timing marks are in alignment.

14. Install the three timing belt covers.

15. Install the dipstick tube.

16. Connect the electrical connector to the oil pressure switch.

17. Install the crankshaft pulley.

18. Install the water pump pulley and pulley mounting bolts.

19. Install the drive belt and tension to specification.

20. Tighten the water pump pulley mounting bolts.

21. Connect the negative battery cable.

3.3L Engine

▶ **See Figure 151**

1. Disconnect the negative battery cable.

2. Remove the timing belt covers.

3. Matchmark the timing belt to the sprocket, cover and block marks as follows:

a. Turn the crankshaft to align the timing marks on the crankshaft sprocket with the mark on the block.

b. With the crankshaft marks aligned make sure the left and right camshaft sprocket marks are lined up with marks on the timing covers.

c. If all the marks are in line, use white paint to mark the direction of rotation of the belt as well as mark the spots on the belt where it crosses over the timing marks on the pulleys.

4. Loosen the belt tensioner bolts.

5. Remove belt idler pulley No. 1.

6. Remove belt idler pulley No. 2.

7. Remove the timing belt.

8. Remove the tensioner pulley bolt and remove the ten-sioner pulley.

9. Remove the two bolts and the tensioner assembly.

10. Remove the left side camshaft mounting bolt. To keep the camshaft from turning use camshaft sprocket wrench 499207100 or equivalent. Remove the sprocket.

11. Remove the right side camshaft mounting bolt. To keep the camshaft from turning use camshaft sprocket wrench 499207100 or equivalent. Remove the sprocket.

12. Remove the crankshaft sprocket.

To install:

13. Install the crankshaft sprocket.

14. Install the right side camshaft sprocket and mounting bolt. Tighten the mounting bolt to 29 ft. lbs. (39 Nm).

15. Install the left side camshaft sprocket and mounting bolt. Tighten the mounting bolt to 29 ft. lbs. (39 Nm).

16. Insert a 0.059 in. (1.5mm) diameter stopper pin into place while pushing the tension adjuster rod into the tensioner body.

17. Install the tensioner and tighten the bolts to 18 ft. lbs. (24 Nm), while the tensioner is pushed all the way to the right.

18. Install the tensioner pulley and mounting bolt. DO NOT tighten the idler pulley bolt completely.

19. Make sure the crankshaft and both camshaft sprockets are still lined up with their respective timing marks.

20. Install the timing belt onto the sprockets with the direc-tion of rotation arrow in the correct direction and the timing marks on the belt in line with the marks on the sprockets.

21. Install the number 1 and 2 idler pulleys and tighten the mounting bolts to 29 ft. lbs. (39 Nm).

22. Loosen the tensioner pulley bolt and the tensioner as-sembly mounting bolts. Slide the tensioner assembly all the way to the left and tighten the bolts to 18 ft. lbs. (24 Nm).

23. Check again that all the timing marks are still in align-ment. If they are remove the stopper pin from the tensioner assembly.

24. Install the timing belt covers.

25. Connect the negative battery cable.

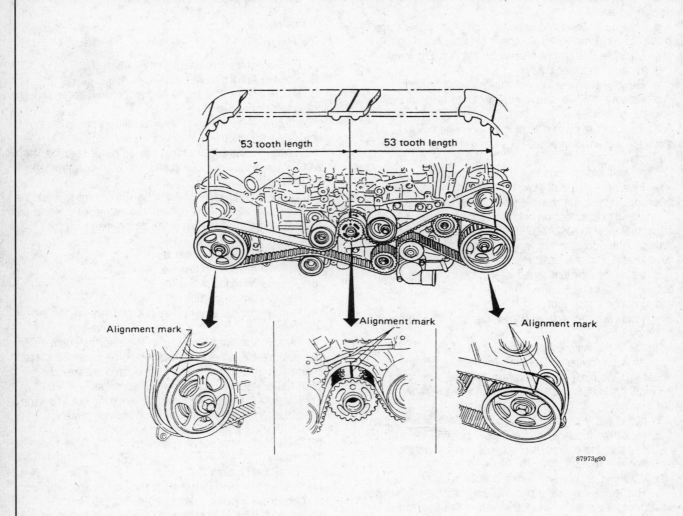

Fig. 151 Timing belt routing and alignment marks — 3.3L engine

ADJUSTMENT

A timing belt should not be viewed as an adjustable component. It is very highly recommended that a timing belt be replaced any time its tension is released.

The timing belt's tension cannot be increased to compensate for wear. If the engine has been disassembled for mechanical work, a new timing belt should always be installed. The small cost of a new timing belt is cheap insurance against expensive engine damage caused by the failure of a re-used timing belt.

Camshaft Sprocket (OHC Engines)

REMOVAL & INSTALLATION

The procedure for removing and installing the camshaft sprockets is covered in the Timing Belt removal and installation procedure, earlier in this section.

Camshaft and Bearings

On some models, it may be necessary to remove the engine from the vehicle to perform this service.

REMOVAL & INSTALLATION

1.2L Engine
▶ See Figures 152, 153 and 154

1. Disconnect the negative battery cable.
2. Remove the rocker arm cover.
3. Place matchmarks on the distributor body and cylinder head, then remove the distributor hold-down bolt and distributor.
4. Remove the timing belt cover and timing belt. Refer to the procedure earlier in this section.
5. Loosen the rocker arm lash adjusters until the rocker arms move freely.

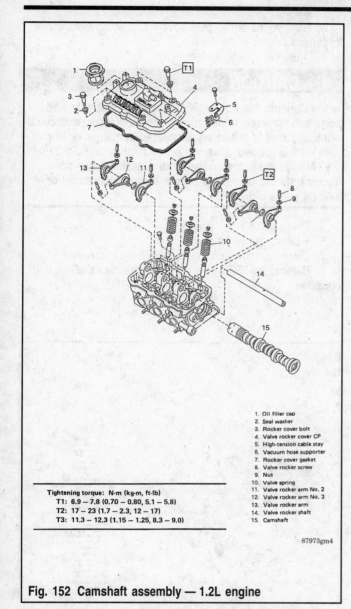

Fig. 152 Camshaft assembly — 1.2L engine

Tightening torque: N·m (kg-m, ft-lb)
T1: 6.9 – 7.8 (0.70 – 0.80, 5.1 – 5.8)
T2: 17 – 23 (1.7 – 2.3, 12 – 17)
T3: 11.3 – 12.3 (1.15 – 1.25, 8.3 – 9.0)

1. Oil filler cap
2. Seal washer
3. Rocker cover bolt
4. Valve rocker cover CP
5. High-tension cable stay
6. Vacuum hose supporter
7. Rocker cover gasket
8. Valve rocker screw
9. Nut
10. Valve spring
11. Valve rocker arm No. 2
12. Valve rocker arm No. 3
13. Valve rocker arm
14. Valve rocker shaft
15. Camshaft

87973gm4

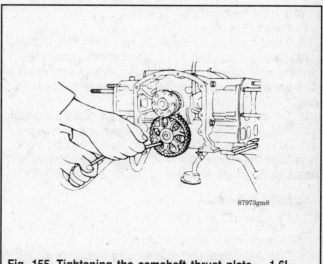

Fig. 153 Removing the valve rocker assembly

87973g91

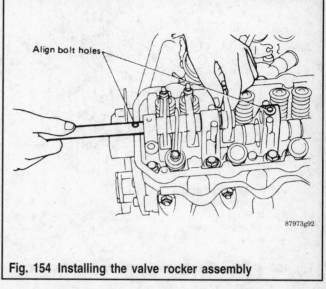

Fig. 154 Installing the valve rocker assembly

87973g92

6. Remove the rocker arm shaft and rocker arms.
7. Carefully remove the camshaft from the cylinder head.

To install:

8. Coat the camshaft lobes with clean engine oil and carefully install the camshaft into the cylinder head.
9. Install the rocker arms and shaft. Adjust the valve lash.
10. Installing the timing belt and cover. Refer to the procedure in this section for installation details.
11. Install the distributor.
12. Install the rocker arm cover.
13. Connect the negative battery cable.
14. Start the vehicle and check the ignition timing and adjust as necessary.

1.6L Engine

▶ See Figures 155 and 156

The camshaft turns on journals that are machined directly into the crankcase.

1. Refer to the engine removal and Installation procedures in this section and remove the engine from the vehicle, then separate the transaxle from the engine.

Fig. 155 Tightening the camshaft thrust plate — 1.6L engine

87973gm8

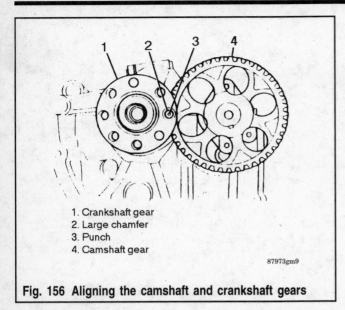

1. Crankshaft gear
2. Large chamfer
3. Punch
4. Camshaft gear

87973gm9

Fig. 156 Aligning the camshaft and crankshaft gears

2. Remove the clutch assembly/flywheel (MT) or the torque converter drive plate (AT).

3. Remove the flywheel housing-to-engine bolts and the housing from the engine.

4. Remove the crankshaft gear from the crankshaft.

5. Straighten the lockwashers and remove the camshaft thrust plate-to-engine bolts.

➡**The lockwashers are straightened and the bolts removed through the access holes in the camshaft gear.**

6. Remove the rocker arm-to-cylinder head covers, the rocker arm-to-cylinder head assemblies, the pushrods and valve lifters.

➡**When removing the pushrods and valve lifters, be sure to keep the items in order for reassembly purposes.**

7. Pull the camshaft toward the rear of the engine and remove it from the engine; be careful not to damage the bearing journals and/or the camshaft lobes.

➡**Remove the oil seal; be sure to replace it with a new one when reassembling the engine.**

8. Inspect the camshaft.
To install:
9. Using a putty knife, clean the gasket mounting surfaces.
10. Install the camshaft and tighten the thrust plate bolts. Using a feeler gauge or a dial indicator, move the camshaft (fore and aft), then measure the end-play, it should be 0.008 in. (0.2032mm) or less.
11. To complete the installation, use new gaskets and sealant where necessary. Assemble the engine and reverse the removal procedures. Refill the cooling system and the crankcase. Start the engine, allow it to reach normal operating temperatures and check for leaks.

1.8L and 2.7L Engines

▶ **See Figures 157 and 158**

1. Disconnect the negative battery cable.
2. Tag and disconnect the spark plug wires from the distributor cap. Matchmark the distributor to the engine and remove the distributor.

3. Remove the timing belts covers and timing belts. Refer to the procedures in the section.
4. Drain the cooling system.

❋❋CAUTION

When draining the coolant, keep in mind that cats and dogs are attracted to ethylene glycol antifreeze, and could drink any that is left in an uncovered container or in puddles on the ground. This will prove fatal in sufficient quantity. Always drain the coolant into a sealable container. Coolant should be reused unless it is contaminated or several years old.

5. Remove the water pipe.
6. Remove the oil fill pipe.
7. Disconnect the PCV hoses from the valve covers.
8. Remove the EGR pipe cover, clamps and EGR pipe, if equipped.

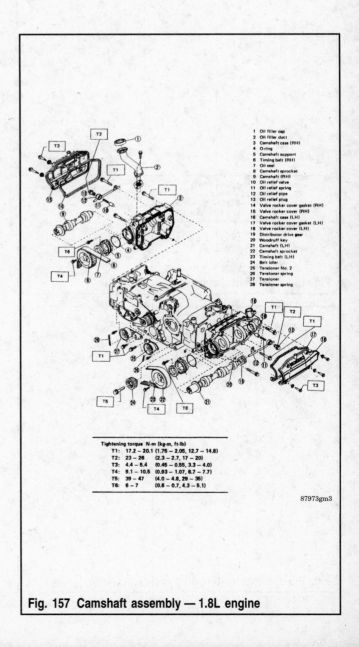

1 Oil filler cap
2 Oil filler duct
3 Camshaft case (RH)
4 O-ring
5 Camshaft support
6 Timing belt (RH)
7 Oil seal
8 Camshaft sprocket
9 Camshaft (RH)
10 Oil relief valve
11 Oil relief spring
12 Oil relief pipe
13 Oil relief plug
14 Valve rocker cover gasket (RH)
15 Valve rocker cover (RH)
16 Camshaft case (LH)
17 Valve rocker cover gasket (LH)
18 Valve rocker cover (LH)
19 Distributor drive gear
20 Woodruff key
21 Camshaft (LH)
22 Camshaft sprocket
23 Timing belt (LH)
24 Belt idler
25 Tensioner No. 2
26 Tensioner spring
27 Tensioner
28 Tensioner spring

Tightening torque N·m (kg·m, ft·lb)	
T1:	17.2 – 20.1 (1.75 – 2.05, 12.7 – 14.8)
T2:	23 – 26 (2.3 – 2.7, 17 – 20)
T3:	4.4 – 5.4 (0.45 – 0.55, 3.3 – 4.0)
T4:	9.1 – 10.5 (0.93 – 1.07, 6.7 – 7.7)
T5:	39 – 47 (4.0 – 4.8, 29 – 35)
T6:	6 – 7 (0.6 – 0.7, 4.3 – 5.1)

87973gm3

Fig. 157 Camshaft assembly — 1.8L engine

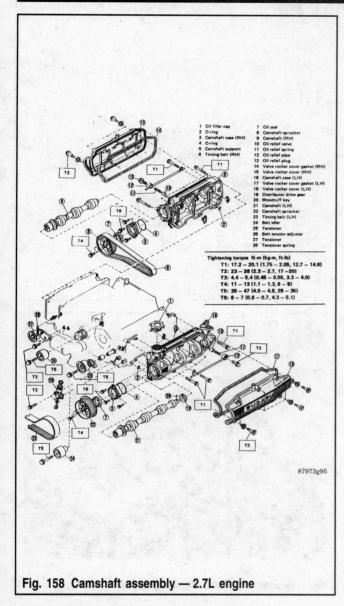

1 Oil filler cap	7 Oil seal
2 O-ring	8 Camshaft sprocket
3 Camshaft case (RH)	9 Camshaft (RH)
4 O-ring	10 Oil relief valve
5 Camshaft support	11 Oil relief spring
6 Timing belt (RH)	12 Oil relief pipe
	13 Oil relief plug
	14 Valve rocker cover gasket (RH)
	15 Valve rocker cover (RH)
	16 Camshaft case (LH)
	17 Valve rocker cover gasket (LH)
	18 Valve rocker cover (LH)
	19 Distributor drive gear
	20 Woodruff key
	21 Camshaft (LH)
	22 Camshaft sprocket
	23 Timing belt (LH)
	24 Belt Idler
	25 Tensioner
	26 Belt tension adjuster
	27 Tensioner
	28 Tensioner spring

Tightening torque N·m (kg-m, ft-lb)
T1: 17.2 – 20.1 (1.75 – 2.05, 12.7 – 14.8)
T2: 23 – 28 (2.3 – 2.7, 17 –20)
T3: 4.4 – 5.4 (0.45 – 0.55, 3.3 – 4.0)
T4: 11 – 13 (1.1 – 1.3, 8 – 9)
T5: 39 – 47 (4.0 – 4.8, 29 – 35)
T6: 6 – 7 (0.6 – 0.7, 4.3 – 5.1)

87973g95

Fig. 158 Camshaft assembly — 2.7L engine

9. Remove the rocker arm covers.

➡**When removing the camshaft carrier the rocker arms may fall off the lash adjusters. Place a suitable container beneath the cylinder head to catch the rocker arms.**

10. Remove the camshaft case mounting bolts.
11. Remove the camshaft case and place on a clean surface.
12. Remove the camshaft retainer from the front of the camshaft carrier.
13. Slide the camshaft out from the carrier.
   To install:
14. Slide the camshaft into the carrier and install the camshaft retainer and bolts. Tighten the retainer bolts to 5 ft. lbs. (7 Nm).
15. Apply grease to the spherical and sliding surface of each valve rocker, then secure the rockers to the valve lash adjusters and valves.

➡**Failure to apply grease to the rocker arms will result in the rocker arms falling off.**

16. Apply sealer to the groove of the camshaft carrier.
17. Install the carrier assembly using the mounting bolts. Tighten the bolts to 14 ft. lbs. (19 Nm).
18. Coat the camshaft with clean engine oil.
19. Install the rocker arm covers using new gaskets. Install the mounting bolts and tighten to 4 ft. lbs. (5 Nm).
20. Connect the PCV hose to the rocker arm cover.
21. Install the EGR pipe, clamps, and EGR pipe cover, if removed.
22. Install the oil filler pipe.
23. Install the water pipe.
24. Install the timing belts and timing belt covers. Refer to the procedures in this section.
25. Install the distributor and mounting bolts remembering to align the marks made during removal.
26. Connect the plug wires to the distributor.
27. Connect the negative battery cable.
28. Start the vehicle, adjust the ignition timing if needed and check for fluid leaks.

2.2L Engine

▶ **See Figures 159, 160, 161, 162 and 163**

1. Disconnect the negative battery cable.
2. Remove the timing belt covers, timing belt and camshaft sprockets.
3. Remove the valve rocker covers.
4. Remove the rocker arm assemblies.
5. To remove the left camshaft:
   a. Remove the cam angle sensor.
   b. Remove the oil dipstick tube attaching bolt.
   c. Remove the camshaft support.
   d. Remove the camshaft O-ring.
   e. Remove the camshaft and rear seal.
6. To remove the right camshaft:
   a. Remove the camshaft support on the right side.
   b. Remove the camshaft O-ring.
   c. Remove the camshaft and rear seal. Remove the oil seal from the camshaft support.
To install:
7. To install the left camshaft:
   a. Lubricate the camshaft journals with clean engine oil. Install the rear oil seal, then install the camshaft into the cylinder head.
   b. Install the O-ring into the camshaft support and install the support. Tighten the front retainer bolts to 7 ft. lbs. (9 Nm), and the rear bolts to 12 ft. lbs. (16 Nm).
   c. Install oil seal into the camshaft support.
   d. Install the bolt into the dipstick tube and tighten to 10 ft. lbs. (13 Nm). Install the camshaft sensor.
8. To install the right camshaft:
   a. Lubricate the camshaft journals with clean engine oil and install the right camshaft.
   b. Install the O-ring into the camshaft support and install the support. Tighten the retainer bolts to 12 ft. lbs. (16 Nm).
   c. Install a new oil seal in the rear of the cylinder head.
9. Install the rocker arm assemblies, tightening the retainer bolts to 9 ft. lbs. (12 Nm).
10. Install the camshaft sprockets, timing belt, timing belt covers and related components.
11. Connect the negative battery cable.
12. Check the fluid levels and start the engine.

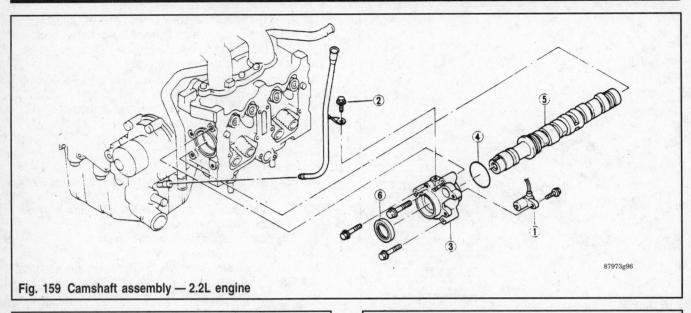

Fig. 159 Camshaft assembly — 2.2L engine

Fig. 160 With the valve cover removed, the camshaft assembly is clearly visible — 2.2L engine

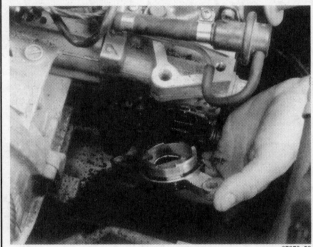

Fig. 162 Remove the camshaft support

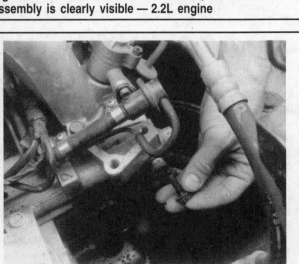

Fig. 161 Remove the retainer bolt securing the camshaft support in place

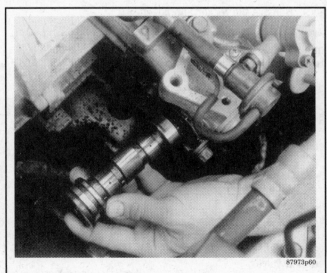

Fig. 163 Carefully slide the camshaft out

13. Allow the engine to reach normal operating temperature and check for leaks.

2.5L Engine

▶ See Figure 164

1. Disconnect the negative battery cable.
2. Remove the timing belt covers, timing belt and camshaft sprockets.
3. Remove the camshaft position sensor.
4. Remove the ignition coils.
5. Remove the valve rocker covers and gaskets.
6. Loosen the intake camshaft cap bolts in sequence, in small increments.
7. Paint alignment marks on the camshafts for installation.

➡ **Be sure to keep the intake and exhaust bearing caps and camshafts in proper order for reassembly. Also note the positioning and location of the camshafts for reinstallation.**

8. Remove the intake camshaft bearing caps, then remove the camshaft.
9. Loosen the exhaust camshaft cap bolts in sequence, in small increments.
10. Remove the exhaust camshaft bearing caps, then remove the camshaft.

To install:

➡**Lubricate the camshaft bearings prior to camshaft installation.**

11. Install the camshafts so the base circle (non-lobe portion) of the camshafts are in contact with the lash adjusters. This will position the lobes of the camshafts away from the valves.

➡**The left camshaft will need to be rotated for timing belt alignment.**

12. Apply liquid sealant to the front bearing cap mating surfaces, then install the bearing caps. Tighten the caps in sequence in two progressive steps to 14.5 ft. lbs. (20 Nm).

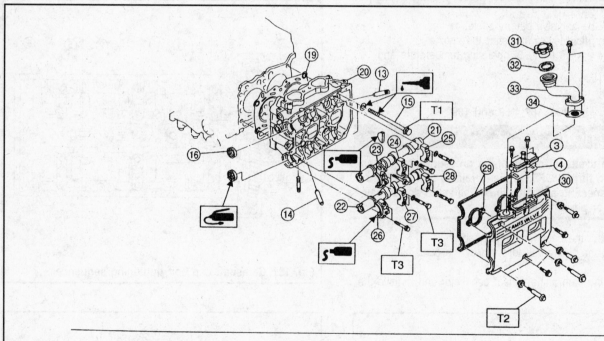

① Rocker cover (RH)
② Rocker cover gasket (RH)
⑨ Exhaust camshaft cap (Front RH)
⑩ Exhaust camshaft cap (Center RH)
⑫ Exhaust camshaft (RH)
⑮ Cylinder head bolt
⑯ Oil seal
⑲ Cylinder head gasket (LH)
⑳ Cylinder head (LH)
㉑ Intake camshaft (LH)
㉒ Exhaust camshaft (LH)
㉓ Intake camshaft cap (Front LH)
㉔ Intake camshaft cap (Center LH)
㉕ Intake camshaft cap (Rear LH)
㉖ Exhaust camshaft (Front LH)
㉗ Exhaust camshaft cap (Center LH)
㉘ Exhaust camshaft cap (Rear LH)
㉙ Rocker cover gasket (LH)
㉚ Rocker cover (LH)
㉛ Oil filler cap
㉜ Gasket
㉝ Oil filler duct
㉞ Gasket

Tightening torque: N·m (kg-m, ft-lb)
T1: Refer to [W4E1]☆2.
T2: 5 (0.5, 3.6)
T3: 10 (1.0, 7)

Fig. 164 Camshaft and cylinder head assembly — 2.5L engine

13. Install new oil seals to the camshafts using a suitable seal installation tool.

❋❋WARNING

Only rotate camshafts the specified amount. If the camshafts are rotated beyond the specified amount, the valves will contact each other and cause severe internal damage.

14. For correct timing belt alignment, rotate the intake camshaft 80 degrees clockwise and the exhaust camshaft 45 degrees counterclockwise.

15. Using a new gasket, install the rocker covers. Be sure to apply liquid sealant to the front edges of the gasket at the camshaft opening.

16. Install the ignition coils.

17. Install the camshaft position sensor.

18. Install the camshaft sprockets and tighten the retaining bolts to 58 ft. lbs. (78 Nm). Be sure to secure the sprockets when tightening the bolts.

19. Check the timing sprockets for proper alignment and install the timing belt.

20. Connect the negative battery cable.

21. Check the fluid levels and start the engine.

22. Allow the engine to reach operating temperature and check for leaks.

3.3L Engine

▶ See Figures 165, 166, 167, 168 and 169

❋❋CAUTION

Fuel injection systems remain under pressure after the engine has been turned OFF. Properly relieve fuel pressure before disconnecting any fuel lines. Failure to do so may result in fire or personal injury.

1. Disconnect the negative battery cable.

2. Remove the timing belt followed by the camshaft sprockets.

3. Detach the cam angle sensor connector and remove the bracket.

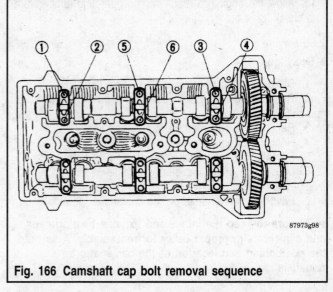

Fig. 166 Camshaft cap bolt removal sequence

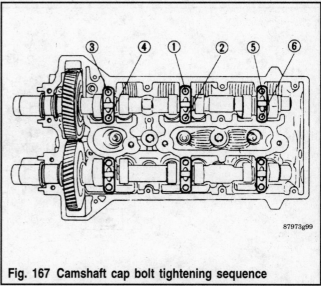

Fig. 167 Camshaft cap bolt tightening sequence

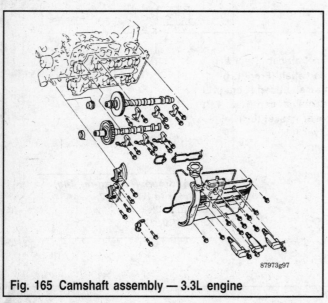

Fig. 165 Camshaft assembly — 3.3L engine

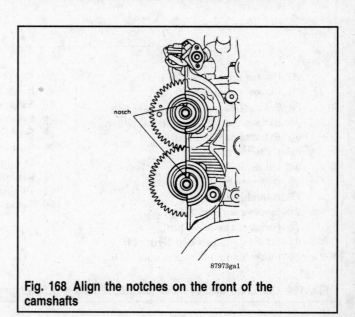

Fig. 168 Align the notches on the front of the camshafts

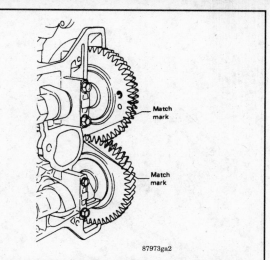

Fig. 169 There are also alignment marks on the rear of the camshaft gears

4. Disconnect the ignition coil harness and remove the individual ignition coils.

5. Disconnect the blow-by hose and remove the cylinder head cover and gasket.

6. Remove the front camshaft cap.

7. Remove the camshaft oil seal and plug.

❊❊WARNING

Since the camshaft thrust clearance is small, the camshaft must be removed by holing it parallel to the cylinder head. If the camshaft is not parallel to the cylinder head, the cylinder head thrust bearing journal may be damaged.

8. Rotate the intake (upper) and exhaust (lower) camshafts until the notch at the front of the camshafts face the 6 o'clock position on the left cylinder head, and the 12 o'clock position on the right cylinder head.

9. Inspect the rear of the camshaft and check that the matchmarks on the rear gears are aligned.

10. Install a service bolt to the sub-gear mounting bolt hole of the intake camshaft gear to lock the sub-gear and driven gear.

11. Loosen the intake camshaft bolt caps in sequence. Make sure that, as the bolts are turned, the clearance between the camshaft journal and the cylinder head journal bearing increase evenly. If not, tighten the bolts and repeat the loosening procedure.

12. Remove the camshaft caps while securing the intake camshaft with one hand. When the caps are removed, then lift out the intake camshaft.

13. Arrange the camshaft caps in the order they were removed. They must be installed to their original positions.

14. If you are removing the exhaust camshaft, rotate the camshaft clockwise for additional access.

15. Loosen the exhaust camshaft bolt caps in sequence. Make sure that, as the bolts are turned, the clearance between the camshaft journal and the cylinder head journal bearing increase evenly. If not, tighten the bolts and repeat the loosening procedure.

16. Remove the camshaft caps while securing the exhaust camshaft with one hand. When the caps are removed, then lift out the intake camshaft.

17. Arrange the camshaft caps in the order they were removed. They must be installed to their original positions.

18. Remove the hydraulic lash adjusters. Keep the lash adjusters in the order they were removed. They must be installed into their original positions.

To install:

19. Measure the thrust clearance of the camshaft with the hydraulic lash adjusters not installed. If thrust clearance exceeds 0.0051 in. (0.13mm) for the intake and 0.0047 in. (0.12mm) for the exhaust, replace the camshaft caps and the cylinder head as an assembly. If necessary replace the camshaft.

20. Measure the camshaft journal oil clearance with the lash adjusters not installed. If clearance exceeds 0.0039 in. (0.10mm), replace the camshaft.

21. Measure the camshaft gear backlash with the intake sub-gear not installed. If backlash exceeds 0.0118 in. (0.30mm), replace the camshafts as a set.

22. Lubricate and install the hydraulic lash adjusters.

23. Lubricate and install the camshafts with the notch on the front facing the 6 o'clock position for the left cylinder head camshafts and the 12 o'clock position for the right cylinder head camshafts. Ensure that the marks for both camshafts are facing the same position.

24. Install the camshaft caps and and bolts and hand-tight.

25. Tighten the camshaft bolts on the caps equally, in small increments, in the correct sequence. Make sure that, as the bolts are turned, the clearance between the camshaft journal and the cylinder head journal bearing decreases evenly. If not, loosen the bolts and repeat the tightening procedure.

26. Tighten the camshaft cap bolts to a final torque of 7 ft. lbs. (10 Nm).

27. Ensure that the matchmarks on the rear side of the camshaft gears are aligned.

28. Remove the sub-gear securing bolt from the camshaft.

29. Install the front camshaft cover using new gaskets.

30. Lubricate and install new oil seals.

31. Install the camshaft plug.

32. Install the camshaft cover and connect the blow-by hose.

33. Connect the ignition coil harnesses and coils.

34. Connect the cam angle sensor and bracket.

35. Install the timing belt and camshaft sprockets.

36. Connect the negative battery cable.

INSPECTION

1. Put the camshaft in V-blocks and have a dial indicator contact the inside face of the cam gear. If run-out exceeds 0.0098 in. (0.24892mm), replace the gear.

2. Using a dial micrometer and a set of V-blocks, measure the camshaft bearing wear and the camshaft bend; the bend limit is 0.002 in. (0.0508mm)

3. Measure the cam gear-to-crankshaft backlash. Mount a dial indicator with its stem resting on a tooth of the camshaft gear. Rotate the gear until all slack is removed, and zero the indicator. Rotate the gear in the opposite direction until slack is removed, and record gear backlash. Mount the indicator with its stem resting on the edge of the camshaft gear, parallel to

the axis of the camshaft. Zero the indicator, then turn the camshaft gear one full turn and record the run-out. If either backlash or run-out exceeds specifications, replace the worn gear(s).

Balance Shaft

A balance shaft is fitted to the 1.2L engine only. The balance shaft, spinning in the opposite direction of engine rotation, counters engine vibration and provides a smoother running engine. To service the balance shaft, the engine must be completely disassembled. Refer to the Crankshaft and Main Bearings portion of this section for removal and installation procedures.

REMOVAL & INSTALLATION

1.2L Engine

▶ See Figures 170 and 171

1. Disconnect the negative battery cable.
2. Remove the engine from the vehicle. Refer to the procedure in this section.
3. Remove the cylinder head from the engine using the steps outlined in the cylinder head removal procedure in this section.
4. Remove the oil filter and discard.
5. Tag and disconnect the alternator wires and remove the alternator and retainer bracket.
6. Remove the engine mount and engine mount stay.
7. Remove the dipstick, tube and seal.
8. Remove the flywheel housing cover.
9. Remove the oil pan assembly.
10. Remove the water pump cover and impeller.
11. Remove the water pipe.
12. Remove the crankcase cover.
13. Remove the connecting rod caps followed by the connecting rod and piston assemblies.
14. Remove the crankshaft main caps, crankshaft and oil seal.
15. Remove the chain and chain guide.
16. Remove the oil pump sprocket.
17. Remove the balance shaft.
   To install:
18. Install the balance shaft.
19. Rotate the balance shaft so the timing mark is pointing toward the base of the engine block.
20. Install the oil pump sprocket so the notch is straight up and down.
21. Install the timing chain with the single gold link over the timing mark on the balance shaft sprocket.
22. Install the crankshaft with the timing mark on the sprocket facing straight up the engine block.
23. Install the crankshaft main bearing caps. Tighten the bolts in order to 29-33 ft. lbs. (38-43 Nm).
24. Tighten the chain guide bolts to 4-5 ft. lbs. (5-6 Nm).
25. Install the piston and connecting rod assemblies following the recommended procedures in this section.
26. Install the rear main oil seal.

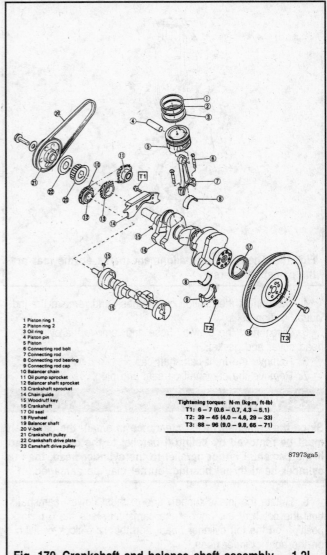

1 Piston ring 1
2 Piston ring 2
3 Oil ring
4 Piston pin
5 Piston
6 Connecting rod bolt
7 Connecting rod
8 Connecting rod bearing
9 Connecting rod cap
10 Balancer chain
11 Oil pump sprocket
12 Balancer shaft sprocket
13 Crankshaft sprocket
14 Chain guide
15 Woodruff key
16 Crankshaft
17 Oil seal
18 Flywheel
19 Balancer shaft
20 V-belt
21 Crankshaft pulley
22 Crankshaft drive plate
23 Camshaft drive pulley

Tightening torque: N·m (kg·m, ft-lb)		
T1:	6 – 7	(0.6 – 0.7, 4.3 – 5.1)
T2:	39 – 45	(4.0 – 4.6, 29 – 33)
T3:	88 – 96	(9.0 – 9.8, 65 – 71)

87973ga5

Fig. 170 Crankshaft and balance shaft assembly — 1.2L engine

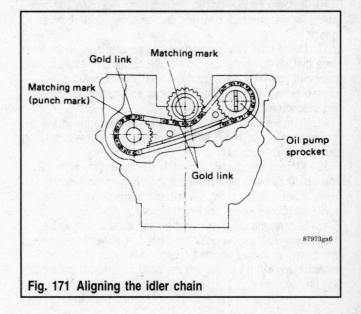

87973ga6

Fig. 171 Aligning the idler chain

27. Install the crankcase cover using a new gasket. Install the suction manifold bracket, then secure the cover and bracket in place with the retainer bolts tightened to 7-8 ft. lbs. (9-10 Nm).

28. Install the water pump impeller into the crankcase cover and connect it to the balance shaft. Tighten the retainer bolts to 7-8 ft. lbs. (9-10 Nm).

29. Install the water pump cover. Tighten the cover bolts to 7-8 ft. lbs. (9-10 Nm).

30. Install the oil pan using a new gasket. Refer to the procedure in this section for installation steps.

31. Install the flywheel housing cover.

32. Install the dipstick, dipstick tube and seal.

33. Install the flywheel. Tighten the bolts to 65-71 ft. lbs. (84-92 Nm).

34. Install a new oil filter.

35. Install the engine mount and engine mount stay.

36. Install the alternator bracket and alternator. Connect the alternator electrical harness.

37. Install the cylinder head following the recommended procedure in this section.

38. Connect the negative battery cable.

39. Start the engine and check for leaks.

Pistons, Connecting Rods, Crankshaft and Bearings

All engines except the 1.2L are of the split case design. In order to remove any of the internal components, the case halves must be split. In other words, for the piston and connecting rod combination to be removed, the crankshaft must be removed and vise-versa.

REMOVAL

Except 1.2L Engine

▶ See Figures 172, 173, 174, 175 and 176

1. Remove the engine from the vehicle. Separate the engine from the transaxle.

2. Remove the intake manifold. Remove the oil pan and oil strainer. Remove the flywheel assembly.

3. Remove the timing belt, timing covers and related components.

4. Remove the cylinder head-to-engine bolts, in the reverse order of the torquing sequence. Remove the cylinder heads and gaskets.

5. Using an Allen wrench, remove the crankcase plugs of No. 1 and No. 2 pistons from the cylinder block.

6. Using a wrench on the crankshaft pulley bolt, rotate the crankshaft so that the No. 1 and No. 2 pistons are at the Bottom Dead Center (BDC) of the their compression stroke.

7. Using needlenose pliers, inserted through the crankcase plug holes, remove the wrist pin-to-pistons circlips.

8. Using a Wrist Pin Removal tool No. 399094310 or equivalent, through the rear service holes, remove the wrist pins through the crankcase plug holes.

➡Keep the circlips and the wrist pins together for each cylinder so that they DO NOT become mixed up.

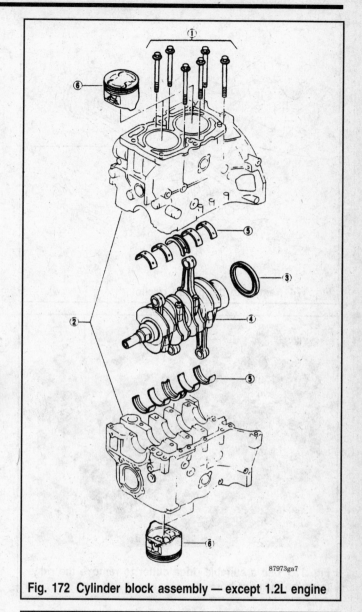

Fig. 172 Cylinder block assembly — except 1.2L engine

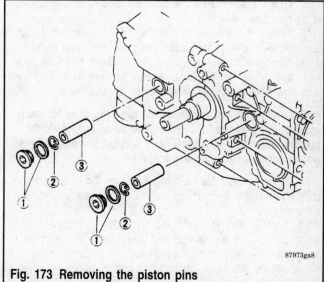

Fig. 173 Removing the piston pins

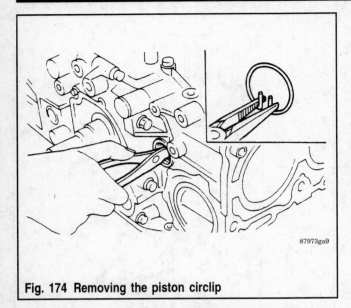

Fig. 174 Removing the piston circlip

Fig. 175 Use a suitable ridge cutter to remove the ridge from the cylinder bore

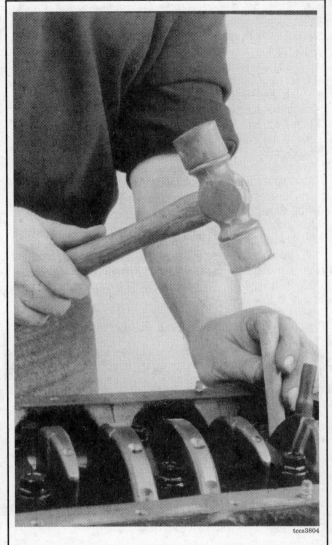

Fig. 176 Carefully tap the piston out of the bore using a wooden dowel

9. In the same manner, remove the piston pins from the other cylinders.

10. Rotate the engine, so that the No. 1 piston side is facing upward, then remove the crankcase halve nuts and bolts.

11. Separate the crankcase halves. Remove the front oil seal, the O-ring and the back-up ring; be sure to replace them with new ones when reassembling the engine.

➡Keep the pistons and the wrist pins together for each cylinder so that they DO NOT become mixed. Mark the pistons and the connecting rods so that the direction is not changed when they are installed.

12. Remove the crankshaft together with the connecting rods, the distributor gear and the crankshaft gear as an assembly.

13. Remove the ridge from the top of the cylinder (unworn area), using a Ridge Reamer tool, to facilitate the removal of the pistons by performing the following procedures:

a. Place the piston at the bottom of its bore and cover it with a rag.

b. Cut the ridge away using a ridge reamer, exercising extreme care to avoid cutting too deeply.

c. Remove the rag and remove the cuttings that remain on the piston.

14. Using a hammer handle or a wooden bar, force the pistons out through the top of the cylinder block.

1.2L Engine

◢ See Figures 170 and 177

1. Remove the engine from the vehicle.

2. Remove the timing belt, belt covers and related components. Remove the cylinder heads.

3. Remove the oil pan and the oil strainer assembly.

4. Stamp the cylinder number on the machined surfaces of the bolt bosses of the connecting rod and cap for identification when reinstalling. If the pistons are to be removed from the connecting rod, mark the cylinder number on the piston with a silver pencil or quick drying paint for proper cylinder identification and cap to rod location.

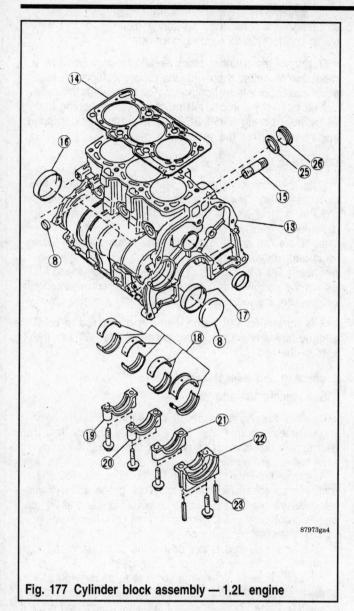

Fig. 177 Cylinder block assembly — 1.2L engine

5. Examine the cylinder bore above the ring travel. If a ridge exists, remove it with a ridge reamer before attempting to remove the piston and rod assembly.

6. Remove the rod bearing cap and bearing.

7. Install a guide hose over the rod bolt threads; this will prevent damage to the bearing journal and rod bolt threads.

8. Using a hammer handle, remove the rod/piston assemblies through the top of the cylinder bore

CLEANING AND INSPECTION

❊❊WARNING

Do not hot tank clean any aluminum parts or they will be ruined. Use carburetor solvent for cleaning.

Pistons

▶ **See Figures 178 and 179**

Using a piston ring expanding tool, remove the piston rings from the pistons; any other method (screwdriver blades, pliers, etc.) usually results in the rings being bent, scratched or distorted and/or the piston itself being damaged.

Clean the varnish from the piston skirts and pins with a cleaning solvent. DO NOT WIRE BRUSH ANY PART OF THE PISTON. Clean the ring grooves with a groove cleaner and make sure that the oil ring holes and slots are clean.

Inspect the piston for cracked ring lands, scuffed or damaged skirts, eroded areas at the top of the piston. Replace the pistons that are damaged or show signs of excessive wear. Inspect the piston ring grooves for nicks or burrs that might cause the rings to hang up.

Measure the piston skirt perpendicular to the piston pin axis and note this figure for the piston clearance check. If installing replacement pistons, follow the manufacturers recommendations on where to measure the piston.

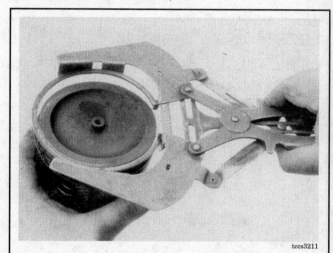

Fig. 178 Use a ring expander to remove the piston rings

Fig. 179 Clean the piston using a ring groove cleaner

Cylinder Bores

▶ See Figures 180 and 181

Using a telescoping gauge or an inside micrometer, measure the diameter of the cylinder bore, perpendicular (90°) to the piston pin, at 1-2½ in. (25-64mm) below the surface of the cylinder block. The difference between the two measurements is the piston clearance.

If the clearance is within specifications or slightly below (after the cylinders have been bored or honed), finish honing is all that is necessary, If the clearance is excessive, try to obtain a slightly larger piston to bring the clearance within specifications. If this is not possible, obtain the first oversize piston and hone the cylinder or (if necessary) bore the cylinder to size.

When measuring the cylinder bore, take measurements in several places. If the cylinder bore is tapered or is out-of-round, it is advisable to rebore for the smallest possible oversize piston and rings. After measuring, mark the pistons with a felt-tip pen for reference during assembly.

➡**Boring of the cylinder block should be performed by a reputable machine shop with the proper equipment. In some cases, clean-up honing can be done with the cylinder block in the vehicle, but most excessive honing and all cylinder boring MUST BE done with the block stripped and removed from the vehicle.**

Connecting Rods

Wash the connecting rods in cleaning solvent and dry with compressed air. Check for twisted or bent rods and inspect for nicks or cracks. Replace the connecting rods that are damaged.

Install the cap on the rod and torque to specification. Using an inside micrometer, measure the inside bore diameter perpendicular (90°) to the axis of rod and once again along the axis of the rod. If the two measurements are not within specification, have the rod resized by a competent machine shop.

➡**It is normal for the inside diameter of the rod to be slightly larger when measured perpendicular (90°) to the axis of the rod.**

Crankshaft and Main Bearings

▶ See Figures 182 and 183

Measure the bearing journals using a micrometer, to determine diameter, journal taper and eccentricity. If crankshaft journals appear defective, or do not meet tolerances, the crankshaft will require grinding.

Assemble the case halves with the bearings installed and torque to specification. Using a telescope gauge and micrometer, measure bearing I.D. parallel to piston axis and at 30° on each side of piston axis. Subtract journal O.D. from bearing I.D. to determine oil clearance.

An alternate method is to measure the oil clearance on each crankshaft bearing by means of Plastigage®.

Wipe off oil, dust, etc. on the surfaces to be measured. Install the bearings in the crankcase and set the crankshaft in position. Cut the Plastigage® to the bearing width and place it

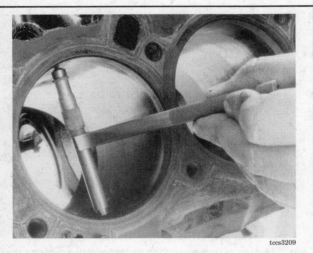

Fig. 180 A telescoping gauge may be useful to measure the cylinder bore diameter

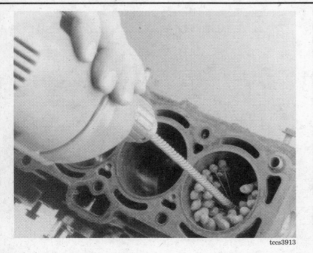

Fig. 181 Using a ball type honer is an easy way to hone the cylinder bore

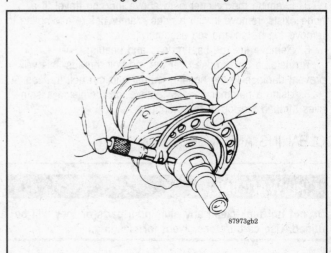

Fig. 182 Checking the bearing journal outside diameter with a micrometer

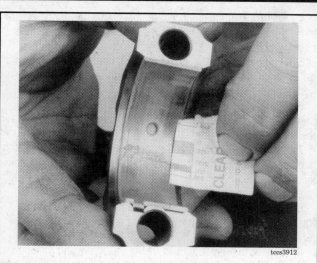

Fig. 183 After the cap is removed, use the scale supplied with the gauge to check clearances

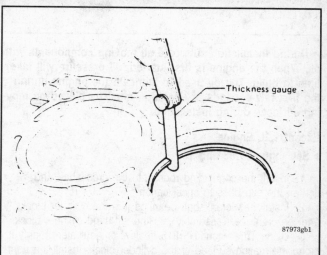

Fig. 184 Checking the piston ring end-gap with a feeler gauge

on the journal parallel with the crankshaft axis. Be careful not to put it on the oil hole or groove. Bring together the crankcase halves and tighten the bolts and nut to the specified torque.

✳✳WARNING

During the work, the crankshaft must not be turned, nor the crankcase inverted.

Remove all the bolts and nut and separate the crankcase. Measure the Plastigage® width with the scale printed on the Plastigage® case. If the measurement is not within the specification, replace the defective bearing with an undersize one, and replace or recondition the crankshaft as necessary.

CHECKING RING END-GAP

▶ See Figure 184

The piston ring end-gap should be checked while the rings are removed from the pistons. Incorrect end-gap indicates that the wrong size rings are being used; ring breakage could result if not corrected.

1. Compress the new piston ring into a cylinder (one at a time).

2. Squirt some clean oil into the cylinder so that the ring and the top 2 in. (51mm) of the cylinder wall are coated.

3. Using an inverted piston, push the ring approximately 1 in. (25mm) below the top of the cylinder.

4. Using a feeler gauge, measure the ring gap and compare it to specification. Carefully remove the ring from the cylinder.

5. If the gap is smaller than specification, file the ring ends using an appropriate piston ring file. If the gap is greater, the cylinder bore must be honed to the next oversize or the piston rings are incorrect.

CONNECTING ROD BEARING REPLACEMENT

Replacement bearings are available in standard size and undersize (for reground crankshafts). Connecting rod-to-crankshaft bearing clearance is checked using Plastigage® at either the top or the bottom of each crank journal. The Plastigage® has a range of 0.001-0.003 in. (0.0254-0.0762mm).

1. Remove the rod cap with the bearing shell. Completely clean the bearing shell and the crank journal, blow any oil from the oil hole in the crankshaft; place the Plastigage® lengthwise along the bottom center of the lower bearing shell, then install the cap with the shell and torque the bolt or nuts to specification. DO NOT turn the crankshaft with the Plastigage® on the bearing.

2. Remove the bearing cap with the shell. The flattened Plastigage® will be found sticking to either the bearing shell or the crank journal. DO NOT remove it yet.

3. Use the scale printed on the Plastigage® envelope to measure the flattened material at its widest point. The number within the scale which most closely corresponds to the width of the Plastigage® indicates the bearing clearance in thousandths of an inch and millimeters.

4. Check the specifications chart in this section for the desired clearance. It is advisable to install a new bearing if the clearance exceeds specification; however, if the bearing is in good condition and is not being checked because of bearing noise, bearing replacement is not necessary.

5. If you are installing new bearings, try a standard size, then each undersize in order until one is found that is within the specified limits when checked for clearance with Plastigage®; each undersize shell has its size stamped on it.

6. When the proper size shell is found, clean off the Plastigage®, oil the bearing thoroughly, reinstall the cap with its shell and torque the rod bolt nuts to specifications.

➡**With the proper bearing selected and the nuts torqued, it should be possible to move the connecting rod back and forth freely on the crank journal as allowed by the specified connecting rod end clearance. If the rod cannot be moved, either the rod bearing is too far undersize or the rod is misaligned.**

INSTALLATION

➡During installation, lubricate all moving components with oil. When the engine is first started, oil pressure will take time to build. The oil used to lubricate the engine during the first few seconds of operation must be placed on moving surfaces during installation.

Except 1.2L Engine
▶ See Figures 185 and 186

1. Install the connecting rods onto the crankshaft and tighten the cap bolts to specification.
2. Install new crankshaft bearings into the cylinder blocks and the crankshaft assembly into the left-hand cylinder block.
3. Using Three-bond® 1215 sealant or equivalent, apply it along the mating surface of the cylinder block. Install the right-hand cylinder block onto the assembly. Tighten the cylinder block bolts to 17-20 ft. lbs. (23-26 Nm) for the 8mm bolts and 29-35 ft. lbs. (39-47 Nm) for the 10mm bolts.

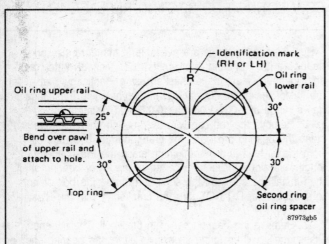

Fig. 185 Piston ring end-gap alignment — except 1.2L engine

Fig. 186 Installing the piston into the bore using a ring compressor and a handle of a hammer

4. Using a dial indicator, check the crankshaft thrust clearance. If not within specification, the crankshaft thrust surface must be corrected.
5. Using a piston ring expander tool, install new rings onto the pistons. Position the piston rings gaps as shown in the illustration.
6. Using engine oil, lubricate the piston assembly. Turn the crankshaft so that the No. 1 and No. 2 connecting rods are positioned at BDC.
7. Using the Piston Ring Compression tool No. 398744300 or equivalent, compress the piston rings into the piston assembly. Then, using a hammer handle, drive the piston assembly into the cylinder block.
8. Using the Piston Pin Guide tool No. 399284300 or equivalent, install the piston pin and the circlip through the service hole.
9. Repeat this procedure to install the remaining pistons.
10. Apply fluid packing to the piston pin plugs and tighten to 46-56 ft. lbs. (62-76 Nm).
11. Install the front and rear oil seals using a driver.
12. Install the oil strainer and oil pan.
13. Install the cylinder heads and torque to specification.
14. Install the timing belt, belt covers and related components.
15. Install the intake manifold and tighten to specification.
16. Join the engine and transaxle. Install the engine in the vehicle.

1.2L Engine
▶ See Figures 186 and 187

1. Install the crankshaft lower bearings and place the crankshaft into the cylinder block after lubricating it with oil. Install the crankshaft so that the chain connecting the balance shaft and oil pump sprocket is as shown in the illustration.
2. Install the upper bearings in the main caps and install the caps on the engine. Tighten the main bearing cap bolts/nuts to specification.
3. Check the crankshaft end-play. If not within specification, the thrust surface of the crankshaft must be corrected prior to assembly.

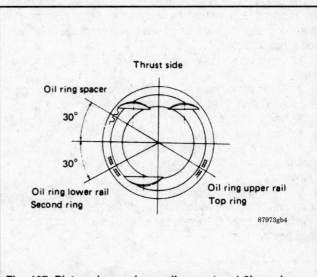

Fig. 187 Piston ring end-gap alignment — 1.2L engine

4. Install the rod bearing on the connecting rod. Install the piston rings on the piston using a ring expander.

5. Position the piston rings as shown in the illustration and install the ring compressor. Install rubber boots over the rod bolts.

6. Install the piston into its cylinder with the Fuji Industries mark facing the front of the engine and tap into place using a wooden hammer handle. Remove the rubber boot, install the rod cap so that the protruding ridge faces the front of the engine and tighten the bolt/nut to specification.

7. Install the oil strainer assembly and oil pan.

8. Install the cylinder heads.

9. Install the timing belt, belt covers and related components. Adjust the valve lash.

10. Install the engine in the vehicle.

BREAK-IN PROCEDURE

Start the engine, and allow it to run at low speed for a few minutes, while checking for leaks. Stop the engine, check the oil level, and fill as necessary. Restart the engine, and fill the cooling system to capacity. Check the point dwell angle and adjust the ignition timing and the valves. Run the engine at low to medium speed (800-2,500 rpm) for approximately ½ hour, and retorque the cylinder head bolts. Road test the car, and check again for leaks.

Follow the manufacturer's recommended engine break-in procedure and maintenance schedule for new engines.

Rear Main Oil Seal

REPLACEMENT

Except 1.2L Engine
▶ See Figure 188

1. Remove the engine from the vehicle. Remove the transaxle-to-engine bolts and separate the transaxle from the engine.

2. Using the Clutch Disc Guide tool 499747000 or equivalent, remove the clutch assembly/flywheel (MT). If equipped with an AT, remove the torque converter flexplate from the crankshaft.

3. Remove the flywheel housing from the engine. Using a small prybar, pry the oil seal from the housing.

To install:

4. Install the new oil seal and press it into the flywheel housing using the appropriate driver.

5. Install the flywheel housing using new gaskets and sealant where necessary. Tighten the bolts to specification.

6. Install the flywheel and tighten the bolts to specification.

7. Join the engine and transaxle. Install the assembly in the vehicle.

1.2L Engine
▶ See Figure 189

1. Remove the engine from the vehicle and separate the engine from the transaxle

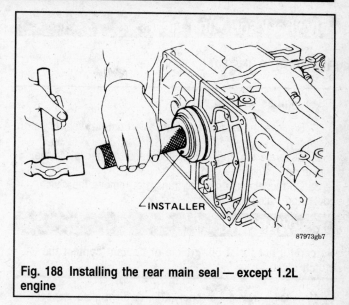

Fig. 188 Installing the rear main seal — except 1.2L engine

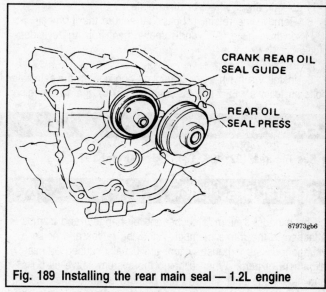

Fig. 189 Installing the rear main seal — 1.2L engine

2. Remove the clutch assembly and the flywheel or torque converter and flexplate from the crankshaft.

3. Using a small prybar, pry the rear oil seal from the crankcase; be careful not to damage the crankshaft or the crankcase housing.

To install:

4. Install the new oil seal and lubricate with engine oil.

5. Using the Crankshaft Rear Oil Seal Guide tool No. 498725600 or equivalent, and the Rear Oil Seal Press tool No. 498725500 or equivalent, drive the new oil seal into the housing until it seats.

6. Install the clutch assembly and flywheel or flexplate and torque converter. Tighten the flywheel/flexplate bolts to specification.

7. Join the engine and transaxle. Install the assembly in the vehicle.

Flywheel and Ring Gear

REMOVAL & INSTALLATION

▶ **See Figures 190 and 191**

1. Remove the engine and transaxle from the vehicle as an assembly.
2. Separate the engine from the transaxle and place the engine on a suitable stand.
3. On models with manual transaxle, remove the clutch cover and clutch disc.

✳✳WARNING

Be careful not to let oil, grease or coolant contact the clutch disc.

4. Install a flywheel stopper (MT), or drive plate stopper (AT), to lock the flywheel or drive plate.
5. Remove the retaining bolts that secure the flywheel (MT), or drive plate (AT), and remove them from the cylinder block.

To install:

6. Install the flywheel or driveplate and tighten the retaining bolts as follows : 65-71 ft. lbs. (88-97 Nm) on the 1.2L engine;

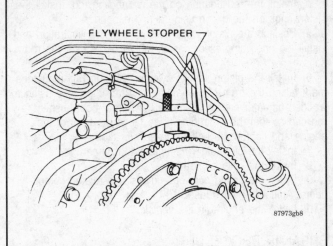

Fig. 190 Installation of the flywheel stopper — manual transaxle equipped models

30-33 ft. lbs. (41-45 Nm) on the 1.6L engine and 51-55 ft. lbs. (69-75 Nm) on all other engines.

7. Install the clutch assembly on manual transaxle vehicles.
8. Join the engine and transaxle assemblies. Install the engine/transaxle assembly in the vehicle.

EXHAUST SYSTEM

▶ **See Figures 192, 193, 194, 195, 196 and 197**

General Description

The exhaust system is suspended by hangers and clamps attached to the frame member. Annoying rattles and noise vibrations in the exhaust system are usually caused by misalignment of parts. When aligning the system, leave all bolts and nuts loose until all parts are properly aligned, then tighten from front to rear. Make sure that you are wearing some form of eye protection when removing or installing the exhaust system, to prevent eye injury. Never work on the exhaust system of a vehicle that has been recently used. Exhaust systems reach very high temperatures and can cause severe burns. Always allow the car to cool down before starting any repairs to the exhaust.

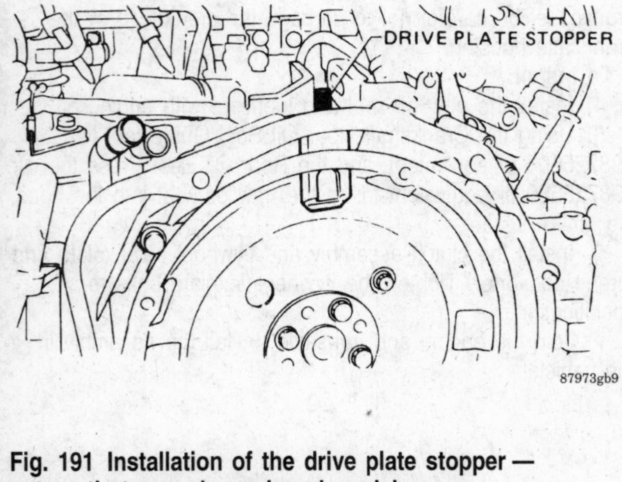

The catalytic converter is an emission control device added to a gasoline engines exhaust system to reduce hydrocarbon and carbon monoxide pollutants in the exhaust gas stream. The catalyst in the converter is not serviceable.

Periodic maintenance of the exhaust system is not required. However, if the vehicle is raised for other service, it is advisable to check the general condition of the catalytic converter, exhaust pipes and muffler.

Testing for leaks in the exhaust system is not a difficult task. Look for black sooty deposits around joints, on the pipes and on the muffler. The presence of black soot indicates a leak. If a leak is suspected but cannot be found, pour a tiny amount of mineral spirits into the carburetor or throttle body with the engine running. The smoke created by the mineral spirits will be seen escaping from the area of the exhaust leak.

Fig. 191 Installation of the drive plate stopper — automatic transaxle equipped models

Front Exhaust Pipe

REMOVAL & INSTALLATION

Turbocharged Models

1. Disconnect the oxygen sensor harness.

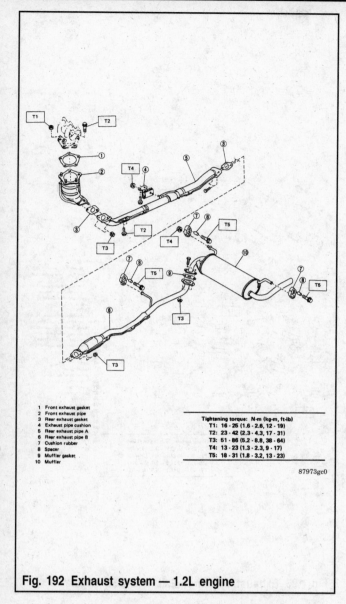

Fig. 192 Exhaust system — 1.2L engine

1 Front exhaust gasket
2 Front exhaust pipe
3 Rear exhaust gasket
4 Exhaust pipe cushion
5 Rear exhaust pipe A
6 Rear exhaust pipe B
7 Cushion rubber
8 Spacer
9 Muffler gasket
10 Muffler

Tightening torque: N-m (kg-m, ft-lb)
T1: 16 - 25 (1.6 - 2.6, 12 - 19)
T2: 23 - 42 (2.3 - 4.3, 17 - 31)
T3: 51 - 86 (5.2 - 8.8, 38 - 64)
T4: 13 - 23 (1.3 - 2.3, 9 - 17)
T5: 18 - 31 (1.8 - 3.2, 13 - 23)

87973gc0

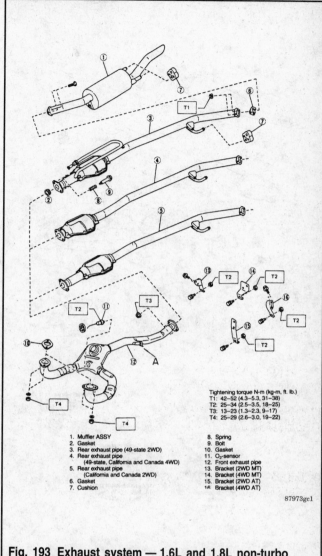

Fig. 193 Exhaust system — 1.6L and 1.8L non-turbo engines

1. Muffler ASSY
2. Gasket
3. Rear exhaust pipe (49-state 2WD)
4. Rear exhaust pipe (49-state, California and Canada 4WD)
5. Rear exhaust pipe (California and Canada 2WD)
6. Gasket
7. Cushion
8. Spring
9. Bolt
10. Gasket
11. O₂-sensor
12. Front exhaust pipe
13. Bracket (2WD MT)
14. Bracket (4WD MT)
15. Bracket (2WD AT)
16. Bracket (4WD AT)

Tightening torque N-m (kg-m, ft. lb.)
T1: 42–52 (4.3–5.3, 31–38)
T2: 25–34 (2.5–3.5, 18–25)
T3: 13–23 (1.3–2.3, 9–17)
T4: 25–29 (2.6–3.0, 19–22)

87973gc1

2. As required, remove the air duct from the upper shell cover.

3. Loosen (do not remove) the nuts which hold the front exhaust pipe to the exhaust port of the engine.

4. Disconnect the front and rear exhaust pipes.

5. Disconnect the front exhaust pipe and bracket.

6. While holding the front exhaust pipe with one hand, remove the nuts which hold the front exhaust pipe to the exhaust port. The front exhaust pipe can then be disconnected.

➥**During installation, do not tighten any connections more then hand tight until the entire exhaust system has been installed. Be sure to install a new gasket at the exhaust port. Use only nuts specified by the manufacturer. Do not remove the gasket placed between the front and rear exhaust pipes. When the front exhaust pipe needs to be replaced, the gasket must be replaced also.**

To install:

7. Install the front exhaust pipe and bracket.

8. Connect the front and rear exhaust pipes.

9. Align exhaust system and tighten all exhaust system nuts and bolts to specification. Work from front to rear.

10. Connect the oxygen sensor harness.

11. Start the engine and allow it to reach operating temperature. Check for leaks.

Non-Turbocharged Models

1. Remove the turbocharger covers, and disconnect the center exhaust pipe. Remove the turbocharger unit.

2. Remove the nuts which hold the turbocharger bracket to the front exhaust pipe.

3. Remove the underguard and right undercover.

4. Loosen the engine mount bracket and pitching stopper. Then slightly raise the engine until the bolts protrude beyond the surface of the crossmember.

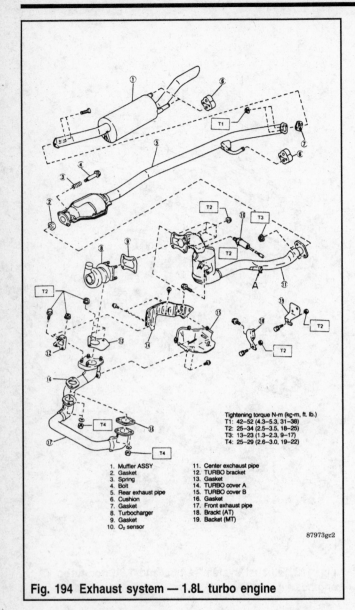

Tightening torque N·m (kg-m, ft. lb.)
T1: 42–52 (4.3–5.3, 31–38)
T2: 25–34 (2.5–3.5, 18–25)
T3: 13–23 (1.3–2.3, 9–17)
T4: 25–29 (2.6–3.0, 19–22)

1. Muffler ASSY	11. Center exhaust pipe
2. Gasket	12. TURBO bracket
3. Spring	13. Gasket
4. Bolt	14. TURBO cover A
5. Rear exhaust pipe	15. TURBO cover B
6. Cushion	16. Gasket
7. Gasket	17. Front exhaust pipe
8. Turbocharger	18. Brackt (AT)
9. Gasket	19. Backet (MT)
10. O₂ sensor	

87973gc2

Fig. 194 Exhaust system — 1.8L turbo engine

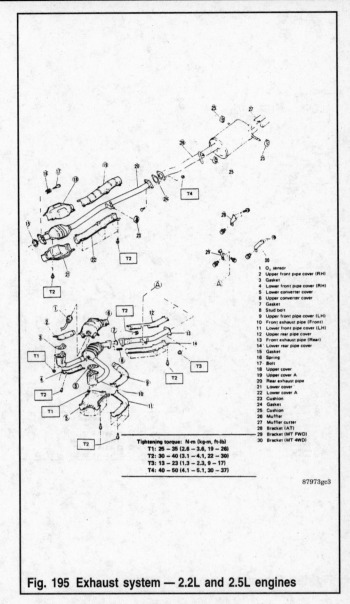

1. O₁ sensor	
2. Upper front pipe cover (RH)	
3. Gasket	
4. Lower front pipe cover (RH)	
5. Lower converter cover	
6. Upper converter cover	
7. Gasket	
8. Stud bolt	
9. Upper front pipe cover (LH)	
10. Front exhaust pipe (Front)	
11. Lower front pipe cover (LH)	
12. Upper rear pipe cover	
13. Front exhaust pipe (Rear)	
14. Lower rear pipe cover	
15. Gasket	
16. Spring	
17. Bolt	
18. Upper cover	
19. Upper cover A	
20. Rear exhaust pipe	
21. Lower cover	
22. Lower cover A	
23. Cushion	
24. Gasket	
25. Cushion	
26. Muffler	
27. Muffler cutter	
28. Bracket (AT)	
29. Bracket (MT FWD)	
30. Bracket (MT 4WD)	

Tightening torque: N·m (kg-m, ft-lb)
T1: 25 – 35 (2.6 – 3.6, 19 – 26)
T2: 30 – 40 (3.1 – 4.1, 22 – 30)
T3: 13 – 23 (1.3 – 2.3, 9 – 17)
T4: 40 – 50 (4.1 – 5.1, 30 – 37)

87973gc3

Fig. 195 Exhaust system — 2.2L and 2.5L engines

5. Disconnect the front exhaust pipe from the engines exhaust port, and remove through the clearance between the crossmember and the cylinder head.

✳✳WARNING

Be sure to remove the bolts only after the engine has cooled off. Before disassembling parts, spray with penetrating lubricant to loosen rust deposits.

To install:

6. Install the gasket onto the stud bolts at the engine's exhaust port with its flat surface facing the engine. If the gasket is tilted, it may catch on a thread and then will not drop down over the bolt.

7. Temporarily tighten the front exhaust pipe to engine's exhaust port with the nuts.

8. Lower the engine. Tighten the engine mount bracket and properly adjust the pitching stopper.

9. Install the underguard and right undercover.

10. Connect the front exhaust pipe to the turbocharger bracket.

11. Properly tighten the front exhaust pipe at the engine's exhaust port.

12. Connect the oxygen sensor connector.

13. Install the turbocharger unit, center the exhaust pipe and turbocharger covers.

Center Exhaust Pipe

REMOVAL & INSTALLATION

Turbocharged Models

1. Remove the turbocharger covers.
2. Disconnect the oxygen sensor connector.

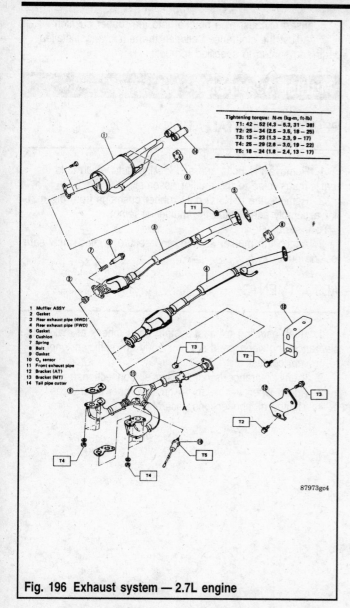

Tightening torque: N·m (kg-m, ft-lb)
T1: 42 — 52 (4.3 — 5.3, 31 — 38)
T2: 25 — 34 (2.5 — 3.5, 18 — 25)
T3: 13 — 23 (1.3 — 2.3, 9 — 17)
T4: 25 — 29 (2.6 — 3.0, 19 — 22)
T5: 18 — 24 (1.8 — 2.4, 13 — 17)

1 Muffler ASSY
2 Gasket
3 Rear exhaust pipe (4WD)
4 Rear exhaust pipe (FWD)
5 Gasket
6 Cushion
7 Spring
8 Bolt
9 Gasket
10 O₂ sensor
11 Front exhaust pipe
12 Bracket (AT)
13 Bracket (MT)
14 Tail pipe cutter

Fig. 196 Exhaust system — 2.7L engine

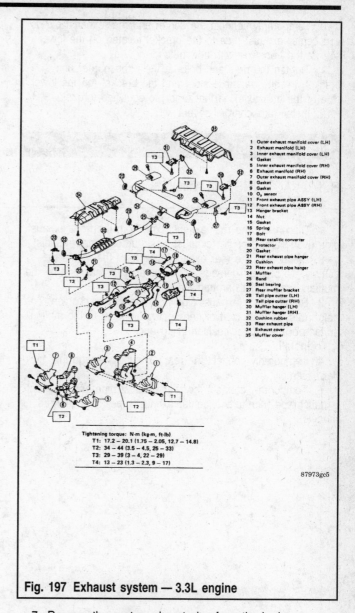

1 Outer exhaust manifold cover (LH)
2 Exhaust manifold (LH)
3 Inner exhaust manifold cover (LH)
4 Gasket
5 Inner exhaust manifold cover (RH)
6 Exhaust manifold (RH)
7 Outer exhaust manifold cover (RH)
8 Gasket
9 Gasket
10 O₂ sensor
11 Front exhaust pipe ASSY (LH)
12 Front exhaust pipe ASSY (RH)
13 Hanger bracket
14 Nut
15 Gasket
16 Spring
17 Bolt
18 Rear catalitic converter
19 Protector
20 Gasket
21 Rear exhaust pipe hanger
22 Cushion
23 Rear exhaust pipe hanger
24 Muffler
25 Band
26 Seal bearing
27 Rear muffler bracket
28 Tail pipe cutter (LH)
29 Tail pipe cutter (RH)
30 Muffler hanger (LH)
31 Muffler hanger (RH)
32 Cushion rubber
33 Rear exhaust pipe
34 Exhaust cover
35 Muffler cover

Tightening torque: N·m (kg-m, ft-lb)
T1: 17.2 — 20.1 (1.75 — 2.05, 12.7 — 14.8)
T2: 34 — 44 (3.5 — 4.5, 25 — 33)
T3: 29 — 39 (3 — 4, 22 — 29)
T4: 13 — 23 (1.3 — 2.3, 9 — 17)

Fig. 197 Exhaust system — 3.3L engine

3. Remove the flange nuts which hold the center exhaust pipe to turbocharger unit.

❊❊WARNING

Be sure to remove the bolts only after the engine has cooled off. Before disassembling parts, spray with penetrating lubricant to loosen rust deposits.

4. Remove the flange nuts from the transaxle side.
5. Disconnect the center and rear exhaust pipes.
6. Disconnect the center exhaust pipe from the bracket located on the lower side of the transaxle.

7. Remove the center exhaust pipe from the body.

❊❊CAUTION

Do not allow the turbocharger cover mounting bracket to interfere with the brake pipe cover located in the front toeboard. Be sure not to damage the steering universal joint. Do not damage the gasket used on the lower side of the turbocharger unit or turbocharger cover.

To install:

8. Install the gasket onto the stud bolts on the turbocharger unit. Connect the center exhaust pipe flange and temporarily tighten it with nuts.

❊❊CAUTION

Be sure not to damage the gasket used on the lower side of the turbocharger unit and turbocharger cover.

9. Temporarily connect the center exhaust pipe and bracket located on the transaxle side.

10. Temporarily connect the center and rear exhaust pipes, and center exhaust pipe to the bracket located on the lower side of the transaxle with new nuts.

11. Tighten the nuts and bolts at the turbocharger unit bracket, (on the transaxle side) and the bracket (on the lower side of the transaxle), in that order, to specified torque.

12. Install turbocharger covers.

Rear Exhaust Pipe

REMOVAL & INSTALLATION

1. Disconnect the rear exhaust pipe from the front exhaust pipe (Non-Turbo), center exhaust pipe (turbocharged models).

2. Disconnect the rear exhaust pipe from the muffler assembly. To prevent damage to the bumper or rear skirt by the muffler, wrap a cloth around the tail pipe.

3. Remove rear exhaust pipe from the rubber cushion. To help in its, apply a coat of penetrating lubricant to the mating surface of the rubber cushion in advance.

To install:

4. Temporarily connect the rear exhaust pipe and the muffler assembly.

5. Temporarily connect the rear exhaust pipe and the front exhaust pipe (non-turbo), center exhaust pipe (turbocharged models).

6. Insert exhaust pipe bracket into the rubber cushion.

7. Adjust the clearance between the temporarily installed parts and tighten to specified torque.

Muffler Assembly

REMOVAL & INSTALLATION

1. Remove the bolts and self locking nuts which hold the rear exhaust pipe to the muffler assembly.

2. Remove the left and right rubber cushions from the muffler assembly and detach the muffler assembly.

To install:

3. Attach the muffler section, and secure in place new safe locking nuts.

ADJUSTMENTS

1. After installing exhaust system parts, check to make sure clearances between parts and car body are sufficient enough to prevent contact.

2. If any clearance is not, loosen all connections.

3. Adjust when necessary to obtain proper clearances.

4. Tighten all connections securely.

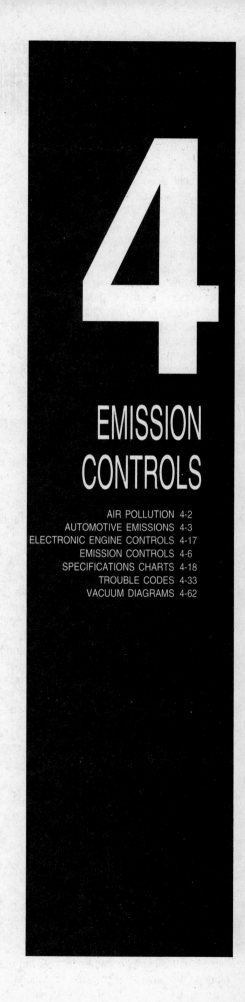

4

EMISSION CONTROLS

AIR POLLUTION

The earth's atmosphere, at or near sea level, consists approximately of 78 percent nitrogen, 21 percent oxygen and 1 percent other gases. If it were possible to remain in this state, 100 percent clean air would result. However, many varied sources allow other gases and particulates to mix with the clean air, causing our atmosphere to become unclean or polluted.

Some of these pollutants are visible while others are invisible, with each having the capability of causing distress to the eyes, ears, throat, skin and respiratory system. Should these pollutants become concentrated in a specific area and under certain conditions, death could result due to the displacement or chemical change of the oxygen content in the air. These pollutants can also cause great damage to the environment and to the many man-made objects that are exposed to the elements.

To better understand the causes of air pollution, the pollutants can be categorized into 3 separate types: natural, industrial and automotive.

Natural Pollutants

Natural pollution has been present on earth since before man appeared and continues to be a factor when discussing air pollution, although it causes only a small percentage of the overall pollution problem. It is the direct result of decaying organic matter, wind born smoke and particulates from such natural events as plain and forest fires (ignited by heat or lightning), volcanic ash, sand and dust which can spread over a large area of the countryside.

Such a phenomenon of natural pollution has been seen in the form of volcanic eruptions, with the resulting plume of smoke, steam and volcanic ash blotting out the sun's rays as it spreads and rises higher into the atmosphere. As it travels into the atmosphere the upper air currents catch and carry the smoke and ash, while condensing the steam back into water vapor. As the water vapor, smoke and ash travel on their journey, the smoke dissipates into the atmosphere while the ash and moisture settle back to earth in a trail hundreds of miles long. In some cases, lives are lost and millions of dollars of property damage result.

Industrial Pollutants

Industrial pollution is caused primarily by industrial processes, the burning of coal, oil and natural gas, which in turn produce smoke and fumes. Because the burning fuels contain large amounts of sulfur, the principal ingredients of smoke and fumes are sulfur dioxide and particulate matter. This type of pollutant occurs most severely during still, damp and cool weather, such as at night. Even in its less severe form, this pollutant is not confined to just cities. Because of air movements, the pollutants move for miles over the surrounding countryside, leaving in its path a barren and unhealthy environment for all living things.

Working with Federal, State and Local mandated regulations and by carefully monitoring emissions, big business has greatly reduced the amount of pollutant introduced from its industrial sources, striving to obtain an acceptable level. Because of the mandated industrial emission clean up, many land areas and streams in and around the cities that were formerly barren of vegetation and life, have now begun to move back in the direction of nature's intended balance.

Automotive Pollutants

The third major source of air pollution is automotive emissions. The emissions from the internal combustion engines were not an appreciable problem years ago because of the small number of registered vehicles and the nation's small highway system. However, during the early 1950's, the trend of the American people was to move from the cities to the surrounding suburbs. This caused an immediate problem in transportation because the majority of suburbs were not afforded mass transit conveniences. This lack of transportation created an attractive market for the automobile manufacturers, which resulted in a dramatic increase in the number of vehicles produced and sold, along with a marked increase in highway construction between cities and the suburbs. Multi-vehicle families emerged with a growing emphasis placed on an individual vehicle per family member. As the increase in vehicle ownership and usage occurred, so did pollutant levels in and around the cities, as suburbanites drove daily to their businesses and employment, returning at the end of the day to their homes in the suburbs.

It was noted that a smoke and fog type haze was being formed and at times, remained in suspension over the cities, taking time to dissipate. At first this "smog," derived from the words "smoke" and "fog," was thought to result from industrial pollution but it was determined that automobile emissions shared the blame. It was discovered that when normal automobile emissions were exposed to sunlight for a period of time, complex chemical reactions would take place.

It is now known that smog is a photo chemical layer which develops when certain oxides of nitrogen (NOx) and unburned hydrocarbons (HC) from automobile emissions are exposed to sunlight. Pollution was more severe when smog would become stagnant over an area in which a warm layer of air settled over the top of the cooler air mass, trapping and holding the cooler mass at ground level. The trapped cooler air would keep the emissions from being dispersed and diluted through normal air flows. This type of air stagnation was given the name "Temperature Inversion."

TEMPERATURE INVERSION

In normal weather situations, surface air is warmed by heat radiating from the earth's surface and the sun's rays. This causes it to rise upward, into the atmosphere. Upon rising it will cool through a convection type heat exchange with the cooler upper air. As warm air rises, the surface pollutants are carried upward and dissipated into the atmosphere.

When a temperature inversion occurs, we find the higher air is no longer cooler, but is warmer than the surface air, causing the cooler surface air to become trapped. This warm air blanket can extend from above ground level to a few hundred or even a few thousand feet into the air. As the surface air is trapped, so are the pollutants, causing a severe smog condition. Should this stagnant air mass extend to a few thousand feet high, enough air movement with the inversion takes place to allow the smog layer to rise above ground level but the pollutants still cannot dissipate. This inversion can remain for days over an area, with the smog level only rising or lowering from ground level to a few hundred feet high. Meanwhile, the pollutant levels increase, causing eye irritation, respiratory problems, reduced visibility, plant damage and in some cases, even disease.

This inversion phenomenon was first noted in the Los Angeles, California area. The city lies in terrain resembling a basin and with certain weather conditions, a cold air mass is held in the basin while a warmer air mass covers it like a lid.

Because this type of condition was first documented as prevalent in the Los Angeles area, this type of trapped pollution was named Los Angeles Smog, although it occurs in other areas where a large concentration of automobiles are used and the air remains stagnant for any length of time.

HEAT TRANSFER

Consider the internal combustion engine as a machine in which raw materials must be placed so a finished product comes out. As in any machine operation, a certain amount of wasted material is formed. When we relate this to the internal combustion engine, we find that through the input of air and fuel, we obtain power during the combustion process to drive the vehicle. The by-product or waste of this power is, in part, heat and exhaust gases with which we must dispose.

The heat from the combustion process can rise to over 4000°F (2204°C). The dissipation of this heat is controlled by a ram air effect, the use of cooling fans to cause air flow and a liquid coolant solution surrounding the combustion area to transfer the heat of combustion through the cylinder walls and into the coolant. The coolant is then directed to a thin-finned, multi-tubed radiator, from which the excess heat is transferred to the atmosphere by 1 of the 3 heat transfer methods, conduction, convection or radiation.

The cooling of the combustion area is an important part in the control of exhaust emissions. To understand the behavior of the combustion and transfer of its heat, consider the air/fuel charge. It is ignited and the flame front burns progressively across the combustion chamber until the burning charge reaches the cylinder walls. Some of the fuel in contact with the walls is not hot enough to burn, thereby snuffing out or quenching the combustion process. This leaves unburned fuel in the combustion chamber. This unburned fuel is then forced out of the cylinder and into the exhaust system, along with the exhaust gases.

Many attempts have been made to minimize the amount of unburned fuel in the combustion chambers due to quenching, by increasing the coolant temperature and lessening the contact area of the coolant around the combustion area. However, design limitations within the combustion chambers prevent the complete burning of the air/fuel charge, so a certain amount of the unburned fuel is still expelled into the exhaust system, regardless of modifications to the engine.

AUTOMOTIVE EMISSIONS

Before emission controls were mandated on internal combustion engines, other sources of engine pollutants were discovered along with the exhaust emissions. It was determined that engine combustion exhaust produced approximately 60 percent of the total emission pollutants, fuel evaporation from the fuel tank and carburetor vents produced 20 percent, with the final 20 percent being produced through the crankcase as a by-product of the combustion process.

Exhaust Gases

The exhaust gases emitted into the atmosphere are a combination of burned and unburned fuel. To understand the exhaust emission and its composition, we must review some basic chemistry.

When the air/fuel mixture is introduced into the engine, we are mixing air, composed of nitrogen (78 percent), oxygen (21 percent) and other gases (1 percent) with the fuel, which is 100 percent hydrocarbons (HC), in a semi-controlled ratio. As the combustion process is accomplished, power is produced to move the vehicle while the heat of combustion is transferred to the cooling system. The exhaust gases are then composed of nitrogen, a diatomic gas (N_2), the same as was introduced in the engine, carbon dioxide (CO_2), the same gas that is used in beverage carbonation, and water vapor (H_2O). The nitrogen (N_2), for the most part, passes through the engine unchanged, while the oxygen (O_2) reacts (burns) with the hydrocarbons (HC) and produces the carbon dioxide (CO_2) and the water vapors (H_2O). If this chemical process would be the only process to take place, the exhaust emissions would be harmless. However, during the combustion process, other compounds are formed which are considered dangerous. These pollutants are hydrocarbons (HC), carbon monoxide (CO), oxides of nitrogen (NOx) oxides of sulfur (SOx) and engine particulates.

HYDROCARBONS

Hydrocarbons (HC) are essentially fuel which was not burned during the combustion process or which has escaped into the atmosphere through fuel evaporation. The main sources of incomplete combustion are rich air/fuel mixtures, low engine temperatures and improper spark timing. The main sources of hydrocarbon emission through fuel evaporation on most vehicles used to be the vehicle's fuel tank and carburetor float bowl.

To reduce combustion hydrocarbon emission, engine modifications were made to minimize dead space and surface area in the combustion chamber. In addition, the air/fuel mixture was made more lean through the improved control which feedback carburetion and fuel injection offers and by the addition of external controls to aid in further combustion of the hydrocarbons outside the engine. Two such methods were the addition of air injection systems, to inject fresh air into the exhaust manifolds and the installation of catalytic converters, units that are able to burn traces of hydrocarbons without affecting the internal combustion process or fuel economy.

To control hydrocarbon emissions through fuel evaporation, modifications were made to the fuel tank to allow storage of the fuel vapors during periods of engine shut-down. Modifications were also made to the air intake system so that at specific times during engine operation, these vapors may be purged and burned by blending them with the air/fuel mixture.

CARBON MONOXIDE

Carbon monoxide is formed when not enough oxygen is present during the combustion process to convert carbon (C) to carbon dioxide (CO_2). An increase in the carbon monoxide (CO) emission is normally accompanied by an increase in the hydrocarbon (HC) emission because of the lack of oxygen to completely burn all of the fuel mixture.

Carbon monoxide (CO) also increases the rate at which the photo chemical smog is formed by speeding up the conversion of nitric oxide (NO) to nitrogen dioxide (NO_2). To accomplish this, carbon monoxide (CO) combines with oxygen (O_2) and nitric oxide (NO) to produce carbon dioxide (CO_2) and nitrogen dioxide (NO_2). ($CO + O_2 + NO = CO_2 + NO_2$).

The dangers of carbon monoxide, which is an odorless and colorless toxic gas are many. When carbon monoxide is inhaled into the lungs and passed into the blood stream, oxygen is replaced by the carbon monoxide in the red blood cells, causing a reduction in the amount of oxygen supplied to the many parts of the body. This lack of oxygen causes headaches, lack of coordination, reduced mental alertness and, should the carbon monoxide concentration be high enough, death could result.

NITROGEN

Normally, nitrogen is an inert gas. When heated to approximately 2500°F (1371°C) through the combustion process, this gas becomes active and causes an increase in the nitric oxide (NO) emission.

Oxides of nitrogen (NOx) are composed of approximately 97-98 percent nitric oxide (NO). Nitric oxide is a colorless gas but when it is passed into the atmosphere, it combines with oxygen and forms nitrogen dioxide (NO_2). The nitrogen dioxide then combines with chemically active hydrocarbons (HC) and when in the presence of sunlight, causes the formation of photo-chemical smog.

Ozone

To further complicate matters, some of the nitrogen dioxide (NO_2) is broken apart by the sunlight to form nitric oxide and oxygen. (NO_2 + sunlight = NO + O). This single atom of oxygen then combines with diatomic (meaning 2 atoms) oxygen (O_2) to form ozone (O_3). Ozone is one of the smells associated with smog. It has a pungent and offensive odor, irritates the eyes and lung tissues, affects the growth of plant life and causes rapid deterioration of rubber products. Ozone

can be formed by sunlight as well as electrical discharge into the air.

The most common discharge area on the automobile engine is the secondary ignition electrical system, especially when inferior quality spark plug cables are used. As the surge of high voltage is routed through the secondary cable, the circuit builds up an electrical field around the wire, which acts upon the oxygen in the surrounding air to form the ozone. The faint glow along the cable with the engine running that may be visible on a dark night, is called the "corona discharge." It is the result of the electrical field passing from a high along the cable, to a low in the surrounding air, which forms the ozone gas. The combination of corona and ozone has been a major cause of cable deterioration. Recently, different and better quality insulating materials have lengthened the life of the electrical cables.

Although ozone at ground level can be harmful, ozone is beneficial to the earth's inhabitants. By having a concentrated ozone layer called the "ozonosphere," between 10 and 20 miles (16-32 km) up in the atmosphere, much of the ultra violet radiation from the sun's rays are absorbed and screened. If this ozone layer were not present, much of the earth's surface would be burned, dried and unfit for human life.

OXIDES OF SULFUR

Oxides of sulfur (SOx) were initially ignored in the exhaust system emissions, since the sulfur content of gasoline as a fuel is less than $1/10$ of 1 percent. Because of this small amount, it was felt that it contributed very little to the overall pollution problem. However, because of the difficulty in solving the sulfur emissions in industrial pollutions and the introduction of catalytic converter to the automobile exhaust systems, a change was mandated. The automobile exhaust system, when equipped with a catalytic converter, changes the sulfur dioxide (SO_2) into sulfur trioxide (SO_3).

When this combines with water vapors (H_2O), a sulfuric acid mist (H_2SO_4) is formed and is a very difficult pollutant to handle since it is extremely corrosive. This sulfuric acid mist that is formed, is the same mist that rises from the vents of an automobile battery when an active chemical reaction takes place within the battery cells.

When a large concentration of vehicles equipped with catalytic converters are operating in an area, this acid mist may rise and be distributed over a large ground area causing land, plant, crop, paint and building damage.

PARTICULATE MATTER

A certain amount of particulate matter is present in the burning of any fuel, with carbon constituting the largest percentage of the particulates. In gasoline, the remaining particulates are the burned remains of the various other compounds used in its manufacture. When a gasoline engine is in good internal condition, the particulate emissions are low but as the engine wears internally, the particulate emissions increase. By visually inspecting the tail pipe emissions, a determination can be made as to where an engine defect may exist. An engine with light gray or blue smoke emitting from the tail pipe normally indicates an increase in the oil consumption through burning due to internal engine wear. Black smoke would indicate a defective fuel delivery system, causing the engine to operate in a rich mode. Regardless of the color of the smoke, the internal part of the engine or the fuel delivery system should be repaired to prevent excess particulate emissions.

Diesel and turbine engines emit a darkened plume of smoke from the exhaust system because of the type of fuel used. Emission control regulations are mandated for this type of emission and more stringent measures are being used to prevent excess emission of the particulate matter. Electronic components are being introduced to control the injection of the fuel at precisely the proper time of piston travel, to achieve the optimum in fuel ignition and fuel usage. Other particulate afterburning components are being tested to achieve a cleaner emission.

Good grades of engine lubricating oils should be used, which meet the manufacturers specification. Cut-rate oils can contribute to the particulate emission problem because of their low flash or ignition temperature point. Such oils burn prematurely during the combustion process causing emission of particulate matter.

The cooling system is an important factor in the reduction of particulate matter. The optimum combustion will occur, with the cooling system operating at a temperature specified by the manufacturer. The cooling system must be maintained in the same manner as the engine oiling system, as each system is required to perform properly in order for the engine to operate efficiently for a long time.

Crankcase Emissions

Crankcase emissions are made up of water, acids, unburned fuel, oil fumes and particulates. These emissions are classified as hydrocarbons (HC) and are formed by the small amount of unburned, compressed air/fuel mixture entering the crankcase from the combustion area (between the cylinder walls and piston rings) during the compression and power strokes. The head of the compression and combustion help to form the remaining crankcase emissions.

Since the first engines, crankcase emissions were allowed into the atmosphere through a road draft tube, mounted on the lower side of the engine block. Fresh air came in through an open oil filler cap or breather. The air passed through the crankcase mixing with blow-by gases. The motion of the vehicle and the air blowing past the open end of the road draft tube caused a low pressure area (vacuum) at the end of the tube. Crankcase emissions were simply drawn out of the road draft tube into the air.

To control the crankcase emission, the road draft tube was deleted. A hose and/or tubing was routed from the crankcase to the intake manifold so the blow-by emission could be burned with the air/fuel mixture. However, it was found that

intake manifold vacuum, used to draw the crankcase emissions into the manifold, would vary in strength at the wrong time and not allow the proper emission flow. A regulating valve was needed to control the flow of air through the crankcase.

Testing, showed the removal of the blow-by gases from the crankcase as quickly as possible, was most important to the longevity of the engine. Should large accumulations of blow-by gases remain and condense, dilution of the engine oil would occur to form water, soots, resins, acids and lead salts, resulting in the formation of sludge and varnishes. This condensation of the blow-by gases occurs more frequently on vehicles used in numerous starting and stopping conditions, excessive idling and when the engine is not allowed to attain normal operating temperature through short runs.

Evaporative Emissions

Gasoline fuel is a major source of pollution, before and after it is burned in the automobile engine. From the time the fuel is refined, stored, pumped and transported, again stored until it is pumped into the fuel tank of the vehicle, the gasoline gives off unburned hydrocarbons (HC) into the atmosphere. Through the redesign of storage areas and venting systems, the pollution factor was diminished, but not eliminated, from the refinery standpoint. However, the automobile still remained the primary source of vaporized, unburned hydrocarbon (HC) emissions.

Fuel pumped from an underground storage tank is cool but when exposed to a warmer ambient temperature, will expand. Before controls were mandated, an owner might fill the fuel tank with fuel from an underground storage tank and park the vehicle for some time in warm area, such as a parking lot. As the fuel would warm, it would expand and should no provisions or area be provided for the expansion, the fuel would spill out of the filler neck and onto the ground, causing hydrocarbon (HC) pollution and creating a severe fire hazard. To correct this condition, the vehicle manufacturers added overflow plumbing and/or gasoline tanks with built in expansion areas or domes.

However, this did not control the fuel vapor emission from the fuel tank. It was determined that most of the fuel evaporation occurred when the vehicle was stationary and the engine not operating. Most vehicles carry 5-25 gallons (19-95 liters) of gasoline. Should a large concentration of vehicles be parked in one area, such as a large parking lot, excessive fuel vapor emissions would take place, increasing as the temperature increases.

To prevent the vapor emission from escaping into the atmosphere, the fuel systems were designed to trap the vapors while the vehicle is stationary, by sealing the system from the atmosphere. A storage system is used to collect and hold the fuel vapors from the carburetor (if equipped) and the fuel tank when the engine is not operating. When the engine is started, the storage system is then purged of the fuel vapors, which are drawn into the engine and burned with the air/fuel mixture.

EMISSION CONTROLS

Crankcase Ventilation System

OPERATION

▶ **See Figures 1, 2, 3 and 4**

A Positive Crankcase Ventilation (PCV) system is used to help reduce emission of blow-by gasses into the atmosphere. The system consists of a sealed oil filler cap, rocker covers with an emission outlet and fresh air inlet, connecting hoses, PCV valve and air cleaner.

At part throttle, blow-by gas in the crankcase flows into the intake manifold through the PCV valve by the strong vacuum of the intake manifold. Under this condition, the fresh air is introduced into the crankcase through the rocker cover fresh air inlet.

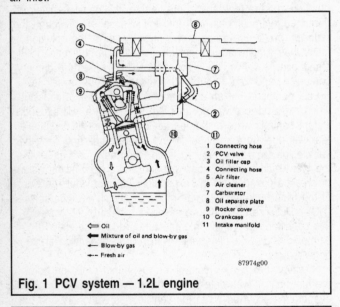

1	Connecting hose
2	PCV valve
3	Oil filler cap
4	Connecting hose
5	Air filter
6	Air cleaner
7	Carburetor
8	Oil separate plate
9	Rocker cover
10	Crankcase
11	Intake manifold

⟸ Oil
◀ Mixture of oil and blow-by gas
◀ Blow-by gas
◀-- Fresh air

87974g00

Fig. 1 PCV system — 1.2L engine

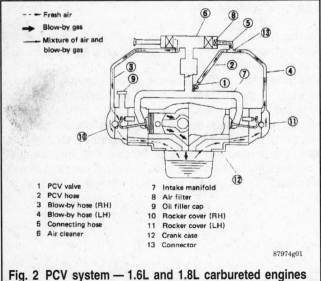

--- Fresh air
➡ Blow-by gas
— Mixture of air and blow-by gas

1	PCV valve	7	Intake manifold
2	PCV hose	8	Air filter
3	Blow-by hose (RH)	9	Oil filler cap
4	Blow-by hose (LH)	10	Rocker cover (RH)
5	Connecting hose	11	Rocker cover (LH)
6	Air cleaner	12	Crank case
		13	Connector

87974g01

Fig. 2 PCV system — 1.6L and 1.8L carbureted engines

--- Fresh air
➡ Blow-by gas
— Mixture of air and blow-by gas

1	PCV valve	8	Connector
2	PCV hose	9	Oil filler cap
3	Blow-by hose (RH)	10	Rocker cover (RH)
4	Blow-by hose (LH)	11	Rocker cover (LH)
5	Blow-by hose (CTR) (MPFI only)	12	Crank case
6	Intake duct	13	Connecting hose
7	Intake manifold	14	Connecting hose
		15	Connector

87974g03

Fig. 3 PCV system — fuel injected engine

Case
Valve
Spring

To intake manifold

87974g04

Fig. 4 Cutaway view of a PCV valve

At wide open throttle, a part of the blow-by gas flows into the air intake duct through the connecting hose and is drawn to the throttle chamber. The system uses this route because the reduced intake manifold vacuum is not able to draw the increased amount of blow-by gases generated by the wide open throttle condition through the PCV valve.

TESTING

PCV Valve
▶ **See Figure 5**

The PCV valve should be checked at regular intervals and replaced as required. If the valve is found to be defective, do not clean, replace it. Connection and system hoses can be

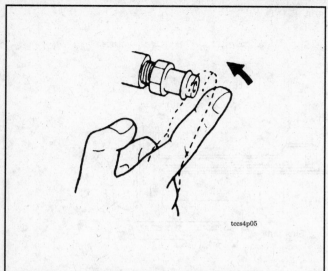

Fig. 5 Check the PCV valve for vacuum at idle

cleaned by using compressed air. Check all hoses for clogging, split or hardening condition. Replace as necessary.

1. With the engine running, remove the valve from its mounting. A hissing sound should be heard and vacuum should be felt from the inlet side of the valve.

2. Reinstall the valve. Remove the crankcase inlet air cleaner. Loosely hold a piece of stiff paper over the opening in the rocker cover. Allow one minute for the crankcase pressure to reduce. The paper should then be pulled against the rocker cover with noticeable force. Replace the inlet air cleaner in the rocker cover.

3. With the engine stopped, remove the PCV valve and shake. A clicking sound should be heard indicating that the valve is not stuck.

4. If the valve fails any of the above tests, it should be replaced.

Regulating Orifice System

Clean the hoses and calibrating orifice internally. Blow away foreign matter with compressed air. Check the hoses for cracks, fatigue and swelling. Replace if necessary.

REMOVAL & INSTALLATION

1. Label the PCV valve or regulating orifice hoses before removing.

2. Disconnect the hoses and remove the valve/orifice.

3. Connect the hoses to the new valve/orifice and install the valve/orifice.

Evaporative Emission Controls

OPERATION

▶ **See Figures 6, 7, 8, 9 and 10**

The evaporative emission control system is employed to prevent evaporated fuel in the fuel tank or carburetor bowl (carbu-

reted engines only) from being discharged into the atmosphere. System components differ slightly according to the model of the vehicle and the type of fuel system, but all systems function in the same manner.

Gasoline vapor from the fuel tank (and carburetor bowl) is introduced into a canister mounted in the engine compartment. This canister is filled with activated charcoal which absorbs the vapors and stores them. This function of the canister is continuous and is performed whether the engine is running or stopped; the function of the float chamber ventilation valve is only performed when the engine is stopped.

In order to clear the charcoal canister of vapors, the system purges the canister while the engine is running. When predetermined engine conditions are met, usually when the engine is at normal operating temperature and running at a speed greater than idle, a purge control valve opens to allow the stored vapors to enter the intake tract. The purge control valve can be vacuum or electrically controlled.

Once the purge control valve is open, the stored vapors in the canister are drawn, along with the incoming air/fuel charge, into the combustion chamber and burned. Fresh air is allowed to enter the canister through a filter in the bottom to fully purge the system.

Most models use a fuel separator, mounted on the fuel tank, to prevent liquid fuel from being transferred to the charcoal canister in the event of severe cornering or abrupt stops. Liquid fuel in the separator is returned to the fuel tank through a hose at the rear of the tank. On some models, a fuel cut valve is used to control liquid fuel from entering the vapor pipe. The rising level of the fuel from the tank causes a float to move up and close the cap hole to prevent fuel from entering the pipe.

A two-way valve is used on all vehicles to allow the fuel tank to breathe. When a vacuum is created in the fuel tank due to the fuel pump suck fuel, the two-way valve opens to allow a flow of air from the vapor canister to the tank. When pressure is built up in the tank, the valve opens in the opposite direction to allow the pressure to be vented into the charcoal canister. In the event of a two-way valve failure, the fuel cap is fitted with a valve to allow the tank to ingest air. This will prevent a collapse of the tank.

TESTING

There are several things which should be checked if a malfunction of the evaporative emission control system is suspected. These include deterioration of the vacuum lines, deteriorated, disconnected or pinched hoses, improperly routed hoses and/or a defective filler cap.

In the most severe cases of evaporative emissions system failure, the fuel tank may collapse. This condition is caused by a clogged or pinched vent line, a defective vapor separator, or a plugged or incorrect filler cap. The incorrect or faulty components do not allow the fuel tank to breathe and thus create a vacuum in the tank, causing it to collapse.

System Operation

Visually inspect the entire system for kinked, cracked, swollen, plugged or fatigued hoses. Replace the vapor canister if cracked, damaged or if fuel is leaking from the bottom.

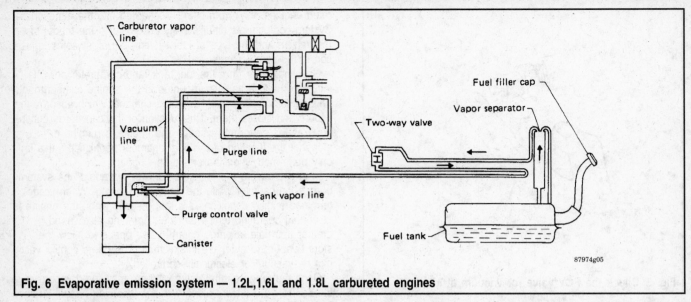

Fig. 6 Evaporative emission system — 1.2L, 1.6L and 1.8L carbureted engines

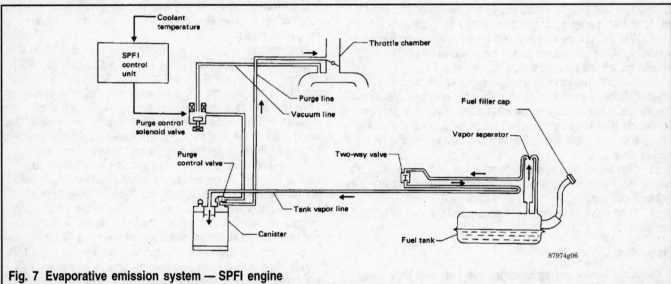

Fig. 7 Evaporative emission system — SPFI engine

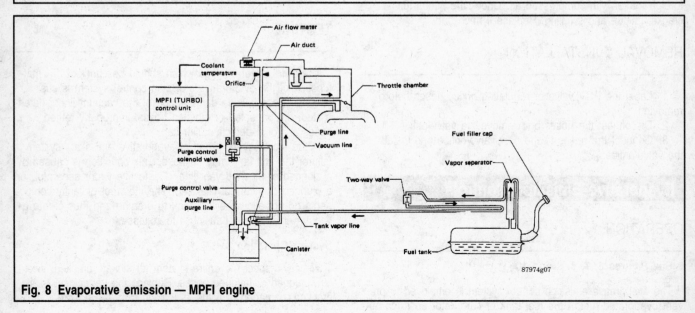

Fig. 8 Evaporative emission — MPFI engine

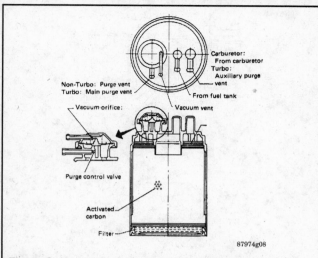

Fig. 9 Cutaway view of an evaporative emission canister

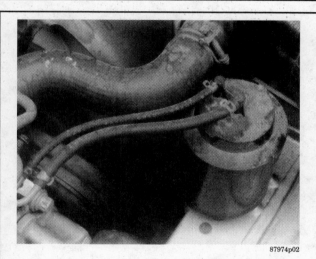

Fig. 10 Evaporative emission canister in the engine compartment — Legacy

Purge Lines and Canister

1. Remove the fuel filler cap.
2. Disconnect the evaporation line at the evaporation pipe.
3. Check for an unobstructed evaporation line on the fuel tank side by blowing air into the hose. A little resistance should be felt due to the two-way valve.

➡**Take care not to suck on the hose as this causes fuel evaporation vapors to enter your mouth. This may cause serious injury.**

4. Check for an unobstructed evaporation line on the canister side by blowing air into the hose. A little resistance should be felt due to the two-way valve.
5. If an obstruction is found, remove the two-way valve and retest. If the obstruction is still present, clean or replace the line. If not, test the two-way valve and replace as necessary.
6. Check all lines for cracks or deterioration. Replace as necessary.

7. Check the exterior of the canister for damage and replace as necessary.

Two-Way Valve

1. Remove the two-way valve.
2. Check for air passage by blowing air into the lower nipple. A little resistance should be felt due to the functioning of the valve.
3. Repeat the test blowing into the upper nipple.
4. Check the valve case for cracks for deterioration.
5. Replace the valve if it fails any of the above tests.

Float Chamber Ventilation Valve

This valve is used on carbureted engines only.
1. Check the resistance between the positive and negative terminals. Resistance should be 16-20 ohms for the Justy and 32.7-39.9 for all other vehicles. If not, replace the solenoid valve.
2. Check the resistance between the Positive and negative terminals and the solenoid valve body. Resistance should be 1M ohm or more. If not, replace the solenoid valve.
3. Check the vacuum passage for opening and closing operation while applying electric current to both positive and negative terminals. If the vacuum passage fails to open when current is not applied or fails to close when current is applied, replace the solenoid valve.

Fuel Filler Cap

1. To test the filler cap, if it is the safety valve type, clean it and place it against your palm.
2. Blow into the relief valve housing.
3. If the cap passes pressure with light blowing or if it fails to release with hard blowing, it is defective and must be replaced.

REMOVAL & INSTALLATION

Components of the evaporative system are all removed in the same basic manner. First label, then unplug any vacuum and electrical connections from the component. Remove any hardware retaining the component to the vehicle, then remove the component from the vehicle.

➡**When replacing any evaporative emission system hoses, always use hoses that are fuel resistant.**

Canister

1. Label and disconnect the vacuum lines from the canister.
2. Loosen and remove the retainer screws holding the canister in place.
3. Remove the canister assembly from the engine compartment.
4. Inspect and replace any vacuum hoses that show signs of deterioration.
5. Inspect the canister for signs of damage and replace as required.
   To install:
6. Install the canister into the retainer clamp, and tighten the screws.
7. Connect the vacuum lines.

Two-Way Valve

➡️The two-way valve is located on the fuel line, either near the fuel tank or in the engine compartment.

1. On fuel injected vehicles, properly relieve the fuel system pressure.
2. Raise and support the vehicle safely on jackstands, and locate the two-way valve.
3. Loosen the hose clamps and slide them out of the way.
4. Note the direction of the valve, then disconnect it from the fuel lines.

✳️✳️CAUTION

The valve will be filled with fuel. Take care not to spill the fuel into your eyes.

To install:
5. Install the valve, making sure the flow direction is correct.
6. Install the hose clamps and tighten securely.
7. Lower the vehicle. Start the vehicle and check for fuel leaks.

Float Chamber Ventilation Valve

1. Tag and disconnect vacuum hoses attached to the float chamber valve.
2. Loosen the clamps, and remove the valve.
To install:
3. Check the condition of the vacuum hoses and replace as required.
4. Install the valve, tightening the hose clamps.
5. Attach the vacuum lines.
6. Start the engine and check for leaks.

Exhaust Gas Recirculation (EGR) System

OPERATION

▶ See Figures 11, 12, 13, 14 and 15

The function of the Exhaust Gas Recirculation (EGR) system is the reduction of NOx (oxides of nitrogen) by reducing the combustion temperature through recirculating a part of the exhaust gas into the cylinders.

The EGR valve opens in response engine vacuum. A thermo-valve, or on computer controlled engines a solenoid valve, is used to control the amount of vacuum reaching the EGR valve. When engine performance would suffer due to the recirculating gasses, normally during start-up, the valves remained closed to not allow vacuum to reach the EGR valve. When predetermined conditions are met, the valves open to allow the EGR valve to function according engine vacuum.

TESTING

➡️The EGR system on the Legacy, Impreza and SVX is diagnosed and tested via the on-board diagnostics.

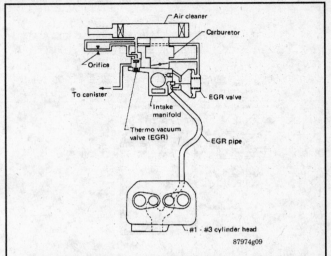

Fig. 11 EGR system — carbureted vehicle without a computer controlled engine

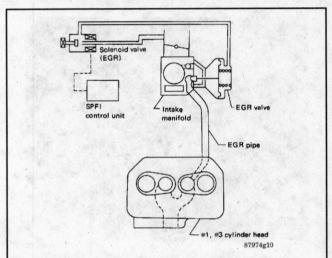

Fig. 12 EGR system — fuel injected vehicle with a computer controlled engine

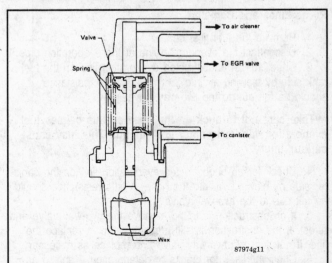

Fig. 13 Cutaway view of an EGR thermo-vacuum valve assembly

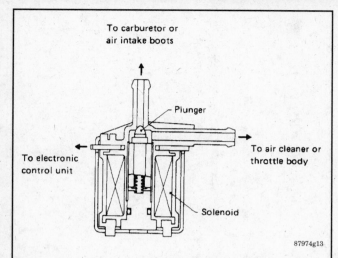

**Fig. 14 Cutaway view of an EGR solenoid valve —
carbureted and SPFI engines**

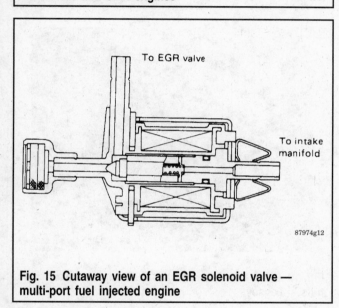

**Fig. 15 Cutaway view of an EGR solenoid valve —
multi-port fuel injected engine**

EGR Valve and Flow Passages

▶ See Figure 16

1. Start the engine and allow it to reach normal operating
temperature.

2. Looking through the opening in the EGR valve body,
check if the valve shaft moves when the engine is revved to
3000-3500 rpm under a no load condition. If the shaft moves,
proceed to Step 4.

➡**During the test in Step 2, the EGR solenoid valve
should be removed from SPFI engines.**

3. If the shaft does not move, check the EGR valve with a
hand vacuum pump. Apply 8 in. Hg (27 kPa) of vacuum and
see if the shaft moves. If not, remove the valve and clean or
replace as needed. If the valve functions properly, check for
leaks in the EGR vacuum lines.

4. With the engine idling, connect a hand vacuum pump to
the EGR valve. Apply 8 in. Hg (27 kPa) of vacuum to the
valve. The engine should stall or idle roughly. If not, clean the

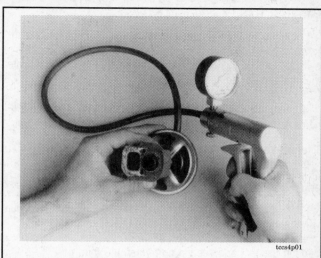

**Fig. 16 Checking the EGR valve with a vacuum pump.
This can be done with the valve on or off the engine**

obstruction from the exhaust gas passages in the cylinder
head.

EGR VALVE CLEANING

▶ See Figure 17

➡**Do not wash the EGR valve in solvent, as permanent
damage could result.**

1. Hold the valve assembly in hand and lightly tap with a
plastic hammer to remove the exhaust deposits from the valve
seat.

2. With a wire brush, remove the deposits from the mounting surfaces of the valve.

3. Depress the valve and look at the seat area. If valve
and seat are not clean, repeat the cleaning procedure.

4. Look for deposits in the valve outlet and remove with an
appropriate tool.

5. Blow any remaining deposits from the valve with compressed air.

6. Check the EGR valve for proper operation using a hand
vacuum pump.

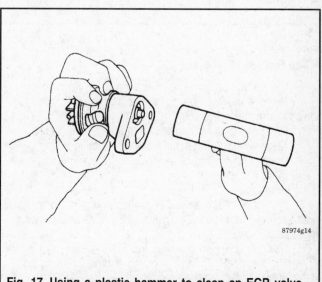

Fig. 17 Using a plastic hammer to clean an EGR valve

EXHAUST GAS PASSAGE CLEANING

1. Inspect the EGR gas inlet to intake manifold for carbon or oil deposits. Remove any deposits present with a hooked awl, taking care to minimize the amount of material falling into the intake manifold.

2. Remove all deposits using a vacuum.

3. Remove the EGR pipe and lightly tap with a plastic hammer to loosen deposits. Blow clean using compressed air.

Thermo-Vacuum Valve

➡ **This valve is used only on non-computer controlled engines.**

1. Drain the cooling system and remove the thermo-vacuum valve.

2. With the valve at 86°F (30°C) or less, air should pass through the first and second port when the third port is plugged. Air should pass through the second and third port when the first port is plugged.

3. Heat the valve to 104°F (40°C) and repeat the tests in Step 2. Air should not pass any of the ports.

4. If the valve does not function properly, remove and replace it.

Vacuum Solenoid Valve

1. Disconnect the electrical harness.

2. Check the resistance between the positive and negative terminals of the valve. Resistance should be 33-40 ohms.

3. Check the resistance between the positive or negative terminals and the body. Resistance should be 1M ohm or more.

4. Check the vacuum passage for opening and closing operation while applying electric current on both the positive and negative terminals. With no electricity applied, the passage between the EGR and intake manifold ports should be open. When the electricity is applied, the passage between the EGR and intake manifold ports should be closed.

5. If the valve does not function properly, it should be replaced.

REMOVAL & INSTALLATION

EGR Valve

▶ **See Figures 18 and 19**

1. Detach the vacuum hose from the EGR valve.

2. Remove the two nuts which secure the EGR valve to the intake manifold assembly.

3. Remove the valve and gasket from the manifold.

4. Clean all gasket material from both mating surfaces.

5. Check the vacuum hose for deterioration and replace as necessary.

To install:

6. Inspect the exhaust gas passages in the intake manifold and clean as necessary. Clean the EGR valve assembly as necessary.

7. Using a new gasket, install the EGR valve.

8. Tighten the EGR valve securing nuts to 17-19 ft. lbs. (22-25 Nm).

9. Install the hose on the EGR valve.

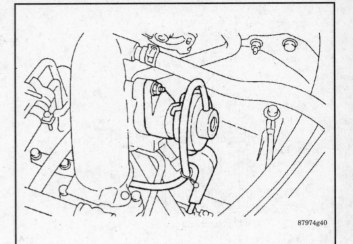

87974g40

Fig. 18 EGR valve attached to the side of the intake manifold — Loyale

87974p03

Fig. 19 Loosen and remove the EGR valve retainer nuts — Legacy

Thermo-Vacuum Valve

1. Drain the cooling system below the level of the thermo-vacuum valve.

2. Tag and disconnect the vacuum hoses from the valve assembly.

3. Remove the thermo-valve using an appropriately sized wrench.

4. Inspect the vacuum hoses for signs of deterioration and replace as necessary.

To install:

5. Install the thermo-vacuum valve after coating the threads with sealant. Tighten the valve securely.

6. Connect the vacuum hoses.

7. Refill the cooling system.

Vacuum Solenoid Valve

1. Disconnect the negative battery cable.

2. Disconnect the vacuum solenoid wiring harness.

3. Tag and disconnect the vacuum hoses from the valve assembly.

4. Remove the solenoid valve attaching screws, then remove the solenoid valve.

To install:

5. Position the valve assembly, securing in place with the retainer screws.

6. Inspect the vacuum hoses for signs of deterioration and replace as necessary.

7. Connect the vacuum hoses to the valve.

8. Connect the vacuum solenoid wiring harness.

9. Connect the negative battery cable.

Air Injection (AI) System

OPERATION

▶ **See Figures 20 and 21**

The Air Injection (AI) system utilizes the vacuum created by exhaust gas pulsation and normal intake manifold vacuum. Each exhaust port is connected to the air suction valve by air suction manifolds. When a vacuum is created in the exhaust ports, a reed in the suction valve opens allowing fresh air to be sucked into the exhaust ports. When there is pressure rather than vacuum in the exhaust ports, the reed in the air suction valve closes, preventing the flow of exhaust gases.

The fresh air sucked through the air suction valve is used for oxidation of HC and CO in the exhaust passages and partly for combustion in the cylinders

The system incorporates an electronically controlled solenoid that either deactivates this system entirely, or partially a short time after the engine is started cold. The only way to determine that there is a problem with this system is to remove the solenoid and test it electrically.

Models equipped with an AI system incorporate an Air Suction Valve (ASV), which can be disassembled and serviced.

Various models have an exhaust port liner made from stainless steel plate built into the cylinder head as one unit. The port liner has a built in air layer which decreases heat transfer to the cylinder head while keeping the exhaust port at a higher temperature. The insulation of the exhaust port helps oxidation of residual HC and CO with the help of the remaining air in the exhaust gases.

The anti-afterburn valve prevents afterburning that occurs on cold starts. Below 122°F (50°C), the temperature valve has an open passage connecting the afterburning valve with the intake manifold via a vacuum line. The vacuum line remains opened, and the afterburning valve in operation until the coolant temperature becomes hot enough to shut off the vacuum and override the afterburning system.

TESTING

Air Suction Valve

1. Remove the air suction valve assembly.

2. Blow air through the air inlet to see if air flows smoothly through the outlet while emitting a hissing sound. If air does

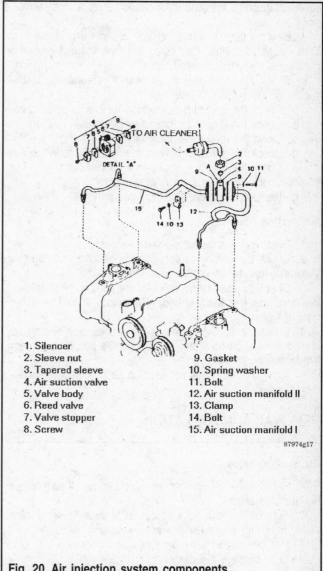

1. Silencer
2. Sleeve nut
3. Tapered sleeve
4. Air suction valve
5. Valve body
6. Reed valve
7. Valve stopper
8. Screw
9. Gasket
10. Spring washer
11. Bolt
12. Air suction manifold II
13. Clamp
14. Bolt
15. Air suction manifold I

87974g17

Fig. 20 Air injection system components

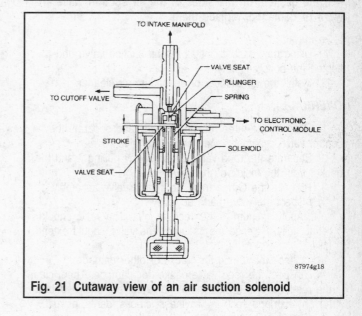

87974g18

Fig. 21 Cutaway view of an air suction solenoid

not flow smoothly, the read valve could be stuck closed. Replace the reed valve.

3. Blow air through the outlet side of the valve to see if air flows through the inlet. If air flows, the reed valve is broken or stuck open. Replace the reed valve.

4. Check the valve after it has been disassembled. To disassemble, proceed as follows:

    a. Check the inlet and outlet case for cracks or damage.

    b. Check the gasket for cracks or damage.

    c. Clean the reed valve thoroughly.

    d. Check for check for waves, cracks or dents in the seat.

    e. Check the reed for cracks or a broken point.

    f. Check the valve for a rusty stopper.

    g. Replace any broken or damaged part.

Air Suction Solenoid

1. Remove the solenoid electrical harness.

2. Check the resistance between the positive and negative terminals. Resistance should be 33-40 ohms.

3. Check the resistance between the positive or negative terminals, and the solenoid body. Resistance should be at least 1M ohm.

4. Check the vacuum passage for opening and closing operation while applying battery voltage to the positive and negative terminals.

5. If the solenoid does not function as specified, replace the solenoid.

REMOVAL & INSTALLATION

Air Suction Valve

1. Remove the air silencer or secondary air cleaner assembly from the engine.

2. Remove the four bolts which run through the air suction valve, mounting it between the two air suction manifolds.

3. Pull the suction valve from between the manifolds. Take care not to damage the reeds.

➡**If the gaskets on the sides of the air suction valve are worn or damaged, replace them.**

To install:

4. Using new gaskets install the air suction valve and tighten the bolts securely.

5. Install the air silencer or secondary air cleaner.

OVERHAUL

1. Remove the three retainer screws, and separate the control valve assembly, seat, and reed valve cover.

2. Separate the reed valve assembly by pulling it and the gasket from the inside of the valve cover.

3. Remove the O-ring from the control valve assembly.

4. Inspect the valve parts as follows:

    a. Apply vacuum to the vacuum inlet. The valve should retract fully. Release the vacuum. The valve should extend fully.

    b. Check the O-ring for cracks or other damage.

    c. Inspect the reed valve gasket for damage. Then, clean the reed valve in a safe, non-volatile solvent and inspect it for any damage such as waviness, cracks, dents, or rust.

5. Replace all damaged or worn parts.

To assemble:

6. Install the O-ring on the control valve assembly.

7. Join the reed valve assembly making sure the gasket stays inside of the valve cover.

8. Install the three screws, joining the control valve assembly, seat, and reed valve cover.

Air Suction Manifolds

1. Remove the air silencer or secondary air cleaner and the air suction valve from the engine compartment.

2. Remove the clamp which supports the right side suction manifold by loosening the mounting bolt.

3. Loosen the threaded sleeves (two on each manifold), which mount the suction manifolds to the engine. Lift off the manifolds.

To install:

4. Lightly oil the threaded sleeves before mounting the suction manifold to the engine.

5. Install the manifolds and tighten the sleeves securely.

6. Install the clamp which supports the right side suction manifold.

7. Install the air silencer or secondary air cleaner and the air suction valve.

Hot Air Control System

▶ **See Figure 22**

The hot air control system is used on carbureted vehicles only. The purpose of the system is to reduce HC emissions and improve engine performance during warm-up. This is accomplished by deflecting either cool outside air or warm engine heated air into the carburetor, depending upon engine operating conditions.

The system works automatically be means of a temperature sensor and vacuum motor. The temperature sensor detects the inlet air temperature, and controls the flow of vacuum to the vacuum motor. Together they regulate the air control valve, mounted in the air horn of the air cleaner.

The possible combinations of inlet (underhood) air temperatures and vacuum readings, and the resulting valve operation, are as follows:

• Underhood temperature below 100°F (38°C) with vacuum below 1.57 in. Hg (5.30 kPa) at motor diaphragm: valve closed and cold air admitted.

• Underhood temperature below 100°F (38°C) with vacuum above 6.30 in. Hg (21.27 kPa) at motor diaphragm: valve closed and hot air admitted.

• Underhood temperature between 100-127°F (38-53°C) with varying vacuum at motor diaphragm: valve open and hot/cold air mixture admitted.

• Underhood temperature above 127°F (53°C) with no vacuum at motor diaphragm: valve open and cold air admitted.

TESTING

Air Control Valve

▶ **See Figure 23**

1. If the car is running, turn off the engine.

2. Place a mirror at the end of the air cleaner assembly.

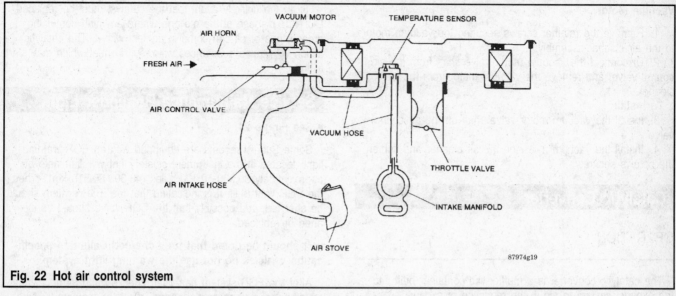

Fig. 22 Hot air control system

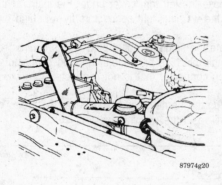

87974g20

Fig. 23 Using a mirror to inspect the air control valve assembly

3. Inspect the position of the air control valve. The proper position is with the fresh air vent open and the hot air inlet closed.

4. If the position is not as described, check the air control valve linkage for any sticking.

Vacuum Motor

1. Keeping the inspection mirror in position, make sure the engine is off.

2. Remove the vacuum hose from the vacuum motor assembly.

3. Connect a separate piece of the same diameter and type of hose to the now vacant vacuum motor. Insert the other end of the new hose into your mouth and draw in a breath, creating a vacuum in the vacuum motor.

4. Check the position of the air control valve. The fresh air vent should be closed and the hot air inlet open.

5. Now, pinch the hose attached to the vacuum motor so that the vacuum is not instantly lost. The valve position should be maintained for more than 30 seconds.

6. If the motor does not function properly, it should be replaced.

Temperature Sensor

> ✳✳**WARNING**
>
> **Engine must be cold before starting this test.**

1. Keep the mirror in position, as described above.

2. Start the engine, and keep it idling.

3. Check the position of the air control valve immediately after starting. The fresh air vent should be closed and the hot air inlet open.

4. Continue to watch the air control valve as the engine warms up to normal operating temperature. The fresh air vent should gradually open.

5. If the sensor does not function properly, replace it.

REMOVAL & INSTALLATION

Temperature Sensor

1. Remove the air cleaner cover and filter assembly.

2. Using a pair of pliers, flatten the clip securing the vacuum hose to the temperature sensor and remove the hose.

3. Now pull the same clip completely away from the sensor. Lift the sensor off the air cleaner.

➡ **The gasket between the sensor and air cleaner is glued to the air cleaner and should be removed.**

4. Remove and discard the gasket. Clean both mating surfaces.

To install:

➡ **Always install a new clip when the temperature sensor is reinstalled.**

5. Install a new gasket to the air cleaner surface.

6. Install the sensor and attach a new clip.

7. Install the air cleaner cover and filter.

Vacuum Motor

1. Remove the retainer screws securing the vacuum motor to the air cleaner assembly.

2. Disconnect the vacuum motor valve shaft from the air control valve, and remove the vacuum motor from the air cleaner.

To install:

3. Install the vacuum motor valve shaft on the air control valve.

4. Install the vacuum motor on the air cleaner and tighten the screws securely.

Catalytic Converter

OPERATION

The catalytic converter is a muffler-like container built into the exhaust system to aid in the reduction of exhaust emissions. The catalyst element is coated with a noble metal such as platinum, palladium, rhodium or a combination of them. When the exhaust gases come into contact with the catalyst, a chemical reaction occurs which reduces the pollutants into harmless substances such as water and carbon dioxide.

There are two types of catalytic converters: an oxidizing type and a three-way type. The oxidizing catalyst requires the addition of oxygen to spur the catalyst into reducing the engine's HC and CO emissions into H_2O and CO_2.

PRECAUTIONS

1. Use only unleaded fuel.

2. Avoid prolonged idling; the engine should run no longer than 20 minutes at curb idle and no longer than 10 minutes at fast idle.

3. Do not disconnect any of the spark plug leads while the engine is running. If any engine testing procedure requires disconnecting or bypassing a control component, perform the procedure as quickly as possible. A misfiring engine can overheat the catalyst and damage the oxygen sensor.

4. Make engine compression checks as quickly as possible.

5. Whenever under the vehicle or around the catalytic converter, remember that it has a very high outside or skin temperature. During operation, the catalyst must reach very high temperatures to work efficiently. Be very wary of burns, even after the engine has been shut off for a while. Additionally, because of the heat, never park the vehicle on or over flammable materials, particularly dry grass or leaves. Inspect the heat shields frequently and correct any bends or damage.

6. In the unlikely event that the catalyst must be replaced, DO NOT dispose of the old one where anything containing grease, gas or oil can come in contact with it. The catalytic action with these substances will result in heat which may start a fire.

Service Maintenance Reminder Light

▶ **See Figure 24**

Some Subaru models are equipped with an EGR warning light, located in the instrument cluster, that will illuminate at approximately 30,000-50,000 miles (48,309-80,515 km). When the EGR light is lit, it is indicating that the EGR system should be checked, and possibly that the EGR valve should be cleaned or replaced.

➡ **It should be noted that turbocharged California specification vehicles do not use the warning light system.**

After the EGR system has been checked and all necessary maintenance or service performed, reset the warning light as follows:

1. Remove the left trim cover under the instrument panel. Pull down the warning light connectors from behind the fuse panel.

2. Locate the single pin blue plug that is connected to another single pin blue plug. Near the blue connectors is a single green connector that is not connected to any wire terminal.

3. Unplug the harness, and plug it into the green connector. This will reset the warning light.

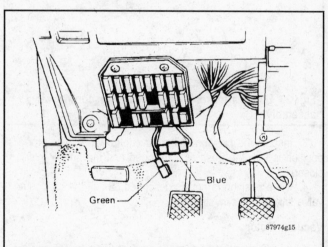

87974g15

Fig. 24 Access the service maintenance reminder harness behind the fuse box at the lower portion of the driver's trim panel

ELECTRONIC ENGINE CONTROLS

Electronic Control Unit (ECU)

OPERATION

The Electronic Control Unit (ECU) is required to maintain the exhaust emissions at acceptable levels. The module is a small, solid state computer which receives signals from many sources and sensors; it uses these data to make judgments about operating conditions and then control output signals to the fuel and emission systems to match the current requirements.

Engines coupled to electronically controlled transaxles employ a Vehicle Control Module (VCM) to oversee both engine and transaxle operation. The integrated functions of engine and transaxle control allow accurate gear selection and improved fuel economy.

In the event of an ECU failure, the system will default to a pre-programmed set of values. These are compromise values which allow the engine to operate, although at a reduced efficiency. This is variously known as the default, limp-in or back-up mode. Driveability is always affected when the ECU enters this mode.

REMOVAL & INSTALLATION

Except SVX

1. Disconnect the negative battery cable.
2. If equipped with an air bag system, allow at least 10 minutes between the time the battery is disconnected and removing the ECU. This will allow time for the air bag module to power down.
3. Remove the lower trim panel retainer screws from below the steering column. Lift the panel off and place aside.
4. If equipped, remove the metal knee panel behind the trim panel, by removing the retainer screws.
5. Remove the retainer screws securing the ECU to the bracket next to or below the steering column.
6. Lower the ECU enough to access the control harnesses attached.
7. Disengage the harnesses from the ECU, by pushing in the lock tab and pulling the pug out of the ECU.
8. Remove the ECU.
   To install:
9. Attach the harnesses to the ECU. Make sure the lock tab engages into place.
10. Position the ECU to the bracket, and secure in place with the retainer screws.
11. Install the metal knee panel, if equipped, using the retainer screws..

12. Install the trim panel and retainer screws.
13. Connect the negative battery cable.

SVX
▶ **See Figure 25**

1. Disconnect the negative battery cable.
2. If equipped with an air bag system, allow at least 10 minutes between the time the battery is disconnected and removing the ECU. This will allow time for the air bag module to power down.
3. Remove the lower trim panel retainer screws from below the steering column. Lift the panel off and place aside.
4. Remove the metal knee panel behind the trim panel, by removing the retainer screws.
5. Remove the retainer screws securing the ECU to the bracket to the left of the steering column.
6. Lower the ECU enough to access the control harnesses attached.
7. Disengage the harnesses from the ECU, by pushing in the lock tab and pulling the pug out of the ECU.
8. Remove the ECU.
   To install:
9. Attach the harnesses to the ECU. Make sure the lock tab engages into place.
10. Position the ECU to the bracket, and secure in place with the retainer screws.
11. Install the metal knee panel, if equipped, using the retainer screws.
12. Install the trim panel and retainer screws.
13. Connect the negative battery cable.

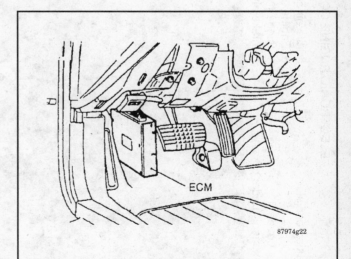

Fig. 25 The ECU is located next to the driver's kick panel — SVX

ELECTRONIC ENGINE CONTROL COMPONETS - 2.2L ENGINE SHOWN

1. Evaporative emission canister
2. Mass air flow
3. EGR valve (under cover)
4. Throttle position sensor (under cover)
5. Idle air control valve (under cover)
6. Engine coolant temperature sensor (side of intake manifold)
7. Intake air sensor
8. MAP sensor (under cover)
9. Camshaft position sensor (under belt cover)
10. Crankshaft position sensor (under belt cover)
11. Knock sensor (lower front of engine block)

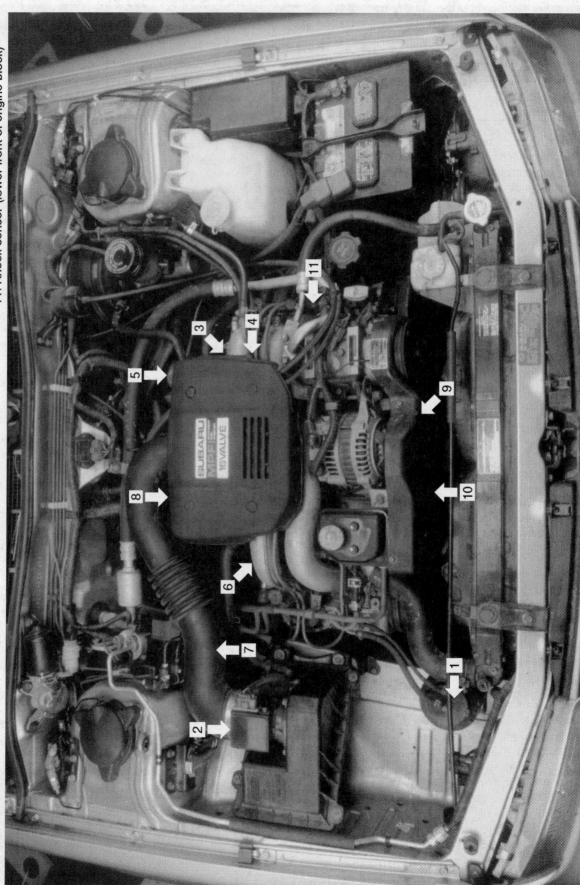

87974p10

Oxygen Sensor

OPERATION

▶ **See Figure 26**

There are two types of oxygen sensor's used in these vehicles. They are the single wire oxygen sensor (02S) and the heated oxygen sensor (H02S). The oxygen sensor is a spark plug shaped device that is screwed into the exhaust manifold. It monitors the oxygen content of the exhaust gases and sends a voltage signal to the Electronic Control Module (ECU). The ECU monitors this voltage and, depending on the value of the received signal, issues a command to the mixture control solenoid on the carburetor to adjust for rich or lean conditions.

The heated oxygen sensor has a heating element incorporated into the sensor to aid in the warm up to the proper operating temperature and to maintain that temperature.

The proper operation of the oxygen sensor depends upon four basic conditions:

1. Good electrical connections. Since the sensor generates low currents, good clean electrical connections at the sensor are a must.

2. Outside air supply. Air must circulate to the internal portion of the sensor. When servicing the sensor, do not restrict the air passages.

3. Proper operating temperatures. The ECU will not recognize the sensor's signals until the sensor reaches approximately 600°F (316°C).

4. Non-leaded fuel. The use of leaded gasoline will damage the sensor very quickly.

TESTING

Single Wire Sensor

1. Start the engine and bring it to normal operating temperature, then run the engine above 1200 rpm for two minutes.

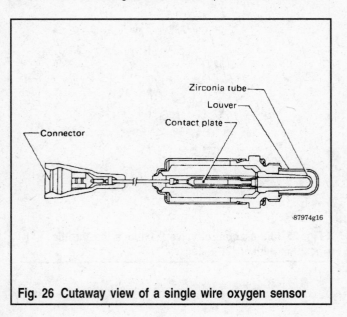

Fig. 26 Cutaway view of a single wire oxygen sensor

2. Backprobe with a high impedance averaging voltmeter or multimeter, set to the DC voltage scale, between the oxygen sensor (02S) and battery ground.

3. Verify that the 02S voltage fluctuates rapidly between 0.40-0.60 volts.

4. If the 02S voltage is stabilized at the middle of the specified range (approximately 0.45-0.55 volts) or if the 02S voltage fluctuates very slowly between the specified range (02S signal crosses 0.5 volts less than 5 times in ten seconds), the 02S may be faulty.

5. If the 02S voltage stabilizes at either end of the specified range, the ECU is probably not able to compensate for a mechanical problem such as a vacuum leak, faulty pressure regulator or high float level. These types of mechanical problems will cause the 02S to sense a constant lean or constant rich mixture. The mechanical problem will first have to be repaired, then the 02S test repeated.

6. Pull a vacuum hose located after the throttle plate. Voltage should drop to approximately 0.12 volts (while still fluctuating rapidly). This tests the ability of the 02S to detect a lean mixture condition. Reattach the vacuum hose.

7. Richen the mixture using a propane enrichment tool. Voltage should rise to approximately 0.90 volts (while still fluctuating rapidly). This tests the ability of the 02S to detect a rich mixture condition.

8. If the 02S voltage is above or below the specified range, the 02S and/or the O2S wiring may be faulty. Check the wiring for any breaks, repair as necessary and repeat the test.

Heated Oxygen Sensor

1. Start the engine and bring it to normal operating temperature, then run the engine above 1200 rpm for two minutes.

2. Turn the ignition **OFF**, and disengage the H02S harness connector.

3. Check for battery voltage at the wires with the ignition switch **ON** and the engine off. If not, there is a problem in the wiring. Check the H02S wiring and the fuse.

4. Next, connect a high impedance ohmmeter between the black wire and white wire. Verify that the resistance is 3.5-14.0 ohms.

5. If the H02S heater resistance is not as specified, the H02S may be faulty.

6. Start the engine and bring it to normal operating temperature, then run the engine above 1200 rpm for two minutes.

7. Backprobe with a high impedance averaging voltmeter or multimeter, set to the DC voltage scale between the oxygen sensor (02S) and battery ground.

8. Verify that the 02S voltage fluctuates rapidly between 0.40-0.60 volts.

9. If the 02S voltage is stabilized at the middle of the specified range (approximately 0.45-0.55 volts) or if the 02S voltage fluctuates very slowly between the specified range (02S signal crosses 0.5 volts less than 5 times in ten seconds), the 02S may be faulty.

10. If the 02S voltage stabilizes at either end of the specified range, the ECU is probably not able to compensate for a mechanical problem such as a vacuum leak or a faulty fuel pressure regulator. These types of mechanical problems will cause the 02S to sense a constant lean or constant rich mixture. The mechanical problem will first have to be repaired and then the 02S test repeated.

11. Pull a vacuum hose located after the throttle plate. Voltage should drop to approximately 0.12 volts (while still fluctuating rapidly). This tests the ability of the 02S to detect a lean mixture condition. Reattach the vacuum hose.

12. Richen the mixture using a propane enrichment tool. Voltage should rise to approximately 0.90 volts (while still fluctuating rapidly). This tests the ability of the 02S to detect a rich mixture condition.

13. If the 02S voltage is above or below the specified range, the 02S and/or the O2S wiring may be faulty. Check the wiring for any breaks, repair as necessary and repeat the test.

REMOVAL & INSTALLATION

▶ See Figure 27

❋❋WARNING

The sensor uses a permanently attached pigtail and connector. This pigtail should not be removed from the sensor. Damage or removal of the pigtail or connector could affect the proper operation of the sensor. Keep the electrical connector and louvered end of the sensor clean and free of grease. NEVER use cleaning solvents of any type on the sensor!

➡**The oxygen sensor may be difficult to remove when the temperature of the engine is below 120°F (49°C). Excessive force may damage the threads in the exhaust manifold or exhaust pipe.**

1. Disconnect the negative battery cable.
2. Remove the exhaust manifold plate, as required.
3. Unplug the electrical harness.
4. Loosen and remove the sensor.

To install:

5. Coat the threads of the sensor with an anti-seize compound before installation. New sensors are precoated with this compound.

➡**DO NOT use a conventional anti-seize paste. The use of a regular paste may electrically insulate the sensor, rendering it useless. The threads MUST be coated with the proper electrically conductive anti-seize compound.**

6. Install the sensor into the exhaust manifold and tighten it 18-25 ft. lbs. (24-34 Nm).
7. Install the exhaust manifold plate, as required.
8. Engage the electrical harness.
9. Connect the negative battery cable.

Idle Air Control (IAC) Valve

OPERATION

▶ See Figure 28

The IAC valve increases engine speed when engine temperature is low by venting air into the air duct behind the throttle plate.

On the Loyale, the IAC valve is located on top of the engine, in front of intake air duct. On the Justy, it is in-line between the air filter housing and the intake manifold. On the Impreza, Legacy and SVX, the IAC valve is incorporated into the throttle body.

TESTING

Electrical Type

1. Disconnect the electrical harness to the IAC valve while the engine is idling. Check to see that the rpm drops.

87974p04

Fig. 27 Loosening the oxygen sensor connection — Legacy

87974g30

Fig. 28 Idle air control valve (1) above the throttle position sensor (2) — Legacy

2. Connect the IAC valve connector and check to see that engine rpm resumes its original speed.

➡**Disconnecting the harness causes a change in engine rpm when the engine is cold. However, when the engine is warm, it causes a smaller change, or almost no change at all.**

3. Stop the engine, then disconnect the electrical harness from the IAC valve.

4. Turn the ignition switch to the **ON** position.

5. Using a voltmeter, measure the voltage across power terminal **BW** on the IAC valve connector and ground. Voltmeter should read 10 volts. If the voltage obtained is less than specified, check the harness.

6. Turn the ignition switch to the **OFF** position. Using an ohmmeter, measure the resistance between each terminal of the connector on the IAC valve. The ohmmeter should read 7.3-13 ohms at -4°F-176°F (-20°C-80°C). If specifications are not as specified, replace the IAC valve.

7. Using an ohmmeter, measure the insulation resistance between each terminal of the connector on the IAC valve and ground. The ohmmeter should read 1 mega-ohm. If specifications are not as specified, replace the IAC valve.

8. Connect the IAC valve harness, then disconnect the control unit electrical harness.

9. Turn the ignition switch to the **ON** position. Using a voltmeter, measure the voltage between terminal **45** (GR) of the control unit harness and ground. Voltmeter should read 10 volts. If specifications are not as specified, check the harness between the IAC valve and the control unit.

10. Turn the ignition switch to the **OFF** position, then connect the control unit harness.

11. Monitor the voltage across terminal **45** (GR) on the control unit harness and ground, when the ignition switch is turned to the **ON** position. Voltmeter should read 1 volt for approximately 1 minute after the ignition switch is turned **ON** and 10 volts after 1 minute. If specifications are not as specified, check for poor contact of the terminal or a faulty control unit.

12. Turn the ignition switch to the **OFF** position, then disconnect the IAC valve hose.

13. Turn the ignition switch to the **ON** position. Look through the open end of the pipe (from which the air control pipe was disconnected) and check that the valve moves from the fully closed position to the fully opened position, 1 minute after the ignition switch is turned to the **ON** position.

REMOVAL & INSTALLATION

1. Disconnect the negative battery cable.
2. Disconnect the injector lead wire from the clamp.
3. Remove the IAC valve, gasket and lead wire from the venturi chamber.
   To install:
4. Using a new gasket, install the IAC valve.
5. Connect the injector lead wire.
6. Connect the negative battery cable.

Engine Coolant Temperature (ECT) Sensor

OPERATION

▶ **See Figure 29**

The ECT sensor is installed on the coolant passage wall of the intake manifold. The thermistor inside changes resistance with to coolant temperature changes. The ECT sensor sends the coolant temperature signal to the ECU, which determines the fuel quantity to be injected and the ignition timing.

TESTING

▶ **See Figure 30**

1. Remove the temperature sensor from the thermostat housing.
2. Place the sensor in water of various temperatures and measure the resistance between the terminals with an ohmmeter.
3. For all models, the resistance should be 3.0 kilo-ohms at 68°F (20°C).
4. At 122°F (50°C), the resistance should be 0.7-1.0 kilo-ohms,
5. At 176°F (80°C), the resistance should be 0.3-0.4 kilo-ohms.
6. If the resistance is not within specification, replace the ECT sensor.

REMOVAL & INSTALLATION

1. Disconnect the negative battery cable.
2. Drain the engine coolant below the level of the intake manifold.

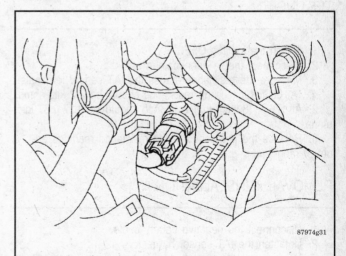

Fig. 29 Engine coolant temperature sensor in the intake manifold — Impreza

87974g31

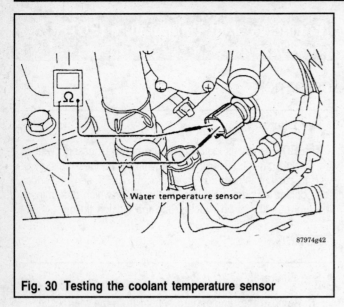

Fig. 30 Testing the coolant temperature sensor

3. Locate the temperature sensor at the water housing on the intake manifold and remove the ECT sensor with a suitable wrench.

To install:

4. Coat the ECT sensor threads with sealant and install. Tighten the sensor securely.

5. Connect the electrical connector.
6. Fill the engine with coolant.
7. Connect the negative battery cable.

Intake Air Temperature (IAT) Sensor

OPERATION

Located on the air cleaner housing, the IAT sensor varies resistance as air temperature changes.

TESTING

1. Switch the ignition **OFF**.
2. Disconnect the IAT sensor harness.
3. Measure the resistance across the IAT sensor terminals.
4. At 68°F (20°C), the resistance should be 2-3 kilo-ohms.
5. At 176°F (80°C), the resistance should be 0.27-0.37 kilo-ohms.
6. Replace the IAT sensor if the resistance readings are out of range.

REMOVAL & INSTALLATION

1. Disconnect the negative battery cable.
2. Unfasten the IAT sensor harness.
3. Using a suitable wrench, loosen and remove the sensor from the side of the air cleaner housing.

To install:

4. Apply a layer of Teflon® tape around the threads of the sensor.

5. Install the sensor, and tighten snugly.
6. Connect the sensor harness.
7. Connect the negative battery cable.

Mass Airflow Sensor

OPERATION

▶ **See Figure 31**

The EFI system incorporates a hot wire type MAF sensor with turbocharger (TC) equipped vehicles or a hot film type with non-TC vehicles. The meter converts the amount of air taken into the engine into an electrical signal by using the heat transfer between the incoming air and a heating resistor (hot wire) located in the air intake. Features of the MAF sensor include:

• Automatic high altitude compensation
• Quick response
• No moving parts
• Compact

TESTING

1985-86 Sedan, Coupe and Wagon

WITH SPFI

▶ **See Figure 32**

1. Switch the ignition **OFF**.
2. Disconnect the electrical harness from the MAF sensor and remove the rubber cover from the MAF sensor connector.

✳✳WARNING

Be careful not to short-circuit the power source. Do not apply voltage greater than 12V.

3. Connect a voltage of 12V to the MAF sensor's positive terminal B and negative terminal C.

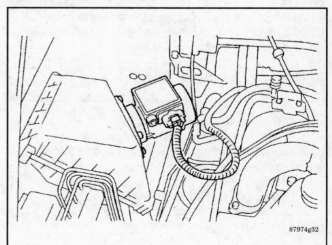

Fig. 31 Mass airflow sensor mounted in the air filter housing

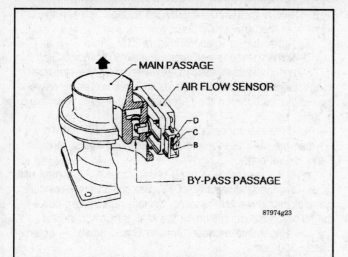

Fig. 32 MAF sensor terminal identification — 1985-86 models with SPFI

4. Using a voltmeter, measure the voltage between terminal C and terminal D of the MAF sensor; it should be 0.1-0.5V.

5. Blow air through the MAF sensor's by-pass passage. If the reading does not change, replace the MAF sensor.

1987-89 Sedan, Coupe and Wagon

WITH SPFI

▶ See Figure 33

1. Switch the ignition **OFF**.

2. Disconnect the electrical connector from the MAF sensor and remove the rubber cover from the MAF sensor connector.

3. Using an ohmmeter, make the following measurements at the MAF sensor connector:
   - Terminal B and ground — less than 10 ohms.

➡**If resistance is greater than 10 ohms, check the harness and internal circuits of the control unit for discontinuity.**

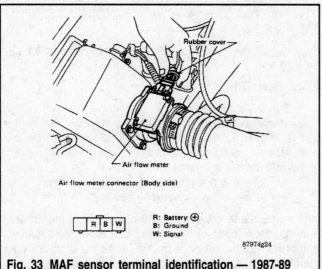

R: Battery ⊕
B: Ground
W: Signal

Fig. 33 MAF sensor terminal identification — 1987-89 models with SPFI

4. Switch the ignition **ON**.

5. Using a voltmeter, measure the voltage between terminal R of the MAF sensor harness and ground; it should be 10V or more.

➡**If the voltage is not within specifications, check the condition of the battery, fuse, control unit harness and/or connector in the power line.**

6. Connect the electrical connector to the MAF sensor.

7. Using a voltmeter, measure the voltage between terminal W and terminal B of the MAF sensor connector; it should be 0.1-0.5V.

➡**If the voltage is not within specifications, replace the mass airflow sensor.**

8. Remove the upper section the air cleaner.

9. Blow air through the MAF sensor, from the air cleaner side, while measuring the voltage between terminal W and terminal B of the MAF sensor connector. If the reading is not 0.1-0.5V, replace the mass airflow sensor.

1988-89 STD, DL and GL

WITH MPFI

▶ See Figure 34

1. Switch the ignition **OFF**.

2. Disconnect the electrical connector from the MAF sensor and remove the rubber cover from the MAF sensor connector.

3. Using an ohmmeter, make the following measurements at the MAF sensor connector:
   - Terminal B and ground — less than 10 ohms.
   - Terminal BR and ground — less than 10 ohms.

➡**If resistance is greater than 10 ohms, check the harness and internal circuits of the control unit for discontinuity and/or the ground terminal on the intake manifold for poor contact.**

4. Switch the ignition **ON** and connect the electrical connector to the MAF sensor.

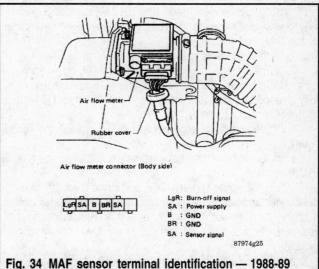

LgR: Burn-off signal
SA : Power supply
B : GND
BR : GND
SA : Sensor signal

Fig. 34 MAF sensor terminal identification — 1988-89 models with MPFI

5. Using a voltmeter, measure the voltage between the SA terminal of the MAF sensor connector and ground; it should be 10V or more.

➡️**If the voltage is not within specifications, check the condition of the battery, fuse, control unit harness and/or connector in the power line.**

6. Using a voltmeter, measure the voltage between the SA terminal and the BR terminal of the MAF sensor connector; it should be 1-2V.

➡️**If the voltage is not within specifications, replace the mass airflow sensor.**

7. Disconnect MAF sensor from air cleaner.
8. Blow air through the MAF sensor, from the air cleaner side, while measuring the voltage between the SA terminal and the BR terminal of the MAF sensor connector. If the reading is not 1-2V, replace the mass airflow sensor.
9. Install the MAF sensor onto the air cleaner.
10. Start and warm the engine.
11. Drive the vehicle at 15 mph for at least 1 minute.
12. Rev the engine above 2000 rpm and allow it to idle.
13. Using a voltmeter, measure the voltage between the light red wire terminal of the MAF sensor and ground; it should be 0V.
14. Turn the ignition switch **OFF**.
15. Using a voltmeter, measure the voltage, within 1 second after turning the engine **OFF**, between the light red wire terminal of the MAF sensor and ground; it should be 12V.

➡️**If the voltage is not within specifications, check the harness from the control unit to the MAF sensor for discontinuity.**

1985-86 Sedan, Coupe, Wagon and XT With MPFI

1. Switch the ignition to **ON**.
2. Using a voltmeter, measure the voltage between the LY terminal of the MAF and ground.
   a. If the voltage is approximately 5.0V, go to Step 3.
   b. If the voltage is not approximately 5.0V, go to Step 6.
3. Using a voltmeter, make sure the MAF sensor flap is fully closed and measure the voltage between the YR terminal of the MAF and ground.
   a. If the voltage is approximately 1.0V, go to Step 4.
   b. If the voltage is not approximately 1.0V, go to Step 5.
4. Using a voltmeter, make sure the MAF sensor flap is fully opened and measure the voltage between the YR terminal of the MAF and ground.
   a. If the voltage is approximately 5.0V, replace the control unit.
   b. If the voltage is not approximately 5.0V, replace the MAF sensor.
5. Turn the ignition switch **OFF** and disconnect the electrical connector from the MAF sensor. Using a ohmmeter, make sure the MAF sensor flap is fully closed and measure the resistance between the YR terminal of the MAF sensor and ground.
   a. If the resistance is approximately 50 ohms, repair YR (US) wire between the MAF sensor and the control unit.
   b. If the resistance is not approximately 50 ohms, replace the MAF sensor.

6. Using a voltmeter, measure the voltage between the G terminal of the MAF and ground.
   a. If the voltage is approximately 8.0V, go to Step 8.
   b. If the voltage is not approximately 8.0V, go to Step 7.
7. Turn the ignition switch **OFF**. Disconnect the electrical connector from the control unit. Using a ohmmeter, measure the resistance between the G terminal of the MAF sensor and ground.
   a. If the resistance is 0 ohms, repair G (UB) wire between the MAF sensor and the control unit and/or replace the control unit.
   b. If the resistance is not 0 ohms, replace the control unit.
8. Turn the ignition switch **OFF**. Disconnect the electrical connector from the MAF sensor. Using an ohmmeter, make the following measurements at the MAF sensor connector:
   • Resistance between terminal G and ground — approximately 300 ohms
   • Resistance between terminal LY and ground — approximately 200 ohms
   • Resistance between terminal YR and ground (from flaps closing to opening) — approximately 50-300 ohms
   a. If all of the above resistances are met, go to Step 9.
   b. If all of the above resistances are not met, replace the MAF sensor.
9. Using an ohmmeter, measure the resistance between terminal YL of the MAF sensor connector and ground.
   a. If the resistance is 0 ohms, go to Step 10.
   b. If the resistance is not 0 ohms, repair the ground wire.
10. Disconnect the electrical connector from the control unit. Using an ohmmeter, measure the resistance between terminal LY of the MAF sensor connector and ground.
   a. If the resistance is 0 ohms, repair the shorted wiring harness.
   b. If the resistance is not 0 ohms, go to Step 11.
11. Using an ohmmeter, measure the resistance between terminal LR of the MAF sensor connector and ground.
   a. If the resistance is 0 ohms, repair the shorted wiring harness.
   b. If the resistance is not 0 ohms, repair the wiring harness between the MAF sensor and the control unit.
12. Reconnect the electrical harness connectors between the control unit and the MAF sensor.

1987 Sedan, Coupe and Wagon With MPFI, 1987-89 XT and 1988-89 XT6

▶ See Figure 35

1. Switch the ignition **OFF**.
2. Disconnect the electrical connector from the MAF sensor and remove the rubber cover from the MAF sensor connector.
3. Using an ohmmeter, make the following measurements at the MAF sensor connector:
   • Terminal B and ground — less than 10 ohms.
   • Terminal BR and ground — less than 10 ohms.

➡️**If resistance is greater than 10 ohms, check the harness and internal circuits of the control unit for discontinuity and/or the ground terminal on the intake manifold for poor contact.**

4. Switch the ignition **ON** and connect the electrical connector to the MAF sensor.

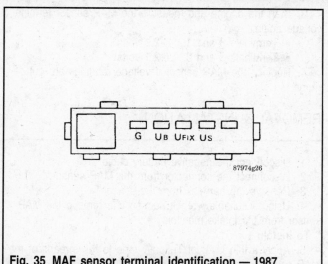

87974g26

Fig. 35 MAF sensor terminal identification — 1987 Sedan, Coupe and Wagon With MPFI, 1987-89 XT and 1988-89 XT6

5. Using a voltmeter, measure the voltage between the R terminal of the MAF sensor connector and ground; it should be 10V or more.

➡**If the voltage is not within specifications, check the condition of the battery, fuse, control unit harness and/or connector in the power line.**

6. Using a voltmeter, measure the voltage between the W terminal and the BR terminal of the MAF sensor connector; it should be 1-2V.

➡**If the voltage is not within specifications, replace the mass airflow sensor.**

7. Disconnect MAF sensor from air cleaner.
8. Blow air through the MAF sensor, from the air cleaner side, while measuring the voltage between the W terminal and the BR terminal of the MAF sensor connector. If the reading is not 1-2V, replace the mass airflow sensor.
9. Install the MAF sensor onto the air cleaner.
10. Start and warm the engine.
11. Drive the vehicle at 15 mph for at least 1 minute.
12. Rev the engine above 2000 rpm and allow it to idle.
13. Using a voltmeter, measure the voltage between the light red wire terminal of the MAF sensor and ground; it should be 0V.
14. Turn the ignition switch **OFF**.
15. Using a voltmeter, measure the voltage, within 1 second after turning the engine **OFF**, between the light red wire terminal of the MAF sensor and ground; it should be 12V.

➡**If the voltage is not within specifications, check the harness from the control unit to the MAF sensor for discontinuity.**

Loyale

1. Remove the MAF sensor. Inspect the air boot and check for leaks.
2. Inspect for obvious signs of contamination such as dust, dirt, water and other foreign matter. Clean out any contamination found.

3. Install the MAF sensor and unplug the connector. Switch the ignition **OFF**.
4. Measure the resistance between terminal BR and ground. If resistance exceeds 10 ohms, check the harness for proper continuity and ground terminal on the intake manifold for poor contact.
5. Switch the ignition **ON** but do not start the engine.
6. Plug the MAF sensor connector back in and measure voltage between terminal SA and ground. It should be at least 10 volts. If not, check the power feed circuit for poor connections, melted fuses, etc.
7. Connect voltmeter positive (+) lead to terminal SA and voltmeter negative (-) lead to terminal BR. Measure the voltage; it should be 1-2 volts. Replace the MAF sensor if not within 1-2 volts.

Impreza

1. Turn the ignition **ON**.
2. Backprobe ECU connector terminal B5 with a high-impedance voltmeter.
   If the voltage is more than 0.3 volt, check the wiring between terminal B5 and the MAF sensor.
   If the voltage is less than 0.3 volt, substitute a known good ECU and retest.
3. Backprobe ECU terminal C1 with a high-impedance voltmeter. The voltage should be 0 volts.
   If the voltage is more than 0 volts, check for a short between C1 and a voltage carrying wire.
   If no short is present, substitute a known good ECU and retest.
4. Start the engine and backprobe terminal B5 on the ECU. The voltage should be between 0.8-1.2 volts.
   If the voltage is not within 0.8-1.2 volts, repair wiring between terminal B5 of the ECU and the MAF sensor.
   If voltage is within 0.8-1.2 volts, continue testing to next step.
5. Backprobe terminal C1 on the ECU. The voltage should be 0 volts.
   If voltage is present, inspect terminal C1 wiring to the MAF sensor for a short to voltage.
   If no short is present, substitute a known good ECU and retest.
6. Turn the ignition switch **OFF** and unplug the MAF sensor. Turn the ignition switch **ON** and check for system voltage at terminal 1 of the MAF connector.
   If voltage is not present, repair wiring.
   If voltage is present, continue testing to next step.
7. Turn the ignition switch **OFF** and unplug the ECU connector. Check all wiring between the ECU and the MAF sensor for shorts, opens and ground. Repair as required.
8. If the wires check out OK, replace the MAF sensor.

Legacy

1. Unplug the MAF sensor connector.
2. Measure the resistance between the MAF sensor terminals and chassis ground.
3. Terminals 1, 2 and 4 should have 1 mega-ohm of resistance to ground.
4. Terminal 3 should have 0 ohms to ground.
5. Replace the MAF sensor if any of the resistance readings are out of range.

SVX

1. Switch the ignition **ON**.
2. Take the following voltage readings:

Measure the voltage between terminal 10 and body ground; it should be between 10-13 volts.

Measure the voltage between terminal 5 and body ground; it should be between 0-0.3 volt.

Measure the voltage between terminal 6 and body ground; it should be 0 volts.

3. Start the engine and take the following readings:

Measure the voltage between terminal 11 and body ground; it should be 13-14 volts.

Measure the voltage between terminal 5 and body ground; it should be 0.8-1.2 volts.

Measure the voltage between terminal 6 and body ground; it should be 0 volts.

4. If any of the MAF readings is out of range, check the harness and power supply. If the readings are still out of range, replace the MAF sensor.

REMOVAL & INSTALLATION

1. Disconnect the negative battery cable.
2. Disconnect the connector from the MAF.
3. Remove the engine harness from the clip.
4. Loosen the hose clamps securing the air intake boot and remove the air intake boot assembly.
5. Loosen the MAF-to-air cleaner assembly bolts and remove the MAF.

To install:

6. Install the MAF and tighten the bolts to 3-5 ft. lbs. (47 Nm).
7. Install the air intake boot assembly and tighten the attaching clamps to secure.
8. Install the engine harness on the clip and connect the airflow meter connector.
9. Connect the negative battery cable.

Manifold Air Pressure (MAP) Sensor

OPERATION

The MAP sensor is connected to the intake plenum with a hose and constantly measures the internal collector pressure. The measured amount of manifold air pressure is converted into an electrical signal and sent to the control unit. The control unit uses this signal, in conjunction with a signal from the CMP sensor, to calculate the amount of intake air.

TESTING

1. Switch the ignition **ON**.
2. Measure the voltage at the MAP sensor terminals with the harness plugged in. Measure the voltage from the harness side.

- Terminals 3 and 1: 3.4-3.8 volts.
- Terminals 3 and 2: 3.4-3.8 volts.

3. Start the engine and measure the MAP sensor terminal voltage again.

- Terminals 3 and 1: 1.6-2.1 volts.
- Terminals 3 and 2: 1.6-2.1 volts.

4. Replace the MAP sensor if voltage readings are out of range.

REMOVAL & INSTALLATION

1. Disconnect the negative battery cable.
2. Disconnect the connector from the MAP sensor.
3. Remove the harness from the sensor.
4. Using a suitable wrench, loosen and remove the MAP sensor from the intake manifold.

To install:

5. Apply a thin layer of Teflon® tape to the threads of the MAP sensor.
6. Install the MAP sensor to the manifold assembly, and tighten to 3-5 ft. lbs. (47 Nm).
7. Attach the harness to the sensor.
8. Connect the negative battery cable.

Barometric Pressure (BARO) Sensor

OPERATION

Unlike many of the electronic sensor, this sensor is built into the ECU.

The BARO sensor detects barometric pressure. The ECU adjusts fuel mixture to compensate for changes in altitude and shift point adjustment at high altitude.

TESTING

Separate component testing is not possible without ECU disassembly. If the vehicle exhibits stalling, unstable idle and poor performance, check the electrical and fuel system. Replace the ECU when all other possibilities have been exhausted.

REMOVAL & INSTALLATION

The BARO sensor, located inside the ECU is not serviceable. The ECU should be replaced if the BARO sensor is found to be defective.

Throttle Position (TP) Sensor

OPERATION

▶ **See Figure 36**

This sensor sends the ECU an output signal which corresponds to the opening of the throttle valve. Using this output signal, the ECU precisely controls the air/fuel ratio during acceleration, deceleration and idling. The TP sensor and the

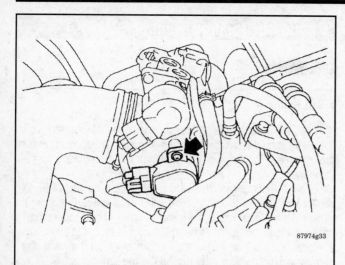

Fig. 36 Throttle position sensor attached to the side of the throttle body assembly — Impreza

throttle switch are combined as part of an assembly. The switch signal turns ON only when the throttle is opened to the idle position or at Wide Open Throttle (WOT) acceleration.

TESTING

Idle Contact

EXCEPT LEGACY, IMPREZA AND SVX

1. Using an ohmmeter, check that continuity exists between terminals A and C when the throttle is fully closed and that no continuity exists when the throttle is opened.
2. Insert a feeler gauge (thickness gauge) of 0.0217 in. (0.55mm) between the stopper screw on the throttle chamber and the stopper (this corresponds to the throttle opening of 1.5 degrees). Ensure that continuity exists between terminals A and C.
3. Insert a feeler gauge (thickness gauge) of 0.0362 in. (0.92mm) between the stopper screw on throttle chamber and the stopper (this corresponds to a throttle opening of 2.5 degrees). Ensure that continuity exists between terminals A and C.

LEGACY, IMPREZA AND SVX

1. Disconnect the TP sensor harness.
2. Measure the resistance with an ohmmeter between terminals 2 and 3.
   a. With the throttle fully closed, the resistance should be 12 kilo-ohms.
   b. With the throttle fully opened, the resistance should be 5 kilo-ohms.
3. The resistance should change smoothly as the throttle plates are moved open and closed.
4. If the TP sensor checks out satisfactorily, check the TP sensor harness for continuity and ground path.
5. Check the idle switch by disconnecting it from the ECU harness.

6. Connect an ohmmeter between terminals 1 and 2.
   a. With the throttle fully closed, the idle switch should be 0 ohms.
   b. With the throttle fully opened, the idle switch resistance should be 1 mega-ohm or more.

Throttle Opening Signal

EXCEPT LEGACY, IMPREZA AND SVX

1. Unplug the throttle sensor and measure the resistance between terminals 1 and 2.
2. The resistance should be 6-18 kilo-ohms. Replace the sensor if the resistance measurement is out of range.
3. Measure the resistance between terminals 1 and 3. It should be:
   - 5.8-17.8 kilo-ohms with the throttle closed
   - 1.5-5.1 kilo-ohms with the throttle open
4. The resistance must change smoothly through its entire range. If the resistances are either out of range or the resistance change is not smooth, replace the throttle sensor.

REMOVAL & INSTALLATION

▶ **See Figures 37, 38, 39 and 40**

1. Disconnect the negative battery cable.
2. Disconnect the throttle sensor electrical harness.
3. Place a matchmark on the throttle position sensor and throttle body mounting surface, so that during installation, the sensor can be properly aligned.
4. Remove the 2 screws securing the throttle sensor to the throttle body assembly.
5. Remove the throttle sensor by pulling it in the axial direction of the throttle shaft.
6. Remove the throttle sensor O-ring and discard.
To install:
7. Using a new throttle O-ring, install the throttle sensor, aligning the matchmarks. Install and hand-tighten the retainer screw.
8. Connect the throttle sensor electrical harness.
9. Connect the negative battery cable.

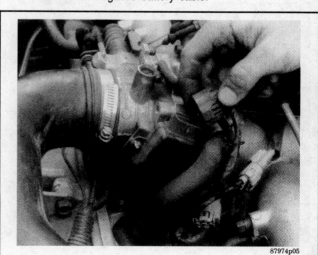

Fig. 37 Disconnect the wire harness from the throttle position sensor — Legacy

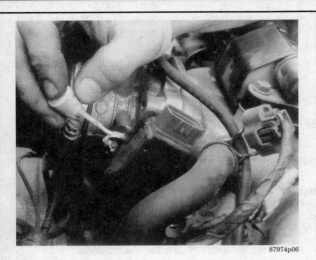

Fig. 38 Paint a matchmark on the sensor and throttle body for ease of installation and adjustment

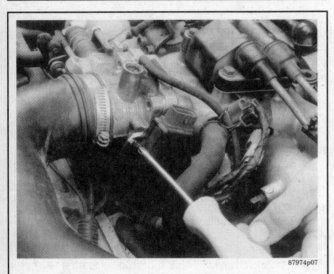

Fig. 39 Remove the sensor retainer screws

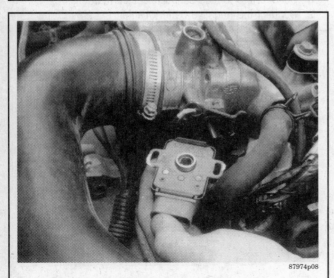

Fig. 40 Lift off the throttle position sensor

Camshaft Position Sensor (CMP)

OPERATION

▶ See Figure 41

The CMP sensor located on the side camshaft support, or in the distributor, detects the number of pulses which occur when protrusions at the back of the camshaft drive sprocket cross the sensor.

The reference signal detected by the photoelectric CMP sensor are sent to the ECU. The ECU determines the optimum ignition timing from these signals and other engine operating parameters and transmits an ignition signal to the ignition coil igniter. The igniter amplifies the ignition signal and causes the primary current to flow intermittently in the ignition coil.

TESTING

Justy and Loyale

The CMP sensor in the distributor is not serviceable. The distributor should be replaced if the CMP sensor is found to be defective.

Except SVX

1. Disconnect the CMP sensor connector.
2. Connect a voltmeter across the CMP sensor terminals.
3. Crank the engine. Voltage should vary around 0.1 volt alternating current and in time with engine movement.
4. If the CMP sensor tests satisfactorily, check the CMP sensor harness.

SVX

1. Remove the CMP sensor from the engine.
2. Connect a lab-type oscilloscope across the CMP terminals. Set the voltage scale to low level.

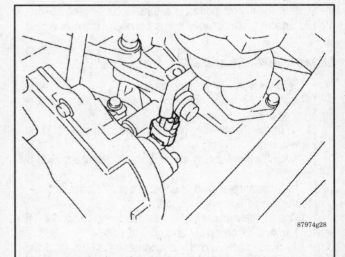

Fig. 41 Camshaft position sensor at the side of the camshaft support — Impreza

3. Wave a magnet past the CMP pickup area. The magnet should pass as close as possible without contacting the CMP sensor.

4. Examine the waveform on the oscilloscope as the magnet passes pickup. A waveform should appear as the magnet passes. If no waveform is present, replace the CMP sensor.

REMOVAL & INSTALLATION

Justy and Loyale

The CMP in these models cannot be replaced independently. the entire distributor assembly most be replaced. Refer to the distributor removal and installation procedure in Section 2 for details.

Impreza

1. Disconnect the negative battery cable.
2. Remove the camshaft position sensor-to-camshaft support bolt.
3. Disconnect the electrical harness, and remove the camshaft position sensor from the engine.
   To install:
4. Install the camshaft position sensor to the camshaft support and tighten the bolt to 36 ft. lbs. (49 Nm).
5. Connect the camshaft position sensor electrical harness.
6. Connect the negative battery cable.

Legacy

1. Disconnect the negative battery cable.
2. Remove the timing belt.
3. Remove the left camshaft sprocket-to-camshaft bolt and the sprocket. Remove the left side-rear belt cover.
4. Remove the left camshaft support-to-cylinder head bolts.
5. Pull the camshaft support forward; be careful not to damage the camshaft position sensor wiring. Remove and discard the O-ring from the camshaft support.
6. Remove the camshaft position sensor-to-camshaft support bolt.
7. Disconnect the electrical harness and remove the camshaft position sensor from the engine.
   To install:
8. Install a new O-ring into the camshaft support. Lubricate the camshaft support oil seal lips with grease.
9. Install the camshaft position sensor to the camshaft support, and tighten the bolt to 3.6 ft. lbs. (5 Nm).
10. Install the camshaft support to the cylinder head. Tighten the large bolt to 12 ft. lbs. (16 Nm) and the 2 smaller bolts to 7 ft. lbs. (10 Nm).
11. Install the camshaft sprocket, and tighten the sprocket-to-camshaft bolt to 47-54 ft. lbs. (64-74 Nm).
12. Install the timing belt.
13. Connect the camshaft position sensor electrical harness.
14. Connect the negative battery cable.

SVX

1. Disconnect the negative battery cable.
2. Remove the timing belt.

3. Remove the left camshaft sprocket-to-camshaft bolt and the sprocket. Remove the left-side rear belt cover.
4. Remove the camshaft position sensor-to-cylinder head bolts.
5. Disconnect the electrical harness, and remove the camshaft position sensor from the engine.
   To install:
6. Install the camshaft position sensor to the cylinder head, and tighten the bolts to 3.6 ft. lbs. (5 Nm).
7. Install the camshaft sprocket, and tighten the sprocket-to-camshaft bolt to 80-94 ft. lbs. (108-127 Nm).
8. Install the timing belt.
9. Connect the camshaft position sensor harness.
10. Connect the negative battery cable.

Crankshaft Position Sensor (CKP)

TESTING

◆ **See Figure 42**

Except SVX

1. Disconnect the CKP sensor harness.
2. Connect a voltmeter across the CKP sensor terminals.
3. Crank the engine. Voltage should vary around 0.1 volt alternating current and in time with engine movement.
4. If the CKP sensor tests satisfactorily, check the CKP sensor harness.

SVX

1. Remove the CKP sensor from the engine.
2. Connect a lab-type oscilloscope across the CKP terminals. Set the voltage scale to low level.
3. Wave a magnet past the CKP pickup area. The magnet should pass as close as possible without contacting the CKP sensor.
4. Examine the waveform on the oscilloscope as the magnet passes pickup. A waveform should appear as the magnet passes. If no waveform is present, replace the CKP sensor.

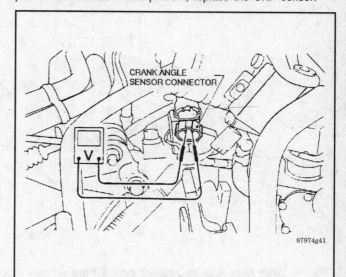

Fig. 42 Testing a crankshaft position sensor

REMOVAL & INSTALLATION

Impreza

▶ **See Figures 43 and 44**

1. Disconnect the negative battery cable.
2. Disconnect the electrical harness from the crankshaft position sensor.
3. Remove the crankshaft position sensor-to-engine bolt, then the crankshaft position sensor from the engine; be careful not damage the electrical wiring.

To install:

4. Install the crankshaft position sensor to the engine, and tighten the bolt to 36 ft. lbs. (49 Nm).
5. Connect the crankshaft position sensor harness.
6. Connect the negative battery cable.

Fig. 43 Crankshaft position sensor attached to the cylinder block — Impreza

Fig. 44 After removing the retainer bolt, lift the sensor out — Impreza

Legacy

1. Disconnect the negative battery cable.
2. Remove the timing belt.
3. Remove the crankshaft position sensor-to-cylinder block bolt, then the crankshaft position sensor from the engine; be careful not damage the electrical wiring.
4. Disconnect the electrical harness, and remove the crankshaft position sensor from the engine.

To install:

5. Install the crankshaft position sensor to the engine, and tighten the bolt to 4 ft. lbs. (5 Nm).
6. Install the timing belt.
7. Connect the crankshaft position sensor harness.
8. Connect the negative battery cable.

SVX

This vehicle is equipped with 2 crankshaft position sensors.
1. Disconnect the negative battery cable.
2. Remove the timing belt.
3. Remove the crankshaft position sensor-to-oil pump bolt, then the crankshaft position sensor from the engine; be careful not damage the electrical wiring.
4. Disconnect the electrical harness and remove the crankshaft position sensor from the engine.

To install:

5. Install the crankshaft position sensor to the oil pump, and tighten the bolt to 4 ft. lbs. (5 Nm).
6. Install the timing belt.
7. Connect the crankshaft position sensor harness.
8. Connect the negative battery cable.

Vehicle Speed Sensor (VSS)

OPERATION

The VSS consists of a magnetic rotor which is rotated by the speedometer cable and a reed switch. Rotation of the magnet rotor pulses the reed switch OFF/ON to produce a digital signal. The signal is used as a vehicle speed coefficient in ECU calculation.

The Impreza has 2 Vehicle Speed Sensors (VSS): VSS1 is located on the right side of the transaxle case housing; VSS2 is located in the combination meter assembly.

The Legacy has 2 Vehicle Speed Sensors (VSS): VSS1 is located inside of the transaxle; VSS2 is located in the combination meter assembly.

The SVX has 2 Vehicle Speed Sensors (VSS): VSS1 is located on the right side of the transaxle case; VSS2 is located on the right side of the torque converter case. The VSS1 detects rear wheel speed and the VSS2 detects front wheel speed.

TESTING

Justy and Loyale

1. Switch the ignition **ON** and check the voltage on VSS terminal 29 of the ECU.

2. The voltage should vary above and below 2 volts with the vehicle moving slowly.

If the voltage varies above and below 2 volts, the VSS is functioning.

If there is no response, check for VSS signal at the rear of the instrument panel. If no VSS signal is present, replace the VSS. If VSS signal is present at the instrument panel, repair the harness.

Impreza

VSS1

1. Disconnect the electrical harness from the transaxle.
2. Connect an ohmmeter across the transaxle's electrical harness terminals 9 and 16.
3. The resistance should be 450-650 ohms.
4. After testing, reconnect the electrical harness.

VSS2

1. Remove the instrument cluster from the instrument panel.
2. Disconnect the electrical harnesses and the speedometer cable from the instrument cluster.
3. Connect an ohmmeter or continuity tester across the combination meter terminals 8 and 15.
4. Insert a small screwdriver in the speedometer cable drive socket.
5. Rotate the speedometer drive and note the continuity across the VSS terminal. Continuity should turn ON/OFF 4 times per speedometer drive revolution.

Legacy

VSS1

1. Disconnect the electrical harness from the transaxle.
2. Connect an ohmmeter across the transaxle's electrical harness terminals 9 and 16.
3. The resistance should be 450-650 ohms.
4. After testing, reconnect the electrical harness.

VSS2

1. Remove the instrument cluster from the instrument panel.
2. Disconnect the electrical connectors and the speedometer cable from the instrument cluster.
3. Connect an ohmmeter or continuity tester across the combination meter terminals 7 and 11.
4. Insert a small screwdriver in the speedometer cable drive socket.
5. Rotate the speedometer drive and note the continuity across the VSS terminal. Continuity should turn ON/OFF 4 times per speedometer drive revolution.

SVX

▶ **See Figure 45**

VSS1

1. Disconnect the electrical harness from the transaxle.
2. Connect an ohmmeter across the transaxle's electrical harness terminals 6 and 13.
3. The resistance should be 450-650 ohms.
4. After testing, reconnect the electrical harness.

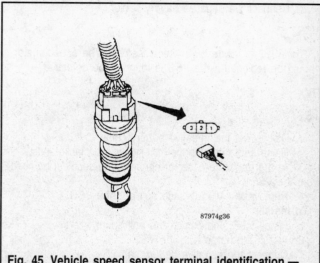

87974g36

Fig. 45 Vehicle speed sensor terminal identification — SVX

VSS2

1. Remove the VSS from the vehicle.
2. Connect the VSS harness to the VSS. Backprobe the harness side of VSS connector terminals with a high-impedance voltmeter.
3. Turn the VSS gear by hand. The voltmeter should show 0-5 volts switching ON/OFF 4 times per revolution.
4. If there is no response, check the electrical connections, the ECU VSS signal terminal connection, the voltmeter setting and the harness. If all these items check out OK, replace the VSS.

REMOVAL & INSTALLATION

Justy and Loyale

The VSS is inside the meter assembly. The speedometer should be replaced if the VSS is found to be defective.

Impreza

VSS1

The VSS1 is located inside the transaxle; no removal and installation is possible.

VSS2

The VSS2 is inside the meter assembly. The speedometer should be replaced if the VSS is found to be defective.

Legacy

VSS1

1. Disconnect the negative battery cable.
2. Raise and safely support the vehicle on jackstands.
3. At the transaxle case, disconnect the electrical harness from the VSS1.
4. Remove the VSS-to-case bolt and the VSS.

To install:
5. Install the VSS, and tighten the bolt snugly.
6. Attach the harness to the VSS.

7. Connect the negative battery cable.

VSS2

The VSS2 is inside the meter assembly. The speedometer should be replaced if the VSS is found to be defective.

SVX

VSS1

1. Disconnect the negative battery cable.
2. Raise and safely support the vehicle on jackstands.
3. At the transaxle case, disconnect the electrical harness from the VSS1.
4. Remove the VSS-to-case bolt and the VSS.
To install:
5. Install VSS, and tighten the bolt snugly.
6. Attach the harness to the VSS.
7. Connect the negative battery cable.

VSS2

1. Disconnect the negative battery cable.
2. Disconnect the electrical harness from the VSS2.
3. Pull the VSS from the torque converter case.
To install:
4. Install VSS into the torque converter case.
5. Attach the wire harness to the sensor.
6. Connect the negative battery cable.

Knock Sensor (KS)

OPERATION

When knocking occurs, the weight in the cylinder case moves, causing the piezo electric element in the KS to translate the vibration into an electric voltage. A signal is then transmitted from the KS to the ECU. In response, the control unit retards spark timing to prevent engine knocking.

On the Loyale with Multi-Point Fuel Injection (MPFI), the KS is located on top right-side of the cylinder block and senses knock signals from each cylinder.

On the Legacy and Impreza, the KS is installed on top left-side of the cylinder block and senses knock signals from each cylinder.

The SVX is equipped with 2 knock sensors; both are located on top of the cylinder block — one on the right side and one on the left side.

TESTING

Legacy, Impreza and SVX
▶ **See Figure 46**

1. Disconnect the KS harness.
2. Measure the resistance across the KS terminals.
3. The resistance should be approximately 560 kilo-ohms.
4. Replace the KS if the resistance is out of range.

REMOVAL & INSTALLATION

1. Disconnect the negative battery cable.
2. Disconnect the KS wire harness.
3. Loosen and remove the sensor retainer bolt, then remove the sensor.
To install:
4. Position the KS on the engine block, and secure in place with the retainer bolt. Tighten the bolt snugly.
5. Connect the sensor wire harness.
6. Connect the negative battery cable.

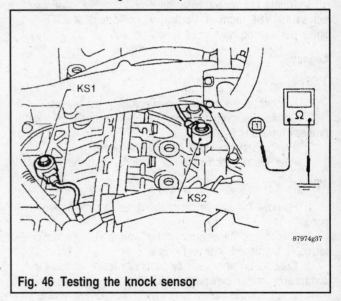

87974g37

Fig. 46 Testing the knock sensor

TROUBLE CODES

General Information

Listings of the trouble for the various engine control system covered in this manual are located in this section. Remember that a code only points to the faulty circuit, NOT necessarily to a faulty component. Loose, damaged or corroded connections may contribute to a fault code on a circuit when the sensor or component is operating properly. Be sure that the components are faulty before replacing them, especially the expensive ones.

Reading Codes

Codes are displayed by the MIL flashing **ON** and **OFF**. The time duration of the flash identifies the significance of the digit. Three flash durations are used:
- A flash duration of 0.5 seconds indicates no malfunction (OK).
- A flash duration of 1.3 seconds indicates that it is a 10's digit.
- A flash duration of 0.2 seconds indicates that it is a 1's digit.

For example, if 3 flashes — 1.3 seconds long — are followed by 4 flashes — 0.2 seconds long — a Code 34 is indicated.

These code sequences are separated by 1.8 seconds to avoid confusing tens and ones digits.
- **Read Memory Mode**: used to pull codes which have been stored in memory. It is most effective in detecting poor contact of wiring harness connectors. To enter this mode, connect the read memory connector with the ignition **ON**.
- **D Mode**: used to diagnose and test the entire injection system. To enter this mode connect the test mode connector with the ignition **ON**. On the Legacy and SVX, the ignition must be **ON** with the engine running.
- **F-Check Mode**: used to measure the performance characteristics of the injection system components. When working in this mode, a Select Monitor or equivalent scan tool is required.
- **U Check Mode**: operates during normal engine operation. It signals the driver using the MIL only when components necessary for start-up and drive are faulty. The read memory and test connectors must be disconnected with the ignition **ON** for this mode to be operational.

Clearing Codes

With the ignition **ON** and the engine running, connect both the read memory terminal and the test mode terminal.

Year – 1985
Model – 1800 Series (4WD)
Engine – 1.8L (109 cid) MPFI 4 cyl
Engine Code – VIN 5

ECM TROUBLE CODES

Code	Explanation
11	No ignition pulse
12	Starter switch in OFF mode
13	Starter switch in ON mode
14	Abnormal air flow meter signal
21	Seized air flow meter flap
22	Pressure or vacuum switch fixed in ON or OFF position
23	Idle switch fixed in ON or OFF position
24	Wide Open Throttle (WOT) switch fixed in ON or OFF position
31	Abnormal speed sensor signal
32	Abnormal oxygen sensor signal
33	Abnormal coolant thermosensor signal
34	Abnormal aspirated air thermosensor signal
35	Exhaust Gas Recirculation (EGR) solenoid switch fixed in ON or OFF position
41	Abnormal atmospheric pressure sensor signal
42	Fuel injector fixed in ON or OFF position
43	Kickdown Low Hold (KDLH) relay fixed in ON or OFF position

87974c00

Year — 1985
Model — XT Series (2WD)
Engine — 1.8L (109 cid) MPFI 4 cyl
Engine Code — VIN 4

ECM TROUBLE CODES

Code	Explanation
11	No ignition pulse
12	Starter switch in OFF mode
13	Starter switch in ON mode
14	Abnormal air flow meter signal
21	Seized air flow meter flap
22	Pressure or vacuum switch fixed in ON or OFF position
23	Idle switch fixed in ON or OFF position
24	Wide Open Throttle (WOT) switch fixed in ON or OFF position
31	Abnormal speed sensor signal
32	Abnormal oxygen sensor signal
33	Abnormal coolant thermosensor signal
34	Abnormal aspirated air thermosensor signal
35	Exhaust Gas Recirculation (EGR) solenoid switch fixed in ON or OFF position
41	Abnormal atmospheric pressure sensor signal
42	Fuel injector fixed in ON or OFF position
43	Kickdown Low Hold (KDLH) relay fixed in ON or OFF position

87974c01

Year — 1985
Model — XT Series (4WD)
Engine — 1.8L (109 cid) MPFI 4 cyl
Engine Code — VIN 7

ECM TROUBLE CODES

Code	Explanation
11	No ignition pulse
12	Starter switch in OFF mode
13	Starter switch in ON mode
14	Abnormal air flow meter signal
21	Seized air flow meter flap
22	Pressure or vacuum switch fixed in ON or OFF position
23	Idle switch fixed in ON or OFF position
24	Wide Open Throttle (WOT) switch fixed in ON or OFF position
31	Abnormal speed sensor signal
32	Abnormal oxygen sensor signal
33	Abnormal coolant thermosensor signal
34	Abnormal aspirated air thermosensor signal
35	Exhaust Gas Recirculation (EGR) solenoid switch fixed in ON or OFF position
41	Abnormal atmospheric pressure sensor signal
42	Fuel injector fixed in ON or OFF position
43	Kickdown Low Hold (KDLH) relay fixed in ON or OFF position

87974c02

DIAGNOSTIC TROUBLE CODE INFORMATION — 1985–87 BRAT, DL, GL, STD AND STATION WAGON WITH 2BC

LIST OF TROUBLE CODES

Trouble code	Item	Remarks		
11	Ignition pulse sys. (NG) (Engine in OFF)	5MT	FF	49-State
12		AT		
15		4MT		
71		5MT	FF	California
72		AT		
73		5MT	4WD	
74		AT		
22	Car speed sensor sys. (NG)			
23	O₂ sensor sys. (NG)			
24	Thermo sensor sys. (NG)			
25	Pressure sensor sys. (NG)			
32	Duty solenoid valve sys. (NG)			
33	Main system in feedback sys. (NG)	In test mode only.		
34	Back-up sys. (NG)			
42	Clutch switch sys. (NG)	Excluding AT and 4WD.		
52	Solenoid valve (ASV) control sys. (NG)			
53	Fuel pump control sys. (NG)			
54	Auto choke control sys. (NG)			
55	Shift-up control sys. (NG)	AT only.		
62	Solenoid valve (EGR) control sys. (NG)			
63	Solenoid valve (CP) control sys. (NG)			
64	Solenoid valve (VLC) control sys. (NG)			
65	Solenoid valve (FCV) control sys. (NG)			

87974c36

Year — 1986
Model — 1800 Series (2WD)
Engine — 1.8L (109 cid) MPFI 4 cyl
Engine Code — VIN 4

ECM TROUBLE CODES

Code	Explanation
11	No ignition pulse
12	Starter switch in OFF mode
13	Starter switch in ON mode
14	Abnormal air flow meter signal
21	Seized air flow meter flap
22	Pressure or vacuum switch fixed in ON or OFF position
23	Idle switch fixed in ON or OFF position
24	Wide Open Throttle (WOT) switch fixed in ON or OFF position
31	Abnormal speed sensor signal
32	Abnormal oxygen sensor signal
33	Abnormal coolant thermosensor signal
34	Abnormal aspirated air thermosensor signal
35	Exhaust Gas Recirculation (EGR) solenoid switch fixed in ON or OFF position
41	Abnormal atmospheric pressure sensor signal
42	Fuel injector fixed in ON or OFF position
43	Kickdown Low Hold (KDLH) relay fixed in ON or OFF position

87974c03

Year — 1986
Model — 1800 Series (4WD)
Engine — 1.8L (109 cid) MPFI 4 cyl
Engine Code — VIN 5

ECM TROUBLE CODES

Code	Explanation
11	No ignition pulse
12	Starter switch in OFF mode
13	Starter switch in ON mode
14	Abnormal air flow meter signal
15	Pressure switch fixed in ON or OFF position
21	Seized air flow meter flap
22	Pressure or vacuum switch fixed in ON or OFF position
23	Idle switch fixed in ON or OFF position
24	Wide Open Throttle (WOT) switch fixed in ON or OFF position
31	Abnormal speed sensor signal
32	Abnormal oxygen sensor signal
33	Abnormal coolant thermosensor signal
34	Abnormal aspirated air thermosensor signal
35	Exhaust Gas Recirculation (EGR) solenoid switch fixed in ON or OFF position
41	Abnormal atmospheric pressure sensor signal
42	Fuel injector fixed in ON or OFF position
43	Kickdown Low Hold (KDLH) relay fixed in ON or OFF position

87974c04

Year — 1986
Model — 1800 Series (2WD)
Engine — 1.8L (109 cid) SPFI 4 cyl
Engine Code — VIN 4

ECM TROUBLE CODES

Code	Explanation
11	Ignition pulse
16	Crank angle sensor
17	Stater switch — indicates items which develop problems after operating in excess of 1500 rpm for a specified time. With other items, problems are indicated immediately after detection
25	Throttle sensor — idle switch — indicates items which develop problems after operating in excess of 1500 rpm for a specified time. With other items, problems are indicated immediately after detection
31	Car speed sensor — indicates items which develop problems after operating in excess of 1500 rpm for a specified time. With other items, problems are indicated immediately after detection
32	O_2 sensor — indicates items which develop problems after operating in excess of 1500 rpm for a specified time. With other items, problems are indicated immediately after detection
33	Coolant thermosensor
35	Air flow meter
42	Fuel injector
46	Neutral switch — parking switch — indicates items which develop problems after operating in excess of 1500 rpm for a specified time. With other items, problems are indicated immediately after detection
53	Fuel pump
55	Kickdown Low Hold (KDLH) control system — indicates items which develop problems after operating in excess of 1500 rpm for a specified time. With other items, problems are indicated immediately after detection
57	Canister control system — indicates items which develop problems after operating in excess of 1500 rpm for a specified time. With other items, problems are indicated immediately after detection
58	Air control valve — indicates items which develop problems after operating in excess of 1500 rpm for a specified time. With other items, problems are indicated immediately after detection
62	Exhaust Gas Recirculation (EGR) control system — indicates items which develop problems after operating in excess of 1500 rpm for a specified time. With other items, problems are indicated immediately after detection
88	Single Point Fuel Injection (SPFI) control unit-indicates items which develop problems after operating in excess of 1500 rpm for a specified time. With other items, problems are indicated immediately after detection

87974c05

Year – 1986
Model – 1800 Series (4WD)
Engine – 1.8L (109 cid) SPFI 4 cyl
Engine Code – VIN 5

ECM TROUBLE CODES

Code	Explanation
11	Ignition pulse
16	Crank angle sensor
17	Stater switch – indicates items which develop problems after operating in excess of 1500 rpm for a specified time. With other items, problems are indicated immediately after detection
25	Throttle sensor – idle switch – indicates items which develop problems after operating in excess of 1500 rpm for a specified time. With other items, problems are indicated immediately after detection
31	Car speed sensor – indicates items which develop problems after operating in excess of 1500 rpm for a specified time. With other items, problems are indicated immediately after detection
32	O_2 sensor – indicates items which develop problems after operating in excess of 1500 rpm for a specified time. With other items, problems are indicated immediately after detection
33	Coolant thermosensor
35	Air flow meter
42	Fuel injector
46	Neutral switch – parking switch – indicates items which develop problems after operating in excess of 1500 rpm for a specified time. With other items, problems are indicated immediately after detection
53	Fuel pump
55	Kickdown Low Hold (KDLH) control system – indicates items which develop problems after operating in excess of 1500 rpm for a specified time. With other items, problems are indicated immediately after detection
57	Canister control system – indicates items which develop problems after operating in excess of 1500 rpm for a specified time. With other items, problems are indicated immediately after detection
58	Air control valve – indicates items which develop problems after operating in excess of 1500 rpm for a specified time. With other items, problems are indicated immediately after detection
62	Exhaust Gas Recirculation (EGR) control system – indicates items which develop problems after operating in excess of 1500 rpm for a specified time. With other items, problems are indicated immediately after detection
88	Single Point Fuel Injection (SPFI) control unit-indicates items which develop problems after operating in excess of 1500 rpm for a specified time. With other items, problems are indicated immediately after detection

87974c08

Year — 1986
Model — XT Series (4WD)
Engine — 1.8L (109 cid) MPFI 4 cyl
Engine Code — VIN 7

ECM TROUBLE CODES

Code	Explanation
11	No ignition pulse
12	Starter switch in OFF mode
13	Starter switch in ON mode
14	Abnormal air flow meter signal
15	Pressure switch fixed in ON or OFF position
21	Seized air flow meter flap
22	Pressure or vacuum switch fixed in ON or OFF position
23	Idle switch fixed in ON or OFF position
24	Wide Open Throttle (WOT) switch fixed in ON or OFF position
31	Abnormal speed sensor signal
32	Abnormal oxygen sensor signal
33	Abnormal coolant thermosensor signal
34	Abnormal aspirated air thermosensor signal
35	Exhaust Gas Recirculation (EGR) solenoid switch fixed in ON or OFF position
41	Abnormal atmospheric pressure sensor signal
42	Fuel injector fixed in ON or OFF position
43	Kickdown Low Hold (KDLH) relay fixed in ON or OFF position

87974c07

Year — 1986
Model — 1800 Series (2WD)
Engine — 1.8L (109 cid) MPFI 4 cyl
Engine Code — VIN 4

ECM TROUBLE CODES

Code	Explanation
11	No ignition pulse
12	Starter switch in OFF mode
13	Starter switch in ON mode
14	Abnormal air flow meter signal
15	Pressure switch fixed in ON or OFF position
21	Seized air flow meter flap
22	Pressure or vacuum switch fixed in ON or OFF position
23	Idle switch fixed in ON or OFF position
24	Wide Open Throttle (WOT) switch fixed in ON or OFF position
31	Abnormal speed sensor signal
32	Abnormal oxygen sensor signal
33	Abnormal coolant thermosensor signal
34	Abnormal aspirated air thermosensor signal
35	Exhaust Gas Recirculation (EGR) solenoid switch fixed in ON or OFF position
41	Abnormal atmospheric pressure sensor signal
42	Fuel injector fixed in ON or OFF position
43	Kickdown Low Hold (KDLH) relay fixed in ON or OFF position

87974c09

DIAGNOSTIC TROUBLE CODE INFORMATION — 1986–89 DL, GL, STD AND STATION WAGON WITH MFI

List of Trouble Codes

Trouble code	Item
11	Crank angle sensor (No reference pulse)
12	Starter switch (Continuously in ON or OFF position while cranking)
13	Crank angle sensor (No position pulse)
14	Fuel injector (Abnormal injector output)
21	Water temperature sensor (Open or shorted circuit)
23	Air flow meter (Open or shorted circuit)
24	Air control valve (Open or shorted circuit)
31	Throttle sensor (Open or shorted circuit)
32	O_2 sensor (Abnormal sensor signal)
33	Car-speed sensor (No signal is present during operation)
34	EGR solenoid valve (Solenoid switch continuously in ON or OFF position, or *clogged EGR line)
35	Purge control solenoid valve (Solenoid switch continuously in ON or OFF position)
42	Idle switch (Abnormal idle switch signal in relation to throttle sensor output)
45	Kick-down control relay (Continuously in ON or OFF position)
51	Neutral switch (Continuously in ON position)
*55	EGR gas temperature sensor (Open or short circuit)
61	Parking switch (Continuously in ON position)

*: California model only

87974c37

DIAGNOSTIC TROUBLE CODE INFORMATION — 1986–87 XT

Trouble code	Item
11	Crank angle sensor (No reference pulse)
12	Starter switch (Continuously in ON position or continuously in OFF position while cranking)
13	Crank angle sensor (No position pulse)
14	Fuel injectors #1 and #2 (Abnormal injector output)
15	Fuel injectors #3 and #4 (Abnormal injector output)
21	Water temperature sensor (Open or shorted circuit)
22	Knock sensor (Open or shorted circuit)
23	Air flow meter (Open or shorted circuit)
31	Throttle sensor (Open or shorted circuit)
32	O_2 sensor (Abnormal sensor signal)
33	Car-speed sensor (No signal is present during operation)
34	EGR solenoid valve (Solenoid switch continuously in ON or OFF position)
35	Purge control solenoid valve (Solenoid switch continuously in ON or OFF position)
41	System too lean
42	Idle switch (Abnormal idle switch signal in relation to throttle sensor output)
44	Duty solenoid valve (Waste gate control)
51	Neutral switch (Continuously in ON position)

87974c38

DIAGNOSTIC TROUBLE CODE INFORMATION — 1988–89 XT

Trouble code	Item	U-check	D-check
11	Crank angle sensor (No reference pulse)	O	O
12	Starter switch (Continuously in ON position or continuously in OFF position while cranking)	O	O
13	Crank angle sensor (No position pulse)	O	O
14	Fuel injectors *#1 and #2, **#5 and #6 (Abnormal injector output)	O	O
15	Fuel injectors *#3 and #4, **#1 and #2 (Abnormal injector output)	O	O
21	Water temperature sensor (Open or shorted circuit)	O	O
**22	Knock sensor (Open or shorted circuit)	O	O
23	Air flow meter (Open or shorted circuit)	O	O
**24	By-pass air control valve (Open or shorted circuit)	O	O
**25	Fuel injectors #3 and #4 (Abnormal injector output)	O	O
31	Throttle sensor (Open or shorted circuit)	O	O
32	O_2 sensor (Abnormal sensor signal)	O	O
33	Car-speed sensor (No signal is present during operation)	O	O
35	Purge control solenoid valve (Solenoid switch continuously in ON or OFF position)	–	O
41	System too lean	O	O
42	Idle switch (Abnormal idle switch signal in relation to throttle sensor output)	–	O
51	Neutral switch (No signal is present)	–	O

*: 1800 cc model   **: 2700 cc model

87974c39

DIAGNOSTIC TROUBLE CODE INFORMATION — 1987–89 JUSTY

Trouble Code	U	D	Item	Remarks
14	O	O	Duty solenoid valve control system	
15	O	O	CFC system	MT only
16		O	Feed back system	
17	O	O	Fuel pump & Auto choke	
21	O	O	Thermosensor	
22	O	O	VLC solenoid valve	
23	O	O	Pressure sensor	
24	O	O	Idle-up solenoid valve	
25	O	O	FCV solenoid valve	
32	O	O	O_2 sensor	
33	O	O	Car speed sensor	
34	O	O	EGR solenoid valve	
35	O	O	CPC solenoid valve	
41	O	O	Feed back system	Cal. only
46	O	O	Radiator fan control system	
52		O	Clutch switch	FWD/MT only
53	O	O	HAC solenoid valve	
55	O	O	EGR sensor	Cal. only
56	O	O	EGR system	Cal. only
62		O	Idle-up system (1)	
63		O	Idle-up system (2)	

87974c40

SUBARU

Year—1987
Model—1800 Series
Body VIN—C, N, G
Engine—1.8L (1781cc) **Cylinders**—4
Fuel System—Single Point Fuel Injection
Engine VIN—4, 5

ENGINE CODES

Code	Explanation
11	Crank angle sensor—no reference pulse
12	Starter switch—continuously in ON or OFF position while cranking
13	Crank angle sensor—no position pulse
14	Fuel injector—abnormal injector output
21	Water temperature sensor—open or shorted circuit
23	Air flow meter—open or shorted circuit
24	Air control valve—open or shorted circuit
31	Throttle sensor—open or shorted circuit
32	Oxygen sensor—abnormal sensor signal
33	Car speed sensor—no signal is present during operation
34	Exhaust Gas Recirculation (EGR) solenoid valve—solenoid switch continuously in ON or OFF position
35	Purge control solenoid valve—solenoid switch continuously in ON or OFF position
42	Idle switch—abnormal idle switch signal in relation to throttle sensor output
45	Kickdown control relay—continuously in ON or OFF position
51	Neutral switch—continuously in ON position
61	Parking switch—continuously in ON position

87974c10

Year—1987
Model—1800 Series
Body VIN—C, N, G
Engine—1.8L (1781cc) **Cylinders**—4
Fuel System—Multi-Point Fuel Injection
Engine VIN—4, 5

ENGINE CODES

Code	Explanation
11	Crank angle sensor—no reference pulse
12	Starter switch—continuously in ON or OFF position while cranking
13	Crank angle sensor—no position pulse
14	Fuel injectors No. 1 and No. 2—abnormal injector output
15	Fuel injectors No. 3 and No. 4—abnormal injector output
21	Water temperature sensor—open or shorted circuit
22	Knock sensor—open or shorted circuit
23	Air flow meter—open or shorted circuit
31	Throttle sensor—open or shorted circuit
32	Oxygen sensor—abnormal sensor signal
33	Car speed sensor—no signal is present during operation
34	Exhaust Gas Recirculation (EGR) solenoid valve—solenoid switch continuously in ON or OFF position
35	Purge control solenoid valve—solenoid switch continuously in ON or OFF position
41	System too lean
42	Idle switch—abnormal idle switch signal in relation to throttle sensor output
51	Neutral switch—continuously in ON position

87974c11

Year—1987
Model—XT
Body VIN—X
Engine—1.8L (1781cc)   **Cylinders**—4
Fuel System—Multi-Point Fuel Injection
Engine VIN—4, 7

ENGINE CODES

Code	Explanation
11	Crank angle sensor—no reference pulse
12	Starter switch—continuously in ON or OFF position while cranking
13	Crank angle sensor—no position pulse
14	Fuel injectors No. 1 and No. 2—abnormal injector output
15	Fuel injectors No. 3 and No. 4—abnormal injector output
21	Water temperature sensor—open or shorted circuit
22	Knock sensor—open or shorted circuit
23	Air flow meter—open or shorted circuit
31	Throttle sensor—open or shorted circuit
32	Oxygen sensor—abnormal sensor signal
33	Car speed sensor—no signal is present during operation
34	Exhaust Gas Recirculation (EGR) solenoid valve—solenoid switch continuously in ON or OFF position
35	Purge control solenoid valve—solenoid switch continuously in ON or OFF position
41	System too lean
42	Idle switch—abnormal idle switch signal in relation to throttle sensor output
44	Duty solenoid valve (wastegate control)
51	Neutral switch—continuously in ON position

87974c12

Year—1987
Model—Justy
Body VIN—A
Engine—1.2L (1189cc)   **Cylinders**—3
Fuel System—Feedback Carburetor
Engine VIN—7, 8

ENGINE CODES

Code	Explanation
14	Duty solenoid valve control system
21	Water temperature sensor
22	Vacuum Line Charging (VLC) solenoid control system
23	Pressure sensor system
24	Idle-up solenoid valve control system
25	Float Chamber Ventilation (FCV) solenoid valve control system
32	Oxygen sensor system
33	Car speed sensor system
35	Purge control solenoid valve system
41	Improper tachometer used or fuel mixture too rich/lean
52	Clutch switch system—Front Wheel Drive (FWD) model only
62	Idle-up system—clearance light and rear defogger
63	Idle-up system—heater fan and radiator fan

87974c13

Year — 1988
Model — XT
Body VIN — X
Engine — 1.8L (1781cc) **Cylinders** — 4
Fuel System — Multi-Point Fuel Injection
Engine VIN — 4, 7

ENGINE CODES

Code	Explanation
11	Crank angle sensor — no reference pulse
12	Starter switch — continuously in ON or OFF position while cranking
13	Crank angle sensor — no position pulse
14	Fuel injectors No. 1 and No. 2 — abnormal injector output
15	Fuel injectors No. 3 and No. 4 — abnormal injector output
21	Water temperature sensor — open or shorted circuit
23	Air flow meter — open or shorted circuit
31	Throttle sensor — open or shorted circuit
32	Oxygen sensor — abnormal sensor signal
33	Car speed sensor — no signal is present during operation
35	Purge control solenoid valve — solenoid switch continuously in ON or OFF position
41	System too lean
42	Idle switch — abnormal idle switch signal in relation to throttle sensor output
51	Neutral switch — continuously in ON position

87974c14

Year — 1988
Model — XT6
Body VIN — X
Engine — 2.7L (2672cc) **Cylinders** — 6
Fuel System — Multi-Point Fuel Injection
Engine VIN — 8, 9

ENGINE CODES

Code	Explanation
11	Crank angle sensor — no reference pulse
12	Starter switch — continuously in ON or OFF position while cranking
13	Crank angle sensor — no position pulse
14	Fuel injectors No. 5 and No. 6 — abnormal injector output
15	Fuel injectors No. 1 and No. 2 — abnormal injector output
21	Water temperature sensor — open or shorted circuit
22	Knock sensor — open or shorted circuit
23	Air flow meter — open or shorted circuit
24	By-pass air control valve — open or shorted circuit
25	Fuel injectors No. 3 and No. 4 — abnormal injector output
31	Throttle sensor — open or shorted circuit
32	Oxygen sensor — abnormal sensor signal
33	Car speed sensor — no signal is present during operation
35	Purge control solenoid valve — solenoid switch continuously in ON or OFF position
41	System too lean
42	Idle switch — abnormal idle switch signal in relation to throttle sensor output
51	Neutral switch — continuously in ON position

87974c15

Year — 1988
Model — 1800 Series
Body VIN — C, N, G
Engine — 1.8L (1781cc) **Cylinders** — 4
Fuel System — Single Point Fuel Injection
Engine VIN — 4, 5

ENGINE CODES

Code	Explanation
11	Crank angle sensor — no reference pulse
12	Starter switch — continuously in ON or OFF position while cranking
13	Crank angle sensor — no position pulse
14	Fuel injector — abnormal injector output
21	Water temperature sensor — open or shorted circuit
23	Air flow meter — open or shorted circuit
24	Air control valve — open or shorted circuit
31	Throttle sensor — open or shorted circuit
32	Oxygen sensor — abnormal sensor signal
33	Car speed sensor — no signal is present during operation
34	Exhaust Gas Recirculation (EGR) solenoid valve — solenoid switch continuously in ON or OFF position or (California only) clogged EGR line
35	Purge control solenoid valve — solenoid switch continuously in ON or OFF position
42	Idle switch — abnormal idle switch signal in relation to throttle sensor output
45	Kickdown control relay — continuously in ON or OFF position
51	Neutral switch — continuously in ON position
55	Exhaust Gas Recirculation (EGR) gas temperature sensor — open or short circuit (California only)
61	Parking switch — continuously in ON position

87974c16

Year — 1988
Model — 1800 Series
Body VIN — C, N, G
Engine — 1.8L (1781cc) **Cylinders** — 4
Fuel System — Multi-Point Fuel Injection
Engine VIN — 4, 5, 7

ENGINE CODES

Code	Explanation
11	Crank angle sensor — no reference pulse
12	Starter switch — continuously in ON or OFF position while cranking
13	Crank angle sensor — no position pulse
14	Fuel injectors No. 1 and No. 2 — abnormal injector output
15	Fuel injectors No. 3 and No. 4 — abnormal injector output
21	Water temperature sensor — open or shorted circuit
22	Knock sensor — open or shorted circuit
23	Air flow meter — open or shorted circuit
31	Throttle sensor — open or shorted circuit
32	Oxygen sensor — abnormal sensor signal
33	Car speed sensor — no signal is present during operation
34	Exhaust Gas Recirculation (EGR) solenoid valve — solenoid switch continuously in ON or OFF position (49 states)
35	Purge control solenoid valve — solenoid switch continuously in ON or OFF position
41	System too lean
42	Idle switch — abnormal idle switch signal in relation to throttle sensor output
51	Neutral switch — continuously in ON position

87974c17

Year—1988
Model—Justy
Body VIN—A
Engine—1.2L (1189cc) **Cylinders**—3
Fuel System—Feedback Carburetor
Engine VIN—7, 8

ENGINE CODES

Code	Explanation
14	Duty solenoid valve control system
15	Coasting Fuel Cut (CFC) system
21	Water temperature sensor
22	Vacuum Line Charging (VLC) solenoid control system
23	Pressure sensor system
24	Idle-up solenoid valve control system
25	Float Chamber Ventilation (FCV) solenoid valve control system
32	Oxygen sensor system
33	Car speed sensor system
35	Purge control solenoid valve control system
52	Clutch switch system—Front Wheel Drive (FWD) model only
62	Idle-up system
63	Idle-up system

87974c06

Year—1989
Model—DL, GL, GL-10
Body VIN—C, N, G, K
Engine—1.8L (1781cc) **Cylinders**—4
Fuel System—Single Point Fuel Injection
Engine VIN—4, 5

ENGINE CODES

Code	Explanation
11	Crank angle sensor—no reference pulse
12	Starter switch—continuously in ON or OFF position while cranking
13	Crank angle sensor—no position pulse
14	Fuel injector—abnormal injector output
21	Water temperature sensor—open or shorted circuit
23	Air flow meter—open or shorted circuit
24	Air control valve—open or shorted circuit
31	Throttle sensor—open or shorted circuit
32	Oxygen sensor—abnormal sensor signal
33	Car speed sensor—no signal is present during operation
34	Exhaust Gas Recirculation (EGR) solenoid valve—solenoid switch continuously in ON or OFF position or (California only) clogged EGR line
35	Purge control solenoid valve—solenoid switch continuously in ON or OFF position
42	Idle switch—abnormal idle switch signal in relation to throttle sensor output
45	Kickdown control relay—continuously in ON or OFF position
51	Neutral switch—continuously in ON position
55	Exhaust Gas Recirculation (EGR) gas temperature sensor—open or short circuit (California only)
61	Parking switch—continuously in ON position

87974c18

Year—1989
Model—GL, GL-10, RX
Body VIN—C, N, G, K
Engine—1.8L (1781cc) Cylinders—4
Fuel System—Multi-Point Fuel Injection
Engine VIN—4, 5, 7

ENGINE CODES

Code	Explanation
11	Crank angle sensor—no reference pulse
12	Starter switch—continuously in ON or OFF position while cranking
13	Crank angle sensor—no position pulse
14	Fuel injectors No. 1 and No. 2—abnormal injector output
15	Fuel injectors No. 3 and No. 4—abnormal injector output
21	Water temperature sensor—open or shorted circuit
22	Knock sensor—open or shorted circuit
23	Air flow meter—open or shorted circuit
31	Throttle sensor—open or shorted circuit
32	Oxygen sensor—abnormal sensor signal
33	Car speed sensor—no signal is present during operation
34	Exhaust Gas Recirculation (EGR) solenoid valve—solenoid switch continuously in ON or OFF position (49 states)
35	Purge control solenoid valve—solenoid switch continuously in ON or OFF position
41	System too lean
42	Idle switch—abnormal idle switch signal in relation to throttle sensor output
44	Duty solenoid valve—wastegate control
51	Neutral switch—continuously in ON position

87974c19

Year—1989
Model—XTDL, XTGL
Body VIN—X
Engine—1.8L (1781cc) Cylinders—4
Fuel System—Multi-Point Fuel Injection
Engine VIN—4, 7

ENGINE CODES

Code	Explanation
11	Crank angle sensor—no reference pulse
12	Starter switch—continuously in ON or OFF position while cranking
13	Crank angle sensor—no position pulse
14	Fuel injectors No. 1 and No. 2—abnormal injector output
15	Fuel injectors No. 3 and No. 4—abnormal injector output
21	Water temperature sensor—open or shorted circuit
23	Air flow meter—open or shorted circuit
31	Throttle sensor—open or shorted circuit
32	Oxygen sensor—abnormal sensor signal
33	Car speed sensor—no signal is present during operation
35	Purge control solenoid valve—solenoid switch continuously in ON or OFF position
41	System too lean
42	Idle switch—abnormal idle switch signal in relation to throttle sensor output
51	Neutral switch—continuously in ON position

87974c20

Year—1989
Model—XT6
Body VIN—X
Engine—2.7L (2672cc)   **Cylinders**—6
Fuel System—Multi-Point Fuel Injection
Engine VIN—8, 9

ENGINE CODES

Code	Explanation
11	Crank angle sensor—no reference pulse
12	Starter switch—continuously in ON or OFF position while cranking
13	Crank angle sensor—no position pulse
14	Fuel injectors No. 5 and No. 6—abnormal injector output
15	Fuel injectors No. 1 and No. 2—abnormal injector output
21	Water temperature sensor—open or shorted circuit
22	Knock sensor—open or shorted circuit
23	Air flow meter—open or shorted circuit
24	By-pass air control valve—open or shorted circuit
25	Fuel injectors No. 3 and No. 4—abnormal injector output
31	Throttle sensor—open or shorted circuit
32	Oxygen sensor—abnormal sensor signal
33	Car speed sensor—no signal is present during operation
35	Purge control solenoid valve—solenoid switch continuously in ON or OFF position
41	System too lean
42	Idle switch—abnormal idle switch signal in relation to throttle sensor output
51	Neutral switch—continuously in ON position

87974c21

Year—1989
Model—Justy DL, GL
Body VIN—A
Engine—1.2L (1189cc)   **Cylinders**—3
Fuel System—Feedback Carburetor
Engine VIN—7, 8

ENGINE CODES

Code	Explanation
14	Duty solenoid valve control system
15	Coasting Fuel Cut (CFC) system—manual transaxle only
16	Feedback system
17	Fuel pump and automatic choke
21	Thermosensor
22	Vacuum Line Charging (VLC) solenoid valve
23	Pressure sensor
24	Idle-up solenoid
25	Float Chamber Ventilation (FCV) solenoid valve
32	Oxygen sensor
33	Car speed sensor
34	Exhaust Gas Recirculation (EGR) solenoid valve
35	CPC solenoid valve
41	Feedback system (California only)
46	Radiator fan control system
52	Clutch switch system—Front Wheel Drive (FWD)/manual transaxle only
53	High Altitude Compensator (HAC) solenoid valve
55	Exhaust Gas Recirculation (EGR) sensor (California only)
56	Exhaust Gas Recirculation (EGR) system (California only)
62	Idle-up system
63	Idle-up system

87974c22

SUBARU

Year — 1990
Model — Loyale
Body VIN — C, N, G, K
Engine — 1.8L (1781cc)   **Cylinders** — 4
Fuel System — SPFI
Engine VIN — 4, 5

ENGINE CODES

Code	Explanation
11	Crank angle sensor — no reference pulse
12	Starter switch — continuously in ON or OFF position while cranking
13	Crank angle sensor — no position pulse
14	Fuel injector — abnormal injector output
21	Water temperature sensor — open or shorted circuit
23	Air flow meter — open or shorted circuit
24	Air control valve — open or shorted circuit
31	Throttle sensor — open or shorted circuit
32	Oxygen sensor — abnormal sensor signal
33	Car speed sensor — no signal is present during operation
34	Exhaust Gas Recirculation (EGR) solenoid valve — solenoid switch continuously in ON or OFF position or (California only) clogged EGR line
35	Purge control solenoid valve — solenoid switch continuously in ON or OFF position
42	Idle switch — abnormal idle switch signal in relation to throttle sensor output
45	Kickdown control relay — continuously in ON or OFF position
51	Neutral switch — continuously in ON position
55	Exhaust Gas Recirculation (EGR) gas temperature sensor — open or short circuit (California only)
61	Parking switch — continuously in ON position

87974c23

Year — 1990
Model — Loyale
Body VIN — C, N, G, K
Engine — 1.8L (1781cc)   **Cylinders** — 4
Fuel System — MPFI
Engine VIN — 4, 5

ENGINE CODES

Code	Explanation
11	Crank angle sensor — no reference pulse
12	Starter switch — continuously in ON or OFF position while cranking
13	Crank angle sensor — no position pulse
14	Fuel injectors No. 1 and No. 2 — abnormal injector output
15	Fuel injectors No. 3 and No. 4 — abnormal injector output
21	Water temperature sensor — open or shorted circuit
22	Knock sensor — open or shorted circuit
23	Air flow meter — open or shorted circuit
31	Throttle sensor — open or shorted circuit
32	Oxygen sensor — abnormal sensor signal
33	Car speed sensor — no signal is present during operation
35	Purge control solenoid valve — solenoid switch continuously in ON or OFF position
41	System too lean
42	Idle switch — abnormal idle switch signal in relation to throttle sensor output
44	Duty solenoid valve — wastegate control

87974c24

Year — 1990
Model — XT GL
Body VIN — X
Engine — 1.8L (1781cc)   **Cylinders** — 4
Fuel System — MPFI
Engine VIN — 4, 7

ENGINE CODES

Code	Explanation
11	Crank angle sensor — no reference pulse
12	Starter switch — continuously in ON or OFF position while cranking
13	Crank angle sensor — no position pulse
14	Fuel injectors No. 1 and No. 2 — abnormal injector output
15	Fuel injectors No. 3 and No. 4 — abnormal injector output
21	Water temperature sensor — open or shorted circuit
23	Air flow meter — open or shorted circuit
31	Throttle sensor — open or shorted circuit
32	Oxygen sensor — abnormal sensor signal
33	Car speed sensor — no signal is present during operation
35	Purge control solenoid valve — solenoid switch continuously in ON or OFF position
41	System too lean
42	Idle switch — abnormal idle switch signal in relation to throttle sensor output
51	Neutral switch — continuously in ON position

87974c25

Year — 1990
Model — XT6
Body VIN — X
Engine — 2.7L (2672cc)   **Cylinders** — 6
Fuel System — MPFI
Engine VIN — 8, 9

ENGINE CODES

Code	Explanation
11	Crank angle sensor — no reference pulse
12	Starter switch — continuously in ON or OFF position while cranking
13	Crank angle sensor — no position pulse
14	Fuel injectors No. 5 and No. 6 — abnormal injector output
15	Fuel injectors No. 1 and No. 2 — abnormal injector output
21	Water temperature sensor — open or shorted circuit
22	Knock sensor — open or shorted circuit
23	Air flow meter — open or shorted circuit
24	By-pass air control valve — open or shorted circuit
25	Fuel injectors No. 3 and No. 4 — abnormal injector output
31	Throttle sensor — open or shorted circuit
32	Oxygen sensor — abnormal sensor signal
33	Car speed sensor — no signal is present during operation
35	Purge control solenoid valve — solenoid switch continuously in ON or OFF position
41	System too lean
42	Idle switch — abnormal idle switch signal in relation to throttle sensor output
51	Neutral switch — continuously in ON position

87974c26

Year — 1990
Model — Justy DL
Body VIN — A
Engine — 1.2L (1189cc)   **Cylinders** — 3
Fuel System — Carburetor
Engine VIN — 7

ENGINE CODES

Code	Explanation
14	Duty solenoid valve control system
15	Coasting Fuel Cut (CFC) system
16	Feedback system
17	Fuel pump and automatic choke
21	Water temperature sensor
22	Vacuum Line Charging (VLC) solenoid valve
23	Pressure sensor
24	Idle-up solenoid valve
25	Float Chamber Ventilation (FCV) solenoid valve
32	Oxygen sensor
33	Car speed sensor
34	Exhaust Gas Recirculation (EGR) solenoid valve
35	CPC solenoid valve
46	Radiator fan control system
52	Clutch switch
53	High Altitude Compensator (HAC) solenoid valve
62	Idle-up system (1)
63	Idle-up system (2)

87974c27

Year — 1990
Model — Justy DL, GL
Body VIN — A
Engine — 1.2L (1189cc)   **Cylinders** — 3
Fuel System — MPFI
Engine VIN — 7, 8

ENGINE CODES

Code	Explanation
11	Crank angle sensor — no signal from sensor, but signal entered from starter switch
12	Starter switch — continuously in ON or OFF position while cranking
13	Cylinder distinction sensor — no signal from sensor, but signal from crank angle sensor
14	Fuel injector No. 1 — abnormal injector output
15	Fuel injector No. 2 — abnormal injector output
16	Fuel injector No. 3 — abnormal injector output
21	Water temperature sensor — abnormal signal
23	Pressure sensor — abnormal signal
24	ISC solenoid valve — valve inoperative, abnormal signal
26	Air temperature sensor — abnormal signal
32	Oxygen sensor — sensor inoperative
33	Car speed sensor — no signal is present during operation
35	CPC solenoid valve — valve inoperative, abnormal signal
36	Igniter — abnormal signal
41	A/F learning control — faulty learning control function
42	Idle switch — abnormal signal
43	Power switch — abnormal signal
45	Atmospheric pressure sensor — abnormal signal
52	Clutch switch — signal remains ON or OFF (Front Wheel Drive/Manual Transaxle only)
62	Electric load signal — headlight HI/LO signal or rear defogger signal remains ON or OFF
63	Blower fan switch — signal remains ON or OFF
65	Vacuum pressure sensor — abnormal signal

87974c28

Year—1990
Model—Legacy
Body VIN—C, J, F
Engine—2.2L (2212cc)   **Cylinders**—4
Fuel System—MPFI
Engine VIN—6

ENGINE CODES

Code	Explanation
11	Crank angle sensor—no signal from sensor, but signal entered from cam angle sensor
12	Starter switch—abnormal signal
13	Cam angle sensor—no signal from sensor, but signal from crank angle sensor
14	Fuel injector No. 1 injector inoperative, abnormal signal
15	Fuel injector No. 2 injector inoperative, abnormal signal
16	Fuel injector No. 3 injector inoperative, abnormal signal
17	Fuel injector No. 4 injector inoperative, abnormal signal
21	Water temperature sensor—abnormal signal
22	Knock sensor—abnormal voltage produced in sensor from monitor circuit
23	Air flow sensor—abnormal voltage input entered from sensor
24	Air control valve—valve inoperative, abnormal signal
31	Throttle sensor—abnormal voltage input entered from sensor
32	Oxygen sensor—sensor inoperative
33	Vehicle speed sensor—abnormal voltage input entered from sensor
35	Canister Purge solenoid valve—solenoid valve inoperative
41	AF (Air/Fuel) learning control—faulty learning control function
42	Idle switch—abnormal voltage input entered from switch
45	Atmospheric sensor—faulty sensor
49	Air flow sensor—use of improper air flow sensor
51	Neutral switch (MT)—abnormal signal from neutral switch
51	Inhibitor switch (AT)—abnormal signal from inhibitor switch
52	Parking switch—abnormal signal from parking switch

87974c29

Year—1991
Model—Loyale
Body VIN—C, N
Engine—1.8L (1781cc)   **Cylinders**—4
Fuel System—SPFI
Engine VIN—4, 5

ENGINE CODES

Code	Explanation
11	Crank angle sensor—no reference pulse
12	Starter switch—continuously in ON or OFF position while cranking
13	Crank angle sensor—no position pulse
14	Fuel injector—abnormal injector output
21	Water temperature sensor—open or shorted circuit
23	Air flow meter—open or shorted circuit
24	Air control valve—open or shorted circuit
31	Throttle sensor—open or shorted circuit
32	Oxygen sensor—abnormal sensor signal
33	Car speed sensor—no signal is present during operation
34	Exhaust Gas Recirculation (EGR) solenoid valve—solenoid switch continuously in ON or OFF position or (California only) clogged EGR line
35	Purge control solenoid valve—solenoid switch continuously in ON or OFF position
42	Idle switch—abnormal idle switch signal in relation to throttle sensor output
45	Kickdown control relay—continuously in ON or OFF position
51	Neutral switch—continuously in ON position
55	Exhaust Gas Recirculation (EGR) gas temperature sensor—open or short circuit (California only)
61	Parking switch—continuously in ON position

87974c30

Year — 1991
Model — XT GL
Body VIN — X
Engine — 1.8L (1781cc)   **Cylinders** — 4
Fuel System — MPFI
Engine VIN — 4, 7

ENGINE CODES

Code	Explanation
11	Crank angle sensor — no reference pulse
12	Starter switch — continuously in ON or OFF position while cranking
13	Crank angle sensor — no position pulse
14	Fuel injectors No. 1 and No. 2 — abnormal injector output
15	Fuel injectors No. 3 and No. 4 — abnormal injector output
21	Water temperature sensor — open or shorted circuit
23	Air flow meter — open or shorted circuit
31	Throttle sensor — open or shorted circuit
32	Oxygen sensor — abnormal sensor signal
33	Car speed sensor — no signal is present during operation
35	Purge control solenoid valve — solenoid switch continuously in ON or OFF position
41	System too lean
42	Idle switch — abnormal idle switch signal in relation to throttle sensor output
51	Neutral switch — no signal is present

87974c31

Year — 1991
Model — XT6
Body VIN — X
Engine — 2.7L (2672cc)   **Cylinders** — 6
Fuel System — MPFI
Engine VIN — 8, 9

ENGINE CODES

Code	Explanation
11	Crank angle sensor — no reference pulse
12	Starter switch — continuously in ON or OFF position while cranking
13	Crank angle sensor — no position pulse
14	Fuel injectors No. 5 and No. 6 — abnormal injector output
15	Fuel injectors No. 1 and No. 2 — abnormal injector output
21	Water temperature sensor — open or shorted circuit
22	Knock sensor — open or shorted circuit
23	Air flow meter — open or shorted circuit
24	By-pass air control valve — open or shorted circuit
25	Fuel injectors No. 3 and No. 4 — abnormal injector output
31	Throttle sensor — open or shorted circuit
32	Oxygen sensor — abnormal sensor signal
33	Car speed sensor — no signal is present during operation
35	Purge control solenoid valve — solenoid switch continuously in ON or OFF position
41	System too lean
42	Idle switch — abnormal idle switch signal in relation to throttle sensor output
51	Neutral switch — no signal is present

87974c32

Year — 1991
Model — Justy DL
Body VIN — A
Engine — 1.2L (1189cc)   **Cylinders** — 3
Fuel System — Carburetor
Engine VIN — 7

ENGINE CODES

Code	Explanation
14	Duty solenoid valve control system
15	Coasting Fuel Cut (CFC) system
16	Feedback system
17	Fuel pump and automatic choke
21	Water temperature sensor
22	Vacuum Line Charging (VLC) solenoid valve
23	Pressure sensor
24	Idle-up solenoid valve
25	Float Chamber Ventilation (FCV) solenoid valve
32	Oxygen sensor
33	Car speed sensor
34	Exhaust Gas Recirculation (EGR) solenoid valve
35	CPC solenoid valve
46	Radiator fan control system
52	Clutch switch
53	High Altitude Compensator (HAC) solenoid valve
62	Idle-up system (1)
63	Idle-up system (2)

87974c33

Year — 1991
Model — Justy DL, GL
Body VIN — A
Engine — 1.2L (1189cc)   **Cylinders** — 3
Fuel System — MPFI
Engine VIN — 7, 8

ENGINE CODES

Code	Explanation
11	Crank angle sensor — no signal from sensor, but signal entered from starter switch
12	Starter switch — continuously in ON or OFF position while cranking
13	Cylinder distinction sensor — no signal from sensor, but signal from crank angle sensor
14	Fuel injector No. 1 — abnormal injector output
15	Fuel injector No. 2 — abnormal injector output
16	Fuel injector No. 3 — abnormal injector output
21	Water temperature sensor — abnormal signal
23	Pressure sensor — abnormal signal
24	ISC solenoid valve — valve inoperative, abnormal signal
26	Air temperature sensor — abnormal signal
32	Oxygen sensor — sensor inoperative
33	Car speed sensor — no signal is present during operation
35	CPC solenoid valve — valve inoperative, abnormal signal
36	Igniter — abnormal signal
41	A/F learning control — faulty learning control function
42	Idle switch — abnormal signal
43	Power switch — abnormal signal
45	Atmospheric pressure sensor — abnormal signal
52	Clutch switch — signal remains ON or OFF (Front Wheel Drive/Manual Transaxle only)
62	Electric load signal — headlight HI/LO signal or rear defogger signal remains ON or OFF
63	Blower fan switch — signal remains ON or OFF
65	Vacuum pressure sensor — abnormal signal

87974c34

Year — 1991
Model — Legacy
Body VIN — C, J, F
Engine — 2.2L (2212cc)   **Cylinders** — 4
Fuel System — MPFI
Engine VIN — 6

ENGINE CODES

Code	Explanation
11	Crank angle sensor — no signal from sensor, but signal entered from cam angle sensor
12	Starter switch — abnormal signal
13	Cam angle sensor — no signal from sensor, but signal from crank angle sensor
14	Fuel injector No. 1 injector inoperative, abnormal signal
15	Fuel injector No. 2 injector inoperative, abnormal signal
16	Fuel injector No. 3 injector inoperative, abnormal signal
17	Fuel injector No. 4 injector inoperative, abnormal signal
21	Water temperature sensor — abnormal signal
22	Knock sensor — abnormal voltage produced in sensor from monitor circuit
23	Air flow sensor — abnormal voltage input entered from sensor
24	Air control valve — valve inoperative, abnormal signal
31	Throttle sensor — abnormal voltage input entered from sensor
32	Oxygen sensor — sensor inoperative
33	Vehicle speed sensor — abnormal voltage input entered from sensor
35	Canister Purge solenoid valve — solenoid valve inoperative
41	AF (Air/Fuel) learning control — faulty learning control function
42	Idle switch — abnormal voltage input entered from switch
44	Duty solenoid valve (wastegate control) — valve inoperative
45	A: Atmospheric pressure sensor — faulty sensor
45	B: Pressure exchange solenoid valve — valve inoperative
49	Air flow sensor — use of improper air flow sensor
51	Neutral switch (MT) — abnormal signal from neutral switch
51	Inhibitor switch (AT) — abnormal signal from inhibitor switch
52	Parking switch — abnormal signal from parking switch

87974c35

DIAGNOSTIC TROUBLE CODE INFORMATION - 1992-94 SUBARU JUSTY

DTC	Description	Items To Check
11	CKP sensor	Harness and connector. If OK, replace the CKP
12	Starter switch	Harness and connector. If OK, replace the starter switch
13	CMP sensor	Harness and connector. If OK, replace the CMP
14	Fuel Injector #1	Harness and connector. If OK, replace the fuel injector
15	Fuel injector #2	Harness and connector. If OK, replace the fuel injector
16	Fuel injector #3	Harness and connector. If OK, replace the fuel injector
21	ECT sensor	Harness and connector. If OK, replace the ECT
23	MAP sensor	MAP sensor
24	IAC valve	IAC valve
26	IAT Sensor	IAT Sensor
32	Oxygen sensor	Harness and connector/ oxygen sensor/fuel pressure/injectors/intake air leaks
33	Vehicle speed sensor 2	Harness and connector. If OK, replace the VSS
35	EVAP purge valve	Harness and connector. If OK, replace the EVAP purge valve
36	ICM	Harness and connector. If OK, replace the ICM
41	Fuel Trim	Harness and connector/ oxygen sensor/fuel pressure/injectors/intake air leaks/ECM
42	TP sensor-Idle switch	Harness and connector. If OK, replace the TPS
43	TP sensor-W+B6OT Throttle switch	Harness and connector. If OK, replace the TPS
45	BARO sensor	Harness and connector. If OK, check for BARO port clogging. Replace the BARO sensor
51	Neutral position switch(M/T)	Harness and connector. If OK, replace the neutral position switch (M/T)
52	Clutch switch (Electronic controlled variable transmission equipped)	Harness and connector. If OK, replace the clutch switch
62	Electrical load signal	Check electrical load circuit
63	Blower fan switch	TPS harness and connector. If OK, replace the TPS.
65	MAP sensor	Damaged or disconnected hose. Check engine manifold vacuum and connections, harness. If OK, replace the MAP sensor

87974c41

DIAGNOSTIC TROUBLE CODE INFORMATION - 1992-94 SUBARU LOYALE

DTC	Description	Items To Check
11	CKP sensor	Harness and connector. If OK, replace the CKP
12	Starter switch	Harness and connector. If OK, replace the starter switch
13	CKP sensor	Harness and connector. If OK, replace the CKP
14	Fuel Injector #1	Harness and connector. If OK, replace the fuel injector
21	ECT sensor	Harness and connector. If OK, replace the ECT
23	MAF sensor	MAF sensor
24	IAC valve	IAC valve
31	TPS	TPS Sensor
32	Oxygen sensor	Harness and connector/ oxygen sensor/fuel pressure/injectors/intake air leaks
33	Vehicle speed sensor 2	Harness and connector. If OK, replace the VSS
34	EGR valve control	EGR valve control circuit
35	EVAP purge valve	Harness and connector. If OK, replace the EVAP purge valve
42	Idle switch	Harness and connector. If OK, replace the TPS
45	Kickdown control relay	Harness and connector. Replace the kickdown control relay
51	Neutral position switch(M/T)	Harness and connector. If OK, replace the neutral position switch (M/T)
55	EGR temperature switch	Harness and connector. If OK, replace the EGR temperature switch
61	Parking brake switch (A/T)	Harness and connector. If OK, replace parking brake switch. If necessary, replace ECM.

87974c42

DIAGNOSTIC TROUBLE CODE INFORMATION - 1993-94 SUBARU IMPREZA

DTC	Description	Items To Check
11	CKP sensor	Harness and connector. If OK, replace the CKP
12	Starter switch	Harness and connector. If OK, replace the starter switch
13	CMP sensor	Harness and connector. If OK, replace the CMP
14	Fuel Injector #1	Harness and connector. If OK, replace the fuel injector
15	Fuel injector #2	Harness and connector. If OK, replace the fuel injector
16	Fuel injector #3	Harness and connector. If OK, replace the fuel injector
17	Fuel injector #4	Harness and connector. If OK, replace the fuel injector
21	ECT sensor	Harness and connector. If OK, replace the ECT
23	MAF sensor	MAF sensor
24	IAC valve	IAC valve
31	Throttle position sensor	Harness and connector. If OK, replace the TPS
32	Oxygen sensor	Harness and connector/heated oxygen sensor/fuel pressure/injectors/intake air leaks
33	Vehicle speed sensor 2	Harness and connector. If OK, replace the VSS
34	EGR solenoid valve	Harness and connector. If OK, replace the EGR solenoid valve
35	EVAP purge valve	Harness and connector. If OK, replace the EVAP purge valve
36	Air suction solenoid valve	Harness and connector. If OK, replace the air suction solenoid valve
41	Fuel Trim	Check harness and air temperature sensor.
51	Neutral position (M/T)/Inhibit (A/T) switch	Injector connections and injection circuit
55	EGR gas temperature sensor	Harness and connector. If OK, replace the EGR temperature sensor
56	EGR system	EGR valve operation and passages for blockage.

87974c43

DIAGNOSTIC TROUBLE CODE INFORMATION - 1992-94 SUBARU LEGACY

DTC	Description	Items To Check
11	CKP sensor	Harness and connector. If OK, replace the CKP
12	Starter switch	Harness and connector. If OK, replace the starter switch
13	CMP sensor	Harness and connector. If OK, replace the CMP
14	Fuel Injector #1	Harness and connector. If OK, replace the fuel injector
15	Fuel injector #2	Harness and connector. If OK, replace the fuel injector
16	Fuel injector #3	Harness and connector. If OK, replace the fuel injector
17	Fuel injector #4	Harness and connector. If OK, replace the fuel injector
21	ECT sensor	Harness and connector. If OK, replace the ECT
22	Knock sensor	Harness and connector. If OK, replace the knock sensor
23	MAF sensor	MAF sensor
24	IAC valve	IAC valve
31	TPS	TPS Sensor
32	Oxygen sensor	Harness and connector/ oxygen sensor/fuel pressure/injectors/intake air leaks
33	Vehicle speed sensor 2	Harness and connector. If OK, replace the VSS
35	EVAP purge valve	Harness and connector. If OK, replace the EVAP purge valve
41	Fuel Trim	Harness and connector/ oxygen sensor/fuel pressure/injectors/intake air leaks/ECM
42	Idle switch	Harness and connector. If OK, replace the TPS
44	Turbocharger wastegate regulating valve	Turbocharger boost pressure
45	Press sensor duty solenoid (TURBO)/BARO sensor (NON-TURBO)	Harness and connector. If OK, check for BARO port clogging. Replace the BARO sensor
49	MAF	MAF sensor and harness
51	Neutral position switch(M/T)	Harness and connector. If OK, replace the neutral position switch (M/T)
52	Clutch switch (Electronic controlled variable transmission equipped)	Harness and connector. If OK, replace the clutch switch

87974c44

DIAGNOSTIC TROUBLE CODE INFORMATION - 1992-94 SUBARU SVX

DTC	Description	Items To Check
11	CKP sensor	Harness and connector. If OK, replace the CKP
12	Starter switch	Harness and connector. If OK, replace the starter switch
13	CKP sensor	Harness and connector. If OK, replace the CKP
14	Fuel Injector #1	Harness and connector. If OK, replace the fuel injector
15	Fuel Injector #2	Harness and connector. If OK, replace the fuel injector
16	Fuel Injector #3	Harness and connector. If OK, replace the fuel injector
17	Fuel Injector #4	Harness and connector. If OK, replace the fuel injector
18	Fuel Injector #5	Harness and connector. If OK, replace the fuel injector
19	Fuel Injector #6	Harness and connector. If OK, replace the fuel injector
21	ECT sensor	Harness and connector. If OK, replace the ECT
22	Knock sensor (RIGHT)	Harness and connector. If OK, replace the knock sensor
23	MAF sensor	MAF sensor
24	IAC valve	IAC valve
28	Knock sensor (LEFT)	Harness and connector. If OK, replace the knock sensor
29	CKP #2	Harness and connector. If OK, replace the CKP
31	TPS	TPS Sensor
32	Oxygen sensor #1 (right)	Harness and connector/ oxygen sensor/fuel pressure/injectors/intake air leaks
33	Vehicle speed sensor 2	Harness and connector. If OK, replace the VSS
34	EGR valve control	EGR valve control circuit
35	EVAP purge valve	Harness and connector. If OK, replace the EVAP purge valve
37	Oxygen sensor #2 (left)	Harness and connector/ oxygen sensor/fuel pressure/injectors/intake air leaks
38	Engine torque control	Check harness. If OK, replace transaxle control unit.
41	Fuel trim	Harness and connector. If OK, replace the TPS
45	BARO sensor	Harness and connector. If OK, check for BARO port clogging. Replace the BARO sensor
51	Neutral position switch	Harness and connector. If OK, replace the neutral position switch (M/T)
55	EGR temperature switch	Harness and connector. If OK, replace the EGR temperature switch
56	EGR system	EGR valve ,operation and passages for blockage.

87974c45

VACUUM DIAGRAMS

Following are vacuum diagrams for most of the engine and emissions package combinations covered by this manual. Because vacuum circuits will vary based on various engine and vehicle options, always refer first to the vehicle emission control information label, if present. Should the label be missing, or should the vehicle be equipped with a different engine than the vehicle's original equipment, refer to the following diagrams for the same or similar configuration.

If you wish to obtain a replacement emissions label, most manufacturers make the labels available for purchase. The labels can usually be ordered from a local dealer.

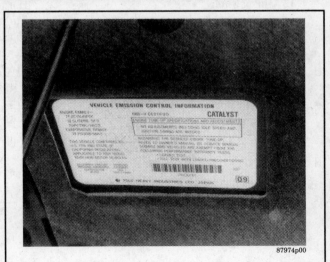

87974p00

Fig. 47 An example of an emission control label on the inside of the hood

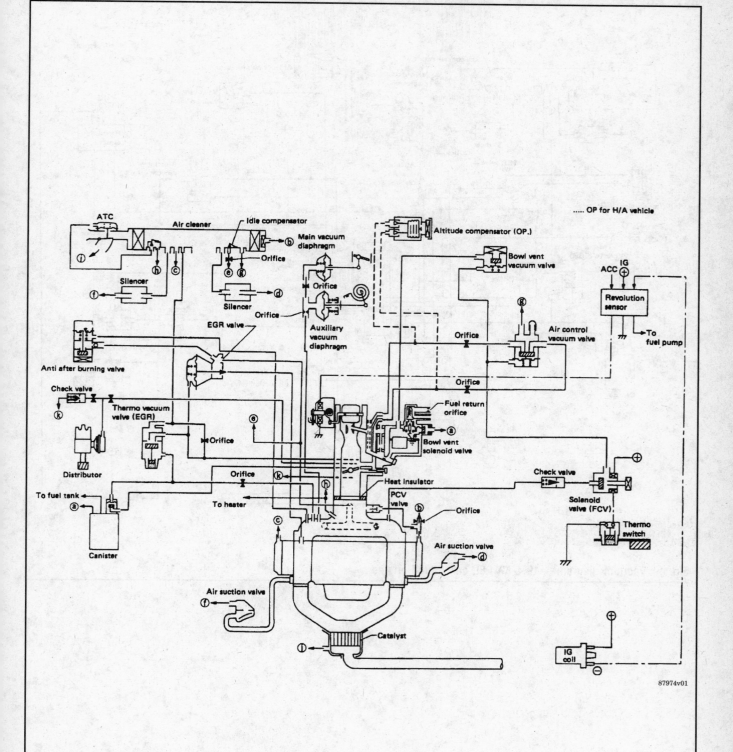

Fig. 48 Vacuum diagram — 1986-87 1.6L and 1.8L carbureted engines

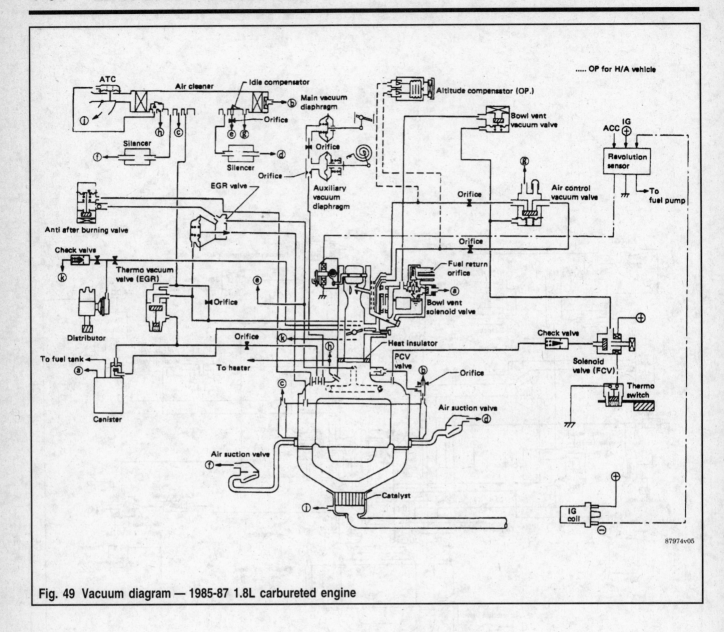

Fig. 49 Vacuum diagram — 1985-87 1.8L carbureted engine

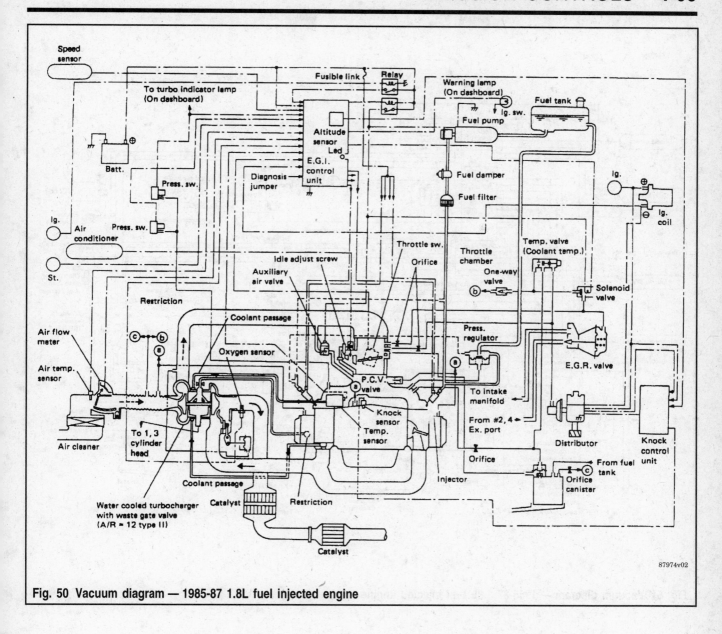

Fig. 50 Vacuum diagram — 1985-87 1.8L fuel injected engine

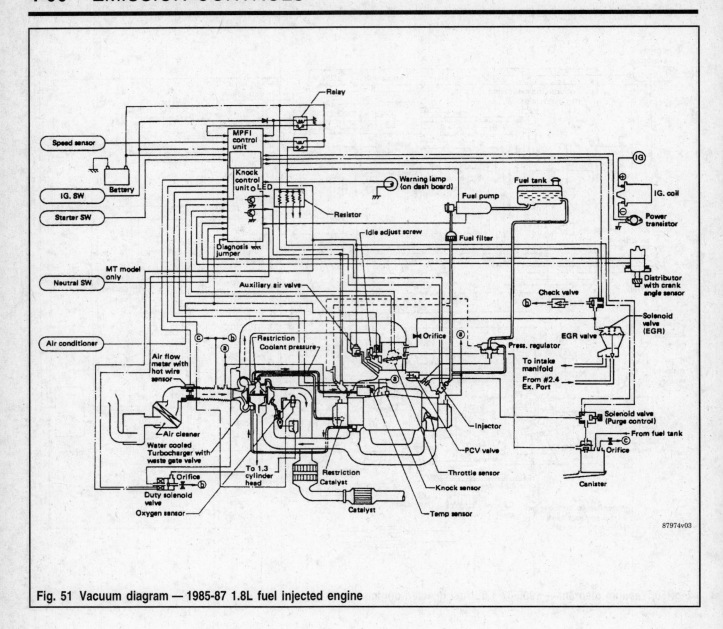

Fig. 51 Vacuum diagram — 1985-87 1.8L fuel injected engine

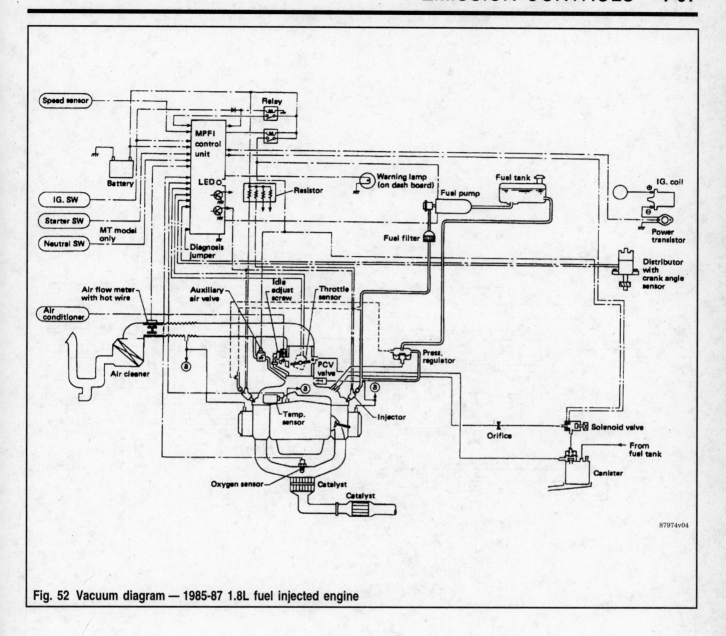

Fig. 52 Vacuum diagram — 1985-87 1.8L fuel injected engine

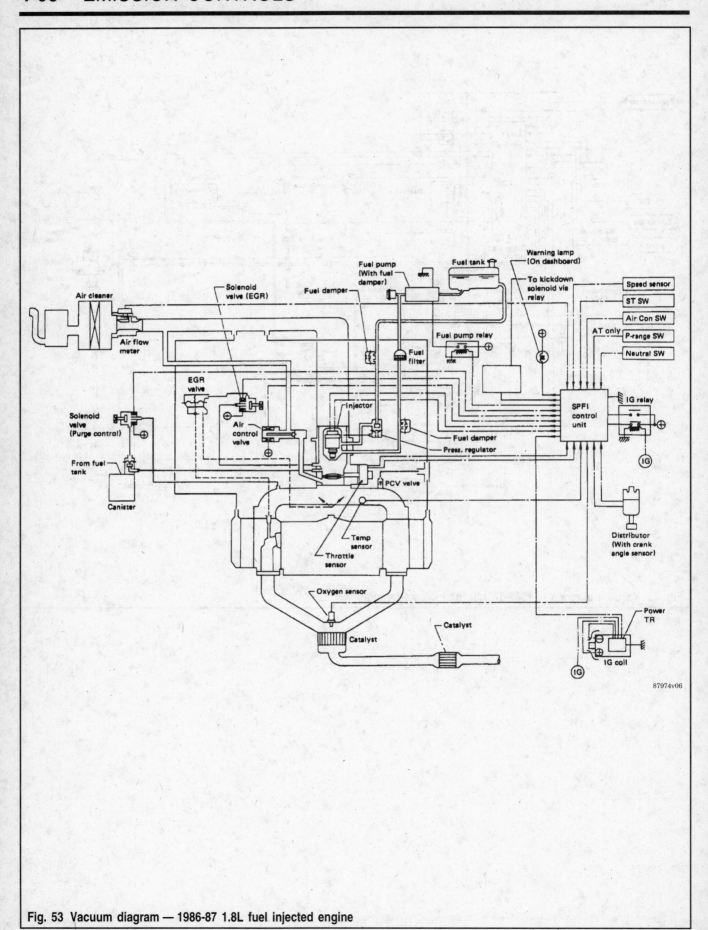

Fig. 53 Vacuum diagram — 1986-87 1.8L fuel injected engine

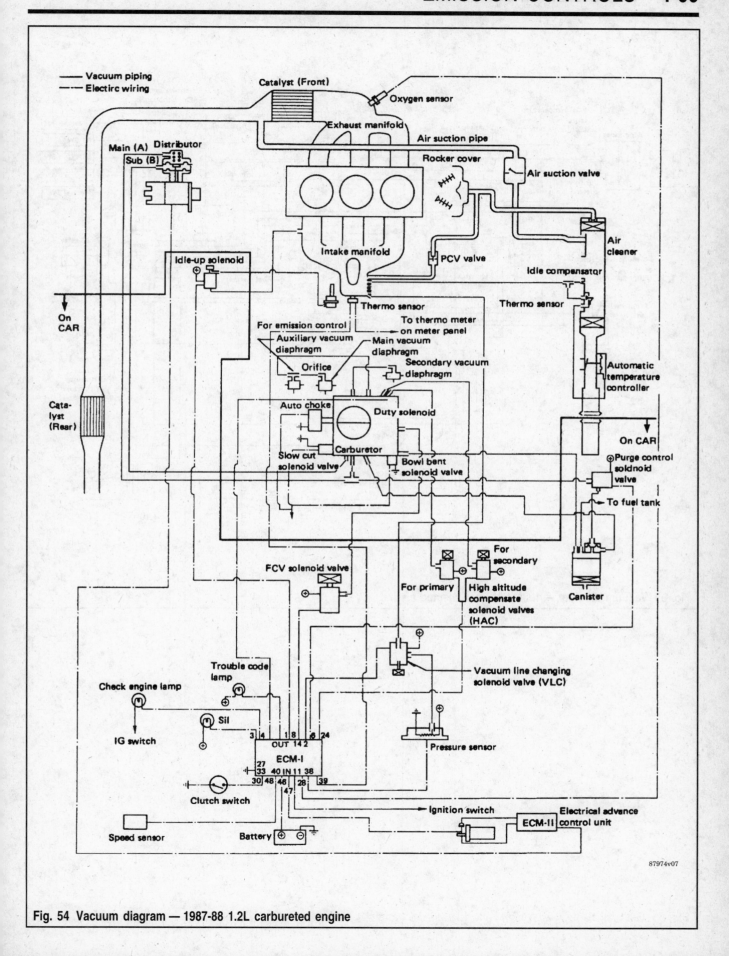

Fig. 54 Vacuum diagram — 1987-88 1.2L carbureted engine

87974v07

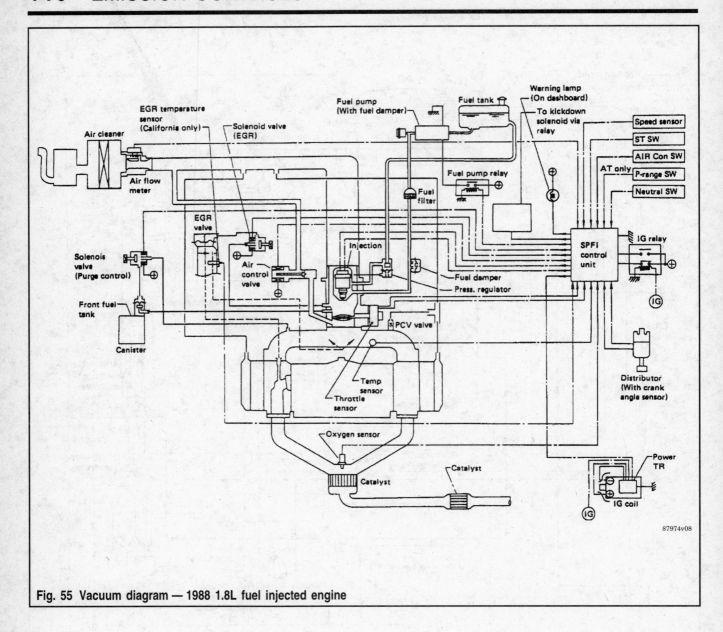

Fig. 55 Vacuum diagram — 1988 1.8L fuel injected engine

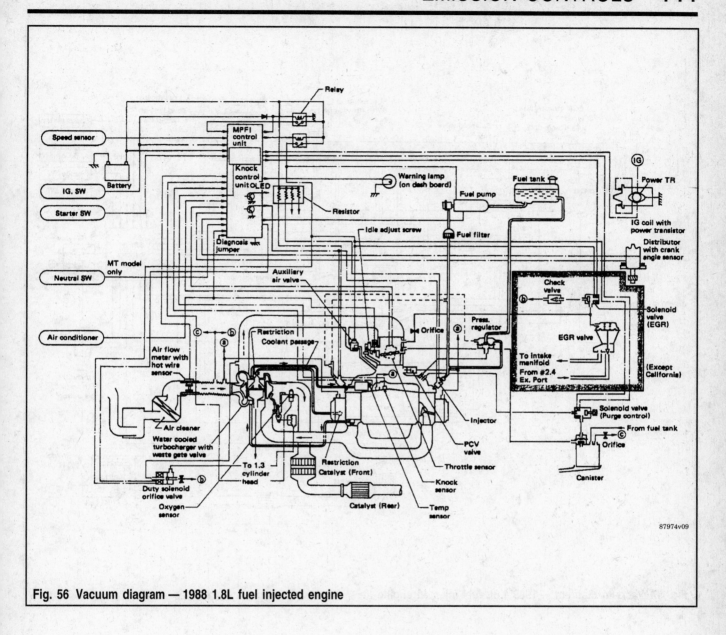

Fig. 56 Vacuum diagram — 1988 1.8L fuel injected engine

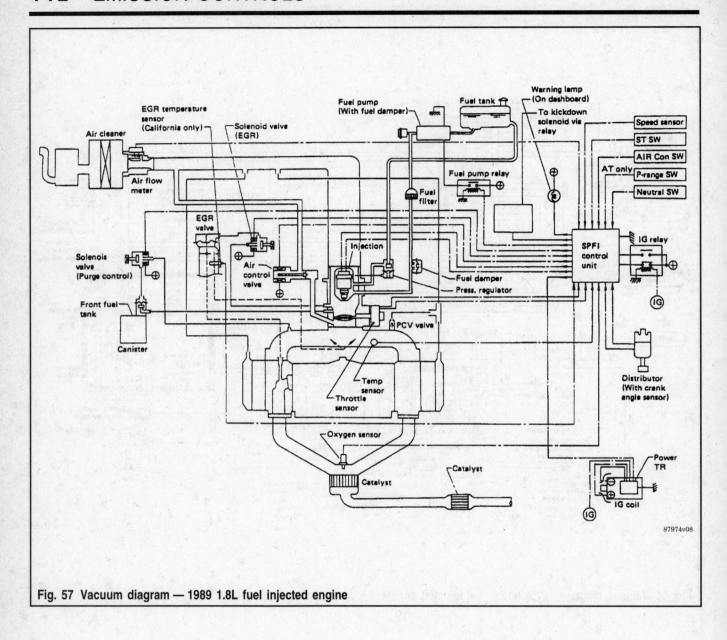

Fig. 57 Vacuum diagram — 1989 1.8L fuel injected engine

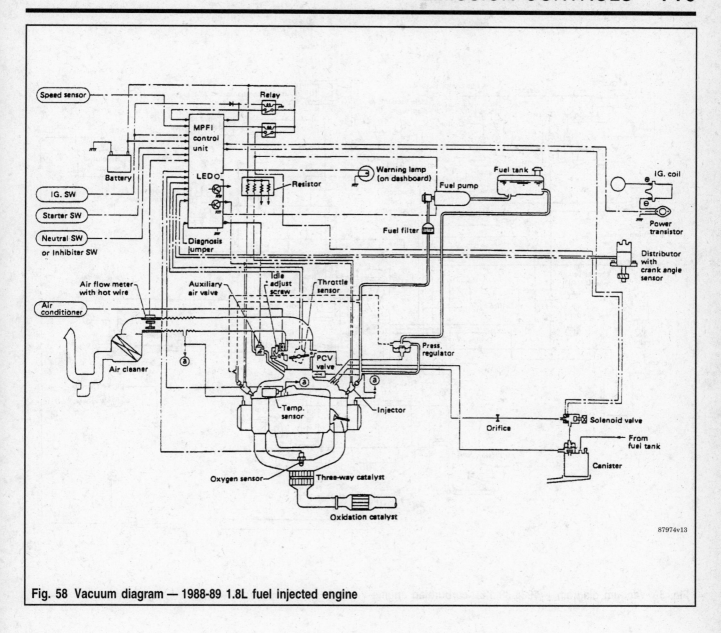

Fig. 58 Vacuum diagram — 1988-89 1.8L fuel injected engine

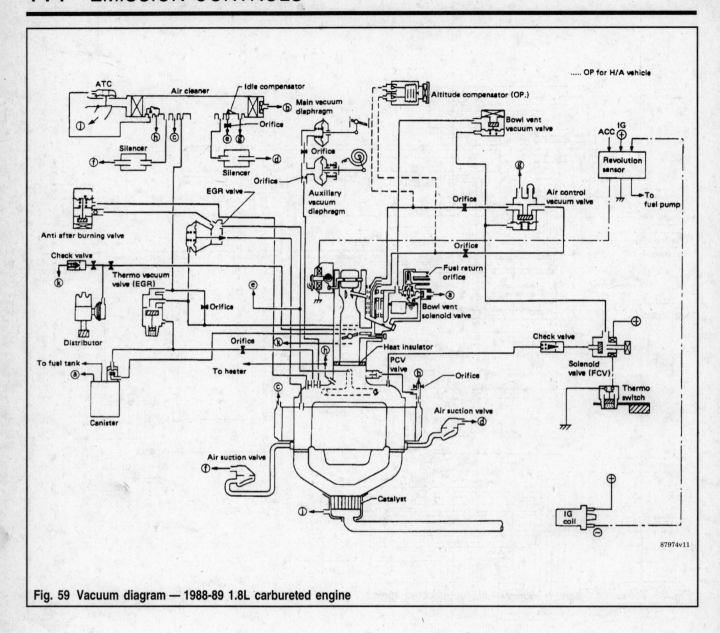

Fig. 59 Vacuum diagram — 1988-89 1.8L carbureted engine

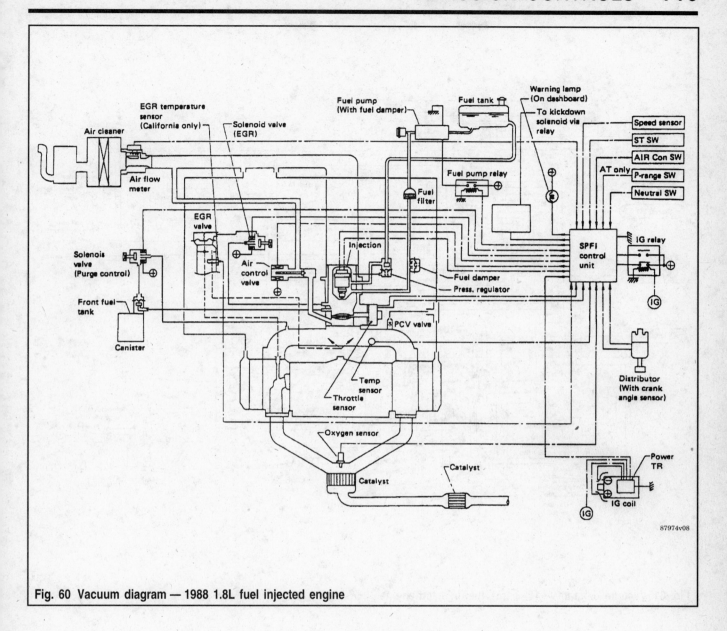

Fig. 60 Vacuum diagram — 1988 1.8L fuel injected engine

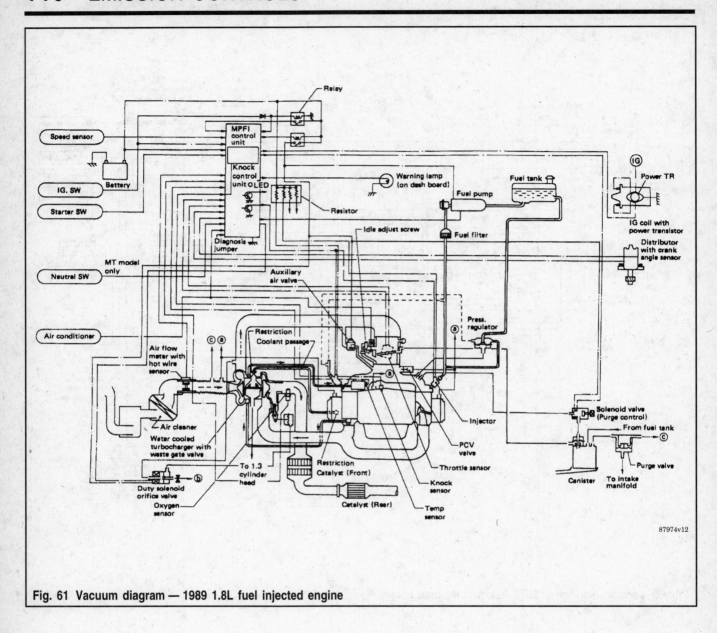

Fig. 61 Vacuum diagram — 1989 1.8L fuel injected engine

87974v12

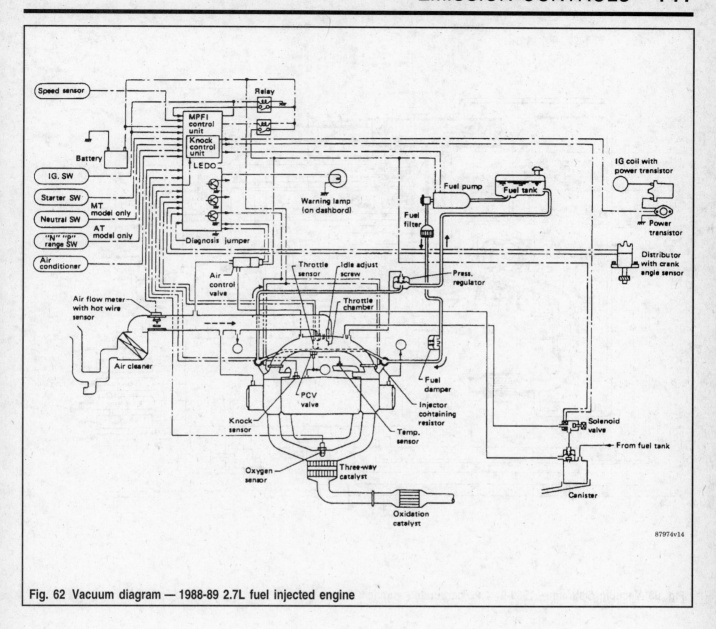

87974v14

Fig. 62 Vacuum diagram — 1988-89 2.7L fuel injected engine

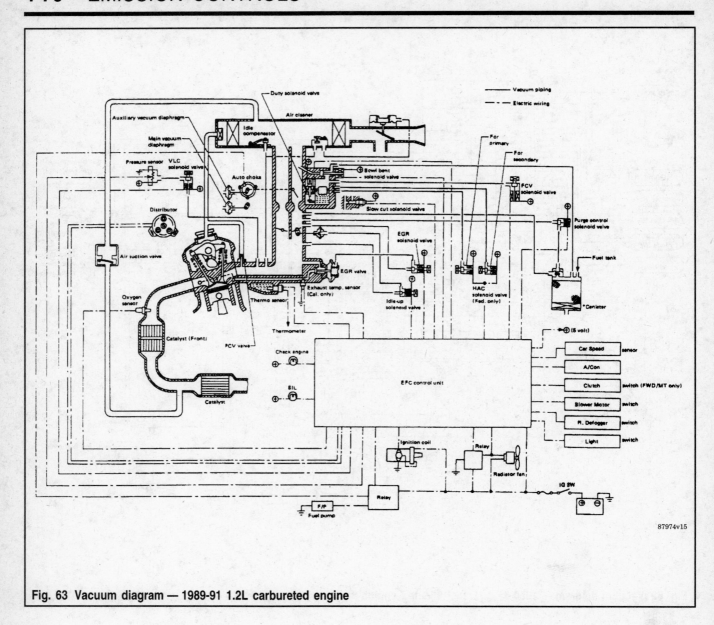

Fig. 63 Vacuum diagram — 1989-91 1.2L carbureted engine

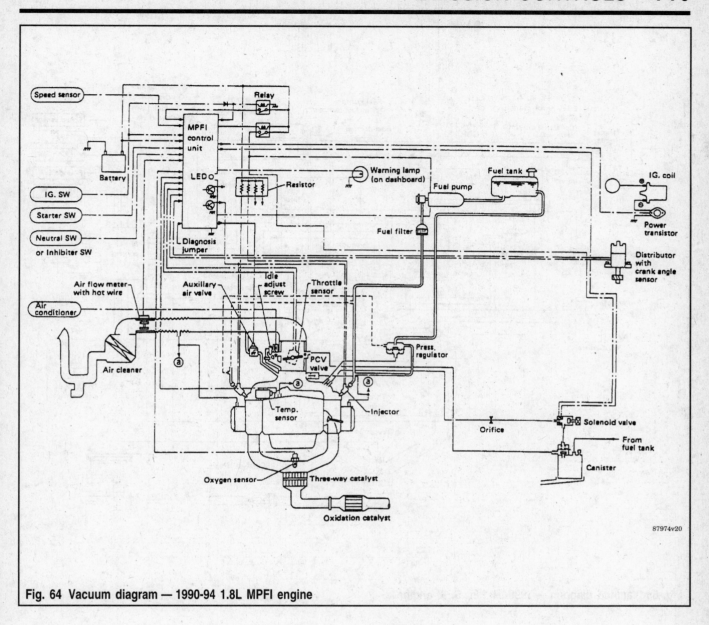

Fig. 64 Vacuum diagram — 1990-94 1.8L MPFI engine

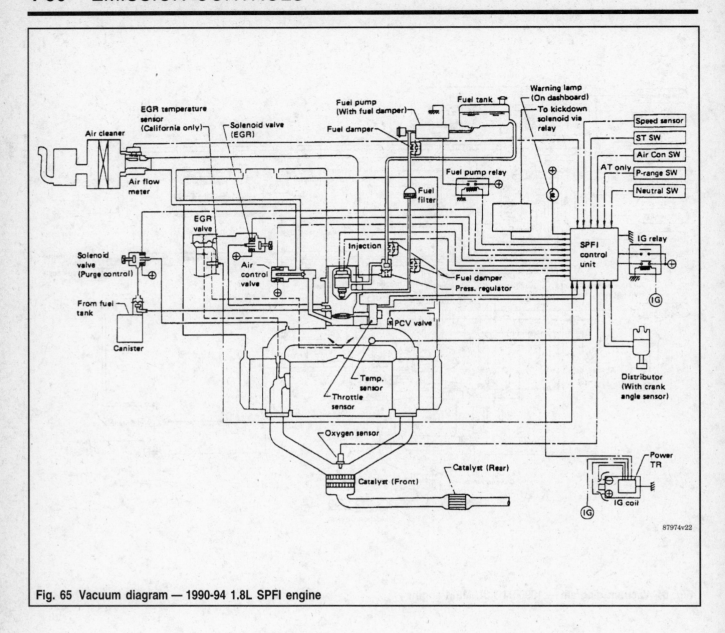

Fig. 65 Vacuum diagram — 1990-94 1.8L SPFI engine

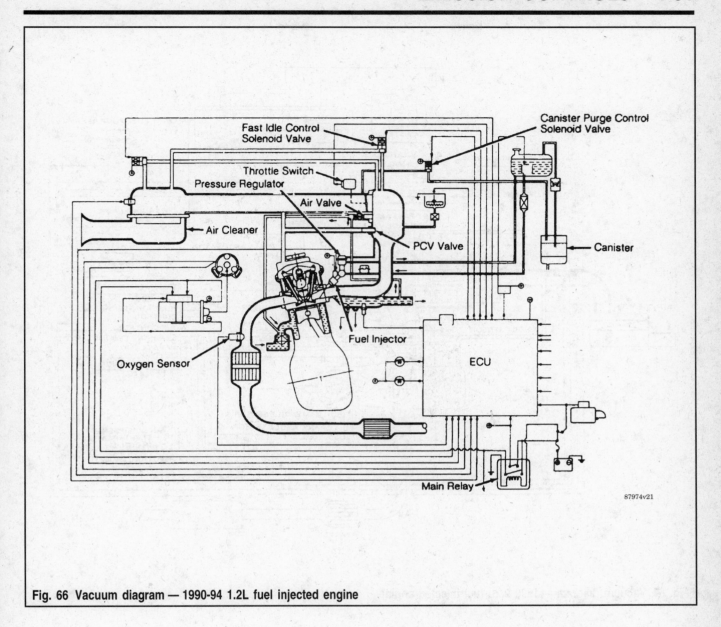

Fig. 66 Vacuum diagram — 1990-94 1.2L fuel injected engine

87974v21

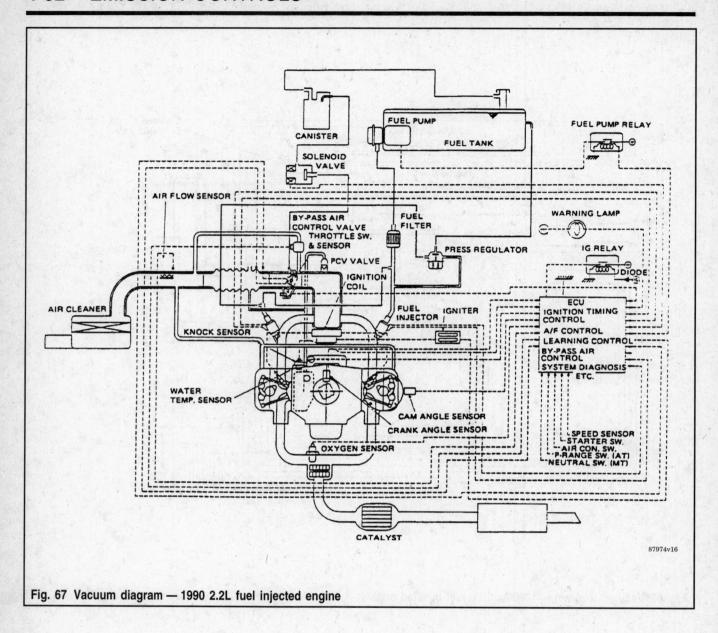

Fig. 67 Vacuum diagram — 1990 2.2L fuel injected engine

87974v16

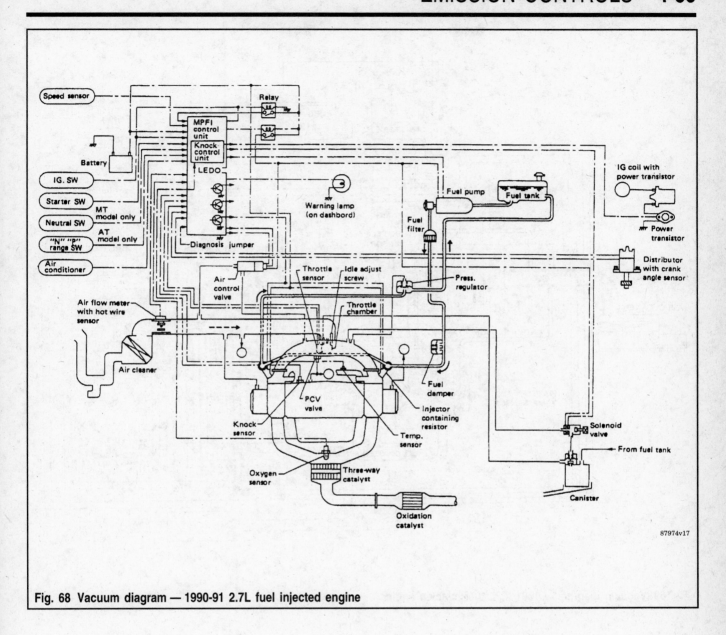

Fig. 68 Vacuum diagram — 1990-91 2.7L fuel injected engine

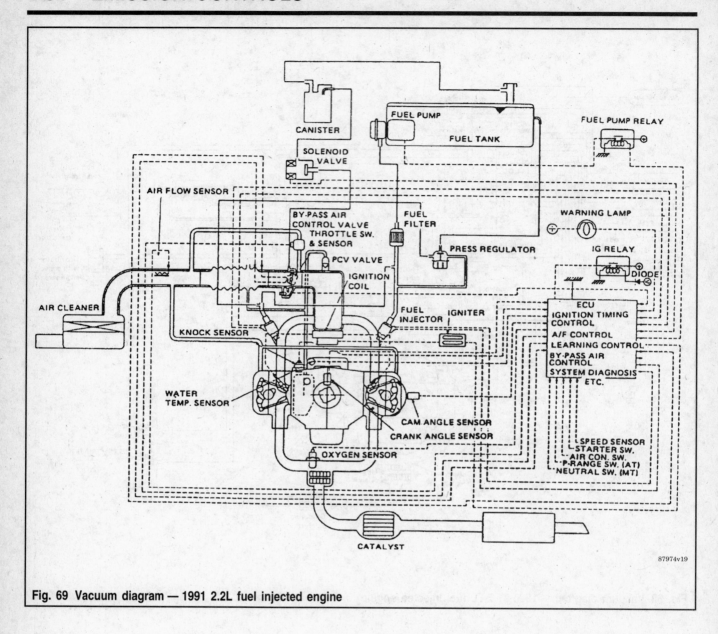

Fig. 69 Vacuum diagram — 1991 2.2L fuel injected engine

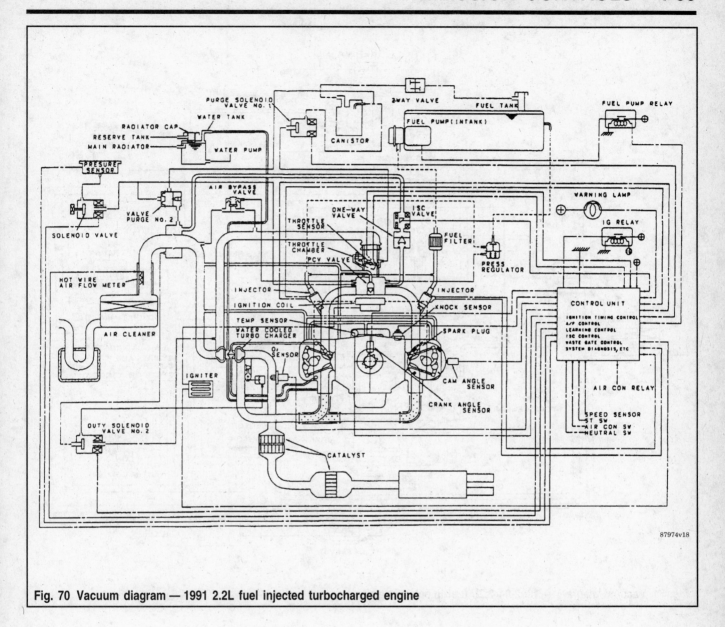

Fig. 70 Vacuum diagram — 1991 2.2L fuel injected turbocharged engine

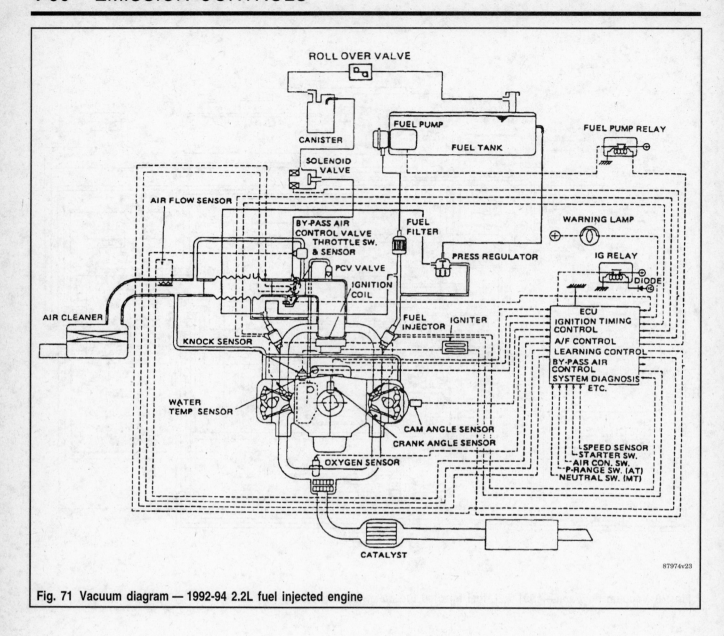

Fig. 71 Vacuum diagram — 1992-94 2.2L fuel injected engine

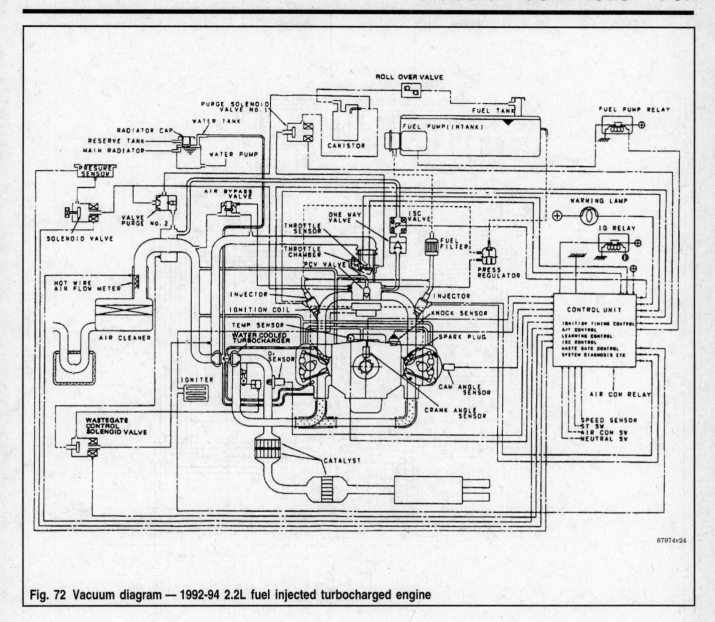

Fig. 72 Vacuum diagram — 1992-94 2.2L fuel injected turbocharged engine

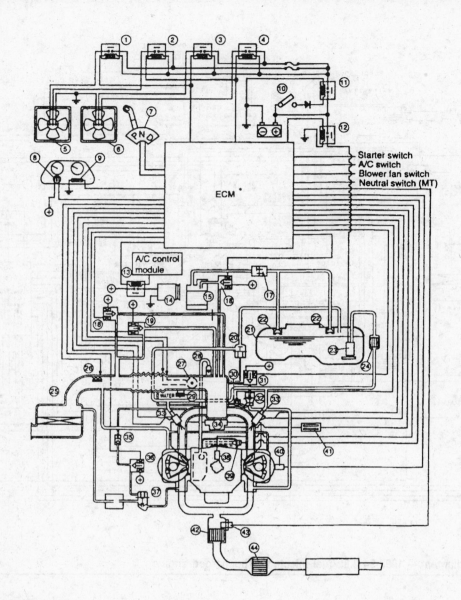

① Radiator main fan relay 1	⑰ Two way valve	㉜ EGR valve
② Radiator main fan relay 2	⑱ FICD solenoid valve (With A/C)	㉝ Fuel injector
③ Radiator sub fan relay 1	⑲ Idle air control solenoid valve	㉞ Ignition coil
④ Radiator sub fan relay 2	⑳ Pressure regulator	㉟ Check valve (All models)
⑤ Radiator main fan	㉑ Fuel tank	㊱ Air suction solenoid valve (All
⑥ Radiator sub fan	㉒ Fuel cut valve	models)
⑦ Inhibitor switch	㉓ Fuel pump	㊲ Air suction valve (All models)
⑧ CHECK ENGINE light	㉔ Fuel filter	㊳ Crankshaft position sensor
⑨ Vehicle speed sensor 2	㉕ Air cleaner	㊴ Engine coolant temperature sen-
⑩ Ignition switch	㉖ Mass air flow sensor	sor
⑪ Main relay	㉗ Throttle position sensor	㊵ Camshaft position sensor
⑫ Fuel pump relay	㉘ PCV valve	㊶ Igniter
⑬ A/C cut relay	㉙ Throttle opener	㊷ Front catalytic converter
⑭ A/C compressor	㉚ Recirculation gas temperature	㊸ Oxygen sensor
⑮ Canister	sensor (All models)	㊹ Rear catalytic converter
⑯ Purge control solenoid valve	㉛ EGR solenoid valve	

87974v26

Fig. 73 Vacuum diagram — 1992-95 1.8L fuel injected engine

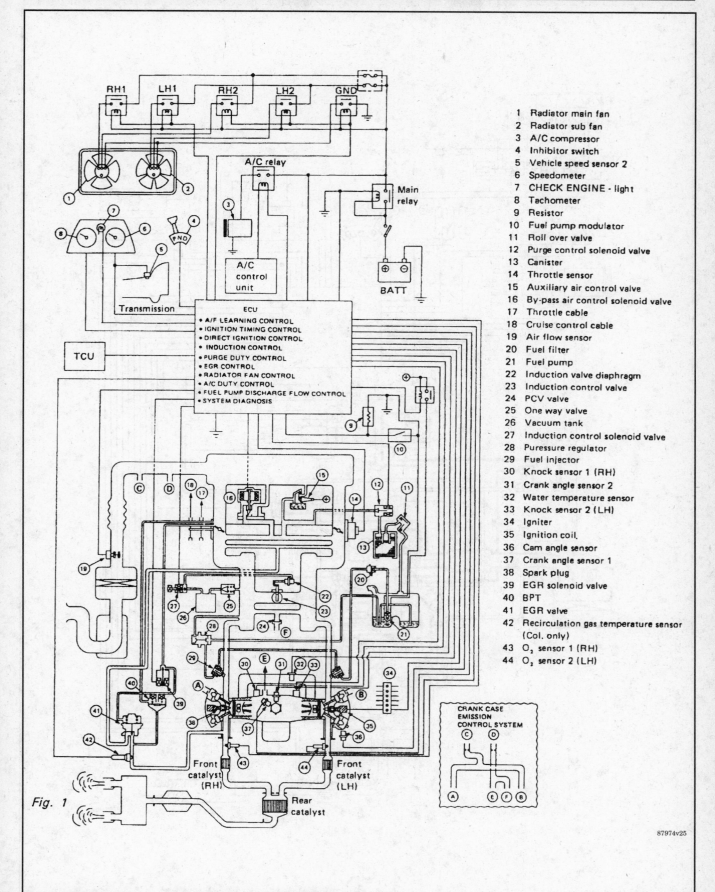

1 Radiator main fan
2 Radiator sub fan
3 A/C compressor
4 Inhibitor switch
5 Vehicle speed sensor 2
6 Speedometer
7 CHECK ENGINE - light
8 Tachometer
9 Resistor
10 Fuel pump modulator
11 Roll over valve
12 Purge control solenoid valve
13 Canister
14 Throttle sensor
15 Auxiliary air control valve
16 By-pass air control solenoid valve
17 Throttle cable
18 Cruise control cable
19 Air flow sensor
20 Fuel filter
21 Fuel pump
22 Induction valve diaphragm
23 Induction control valve
24 PCV valve
25 One way valve
26 Vacuum tank
27 Induction control solenoid valve
28 Puressure regulator
29 Fuel injector
30 Knock sensor 1 (RH)
31 Crank angle sensor 2
32 Water temperature sensor
33 Knock sensor 2 (LH)
34 Igniter
35 Ignition coil.
36 Cam angle sensor
37 Crank angle sensor 1
38 Spark plug
39 EGR solenoid valve
40 BPT
41 EGR valve
42 Recirculation gas temperature sensor (Col. only)
43 O₂ sensor 1 (RH)
44 O₂ sensor 2 (LH)

Fig. 74 Vacuum diagram — 1992-95 3.3L fuel injected engine

87974v25

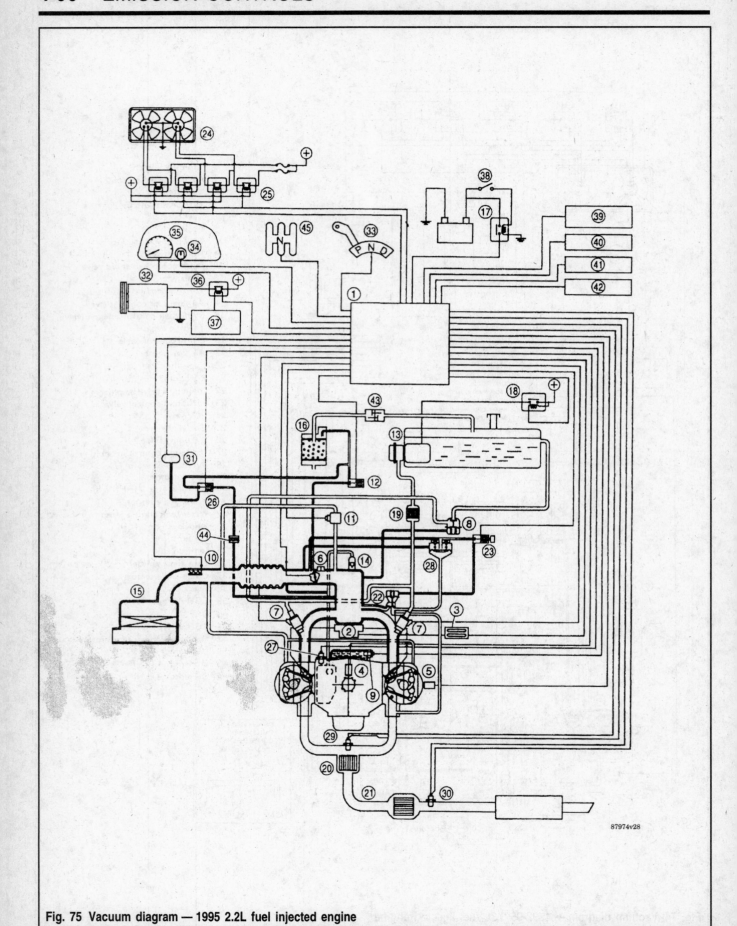

Fig. 75 Vacuum diagram — 1995 2.2L fuel injected engine

87974v28

① Engine control module (ECM)
② Ignition coil
③ Ignitor
④ Crankshaft position sensor
⑤ Camshaft position sensor
⑥ Throttle position sensor
⑦ Fuel injectors
⑧ Pressure regulator
⑨ Engine coolant temperature sensor
⑩ Mass air flow sensor
⑪ Idle air control solenoid valve
⑫ Purge control solenoid valve
⑬ Fuel pump
⑭ PCV valve
⑮ Air cleaner
⑯ Canister
⑰ Main relay
⑱ Fuel pump relay
⑲ Fuel filter
⑳ Front catalytic converter
㉑ Rear catalytic converter
㉒ EGR valve (AT vehicles only)
㉓ EGR control solenoid valve (AT vehicles only)

㉔ Radiator fan
㉕ Radiator fan relay
㉖ Pressure sources switching solenoid valve
㉗ Knock sensor
㉘ Back-pressure transducer
㉙ Front oxygen sensor
㉚ Rear oxygen sensor
㉛ Pressure sensor
㉜ A/C compressor
㉝ Inhibitor switch (AT vehicles)
㉞ CHECK ENGINE malfunction indicator lamp (MIL)
㉟ Tachometer
㊱ A/C relay
㊲ A/C control module
㊳ Ignition switch
㊴ Transmission control module (TCM)
㊵ Vehicle speed sensor
㊶ Data link connector (Subaru select monitor)
㊷ Data link connector (OBD-II general scan tool)
㊸ Two way valve
㊹ Filter
㊺ Neutral position switch (MT vehicles)

87974v29

Fig. 76 Vacuum diagram — 1995 2.2L fuel injected engine — continued

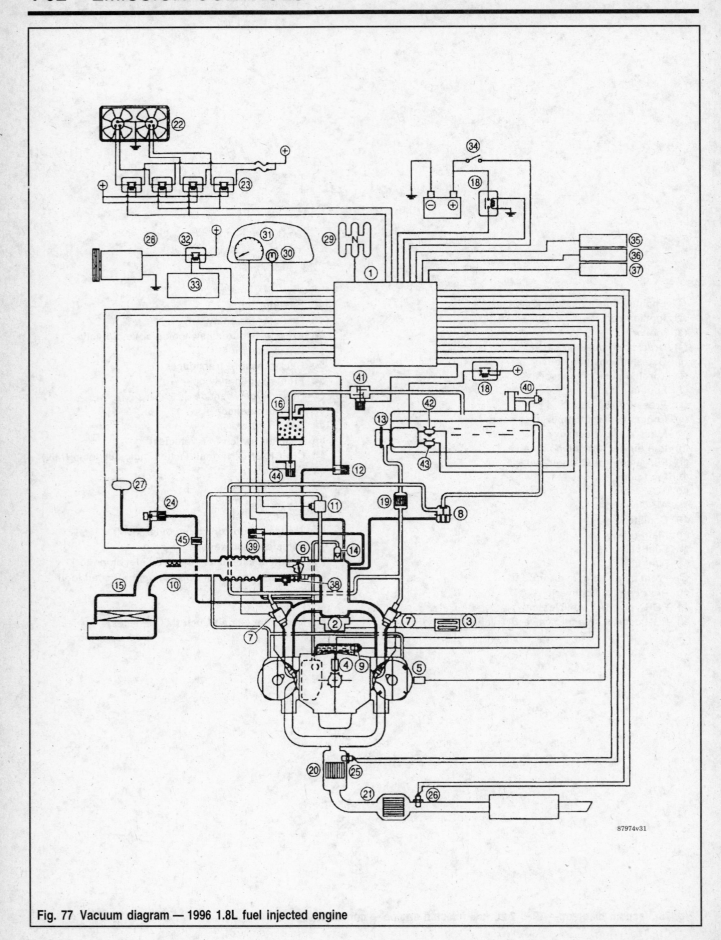

Fig. 77 Vacuum diagram — 1996 1.8L fuel injected engine

① Engine control module (ECM)
② Ignition coil
③ Ignitor
④ Crankshaft position sensor
⑤ Camshaft position sensor
⑥ Throttle position sensor
⑦ Fuel injectors
⑧ Pressure regulator
⑨ Engine coolant temperature sensor
⑩ Mass air flow sensor
⑪ Idle air control solenoid valve
⑫ Purge control solenoid valve
⑬ Fuel pump
⑭ PCV valve
⑮ Air cleaner
⑯ Canister
⑰ Main relay
⑱ Fuel pump relay
⑲ Fuel filter
⑳ Front catalytic converter
㉑ Rear catalytic converter
㉒ Radiator fan
㉓ Radiator fan relay

㉔ Pressure sources switching solenoid valve
㉕ Front oxygen sensor
㉖ Rear oxygen sensor
㉗ Pressure sensor
㉘ A/C compressor (With A/C models)
㉙ Neutral position switch
㉚ CHECK ENGINE malfunction indicator lamp (MIL)
㉛ Tachometer
㉜ A/C relay (With A/C models)
㉝ A/C control module (With A/C models)
㉞ Ignition switch
㉟ Vehicle speed sensor
㊱ Data link connector (For Subaru select monitor)
㊲ Data link connector (For Subaru select monitor and OBD-II general scan tool)
㊳ Throttle opener
㊴ FICD solenoid valve (With A/C models)
㊵ Fuel tank pressure sensor
㊶ Pressure control solenoid valve
㊷ Fuel temperature sensor
㊸ Fuel level sensor
㊹ Vent control solenoid valve
㊺ Filter

87974v37

Fig. 78 Vacuum diagram — 1996 1.8L fuel injected engine (continued)

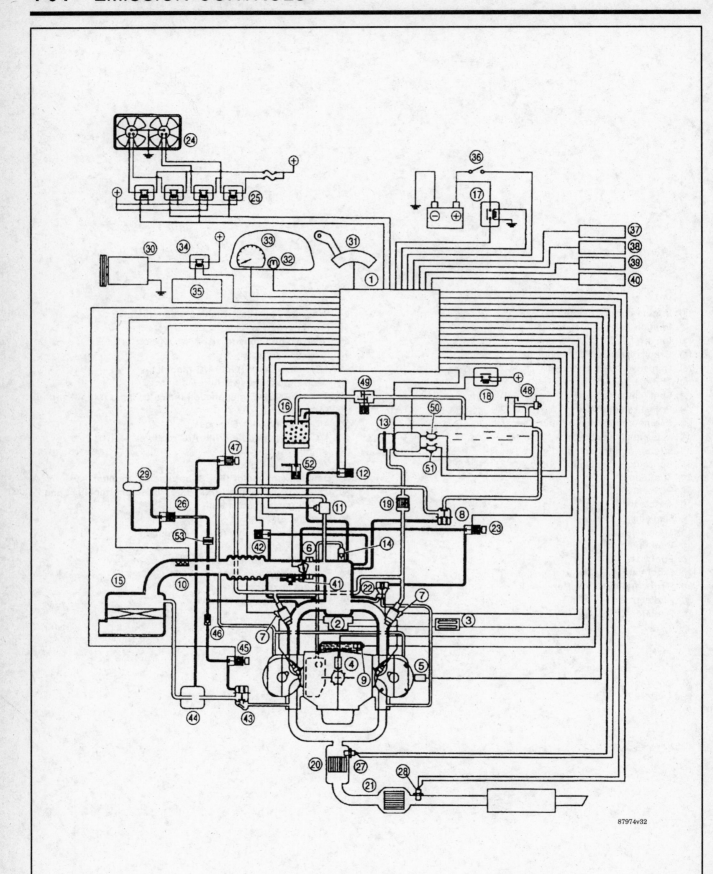

Fig. 79 Vacuum diagram — 1996 1.8L fuel injected engine

87974v32

① Engine control module (ECM)
② Ignition coil
③ Ignitor
④ Crankshaft position sensor
⑤ Camshaft position sensor
⑥ Throttle position sensor
⑦ Fuel injectors
⑧ Pressure regulator
⑨ Engine coolant temperature sensor
⑩ Mass air flow sensor
⑪ Idle air control solenoid valve
⑫ Purge control solenoid valve
⑬ Fuel pump
⑭ PCV valve
⑮ Air cleaner
⑯ Canister
⑰ Main relay
⑱ Fuel pump relay
⑲ Fuel filter
⑳ Front catalytic converter
㉑ Rear catalytic converter
㉒ EGR valve
㉓ EGR control solenoid valve
㉔ Radiator fan
㉕ Radiator fan relay
㉖ Pressure sources switching solenoid valve
㉗ Front oxygen sensor

㉘ Rear oxygen sensor
㉙ Pressure sensor
㉚ A/C compressor (With A/C models)
㉛ Inhibitor switch
㉜ CHECK ENGINE malfunction indicator lamp (MIL)
㉝ Tachometer
㉞ A/C relay (With A/C models)
㉟ A/C control module (With A/C models)
㊱ Ignition switch
㊲ Transmission control module (TCM)
㊳ Vehicle speed sensor
㊴ Data link connector (For Subaru select monitor)
㊵ Data link connector (For Subaru select monitor and OBD-II general scan tool)
㊶ Throttle opener
㊷ FICD solenoid valve (With A/C models)
㊸ Air suction valve
㊹ ASV silencer
㊺ ASV solenoid valve
㊻ Check valve
㊼ Air injection system diagnosis solenoid valve
㊽ Fuel tank pressure sensor
㊾ Pressure control solenoid valve
㊿ Fuel temperature sensor
51 Fuel level sensor
52 Vent control solenoid valve
53 Filter

87974v33

Fig. 80 Vacuum diagram — 1996 1.8L fuel injected engine (continued)

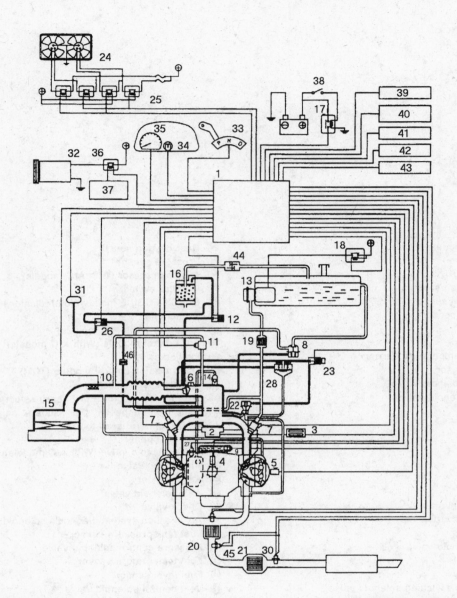

1. Engine control module (ECM)
2. Ignition coil
3. Ignitor
4. Crankshaft position sensor
5. Camshaft position sensor
6. Throttle position sensor
7. Fuel injectors
8. Pressure regulator
9. Engine coolant temperature sensor
10. Mass air flow sensor
11. Idle air control solenoid valve
12. Purge control solenoid valve
13. Fuel pump
14. PCV valve
15. Air cleaner
16. Canister
17. Main relay
18. Fuel pump relay
19. Fuel filter

20. Front catalytic converter
21. Rear catalytic converter
22. EGR valve (AT vehicles only)
23. EGR control solenoid valve (AT vehicles only)
24. Radiator fan
25. Radiator fan relay
26. Pressure sources switching solenoid valve
27. Knock sensor
28. Back-pressure transducer (AT vehicles only)
29. Front oxygen sensor
30. Rear oxygen sensor (Except 2200 cc California model)
31. Pressure sensor
32. A/C compressor
33. Inhibitor switch

34. CHECK ENGINE malfunction indicator lamp (MIL)
35. Tachometer
36. A/C relay
37. A/C control module
38. Ignition switch
39. Transmission control module (TCM) (AT vehicles only)
40. ABS/TCS control module (TCS equipped models)
41. Vehicle speed sensor
42. Data link connector (For Subaru select monitor)
43. Data link connector (For Subaru select monitor and OBD-II general scan tool)
44. Two way valve
45. Rear oxygen sensor (2200 cc California model only)
46. Filter

87974v30

Fig. 81 Vacuum diagram — 1996 2.2L fuel injected engine

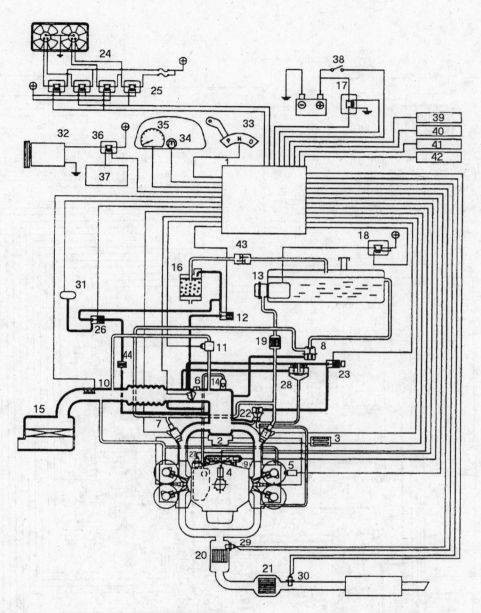

1. Engine control module (ECM)
2. Ignition coil
3. Ignitor
4. Crankshaft position sensor
5. Camshaft position sensor
6. Throttle position sensor
7. Fuel injectors
8. Pressure regulator
9. Engine coolant temperature sensor
10. Mass air flow sensor
11. Idle air control solenoid valve
12. Purge control solenoid valve
13. Fuel pump
14. PCV valve
15. Air cleaner
16. Canister

17. Main relay
18. Fuel pump relay
19. Fuel filter
20. Front catalytic converter
21. Rear catalytic converter
22. EGR valve
23. EGR control solenoid valve
24. Radiator fan
25. Radiator fan relay
26. Pressure sources switching
    solenoid valve
27. Knock sensor
28. Back-pressure transducer
29. Front oxygen sensor
30. Rear oxygen sensor
31. Pressure sensor

32. A/C compressor
33. Inhibitor switch
34. CHECK ENGINE malfunction indicator
    lamp (MIL)
35. Tachometer
36. A/C relay
37. A/C control module
38. Ignition switch
39. Transmission control module (TCM)
40. Vehicle speed sensor
41. Data link connector (Subaru select monitor)
42. Data link connector (OBD-II general
    scan tool)
43. Two way valve
44. Filter

87974v34

Fig. 82 Vacuum diagram — 1996 2.5L fuel injected engine

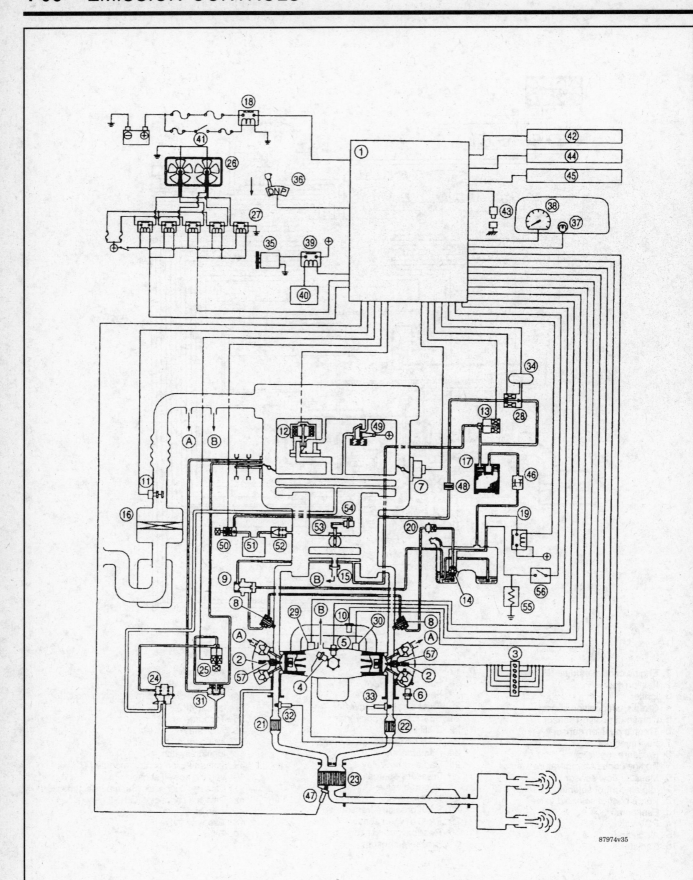

Fig. 83 Vacuum diagram — 1996 3.3L fuel injected engine

87974v35

① Engine control module (ECM)
② Ignition coil
③ Ignitor
④ Crankshaft position sensor 1
⑤ Crankshaft position sensor 2
⑥ Camshaft position sensor
⑦ Throttle position sensor
⑧ Fuel injectors
⑨ Pressure regulator
⑩ Engine coolant temperature sensor
⑪ Mass air flow sensor
⑫ Idle air control solenoid valve
⑬ Purge control solenoid valve
⑭ Fuel pump
⑮ PCV valve
⑯ Air cleaner
⑰ Canister
⑱ Main relay
⑲ Fuel pump relay
⑳ Fuel filter
㉑ Front catalytic converter (RH)
㉒ Front catalytic converter (LH)
㉓ Rear catalytic converter
㉔ EGR valve
㉕ EGR control solenoid valve
㉖ Radiator fan
㉗ Radiator fan relay
㉘ Pressure sources switching solenoid valve
㉙ Knock sensor 1

㉚ Knock sensor 2
㉛ Back-pressure transducer (BPT)
㉜ Front oxygen sensor 1 (RH)
㉝ Front oxygen sensor 2 (LH)
㉞ Pressure sensor
㉟ A/C compressor
㊱ Inhibitor switch
㊲ CHECK ENGINE malfunction indicator lamp (MIL)
㊳ Tachometer
㊴ A/C relay
㊵ A/C control module
㊶ Ignition switch
㊷ Transmission control module (TCM)
㊸ Vehicle speed sensor 2
㊹ Data link connector (For Subaru select monitor)
㊺ Data link connector (For Subaru select monitor and OBD-II general scan tool)
㊻ Two-way valve
㊼ Rear oxygen sensor
㊽ Filter
㊾ Auxiliary air control valve
㊿ Induction control solenoid valve
51 Vacuum tank
52 Check valve
53 Induction control valve
54 Induction valve diaphragm
55 Resistor
56 Fuel pump modulator
57 Spark plug

87974v36

Fig. 84 Vacuum diagram — 1996 3.3L fuel injected engine (continued)

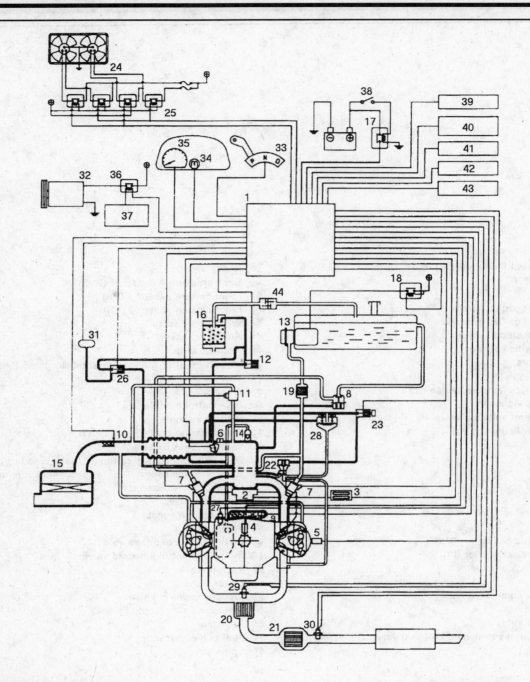

1. Engine control module (ECM)
2. Ignition coil
3. Igniter
4. Crankshaft position sensor
5. Camshaft position sensor
6. Throttle position sensor
7. Fuel injectors
8. Pressure regulator
9. Engine coolant temperature sensor
10. Mass air flow sensor
11. Idle air control solenoid valve
12. Purge control solenoid valve
13. Fuel pump
14. PCV valve
15. Air cleaner
16. Canister
17. Main relay
18. Fuel pump relay
19. Fuel filter
20. Front catalytic converter
21. Rear catalytic converter
22. EGR valve
23. EGR control solenoid valve
24. Radiator fan
25. Radiator fan relay
26. Pressure sources switching solenoid valve (AT model only)
27. Knock sensor
28. Back-pressure transducer (AT model only)
29. Front oxygen sensor
30. Rear oxygen sensor
31. Pressure sensor (AT model only)
32. A/C compressor
33. Inhibitor switch
34. Malfunction indicator lamp (ENGINE CHECK light)
35. Tachometer
36. A/C relay
37. A/C control module
38. Ignition switch
39. Transmission control module (TCM) (AT model only)
40. TCS control module (TCS equipped models)
41. Vehicle speed sensor
42. Data link connector (Subaru select monitor)
43. Data link connector (OBD-II general scan tool)
44. Two way valve

87974v27

Fig. 85 Vacuum diagram — 1995 2.2L fuel injected engine

5

FUEL
SYSTEM

BASIC FUEL SYSTEM DIAGNOSIS

When there is a problem starting or driving a vehicle, two of the most important checks involve the ignition and the fuel systems. The questions most mechanics attempt to answer first, "is there spark?" and "is there fuel?" will often lead to solving most basic problems. For ignition system diagnosis and testing, please refer to the information on engine electrical components and ignition systems found earlier in this manual. If the ignition system checks out (there is spark), then you must determine if the fuel system is operating properly (is there fuel?).

CARBURETED FUEL SYSTEM

Electric Fuel Pump

REMOVAL & INSTALLATION

1.2L Engine

▶ See Figures 1, 2 and 3

1. Disconnect the negative battery cable.
2. Remove the three fuel pump/filter bracket bolts.
3. Place a drip pan beneath the fuel pump to catch any spilled fuel.
4. Pinch off the fuel lines from the fuel pump.
5. Disconnect the fuel pump electrical harness.
6. Remove the fuel pump-to-bracket bolts and remove the fuel pump.

To install:

7. Position the fuel pump on the bracket and install the mounting bolts.
8. Connect the electrical harness to the fuel pump.
9. Connect the fuel lines to the fuel pump.
10. Position the fuel pump/filter bracket and install the three mounting bolts.
11. Connect the negative battery cable.

1.6L and 1.8L Engines

▶ See Figure 4

1. Disconnect the negative battery cable.

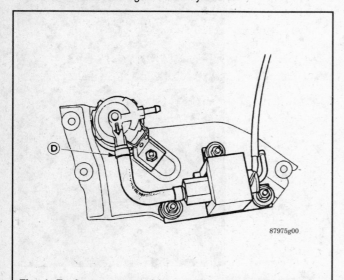

Fig. 1 Fuel pump assembly — 1.2L carbureted engine

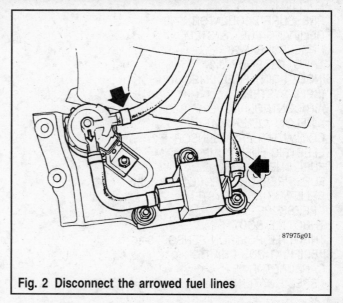

Fig. 2 Disconnect the arrowed fuel lines

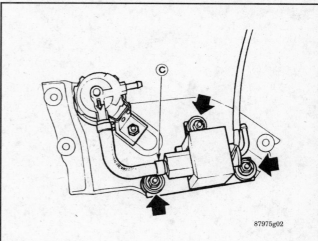

Fig. 3 Unfasten the indicated nuts to remove the fuel pump

2. Raise and safely support the vehicle.
3. Place a drip pan beneath the inlet side fuel connection.
4. Pinch off the inlet side of the fuel filter to minimize fuel loss.
5. Disconnect the electrical harness from the fuel pump.
6. Remove the three screws securing the fuel bracket to the vehicle and pull the bracket and pump down as a unit.
7. Remove the three nuts securing the fuel pump to the bracket.

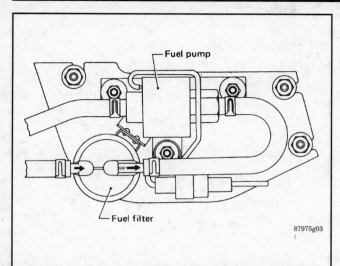

Fig. 4 Fuel pump assembly — 1.6L and 1.8L carbureted engines

8. Disconnect the inlet and outlet hoses from the fuel pump.

9. Remove the pump from the vehicle.

10. Remove the fuel pump-to-bracket bolts and remove the fuel pump.

To install:

11. Install the mounting cushions to the fuel pump.

12. Position the fuel pump on the mounting bracket and install the three mounting nuts and washers.

13. Connect the inlet and outlet lines to the fuel pump.

14. Position the pump and bracket assembly to the frame and install the three mounting bolts.

15. Install the clips securing the fuel pipes to the fuel line assembly.

16. Connect the electrical harness to the fuel pump.

17. Unclamp the fuel inlet line.

18. Lower the vehicle.

19. Connect the negative battery cable.

20. Pressurize the fuel system and verify that there are no leaks.

PRESSURE TESTING

1. Raise and support the vehicle safely on jackstands.

2. Disconnect the fuel line at the outlet side of the fuel pump, then connect a fuel pressure gauge to the fuel pump.

3. Turn the ignition switch **ON** and observe the fuel pressure; it should be 2.6-3.3 psi (5.2-6.6 in Hg). If the fuel pump does not meet this specification, replace the pump.

4. After testing, disconnect the pressure gauge and reconnect the fuel line.

5. Lower the vehicle.

Carburetor

Three types of carburetor are used on Subaru vehicles. All 1.2L engines use a DFC-328 carburetor; 1.6L engines use a DCP-306 carburetor and 1.8L engines use a DCZ-328 carburetor.

The carburetor supplies the correct mixture of fuel and air to the engine under varying conditions. Despite their complexity in design, carburetors function because of a simple physical principle (the venturi principle). Air is drawn into the engine by the pumping action of the pistons. As air enters the top of the carburetor it passes through a venturi, which is nothing more than a restriction in the throttle bore. The air speeds up as it passes through the venturi, causing a slight drop in pressure. The pressure drop pulls fuel from the float bowl through a nozzle into the throttle bore, where it mixes with the air and forms a fine mist which is distributed to the cylinders through the intake manifold.

The carburetor uses a progressive linkage between the primary and secondary circuit. For optimum performance plus fuel economy, the secondary circuit of the carburetor is used only at high engine rpm. Normal low speed operation is handled by the primary circuit.

On later models, the carburetor is provided with a coasting bypass system which helps control exhaust emissions during deceleration.

An automatic control choke is used on all carburetors. The automatic choke and a throttle chamber are heated by engine coolant to prevent throttle bore icing, help the engine start and run well in the coldest conditions.

The basic systems of the carburetor are:

1. The float system
2. The primary side
   a. Slow system
   b. Main system
   c. Accelerator pump
   d. Power system
   e. Choke system
   f. Slow float shutoff system
3. Secondary side
   a. Step system
   b. Main system
4. Coasting bypass system.

➡**If you are planning to clean, rebuild or replace your carburetor, be sure you understand what is necessary. Read all instructions, have all parts and tools on hand and keep everything as clean as possible. Remember that gasoline mileage and performance depend on how well you do the job.**

ADJUSTMENTS

Automatic Choke Mechanism

▶ **See Figures 5 and 6**

1. With the carburetor removed from the engine, set the fast idle cam adjusting lever on the fourth highest step of the fast idle cam.

2. Check to be sure that the choke valve is fully closed.

3. Measure the clearance between the lower edge of the primary throttle valve and the bore.

4. Measurement should be as follows:
   - DFC-328: 0.0303 in. (0.77mm)
   - DCZ-328: 0.0472-0.0587 in. (1.20-1.49mm)
   - DCP-306: 0.0386-0.0528 in. (0.98-1.34mm)

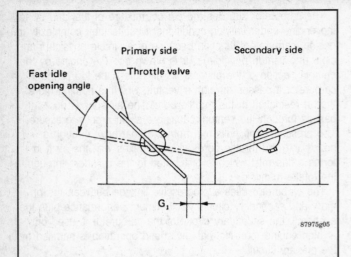

Fig. 5 Throttle valve measurement — 1.2L carbureted engine

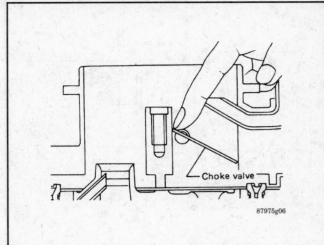

Fig. 7 Using a finger to hold the choke valve closed — 1.2L carbureted engine

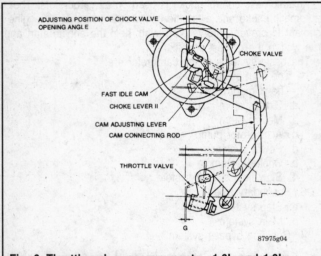

Fig. 6 Throttle valve measurement — 1.6L and 1.8L carbureted engines

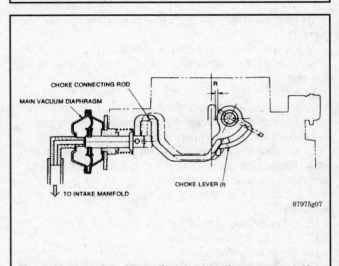

Fig. 8 Vacuum break opening angle adjustment — 1.6L and 1.8L carbureted engines

5. If not within specification, turn the fast idle adjusting screw.

Vacuum Break Opening Angle
▶ **See Figures 7 and 8**

1. Move the throttle lever while lightly holding the choke valve with your hand, to keep it fully closed. Release your hand to make sure the choke valve is fully closed.

2. With the choke valve closed, connect a portable vacuum pump to the vacuum break diaphragm and continue to apply vacuum pressure until the diaphragm shaft moves a complete stroke toward the diaphragm.

3. Measure the clearance (R) while lightly holding the choke valve with your hand. Clearance should be as follows:
- DFC-328: 0.063 in. (1.6mm)
- DCZ-328: 0.059-0.075 in. (1.5-1.9mm)
- DCP-306: 0.059-0.075 in. (1.5-1.9mm)

4. If not within specification, adjust by bending the pawl at the tip of the lever.

Float and Fuel Level
▶ **See Figures 9, 10, 11 and 12**

The float level may be adjusted with the carburetor installed on the engine, by removing the air horn as follows:

1. Disconnect the accelerator pump actuating rod from the pump lever.

2. Remove the throttle return spring.

3. Disconnect the choke cable from the choke lever, and remove it from the spring hanger.

4. Remove the spring hanger, the choke bellcrank and the remaining air horn retaining screws.

5. Lift the air horn slightly, disconnect the choke connecting rod, and remove the air horn.

6. Invert the air horn (float up), and measure the distance between the surface of the air horn and the float.

7. Clearance should be as follows:
- DFC-328: 0.437 in. (11.1mm)
- DCZ-328: 0.435-0.492 in. (11.5-12.5mm)
- DCP-306: 0.393 in. (10mm)

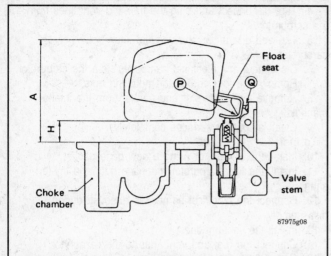

Fig. 9 Float and fuel level adjustment — 1.2L carbureted engine

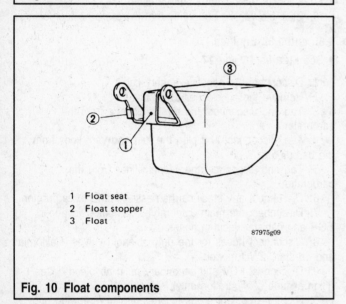

1 Float seat
2 Float stopper
3 Float

Fig. 10 Float components

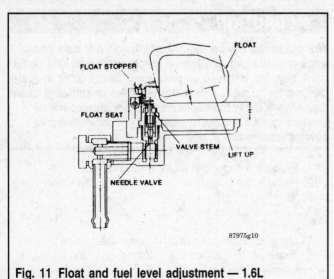

Fig. 11 Float and fuel level adjustment — 1.6L carbureted engine

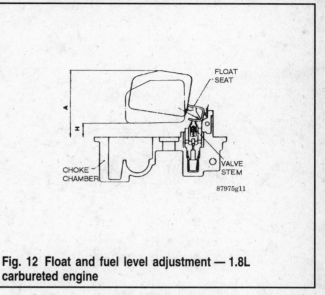

Fig. 12 Float and fuel level adjustment — 1.8L carbureted engine

8. If not within specification, bend the float arm until the clearance is correct.

9. Invert the air horn to its installed position.

10. On the DCZ-328 and DCP-306 carburetors, measure the distance between the float arm and the needle valve seat. On the DFC-328 carburetor, measure the distance between the choke chamber and the bottom of the float.

11. Clearance should be as follows:
- DCF-328: 1.835 in. (46.6mm)
- DCZ-328: 0.059-0.075 in. (1.5-1.9mm)
- DCP-306: 0.051-0.067 in. (1.3-1.7mm)

12. If not within specification, adjust by bending the float stops.

Primary/Secondary Throttle Linkage
▶ **See Figures 13 and 14**

1. With the carburetor removed from the engine, operate the linkage so that the connecting rod contacts the groove on the end of the secondary actuating lever.

2. Measure the clearance between the lower end of the primary throttle valve and its bore.

3. Clearance should be as follows:
- DFC-328: 0.236 in. (6.0mm)
- DCZ-328: 0.271-0.275 in. (6.89-6.99mm)
- DCP-306: 0.236 in. (6.0mm)

4. If not within specification, adjust the clearance by bending the connecting rod.

5. Check to make sure that the linkage operates smoothly after performing the adjustment.

REMOVAL & INSTALLATION

1.2L Engine
▶ **See Figure 15**

1. Disconnect the negative battery cable.
2. Remove the air cleaner assembly.
3. Tag and disconnect the throttle linkage from the carburetor.

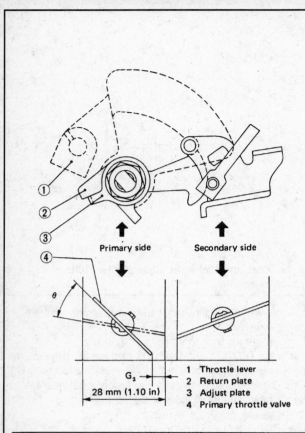

1	Throttle lever
2	Return plate
3	Adjust plate
4	Primary throttle valve

| Clearance G₂ | 6.0 mm (0.236 in) |
| Opening angle θ | 47° |

87975g13

Fig. 13 Measuring throttle valve opening — 1.2L carbureted engine

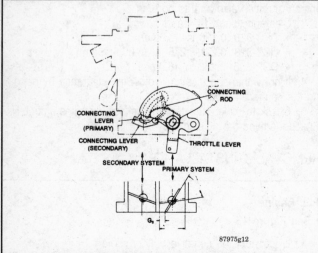

87975g12

Fig. 14 Measuring throttle valve opening — 1.6L and 1.8L carbureted engines

4. Tag, disconnect and plug the fuel and vent lines from the carburetor.

5. Tag and disconnect the vacuum lines from the carburetor.

6. Disconnect any electrical harnesses from the carburetor.

7. Remove the four carburetor mounting nuts.

8. Remove the carburetor and gasket from the intake manifold.

9. Clean all gasket surfaces completely.

To install:

10. Install the carburetor using a new base gasket.

11. Install the four carburetor mounting nuts and tighten snugly.

12. Connect the electrical harnesses removed during disassembly.

13. Install the vacuum lines.

14. Connect the fuel and vent lines to the carburetor.

15. Connect the throttle linkage.

16. Install the air cleaner assembly.

17. Connect the negative battery cable.

18. Start the vehicle and verify that there are no fuel leaks.

1.6L and 1.8L Engines

▶ See Figures 16 and 17

1. Disconnect the negative battery cable.

2. Remove the air cleaner assembly.

3. Tag and disconnect the throttle linkage from the carburetor.

4. Tag, disconnect and plug the fuel and vent lines from the carburetor.

5. Tag and disconnect the vacuum lines from the carburetor.

6. Disconnect any electrical harnesses from the carburetor.

7. Disconnect the main diaphragm, distributor advancer, EGR and canister vacuum hoses.

8. Disconnect hoses for the duty solenoid valves (California and 49 state 2WD models).

9. Disconnect FCV and secondary main air bleed hoses (High altitude configuration only).

10. Drain the coolant so as to prevent it from flowing out.

✳✳CAUTION

When draining the coolant, keep in mind that cats and dogs are attracted to ethylene glycol antifreeze, and could drink any that is left in an uncovered container or in puddles on the ground. This will prove fatal in sufficient quantity. Always drain the coolant into a sealable container. Coolant should be reused unless it is contaminated or several years old.

11. Remove the four carburetor mounting nuts.

12. Remove the carburetor and gasket from the intake manifold.

13. Clean all gasket surfaces completely.

To install:

14. Install the carburetor using a new base gasket.

15. Install the four carburetor mounting nuts, and tighten them snugly.

16. Connect the electrical harnesses removed during disassembly.

17. Install the vacuum lines.

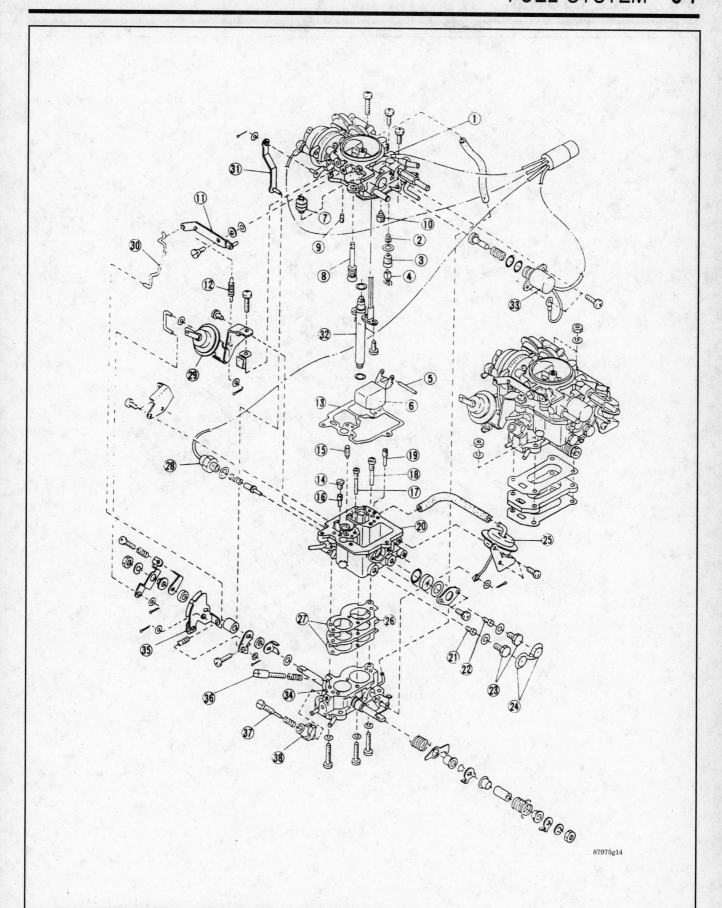

Fig. 15 Exploded view of carburetor assembly — 1.2L carbureted engine

87975g14

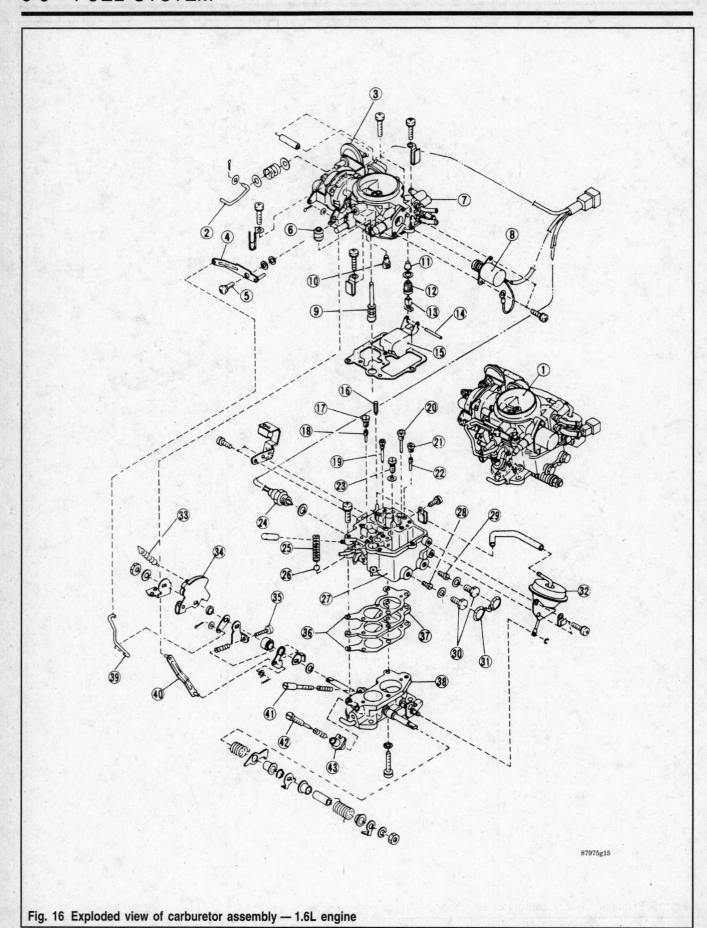

Fig. 16 Exploded view of carburetor assembly — 1.6L engine

87975g15

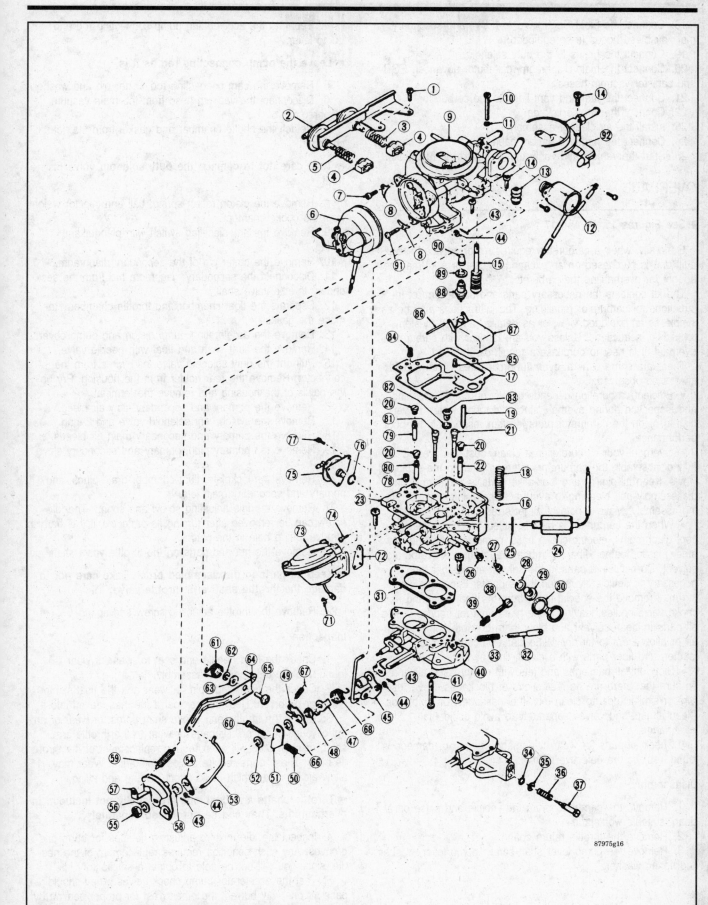

Fig. 17 Exploded view of carburetor assembly — 1.8L engine

87975g16

18. Connect the Float Control Valve (FCV) and secondary main air bleed hoses (if so equipped).
19. Connect the hoses to the duty solenoid.
20. Connect the main diaphragm, distributor advancer, EGR and canister vacuum hoses.
21. Connect the fuel and vent lines to the carburetor.
22. Connect the throttle linkage.
23. Install the air cleaner assembly.
24. Connect the negative battery cable.
25. Start the vehicle and verify that there are no fuel leaks.

OVERHAUL

▶ **See Figures 15, 16 and 17**

Generally, when a carburetor requires major service, a rebuilt one is purchased on an exchange basis, or a kit may be bought for overhauling the carburetor.

The kit contains the necessary parts and some form of instructions for carburetor rebuilding. The instructions may be as simple as an exploded view, or as detailed as step-by-step rebuilding instructions. Unless you are familiar with carburetor overhaul, it is best to purchase a rebuilt carburetor.

There are some general overhaul procedures which should always be observed:

• Efficient carburetion depends greatly on careful cleaning and inspection during overhaul since dirt, gum, water, or varnish in or on the carburetor parts is often responsible for poor performance.

• Overhaul your carburetor in a clean, dust-free area. Carefully disassemble the carburetor, referring often to the exploded views. Keep all similar and look-alike parts segregated during disassembly and cleaning to avoid accidental interchange during assembly. Make a note of all jet sizes.

• When the carburetor is disassembled, wash all parts (except diaphragms, electric choke units, pump plunger, and any other plastic, leather, fiber, or rubber parts) in clean carburetor solvent. Do not leave parts in the solvent any longer than is necessary to sufficiently loosen the deposits. Excessive cleaning may remove the special finish from the float bowl and choke valve bodies, leaving these parts unfit for service. Rinse all parts in clean solvent and blow them dry with compressed air or allow them to air dry. Wipe clean all cork, plastic, leather, and fiber parts with a clean, lint-free cloth.

• Blow out all passages and jets with compressed air and be sure that there are no restrictions or blockages. Never use wire or similar tools to clean jets, fuel passages, or air bleeds. Clean all jets and valves separately to avoid accidental interchange.

• Check all parts for wear or damage. If wear or damage is found, replace the defective parts.

Disassembly

1. Remove the carburetor from the vehicle and place on a clean, suitable workstand.
2. Remove the throttle return spring.
3. Remove the pump lever shaft screw, pump lever, washer and spring washer.

4. Separate the accelerating pump connecting rod and pump lever.

➡**Leave the pump connecting rod as it is.**

5. Remove the cam connecting rod, cotter pin and washer.
6. Disconnect the vacuum hose from the main vacuum diaphragm.
7. Detach the choke chamber and gasket from the float chamber.

➡**Take care not to damage the duty solenoid valve or float.**

8. Remove the piston return spring, ball and injector weight from the choke chamber.
9. Remove the anti-dieseling switch with plunger and spring.
10. Remove the cotter pin of the secondary diaphragm.
11. Disconnect the secondary diaphragm rod from the secondary throttle valve shaft.
12. Separate the float chamber and throttle chamber. Remove the gasket.
13. Remove the accelerating pump piston and pump cover.
14. Remove the float shaft and float with needle valve.
15. Pull out the duty solenoid valve lead wires from the connector. Remove the rear holder from the housing. Pry up the pawls of the housing and remove the terminal.
16. Remove the primary and secondary slow air bleed.
17. Remove the switch vent solenoid valve and O-ring.
18. Remove the primary and secondary main air bleeds.
19. Remove the primary plug, primary and secondary slow jets.
20. Remove the lockplate, float chamber drain plugs, and primary and secondary main jets.
21. Remove the idle adjusting screw and spring. The idle screw can be removed after turning its protector. If it is hard to remove, drill a hole in the plug.
22. Remove the nut and parts on the throttle valve shaft.

➡**Keep all parts in disassembled order. Take care not to damage the throttle shaft and throttle valve.**

23. Remove the throttle adjusting screw and spring.

Inspection

1. Check the float needle and seat for wear. If wear is found, replace the complete assembly.
2. Check the float hinge pin for wear and the float(s) for dents or distortion. Replace the float if fuel has leaked into it.
3. Check the throttle and choke shaft bores for wear or an out-of-round condition. Damage or wear to the throttle arm, shaft, or shaft bore will often require replacement of the throttle body. These parts require a close tolerance. Wear may allow air leakage, which could affect starting and idling.

➡**Throttle shafts and bushings are usually not included in overhaul kits. They can be purchased separately.**

4. Inspect the idle mixture adjusting needles for burrs or grooves. Any such condition requires replacement of the needle, since you will not be able to obtain a satisfactory idle.
5. Test the accelerator pump check valves. They should pass air one way but not the other. Test for proper seating by blowing and sucking on the valve. Replace the valve if neces-

sary. If the valve is satisfactory, clean the valve with solvent and dry with compressed to remove any moisture.

6. Check the bowl cover for warped surfaces with a straightedge.

7. Closely inspect the valves and seats for wear and damage, replacing as necessary.

8. After the carburetor is assembled, check the choke valve for freedom of operation.

Assembly

1. Attach the switch vent solenoid valve with O-rings.
2. Install the primary and secondary slow air bleeds.
3. Connect the duty solenoid valve.

➡**Apply silicone grease to the O-ring of the duty solenoid valve.**

4. Install the needle valve case washer.
5. Attach the float with needle valve and float shaft, and adjust the float level.
6. Position the accelerating pump piston and pump cover.
7. Attach the primary and secondary main jets and float chamber drain plugs with washers and install the lock plate.
8. Position the primary slow jet and then install the plug.
9. Install the secondary slow jet and then connect the air bleed.
10. Install the primary and secondary main air bleeds.
11. Secure the throttle adjusting screw and spring.
12. Install the adjusting plate, lever, washer, sleeve, etc. onto the throttle valve shaft.
13. Put the flat chamber and throttle chamber together with new gaskets.

➡**Be sure to attach the throttle valve shaft spring to the float chamber body. After installation, check that both the primary and secondary throttle valve move properly.**

14. Install the idle adjusting screw, spring and screw case. Do not attach the plug at this time.
15. Connect the secondary diaphragm rod to the secondary throttle valve shaft.
16. Position the injector weight. Install the ball and piston return spring.

➡**Install the return spring with its hook portion facing downward.**

17. Install the anti-dieseling switch with plunger, spring and washer.
18. Position the throttle chamber on the float chamber with gasket and clamps.
19. Attach the cam connecting rod with cotter pins and plain washers.
20. Connect the accelerating pump connecting rod to the pump lever by inserting the rod end into the hole in the pump lever.
21. Install the pump lever with the pump lever shaft screw, plain washer and spring washer.
22. Connect the idle-up actuator.

➡**When installing the idle-up actuator, securely tighten the idle adjusting screw so that the throttle valve does not gouge the throttle bore surface.**

23. Attach the throttle return spring.
24. Connect the vacuum hose to the main vacuum diaphragm.
25. Make sure that all linkages operate smoothly and all lead wires are routed properly.
26. Install the carburetor and adjust the idle speed and idle mixture.

| | 1985-86 | | | | | | | | | |
| | DCP306-17 ① | | DCP306-18 ② | | DCP306-19 ③ | | DCP306-21 ④ | | DCP306-22 ⑤ | |
	Primary	Secondary	Primary	Secondary	Primary	Secondary	Primary	Secondary	Primary	Secondary
Main jet	#116	#145	#114	#145	#114	#145	#109	#140	#109	#145
Slow jet	#43	#80	#43	#80	#43	#80	#43	#80	#43	#80
Main air bleed	#60	#80	#60	#80	#60	#80	#70	#80	#70	#80
Slow air bleed	#50	#150	#50	#150	#50	#150	#160	#90	#150	#90
Power valve	#50		#50		#50		#35		plugged	
Econ. Bleed	#95	#90	#95	#90	#95	#90	#95	#90	#95	#90
Acc. Pump Nozzle	.020		.020		.020		.020		.020	

① 1600 engines only
② 1800 man. Cal and 2WD 49 states
③ 1800 auto. Cal and 2WD 49 states
④ 1800 man. Canada and 4WD 49 states
⑤ 1800 auto. Canada and 4WD 49 states

87975c01

SINGLE POINT FUEL INJECTION (SPFI) SYSTEM

◆ **See Figures 18 and 19**

The Single Point Fuel Injection (SPFI) system is used on the 1.8L engine only. The system electronically controls the amount of injection from the fuel injector, and supplies the optimum air/fuel mixture under all operating conditions of the engine. Features of the SPFI system are as follows:

• Precise control of the air/fuel mixture is accomplished by an increased number of input signals transmitting engine operating conditions to the control unit.

• The use of hot a wire type airflow meter not only eliminates the need for high altitude compensation, but improves driving performance at high altitudes.

• The air control valve automatically regulates the idle speed to the set value under all engine operating conditions.

• Ignition timing is electrically controlled, thereby allowing the use of complicated spark advance characteristics.

• Wear of the airflow meter and fuel injector is automatically corrected so that they maintain their original performance.

• Troubleshooting can easily be accomplished by the built-in self-diagnosis function.

Relieving Fuel System Pressure

➡**This procedure must be performed prior to servicing any component of the fuel injection system.**

1. Disconnect the fuel pump harness at the fuel pump.
2. Crank the engine for 5 seconds or more to relieve the fuel pressure. If the engine starts during this time, allow it to run until it stalls.
3. Connect the fuel pump harness.

Electric Fuel Pump

REMOVAL & INSTALLATION

◆ **See Figure 20**

1. Release the fuel system pressure. Do not reconnect the fuel pump harness.
2. Disconnect the negative battery cable.
3. Raise and support the vehicle safely on jackstands.
4. Clamp the middle portion of the hose connecting the fuel tank pipe and the pump to prevent fuel from flowing out of the tank when unfastened.
5. Loosen the hose clamp and disconnect the hose.
6. Remove the three pump bracket mounting bolts and remove the pump together with the pump damper.

To install:

7. Install the fuel pump and damper, and tighten the bolts securely.
8. Install the hose and tighten the clamp screw to 9-13 inch lbs. (1.0-1.5 Nm).

9. Install the pump bracket in position to the vehicle body and secure it with the bolts.

➡**Take care to position the rubber cushion properly.**

10. Connect the pump harness.
11. Connect the negative battery cable and test the fuel pump for proper operation.
12. Check for fuel leaks.

TESTING

1. Turn the ignition **ON** and listen for the fuel pump to make a growling sound. Turn the ignition **OFF**.
2. Release the fuel system pressure. Disconnect the pump harness and crank the engine for 5 seconds or more. If the engine starts, allow it to run until it stops. Turn the ignition **OFF** and install the fuel pump connector.
3. Disconnect the fuel hose at the fuel pump.
4. Connect a gauge in-line using a T-fitting.
5. Start the engine and measure the fuel pressure. If the fuel pressure is not 36-50 psi (248-344 kPa), replace the pump.
6. Release the fuel system pressure and remove the gauge.

Throttle Body

REMOVAL & INSTALLATION

◆ **See Figure 21**

1. Disconnect the negative battery cable.
2. Remove the air intake duct.
3. Remove the air control valve inlet hose.
4. Remove the PCV hoses.
5. Label and disconnect all electrical harnesses attached to or on the throttle body.
6. Loosen the throttle body attaching nuts evenly as to not warp the throttle body assembly.
7. Remove the throttle body.
8. Remove and discard the throttle body gasket. Clean any remaining gasket material from both mating surfaces.

To install:

9. Install the throttle body using a new gasket. Tighten the retainer nuts to 13-15 ft. lbs. (18-21 Nm).
10. Connect the electrical harnesses.
11. Install the air control valve inlet hose and PCV hoses.
12. Install the air intake duct.
13. Connect the negative battery cable.
14. Start the engine and listen for leaks. Correct as necessary.

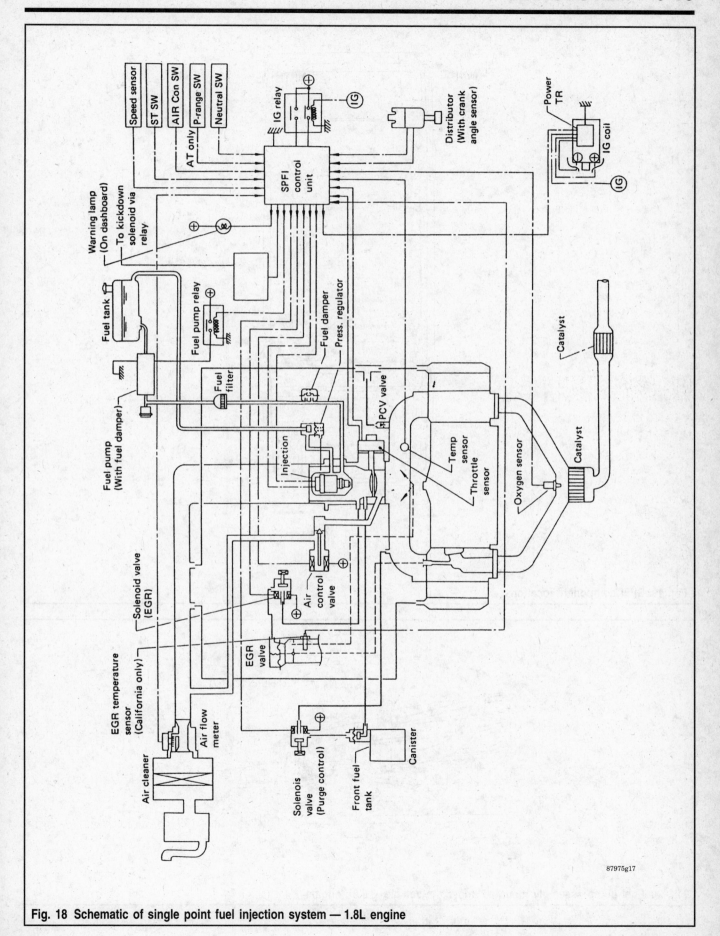

Fig. 18 Schematic of single point fuel injection system — 1.8L engine

87975g17

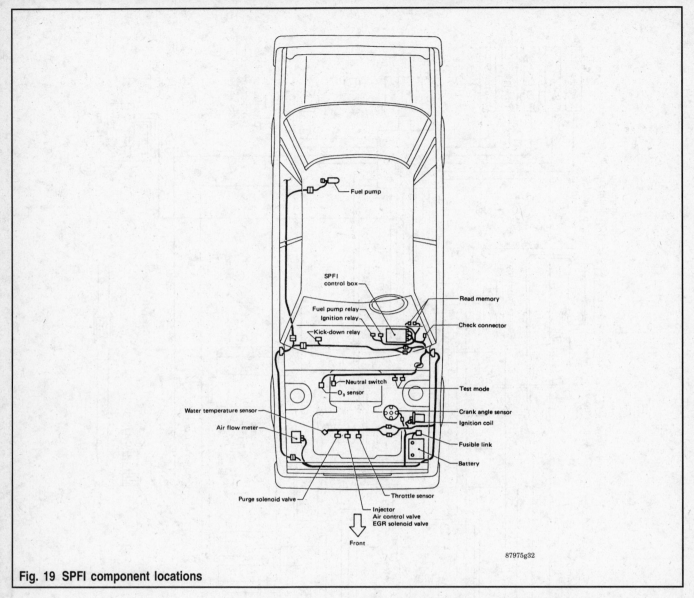

Fig. 19 SPFI component locations

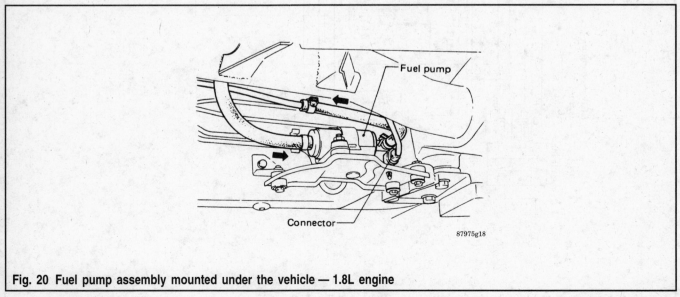

Fig. 20 Fuel pump assembly mounted under the vehicle — 1.8L engine

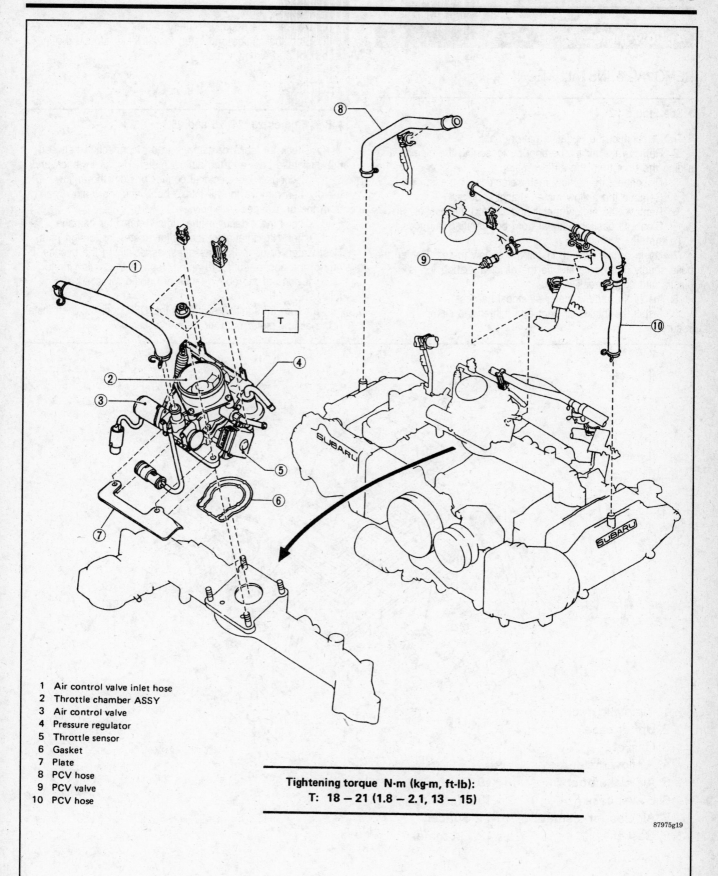

1 Air control valve inlet hose
2 Throttle chamber ASSY
3 Air control valve
4 Pressure regulator
5 Throttle sensor
6 Gasket
7 Plate
8 PCV hose
9 PCV valve
10 PCV hose

Tightening torque N·m (kg-m, ft-lb):
   T: 18 — 21 (1.8 — 2.1, 13 — 15)

Fig. 21 Throttle body assembly — 1.8L engine

87975g19

Airflow Meter

REMOVAL & INSTALLATION

▶ **See Figure 22**

1. Disconnect the negative battery cable.
2. Remove the air intake boot by loosening the clamps and sliding the boot from the airflow meter.
3. Disconnect the airflow meter electrical harness.
4. Remove the airflow meter attaching bolts.
5. Remove the airflow meter and discard the gasket.
6. Clean all gasket material from both mating surfaces.

To install:

7. Using a new gasket, install the airflow meter. Tighten the bolts snugly, but be careful as the air cleaner housing is plastic and could break easily.
8. Install the airflow meter electrical harness.
9. Install the intake air boot and tighten the clamps securely.
10. Connect the negative battery cable.
11. Start the engine and listen for air leaks around the intake boot and airflow meter.

TESTING

▶ **See Figures 23, 24, 25 and 26**

1. Check for leaks or damage in the connection between the air intake boot and the airflow meter. Repair if necessary.
2. Disconnect the electrical connector from the airflow meter, then remove the air intake boot, and the airflow meter from the air cleaner assembly.
3. Check the exterior of the airflow meter for damage.
4. Check the interior of the airflow meter for foreign particles, water, or oil in the passages, especially in the bypass. If any of the above faults are noted, replace the airflow meter.
5. If none of the above faults are noted, proceed as follows:
   a. Turn the ignition switch to the **OFF** position, then install the airflow meter onto air cleaner assembly.

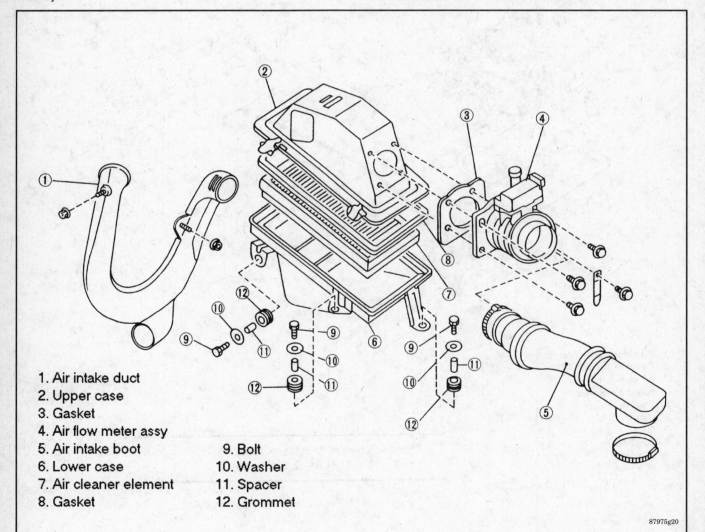

1. Air intake duct
2. Upper case
3. Gasket
4. Air flow meter assy
5. Air intake boot
6. Lower case
7. Air cleaner element
8. Gasket
9. Bolt
10. Washer
11. Spacer
12. Grommet

87975g20

Fig. 22 Airflow meter assembly — 1.8L engine

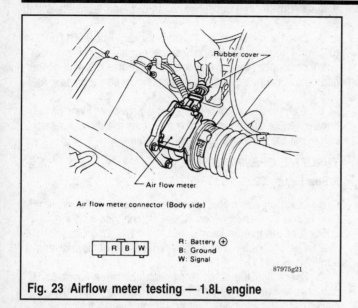

Fig. 23 Airflow meter testing — 1.8L engine

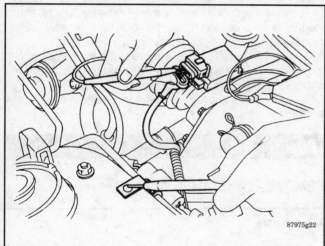

Fig. 24 Testing the resistance between terminal B and ground

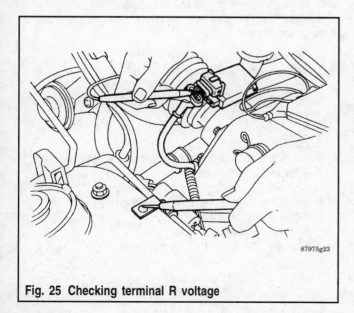

Fig. 25 Checking terminal R voltage

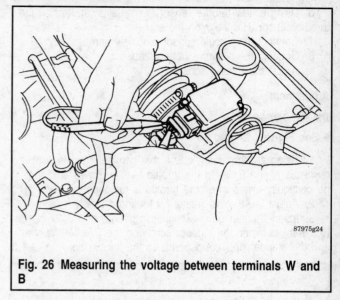

Fig. 26 Measuring the voltage between terminals W and B

b. Disconnect the airflow meter electrical connector, then slide back the rubber boot.

➡Conduct the following test by connecting the tester pins to the connector terminals on the side from which the rubber boot was removed.

c. Using an ohmmeter, measure the resistance between terminal B on the connector and ground. The ohmmeter should read 10 ohms. If the ohmmeter reading exceeds 10 ohms, check the harness and internal circuits of the control unit for discontinuity.

d. Turn the ignition switch to the **ON** position.

e. Using a voltmeter, measure voltage across power terminal R and ground. The voltmeter should read 10 volts. If specifications are not as specified, check the power line (battery, fuse, control unit, harness connector, etc).

f. Connect the airflow meter electrical connector. Using a voltmeter, connect the positive lead of the tester to terminal W and the negative lead of the tester to terminal B, and measure voltage across the 2 terminals. The voltmeter should read 0.1-0.5 volts. If the readings are not as specified, replace the airflow meter.

g. Remove the upper section of the air cleaner assembly, then blow air in from the air cleaner side and check if voltage across terminals W and B is higher than the reading obtained in Step f. If not, replace the airflow meter.

Throttle Position Sensor

REMOVAL & INSTALLATION

1. Disconnect the negative battery cable.
2. Scribe alignment marks on the sensor and throttle body assembly. Remove the 2 screws securing the throttle sensor to the throttle body.
3. Disconnect the throttle sensor electrical harness.
4. Remove the throttle sensor by pulling it in the axial direction of the throttle shaft.
5. Remove the throttle sensor O-ring and discard.

To install:

6. Using a new throttle sensor O-ring, align and install the throttle sensor. Hand-tighten the screw.

7. Connect the throttle sensor electrical harness.

8. Connect the negative battery cable.

9. Adjust the throttle sensor.

Adjustment

IDLE CONTACT

▶ See Figures 27 and 28

1. Using an ohmmeter, check that continuity exists between terminals A and B, when the throttle is fully closed, and that no continuity exists when the throttle is fully opened.

2. Adjust the throttle sensor by turning it slowly.

3. Insert a feeler gauge (thickness gauge) of 0.0122 in. (0.31mm) between the stopper screw on the throttle chamber and the stopper (this corresponds to the throttle opening of 1.0

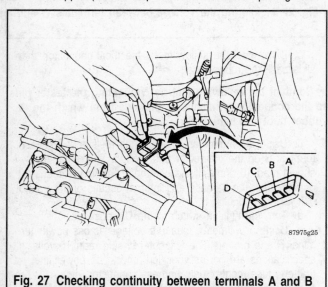

87975g25

Fig. 27 Checking continuity between terminals A and B

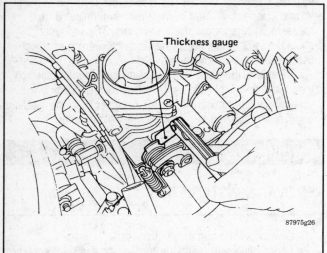

Thickness gauge

87975g26

Fig. 28 Check for continuity after inserting a thickness gauge between the stopper screw and stopper

degree). Ensure that continuity exists between terminals A and B.

4. Insert a feeler gauge (thickness gauge) of 0.0311 in. (0.79mm) between the stopper screw on the throttle chamber and the stopper (this corresponds to a throttle opening of 2.5 degrees). Ensure that continuity exists between terminals A and B.

5. If above specifications are not as specified, loosen the throttle sensor attaching screws, then turn the throttle sensor body until the correct adjustment is obtained.

THROTTLE OPENING SIGNAL

▶ See Figure 29

1. Using an ohmmeter, measure resistance between terminals B and D, then between B and C (changes with the opening of the throttle valve).

2. The ohmmeter should read 3.5-6.5 kilo-ohms between terminals B and D.

3. Check that the ohmmeter reading between terminals B and C is less than 1 kilo-ohm with the throttle valve fully closed, and 2.4 kilo-ohms with the throttle valve fully opened.

4. When the throttle valve is moved from the fully closed to the fully opened position, check that resistance between terminals B and C increases continuously.

5. When the throttle valve is moved from the fully opened to the fully closed position, check that resistance between terminals B and C decreases continuously.

6. If any of the above faults are noted, replace the throttle sensor.

Fuel Injector

REMOVAL & INSTALLATION

▶ See Figure 30

1. Disconnect the negative battery cable.

➡This procedure may be performed with the throttle body mounted on the intake manifold or removed. If the throttle body is mounted on the intake manifold during servicing, ensure that debris does not fall into the intake manifold through the throttle body.

2. Remove the air intake boot.

3. Remove the injector cap and gasket.

4. Disconnect the injector electrical harness.

5. Hold the injector body using pliers to avoid risk, then pull the injector from the throttle body.

6. Remove the O-ring and discard.

To install:

7. Using a new O-ring coated with clean engine oil, install the injector in the throttle body.

8. Connect the injector electrical harness.

9. Install the injector cap using a new gasket.

10. Install the air intake boot.

11. Connect the negative battery cable.

12. Start the vehicle and check for leaks.

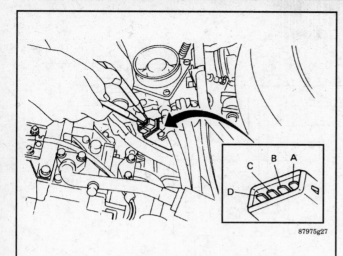

Fig. 29 Check continuity between terminals B and D, then terminals B and C

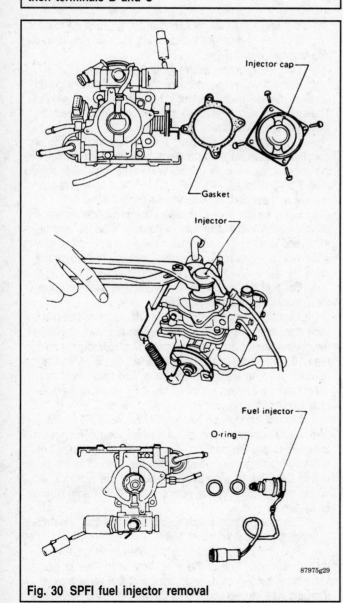

Fig. 30 SPFI fuel injector removal

TESTING

▶ **See Figures 31 and 32**

1. Using a stethoscope, ensure that a clicking sound is heard at the injector (when idling or cranking the engine). If a clicking noise is not heard, proceed as follows:

a. Turn the ignition switch to the **OFF** position, then disconnect the control unit connector.

b. Using an ohmmeter, measure resistance between terminal 43 (RW) and terminal 48 (RB) on the harness connector. The ohmmeter should read 0.5-2 ohms.

2. Check the injector for discontinuity as follows:

a. Disconnect the electrical connector from the injector.

b. Using an ohmmeter, measure the resistance between the terminals of the connector. The ohmmeter should read 0.5-2 ohms.

c. If the readings are not as specified, replace the injector.

3. Check the injector for insulation as follows:

a. Using an ohmmeter, measure resistance between each terminal of the connector on the injector side and ground. The ohmmeter should read 1 mega-ohm.

b. If the readings are not as specified, replace the injector.

4. If specifications obtained in Step 1 are not as specified, but those obtained in Steps 2 and 3 are within specifications, check the harness for discontinuity and the connector for poor connection.

Air Control Valve

REMOVAL & INSTALLATION

▶ **See Figure 33**

1. Disconnect the negative battery cable.
2. Disconnect the injector lead wire from the clamp.
3. Remove the air control valve retainer screws and valve assembly, gasket and lead wire from the venturi chamber.
4. Remove all gasket material from both mating surfaces.
To install:
5. Using a new gasket, install the air control valve. Secure in place using the retainer screws tightened snugly.
6. Connect the injector lead wire.
7. Connect the negative battery cable.

TESTING

1. Disconnect the electrical harness to the air control valve while the engine is idling. Check and make sure the engine rpm drops.

2. Connect the air control valve harness, and make sure that the engine rpm returns to the original level.

➡ Detaching the connector causes a change in the engine rpm when the engine is cold. However, when the engine is warm, it causes a smaller change or almost no change at all.

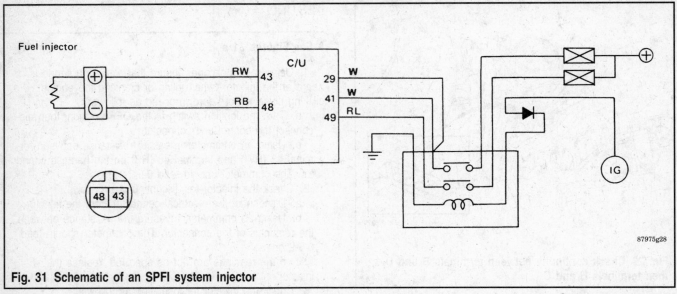

Fig. 31 Schematic of an SPFI system injector

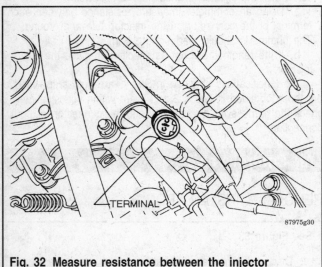

Fig. 32 Measure resistance between the injector terminals

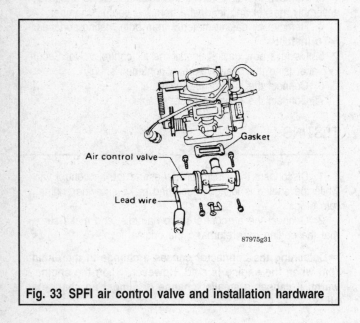

Fig. 33 SPFI air control valve and installation hardware

3. If the engine shows no rpm change, proceed as follows:

a. Stop the engine, then disconnect the electrical harness from the air control valve.

b. Turn the ignition switch to the **ON** position.

c. Using a voltmeter, measure the voltage across power terminal BW on the air control valve connector and ground. The voltmeter should read 10 volts. If voltage obtained is less than specified, check the harness.

d. Turn the ignition switch to the **OFF** position. Using an ohmmeter, measure the resistance between each terminal of the connector on the air control valve. The ohmmeter should read 7.3-13 ohms at -4-176°F (-20-80°C). If specifications are not as specified, replace the air control valve.

e. Using an ohmmeter, measure the insulation resistance between each terminal of the connector on the air control valve and ground. The ohmmeter should read 1 mega-ohm. If the readings are not as specified, replace the air control valve.

f. Connect the air control valve harness, then unfasten the control unit electrical harness.

g. Turn the ignition switch to the **ON** position. Using a voltmeter, measure the voltage between terminal 45 (GR) of the control unit harness and ground. The voltmeter should read 10 volts. If the readings are not as specified, check the harness between the air control valve and the control unit.

h. Turn the ignition switch to the **OFF** position, then attach the control unit connector.

i. Monitor the voltage across terminal 45 (GR) on the control unit connector and ground, when the ignition switch is turned to the **ON** position. The voltmeter should read 1 volt for approximately 1 minute after the ignition switch is turned **ON**, and 10 volts after 1 minute. If the readings are not as specified, check for poor contact of the terminal or a faulty control unit.

j. Turn the ignition switch to the **OFF** position, then disconnect the air control valve hose.

k. Turn the ignition switch to the **ON** position. Look through the open end of the pipe (from which the air control valve was disconnected) and check that the valve moves from the fully closed position to the fully opened position, 1 minute after the ignition switch is turned to the **ON** position.

Fuel Pressure Regulator

REMOVAL & INSTALLATION

1. Relieve the fuel system pressure.
2. Disconnect the negative battery cable.
3. Disconnect the fuel line from the regulator.
4. Remove the 2 screws securing the pressure regulator to the venturi chamber.
5. Pull the pressure regulator upward to remove.
To install:
6. Install the pressure regulator and tighten the screws securely.
7. Connect the fuel line to the regulator, and tighten the hose clamp.
8. Connect the negative battery cable.
9. Start the engine and check for fuel leaks.

TESTING

1. Relieve the fuel system pressure.
2. Disconnect the fuel hose from the fuel delivery pipe of the throttle chamber, then install a suitable fuel gauge.

➡**Before disconnecting the fuel hose, disconnect the fuel pump connector and crank the engine for approximately 5 seconds to release the pressure in the fuel system. If the engine starts, let it run until it stops.**

3. Measure fuel pressure with the engine idling. The fuel gauge should read 20-24 psi (136-163 kPa). If not within specification, replace the pressure regulator.

Coolant Thermosensor

REMOVAL & INSTALLATION

▶ **See Figure 34**

1. Disconnect the negative battery cable.
2. Drain the engine coolant below the level of the intake manifold.
3. Locate the thermosensor (water temperature sensor) at the water housing on the intake manifold and disconnect the thermosensor electrical fastener.
4. Remove the thermosensor with a suitable wrench.
To install:
5. Coat the sensor threads with sealant and install. Tighten the sensor securely.
6. Connect the electrical fastener.
7. Fill the engine with coolant.
8. Connect the negative battery cable.
9. Start the engine and check for leaks.

TESTING

1. Remove the thermosensor from the thermostat housing.
2. Place the sensor in water of various temperatures and measure the resistance between the terminals with an ohmmeter.
3. Resistance should be 7-11.5 kilo-ohms at 14°F (-10°C), 2-3 kilo-ohms at 68°F (20°C), and 700-1000 ohms at 122°F (50°C).
4. If the resistance is not within specification, replace the thermosensor.

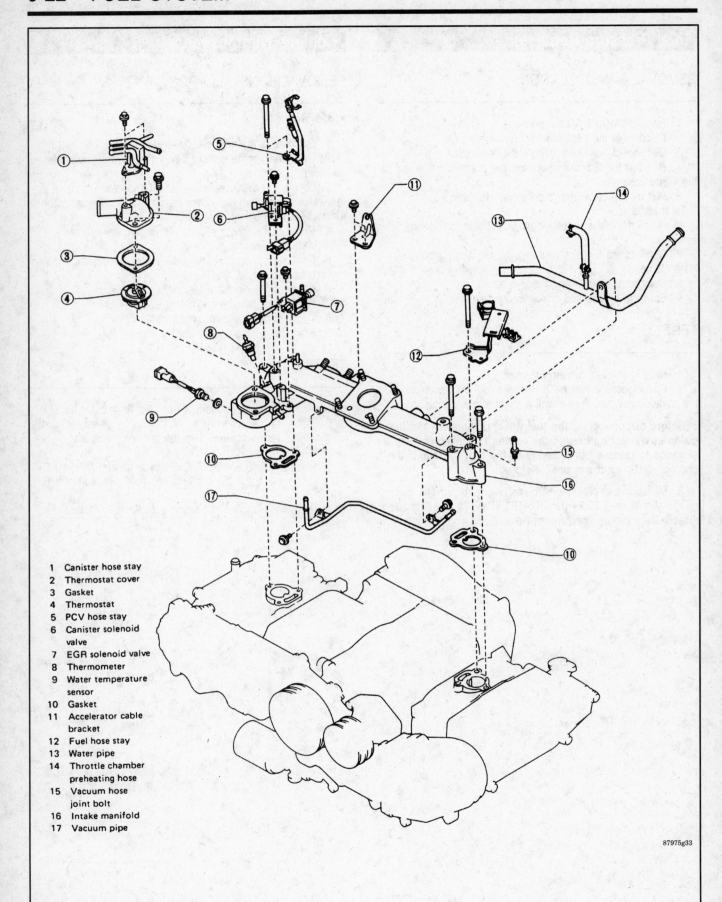

1 Canister hose stay
2 Thermostat cover
3 Gasket
4 Thermostat
5 PCV hose stay
6 Canister solenoid valve
7 EGR solenoid valve
8 Thermometer
9 Water temperature sensor
10 Gasket
11 Accelerator cable bracket
12 Fuel hose stay
13 Water pipe
14 Throttle chamber preheating hose
15 Vacuum hose joint bolt
16 Intake manifold
17 Vacuum pipe

87975g33

Fig. 34 SPFI intake assembly — 1.8L engine

MULTI-POINT FUEL INJECTION (MPFI) SYSTEM

◆ **See Figures 35 and 36**

The MPFI system supplies the optimum air/fuel mixture to the engine under various operating conditions. System fuel, which is pressurized at a constant pressure, is injected into the intake air passage of the cylinder head. The amount of fuel injected is controlled by the intermittent injection system, whereby the electro-magnetic injection valve (fuel injector) opens only for a short period of time, depending on the amount of air required for 1 cycle of operation. During system operation, the amount of injection is determined by the duration of an electric pulse sent to the fuel injector, which permits precise metering of the fuel.

All the operating conditions of the engine are converted into electric signals, resulting in additional features of the system, such as improved adaptability and easier addition of compensating elements like ignition timing. The MPFI system also incorporates the following features:
- Reduced emission of exhaust gases
- Reduction in fuel consumption
- Increased engine output
- Superior acceleration and deceleration
- Superior starting and warm-up performance in cold weather since compensation is made for coolant and intake air temperature
- Good performance with turbocharger, if so equipped

Relieving Fuel System Pressure

➡**This procedure must be performed prior to servicing any component of the fuel injection system which contains fuel.**

1. Disconnect the fuel pump harness at the fuel pump.
2. Crank the engine for 5 seconds or more to relieve the fuel pressure. If the engine starts during this time, allow it to run until it stalls.
3. Connect the fuel pump harness.

Electric Fuel Pump

REMOVAL & INSTALLATION

1.2L Engine

1. Disconnect the negative battery cable.
2. Remove the rear seat back and bottom cushion.
3. Remove the fuel sender access hole cover plate.
4. Relieve the fuel system pressure.
5. Disconnect the electrical harness from the fuel pump.
6. Disconnect and cap the fuel lines from the fuel sender assembly.
7. Remove the eight screws securing the fuel assembly into the fuel tank.
8. Remove the fuel sender assembly.
9. Remove the filter strainer from the fuel pump.
10. Disconnect the electrical harness from the fuel pump.

11. Disconnect the fuel lines from the pump.
12. Remove the pump from the sender assembly.
To install:
13. Connect the fuel lines to the pump, then install the pump on the sender assembly.
14. Connect the electrical harness to the fuel pump.
15. Install a **new** fuel strainer on the pump.
16. Install the fuel sender assembly in the fuel tank and install the eight mounting screws.
17. Connect the fuel lines to the fuel sender.
18. Connect the electrical harness to the fuel sender.
19. Install the fuel sender access hole cover.
20. Install the rear seat bottom and back.
21. Connect the negative battery cable.
22. Start the vehicle and check for leaks.

1.8L Engine
◆ **See Figure 37**

1. Release the fuel system pressure.
2. Disconnect the negative battery cable.
3. Keep the fuel pump harness disconnected after releasing the fuel system pressure.
4. Raise and support the vehicle safely on jackstands.
5. Clamp the middle portion of the hose connecting the pipe to the fuel pump to prevent fuel from flowing out of the tank.
6. Loosen the hose clamp and disconnect the hose.
7. Remove the three pump bracket mounting bolts and remove the pump together with the pump damper.
To install:
8. If the pump and damper have been removed from the bracket, reinstall and tighten the bolts securely.
9. Install the hose and tighten the clamp screw to 9-13 inch lbs. (1.0-1.5 Nm).
10. Install the pump bracket in position to the vehicle body and secure it with the bolts.

➡**Take care to position the rubber cushion properly.**

11. Connect the pump harness connector.
12. Connect the negative battery cable and test the fuel pump for proper operation.
13. Check for leaks.

2.2L, 2.5L and 2.7L Engines
◆ **See Figure 38**

✳✳CAUTION

Fuel injection systems remain under pressure after the engine has been turned OFF. Properly relieve fuel pressure before disconnecting any fuel lines. Failure to do so may result in fire or personal injury.

1. Relieve the fuel system pressure.
2. Disconnect the negative battery cable.
3. Remove the rear seat bottom to reach the fuel pump access cover.

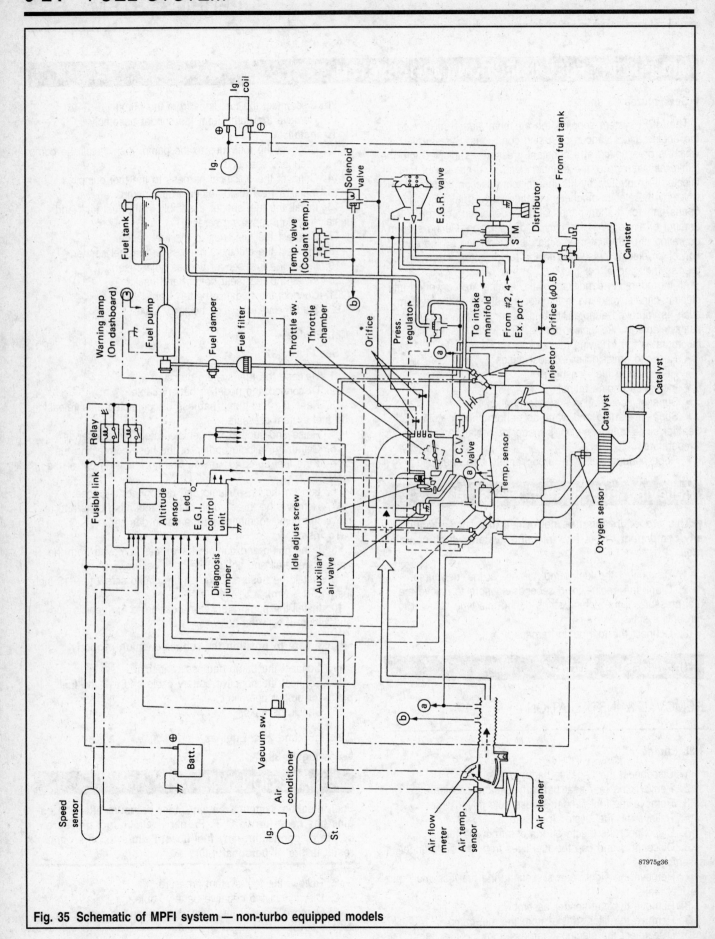

Fig. 35 Schematic of MPFI system — non-turbo equipped models

87975g36

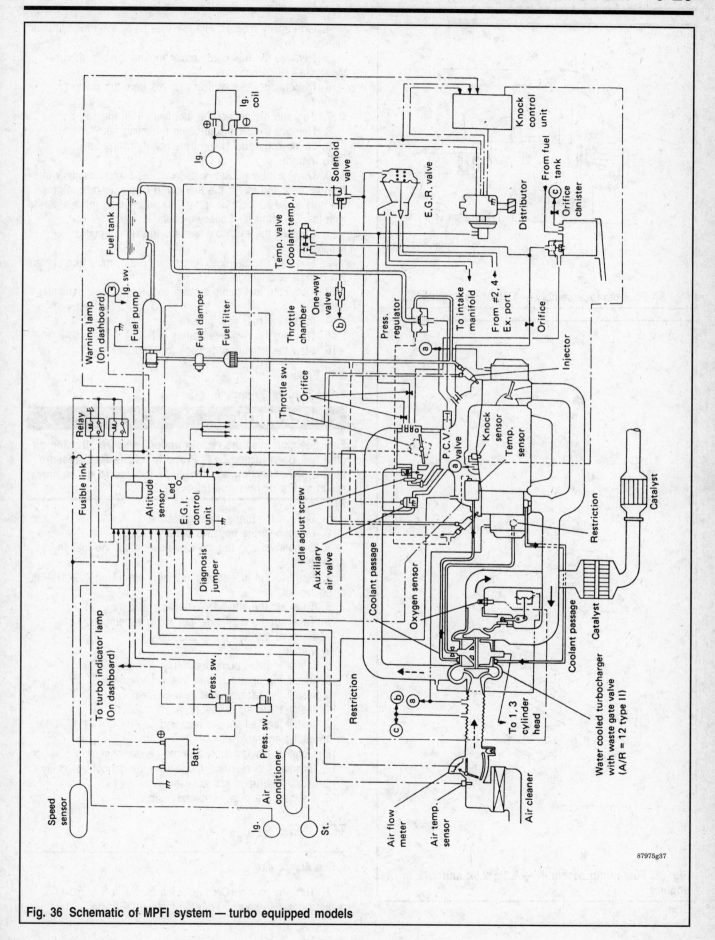

Fig. 36 Schematic of MPFI system — turbo equipped models

87975g37

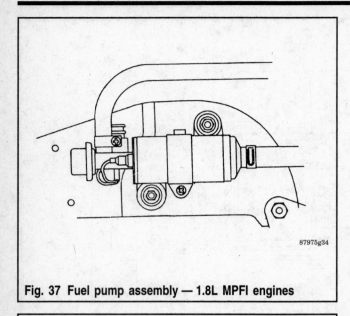

87975g34

Fig. 37 Fuel pump assembly — 1.8L MPFI engines

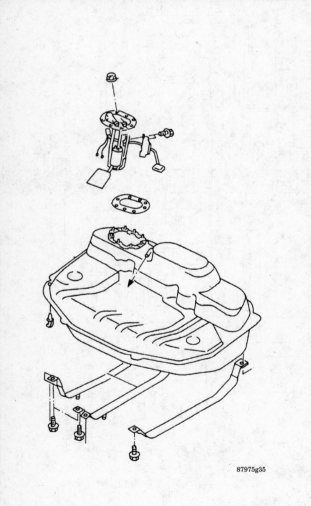

87975g35

Fig. 38 Fuel pump assembly — 2.2L, 2.5L and 2.7L engines

4. On Legacy models, fold the seat back, then roll the floor mat back.

5. Remove the fuel pump cover mounting bolts, then remove the fuel pump cover.

6. Disconnect the electrical harness from the pump assembly.

7. Tag and disconnect the fuel lines from the fuel pump.

8. Remove the eight fuel pump mounting nuts.

9. Remove the fuel pump assembly from the tank.

To install:

10. Using a new gasket, install the fuel pump assembly into the fuel tank and install the fuel pump mounting nuts. Tighten the nuts to 20-33 inch lbs. (2-4 Nm) on Impreza models, 24-48 inch lbs. (3-6 Nm) for Legacy models.

11. Connect the electrical harness to the fuel pump assembly.

12. Connect the fuel lines to the pump assembly and tighten the clamps and fittings.

13. Install the fuel pump service cover and cover mounting bolts.

14. Install the rear seat bottom.

15. Connect the negative battery cable.

16. Start the engine and check for leaks.

3.3L Engine

▶ **See Figures 39 and 40**

※※CAUTION

Fuel injection systems remain under pressure after the engine has been turned OFF. Properly relieve fuel pressure before disconnecting any fuel lines. Failure to do so may result in fire or personal injury.

1. Relieve the fuel system pressure.

2. Disconnect the negative battery cable.

3. Disconnect and tag the four hoses from the fuel sender assembly.

4. Remove the fuel sender retaining cap using 42911PA000 or equivalent.

5. Take out the left side fuel meter assembly.

6. Take out the right side fuel meter assembly.

7. Remove the fuel pump assembly.

To install:

8. Install the fuel pump assembly.

9. Install the right side fuel meter assembly.

10. Install the left side fuel meter assembly.

11. Install the bracket covers.

12. Install the fuel sender retaining cap using 42911PA000, or an equivalent replacer.

13. Connect the four hoses to the sender assembly.

14. Connect the electrical harness to the sender assembly.

15. Install the fuel pump access cover.

16. Connect the negative battery cable.

TESTING

▶ **See Figure 41**

1. Turn the ignition **ON** and listen for the fuel pump to make a growling sound. Turn the ignition **OFF**.

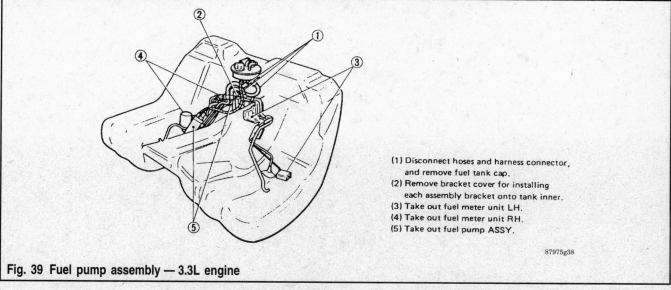

(1) Disconnect hoses and harness connector, and remove fuel tank cap.
(2) Remove bracket cover for installing each assembly bracket onto tank inner.
(3) Take out fuel meter unit LH.
(4) Take out fuel meter unit RH.
(5) Take out fuel pump ASSY.

87975g38

Fig. 39 Fuel pump assembly — 3.3L engine

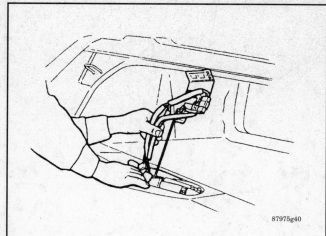

Fig. 40 Carefully remove the fuel pump assembly from the tank

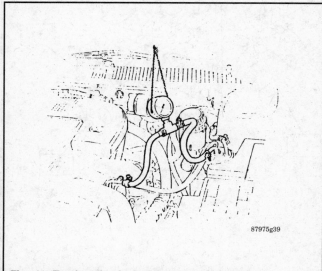

87975g39

Fig. 41 Testing the fuel pressure with a gauge

2. Release the fuel system pressure. Disconnect the pump connector and crank the engine for 5 seconds or more. If the engine starts, allow it to run until it stops. Turn the ignition **OFF** and install the fuel pump connector.

3. Disconnect the fuel hose at the fuel pump.

4. Connect a gauge in-line using a T-fitting.

5. Start the engine and measure the fuel pressure. The pressure should be 2.6-3.3 psi (5.2-6.6 in Hg). If the fuel pump does not meet this specification, replace the pump.

6. After testing, disconnect the pressure gauge and reconnect the fuel line.

Throttle Body

REMOVAL & INSTALLATION

1.2L Engine
▶ See Figure 42

1. Disconnect the negative battery cable.

2. Drain the coolant from the radiator to a level below the throttle body.

3. Remove the air intake duct from the throttle body.

4. If equipped with cruise control, disconnect the cable from the throttle body.

5. Disconnect the accelerator cable from the throttle body.

6. Disconnect the idle air control solenoid and throttle position sensor harnesses.

7. Disconnect the coolant hoses from the throttle body.

8. Remove the four throttle body mounting bolts and remove the throttle body from the collector chamber.

9. Clean all gasket material from both mating surfaces.

To install:

10. Using a new gasket, install the throttle body to the collector. Tighten the mounting bolts to 17-20 ft. lbs. (22-26 Nm).

11. Using new clamps, connect the coolant hoses to the throttle body.

12. Connect the throttle position sensor and the air idle control solenoid harnesses.

13. Connect the accelerator cable to the throttle body.

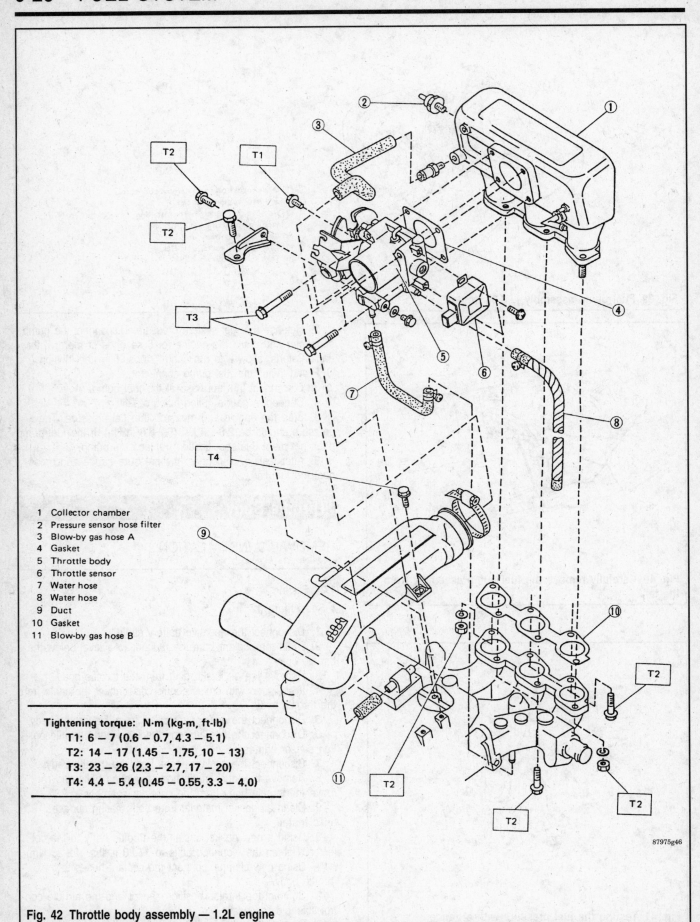

1 Collector chamber
2 Pressure sensor hose filter
3 Blow-by gas hose A
4 Gasket
5 Throttle body
6 Throttle sensor
7 Water hose
8 Water hose
9 Duct
10 Gasket
11 Blow-by gas hose B

Tightening torque: N·m (kg-m, ft-lb)
   T1: 6 – 7 (0.6 – 0.7, 4.3 – 5.1)
   T2: 14 – 17 (1.45 – 1.75, 10 – 13)
   T3: 23 – 26 (2.3 – 2.7, 17 – 20)
   T4: 4.4 – 5.4 (0.45 – 0.55, 3.3 – 4.0)

87975g46

Fig. 42 Throttle body assembly — 1.2L engine

14. If equipped with cruise control, connect the cable to the throttle body.

15. Install the air intake duct.

16. Refill the radiator with coolant.

17. Connect the negative battery cable and bleed the cooling system.

1.8L, 2.2L, 2.5L and 2.7L Engines
▶ **See Figures 43 and 44**

1. Disconnect the negative battery cable.

2. Drain the coolant from the radiator to a level below the throttle body.

3. Remove the air intake duct from the throttle body.

4. If equipped with cruise control, disconnect the cable from the throttle body.

5. Disconnect the accelerator cable from the throttle body.

6. Disconnect the idle air control solenoid and throttle position sensor harnesses.

7. Disconnect the coolant hoses from the throttle body.

8. Remove the four throttle body mounting bolts and remove the throttle body from the collector chamber.

9. Clean all gasket material from both mating surfaces.

To install:

10. Using a new gasket, install the throttle body to the collector. Tighten the mounting bolts to 14-17 ft. lbs. (19-23 Nm).

11. Using new clamps, connect the coolant hoses to the throttle body.

12. Connect the throttle position sensor and the air idle control solenoid harnesses.

13. Connect the accelerator cable to the throttle body.

14. If equipped with cruise control, connect the cable to the throttle body.

15. Install the air intake duct.

16. Refill the radiator with coolant.

17. Connect the negative battery cable and bleed the cooling system.

SVX
▶ **See Figure 45**

1. Disconnect the negative battery cable.

2. Drain the engine coolant to a level below the throttle body.

3. Remove the intake collector cover.

4. Disconnect the cruise control and accelerator cables from the throttle body.

5. Remove the air intake duct from the throttle body.

6. Disconnect the coolant and vacuum hoses from the throttle body. Tag them if necessary for installation.

7. Disconnect the throttle position sensor and idle air control solenoid valve connectors.

8. Remove the six bolts attaching the throttle body to the intake collector and remove the throttle body.

9. Clean all gasket material from both mating surfaces.

To install:

10. Use a new gasket and install the throttle body to the intake collector. Tighten the mounting bolts to 14-16 ft. lbs. (20-22 Nm).

11. Connect the throttle position sensor and idle air control solenoid valve connectors.

12. Connect the coolant and vacuum hoses to the throttle body.

13. Install the air intake duct.

14. Connect the cruise control and accelerator cables.

15. Install the intake collector cover.

16. Connect the negative battery cable.

17. Refill and bleed the cooling system.

TESTING

1.2L and 1.8L Engines
▶ **See Figure 46**

1. Insert a feeler gauge between the stopper screw of the throttle body and the stopper, and check for continuity between the following terminals:
   - 1.8L engines except XT: terminals A and C
   - 1.8L XT: terminals 4 and 3

2. Check that there is continuity between the terminals when the throttle is fully closed.

3. Check that there is continuity between the terminals when a 0.0217 in. (0.55mm) feeler gauge is inserted between the throttle body screw and the stopper.

4. Check that there is no continuity between the terminals when a 0.0362 in. (0.92mm) feeler gauge is inserted between the throttle body screw and the stopper.

5. If not within specifications, loosen the screws securing the throttle switch and adjust until all specifications are met.

6. Measure the resistance between the sensor signal and ground on the throttle sensor connector terminals as follows:
   - 1.2L and 1.8L engines except XT: terminals 1 and 2
   - 1.8L XT: terminals 3 and 2

7. Resistance should be 6-18 kilo-ohms. If not, replace the throttle opening sensor.

8. Measure the resistance between the throttle sensor terminals 1 and 3. Resistance should be 5.8-17.8 kilo-ohms when the throttle valve is fully closed and 1.5-5.1 kilo-ohms when the throttle valve is fully open.

9. Ensure that the resistance changes smoothly between the fully closed and fully open positions. If resistance is not within specifications, replace the sensor.

10. Start the engine and allow it to reach normal operating temperature. Check the idle speed.

11. Under a non-loaded state, turn the throttle lever by hand to increase engine rpm until the end of the dashpot comes off the throttle cam.

12. Gradually return the throttle lever, then check engine rpm when the throttle cam contacts the end of the dashpot. Engine rpm should be 2800-3400.

13. If rpm is not as specified, loosen the dashpot locknut, then turn the dashpot until engine rpm is within specification. Tighten the locknut.

14. After adjustment, rev the engine to ensure that the idle speed returns correctly as the throttle is released.

2.2L and 2.5L Engines
▶ **See Figure 47**

1. Turn the ignition switch **ON**.

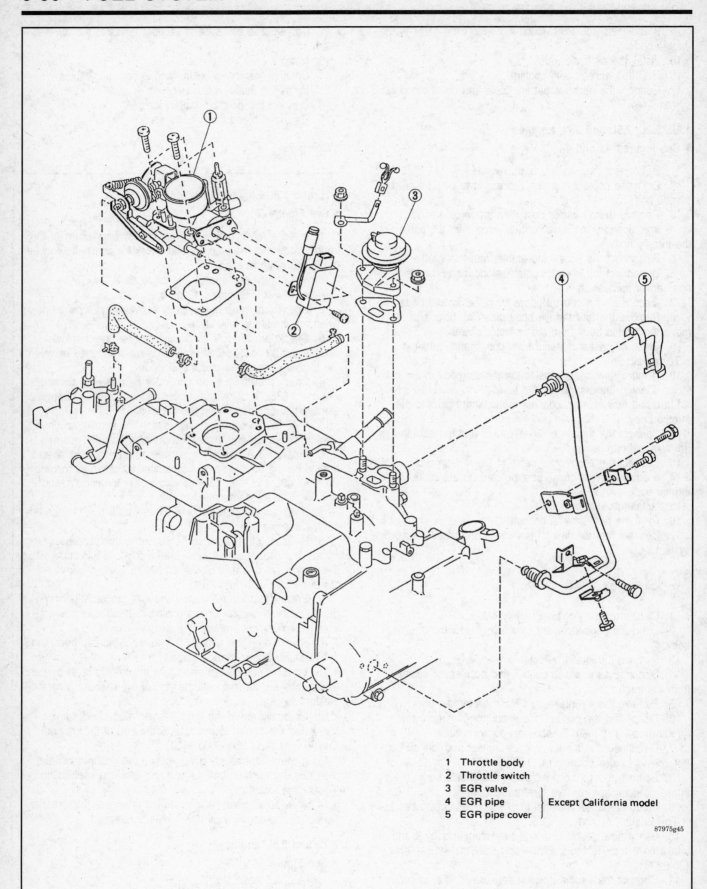

1 Throttle body
2 Throttle switch
3 EGR valve
4 EGR pipe
5 EGR pipe cover
} Except California model

87975g45

Fig. 43 Throttle body assembly — 1.8L engine

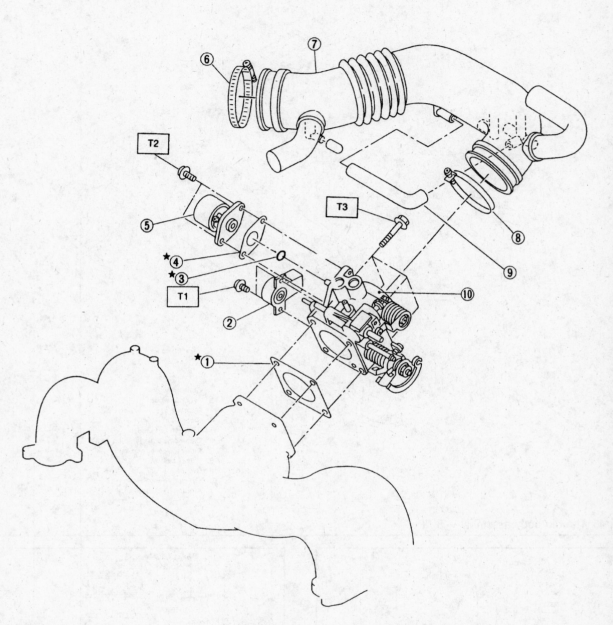

① Gasket
② Throttle position sensor
③ O-ring
④ Gasket
⑤ Idle air control solenoid valve
⑥ Clamp
⑦ Air intake duct
⑧ Clamp

⑨ By-pass hose
⑩ Throttle body

Tightening torque: N·m (kg-m, ft-lb)
   T1: 2.0 — 2.4 (0.20 — 0.24, 1.5 — 1.8)
   T2: 5.2 — 6.8 (0.53 — 0.69, 3.8 — 5.0)
   T3: 14 — 24 (1.4 — 2.4, 10 — 18)

87975g42

Fig. 44 Throttle body assembly — 2.2L and 2.5L engines

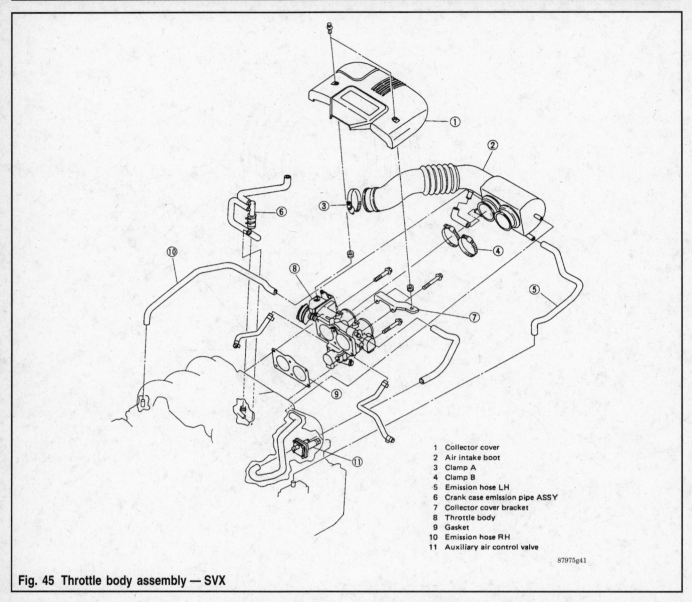

1 Collector cover
2 Air intake boot
3 Clamp A
4 Clamp B
5 Emission hose LH
6 Crank case emission pipe ASSY
7 Collector cover bracket
8 Throttle body
9 Gasket
10 Emission hose RH
11 Auxiliary air control valve

87975g41

Fig. 45 Throttle body assembly — SVX

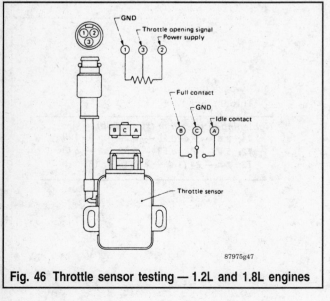

87975g47

Fig. 46 Throttle sensor testing — 1.2L and 1.8L engines

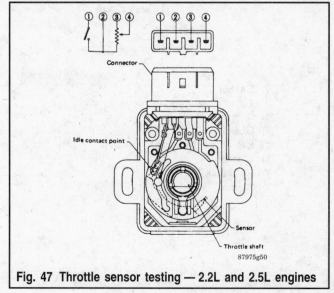

87975g50

Fig. 47 Throttle sensor testing — 2.2L and 2.5L engines

2. Measure the voltage between the ECU connector terminal and ground. Voltage should be as follows:
- Terminal 2 and ground: 4.4-4.8 volts with the throttle fully open
- Terminal 2 and ground: 0.7-1.6 volts with the throttle fully closed
- Terminal 3 and ground: 5 volts
- Terminal 1 and ground: 0 volts

3. Ensure that voltage smoothly decreases in response to throttle opening. If measurements are not within specification, check and repair the ECU terminals or harness.

4. Disconnect the harness from the throttle sensor. Measure the resistance between throttle sensor terminals 2 and 3. Resistance should be 12 kilo-ohms.

5. Measure the resistance between terminals while slowly opening the throttle valve from the closed position. Resistance should be as follows:
- Terminals 2 and 4: 10-12 kilo-ohms with the throttle valve fully closed
- Terminals 2 and 4: 3-5 kilo-ohms with the throttle valve fully open

6. Ensure resistance smoothly increases in response to throttle opening. If measurements are not within specification, replace the throttle sensor.

7. Detach connectors from the ECU and throttle sensor.

8. Measure resistance between the ECU connector and throttle sensor connectors. Resistance should be as follows:
- ECU terminal 1 and throttle sensor terminal 2: 0 ohms
- ECU terminal 2 and throttle sensor terminal 4: 0 ohms
- ECU terminal 3 and throttle sensor terminal 3: 0 ohms

9. Measure resistance between the throttle sensor connectors and ground. Resistance should be as follows:
- Terminal 2 and ground: 1 mega-ohm minimum
- Terminal 4 and ground: 1 mega-ohm minimum
- Terminal 3 and ground: 1 mega-ohm minimum

10. If resistance is not within specification, check and repair the harness or connector.

2.7L Engine
▶ See Figure 48

1. Disconnect the throttle sensor connector.

2. Insert a feeler gauge between the stopper screw of the throttle body and the stopper, and check for continuity between terminals 4 and 3.

3. Check that there is 5 a maximum of kilo-ohms resistance between the terminals when a 0.0138 in. (0.35mm) feeler gauge is inserted between the throttle body screw and the stopper.

4. Check that there is 1 mega-ohm resistance minimum between the terminals when a 0.0295 in. (0.75mm) feeler gauge is inserted between the throttle body screw and the stopper.

5. If not within specifications, loosen the screws securing the throttle switch and adjust until all specifications are met.

6. Measure the resistance between terminals 1 and 4. Resistance should be 3-7 kilo-ohms.

7. Measure the resistance between terminals 2 and 4. Resistance should be 2 kilo-ohms.

8. Ensure that the resistance changes smoothly between the fully closed and fully open positions. If resistance is not within specifications, replace the sensor.

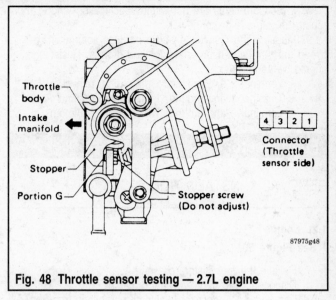

Fig. 48 Throttle sensor testing — 2.7L engine

3.3L Engine
▶ See Figure 49

1. Turn the ignition switch **OFF**.

2. Disconnect the throttle sensor connector.

3. Measure the resistance between throttle sensor connector terminals 1 and 3. Resistance should be 5 kilo-ohms.

4. Measure the resistance between terminals 2 and 3 while slowly opening the throttle valve from the closed position.

5. Resistance should be 10-12 kilo-ohms when the throttle valve is closed and 3-5 kilo-ohms when the throttle is open. Ensure that the resistance increases in response to throttle valve opening.

6. If the throttle body fails the checks up to this point, replace it.

7. Disconnect the ECU connectors and measure the resistance of the harness connector between the ECU and the throttle sensor. Resistance should be as follows:
- ECU terminal 3 and throttle sensor terminal 2: 0 ohms
- ECU terminal 2 and throttle sensor terminal 1: 0 ohms
- ECU terminal 1 and throttle sensor terminal 3: 0 ohms

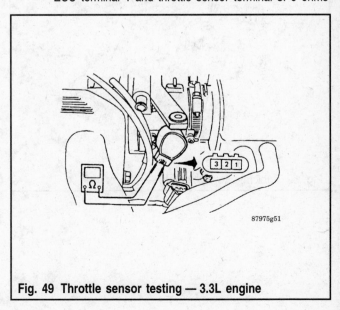

Fig. 49 Throttle sensor testing — 3.3L engine

8. If measurements are not within specification, check and repair the harness or connector.

9. Measure the resistance of the harness connector between the throttle sensor connector and ground. Resistance should be as follows:
- Terminal 2 and ground: 1 mega-ohm minimum
- Terminal 1 and ground: 1 mega-ohm minimum
- Terminal 3 and ground: 1 mega-ohm minimum

Fuel Injector

REMOVAL & INSTALLATION

1.2L Engine

▶ **See Figure 50**

1. Relieve the fuel system pressure.
2. Disconnect the negative battery cable.
3. Tag and disconnect the electrical harnesses from the fuel injectors.
4. Disconnect and tag the hoses attached to the fuel rail.
5. Remove the fuel rail mounting bolts, then remove the fuel rail assembly carefully.
6. Remove the individual injectors from the rail by pulling lightly with a slight twist.
7. Remove the fuel injector O-rings and discard.

To install:

8. Install the injectors using new gaskets and O-rings. Lubricate the O-rings with fuel before installation.
9. Carefully install the fuel rail on the engine and install the mounting bolts.
10. Connect the electrical harnesses to the fuel rail.

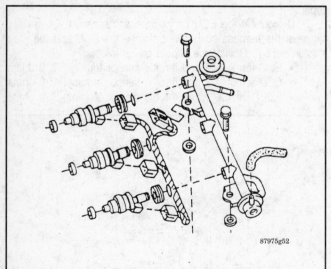

Fig. 50 Fuel injector assembly — 1.2L engine

87975g52

11. Connect the hoses to the fuel rail.
12. Connect the negative battery cable.
13. Pressurize the fuel system and verify that there are no fuel leaks.

1.8L and 2.7L Engines

▶ **See Figures 51 and 52**

1. Relieve the fuel system pressure.
2. Disconnect the negative battery cable.

➡ **On some engines, it may be necessary to remove the intake plenum to gain access to the fuel lines connecting the injectors.**

3. Remove the fuel lines connecting the injectors.
4. Disconnect the fuel injector electrical harnesses.
5. Remove the injectors by pulling with a slight twist. Discard the gaskets and O-rings.
6. Remove the injector holder plate, insulator, holder and seal. Discard the insulator and seal.

To install:

7. Install the injectors using new gaskets, seals, insulators and O-rings. Lubricate the O-rings with clean engine oil prior to installation.
8. Install the fuel lines connecting the injectors.
9. Connect the injector electrical harnesses.
10. Install the intake plenum if removed.
11. Connect the negative battery cable.
12. Start the engine and check for leaks.

2.2L and 2.5L Engines

▶ **See Figures 53, 54, 55, 56, 57, 58, 59, 60, 61 and 62**

✳✳CAUTION

Fuel injection systems remain under pressure after the engine has been turned OFF. Properly relieve fuel pressure before disconnecting any fuel lines. Failure to do so may result in fire or personal injury.

1. Relieve the fuel system pressure.
2. Disconnect the negative battery cable.
3. Disconnect the fuel injector electrical harness.
4. Remove the fuel injection cover.
5. Remove the fuel injector from the fuel pipe assembly.
6. Remove and discard the fuel injector O-rings and insulators,

To install:

7. Install the injector with two new O-rings and a new insulator. Tighten the bolts to 24 inch lbs. (3 Nm).
8. Install the fuel injector cover.
9. Connect the fuel injector electrical harness.
10. Connect the negative battery cable.
11. Start the engine and check for leaks.

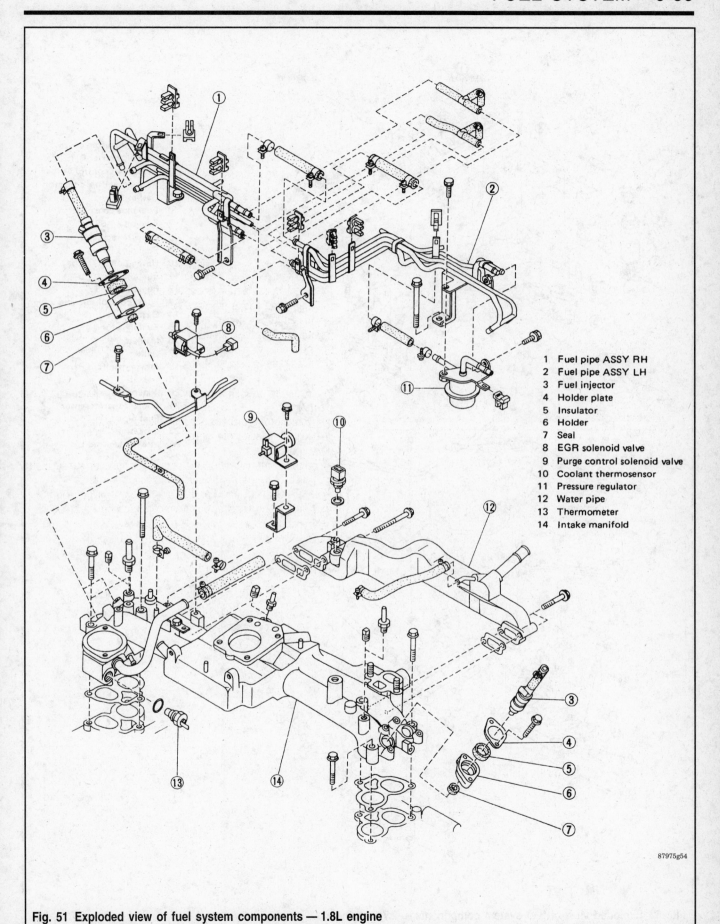

1   Fuel pipe ASSY RH
2   Fuel pipe ASSY LH
3   Fuel injector
4   Holder plate
5   Insulator
6   Holder
7   Seal
8   EGR solenoid valve
9   Purge control solenoid valve
10 Coolant thermosensor
11 Pressure regulator
12 Water pipe
13 Thermometer
14 Intake manifold

87975g54

Fig. 51 Exploded view of fuel system components — 1.8L engine

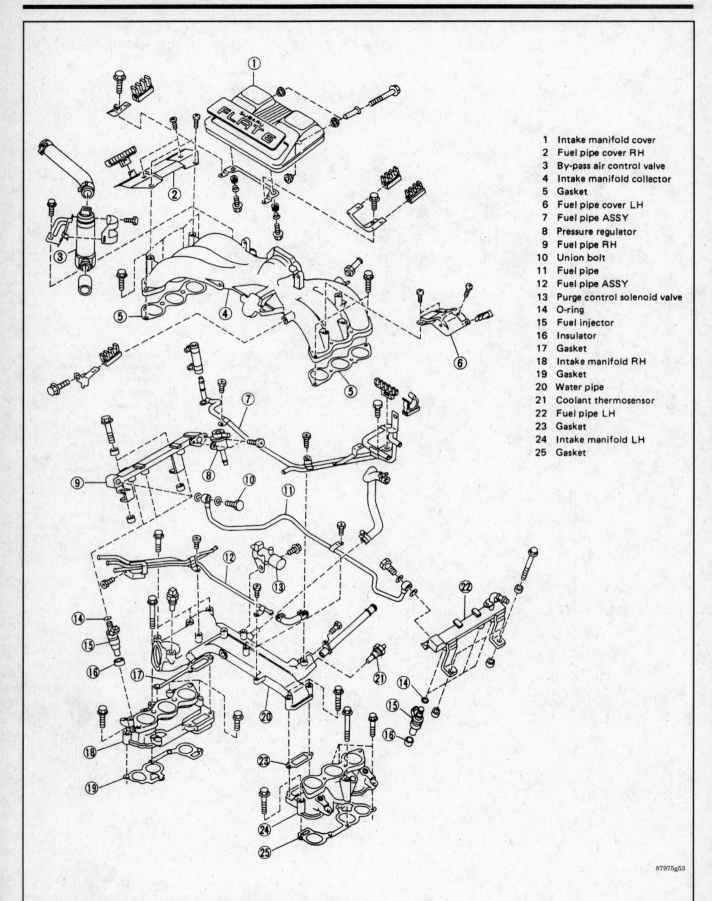

1 Intake manifold cover
2 Fuel pipe cover RH
3 By-pass air control valve
4 Intake manifold collector
5 Gasket
6 Fuel pipe cover LH
7 Fuel pipe ASSY
8 Pressure regulator
9 Fuel pipe RH
10 Union bolt
11 Fuel pipe
12 Fuel pipe ASSY
13 Purge control solenoid valve
14 O-ring
15 Fuel injector
16 Insulator
17 Gasket
18 Intake manifold RH
19 Gasket
20 Water pipe
21 Coolant thermosensor
22 Fuel pipe LH
23 Gasket
24 Intake manifold LH
25 Gasket

87975g53

Fig. 52 Exploded view of fuel system components — 2.7L engine

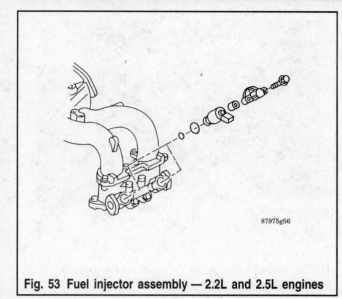

Fig. 53 Fuel injector assembly — 2.2L and 2.5L engines

Fig. 54 Unfasten the fuel injector wire harness from the top of the injector assembly

Fig. 55 Remove the fuel injector cover retainer screw from one side of the injector . . .

Fig. 56 . . . then unfasten the other retainer screw

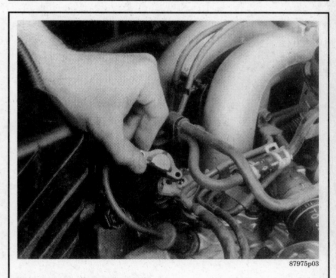

Fig. 57 Lift the cover off . . .

Fig. 58 . . . and remove the seal

Fig. 59 Carefully remove the fuel injector from the cylinder head

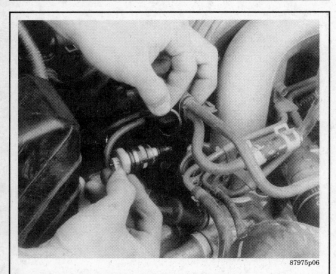

Fig. 60 Remove the lower injector O-ring

Fig. 61 If necessary, remove a stuck O-ring with a pick tool

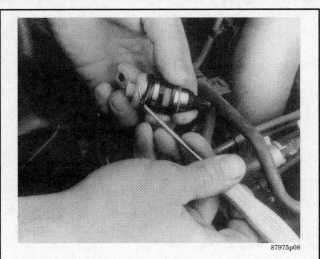

Fig. 62 Remove the upper O-ring from the injector. Discard all used O-rings

3.3L Engine

▶ See Figure 63

✳✳CAUTION

Fuel injection systems remain under pressure after the engine has been turned OFF. Properly relieve fuel pressure before disconnecting any fuel lines. Failure to do so may result in fire or personal injury.

1. Relieve the fuel system pressure.
2. Disconnect the negative battery cable.
3. Remove the collector cover.
4. Remove the air duct between the throttle body and mass airflow sensor.
5. Remove the retainer bolts attaching the power steering hose to the collector and position the hose out of the way.
6. Disconnect the fuel injector electrical harness.
7. Remove the two screws securing the injector cover, then remove the cover.
8. Pull the injector out while rotating it.
9. Remove and discard the fuel injector O-rings.

To install:

10. Install the fuel injector using O-rings coated with clean engine oil.
11. Install the injector cover and cover bolts.
12. Connect the electrical harness to the fuel injector.
13. Install the power steering hose to the intake collector.
14. Install the air intake duct.
15. Install the intake collector cover.
16. Connect the negative battery cable.
17. Pressurize the fuel system and verify that there are no leaks.

TESTING

1.2L Engine

1. Using a stethoscope, ensure that a clicking sound is heard at each injector (when idling or cranking the engine).

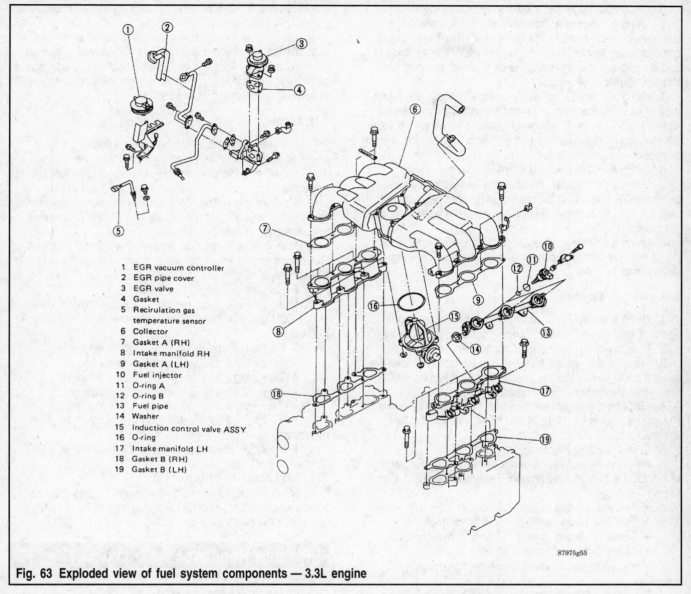

1 EGR vacuum controller
2 EGR pipe cover
3 EGR valve
4 Gasket
5 Recirulation gas
  temperature sensor
6 Collector
7 Gasket A (RH)
8 Intake manifold RH
9 Gasket A (LH)
10 Fuel injector
11 O-ring A
12 O-ring B
13 Fuel pipe
14 Washer
15 Induction control valve ASSY
16 O-ring
17 Intake manifold LH
18 Gasket B (RH)
19 Gasket B (LH)

87975g55

Fig. 63 Exploded view of fuel system components — 3.3L engine

2. Turn the ignition switch to the **OFF** position, then unfasten the control unit connector.

3. Measure the voltage between fuel injector connector terminal 1 and ground. Resistance should be 9 volts or above. If not, repair the fuel injector power circuit.

4. Measure resistance between the fuel injector connector terminals. Resistance should be as follows:
  • Terminals 1 and 2: 10-18 ohms
  • Terminals 1 and 3: 10-18 ohms
  • Terminals 1 and 4: 10-18 ohms

5. If resistance is not within specification, repair the engine harness. If the engine harness is good, replace the fuel injector.

6. Connect the fuel injector connector. Turn the ignition **ON**.

7. Measure the resistance between ECU connector terminals and ground. Resistance should be as follows:
  • Terminal 12 and ground: 8 volts or more
  • Terminal 25 and ground: 8 volts or more
  • Terminal 11 and ground: 8 volts or more

8. If not within specification, repair the harness connector between ECU and fuel injectors.

9. Turn the ignition **OFF** and disconnect the ECU connector.

10. Measure resistance between the ECU connector terminal and ground. Resistance should be as follows:
  • Terminal 13 and ground: below 10 mega-ohms
  • Terminal 26 and ground: below 10 mega-ohms

11. If not within specification, repair the harness connector between the ECU and ground.

1.8L Engine

1. Using a stethoscope, ensure that a clicking sound is heard at each injector (when idling or cranking the engine).

2. Turn the ignition switch to the **OFF** position, then disconnect the control unit connector.

3. Using a voltmeter, measure voltage between ground and terminals 49 (W), 50 (W), 51 (WR) (WL on XT models), and 52 (WR) (WL on XT models) on the control unit connector.

4. The voltmeter should read 12 volts at all terminals.
  a. If the voltmeter reads below 10 volts in any line, the harness from the battery to the control unit through the resistor and injector is broken or shorted.

5. Disconnect each fuel injector electrical connector.

6. Using an ohmmeter, measure resistance between the terminals of each injector. The ohmmeter should read 2-3 ohms at each injector. If the ohmmeter reads infinity, the circuit is broken. If the ohmmeter reads 0 ohms, the circuit is shorted. Replace the injector.

7. Using a voltmeter, measure voltage between the terminals of each injector connector and ground. The voltmeter should read 12 volts. If voltage obtained is less than 10 volts, the harness from the battery to the injector through the resistor is disconnected or shorted.

8. Disconnect the electrical harness from the resistor.

9. Using an ohmmeter, measure the resistance between terminals (W) and (B) of the resistor. The ohmmeter should read 5.8-6.5 ohms. If the reading are not as specified, replace the resistor.

10. Using a voltmeter, measure voltage between terminal 5 (R) of the body harness connector and ground. The voltmeter should read 12 volts.

2.2L and 2.5L Engines

1. Using a stethoscope, ensure that a clicking sound is heard at each injector (when idling or cranking the engine).

2. Disconnect the fuel injector connector.

3. Measure the voltage between fuel injector connector terminal 2 and ground. Voltage should be 10 volts minimum. If not, repair the harness or connector.

4. Measure the resistance between the injector terminals. Resistance should be 10-12 ohms. If not, replace the fuel injector.

5. Fasten the fuel injector connector.

6. Measure the voltage between each fuel injector terminal of the ECU connector and ground. Resistance should be as follows:

- Terminal 11 and ground: 10 volts minimum
- Terminal 12 and ground: 10 volts minimum
- Terminal 13 and ground: 10 volts minimum
- Terminal 26 and ground: 10 volts minimum

7. If not within specification, repair the harness or connector.

8. Disconnect ECU connector.

9. Measure the resistance between ground and ECU connector terminals 24 and 25. Resistance should be 0 ohms, if not, repair the harness or connector.

2.7L Engine

1. Using a stethoscope, ensure that a clicking sound is heard at each injector (when idling or cranking the engine).

2. Disconnect the control unit connector.

3. Using a voltmeter, measure voltage between ground and terminals 49 (W), 50 (W), 51 (WR), 52 (WR), 53 (WY) and 54 (WY) on the control unit connector.

4. The voltmeter should read 12 volts at all terminals.

5. If the voltmeter reads below 10 volts in any line, the harness from the battery to the control unit through the resistor and injector is broken or shorted.

6. Disconnect each fuel injector electrical connector.

7. Using an ohmmeter, measure resistance between the terminals of each injector. The ohmmeter should read 13.8 ohms at each injector. If the ohmmeter reads infinity, the cir-

cuit is broken. If the ohmmeter reads 0 ohm, the circuit is shorted. Replace injector.

8. Using a voltmeter, measure voltage between the terminals of each injector and ground. The voltmeter should read 12 volts at each injector. If the voltage obtained is less than 10 volts at any injector, the harness from the battery to the injector is disconnected or shorted.

3.3L Engine

1. Using a stethoscope, ensure that a clicking sound is heard at each injector (when idling or cranking the engine).

2. Turn the ignition switch **OFF**. Disconnect the fuel injector connector.

3. Measure the voltage between fuel injector connector terminal 2 and ground. Voltage should be 10 volts minimum. If not, repair the harness or connector.

4. Measure the resistance between the injector terminals. Resistance should be 11-12 ohms. If not, replace the fuel injector.

5. Fasten the fuel injector connector.

6. Measure the voltage between each fuel injector terminal of the ECU connector and ground. Resistance should be as follows:

- Terminal 1 and ground: 10 volts minimum
- Terminal 11 and ground: 10 volts minimum
- Terminal 12 and ground: 10 volts minimum
- Terminal 13 and ground: 10 volts minimum
- Terminal 26 and ground: 10 volts minimum
- Terminal 12 (connector E59) and ground: 10 volts minimum

7. If not within specification, repair the harness or connector.

8. Disconnect the ECU harness.

9. Measure the resistance between ground and ECU connector terminals 24 and 25. Resistance should be 0 ohms, if not, repair the harness or connector.

Pressure Regulator

REMOVAL & INSTALLATION

▶ See Figures 64, 65, 66, 67 and 68

1. Locate the pressure regulator on the fuel rail near the injectors.

2. Relieve the fuel system pressure.

3. Disconnect the negative battery cable.

4. Remove the vacuum line leading to the regulator.

5. Loosen the fuel line nuts and remove the regulator.

6. Disconnect the fuel hose and clamp from the regulator assembly.

7. Remove and discard the rubber O-ring from the regulator.

To install:

8. Install the regulator and tighten the fuel line nuts securely.

9. Install the vacuum line on the regulator.

10. Connect the fuel hose to the regulator, and secure in place with a hose clamp.

11. Connect the negative battery cable.

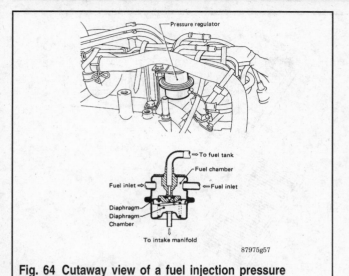

Fig. 64 Cutaway view of a fuel injection pressure regulator

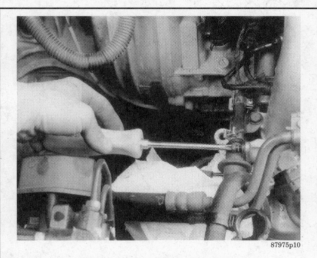

Fig. 66 Remove the retainer bolts securing the regulator in place

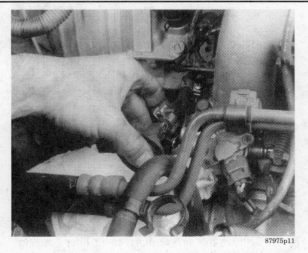

Fig. 67 Disconnect the regulator from the fuel rail by pulling outward

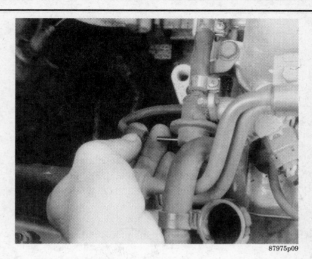

Fig. 65 Disconnect the vacuum line from the pressure regulator

12. Start the engine and check for leaks.
13. Check for correct fuel pressure.

Airflow Meter

REMOVAL & INSTALLATION

▶ **See Figures 69, 70, 71 and 72**

1. Disconnect the negative battery cable.
2. Unfasten the connector from the airflow meter.
3. Loosen the hose clamps securing the air intake boot and remove the air intake boot assembly.
4. Loosen the bolts attaching the airflow meter to the air cleaner assembly, then remove the airflow meter and gasket, if equipped. Discard the gasket.
   To install:
5. Install the airflow meter using a new gasket between the meter assembly and air filter housing. Tighten the retainer bolts to 26-44 ft. lbs. (4-7 Nm).

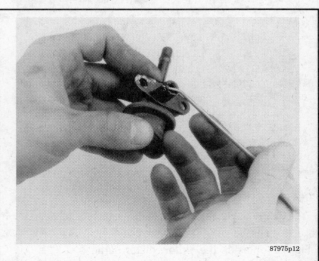

Fig. 68 With the regulator completely removed, detach the O-ring from the regulator-to-fuel rail connector

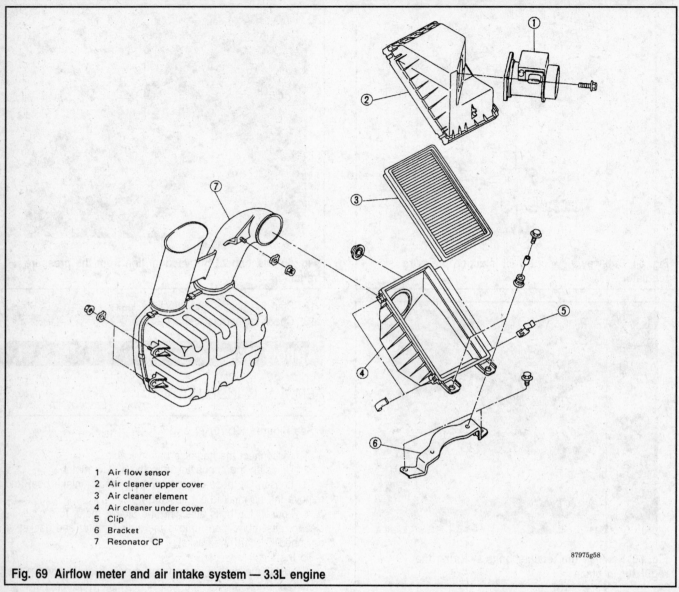

1 Air flow sensor
2 Air cleaner upper cover
3 Air cleaner element
4 Air cleaner under cover
5 Clip
6 Bracket
7 Resonator CP

87975g58

Fig. 69 Airflow meter and air intake system — 3.3L engine

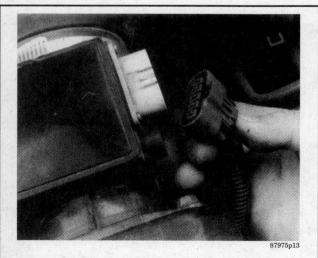

87975p13

Fig. 70 Unfasten the airflow meter harness — 2.2L engine

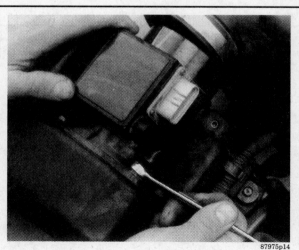

87975p14

Fig. 71 Remove the airflow meter-to-air filter housing retainer screws

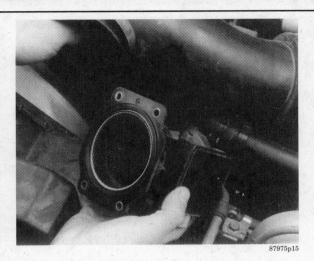

Fig. 72 Detach the airflow meter from the air filter housing

6. Install the air intake boot assembly and tighten the attaching clamps to secure.
7. Attach the airflow meter connector.
8. Connect the negative battery cable.
9. Start the engine and listen for air flow leaks and correct engine operation.

FUEL TANK

Tank Assembly

REMOVAL & INSTALLATION

Justy

▶ See Figures 73, 74 and 75

1. Disconnect the negative battery cable.
2. Release the fuel system pressure, if equipped with fuel injection.
3. Drain any fuel from the tank into a suitable container. Observe all fire precautions.
4. Remove the rear seat back and lower cushion assemblies.
5. Remove the left side sill trim, then remove the filler pipe cover.
6. Remove the separator and roll-over valve, and disconnect the tube from the separator by moving the clip out of place.
7. Remove the access hole plate, and disconnect the electrical harness from the sender unit.
8. Disconnect the fuel filler hose from the fuel tank.
9. Disconnect the air vent hose from the filler pipe.
10. Raise and safely support the vehicle on jackstands.
11. Remove the two parking brake cable mounting bolts and lower the cable assembly.
12. Remove the fuel filter bracket mounting bolts.
13. Disconnect and cap the fuel lines from the tank-to-fuel filter and fuel tank-to-return pipe.
14. Support the tank with a suitable jack.
15. Remove the six tank mounting bolts and lower the tank from the vehicle.

To install:

16. Raise the fuel tank into position and install the six mounting bolts. Tighten the mounting bolts to 13 ft. lbs. (18 Nm).
17. Connect the fuel lines from the fuel filter-to-fuel tank and the fuel tank-to-return pipe.
18. Position the fuel filter bracket and install the mounting bolts.
19. Position the parking brake cable assembly and install the mounting bolts.
20. Lower the vehicle.
21. Connect the air vent hose to the filler neck.
22. Connect the fuel filler hose to the tank.
23. Connect the electrical harness to the sender unit and install the access plate.
24. Install the separator and roll-over valve, and connect the tube to the separator with the clip.
25. Install the filler pipe cover and install the left side sill trim.
26. Install the rear seat back and lower cushion.
27. Connect the negative battery cable.
28. Start the vehicle and check for leaks.

Coupe, XT, Sedan, Wagon, Loyale and Brat

▶ See Figure 76

1. Release the fuel system pressure, if equipped with fuel injection.
2. Disconnect the negative battery cable.
3. Raise and safely support the vehicle on jackstands.
4. Remove the muffler and differential assembly, if equipped with 4WD.
5. Remove the fuel filler cap and drain the fuel tank into a suitable container.
6. Remove the fuel filler pipe protector.
7. Remove the clamp and disconnect the fuel filler hose from the filler pipe.

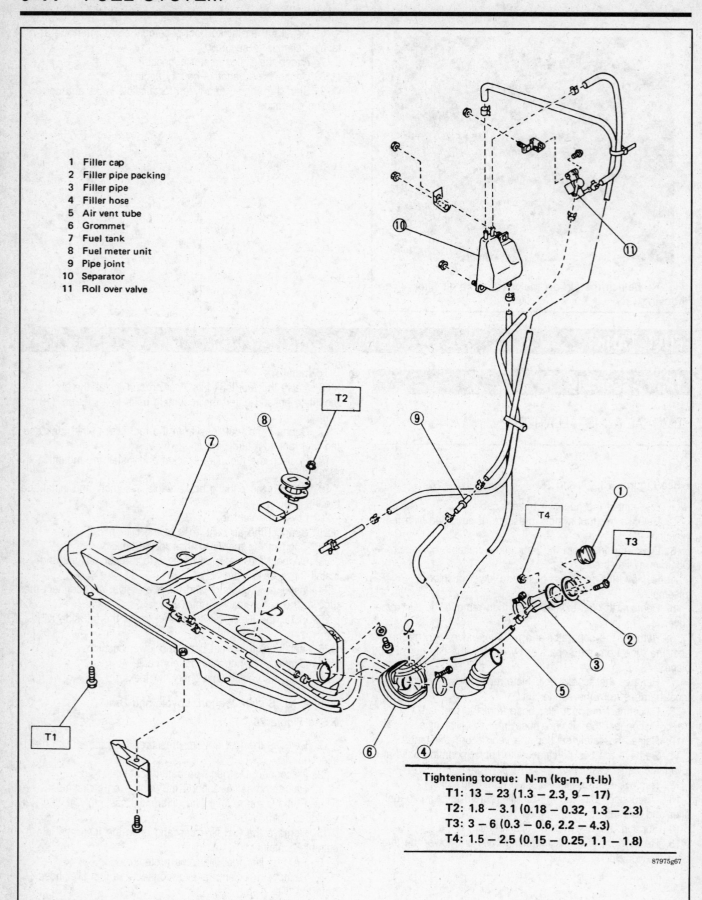

1 Filler cap
2 Filler pipe packing
3 Filler pipe
4 Filler hose
5 Air vent tube
6 Grommet
7 Fuel tank
8 Fuel meter unit
9 Pipe joint
10 Separator
11 Roll over valve

Tightening torque: N·m (kg-m, ft-lb)
   T1: 13 — 23 (1.3 — 2.3, 9 — 17)
   T2: 1.8 — 3.1 (0.18 — 0.32, 1.3 — 2.3)
   T3: 3 — 6 (0.3 — 0.6, 2.2 — 4.3)
   T4: 1.5 — 2.5 (0.15 — 0.25, 1.1 — 1.8)

87975g67

Fig. 73 Fuel tank assembly — Justy with carbureted engine

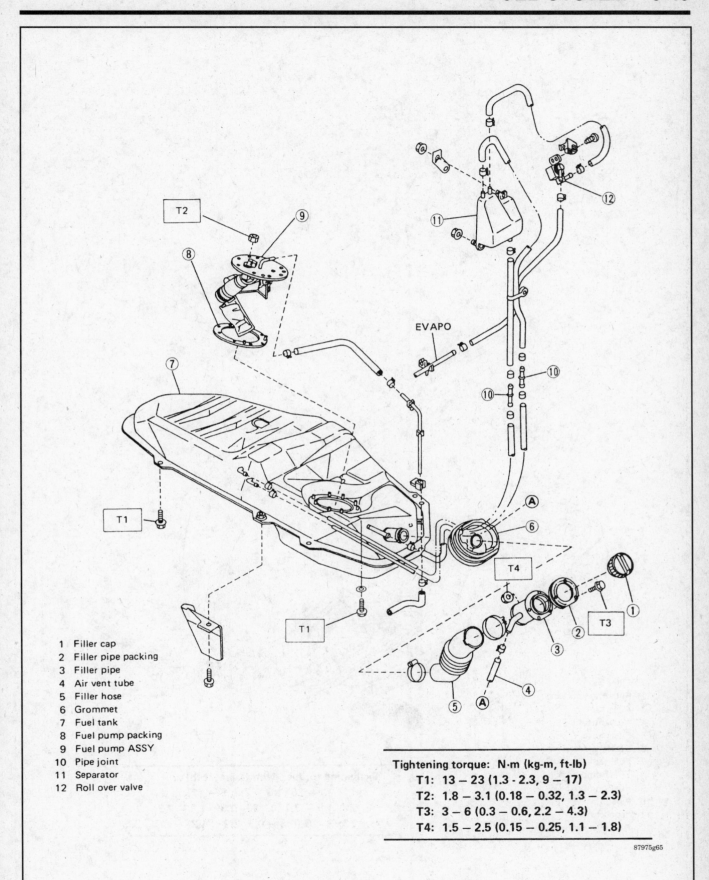

1 Filler cap
2 Filler pipe packing
3 Filler pipe
4 Air vent tube
5 Filler hose
6 Grommet
7 Fuel tank
8 Fuel pump packing
9 Fuel pump ASSY
10 Pipe joint
11 Separator
12 Roll over valve

Tightening torque: N·m (kg-m, ft-lb)
  T1: 13 — 23 (1.3 - 2.3, 9 — 17)
  T2: 1.8 — 3.1 (0.18 — 0.32, 1.3 — 2.3)
  T3: 3 — 6 (0.3 — 0.6, 2.2 — 4.3)
  T4: 1.5 — 2.5 (0.15 — 0.25, 1.1 — 1.8)

87975g65

Fig. 74 Fuel tank assembly — 3-door Justy with fuel injection

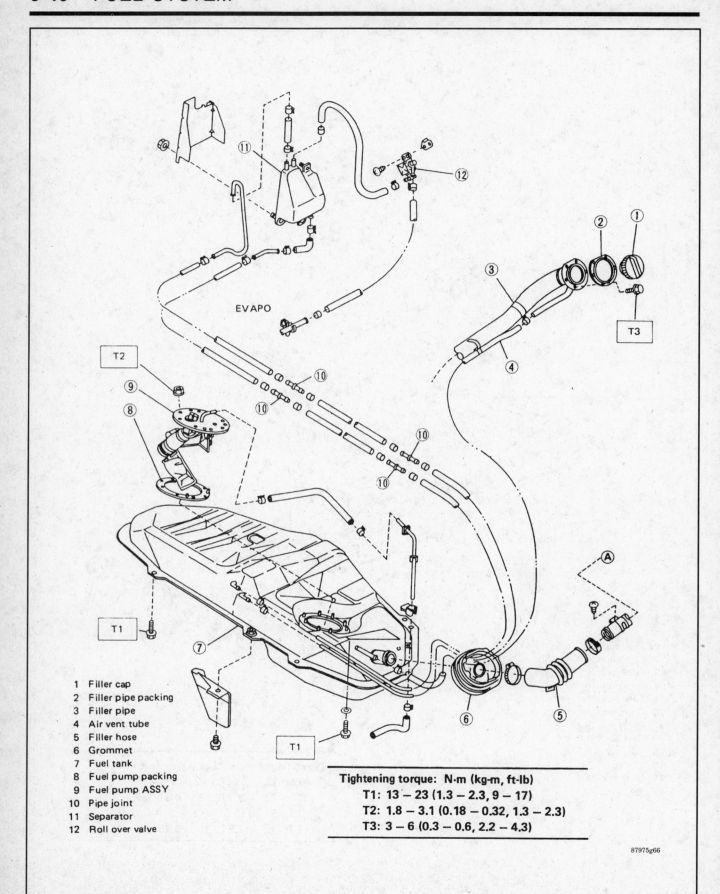

EVAPO

1 Filler cap
2 Filler pipe packing
3 Filler pipe
4 Air vent tube
5 Filler hose
6 Grommet
7 Fuel tank
8 Fuel pump packing
9 Fuel pump ASSY
10 Pipe joint
11 Separator
12 Roll over valve

Tightening torque: N·m (kg-m, ft-lb)
  T1: 13 — 23 (1.3 — 2.3, 9 — 17)
  T2: 1.8 — 3.1 (0.18 — 0.32, 1.3 — 2.3)
  T3: 3 — 6 (0.3 — 0.6, 2.2 — 4.3)

87975g66

Fig. 75 Fuel tank assembly — 5-door Justy with fuel injection

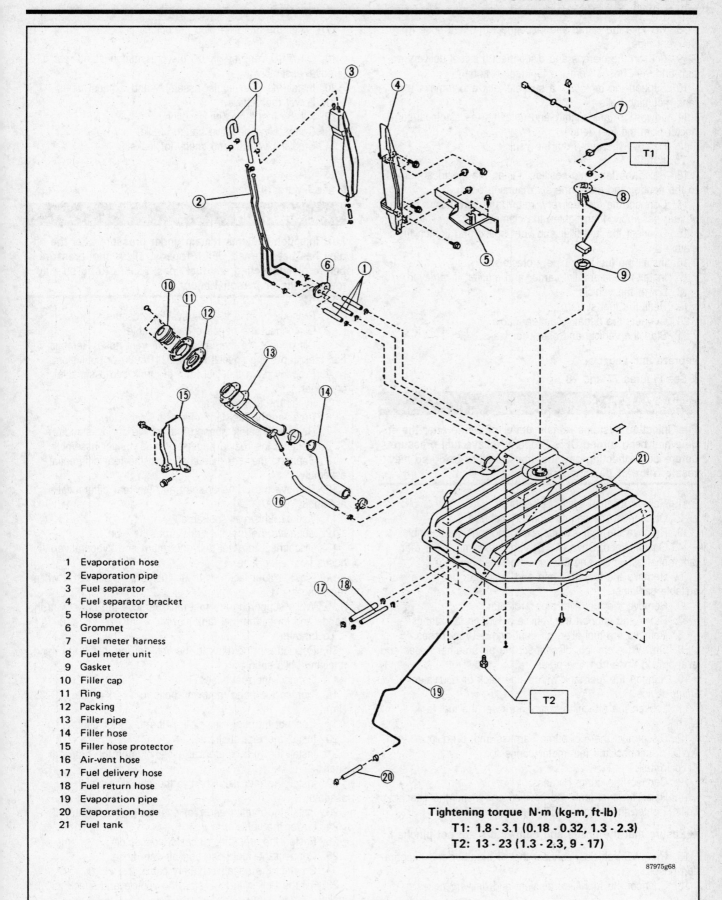

1   Evaporation hose
2   Evaporation pipe
3   Fuel separator
4   Fuel separator bracket
5   Hose protector
6   Grommet
7   Fuel meter harness
8   Fuel meter unit
9   Gasket
10 Filler cap
11 Ring
12 Packing
13 Filler pipe
14 Filler hose
15 Filler hose protector
16 Air-vent hose
17 Fuel delivery hose
18 Fuel return hose
19 Evaporation pipe
20 Evaporation hose
21 Fuel tank

Tightening torque N·m (kg-m, ft-lb)
T1: 1.8 - 3.1 (0.18 - 0.32, 1.3 - 2.3)
T2: 13 - 23 (1.3 - 2.3, 9 - 17)

87975g68

Fig. 76 Fuel tank assembly — Coupe, XT, Sedan, Wagon, Loyale and Brat

8. Remove the clamp and disconnect the vent hose from the vent pipe.

9. Loosen the clamps and disconnect the fuel delivery, return and vent hoses from the tank sender unit.

10. Support the tank with a suitable jack and remove the tank mounting bolts.

11. Lower the tank slightly and unfasten the electrical connector from the fuel sender.

12. Remove the tank from the vehicle.

To install:

13. Raise the tank into position, fasten the electrical harness to the sender and install the six mounting bolts.

14. Connect the fuel delivery, return and vent hoses to the sender assembly, then tighten the clamps.

15. Connect the fuel filler and vent hoses and tighten the clamps.

16. Install the fuel filler pipe protector.

17. Install the differential carrier and muffler, if removed.

18. Lower the vehicle.

19. Refill the fuel system.

20. Connect the negative battery cable.

21. Start the vehicle and check for leaks.

Impreza and Legacy

▶ **See Figures 77 and 78**

✴✴CAUTION

Fuel injection systems remain under pressure after the engine has been turned OFF. Properly relieve fuel pressure before disconnecting any fuel lines. Failure to do so may result in fire or personal injury.

1. Relieve the fuel system pressure.

2. Disconnect the negative battery cable.

3. Remove the rear exhaust pipe and muffler assembly.

4. On All Wheel Drive (AWD) vehicles, remove the rear differential assembly and the rear crossmember.

5. Remove the fuel filler cap and drain the fuel into a suitable container.

6. Remove the fuel filler pipe protector.

7. Raise and support the vehicle safely on jackstands.

8. Remove the fuel filler, air vent and delivery hoses.

9. On AWD vehicles, disconnect the air breather hoses and evaporation hose from the pipes.

10. Support the fuel tank with a floor jack or equivalent lifting device.

11. Loosen the attaching bolts and lower the fuel tank slightly.

12. Disconnect the fuel pump harness and, if equipped with AWD, disconnect the fuel meter connector.

To install:

13. Connect the pump harness.

14. Raise the fuel tank into position and install the attaching bolts. Tighten the bolts to 9-17 ft. lbs. (13-23 Nm).

➡**Ensure that the hoses and connectors are not pinched.**

15. On AWD vehicles, connect the air breather and evaporation hoses.

16. Connect the fuel filler, air vent and delivery hoses.

17. Install the fuel filler pipe protector.

18. Install the fuel filler cap.

19. On AWD vehicles, install the crossmember and rear differential assembly.

20. Install the rear muffler assembly and exhaust pipe.

21. Lower the vehicle.

22. Fill the fuel tank with gasoline.

23. Connect the negative battery cable.

24. Start the vehicle and check for leaks.

SVX

▶ **See Figure 79**

✴✴CAUTION

Fuel injection systems remain under pressure after the engine has been turned OFF. Properly relieve fuel pressure before disconnecting any fuel lines. Failure to do so may result in fire or personal injury.

1. Properly release the fuel system pressure.

2. Disconnect the negative battery cable.

3. Disconnect the fuel hose and air vent hose. Remove the fuel tank cap using special tool 42911PA000 or equivalent.

4. Properly drain the fuel from the tank into a suitable container.

5. Install the fuel tank cap.

6. Unfasten the fuel tank electrical connector.

7. Raise and safely support the vehicle on jackstands.

8. Remove the rear exhaust pipe and muffler assembly.

9. Separate the rear axle shaft from the rear differential assembly.

10. Remove the propeller shaft and the rear differential assembly.

11. Remove the rear subframe.

12. Separate the fuel filler duct from the pipe.

13. Disconnect the fuel delivery, return and evaporative hoses from each pipe.

14. Place a floor jack under the fuel tank to support it while removing it.

15. While supporting the fuel tank, remove the bolts from the bands and lower the fuel tank slowly.

To install:

16. Position the fuel tank to the vehicle and install the band retaining bolts snugly.

17. Connect the fuel hoses.

18. Tighten the band mounting bolts to 17-31 ft. lbs. (23-42 Nm).

19. Connect the fuel filler pipe to the fuel filler duct.

20. Install the rear subframe.

21. Install the rear differential assembly and the propeller shaft.

22. Install the rear axle shaft to the rear differential assembly.

23. Install the muffler and rear exhaust pipe assembly.

24. Lower the vehicle.

25. Fasten the fuel tank electrical connector.

26. Connect the fuel hose and air vent hose.

27. Connect the negative battery cable.

28. Fill the tank with fuel, start the vehicle and check for leaks.

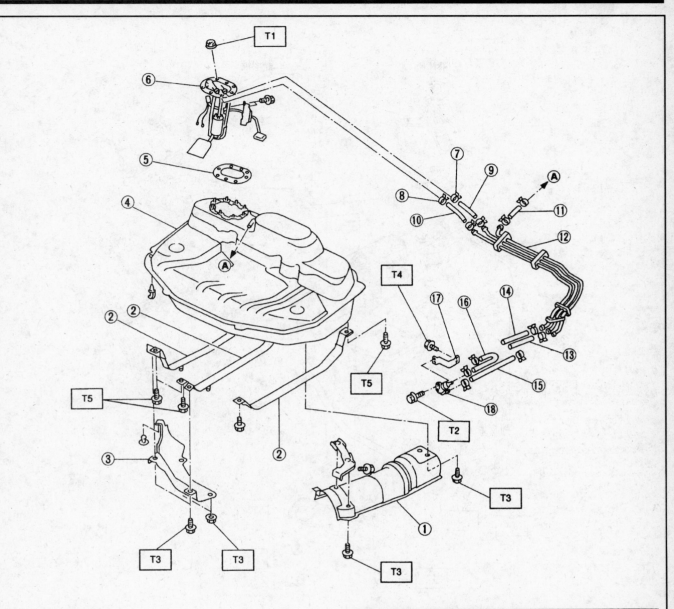

① Heat seated cover
② Fuel tank band
③ Protector
④ Fuel tank
⑤ Fuel pump gasket
⑥ Fuel pump ASSY
⑦ Clamp
⑧ Clip
⑨ Fuel delivery hose A
⑩ Fuel return hose A
⑪ Evaporation hose A
⑫ Fuel pipe ASSY
⑬ Fuel delivery hose B
⑭ Fuel return hose B
⑮ Evaporation hose B
⑯ Evaporation hose C
⑰ Roll over valve bracket
⑱ Roll over valve

Tightening torque: N·m (kg-m, ft-lb)
  T1: 3 — 6 (0.3 — 0.6, 2.2 — 4.4)
  T2: 5 — 8 (0.5 — 0.8, 3.7 — 5.9)
  T3: 5.5 — 9.5 (0.56 — 0.97, 4.1 — 7.0)
  T4: 13 — 23 (1.3 — 2.3, 10 — 17)
  T5: 23 — 43 (2.3 — 4.4, 17 — 32)

87975g71

Fig. 77 Fuel tank assembly — FWD Impreza and Legacy

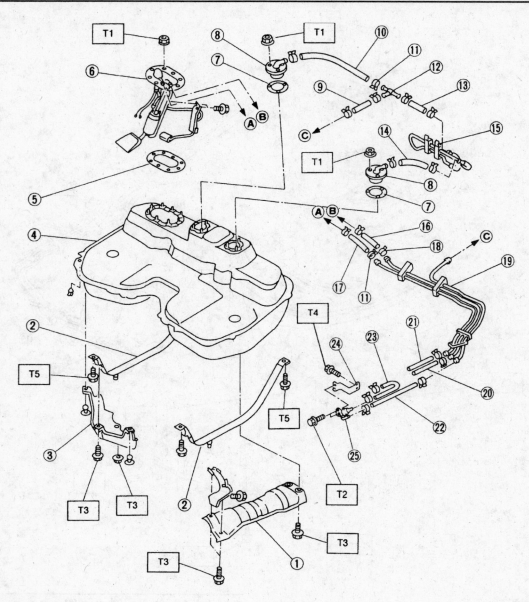

1. Heat sealed cover
2. Fuel tank band
3. Protector
4. Fuel tank
5. Fuel pump gasket
6. Fuel pump ASSY
7. Fuel cut valve gasket
8. Fuel cut valve
9. Evaporation hose C
10. Evaporation hose A
11. Clip
12. Joint pipe
13. Evaporation hose B
14. Evaporation hose D
15. Evaporation pipe ASSY
16. Fuel delivery hose A
17. Fuel return hose A

18. Clamp
19. Fuel pipe ASSY
20. Fuel delivery hose B
21. Fuel return hose B
22. Evaporation hose E
23. Evaporation hose F
24. Roll cover valve bracket
25. Roll over valve

Tightening torque: N·m (kg-m, ft-lb)
T1: 3 — 6 (0.3 — 0.6, 2.2 — 4.4)
T2: 5 — 8 (0.5 — 0.8, 3.7 — 5.9)
T3: 5.5 — 9.5 (0.56 — 0.97, 4.1 — 7.0)
T4: 13 — 23 (1.3 — 2.3, 10 — 17)
T5: 23 — 43 (2.3 — 4.4, 17 — 32)

Fig. 78 Fuel tank assembly — AWD Impreza and Legacy

87975g70

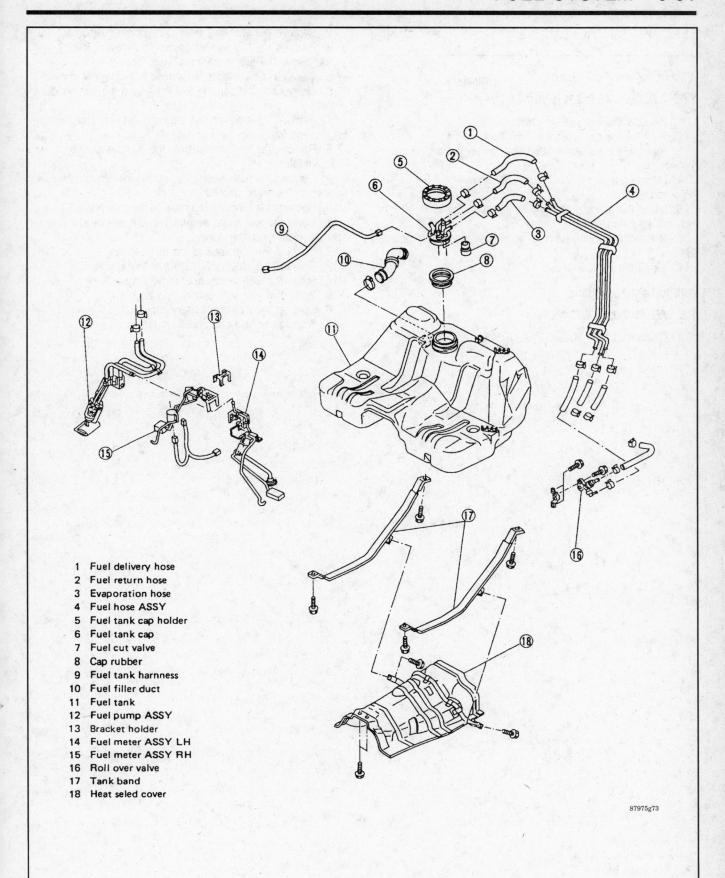

1 Fuel delivery hose
2 Fuel return hose
3 Evaporation hose
4 Fuel hose ASSY
5 Fuel tank cap holder
6 Fuel tank cap
7 Fuel cut valve
8 Cap rubber
9 Fuel tank harnness
10 Fuel filler duct
11 Fuel tank
12 Fuel pump ASSY
13 Bracket holder
14 Fuel meter ASSY LH
15 Fuel meter ASSY RH
16 Roll over valve
17 Tank band
18 Heat seled cover

87975g73

Fig. 79 Fuel tank assembly — SVX

SENDING UNIT REPLACEMENT

Without In-Tank Fuel Pump

1.8L, 2.2L, 2.5L AND 2.7L ENGINES

1. Release the fuel system pressure.
2. Remove the mat from the trunk floor.
3. Remove the access hole lid and disconnect the wiring harness.
4. Loosen the sending unit nuts and remove.
   To install:
5. Install the sending unit and tighten the nuts to 16-28 inch lbs. (2-3 Nm) in a star pattern.
6. Connect the wiring harness and install the access hole lid.
7. Install the trunk floor mat.

With In-Tank Fuel Pump

1.2L MFI AND 3.3L ENGINES

1. Disconnect the negative battery cable.
2. Remove the rear seat back and bottom cushion.
3. Remove the fuel sender access hole cover plate.
4. Relieve the fuel system pressure.
5. Disconnect the electrical harness from the fuel pump.
6. Disconnect and cap the fuel lines from the fuel sender assembly.
7. Remove the eight screws securing the fuel pump assembly into the fuel tank.
8. Remove the fuel sender from the pump assembly.
   To install:
9. Connect the fuel lines to the pump, then install the fuel sender on the pump assembly.
10. Connect the electrical harness to the fuel pump.
11. Install the fuel pump assembly in the fuel tank and install the eight mounting screws.
12. Connect the fuel lines to the fuel sender.
13. Connect the electrical harness to the fuel sender.
14. Install the fuel sender access hole cover.
15. Install the rear seat bottom and back.
16. Connect the negative battery cable.
17. Start the vehicle and check for leaks.

6

CHASSIS ELECTRICAL

UNDERSTANDING AND TROUBLESHOOTING ELECTRICAL SYSTEMS

Over the years import and domestic manufacturers have incorporated electronic control systems into their production lines. In fact, electronic control systems are so prevalent that all new cars and trucks built today are equipped with at least 1 on-board computer. These electronic components (with no moving parts) should theoretically last the life of the vehicle, provided that nothing external happens to damage the circuits or memory chips.

While it is true that electronic components should never wear out, in the real world malfunctions do occur. It is also true that any computer-based system is extremely sensitive to electrical voltages and cannot tolerate careless or haphazard testing/service procedures. An inexperienced individual can literally cause major damage looking for a minor problem by using the wrong kind of test equipment or connecting test leads/connectors with the ignition switch **ON**. When selecting test equipment, make sure the manufacturer's instructions state that the tester is compatible with whatever type of system is being serviced. Read all instructions carefully and double check all test points before installing probes or making any test connections.

The following section outlines basic diagnosis techniques for dealing with automotive electrical systems. Along with a general explanation of the various types of test equipment available to aid in servicing modern automotive systems, basic repair techniques for wiring harnesses and connectors are also given. Read the basic information before attempting any repairs or testing. This will provide the background of information necessary to avoid the most common and obvious mistakes that can cost both time and money. Although the replacement and testing procedures are simple in themselves, the systems are not, and unless one has a thorough understanding of all components and their function within a particular system, the logical test sequence these systems demand cannot be followed. Minor malfunctions can make a big difference, so it is important to know how each component affects the operation of the overall system in order to find the ultimate cause of a problem without replacing good components unnecessarily. It is not enough to use the correct test equipment; the test equipment must be used correctly.

Safety Precautions

✳✳CAUTION

Whenever working on or around any electrical or electronic systems, always observe these general precautions to prevent the possibility of personal injury or damage to electronic components.

- Never install or remove battery cables with the key **ON** or the engine running. Jumper cables should be connected with the key **OFF** to avoid power surges that can damage electronic control units. Engines equipped with computer controlled systems should avoid both giving and getting jump starts due to the possibility of serious damage to components from arcing in the engine compartment if connections are made with the ignition **ON**.

- Always remove the battery cables before charging the battery. Never use a high output charger on an installed battery or attempt to use any type of "hot shot" (24 volt) starting aid.

- Exercise care when inserting test probes into connectors to insure good contact without damaging the connector or spreading the pins. Always probe connectors from the rear (wire) side, NOT the pin side, to avoid accidental shorting of terminals during test procedures.

- Never remove or attach wiring harness connectors with the ignition switch **ON**, especially to an electronic control unit.

- Do not drop any components during service procedures and never apply 12 volts directly to any component (like a solenoid or relay) unless instructed specifically to do so. Some component electrical windings are designed to safely handle only 4 or 5 volts and can be destroyed in seconds if 12 volts are applied directly to the connector.

- Remove the electronic control unit if the vehicle is to be placed in an environment where temperatures exceed approximately 176°F (80°C), such as a paint spray booth or when arc/gas welding near the control unit location.

Understanding Basic Electricity

Understanding the basic theory of electricity makes electrical troubleshooting much easier. Several gauges are used in electrical troubleshooting to see inside the circuit being tested. Without a basic understanding, it will be difficult to understand testing procedures.

THE WATER ANALOGY

Electricity is the flow of electrons — hypothetical particles thought to constitute the basic stuff of electricity. Many people have been taught electrical theory using an analogy with water. In a comparison with water flowing in a pipe, the electrons would be the water. As the flow of water can be measured, the flow of electricity can be measured. The unit of measurement is amperes, frequently abbreviated amps. An ammeter will measure the actual amount of current flowing in the circuit.

Just as the water pressure is measured in units such as pounds per square inch, electrical pressure is measured in volts. When a voltmeter's 2 probes are placed on 2 live portions of an electrical circuit with different electrical pressures, current will flow through the voltmeter and produce a reading which indicates the difference in electrical pressure between the 2 parts of the circuit.

While increasing the voltage in a circuit will increase the flow of current, the actual flow depends not only on voltage, but on the resistance of the circuit. The standard unit for measuring circuit resistance is an ohm, measured by an ohmmeter. The ohmmeter is somewhat similar to an ammeter, but incorporates its own source of power so a standard voltage is always present.

CIRCUITS

An actual electric circuit consists of 4 basic parts. These are: the power source, such as a generator or battery; a hot wire, which conducts the electricity under a relatively high voltage to the component supplied by the circuit; the load, such as a lamp, motor, resistor or relay coil; and the ground wire, which carries the current back to the source under very low voltage. In such a circuit the bulk of the resistance exists between the point where the hot wire is connected to the load, and the point where the load is grounded. In an automobile, the vehicle's frame or body, which is made of steel, is used as a part of the ground circuit for many of the electrical devices.

Remember that, in electrical testing, the voltmeter is connected in parallel with the circuit being tested (without disconnecting any wires) and measures the difference in voltage between the locations of the 2 probes; that the ammeter is connected in series with the load (the circuit is separated at 1 point and the ammeter inserted so it becomes a part of the circuit); and the ohmmeter is self-powered, so all the power in the circuit should be OFF and the portion of the circuit to be measured contacted at either end by 1 of the probes of the meter.

For any electrical system to operate, it must make a complete circuit. This simply means that the power flow from the battery must make a complete circle. When an electrical component is operating, power flows from the battery to the component, passes through the component causing it to perform it to function (such as lighting a light bulb) and then returns to the battery through the ground of the circuit. This ground is usually (but not always) the metal part of the vehicle on which the electrical component is mounted.

Perhaps the easiest way to visualize this is to think of connecting a light bulb with 2 wires attached to it to your vehicle's battery. The battery in your vehicle has 2 posts (negative and positive). If 1 of the 2 wires attached to the light bulb was attached to the negative post of the battery and the other wire was attached to the positive post of the battery, you would have a complete circuit. Current from the battery would flow out 1 post, through the wire attached to it and then to the light bulb, where it would pass through causing it to light. It would then leave the light bulb, travel through the other wire, and return to the other post of the battery.

AUTOMOTIVE CIRCUITS

The normal automotive circuit differs from this simple example in 2 ways. First, instead of having a return wire from the bulb to the battery, the light bulb return the current to the battery through the chassis of the vehicle. Since the negative battery cable is attached to the chassis and the chassis is made of electrically conductive metal, the chassis of the vehicle can serve as a ground wire to complete the circuit. Secondly, most automotive circuits contain switches to turn components ON and OFF.

Some electrical components which require a large amount of current to operate also have a relay in their circuit. Since these circuits carry a large amount of current, the thickness of the wire in the circuit (gauge size) is also greater. If this large wire were connected from the component to the control switch on the instrument panel, and then back to the component, a voltage drop would occur in the circuit. To prevent this potential drop in voltage, an electromagnetic switch (relay) is used. The large wires in the circuit are connected from the vehicle battery to 1 side of the relay, and from the opposite side of the relay to the component. The relay is normally open, preventing current from passing through the circuit. An additional, smaller wire is connected from the relay to the control switch for the circuit. When the control switch is turned ON, it grounds the smaller wire from the relay and completes the circuit.

SHORT CIRCUITS

If you were to disconnect the light bulb (from the previous example of a light-bulb being connected to the battery by 2 wires) from the wires and touch the 2 wires together (please take our word for this; don't try it), the result will be a shower of sparks. A similar thing happens (on a smaller scale) when the power supply wire to a component or the electrical component itself becomes grounded before the normal ground connection for the circuit. To prevent damage to the system, the fuse for the circuit blows to interrupt the circuit — protecting the components from damage. Because grounding a wire from a power source makes a complete circuit — less the required component to use the power — the phenomenon is called a short circuit. The most common causes of short circuits are: the rubber insulation on a wire breaking or rubbing through to expose the current carrying core of the wire to a metal part of the car, or a shorted switch.

Some electrical systems on the vehicle are protected by a circuit breaker which is, basically, a self-repairing fuse. When either of the described events takes place in a system which is protected by a circuit breaker, the circuit breaker opens the circuit the same way a fuse does. However, when either the short is removed from the circuit or the surge subsides, the circuit breaker resets itself and does not have to be replaced as a fuse does.

Troubleshooting

When diagnosing a specific problem, organized troubleshooting is a must. The complexity of a modern automobile demands that you approach any problem in a logical, organized manner. There are certain troubleshooting techniques that are standard:

1. Establish when the problem occurs. Does the problem appear only under certain conditions? Were there any noises, odors, or other unusual symptoms?

2. Isolate the problem area. To do this, make some simple tests and observations; then eliminate the systems that are working properly. Check for obvious problems such as broken wires, dirty connections or split/disconnected vacuum hoses. Always check the obvious before assuming something complicated is the cause.

3. Test for problems systematically to determine the cause once the problem area is isolated. Are all the components functioning properly? Is there power going to electrical switches and motors? Is there vacuum at vacuum switches and/or actuators? Is there a mechanical problem such as bent linkage

or loose mounting screws? Performing careful, systematic checks will often turn up most causes on the first inspection without wasting time checking components that have little or no relationship to the problem.

4. Test all repairs after the work is done to make sure the problem is fixed. Some causes can be traced to more than 1 component, so a careful verification of repair work is important in order to pick up additional malfunctions that may cause a problem to reappear or a different problem to arise. A blown fuse, for example, is a simple problem that may require more than another fuse to repair. If you don't look for a problem that caused a fuse to blow, a shorted wire (for example) may go undetected.

Experience has shown that most problems tend to be the result of a fairly simple and obvious cause, such as loose or corroded connectors or air leaks in the intake system. This makes careful inspection of components during testing essential to quick and accurate troubleshooting.

BASIC TROUBLESHOOTING THEORY

Electrical problems generally fall into 1 of 3 areas:
- The component that is not functioning is not receiving current.
- The component itself is not functioning.
- The component is not properly grounded.

Problems that fall into the first category are by far the most complicated. It is the current supply system to the component which contains all the switches, relay, fuses, etc.

The electrical system can be checked with a test light and a jumper wire. A test light is a device that looks like a pointed screwdriver with a wire attached to it. It has a light bulb in its handle. A jumper wire is a piece of insulated wire with an alligator clip attached to each end.

If a light bulb is not working, you must follow a systematic plan to determine which of the 3 causes is the villain.

1. Turn ON the switch that controls the inoperable bulb.
2. Disconnect the power supply wire from the bulb.
3. Attach the ground wire to the test light to a good metal ground.
4. Touch the probe end of the test light to the end of the power supply wire that was disconnected from the bulb. If the bulb is receiving current, the test light will go ON.

➡️**If the bulb is one which works only when the ignition key is turned ON (turn signal), make sure the key is turned ON.**

If the test light does not go ON, then the problem is in the circuit between the battery and the bulb. As mentioned before, this includes all the switches, fuses, and relays in the system. Turn to a wiring diagram and find the bulb on the diagram. Follow the wire that runs back to the battery. The problem is an open circuit between the battery and the bulb. If the fuse is blown and, when replaced, immediately blows again, there is a short circuit in the system which must be located and repaired. If there is a switch in the system, bypass it with a jumper wire. This is done by connecting 1 end of the jumper wire to the power supply wire into the switch and the other end of the jumper wire to the wire coming out of the switch. If the test

light illuminates with the jumper wire installed, the switch or whatever was bypassed is defective.

➡️**Never substitute the jumper wire for the bulb, as the bulb is the component required to use the power from the power source.**

5. If the bulb in the test light goes ON, then the current is getting to the bulb that is not working in the car. This eliminates the first of the 3 possible causes. Connect the power supply wire and connect a jumper wire from the bulb to a good metal ground. Do this with the switch which controls the bulb works with jumper wire installed, then it has a bad ground. This is usually caused by the metal area on which the bulb mounts to the vehicle being coated with some type of foreign matter.

6. If neither test located the source of the trouble, then the light bulb itself is defective.

The above test procedure can be applied to any of the components of the chassis electrical system by substituting the component that is not working for the light bulb. Remember that for any electrical system to work, all connections must be clean and tight.

TEST EQUIPMENT

➡️**Pinpointing the exact cause of trouble in an electrical system can sometimes only be accomplished by the use of special test equipment. The following describes different types of commonly used test equipment and explains how to use them in diagnosis. In addition to the information covered below, the tool manufacturer's instructions booklet (provided with the tester) should be read and clearly understood before attempting any test procedures.**

Jumper Wires

Jumper wires are simple, yet extremely valuable, pieces of test equipment. They are basically test wires which are used to bypass sections of a circuit. The simplest type of jumper wire is a length of multi-strand wire with an alligator clip at each end. Jumper wires are usually fabricated from lengths of standard automotive wire and whatever type of connector (alligator clip, spade connector or pin connector) that is required for the particular vehicle being tested. The well equipped tool box will have several different styles of jumper wires in several different lengths. Some jumper wires are made with 3 or more terminals coming from a common splice for special purpose testing. In cramped, hard-to-reach areas it is advisable to have insulated boots over the jumper wire terminals in order to prevent accidental grounding, sparks, and possible fire, especially when testing fuel system components.

Jumper wires are used primarily to locate open electrical circuits, on either the ground (-) side of the circuit or on the hot (+) side. If an electrical component fails to operate, connect the jumper wire between the component and a good ground. If the component operates only with the jumper installed, the ground circuit is open. If the ground circuit is good, but the component does not operate, the circuit between the power feed and component may be open. By moving the jumper wire successively back from the lamp toward the power source, you can isolate the area of the circuit where the open is located. When the component stops functioning, or the power is cut off, the open is in the segment of wire between the jumper and the point previously tested.

You can sometimes connect the jumper wire directly from the battery to the hot terminal of the component, but first make sure the component uses 12 volts in operation. Some electrical components, such as fuel injectors, are designed to operate on about 4 volts and running 12 volts directly to the injector terminals can cause damage.

By inserting an in-line fuse holder between a set of test leads, a fused jumper wire can be used for bypassing open circuits. Use a 5 amp fuse to provide protection against voltage spikes. When in doubt, use a voltmeter to check the voltage input to the component and measure how much voltage is normally being applied.

✳✳CAUTION

Never use jumpers made from wire that is of lighter gauge than that which is used in the circuit under test. If the jumper wire is of too small a gauge, it may overheat and possibly melt. Never use jumpers to bypass high resistance loads in a circuit. Bypassing resistances, in effect, creates a short circuit. This may, in turn, cause damage and fire. Jumper wires should only be used to bypass lengths of wire.

Unpowered Test Lights

The 12 volt test light is used to check circuits and components while electrical current is flowing through them. It is used for voltage and ground tests. Twelve volt test lights come in different styles but all have 3 main parts; a ground clip, a probe, and a light. The most commonly used 12 volt test lights have pick-type probes. To use a 12 volt test light, connect the ground clip to a good ground and probe wherever necessary with the pick. The pick should be sharp so it can be probed into tight spaces.

✳✳CAUTION

Do not use a test light to probe electronic ignition spark plug or coil wires. Never use a pick-type test light to probe wiring on computer controlled systems unless specifically instructed to do so. Any wire insulation that is pierced by the test light probe should be taped and sealed with silicone after testing.

Like the jumper wire, the 12 volt test light is used to isolate opens in circuits. But, whereas the jumper wire is used to bypass the open to operate the load, the 12 volt test light is used to locate the presence of voltage in a circuit. If the test light glows, you know that there is power up to that point; if the 12 volt test light does not glow when its probe is inserted into the wire or connector, you know that there is an open circuit (no power). Move the test light in successive steps back toward the power source until the light in the handle does

glow. When it glows, the open is between the probe and point which was probed previously.

➡**The test light does not detect that 12 volts (or any particular amount of voltage) is present; it only detects that some voltage is present. It is advisable before using the test light to touch its terminals across the battery posts to make sure the light is operating properly.**

Self-Powered Test Lights

The self-powered test light usually contains a 1.5 volt penlight battery. One type of self-powered test light is similar in design to the 12 volt unit. This type has both the battery and the light in the handle, along with a pick-type probe tip. The second type has the light toward the open tip, so the light illuminates the contact point. The self-powered test light is a dual purpose piece of test equipment. It can be used to test for either open or short circuits when power is isolated from the circuit (continuity test). A powered test light should not be used on any computer controlled system or component unless specifically instructed to do so. Many engine sensors can be destroyed by even this small amount of voltage applied directly to the terminals.

Voltmeters

A voltmeter is used to measure voltage at any point in a circuit, or to measure the voltage drop across any part of a circuit. It can also be used to check continuity in a wire or circuit by indicating current flow from 1 end to the other. Analog voltmeters usually have various scales on the meter dial and a selector switch to allow the selection of different voltages. The voltmeter has a positive and a negative lead. To avoid damage to the meter, always connect the negative lead to the negative (-) side of the circuit (to ground or nearest the ground side of the circuit) and connect the positive lead to the positive (+) side of the circuit (to the power source or the nearest power source). Note that the negative voltmeter lead will always be black and that the positive voltmeter will always be some color other than black (usually red).

Depending on how the voltmeter is connected into the circuit, it has several uses. A voltmeter can be connected either in parallel or in series with a circuit and it has a very high resistance to current flow. When connected in parallel, only a small amount of current will flow through the voltmeter current path; the rest will flow through the normal circuit current path and the circuit will work normally. When the voltmeter is connected in series with a circuit, only a small amount of current can flow through the circuit. The circuit will not work properly, but the voltmeter reading will show if the circuit is complete or not.

Ohmmeters

The ohmmeter is designed to read resistance (which is measured in ohms or Ω) in a circuit or component. Although there are several different styles of ohmmeters, all analog meters will usually have a selector switch which permits the measurement of different ranges of resistance (usually the selector switch allows the multiplication of the meter reading by 10, 100, 1000, and 10,000). A calibration knob allows the meter to be set at zero for accurate measurement. Since all ohmmeters are powered by an internal battery, the ohmmeter can be used as a self-powered test light. When the ohmmeter is connected, current from the ohmmeter flows through the circuit or component being tested. Since the ohmmeter's internal resistance and voltage are known values, the amount of current flow through the meter depends on the resistance of the circuit or component being tested.

The ohmmeter can be used to perform a continuity test for opens or shorts (either by observation of the meter needle or as a self-powered test light), and to read actual resistance in a circuit. It should be noted that the ohmmeter is used to check the resistance of a component or wire while there is no voltage applied to the circuit. Current flow from an outside voltage source (such as the vehicle battery) can damage the ohmmeter, so the circuit or component should be isolated from the vehicle electrical system before any testing is done. Since the ohmmeter uses its own voltage source, either lead can be connected to any test point.

➡ **When checking diodes or other solid state components, the ohmmeter leads can only be connected one way in order to measure current flow in a single direction. Make sure the positive (+) and negative (-) terminal connections are as described in the test procedures to verify the one-way diode operation.**

In using the meter for making continuity checks, do not be concerned with the actual resistance readings. Zero resistance, or any ohm reading, indicates continuity in the circuit. Infinite resistance indicates an open in the circuit. A high resistance reading where there should be none indicates a problem in the circuit. Checks for short circuits are made in the same manner as checks for open circuits except that the circuit must be isolated from both power and normal ground. Infinite resistance indicates no continuity to ground, while zero resistance indicates a dead short to ground.

Ammeters

An ammeter measures the amount of current flowing through a circuit in units called amperes or amps. Amperes are units of electron flow which indicate how fast the electrons are flowing through the circuit. Since Ohms Law dictates that current flow in a circuit is equal to the circuit voltage divided by the total circuit resistance, increasing voltage also increases the current level (amps). Likewise, any decrease in resistance will increase the amount of amps in a circuit. At normal operating voltage, most circuits have a characteristic amount of amperes, called "current draw" which can be measured using an ammeter. By referring to a specified current draw rating, measuring the amperes, and comparing the 2 values, one can determine what is happening within the circuit to aid in diagnosis. An open circuit, for example, will not allow any current to flow so the ammeter reading will be zero. More current flows through a heavily loaded circuit or when the charging system is operating.

An ammeter is always connected in series with the circuit being tested. All of the current that normally flows through the circuit must also flow through the ammeter; if there is any other path for the current to follow, the ammeter reading will not be accurate. The ammeter itself has very little resistance to current flow and therefore will not affect the circuit, but it will measure current draw only when the circuit is closed and electricity is flowing. Excessive current draw can blow fuses and drain the battery, while a reduced current draw can cause motors to run slowly, lights to dim and other components to not operate properly. The ammeter can help diagnose these conditions by locating the cause of the high or low reading.

Multimeters

Different combinations of test meters can be built into a single unit designed for specific tests. Some of the more common combination test devices are known as Volt/Amp testers, Tach/Dwell meters, or Digital Multimeters. The Volt/Amp tester is used for charging system, starting system or battery tests and consists of a voltmeter, an ammeter and a variable resistance carbon pile. The voltmeter will usually have at least 2 ranges for use with 6, 12 and/or 24 volt systems. The ammeter also has more than 1 range for testing various levels of battery loads and starter current draw. The carbon pile can be adjusted to offer different amounts of resistance. The Volt/Amp tester has heavy leads to carry large amounts of current and many later models have an inductive ammeter pickup that clamps around the wire to simplify test connections. On some models, the ammeter also has a zero-center scale to allow testing of charging and starting systems without switching leads or polarity. A digital multimeter is a voltmeter, ammeter and ohmmeter combined in an instrument which gives a digital readout. These are often used when testing solid state circuits because of their high input impedance (usually 10 megohms or more).

The tach/dwell meter that combines a tachometer and a dwell (cam angle) meter is a specialized kind of voltmeter. The tachometer scale is marked to show engine speed in rpm and the dwell scale is marked to show degrees of distributor shaft rotation. In most electronic ignition systems, dwell is determined by the control unit, but the dwell meter can also be used to check the duty cycle (operation) of some electronic engine control systems. Some tach/dwell meters are powered by an internal battery, while others take their power from the vehicle battery in use. The battery powered testers usually require calibration (much like an ohmmeter) before testing.

TESTING

Open Circuits

To use the self-powered test light or a multimeter to check for open circuits, first isolate the circuit from the vehicle's 12 volt power source by disconnecting the battery or wiring harness connector. Connect the test light or ohmmeter ground clip to a good ground and probe sections of the circuit sequentially with the test light. (start from either end of the circuit). If the light is out/or there is infinite resistance, the open is between the probe and the circuit ground. If the light is ON/or the meter shows continuity, the open is between the probe and end of the circuit toward the power source.

Short Circuits

By isolating the circuit both from power and from ground, and using a self-powered test light or multimeter, you can check for shorts to ground in the circuit. Isolate the circuit from power and ground. Connect the test light or ohmmeter ground clip to a good ground and probe any easy-to-reach test point in the circuit. If the light comes ON or there is continuity, there is a short somewhere in the circuit. To isolate the short, probe a test point at either end of the isolated circuit (the light should be ON/there should be continuity). Leave the test light probe engaged and open connectors, switches, remove parts, etc., sequentially, until the light goes out/continuity is broken. When the light goes out, the short is between the last circuit component opened and the previous circuit opened.

➡The battery in the test light and does not provide much current. A weak battery may not provide enough power to illuminate the test light even when a complete circuit is made (especially if there are high resistances in the circuit). Always make sure the test battery is strong. To check the battery, briefly touch the ground clip to the probe; if the light glows brightly the battery is strong enough for testing. Never use a self-powered test light to perform checks for opens or shorts when power is applied to the electrical system under test. The 12 volt vehicle power will quickly burn out the light bulb in the test light.

Available Voltage Measurement

Set the voltmeter selector switch to the 20V position and connect the meter negative lead to the negative post of the battery. Connect the positive meter lead to the positive post of the battery and turn the ignition switch ON to provide a load. Read the voltage on the meter or digital display. A well charged battery should register over 12 volts. If the meter reads below 11.5 volts, the battery power may be insufficient to operate the electrical system properly. This test determines voltage available from the battery and should be the first step in any electrical trouble diagnosis procedure. Many electrical problems, especially on computer controlled systems, can be caused by a low state of charge in the battery. Excessive corrosion at the battery cable terminals can cause a poor contact that will prevent proper charging and full battery current flow.

Normal battery voltage is 12 volts when fully charged. When the battery is supplying current to 1 or more circuits it is said to be "under load." When everything is OFF the electrical system is under a "no-load" condition. A fully charged battery may show about 12.5 volts at no load; will drop to 12 volts under medium load; and will drop even lower under heavy load. If the battery is partially discharged the voltage decrease under heavy load may be excessive, even though the battery shows 12 volts or more at no load. When allowed to discharge further, the battery's available voltage under load will decrease more severely. For this reason, it is important that the battery be fully charged during all testing procedures to avoid errors in diagnosis and incorrect test results.

Voltage Drop

When current flows through a resistance, the voltage beyond the resistance is reduced (the larger the current, the greater the reduction in voltage). When no current is flowing, there is no voltage drop because there is no current flow. All points in the circuit which are connected to the power source are at the same voltage as the power source. The total voltage drop always equals the total source voltage. In a long circuit with many connectors, a series of small, unwanted voltage drops due to corrosion at the connectors can add up to a total loss of voltage which impairs the operation of the normal loads in the circuit. The maximum allowable voltage drop under load is critical, especially if there is more than 1 high resistance problem in a circuit because all voltage drops are cumulative. A small drop is normal due to the resistance of the conductors.

INDIRECT COMPUTATION OF VOLTAGE DROPS

1. Set the voltmeter selector switch to the 20 volt position.
2. Connect the meter negative lead to a good ground.
3. While operating the circuit, probe all loads in the circuit with the positive meter lead and observe the voltage readings. A drop should be noticed after the first load. But, there should be little or no voltage drop before the first load.

DIRECT MEASUREMENT OF VOLTAGE DROPS

1. Set the voltmeter switch to the 20 volt position.
2. Connect the voltmeter negative lead to the ground side of the load to be measured.
3. Connect the positive lead to the positive side of the resistance or load to be measured.
4. Read the voltage drop directly on the 20 volt scale.

Too high a voltage indicates too high a resistance. If, for example, a blower motor runs too slowly, you can determine if perhaps there is too high a resistance in the resistor pack. By taking voltage drop readings in all parts of the circuit, you can isolate the problem. Too low a voltage drop indicates too low a resistance. Take the blower motor for example again. If a blower motor runs too fast in the MED and/or LOW position, the problem might be isolated in the resistor pack by taking voltage drop readings in all parts of the circuit to locate a possibly shorted resistor.

HIGH RESISTANCE TESTING

1. Set the voltmeter selector switch to the 4 volt position.
2. Connect the voltmeter positive lead to the positive post of the battery.
3. Turn ON the headlights and heater blower to provide a load.
4. Probe various points in the circuit with the negative voltmeter lead.
5. Read the voltage drop on the 4 volt scale. Some average maximum allowable voltage drops are:
   - FUSE PANEL: 0.7 volts
   - IGNITION SWITCH: 0.5 volts
   - HEADLIGHT SWITCH: 0.7 volts
   - IGNITION COIL (+): 0.5 volts
   - ANY OTHER LOAD: 1.3 volts

➡Voltage drops are all measured while a load is operating; without current flow, there will be no voltage drop.

Resistance Measurement

The batteries in an ohmmeter will weaken with age and temperature, so the ohmmeter must be calibrated or "zeroed" before taking measurements. To zero the meter, place the selector switch in its lowest range and touch the 2 ohmmeter leads together. Turn the calibration knob until the meter needle is exactly on zero.

➡**All analog (needle) type ohmmeters must be zeroed before use, but some digital ohmmeter models are automatically calibrated when the switch is turned ON. Self-calibrating digital ohmmeters do not have an adjusting knob, but its a good idea to check for a zero readout before use by touching the leads together. All computer controlled systems require the use of a digital ohmmeter with at least 10 megohms impedance for testing. Before any test procedures are attempted, make sure the ohmmeter used is compatible with the electrical system or damage to the on-board computer could result.**

To measure resistance, first isolate the circuit from the vehicle power source by disconnecting the battery cables or the harness connector. Make sure the key is **OFF** when disconnecting any components or the battery. Where necessary, also isolate at least 1 side of the circuit to be checked in order to avoid reading parallel resistances. Parallel circuit resistances will always give a lower reading than the actual resistance of either of the branches. When measuring the resistance of parallel circuits, the total resistance will always be lower than the smallest resistance in the circuit. Connect the meter leads to both sides of the circuit (wire or component) and read the actual measured ohms on the meter scale. Make sure the selector switch is set to the proper ohm scale for the circuit being tested to avoid misreading the ohmmeter test value.

✳✳WARNING

Never use an ohmmeter with power applied to the circuit. Like the self-powered test light, the ohmmeter is designed to operate on its own power supply. The normal 12 volt automotive electrical system current could damage the meter!

Wiring Harnesses

The average automobile contains about ½ mile of wiring, with hundreds of individual connections. To protect the many wires from damage and to keep them from becoming a confusing tangle, they are organized into bundles, enclosed in plastic or taped together and called wiring harnesses. Different harnesses serve different parts of the vehicle. Individual wires are color coded to help trace them through a harness where sections are hidden from view.

Automotive wiring or circuit conductors can be in any 1 of 3 forms:
1. Single strand wire
2. Multi-strand wire
3. Printed circuitry

Single strand wire has a solid metal core and is usually used inside such components as alternators, motors, relays and other devices. Multi-strand wire has a core made of many small strands of wire twisted together into a single conductor. Most of the wiring in an automotive electrical system is made up of multi-strand wire, either as a single conductor or grouped

together in a harness. All wiring is color coded on the insulator, either as a solid color or as a colored wire with an identification stripe. A printed circuit is a thin film of copper or other conductor that is printed on an insulator backing. Occasionally, a printed circuit is sandwiched between 2 sheets of plastic for more protection and flexibility. A complete printed circuit, consisting of conductors, insulating material and connectors for lamps or other components is called a printed circuit board. Printed circuitry is used in place of individual wires or harnesses in places where space is limited, such as behind instrument panels.

Since automotive electrical systems are very sensitive to changes in resistance, the selection of properly sized wires is critical when systems are repaired. A loose or corroded connection or a replacement wire that is too small for the circuit will add extra resistance and an additional voltage drop to the circuit. A 10 percent voltage drop can result in slow or erratic motor operation, for example, even though the circuit is complete. The wire gauge number is an expression of the cross-section area of the conductor. The most common system for expressing wire size is the American Wire Gauge (AWG) system.

Gauge numbers are assigned to conductors of various cross-section areas. As gauge number increases, area decreases and the conductor becomes smaller. A 5 gauge conductor is smaller than a 1 gauge conductor and a 10 gauge is smaller than a 5 gauge. As the cross-section area of a conductor decreases, resistance increases and so does the gauge number. A conductor with a higher gauge number will carry less current than a conductor with a lower gauge number.

➡**Gauge wire size refers to the size of the conductor, not the size of the complete wire. It is possible to have 2 wires of the same gauge with different diameters because 1 may have thicker insulation than the other.**

12 volt automotive electrical systems generally use 10, 12, 14, 16 and 18 gauge wire. Main power distribution circuits and larger accessories usually use 10 and 12 gauge wire. Battery cables are usually 4 or 6 gauge, although 1 and 2 gauge wires are occasionally used. Wire length must also be considered when making repairs to a circuit. As conductor length increases, so does resistance. An 18 gauge wire, for example, can carry a 10 amp load for 10 feet without excessive voltage drop; however if a 15 foot wire is required for the same 10 amp load, it must be a 16 gauge wire.

An electrical schematic shows the electrical current paths when a circuit is operating properly. It is essential to understand how a circuit works before trying to figure out why it doesn't. Schematics break the entire electrical system down into individual circuits and show only 1 particular circuit. In a schematic, no attempt is made to represent wiring and components as they physically appear on the vehicle; switches and other components are shown as simply as possible. Face views of harness connectors show the cavity or terminal locations in all multi-pin connectors to help locate test points.

If you need to backprobe a connector while it is on the component, the order of the terminals must be mentally reversed. The wire color code can help in this situation, as well as a keyway, lock tab or other reference mark.

WIRING REPAIR

Soldering is a quick, efficient method of joining metals permanently. Everyone who has the occasion to make wiring repairs should know how to solder. Electrical connections that are soldered are far less likely to come apart and will conduct electricity much better than connections that are only "pig-tailed" together. The most popular (and preferred) method of soldering is with an electrical soldering gun. Soldering irons are available in many sizes and wattage ratings. Irons with higher wattage ratings deliver higher temperatures and recover lost heat faster. A small soldering iron rated for no more than 50 watts is recommended, especially on electrical systems where excess heat can damage the components being soldered.

There are 3 ingredients necessary for successful soldering; proper flux, good solder and sufficient heat. A soldering flux is necessary to clean the metal of tarnish, prepare it for soldering and to enable the solder to spread into tiny crevices. When soldering, always use a rosin core solder which is non-corrosive and will not attract moisture once the job is finished. Other types of flux (acid core) will leave a residue that will attract moisture and cause the wires to corrode. Tin is a unique metal with a low melting point. In a molten state, it dissolves and alloys easily with many metals. Solder is made by mixing tin with lead. The most common proportions are 40/60, 50/50 and 60/40, with the percentage of tin listed first. Low priced solders usually contain less tin, making them very difficult for a beginner to use because more heat is required to melt the solder. A common solder is 40/60 which is well suited for all-around general use, but 60/40 melts easier and is preferred for electrical work.

Soldering Techniques

Successful soldering requires that the metals to be joined be heated to a temperature that will melt the solder, usually 360-460°F (182-238°C). Contrary to popular belief, the purpose of the soldering iron is not to melt the solder itself, but to heat the parts being soldered to a temperature high enough to melt the solder when it is touched to the work. Melting flux-cored solder on the soldering iron will usually destroy the effectiveness of the flux.

➡**Soldering tips are made of copper for good heat conductivity, but must be "tinned" regularly for quick transference of heat to the project and to prevent the solder from sticking to the iron. To "tin" the iron, simply heat it and touch the flux-cored solder to the tip; the solder will flow over the hot tip. Wipe the excess off with a clean rag, but be careful as the iron will be hot.**

After some use, the tip may become pitted. If so, simply dress the tip smooth with a smooth file and "tin" the tip again. Flux-cored solder will remove oxides but rust, bits of insulation and oil or grease must be removed with a wire brush or emery cloth. For maximum strength in soldered parts, the joint must start off clean and tight. Weak joints will result in gaps too wide for the solder to bridge.

If a separate soldering flux is used, it should be brushed or swabbed on only those areas that are to be soldered. Most solders contain a core of flux and separate fluxing is unnecessary. Hold the work to be soldered firmly. It is best to solder on a wooden board, because a metal vise will only rob the piece to be soldered of heat and make it difficult to melt the solder. Hold the soldering tip with the broadest face against the work to be soldered. Apply solder under the tip close to the work, using enough solder to give a heavy film between the iron and the piece being soldered, while moving slowly and making sure the solder melts properly. Keep the work level or the solder will run to the lowest part and favor the thicker parts, because these require more heat to melt the solder. If the soldering tip overheats (the solder coating on the face of the tip burns up), it should be retinned. Once the soldering is completed, let the soldered joint stand until cool. Tape and seal all soldered wire splices after the repair has cooled.

Wire Harness Connectors

Most connectors in the engine compartment or that are otherwise exposed to the elements are protected against moisture and dirt which could create oxidation and deposits on the terminals.

These special connectors are weather-proof. All repairs require the use of a special terminal and the tool required to service it. This tool is used to remove the pin and sleeve terminals. If removal is attempted with an ordinary pick, there is a good chance that the terminal will be bent or deformed. Unlike standard blade type terminals, these weather-proof terminals cannot be straightened once they are bent. Make certain that the connectors are properly seated and all of the sealing rings are in place when connecting leads. On some models, a hinge-type flap provides a backup or secondary locking feature for the terminals. Most secondary locks are used to improve connector reliability by retaining the terminals if the small terminal lock tangs are not positioned properly.

Molded-on connectors require complete replacement of the connection. This means splicing a new connector assembly into the harness. All splices should be soldered to insure proper contact. Use care when probing the connections or replacing terminals in them as it is possible to short between opposite terminals. If this happens to the wrong terminal pair, it is possible to damage certain components. Always use jumper wires between connectors for circuit checking and never probe through weatherproof seals.

Open circuits are often difficult to locate by sight because corrosion or terminal misalignment are hidden by the connectors. Merely wiggling a connector on a sensor or in the wiring harness may correct the open circuit condition. This should always be considered when an open circuit or a failed sensor is indicated. Intermittent problems may also be caused by oxidized or loose connections. When using a circuit tester for diagnosis, always probe connections from the wire side. Be careful not to damage sealed connectors with test probes.

All wiring harnesses should be replaced with identical parts, using the same gauge wire and connectors. When signal wires are spliced into a harness, use wire with high temperature insulation only. It is seldom necessary to replace a complete harness. If replacement is necessary, pay close attention to insure proper harness routing. Secure the harness with suitable plastic wire clamps to prevent vibrations from causing the harness to wear in spots or contact any hot components.

➡Weatherproof connectors cannot be replaced with standard connectors. Instructions are provided with replacement connector and terminal packages. Some wire harnesses have mounting indicators (usually pieces of colored tape) to mark where the harness is to be secured.

In making wiring repairs, its important that you always replace damaged wires with wiring of the same gauge as the wire being replaced. The heavier the wire, the smaller the gauge number. Wires are color-coded to aid in identification and whenever possible the same color coded wire should be used for replacement. A wire stripping and crimping tool is necessary to install solderless terminal connectors. Test all crimps by pulling on the wires; it should not be possible to pull the wires out of a good crimp.

Wires which are open, exposed or otherwise damaged are repaired by simple splicing. Where possible, if the wiring harness is accessible and the damaged place in the wire can be located, it is best to open the harness and check for all possible damage. In an inaccessible harness, the wire must be bypassed with a new insert, usually taped to the outside of the old harness.

When replacing fusible links, be sure to use fusible link wire, NOT ordinary automotive wire. Make sure the fusible segment is of the same gauge and construction as the one being replaced and double the stripped end when crimping the terminal connector for a good contact. The melted (open) fusible link segment of the wiring harness should be cut off as close to the harness as possible, then a new segment spliced in as described. In the case of a damaged fusible link that feeds 2 harness wires, the harness connections should be replaced with 2 fusible link wires so each circuit will have its own separate protection.

➡Most of the problems caused in the wiring harness are due to bad ground connections. Always check all vehicle ground connections for corrosion or looseness before performing any power feed checks to eliminate the chance of a bad ground affecting the circuit.

Hard-Shell Connectors

Unlike molded connectors, the terminal contacts in hard-shell connectors can be replaced. Weatherproof hard-shell connectors with the leads molded into the shell have non-replaceable terminal ends. Replacement usually involves the use of a special terminal removal tool that depresses the locking tangs (barbs) on the connector terminal and allows the connector to be removed from the rear of the shell. The connector shell should be replaced if it shows any evidence of burning, melting, cracks, or breaks. Replace individual terminals that are burnt, corroded, distorted or loose.

➡The insulation crimp must be tight to prevent the insulation from sliding back on the wire when the wire is pulled. The insulation must be visibly compressed under the crimp tabs, and the ends of the crimp should be turned in for a firm grip on the insulation.

The wire crimp must be made with all wire strands inside the crimp. The terminal must be fully compressed on the wire strands with the ends of the crimp tabs turned in to make a

firm grip on the wire. Check all connections with an ohmmeter to insure a good contact. There should be no measurable resistance between the wire and the terminal when connected.

Fusible Links

The fuse link is a short length of special, Hypalon (high temperature) insulated wire, integral with the engine compartment wiring harness and should not be confused with standard wire. It is several wire gauges smaller than the circuit which it protects. Under no circumstances should a fuse link replacement repair be made using a length of standard wire cut from bulk stock or from another wiring harness.

To repair any blown fuse link use the following procedure:
1. Determine which circuit is damaged, its location and the cause of the open fuse link. If the damaged fuse link is 1 of 3 fed by a common No. 10 or 12 gauge feed wire, determine the specific affected circuit.
2. Disconnect the negative battery cable.
3. Cut the damaged fuse link from the wiring harness and discard it. If the fuse link is 1 of 3 circuits fed by a single feed wire, cut it out of the harness at each splice end and discard it.
4. Identify and procure the proper fuse link with butt connectors for attaching the fuse link to the harness.

➡Heat shrink tubing must be slipped over the wire before crimping and soldering the connection.

5. To repair any fuse link in a 3-link group with 1 feed:
   a. After cutting the open link out of the harness, cut each of the remaining undamaged fuse links close to the feed wire weld.
   b. Strip approximately ½ in. (13mm) of insulation from the detached ends of the 2 good fuse links. Insert 2 wire ends into 1 end of a butt connector, then carefully push 1 stripped end of the replacement fuse link into the same end of the butt connector and crimp all 3 firmly together.

➡Care must be taken when fitting the 3 fuse links into the butt connector as the internal diameter is a snug fit for 3 wires. Make sure to use a proper crimping tool. Pliers, side cutters, etc. will not apply the proper crimp to retain the wires and withstand a pull test.

   c. After crimping the butt connector to the 3 fuse links, cut the weld portion from the feed wire and strip approximately ½ in. (13mm) of insulation from the cut end. Insert the stripped end into the open end of the butt connector and crimp very firmly.
   d. To attach the remaining end of the replacement fuse link, strip approximately ½ in. (13mm) of insulation from the wire end of the circuit from which the blown fuse link was removed, and firmly crimp a butt connector or equivalent to the stripped wire. Then, insert the end of the replacement link into the other end of the butt connector and crimp firmly.
   e. Using rosin core solder with a consistency of 60 percent tin and 40 percent lead, solder the connectors and the wires at the repairs then insulate with electrical tape or heat shrink tubing.
6. To replace any fuse link on a single circuit in a harness, cut out the damaged portion, strip approximately ½ in. (13mm) of insulation from the 2 wire ends and attach the appropriate replacement fuse link to the stripped wire ends with 2 proper

size butt connectors. Solder the connectors and wires, then insulate.

7. To repair any fuse link which has an eyelet terminal on 1 end such as the charging circuit, cut off the open fuse link behind the weld, strip approximately ½ in. (13mm) of insulation from the cut end and attach the appropriate new eyelet fuse link to the cut stripped wire with an appropriate size butt connector. Solder the connectors and wires at the repair, then insulate.

8. Connect the negative battery cable to the battery and test the system for proper operation.

➡**Do not mistake a resistor wire for a fuse link. The resistor wire is generally longer and has print stating, "Resistor-don't cut or splice."**

When attaching a single No. 16, 17, 18 or 20 gauge fuse link to a heavy gauge wire, always double the stripped wire end of the fuse link before inserting and crimping it into the butt connector for positive wire retention.

Add-On Electrical Equipment

The electrical system in your vehicle is designed to perform under reasonable operating conditions without interference between components. Before any additional electrical equipment is installed, it is recommended that you consult your dealer or a reputable repair facility that is familiar with the vehicle and its systems.

If the vehicle is equipped with mobile radio equipment and/or mobile telephone, it may have an effect upon the operation of any on-board computer control modules. Radio Frequency Interference (RFI) from the communications system can be picked up by the vehicle's wiring harnesses and conducted into the control module, giving it the wrong messages at the wrong time. Although well shielded against RFI, the computer should be further protected by taking the following measures:

• Install the antenna as far as possible from the control module. For instance, if the module is located behind the center console area, then the antenna should be mounted at the rear of the vehicle.

• Keep the antenna wiring a minimum of 8 inches away from any wiring running to control modules and from the module itself. NEVER wind the antenna wire around any other wiring.

• Mount the equipment as far from the control module as possible. Be very careful during installation not to drill through any wires or short a wire harness with a mounting screw.

• Insure that the electrical feed wire(s) to the equipment are properly and tightly connected. Loose connectors can cause interference.

• Make certain that the equipment is properly grounded to the vehicle. Poor grounding can damage expensive equipment.

BATTERY CABLES

When disconnecting the battery cables from the battery it is important to remove the cables in a particular order to minimize the chance of personal injury and component damage. The negative (-) battery cable should be removed first to stop the body of the car from being an active ground. After the negative cable is removed and set aside, the positive cable can be removed from the battery. The cables, once removed, can be cleaned with a solution of water and baking soda to remove any corrosion.

If the positive (+) battery cable is disconnected first, the chance of grounding the positive terminal against the negatively charged car body with a wrench or other metal tool is much greater. If the battery is so grounded, the battery, alternator, ECU or other fragile electronic components may be damaged by electrical surges, or any flammable gases may be ignited by the sparks produced by the electrical arcing, leading to possible fatal personal injury.

The battery cables should also not be disconnected with the ignition in the **ON** position. The sudden removal of the electric current can cause numerous electrical surges throughout the electrical system. These surges can damage any of the various voltage sensitive components such as the ECU. Always make certain that the ignition switch is turned **OFF**.

SEAT BELT/STARTER INTERLOCK

General Information

▶ **See Figure 1**

In addition to the light and buzzer, a starter interlock was incorporated into the seat belt warning system on some 1974-85 models.

The car cannot be started unless the seat belts are fastened in a specific order. The driver (and front seat passenger) must get into the car, close the door(s), sit down, and then fasten the seat belts. If the seat belts are not fastened, or if they are fastened before the driver (and passenger) sit down, the car will not start, and the light and buzzer will operate. This prevents the belts from being permanently fastened and shoved behind the seats.

In case of a system failure and to make it easier for mechanics working on a car, a manual bypass button is located under the hood. Pushing this button allows 1 free start, that is, without fastening the seat belt. Each additional free start requires that the button be pushed again.

➡**If a package, handbag, etc., is placed on the passenger's seat, the car may not start, and the light and buzzer may come ON as well, even if there is no one sitting in the seat. Either fasten the seat belt or remove the item.**

The following components are used for the seat belt/starter interlock system: a logic module (transistorized), 2 pressure sensitive front seat switches, a starter relay, a bypass (emergency start button, 2 seat belt buckle switches, a warning buzzer, and a warning light.

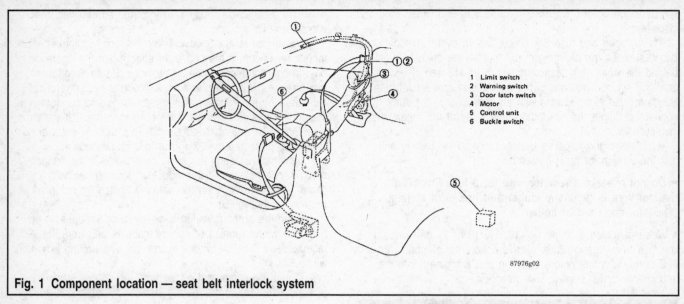

Fig. 1 Component location — seat belt interlock system

1 Limit switch
2 Warning switch
3 Door latch switch
4 Motor
5 Control unit
6 Buckle switch

87976g02

SERVICE

Repair of the seat belt interlock components is limited to their replacement. Testing the system requires the use of a special tester, which connects to the seat belt/starter interlock system at several points. About the only place that you are likely to find the tester is at your local Subaru dealer. Because of this, repair and testing are best left to a dealer.

If the warning light bulb burns out, access to it may be gained by removing the instrument cluster.

SUPPLEMENTAL RESTRAINT SYSTEM (AIR BAG)

General Information

▶ **See Figure 2**

Some late model Subaru vehicles are equipped with an air bag system, to supplement the safety belts. When an impact at the front of the vehicle is greater than a set level in the air bag sensor, the sensor senses it and generates an electrical pulse to inflate the bag in the air bag module, preventing the drivers body from contacting the steering wheel.

The SRS air bag consists of an control unit, left and right front sensors, 2 safety sensors built into the control unit and an air bag module containing an air bag and inflator. The left and right front sensors and the 2 safety sensors are connected in parallel respectively, and the front sensors and safety sensors are connected in series, so the air bag will inflate if at least 1 front sensor and 1 safety sensor sense an impact at the same time.

The components of the SRS system are not owner serviceable and no attempts should be made to repair the system, however, when working on any of the electrical systems inside of the vehicle, the air bag system must be disarmed. This can be accomplished by following the disarming procedure given in this section.

➡ **All SRS electrical wiring harnesses and connections are covered with yellow outer insulation.**

SYSTEM OPERATION

▶ **See Figures 3, 4 and 5**

The SRS is designed to deploy the air bag when the safing sensor and any of the 4 sensors (front crash zone sensor, center crash zone sensor, left crash zone sensor or tunnel sensor) simultaneously make contact, with the ignition switch in the **ON** position. Air bag deployment will occur in a frontal or near frontal impact of moderate to severe force.

The diagnostic unit monitors the SRS system and stores data, should any faults be detected in the system. When the engine is started or the ignition switch is in the **ON** or **START** position, the SRS warning light should illuminate for approximately 7 seconds and then turn OFF. This indicates that the system is operational.

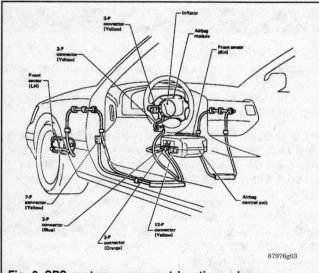

3-P connector (Yellow)
Inflator
Airbag module
3-P connector (Yellow)
Front sensor (RH)
Front sensor (LH)
7-P connector (Yellow)
2-P connector (Blue)
2-P connector (Orange)
12-P connector (Yellow)
Airbag control unit

87976g03

Fig. 2 SRS system component location — Legacy

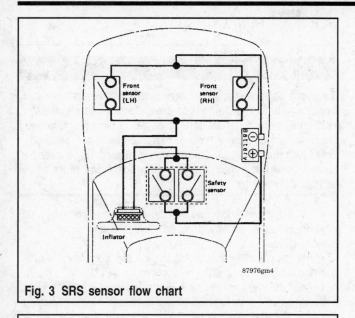

Fig. 3 SRS sensor flow chart

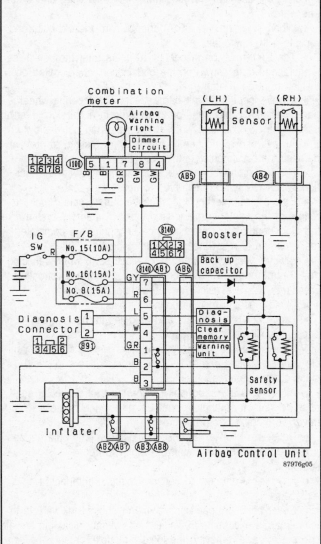

Fig. 4 SRS wiring diagram — Legacy, Impreza and SVX

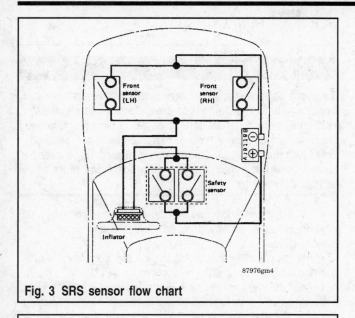

Fig. 5 SRS wiring locations — Legacy, Impreza and SVX

Connector No.	AB1	AB2	AB3	AB4	AB5	AB6
Pole	7	3	3	2	2	12
Color	Yellow	Yellow	Yellow	Blue	Orange	Yellow

SYSTEM COMPONENTS

▶ See Figure 6

Air Bag Module

The air bag module, located in the center of the steering wheel, contains a folded air bag and an inflator unit.

Spiral Cable

The spiral cable, located in the steering column, ensures an uninterrupted electrical circuit to the air bag module, while allowing rotation of the steering wheel. This cable is sometimes referred to as a clockspring.

Warning Lamp

The warning lamp, located in the instrument panel, indicates operational status of the SRS.

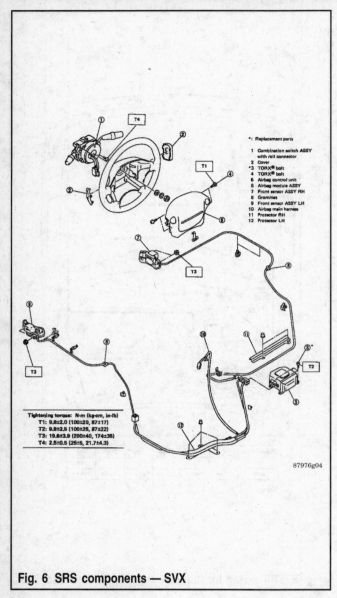

*: Replacement parts

1 Combination switch ASSY with roll connector
2 Cover
*3 TORX® bolt
4 TORX® bolt
5 Airbag control unit
6 Airbag module ASSY
7 Front sensor ASSY RH
8 Grommet
9 Front sensor ASSY LH
10 Airbag main harness
11 Protector RH
12 Protector LH

Tightening torque: N-m (kg-cm, in-lb)
T1: 9.8±2.0 (100±20, 87±17)
T2: 9.8±2.5 (100±25, 87±22)
T3: 19.6±3.9 (200±40, 174±35)
T4: 2.5±0.5 (25±5, 21.7±4.3)

87976g04

Fig. 6 SRS components — SVX

SRS Control Unit

The SRS control unit, monitors the SRS system and stores data, should any faults be detected in the system.

Air Bag Connector

The SRS system connectors use a double lock mechanism and a coupling error detection system. If the connector is not properly connected, the air bag warning light will illuminate on the instrument cluster.

The proper method for using these connectors is to press the release tab on the connector until the green lever pops up, this will unlock the connector. Then pull the connector apart while pushing the lever down. To reconnect the connectors, push the halves together until a click is heard then push the green lever down until another click is heard.

SERVICE PRECAUTIONS

✻✻CAUTION

To avoid deployment when servicing the SIR system or components in the immediate area, do not use electrical test equipment such as battery or AC powered voltmeter, ohmmeter, etc. or any type of tester other than specified on the air bag system. Do not use a non-powered probe tester. To avoid personal injury all precautions must be strictly adhered to.

- Do not disassemble any air bag system components.
- Always carry an inflator module with the trim cover pointed away.
- Always place an inflator module on the workbench with the pad side facing upward, away from loose objects.
- After deployment, the air bag surface may contain sodium hydroxide dust. Always wear gloves and safety glasses when handling the assembly. Wash hands with mild soap and water afterwards.
- When servicing any SRS parts, discard the old bolts and replace with new ones.
- The SRS must be inspected 10 years after the vehicle's manufacture date shown on the certification label located on the left front door latch post.
- Always inspect the air bag sensors and steering wheel pad, when the vehicle has been involved in a collision (even in cases of minor collision) where the air bag did not deploy.
- Always use a fine needle test lead for testing, to prevent damaging the connector terminals.
- Never disconnect any electrical connection with the ignition switch **ON** unless instructed to do so in a test.
- Before disconnecting the negative battery cable, make a record of the contents memorized by each memory system like the clock, audio, etc., when service or repairs are completed make certain to reset these memory systems.
- Always wear a grounded wrist static strap when servicing any control module or component labeled with a Electrostatic Discharge (ESD) sensitive device symbol.
- Avoid touching module connector pins.
- Leave new components and modules in the shipping package until ready to install them.
- Always touch a vehicle ground after sliding across a vehicle seat or walking across vinyl or carpeted floors to avoid static charge damage.
- All sensors are specifically calibrated to a particular series.The sensors, mounting brackets and wiring harness must never be modified from original design.
- Never strike or jar a sensor, or deployment could happen.
- The inflator module must be deployed before it is scrapped.
- Any visible damage to sensors requires component replacement.
- Never bake dry paint on vehicle or subject the vehicle to temperatures exceeding 200°F (93°C), without disabling the air bag system and removing the inflator module, crash zone sensors, SRS diagnosis unit and the spiral cable.
- Do not interchange sensors between models or years.
- Do not install used air bag system parts from another vehicle.

- Never allow welding cables to lay on, near or across any vehicle electrical wiring.
- When ever any SRS parts are removed, always use new retaining bolts.
- Caution labels are important when servicing the air bag system in the field. If they are dirty or damaged, replace them with new ones.

DISARMING THE SYSTEM

▶ See Figures 7, 8 and 9

➡Be sure to properly disconnect and connect the air bag connector.

1. Turn the ignition switch to the **OFF** position.
2. Disconnect the negative battery cable.

❋❋CAUTION

Wait at least 10 minutes after disconnecting the battery cable before doing any further work. The SRS system is designed to retain enough voltage to deploy the air bag for a short time, even after the battery has been disconnected. Serious injury may result from unintended air bag deployment, if work is done on the SRS system immediately after the battery cable is disconnected.

3. Remove the lower lid from the steering column and disconnect the harness between the air bag module and spiral cable.

ENABLING THE SYSTEM

1. Reconnect the connector between the air bag module and spiral cable. Then install the lower steering column lid.
2. Reconnect the negative battery cable.
3. Turn the ignition switch to the **ON** position and observe the SRS warning light. The SRS warning light should illuminate for approximately 7 seconds, turn OFF and remain OFF for at least 45 seconds.
4. If the SRS warning light function as indicated in Step 3, the SRS system is functioning properly.

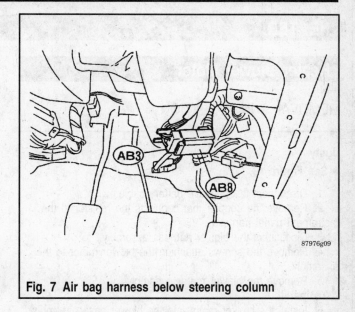

87976g09

Fig. 7 Air bag harness below steering column

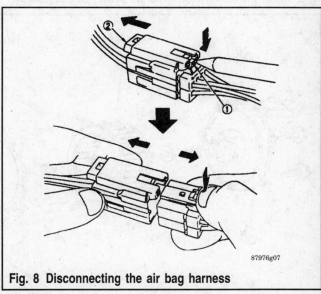

87976g07

Fig. 8 Disconnecting the air bag harness

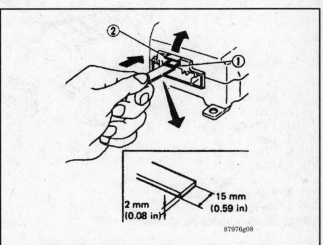

2 mm (0.08 in)   15 mm (0.59 in)

87976g08

Fig. 9 If disconnecting the harness from the control unit, construct a tab removal tool, and depress the tab until the green lever pops up

HEATER

Heater Blower Motor

REMOVAL & INSTALLATION

Justy

▶ **See Figure 10**

1. Disconnect the negative battery cable.
2. Remove the coupler that connects the resistor to the instrument panel harness.
3. Disconnect the blower harness assembly.
4. Remove the screws attaching the blower motor to the assembly.
5. Remove the blower motor assembly.

To install:

6. Install the blower motor into the blower case assembly.

7. Install the mounting screws to secure the blower motor in place.
8. Install the coupler that connects the resistor to the instrument panel harness.
9. Connect the negative battery cable.
10. Test for proper blower motor operation.

Sedan, Coupe, Wagon and Brat

▶ **See Figure 11**

1. Disconnect the negative battery cable.
2. Remove the trim panel from under the passenger dash panel, by removing the retainer screws.
3. Remove the glove box assembly.
4. Remove the glove box frame.
5. Remove the heater duct on vehicles equipped without A/C, or separate the evaporator from the blower motor assembly on A/C equipped vehicles.

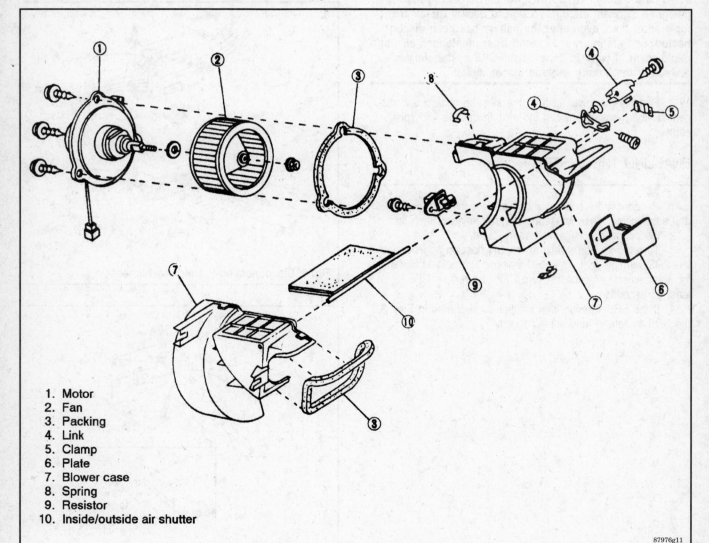

1. Motor
2. Fan
3. Packing
4. Link
5. Clamp
6. Plate
7. Blower case
8. Spring
9. Resistor
10. Inside/outside air shutter

87976g11

Fig. 10 Blower motor and heater case assembly — Justy

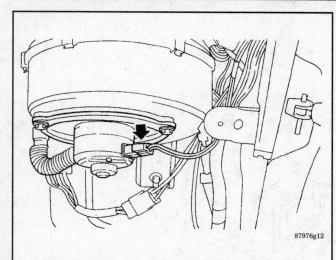

Fig. 11 Blower motor harness connection — Sedan, Coupe, Wagon, Brat and XT

6. Disconnect the blower motor vacuum hose from the instrument panel hose assembly.

7. Disconnect the blower motor electrical harness at the motor.

8. Disconnect the blower motor resistor harness.

9. Remove the blower motor mounting screws.

10. Remove the ventilation duct bracket.

11. Remove the blower motor from the heater case assembly.

To install:

12. Install the blower motor to the case assembly, and secure in place with the retainer screws.

13. Install the ventilation duct bracket.

14. Connect the electrical harness to the blower motor resistor.

15. Connect the electrical harness to the blower motor.

16. Connect the blower motor vacuum hose.

17. Connect the evaporator to the blower motor assembly on A/C equipped vehicles or install the heater duct on vehicles without A/C.

18. Install the glove box frame.

19. Install the glove box assembly.

20. Install the under dash panel.

21. Connect the negative battery cable.

22. Test the blower motor for proper operation.

XT

▶ **See Figures 11 and 12**

1. Disconnect the negative battery cable.

2. Remove the lower instrument panel cover on the passenger side.

3. Remove the glove box assembly.

4. Remove the heater duct on non-A/C vehicles or separate the evaporator from the blower assembly on A/C vehicles.

5. Disconnect the blower motor harness and resistor harness.

6. Remove the blower motor mounting bolts and remove the blower motor.

To install:

7. Install the blower motor and install the mounting bolts.

8. Connect the electrical harnesses to the blower motor and resistor.

9. Install the heater duct or connect the evaporator to the blower assembly.

10. Install the glove box.

11. Install the lower instrument panel cover.

12. Connect the negative battery cable.

13. Test for proper blower motor operation.

Loyale

➡**Depending upon working clearance, the air conditioning system may have to be discharged in order to service the blower motor. If this is the case, be sure to observe all the required safety precautions when discharging and recharging the air conditioning system, and use an approved recovery/recycling machine.**

1. Disconnect the negative battery cable.

2. Remove the lower instrument panel cover on the passenger side of the vehicle. Remove the glove box assembly, as required for working clearance.

3. If equipped with a vacuum actuator, set the control lever to the **CIRC** position and disconnect the vacuum hose from the assembly. Remove the actuator from its mounting.

4. Remove the heater duct, if not equipped with air conditioning.

5. If equipped with air conditioning, separate the evaporator from the blower assembly.

6. Disconnect the blower motor harness and the resistor electrical harness.

7. Remove the blower motor retaining bolts. Remove the blower motor assembly from its mounting. As required, separate the fan from the blower motor.

To install:

8. If the fan was removed, attach to the motor and secure in place.

9. Install the blower motor and tighten the retaining bolts. Connect the blower motor harness and the resistor electrical harness connector.

10. Install the evaporator to the blower assembly as required. Install the heater duct as required. Install the glove box.

11. Install the vacuum actuator and connect the vacuum line. Install the lower instrument panel cover and connect the negative battery cable.

Legacy and Impreza

▶ **See Figure 12**

1. Disconnect the negative battery cable.

2. Remove the glove box and lower metal bracket.

3. Disconnect the blower motor electrical harness.

4. Disconnect the flexible aspirator pipe from the blower motor base.

5. Remove the retainer screws, then lower the blower motor out.

To install:

6. Install the blower motor and secure in place with the retainer screws.

7. Connect the aspirator pipe to the blower motor.

8. Connect the blower motor electrical harness.

9. Install the glove box.

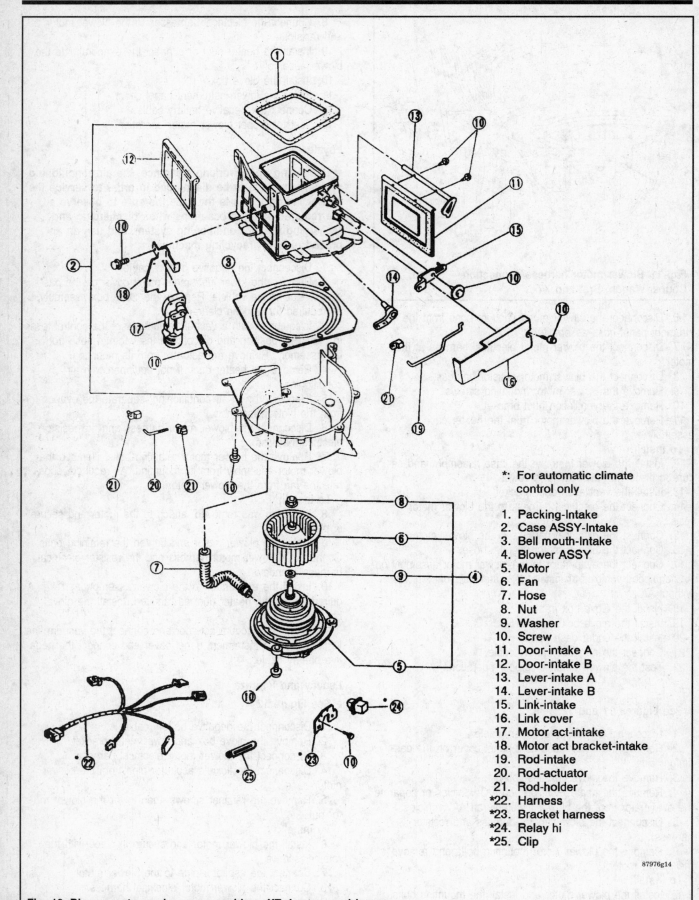

*: For automatic climate control only

1. Packing-Intake
2. Case ASSY-Intake
3. Bell mouth-Intake
4. Blower ASSY
5. Motor
6. Fan
7. Hose
8. Nut
9. Washer
10. Screw
11. Door-intake A
12. Door-intake B
13. Lever-intake A
14. Lever-intake B
15. Link-intake
16. Link cover
17. Motor act-intake
18. Motor act bracket-intake
19. Rod-intake
20. Rod-actuator
21. Rod-holder
*22. Harness
*23. Bracket harness
*24. Relay hi
*25. Clip

87976g14

Fig. 12 Blower motor and case assembly — XT, Legacy and Impreza

10. Connect the negative battery cable.
11. Test for proper blower motor operation.

SVX

▶ See Figure 13

❋❋CAUTION

The air bag system (SRS) must be disarmed before removing the glove compartment. Failure to do so may cause accidental deployment and/or personal injury.

1. Disconnect the negative battery cable. If equipped with a passenger side air bag, wait at least 10 minutes before doing any work on the vehicle to allow the air bag time to disarm.
2. Remove the glove box.
3. Remove the glove box lower support bracket.
4. Disconnect the blower motor electrical harness.
5. Remove the blower motor flexible vent tube.
6. Remove the blower motor mounting screws.
7. Remove the blower motor.
   To install:
8. Install the blower motor and blower motor mounting screws.
9. Connect the blower motor vent tube.
10. Connect the blower motor electrical harness.
11. Install the glove box lower support bracket.
12. Install the glove box.
13. Connect the negative battery cable.
14. Test for proper blower motor operation.

Heater Core

REMOVAL & INSTALLATION

❋❋CAUTION

Properly disarm the air bag on vehicles equipped with the SRS system. Failure to do so can cause serious injury.

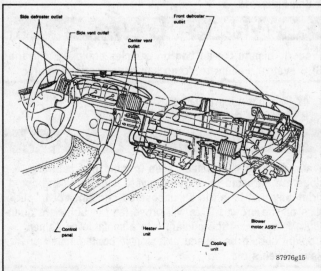

Fig. 13 Climate control components — SVX

Justy

▶ See Figure 14

1. Disconnect the negative battery cable.
2. Drain the cooling system into a suitable container.
3. Tag and disconnect the heater hoses from the heater core assembly.
4. Remove the right and left defroster ducts from the defroster nozzles. Pull the ducts from the heater case.
5. Disconnect the electrical wires from the fan switch and the blower motor.
6. Disconnect the air mix cable from the heater unit. Disconnect the mode cable from the heater unit. Tag each cable for identification before removing.
7. Remove the bolts that retain the heater unit to the instrument panel assembly.
8. Remove the glove box assembly for additional working space.
9. Disconnect the inside/outside air control cable from the blower assembly.
10. Remove the instrument panel assembly. Refer to Section 10 for removal and installation steps.
11. Remove the heater unit retaining bolts. Remove the heater unit from the vehicle.
12. Remove the heater core cushion. Loosen the heater core holder and remove. Pull the heater core from the mounting and remove from the heater case.
    To install:
13. Install the heater core into the heater case and install the core holder. Tighten the heater core holder and install the cushion.
14. Install the heater unit in the vehicle and install the mounting hardware.
15. Install the instrument panel assembly.
16. Connect the inside/outside air control cable to the blower assembly.
17. If removed, install the glove box door assembly.
18. Install the heater assembly-to-instrument panel bolts.
19. Connect the mode cable and air mix cables to the heater unit.
20. Connect the harness to the blower motor and fan switch.
21. Install the left and right defroster vents.
22. Connect the heater hoses.
23. Refill the cooling system.
24. Connect the negative battery cable.
25. Check for coolant leaks from the heater core and hose connections.

Sedan, Coupe, Wagon and Brat

1. Disconnect the negative battery cable.
2. Drain the coolant into a suitable container.
3. Tag and disconnect the heater hoses from the heater core pipes under the hood.
4. Remove the instrument panel from the vehicle. Refer to Section 10 for removal and installation steps.
5. Remove the steering support beam.
6. Disconnect the door motor joint harnesses.
7. Remove the breather hose.
8. Discharge the A/C system using an approved recovery/recycling machine.
9. Remove the evaporator.
10. Remove the heater unit.

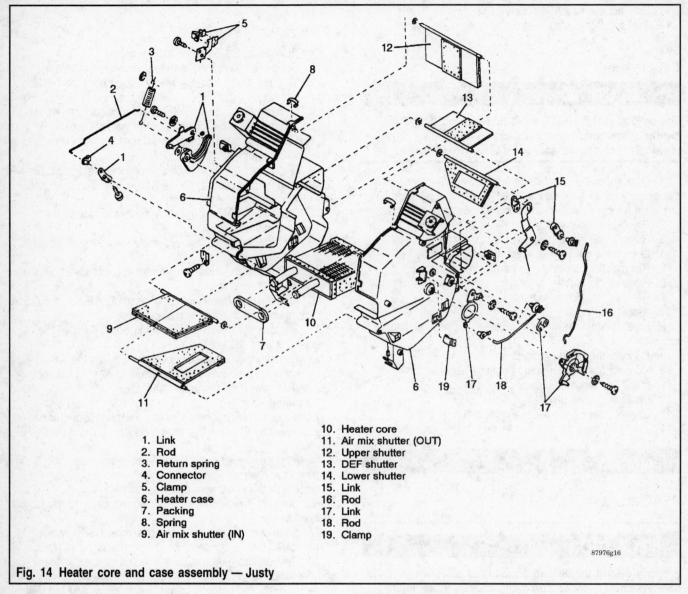

1. Link	10. Heater core
2. Rod	11. Air mix shutter (OUT)
3. Return spring	12. Upper shutter
4. Connector	13. DEF shutter
5. Clamp	14. Lower shutter
6. Heater case	15. Link
7. Packing	16. Rod
8. Spring	17. Link
9. Air mix shutter (IN)	18. Rod
	19. Clamp

87976g16

Fig. 14 Heater core and case assembly — Justy

11. Remove the heater core from the case.
To install:
12. Install the heater in the case.
13. Install the heater case in the vehicle.
14. Install the evaporator assembly.
15. Recharge the A/C system using an approved recovery/recycling machine.
16. Connect the breather hose.
17. Connect the door joint harnesses.
18. Install the steering support beam.
19. Install the instrument panel.
20. Connect the heater hoses to the heater core.
21. Refill the cooling system.
22. Connect the negative battery cable.
23. Check for coolant leaks from the core and hose connections.

Loyale and XT
◗ See Figure 15

> ✻✻**CAUTION**
>
> **Properly disarm the air bag on vehicles equipped with the SRS system. Failure to do so can cause serious injury.**

1. Disconnect the negative battery cable.
2. Drain the engine coolant into a suitable container.

> ✻✻**CAUTION**
>
> **When draining the coolant, keep in mind that cats and dogs are attracted to ethylene glycol antifreeze, and could drink any that is left in an uncovered container or in puddles on the ground. This will prove fatal in sufficient quantity. Always drain the coolant into a sealable container. Coolant should be reused unless it is contaminated or several years old.**

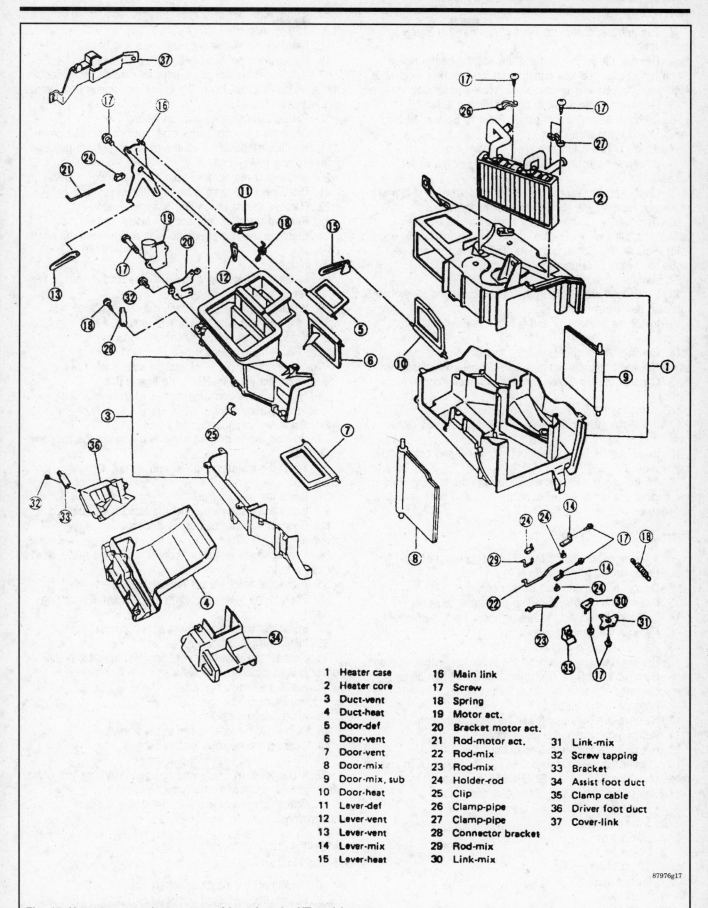

1	Heater case	16	Main link		
2	Heater core	17	Screw		
3	Duct-vent	18	Spring		
4	Duct-heat	19	Motor act.		
5	Door-def	20	Bracket motor act.		
6	Door-vent	21	Rod-motor act.	31	Link-mix
7	Door-vent	22	Rod-mix	32	Screw tapping
8	Door-mix	23	Rod-mix	33	Bracket
9	Door-mix, sub	24	Holder-rod	34	Assist foot duct
10	Door-heat	25	Clip	35	Clamp cable
11	Lever-def	26	Clamp-pipe	36	Driver foot duct
12	Lever-vent	27	Clamp-pipe	37	Cover-link
13	Lever-vent	28	Connector bracket		
14	Lever-mix	29	Rod-mix		
15	Lever-heat	30	Link-mix		

87976g17

Fig. 15 Heater core and case assembly — Loyale, XT and Legacy

3. Tag and disconnect the heater hoses in the engine compartment.

4. Remove the rubber grommet around the heater hoses which run through the kick panel inside the car. The location is slightly above, and to the right of the accelerator pedal.

5. Remove the radio box or center console assembly.

6. Remove the instrument panel. Refer to Section 10 for removal and installation steps.

7. If the car has a luggage shelf, remove it.

8. Disconnect the heater control cables and fan motor harness.

9. Disconnect the duct between the heater unit and blower assembly. Remove the right and left defroster nozzles.

10. Remove the mounting bolts at the top sides of the heater unit. Lift the heater core up and out on the heater unit.

11. Remove the heater core retaining connectors and remove the heater core from the mounting.

To install:

12. Install the heater core in the heater case and install the retaining hardware.

13. Install the heater unit and tighten the mounting bolts securely.

14. Connect the duct between the heater unit and blower assembly and install the left and right defroster nozzles.

15. Connect the fan motor harness and heater control cables.

16. Install the luggage shelf, if equipped.

17. Install the instrument panel, center console and radio box.

18. Install the heater hose rubber grommets and connect the heater hoses.

19. Fill the radiator with coolant. Connect the battery, start the engine and check for leaks at the core and hose connections.

Impreza

1. If equipped, discharge the A/C system using an approved recovery/recycling machine.

2. Disconnect the negative battery cable.

3. Drain the cooling system into a suitable container.

4. Tag and disconnect the heater hoses from the firewall.

5. Remove the center console box.

6. Remove the cup holder.

7. Remove the radio. Refer to the procedure in this section.

8. Remove the drivers side lower instrument trim panel, then disconnect the seat belt timer harness.

9. Remove the glove box.

10. Remove the bolts and lower the steering column.

11. Remove the steering column covers.

12. Remove the hood release handle.

13. Set the temperature control switch to MAX. COLD, and mode selector switch to the DEFROSTER position.

14. Unfasten the following underdash connectors:
   a. 15-pin gray
   b. 5-pin natural
   c. 20-pin white
   d. 20-pin blue
   e. 12-pin black
   f. 8-pin natural
   g. 1-pin blue
   h. 6-pin black

   i. 20-pin natural

15. Remove the instrument panel nuts and bolts.

16. Remove the defroster grilles.

17. Pull the instrument panel outward carefully, disconnect the speedometer cable from the instrument cluster and remove the instrument panel.

18. Remove the steering support beam.

19. Disconnect the discharge pipe, suction pipe and grommets from the evaporator. Cap the hoses to prevent moisture from entering the system.

20. Disconnect the harness from the evaporator.

21. Disconnect the drain hose from the evaporator.

22. Remove the mounting nut, bolt and evaporator.

23. Remove the bolt, nuts and the heater unit.

24. Separate the heater unit housing and remove the heater core.

To install:

25. Install the heater core into the case, and assemble the heater unit.

26. Install the heater unit. Attach the retainer bolts, and tighten the bolt and nuts to 6 ft. lbs. (8 Nm).

27. If equipped with A/C perform the following:
   a. Install the evaporator.
   b. Connect the drain hose to the evaporator case.
   c. Connect the harness to the evaporator.
   d. Connect the discharge pipe, suction pipe and grommets to the evaporator.

28. Install the steering support beam.

29. Position the instrument panel and connect the speedometer cable.

30. Install the instrument panel and ensure it engages the 3 body clips.

31. Install the defroster grille.

32. Install the instrument panel mounting bolts and nuts.

33. Connect the wire harnesses disconnected during removal.

34. Connect the temperature control cable and mode selector cable to the link.

35. Install the hood release handle.

36. Position the steering column and install the mounting bolts.

37. Install the center instrument panel console.

38. Install the glove box.

39. Connect the seat belt timer harness, then install the driver lower instrument trim panel.

40. Install the radio.

41. Install the center console.

42. Install the cup holder.

43. Connect the heater hoses to the firewall.

44. Connect the negative battery cable.

45. Fill and bleed the cooling system.

46. If equipped, evacuate and charge the A/C system using an approved recovery/recycling machine.

47. Check for coolant leaks at the core and hose connections.

Legacy
▶ **See Figure 15**

1. Disconnect the negative battery cable.

2. Disarm the air bag, if equipped.

3. Drain the engine coolant into a suitable container.

4. In the engine compartment, tag and disconnect the heater hoses at the firewall. Plug the openings to prevent spillage inside the vehicle.

5. Remove the front side sill cover and disconnect the air bag connector (AB9) and (AB10).

6. Remove the shift knob, if equipped with a manual transaxle.

7. Remove the center console assembly.

8. Remove the front pillar lower trim panel from the body.

9. Remove the trim panel that secures the hood release cable in place.

10. Remove the trim cover below the steering column.

11. Remove the instrument panel, disconnecting the speedometer cable and wire harnesses. Refer to Section 10 for removal and installation steps.

12. Remove the glove box and back panel assembly.

13. Disconnect the blower motor harness.

14. Remove the bolts and lower the steering column. Tag and disconnect the necessary wire harnesses.

15. Disconnect the temperature control cable from the link of the heater case.

16. Remove ash tray, radio and temperature control unit from the dash.

17. Disconnect the dashboard harness connectors.

18. Remove the dashboard mounting bolts.

19. Remove the front defroster grille and 2 mounting bolts.

20. Remove the dashboard from the body. Refer to Section 10 for removal and installation steps.

➡**When storing the removed dashboard, place in an upright position on a workbench or floor.**

21. Remove the steering support beam.

22. Properly evacuate the A/C refrigerant from the system using an approved recovery/recycling machine.

23. Disconnect the discharge pipe, suction pipe and grommets. Cap the openings of the A/C pipes to prevent contamination of the system.

24. Disconnect the harness from the evaporator.

25. Disconnect the drain hose.

26. Remove the evaporator unit mounting nut and bolt, remove the evaporator unit.

27. Remove the heater unit and separate the case halves. Remove the heater core from the heater unit.

To install:

28. Install the heater core into the heater unit. Connect the case halves. Install the heater unit to the vehicle.

29. Install the evaporator unit and secure.

30. Connect the drain hose and the harness to the evaporator.

31. Connect the grommets, suction pipe and discharge pipe to the evaporator. Be sure to use new O-rings for the A/C connections

32. Install the center support beam.

33. Install the dashboard to the body. Push the 2 pins into the grommets on the body panel and set the clips located at both inside ends of the instrument panel onto the body side.

34. Install the 2 mounting bolts at the front defroster grille and install the grille.

35. Install the dashboard mounting bolts.

36. Connect the dashboard harnesses.

37. Install the temperature control unit, radio and ashtray to the dash.

38. Connect the temperature control cable to the link of the heater case.

39. Raise the steering column and install the mounting bolts. Connect the wiring harnesses.

40. Connect the blower motor harness.

41. Install the glove box back panel and the glove box assembly.

42. Install the instrument panel, connecting the speedometer cable and harnesses.

43. Install the cover below the steering column.

44. Install the trim panel that secures the hood release cable.

45. Install the front pillar lower trim panel to the body.

46. Install the center console.

47. If removed, install the shift knob.

48. Connect the air bag connectors (AB9) and (AB10) and install the front side sill cover.

49. Using new clamps, connect the heater hoses to the heater core.

50. Connect the negative battery cable.

51. Fill the cooling system with coolant.

52. Properly charge the A/C system, using an approved recovery/recycling machine.

53. Run vehicle to normal operating temperature and check for leaks. Check the heating and A/C system for proper operation.

SVX

1. Disconnect the negative battery cable.

2. Disarm the air bag.

3. Drain the cooling system into a suitable container.

4. Tag and disconnect the heater hoses from the heater core in the engine compartment.

5. Remove the center console box assembly.

6. Remove the front pillar upper trim.

7. Remove the radio grounding wire.

8. Remove the remote controlled rearview mirror switch and internal bolt.

9. Remove the lower trim cover by removing the clips and bolts.

10. Disconnect the air bag harness at the harness spool.

11. Remove the plastic trim caps from both ends of the instrument panel, and remove the bolts.

12. Remove, tag and disconnect the instrument panel switches.

13. Remove the visor by removing the retainer screws. Disconnect the clock harness.

14. Remove the combination switch assembly.

15. Remove the glove box assembly.

16. Disconnect the instrument and body harnesses, as well as the antenna lead.

17. Cover the automatic transaxle select lever with cloth to avoid damage, if equipped with an automatic transaxle.

18. Remove the instrument panel by pulling it forward. Refer to Section 10 for removal and installation steps.

19. Remove the steering support beam.

20. Disconnect the door motor joint harnesses (mode, air mix door and sensor) from the heater unit.

21. Remove the aspirator hose.

22. Remove the evaporator.

23. Remove the heater unit.

24. Remove the heater core from the case.
To install:
25. Install the heater core to the heater unit, and install the case assembly.
26. Install the evaporator and the evaporator hose.
27. Connect the door motor joint harnesses.
28. Install the steering support beam.
29. Install the instrument panel and connect the harnesses and antenna leads.
30. Install the glove box and retainer screws.
31. Install the combination meter.
32. Connect the clock harness.
33. Install the instrument panel switches, attaching the harnesses to each.
34. At the ends of the instrument panel, install the bolts and trim covers.
35. Install the 2 screws to the left and right sides.
36. Connect the air bag harness at the harness spool.
37. Install the panel lower cover.
38. Install the lower cover (six clips and 3 connectors).
39. Install the internal bolt and the remote controlled mirror switch.
40. Connect the radio grounding wire.
41. Install the front pillar upper trim.
42. Install the center console box.
43. Connect the heater hoses.
44. Fill the cooling system with coolant, check for leaks.
45. Connect the negative battery cable.

Control Cables

REMOVAL & INSTALLATION

Air Mix, Temperature Control and Ram Ventilation Cables
◗ **See Figures 16, 17 and 18**

1. Disconnect the negative battery cable.
2. Place the control lever in the FULLY OPEN position.
3. Remove the lower trim panel from the passenger side.

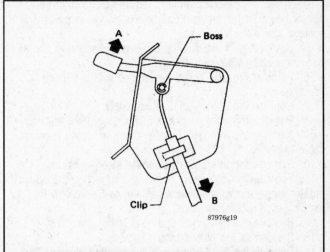

Fig. 17 Ram ventilation cable connection — Sedan, Coupe, Wagon and Brat

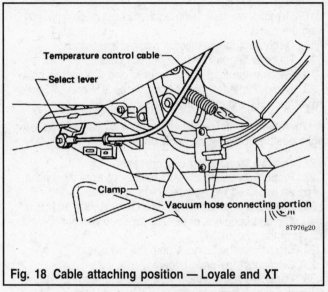

Fig. 18 Cable attaching position — Loyale and XT

4. Detach the control cable retainer clips from the side of the heater case assembly.
5. Unfasten the control cable from the cable attaching boss on the case assembly.
6. Remove the control panel assembly from the dash. Lift the control panel out enough to access the control cable.
7. Detach the control cable retainer clip from the control panel assembly.
8. Unfasten the control cable from the lever on the control panel.
9. Slowly remove the cable from the control panel opening.
To install:
10. Feed the control cable through the control panel opening in the dash panel, and route the cable to the heater case assembly. Be careful not to route the cable in such a manner that sharp bends are created in the cable.
11. Attach the cable to the control panel lever. Secure the cable in place with the retainer clip.
12. Position the control panel in the dash panel, and secure in place with the retainer screws.

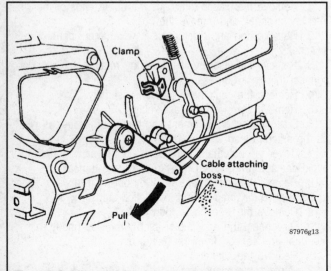

Fig. 16 Cable attaching boss on heater case — Justy

13. Fasten the control cable to the heater case attaching boss. Secure the cable to the case assembly with the retainer clip.
14. Install the lower trim using the retainer screws.
15. Connect the negative battery cable.
16. Test the control cable for smooth operation.

Control Panel

REMOVAL & INSTALLATION

Justy

▶ See Figures 19, 20 and 21

1. Disconnect the negative battery cable.
2. Remove the control knobs by grasping the knob and pulling toward you.

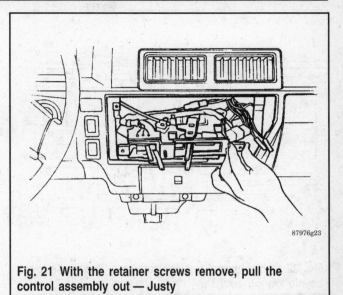
Fig. 21 With the retainer screws remove, pull the control assembly out — Justy

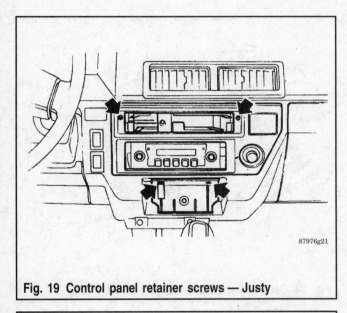
Fig. 19 Control panel retainer screws — Justy

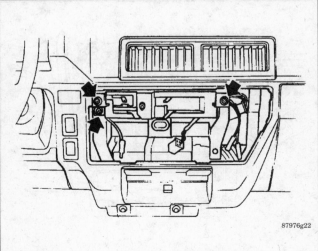
Fig. 20 Control assembly retainer screws — Justy

3. Remove the center pocket from the dash assembly. Insert your hand through the open hole, and push the control panel plate out.
4. Loosen the center panel attaching screws and remove the center panel.
5. Remove the control assembly attaching screws. Pull the assembly toward you, and disconnect the control cables, and fan switch harness.
6. Remove the control assembly.
To install:
7. Attach the fan switch harness and control cable to the control assembly.
8. Install the control assembly to the dash panel, and secure in place with the retainer screws.
9. Install the center panel, and secure in place with the attaching screws.
10. Install the control panel plate and press into position.
11. Attach the control knobs.
12. Connect the negative battery cable.
13. Test the control panel levers and knobs for proper operation.

Sedan, Coupe, Loyale Wagon and Brat
▶ See Figure 22

1. Disconnect the negative battery cable.
2. Remove the temperature control cable from the heater case assembly.
3. Using a suitable prytool, remove the individual control knobs from the control assembly.
4. Remove the control panel retainer screws and lift out the control assembly enough to access the control cables, vacuum lines and harness.
5. Detach the control cables from the rear of the control panel. Tag each cable for identification.
6. Tag and disconnect the vacuum lines from the rear of the control panel.
7. Disconnect the fan switch harness from the control panel.
To install:
8. Fasten the fan switch harness to the control panel.
9. Attach the vacuum lines to the control panel.

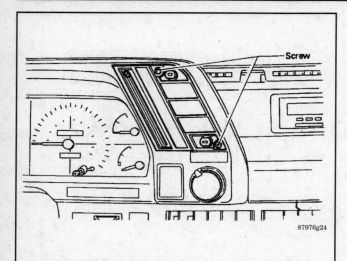

Fig. 22 Control panel retainer screws — Sedan, Coupe, Loyale Wagon and Brat

10. Attach the control cables to the rear of the control panel.
11. Install the control knobs.
12. Attach the temperature control cable to the heater case assembly.
13. Connect the negative battery cable.
14. Test the control panel for proper operation.

XT

▶ See Figure 23

1. Disconnect the negative battery cable.
2. Remove the console box retainer screws followed by the console box.
3. Using a suitable prytool, remove the individual control knobs.
4. Remove the retainer screws from the rear of the console box. Lift out the temperature control lever and fan switch lever.
5. Unfasten and tag the control levers and vacuum lines from the temperature control lever.

To install:

6. Attach the control cables and vacuum lines to the temperature control lever assembly.

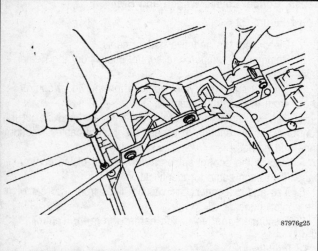

Fig. 23 Removing the retainer screws from the back side of the console box — XT

7. Position the temperature control lever and fan switch lever in the console box, and secure in place using the retainer screws.
8. Install the control knobs.
9. Install the console box using the retainer screws.
10. Connect the negative battery cable.
11. Test the control panel for proper operation.

Legacy and Impreza

▶ See Figures 24 and 25

1. Disconnect the negative battery cable.
2. Remove the temperature control cable from the heater case assembly.
3. Remove the trim panel around the control panel assembly.
4. Remove the control panel retainer screws and lift out the control assembly enough to access the cable and harnesses at the rear of the panel.
5. Unfasten the control cable and wire harnesses from the rear of the control panel.

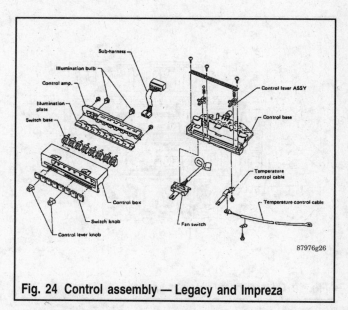

Fig. 24 Control assembly — Legacy and Impreza

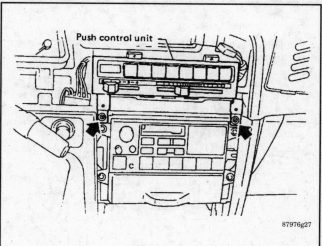

Fig. 25 Control panel retainer screws — Legacy and Impreza

To install:

6. Attach the control cable and wire harnesses to the rear of the control panel.

7. Position the control panel in the dash, and secure in place with the retainer screws.

8. Install the trim panel around the control panel assembly.

9. Attach the control cable to the heater case assembly.

10. Connect the negative battery cable.

11. Test the control panel for proper operation.

SVX

▶ **See Figures 26 and 27**

1. Disconnect the negative battery cable.

2. Remove the dash panel trim plate around the control assembly.

3. Remove the control panel retainer screws, and lift out the assembly.

4. Disconnect the aspirator duct from the rear of the control panel.

5. Unfasten the wire harness from the control panel.

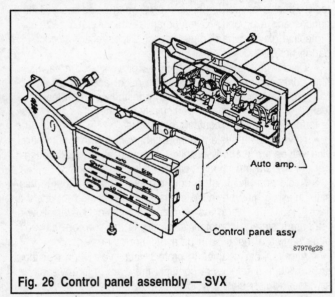

Fig. 26 Control panel assembly — SVX

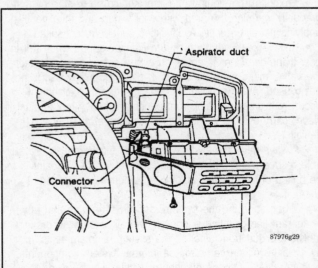

Fig. 27 Control panel and aspirator duct — SVX

To install:

6. Fasten the wire harness to the control panel.

7. Attach the aspirator duct to the control panel.

8. Position the control panel in the dash, and secure with retainer screws.

9. Install the dash panel trim plate around the control assembly.

10. Connect the negative battery cable.

11. Test the control panel for proper operation.

Blower Switch

REMOVAL & INSTALLATION

Justy

1. Disconnect the negative battery cable

2. Remove the blower switch control knob.

3. Remove the control panel from the dash assembly.

4. Disconnect the wire harness and cables from the control panel.

5. Remove the blower switch retainer screws from the rear of the control panel. Lift the blower switch out from the control panel.

To install:

6. Position the blower switch in the control panel.

7. Secure the blower switch to the control panel using the retainer screws.

8. Attach the wire harness and cables to the control panel.

9. Install the control panel to the dash assembly.

10. Install the blower switch control knob.

11. Connect the negative battery cable.

12. Test the fan switch for proper operation on all speeds.

Sedan, Coupe, Loyale, Wagon and Brat

1. Disconnect the negative battery cable.

2. Remove the blower switch control knob.

3. Loosen and remove the blower switch retainer nut.

4. Remove the control panel from the dash.

5. Remove the blower switch from the rear of the control panel.

6. Unfasten the wire harness from the blower switch.

To install:

7. Fasten the wire harness to the blower switch.

8. Position the blower switch in the rear of the control panel.

9. Install the blower switch retainer nut, and tighten snugly.

10. Install the control panel to the dash assembly.

11. Connect the negative battery cable.

12. Test the blower switch to make sure it functions at all speeds.

XT

1. Disconnect the negative battery cable.

2. Remove the console box and control panel assembly.

3. Remove the blower switch retainer screws, and lift out the blower switch and control knobs.

4. Unfasten the wire harness from the blower switch.

5. Remove the control knobs from the switch assembly.

To install:

6. Attach the knobs to the switch assembly.

7. Connect the wire harness to the blower switch.

8. Install the blower switch, and secure in place with the retainer screws.

9. Install the control panel and console box.

10. Connect the negative battery cable.

11. Test the blower switch to make sure it functions correctly on all speeds.

Legacy and Impreza

1. Disconnect the negative battery cable.

2. Remove the control panel, and disconnect the wire harness from the rear of the assembly.

3. Remove the blower switch retainer screws, and lift out the switch assembly.

To install:

4. Install the blower switch, and secure in place with the retainer screws.

5. Attach the wire harness to the control panel. Install the control panel to the dash panel.

6. Connect the negative battery cable.

7. Test the blower switch on all speed setting to make sure it functions correctly.

SVX

The blower switch is an integral part of the control panel assembly, and is not replaceable or serviceable by itself. In the event the fan switch requires service, the entire control panel must be replaced.

AIR CONDITIONER

General Precautions

➡**Be sure to consult the laws in your area before servicing the air conditioning system. In most areas, it is illegal to perform repairs involving refrigerant unless the work is done by a certified technician. Also, it is quite likely that you will not be able to purchase refrigerant without proof of certification.**

SAFETY PRECAUTIONS

There are 2 major hazards associated with air conditioning systems and they both relate to the refrigerant gas. First, the refrigerant gas (R-12 or R-134a) is an extremely cold substance. When exposed to air, it will instantly freeze any surface it comes in contact with, including your eyes. The other hazard relates to fire (if your vehicle is equipped with R-12. Although normally non-toxic, the R-12 gas becomes highly poisonous in the presence of an open flame. One good whiff of the vapor formed by burning R-12 can be fatal. Keep all forms of fire (including cigarettes) well clear of the air conditioning system.

Because of the inherent dangers involved with working on air conditioning systems, these safety precautions must be strictly followed.

• Avoid contact with a charged refrigeration system, even when working on another part of the air conditioning system or vehicle. If a heavy tool comes into contact with a section of tubing or a heat exchanger, it can easily cause the relatively soft material to rupture.

• When it is necessary to apply force to a fitting which contains refrigerant, as when checking that all system couplings are securely tightened, use a wrench on both parts of the fitting involved, if possible. This will avoid putting torque on refrigerant tubing. (It is also advisable to use tube or line wrenches when tightening these flare nut fittings.)

➡**R-12 refrigerant is a chlorofluorocarbon which, when released into the atmosphere, can contribute to the depletion of the ozone layer in the upper atmosphere. Ozone filters out harmful radiation from the sun.**

• Do not attempt to discharge the system without the proper tools. Precise control is possible only when using the service gauges and a proper A/C refrigerant recovery station. Wear protective gloves when connecting or disconnecting service gauge hoses.

• Discharge the system only in a well ventilated area, as high concentrations of the gas which might accidentally escape can exclude oxygen and act as an anesthetic. When leak testing or soldering, this is particularly important, as toxic gas is formed when R-12 contacts any flame.

• Never start a system without first verifying that both service valves are properly installed, and that all fittings throughout the system are snugly connected.

• Avoid applying heat to any refrigerant line or storage vessel. Charging may be aided by using water heated to less than 125°F (50°C) to warm the refrigerant container. Never allow a refrigerant storage container to sit out in the sun, or near any other source of heat, such as a radiator or heater.

• Always wear goggles to protect your eyes when working on a system. If refrigerant contacts the eyes, it is advisable in all cases to consult a physician immediately.

• Frostbite from liquid refrigerant should be treated by first gradually warming the area with cool water, and then gently applying petroleum jelly. A physician should be consulted.

• Always keep refrigerant drum fittings capped when not in use. If the container is equipped with a safety cap to protect the valve, make sure the cap is in place when the can is not being used. Avoid sudden shock to the drum, which might occur from dropping it, or from banging a heavy tool against it. Never carry a drum in the passenger compartment of a vehicle.

• Always have the system completely discharged into a suitable recovery unit before painting the vehicle (if the paint is to be baked on), or before welding anywhere near refrigerant lines.

• When servicing the system, minimize the time that any refrigerant line or fitting is open to the air in order to prevent moisture or dirt from entering the system. Contaminants such as moisture or dirt can damage internal system components. Always replace O-rings on lines or fittings which are disconnected. Prior to installation coat, but do not soak, replacement O-rings with suitable compressor oil.

Compressor

REMOVAL & INSTALLATION

Justy

The Justy was never factory equipped with air conditioning. A/C on these models was a dealer installed option.

Several different companies offered A/C parts for this model. It is recommended that any A/C service on the Justy be referred to a local dealer.

Sedan, Coupe, Loyale, Wagon and Brat

▶ See Figures 28, 29, 30 and 31

1. Remove the spare tire from the engine compartment.
2. Disconnect the negative battery cable.
3. Remove the air cleaner, if removing a Hitachi compressor.

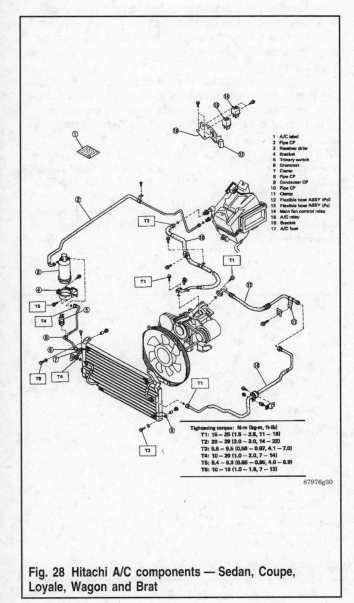

Tightening torque: N·m (kg-m, ft-lb)
T1: 15 – 25 (1.5 – 2.5, 11 – 18)
T2: 20 – 29 (2.0 – 3.0, 14 – 22)
T3: 6.5 – 9.5 (0.56 – 0.97, 4.1 – 7.0)
T4: 10 – 20 (1.0 – 2.0, 7 – 14)
T5: 5.4 – 9.3 (0.55 – 0.95, 4.0 – 6.9)
T6: 10 – 18 (1.0 – 1.8, 7 – 13)

87976g30

Fig. 28 Hitachi A/C components — Sedan, Coupe, Loyale, Wagon and Brat

1 A/C label
2 Pipe CP
3 Receiver drier
4 Bracket
5 Trinary switch
6 Grommet
7 Clamp
8 Pipe CP
9 Condenser CP
10 Pipe CP
11 Clamp
12 Flexible hose ASSY (Pd)
13 Flexible hose ASSY (Ps)
14 Main fan control relay
15 A/C relay
16 Bracket
17 A/C fuse

Tightening torque: N·m (kg-m, ft-lb)
T1: 20 – 29 (2.0 – 3.0, 14 – 22)
T2: 15 – 25 (1.5 – 2.5, 11 – 18)
T3: 10 – 20 (1.0 – 2.0, 7 – 14)
T4: 9 – 11 (0.9 – 1.1, 6.5 – 8.0)
T5: 10 – 18 (1.0 – 1.8, 7 – 13)
T6: 5.5 – 9.5 (0.56 – 0.97, 4.1 – 7.0)

1 Compressor
2 Condenser
3 Receiver drier
4 Condenser cooling fan (Sub-fan)
5 Compressor bracket
6 Belt
7 Hose Pd
8 Hose Ps
9 Relay
10 Idler pulley
11 Evaporator
12 Drain hose
13 Grommet
14 Pipe (Condenser-Receiver drier)
15 Pipe (Receiver drier-Evaporator)
16 Pipe (Hose Pd-condenser)
17 Shroud
18 Pulser amplifier
19 Band
20 Band

87976g31

Fig. 29 Matsushita A/C components — Sedan, Coupe, Loyale, Wagon and Brat

4. Properly discharge the air conditioning system using an approved recovery/recycling machine.
5. Disconnect both of the refrigerant lines from the compressor and plug the openings. Remove the O-rings and discard.
6. Remove the bolts from the alternator and compressor belt cover and remove the cover.
7. Remove the alternator drive belt.
8. Loosen the lock bolt on the idler pulley and remove the compressor belt.
9. Disconnect the alternator harness from the alternator.
10. Disconnect the compressor wire harness.
11. On some models, remove the compressor-to-lower bracket mounting bolts, then remove the lower bracket. Remove the compressor-to-upper bracket mounting bolts, then remove the compressor from the engine.
12. On other models, remove the compressor-to-bracket bolts, then remove the compressor from the engine.
  To install:
13. Install the compressor in position on the engine. Tighten the compressor mounting bolts to 14-22 ft. lbs. (20-30 Nm).

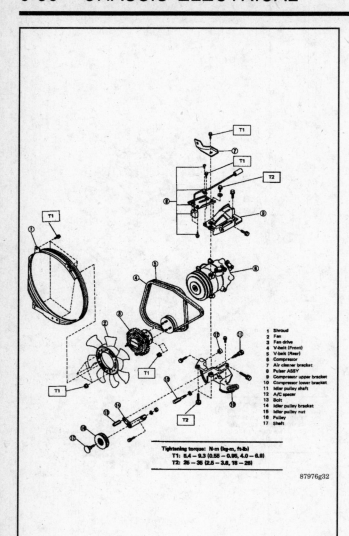

1 Shroud
2 Fan
3 Fan drive
4 V-belt (Front)
5 V-belt (Rear)
6 Compressor
7 Air cleaner bracket
8 Pulser ASSY
9 Compressor upper bracket
10 Compressor lower bracket
11 Idler pulley shaft
12 A/C spacer
13 Bolt
14 Idler pulley bracket
15 Idler pulley nut
16 Pulley
17 Shaft

Tightening torque: N·m (kg-m, ft-lb)
T1: 5.4 – 9.3 (0.55 – 0.95, 4.0 – 6.9)
T2: 25 – 35 (2.5 – 3.6, 18 – 26)

87976g32

Fig. 30 Hitachi compressor, fan and belt — Sedan, Coupe, Loyale, Wagon and Brat

14. Reconnect the electrical leads to the compressor and alternator.

15. Apply a coating of compressor oil to the new O-rings, and install them on the refrigerant lines, then connect the lines to the compressor. Tighten the lines to 7-14 ft. lbs. (10-20 Nm).

16. Install the air cleaner, if removed.

17. Connect the negative battery cable. Properly evacuate and charge the air conditioning system using an approved recovery/recycling machine.

18. Install the spare tire.

XT

▶ **See Figures 32 and 33**

1. Disconnect the negative battery cable.

2. Properly discharge the air conditioning system using an approved recovery/recycling machine.

3. Disconnect both of the refrigerant lines from the compressor and plug the openings. Remove the O-rings and discard.

4. Remove the alternator drive belt and compressor belt.

5. Disconnect the compressor harness.

6. Remove the compressor-to-bracket bolts, then remove the compressor from the engine.

To install:

7. Install the compressor in position on the engine. Tighten the compressor mounting bolts to 25-33 ft. lbs. (34-44 Nm).

8. Reconnect the electrical leads to the compressor.

9. Install the compressor and alternator belts. Adjust to the proper tension.

10. Apply a coating of compressor oil to the new O-rings, and install them on the refrigerant lines, then connect the lines to the compressor. Tighten the lines to 7-14 ft. lbs. (10-20 Nm).

11. Connect the negative battery cable. Properly evacuate and charge the air conditioning system using an approved recovery/recycling machine.

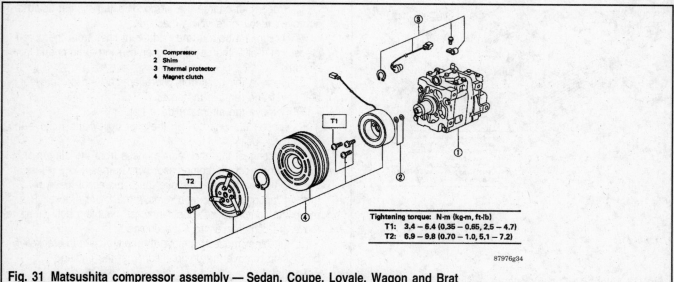

1 Compressor
2 Shim
3 Thermal protector
4 Magnet clutch

Tightening torque: N·m (kg-m, ft-lb)
T1: 3.4 – 6.4 (0.35 – 0.65, 2.5 – 4.7)
T2: 6.9 – 9.8 (0.70 – 1.0, 5.1 – 7.2)

87976g34

Fig. 31 Matsushita compressor assembly — Sedan, Coupe, Loyale, Wagon and Brat

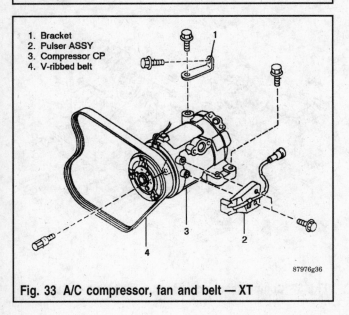

Fig. 32 Zexel A/C system components — XT, Legacy and Impreza

1 A/C fuse
2 Radiator fan relay
3 A/C relay
4 Clamp
5 Bracket A
6 Bracket B
7 Pipe CP
8 Flexible hose ASSY (Ps)
9 Flexible hose ASSY (Pd)
10 Pressure switch
11 Bracket (RH)
12 Bracket (LH)
13 Rubber cushion
14 Condenser
15 Pipe CP
16 Bracket
17 Receiver drier
18 Condenser fan relay

Tightening torque: N-m (kg-m, ft-lb)
T1: 10 — 20 (1.0 — 2.0, 7 — 14)
T2: 15 — 25 (1.5 — 2.5, 11 — 18)
T3: 5 — 10 (0.5 — 1.0, 3.6 — 7.2)
T4: 3 — 6 (0.3 — 0.6, 2.2 — 4.3)
T5: 20 — 29 (2.0 — 3.0, 14 — 22)
T6: 5.4 — 8.3 (0.55 — 0.85, 4.0 — 6.1)
T7: 15 — 18 (1.5 — 1.8, 11 — 13)

87976g35

1. Bracket
2. Pulser ASSY
3. Compressor CP
4. V-ribbed belt

87976g36

Fig. 33 A/C compressor, fan and belt — XT

Legacy and Impreza

▶ See Figures 32, 34 and 35

1. Disconnect the negative battery cable.
2. Properly discharge the air conditioning system using an approved recovery/recycling machine.
3. Disconnect both of the refrigerant lines from the compressor and plug the openings. Remove the O-rings and discard.
4. Remove the drive belt cover, then remove the alternator drive belt and compressor belts.
5. Disconnect the compressor and alternator harness harness.
6. Remove the compressor-to-bracket bolts, then remove the compressor from the engine.

To install:

7. Install the compressor in position on the engine. Tighten the compressor mounting bolts to 17-31 ft. lbs. (23-42 Nm).
8. Reconnect the electrical leads to the compressor.
9. Install the compressor and alternator belts. Adjust to the proper tension. Install the drive belt cover.

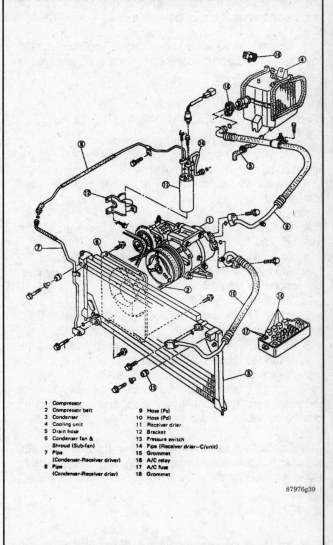

1 Compressor
2 Compressor belt
3 Condenser
4 Cooling unit
5 Drain hose
6 Condenser fan &
   Shroud (Sub-fan)
7 Pipe
   (Condenser-Receiver drier)
8 Pipe
   (Condenser-Receiver drier)
9 Hose (Ps)
10 Hose (Pd)
11 Receiver drier
12 Bracket
13 Pressure switch
14 Pipe (Receiver drier—C/unit)
15 Grommet
16 A/C relay
17 A/C fuse
18 Grommet

87976g39

Fig. 34 Calsonic A/C system components — Legacy and Impreza

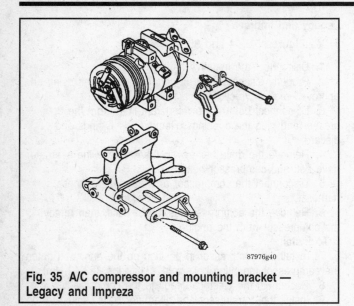

Fig. 35 A/C compressor and mounting bracket — Legacy and Impreza

10. Apply a coating of compressor oil to the new O-rings, and install them on the refrigerant lines, then connect the lines to the compressor. Tighten the lines to 7-14 ft. lbs. (10-20 Nm).

11. Connect the negative battery cable. Properly evacuate and charge the air conditioning system using an approved recovery/recycling machine.

SVX

▶ See Figures 36 and 37

1. Disconnect the negative battery cable.
2. Properly discharge the air conditioning system using an approved recovery/recycling machine.
3. Disconnect both of the refrigerant lines from the compressor and plug the openings. Remove the O-rings and discard.
4. Remove the drive belt cover, the n remove the alternator drive belt and compressor belts.
5. Disconnect the compressor and alternator harness.
6. Remove the compressor-to-bracket bolts, then remove the compressor from the engine.

To install:

7. Install the compressor in position on the engine. Tighten the compressor mounting bolts to 23-29 ft. lbs. (31-39 Nm).
8. Reconnect the electrical leads to the compressor.
9. Install the compressor and alternator belts. Adjust to the proper tension. Install the drive belt cover.
10. Apply a coating of compressor oil to the new O-rings, and install them on the refrigerant lines, then connect the lines to the compressor. Tighten the lines to 7-14 ft. lbs. (10-20 Nm).
11. Connect the negative battery cable. Properly evacuate and charge the air conditioning system using an approved recovery/recycling machine.

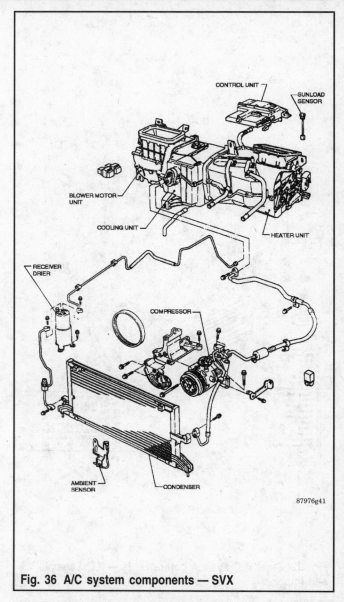

Fig. 36 A/C system components — SVX

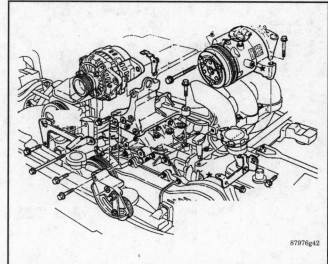

Fig. 37 Compressor and alternator mounting — SVX

Condenser

REMOVAL & INSTALLATION

Justy

Consult an authorized Subaru dealer for Justy A/C service. Because the air conditioner on the Justy is dealer installed as opposed to factory installed, there are several different A/C systems in these vehicles, each requiring a different removal and installation technique.

Sedan, Coupe, Loyale, Wagon and Brat
▶ See Figures 38 and 39

1. Disconnect the negative battery cable.
2. Properly discharge the air conditioning system using an approved recovery/recycling machine.
3. Remove the front grille assembly.

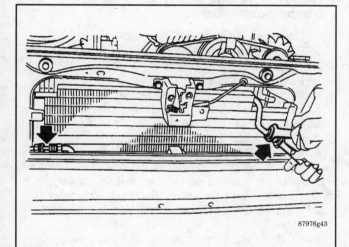

Fig. 38 Condenser line disconnect points — Sedan, Coupe, Loyale, Wagon and Brat

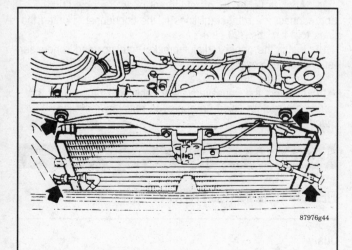

Fig. 39 Condenser retainer bolt on radiator support — Sedan, Coupe, Loyale, Wagon and Brat

4. Disconnect and plug the refrigerant lines from the condenser. Remove and discard the O-rings.
5. Remove the upper and lower condenser mounting bolts, then pull the condenser out of the vehicle.
   To install:
6. Install the condenser in position and install the retaining bolts. Tighten the retaining bolts to 4-7 ft. lbs. (5-10 Nm)
7. Apply a light coat of refrigerant oil to the new O-rings, and connect the refrigerant lines to the condenser. Tighten the lines to 7-14 ft. lbs. (9-20 Nm) for right-hand thread lines, 11-18 ft. lbs. (14-23 Nm) for left-hand thread lines.
8. Install the front grille.
9. Connect the negative battery cable and properly fill the refrigerant system using an approved recovery/recycling machine.

XT
▶ See Figures 40 and 41

1. Disconnect the negative battery cable.
2. Properly discharge the air conditioning system using an approved recovery/recycling machine.
3. If equipped with and air guide, remove it.
4. Disconnect and plug the refrigerant lines from the condenser. Remove and discard the O-rings.
5. Remove the upper condenser mounting bolts, then pull out the condenser from the vehicle.
   To install:
6. Install the condenser in position and install the retaining bolts. Tighten the retaining bolts to 11-18 ft. lbs. (14-23 Nm).
7. Apply a light coat of refrigerant oil to the new O-rings, and connect the refrigerant lines to the condenser. Tighten the lines to 7-14 ft. lbs. (9-20 Nm) for right-hand thread lines, 11-18 ft. lbs. (14-23 Nm) for left-hand thread lines.
8. Connect the negative battery cable and properly fill the refrigerant system using an approved recovery/recycling machine.

Legacy and Impreza
▶ See Figures 42 and 43

1. Disconnect the negative battery cable.

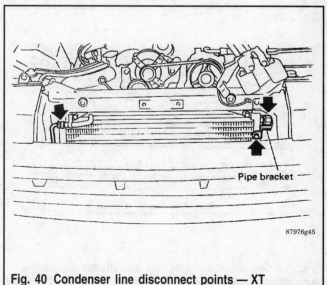

Pipe bracket

Fig. 40 Condenser line disconnect points — XT

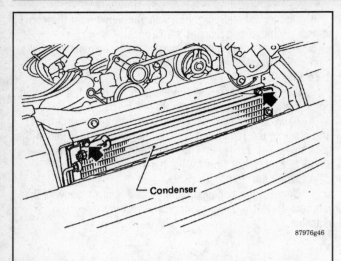

Fig. 41 Condenser retainer bolt on radiator support —
XT

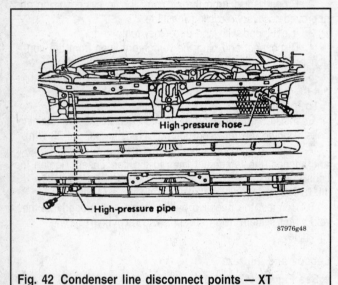

Fig. 42 Condenser line disconnect points — XT

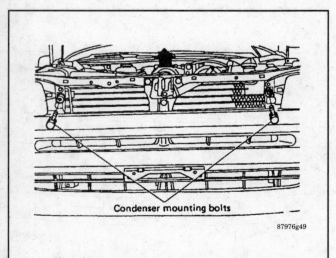

Fig. 43 Condenser retainer bolt on radiator support —
Legacy and Impreza

2. Properly discharge the air conditioning system using an approved recovery/recycling machine.
3. Remove the radiator bracket.
4. Disconnect and plug the refrigerant lines from the condenser. Remove and discard the O-rings.
5. Remove the upper condenser mounting bolts, then pull out the condenser from the vehicle.

To install:
6. Install the condenser in position and install the retaining bolts. Tighten the retaining bolts to 4-6 ft. lbs. (5-8 Nm).
7. Apply a light coat of refrigerant oil to the new O-rings, and connect the refrigerant lines to the condenser. Tighten the lines to 7-14 ft. lbs. (9-20 Nm).
8. Install the radiator support.
9. Connect the negative battery cable and properly fill the refrigerant system using an approved recovery/recycling machine.

SVX

▶ See Figure 44

➡The vehicle will have to be raised to remove the 2 lower condenser mounting bolts.

1. Disconnect the negative battery cable.
2. Properly discharge the air conditioning system using an approved recovery/recycling machine.
3. Remove the front grille.
4. If equipped with an air guide, remove it.
5. Remove the belt cover and upper radiator bracket.
6. Disconnect and plug the refrigerant lines from the condenser. Remove and discard the O-rings.
7. Remove the radiator and condenser fans.
8. Raise and support the front of the vehicle on jackstands, and remove the under cover, remove the lower condenser mounting bolts. Lower the vehicle. Remove the condenser by pushing the radiator back to the engine and pulling it out.

To install:
9. Install the condenser in position and install the retaining bolts. Tighten the retaining bolts to 7 ft. lbs. (10 Nm).
10. Raise the vehicle and install the lower bolts and the under cover.
11. Apply a light coat of refrigerant oil to the new O-rings and connect the refrigerant lines to the condenser. Tighten the lines to 14 ft. lbs. (20 Nm).
12. Install the upper radiator bracket, radiator and condenser fans, and belt cover.
13. Install the front grille.
14. Connect the negative battery cable and properly fill the refrigerant system using an approved recovery/recycling machine.

Evaporator Core

REMOVAL & INSTALLATION

Justy

Consult an authorized Subaru dealer for Justy A/C service. Because the air conditioner on the Justy is dealer installed as opposed to factory installed, there are several different A/C

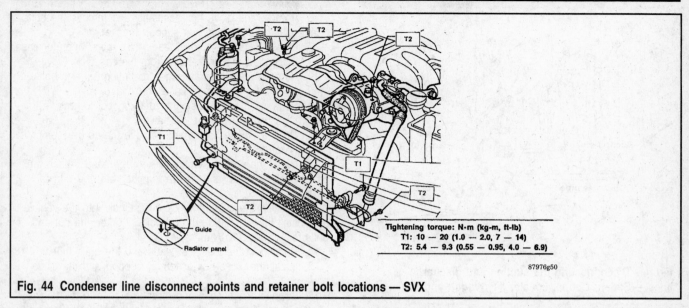

Tightening torque: N·m (kg-m, ft-lb)
T1: 10 — 20 (1.0 — 2.0, 7 — 14)
T2: 5.4 — 9.3 (0.55 — 0.95, 4.0 — 6.9)

87976g50

Fig. 44 Condenser line disconnect points and retainer bolt locations — SVX

systems in these vehicles, each requiring a different removal and installation technique.

Sedan, Coupe, Loyale, XT, Wagon and Brat

▶ See Figures 45, 46 and 47

1. Open the hood and remove the spare tire, if necessary.
2. Disconnect the negative battery cable.
3. Properly discharge the air conditioning system using an approved recovery/recycling machine.
4. Tag and disconnect the evaporator discharge pipe, suction pipe and grommets. Remove and discard the rubber O-rings.
5. Remove the evaporator core under cover.
6. Remove the pocket assembly from the dash.
7. Disconnect the wire harness from the evaporator case.
8. Remove the 2 retaining bands and remove the evaporator case.
9. Using a suitable prytool, remove the retainer clips around the evaporator case halves, then separate the sections to access the evaporator assembly.

To install:

10. Position the evaporator core in one of the halves of the case assembly. Close the evaporator case halves, and install the retainer clips around the assembly to secure the sections together.
11. Install the evaporator case in the vehicle, and secure in place using the retainer bands.

➡**When installing the evaporator into the car body, make sure the wiring harness and any vacuum hoses do not get caught between the body parts.**

12. Attach the wire harness to the evaporator case.
13. Install the pocket to the dash panel.
14. Install the suction and discharge pipes, using new O-rings coated with clean refrigerant oil. Tighten the discharge pipe to 7-14 ft. lbs. (10-20 Nm), the nut on the suction side to 14-22 ft. lbs. (20-29 Nm).
15. Connect the negative battery cable.
16. Properly charge the A/C system using an approved recovery/recycling machine.

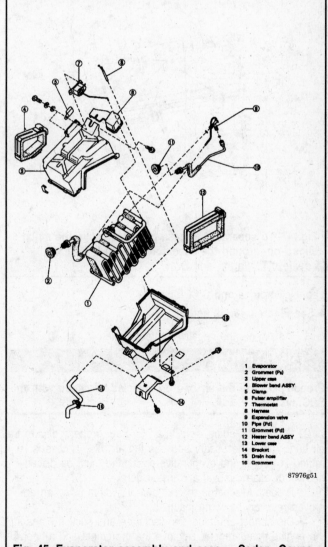

1 Evaporator
2 Grommet (Ps)
3 Upper case
4 Blower band ASSY
5 Clamp
6 Pulser amplifier
7 Thermostat
8 Harness
9 Expansion valve
10 Pipe (Pd)
11 Grommet (Pd)
12 Heater band ASSY
13 Lower case
14 Bracket
15 Drain hose
16 Grommet

87976g51

Fig. 45 Evaporator assembly and case — Sedan, Coupe, Loyale, XT, Wagon and Brat

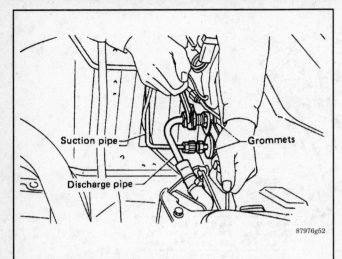

Fig. 46 Disconnecting the suction and discharge lines — Sedan, Coupe, Loyale, XT, Wagon and Brat

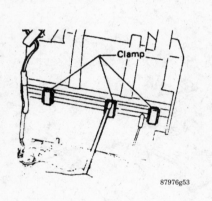

Fig. 47 To separate the case halves, remove the metal clips from around the assembly — Sedan, Coupe, Loyale, XT, Wagon and Brat

Legacy, Impreza and SVX
▶ **See Figures 48, 49 and 50**

1. Disconnect the negative battery cable.

✳✳CAUTION

Properly disarm the air bag on vehicles equipped with the SRS system.

2. On models equipped with an air bag, properly disarm the air bag. This is necessary because the air bag harness is routed in front of the evaporative case, and must be disconnected for case removal and installation.
3. Properly discharge the refrigerant system using an approved recovery/recycling machine.
4. Disconnect and plug the discharge and suction pipes in the engine compartment. Remove the grommets and rubber O-rings. Discard the O-rings
5. Disconnect the air bag harness routed in front of evaporator case.

6. Remove the glove box assembly and remove the bolts retaining the metal glove box support bracket.
7. Disconnect the electrical leads from the evaporator case.
8. Disconnect the drain hose from the case.
9. Remove the evaporator case mounting nut and bolts, then remove the evaporator case from the vehicle.
10. Separate the case using a small prytool to remove the metal clips that retain the case halves.
11. Open the case halves and remove the core assembly.
To install:
12. Install the core assembly in ½ of the case. Attach the other ½ of the case, and secure together with the retainer clips.
13. Position the evaporator case assembly into the vehicle and install the mounting nut and bolts. Tighten the nut and bolts to 7 ft. lbs. (10 Nm).
14. Reconnect the electrical leads and the drain tube.
15. Install the glove box assembly support and the glove box.
16. Connect the suction and discharge lines in the engine compartment. Coat the new O-rings lightly with refrigerant oil and tighten the connections. Tighten the nut on the discharge side to 18 ft. lbs. (25 Nm) and the nut on the suction side to 7 ft. lbs. (10 Nm).
17. Connect the negative battery cable and properly charge the air conditioning system. Using an approve recovery/recycling machine.

Control Panel

REMOVAL & INSTALLATION

The A/C control panel is part of the heater control panel assembly. Refer to the control panel removal and installation steps in the heater section for details.

Expansion Valve

REMOVAL & INSTALLATION

Except Justy
▶ **See Figures 51 and 52**

The expansion valve is located inside the evaporator case attached to the evaporator core.

1. Disconnect the negative battery cable.
2. Properly discharge the air conditioning system using an approved recovery/recycling machine.
3. Disarm the air bag on equipped models.
4. Disconnect and plug the refrigerant lines at the evaporator.
5. Disconnect the air bag harness routed in front of the evaporative case on equipped models.
6. Remove the glove box and support brackets.
7. Loosen and remove the evaporator case retainer bands or nut and bolts.
8. Disconnect the harness attached to the case assembly.

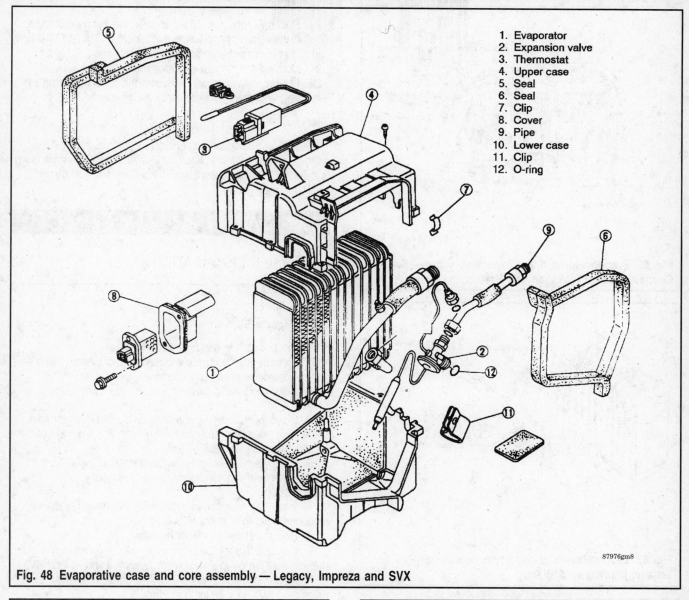

1. Evaporator
2. Expansion valve
3. Thermostat
4. Upper case
5. Seal
6. Seal
7. Clip
8. Cover
9. Pipe
10. Lower case
11. Clip
12. O-ring

87976gm8

Fig. 48 Evaporative case and core assembly — Legacy, Impreza and SVX

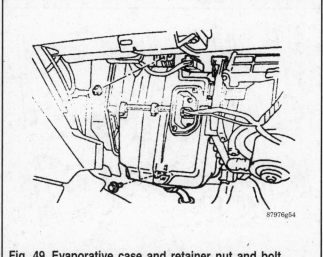

87976g54

Fig. 49 Evaporative case and retainer nut and bolt under dash panel — Legacy and Impreza

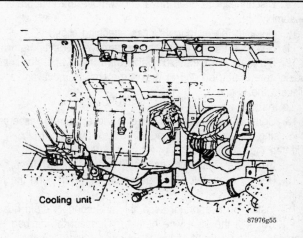

Cooling unit

87976g55

Fig. 50 Evaporative case and retainer nut and bolts — SVX

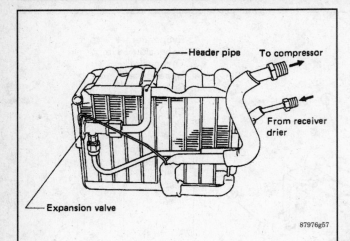

Fig. 51 Evaporative core and expansion valve — Sedan, Coupe, Loyale, XT, Wagon and Brat

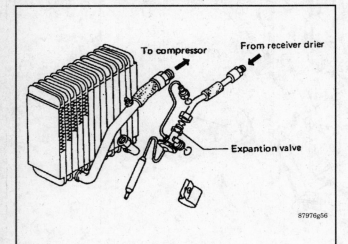

Fig. 52 Evaporative core and expansion valve — Legacy, Impreza and SVX

9. Disconnect the drain hose and remove the evaporator assembly.

10. Remove the evaporator case attaching clips.

11. Separate the case halves and remove the evaporator.

12. Separate the expansion valve from the evaporator line, being careful not to bend or distort the line. Remove and discard the O-ring.

To install:

13. Connect the expansion valve to the evaporator assembly, using a new O-ring coated with clean refrigerant oil. Tighten the retainer nut to 14-22 ft. lbs. (20-29 Nm).

14. Install the evaporator assembly into the case halves.

15. Secure evaporator case assembly together using the retainer clips.

16. Install the evaporator assembly and connect drain hose.

17. Connect the case wire harness. Connect the air bag harness routed in front of the evaporative case assembly.

18. Install the evaporator housing securing bands or nut and bolts.

19. Install the glove box assembly.

20. Reconnect the refrigerant lines at the evaporator case. Tighten the suction hose-to-the evaporator to 7 ft. lbs. (10 Nm) and the receiver pip-to-evaporator to 18 ft. lbs. (25 Nm).

21. Connect the negative battery cable.

22. Charge, evacuate and leak test the air conditioning system using an approved recovery/recycling machine.

Justy

Consult an authorized Subaru dealer for expansion valve removal and installation. Because the A/C system on the Justy is a dealer installed option, many locations and installation variations may occur.

Receiver/Drier

REMOVAL & INSTALLATION

Except Justy

▶ **See Figures 53, 54 and 55**

1. Disconnect the negative battery cable.

2. Properly discharge the air conditioning system using an approved recovery/recycling machine.

3. Disconnect the receiver/drier pressure switch wire harness.

4. Disconnect and plug the receiver/drier refrigerant lines. Depending on model and production year, the lines are attached with nuts or bolts.

5. Remove the receiver/drier bracket attaching bolts.

6. Remove the receiver/drier assembly.

To install:

7. Install the receiver/drier in position and tighten the mounting bolts to 7 ft. lbs. (10 Nm).

8. Reconnect the electrical harness.

9. Connect the refrigerant lines to the receiver/drier. Tighten the line nuts on all models except Legacy, Impreza and SVX to 12 ft. lbs. (17 Nm). Tighten the line bolts on Legacy, Impreza and SVX to 7 ft. lbs. (10 Nm).

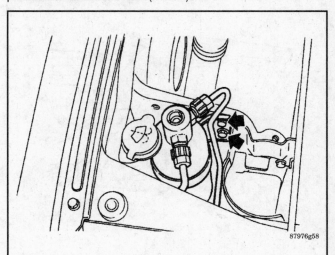

Fig. 53 Receiver/drier assembly — Sedan, Coupe, Loyale, Wagon and Brat

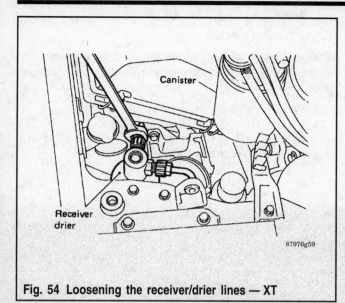

Fig. 54 Loosening the receiver/drier lines — XT

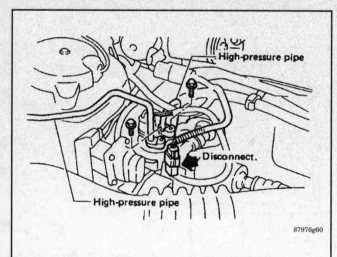

Fig. 55 Receiver/drier and refrigerant lines — Legacy, Impreza and SVX

10. Properly recharge the refrigerant system using an approved recovery/recycling machine.

11. Connect the negative battery cable and check the operation of the A/C system.

Justy

Consult an authorized Subaru dealer for receiver/drier location and removal and installation steps. Because the A/C system on the Justy was a dealer installed option, variations in installation and service procedures occur.

Refrigerant Lines

REMOVAL & INSTALLATION

▶ **See Figures 56, 57, 58 and 59**

1. Disconnect the negative battery cable.

2. Properly discharge the air conditioning system using an approved recovery/recycling machine.

3. Remove chassis, engine or body parts, if required for line removal.

4. If removing a line secured with a nut, use a suitable flare-end or backup wrench loosen, disconnect and immediately plug the refrigerant line.

5. If removing a line attached with a retainer bolt, loosen and remove the retainer bolt using a suitable wrench or socket. Immediately plug the open connection.

6. Remove and discard the sealing O-ring.

7. Disconnect the pressure switch wire connectors, if required.

8. Remove all attaching brackets and bolts.

9. Remove the refrigerant lines.

To install:

10. Apply a light coat of refrigerant oil to new O-rings, and install on the refrigerant line.

11. If the line is secured with a nut, tighten the nut to 14-22 ft. lbs. (20-29 Nm).

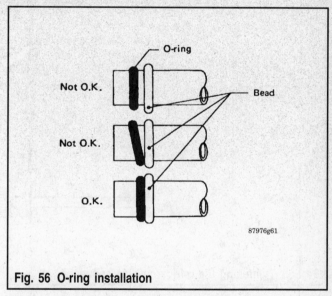

Fig. 56 O-ring installation

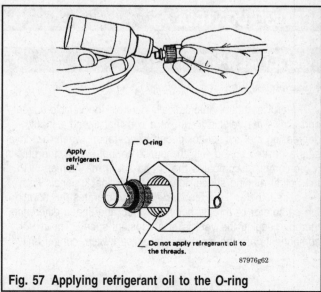

Fig. 57 Applying refrigerant oil to the O-ring

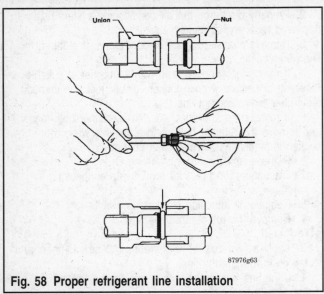

Fig. 58 Proper refrigerant line installation

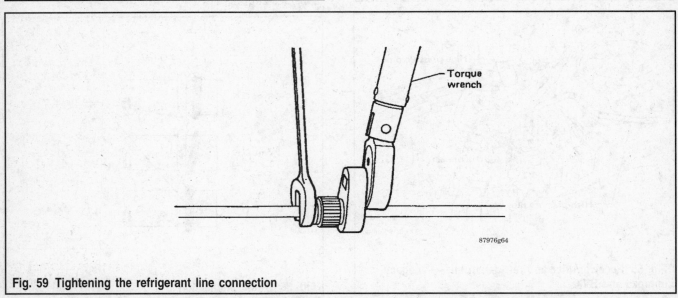

Fig. 59 Tightening the refrigerant line connection

12. If the line is secured with a retainer bolt, tighten the bolt to 7-14 ft. lbs. (10-20 Nm).

➡ **Tighten the refrigerant line to the previously given valves, unless the procedure requires a different tightening value.**

13. Route refrigerant lines in the original locations.
14. Use original securing brackets and bolts.
15. Evacuate, charge and check system for leaks using an approved recovery/recycling machine.

CRUISE CONTROL

GENERAL INFORMATION

▶ **See Figure 60**

The cruise control automatically controls the vehicle speed and allows the vehicle to run at a constant speed without depressing the accelerator pedal. In operation, when the driver sets a desired speed with the cruise control switch, the built-in micro-computer compares the speed set in the memory with the actual running speed detected by feedback signals from the speedometer. This feedback system operates the throttle of the carburetor or throttle body to correct the speed difference, thereby keeping the vehicle at a constant speed. The major components are the main switch, cruise switch, control unit, vacuum pump and valve assembly, actuator, clutch switch and stop and brake switch.

➡ **The use of the speed control is not recommended when driving conditions do not permit maintaining a constant speed, such as in heavy traffic or on roads that are winding, icy, snow covered or slippery.**

SYSTEM OPERATION

Cruise control unit compares the actual vehicle speed detected by feedback signals from the speed sensor incorporated in the speedometer with the speed set in the memory memorized when the set switch was turned **ON**. A signal is then transmitted according to the difference between the 2 speeds.

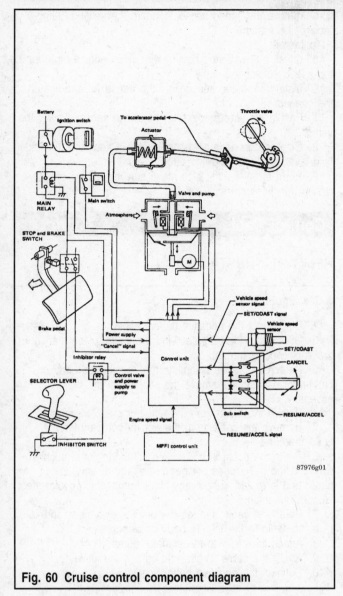

Fig. 60 Cruise control component diagram

This signal is transmitted to the solenoid valves of the valve assembly located in the engine compartment. The movement of the actuator operates the throttle valve through the accelerator pedal and cable, thereby keeping the vehicle's speed constant.

SYSTEM COMPONENTS

Vacuum Pump

The vacuum pump is controlled by the vacuum switch built into the valve assembly tank, and is used to supply the vacuum to the tank. Power to the pump is fed when the vacuum switch is turned **ON**, and the diaphragm is moved up and down by the rotation of the offset shaft fixed to the motor shaft.

Vacuum Valve Assembly

The vacuum valve, vent valve, and safety valve provide the open-close operation which leads to the vacuum/atmospheric

pressure to the actuator. Also attached to this assembly is the tank for storing vacuum generated by the pump, and the vacuum switch for controlling the pump to maintain a constant vacuum level in the tank.

If the cruise control is turned **ON** and a constant vehicle speed is attained, the safety valve connected to the atmosphere is closed. Also, the vacuum valve connected to the tank and the vent valve connected to the atmosphere operate to lead the atmosphere/vacuum to the actuator. When the cruise control is canceled, the vacuum valve closes to shut off the tank vacuum, and the safety valve opens to allow atmospheric pressure to enter the actuator.

The vacuum in the tank is consumed by the operation of the vacuum valve. If the vacuum in the tank reaches 13 in. Hg (43 kPa) the vacuum switch is turned **ON**, and the pump feeds the vacuum into the tank. When the vacuum in the tank reaches 15 in. Hg (52 kPa) the vacuum switch turns **OFF** to stop the pump.

Actuator

The diaphragm is operated by vacuum or atmospheric pressure led by each valve, and this diaphragm movement actuates the wire cable through the link assembly to open or close the throttle valve. With the cruise control set to **OFF** (system **OFF** state), no diaphragm operation occurs as the atmospheric pressure is kept inside the actuator.

Engine Throttle

The throttle body or carburetor is equipped with 2 throttle cams. One cam is used during acceleration and the other during cruising, in order to open or close the throttle valve. These cams operate independently of each other. In other words, while 1 cam operates, the other does not.

SERVICE PRECAUTIONS

❊❊CAUTION

Properly disarm the air bag on vehicles equipped with the SRS system. Failure to do so can cause serious injury and/or damage.

- Never disconnect any electrical connection with the ignition switch **ON** unless instructed to do so in a test.
- Always wear a grounded wrist static strap when servicing any control module or component labeled with a Electrostatic Discharge (ESD) sensitive device symbol.
- Avoid touching module connector pins.
- Leave new components and modules in the shipping package until ready to install them.
- Always touch a vehicle ground after sliding across a vehicle seat or walking across vinyl or carpeted floors to avoid static charge damage.
- Never allow welding cables to lie on, near or across any vehicle electrical wiring.
- Do not allow extension cords for power tools or drop lights to lie on, near or across any vehicle electrical wiring.
- Do not operate the cruise control or the engine with the drive wheels off the ground unless specifically instructed to do so by a test procedure.

Control Switches

REMOVAL & INSTALLATION

Steering Column Control Switch

The cruise control switches in all models are mounted on a stalk on the steering column combination switch assembly. Refer to the combination switch removal and installation procedure in Section 8 for details.

Brake Switch

1. Disconnect the negative battery cable.
2. Remove the driver side lower trim panel.
3. Unfasten the brake switch harness connector.
4. Remove the lock nut and unscrew the switch.

To install:

5. Screw the switch into position on the bracket, and install the lock nut. Do not tighten the locknut until an adjustment is made.
6. Adjust the switch by turning the switch clockwise until tip of the screw portion of the brake pedal hits the pedal arm.
7. Turn the switch counterclockwise unit the clearance is about 0.02-0.04 in. (0.5-1.0mm).
8. Tighten the locknut and install the harness.
9. Connect the negative battery cable. Test the cruise control system.

Clutch Switch

1. Disconnect the negative battery cable.
2. Disconnect the clutch switch wire harness.
3. Remove the lock nut and unscrew the switch.

To install:

4. Screw the switch into position, and install the locknut. Do not tighten the nut until the switch is adjusted.
5. Push the switch by hand until the pushrod cannot be seen from the tip of the switch.
6. Give the switch 1 reverse rotation turn and tighten the locknut.
7. Install the wire harness.
8. Connect the negative battery cable.
9. Test the cruise control system.

Speed Sensor

REMOVAL & INSTALLATION

The speed sensor is located on the transaxle assembly of the vehicle.

1. Disconnect the negative battery cable.
2. Raise and support the front of the vehicle safely on jackstands.
3. Disconnect the wire harness attached to the speed sensor.
4. Place a suitable drip pan below the speed sensor to catch any fluid which may spill out during removal and installa-

tion. Remove the speed sensor. Discard the sealing O-ring around the assembly.

To install:

5. Install a new O-ring coated with clean engine oil around the speed sensor assembly.
6. Install the speed sensor into the transaxle, and tighten the connection.
7. Fasten the wire harness to the speed sensor. Lower the vehicle.
8. Connect the negative battery cable. Check the transaxle fluid level, and add fluid if needed.
9. Road test the vehicle to make sure the cruise control system functions correctly.

Control Cable

REMOVAL & INSTALLATION

▶ See Figure 61

1. Disconnect the negative battery cable.
2. Loosen the locknuts securing the cable to the bracket in the engine compartment.
3. Detach the cable assembly from the throttle body or carburetor assembly. Remove the cable from the bracket assembly.
4. Detach the cable from the actuator pump assembly.
5. Remove the cable from the engine compartment.

To install:

6. Route the cable in the engine compartment in such a way that the cable does not get in the way of any moving parts, and is routed without any sharp turns which could effect smooth operation.
7. Route the cable through the bracket assembly, and attach the cable to the throttle body or carburetor.
8. Attach the cable to the actuator pump.
9. Adjust the cable length, and tighten the locknuts.
10. Connect the negative battery cable.

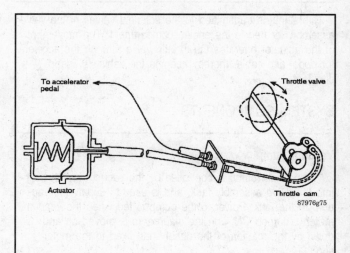

87976g75

Fig. 61 Cruise control cable between the actuator and throttle cam

ADJUSTMENT

Sedan, Coupe, Loyale, Wagon and Brat
▶ See Figure 62

The actuator wire cable sagging can be adjusted by changing the position of the actuator-to-pedal bracket mounting bolt. Adjust the bracket so the control cable play is 0.04-0.08 in. (1-2mm). Be sure to adjust the accelerator when the pedal is held in the fully returned position. Be careful not to apply excessive load to the wire cable when adjusting or installing; otherwise the actuator may be deformed or damaged.

XT
▶ See Figure 63

When securing the cable outer end, adjust the clearance between the throttle cam and stop to 0-0.08 in. (0-2mm) using the adjusting nut. Ensure that there is no free play between the throttle cam and the cable.

➡ Do not bend the control cable too sharply; otherwise, it will not operate smoothly. When installing the cam to the inner end of the control cable, do not bend or crush the inner cable.

Legacy and Impreza
▶ See Figure 64

When securing the cable outer end, adjust the clearance between the throttle cam and the lever to 0.04-0.08 in. (1-2mm) using the adjusting nut. Ensure that there is no free play between the throttle cam and the cable.

➡ Do not bend the control cable too sharply; otherwise, it will not operate smoothly. When installing the cam to the inner end of the control cable, do not bend or crush the inner cable.

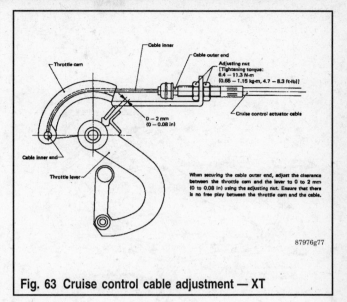

Fig. 63 Cruise control cable adjustment — XT

SVX
▶ See Figure 65

When securing the cable outer end, adjust the clearance between the throttle cam and the lever to 0.04-0.08 in. (1-2mm) using the adjusting nut. Ensure that there is no free play between the throttle cam and the cable.

➡ Do not bend the control cable too sharply; otherwise, it will not operate smoothly. When installing the cam to the inner end of the control cable, do not bend or crush the inner cable.

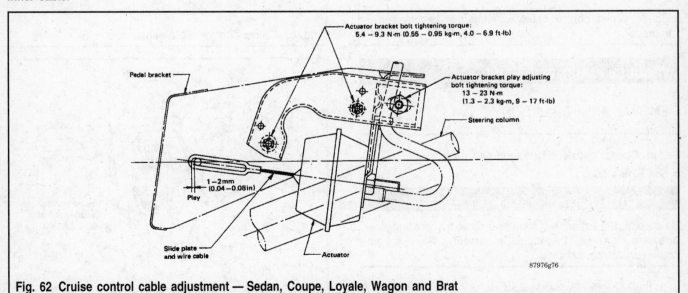

Fig. 62 Cruise control cable adjustment — Sedan, Coupe, Loyale, Wagon and Brat

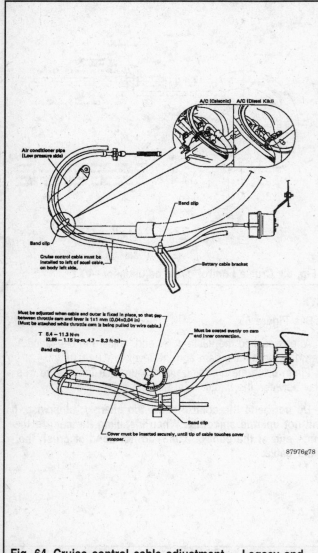

Fig. 64 Cruise control cable adjustment — Legacy and Impreza

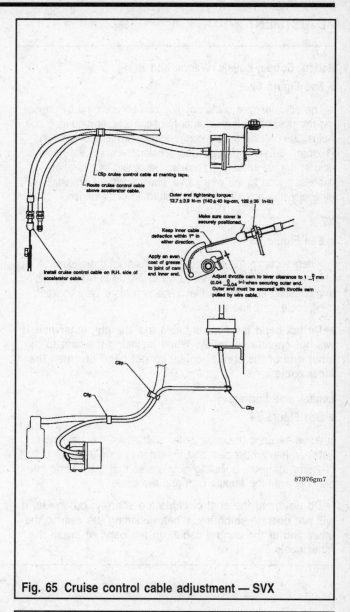

Fig. 65 Cruise control cable adjustment — SVX

Vacuum Pump and Valve

REMOVAL & INSTALLATION

Sedan, Coupe, Loyale, XT, Wagon and Brat

▶ See Figure 66

> **✳✳CAUTION**
>
> Be careful, the exhaust system and turbocharger temperatures are high while the engine is operating. Serious burns could result from contact.

1. Ensure that the ignition is **OFF**.
2. Remove the air cleaner and air flow meter:
   a. Loosen the hose clamp.
   b. Remove the boot from the air cleaner cover.
   c. Release the clips on the air cleaner cover.

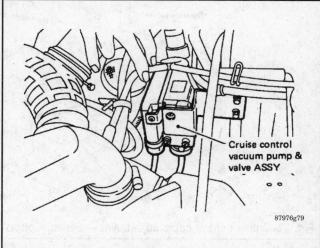

Fig. 66 Vacuum pump assembly bolts — Sedan, Coupe, Loyale, XT, Wagon, and Brat

d. Place the air cleaner cover together with the air flow meter on the engine.

➡**Always keep air cleaner, vacuum hose, etc. free from dirt and dust.**

3. Disconnect the wiring harness and hose from the vacuum pump assembly.

4. Remove the vacuum pump assembly and the valve assembly as a unit. Tighten the mounting nuts to 65 inch lbs. (7 Nm).

To install:

5. Position and secure the vacuum pump assembly using the retainer nuts and bolts. Tighten the mounting nuts and bolts to 65 inch lbs. (7 Nm).

6. Attach the wire harness and vacuum hose assembly to the pump.

7. Install the air flow meter and air cleaner assemblies.

8. Test drive the vehicle to make sure the cruise control system functions correctly.

Legacy, Impreza and SVX

▶ **See Figure 67**

1. Disconnect the negative battery cable.

2. Disconnect the wiring harness and hose. Be sure to always disconnect the hose at the body pipe side.

3. Remove the attaching nuts, then disconnect the ABS sensor connector clip from the bracket and remove the vacuum pump assembly.

To install:

4. Install the vacuum pump to the bracket and tighten the mounting nuts to 65 inch lbs. (7.4 Nm). Connect the ABS sensor clip.

5. Attach the wire harness and vacuum line.

6. Connect the negative battery cable. Test the cruise control system.

Actuator Assembly

REMOVAL & INSTALLATION

Sedan, Coupe, Loyale, XT, Wagon and Brat

▶ **See Figure 68**

1. Disconnect the negative battery cable.

2. Remove the nut which secures the control cable end to throttle cam, and remove control cable end.

3. Remove the attaching bolts and actuator assembly.

4. Remove the clip bands from the control cable. Disconnect the vacuum pipe and vacuum hose.

To install:

5. Attach the vacuum pipe and hose. Install the clip bands to the control cable.

6. Install the actuator assembly, and tighten the mounting nuts to 65 inch lbs. (7 Nm).

7. Install the control cable, and adjust.

8. Connect the negative battery cable, and test the cruise control system.

Legacy, Impreza and SVX

▶ **See Figure 69**

1. Disconnect the negative battery cable.

2. Remove the intake manifold cover. Remove the nut which secures the control cable end to throttle cam, and remove control cable end.

3. Remove the attaching bolts and actuator assembly.

4. Remove the clip bands from the control cable. Disconnect the vacuum pipe and vacuum hose.

To install:

5. Attach the vacuum pipe and hose. Install the clip bands to the control cable.

6. Install the actuator assembly, and tighten the mounting nuts to 65 inch lbs. (7 Nm).

7. Install the control cable, and adjust.

8. Install the intake manifold cover.

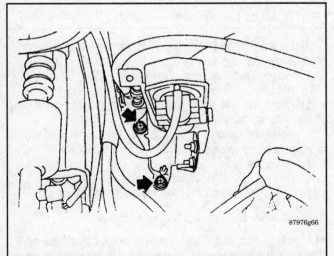

87976g66

Fig. 67 Vacuum pump retainer bolts — Legacy, Impreza and SVX

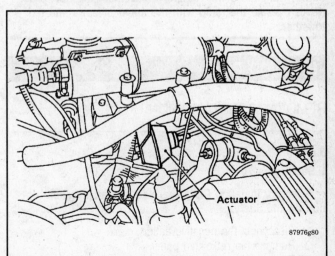

87976g80

Fig. 68 Actuator pump assembly bolts — Sedan, Coupe, Loyale, XT, Wagon, and Brat

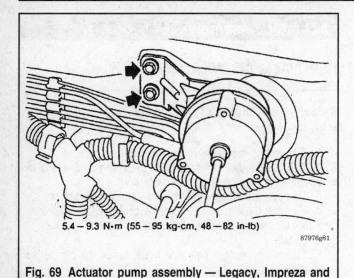

5.4 — 9.3 N•m (55 — 95 kg-cm, 48 — 82 in-lb)

87976g81

Fig. 69 Actuator pump assembly — Legacy, Impreza and SVX

9. Connect the negative battery cable, and test the cruise control system.

ENTERTAINMENT SYSTEMS

The radio is mounted in the center portion of the dashboard, with speakers mounted in various locations through out the vehicle. Most models contain 2, 4 or 6 speakers, 2 or 4 mounted in the front of the vehicle (usually in the door panels or in the lower portion of the dash board) and 2 mounted in the rear of the vehicle. The SVX is equipped with 6 speakers, 2 tweeters mounted in the top of the dash board, 2 full range speakers mounted in the front doors and 2 larger speakers mounted in the rear shelf. The Legacy, Impreza and SVX can also be equipped with a compact disc player mounted below the radio.

✳✳CAUTION

Never operate the radio without a speaker. Damage to the output transistors will result. If the speaker must be replaced, use a speaker of correct impedance (ohms) or the output transistors will require replacement in short order. Never operate the radio with the speaker leads shorted together.

Radio/CD Player

REMOVAL & INSTALLATION

Justy

▶ See Figure 70

➡A factory installed CD player was not an available option on the Justy.

1. Disconnect the negative battery cable.
2. Remove the radio trim panel.
3. Remove the radio attaching screws and pull the radio body forward out of the dash assembly.

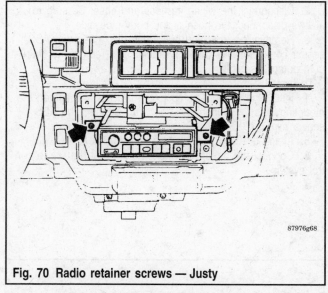

87976g68

Fig. 70 Radio retainer screws — Justy

4. Disconnect the power and speaker harness and the antenna cable from the rear of the radio assembly.
5. Remove the radio from the vehicle.

To install:

6. Attach the wire harnesses and antenna cable to the rear of the radio assembly.
7. Install the radio in position in the dash panel, and secure in place with the retainer screws.
8. Install the radio trim panel.
9. Connect the negative battery cable.
10. Check the operation of the radio and speakers.

Sedan Coupe, XT, Loyale, Wagon and Brat

➡A factory installed CD player was not an available option on the Sedan, sedan, coupe, XT, Loyale, Wagon or Brat.

1. Disconnect the negative battery cable.
2. Remove the clock assembly from the dash panel on XT models.
3. Remove the trim panel that surrounds the radio and pocket assembly.
4. Remove the radio attaching screws and pull the radio body out enough to access the wire harness and antenna cable at the back of the assembly.
5. Disconnect the wire harnesses and antenna cable.
6. Remove the radio from the vehicle.

To install:

7. Attach the speaker and power harnesses to the rear of the radio. Install the antenna cable into the radio.
8. Position the radio in the dash panel and secure in place with the retainer screws.
9. Install the trim panel around the radio assembly.
10. Install the clock assembly.
11. Connect the negative battery cable.
12. Check the operation of the radio and speakers.

Legacy and Impreza

1. Disconnect the negative battery cable.
2. Remove the cup holder above the radio.
3. Remove the ashtray holder retainer screws from below the radio, and lower the holder.
4. Remove the center panel around the radio.
5. Remove the radio attaching screws and pull the radio body forward to access the antenna and wire harnesses.
6. Disconnect the wire harnesses and antenna cable from the radio.
7. Remove the radio from the vehicle.
8. To separate the CD player, if equipped, from the radio, remove the retainer screws from both sides of the radio and CD assemblies securing the brackets to the radio case, and separate the CD player from the radio. Disconnect the DIN cable from the rear of the radio, and remove the CD player.

To install:

9. If equipped, and if removed, place the CD player beneath the radio assembly, and attach the brackets to the sides of the radio and CD player using the retainer screws. Attach the DIN cable from the CD player to the rear of the radio.
10. Attach the wire harnesses and antenna cable to the rear of the radio assembly.
11. Install the radio into the dash panel and secure in place with the retainer screws
12. Install the center trim panel and secure in place with the retainer screws.
13. Install the cup holder above the radio, and the ashtray below the radio assembly.
14. Connect the negative battery cable.
15. Check the operation of the radio, speakers and CD player if equipped.

SVX

▶ **See Figures 71 and 72**

1. Disconnect the negative battery cable.
2. Place the steering wheel in the lowest position.
3. Remove the lower instrument cluster trim panel.
4. Remove the instrument cluster visor retaining screws and remove the visor. Disconnect the clock when removing the visor.

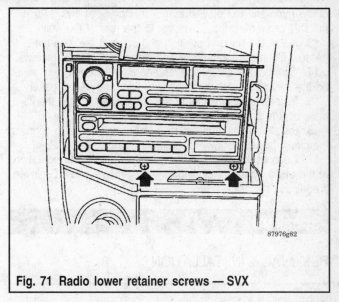

Fig. 71 Radio lower retainer screws — SVX

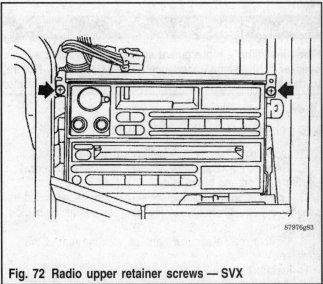

Fig. 72 Radio upper retainer screws — SVX

5. Remove the center ventilation grille from above the radio housing.
6. Remove the ventilation control panel. Open the radio housing cover and carefully pry its back panel off with a small prybar.
7. Remove the center trim panel. Remove the left console panel and disconnect the antenna cables.
8. Remove the ashtray and holder.
9. Remove the radio mounting screws, close the radio cover door and remove the radio body.
10. Disconnect the wire harnesses from the rear of the radio.
11. To separate the CD player, if equipped, from the radio, remove the retainer screws from both sides of the radio and CD assemblies securing the brackets to the radio case, and separate the CD player from the radio. Disconnect the DIN cable from the rear of the radio, and remove the CD player.

To install:

12. If equipped, and if removed, place the CD player beneath the radio assembly, and attach the brackets to the sides

of the radio and CD player using the retainer screws. Attach the DIN cable from the CD player to the rear of the radio.

13. Install the radio in position and connect the wire harnesses. Open the radio cover and install the retaining screws.

14. Connect the antenna wires and install the left side panel on the console. Install the ashtray, holder and center panel.

15. Install the inner panel to the radio cover. Install the climate control panel and the center ventilation grille.

16. Install the instrument cluster visor, make sure to connect the clock. Install the lower instrument cluster trim panel.

17. Connect the negative battery cable. Check the operation of the audio system, including all the speakers and CD player, if equipped.

Speakers

REMOVAL & INSTALLATION

Front

> **✳✳WARNING**
>
> **When installing a replacement speaker, always use a speaker of the same impedance as the 1 removed. Failure to use the correct speaker will cause damage to the radio.**

JUSTY

▶ **See Figure 73**

1. Disconnect the negative battery cable.

2. Remove the dash panel speaker grille retainer screws. Lift the grille off and place aside.

3. Loosen and remove the speaker retainer screws. Lift the speaker out enough to access the wire harness at the back of the speaker.

4. Disconnect the speaker harness from the rear of the speaker.

To install:

5. Attach the speaker wire harness to the back of the speaker assembly.

6. Position the speaker in the opening in the dash, and secure in place with the retainer screws.

7. Position the grille in place, and secure with the retainer screws.

8. Connect the negative battery cable.

9. Test the radio to make sure all speakers function correctly.

SEDAN, COUPE, XT, LOYALE, WAGON AND BRAT

1. Disconnect the negative battery cable.

2. Remove the dash lower trim panel, if removing the driver side dash speaker. Remove the glove box if removing the passenger side dash speaker.

3. Remove the speaker retainer nuts from the underside of the dash panel. Remove the speaker from the dash studs.

4. Disconnect the speaker harness.

5. Remove the speaker.

To install:

6. Attach the wire harness to the speaker.

7. Position the speakers on the retainer studs on the underside of the dash panel.

8. Secure the speaker in place with the retainer nuts.

9. Install the lower trim panel, and/or glove box.

10. Connect the negative battery cable.

11. Test the radio to make sure all speakers function correctly.

LEGACY AND IMPREZA

▶ **See Figures 74 and 75**

1. Disconnect the negative battery cable.

2. Remove the door panel assembly.

3. Disconnect the speaker harness located between the door panel and inner door metal.

4. Loosen and remove the speaker retainer screws. Lift the speaker out.

To install:

5. Position the speaker in the opening in the dash, and secure in place with the retainer screws.

6. Attach the speaker harness.

7. Install the door panel and trim pieces.

8. Connect the negative battery cable.

87976g84

Fig. 73 Front dash speaker grille — Justy

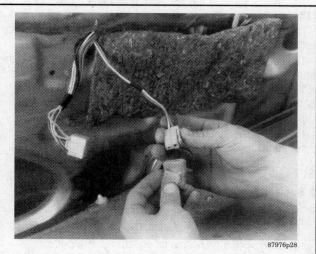

87976p28

Fig. 74 Disconnect the speaker harness — Legacy shown

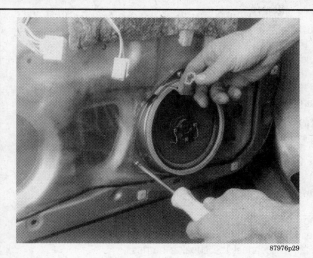

87976p29

Fig. 75 Remove the speaker retainer screws, and lift the speaker out — Legacy shown

9. Test the radio to make sure all speaker function correctly.

SVX

1. Disconnect the negative battery cable.
2. Remove the door panel assembly.
3. Disconnect the speaker harness located between the door panel and inner door metal.
4. Loosen and remove the speaker retainer screws. Lift the speaker out.

To install:

5. Position the speaker in the opening in the dash, and secure in place with the retainer screws.
6. Attach the speaker harness.
7. Install the door panel and trim pieces.
8. Connect the negative battery cable.
9. Test the radio to make sure all speakers function correctly.

Front Tweeters

LEGACY AND IMPREZA

1. Disconnect the negative battery cable.
2. Remove the door panel assembly.
3. Remove the tweeter assembly from the front corner of the window assembly by unfastening the retainer screw at the base of the tweeter. Lift the speaker out enough to access to wire harness.
4. Disconnect the harness at the back side of the tweeter.

To install:

5. Attach the harness to the rear of the tweeter.
6. Position the tweeter in the corner of the from window, and secure in place with the retainer screw.
7. Install the door panel and trim pieces.
8. Connect the negative battery cable.
9. Test the radio to make sure all speakers function correctly.

SVX

1. Disconnect the negative battery cable.

2. Use a small prytool to remove the tweeter from the dash panel. Be careful not to damage the dash panel surface.
3. Disconnect the harness at the back side of the tweeter.

To install:

4. Attach the harness to the rear of the tweeter.
5. Insert the tweeter into the hole in the dash panel, and press into place.
6. Connect the negative battery cable.
7. Test the radio to make sure all speakers function correctly.

Rear

JUSTY

1. Disconnect the negative battery cable.
2. Remove the speaker grille retainer screws. Lift the grille off and place aside.
3. Loosen and remove the speaker retainer screws. Lift the speaker out enough to access the wire harness at the back of the speaker.
4. Disconnect the speaker harness from the rear of the speaker.

To install:

5. Attach the speaker wire harness to the back of the speaker assembly.
6. Position the speaker in the opening, and secure in place with the retainer screws.
7. Position the grille in place, and secure with the retainer screws.
8. Connect the negative battery cable.
9. Test the radio to make sure all speakers function correctly.

SEDAN, COUPE, XT, LOYALE AND WAGON

1. Disconnect the negative battery cable.
2. Remove the rear door panel on 4-door sedan and wagon models. Unfasten the rear speaker grille retainer screws on all other models, and remove the grille assembly.
3. Loosen and remove the speaker retainer screws securing the speaker to the door or rear deck, depending on model. Lift the speaker out enough to access the wire harness at the rear of the assembly.
4. Disconnect the speaker harness.
5. Remove the speaker.

To install:

6. Attach the wire harness to the speaker.
7. Position the speakers on the door or rear deck assembly, depending on model.
8. Secure the speaker in place with the retainer screws.
9. Install the door panel on 4-door Sedan and Wagon models. Position the speaker grille in place on the rear deck on all other models, and secure in place with the retainer screws.
10. Connect the negative battery cable.
11. Test the radio to make sure all speakers function correctly.

LEGACY AND IMPREZA

▶ See Figures 76 and 77

1. Disconnect the negative battery cable.
2. On Wagon and Hatchback models, remove the luggage cover and holder assembly. Fold the backrest forward.

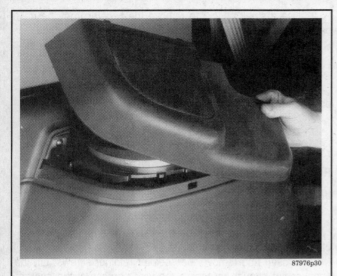

Fig. 76 Remove the speaker grille — Legacy wagon

Fig. 77 Remove the speaker retainer screws — Legacy shown

3. On Sedan models, remove the rear seat cushion and backrest assembly.

4. On Wagon and Hatchback models, remove the speaker cover retainer nuts and screws securing the cover in place over the speaker assembly.

5. On Sedan models, remove the rear right and left quarter trim panels, followed by the rear shelf assembly.

6. Loosen and remove the speaker retainer screws securing the speaker in place. Lift the speaker out enough to access the wire harness at the rear of the assembly.

7. Disconnect the speaker harness.

8. Remove the speaker.

To install:

9. Attach the wire harness to the speaker.

10. Position the speakers in place, and secure with the retainer screws.

11. On Sedan models, install the rear shelf assembly followed by the right and left rear quarter trim panels.

12. On Wagon and Hatchback models, install the speaker cover, and secure in place with the retainer nuts and screws.

13. On Sedan models, install the rear seat backrest and cushion.

14. On Wagon and Hatchback models, fold the seat back, and install the luggage cover and holder.

15. Connect the negative battery cable.

16. Test the radio to make sure all speakers function correctly.

SVX

1. Disconnect the negative battery cable.

2. Remove the rear seat cushion and backrest assembly.

3. Remove the rear right and left quarter trim panels, followed by the rear shelf assembly.

4. Loosen and remove the speaker retainer screws securing the speaker in place. Lift the speaker out enough to access the wire harness at the rear of the assembly.

5. Disconnect the speaker harness.

6. Remove the speaker.

To install:

7. Attach the wire harness to the speaker.

8. Position the speakers in place, and secure with the retainer screws.

9. Install the rear shelf assembly followed by the right and left rear quarter trim panels.

10. Install the rear seat backrest and cushion.

11. Connect the negative battery cable.

12. Test the radio to make sure all speakers function correctly.

TESTING

If a speaker in the vehicle will not work, a small battery can be used to determine if the speaker has failed, or if the problem is in the radio itself or in the speaker wiring. Proceed with the following steps to test a speaker.

1. Remove the speaker from the vehicle. Refer to the appropriate procedure in this section for speaker removal and installation. When removed, place the speaker face down on a clean flat surface.

2. Purchase a AA or AAA-size (1.5V) battery and solder a length wire to both the positive and negative side of the battery.

3. Strip 1/2-1 in. (1-2cm) of insulation off the ends of each wire.

4. To test the speaker, touch 1 end of each wire attached to the battery to each terminal of the speaker. If the speaker is functioning correctly, you will hear a crackling sound from the speaker when the battery makes contact with the speaker terminals. A dead speaker will make no sound when touched with the battery. Replace a dead speaker. If after testing the speaker and learning that it does function correctly, there is a problem with either the speaker wiring or the radio.

A battery can also be used to check the polarity of a speaker. Each speaker has a positive side and a negative side, which are needed to produce the sound you hear when playing the radio. Even though a speaker will function if the positive and negative wires are reversed, the sound will not be as loud or as clear compared to when they are installed correctly. To determine the polarity of the speaker terminals, touch the wires of the battery to the speaker and watch the cone of the speaker as contact is made. With the speaker face down, if the cone moves towards you when the wires touch the speaker terminals, the positive and negative side of the battery are contacting the opposite terminals on the speaker. Reverse the wires and try again. A properly polarized speaker will move the cone away from you when touched with the battery.

Although this procedure is not as important with speakers that have their respective terminals marked with a plus (+) or a minus (-), many factory speakers do not identify the individual terminals or wires attached to them. This procedure will be most helpful when installing aftermarket speakers into a vehicle using the factory wire harness.

WINDSHIELD WIPERS AND WASHERS

Windshield Wiper Blade and Arm

REMOVAL & INSTALLATION

➡Refer to Section 1 for wiper blade and rubber insert removal and installation.

Justy

▶ See Figure 78

1. Disconnect the negative battery cable.
2. Use a suitable prytool to remove the wiper arm retainer nut cover at the base of the wiper arm assembly.
3. Paint an alignment mark on the linkage or motor stud and wiper arm. Loosen and remove the wiper arm retainer nut.
4. Apply upward pressure to remove the wiper arm.

To install:

5. Place the wiper arm in position on the stud aligning the painted marks. Install the retainer nut, and tighten to 65 inch lbs. (7 Nm).
6. Install the retainer nut cover.
7. Connect the negative battery cable.
8. Test the wipers for proper wiper arm alignment and smooth operation.

Sedan, Coupe, Loyale, XT, Wagon and Brat

▶ See Figure 79

1. Disconnect the negative battery cable.
2. Open the hood to access the wiper arm assembly.

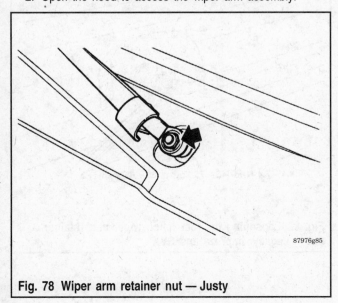

Fig. 78 Wiper arm retainer nut — Justy

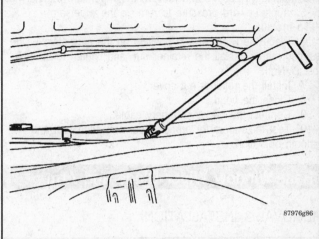

Fig. 79 Loosening and removing the wiper arm retainer nut — Sedan, Coupe, Loyale, XT, Wagon and Brat

3. Use a suitable prytool to remove the wiper arm retainer nut cover at the base of the wiper arm assembly, if equipped.
4. Paint an alignment mark on the linkage or motor stud and wiper arm. Loosen and remove the wiper arm retainer nut.
5. Apply upward pressure to remove the wiper arm.

To install:

6. Place the wiper arm in position on the stud aligning the painted marks. Install the retainer nut, and tighten to 65 inch lbs. (7 Nm).
7. Install the retainer nut cover.
8. Close the hood.
9. Connect the negative battery cable.
10. Test the wipers for proper wiper arm alignment and smooth operation.

Legacy and Impreza

1. Disconnect the negative battery cable.
2. Open the hood to access the wiper arm assembly.
3. Use a suitable prytool to remove the wiper arm retainer nut cover at the base of the wiper arm assembly, if equipped.
4. Paint an alignment mark on the linkage or motor stud and wiper arm. Loosen and remove the wiper arm retainer nut.
5. Apply upward pressure to remove the wiper arm.

To install:

6. Place the wiper arm in position on the stud aligning the painted marks. Install the retainer nut, and tighten to 65 inch lbs. (7 Nm).
7. Install the retainer nut cover.
8. Close the hood.
9. Connect the negative battery cable.

10. Test the wipers for proper wiper arm alignment and smooth operation.

SVX

▶ **See Figure 80**

1. Disconnect the negative battery cable.
2. Open the hood to access the wiper arm assembly.
3. Use a suitable prytool to remove the wiper arm retainer nut cover at the base of the wiper arm assembly, if equipped.
4. Paint an alignment mark on the linkage or motor stud and wiper arm. Loosen and remove the wiper arm retainer nut.
5. Apply upward pressure to remove the wiper arm.

To install:

6. Place the wiper arm in position on the stud aligning the painted marks. Install the retainer nut, and tighten to 65 inch lbs. (7 Nm).
7. Install the retainer nut cover.
8. Close the hood.
9. Connect the negative battery cable.
10. Test the wipers for proper wiper arm alignment and smooth operation.

Rear Window Wiper Blade and Arm

REMOVAL & INSTALLATION

➡ Refer to Section 1 for wiper blade and rubber insert removal and installation.

Justy

1. Disconnect the negative battery cable.
2. Pull the wiper arm upward slightly, and depress the clip at the base to remove the retainer nut cover.
3. Paint an alignment mark on the linkage or motor stud and wiper arm. Loosen and remove the wiper arm retainer nut.
4. Apply upward pressure to remove the wiper arm.

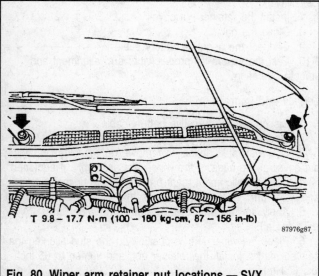

Fig. 80 Wiper arm retainer nut locations — SVX

To install:

5. Place the wiper arm in position on the stud aligning the painted marks. Install the retainer nut, and tighten to 65 inch lbs. (7 Nm).
6. Install the retainer nut cover.
7. Connect the negative battery cable.
8. Test the wipers for proper wiper arm alignment and smooth operation.

Except Justy

▶ **See Figures 81 and 82**

1. Disconnect the negative battery cable.
2. Use a suitable prytool to remove the wiper arm retainer nut cover at the base of the wiper arm assembly, if equipped.
3. Paint an alignment mark on the linkage or motor stud and wiper arm. Loosen and remove the wiper arm retainer nut.
4. Apply upward pressure to remove the wiper arm.

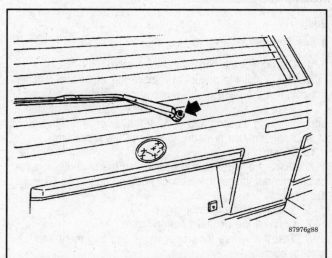

Fig. 81 Rear hatch wiper arm retainer nut — Coupe, Loyale, XT and Wagon

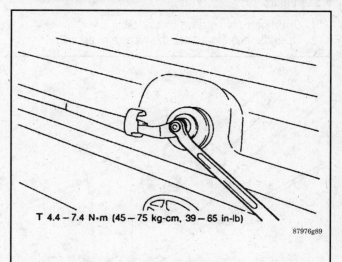

Fig. 82 Loosening the rear hatch wiper arm retainer nut — Legacy, Impreza and SVX

To install:

5. Place the wiper arm in position on the stud aligning the painted marks. Install the retainer nut, and tighten to 65 inch lbs. (7 Nm).

6. Install the retainer nut cover.

7. Connect the negative battery cable.

8. Test the wipers for proper wiper arm alignment and smooth operation.

Windshield Wiper Motor

REMOVAL & INSTALLATION

Justy

▶ See Figure 83

1. Disconnect the negative battery cable.
2. Remove the front wiper arm assembly.
3. At the wiper motor, disconnect the electrical harness.
4. Remove the wiper motor-to-cowl retainer bolts.
5. Using a suitable prytool, separate the wiper link from the motor assembly.

To install:

6. Attach the wiper motor to the link assembly.
7. Install the wiper motor and tighten the cowl bolts to 65 inch lbs. (7.4 Nm).
8. Install the wiper arm assembly.
9. Connect the wiper motor harness.
10. Connect the negative battery cable. Check for proper wiper operation.

Sedan, Coupe, Loyale, XT, Wagon and Brat

▶ See Figure 84

1. Disconnect the negative battery cable.
2. Remove the wiper arm.
3. At the wiper motor, disconnect the electrical harness.
4. Remove the wiper motor-to-cowl retainer bolts.
5. Find or fabricate a ring which has the same diameter as the outer diameter of the plastic joint that retains the linkage to

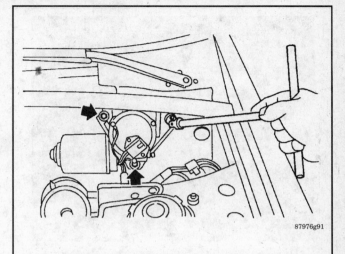

Fig. 84 Loosen the indicated front wiper motor retainer bolts — Sedan, Coupe, Loyale, XT, Wagon and Brat

the wiper motor. Force the ring down over the joint to force the 4 plastic retaining jaws inward, then disconnect and remove the linkage.

6. Remove the wiper motor.

To install:

7. Attach the wiper motor to the link assembly.
8. Install the wiper motor and tighten the cowl bolts to 65 inch lbs. (7.4 Nm).
9. Install the wiper arm assembly.
10. Connect the wiper motor harness.
11. Connect the negative battery cable. Check for proper wiper operation.

Legacy, Impreza and SVX

▶ See Figures 85, 86, 87 and 88

1. Disconnect the negative battery cable.
2. Remove the wiper arm.
3. At the wiper motor, disconnect the electrical harness.
4. Remove the wiper motor-to-cowl retainer bolts.
5. Find or fabricate a ring which has the same diameter as the outer diameter of the plastic joint that retains the linkage to

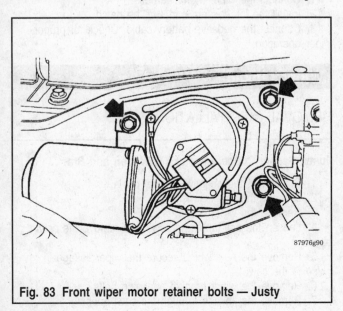

Fig. 83 Front wiper motor retainer bolts — Justy

Fig. 85 Disconnect the wiper motor wire harness — Legacy shown

Fig. 86 Loosen and remove the wiper motor retainer bolts — Legacy shown

Fig. 87 After separating the linkage assembly, remove the motor — Legacy shown

the wiper motor. Force the ring down over the joint to force the 4 plastic retaining jaws inward, then disconnect and remove the linkage.

6. Remove the wiper motor.

To install:

7. Attach the wiper motor to the link assembly.

8. Install the wiper motor and tighten the cowl bolts to 39-65 inch lbs. (4-7 Nm).

9. Install the wiper arm assembly.

10. Connect the wiper motor harness.

11. Connect the negative battery cable. Check for proper wiper operation.

Rear Window Wiper Motor

REMOVAL & INSTALLATION

Justy, Coupe, Loyale, XT and Wagon
▶ See Figures 89 and 90

1. Disconnect the negative battery cable.
2. Remove the wiper arm.
3. Remove the wiper shaft cap nut and cushion.
4. Remove the rear hatch interior trim cover.
5. At the wiper motor, disconnect the electrical harness.
6. Remove the wiper motor retainer bolts.
7. Remove the wiper motor.

To install:

8. Install the wiper motor inside the hatch assembly. Insert and tighten the retainer bolts to 52 inch lbs. (6 Nm).

9. Install the cushion, nut and cap. Tighten the nut snugly.

10. Install the wiper arm assembly.

11. Connect the wiper motor harness.

12. Install the interior trim panel to the hatch.

13. Connect the negative battery cable. Check for proper wiper operation.

Legacy, Impreza and SVX
▶ See Figures 91 and 92

1. Disconnect the negative battery cable.
2. Remove the wiper arm.
3. Remove the wiper shaft cap and nut.
4. Remove the rear hatch interior trim cover.
5. At the wiper motor, disconnect the electrical harness.
6. Remove the wiper motor retainer bolts.
7. Remove the wiper motor.

To install:

8. Install the wiper motor inside the hatch assembly. Insert and tighten the retainer bolts to 39-62 inch lbs. (4-7 Nm).

9. Install the nut and cap. Tighten the nut snugly.

10. Install the wiper arm assembly.

11. Connect the wiper motor harness.

12. Install the interior trim panel to the hatch.

13. Connect the negative battery cable. Check for proper wiper operation.

Wiper Linkage

REMOVAL & INSTALLATION

Justy, Sedan, Coupe, Loyale, XT, Wagon and Brat

1. Disconnect the negative battery cable.
2. Remove the wiper arms.
3. Remove the wiper motor.
4. Loosen the self-tapping screws and remove the cowl panel.
5. Remove the nuts which secure the wiper linkage in place to the cowl.
6. Remove the wiper bracket attaching bolts.
7. Remove the linkage through the cowl opening.

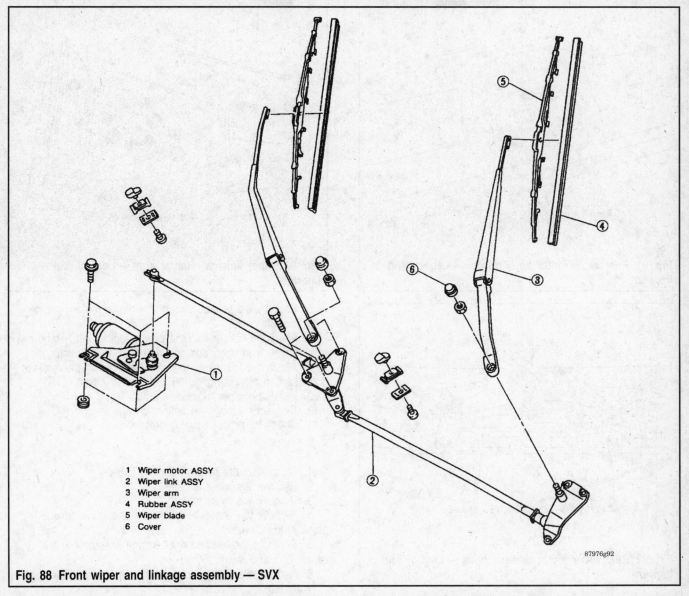

1 Wiper motor ASSY
2 Wiper link ASSY
3 Wiper arm
4 Rubber ASSY
5 Wiper blade
6 Cover

87976g92

Fig. 88 Front wiper and linkage assembly — SVX

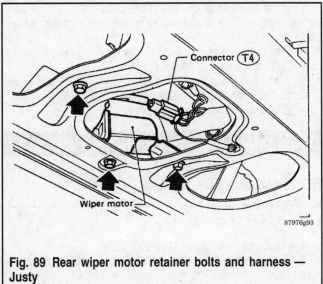

Connector T4

Wiper motor

87976g93

Fig. 89 Rear wiper motor retainer bolts and harness — Justy

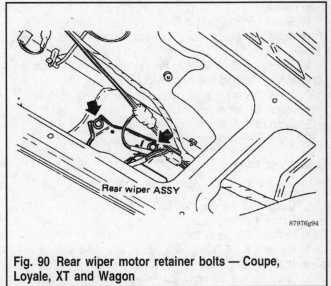

Rear wiper ASSY

87976g94

Fig. 90 Rear wiper motor retainer bolts — Coupe, Loyale, XT and Wagon

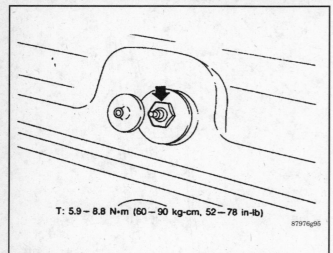

T: 5.9 – 8.8 N·m (60 – 90 kg-cm, 52 – 78 in-lb)

87976g95

Fig. 91 Rear wiper motor cap and nut — Legacy and Impreza

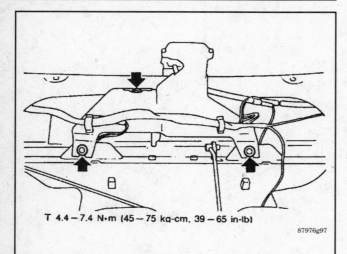

T 4.4 – 7.4 N·m (45 – 75 kg-cm, 39 – 65 in-lb)

87976g97

Fig. 92 Rear wiper motor retainer bolts — Legacy and Impreza

To install:

8. Place the linkage into the cowl opening and secure in place using the retainer bolts. Tighten the bolts to 65 inch lbs. (7 Nm).

9. Attach the cowl panel to the linkage assembly using the retainer nuts. Tighten the nuts snugly.

10. Install the cowl panel using the self-tapping screws.

11. Install the wiper motor and arms.

12. Connect the negative battery cable.

13. Check for proper wiper operation.

Legacy and Impreza

♦ See Figure 93

1. Disconnect the negative battery cable.
2. Remove the wiper arms.
3. Remove the wiper motor.
4. Remove the 6 nuts which secure the wiper linkage in place to the cowl.
5. Separate the left and right linkage assembly at the center joint.

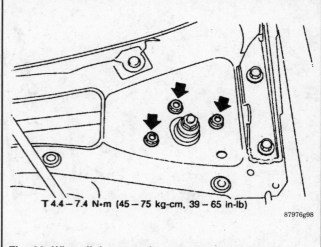

T 4.4 – 7.4 N·m (45 – 75 kg-cm, 39 – 65 in-lb)

87976g98

Fig. 93 Wiper linkage retainer nuts — Legacy and Impreza

6. Remove the linkage through the wiper motor opening.

To install:

7. Place the linkage into the cowl opening, left linkage assembly first, then right, and secure attach at the center joint.

8. Attach the linkage to the cowl panel using the retainer nuts. Tighten the nuts to 39-65 inch lbs. (4-7 Nm).

9. Install the wiper motor and arms.

10. Connect the negative battery cable.

11. Check for proper wiper operation.

SVX

1. Disconnect the negative battery cable.
2. Remove the wiper arms.
3. Remove the wiper motor.
4. Remove the 6 nuts which secure the wiper linkage in place to the cowl.
5. Separate the left and right linkage assembly at the center joint and motor.
6. Remove the linkage through the wiper motor opening.

To install:

7. Place the linkage into the cowl opening, left linkage assembly first, then right, and secure attach at the center joint and motor joint.

8. Attach the linkage to the cowl panel using the retainer nuts. Tighten the nuts to 39-65 inch lbs. (4-7 Nm).

9. Install the wiper motor and arms.

10. Connect the negative battery cable.

11. Check for proper wiper operation.

Windshield Washer Fluid Reservoir

REMOVAL & INSTALLATION

♦ See Figures 94 and 95

1. Disconnect the negative battery cable.
2. Disconnect the electrical lead from the washer pump.
3. Remove the washer tank cover, if equipped.
4. Disconnect the washer fluid lines.

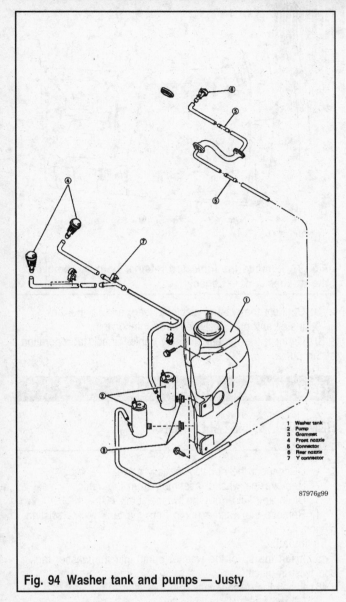

Fig. 94 Washer tank and pumps — Justy

1	Washer tank
2	Pump
3	Grommet
4	Front nozzle
5	Connector
6	Rear nozzle
7	Y connector

87976g99

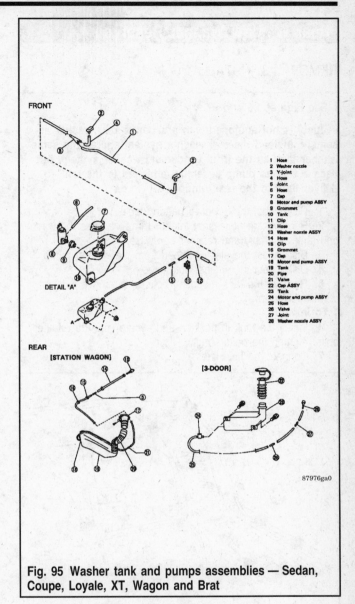

Fig. 95 Washer tank and pumps assemblies — Sedan, Coupe, Loyale, XT, Wagon and Brat

1	Hose
2	Washer nozzle
3	Y-joint
4	Hose
5	Joint
6	Hose
7	Cap
8	Motor and pump ASSY
9	Grommet
10	Tank
11	Clip
12	Hose
13	Washer nozzle ASSY
14	Hose
15	Clip
16	Grommet
17	Cap
18	Motor and pump ASSY
19	Tank
20	Pipe
21	Valve
22	Cap ASSY
23	Tank
24	Motor and pump ASSY
25	Hose
26	Valve
27	Joint
28	Washer nozzle ASSY

87976ga0

5. Remove the tank mounting bolts and remove the tank from the vehicle.

To install:

6. Install the tank in position and secure with the retainer bolts. Tighten the bolts snugly.

7. Connect the fluid lines.

8. Install the washer tank cover, if equipped.

9. Connect the washer electrical lead, and fill the tank.

10. Connect the negative battery cable. Check the operation of the pump.

Windshield Washer Motor

REMOVAL & INSTALLATION

1. Disconnect the negative battery cable.

2. Remove the washer assembly from the vehicle.

3. Drain any fluid from the washer tank.

4. Remove the washer pump from the tank with a twisting motion.

To install:

5. Insert the tip of the washer pump into the washer tank and twist in place.

6. Install the washer tank into the vehicle.

7. Fill the tank with washer fluid.

8. Connect the negative battery cable.

9. Test the washer system for proper operation.

Rear Window Washer Reservoir

REMOVAL & INSTALLATION

▶ See Figures 96 and 97

➡Justy is not equipped with a separate rear washer assembly. Instead the rear washer system shares the same washer tank as the front windshield washer system, but uses a second pump assembly attached to the tank to deliver fluid to the rear window.

1. Disconnect the negative battery cable.
2. Remove the necessary interior trim to access the washer and tank assembly and retainer hardware.
3. Disconnect the electrical lead from the washer pump.
4. Disconnect the washer fluid lines.
5. Remove the tank mounting bolts and remove the tank from the vehicle.

To install:

6. Install the tank in position and secure with the retainer bolts. Tighten the bolts snugly.
7. Connect the fluid lines.

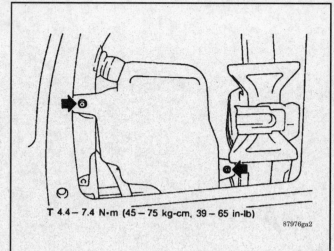

T 4.4 – 7.4 N·m (45 – 75 kg-cm, 39 – 65 in-lb)

87976ga2

Fig. 97 Remove the indicated retainer bolts to remove the washer tank — Legacy

8. Connect the washer electrical lead, and fill the tank.
9. Install any previously removed interior trim.
10. Connect the negative battery cable. Check the operation of the pump.

Rear Window Washer Motor

REMOVAL & INSTALLATION

1. Disconnect the negative battery cable.
2. Remove the washer assembly from the vehicle.
3. Drain any fluid from the washer tank.
4. Remove the washer pump from the tank with a twisting motion.

To install:

5. Insert the tip of the washer pump into the washer tank and twist in place.
6. Install the washer tank into the vehicle.
7. Fill the tank with washer fluid.
8. Connect the negative battery cable.
9. Test the washer system for proper operation.

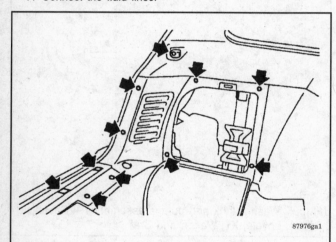

87976ga1

Fig. 96 Unfasten the indicated retainer screws to remove interior trim panel to access the washer and pump assembly — Legacy

INSTRUMENTS AND SWITCHES

Instrument Cluster

✳✳CAUTION

Properly disarm the air bag on vehicles equipped with the SRS system. Failure to do so can cause serious injury.

REMOVAL & INSTALLATION

Justy

1. Disconnect the negative battery cable.

2. Remove the retainer clips and choke knob and nut, if equipped.
3. Remove the instrument cluster trim cover retainer screws and clips.
4. Remove the trim cover, and place aside.
5. Remove the defroster duct assembly.
6. Disconnect the heater control cable from the air selector rod at the heater unit.
7. Remove the instrument cluster retaining screws, and carefully pull the cluster assembly forward enough to access the rear of the assembly.
8. Disconnect the speedometer cable from the rear of the instrument cluster. Disconnect the electrical harnesses from the cluster assembly.

9. Remove the instrument cluster from the mounting tabs.

To install:

10. Connect the speedometer cable and electrical harnesses to the rear of the instrument cluster.

11. Position the instrument cluster in the mounting tabs.

12. Install the instrument cluster and tighten the retaining screws securely.

13. Install the heater control cable and the defroster duct assembly.

14. Install the trim panel using the retainer screws.

15. Attach the trim panel retainer clips. Install the choke nut and knob, if equipped.

16. Connect the negative battery cable.

17. Test all instrument functions, including the gauges and dash light to make them work correctly.

Sedan, Coupe, Loyale, Wagon and Brat

▶ **See Figures 98 and 99**

1. Disconnect the negative battery cable.

Fig. 98 Remove the retainer screws from the heater panel to remove the instrument cluster visor — Sedan, Coupe, Loyale, Wagon and Brat

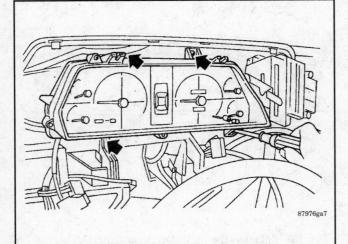

Fig. 99 Remove the instrument cluster retainer screws — Sedan, Coupe, Loyale, Wagon and Brat

2. Remove the steering column retainer bolts, and lower the column.

3. Remove the retainer screws securing the instrument cluster visor in place. Lift the visor forward and unfasten the harnesses attached to the switches in the panel. Place the panel aside.

4. Remove the instrument cluster retainer screws. Pull the cluster assembly out enough to access the wire harnesses and speedometer cable at the rear of the assembly.

5. Disconnect the speedometer cable and wire harnesses from the rear of the cluster.

6. Remove the cluster from the vehicle.

To install:

7. Attach the wire harnesses and speedometer cable to the rear of the cluster assembly.

8. Position the cluster in the dash panel, and secure in place with the retainer screws.

9. Attach the harnesses to the visor mounted switches, then install the instrument cluster visor. Secure the visor in place using the retainer screws.

10. Raise the steering column up, and secure in place with the retainer bolts.

11. Connect the negative battery cable.

12. Test all instrument functions, including the gauges and dash light to make them work correctly.

XT

▶ **See Figure 100**

1. Disconnect the negative battery cable.

2. Remove the lower trim panel on the driver's side. Remove the side ventilation duct.

3. Open the fuse box lid. Remove the fuse box-to-instrument panel screws, then remove the fuse box.

4. Using a suitable prytool.carefully separate the upper cover, at 3 points, from the instrument panel.

5. Remove the steering column assembly, combination meter and the control wing as a unit. Refer to Section 8 for steering column removal and installation.

6. Disconnect the instrument panel electrical harnesses from the steering column assembly.

7. Remove the instrument cluster to steering column screws, and separate the cluster from the column.

To install:

8. Install the instrument cluster to the steering column, and secure in place using the retainer screws.

9. Connect the electrical harnesses from the cluster assembly and steering column to the dash panel harnesses.

10. Install the steering column.

11. Install the lower and upper instrument panel covers.

12. Install the fuse box, the side ventilation duct and the lower instrument panel covers. Connect the negative battery cable.

13. Test all instrument functions, including the gauges and dash light to make them work correctly.

Legacy and Impreza

▶ **See Figures 101 and 102**

1. Disconnect the negative battery cable. Properly disarm the air bag.

2. Remove the bolts securing the steering column and lower it down.

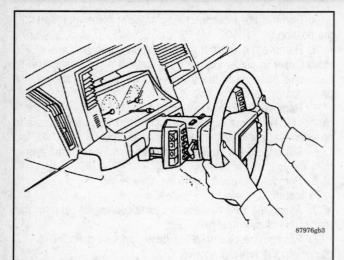

Fig. 100 Lower the steering column to remove the instrument cluster — XT

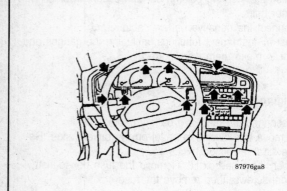

Fig. 101 Unfasten the indicated retainer screws to remove the dash trim panel around the instrument cluster — Legacy and Impreza

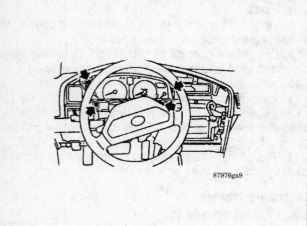

Fig. 102 Unfasten the indicated retainer screws to remove the instrument cluster — Legacy and Impreza

3. Remove the center ventilator control lever by pulling it. Remove the 3 screws accessible through the ventilator grille to the right of the cluster and the 1 screw accessible through the grille on the left. Remove the vent.

4. Remove the dash panel retainer screws around the instrument cluster.

5. Carefully pull the trim panel forward and disconnect the electrical harnesses attached to the switches in the trim panel. Remove the trim panel and place aside.

6. Remove the cluster retaining screws, then pull the cluster out far enough to disconnect the speedometer cable and electrical harnesses from behind, then remove the cluster assembly from the vehicle.

To install:

7. Connect the electrical harnesses and the speedometer cable to the rear of the cluster assembly.

8. Install the cluster assembly, and tighten the attaching screws securely.

9. Install the cluster visor and the visor screws.

10. Install the ventilator vent, control lever and retainer screws.

11. Lift the steering column up, instal and tighten the retainer bolts.

12. Connect the negative battery cable.

13. Test all instrument functions, including the gauges and dash light to make them work correctly.

SVX

▶ **See Figures 103, 104 and 105**

1. Disconnect the negative battery cable. Properly disarm the air bag.

2. Move the steering wheel to its lowest tilt position. Remove the lower steering column cover.

3. Remove the lower cluster cover and the screws that retain the cluster visor around the instrument cluster.

4. Disconnect the clock while pulling the visor away from the cluster.

5. Remove the screws that retain the cluster and tilt the cluster forward. Disconnect the electrical harnesses and speedometer cable.

6. Remove the cluster from the vehicle.

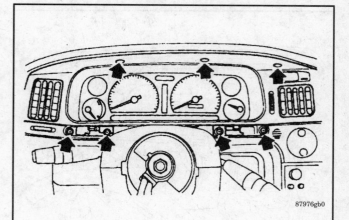

Fig. 103 Unfasten the indicated retainer screws to remove the dash trim panel around the instrument cluster — SVX

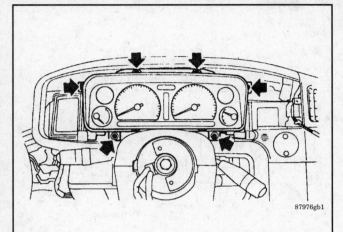

Fig. 104 Unfasten the indicated retainer screws to remove the instrument cluster — SVX

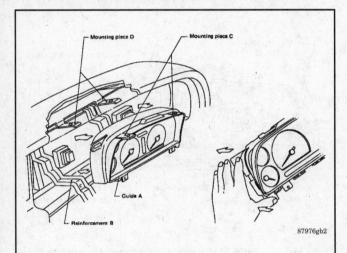

Fig. 105 Instrument cluster removal and installation — SVX

To install:

7. Connect the electrical leads and speedometer cable to the rear of the instrument cluster assembly.

8. Install the cluster in position in the dash panel.

9. Install the cluster retaining screws.

10. Install the cluster visor, making sure to connect the clock harness. Secure in place with the retainer screws

11. Install the lower cluster cover panel and the lower steering column cover.

12. Raise the steering column up to the original position.

13. Connect the negative battery cable.

14. Test all instrument functions, including the gauges and dash light to make them work correctly.

Speedometer

REMOVAL & INSTALLATION

Justy

◆ **See Figures 106, 107 and 108**

1. Disconnect the negative battery cable.

2. Remove the instrument cluster, and place on a flat, clean, well lighted surface.

3. Turn the cluster upside down and remove the case and circuit board retainer screws.

4. Remove the gauge-to-circuit board retainer nuts.

5. Carefully remove the circuit board assembly.

6. Lift the speedometer assembly out of the cluster.

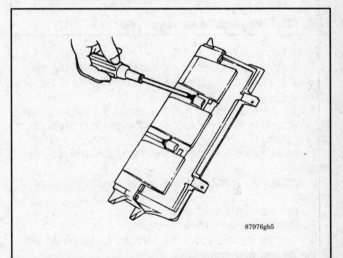

Fig. 106 Remove the circuit board-to-gauge and cluster retainer screws — Justy

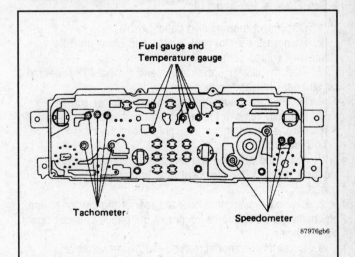

Fig. 107 Remove the indicated retainer nuts to remove the circuit board — Justy

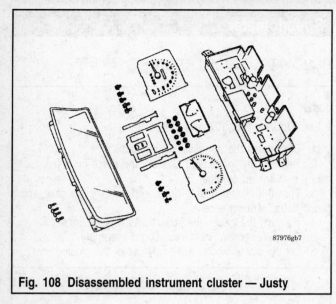

Fig. 108 Disassembled instrument cluster — Justy

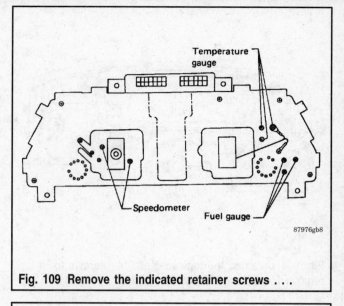

Fig. 109 Remove the indicated retainer screws . . .

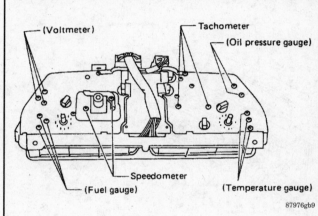

Fig. 110 . . . plus these indicated screws to remove the circuit board from the rear of the instrument cluster — Sedan, Coupe, Loyale, Wagon and Brat

To install:

7. Install the speedometer into the cluster assembly, making sure to insert the alignment tabs at the corners of the gauge.

8. Lay the circuit board over the rear of the cluster assembly, making sure to proper alignment the gauge-to-circuit board contact studs.

9. Install the retainer nuts to the gauge studs, and tighten snugly.

10. Install the circuit board and cluster assembly retainer screws.

11. Install the instrument cluster.

12. Connect the negative battery cable.

13. Start the vehicle, and make sure the speedometer and all the gauges work correctly.

Sedan, Coupe, Loyale, Wagon and Brat

◆ **See Figures 109 and 110**

1. Disconnect the negative battery cable.

2. Remove the instrument cluster, and place on a flat, clean, well lighted surface.

3. Turn the cluster upside down and remove the case and circuit board retainer screws.

4. Remove the gauge-to-circuit board retainer screws.

5. Carefully remove the circuit board assembly.

6. Lift the speedometer assembly out of the cluster.

To install:

7. Install the speedometer into the cluster assembly, making sure to insert the alignment tabs at the corners of the gauge.

8. Lay the circuit board over the rear of the cluster assembly, making sure to proper alignment the gauge-to-circuit board contact holes.

9. Install the retainer screws to the gauge holes, and tighten snugly.

10. Install the circuit board and cluster assembly retainer screws.

11. Install the instrument cluster.

12. Connect the negative battery cable.

13. Start the vehicle, and make sure the speedometer and all the gauges work correctly.

XT

◆ **See Figures 111 and 112**

1. Disconnect the negative battery cable.

2. Remove the instrument cluster, and place on a flat, clean, well lighted surface.

3. Turn the cluster upside down and remove the case and circuit board retainer screws.

4. Remove the telltale monitor retainer screws, and lift the monitor assembly out of the cluster assembly.

5. Remove the gauge-to-circuit board retainer screws.

6. Carefully remove the circuit board assembly.

7. Lift the speedometer assembly out of the cluster.

To install:

8. Install the speedometer into the cluster assembly, making sure to insert the alignment tabs at the corners of the gauge.

9. Lay the circuit board over the rear of the cluster assembly, making sure to proper alignment the gauge-to-circuit board contact holes.

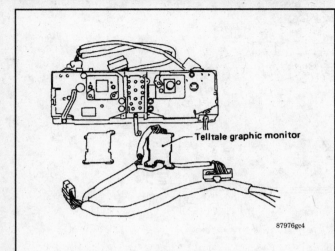

Fig. 111 Remove the telltale monitor from the rear of the cluster assembly — XT

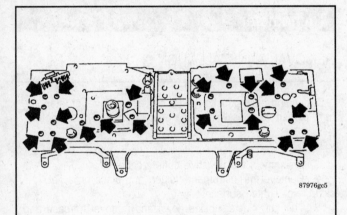

Fig. 112 Remove the indicated screws to remove the circuit board from the rear of the instrument cluster — XT

10. Install the retainer screws to the gauge holes, and tighten snugly.

11. Install the telltale monitor, and secure in place with the retainer screws.

12. Install the circuit board and cluster assembly retainer screws.

13. Install the instrument cluster.

14. Connect the negative battery cable.

15. Start the vehicle, and make sure the speedometer and all the gauges work correctly.

Legacy and Impreza

▶ See Figures 113 and 114

1. Disconnect the negative battery cable.

2. Remove the instrument cluster, and place on a flat, clean, well lighted surface.

3. Turn the cluster upside down and remove the case and circuit board retainer screws.

4. Remove the gauge-to-circuit board retainer screws.

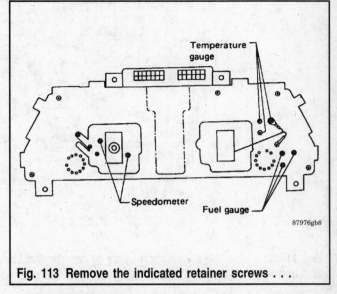

Fig. 113 Remove the indicated retainer screws . . .

5. Remove the cluster illumination bulbs by turning ¼ turn and lifting the bulbs out.

6. Carefully remove the circuit board assembly.

7. Lift the speedometer assembly out of the cluster.

To install:

8. Install the speedometer into the cluster assembly, making sure to insert the alignment tabs at the corners of the gauge.

9. Lay the circuit board over the rear of the cluster assembly, making sure to proper alignment the gauge-to-circuit board contact holes.

10. Install the retainer screws to the gauge holes, and tighten snugly.

11. Install the illumination bulbs, and turn ¼ turn to lock in place.

12. Install the circuit board and cluster assembly retainer screws.

13. Install the instrument cluster.

14. Connect the negative battery cable.

15. Start the vehicle, and make sure the speedometer and all the gauges work correctly.

SVX

▶ See Figure 115

1. Disconnect the negative battery cable.

2. Remove the instrument cluster, and place on a flat, clean, well lighted surface.

3. Turn the cluster upside down and remove the case and circuit board retainer screws.

4. Remove the cluster illumination bulbs by turning ¼ turn and lifting the bulbs out.

5. Carefully detach the individual gauge contact tabs from the circuit board.

6. Carefully remove the circuit board assembly.

7. Remove the retainer screws securing the gauges to the cluster case.

8. Lift the speedometer assembly out of the cluster.

To install:

9. Install the speedometer into the cluster assembly, making sure to insert the alignment tabs at the corners of the gauge.

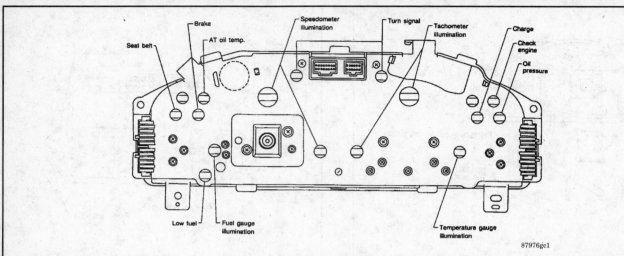

Fig. 114 . . . plus the illumination bulbs to remove the circuit board from the rear of the instrument cluster — Legacy and Impreza

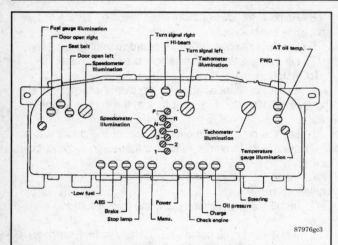

Fig. 115 Remove the indicated illumination bulbs and contact tabs to detach the circuit board from the back of the cluster assembly — SVX

10. Install the gauge retainer screws.
11. Lay the circuit board over the rear of the cluster assembly, making sure to proper alignment the gauge-to-circuit board contact holes.
12. Press the contact tabs on to the gauge connection tabs.
13. Install the illumination bulbs, and turn 1/4 turn to lock in place.
14. Install the circuit board and cluster assembly retainer screws.
15. Install the instrument cluster.
16. Connect the negative battery cable.
17. Start the vehicle, and make sure the speedometer and all the gauges work correctly.

Tachometer

REMOVAL & INSTALLATION

Depending on production date, model and level of interior trim, certain vehicles will not be equipped with a tachometer.

Justy

1. Disconnect the negative battery cable.
2. Remove the instrument cluster, and place on a flat, clean, well lighted surface.
3. Turn the cluster upside down and remove the case and circuit board retainer screws.
4. Remove the gauge-to-circuit board retainer nuts.
5. Carefully remove the circuit board assembly.
6. Lift the tachometer assembly out of the cluster.
To install:
7. Install the tachometer into the cluster assembly, making sure to insert the alignment tabs at the corners of the gauge.
8. Lay the circuit board over the rear of the cluster assembly, making sure to proper alignment the gauge-to-circuit board contact studs.
9. Install the retainer nuts to the gauge studs, and tighten snugly.
10. Install the circuit board and cluster assembly retainer screws.
11. Install the instrument cluster.
12. Connect the negative battery cable.
13. Start the vehicle, and make sure the tachometer and all the gauges work correctly.

Sedan, Coupe, Loyale, Wagon and Brat

1. Disconnect the negative battery cable.
2. Remove the instrument cluster, and place on a flat, clean, well lighted surface.
3. Turn the cluster upside down and remove the case and circuit board retainer screws.
4. Remove the gauge-to-circuit board retainer screws.
5. Carefully remove the circuit board assembly.

6. Lift the tachometer assembly out of the cluster.

To install:

7. Install the tachometer into the cluster assembly, making sure to insert the alignment tabs at the corners of the gauge.

8. Lay the circuit board over the rear of the cluster assembly, making sure to proper alignment the gauge-to-circuit board contact holes.

9. Install the retainer screws to the gauge holes, and tighten snugly.

10. Install the circuit board and cluster assembly retainer screws.

11. Install the instrument cluster.

12. Connect the negative battery cable.

13. Start the vehicle, and make sure the tachometer and all the gauges work correctly.

XT

▶ **See Figure 116**

1. Disconnect the negative battery cable.

2. Remove the instrument cluster, and place on a flat, clean, well lighted surface.

3. Turn the cluster upside down and remove the case and circuit board retainer screws.

4. Remove the telltale monitor retainer screws, and lift the monitor assembly out of the cluster assembly.

5. Remove the gauge-to-circuit board retainer screws.

6. Carefully remove the circuit board assembly.

7. Lift the tachometer assembly out of the cluster.

To install:

8. Install the tachometer into the cluster assembly, making sure to insert the alignment tabs at the corners of the gauge.

9. Lay the circuit board over the rear of the cluster assembly, making sure to proper alignment the gauge-to-circuit board contact holes.

10. Install the retainer screws to the gauge holes, and tighten snugly.

11. Install the telltale monitor, and secure in place with the retainer screws.

12. Install the circuit board and cluster assembly retainer screws.

13. Install the instrument cluster.

14. Connect the negative battery cable.

15. Start the vehicle, and make sure the tachometer and all the gauges work correctly.

Legacy and Impreza

1. Disconnect the negative battery cable.

2. Remove the instrument cluster, and place on a flat, clean, well lighted surface.

3. Turn the cluster upside down and remove the case and circuit board retainer screws.

4. Remove the gauge-to-circuit board retainer screws.

5. Remove the cluster illumination bulbs by turning ¼ turn and lifting the bulbs out.

6. Carefully remove the circuit board assembly.

7. Lift the tachometer assembly out of the cluster.

To install:

8. Install the tachometer into the cluster assembly, making sure to insert the alignment tabs at the corners of the gauge.

9. Lay the circuit board over the rear of the cluster assembly, making sure to proper alignment the gauge-to-circuit board contact holes.

10. Install the retainer screws to the gauge holes, and tighten snugly.

11. Install the illumination bulbs, and turn ¼ turn to lock in place.

12. Install the circuit board and cluster assembly retainer screws.

13. Install the instrument cluster.

14. Connect the negative battery cable.

15. Start the vehicle, and make sure the tachometer and all the gauges work correctly.

SVX

1. Disconnect the negative battery cable.

2. Remove the instrument cluster, and place on a flat, clean, well lighted surface.

3. Turn the cluster upside down and remove the case and circuit board retainer screws.

4. Remove the cluster illumination bulbs by turning ¼ turn and lifting the bulbs out.

5. Carefully detach the individual gauge contact tabs from the circuit board.

6. Carefully remove the circuit board assembly.

7. Remove the retainer screws securing the gauges to the cluster case.

8. Lift the tachometer assembly out of the cluster.

To install:

9. Install the tachometer into the cluster assembly, making sure to insert the alignment tabs at the corners of the gauge.

10. Install the gauge retainer screws.

11. Lay the circuit board over the rear of the cluster assembly, making sure to proper alignment the gauge-to-circuit board contact holes.

12. Press the contact tabs on to the gauge connection tabs.

13. Install the illumination bulbs, and turn ¼ turn to lock in place.

14. Install the circuit board and cluster assembly retainer screws.

15. Install the instrument cluster.

16. Connect the negative battery cable.

17. Start the vehicle, and make sure the tachometer and all the gauges work correctly.

Speedometer Cable

REMOVAL & INSTALLATION

1. Disconnect the negative battery cable.

2. Raise the vehicle and support it safely on jackstands.

3. Disengage the cable assembly from the transaxle by removing the retainer bolt and bracket, or loosening the retainer nut, depending on model and production date. Once the retainer is removed, slowly pull the cable from the transaxle.

4. Disengage all remaining cable securing clips.

5. Push the grommet out of the firewall and feed the cable through the opening into the interior.

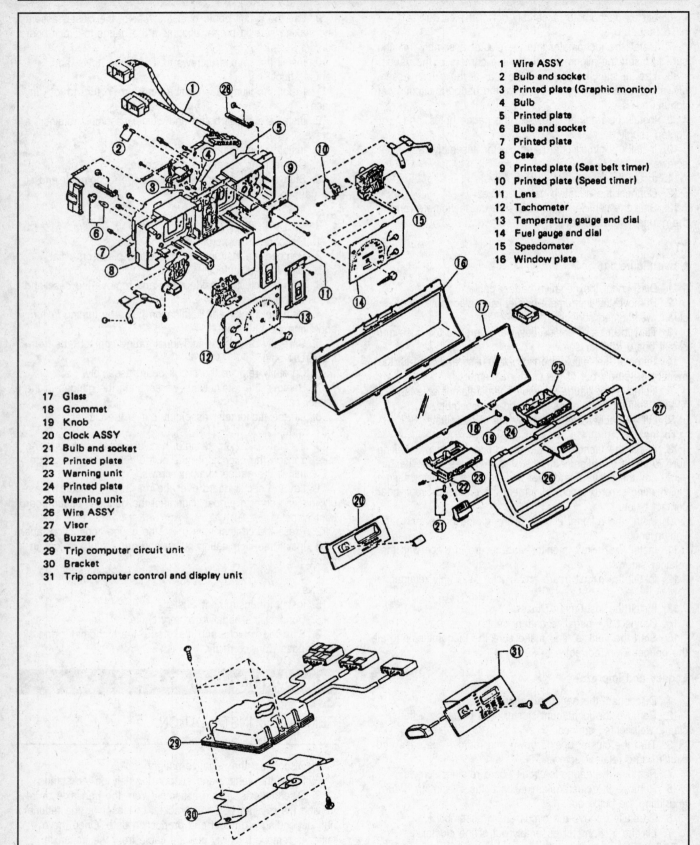

1 Wire ASSY
2 Bulb and socket
3 Printed plate (Graphic monitor)
4 Bulb
5 Printed plate
6 Bulb and socket
7 Printed plate
8 Case
9 Printed plate (Seat belt timer)
10 Printed plate (Speed timer)
11 Lens
12 Tachometer
13 Temperature gauge and dial
14 Fuel gauge and dial
15 Speedometer
16 Window plate

17 Glass
18 Grommet
19 Knob
20 Clock ASSY
21 Bulb and socket
22 Printed plate
23 Warning unit
24 Printed plate
25 Warning unit
26 Wire ASSY
27 Visor
28 Buzzer
29 Trip computer circuit unit
30 Bracket
31 Trip computer control and display unit

87976gc7

Fig. 116 Disassembled cluster assembly — XT

6. Remove any screws holding the cable clip to dash brackets.

7. Remove the instrument cluster. Lift the cluster out enough to access the speedometer cable.

8. Disconnect the speedometer cable from the speedometer and remove the cable.

To install:

✳✳WARNING

The speedometer cable routing should avoid sharp bends.

9. Feed the speedometer cable through the dash panel to the firewall of the vehicle.

10. Connect the speedometer cable to the speedometer head.

11. Attach the clip to the steering column bracket.

12. Feed the cable through the firewall hole to the transaxle. Install the rubber grommet around the hole.

13. Lubricate the cable core exposed at the transmission ferrule with silicone grease.

14. Secure the cable with the clips and clamps.

15. Attach the speedometer cable to the transaxle using the bracket and retainer bolt, or tighten the nut on the cable.

16. Connect the negative battery cable.

17. Road test the vehicle to make sure the speedometer is functioning correctly.

Oil Pressure Gauge

REMOVAL & INSTALLATION

Depending on production date, model and level of interior trim, certain vehicles will not be equipped with an oil pressure gauge.

Also some models incorporate an oil pressure gauge with another gauge like a fuel, voltmeter or temperature gauge. If 1 of these gauges fails, the entire combination gauge assembly must be replaced.

Justy

1. Disconnect the negative battery cable.

2. Remove the instrument cluster, and place on a flat, clean, well lighted surface.

3. Turn the cluster upside down and remove the case and circuit board retainer screws.

4. Remove the gauge-to-circuit board retainer nuts.

5. Carefully remove the circuit board assembly.

6. Lift the combination gauge assembly out of the cluster.

To install:

7. Install the combination gauge into the cluster assembly, making sure to insert the alignment tabs at the corners of the gauge.

8. Lay the circuit board over the rear of the cluster assembly, making sure to proper alignment the gauge-to-circuit board contact studs.

9. Install the retainer nuts to the gauge studs, and tighten snugly.

10. Install the circuit board and cluster assembly retainer screws.

11. Install the instrument cluster.

12. Connect the negative battery cable.

13. Start the vehicle, and make sure all the gauges work correctly.

Sedan, Coupe, Loyale, Wagon and Brat

1. Disconnect the negative battery cable.

2. Remove the instrument cluster, and place on a flat, clean, well lighted surface.

3. Turn the cluster upside down and remove the case and circuit board retainer screws.

4. Remove the gauge-to-circuit board retainer screws.

5. Carefully remove the circuit board assembly.

6. Lift the oil pressure/combination gauge assembly out of the cluster.

To install:

7. Install the oil pressure/combination gauge into the cluster assembly, making sure to insert the alignment tabs at the corners of the gauge.

8. Lay the circuit board over the rear of the cluster assembly, making sure to proper alignment the gauge-to-circuit board contact holes.

9. Install the retainer screws to the gauge holes, and tighten snugly.

10. Install the circuit board and cluster assembly retainer screws.

11. Install the instrument cluster.

12. Connect the negative battery cable.

13. Start the vehicle, and make sure all the gauges work correctly.

XT

1. Disconnect the negative battery cable.

2. Remove the instrument cluster, and place on a flat, clean, well lighted surface.

3. Turn the cluster upside down and remove the case and circuit board retainer screws.

4. Remove the telltale monitor retainer screws, and lift the monitor assembly out of the cluster assembly.

5. Remove the gauge-to-circuit board retainer screws.

6. Carefully remove the circuit board assembly.

7. Lift the oil pressure/combination gauge assembly out of the cluster.

To install:

8. Install the oil pressure/combination gauge into the cluster assembly, making sure to insert the alignment tabs at the corners of the gauge.

9. Lay the circuit board over the rear of the cluster assembly, making sure to proper alignment the gauge-to-circuit board contact holes.

10. Install the retainer screws to the gauge holes, and tighten snugly.

11. Install the telltale monitor, and secure in place with the retainer screws.

12. Install the circuit board and cluster assembly retainer screws.

13. Install the instrument cluster.

14. Connect the negative battery cable.

15. Start the vehicle, and make sure all the gauges work correctly.

Legacy and Impreza

1. Disconnect the negative battery cable.
2. Remove the instrument cluster, and place on a flat, clean, well lighted surface.
3. Turn the cluster upside down and remove the case and circuit board retainer screws.
4. Remove the gauge-to-circuit board retainer screws.
5. Remove the cluster illumination bulbs by turning 1/4 turn and lifting the bulbs out.
6. Carefully remove the circuit board assembly.
7. Lift the oil pressure/combination gauge assembly out of the cluster.

To install:

8. Install the oil pressure/combination gauge into the cluster assembly, making sure to insert the alignment tabs at the corners of the gauge.
9. Lay the circuit board over the rear of the cluster assembly, making sure to proper alignment the gauge-to-circuit board contact holes.
10. Install the retainer screws to the gauge holes, and tighten snugly.
11. Install the illumination bulbs, and turn 1/4 turn to lock in place.
12. Install the circuit board and cluster assembly retainer screws.
13. Install the instrument cluster.
14. Connect the negative battery cable.
15. Start the vehicle, and make sure the all the gauges work correctly.

SVX

1. Disconnect the negative battery cable.
2. Remove the instrument cluster, and place on a flat, clean, well lighted surface.
3. Turn the cluster upside down and remove the case and circuit board retainer screws.
4. Remove the cluster illumination bulbs by turning 1/4 turn and lifting the bulbs out.
5. Carefully detach the individual gauge contact tabs from the circuit board.
6. Carefully remove the circuit board assembly.
7. Remove the retainer screws securing the gauges to the cluster case.
8. Lift the oil pressure/combination gauge assembly out of the cluster.

To install:

9. Install the oil pressure/combination gauge into the cluster assembly, making sure to insert the alignment tabs at the corners of the gauge.
10. Install the gauge retainer screws.
11. Lay the circuit board over the rear of the cluster assembly, making sure to proper alignment the gauge-to-circuit board contact holes.
12. Press the contact tabs on to the gauge connection tabs.
13. Install the illumination bulbs, and turn 1/4 turn to lock in place.
14. Install the circuit board and cluster assembly retainer screws.
15. Install the instrument cluster.
16. Connect the negative battery cable.

17. Start the vehicle, and make sure all the gauges work correctly.

Fuel Gauge

REMOVAL & INSTALLATION

Some models incorporate a fuel gauge with another gauge like an oil pressure, voltmeter or temperature gauge. If 1 of these gauges fails, the entire combination gauge assembly must be replaced.

Justy

1. Disconnect the negative battery cable.
2. Remove the instrument cluster, and place on a flat, clean, well lighted surface.
3. Turn the cluster upside down and remove the case and circuit board retainer screws.
4. Remove the gauge-to-circuit board retainer nuts.
5. Carefully remove the circuit board assembly.
6. Lift the combination gauge assembly out of the cluster.

To install:

7. Install the combination gauge into the cluster assembly, making sure to insert the alignment tabs at the corners of the gauge.
8. Lay the circuit board over the rear of the cluster assembly, making sure to proper alignment the gauge-to-circuit board contact studs.
9. Install the retainer nuts to the gauge studs, and tighten snugly.
10. Install the circuit board and cluster assembly retainer screws.
11. Install the instrument cluster.
12. Connect the negative battery cable.
13. Start the vehicle, and make sure all the gauges work correctly.

Sedan, Coupe, Loyale, Wagon and Brat

1. Disconnect the negative battery cable.
2. Remove the instrument cluster, and place on a flat, clean, well lighted surface.
3. Turn the cluster upside down and remove the case and circuit board retainer screws.
4. Remove the gauge-to-circuit board retainer screws.
5. Carefully remove the circuit board assembly.
6. Lift the fuel/combination gauge assembly out of the cluster.

To install:

7. Install the fuel/combination gauge into the cluster assembly, making sure to insert the alignment tabs at the corners of the gauge.
8. Lay the circuit board over the rear of the cluster assembly, making sure to proper alignment the gauge-to-circuit board contact holes.
9. Install the retainer screws to the gauge holes, and tighten snugly.
10. Install the circuit board and cluster assembly retainer screws.
11. Install the instrument cluster.

12. Connect the negative battery cable.

13. Start the vehicle, and make sure all the gauges work correctly.

XT

1. Disconnect the negative battery cable.

2. Remove the instrument cluster, and place on a flat, clean, well lighted surface.

3. Turn the cluster upside down and remove the case and circuit board retainer screws.

4. Remove the telltale monitor retainer screws, and lift the monitor assembly out of the cluster assembly.

5. Remove the gauge-to-circuit board retainer screws.

6. Carefully remove the circuit board assembly.

7. Lift the fuel/combination gauge assembly out of cluster.

To install:

8. Install the fuel/combination gauge into the cluster assembly, making sure to insert the alignment tabs at the corners of the gauge.

9. Lay the circuit board over the rear of the cluster assembly, making sure to proper alignment the gauge-to-circuit board contact holes.

10. Install the retainer screws to the gauge holes, and tighten snugly.

11. Install the telltale monitor, and secure in place with the retainer screws.

12. Install the circuit board and cluster assembly retainer screws.

13. Install the instrument cluster.

14. Connect the negative battery cable.

15. Start the vehicle, and make sure all the gauges work correctly.

Legacy and Impreza

1. Disconnect the negative battery cable.

2. Remove the instrument cluster, and place on a flat, clean, well lighted surface.

3. Turn the cluster upside down and remove the case and circuit board retainer screws.

4. Remove the gauge-to-circuit board retainer screws.

5. Remove the cluster illumination bulbs by turning 1/4 turn and lifting the bulbs out.

6. Carefully remove the circuit board assembly.

7. Lift the fuel/combination gauge assembly out of cluster.

To install:

8. Install the fuel/combination gauge into the cluster assembly, making sure to insert the alignment tabs at the corners of the gauge.

9. Lay the circuit board over the rear of the cluster assembly, making sure to proper alignment the gauge-to-circuit board contact holes.

10. Install the retainer screws to the gauge holes, and tighten snugly.

11. Install the illumination bulbs, and turn 1/4 turn to lock in place.

12. Install the circuit board and cluster assembly retainer screws.

13. Install the instrument cluster.

14. Connect the negative battery cable.

15. Start the vehicle, and make sure the all the gauges work correctly.

SVX

1. Disconnect the negative battery cable.

2. Remove the instrument cluster, and place on a flat, clean, well lighted surface.

3. Turn the cluster upside down and remove the case and circuit board retainer screws.

4. Remove the cluster illumination bulbs by turning 1/4 turn and lifting the bulbs out.

5. Carefully detach the individual gauge contact tabs from the circuit board.

6. Carefully remove the circuit board assembly.

7. Remove the retainer screws securing the gauges to the cluster case.

8. Lift the fuel/combination gauge assembly out of cluster.

To install:

9. Install the fuel/combination gauge into the cluster assembly, making sure to insert the alignment tabs at the corners of the gauge.

10. Install the gauge retainer screws.

11. Lay the circuit board over the rear of the cluster assembly, making sure to proper alignment the gauge-to-circuit board contact holes.

12. Press the contact tabs on to the gauge connection tabs.

13. Install the illumination bulbs, and turn 1/4 turn to lock in place.

14. Install the circuit board and cluster assembly retainer screws.

15. Install the instrument cluster.

16. Connect the negative battery cable.

17. Start the vehicle, and make sure all the gauges work correctly.

Temperature Gauge

REMOVAL & INSTALLATION

Depending on production date, model and level of interior trim, certain vehicles will not be equipped with a temperature gauge.

Also some models incorporate an oil pressure gauge with another gauge like a fuel, voltmeter or temperature gauge. If 1 of these gauges fails, the entire combination gauge assembly must be replaced.

Justy

1. Disconnect the negative battery cable.

2. Remove the instrument cluster, and place on a flat, clean, well lighted surface.

3. Turn the cluster upside down and remove the case and circuit board retainer screws.

4. Remove the gauge-to-circuit board retainer nuts.

5. Carefully remove the circuit board assembly.

6. Lift the combination gauge assembly out of the cluster.

To install:

7. Install the combination gauge into the cluster assembly, making sure to insert the alignment tabs at the corners of the gauge.

8. Lay the circuit board over the rear of the cluster assembly, making sure to proper alignment the gauge-to-circuit board contact studs.

9. Install the retainer nuts to the gauge studs, and tighten snugly.

10. Install the circuit board and cluster assembly retainer screws.

11. Install the instrument cluster.

12. Connect the negative battery cable.

13. Start the vehicle, and make sure all the gauges work correctly.

Sedan, Coupe, Loyale, Wagon and Brat

1. Disconnect the negative battery cable.

2. Remove the instrument cluster, and place on a flat, clean, well lighted surface.

3. Turn the cluster upside down and remove the case and circuit board retainer screws.

4. Remove the gauge-to-circuit board retainer screws.

5. Carefully remove the circuit board assembly.

6. Lift the temperature/combination gauge assembly out of the cluster.

To install:

7. Install the temperature/combination gauge into the cluster assembly, making sure to insert the alignment tabs at the corners of the gauge.

8. Lay the circuit board over the rear of the cluster assembly, making sure to proper alignment the gauge-to-circuit board contact holes.

9. Install the retainer screws to the gauge holes, and tighten snugly.

10. Install the circuit board and cluster assembly retainer screws.

11. Install the instrument cluster.

12. Connect the negative battery cable.

13. Start the vehicle, and make sure all the gauges work correctly.

XT

1. Disconnect the negative battery cable.

2. Remove the instrument cluster, and place on a flat, clean, well lighted surface.

3. Turn the cluster upside down and remove the case and circuit board retainer screws.

4. Remove the telltale monitor retainer screws, and lift the monitor assembly out of the cluster assembly.

5. Remove the gauge-to-circuit board retainer screws.

6. Carefully remove the circuit board assembly.

7. Lift the temperature/combination gauge assembly out of the cluster.

To install:

8. Install the temperature/combination gauge into the cluster assembly, making sure to insert the alignment tabs at the corners of the gauge.

9. Lay the circuit board over the rear of the cluster assembly, making sure to proper alignment the gauge-to-circuit board contact holes.

10. Install the retainer screws to the gauge holes, and tighten snugly.

11. Install the telltale monitor, and secure in place with the retainer screws.

12. Install the circuit board and cluster assembly retainer screws.

13. Install the instrument cluster.

14. Connect the negative battery cable.

15. Start the vehicle, and make sure all the gauges work correctly.

Legacy and Impreza

1. Disconnect the negative battery cable.

2. Remove the instrument cluster, and place on a flat, clean, well lighted surface.

3. Turn the cluster upside down and remove the case and circuit board retainer screws.

4. Remove the gauge-to-circuit board retainer screws.

5. Remove the cluster illumination bulbs by turning 1/4 turn and lifting the bulbs out.

6. Carefully remove the circuit board assembly.

7. Lift the temperature/combination gauge assembly out of the cluster.

To install:

8. Install the temperature/combination gauge into the cluster assembly, making sure to insert the alignment tabs at the corners of the gauge.

9. Lay the circuit board over the rear of the cluster assembly, making sure to proper alignment the gauge-to-circuit board contact holes.

10. Install the retainer screws to the gauge holes, and tighten snugly.

11. Install the illumination bulbs, and turn 1/4 turn to lock in place.

12. Install the circuit board and cluster assembly retainer screws.

13. Install the instrument cluster.

14. Connect the negative battery cable.

15. Start the vehicle, and make sure the all the gauges work correctly.

SVX

1. Disconnect the negative battery cable.

2. Remove the instrument cluster, and place on a flat, clean, well lighted surface.

3. Turn the cluster upside down and remove the case and circuit board retainer screws.

4. Remove the cluster illumination bulbs by turning 1/4 turn and lifting the bulbs out.

5. Carefully detach the individual gauge contact tabs from the circuit board.

6. Carefully remove the circuit board assembly.

7. Remove the retainer screws securing the gauges to the cluster case.

8. Lift the temperature/combination gauge assembly out of the cluster.

To install:

9. Install the temperature/combination gauge into the cluster assembly, making sure to insert the alignment tabs at the corners of the gauge.

10. Install the gauge retainer screws.

11. Lay the circuit board over the rear of the cluster assembly, making sure to proper alignment the gauge-to-circuit board contact holes.

12. Press the contact tabs on to the gauge connection tabs.

13. Install the illumination bulbs, and turn ¼ turn to lock in place.

14. Install the circuit board and cluster assembly retainer screws.

15. Install the instrument cluster.

16. Connect the negative battery cable.

17. Start the vehicle, and make sure all the gauges work correctly.

Printed Circuit Board

REMOVAL & INSTALLATION

1. Disconnect the negative battery cable.

2. Remove the instrument cluster, and place on a flat, clean, well lighted surface.

3. Turn the cluster upside down and remove the case and circuit board retainer screws.

4. Remove the gauge-to-circuit board retainer nuts, if equipped.

5. Remove the gauge-to-circuit board retainer screws, if equipped.

6. Remove the cluster illumination bulbs, if equipped by turning ¼ turn and lifting the bulbs out.

7. Carefully detach the individual gauge contact tabs from the circuit board.

8. Carefully remove the circuit board assembly.

To install:

9. Lay the circuit board over the rear of the cluster assembly, making sure to proper alignment the gauge-to-circuit board contact holes tabs, or studs.

10. Install the illumination bulbs, if equipped, and turn ¼ turn to lock in place.

11. Install the circuit board retainer nuts or screws, if equipped.

12. Install the circuit board and cluster assembly retainer screws.

13. Install the instrument cluster.

14. Connect the negative battery cable.

15. Start the vehicle, and make sure all the gauges work correctly.

Voltmeter

REMOVAL & INSTALLATION

Depending on production date, model and level of interior trim, certain vehicles will not be equipped with a voltmeter.

Also some models incorporate a voltmeter with another gauge like a fuel, oil pressure or temperature gauge. If 1 of these gauges fails, the entire combination gauge assembly must be replaced.

Justy

1. Disconnect the negative battery cable.

2. Remove the instrument cluster, and place on a flat, clean, well lighted surface.

3. Turn the cluster upside down and remove the case and circuit board retainer screws.

4. Remove the gauge-to-circuit board retainer nuts.

5. Carefully remove the circuit board assembly.

6. Lift the combination gauge assembly out of the cluster.

To install:

7. Install the combination gauge into the cluster assembly, making sure to insert the alignment tabs at the corners of the gauge.

8. Lay the circuit board over the rear of the cluster assembly, making sure to proper alignment the gauge-to-circuit board contact studs.

9. Install the retainer nuts to the gauge studs, and tighten snugly.

10. Install the circuit board and cluster assembly retainer screws.

11. Install the instrument cluster.

12. Connect the negative battery cable.

13. Start the vehicle, and make sure all the gauges work correctly.

Sedan, Coupe, Loyale, Wagon and Brat

1. Disconnect the negative battery cable.

2. Remove the instrument cluster, and place on a flat, clean, well lighted surface.

3. Turn the cluster upside down and remove the case and circuit board retainer screws.

4. Remove the gauge-to-circuit board retainer screws.

5. Carefully remove the circuit board assembly.

6. Lift the voltmeter/combination gauge assembly out of the cluster.

To install:

7. Install the voltmeter/combination gauge into the cluster assembly, making sure to insert the alignment tabs at the corners of the gauge.

8. Lay the circuit board over the rear of the cluster assembly, making sure to proper alignment the gauge-to-circuit board contact holes.

9. Install the retainer screws to the gauge holes, and tighten snugly.

10. Install the circuit board and cluster assembly retainer screws.

11. Install the instrument cluster.

12. Connect the negative battery cable.

13. Start the vehicle, and make sure all the gauges work correctly.

XT

1. Disconnect the negative battery cable.

2. Remove the instrument cluster, and place on a flat, clean, well lighted surface.

3. Turn the cluster upside down and remove the case and circuit board retainer screws.

4. Remove the telltale monitor retainer screws, and lift the monitor assembly out of the cluster assembly.

5. Remove the gauge-to-circuit board retainer screws.

6. Carefully remove the circuit board assembly.

7. Lift the voltmeter/combination gauge assembly out of the cluster.

To install:

8. Install the voltmeter/combination gauge into the cluster assembly, making sure to insert the alignment tabs at the corners of the gauge.

9. Lay the circuit board over the rear of the cluster assembly, making sure to proper alignment the gauge-to-circuit board contact holes.

10. Install the retainer screws to the gauge holes, and tighten snugly.

11. Install the telltale monitor, and secure in place with the retainer screws.

12. Install the circuit board and cluster assembly retainer screws.

13. Install the instrument cluster.

14. Connect the negative battery cable.

15. Start the vehicle, and make sure all the gauges work correctly.

Legacy and Impreza

1. Disconnect the negative battery cable.

2. Remove the instrument cluster, and place on a flat, clean, well lighted surface.

3. Turn the cluster upside down and remove the case and circuit board retainer screws.

4. Remove the gauge-to-circuit board retainer screws.

5. Remove the cluster illumination bulbs by turning ¼ turn and lifting the bulbs out.

6. Carefully remove the circuit board assembly.

7. Lift the voltmeter/combination gauge assembly out of the cluster.

To install:

8. Install the voltmeter/combination gauge into the cluster assembly, making sure to insert the alignment tabs at the corners of the gauge.

9. Lay the circuit board over the rear of the cluster assembly, making sure to proper alignment the gauge-to-circuit board contact holes.

10. Install the retainer screws to the gauge holes, and tighten snugly.

11. Install the illumination bulbs, and turn ¼ turn to lock in place.

12. Install the circuit board and cluster assembly retainer screws.

13. Install the instrument cluster.

14. Connect the negative battery cable.

15. Start the vehicle, and make sure the all the gauges work correctly.

SVX

1. Disconnect the negative battery cable.

2. Remove the instrument cluster, and place on a flat, clean, well lighted surface.

3. Turn the cluster upside down and remove the case and circuit board retainer screws.

4. Remove the cluster illumination bulbs by turning ¼ turn and lifting the bulbs out.

5. Carefully detach the individual gauge contact tabs from the circuit board.

6. Carefully remove the circuit board assembly.

7. Remove the retainer screws securing the gauges to the cluster case.

8. Lift the voltmeter/combination gauge assembly out of the cluster.

To install:

9. Install the voltmeter/combination gauge into the cluster assembly, making sure to insert the alignment tabs at the corners of the gauge.

10. Install the gauge retainer screws.

11. Lay the circuit board over the rear of the cluster assembly, making sure to proper alignment the gauge-to-circuit board contact holes.

12. Press the contact tabs on to the gauge connection tabs.

13. Install the illumination bulbs, and turn ¼ turn to lock in place.

14. Install the circuit board and cluster assembly retainer screws.

15. Install the instrument cluster.

16. Connect the negative battery cable.

17. Start the vehicle, and make sure all the gauges work correctly.

Combination Switch

✳✳CAUTION

Properly disarm the air bag on vehicles equipped with the SRS system. Failure to do so can cause serious injury.

REMOVAL & INSTALLATION

▶ See Figures 117, 118 and 119

On all models except the XT, the combination switch contains the switches for the turn signal, headlight and wiper/washer functions of the vehicle. The XT models do not control the headlights from this switch, but retain the other functions. The stalk assemblies are mounted to a main switch body located on the steering column. Once the assembly is removed the individual switches can be removed. On all mod-

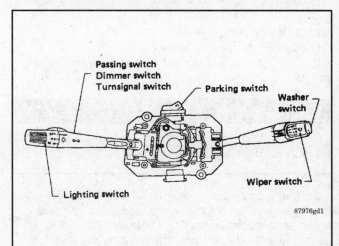

Passing switch
Dimmer switch
Turnsignal switch
Parking switch
Washer switch
Lighting switch
Wiper switch

87976gd1

Fig. 117 Combination switch assembly — Sedan, Coupe, Loyale, Wagon, Brat, Legacy and Impreza

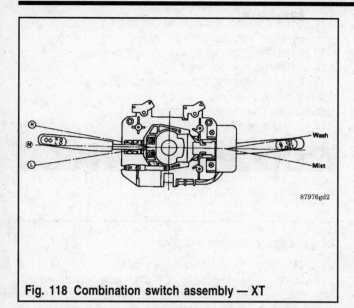

Fig. 118 Combination switch assembly — XT

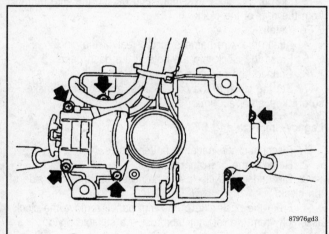

Fig. 119 Remove the combination switch retainer screws

els except the SVX, there are 2 stalk controls; on the SVX, there are 3 stalk controls.

1. Disconnect the negative battery cable.
2. Remove the lower trim cover.
3. Remove the steering column cover screws and the upper and lower column covers.
4. Remove the steering wheel. Refer to Section 8 for removal and installation steps.
5. Remove the electrical harness-to-steering column clip and band fitting,
6. Disconnect the combination switch electrical harnesses.
7. Remove the combination switch-to-control wing bracket screws on XT models.
8. Remove the combination switch mounting screws. Remove the switch assembly from the steering column.
9. If replacing part of the combination switch assembly, remove the switch assembly retainer screws and separate the assembly.

To install:

10. If the switch assembly was separated, attach the sections, and secure in place with the retaining screws.
11. Install the combination switch on the steering column, and tighten the bracket screws securely.
12. On XT models, attach the control wing-to-combination switch bracket, and secure in place with the retainer screws.
13. Connect the combination switch electrical harnesses. Secure in place with the retainer clips and ban fittings.
14. Install the steering wheel assembly and tighten the center nut.
15. Install the steering column covers and the lower instrument panel cover.
16. Connect the negative battery cable. Check for proper operation.

Rear Wiper Switch

REMOVAL & INSTALLATION

Dash Mounted Switch

1. Disconnect the negative battery cable.
2. Using a suitable small prytool, remove the rear wiper switch from the dash trim panel. Remove the switch enough to access the harness at the rear of the switch assembly.
3. Unfasten the switch wire harness.

To install:

4. Attach the rear wiper switch to the wire harness.
5. Install the switch assembly into the dah panel.
6. Connect the negative battery cable.
7. Test the rear wiper to make sure it functions correctly.

Steering Column Mounted

Refer to the combination switch procedure in this section for removal and installation steps for rear wiper control switches incorporated into the combination switch assembly.

Headlight Switch

REMOVAL & INSTALLATION

Except XT

Refer to the combination switch procedure in this section for removal and installation steps for headlight switch assemblies incorporated into the combination switch assembly.

XT

▶ **See Figure 120**

The headlight switch is installed on a control wing at the left side of the steering wheel.

1. Disconnect the negative battery cable.
2. Remove the lower steering column cover retainer screws and the upper and lower trim covers.
3. Remove the steering wheel. Refer to Section 8 for removal and chastallation steps.

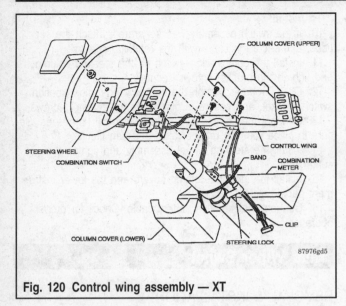

STEERING WHEEL
COMBINATION SWITCH
COLUMN COVER (UPPER)
CONTROL WING
BAND
COMBINATION METER
CLIP
COLUMN COVER (LOWER)
STEERING LOCK

87976gd5

Fig. 120 Control wing assembly — XT

4. Disconnect the electrical harness-to-steering column clip and band.

5. Remove the combination switch-to-steering column screws and the switch assembly from the steering wheel.

6. Remove the left control wing-to-steering column screws, then remove the left control wing from the steering column.

7. Remove the control wing case screws and separate the case halves from each other; this will provide access to the headlight switch.

8. To replace the headlight switch knob, use a pin rod to lightly push the pawl (inside the switch knob) inward, and pull the knob outward.

9. Remove the headlight switch retainer screws, and remove the switch from the case.

To install:

10. Position the headlight switch in the case, and secure in place with the retainer screws. To install the knob onto the switch, place the knob on the switch, place your finger on the back side of the switch, and squeeze the knob onto the switch.

➡**When reassembling the control wing cases, be careful not to get the electrical harness caught between the cases.**

11. Attach the wing case halves together, and install the retainer screws.

LIGHTING

Headlights

REMOVAL & INSTALLATION

Justy

▶ **See Figure 121**

The Justy is equipped with halogen headlamps, where the bulb can be replaced without removing the headlight assembly.

1. Disconnect the negative battery cable.

12. Install the wing assembly to the steering column, and secure in place with the retainer screws.

13. Install the combination switch and harnesses.

14. Install the steering wheel.

15. Install the steering column covers, and attach using the retainer screws.

16. Connect the negative battery cable.

17. Test the headlight switch to make sure it works correctly.

Clock

REMOVAL & INSTALLATION

Except Legacy, Impreza and SVX

1. Disconnect the negative battery cable.

2. Using a small prytool, pry the clock assembly from the dash panel.

3. Lift out the clock assembly, and detach the wire harness from the rear of the clock.

To install:

4. Attach the wire harness to the rear of the clock.

5. Press the clock into the hole in the dash panel.

6. Connect the negative battery cable.

7. Set the clock to the correct time, and check to make sure it keeps correct time.

Legacy, Impreza and SVX

1. Disconnect the negative battery cable.

2. Remove the dash trim panel.

3. Disconnect the clock wire harness from the back side of the clock.

4. From the back side of the trim panel, remove the clock assembly from the retainer tabs, using a suitable prytool.

To install:

5. Install the clock into the rear of the dash panel. Make sure all retainer tabs engage.

6. Attach the wire harness to the rear of the clock assembly.

7. Install the dash trim panel into the dash assembly.

8. Connect the negative battery cable.

9. Set the clock to the correct time, and check to make sure it keeps correct time.

2. Remove the front grille retaining screws and remove the grille assembly.

3. Remove the screws that secure the front combination light assembly.

4. Disconnect the electrical harness from the combination light and headlight assemblies.

5. Remove the headlight assembly retaining nuts and bolts, then remove the assembly from the vehicle.

To install:

6. Install the headlight assembly and tighten the nuts and bolts to 61 inch lbs. (6.9 Nm).

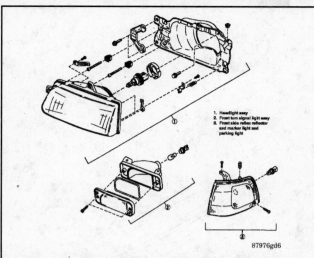

1. Headlight assy
2. Front turn signal light assy
3. Front side reflex reflector and marker light and parking light

87976gd6

Fig. 121 Headlight and combination light assembly — Justy

7. Attach the wire harnesses to the headlight and combination light assemblies.

8. Install the combination light, using the retainer screws.

9. Install the front grille, and secure with the retainer screws.

10. Connect the negative battery cable.

11. Test to make sure the headlight work correctly. Check the headlight alignment. Adjust if needed.

Sedan, Coupe, Loyale, Wagon and Brat
♦ See Figure 122

WITH 4 HEADLIGHTS

These vehicles are equipped with 4 5 inch rectangular headlights. These headlight do not have replaceable bulbs. The entire headlight must be removed and replaced.

1. Disconnect the negative battery cable.

2. Remove the retainer screws securing the bezel around the headlight assembly. Remove the bezel and place aside.

3. Pull the headlight out enough to access the wire harness at the rear of the light assembly.

4. Disconnect the electrical harness from the headlight assembly.

To install:

5. Attach the wire harness to the rear of the headlight assembly.

6. Position the headlight into the bracket assembly. Make sure the tabs on the headlight seat within the grooves in the bracket assembly.

7. Install the bezel around the headlight, and secure in place with the retainer screws.

8. Connect the negative battery cable.

9. Test to make sure the headlight work correctly. Check the headlight alignment. Adjust if needed.

WITH 2 HEADLIGHTS

These models are equipped with halogen headlamps, where the bulb can be replaced without removing the headlight assembly.

1. Disconnect the negative battery cable.

2. Remove the front grille retaining screws and remove the grille assembly.

3. Remove the screws that secure the front combination light assembly.

4. Disconnect the electrical harness from the combination light and headlight assemblies.

5. Remove the headlight assembly retaining nuts and bolts, then remove the assembly from the vehicle.

To install:

6. Install the headlight assembly and tighten the nuts and bolts to 61 inch lbs. (7 Nm).

7. Attach the wire harnesses to the headlight and combination light assemblies.

8. Install the combination light, using the retainer screws.

9. Install the front grille, and secure with the retainer screws.

10. Connect the negative battery cable.

11. Test to make sure the headlight work correctly. Check the headlight alignment. Adjust if needed.

XT
♦ See Figures 123, 124 and 125

The XT is equipped with pop-up headlamps. The headlamp motors are actuated by a switch on the left control wing. If the light fails to raise, it can be manually raised by means of a knob on top of the motor. The knob is covered by a rubber boot. Remove the boot and turn the knob in the direction of the arrow on top of the motor, this will raise the light.

➡ **The XT is equipped with a sealed beam type headlight. If the light fails, the entire lens assembly must be replaced.**

1. Disconnect the negative battery cable.

2. Disconnect the electrical harnesses from the light and the retractor motor.

3. Remove the front grille assembly.

4. Remove the screws that retain the lid on the light assembly and remove the lid.

5. Remove the headlight cover, by removing the retainer screws.

6. Remove the bolts that retain the headlight assembly and motor, and remove the assembly from the vehicle.

7. If needed, remove the motor from the assembly.

8. To remove the headlight, proceed as follows;

   a. Remove the retainer screws securing the bezel around the headlight assembly. Remove the bezel and place aside.

   b. Pull the headlight out enough to access the wire harness at the rear of the light assembly.

   c. Disconnect the electrical harness from the headlight assembly.

   d. To install, attach the wire harness to the rear of the headlight assembly.

   e. Position the headlight into the bracket assembly. Make sure the tabs on the headlight seat within the grooves in the bracket assembly.

   f. Install the bezel around the headlight, and secure in place with the retainer screws.

To install:

9. Install the headlight motor if removed.

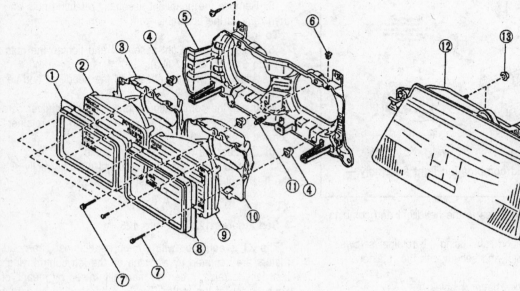

FOR DL MODEL

EXCEPT DL MODEL

1. Retaining ring
2. Sealed beam unit
3. Mounting ring
4. Screw grommet
5. Housing
6. Screw grommet
7. Adjusting screw

8. Retaining ring
9. Sealed beam unit
10. Mounting ring
11. Spring
12. Lens and body
13. Nut
14. Bulb (Halogen)
15. Cap

87976gd7

Fig. 122 Headlight assemblies — Sedan, Coupe, Loyale, Wagon and Brat

10. Install the assembly in place on the vehicle and secure in place with the retainer bolts. Tighten the bolts to 17 ft. lbs. (23 Nm).

11. Install the cover and lid using the retainer screws.

12. Install the front grille.

13. Connect the motor and headlight wire leads.

14. Connect the negative battery cable.

15. Test the operation of the headlights. Adjust the lights if needed.

Legacy, Impreza and SVX

▶ **See Figures 126 and 127**

1. Disconnect the negative battery cable.

2. Remove the front grille retaining screws, then remove the grille and place aside.

3. Remove the screws that secure the front combination light assembly.

4. Disconnect the electrical connectors from the combination light and headlight assemblies.

5. Remove the headlight assembly retaining nuts and bolts at the top and side of the bracket assembly.

6. Remove the headlight assembly from the vehicle.

To install:

7. Install the headlight assembly and tighten the nuts and bolts to 61 inch lbs. (7 Nm).

8. Attach the wire harnesses to the headlight and combination light assemblies.

9. Install the combination light, using the retainer screws.

10. Install the front grille, and secure with the retainer screws.

11. Connect the negative battery cable.

12. Test to make sure the headlight work correctly. Check the headlight alignment. Adjust if needed.

HALOGEN BULB REPLACEMENT

▶ **See Figures 128 and 129**

➡The 9004 headlight bulb is a halogen type bulb. This type of bulb is very sensitive to oils on the glass lens. When removing or installing a type 9004 bulb, NEVER touch the lens, or bulb life will be severely reduced.

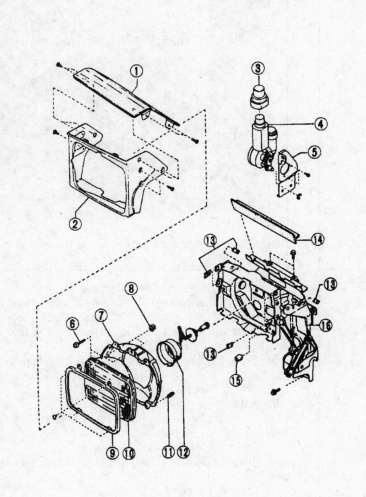

1 Lid
2 Cover
3 Cap
4 Retractable headlight motor
5 Bracket
6 Adjusting screw
7 Mounting ring
8 Screw grommet
9 Retaining ring
10 Sealed beam unit
11 Spring
12 Cord
13 Spring nut
14 Protector
15 Stopper
16 Retractable headlight ASSY

87976gd8

Fig. 123 Retractable headlight system — XT

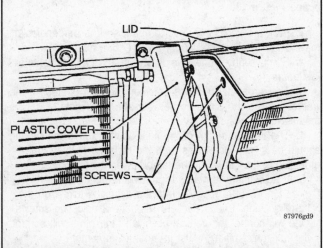

87976gd9

Fig. 124 Remove the retainer screws to access the headlight — XT

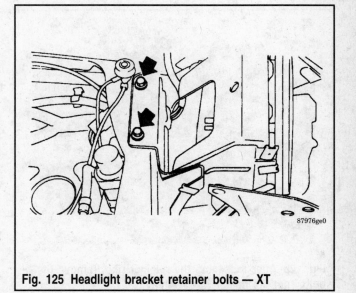

87976ge0

Fig. 125 Headlight bracket retainer bolts — XT

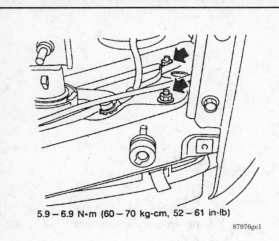

5.9 — 6.9 N·m (60 — 70 kg-cm, 52 — 61 in-lb)

87976ge1

Fig. 126 Headlight bracket retainer nuts on front radiator support — Legacy, Impreza and SVX

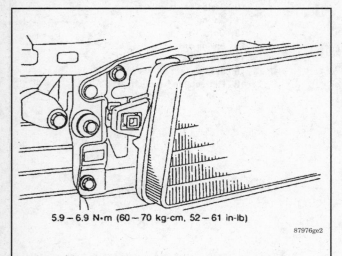

5.9 — 6.9 N·m (60 — 70 kg-cm, 52 — 61 in-lb)

87976ge2

Fig. 127 Headlight bracket retainer bolts behind the grille assembly

87976p35

Fig. 128 After loosening the retainer ring, remove the bulb from the headlight assembly

87976p36

Fig. 129 Disconnect the harness from the rear of the bulb

1. Disconnect the negative battery cable.
2. From inside the engine compartment, slide the protective rubber cap from the rear of the bulb assembly, if equipped.
3. Twist off the headlight bulb retainer ring and slide over the harness plug.
4. Grasp the base of the bulb and pull it out from the headlamp.
5. Unplug the bulb from the harness.
To install:
6. Grasp the base of the bulb with your hand. Plug the wire harness into the bulb.
7. Insert the bulb into the headlamp.
8. Twist the headlight bulb retainer ring on until it locks in place.
9. Connect the negative battery cable.
10. Turn **ON** the headlight switch to make sure all the lights work correctly.

AIMING

▶ **See Figure 130**

1. Park the vehicle on level ground, so it is perpendicular to, and facing a flat wall about 25 ft. (7.6m) away.
2. Remove any stone shields and switch ON the lights to low beam.
3. The horizontal distance between the light beams on the wall should be the same as between the headlights themselves.
4. The vertical height of the light beams above the ground should be 4 in. (10cm) less than the distance between the ground and the center of the lamp lenses for the lights.
5. If adjustment is needed, proceed as follows:
   a. On 1985-93 models, turn the adjusting screw on the headlight ring. Each headlight will have 2 adjusting screws. One will control the vertical plain, and the other will control the horizontal plain. Adjust in small increments.
   b. On 1994-96 models, headlight alignment is made easier because each light assembly is equipped with an adjustment level. Use a suitable wrench or socket to adjust the

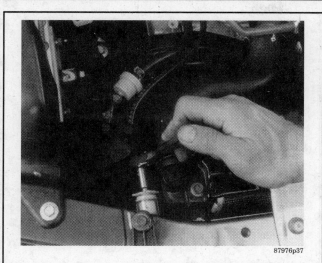

Fig. 130 Using the built-in level to align the headlight — Legacy

level indicator nut at the end of the level, until the bubble is in the middle of the sight glass.

6. Test to make sure the lights work correctly, and the light pattern is even.

Signal and Marker Lights

REMOVAL & INSTALLATION

Front Turn Signal and Parking Lights
▶ See Figure 131

1. Disconnect the negative battery cable.
2. Remove the 2 screws which secure the lens cover and gasket to the vehicle.
3. Pull the assembly out enough to access the lamp wire and plug.
4. Remove the lamp assembly by twisting counterclockwise and pulling out.

5. Depress and twist the bulb approximately ⅛ turn counterclockwise to remove from the socket.
   To install:
6. Install the bulb by inserting it into the light socket and twisting clockwise.
7. Install the light assembly into the light assembly by inserting it into the hole and twisting clockwise slightly.
8. Install the trim light assembly and secure with the retainer screws.
9. Test to make sure the lights work correctly.

Side Marker Lights
▶ See Figure 132

1. Disconnect the negative battery cable.
2. From inside the wheel arch, grasp the bulb and socket assembly and pull out.
3. Remove the lamp assembly by twisting counterclockwise and pulling out.
4. Depress and twist the bulb approximately ⅛ turn counterclockwise to remove from the socket.

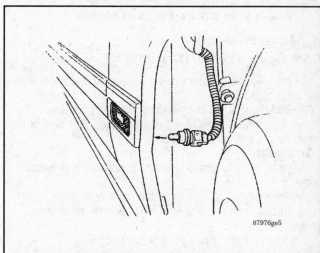

Fig. 132 Side marker light assemblies — Legacy, Impreza

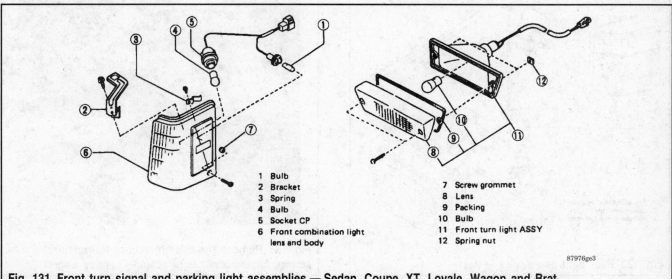

1 Bulb	7 Screw grommet
2 Bracket	8 Lens
3 Spring	9 Packing
4 Bulb	10 Bulb
5 Socket CP	11 Front turn light ASSY
6 Front combination light lens and body	12 Spring nut

Fig. 131 Front turn signal and parking light assemblies — Sedan, Coupe, XT, Loyale, Wagon and Brat

To install:

5. Install the bulb by inserting it into the light socket and twisting clockwise.

6. Install the light and socket assembly into the lens by inserting it into the hole and pressing firmly.

7. Test to make sure the lights work correctly.

Rear Turn Signal, Brake and Parking Lights

▶ See Figures 133 and 134

1. Working from inside the trunk, remove the protective covering from the tail light panel, if equipped.

2. Remove the lamp assembly by twisting counterclockwise and pulling out.

3. Depress and twist the bulb approximately ⅛ turn counterclockwise to remove from the socket.

To install:

4. Install the bulb by inserting it into the light socket and twisting clockwise.

5. Install the light assembly into the bezel by inserting it into the hole and twisting clockwise slightly.

6. Install the cover over the light assembly.

7. Test to make sure the lights work correctly.

High-Mount Brake Light

▶ See Figures 135, 136, 137 and 138

1. Remove the retainer screws securing the lens cover to the lamp housing.

2. Pull the lens cover away from the lamp housing.

3. Pull the bulb straight out of the socket. This type of bulb does not have to be twisted out.

To install:

4. Insert a replacement bulb into the socket and press in place.

5. Attach the lens housing to the lamp assembly.

6. Secure the lamp and lens together with the retainer screws.

7. Test to make sure the lights work correctly.

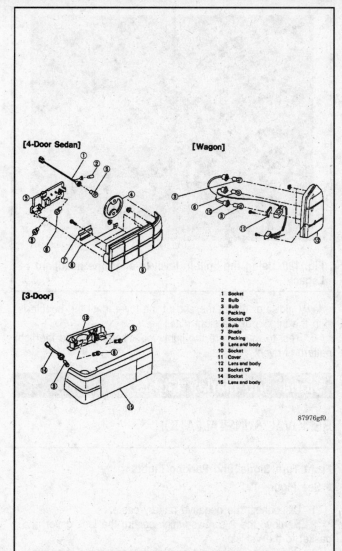

1	Socket
2	Bulb
3	Bulb
4	Packing
5	Socket CP
6	Bulb
7	Shade
8	Packing
9	Lens and body
10	Socket
11	Cover
12	Lens and body
13	Socket CP
14	Socket
15	Lens and body

87976gf0

Fig. 134 Rear light assembly — Sedan, Coupe, XT, Loyale, Wagon and Brat

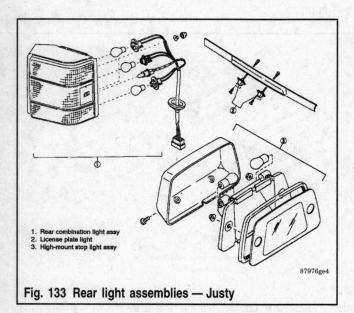

1. Rear combination light assy
2. License plate light
3. High-mount stop light assy

87976ge4

Fig. 133 Rear light assemblies — Justy

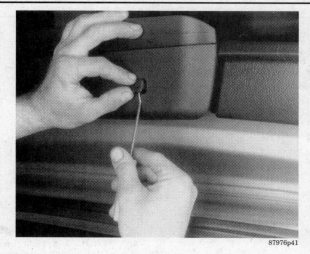

87976p41

Fig. 135 Remove the caps to access the retainer screws for the brake light cover — Legacy wagon

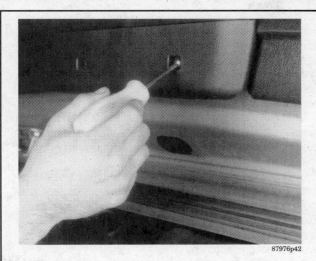

Fig. 136 Loosen and remove the lamp cover retainer screws . . .

Fig. 137 . . . and remove the cover to access the brake light bulbs

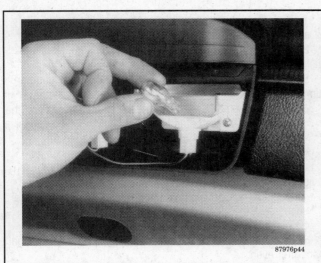

Fig. 138 Remove the bulb by pulling it out of the socket

Dome Light

▶ See Figures 139 and 140

1. Carefully remove the lens from the lamp assembly by prying in on the sides of the lens.
2. Remove the bulb from the retainer clips.

To install:

3. Insert the bulb into the retainer clips, making sure the bulb is seated firmly in each contact point.
4. Snap the lens into place.
5. Test to make sure the light works correctly.

Cargo Lamp

1. Remove the lens by squeezing in on the sides of the lens.
2. Depress the bulb and rotate it counterclockwise to remove it.

To install:

3. Insert a replacement bulb. Depress the bulb and turn clockwise to lock it in place.

Fig. 139 Removing the dome light lens — Legacy

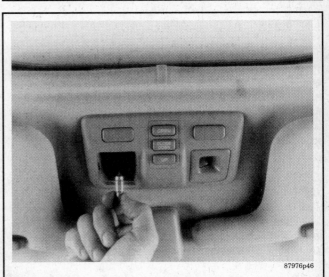

Fig. 140 Remove the bulb from the clips

4. Install the lens.

5. Test to make sure the light works correctly.

License Plate Light

1. Remove the 2 screws retaining the lamp to the rear panel.

2. Pull the lamp assembly out enough to remove the lenses and access the bulb.

3. Rotate the socket 1/4 turn counterclockwise from the backside of the lamp.

4. Pull the bulb straight out from the socket. Twisting is not needed on these type bulbs.

To install:

5. Insert the bulb into the socket. Twisting is not needed on these type bulbs.

6. Insert the socket into the lamp, and rotate it clockwise to lock in place.

7. Position the lens to the door panel and secure using the retainer screws.

8. Test to make sure the lights work correctly.

Fog/Driving Lights

REMOVAL & INSTALLATION

1. Disconnect the negative battery cable.

2. Unfasten the wire harness at the rear of the fog/driving light assembly.

3. Remove the retainer nut securing the fog/driving light to the bracket attached to the bumper reinforcement.

4. Lower the light assembly and remove from the vehicle.

To install:

5. Position the light assembly in the bracket attached to the bumper. Install the retainer nut and washer, then tighten.

6. Connect the wire harness to the rear of the fog/driving light.

7. Connect the negative battery cable.

8. Test to make sure the lights work correctly.

INSTALLING AFTERMARKET AUXILIARY LIGHTS

➡ **Before installing any aftermarket light, make sure it is legal for road use. Most acceptable lights will have a DOT approval number. Also check your local and regional inspection regulations. In certain areas, aftermarket lights must be installed in a particular manner or they may not be legal for inspection.**

1. Disconnect the negative battery cable.

2. Unpack the contents of the light kit purchased. Place the contents in an open space where you can easily retrieve a piece if needed.

3. Choose a location for the lights. If you are installing fog lights, below the bumper and apart from each other is desirable. Most fog lights are mounted below or very close to the

headlights. If you are installing driving lights, above the bumper and close together is desirable. Most driving lights are mounted between the headlights.

4. Drill the needed hole(s) to mount the light. Install the light, and secure using the supplied retainer nut and washer. Tighten the light mounting hardware, but not the light adjustment nut or bolt.

5. Install the relay that came with the light kit in the engine compartment, in a rigid area, like a fender. Always install the relay with the terminals facing down. This will prevent water from entering the relay assembly.

6. Using the wire supplied, locate the ground terminal, or terminal with the number 85 next to it on the relay, and connect a length of wire from this terminal to a good ground source. You can drill a hole and screw this wire to an inside piece of metal; just scrape the paint away from the hole to ensure a good connection.

7. Locate the light terminal, or terminal with the number 87 next to it on the relay; and attach a length of wire between this terminal and the fog/driving lamps.

8. Locate the ignition terminal, or terminal with the number 86 next to it on the relay, and connect a length of wire between this terminal and the light switch.

9. Find a suitable mounting location for the light switch and install. Some examples of mounting areas are a location close to the main light switch, auxiliary light position in the dash panel, if equipped, or in the center of the dash panel.

10. Depending on local and regional regulations, the other end of the switch can be connected to a constant power source like the battery, an ignition opening in the fuse panel, or a parking or headlight wire.

11. Locate the power terminal, or terminal with the No. 30 next to it on the relay, and connect a wire with a fuse of at least 10 amperes in it between the terminal and the battery.

12. With all the wires connected and tied up neatly, connect the negative battery cable.

13. Turn the lights ON and adjust the light pattern if needed.

AIMING

1. Park the vehicle on level ground, so it is perpendicular to and, facing a flat wall about 25 ft. (7.6m) away.

2. Remove any stone shields, if equipped and switch ON the lights.

3. Loosen the mounting hardware of the lights so you can aim them as follows:

   a. The horizontal distance between the light beams on the wall should be the same as between the lights themselves.

   b. The vertical height of the light beams above the ground should be 4 in. (10cm) less than the distance between the ground and the center of the lamp lenses for fog lights. For driving lights, the vertical height should be even with the distance between the ground and the center of the lamp.

4. Tighten the mounting hardware.

5. Test to make sure the lights work correctly, and the light pattern is even.

TRAILER WIRING

Wiring the vehicle for towing is fairly easy. There are a number of good wiring kits available and these should be used, rather than trying to design your own.

All trailers will need brake lights and turn signals, as well as tail lights and side marker lights. Most areas require extra marker lights for overwide trailers. Also, most areas have recently required back-up lights for trailers, and most trailer manufacturers have been building trailers with back-up lights for several years.

Additionally, some Class I, most Class II and just about all Class III trailers will have electric brakes. Add to this number an accessories wire, to operate trailer internal equipment or to charge the trailer's battery, and you can have as many as 7 wires in the harness.

Determine the equipment on your trailer and buy the wiring kit necessary. The kit will contain all the wires needed, plus a plug adapter set which includes the female plug, mounted on the bumper or hitch, and the male plug, wired into, or plugged into the trailer harness.

When installing the kit, follow the manufacturer's instructions. The color coding of the wires is usually standard throughout the industry. One point to note: some domestic vehicles, and most imported vehicles, have separate turn signals. On most domestic vehicles, the brake lights and rear turn signals operate with the same bulb. For those vehicles without separate turn signals, you can purchase an isolation unit so the brake lights won't blink whenever the turn signals are operated, or, you can go to your local electronics supply house and buy 4 diodes to wire in series with the brake and turn signal bulbs. Diodes will isolate the brake and turn signals. The choice is yours. The isolation units are simple and quick to install, but far more expensive than the diodes. The diodes, however, require more work to install properly, since they require the cutting of each bulb's wire and soldering in place of the diode.

One, final point: the best kits are those with a spring loaded cover on the vehicle-mounted socket. This cover prevents dirt and moisture from corroding the terminals. Never let the vehicle socket hang loosely; always mount it securely to the bumper or hitch.

CIRCUIT PROTECTION

Fuse Panel and Fuses

▶ **See Figure 141**

Most of the replaceable fuses for the electrical system are located on the fuse panel under the instrument panel, to the left of the steering column. In addition to the plastic fuses installed in the fuse box, there are 1 or more circuit breakers and a flasher relay.

For access to the fuse panel, remove the fasteners from the lower edge of the cover, then pull the cover downward until the spring clips disengage from the instrument panel. On the base models, the cover simply snaps on and off.

The locations of various fuses are illustrated in the owner's manual, and in some cases, on the cover of the fuse panel.

REPLACEMENT

Fuses are replaced by simply pulling them out. A blown or open fuse can be seen as a break in the metal filament that runs between the blades. The fuse is made with a plastic body so the break can be clearly seen.

Fuses that open (blow) may be replaced, but will continue to open until the cause of the overload condition is corrected. If a fuse needs to be replaced, use only a new fuse rated according to the specifications and of the same amperage number as the 1 removed. At the time of manufacture, 5 spare fuses were located inside the fuse panel cover.

✳✳CAUTION

Always replace a blown fuse or fuse link with the same rating as specified. Never replace a fuse with a higher amperage rating than the 1 removed, or severe wiring damage and a possible fire can result.

Fusible Links

▶ **See Figure 141**

A fusible link is a short length of Hypalon (high temperature) insulated wire, integral with the wiring harness, and should not be confused with standard wire. The fusible link is several wire gauges smaller than the circuit it protects, and is designed to melt and break the circuit should an overload occur. Under no circumstances should a fusible link be replaced with a standard length of wire.

The higher melting temperature properties and additional thickness of the Hypalon insulation will usually allow the undersized internal fuse wire to melt and disintegrate within the Hypalon casing with little damage to the high temperature insu-

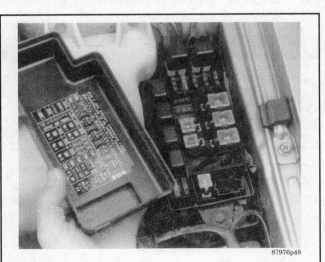

87976p48

Fig. 141 Engine compartment fuse, relay, and fusible link box — 1996 Outback

lation other than discoloration and/or bubbling of the insulation surface. In extreme cases of excessive circuit current, the insulation may separate after the fuse wire has disintegrated, however, the bare wire will seldom be exposed. If it becomes difficult to determine if the fuse link is burnt open, perform a continuity test. When heavy current flows, such as when a booster battery is connected incorrectly or when a short to ground occurs in the wiring harness, the fusible link burns out to protect the alternator and/or wiring.

Production fuse links have a flag moulded on the wire or on the terminal insulator. Color identification of the flag or connector is Blue-20 gauge wire, Red-18 gauge wire, Yellow-17 gauge wire, Orange-16 gauge wire, and Green-14 gauge wire.

➡**Some vehicles have individual fusible links which simply plug into connectors within an underhood fuse box.**

REPLACEMENT

To repair any blown fuse link (other than the plug-in type), use the following procedure:

1. Determine which circuit is damaged, its location and the cause of the open fuse link. If the damaged fuse link is 1 of 3 fed by a common No. 10 or 12 gauge feed wire, determine the specific affected circuit.
2. Disconnect the negative battery cable.
3. Cut the damaged fuse link from the wiring harness and discard it. If the fuse link is 1 of 3 circuits fed by a single feed wire, cut it out of the harness at each splice end and discard it.
4. Identify and procure the proper fuse link and butt connectors for attaching the fuse link in the harness.
5. To repair any fuse link in a 3-link group with 1 feed:
   a. After cutting the open link out of the harness, cut each of the remaining undamaged fuse links close to the feed wire weld.
   b. Strip approximately ½ in. (12.7mm) of insulation from the detached ends of the 2 good fuse links. Then insert 2 wire ends into 1 end of a butt connector, and carefully push 1 stripped end of the replacement fuse link into the same end of the butt connector. Crimp all 3 firmly together.

➡**Care must be taken when fitting the 3 fuse links into the butt connector, as the internal diameter is a snug fit for 3 wires. Make sure to use a proper crimping tool. Pliers, side cutters, etc. will not apply the proper crimp to retain the wires and withstand a pull test.**

   c. After crimping the butt connector to the 3 fuse links, cut the weld portion from the feed wire and strip approximately ½ in. (12.7mm) of insulation from the cut end. Insert the stripped end into the open end of the butt connector and crimp very firmly.
   d. To attach the remaining end of the replacement fuse link, strip approximately ½ in. (12.7mm) of insulation from

the wire end of the circuit from which the blown fuse link was removed, and firmly crimp a butt connector to the stripped wire. Then, insert the end of the replacement link into the other end of the butt connector and crimp firmly.
   e. Using rosin core solder with a consistency of 60 percent tin and 40 percent lead, solder the connectors and the wires at the repairs, and insulate with electrical tape.
6. To replace any fuse link on a single circuit in a harness, cut out the damaged portion, strip approximately ½ in. (12.7mm) of insulation from the 2 wire ends and attach the appropriate replacement fuse link to the stripped wire ends with 2 proper size butt connectors. Solder the connectors and wires, and insulate with tape.
7. To repair any fuse link which has an eyelet terminal on 1 end such as the charging circuit, cut off the open fuse link behind the weld, strip approximately ½ in. (13mm) of insulation from the cut end, and attach the appropriate new eyelet fuse link to the cut stripped wire with an appropriate size butt connector. Solder the connectors and wires at the repair, and insulate with tape.
8. Connect the negative battery cable to the battery and test the system for proper operation.

➡**Do not mistake a resistor wire for a fuse link. The resistor wire is generally longer and has print stating, "Resistor: don't cut or splice." When attaching a single No. 16, 17, 18 or 20 gauge fuse link to a heavy gauge wire, always double the stripped wire end of the fuse link before inserting and crimping it into the butt connector for positive wire retention.**

Circuit Breaker

Selected circuits, such as headlights and windshield wipers, are protected with circuit breakers. A circuit breaker is designed to stop current flow in case of a short circuit or overload. It will automatically restore current flow after a few seconds, but will again interrupt current flow if the overload or short circuit continues. This ON/OFF cycle will continue as long as the overload or short circuit exists, except for the circuit breakers protecting the power door lock and power window circuits, which will not restore current flow until the overload is removed.

Flasher

Both the turn signal and hazard warning flashers are mounted on the fuse panel.

REPLACEMENT

To remove a relay, simple pull the relay out. When installing a relay, make sure the terminals on the relay line up with the terminals in the fuse panel.

WIRING DIAGRAMS

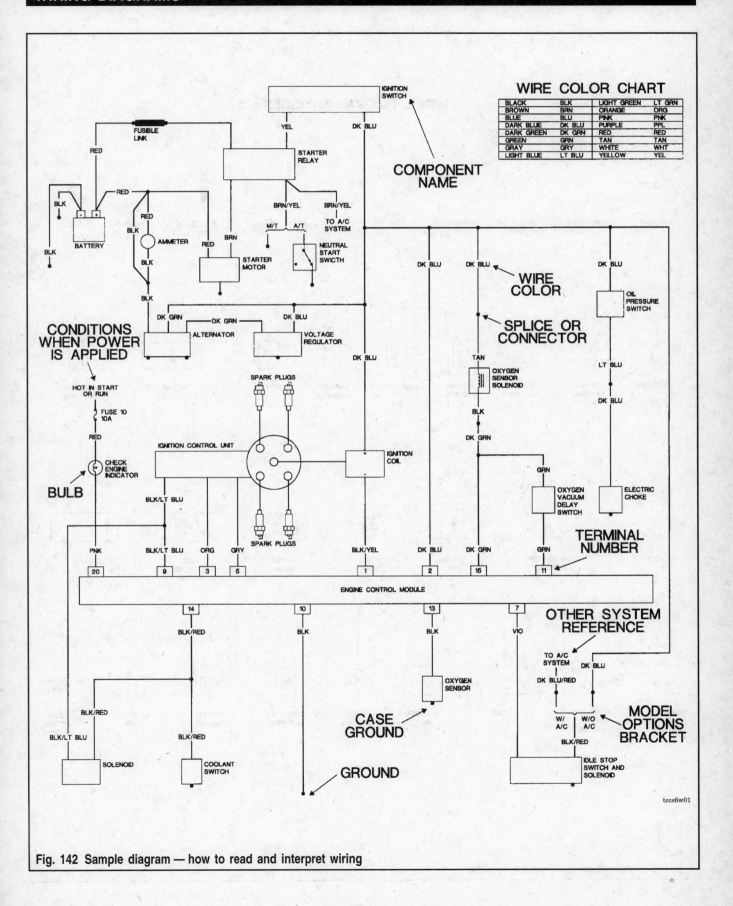

WIRE COLOR CHART

BLACK	BLK	LIGHT GREEN	LT GRN
BROWN	BRN	ORANGE	ORG
BLUE	BLU	PINK	PNK
DARK BLUE	DK BLU	PURPLE	PPL
DARK GREEN	DK GRN	RED	RED
GREEN	GRN	TAN	TAN
GRAY	GRY	WHITE	WHT
LIGHT BLUE	LT BLU	YELLOW	YEL

Fig. 142 Sample diagram — how to read and interpret wiring

tccs6w01

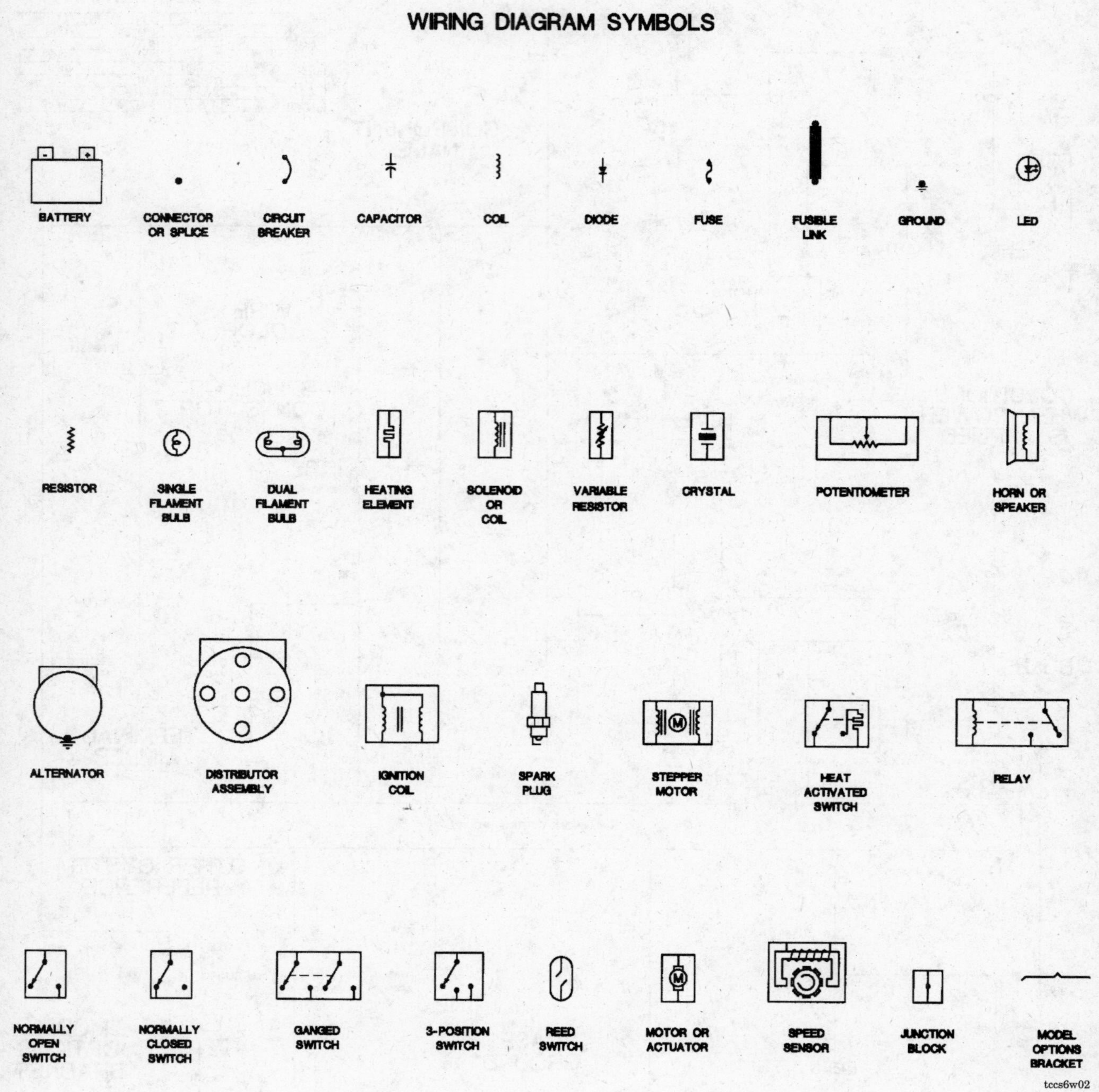

WIRING DIAGRAM SYMBOLS

BATTERY	CONNECTOR OR SPLICE	CIRCUIT BREAKER	CAPACITOR	COIL	DIODE	FUSE	FUSIBLE LINK	GROUND	LED

RESISTOR	SINGLE FILAMENT BULB	DUAL FILAMENT BULB	HEATING ELEMENT	SOLENOID OR COIL	VARIABLE RESISTOR	CRYSTAL	POTENTIOMETER	HORN OR SPEAKER

ALTERNATOR	DISTRIBUTOR ASSEMBLY	IGNITION COIL	SPARK PLUG	STEPPER MOTOR	HEAT ACTIVATED SWITCH	RELAY

NORMALLY OPEN SWITCH	NORMALLY CLOSED SWITCH	GANGED SWITCH	3-POSITION SWITCH	REED SWITCH	MOTOR OR ACTUATOR	SPEED SENSOR	JUNCTION BLOCK	MODEL OPTIONS BRACKET

tccs6w02

Fig. 143 Common wiring diagram symbols

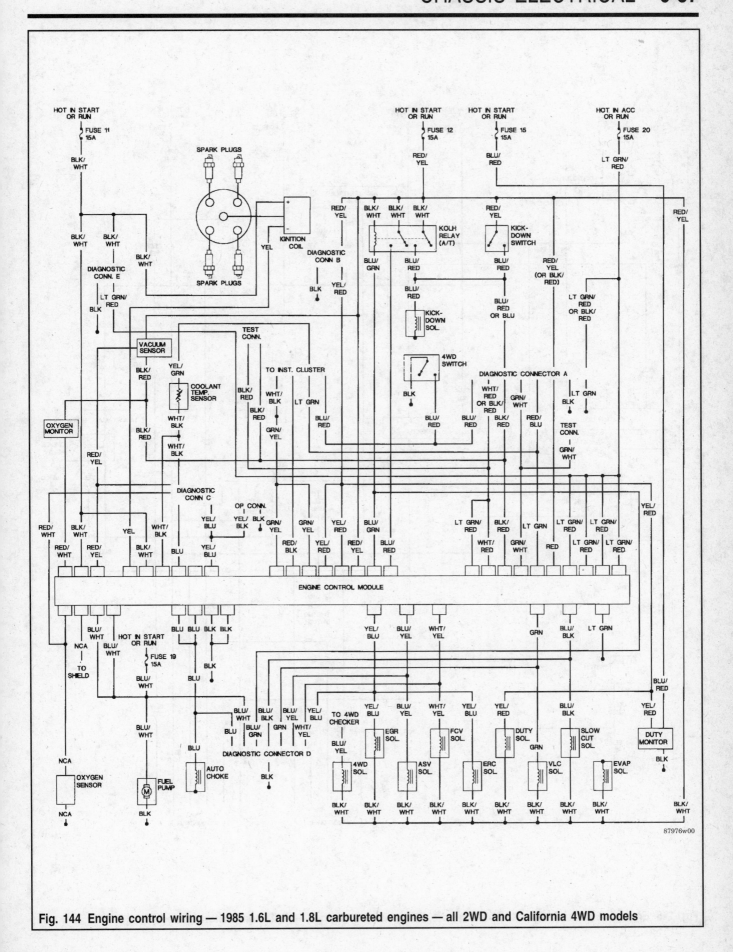

Fig. 144 Engine control wiring — 1985 1.6L and 1.8L carbureted engines — all 2WD and California 4WD models

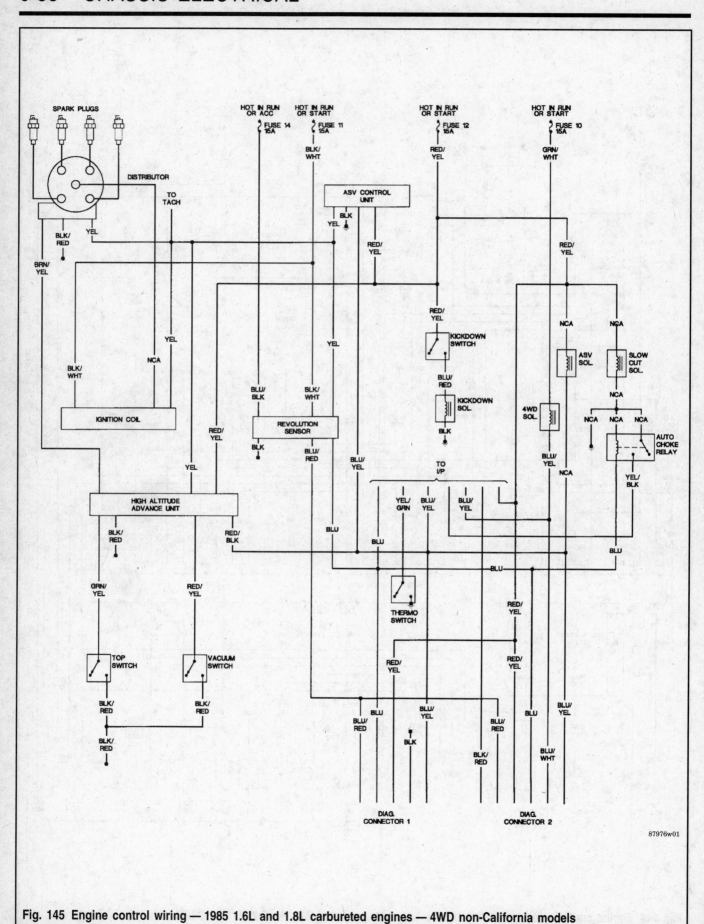

Fig. 145 Engine control wiring — 1985 1.6L and 1.8L carbureted engines — 4WD non-California models

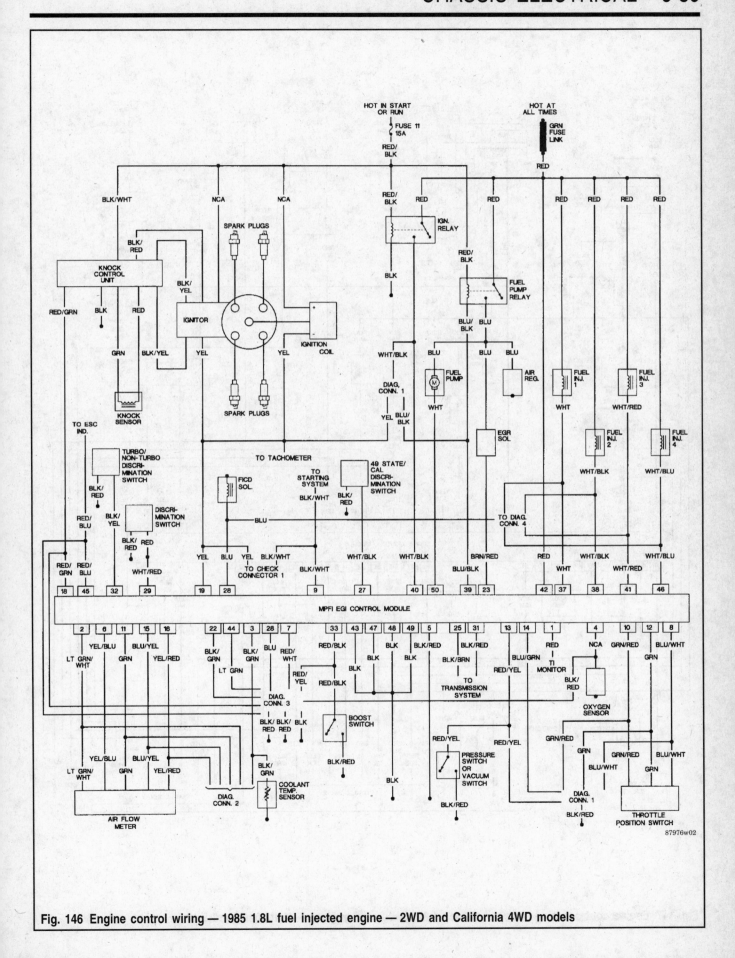

Fig. 146 Engine control wiring — 1985 1.8L fuel injected engine — 2WD and California 4WD models

87976w02

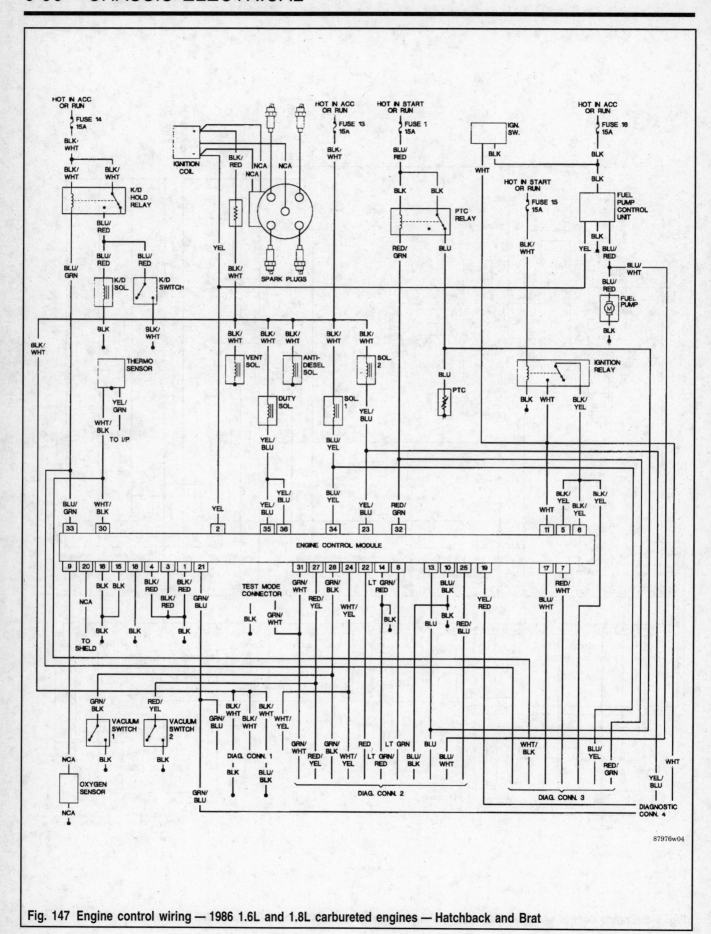

Fig. 147 Engine control wiring — 1986 1.6L and 1.8L carbureted engines — Hatchback and Brat

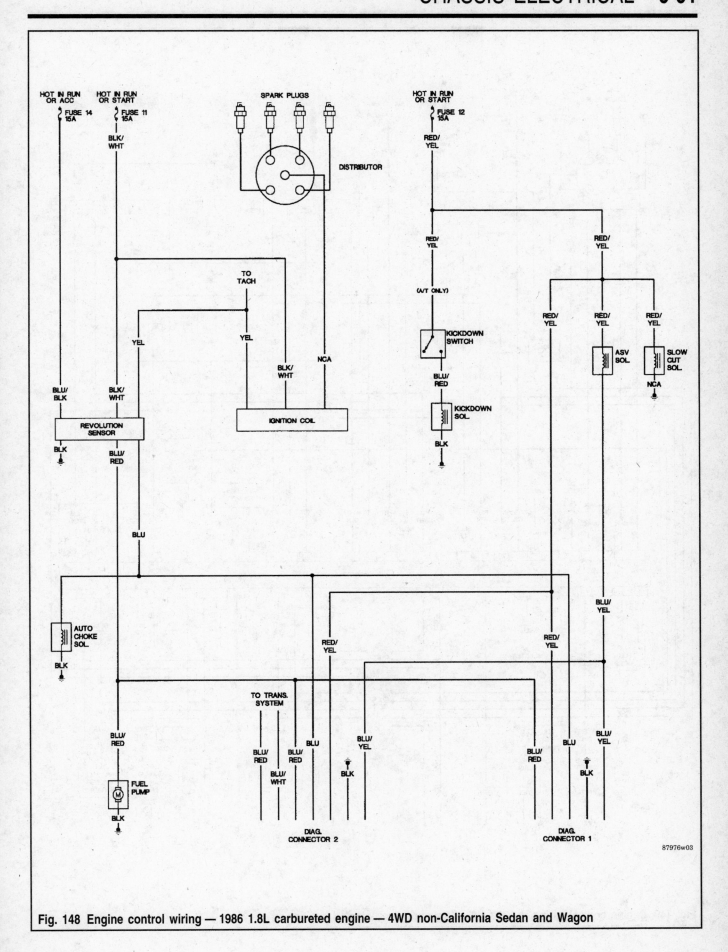

Fig. 148 Engine control wiring — 1986 1.8L carbureted engine — 4WD non-California Sedan and Wagon

87976w03

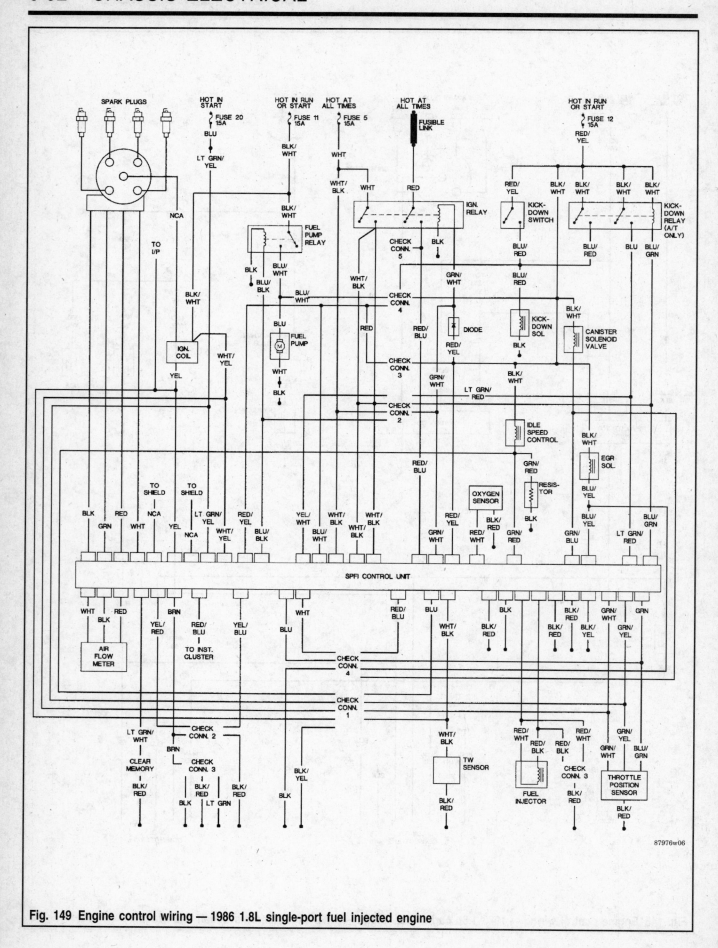

Fig. 149 Engine control wiring — 1986 1.8L single-port fuel injected engine

87976w06

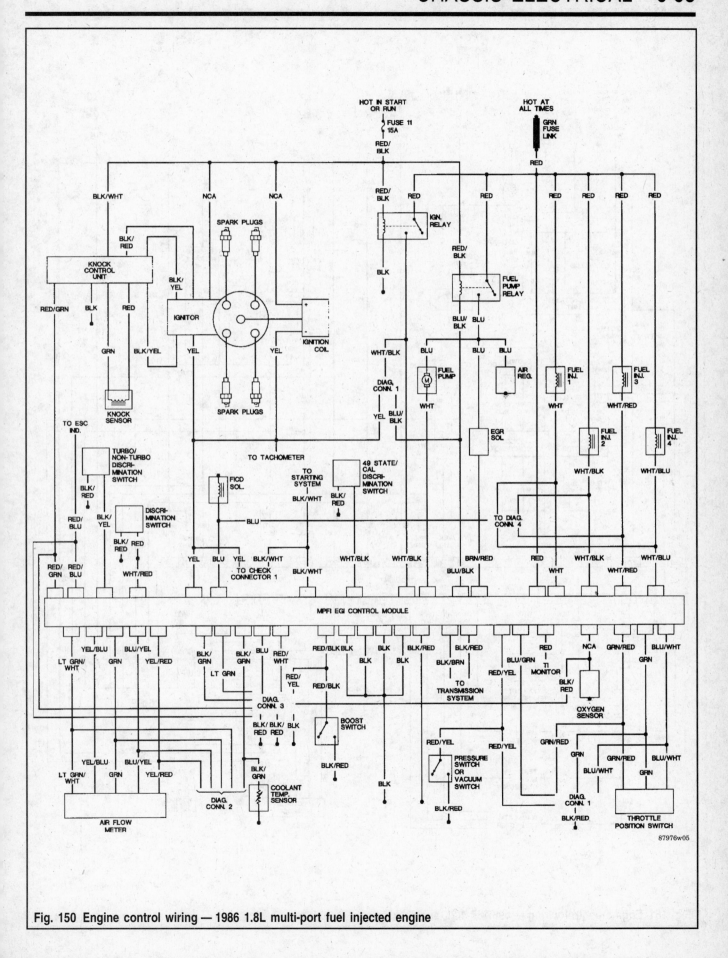

Fig. 150 Engine control wiring — 1986 1.8L multi-port fuel injected engine

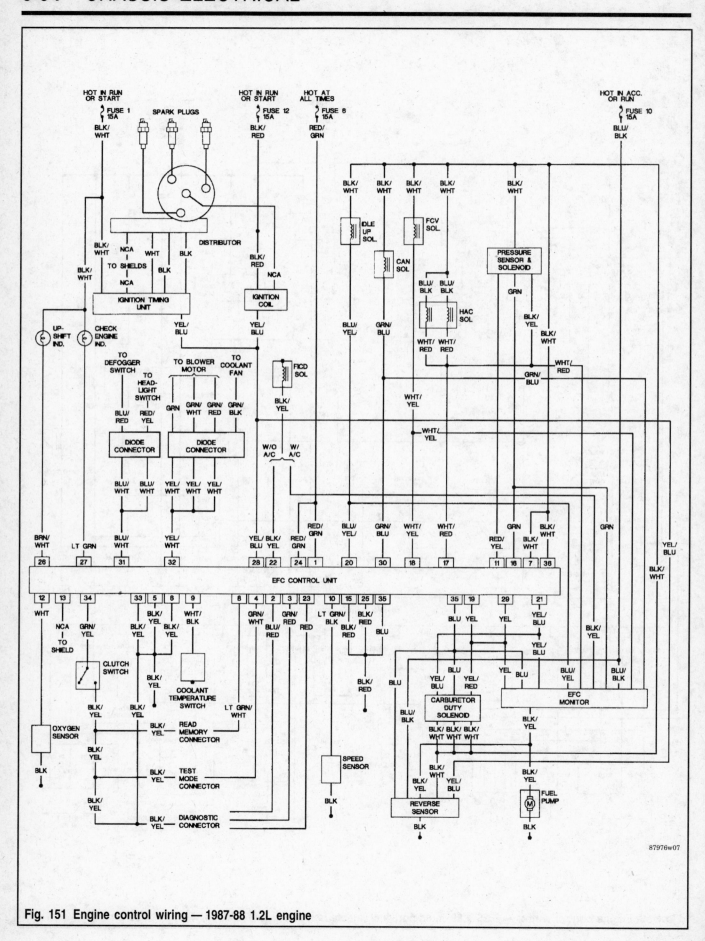

Fig. 151 Engine control wiring — 1987-88 1.2L engine

87976w07

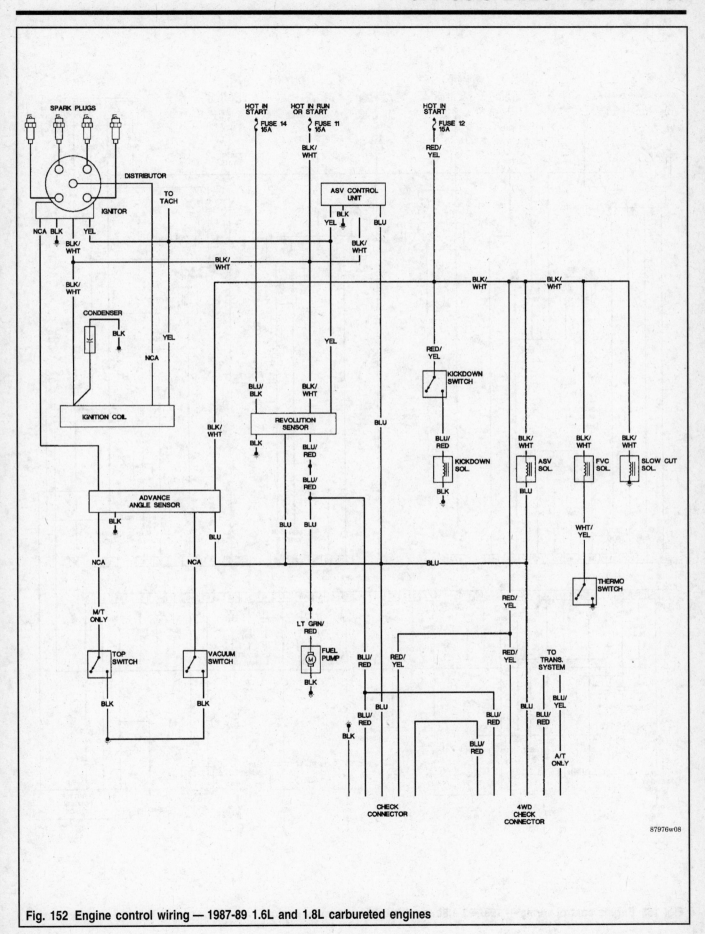

Fig. 152 Engine control wiring — 1987-89 1.6L and 1.8L carbureted engines

87976w08

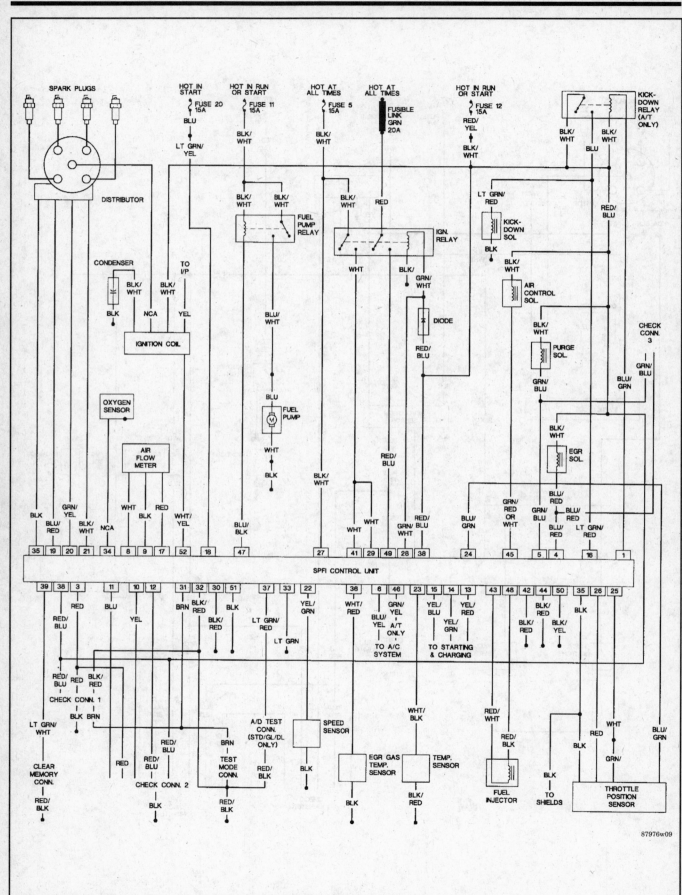

Fig. 153 Engine control wiring — 1987-92 1.8L single-port fuel injected engine

87976w09

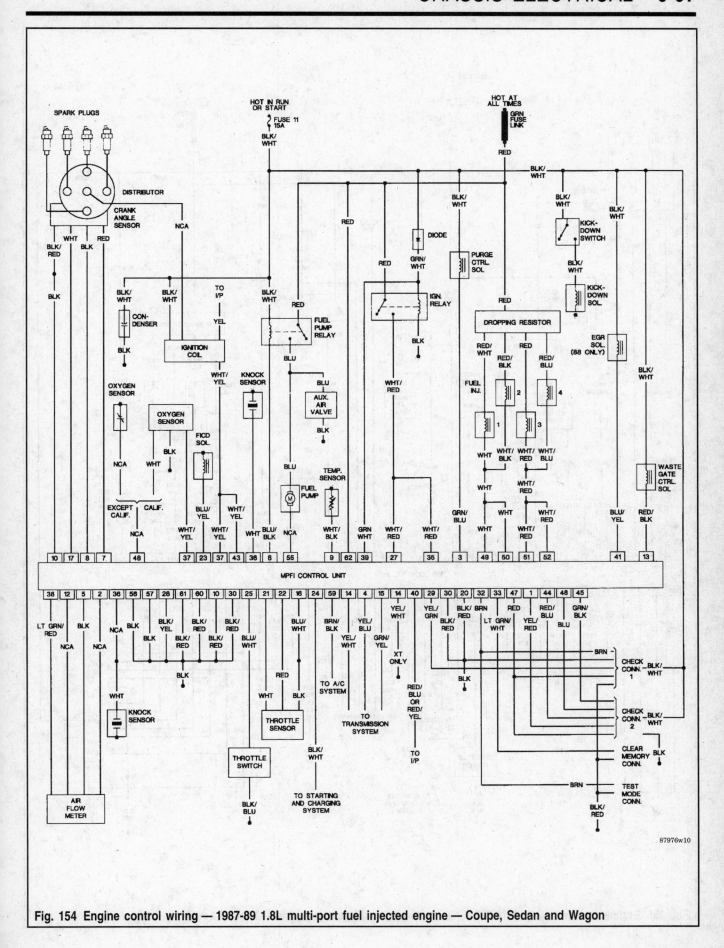

Fig. 154 Engine control wiring — 1987-89 1.8L multi-port fuel injected engine — Coupe, Sedan and Wagon

87976w10

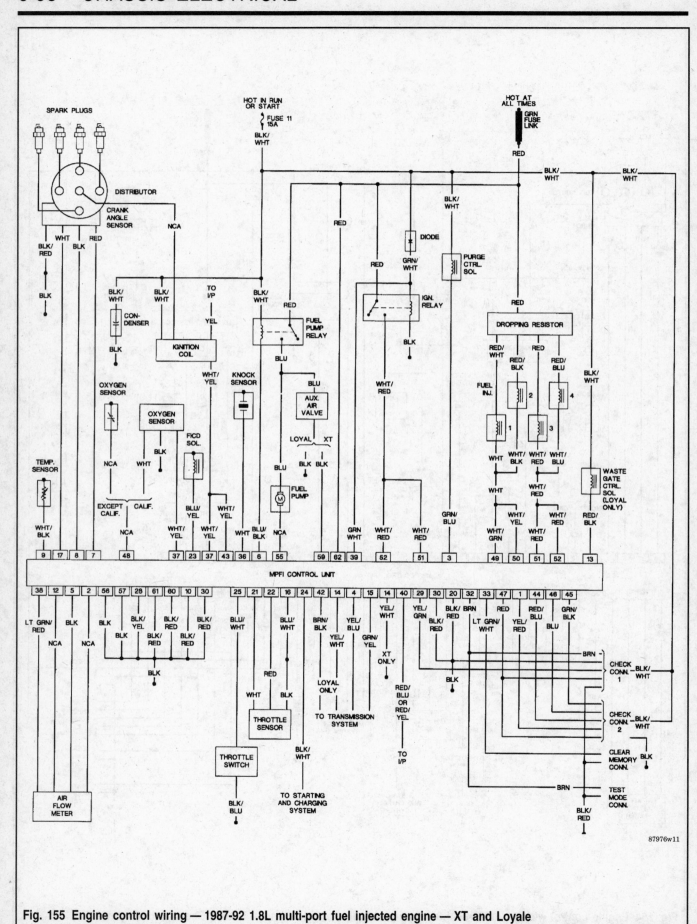

Fig. 155 Engine control wiring — 1987-92 1.8L multi-port fuel injected engine — XT and Loyale

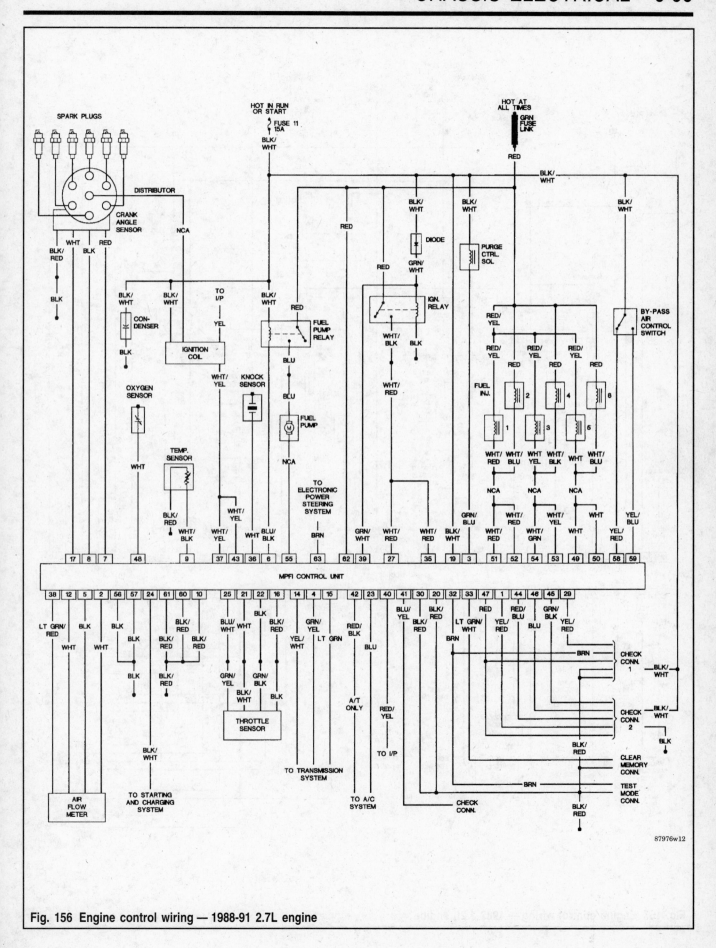

Fig. 156 Engine control wiring — 1988-91 2.7L engine

87976w12

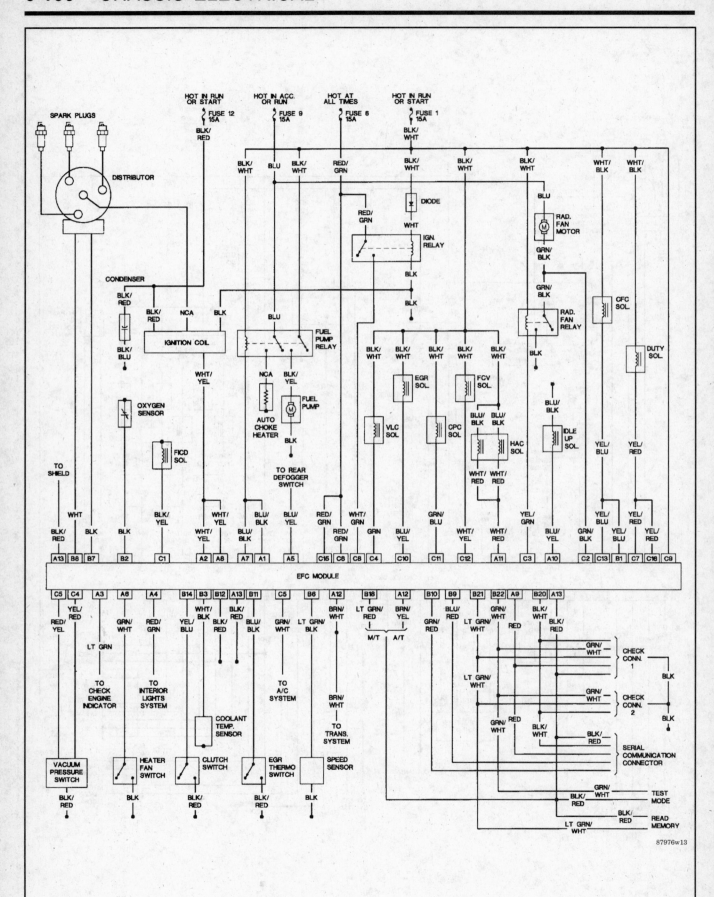

Fig. 157 Engine control wiring — 1989 1.2L engine

87976w13

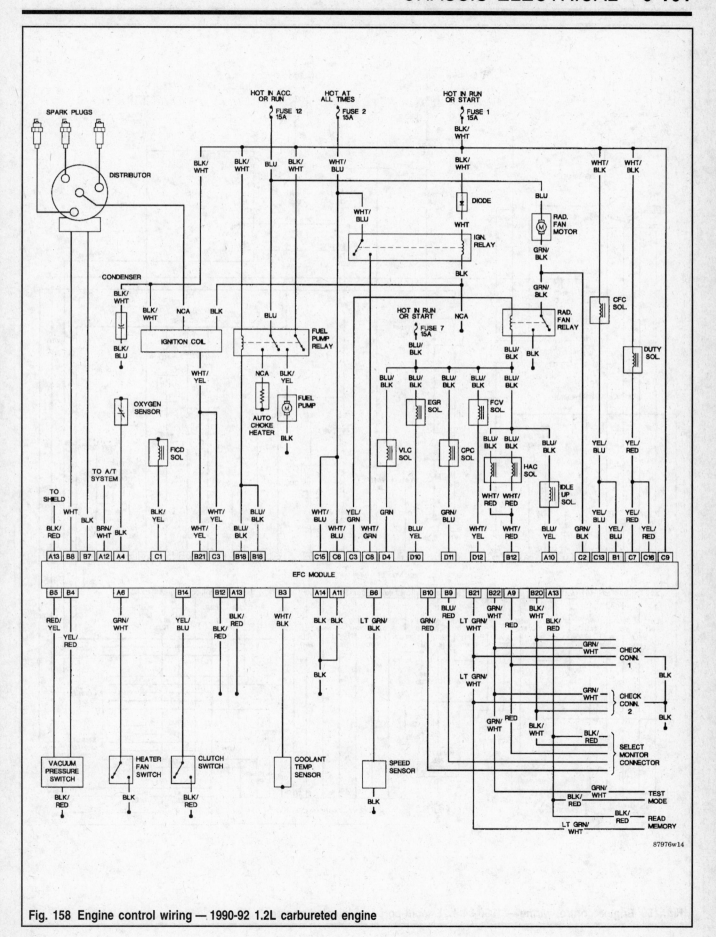

Fig. 158 Engine control wiring — 1990-92 1.2L carbureted engine

87976w14

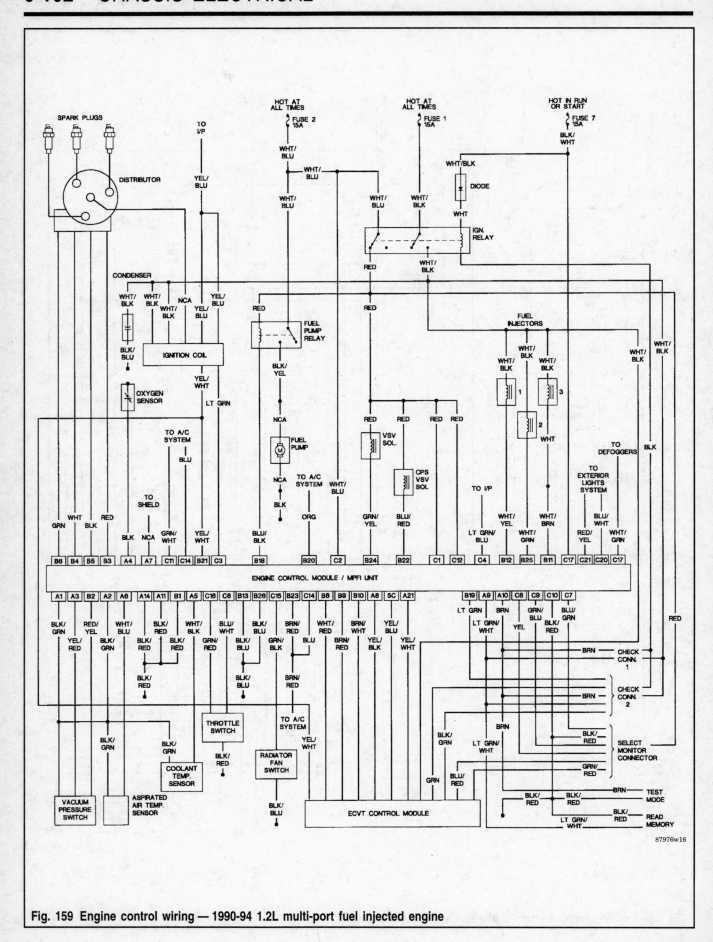

Fig. 159 Engine control wiring — 1990-94 1.2L multi-port fuel injected engine

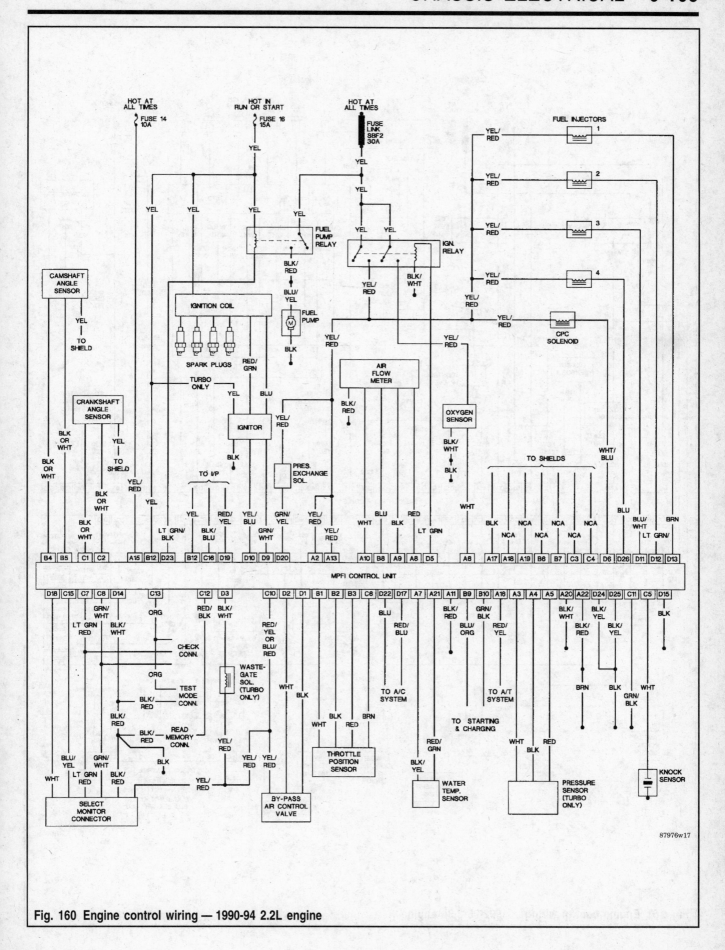

Fig. 160 Engine control wiring — 1990-94 2.2L engine

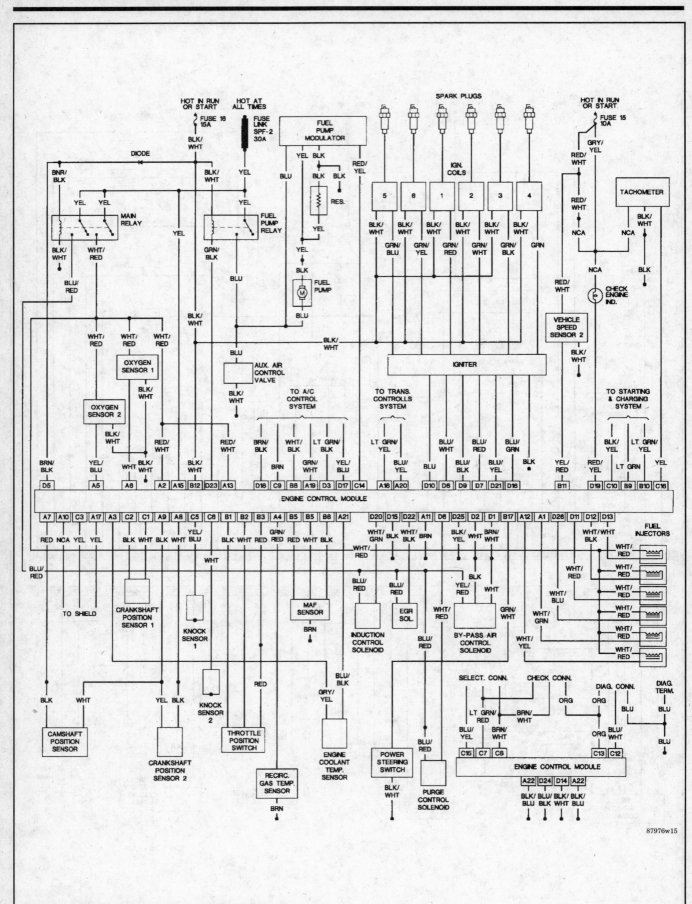

Fig. 161 Engine control wiring — 1992-95 3.3L engine

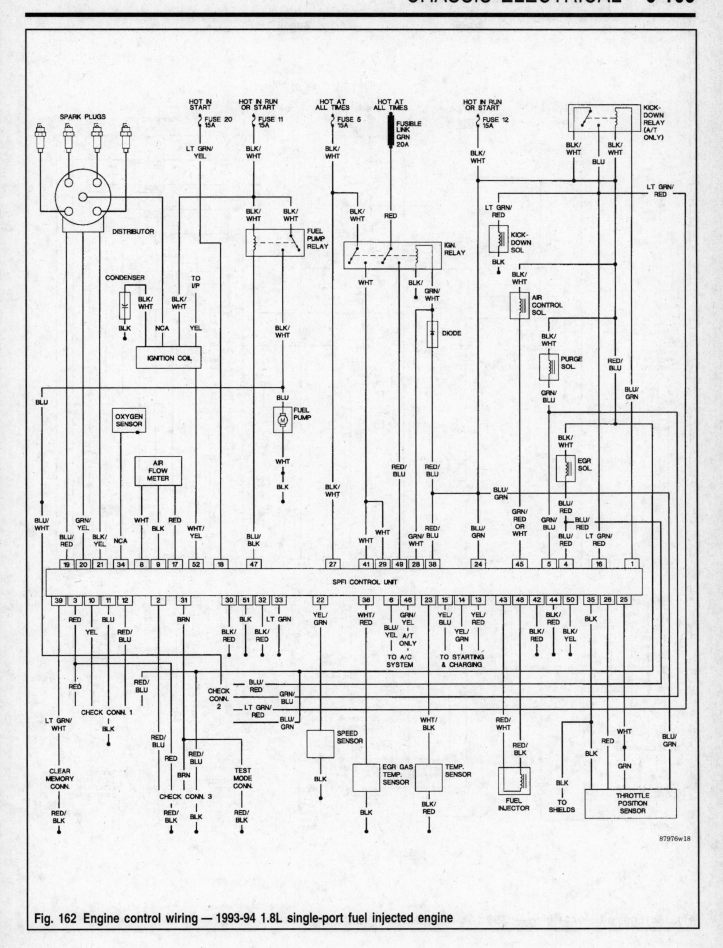

Fig. 162 Engine control wiring — 1993-94 1.8L single-port fuel injected engine

87976w18

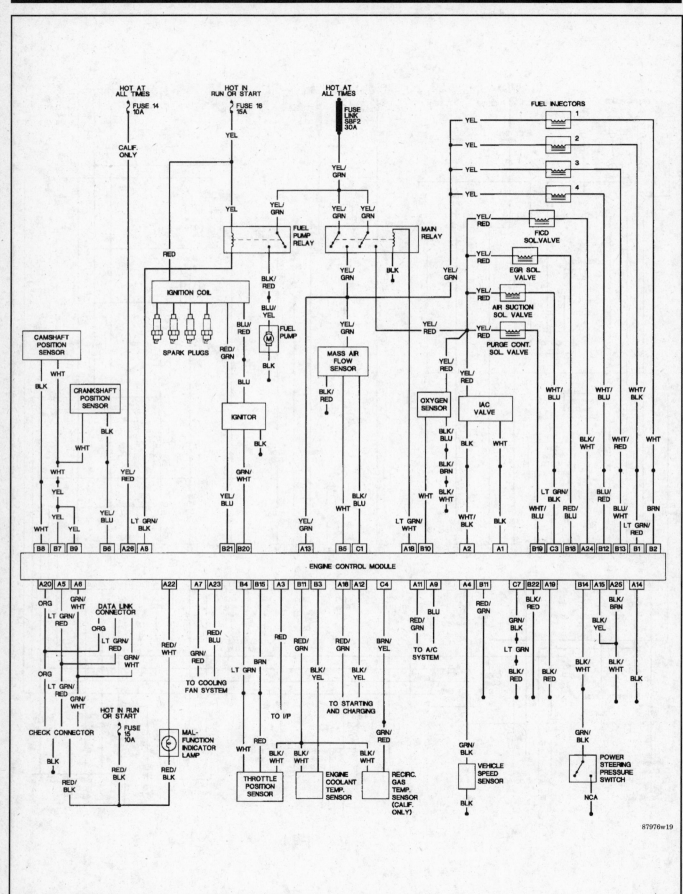

Fig. 163 Engine control wiring — 1993 1.8L multi-port fuel injected engine

87976w19

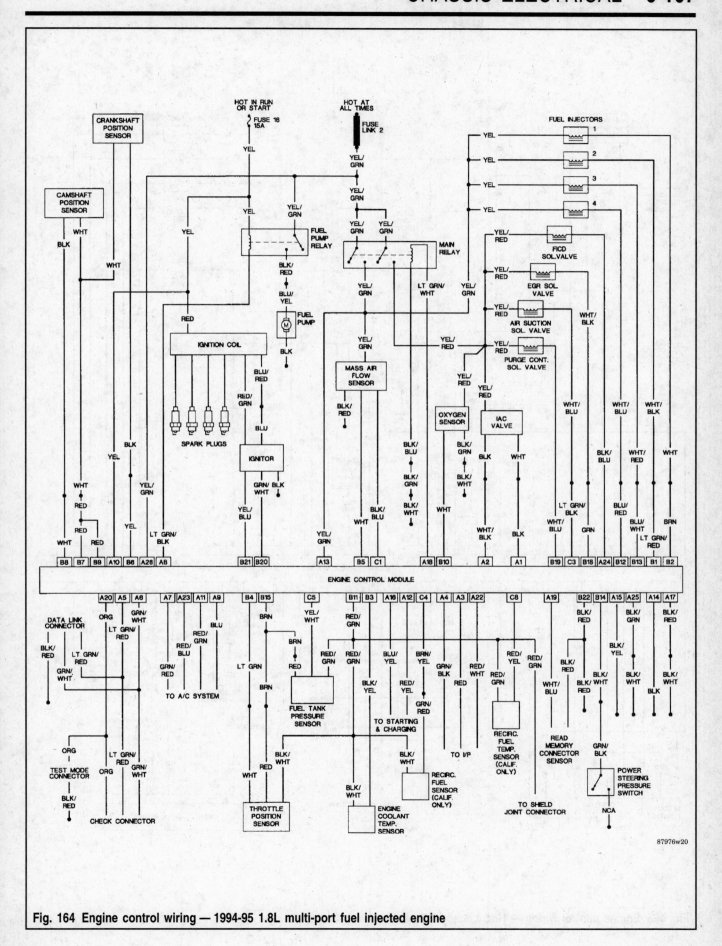

Fig. 164 Engine control wiring — 1994-95 1.8L multi-port fuel injected engine

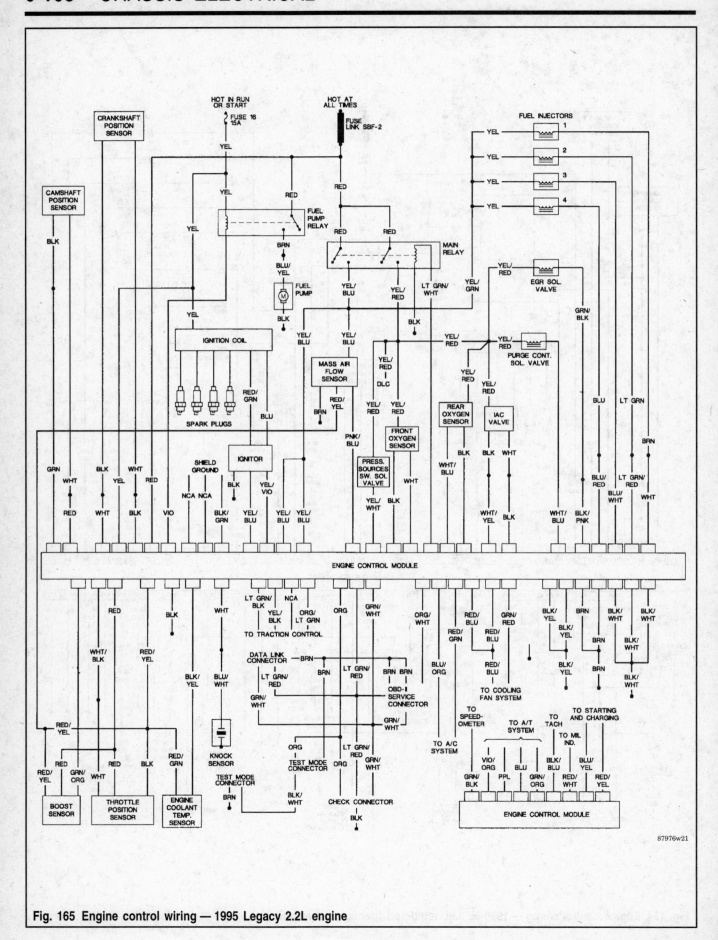

Fig. 165 Engine control wiring — 1995 Legacy 2.2L engine

87976w21

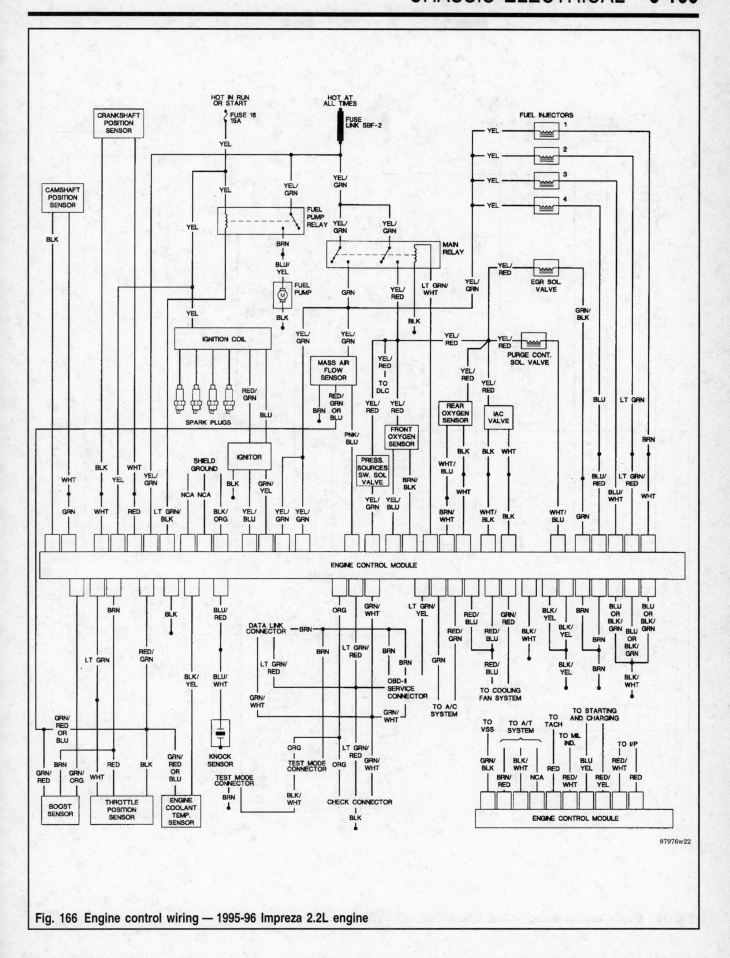

Fig. 166 Engine control wiring — 1995-96 Impreza 2.2L engine

87976w22

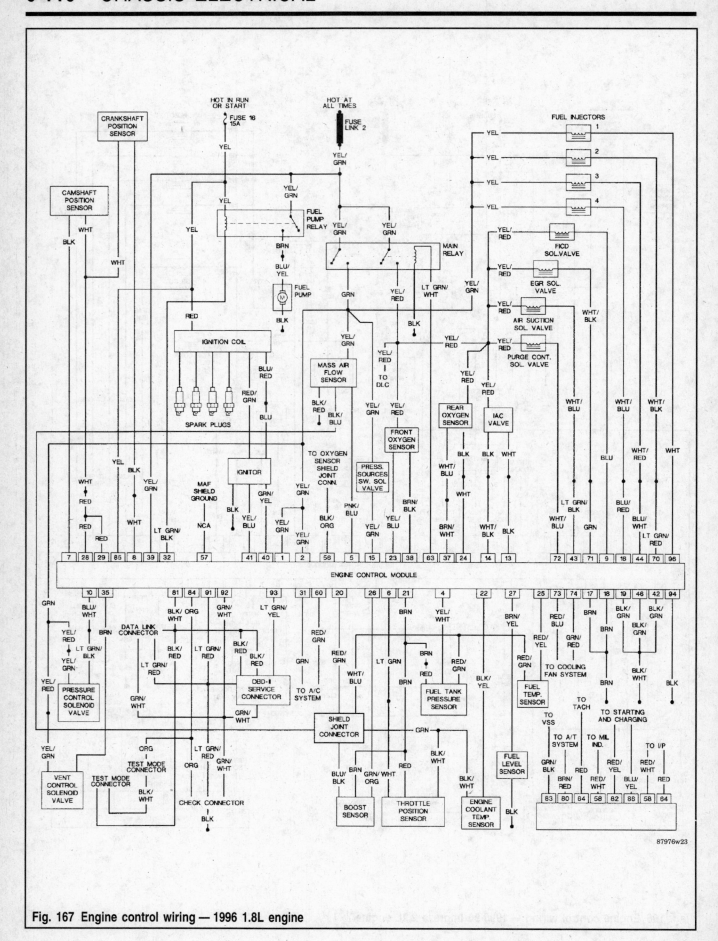

Fig. 167 Engine control wiring — 1996 1.8L engine

87976w23

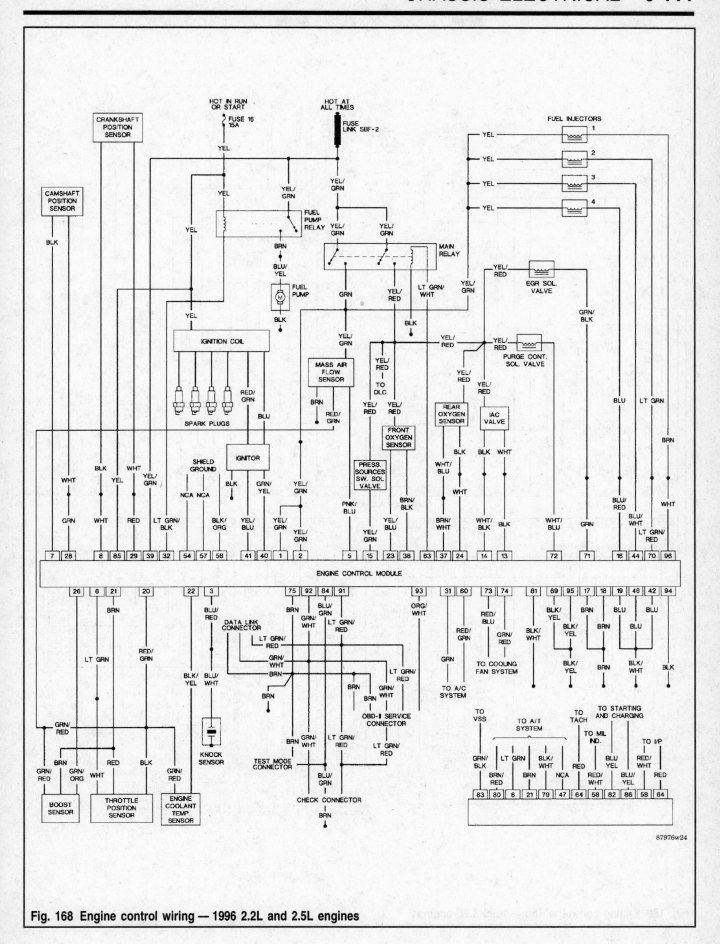

Fig. 168 Engine control wiring — 1996 2.2L and 2.5L engines

87976w24

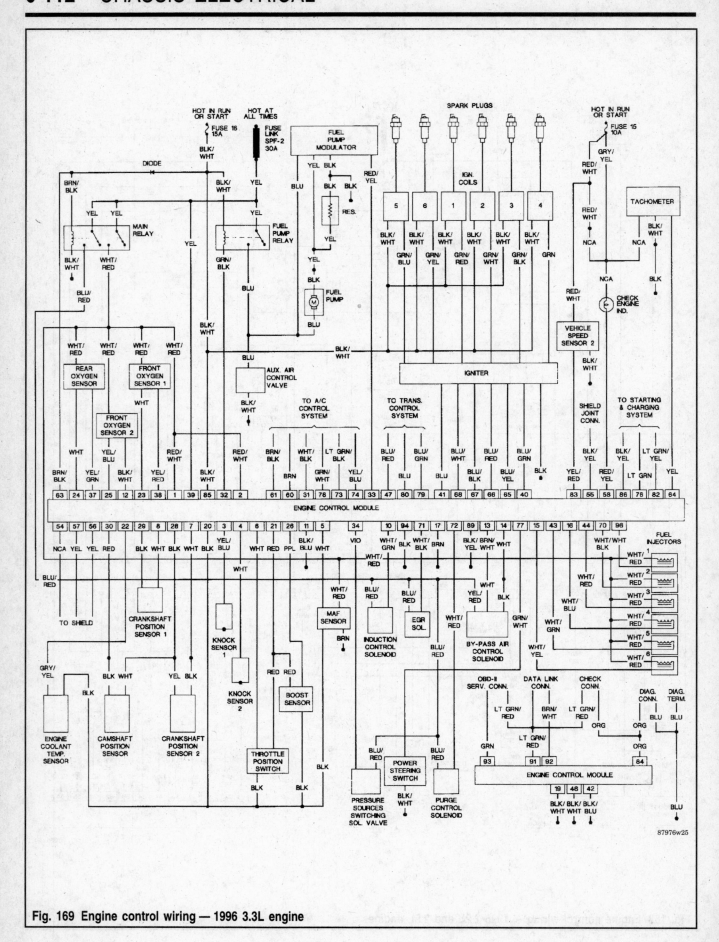

Fig. 169 Engine control wiring — 1996 3.3L engine

87976w25

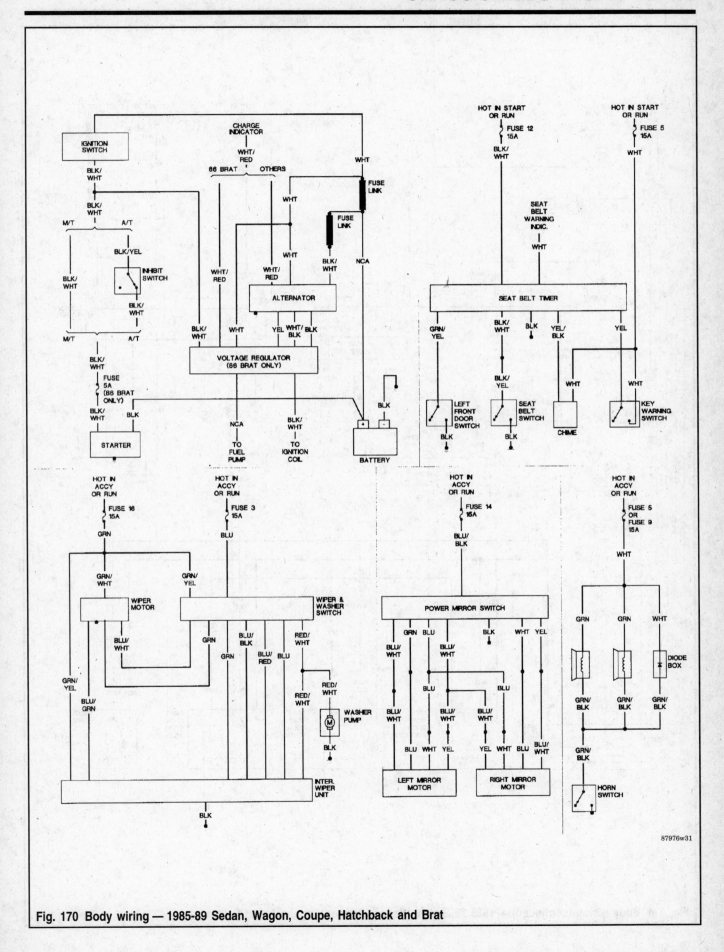

Fig. 170 Body wiring — 1985-89 Sedan, Wagon, Coupe, Hatchback and Brat

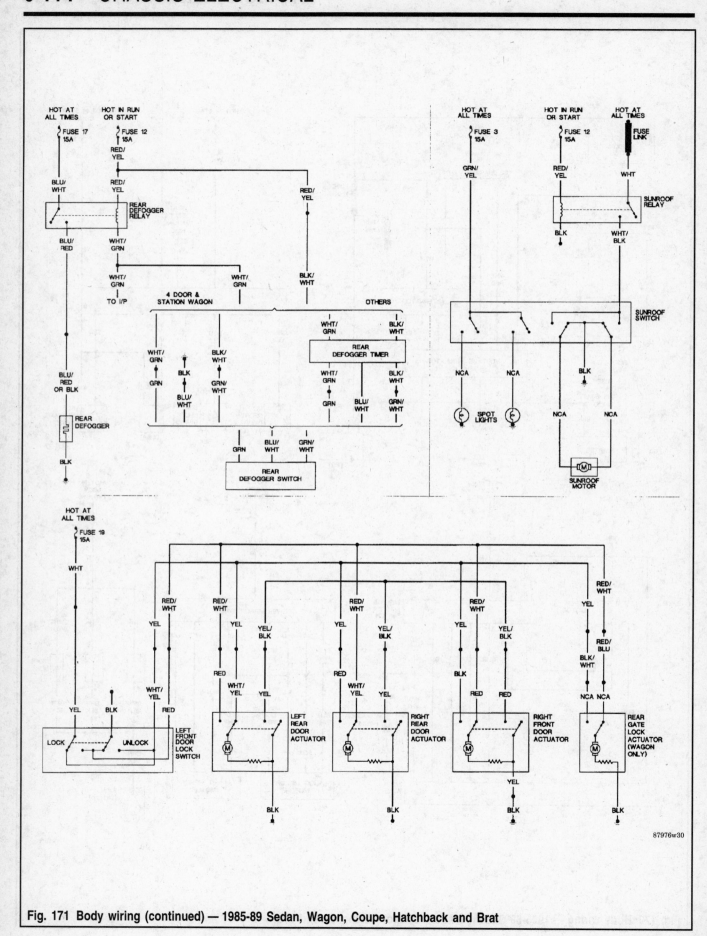

Fig. 171 Body wiring (continued) — 1985-89 Sedan, Wagon, Coupe, Hatchback and Brat

87976w30

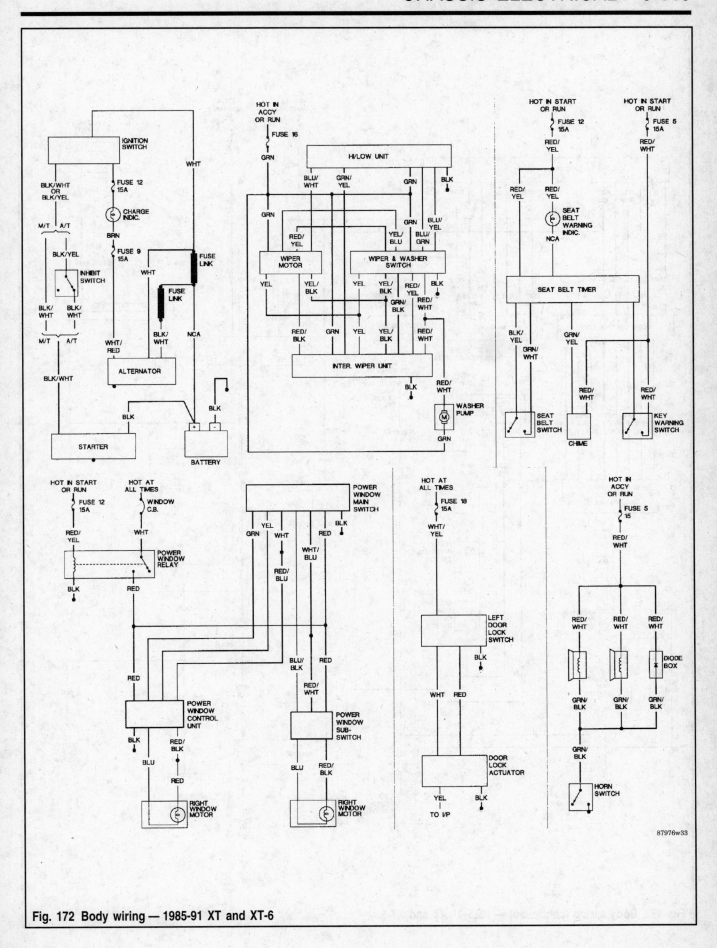

Fig. 172 Body wiring — 1985-91 XT and XT-6

87976w33

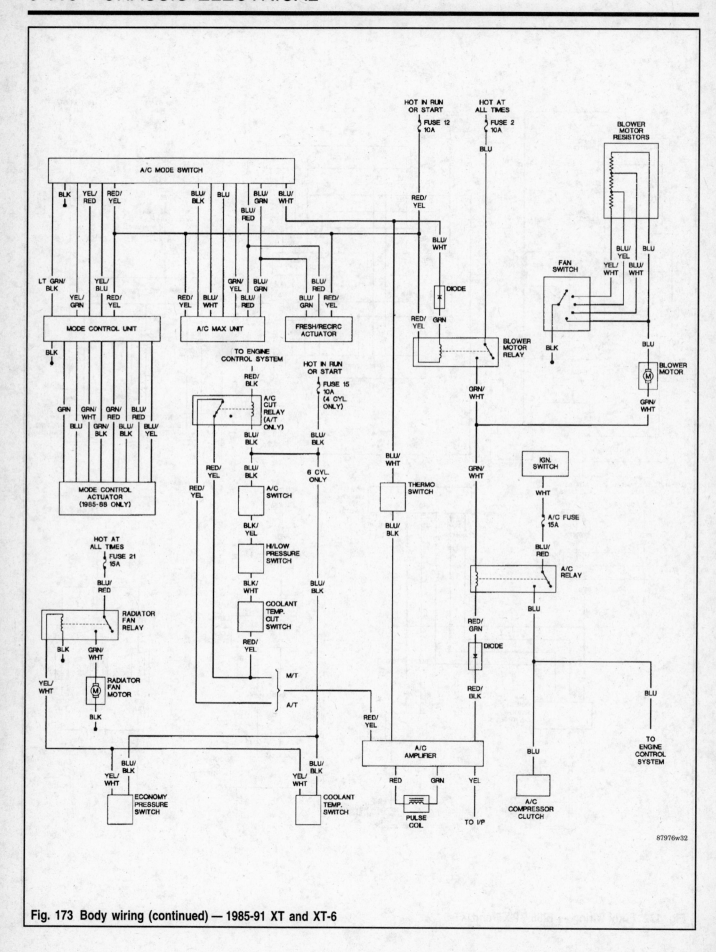

Fig. 173 Body wiring (continued) — 1985-91 XT and XT-6

87976w32

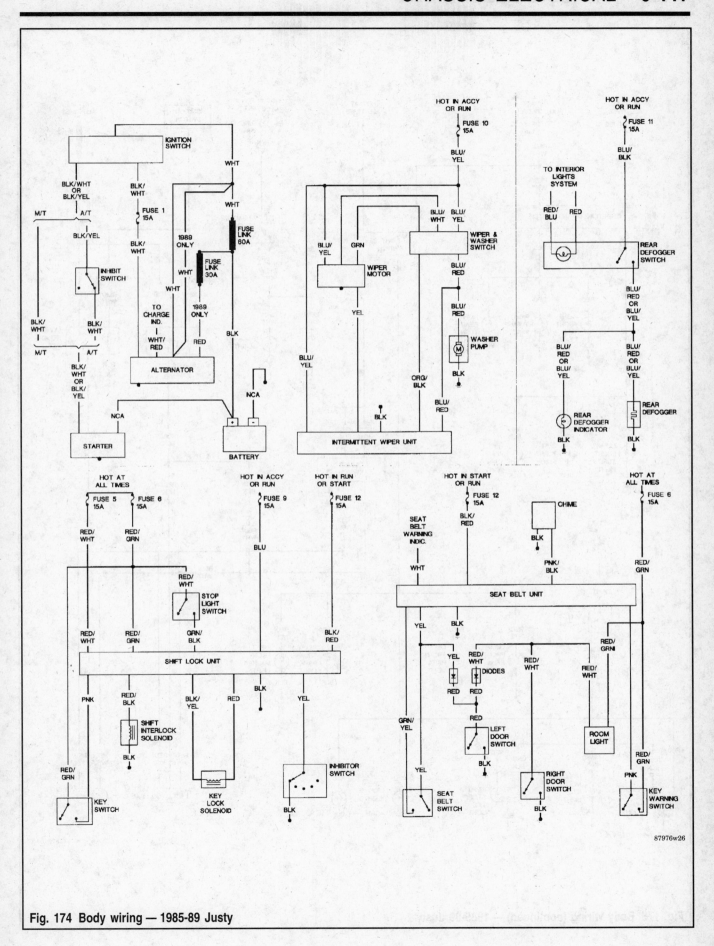

Fig. 174 Body wiring — 1985-89 Justy

87976w26

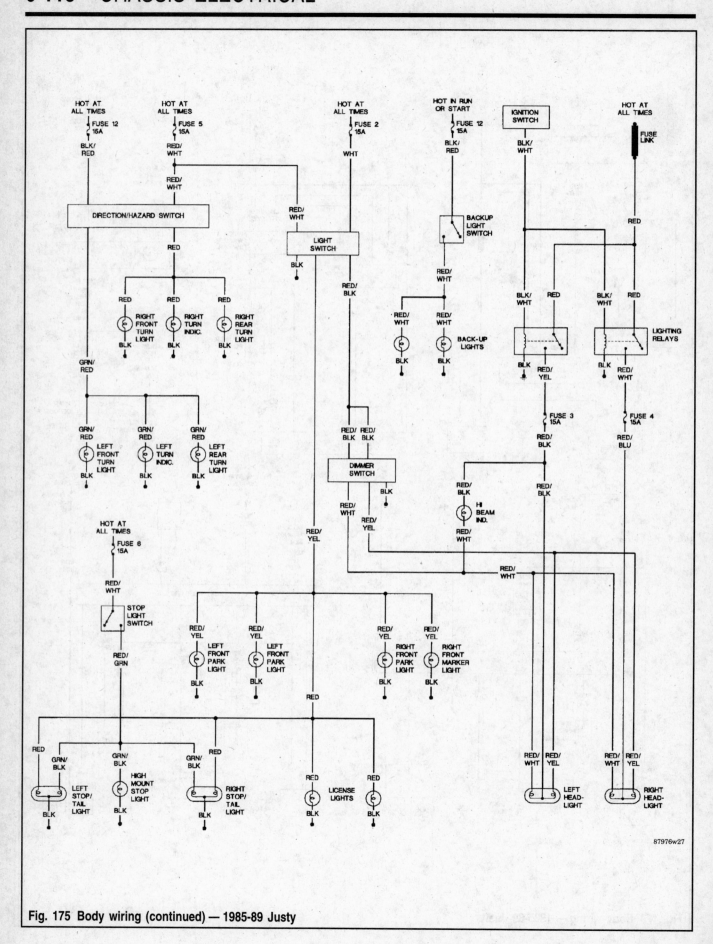

Fig. 175 Body wiring (continued) — 1985-89 Justy

87976w27

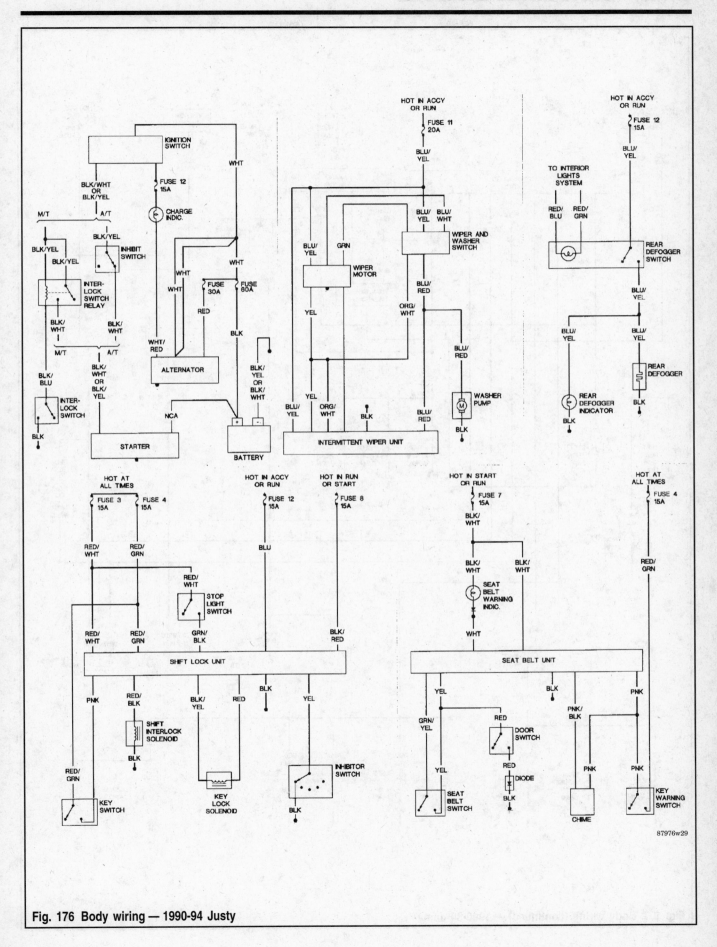

Fig. 176 Body wiring — 1990-94 Justy

87976w29

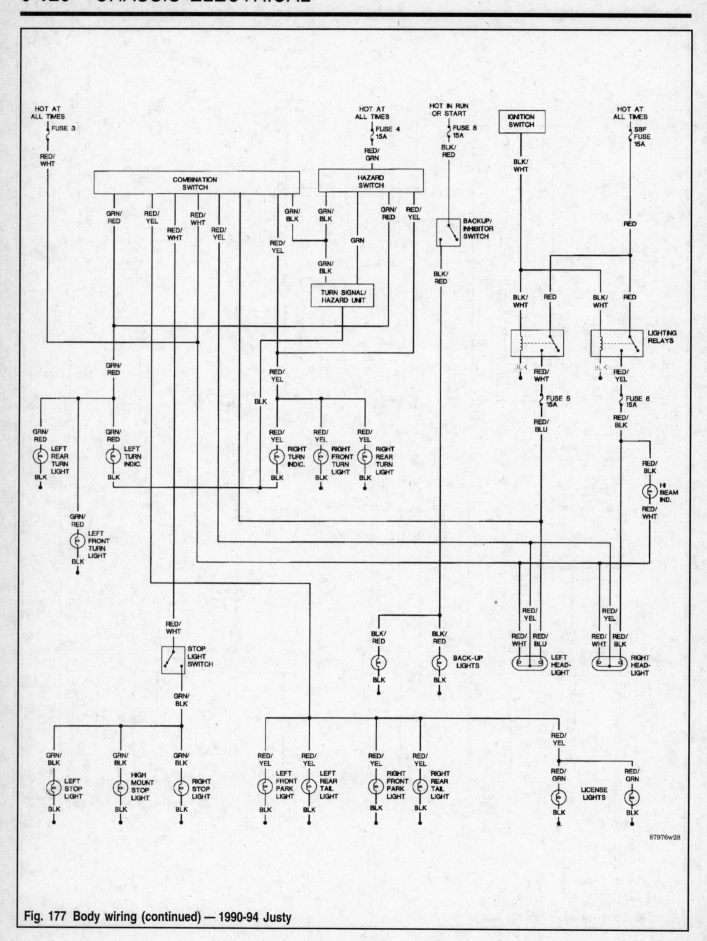

Fig. 177 Body wiring (continued) — 1990-94 Justy

87976w28

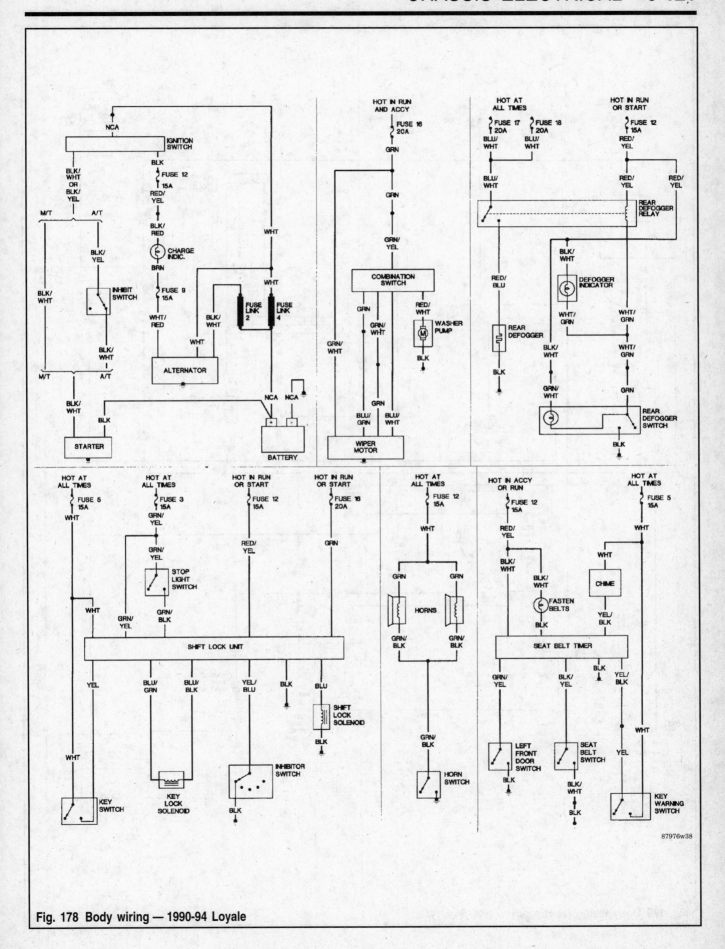

Fig. 178 Body wiring — 1990-94 Loyale

87976w38

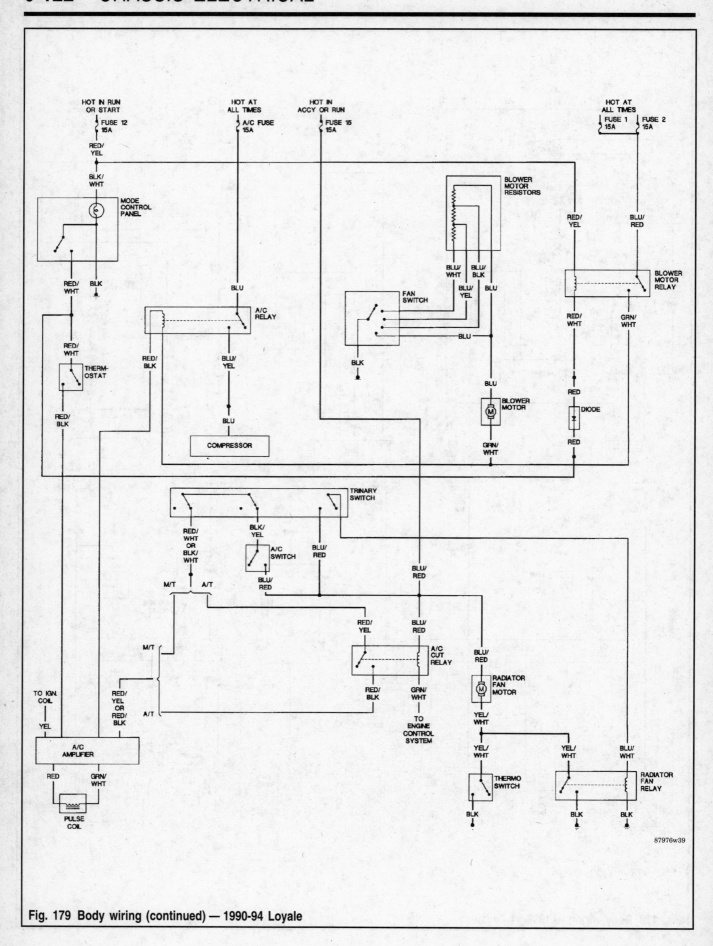

Fig. 179 Body wiring (continued) — 1990-94 Loyale

87976w39

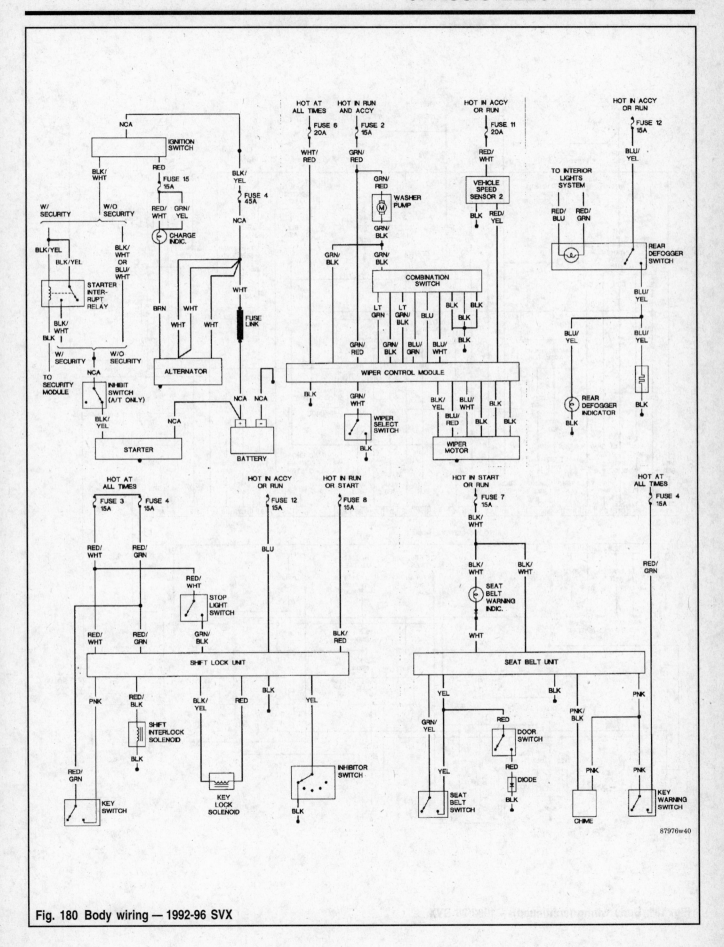

Fig. 180 Body wiring — 1992-96 SVX

87976w40

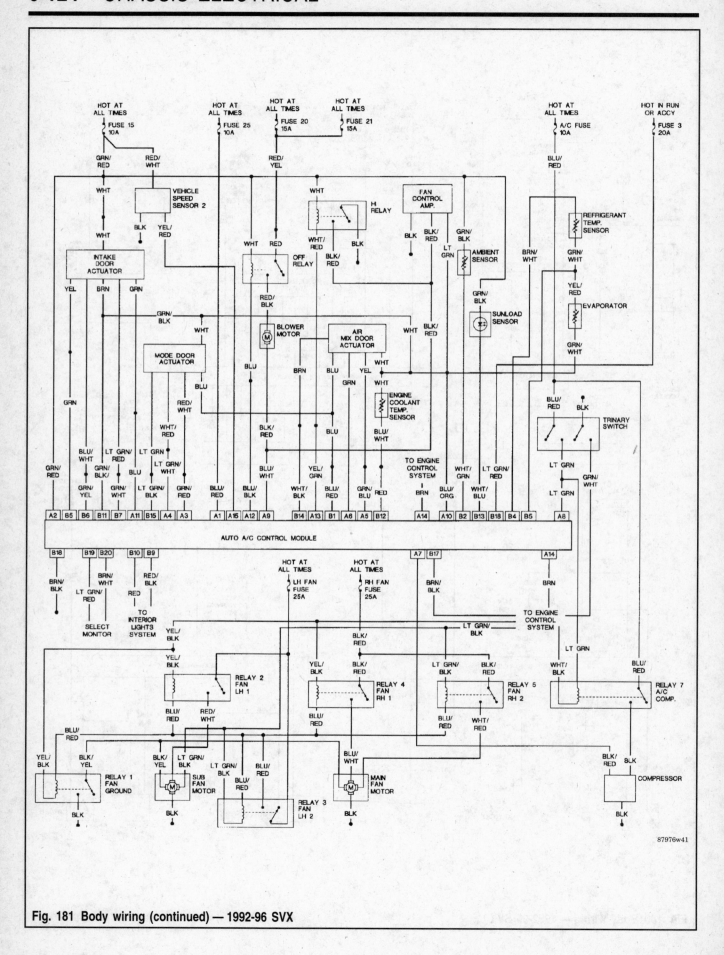

Fig. 181 Body wiring (continued) — 1992-96 SVX

87976w41

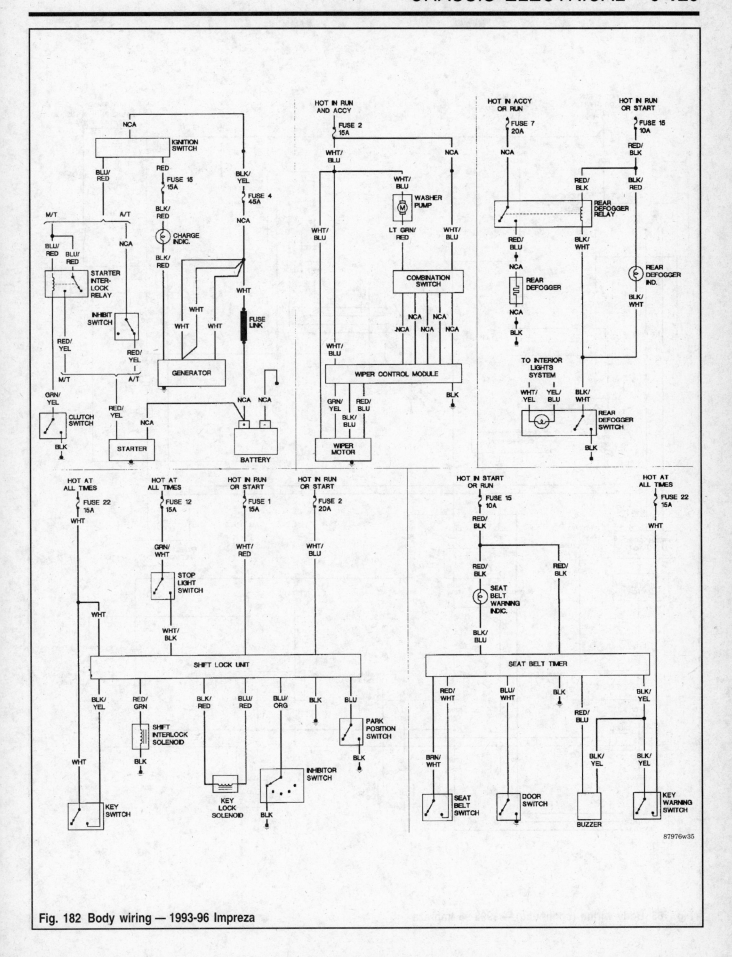

Fig. 182 Body wiring — 1993-96 Impreza

87976w35

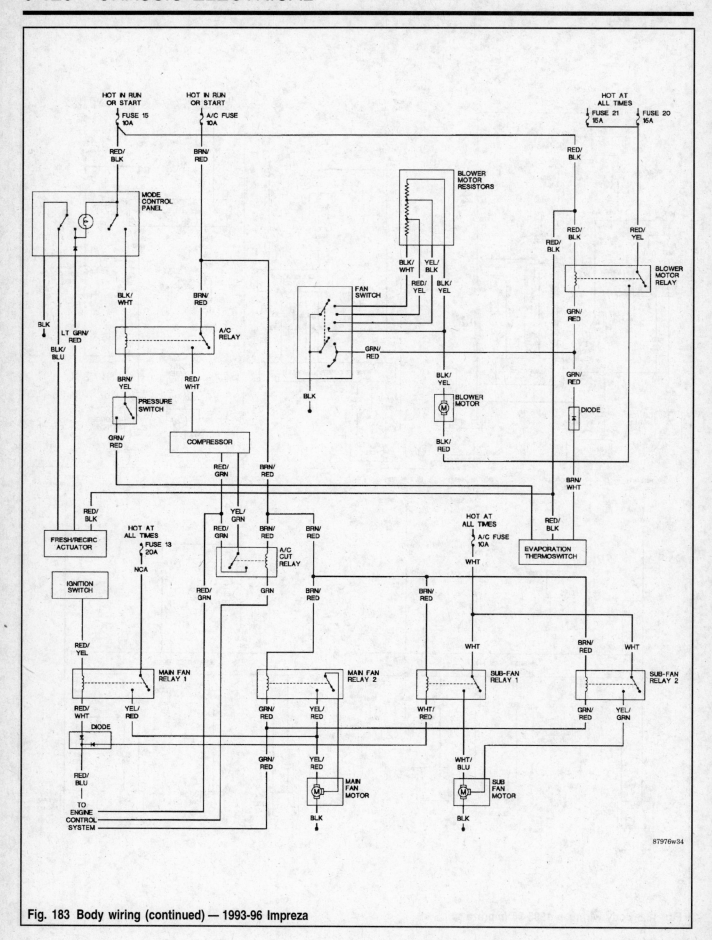

Fig. 183 Body wiring (continued) — 1993-96 Impreza

87976w34

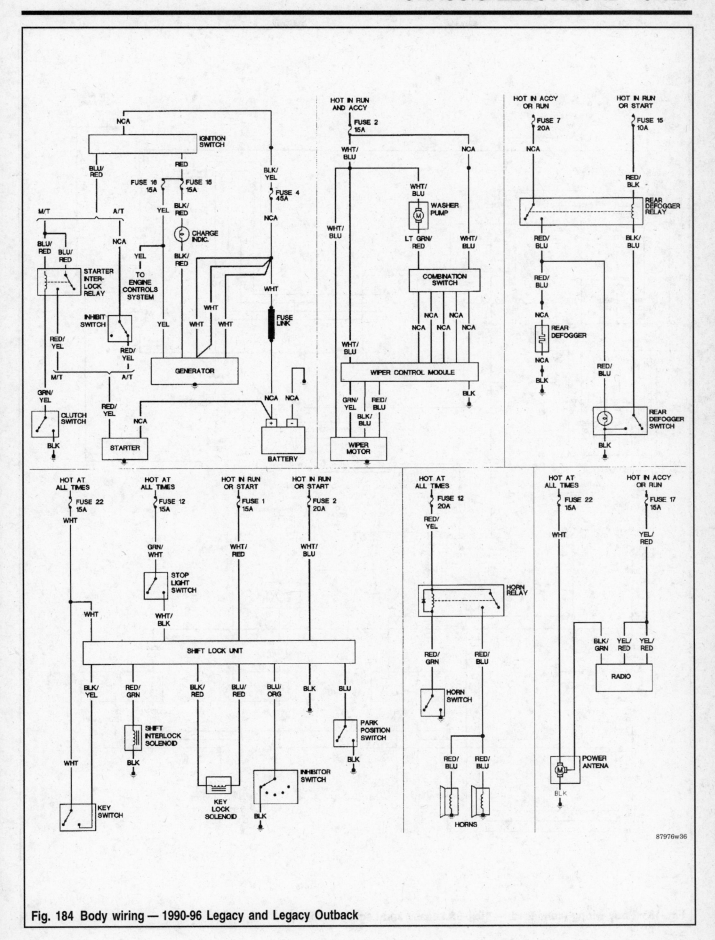

Fig. 184 Body wiring — 1990-96 Legacy and Legacy Outback

87976w36

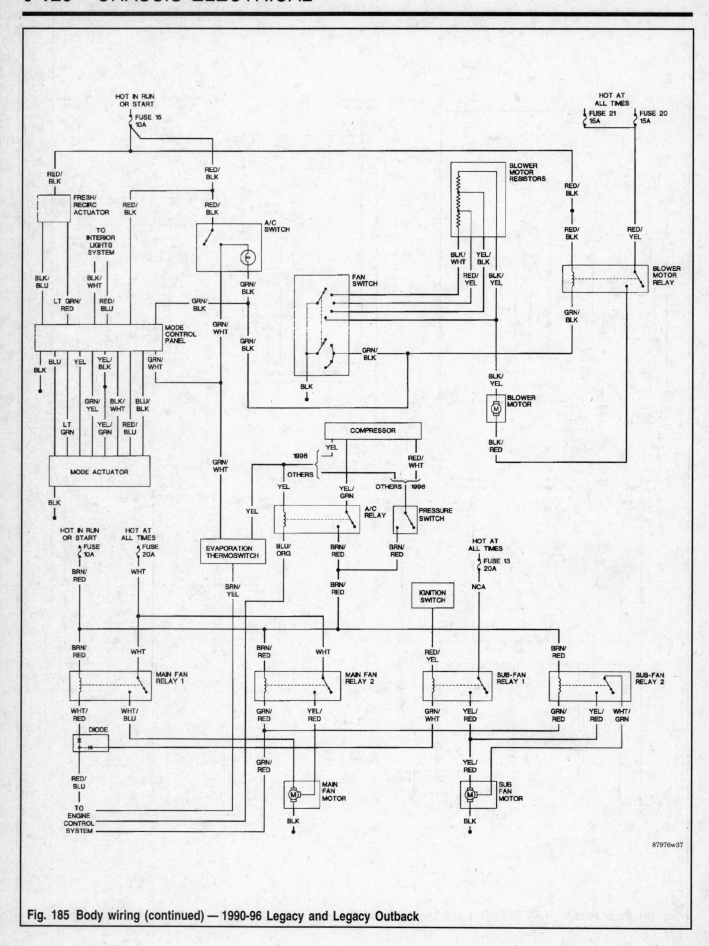

Fig. 185 Body wiring (continued)—1990-96 Legacy and Legacy Outback

87976w37

7

DRIVE

TRAIN

MANUAL TRANSAXLE

Understanding Manual Transaxles

▶ **See Figure 1**

Because of the way an internal combustion engine breathes, it can produce torque, or twisting force, only within a narrow speed range. Most modern, overhead valve pushrod engines must turn at about 2500 rpm to produce their peak torque. By 4500 rpm they are producing so little torque that continued increases in engine speed produce no power increases. The torque peak on overhead camshaft engines is generally much higher, but much narrower.

The manual transaxle and clutch are employed to vary the relationship between engine speed and the speed of the wheels so that adequate engine power can be produced under all circumstances. The clutch allows engine torque to be applied to the transaxle input shaft gradually, due to mechanical slippage. Consequently, the vehicle may be started smoothly from a full stop. The transaxle changes the ratio between the rotating speeds of the engine and the wheels by the use of gears. The gear ratios allow full engine power to be applied to the wheels during acceleration at low speeds and at highway/passing speeds.

In a front wheel drive transaxle, power is usually transmitted from the input shaft to a mainshaft or output shaft located slightly beneath and to the side of the input shaft. The gears of the mainshaft mesh with gears on the input shaft, allowing power to be carried from one to the other. All forward gears are in constant mesh and are free from rotating with the shaft unless the synchronizer and clutch is engaged. Shifting from one gear to the next causes one of the gears to be freed from rotating with the shaft and locks another to it. Gears are locked and unlocked by internal dog clutches which slide between the center of the gear and the shaft. The forward gears employ synchronizers; friction members which smoothly bring

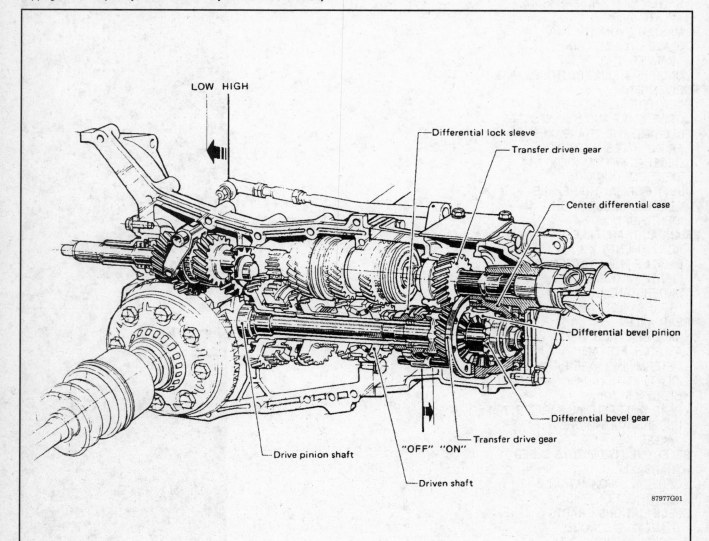

Fig. 1 Cross-sectional view of a typical 4WD transaxle — 1800 series Subaru

87977G01

gear and shaft to the same speed before the toothed dog clutches are engaged.

Identification

Each of the Subaru transaxles can be identified by locating the number on the transaxle housing. For application of the individual transaxles, refer to the procedures in this section.

Adjustments

LINKAGE

Standard Transaxle (Including 4WD)

There are no adjustments that can be made on the shift linkage for standard transaxles or for the rear drive system. If you experience looseness or too much play in shifting, it is a sign of worn parts, which should be replaced.

CLUTCH SWITCH

Except Justy
▶ See Figure 2

This switch is threaded into the clutch pedal bracket and is retained in position by an adjustment nut and a locknut.

With the clutch pedal depressed, measure the clutch switch contact pin length. It should extend 0.197-0.256 in. (5-6.5mm). If not, loosen the locknut and adjust the adjustment nut until the correct length is achieved.

Justy
▶ See Figure 3

This switch is attached to the side of the clutch pedal bracket and retained in place by 2 screws.

Check the clutch pedal free-play. It should be between 1.06-1.30 in. (26-33mm). If not, adjust free-play to specification and then adjust the switch by moving the switch mounting bracket. Ensure that the clutch switch activates when the pedal is depressed 1.06-1.30 in. (26-33mm).

Back-up Light Switch

REMOVAL & INSTALLATION

▶ See Figure 4

This switch is threaded into the side of the transaxle extension housing on 2WD and 4WD transaxles.
1. Disconnect the negative battery cable.
2. Raise and safely support the vehicle.
3. Unplug the electrical connector from the harness. Use an open end wrench to remove the switch.
To install:
4. Install a new switch and tighten to 17-20 ft. lbs. (23-26 Nm). Engage the electrical connector.

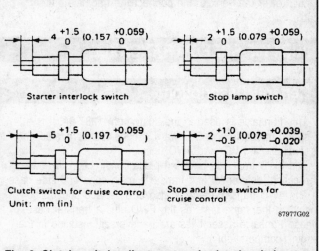
Fig. 2 Clutch switch adjustment and related switches — except Justy

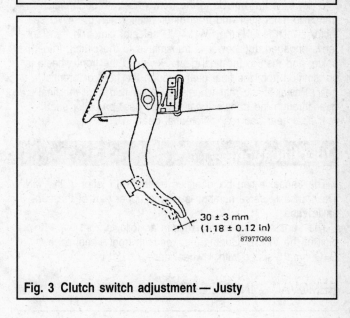
Fig. 3 Clutch switch adjustment — Justy

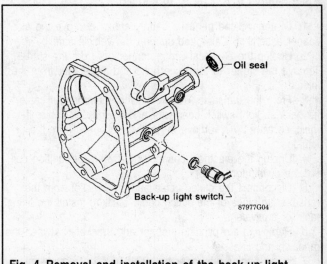
Fig. 4 Removal and installation of the back-up light switch — 4WD manual transaxle shown

5. Lower the vehicle and connect the negative battery cable.

JUSTY 5-SPEED TRANSAXLE

General Description

This transaxle is used in the Justy from 1987-94. It is a 5-speed transaxle with 5 forward speeds and 1 reverse gear. It is available in FWD and 4WD units.

The FWD transaxle is of a 1-piece construction. It houses the clutch, deferential and transaxle main case and side case.

The 4WD transaxle axle is also of a 1-piece construction including the same units as the FWD plus a transfer case. These transaxle assemblies are transversely installed in the engine compartment.

The 4WD operates as follows: when the 4WD switch is OFF, the FWD/4WD selector clutch in the transfer is disengaged, and power is transmitted to the front wheels through clutch transaxle, final gear and front differential. When the 4WD selector switch is ON, the FWD/4WD selector clutch in the transfer is engaged and power is transmitted to the clutch, transaxle, and then to the final gear. Power to the front wheels is transmitted from the final gear through the front differential gear. Power to the rear wheels is transmitted from the final gear through the transfer gear, hypoid gear propeller shaft, rear final gear and rear differential gear.

Identification

The transaxle can be identified by the 11th letter in the VIN. The transaxle serial number is on the upper part of the transaxle case.

The transaxle can be determined as follows from the 11th digit of the VIN: B=Gunma 5-speed with front wheel drive, G=Gunma 5-speed with 4 wheel drive.

REMOVAL & INSTALLATION

▶ See Figures 5, 6, 7, 8, 9, 10 and 11

1. Disconnect the negative battery cable. Remove the air cleaner assembly. Raise and support the vehicle safely.
2. Unplug the electrical wiring connectors from the starter. Remove the starter to transaxle bolts and the starter from the vehicle.
3. From the transaxle, disconnect the speedometer cable, the back-up light switch connector and the ground cable. If equipped with 4WD, remove the activation hoses from the actuator.
4. Unplug the electrical connector between the ignition coil and the distributor.
5. Disconnect the clutch cable and the bracket from the transaxle. In place of the clutch cable bracket, install the lifting hook, or equivalent.
6. Removing the pitching stopper and brackets between the transaxle and chassis.
7. Install engine supporter tool 921540000 or equivalent.
8. Install the vertical hoist to T000100 transaxle lifting hook and raise the transaxle slightly.

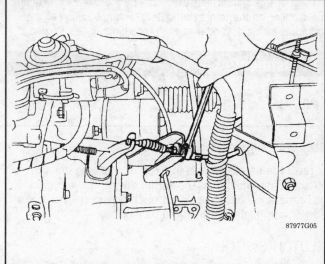

Fig. 5 Disconnecting the clutch cable at the transaxle

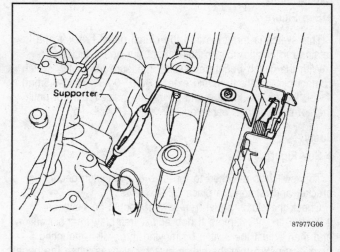

Fig. 6 Supporting the front of the engine using an engine support tool

9. From under the vehicle, remove the under covers.
10. Disconnect the rear exhaust pipe from the front exhaust pipe and the vehicle.
11. Remove the center crossmember to engine/transaxle assembly bolts.
12. Using a pin punch and a hammer, drive out the axle shaft to driveshaft spring pin. Discard the spring pin and separate the axle shaft.
13. Remove the transaxle mounting bracket.
14. Disconnect the gearshift rod and stay from the transaxle.
15. Properly support the engine assembly. Remove the transaxle to engine bolts.
16. Using the vertical hoist, lift the transaxle from the vehicle.

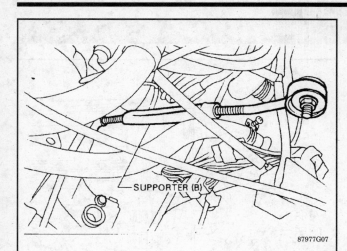

Fig. 7 Supporting the side of the engine using an engine support tool

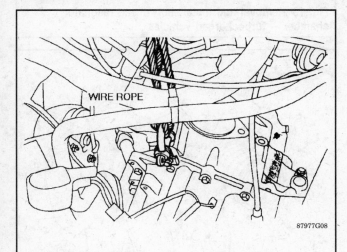

Fig. 8 Raising the transaxle up slightly using a steel cable, engine hook and hoist

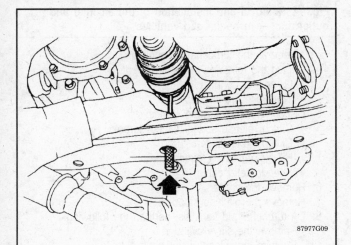

Fig. 9 Disconnecting the halfshaft from the transaxle — removing the roll pin

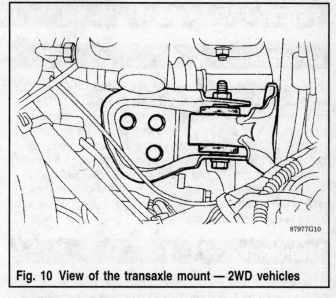

Fig. 10 View of the transaxle mount — 2WD vehicles

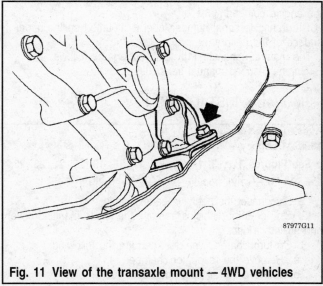

Fig. 11 View of the transaxle mount — 4WD vehicles

To install:

17. Install the transaxle assembly in the vehicle and install the transaxle-to-engine bolts. Install the gearshift rods on the transaxle.

18. Join the axle shaft and the differential. Install a new axle shaft spring pin. Install the center crossmember and tighten bolts to 27-49 ft. lbs. (37-67 Nm). Tighten the center rubber cushion to 20-35 ft. lbs. (27-47 Nm).

19. Install the rear exhaust pipe, engine under covers, pitching stopper and brackets, clutch cable, electrical connectors, speedometer cable, 4WD activation hoses, starter wires and starter-to-transaxle bolts.

20. Tighten the pitching bracket-to-frame bolts to 31-46 ft. lbs. (42-62 Nm). Tighten the pitching bracket-to-engine bolts to 13-23 ft. lbs. (18-31 Nm).

21. Lower the vehicle, connect the negative battery cable, check the transaxle fluid and test drive the vehicle.

5-SPEED FWD TRANSAXLE

General Information

This transaxle is used in the 1993-96 Impreza, 1990-96 Legacy, 1990-94 Loyale, 1985-89 STD., and 1985-91 XT. The Front Wheel Drive (FWD) transaxle has 5 forward speeds and 1 reverse gear. It utilizes a floor shift lever design for gear selection. All forward gears are provided with synchromesh mechanisms that utilize inertia lock-key designs. The transaxle is unitized with the differential and is housed in an aluminum case that is unitized with the clutch housing. The aluminum case is divided into left and right halves. This transaxle is used in front wheel drive only applications.

Identification

The transaxle can be identified by the 11th letter in the vehicle identification number located on the bulkhead panel of the engine compartment.

The transaxle serial number label is mounted on the upper surface of the main case.

The manual transaxle 11th letter code is as follows: B=Gunma 5-speed manual transaxle.

REMOVAL & INSTALLATION

1990-94 Legacy

▶ See Figures 12, 13, 14, 15, 16, 17, 18, 19, 20, 21, 22, 23, 24, 25, 26, 27, 28, 29, 30, 31, 32, 33, 34, 35 and 36

1. Disconnect the negative battery cable.
2. On non-turbo vehicles, remove the intake manifold cover and air intake duct.
3. On turbocharged vehicles, perform the following:
   a. Remove the resonator chamber.
   b. Remove the air inlet and outlet ducts.

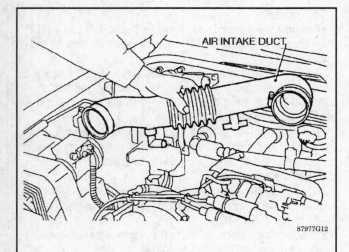

Fig. 12 Removal and installation of the intake air duct — except turbocharged vehicles

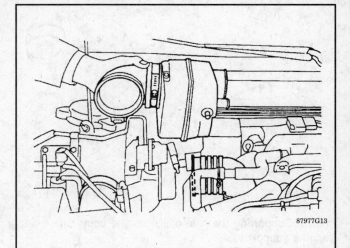

Fig. 13 Removal and installation of the resonator chamber — turbocharged vehicles

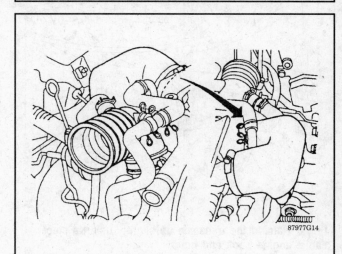

Fig. 14 Removal and installation of the air inlet and outlet duct — turbocharged vehicles

   c. Remove the turbocharger cooling duct.
4. Unplug the following connectors:
   • O_2 sensor connector
   • Transaxle ground cable
5. Disconnect the following cables:
   • Clutch release spring (except turbo)
   • Clutch cable (except turbo)
   • Hill Holder cable (except turbo)
   • Speedometer cable
6. Remove the starter.
7. Remove the pitching stopper.
8. On turbocharged vehicles, perform the following:
   a. Remove the slave cylinder.
   b. Remove the release lever shaft plug.
   c. Screw a 6mm bolt into the bolt hole of the release fork shaft and drive the shaft out.
   d. Raise the fork to release the throwout bearing tabs.

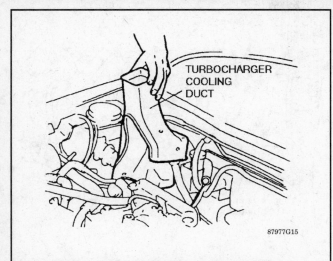

Fig. 15 Removing and installing the cooling duct — turbocharged vehicles

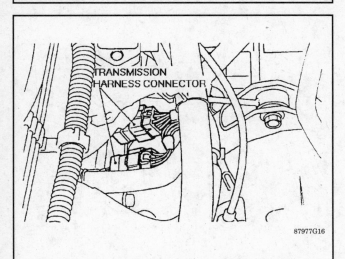

Fig. 16 Unplug the transaxle harness, O₂ connectors and ground terminal

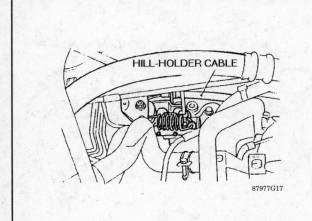

Fig. 17 Disconnect the Hill Holder cable — except turbocharged vehicles

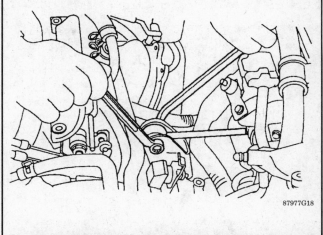

Fig. 18 Removal and installation of the pitching stopper bracket — turbocharged model shown

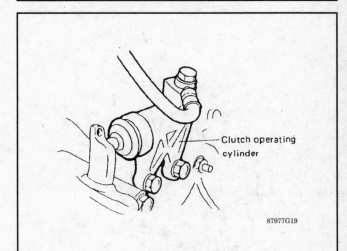

Fig. 19 Removal and installation of the slave cylinder — hydraulically actuated clutch system

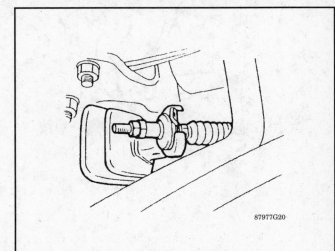

Fig. 20 Disconnect the clutch release lever cable — manually actuated clutch system

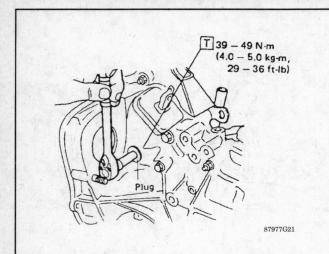

$\boxed{T}$ 39 – 49 N·m
(4.0 – 5.0 kg-m,
29 – 36 ft-lb)

Plug

87977G21

Fig. 21 Using a 10mm hex extension to remove or install the release lever shaft plug

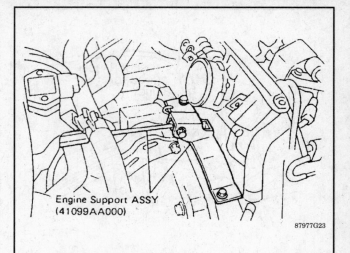

Engine Support ASSY
(41099AA000)

87977G23

Fig. 23 Install a special engine support tool to hold the engine in place

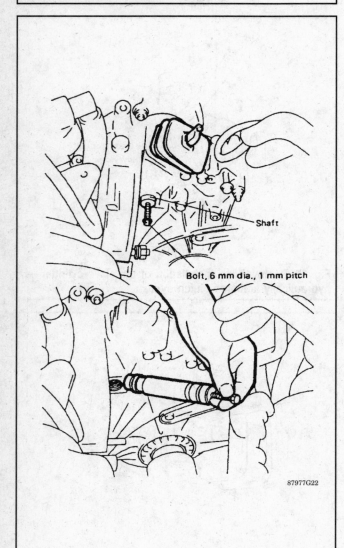

Shaft

Bolt, 6 mm dia., 1 mm pitch

87977G22

Fig. 22 Using a 6mm bolt to remove the release lever shaft

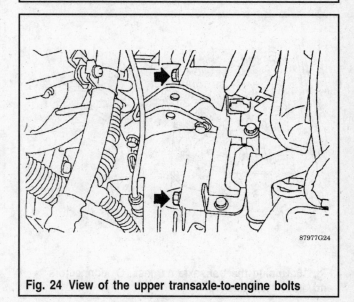

87977G24

Fig. 24 View of the upper transaxle-to-engine bolts

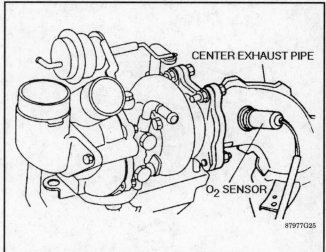

CENTER EXHAUST PIPE

O₂ SENSOR

87977G25

Fig. 25 Disconnect the center exhaust pipe — turbocharged models

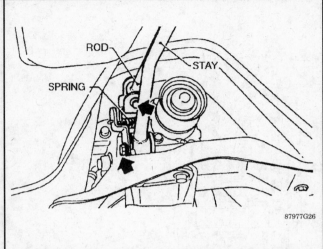

Fig. 26 Disconnect the gear shift rod and stay from the transaxle

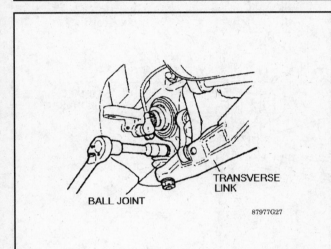

Fig. 27 Removal and installation of the transverse link from the transaxle housing

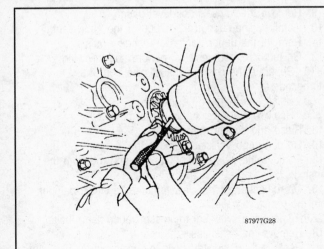

Fig. 28 Drive out the spring pin and remove the halfshafts

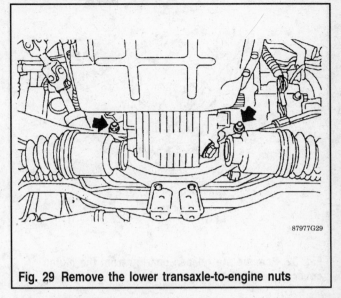

Fig. 29 Remove the lower transaxle-to-engine nuts

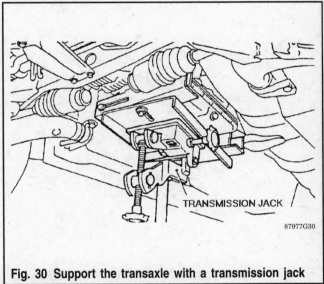

Fig. 30 Support the transaxle with a transmission jack

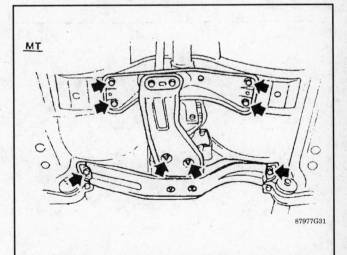

Fig. 31 The rear transaxle crossmember is retained by the indicated fasteners

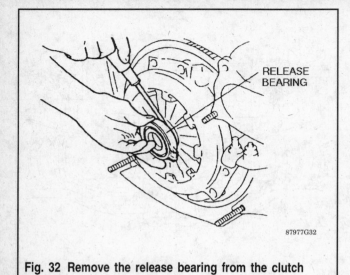

Fig. 32 Remove the release bearing from the clutch cover

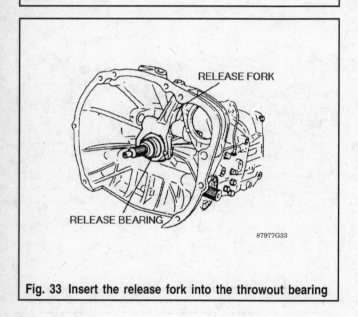

Fig. 33 Insert the release fork into the throwout bearing

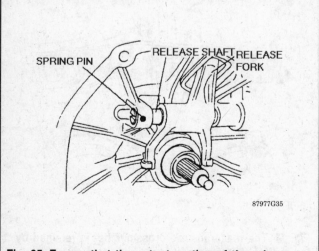

Fig. 35 Ensure that the cutout portion of the release fork shaft contacts the spring pin

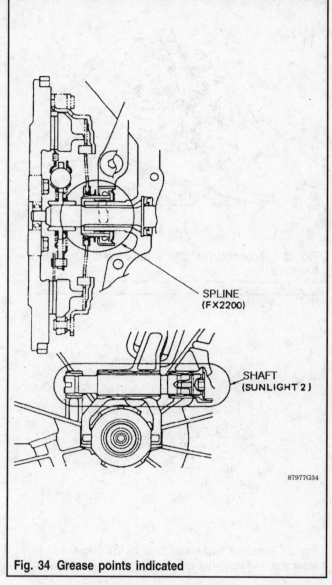

Fig. 34 Grease points indicated

9. Remove the transaxle oil level gauge.
10. Install engine support 92767000 or the equivalent.
11. Remove the upper transaxle-to-engine nuts.
12. On turbocharged vehicles, perform the following:
  a. Separate the center exhaust pipe from the turbocharger.
  b. Raise and support the vehicle.
  c. Remove the lower turbocharger cover.
13. Raise and support the vehicle.
14. On non-turbo vehicles, remove the Y-pipe.
15. Remove the gearshift spring, stay and rod from the transaxle.
16. On turbocharger vehicles, remove the clutch damper from the transaxle case.
17. Remove the sway bar-to-crossmember clamp bolts.
18. Remove the halfshafts.
19. Remove the lower transaxle-to-engine nuts.
20. Support the transaxle with a jack.
21. Remove the rear crossmember.
22. Lower the support jack until the mainshaft is withdrawn from the pressure plate and remove the transaxle.

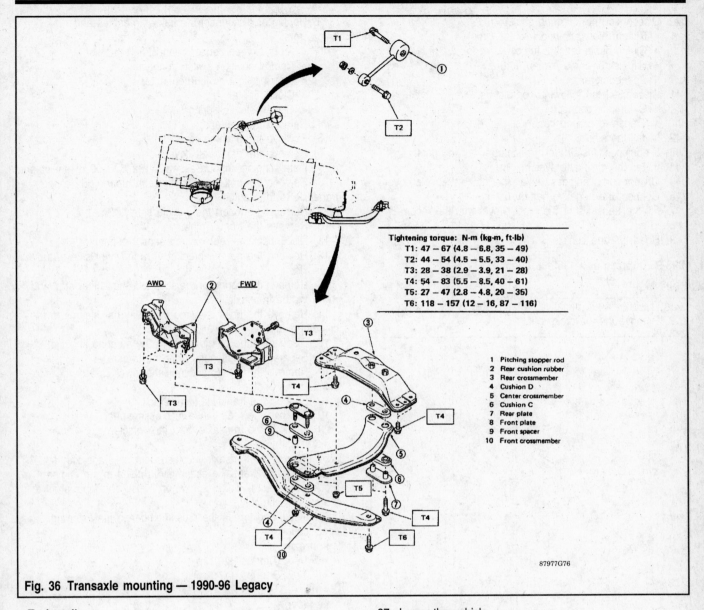

Tightening torque: N·m (kg-m, ft-lb)
T1: 47 — 67 (4.8 — 6.8, 35 — 49)
T2: 44 — 54 (4.5 — 5.5, 33 — 40)
T3: 28 — 38 (2.9 — 3.9, 21 — 28)
T4: 54 — 83 (5.5 — 8.5, 40 — 61)
T5: 27 — 47 (2.8 — 4.8, 20 — 35)
T6: 118 — 157 (12 — 16, 87 — 116)

1 Pitching stopper rod
2 Rear cushion rubber
3 Rear crossmember
4 Cushion D
5 Center crossmember
6 Cushion C
7 Rear plate
8 Front plate
9 Front spacer
10 Front crossmember

87977G76

Fig. 36 Transaxle mounting — 1990-96 Legacy

To install:

23. On turbocharger vehicles, perform the following:
   a. Pry the throwout bearing from the clutch cover.
   b. Install the throwout bearing onto the transaxle.
   c. Insert the release fork into the throwout bearing tab.
   d. Apply Fx2200® or equivalent to the splines of the transaxle and SUNLIGHT 2® or equivalent to the shaft.
   e. Insert the shaft into the release fork.

➡**Ensure the cutout portion of the release fork shaft contacts the spring pin.**

   f. Install the plug and torque it to 36 ft. lbs. (49 Nm).
24. Install the transaxle engaging the splines.
25. Install the rear cushion and crossmember. Tighten cushion bolts to 20-35 ft. lbs. (27-47 Nm); crossmember front bolts to 87-116 ft. lbs. (118-157 Nm), rear 40-61 ft. lbs. (54-83 Nm).
26. Install the lower transaxle-to-engine nuts and torque them to 34-40 ft. lbs. (46-54 Nm).

27. Lower the vehicle.
28. On turbocharged vehicles, push the release fork and assemble the throwout bearing into the clutch cover.
29. Install the upper transaxle-to-engine bolts and torque them to 34-40 ft. lbs. (46-54 Nm).
30. Remove the engine support.
31. Install the pitching stopper bracket onto the transaxle. Install the pitching stopper. Torque the body side bolt to 49 ft. lbs. (67 Nm) and bracket side bolt to 40 ft. lbs. (54 Nm).
32. On turbocharged vehicles, install the slave cylinder.
33. Install the halfshafts.
34. Install the sway bar clamps and torque the bolts to 21 ft. lbs. (28 Nm).
35. Assemble the gear shift assembly.
36. On turbocharged vehicles, install the clutch damper and torque the bolts to 23 ft. lbs. (32 Nm).
37. On 4WD vehicles, install the driveshaft.
38. Install the exhaust system with new gaskets and nuts.
39. Install the transaxle oil level gauge.

40. Disconnect the following cables:
- Clutch release spring (except turbo)
- Clutch cable (except turbo)
- Hill Holder cable (except turbo)
- Speedometer cable

41. Disconnect the following connectors:
- O₂ sensor connector
- Transaxle ground cable

42. Install the starter.
43. If equipped, install the turbocharger cooling duct.
44. Install the air intake system.
45. On non-turbo engines, install the intake manifold cover.
46. Connect the negative battery cable.
47. Fill the transaxle to the proper level with the recommended oil.
48. Road test the vehicle.

1993-96 Impreza and 1995-96 Legacy

▶ See Figure 37

1. Disconnect the negative battery cable.
2. Remove the air intake duct.

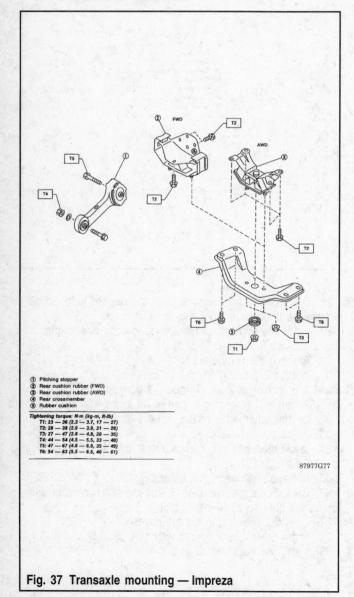

① Pitching stopper
② Rear cushion rubber (FWD)
③ Rear cushion rubber (AWD)
④ Rear crossmember
⑤ Rubber cushion

Tightening torque: N·m (kg-m, ft-lb)
T1: 23 — 36 (2.3 — 3.7, 17 — 27)
T2: 28 — 38 (2.9 — 3.9, 21 — 28)
T3: 27 — 47 (2.8 — 4.8, 20 — 35)
T4: 44 — 54 (4.5 — 5.5, 33 — 40)
T5: 47 — 67 (4.8 — 6.8, 35 — 49)
T6: 54 — 83 (5.5 — 8.5, 40 — 61)

87977G77

Fig. 37 Transaxle mounting — Impreza

3. Unplug or disconnect the following cables and connectors:
- Front oxygen sensor connector
- Neutral position switch connector
- Back-up light switch connector
- Clutch cable
- Clutch release spring

4. Remove the starter.
5. Remove the pitching stopper.
6. Remove the drive belt cover.
7. Install engine support assembly 927670000 or equivalent.
8. Remove the bolt securing the right upper side of the transaxle to the engine.
9. Raise and support the vehicle safely.
10. Remove the front Y-pipe.
11. Disconnect the rear oxygen sensor connector.
12. Remove the hanger bracket from the right side of the transaxle.
13. Remove the spring and disconnect the shifter stay and rod from the transaxle.
14. Remove the bolts securing the sway bar clamps to the crossmember.
15. Disconnect the ball joints from the steering knuckle.
16. Separate the halfshafts from the transaxle.
17. Remove the 2 nuts securing the lower side of the transaxle to the engine.
18. Support the transaxle with a jack.
19. Remove the rear transaxle crossmember.
20. Remove the transaxle from the vehicle.

To install:

21. Secure the transaxle in place onto the transaxle jack.
22. Raise the transaxle assembly in place to the engine block and install it. Take care when mating the input shaft to the clutch assembly.
23. Install and torque the crossmember to the following specifications:

Impreza:
- T1 — 20 ft. lbs. (26 Nm)
- T2 — 35 ft. lbs. (47 Nm)
- T3 — 61 ft. lbs. (83 Nm)

Legacy:
- T1 — 40-62 ft. lbs. (54-84 Nm)
- T2 — 87-115 ft. lbs. (117-157 Nm)

24. Remove the transmission jack.
25. Install the nuts securing the lower portion of the engine to the transaxle and torque them to 40 ft. lbs. (54 Nm).
26. Install the bolt securing the right upper side of the transaxle to the engine and torque it to 40 ft. lbs. (54 Nm).
27. Remove the engine support.
28. Install the drive belt cover.
29. Install the pitching stopper and tighten the bolts to the following specifications:
- T1 — 40 ft. lbs. (54 Nm)
- T2 — 49 ft. lbs. (67 Nm)

30. Insert the halfshafts into the transaxle and install new roll pins.
31. Connect the ball joint to the steering knuckle and torque the bolt to 22 ft. lbs. (29 Nm).
32. Connect the sway bar to the crossmember and torque the clamp bolts to 21 ft. lbs. (28 Nm).
33. Connect the shift control rod and stay to the transaxle and install the spring.

34. Install the heat shield cover, if removed.
35. Install the Y-pipe with new gaskets and nuts.
36. Install the hanger bracket on the right side of the transaxle, if removed.
37. Connect the rear oxygen sensor connector.
38. Install the transaxle connectors bracket.
39. Install the drive belt cover.
40. Install the pitching stopper.
41. Install the starter.
42. Engage or connect the following cables and connectors:
    - Front oxygen sensor connector
    - Neutral position switch connector
    - Back-up light switch connector
    - Clutch cable
    - Clutch release spring
43. Install the air intake duct and connector the airflow sensor connector.
44. Connect the negative battery cable.

Loyale, STD. and XT

1. Disconnect the negative battery cable. Remove the air cleaner assembly.
2. Remove the clutch cable and the Hill Holder cable. Remove the speedometer cable.
3. Remove the oxygen sensor electrical connector and the neutral switch connector.
4. Unplug the electrical connections at the back-up light.
5. Disconnect the starter electrical connections. Remove the starter retaining bolts. Remove the starter from the transaxle case.
6. Remove the air intake boot. Disconnect the pitching stopper rod from its mounting bracket. Remove the right side engine to transaxle mounting bolt.
7. Install engine support bracket 927160000 and engine support tool 927150000 or their equivalents. Remove the buffer rod from the engine and body side bracket.

➡**Before attaching the special engine support tools, connect the adjuster to the buffer rod assembly on the right side of the engine.**

8. Raise and support the vehicle safely.
9. Disconnect the exhaust pipes at the exhaust manifold flange. Remove the exhaust system up to the rear exhaust pipe assembly.
10. Remove the spring and disconnect the shifter stay and rod from the transaxle.
11. Loosen the upper bolt and nut from the plate that secures the transverse link to the stabilizer. Remove the lower bolt and separate the link from the stabilizer.
12. Remove the right brake cable bracket from the transverse link. Remove the bolt retaining the link to the crossmember on each side.
13. Lower the transverse link. Using tool 398791700 or equivalent, remove the spring pin and separate the axle shaft from the driveshaft on each side of the assembly by pushing the rear of the tire outward.
14. Remove the engine to transaxle mounting bolts. Position the proper transaxle jack under the transaxle assembly.
15. Remove the rear cushion rubber mounting bolts. Remove the rear crossmember assembly.
16. Turn the engine support tool adjuster counterclockwise in order to slightly raise the engine.
17. Move the transaxle jack toward the rear of the vehicle until the mainshaft is withdrawn from the clutch cover.
18. Carefully remove the transaxle assembly from the vehicle.

   To install:
19. Carefully raise the transaxle until the mainshaft is aligned with the clutch side. Install the engine to the transaxle and temporarily tighten the mounting bolts.
20. Install the rear crossmember rubber cushion and tighten nuts to 20-35 ft. lbs. (27-47 Nm). Install the rear crossmember and tighten front bolts to 65-87 ft. lbs. (88-118 Nm); rear bolts to 27-49 ft. lbs. (37-67 Nm).
21. Tighten the engine to transaxle nuts to 34-40 ft. lbs. (46-54 Nm). Remove the transaxle jack.
22. Install the halfshaft into the differential and spring pin into place. Install the transverse link and stabilizer temporarily to the front crossmember. Install the brake cable bracket. Lower the vehicle and tighten transverse link bolt to 43-51 ft. lbs. (59-69 Nm); stabilizer bolts to 14-22 ft. lbs. (20-29 Nm).
23. Install the gearshift system. Install the starter, pitching stopper, timing hole plug, air intake boot and speedometer cable. Reconnect all electrical and vacuum connectors.
24. Connect the clutch cable and Hill Holder. Install the front exhaust pipe.
25. Connect the negative battery cable, check the transaxle fluid level and test drive the vehicle.

SELECTIVE (4WD/FWD) 5-SPEED TRANSAXLE

General Information

On this transaxle, a selector switch in the shift lever allows the driver to choose 4WD or front wheel drive. The switch can be operated at any time, regardless of the shifter position. The selective 4WD engagement is accomplished by movement of a shifter fork (inside transfer case) sliding a synchronizer hub in place to engaging the transfer gear. This action results in the rear driveshaft being coupled to the transaxle and movement of the front and rear wheels is established.

The shift fork inside the transfer case is actuated by a vacuum actuator and cable. When the switch in the shift lever is pressed **ON**, the vacuum actuator is energized. Thus engaging the shift fork into transfer lock position. When the switch is switched **OFF**, the actuator moves the shift fork back, uncoupling the rear driveshaft and resumes front wheel drive operation.

Identification

This transaxle is used in the Loyale, STD. and XT.

The transaxle can be identified by the 11th letter in the vehicle identification number located on the bulkhead panel of the engine compartment.

The transaxle serial number label is mounted on the upper surface of the main case.

The manual transaxle 11th letter code is as follows:
D=Gunma 4WD 5-speed manual transaxle
E=Gunma 4WD dual-range (sedan and wagon only)

REMOVAL & INSTALLATION

Loyale, STD. and XT

1. Disconnect the negative battery cable. Remove the air cleaner assembly.

2. Remove the clutch cable and the Hill Holder cable. Remove the speedometer cable.

3. Remove the oxygen sensor electrical connector and the neutral switch connector.

4. If equipped with 4WD, unplug the electrical connections at the back-up light and differential lock indicator switch assembly. Disconnect the differential lock vacuum hose.

5. Disconnect the starter electrical connections. Remove the starter retaining bolts. Remove the starter from the transaxle case.

6. Remove the air intake boot. Disconnect the pitching stopper rod from its mounting bracket. Remove the right side engine to transaxle mounting bolt.

7. Install engine support bracket 927160000 and engine support tool 927150000 or their equivalents. Remove the buffer rod from the engine and body side bracket.

➡Before attaching the special engine support tools, connect the adjuster to the buffer rod assembly on the right side of the engine.

8. Raise and support the vehicle safely.

9. Disconnect the exhaust pipes at the exhaust manifold flange. Remove the exhaust system up to the rear exhaust pipe assembly.

10. If equipped with 4WD, matchmark and remove the driveshaft.

11. Remove the spring and disconnect the shifter stay and rod from the transaxle.

12. Loosen the upper bolt and nut from the plate that secures the transverse link to the stabilizer. Remove the lower bolt and separate the link from the stabilizer.

13. Remove the right brake cable bracket from the transverse link. Remove the bolt retaining the link to the crossmember on each side.

14. Lower the transverse link. Using tool 398791700 or equivalent, remove the spring pin and separate the axle shaft from the driveshaft on each side of the assembly by pushing the rear of the tire outward.

15. Remove the engine to transaxle mounting bolts. Position the proper transaxle jack under the transaxle assembly.

16. Remove the rear cushion rubber mounting bolts. Remove the rear crossmember assembly.

17. Turn the engine support tool adjuster counterclockwise in order to slightly raise the engine.

18. Move the transaxle jack toward the rear of the vehicle until the mainshaft is withdrawn from the clutch cover.

19. Carefully remove the transaxle assembly from the vehicle.

To install:

20. Carefully raise the transaxle until the mainshaft is aligned with the clutch side. Install the engine to the transaxle and temporarily tight the mounting bolts.

21. Install the rear crossmember rubber cushion and tighten nuts to 20-35 ft. lbs. (27-47 Nm). Install the rear crossmember and tighten front bolts to 65-87 ft. lbs. (88-118 Nm); rear bolts to 27-49 ft. lbs. (37-67 Nm).

22. Tighten the engine to transaxle nuts to 34-40 ft. lbs. (46-54 Nm). Remove the transaxle jack.

23. Install the halfshaft into the differential and spring pin into place. Install the transverse link and stabilizer temporarily to the front crossmember. Install the brake cable bracket. Lower the vehicle and tighten transverse link bolt to 43-51 ft. lbs. (59-69 Nm); stabilizer bolts to 14-22 ft. lbs. (20-29 Nm).

24. Connect the shift control rod and stay to the transaxle and install the spring.

25. Install the driveshaft (4WD vehicles). Install the starter, pitching stopper, timing hole plug, air intake boot and speedometer cable. Reconnect all electrical and vacuum connectors.

26. Connect the clutch cable and Hill Holder. Install the front exhaust pipe.

27. Connect the negative battery cable, check the transaxle fluid level and test drive the vehicle.

FULL-TIME 4WD TRANSAXLE

General Information

The full-time 4WD transaxle is based on the selective 5-speed transaxle, the overall case design and operation are the same. The basic difference between the full-time transaxle and the selective transaxle are the components of which are used to accomplish the 4WD action.

As mention previously, the selective transaxle uses a vacuum actuator, transfer shift fork and synchronizer to engage the transfer case. Full-time transaxles use one of two methods of transfer engagement. In Loyale STD., and XT models, the full-time 4WD transaxle is designed on the basis of the selective 4WD unit. However, a center differential unit and locking mechanism was added to the rear end transfer section, (taking the place of the shift fork). The center differential is locked and unlocked by a vacuum actuator when the differential lock switch located on the console box is operated. When the center differential is locked, the driveshaft is coupled directly to the front and rear wheels. This provides a maximum drive equivalent of that of the 4WD mode of the selective 4WD unit.

The second method used by the full-time transaxle is the use of a viscous coupling between the transfer case and center differential. This is used in Impreza and Legacy models. With this form of transfer engagement, the use of a vacuum actuator is not required. This type of transaxle may also be referred to as All Wheel Drive (AWD).

This transaxle is a compact, full-time transaxle that utilizes a center differential provided with a viscous coupling at the rear of a transfer unit. The viscous coupling serves as a differential action control. The center differential utilizes a highly reliable, bevel gear. It not only delivers an equal amount of drive power to both the front and rear, but controls the difference in rotating speed between the front and rear wheels. A viscous coupling and center differential gears are located in the center differential case to connect the front and rear wheel driveshafts. With this arrangement, the transfer system realized a compact construction. In addition, the viscous coupling serves as a differential action control to eliminate a mechanical lock mechanism.

In general terms this particular transaxle provides a constant 4 wheel drive action at all times, controlling distribution of power to all 4 wheels as required under varied driving conditions.

Identification

This transaxle is used in the Legacy, Loyale, STD., and XT.
The transaxle can be identified by the 11th letter in the vehicle identification number located on the bulkhead panel of the engine compartment.

The transaxle serial number label is mounted on the upper surface of the main case.

The manual transaxle 11th letter code is as follows:
G: Gunma manufacturer — full-time 4WD 5-speed

REMOVAL & INSTALLATION

1990-94 Legacy
▶ See Figures 38, 39, 40, 41, 42, 43, 44, 45, 46, 47, 48, 49, 50, 51, 52, 53, 54, 55, 56, 57, 58, 59, 60 and 61

1. Disconnect the negative battery cable.
2. On non-turbo vehicles, remove the intake manifold cover and air intake duct.
3. On turbocharged vehicles perform the following:
   a. Remove the resonator chamber.
   b. Remove the air inlet and outlet ducts.

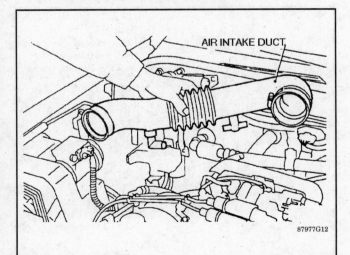

Fig. 38 Removal and installation of the intake air duct — except turbocharged vehicles

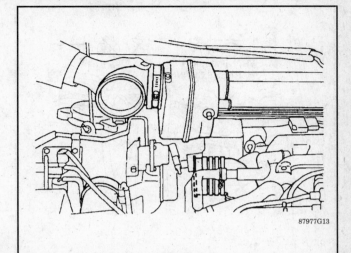

Fig. 39 Removal and installation of the resonator chamber — turbocharged vehicles

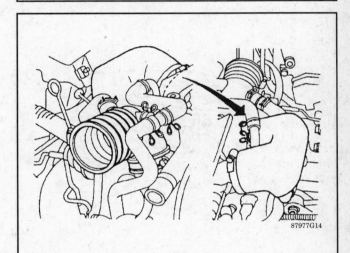

Fig. 40 Removal and installation of the air inlet and outlet duct — turbocharged vehicles

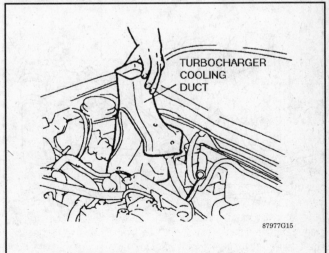

Fig. 41 Removing and installing the cooling duct — turbocharged vehicles

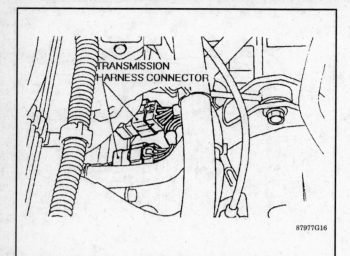

87977G16

Fig. 42 Unplug the transaxle harness, O₂ connectors and ground terminal

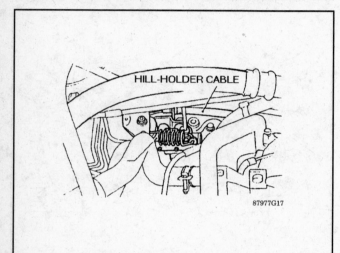

87977G17

Fig. 43 Disconnect the Hill Holder cable — except turbocharged vehicles

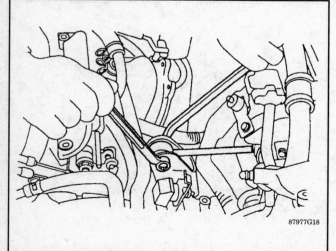

87977G18

Fig. 44 Removal and installation of the pitching stopper bracket — turbocharged model shown

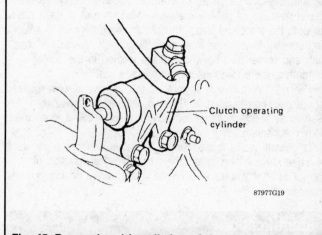

87977G19

Fig. 45 Removal and installation of the slave cylinder — hydraulically actuated clutch system

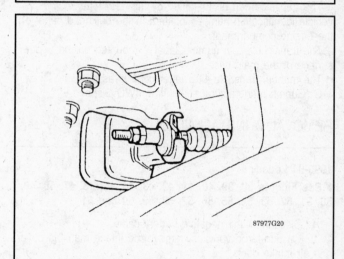

87977G20

Fig. 46 Disconnect the clutch release lever cable — manually actuated clutch system

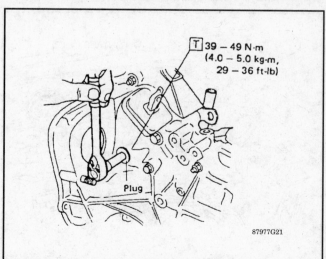

87977G21

Fig. 47 Using a 10mm hex extension to remove or install the release lever shaft plug

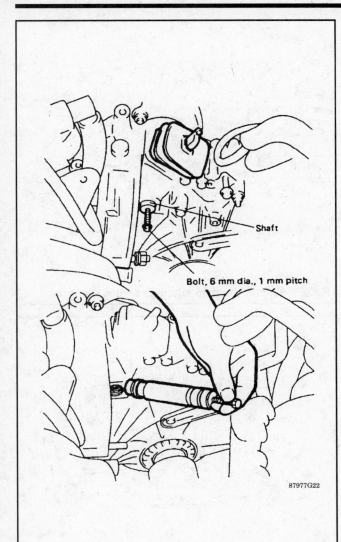

Fig. 48 Using a 6mm bolt to remove the release lever shaft

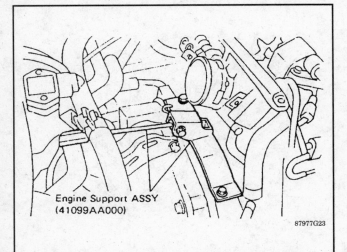

Fig. 49 Install a special engine support tool to hold the engine in place

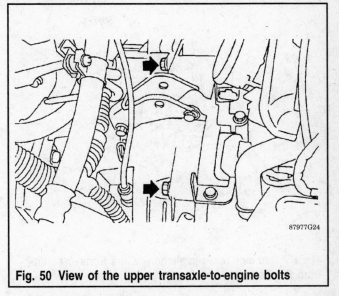

Fig. 50 View of the upper transaxle-to-engine bolts

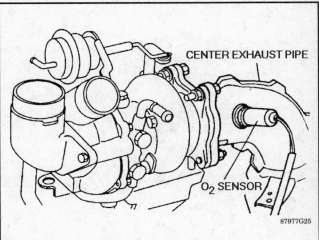

Fig. 51 Disconnect the center exhaust pipe — turbocharged models

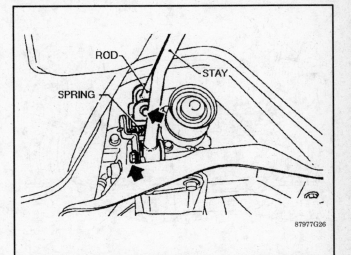

Fig. 52 Disconnect the gear shift rod and stay from the transaxle

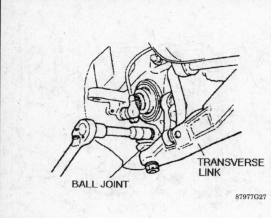

Fig. 53 Removal and installation of the transverse link from the transaxle housing

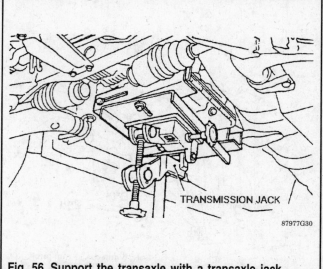

Fig. 56 Support the transaxle with a transaxle jack

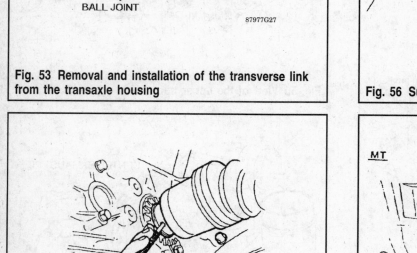

Fig. 54 Drive out the spring pin and remove the halfshafts

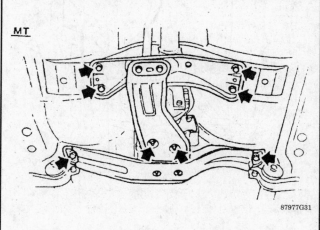

Fig. 57 The rear transaxle crossmember is retained by the indicated fasteners

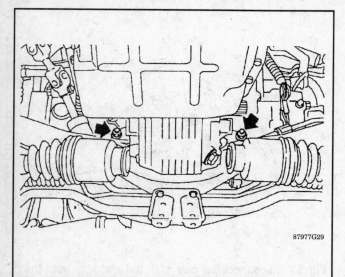

Fig. 55 Remove the lower transaxle-to-engine nuts

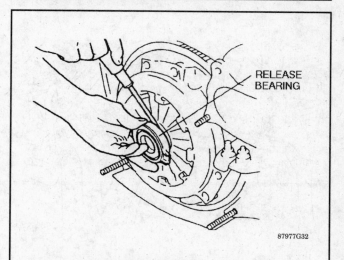

Fig. 58 Remove the release bearing from the clutch cover

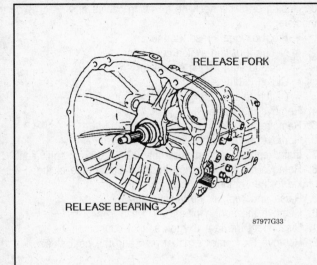

Fig. 59 Insert the release fork into the throwout bearing

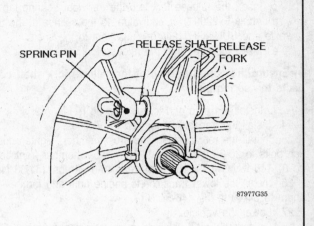

Fig. 61 Ensure that the cutout portion of the release fork shaft contacts the spring pin

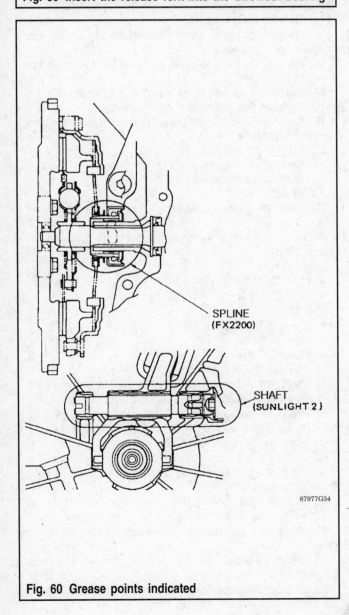

Fig. 60 Grease points indicated

c. Remove the turbocharger cooling duct.
4. Unplug the following connectors:
   - O_2 sensor connector
   - Transaxle ground cable
5. Disconnect the following cables:
   - Clutch release spring (except turbo)
   - Clutch cable (except turbo)
   - Hill Holder cable (except turbo)
   - Speedometer cable
6. Remove the starter.
7. Remove the pitching stopper.
8. On turbocharger vehicles, perform the following:
   a. Remove the slave cylinder.
   b. Remove the release lever shaft plug.
   c. Screw a 6mm bolt into the bolt hole of the release fork shaft and drive the shaft out.
   d. Raise the fork to release the throwout bearing tabs.
9. Remove the transaxle oil level gauge.
10. Install engine support 92767000 or the equivalent.
11. Remove the upper transaxle-to-engine nuts.
12. On turbocharged vehicles, perform the following:
   a. Separate the center exhaust pipe from the turbocharger.
   b. Raise and support the vehicle.
   c. Remove the lower turbocharger cover.
13. Raise and support the vehicle.
14. On non-turbo vehicles, remove the Y-pipe.
15. Remove the gearshift spring, stay and rod from the transaxle.
16. On turbocharger vehicles, remove the clutch damper from the transaxle case.
17. Remove the sway bar-to-crossmember clamp bolts.
18. Remove the halfshafts.
19. Remove the lower transaxle-to-engine nuts.
20. Support the transaxle with a jack.
21. Remove the rear crossmember.
22. Lower the support jack until the mainshaft is withdrawn from the pressure plate and remove the transaxle.
   To install:
23. On turbocharger vehicles, perform the following:
   a. Pry the throwout bearing from the clutch cover.

b. Install the throwout bearing onto the transaxle.

c. Insert the release fork into the throwout bearing tab.

d. Apply Fx2200® or equivalent to the splines of the transaxle and SUNLIGHT 2® or equivalent to the shaft.

e. Insert the shaft into the release fork.

➡**Ensure the cutout portion of the release fork shaft contacts the spring pin.**

f. Install the plug and torque it to 36 ft. lbs. (49 Nm).

24. Install the transaxle engaging the splines.

25. Install the rear cushion and crossmember. Tighten cushion bolts to 20-35 ft. lbs. (27-47 Nm); crossmember front bolts to 87-116 ft. lbs. (118-157 Nm), rear 40-61 ft. lbs. (54-83 Nm).

26. Install the lower transaxle-to-engine nuts and torque them to 34-40 ft. lbs. (46-54 Nm).

27. Lower the vehicle.

28. On turbocharged vehicles, push the release fork and assemble the throwout bearing into the clutch cover.

29. Install the upper transaxle-to-engine bolts and torque them to 34-40 ft. lbs. (46-54 Nm).

30. Remove the engine support.

31. Install the pitching stopper bracket onto the transaxle. Install the pitching stopper. Torque the body side bolt to 49 ft. lbs. (67 Nm) and bracket side bolt to 40 ft. lbs. (54 Nm).

32. On turbocharged vehicles, install the slave cylinder.

33. Install the halfshafts.

34. Install the sway bar clamps and torque the bolts to 21 ft. lbs. (28 Nm).

35. Connect the shift control rod and stay to the transaxle and install the spring.

36. On turbocharged vehicles, install the clutch damper and torque the bolts to 23 ft. lbs. (32 Nm).

37. Install the driveshaft.

38. Install the exhaust system with new gaskets and nuts.

39. Install the transaxle oil level gauge.

40. Disconnect the following cables:
- Clutch release spring (except turbo)
- Clutch cable (except turbo)
- Hill Holder cable (except turbo)
- Speedometer cable

41. Disconnect the following connectors:
- O_2 sensor connector
- Transaxle ground cable

42. Install the starter.

43. If equipped, install the turbocharger cooling duct.

44. Install the air intake system.

45. On non-turbo engines, install the intake manifold cover.

46. Connect the negative battery cable.

47. Fill the transaxle to the proper level with the recommended oil.

48. Road test the vehicle.

1995-96 Legacy and 1993-96 Impreza

1. Disconnect the negative battery cable.

2. Remove the air intake duct.

3. Unplug or disconnect the following cables and connectors:
- Front oxygen sensor connector
- Neutral position switch connector
- Back-up light switch connector
- Clutch cable
- Clutch release spring

4. Remove the starter.

5. Remove the pitching stopper.

6. Remove the drive belt cover.

7. Install engine support assembly 927670000 or equivalent.

8. Remove the bolt securing the right upper side of the transaxle to the engine.

9. Raise and support the vehicle safely.

10. Remove the front Y-pipe.

11. Disconnect the rear oxygen sensor connector.

12. Remove the center exhaust pipe and the heat shield cover.

13. Remove the hanger bracket from the right side of the transaxle.

14. Remove the driveshaft.

15. Remove the spring and disconnect the shifter stay and rod from the transaxle.

16. Remove the bolts securing the sway bar clamps to the crossmember.

17. Disconnect the ball joints from the steering knuckle.

18. Separate the halfshafts from the transaxle.

19. Remove the 2 nuts securing the lower side of the transaxle to the engine.

20. Support the transaxle with a jack.

21. Remove the rear transaxle crossmember.

22. Remove the transaxle from the vehicle.

To install:

23. Install the transaxle assembly and secure to the engine block.

24. Install and torque the crossmember to the following specifications:

Legacy:
- T1 — 40-62 ft. lbs. (54-84 Nm)
- T2 — 87-115 ft. lbs. (117-157 Nm)

Impreza:
- T1 — 20 ft. lbs. (26 Nm)
- T2 — 35 ft. lbs. (47 Nm)
- T3 — 61 ft. lbs. (83 Nm)

25. Remove the transmission jack.

26. Install the nuts securing the lower portion of the engine to the transaxle and torque them to 40 ft. lbs. (54 Nm).

27. Install the bolt securing the right upper side of the transaxle to the engine and torque it to 40 ft. lbs. (54 Nm).

28. Remove the engine support.

29. Install the drive belt cover.

30. Install the pitching stopper and torque the bolts to the following specifications:
- T1 — 40 ft. lbs. (54 Nm)
- T2 — 49 ft. lbs. (67 Nm)

31. Insert the halfshafts into the transaxle and install new roll pins.

32. Connect the ball joint to the steering knuckle and torque the bolt to 22 ft. lbs. (29 Nm).

33. Connect the sway bar to the crossmember and torque the clamp bolts to 21 ft. lbs. (28 Nm).

34. Connect the shift control rod and stay to the transaxle and install the spring.
35. Install the driveshaft.
36. Install the heat shield cover, if removed.
37. Install the Y-pipe with new gaskets and nuts.
38. Install the hanger bracket on the right side of the transaxle, if removed.
39. Connect the rear oxygen sensor connector.
40. Install the transaxle connectors bracket.
41. Install the drive belt cover.
42. Install the pitching stopper.
43. Install the starter.
44. Connect the following cables and connectors:
   - Front oxygen sensor connector
   - Neutral position switch connector
   - Back-up light switch connector
   - Clutch cable
   - Clutch release spring
45. Install the air intake duct and connector the airflow sensor connector.
46. Connect the negative battery cable.

Loyale, STD. and XT

1. Disconnect the negative battery cable. Remove the air cleaner assembly.
2. Remove the clutch cable and the Hill Holder cable. Remove the speedometer cable.
3. Remove the oxygen sensor electrical connector and the neutral switch connector.
4. Unplug the electrical connections at the back-up light and differential lock indicator switch assembly. Disconnect the differential lock vacuum hose.
5. Disconnect the starter electrical connections. Remove the starter retaining bolts. Remove the starter from the transaxle case.
6. Remove the air intake boot. Disconnect the pitching stopper rod from its mounting bracket. Remove the right side engine to transaxle mounting bolt.
7. Install engine support bracket 927160000 and engine support tool 927150000 or their equivalents. Remove the buffer rod from the engine and body side bracket.

➡Before attaching the special engine support tools, connect the adjuster to the buffer rod assembly on the right side of the engine.

8. Raise and support the vehicle safely.
9. Disconnect the exhaust pipes at the exhaust manifold flange. Remove the exhaust system up to the rear exhaust pipe assembly.
10. Matchmark and remove the driveshaft.
11. Remove the spring and disconnect the shifter stay and rod from the transaxle.
12. Loosen the upper bolt and nut from the plate that secures the transverse link to the stabilizer. Remove the lower bolt and separate the link from the stabilizer.
13. Remove the right brake cable bracket from the transverse link. Remove the bolt retaining the link to the crossmember on each side.
14. Lower the transverse link. Using tool 398791700 or equivalent, remove the spring pin and separate the axle shaft

from the driveshaft on each side of the assembly by pushing the rear of the tire outward.
15. Remove the engine to transaxle mounting bolts. Position the proper transaxle jack under the transaxle assembly.
16. Remove the rear cushion rubber mounting bolts. Remove the rear crossmember assembly.
17. Turn the engine support tool adjuster counterclockwise in order to slightly raise the engine.
18. Move the transaxle jack toward the rear of the vehicle until the mainshaft is withdrawn from the clutch cover.
19. Carefully remove the transaxle assembly from the vehicle.
   To install:
20. Carefully raise the transaxle until the mainshaft is aligned with the clutch side. Install the engine to the transaxle and temporarily tight the mounting bolts.
21. Install the rear crossmember rubber cushion and tighten nuts to 20-35 ft. lbs. (27-47 Nm). Install the rear crossmember and tighten front bolts to 65-87 ft. lbs. (88-118 Nm); rear bolts to 27-49 ft. lbs. (37-67 Nm).
22. Tighten the engine to transaxle nuts to 34-40 ft. lbs. (46-54 Nm). Remove the transaxle jack.
23. Install the halfshaft into the differential and spring pin into place. Install the transverse link and stabilizer temporarily to the front crossmember. Install the brake cable bracket. Lower the vehicle and tighten transverse link bolt to 43-51 ft. lbs. (59-69 Nm); stabilizer bolts to 14-22 ft. lbs. (20-29 Nm).
24. Connect the shift control rod and stay to the transaxle and install the spring.
25. Install the driveshaft (4WD vehicles). Install the starter, pitching stopper, timing hole plug, air intake boot and speedometer cable. Reconnect all electrical and vacuum connectors.
26. Connect the clutch cable and Hill Holder. Install the front exhaust pipe.
27. Connect the negative battery cable, check the transaxle fluid level and test drive the vehicle.

Front Halfshafts

REMOVAL & INSTALLATION

Justy

▶ See Figures 62, 63, 64, 65, 66, 67, 68, 69, 70, 71, 72, 73, 74 and 75

1. Remove the wheel cover, cotter pin and loosen the castle nut.
2. Raise and support the vehicle safely. Remove the tire and wheel assembly.
3. Remove the disc brake assembly.
4. Remove the castle nut and conical spring. Remove the center piece, using the proper tools.
5. Pull the hub and disc assembly from the halfshaft (a special puller tool is not required). Remove the disc cover from the housing.
6. Drive out the spring pin connecting the halfshaft to the differential, using the proper tool.
7. Remove the cotter pin and the castle nut from the tie rod end ball joint.

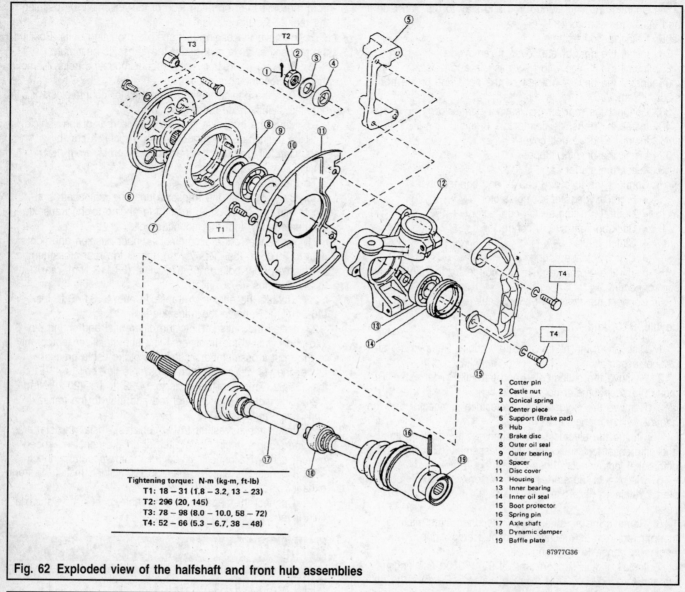

Tightening torque: N·m (kg-m, ft-lb)
T1: 18 − 31 (1.8 − 3.2, 13 − 23)
T2: 296 (20, 145)
T3: 78 − 98 (8.0 − 10.0, 58 − 72)
T4: 52 − 66 (5.3 − 6.7, 38 − 48)

1 Cotter pin
2 Castle nut
3 Conical spring
4 Center piece
5 Support (Brake pad)
6 Hub
7 Brake disc
8 Outer oil seal
9 Outer bearing
10 Spacer
11 Disc cover
12 Housing
13 Inner bearing
14 Inner oil seal
15 Boot protector
16 Spring pin
17 Axle shaft
18 Dynamic damper
19 Baffle plate

87977G36

Fig. 62 Exploded view of the halfshaft and front hub assemblies

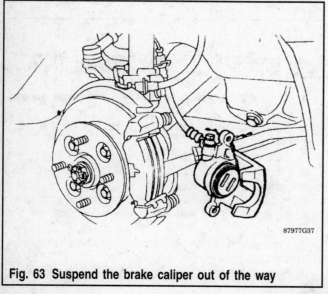

87977G37

Fig. 63 Suspend the brake caliper out of the way

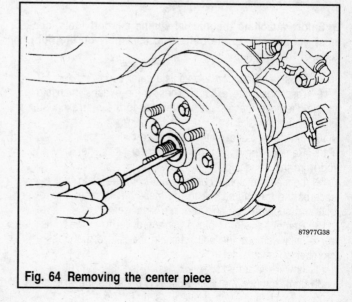

87977G38

Fig. 64 Removing the center piece

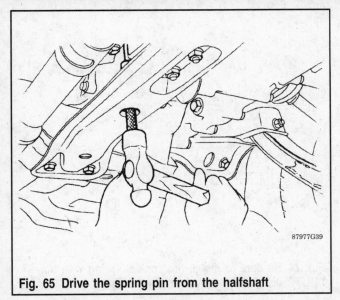

Fig. 65 Drive the spring pin from the halfshaft

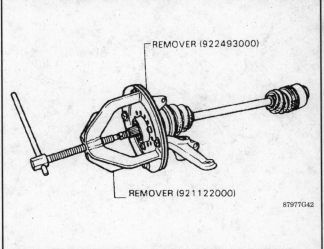

Fig. 68 Using a special tool to separate the halfshaft from the spindle housing

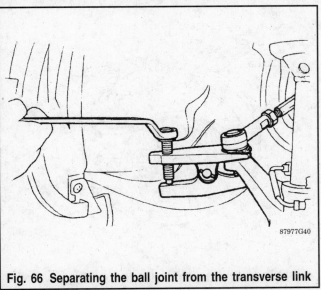

Fig. 66 Separating the ball joint from the transverse link

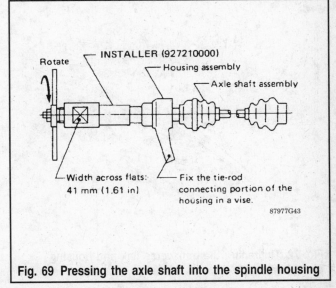

Fig. 69 Pressing the axle shaft into the spindle housing

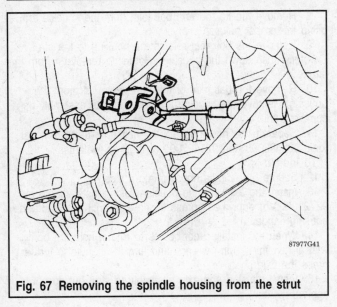

Fig. 67 Removing the spindle housing from the strut

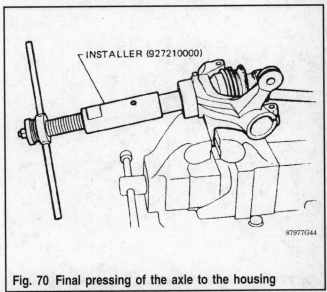

Fig. 70 Final pressing of the axle to the housing

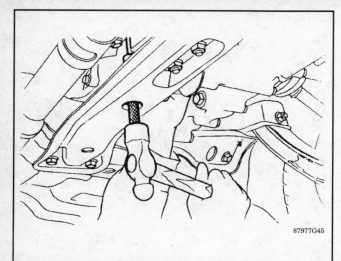

Fig. 71 Driving the spring pin into the double offset joint and differential shaft

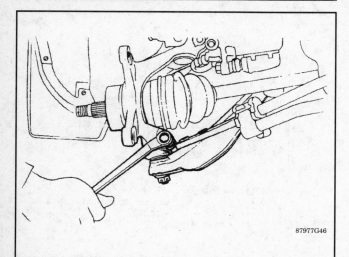

Fig. 72 Tightening the transverse link and housing pinch bolt

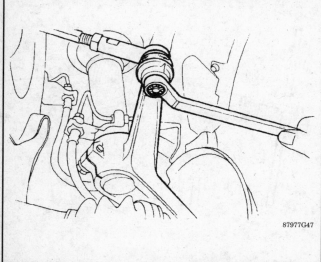

Fig. 73 Tightening the tie rod ball joint-to-knuckle nut

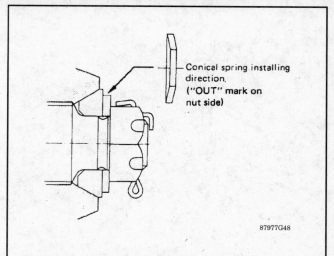

Fig. 74 Be sure to install the conical spring with the "OUT" side facing away from the bearing

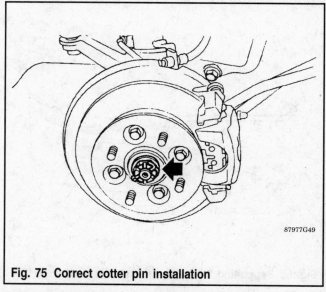

Fig. 75 Correct cotter pin installation

8. Remove the tie rod end ball joint from the knuckle arm, using the proper puller.

9. Remove the bolt that retains the housing to the strut. Carefully push down the housing in order to remove it from the strut.

10. Remove the ball joint of the transverse link from the housing. Remove the housing and the halfshaft assembly as a complete unit.

11. Separate the housing from the halfshaft, using removal tools 922493000 and 921122000 or their equivalents.

To install:

12. Secure the spindle housing into a vice.

13. Install the axle into the housing. Using installation tool 927210000 or equivalent, press fit the axle until it contacts the housing flange.

14. When the installer tool begins to rotate, hold the body with a 1.61 in. (41mm) wrench and turn the handle to further press the axle shaft.

15. Install housing and axle assembly to strut but do not tighten.

16. Install the dust seal on the spindle. Insert the halfshaft into the differential and install a new spring pin. Lubricate the splines with grease.

17. Install the transverse link ball joint to the housing and tighten the nut to 25-33 ft. lbs. (34-44 Nm).

18. Connect the tie rod end ball joint to the knuckle arm an tighten the castle nut to 18-22 ft. lbs. (25-29 Nm). Turn the nut just enough to align the next nut slot and hole. Use a new cotter pin.

19. Tighten the housing-to-strut bolt to 25-33 ft. lbs. (34-44 Nm).

20. Install the disc cover, hub, disc brake assembly and castle nut. Do not tighten at this time.

21. Install the caliper assembly. Tighten bolts to 31-46 ft. lbs. (42-62 Nm).

22. Install the wheel and tire, lower the vehicle. Tighten the castle nut to 130 ft. lbs. (177 Nm) for 1987-88 vehicles or 145 ft. lbs. (196 Nm) for 1989 and later vehicles.

Loyale, STD and XT

1. Disconnect the negative battery cable.
2. Raise and safely support the vehicle.
3. Remove the tire and wheel assembly.
4. Remove the parking brake cable bracket from the lower control arm.
5. Drive out the spring pin from the inner CV-joint.
6. Remove the caliper assembly and mounting bracket. Suspend the caliper assembly from a wire. DO NOT allow the caliper to hang from the brake hose.
7. Remove the brake rotor.
8. Remove the lower ball joint pinch bolt.
9. Remove the tie rod end cotter pin and castle nut and separate tie rod end from the steering knuckle.
10. Remove the strut-to-steering knuckle bolts.
11. Remove the steering knuckle and halfshaft as an assembly.
12. Using tool 926470000 or equivalent, press the axle shaft out of the bearing assembly.

To install:
13. Install the halfshaft through the hub bearing. Using installer tool 925130000 or equivalent, pull the shaft into place.

14. Install the axle and spindle assembly into the vehicle, guiding the halfshaft onto the splined shaft so the spring pin holes are in alignment. Install the lower ball joint stud into the lower control arm. Tighten the castle nut to 25 ft. lbs. (34 Nm) for all except XT6. For XT6, tighten to 69-83 ft. lbs. (93-113 Nm).

15. Install a new spring pin to secure the axle.

16. Connect the strut to the steering knuckle and install the two mounting bolts and tighten to 25 ft. lbs. (34 Nm).

17. Connect the tie rod end to the steering knuckle and tighten the castle nut to 20 ft. lbs. (27 Nm). Install a new cotter pin.

18. Install the brake rotor.

19. Install the caliper assembly onto the steering knuckle and tighten the mounting bracket-to-steering knuckle bolts to 44 ft. lbs. (59 Nm).

20. Connect the parking brake cable to the caliper.

21. Install the center piece, washer and castle nut on the axle and tighten the castle nut to 145 ft. lbs. (196 Nm).

22. Install the tire and wheel assemblies.

23. Lower the vehicle.
24. Connect the negative battery cable.

Impreza and Legacy
▶ **See Figures 76, 77, 78, 79, 80, 81, 82, 83, 84, 85, 86, 87 and 88**

1. Disconnect the negative battery cable.
2. Raise and support the vehicle safely.
3. Remove the wheel.
4. Unstake and remove the axle nut.
5. Remove the transverse link arm from the front crossmember.
6. Remove the halfshaft-to-transaxle roll pin and discard it.
7. Remove the sway bar bracket.
8. Disconnect the halfshaft from the transaxle.
9. Using puller 92707000 or equivalent, remove the halfshaft from the hub.

To install:
10. Insert the halfshaft into the hub.

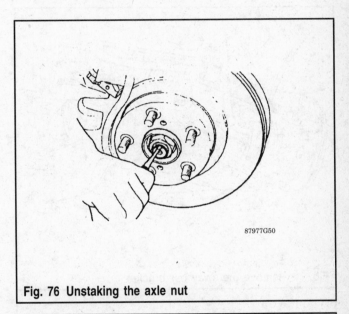

Fig. 76 Unstaking the axle nut

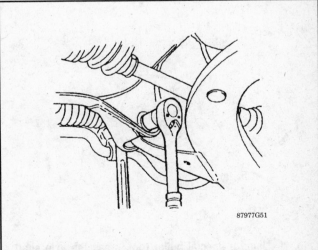

Fig. 77 Remove the transverse link arm from the crossmember

Fig. 78 Drive out the halfshaft-to-transaxle roll pin

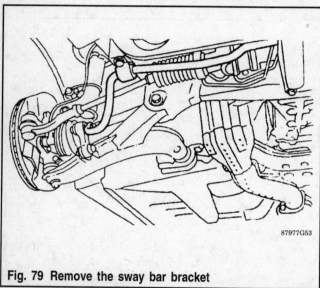

Fig. 79 Remove the sway bar bracket

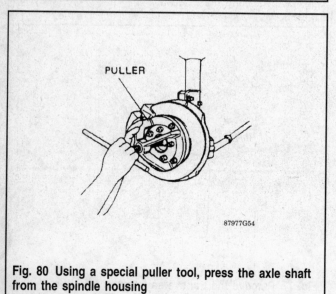

Fig. 80 Using a special puller tool, press the axle shaft from the spindle housing

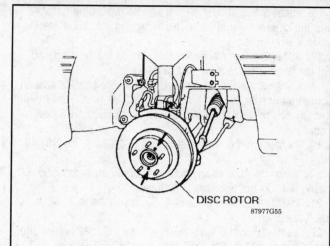

Fig. 81 Use two 8mm bolts to loosen the rotor from the spindle housing

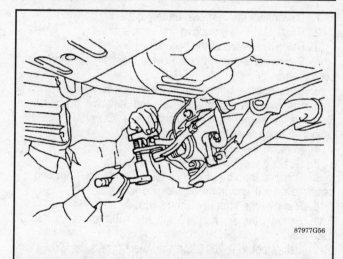

Fig. 82 Using a special tool to separate the tie rod ball joint

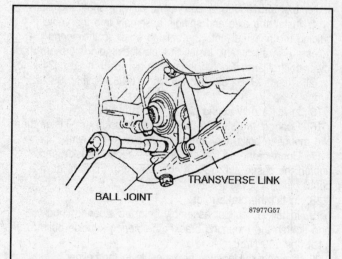

Fig. 83 Remove the transverse link arm from the spindle housing

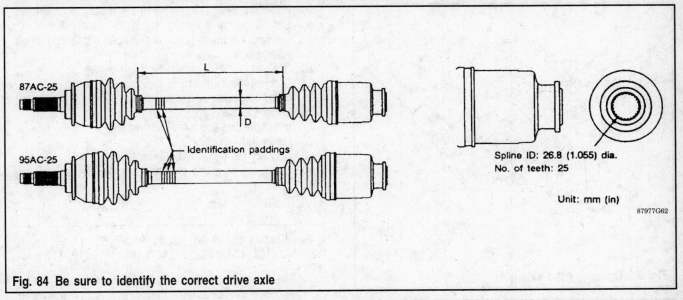

Fig. 84 Be sure to identify the correct drive axle

11. Using installer 922431000 and adapter 927390000 or equivalent, pull the halfshaft through the hub.
12. Install and temporarily tighten a new axle nut.
13. Align the halfshaft roll pin hole and insert the halfshaft onto the transaxle. Install a new roll pin.
14. Connect the lower control arm to the crossmember and tighten a new self-locking nut to 83 ft. lbs. (113 Nm).
15. Install the sway bar bracket.
16. Torque the new axle nut to 152 ft. lbs. (206 Nm) and stake the nut.
17. Install the wheel.
18. Lower the vehicle.
19. Connect the negative battery cable.

SVX

1. Disconnect the negative battery cable.
2. Raise and safely support the vehicle.
3. Remove the tire and wheel assembly.
4. Unstake and remove the axle nut.
5. Disconnect the sway bar link from the sway bar.
6. Disconnect the ABS sensor bracket from the strut.

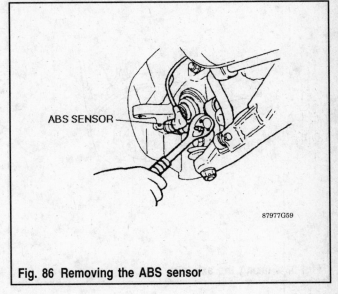

Fig. 86 Removing the ABS sensor

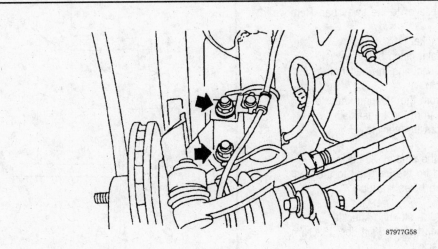

Fig. 85 Before loosening the strut-to-housing bolts, matchmark the camber adjustment bolt and strut

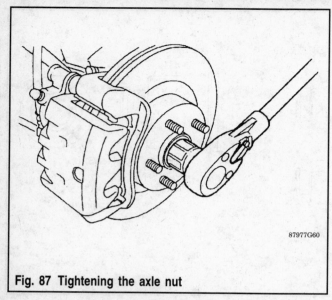

87977G60

Fig. 87 Tightening the axle nut

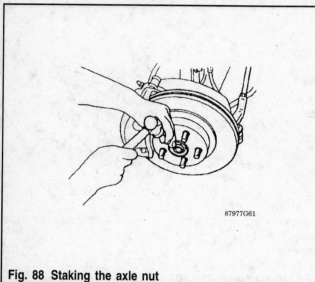

87977G61

Fig. 88 Staking the axle nut

7. Remove the brake hose bracket bolt and bracket from the strut.

8. Matchmark the sway bar lever to the sway bar. Remove the sway bar lever.

9. Loosen the sway bar bracket.

10. Remove the lower ball joint pinch bolt.

11. Drive out the spring pin securing the halfshaft to the transaxle. Discard the spring pin.

12. Separate the ball joint from the steering knuckle.

13. Disconnect the halfshaft from the transaxle.

14. Remove the halfshaft from the vehicle.

To install:

15. Install the halfshaft into the steering knuckle.

16. Connect the inboard end on the halfshaft to the transaxle. Make sure the spring pin holes line up.

17. Install a new spring pin.

18. Connect the ball joint to the steering knuckle.

19. Tighten the ball joint pinch bolt to 38 ft. lbs. (52 Nm).

20. Tighten the sway bar bracket.

21. Install the sway bar lever with the matchmarks in alignment and tighten the mounting bolt to 38 ft. lbs. (52 Nm).

22. Connect the brake hose bracket to the strut and install the mounting bolt.

23. Connect the ABS sensor to strut bracket.

24. Connect the sway bar to the sway bar link.

25. Install the axle nut and tighten to 137 ft. lbs. (187 Nm).

26. Install the dust cap.

27. Install the tire and wheel assembly.

28. Lower the vehicle.

29. Connect the negative battery cable.

30. Check the front end alignment and adjust as necessary.

OVERHAUL

▶ **See Figures 89, 90, 91, 92, 93, 94, 95, 96, 97, 98, 99, 100, 101, 102, 103, 104, 105, 106, 107, 108, 109, 110, 111 and 112**

1. Remove the bands from the boots at both the constant velocity and double offset joints, and slide the boots away from the joints.

2. Pry the circlip out of the double offset joint, and slide the outer race of the joint off the shaft.

3. Remove the balls from the cage, rotate the cage slightly, and slide the cage inward on the axle shaft.

4. Using snapring pliers, remove the outer snapring which retains the inner race to the shaft.

5. Slide the inner race, cage, and boot off the axle shaft.

❊❊WARNING

Exercise care to avoid damaging the boot on the inner snapring.

6. Pull back the constant velocity joint boot and pivot the stub axle around the joint far enough to expose a ball.

7. Remove the exposed ball, and continue this procedure until all balls are removed, at which time the outer race (stub axle) may be removed from the axle shaft.

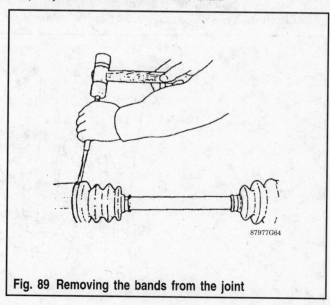

87977G64

Fig. 89 Removing the bands from the joint

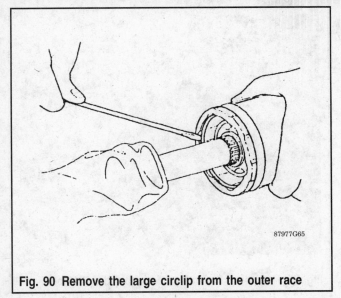

Fig. 90 Remove the large circlip from the outer race

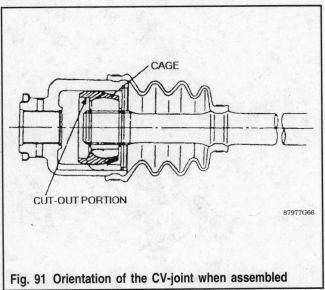

CAGE

CUT-OUT PORTION

Fig. 91 Orientation of the CV-joint when assembled

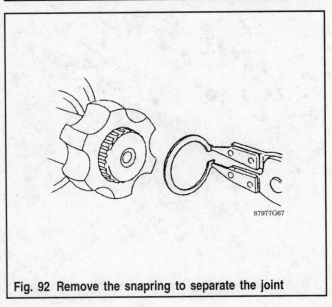

Fig. 92 Remove the snapring to separate the joint

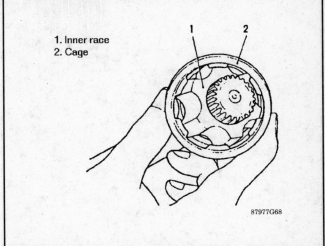

1. Inner race
2. Cage

Fig. 93 Inner race and cage — align the cage with the protruding part of the inner race

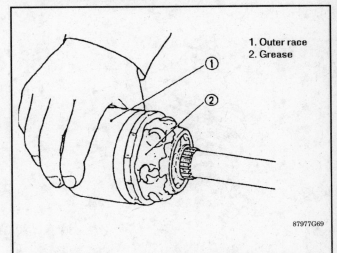

1. Outer race
2. Grease

Fig. 94 Install the inner race and ball assembly into the outer race

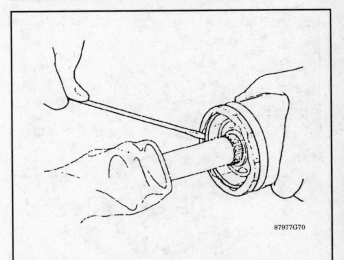

Fig. 95 Make sure the circlip is securely in the outer race, and not in the ball groove

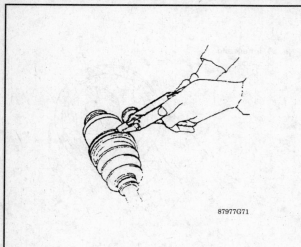

Fig. 96 Install the CV-boot and band — make sure to pull the band snug

Fig. 99 Removing the outer band from the CV-boot

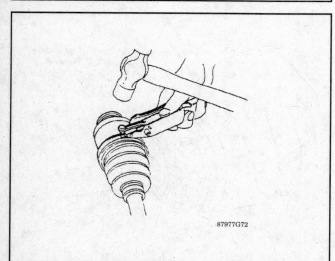

Fig. 97 Use a hammer to tap the band end down until it is snug — use care not to rip the boot

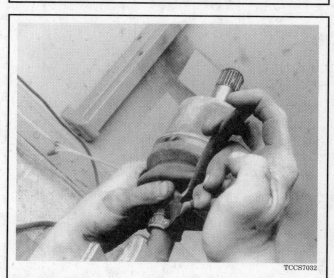

Fig. 100 Removing the inner band from the CV-boot

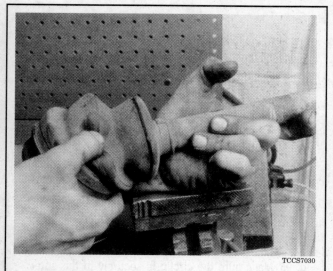

Fig. 98 Check the CV-boot for wear

Fig. 101 Removing the CV-boot from the joint housing

Fig. 102 Clean the CV-joint housing prior to removing the boot

Fig. 103 Removing the CV-joint housing assembly

Fig. 104 Removing the CV-joint

Fig. 105 Inspecting the CV-joint housing

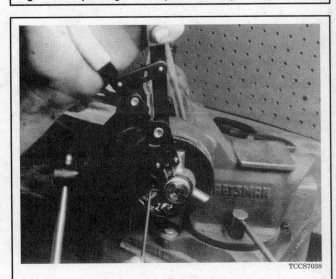
Fig. 106 Removing the CV-joint outer snapring

Fig. 107 Checking the CV-joint snapring for wear

Fig. 108 A typical CV-joint snapring

Fig. 109 Removing the CV-joint assembly

Fig. 110 Removing the CV-joint inner snapring

Fig. 111 Installing a typical CV-joint assembly

8. Remove the retaining snapring, and slide the inner race off the shaft.

9. Inspect the parts of both joints for wear, damage, or corrosion, and replace if necessary. Examine the axle shaft for bending or distortion, and replace if evident. Should the boots be dried out, cracked, or distorted, they must be replaced.

10. Install the constant velocity joint inner race on the axle shaft, and retain with a snapring.

11. Assemble the joint in the opposite order of disassembly.

12. Slide the double offset joint cage onto the shaft, with the counterbore toward the end of the shaft.

13. Install the inner race on the shaft, and install the retaining snapring.

14. Position the cage over the inner race, and fill the cage pockets with grease.

15. Insert the balls into the cage.

16. Fill the well in the outer race with approximately 1 oz. grease, and slide the outer race onto the axle shaft.

17. Align the outer race track and ball positions and place it into the part where the shaft, inner cage and balls were previously installed, then install it into the outer race.

18. Install the retaining circlip in the grove on the outer race.

➡Assure that the balls, cage and inner race are completely fitted in the outer race of the joint. Exercise care not to place the matched position of the circlip in the ball groove of the outer race. Finally, pull lightly on the shaft and assure that the circlip is completely fitted in the groove.

19. Add 1 oz. more grease to the interior of the joint. Fill the boot with approximately 1 oz. grease, and slide it into position over the double offset joint.

20. Fill the constant velocity joint boot with 3 oz. grease, and install the boot over the joint.

21. Band the boots on both joints tightly enough that they cannot be turned by hand.

✳✳WARNING

Use only grease specified for use in constant velocity joints.

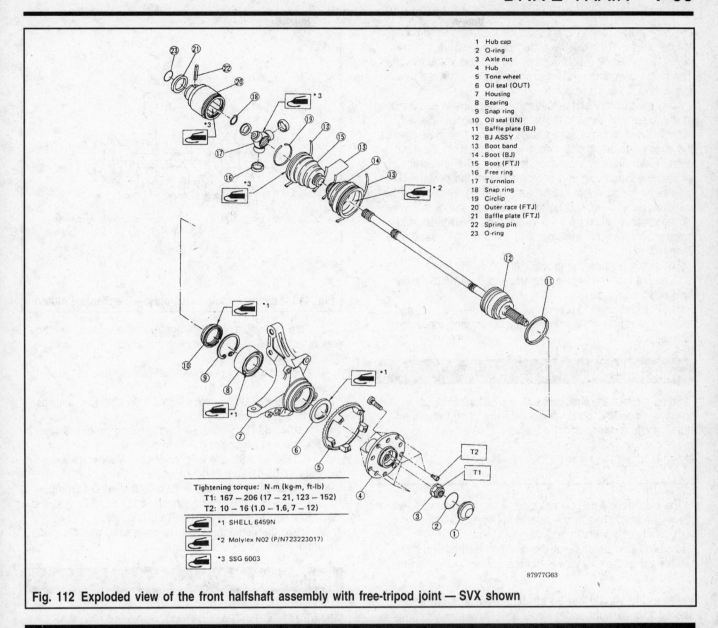

1 Hub cap
2 O-ring
3 Axle nut
4 Hub
5 Tone wheel
6 Oil seal (OUT)
7 Housing
8 Bearing
9 Snap ring
10 Oil seal (IN)
11 Baffle plate (BJ)
12 BJ ASSY
13 Boot band
14 Boot (BJ)
15 Boot (FTJ)
16 Free ring
17 Turnnion
18 Snap ring
19 Circlip
20 Outer race (FTJ)
21 Baffle plate (FTJ)
22 Spring pin
23 O-ring

Tightening torque: N.m (kg-m, ft-lb)
T1: 167 — 206 (17 — 21, 123 — 152)
T2: 10 — 16 (1.0 — 1.6, 7 — 12)

*1 SHELL 6459N

*2 Molylex N02 (P/N723223017)

*3 SSG 6003

87977G63

Fig. 112 Exploded view of the front halfshaft assembly with free-tripod joint — SVX shown

CLUTCH

Understanding Clutches

✻✻CAUTION

The clutch driven disc may contain asbestos, which has been determined to be a cancer causing agent. Never clean clutch surfaces with compressed air! Avoid inhaling any dust from any clutch surface! When cleaning clutch surfaces, use a commercially available brake cleaning fluid.

The purpose of the clutch is to disconnect and connect engine power at the transaxle. A vehicle at rest requires a lot of engine torque to get all that weight moving. An internal combustion engine does not develop a high starting torque (unlike steam engines) so it must be allowed to operate without any load until it builds up enough torque to move the vehicle.

Torque increases with engine rpm. The clutch allows the engine to build up torque by physically disconnecting the engine from the transaxle, relieving the engine of any load or resistance.

The transfer of engine power to the transaxle (the load) must be smooth and gradual; if it weren't, driveline components would wear out or break quickly. This gradual power transfer is made possible by gradually releasing the clutch pedal. The clutch disc and pressure plate are the connecting link between the engine and transaxle. When the clutch pedal is released, the disc and plate contact each other (the clutch is engaged) physically joining the engine and transaxle. When the pedal is pushed inward, the disc and plate separate (the clutch is disengaged) disconnecting the engine from the transaxle.

Most clutches utilize a single plate, dry friction disc with a diaphragm-style spring pressure plate. The clutch disc has a splined hub which attaches the disc to the input shaft. The disc has friction material where it contacts the flywheel and pressure plate. Torsion springs on the disc help absorb engine torque pulses. The pressure plate applies pressure to the clutch disc, holding it tight against the surface of the flywheel. The clutch operating mechanism consists of a release bearing, fork and cylinder assembly.

The release fork and actuating linkage transfer pedal motion to the release bearing. In the engaged position (pedal released) the diaphragm spring holds the pressure plate against the clutch disc, so engine torque is transmitted to the input shaft. When the clutch pedal is depressed, the release bearing pushes the diaphragm spring center toward the flywheel. The diaphragm spring pivots the fulcrum, relieving the load on the pressure plate. Steel spring straps riveted to the clutch cover lift the pressure plate from the clutch disc, disengaging the engine drive from the transaxle and enabling the gears to be changed.

The clutch is operating properly if:

1. It will stall the engine when released with the vehicle held stationary.

2. The shift lever can be moved freely between 1st and reverse gears when the vehicle is stationary and the clutch disengaged.

Adjustments

Some models are equipped with a mechanical clutch system, which is adjustable. Other models are equipped with an hydraulic system, which is not adjustable.

CABLE ADJUSTMENT

The clutch cable can be adjusted at the cable bracket where the cable is attached to the side of the transaxle housing.

1. Remove the circlip and clamp.

2. Slide the cable end in the direction desired and then replace the circlip and clamp into the nearest gutters on the cable end.

➡The cable should not be stretched out straight nor should it have right angle kinks in it. Any straightening should be gradual.

3. Check the clutch for proper operation.

PEDAL HEIGHT

Adjust the pedal with the return stop bolt, so that its pad is on the same level as the brake pedal pad.

Check to be sure that the stroke of the pedal is 5.04-5.43 in. (128-138mm). Check the clutch release fork stroke. It should be 0.67 in. (17mm).

FREE-PLAY ADJUSTMENT

▶ See Figure 113

1. Remove the clutch fork return spring and loosen the locknut on the fork adjusting nut.

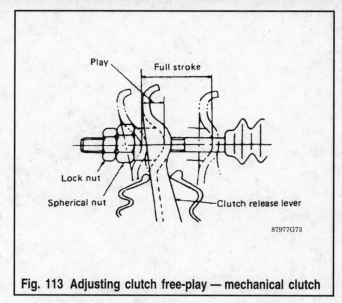

Fig. 113 Adjusting clutch free-play — mechanical clutch

2. Turn the adjusting nut (wingnut) until a release fork free-play of 0.14-0.18 in. (3.5-4.5mm) is obtained.

3. Tighten the locknut.

4. Check the pedal free-play. It should be one of the following:

• 1985-87 (2WD — Non-Turbo, 1.6L and 1.8L engines): 0.12-0.16 in. (3-4mm)

• 1985-87 (2WD/4WD — Turbo, 1.8L engines): 3-4mm

• 1987 (1.2L engine): 2-4mm

• 1988-92 1.8L and 2.7L engines, 2WD except turbocharger — 0.08-0.12 in. (2.0-3.0mm).

• 1988-94 1.2L engine — 0.08-0.16 in. (2.0-4.0mm).

• 1988-96 2WD/4WD turbocharged, 1.8L, 2.2L and the 4WD 2.7L engine — 0.12-0.16 in. (3.0-4.0mm).

5. Adjust the pedal free-play, as necessary, with the pedal adjusting bolt.

Clutch Pedal

REMOVAL & INSTALLATION

Except Legacy
▶ See Figure 114

1. Disconnect the negative battery cable.

2. Disengage the accelerator cable from the throttle body.

3. Disengage and detach the clutch cable from the following parts.

a. Clutch release fork

b. Clamp on the transaxle case.

c. Grommet of the toe board.

4. Detach the rim panel and lower the steering column.

5. Disengage the following parts from the pedal bracket.

a. Operating rod of the brake booster.

b. Electrical connectors for the clutch, cruise control and stop light switches.

c. Accelerator cable.

➡Take care not to kink the accelerator cable.

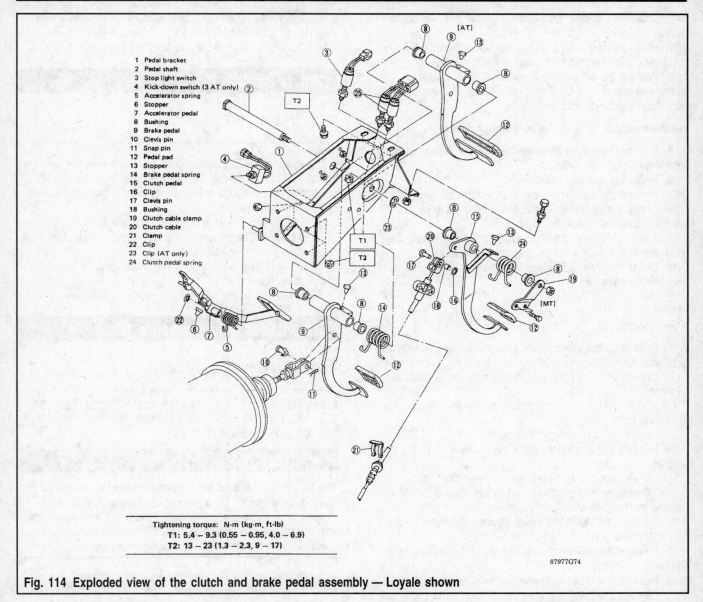

```
1  Pedal bracket
2  Pedal shaft
3  Stop light switch
4  Kick-down switch (3 AT only)
5  Accelerator spring
6  Stopper
7  Accelerator pedal
8  Bushing
9  Brake pedal
10 Clevis pin
11 Snap pin
12 Pedal pad
13 Stopper
14 Brake pedal spring
15 Clutch pedal
16 Clip
17 Clevis pin
18 Bushing
19 Clutch cable clamp
20 Clutch cable
21 Clamp
22 Clip
23 Clip (AT only)
24 Clutch pedal spring
```

Tightening torque: N·m (kg-m, ft-lb)
T1: 5.4 – 9.3 (0.55 – 0.95, 4.0 – 6.9)
T2: 13 – 23 (1.3 – 2.3, 9 – 17)

87977G74

Fig. 114 Exploded view of the clutch and brake pedal assembly — Loyale shown

6. Remove the pedal bracket assembly along with the clutch cable while supporting the brake booster in the engine compartment.

7. Detach the following parts from the pedal bracket assembly.
   a. Accelerator pedal return spring.
   b. Accelerator pedal.
   c. Clutch cable.
   d. Brake pedal return spring.
   e. Clutch pedal return spring, if equipped with Hill Holder.
   f. Circlip retaining pedal shaft
   g. Clutch pedal and brake pedal
   h. Stop light switch

To install:

8. Attach the switches on to the pedal bracket temporarily.

9. Clean inside of the bores of the clutch pedal and brake pedal, apply grease and set the bushing into the bores.

10. Align bores of the pedal bracket, clutch pedal and brake pedal.

11. Attach the brake pedal return spring and clutch pedal return spring (vehicle with a Hill Holder), then install the pedal shaft completely to prevent it from rotating.

➡**Be sure to clean up the bushings and apply grease prior to installing the shaft.**

12. Clean and apply grease to the shaft and inside of the bore of the accelerator pedal. Install the accelerator pedal onto the pedal bracket.

13. Set brake pedal position by adjusting position of the stop light switch.

14. Connect the clutch cable to the clutch pedal by using clevis pin and clip.

15. Insert the clutch cable into the hole on the toe board and set the pedal bracket above the steering column.

➡**Be careful not to bend the clutch cable too much.**

16. Insert bolts of the brake booster into the holes on the toe board, support it form the engine compartment and align the holes of the pedal bracket with the bolts. The operating

rod of the brake booster should be engaged with the brake pedal.

17. While pushing the pedal bracket upward firmly, tighten the 4 nuts and 2 bolts at its upper surface.

18. Pull out the accelerator inner cable to its maximum stroke and attach it to the accelerator pedal. Pull the accelerator cable from the throttle body side.

➡ **Take care not to kink the accelerator cable.**

19. Engage the electrical connectors for the clutch, cruise control and stop light switches.

20. Install the steering column.

21. Engage the accelerator cable to the throttle body.

22. Check the operation of the accelerator cable by operating the accelerator pedal by hand.

23. Attach the clutch cable grommet to the toe board, then engage the clutch cable to the clutch release fork.

24. Cover the outer cable end with the protective boot. Connect the negative battery cable.

Legacy

▶ **See Figure 115**

1. Disengage the clutch cable from the release lever. (non-turbo vehicles).

2. On vehicles equipped with a turbocharger, remove the steering bolts.

   a. Raise and support the vehicle safely and remove the 2 steering bolts.

   b. Lower the vehicle to the floor.

3. Remove the instrument panel lower cover from the pedal bracket.

   a. Disengage the operating rod at the brake booster.

   b. Disengage the electrical connectors for the clutch, cruise control and stop light switches.

4. Remove the clevis pin which secures the pedal to the pushrod, (turbo vehicles).

5. Remove the nut which secures the clutch master cylinder (turbo vehicles).

6. Remove the steering assembly (turbo vehicles).

7. Remove the bolts and nuts which secure the brake and clutch pedals.

8. Remove the pedal assembly and the clutch cable as unit.

➡ **Prior to removing the clutch cable from the toe board, remove the grommet. Slowly remove the clutch cable, being careful not to scratch it.**

9. Insert the clutch cable into the hole on the toe board and set the pedal bracket above the steering column.

➡ **Be careful not to bend the clutch cable too much.**

10. Insert the bolts of the brake booster into holes on the toe board supporting the booster from the engine compartment.

11. Align the holes of the pedal bracket onto the bolts.

12. Engage the operating rod of the brake booster to the brake pedal using the clevis pin and snap pin.

13. Engage the electrical connectors for the clutch, cruise control and stop light switches

14. On vehicles equipped with turbocharger, install the steering assembly and bolts.

15. Attach the clutch cable grommet to the toe board and then connect the clutch cable to the clutch release fork.

16. Cover the outer cable end with the protective boot.

Clutch Cable

REMOVAL & INSTALLATION

The clutch cable is connected to the clutch pedal at one end and to the clutch release lever at the other end. The cable conduit is retained by a bolt and clamp on a bracket mounted on the flywheel housing.

1. If necessary, raise and support the vehicle safely.

2. Disconnect both ends of the cable and the conduit, then remove the assembly from under the vehicle.

3. Using engine oil, lubricate the clutch cable. If the cable is defective, replace it.

4. Installation is the reverse the removal procedure.

Driven Disc and Pressure Plate

REMOVAL & INSTALLATION

▶ **See Figures 116, 117, 118, 119, 120, 121, 122, 123, 124, 125, 126, 127, 128, 129, 130, 131, 132, 133, 134, 135, 136, 137, 138, 139, 140 and 141**

✳✳CAUTION

The clutch driven disc may contain asbestos, which has been determined to be a cancer causing agent. Never clean clutch surfaces with compressed air! Avoid inhaling any dust from any clutch surface! When cleaning clutch surfaces, use a commercially available brake fluid.

1. Disconnect the negative battery cable. Remove the transaxle as outlined earlier in this section.

2. Gradually unscrew the six bolts (6mm) which hold the pressure plate assembly on the flywheel. Loosen the bolts only one turn at a time, working around the pressure plate. Do not unscrew all the bolts on one side at one time.

3. When all of the bolts have been removed, remove the clutch plate and disc.

✳✳WARNING

Do not get oil or grease on the clutch facing.

4. Remove the two retaining springs and remove the throwout bearing and the release fork.

➡ **Do not disassemble either the clutch cover or disc. Inspect the parts for wear or damage and replace any parts as necessary. Replace the clutch disc if there is any oil or grease on the facing. Do not wash or attempt to lubricate the throwout bearing. If it requires replacement, the bearing may be removed and a new one installed in the holder by means of a press.**

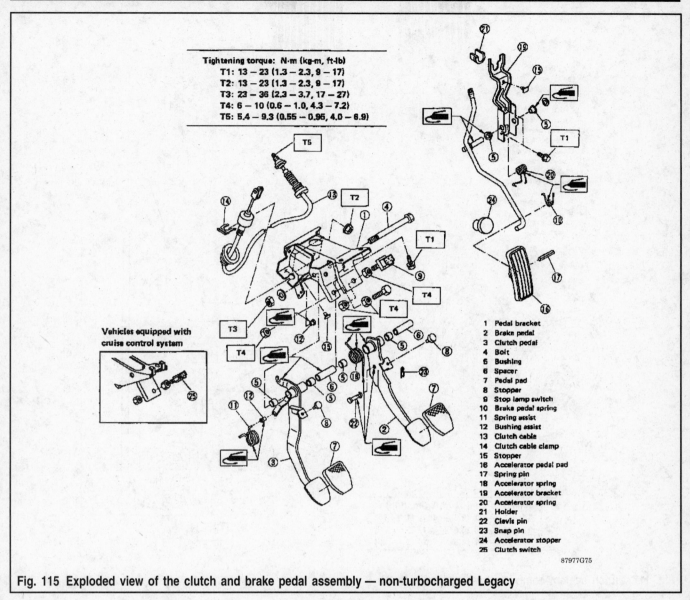

Tightening torque: N·m (kg-m, ft-lb)
T1: 13 — 23 (1.3 — 2.3, 9 — 17)
T2: 13 — 23 (1.3 — 2.3, 9 — 17)
T3: 23 — 36 (2.3 — 3.7, 17 — 27)
T4: 6 — 10 (0.6 — 1.0, 4.3 — 7.2)
T5: 5.4 — 9.3 (0.55 — 0.95, 4.0 — 6.9)

Vehicles equipped with cruise control system

1 Pedal bracket
2 Brake pedal
3 Clutch pedal
4 Bolt
5 Bushing
6 Spacer
7 Pedal pad
8 Stopper
9 Stop lamp switch
10 Brake pedal spring
11 Spring assist
12 Bushing assist
13 Clutch cable
14 Clutch cable clamp
15 Stopper
16 Accelerator pedal pad
17 Spring pin
18 Accelerator spring
19 Accelerator bracket
20 Accelerator spring
21 Holder
22 Clevis pin
23 Snap pin
24 Accelerator stopper
25 Clutch switch

87977G75

Fig. 115 Exploded view of the clutch and brake pedal assembly — non-turbocharged Legacy

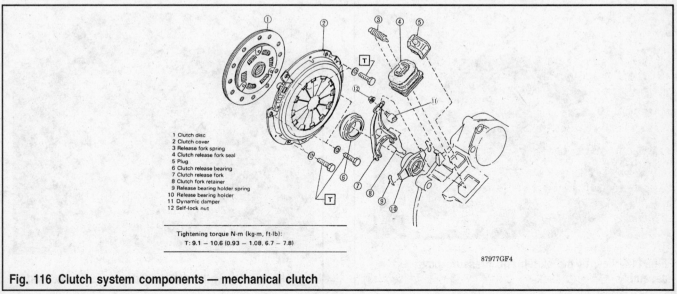

1 Clutch disc
2 Clutch cover
3 Release fork spring
4 Clutch release fork seal
5 Plug
6 Clutch release bearing
7 Clutch release fork
8 Clutch fork retainer
9 Release bearing holder spring
10 Release bearing holder
11 Dynamic damper
12 Self-lock nut

Tightening torque N·m (kg-m, ft-lb):
T: 9.1 — 10.6 (0.93 — 1.08, 6.7 — 7.8)

87977GF4

Fig. 116 Clutch system components — mechanical clutch

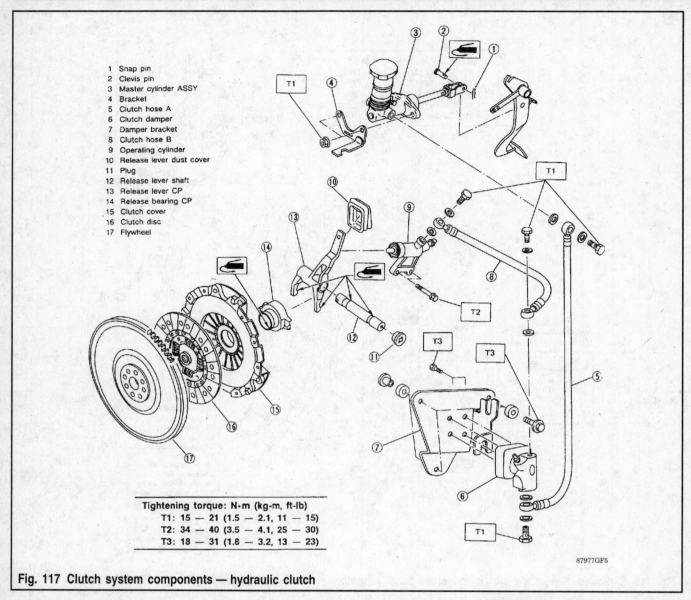

1 Snap pin
2 Clevis pin
3 Master cylinder ASSY
4 Bracket
5 Clutch hose A
6 Clutch damper
7 Damper bracket
8 Clutch hose B
9 Operating cylinder
10 Release lever dust cover
11 Plug
12 Release lever shaft
13 Release lever CP
14 Release bearing CP
15 Clutch cover
16 Clutch disc
17 Flywheel

Tightening torque: N·m (kg-m, ft-lb)
T1: 15 — 21 (1.5 — 2.1, 11 — 15)
T2: 34 — 40 (3.5 — 4.1, 25 — 30)
T3: 18 — 31 (1.8 — 3.2, 13 — 23)

87977GF5

Fig. 117 Clutch system components — hydraulic clutch

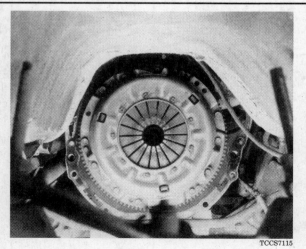

TCCS7115

Fig. 118 View of the clutch and pressure plate assembly

TCCS7116

Fig. 119 Removing the clutch and pressure plate bolts

Fig. 120 Removing the clutch and pressure plate assembly

Fig. 123 Removing the flywheel bolts. Be sure to first lock the flywheel in place

Fig. 121 Removing the clutch and pressure plate

Fig. 124 Removing the flywheel from the crankshaft

Fig. 122 View of the flywheel once the clutch assembly is removed

Fig. 125 Add a threadlocking agent to the flywheel bolts upon installation

TCCS7124

Fig. 126 Be sure that the flywheel surface is clean, before installing the clutch

TCCS7125

Fig. 127 Check across the flywheel surface, it should be flat

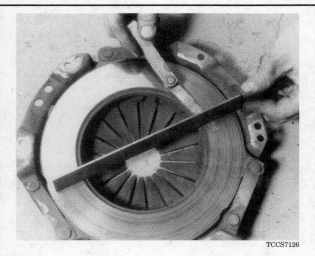

TCCS7126

Fig. 128 Checking the pressure plate for excessive wear

TCCS7142

Fig. 129 View of the clutch alignment arbor, used to install the clutch and pressure plate assembly

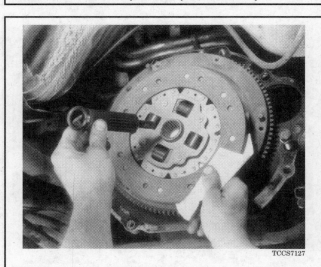

TCCS7127

Fig. 130 Install a clutch alignment arbor, to align the clutch assembly during installation

TCCS7128

Fig. 131 Clutch plate installed with the arbor in place

Fig. 132 The pressure plate-to-flywheel bolt holes should align

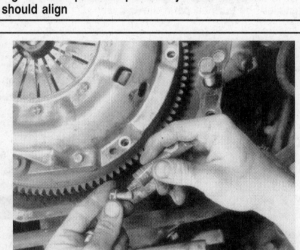

Fig. 133 Apply threadlocking agent to the clutch assembly bolts

Fig. 134 Be sure to use a torque wrench to tighten all bolts

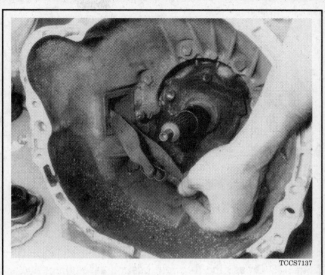

Fig. 135 Removing the clutch release fork

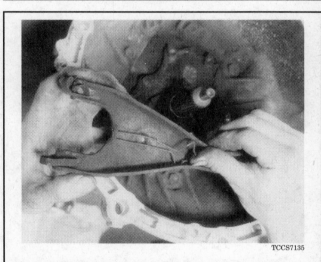

Fig. 136 Check the clutch release fork, including the bearing clips, for signs of damage

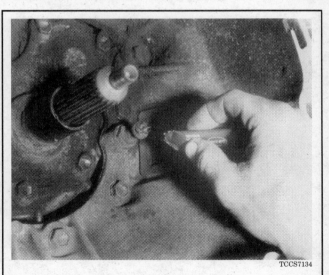

Fig. 137 Grease the clutch release fork ball

Fig. 138 Grease the throwout bearing assembly at the outer contact points

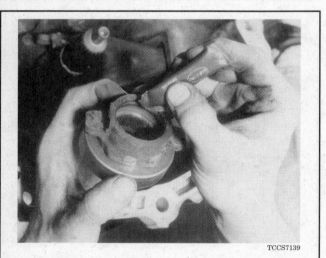

Fig. 139 Grease the throwout bearing assembly at the inner contact points

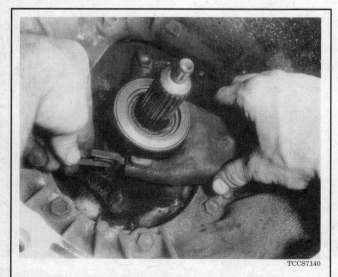

Fig. 140 Installing the clutch release fork bearing clip

Fig. 141 View of the clutch release fork assembly installed; be sure all parts move freely

To install:

5. Fit the release fork boot on the front of the transaxle housing. Install the release fork.

6. Insert the throwout bearing assembly and secure it with the two springs. Coat the inside diameter of the bearing holder and the fork-to-holder contact points with grease.

7. Insert a pilot shaft through the clutch cover and disc, then insert the end of the pilot into the needle bearing.

8. Tighten the pressure plate bolts gradually, one turn at a time, until the proper torque is reached. Tighten to 13 ft. lbs. (17 Nm).

✳✳WARNING

When installing the clutch pressure plate assembly, make sure that the O marks on the flywheel and the clutch pressure plate assembly are at least 120° apart. These marks indicate the direction of residual unbalance. Also, make sure that the clutch disc is installed properly, noting the FRONT and REAR markings.

9. After installation of the transaxle in the car, perform the adjustments outlined above.

Master Cylinder

REMOVAL & INSTALLATION

The clutch master cylinder is located on the firewall near the brake master cylinder. To remove the clutch master cylinder, disconnect and plug the fluid lines. Disconnect the pin retainer at the clutch pedal and remove the mounting bolts. To install, reverse the removal steps and tighten the master cylinder mounting bolts to 15 ft. lbs. (21 Nm). Be sure to bleed the system (as described in the Slave Cylinder procedure) when installation is complete.

Slave Cylinder and Damper

REMOVAL & INSTALLATION

The clutch slave cylinder and damper are located on the top of the transaxle housing. To remove the slave cylinder and damper, disconnect and plug the fluid lines and remove the mounting bolts. To install, reverse the removal steps. Tighten the slave cylinder and damper mounting bolts to 30 ft. lbs. (41 Nm). Tighten the fluid hoses to 13 ft. lbs. (18 Nm). Be sure to bleed the system when installation is complete.

SYSTEM BLEEDING

▶ See Figures 142 and 143

➡To properly bleed the system, it must be bled at the slave cylinder and at the damper. Each of these has an air bleeder on it.

1. Connect a vinyl tube to the air bleeder on the damper and put the other end in a jar with clean clutch fluid.
2. With the help of an assistant depressing the clutch pedal, slowly open the bleeder valve. Close the bleeder valve

and release the pedal. Repeat this process until no air bubbles appear in the jar.

3. Move the tube to the bleeder on the slave cylinder and repeat the process. Check the operation of the clutch after the bleed procedure is complete.

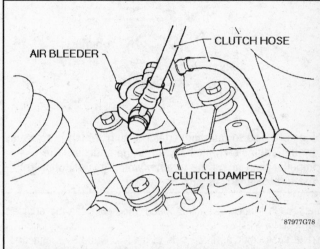

Fig. 142 Bleeding the hydraulic clutch at the clutch damper

AUTOMATIC TRANSAXLE

➡The Justy uses a unique automatic transaxle known as the Electronic Constantly Variable Transaxle (ECVT). This transaxle is considerably different from standard transaxles, as such the following description does not apply to the ECVT. A brief description of the ECVT can be found following this section on automatic transaxles.

Understanding Automatic Transaxles

The automatic transaxle allows engine torque and power to be transmitted to the drive wheels within a narrow range of

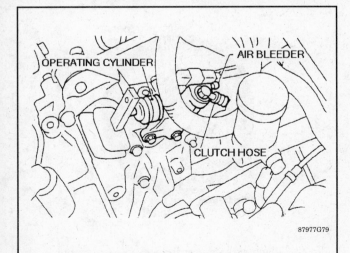

Fig. 143 Bleeding the hydraulic clutch at the slave cylinder

engine operating speeds. The transaxle will allow the engine to turn fast enough to produce plenty of power and torque at very low speeds, while keeping it at a sensible rpm at high vehicle speeds. The transaxle performs this job entirely without driver assistance. The transaxle uses a light fluid as the medium for the transaxle of power. This fluid also works in the operation of various hydraulic control circuits and as a lubricant. Because the transaxle fluid performs all of these three functions, trouble within the unit can easily travel from one part to another. For this reason, and because of the complexity and unusual operating principles of the transaxle, a very sound understanding of the basic principles of operation will simplify troubleshooting.

THE TORQUE CONVERTER

▶ See Figure 144

The torque converter replaces the conventional clutch. It has three functions:

1. It allows the engine to idle with the vehicle at a standstill, even with the transaxle in gear.
2. It allows the transaxle to shift from range to range smoothly, without requiring that the driver close the throttle during the shift.
3. It multiplies engine tighten to an increasing extent as vehicle speed drops and throttle opening is increased. This has the effect of making the transaxle more responsive and reduces the amount of shifting required.

The torque converter is a metal case which is shaped like a sphere that has been flattened on opposite sides. It is bolted to the rear end of the engine's crankshaft. Generally, the entire

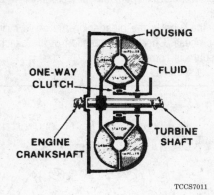

TCCS7011

Fig. 144 The torque converter housing, which is rotated by the engine's crankshaft, turns the impeller. The impeller then spins the turbine, which gives motion to the turbine shaft, driving the gears

metal case rotates at engine speed and serves as the engine's flywheel.

The case contains three sets of blades. One set is attached directly to the case. This set forms the torus or pump. Another set is directly connected to the output shaft, and forms the turbine. The third set is mounted on a hub which, in turn, is mounted on a stationary shaft through a one-way clutch. This third set is known as the stator.

A pump, which is driven by the converter hub at engine speed, keeps the torque converter full of transaxle fluid at all times. Fluid flows continuously through the unit to provide cooling.

Under low speed acceleration, the torque converter functions as follows:

The torus is turning faster than the turbine. It picks up fluid at the center of the converter and, through centrifugal force, slings it outward. Since the outer edge of the converter moves faster than the portions at the center, the fluid picks up speed.

The fluid then enters the outer edge of the turbine blades. It then travels back toward the center of the converter case along the turbine blades. In impinging upon the turbine blades, the fluid loses the energy picked up in the torus.

If the fluid were now to immediately be returned directly into the torus, both halves of the converter would have to turn at approximately the same speed at all times, and torque input and output would both be the same.

In flowing through the torus and turbine, the fluid picks up two types of flow, or flow in two separate directions. It flows through the turbine blades, and it spins with the engine. The stator, whose blades are stationary when the vehicle is being accelerated at low speeds, converts one type of flow into another. Instead of allowing the fluid to flow straight back into the torus, the stator's curved blades turn the fluid almost 90° toward the direction of rotation of the engine. Thus the fluid does not flow as fast toward the torus, but is already spinning when the torus picks it up. This has the effect of allowing the torus to turn much faster than the turbine. This difference in speed may be compared to the difference in speed between the smaller and larger gears in any gear train. The result is that engine power output is higher, and engine torque is multiplied.

As the speed of the turbine increases, the fluid spins faster and faster in the direction of engine rotation. As a result, the ability of the stator to redirect the fluid flow is reduced. Under cruising conditions, the stator is eventually forced to rotate on its one-way clutch in the direction of engine rotation. Under these conditions, the torque converter begins to behave almost like a solid shaft, with the torus and turbine speeds being almost equal.

THE PLANETARY GEARBOX

▶ **See Figures 145, 146 and 147**

The ability of the torque converter to multiply engine torque is limited. Also, the unit tends to be more efficient when the turbine is rotating at relatively high speeds. Therefore, a planetary gearbox is used to carry the power output of the turbine to the halfshafts.

Planetary gears function very similarly to conventional transaxle gears. However, their construction is different in that

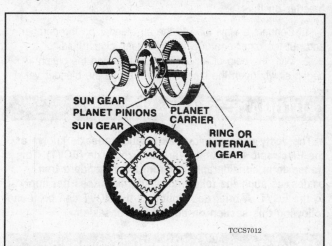

TCCS7012

Fig. 145 Planetary gears work in a similar fashion to manual transmission gears, but are composed of three parts

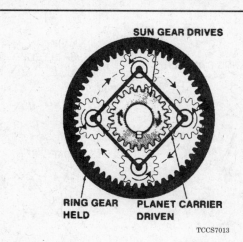

TCCS7013

Fig. 146 Planetary gears in the maximum reduction (low) range. The ring gear is held and a lower gear ratio is obtained

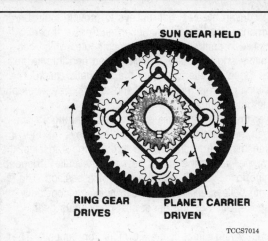

Fig. 147 Planetary gears in the minimum reduction (drive) range. The ring gear is allowed to revolve, providing a higher gear ratio

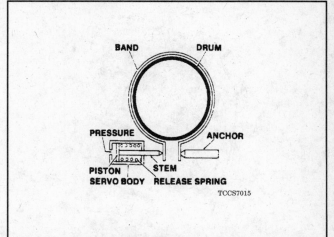

Fig. 148 Servos, operated by pressure, are used to apply or release the bands, to either hold the ring gear or allow it to rotate

three elements make up one gear system, and, in that all three elements are different from one another. The three elements are: an outer gear that is shaped like a hoop, with teeth cut into the inner surface; a sun gear, mounted on a shaft and located at the very center of the outer gear; and a set of three planet gears, held by pins in a ring-like planet carrier, meshing with both the sun gear and the outer gear. Either the outer gear or the sun gear may be held stationary, providing more than one possible torque multiplication factor for each set of gears. Also, if all three gears are forced to rotate at the same speed, the gearset forms, in effect, a solid shaft.

Most modern automatics use the planetary gears to provide either a single reduction ratio of about 1.8:1, or two reduction gears: a low of about 2.5:1, and an intermediate of about 1.5:1. Bands and clutches are used to hold various portions of the gearsets to the transaxle case or to the shaft on which they are mounted. Shifting is accomplished, then, by changing the portion of each planetary gearset which is held to the transaxle case or to the shaft.

THE SERVOS AND ACCUMULATORS

▶ See Figure 148

The servos are hydraulic pistons and cylinders. They resemble the hydraulic actuators used on many familiar machines, such as bulldozers. Hydraulic fluid enters the cylinder, under pressure, and forces the piston to move to engage the band or clutches.

The accumulators are used to cushion the engagement of the servos. The transaxle fluid must pass through the accumulator on the way to the servo. The accumulator housing contains a thin piston which is sprung away from the discharge passage of the accumulator. When fluid passes through the accumulator on the way to the servo, it must move the piston against spring pressure, and this action smooths out the action of the servo.

THE HYDRAULIC CONTROL SYSTEM

The hydraulic pressure used to operate the servos comes from the main transaxle oil pump. This fluid is channeled to the various servos through the shift valves. There is generally a manual shift valve which is operated by the transaxle selector lever and an automatic shift valve for each automatic upshift the transaxle provides.

➡Many new transaxles are electronically controlled. On these models, electrical solenoids are used to better control the hydraulic fluid. Usually, the solenoids are regulated by an electronic control module.

There are two pressures which affect the operation of these valves. One is the governor pressure which is effected by vehicle speed. The other is the modulator pressure which is effected by intake manifold vacuum or throttle position. Governor pressure rises with an increase in vehicle speed, and modulator pressure rises as the throttle is opened wider. By responding to these two pressures, the shift valves cause the upshift points to be delayed with increased throttle opening to make the best use of the engine's power output.

Most transaxles also make use of an auxiliary circuit for downshifting. This circuit may be actuated by the throttle linkage the vacuum line which actuates the modulator, by a cable or by a solenoid. It applies pressure to a special downshift surface on the shift valve or valves.

The transaxle modulator also governs the line pressure, used to actuate the servos. In this way, the clutches and bands will be actuated with a force matching the torque output of the engine.

Electronic Constantly Variable Transaxle (ECVT)

▶ See Figures 149 and 150

The ECVT is used in the Justy. This transaxle combines a electronically controlled magnetic clutch with a variable tran-

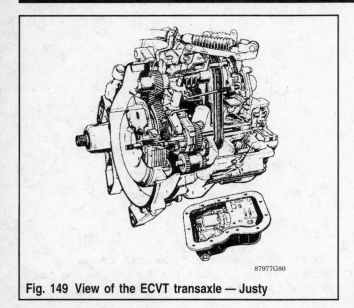

87977G80

Fig. 149 View of the ECVT transaxle — Justy

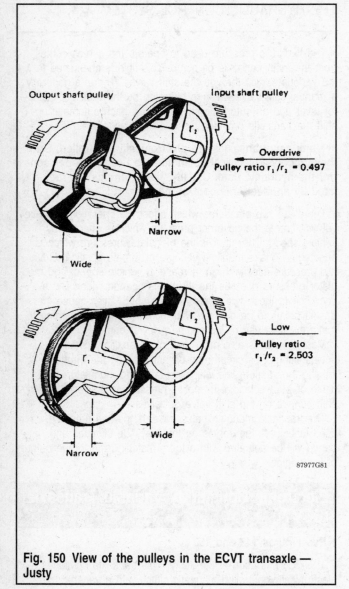

87977G81

Fig. 150 View of the pulleys in the ECVT transaxle — Justy

saxle that is driven by steel belt pulleys to provide high running performance, low fuel consumption and ease of control.

The transaxle is controlled by a microcomputer which constantly monitors engine speed, vehicle speed and throttle position. It uses these signals to control the magnetic clutch. The magnetic clutch controls the width of the drive pulley faces and thus provides the shifting effect.

The power from the transaxle is transmitted through a special steel belt that runs between 2 variable pulleys, as the power is transmitted from the engine through the transaxle, the control computer varies the space between the pulleys depending on engine load, vehicle speed and throttle position. The varying of the pulleys allows the belt to ride in a constantly changing space, this has the effect of a continuous gear change.

The overall driving effect of the ECVT is very smooth. The constant adjustment of the pulleys means that the transaxle works more efficiently to transmit power to the drive wheels.

Oil Pan and Filter

REMOVAL & INSTALLATION

▶ See Figure 151

➡ Normal maintenance does not require removal of the transaxle oil pan, or changing or cleaning of the oil strainer. However, if a leak is detected at the transaxle oil pan gasket it must be replaced.

1. Park the car on a level surface or support it on jack-stands, engine off.
2. Remove the drain plug and drain the transaxle fluid into a suitable container.
3. Remove the mounting bolts and lower the oil pan and gasket.
4. Reverse the above process to install the pan. Always use a new pan gasket.

If you wish to remove the oil strainer, simply unbolt it from the valve body after Step 3 above. It can be cleaned in fresh gasoline and dried with compressed air or allowed to air dry.

87977G82

Fig. 151 Transaxle oil filter screen mounting bolts — the oil filter is located in the oil pan

Adjustments

SHIFT LINKAGE

Except Justy ECVT
▶ **See Figures 152 and 153**

The linkage adjustment is important for the automatic transaxle. Great care should be exercised because improper adjustment will result in damage to the transaxle.

To determine if adjustment is necessary, check the shifting operation with the engine off and the parking brake applied. While holding in the release button with your thumb, move the selector lever forward until you can feel that the transaxle is in PARK. Then move the lever back and feel for the five remaining positions. If the gear selector indicator points to the proper gear at each stop, and if the selector lever does not jump

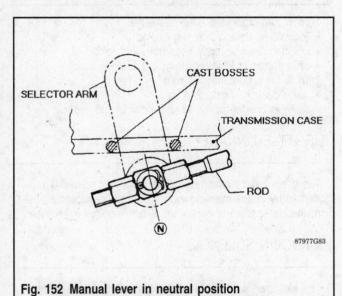

Fig. 152 Manual lever in neutral position

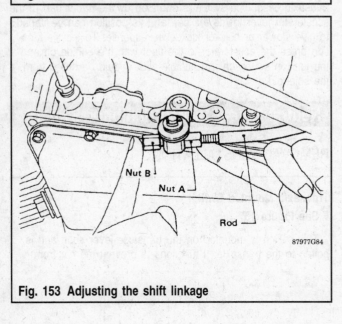

Fig. 153 Adjusting the shift linkage

when the release button is let go, the shift linkage is properly adjusted. If this is not the case adjustment is necessary.

1. Place the gear selector in N position.
2. Loosen the adjusting nuts on the linkage rod.
3. Check that the manual lever on the transaxle is in the **N** detent position. The manual lever is in the neutral position when the selector arm is between the cast bosses of the transaxle case.
4. Set the gear selector lever so that it clicks in the neutral position.
5. Adjust the fitting length of the rod by turning nut **A** until it comes into contact with the connector while pushing the rod lightly with one finger.
6. Tighten the nut **B** with nut **A** kept stationary with wrench.
7. Engage the electrical connector to the neutral safety switch.
8. After adjustment, check the selector operation through all gear ranges.
9. Check operation of the back-up lights when the selector is place in **R**.
10. Check that the engine does not start in any other position except **P** and **N**.

Justy ECVT
▶ **See Figure 154**

ADJUSTMENT AT SHIFTER SIDE

1. Set the gear selector lever so that it clicks in the neutral position.
2. Push cable and nut **A** to the lever end and adjust the inner cable with nut **B**.

➡**Do not move nut C.**

3. After adjustment, check the selector operation through all gear ranges.
4. Check operation of the back-up lights when the selector is place in **R**.
5. Check that the engine does not start in any other position except **P** and **N**.

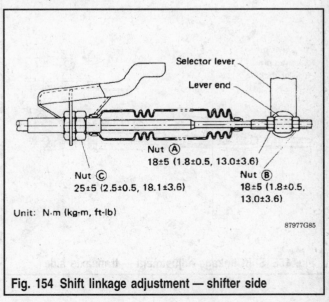

Fig. 154 Shift linkage adjustment — shifter side

ADJUSTMENT AT TRANSAXLE SIDE

▶ See Figure 155

1. Set the gear selector lever so that it clicks in the neutral position.

2. Measure the distance between the turn buckle and cable end link at the transaxle. It should be is less than 0.51 in. (13mm).

3. Adjust the cable by turning the turn buckle on the cable link.

4. If necessary, loosen the cable end at the transaxle side to increase or decrease the length of the inner cable.

5. After adjustment, check the selector operation through all gear ranges.

6. Check operation of the back-up lights when the selector is place in **R**.

7. Check that the engine does not start in any other position except **P** and **N**.

BRAKE BAND ADJUSTMENT

Except Justy ECVT

▶ See Figure 156

This adjustment can be performed on the outside of the transaxle.

1. Park the car on a level surface or support it on jackstands, engine off.

2. Locate the adjusting screw above the pan on the left side of the transaxle.

3. Loosen the locknut.

4. On 1985 and later models, tighten the adjusting screw to 18 ft. lbs. (25 Nm), then turn it back exactly ¾ turn.

5. Tighten the lock nut.

Following the above procedure will adjust the transaxle brake band to the factory specified setting. However, if any of the following conditions are detected the adjusting screw can be moved ¼ turn in either direction:

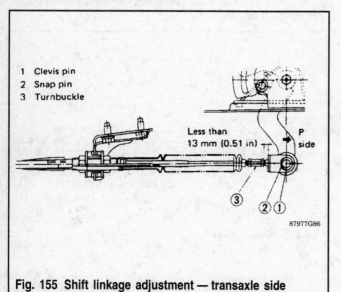

1 Clevis pin
2 Snap pin
3 Turnbuckle

Less than 13 mm (0.51 in)

P side

③ ② ①

87977G86

Fig. 155 Shift linkage adjustment — transaxle side

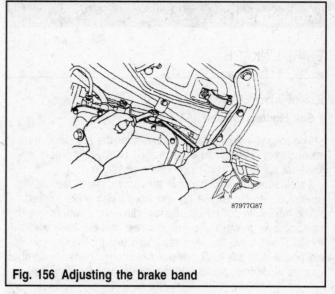

87977G87

Fig. 156 Adjusting the brake band

Turn ¼ turn clockwise if the transaxle:
• jolts when shifting from 1st to 2nd
• engine speed abruptly rises from 2nd to 3rd, or,
• shift delays in kickdown from 3rd to 2nd.
Turn ¼ turn counterclockwise if:
• car slips from 1st to 2nd, or
• there is braking action at shift from 2nd to 3rd.

THROTTLE LINKAGE

The control valve assembly of the automatic transaxle is governed by intake manifold vacuum rather than throttle position, therefore, there is no linkage which requires adjustment.

KICKDOWN SOLENOID

The kickdown solenoid is located on the right side of the transaxle case. The switch is operated by the upper part of the accelerator lever inside the car, and its position can be varied to give slower or quicker kickdown response. To test its function press the accelerator to the floor with the engine off and the ignition switch on. An audible click should be heard from the solenoid.

Neutral Safety Switch (Inhibitor Switch)

REMOVAL & INSTALLATION

Transaxle Mounted Switch

▶ See Figure 157

This switch is mounted on the transaxle lever shaft and is bolted to the transaxle. It functions to prevent the car from

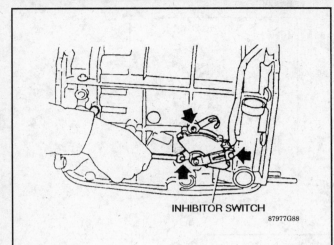

INHIBITOR SWITCH

87977G88

Fig. 157 Removal and installation of the neutral safety switch — transaxle mounted

starting in any gear position but Park or Neutral, and to activate the back-up lights when in reverse.

1. Disconnect the linkage rod from the transaxle manual lever.

➡**Refer to the diagram of the shift linkage system earlier in this Section.**

2. Make sure that the manual lever on the transaxle is in the neutral detent position.

3. Remove the manual lever by taking off the mounting nut.

4. Disengage the wire harness connector from the switch.

5. Remove the two safety switch mounting bolts and the setscrew from the lower face of the switch and remove the switch.

To install:

6. Position the switch over the manual shaft and bolt the switch in place. If a new switch is being installed it will have set pins already in place.

7. If not follow the switch adjustment procedure below.

8. Connect the linkage rod and adjust, if necessary.

Shifter Mounted Switch

▶ **See Figure 158**

This switch is mounted on the shifter assembly. It functions to prevent the car from starting in any gear position but Park or Neutral, and to activate the back-up lights when in reverse. Adjustment is as follows.

1. Disconnect the negative battery cable.

2. Place the selector lever in the **N** position.

3. Remove the hand brake cover and the console.

4. Remove the selector handle by removing the 2 retaining screws on each side of it. Hold the release button in an remove the pull the handle straight up.

5. Disengage the harness connector from the inhibitor switch.

6. Remove the 2 bolts holding the inhibitor switch to the shifter assembly.

To install:

7. If a new switch is being installed, a locating pin will already be in the switch for correct adjustment position.

8. If there is no knock pin in the switch, see adjustment procedure.

9. Install the switch and retaining screws. Engage the harness connector.

10. Install the shift indicator assembly and retaining screws.

11. Assembly the selector handle, spring, 4WD switch and button as follows:

a. Apply grease on the sliding part of the selector handle button and spring. install the selector handle on to the shifter.

b. Insert the spring into the button and insert it into the grip handle from the spring side.

c. Insert the grip handle on the selector lever while pushing the button in the grip.

d. The shifter release button should be on the driver's side. Install the retaining screws securing the handle to the shifter lever.

12. Perform the following steps for 4WD vehicles only:

a. Connect the 4WD harness to the switch so that the lag terminal turns downward.

b. Put the harness into the grip handle to prevent it from getting considerably distorted and subject to any excessive force.

c. Place the 4WD switch into the grip handle and install the retaining screw.

ADJUSTMENT

Transaxle Mounted Switch

▶ **See Figure 159**

1. Loosen the 3 inhibitor switch mounting bolts

2. Shift the select lever to the N position.

3. Insert a 1.5mm drill bit through the set screw hole. Turn the switch slightly so that the drill bit passes through into the back part of the switch.

4. In this position, tighten the switch mounting bolts.

Shifter Mounted Switch

▶ **See Figure 160**

➡**If a new neutral safety switch is being installed, a locating pin (knock pin) is pre-installed for correct switch installation position. Simply install the switch according to replacement procedure and remove the knock pin. If the switch does not have a knock pin installed, perform the following procedure.**

1. Loosen the switch retaining screws.

2. Using a 0.08 in. (2mm) drill bit align the switch knock pin hole, the moving plate and knock pin hole at the case.

3. At the position where the selector lever is shifted in the **N** and pushed to **P** side lightly, align the locator to the bracket hole, the moving plate pin-to-arm hole. Secure with the retaining bolts.

4. Turn the ignition switch **ON** and check the back-up light operation. Check that the engine starts only in park and neutral positions.

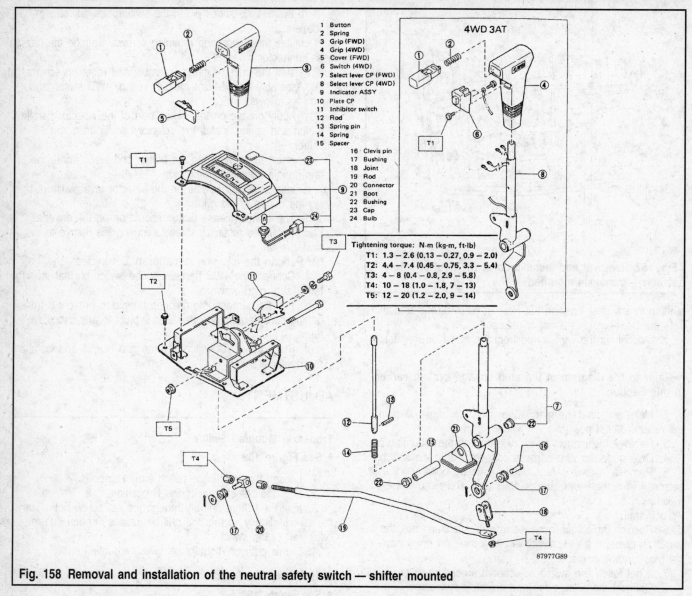

1 Button
2 Spring
3 Grip (FWD)
4 Grip (4WD)
5 Cover (FWD)
6 Switch (4WD)
7 Select lever CP (FWD)
8 Select lever CP (4WD)
9 Indicator ASSY
10 Plate CP
11 Inhibitor switch
12 Rod
13 Spring pin
14 Spring
15 Spacer
16 Clevis pin
17 Bushing
18 Joint
19 Rod
20 Connector
21 Boot
22 Bushing
23 Cap
24 Bulb

4WD 3AT

Tightening torque: N·m (kg-m, ft-lb)
T1: 1.3 – 2.6 (0.13 – 0.27, 0.9 – 2.0)
T2: 4.4 – 7.4 (0.45 – 0.75, 3.3 – 5.4)
T3: 4 – 8 (0.4 – 0.8, 2.9 – 5.8)
T4: 10 – 18 (1.0 – 1.8, 7 – 13)
T5: 12 – 20 (1.2 – 2.0, 9 – 14)

87977G89

Fig. 158 Removal and installation of the neutral safety switch — shifter mounted

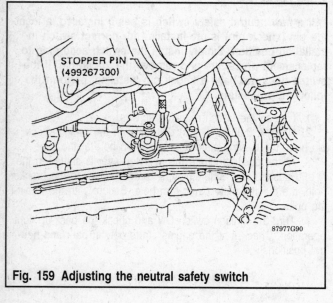

STOPPER PIN
(499267300)

87977G90

Fig. 159 Adjusting the neutral safety switch

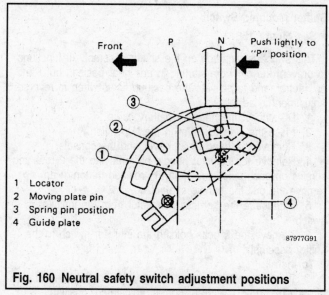

Front

P   N

Push lightly to "P" position

1 Locator
2 Moving plate pin
3 Spring pin position
4 Guide plate

87977G91

Fig. 160 Neutral safety switch adjustment positions

Transaxle

REMOVAL & INSTALLATION

Justy

WITH ECVT TRANSAXLE

▶ **See Figure 161**

➡ **When removing and installing ECVT transaxle, always remove and install the engine and transaxle as an assembly.**

1. Disconnect the negative battery cable. Drain the coolant by removing drain plug from radiator.

2. Remove the grille. Disconnect hoses and electric wiring from radiator and remove the radiator.

3. Remove front hood release cable and remove radiator upper support member. Disconnect horn and remove the air cleaner assembly.

4. Disconnect the following hoses and cables:
   a. Hoses from carburetor
   b. Hoses from the heater unit
   c. Hose for brake booster
   d. Clutch cable
   e. Accelerator cable
   f. Choke cable from carburetor, if equipped
   g. Speedometer cable
   h. Distributor wiring

5. Disconnect selector cable. Set selector lever at **N** position. Remove clip and detach selector cable from bracket. Remove snap pin, clevis pin and separate selector cable from transaxle.

6. Remove the pitching stopper from the bracket.

7. Disconnect the starter cable, engine wiring harness connectors, ground lead terminals and brush holder harness connector.

8. Remove the hanger from the rear of transaxle.

9. Remove under covers and remove the exhaust system.

10. Remove the driveshaft from transaxle.

11. Remove transverse link.

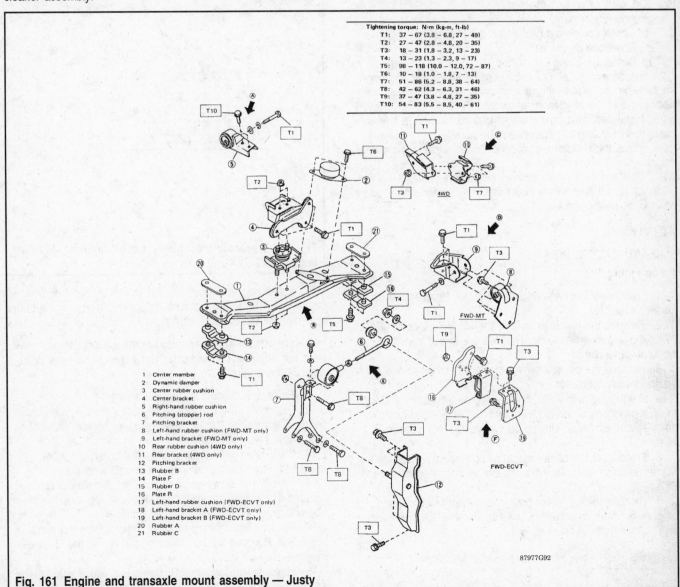

Tightening torque: N·m (kg-m, ft-lb)
T1:	37 – 67 (3.8 – 6.8, 27 – 49)
T2:	27 – 47 (2.8 – 4.8, 20 – 35)
T3:	18 – 31 (1.8 – 3.2, 13 – 23)
T4:	13 – 23 (1.3 – 2.3, 9 – 17)
T5:	98 – 118 (10.0 – 12.0, 72 – 87)
T6:	10 – 18 (1.0 – 1.8, 7 – 13)
T7:	51 – 86 (5.2 – 8.8, 38 – 64)
T8:	42 – 62 (4.3 – 6.3, 31 – 46)
T9:	37 – 47 (3.8 – 4.8, 27 – 35)
T10:	54 – 83 (5.5 – 8.5, 40 – 61)

1	Center member
2	Dynamic damper
3	Center rubber cushion
4	Center bracket
5	Right-hand rubber cushion
6	Pitching (stopper) rod
7	Pitching bracket
8	Left-hand rubber cushion (FWD-MT only)
9	Left-hand bracket (FWD-MT only)
10	Rear rubber cushion (4WD only)
11	Rear bracket (4WD only)
12	Pitching bracket
13	Rubber B
14	Plate F
15	Rubber D
16	Plate R
17	Left-hand rubber cushion (FWD-ECVT only)
18	Left-hand bracket A (FWD-ECVT only)
19	Left-hand bracket B (FWD-ECVT only)
20	Rubber A
21	Rubber C

87977G92

Fig. 161 Engine and transaxle mount assembly — Justy

12. Remove the spring pin retaining the axle shaft by using a suitable tool and separate front axle shaft from the transaxle.

13. Remove engine and transaxle mounting brackets.

14. Raise the engine and remove center member and crossmember.

15. Lift up the engine/transaxle assembly carefully and remove it from the vehicle.

To install:

16. Position the engine/transaxle assembly in the vehicle. Install engine and transaxle mounting brackets.

17. Install center member and crossmember.

18. Install the axle shaft to transaxle with new spring pin.

19. Install gearshift rod and stay to transaxle.

20. Install the exhaust system. Connect driveshaft to transaxle.

21. Install transverse link and under covers to the vehicle.

22. Reconnect the pitching stopper to bracket.

23. Reconnect the following hoses and cables:
   a. Hoses to carburetor
   b. Hoses to the heater unit
   c. Hose to brake booster
   d. Clutch cable to transaxle
   e. Accelerator cable
   f. Choke cable from carburetor, if equipped
   g. Speedometer cable
   h. Distributor wiring

24. Reconnect the starter cable, engine wiring harness connectors, ground lead terminals and brush holder harness connector. Install the air cleaner assembly.

25. Install radiator upper member and connect hood release cable to lock assembly. Reconnect the horn.

26. Install the radiator and connect hoses and electric wiring. Attach grille to the vehicle.

27. Refill the coolant. Reconnect the battery cable.

28. Check all fluid levels. Road test vehicles for proper operation in all driving ranges.

XT Coupe

1.8L AND 2.7L ENGINES

▶ See Figure 162

1. Disconnect the negative battery cable. Remove the air cleaner assembly.

2. Remove the clutch cable and the Hill Holder cable. Remove the speedometer cable. Remove the torque converter from the drive plate.

3. Remove the oxygen sensor electrical connector and the neutral switch connector.

4. If equipped with 4WD, remove the and unplug the electrical connections at the back-up light and differential lock indicator switch assembly. Unplug the differential lock vacuum hose.

5. Disconnect the starter electrical connections. Remove the starter retaining bolts. Remove the starter from the transaxle case.

6. Remove the air intake boot. Disconnect the pitching stopper rod from its mounting bracket. Remove the right side engine to transaxle mounting bolt.

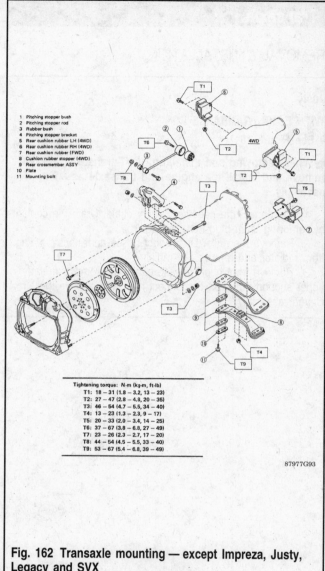

1 Pitching stopper bush
2 Pitching stopper rod
3 Rubber bush
4 Pitching stopper bracket
5 Rear cushion rubber LH (4WD)
6 Rear cushion rubber RH (4WD)
7 Rear cushion rubber (FWD)
8 Cushion rubber stopper (4WD)
9 Rear crossmember ASSY
10 Plate
11 Mounting bolt

Tightening torque: N·m (kg-m, ft-lb)
T1: 18 — 31 (1.8 — 3.2, 13 — 23)
T2: 27 — 47 (2.8 — 4.8, 20 — 35)
T3: 46 — 54 (4.7 — 5.5, 34 — 40)
T4: 13 — 23 (1.3 — 2.3, 9 — 17)
T5: 20 — 33 (2.0 — 3.4, 14 — 25)
T6: 37 — 67 (3.8 — 6.8, 27 — 49)
T7: 23 — 26 (2.3 — 2.7, 17 — 20)
T8: 44 — 54 (4.5 — 5.5, 33 — 40)
T9: 53 — 67 (5.4 — 6.8, 39 — 49)

87977G93

Fig. 162 Transaxle mounting — except Impreza, Justy, Legacy and SVX

7. Install engine support bracket 927160000 and engine support tool 927150000 or their equivalents. Remove the buffer rod from the engine and body side bracket.

➡**Before attaching the special engine support tools, connect the adjuster to the buffer rod assembly on the right side of the engine.**

8. Raise and support the vehicle safely.

9. Disconnect the exhaust pipes at the exhaust manifold flange. Remove the exhaust system up to the rear exhaust pipe assembly.

10. If equipped with 4WD, matchmark and remove the driveshaft. Remove the complete gear shift assembly.

11. Loosen the upper bolt and nut from the plate that secures the transverse link to the stabilizer. Remove the lower bolt and separate the link from the stabilizer.

12. Remove the right brake cable bracket from the transverse link. Remove the bolt retaining the link to the crossmember on each side.

13. Lower the transverse link. Using tool 398791700 or equivalent, remove the spring pin and separate the axle shaft

from the driveshaft on each side of the assembly by pushing the rear of the tire outward.

14. Remove the engine to transaxle mounting bolts. Position the proper transaxle jack under the transaxle assembly. Disconnect the transaxle cooler lines.

15. Remove the rear cushion rubber mounting bolts. Remove the rear crossmember assembly.

16. Turn the engine support tool adjuster counterclockwise in order to slightly raise the engine.

17. Move the transaxle jack toward the rear of the vehicle until the mainshaft is withdrawn from the clutch cover.

18. Carefully remove the transaxle assembly from the vehicle.

To install:

19. Carefully raise the transaxle until the mainshaft is aligned with the clutch side. Install the engine to the transaxle and temporarily tighten the mounting bolts.

20. Install the rear crossmember rubber cushion and tighten nuts to 20-35 ft. lbs. (27-47 Nm). Install the rear crossmember and tighten front bolts to 65-87 ft. lbs. (88-118 Nm); rear bolts to 27-49 ft. lbs. (37-67 Nm).

21. Tighten the engine-to-transaxle nuts to 34-40 ft. lbs. (46-54 Nm). Remove the transaxle jack.

22. Install the halfshaft into the differential and spring pin into place. Install the transverse link and stabilizer temporarily to the front crossmember. Install the brake cable bracket. Lower the vehicle and tighten transverse link bolt to 43-51 ft. lbs. (59-69 Nm); stabilizer bolts to 14-22 ft. lbs. (20-29 Nm).

23. Install the gearshift system. Install the driveshaft (4WD vehicles). Install the starter, pitching stopper, timing hole plug, air intake boot and speedometer cable. Reconnect all electrical and vacuum connectors.

24. Connect the clutch cable and Hill Holder. Install the front exhaust pipe. Connect the oil cooler lines. Install and tighten the torque converter mounting bolts to 17-20 ft. lbs. (23-26 Nm).

25. Connect the negative battery cable, check the transaxle fluid level and test drive the vehicle.

Brat, 1800 Sedan/Station Wagon, Loyale and XT Coupe

2WD AND 4WD NON-ELECTRONIC 3 AND 4-SPEED TRANSAXLES

1. Disconnect the negative battery cable.
2. Remove clamp from spare tire supporter and remove the spare tire.

➡**Use care when removing spare tire assembly from the vehicle.**

3. Remove spare tire supporter and battery clamp.
4. Remove speedometer cable and retaining clip. Before disconnecting speedometer cable, remove front exhaust pipe on 4-speed automatic transaxle.
5. Unplug the following electrical harness connections on the 3-speed automatic transaxle:
   a. Oxygen sensor connector
   b. ATF temperature switch connector
   c. Kickdown solenoid valve connector
   d. 4WD solenoid valve connector on 4WD equipped vehicles

6. Unplug the following electrical harness connections on the 4-speed automatic transaxle:
   a. Oxygen sensor connector
   b. Transaxle harness connector
   c. Inhibitor switch connector
   d. Revolution sensor connector on 4WD equipped vehicles

7. Disconnect the diaphragm vacuum hose on 3-speed automatic transaxle and 4WD vacuum hose on 4WD equipped vehicles.

8. Remove clip band which secures air breather hose to pitching stopper.

9. Remove the pitching stopper rod. Remove the starter.

10. Remove timing hole inspection plug and remove the 4 bolts which hold torque converter to driveplate.

11. Support the engine assembly with special engine support tool 926610000 or equivalent.

12. Remove engine-to-transaxle mounting nut and bolt on the right side.

13. Remove the exhaust system.

➡**Apply a penetrating oil or equivalent to all exhaust retaining nuts in advance to facilitate removal.**

14. On turbocharged vehicles, remove accelerator cable cover and upper and lower turbocharger covers. Remove the center exhaust pipe at turbocharger location and at rear exhaust pipe. Remove any exhaust brackets or hangers that attach to the transaxle, as necessary.

15. On non-turbocharged vehicles, disconnect front exhaust pipe from the engine and from the rear exhaust pipe. Remove any exhaust brackets or hangers that attach to the transaxle as necessary.

16. Drain all transaxle fluid from the oil pan.

17. Remove the driveshaft on 4WD vehicles. Plug the opening at the rear of extension housing to prevent oil from flowing out.

18. Disconnect the linkage rod for a 3-speed or cable for a 4-speed. from the select lever.

19. Remove stabilizer from transverse link by loosening (not removing) nut and bolt on the lower side of plate.

20. Remove parking brake cable bracket from transverse link and bolt holding transverse link to crossmember on each side. Lower the transverse link.

21. Remove spring pin and separate axle shaft from transaxle on each side.

➡**Use a suitable tool to remove spring pin. Discard old spring pin and always install a new pin.**

22. Disconnect the axle shaft from transaxle on each side. Be sure to remove axle shaft from transaxle by pushing the rear of tire outward.

23. Remove engine-to-transaxle mounting nuts.

24. Disconnect oil cooler hoses and oil supply pipe. Be careful not to damage the oil supply pipe O-ring.

25. Place transaxle jack or equivalent under transaxle. Always support transaxle case with a transaxle jack.

➡**Do not place jack under oil pan otherwise oil pan may be damaged.**

26. Remove rear cushion rubber mounting nuts and rear crossmember. Move torque converter and transaxle as a unit away from the engine. Remove the transaxle.

To install:

27. Install transaxle to engine and temporarily tighten engine-to-transaxle mounting nuts.

28. Install rear crossmember to rear cushion rubber mounts. Align rear cushion guide with rear crossmember guide hole and tighten nuts.

29. Install rear crossmember to chassis. Be careful not to damage threads. Tighten rear crossmember bolts to 39-49 ft. lbs. (52-67 Nm).

30. Tighten engine to transaxle nuts on the lower side to 34-40 ft. lbs. (46-54 Nm). Remove transaxle jack from the vehicle.

31. Install axle shaft to transaxle and install spring pin into place.

➡ **Always use new spring pin. Be sure to align the half-shaft and shaft from the transaxle at chamfered holes and engage shaft splines correctly.**

32. Install transverse link temporarily to front crossmember by using bolt and self-locking nut. Do not complete final torque at this point.

33. Install stabilizer temporarily to transverse link. Install parking brake cable bracket to transverse link.

34. Connect the linkage rod for a 3-speed or cable for a 4-speed to the select lever. Make sure the lever operates smoothly all across the operating range.

35. Install propeller shaft on 4WD vehicles. Tighten propeller shaft to rear differential retaining bolts to 13-20 ft. lbs. (18-20 Nm) and center bearing location retaining bolts to 25-33 ft. lbs. (34-44 Nm).

36. Connect oil cooler hoses and oil supply pipe. Lower vehicle to floor.

37. Tighten transverse link to front crossmember mounting bolts and transverse link to stabilizer mounting bolts with the tires placed on the ground when the vehicle is not loaded. Tightening torque for transverse link to front crossmember (self-locking nuts) 43-51 ft. lbs. (58-69 Nm) and transverse link to stabilizer 14-22 ft. lbs. (19-30 Nm).

38. Tighten engine to transaxle nuts on the upper side to 34-40 ft. lbs. (46-54 Nm).

39. Raise vehicle and safely support. Install exhaust system.

➡ **Before installing exhaust system, connect speedometer cable on 4-speed vehicles.**

40. On turbocharged vehicles, install the center exhaust pipe at turbocharger location and at rear exhaust pipe. Install any exhaust brackets or hangers that attach to the transaxle as necessary. Install upper and lower turbocharger covers and accelerator cable cover.

41. On non-turbocharged vehicles, connect front exhaust pipe to the engine and rear exhaust pipe. Install any exhaust brackets or hangers that attach to the transaxle as necessary.

42. Remove the special engine support tool. Install and tighten torque converter to driveplate mounting bolts to 17-20 ft. lbs.

43. Install timing hole inspection plug.

44. Install starter.

45. Install pitching stopper. Be sure to tighten the bolt for the body side first and then the 1 for engine or transaxle side.

Tightening torque for chassis side is 27-49 ft. lbs. and for engine or transaxle side is 33-40 ft. lbs.

46. Engage the following electrical harness connections on the 3-speed automatic transaxle:
   a. Oxygen sensor connector
   b. ATF temperature switch connector
   c. Kickdown solenoid valve connector
   d. 4WD solenoid valve connector on 4WD equipped vehicles

47. Engage the following electrical harness connections on the 4-speed automatic transaxle:
   a. Oxygen sensor connector
   b. Transaxle harness connector
   c. Inhibitor switch connector
   d. Revolution sensor connector on 4WD equipped vehicles

48. Reconnect the diaphragm vacuum hose on 3-speed automatic transaxle and 4WD vacuum hose on 4WD equipped vehicles.

49. Secure air breather hose to pitching stopper with a clip band.

50. Reconnect the speedometer cable. Manually tighten cable nut all the way and then turn it approximately 30 degrees more with a tool.

51. Connect the battery ground cable. Refill and check transaxle oil level.

52. Install spare tire supporter and battery clamp. Install spare tire.

53. Road test vehicle for proper operation across all operating ranges.

Impreza, Legacy, SVX and XT Coupe

4-SPEED ELECTRONIC TRANSAXLE

▶ **See Figures 163 and 164**

1. Disconnect the negative battery cable.

2. Remove speedometer cable or electronic wiring connector from speed sensor.

3. Unplug the following electrical harness connections on the automatic transaxle:
   a. Oxygen sensor connector

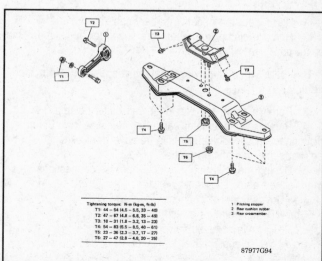

Tightening torque: N·m (kg-m, ft-lb)	
T1: 44 – 54 (4.5 – 5.5, 33 – 40)	
T2: 47 – 67 (4.8 – 6.8, 35 – 49)	
T3: 18 – 31 (1.8 – 3.2, 13 – 23)	
T4: 54 – 83 (5.5 – 8.5, 40 – 61)	
T5: 23 – 36 (2.3 – 3.7, 17 – 27)	
T6: 27 – 47 (2.8 – 4.8, 20 – 35)	

1 Pitching stopper	
2 Rear cushion rubber	
3 Rear crossmember	

87977G94

Fig. 163 Engine and transaxle mounts — Impreza and Legacy

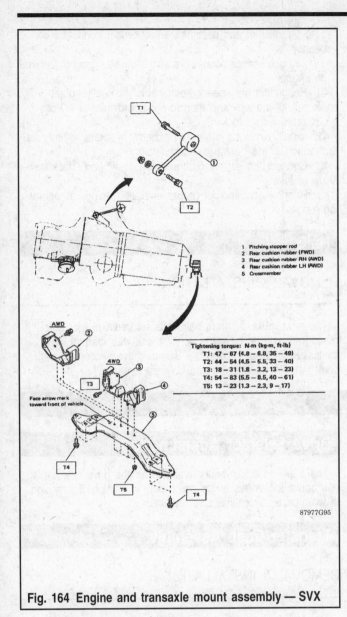

1 Pitching stopper rod
2 Rear cushion rubber (FWD)
3 Rear cushion rubber RH (AWD)
4 Rear cushion rubber LH (AWD)
5 Crossmember

Tightening torque: N-m (kg-m, ft-lb)
T1: 47 — 67 (4.8 — 6.8, 35 — 49)
T2: 44 — 54 (4.5 — 5.5, 33 — 40)
T3: 18 — 31 (1.8 — 3.2, 13 — 23)
T4: 54 — 83 (5.5 — 8.5, 40 — 61)
T5: 13 — 23 (1.3 — 2.3, 9 — 17)

Face arrow mark toward front of vehicle

87977G95

Fig. 164 Engine and transaxle mount assembly — SVX

b. Transaxle harness connector
c. Inhibitor switch connector
d. Revolution sensor connector on 4WD equipped vehicles
e. Crankshaft and camshaft angle sensor connector on Legacy vehicles
f. Knock sensor connectors and transaxle ground terminal on Legacy vehicles
4. Remove clip band which secures air breather hose to pitching stopper.
5. Remove the starter and air intake boot.
6. Remove timing hole inspection plug and remove the 4 bolts which hold torque converter to driveplate.
7. Disconnect pitching stopper rod from bracket.
8. Remove engine to transaxle mounting nut and bolt on the right side.
9. Remove the buffer rod from the vehicle. Support the engine assembly with special engine support tool or equivalent.
10. Remove the exhaust system. Remove exhaust brackets or hangers that attach to the transaxle, as necessary.

11. Matchmark and remove the driveshaft on 4WD vehicles. Plug the opening at the rear of extension housing to prevent oil from flowing out.
12. Disconnect the gear shift cable from the transaxle select lever.
13. Remove stabilizer from transverse link.
14. Remove parking brake cable bracket from transverse link and bolt holding transverse link to crossmember on each side. Lower the transverse link.
15. Remove spring pin and separate halfshaft from transaxle on each side.

➡ **Use a suitable tool to remove spring pin. Discard old spring pin and always install a new pin.**

16. Disconnect the halfshaft from transaxle on each side. Be sure to remove axle shaft from transaxle by pushing the rear of tire outward.
17. Remove engine to transaxle mounting nuts.
18. Disconnect oil cooler hoses.
19. Place transaxle jack or equivalent, under transaxle. Always support transaxle case with a transaxle jack.

➡ **Do not place jack under oil pan otherwise oil pan may be damaged.**

20. Remove rear cushion rubber mounting nuts and rear crossmember.
21. Move torque converter and transaxle as a unit away from the engine. Remove the transaxle.
To install:
22. Install transaxle to engine and temporarily tighten engine to transaxle mounting nuts.
23. Install rear crossmember to rear cushion rubber mounts. Align rear cushion guide with rear crossmember guide hole and tighten nuts.
24. Install rear crossmember to chassis; be careful not to damage threads. Tighten rear crossmember bolts to 39-49 ft. lbs. (53-66 Nm).
25. Tighten engine to transaxle retaining nuts to 34-40 ft. lbs. (46-54 Nm). Remove transaxle jack from the vehicle.
26. Remove the engine support tool and install buffer rod.
27. Install axle shaft to transaxle and install spring pin into place.

➡ **Always use new spring pin. Be sure to align the axle shaft and shaft from the transaxle at chamfered holes and install shaft splines correctly.**

28. Install transverse link temporarily to front crossmember by using bolt and self locking nut. Do not complete final torque at this point.
29. Install stabilizer temporarily to transverse link. Install parking brake cable bracket to transverse link.
30. Lower vehicle to floor. Tighten transverse link to front crossmember mounting bolts and transverse link to stabilizer mounting bolts with the tires placed on the ground when the vehicle is not loaded. Torque the transverse link to front crossmember (self-locking nuts) to 43-51 ft. lbs. (58-69 Nm) and the transverse link to stabilizer to 14-22 ft. lbs. (19-30 Nm).
31. Raise and safely support the vehicle. Reconnect the gear shift cable to the select lever. Make sure the lever operates smoothly all across the operating range.

32. Install propeller shaft on 4WD vehicles. Tighten propeller shaft-to-rear differential retaining bolts to 17-24 ft. lbs. (23-33 Nm) and center bearing location retaining bolts to 25-33 ft. lbs. (34-45 Nm).
33. Connect oil cooler hoses.
34. Tighten engine to transaxle bolts to 34-40 ft. lbs. (46-54 Nm).
35. Install starter.
36. Install pitching stopper. Be sure to tighten the bolt for the body side first and then the 1 for engine or transaxle side. Tightening tighten for chassis side is 27-49 ft. lbs. (37-66 Nm) and for engine or transaxle side is 33-40 ft. lbs. (45-54 Nm).
37. Install and tighten torque converter-to-driveplate mounting bolts to 17-20 ft. lbs. (23-27 Nm).
38. Install timing hole inspection plug, air intake boot and air breather hose to pitching stopper.
39. Engage the following electrical harness connections on the automatic transaxle:
   a. Oxygen sensor connector
   b. Transaxle harness connector
   c. Inhibitor switch connector
   d. Revolution sensor connector on 4WD equipped vehicles

e. Crankshaft and camshaft angle sensor connector on Legacy
   f. Knock sensor connectors and transaxle ground terminal on Legacy
40. Reconnect the speedometer cable. Manually tighten cable nut all the way and then turn it approximately 30 degrees more with a tool.
41. Install exhaust system and exhaust brackets or hangers that attach to the transaxle, as necessary.
42. Connect the battery ground cable. Refill and check transaxle oil level.
43. Road test vehicle for proper operation across all operating ranges.

Halfshafts

REMOVAL & INSTALLATION

The removal of the front halfshafts for vehicles with automatic transaxle is the same as for those with manual transaxles. Refer to the procedure earlier in this section for halfshaft removal, installation and CV-joint overhaul.

TRANSFER CASE (4WD ONLY)

The transfer case for driving the rear wheels mounts directly to the back of the transaxle case and is part of the transaxle. It provides a direct drive (1:1 gear ratio) coupling to the rear differential. This means that when the 4WD unit is engaged, the transaxle provides equal power to the front and rear differentials. When the 4WD unit is not engaged power is transmitted to only the front wheels. In either case shifting of the transaxle remains the same. Late models have dual range 4WD.

The drive selector can be shifted at any time, with or without clutching. However, if you shift the drive selector while the car is moving the steering wheel should be in the straight forward position. This minimizes the load on the rear drive system and shifting is made easier.

➡**You may feel a braking action when turning a sharp corner in four wheel drive. This is a normal phenomenon which arises from the difference in turning radius between the front wheels and the rear wheels, and will not occur when running in front wheel drive.**

Drive Selector Adjustment

There are no adjustments available for the drive selector. If you notice looseness or too much play in shifting, it is a sign of worn parts, which must be replaced.

Transfer Case Assembly

REMOVAL & INSTALLATION

The transfer case must be removed as an assembly with the transaxle. The procedure can be found earlier in this section.

DRIVELINE

Driveshaft and U-Joints

REMOVAL & INSTALLATION

▶ **See Figures 165, 166, 167 and 168**

1. Raise and support the vehicle safely.
2. Remove the differential mount front cover, if so equipped.

3. Remove the exhaust shield, exhaust pipe and muffler if necessary.
4. Remove the driveshaft flange to rear differential flange bolts.

➡**If equipped with a center bearing, remove the center bearing to chassis bolts and lower the assembly from the vehicle. Also note that the SVX uses an double offset type joint at the center of the driveshaft.**

5. Position a drain pan under the rear of the transaxle. Remove the driveshaft from the vehicle.

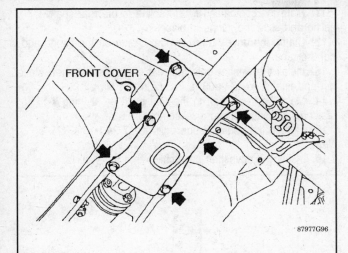

Fig. 165 The rear cover splash shield is secured by the indicated fasteners

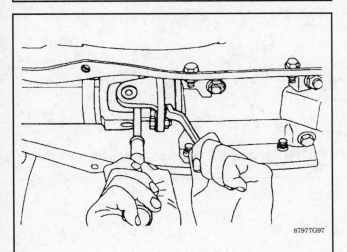

Fig. 166 Removing or installing the driveshaft-to-differential flange bolts

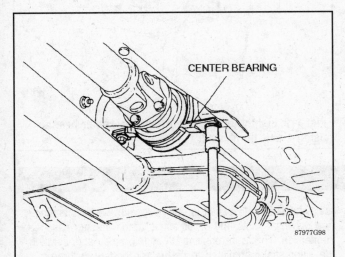

Fig. 167 Removing or installing the center bearing support bolts

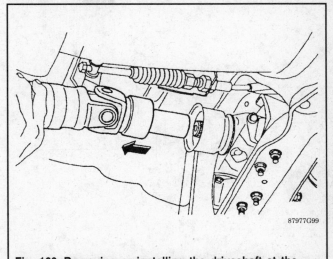

Fig. 168 Removing or installing the driveshaft at the transfer case tailshaft

6. Inspect the driveshafts. Replace the parts as required if any of the following conditions are found:

  a. Driveshaft tube is dented or has cracks on the surface.

  b. Deformation or abnormal wear of the shaft splines.

  c. The driveshaft run-out exceeds 0.024 in. (0.6mm)

  d. U-joints making abnormal noise or rough operation.

7. Inspect the center bearing. Replace the center bearing if any of the following conditions are found:

  a. Center bearing has excessive free-play or makes abnormal noise.

  b. Center bearing oil seals worn or damaged.

  c. Center bearing is broken.

To install:

8. Install the driveshaft and tighten the flange bolts to 17-24 ft. lbs. (24-32 Nm).

9. If equipped with a center bearing, raise the assembly and install the center bearing bolts. Tighten center bearing attaching bolts to 25-33 ft. lbs. (34-44 Nm).

10. Install the exhaust shield, exhaust pipe and muffler if removed.

11. Install the differential mount front cover, if removed.

12. Lower the vehicle, check the transaxle fluid level and test drive.

Center Bearing

REMOVAL & INSTALLATION

▶ See Figures 169, 170, 171 and 172

1. Raise and support the vehicle safely.

2. Remove the front and rear driveshafts as an assembly.

3. Matchmark the flanges, then remove the bolts holding the front and rear driveshafts together and separate the shafts.

4. Secure the rear driveshaft into a vise. Clamp it by the companion shaft.

➡**Never clamp the driveshaft by the tube section. Clamp the flange.**

5. Remove the companion flange stake nut.

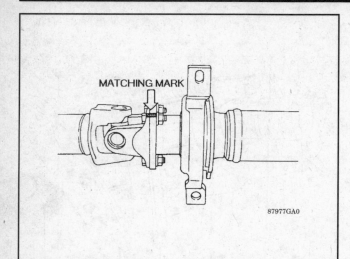

Fig. 169 Matchmark the driveshafts' front, rear and center flanges

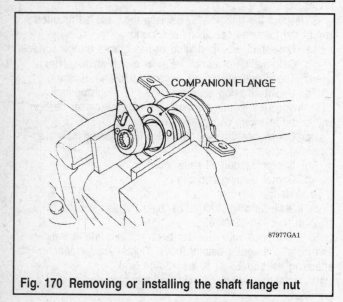

Fig. 170 Removing or installing the shaft flange nut

6. Using flange remover tool 899858600 or equivalent and a press tool, press the flange from the shaft.

7. When the flange is removed, position the shaft in the vise supported by the center bearing.

8. With a soft tip hammer, lightly tap the shaft from the center bearing assembly.

To install:

9. Mount the center bearing onto the rear shaft.

10. Apply a molybdenum disulfide grease to both sides of the washer and place it on the center bearing end face.

11. Mate the companion flange spline to the rear shaft spline and slide the flange in place.

12. Clamp the driveshaft in a vise. Clamp on the flange and not the tube.

13. Install the washer onto the rear shaft. Install a new stake nut and tighten to 174-203 ft. lbs. (235-275 Nm).

14. Mate the front shaft to the rear shaft by aligning the matchmarks made during disassembly.

15. Tighten the center flange bolts to 17-24 ft. lbs. (24-32 Nm).

16. Install the driveshaft assemblies into the vehicle.

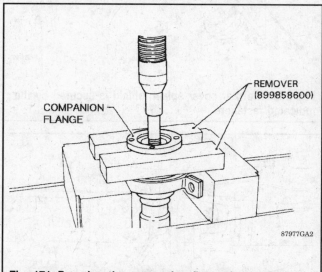

Fig. 171 Pressing the companion flange from the shaft

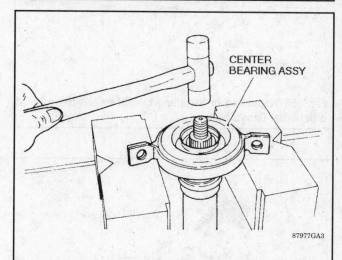

Fig. 172 Lightly tap the shaft from the center bearing using a soft tip hammer

REAR AXLE

Identification

The rear drive system of the four wheel drive models contains a differential unit, a driveshaft connected to the output shaft of the transfer case, and an axle shaft running to each rear wheel. The driveshaft is equipped with two maintenance free universal joints and a ball spline at the transfer case connection. To aid in reducing drive train noise and vibration, the differential is mounted to the vehicle body with three or four rubber bushings, one or two at the front and two at the rear of the differential carrier.

Understanding Drive Axles

▶ **See Figure 173**

Power enters the axle from the driveshaft via the companion flange. The flange is mounted on the drive pinion shaft. The drive pinion shaft and gear which carry the power into the differential turn at engine speed. The gear on the end of the pinion shaft drives a large ring gear the axis of rotation of which is 90° away from the of the pinion. The pinion and gear reduce the gear ratio of the axle, and change the direction of rotation to turn the axle shafts which drive both wheels. The axle gear ratio is found by dividing the number of pinion gear teeth into the number of ring gear teeth.

The ring gear drives the differential case. The case provides the two mounting points for the ends of a pinion shaft on which are mounted two pinion gears. The pinion gears drive the two side gears, one of which is located on the inner end of each axle shaft.

By driving the axle shafts through the arrangement, the differential allows the outer drive wheel to turn faster than the inner drive wheel in a turn.

The main drive pinion and the side bearings, which bear the weight of the differential case, are shimmed to provide proper bearing preload, and to position the pinion and ring gears properly.

❊❊WARNING

The proper adjustment of the relationship of the ring and pinion gears is critical. It should be attempted only by those with extensive equipment and/or experience.

Limited slip differentials include clutches which tend to link each axle shaft to the differential case. Clutches may be engaged either by spring action or by pressure produced by the torque on the axles during a turn. During turning on a dry pavement, the effects of the clutches are overcome, and each wheel turns at the required speed. When slippage occurs at either wheel, however, the clutches will transmit some of the power to the wheel which has the greater amount of traction.

Because of the presence of clutches, limited slip units require a special lubricant.

Determining Axle Ratio

The drive axle is said to have a certain axle ratio. This number (usually a whole number and a decimal fraction) is actually a comparison of the number of gear teeth on the ring gear and the pinion gear. For example, a 4.11 rear means that theoretically, there are 4.11 teeth on the ring gear and one tooth on the pinion gear or, put another way, the driveshaft must turn 4.11 times to turn the wheels once. Actually, on a 4.11 rear, there might be 37 teeth on the ring gear and 9 teeth on the pinion gear. By dividing the number of teeth on the pinion gear into the number of teeth on the ring gear, the numerical axle ratio (4.11) is obtained. This also provides a good method of ascertaining exactly what axle ratio one is dealing with.

Another method of determining gear ratio is to jack up and support the car so that both rear wheels are off the ground. Make a chalk mark on the rear wheel and the driveshaft. Put the transaxle in neutral. Turn the rear wheel one complete turn and count the number of turns that the driveshaft makes. The number of turns that the driveshaft makes in one complete revolution of the rear wheel is an approximation of the rear axle ratio.

Axle Shafts

REMOVAL & INSTALLATION

Justy

2WD

▶ **See Figures 174, 175, 176, 177 and 178**

1. Raise and support the vehicle safely. Remove the tire and wheel assembly.
2. Remove the dust cap. Straighten the locking washer edge. Remove the nut, lockwasher and washer.

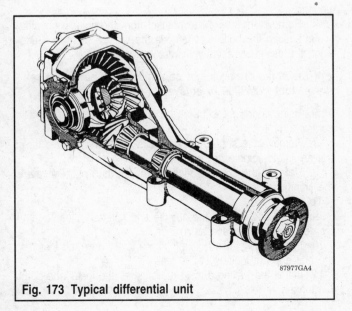

Fig. 173 Typical differential unit

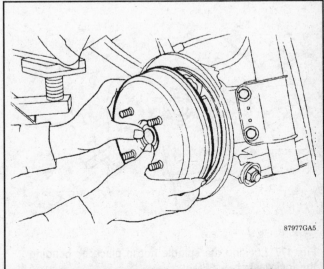

Fig. 174 Removing or installing the rear brake drum

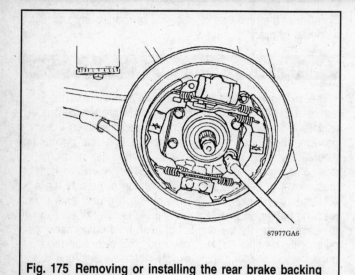

Fig. 175 Removing or installing the rear brake backing plate assembly

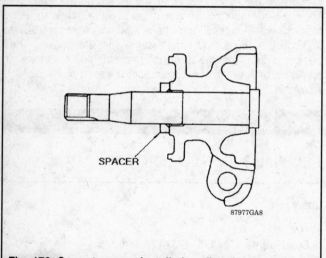

SPACER

Fig. 176 Correct spacer installation direction on the spindle — 2WD

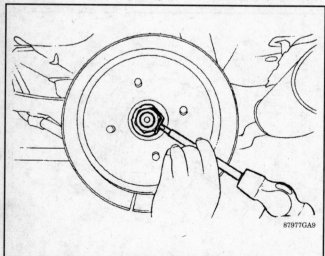

Fig. 177 Locking the spindle nut in place by bending the lockwasher — 2WD

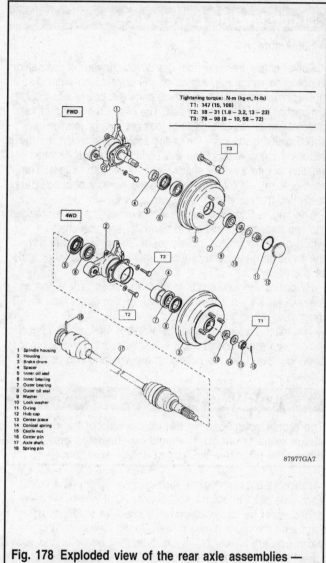

Tightening torque: N-m (kg-m, ft-lb)
T1: 147 (15, 108)
T2: 18 — 31 (1.8 — 3.2, 13 — 23)
T3: 78 — 98 (8 — 10, 58 — 72)

1 Spindle housing
2 Housing
3 Brake drum
4 Spacer
5 Inner oil seal
6 Inner bearing
7 Outer bearing
8 Outer oil seal
9 Washer
10 Lock washer
11 O-ring
12 Hub cap
13 Center piece
14 Conical spring
15 Castle nut
16 Cotter pin
17 Axle shaft
18 Spring pin

Fig. 178 Exploded view of the rear axle assemblies — 2WD and 4WD

3. Remove the brake drum. Be sure not to drop the outer bearing.

4. Remove the brake line bracket from the spindle housing.

5. Loosen the bolts and remove the brake assembly. Suspend the assembly aside with wire.

➡**If the brake drum cannot be removed by hand, use remover tool 92249300 or equivalent to remove the drum.**

6. Using floor jack, support the suspension under the lower control arm.

7. Remove the strut-to-spindle bolts and nuts, remove the trailing link-to-spindle bolt and nut.

8. Remove the spindle-to-lower arm bolt and nut. Remove the spindle.

To install:

9. Clean and inspect the spindle and spacer for damage for deformation. Replace as necessary.

10. Install the spindle housing to the lower arm and install the bolt and nut loosely at this time.

11. Install the trailing arm to the spindle and install the bolt nut loosely at this time.

12. Install the strut to the spindle housing and install the bolts and nuts loosely at this time.

13. Tighten the strut-to-spindle bolts and nuts to 72-87 ft. lbs. (98-118 Nm), the trailing link-to-spindle bolt and nut to 43-58 ft. lbs. (59-78 Nm) and the spindle-to-lower arm bolt and nut to 54-69 ft. lbs. (74-93 Nm).

14. Install the brake backing plate assembly to spindle, tighten the retaining bolts to 13-23 ft. lbs. (18-31 Nm).

15. Install the brake line bracket and brake drum. Install a new lockwasher on the spindle nut and bend it in place.

➡Prior to installing the brake drum, make sure the spacer is installed in the correct direction on the spindle.

16. Install the wheel and tire, lower the vehicle and test drive.

4WD

▶ See Figures 179, 180, 181, 182 and 183

1. Raise and support the vehicle safely. Remove the tire and wheel assembly.

2. Remove the dust cap. Remove the cotter pin and castle nut, conical spring and center piece.

3. Remove the center piece by wedging flat tool between the separation while using a hammer to tap the center piece free.

4. Pull the brake drum off by hand.

5. Remove the brake line bracket from the axle bearing housing.

6. Remove the brake backing plate mounting bolts and remove the backing plate assembly. Suspend the assembly aside with wire.

7. Using the proper tools, drive out the spring pin connecting the halfshaft assembly to the differential.

8. Remove the strut, lower link and trailing link. Pull the housing along with the halfshaft from its mounting.

9. Separate the housing from the halfshaft, using removal tools 922493000 and 921122000 or their equivalent.

To install:

10. Join the housing and halfshaft. Install the strut, lower link and trailing link. Install the spring pin connecting the halfshaft assembly to the differential.

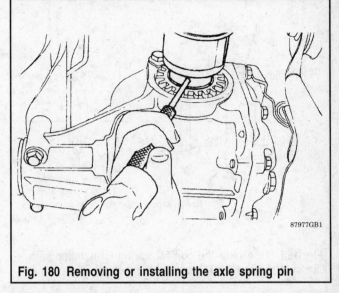

Fig. 180 Removing or installing the axle spring pin

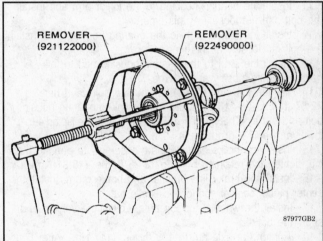

Fig. 181 Separating the halfshaft from the bearing housing

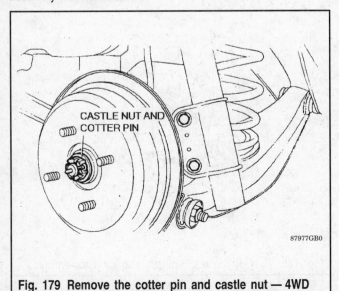

Fig. 179 Remove the cotter pin and castle nut — 4WD

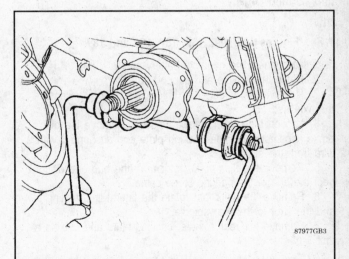

Fig. 182 Removing or installing the lower control arm at the bearing housing

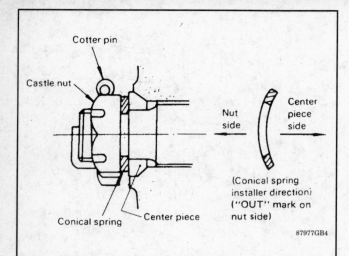

Fig. 183 Make sure the conical spring is installed with the side marked "OUT" toward the nut

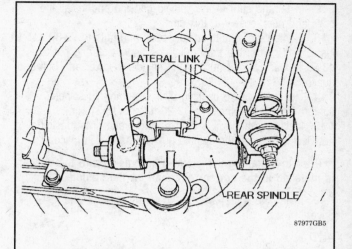

Fig. 184 View of the rear spindle and lateral links — 2WD Impreza and Legacy

11. Install the bearing housing to the lower arm and install the bolt and nut loosely at this time.

12. Install the trailing arm to the bearing housing and install the bolt nut loosely at this time.

13. Install the strut to the bearing housing and install the bolts and nuts loosely at this time.

14. Tighten the strut-to-bearing housing bolts and nuts to 72-87 ft. lbs. (98-118 Nm), the trailing link-to-bearing housing bolt and nut to 43-58 ft. lbs. (59-78 Nm) and the spindle-to-lower arm bolt and nut to 54-69 ft. lbs. (74-93 Nm).

15. Install the brake backing plate assembly to bearing housing, tighten the retaining bolts to 13-23 ft. lbs. (18-31 Nm).

16. Install the brake line bracket and brake drum. Install the center piece, conical spring and castle nut.

17. Install the wheels and lug nuts. Lower the vehicle and apply the brake.

18. Tighten the axle nut to 108 ft. lbs. (147 Nm). After tightening to specifications, tighten the axle shaft nut 30 degrees further. Install and new cotter pin.

19. Test drive the vehicle.

Impreza and Legacy

2WD

▶ **See Figures 184, 185, 186, 187, 188 and 189**

1. Disconnect the negative battery cable.

2. Raise the vehicle and support safely.

3. Remove the wheels and unlock the axle nut. Remove the axle nut.

4. Loosen the parking brake adjuster. Remove the disc brake assembly from the backing plate and suspend it with a wire from the strut.

5. Remove the disc brake rotor from the hub and disconnect the end of the parking brake cable.

6. Remove the bolts that retain the lateral link, trailing link and the strut to the rear spindle.

7. Remove the rear spindle, backing plate and hub as a unit.

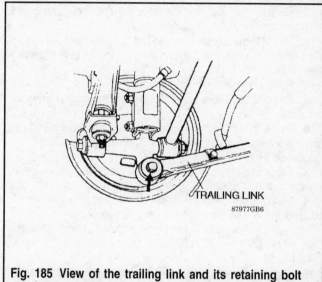

Fig. 185 View of the trailing link and its retaining bolt

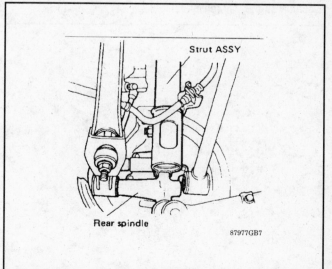

Fig. 186 View of the rear spindle and strut assembly

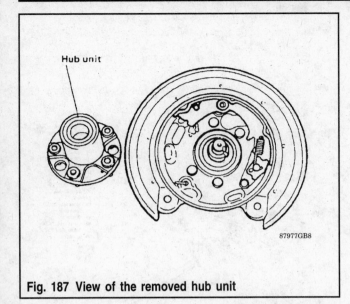

Fig. 187 View of the removed hub unit

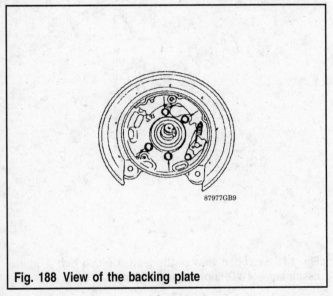

Fig. 188 View of the backing plate

To install:

8. The installation is the reverse of the removal procedure. Use the following torque values during installation.

   a. Rear spindle to strut assembly — 98-119 ft. lbs. (133-161 Nm).

   b. Rear spindle assembly to trailing link — 72-94 ft. lbs. (98-127 Nm).

   c. Rear spindle to lateral link — 87-116 ft. lbs. (118-157 Nm).

   d. Disc brake assembly to backing plate — 34-43 ft. lbs. (46-58 Nm).

   e. Axle nut — 123-152 ft. lbs. (167-206 Nm).

   f. Wheel nuts — 58-72 ft. lbs. (79-98 Nm).

4WD

▶ **See Figures 190, 191, 192, 193 and 194**

1. Disconnect the negative battery cable.
2. Raise and support the vehicle safely.
3. Unstake and remove the axle nut.
4. Remove the sway bar bracket.

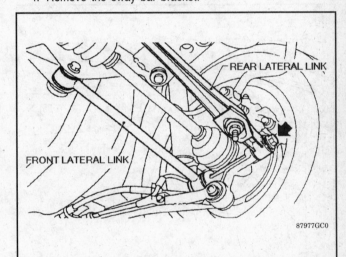

Fig. 190 View of the lateral links and their fasteners — 4WD Impreza and Legacy

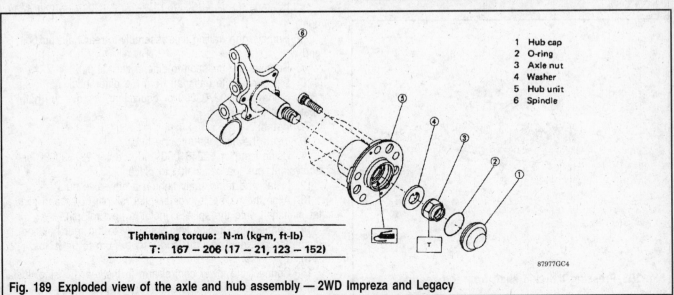

1	Hub cap
2	O-ring
3	Axle nut
4	Washer
5	Hub unit
6	Spindle

Tightening torque: N·m (kg-m, ft-lb)
T: 167 — 206 (17 — 21, 123 — 152)

Fig. 189 Exploded view of the axle and hub assembly — 2WD Impreza and Legacy

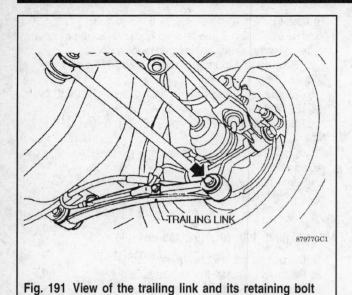

Fig. 191 View of the trailing link and its retaining bolt

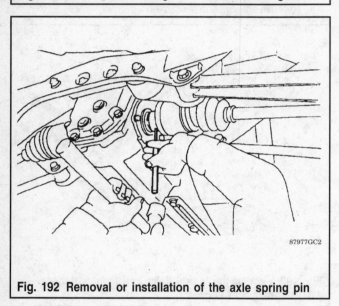

Fig. 192 Removal or installation of the axle spring pin

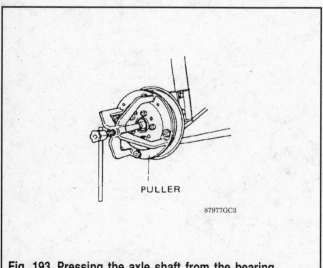

Fig. 193 Pressing the axle shaft from the bearing housing

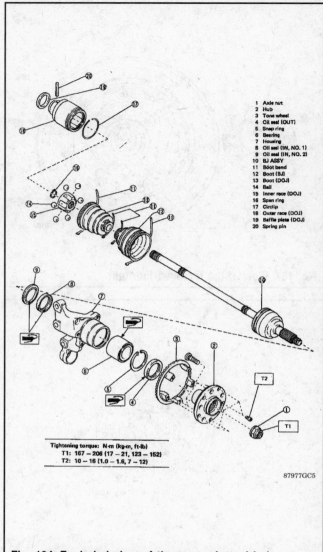

1 Axle nut
2 Hub
3 Tone wheel
4 Oil seal (OUT)
5 Snap ring
6 Bearing
7 Housing
8 Oil seal (IN, NO. 1)
9 Oil seal (IN, NO. 2)
10 BJ ASSY
11 Boot band
12 Boot (BJ)
13 Boot (DOJ)
14 Ball
15 Inner race (DOJ)
16 Span ring
17 Circlip
18 Outer race (DOJ)
19 Baffle plate (DOJ)
20 Spring pin

Tightening torque: N·m (kg·m, ft-lb)
T1: 167 — 206 (17 — 21, 123 — 152)
T2: 10 — 16 (1.0 — 1.6, 7 — 12)

Fig. 194 Exploded view of the rear axle and hub assembly — 4WD Impreza and Legacy

5. Remove the lower control arm-to-rear housing bolt and nut.

6. Remove the trailing link assembly-to-rear housing bolt and nut.

7. Remove the halfshaft-to-differential roll pin.

8. Disconnect the halfshaft from the differential.

9. Using puller 92707000 or equivalent, remove the halfshaft from the hub.

To install:

10. Insert the halfshaft into the hub.

11. Using installer 922431000 and adapter 927390000 or equivalent, pull the halfshaft into place.

12. Install and temporarily tighten a new axle nut.

13. Align the halfshaft-to-differential roll pin holes and slide the halfshaft onto the splines. Install a new roll pin.

14. Connect the trailing link assembly to the rear housing. Install the bolt and new nut and torque them to 94 ft. lbs. (127 Nm).

15. Connect the lower control arm to the rear housing. Install the bolt and new nut and torque them to 116 ft. lbs. (157 Nm).

16. Install the sway bar bracket.

17. Torque the new axle nut to 152 ft. lbs. (206 Nm).
18. Install the wheel.
19. Lower the vehicle.
20. Connect the negative battery cable.

SVX

▶ See Figure 195

1. Disconnect the negative battery cable.
2. Raise and safely support the vehicle.
3. Remove the tire and wheel assembly.
4. Unstake and remove the axle nut.
5. Move the parking brake lever forward.
6. Disconnect the rear exhaust pipe.
7. Remove the sway bar link.
8. Remove the ABS sensor clamp and parking brake cable bracket from the trailing link.
9. Remove the parking brake cable from the floor.
10. Disconnect the brake hose from the strut.
11. Remove the trailing link-to-knuckle through-bolt and nut.
12. Remove the lateral link-to-knuckle through-bolt and nut.

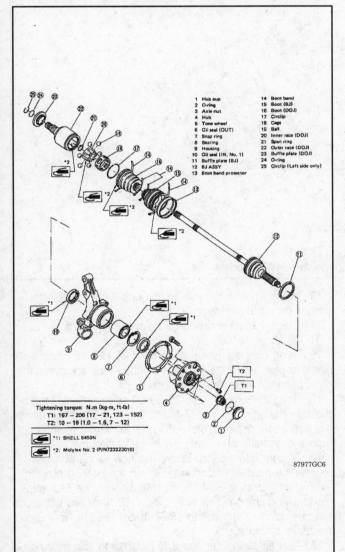

Fig. 195 Exploded view of the rear axle and hub assembly — SVX

13. Disconnect the halfshaft from the differential carrier using a half shaft remover, 28099PA100, or the equivalent.
14. Remove the halfshaft from the rear bearing assembly.
To install:
15. Install a new circlip on the inboard end of the halfshaft.
16. Insert the outer joint through the hub splines. Using a halfshaft installer, pull the shaft into the hub completely.
17. Install the inboard joint into the differential carrier.
18. Once the splines are lined up the inner joint can be seated fully by pushing in on the knuckle.
19. Line up the lateral links and install the through-bolt and nut and tighten to 86 ft. lbs. (118 Nm).
20. Line up the trailing link and install the through-bolt and nut and tighten to 90 ft. lbs. (123 Nm).
21. Connect the brake hose bracket to the strut and install the mounting bolt.
22. Install the parking brake cable bracket to the floor.
23. Install the ABS sensor clamp and parking brake cable bracket to the trailing link.
24. Install the sway bar link.
25. Connect the rear exhaust pipe.
26. Install the axle nut and tighten to 138 ft. lbs. (186 Nm).
27. Install the tire and wheel assembly.
28. Lower the vehicle.
29. Connect the negative battery cable.
30. Check the front end alignment and adjust as necessary.

Brat, Loyale, STD. and XT

2WD

▶ See Figure 196

1. Raise and support the vehicle safely. Remove the tire and wheel assembly.
2. Remove the dust cap. Straighten the lockwasher. Remove the nut, lockwasher and washer.
3. Remove the brake drum. Be sure not to drop the outer bearing.
4. Remove the brake line bracket from the spindle housing.
5. Loosen the bolts and remove the brake assembly. Suspend the assembly aside with wire.
6. Remove the damper strut, lower link and trailing link.
7. Remove the spindle assembly retaining bolts. Remove the spindle from its mounting.
To install:
8. Install the spindle assembly, damper strut, lower link and trailing link. Tighten all bolts to specification.
9. Install the brake assembly and brake line bracket. Install the brake drum.
10. Install wheel and tire, lower the vehicle and test drive.

4WD

▶ See Figure 197

1. Firmly apply the parking brake.
2. Remove the rear wheel cap and the cotter pin, then loosen the castle nut.
3. Disconnect the shock absorber from the inner arm.
4. Loosen the crossmember outer bushing lock bolts. Remove the inner trailing arm to chassis bolt and the inner arm.
5. Raise and support the vehicle safely. Remove the rear wheel assemblies.

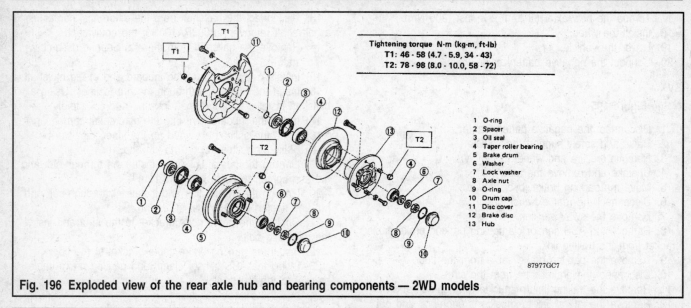

Tightening torque N·m (kg-m, ft-lb)
T1: 46 - 58 (4.7 - 5.9, 34 - 43)
T2: 78 - 98 (8.0 - 10.0, 58 - 72)

1 O-ring
2 Spacer
3 Oil seal
4 Taper roller bearing
5 Brake drum
6 Washer
7 Lock washer
8 Axle nut
9 O-ring
10 Drum cap
11 Disc cover
12 Brake disc
13 Hub

87977GC7

Fig. 196 Exploded view of the rear axle hub and bearing components — 2WD models

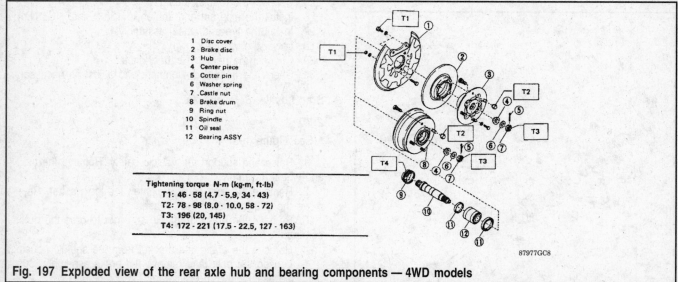

1 Disc cover
2 Brake disc
3 Hub
4 Center piece
5 Cotter pin
6 Washer spring
7 Castle nut
8 Brake drum
9 Ring nut
10 Spindle
11 Oil seal
12 Bearing ASSY

Tightening torque N·m (kg-m, ft-lb)
T1: 46 - 58 (4.7 - 5.9, 34 - 43)
T2: 78 - 98 (8.0 - 10.0, 58 - 72)
T3: 196 (20, 145)
T4: 172 - 221 (17.5 - 22.5, 127 - 163)

87977GC8

Fig. 197 Exploded view of the rear axle hub and bearing components — 4WD models

6. Using a 0.24 in. (6mm) diameter steel rod or a pin punch, drive the inner/outer spring pins from the double offset joints.

7. With the trailing arm fully lowered, remove the ball joint from the trailing arm spindle and the inner double offset joint and the differential spindle.

8. Remove the castle nut and the brake drum or rear wheel caliper If equipped, remove the brake caliper and properly position it aside. Do not disconnect the brake hose from the caliper.

9. Disconnect and plug the brake hose from the inner arm bracket.

10. If equipped with rear brake drums, remove the brake assembly from the trailing arm.

11. Disconnect the inner arm from the outer arm and remove the inner arm from the vehicle.

12. Secure the inner arm in a vise, then using a hammer and a punch, straighten the staked portion of the ring nut or remove the cotter pin from the castled nut. Using the wrench tool 925550000 or equivalent, remove the ring nut.

13. Using a plastic hammer on the outside of the spindle, drive it inward to remove it.

14. Clean, inspect and replace the necessary parts.
To install:

15. Using an arbor press and a piece of 1.38 in. (35mm) diameter pipe, insert the spindle from the inside and press the outer bearing's inner race from outside.

16. Using the wrench tool 925550000 or equivalent, tighten the axle shaft ring nut to 127-163 ft. lbs. (172-221 Nm). Using a punch and a hammer, stake the ring nut, facing the ring nut groove or install a new cotter pin in the castled nut.

17. To complete the installation, use new spring pins and reverse the removal procedures. Tighten the backing plate to axle housing bolts to 34-43 ft. lbs. (46-58 Nm), the axle spindle to axle housing nut to 145 ft. lbs. (196 Nm), and the shock absorber to inner arm bolt to 65-87 ft. lbs. (88-118 Nm). Bleed the brake system.

18. After tightening the rear axle halfshaft to axle housing nut, tighten the axle shaft nut 30 degrees further to align cotter

pin holes as required. Be careful not to install the double offset joint and the constant velocity joint oppositely.

Axle Bearings

REMOVAL & INSTALLATION

2WD

▶ **See Figures 198, 199, 200, 201, 202 and 203**

1. Raise and support the vehicle safely and remove the wheels.
2. Remove the dust cover, lockwasher, nut and remove the brake drum. Take care not to allow the outer bearing to drop on the ground.
3. Remove the inner bearing from the drum.

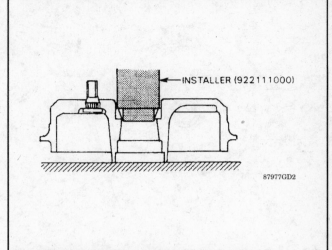

Fig. 200 Pressing the outer bearing race into the drum — 2WD Justy shown

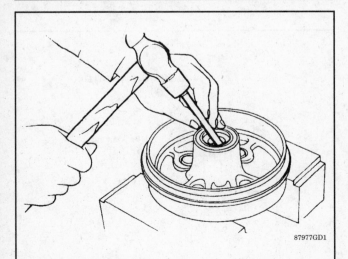

Fig. 198 Driving the inner bearing race from the brake drum — 2WD Justy shown

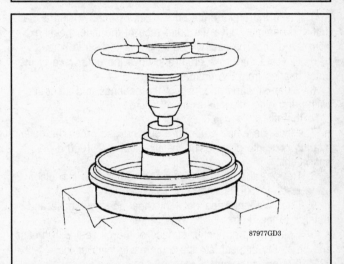

Fig. 201 Pressing the seal into the drum — 2WD Justy shown

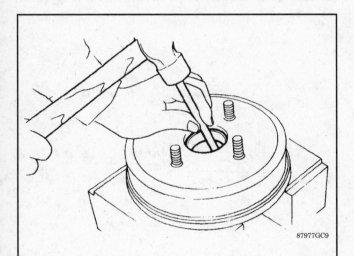

Fig. 199 Driving the outer bearing race from the brake drum — 2WD Justy shown

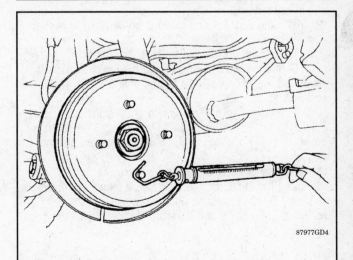

Fig. 202 Checking the brake drum starting torque — 2WD Justy shown

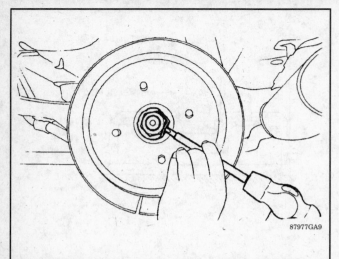

Fig. 203 Bending the locking washer on the spindle nut — 2WD Justy shown

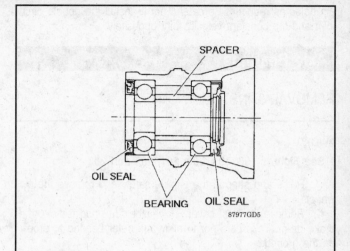

Fig. 204 Position the spacer in a radial position — 4WD Justy shown

4. Place the brake drum on 2 block of wood. Using a brass drift and hammer, drive the outer race of the inner bearing from the drum. The seal will come out at the same time.

5. Reverse the brake drum and drive the outer race of the outer bearing from the drum.

6. Clean all parts and inspect the bearings and races for pitting and other obvious signs of failure.

To install:

7. Place the brake drum on a support and press the outer bearing race into place using installer tool 92211000 or equivalent.

8. Reverse the drum and press the outer race into place using installer tool 92211000 or equivalent.

9. Pack the inner bearing with wheel bearing grease and install it to the drum.

10. Coat the lip and inner surface of the oil seal with grease and press the oil seal into the drum using installer tool 92211000 or equivalent.

11. Install the spacer on the spindle and the brake drum.

12. Pack the outer bearing with wheel bearing grease and install it to the drum.

13. Install the washers and axle nut on the spindle. Adjust the wheel bearing as follows:

   a. Tighten the spindle nut to 29 ft. lbs. (39 Nm).

   b. Rotate the drum clockwise and then counterclockwise several times. Then back the nut off until 0 ft. lbs. (0 Nm) is obtained.

   c. Tighten the spindle nut until a drum starting torque of 0.5-0.7 ft. lbs. (0.7-1.0 Nm) or 3.1-4.4 lbs. (13.7-19.6 N) is obtained. Using a spring gauge tool to check the starting torque.

14. Bend the lockwasher over the spindle nut.

15. Install the O-ring on the dust cap. If damaged replace it with a new O-ring. Install the dust cover.

16. Install the wheels and lower the vehicle. Install the negative battery cable.

4WD

▶ See Figures 204, 205, 206, 207, 208, 209 and 210

1. Raise and support the vehicle safely. Remove the tire and wheel assembly.

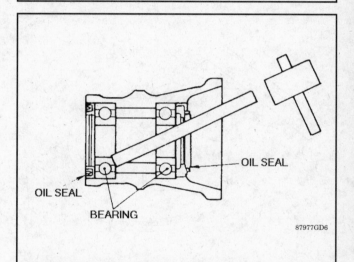

Fig. 205 Driving the bearing and seal out of the housing — 4WD Justy shown

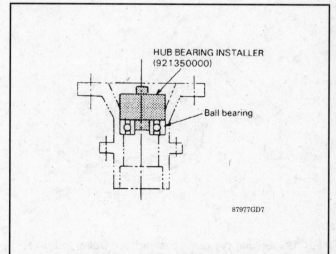

Fig. 206 Pressing the inner bearing into the housing — 4WD Justy shown

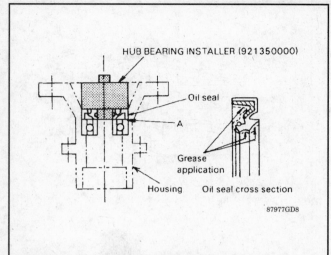

**Fig. 207 Pressing the inner seal into the housing —
4WD Justy shown**

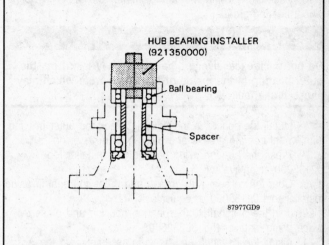

**Fig. 208 Pressing the outer bearing into the housing —
4WD Justy shown**

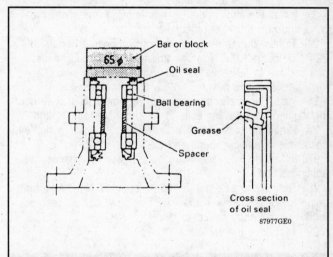

**Fig. 209 Pressing the outer seal into the housing —
4WD Justy shown**

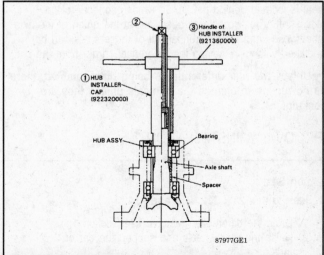

**Fig. 210 Press fitting the halfshaft to the bearing
housing — 4WD Justy shown**

  2. Remove the dust cap. Remove the cotter pin and castle
nut, conical spring and center piece.
  3. Remove the center piece by wedging flat tool between
the separation while using a hammer to tap the center piece
free.
  4. Pull the brake drum off by hand.
  5. Remove the rear axle and bearing housing as an assembly. Press the halfshaft from the housing.
  6. Position the spacer inside the housing in a radial direction to gain access to the outer bearing.
  7. Place a brass drift to the outer bearing inner race. Then
drive out the bearing, together with the oil by lightly tapping
with a hammer.

➡**Do not reuse the old bearing, the old bearing may develop abnormal noise if reinstalled.**

  8. Remove the spacer from the housing.
  9. Reverse the bearing housing and drive out the inner
bearing and seal.

➡**Always tap around the periphery of the bearing outer
race.**

  10. Clean and inspect the bearing inner and outer race for
cracks or damage. Check for noise and binding when the
outer race is turned slowly and while the inner race is held in
position.
  11. Clean and inspect the spacer. Check for damage and
deformation. Replace as necessary.
  12. For the bearing housing, wipe the inner surface with a
clean cloth and check for cracks or damage. Replace as
necessary.
  To install:
  13. Pack the inner bearing with wheel bearing grease.
  14. Install the bearing into the housing. Press the bearing
using bearing hub installer tool 92135000 or equivalent.
  15. Coat the oil seal with grease and press the seal in using
installer tool 92135000 or equivalent.

➡**A gap between the seal lip and bearing changes oil seal
lip interference, resulting in excessive wear on the lip.**

16. Pack the housing with approximately 0.6 oz. (17 g) of wheel bearing grease.

✳✳WARNING

Do not pack excessively, otherwise it may leak from the outer bearing in the inside of the brake drum which may cause brake failure.

17. Install the spacer in the housing. Pack the outer bearing with wheel bearing grease and place into the housing.
18. Press the bearing using bearing hub installer tool 92135000 or equivalent.
19. Coat the oil seal with grease and press the seal in using installer tool 92135000 or equivalent.
20. Join the halfshaft to the bearing housing and press in place using installer tool 92232000.
21. Install the halfshaft and housing assembly into the vehicle.
22. Install the trailing arm to the bearing housing and install the bolt nut loosely at this time.
23. Install the strut to the bearing housing and install the bolts and nuts loosely at this time.
24. Tighten the strut-to-bearing housing bolts and nuts to 72-87 ft. lbs. (98-118 Nm), the trailing link-to-bearing housing bolt and nut to 43-58 ft. lbs. (59-78 Nm) and the spindle-to-lower arm bolt and nut to 54-69 ft. lbs. (74-93 Nm).
25. Install the brake backing plate assembly to bearing housing, tighten the retaining bolts to 13-23 ft. lbs. (18-31 Nm)
26. Install the brake line bracket and brake drum. Install the center piece, conical spring and castle nut.
27. Install the wheels and lug nuts. Lower the vehicle and apply the brake.
28. Tighten the axle nut to 108 ft. lbs. (147 Nm). After tightening to specifications, tighten the axle shaft nut 30 degrees further. Install and new cotter pin.
29. Test drive the vehicle.

Oil Seals

The rear differential carrier has three oil seals. The front oil seal is located behind the flange which connects to the driveshaft. The two side oil seals are at the union of the axle shaft yokes and the differential. All of these seals can be replaced without removing the differential carrier from the car.

➡**Unless the rear differential is being disassembled, there is no reason to change the oil seals unless they are leaking.**

REMOVAL & INSTALLATION

Pinion Seal
▸ **See Figures 211, 212, 213 and 214**

1. Drain the differential gear oil (see Section 1).
2. Raise the rear wheels and support the car on jackstands.
3. Remove the driveshaft as outlined earlier in this section.
4. Measure the turning resistance of the differential companion flange. To do this, attach either a spring scale or an

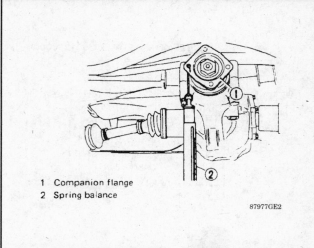

1 Companion flange
2 Spring balance

87977GE2

Fig. 211 Measuring the companion flange turning resistance

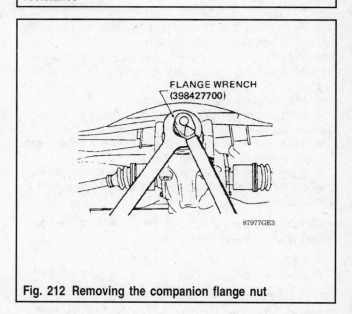

FLANGE WRENCH (398427700)

87977GE3

Fig. 212 Removing the companion flange nut

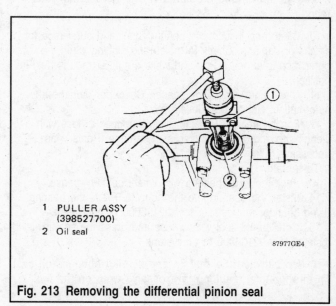

1 PULLER ASSY (398527700)
2 Oil seal

87977GE4

Fig. 213 Removing the differential pinion seal

inch pound torque wrench to one of the mounting holes. Make sure that the flange turns smoothly, and then turn the flange through one complete revolution using the scale or torque wrench. Mark down the reading registered. It will be used during installation.

5. Remove the drive pinion nut while holding the companion flange with a flange or pipe wrench.

6. Remove the companion flange and oil seal with a puller.

7. Using a drift, tap in a new oil seal.

➡**Apply axle grease between the oil seal lips.**

8. Install the companion flange.

9. Tighten the pinion nut to 123-145 ft. lbs. (167-196 Nm). The proper torque has been reached when the turning resistance of the companion flange is the same as it was when measured in Step 4 above.

10. Stake the pinion nut with a punch.

Side Oil Seal

▶ **See Figure 215**

1. Drain the differential oil (see Section 1).

2. Raise the rear wheels and support the car on jackstands.

3. Remove the side yolk retaining bolt and pull the side yolk out of the differential carrier.

4. Extract the oil seal with a puller.

5. Using a drift, tap in a new oil seal.

➡**Apply axle grease between the oil seal lips.**

6. Install the side yoke and tighten the retaining bolt.

Rear Differential Carrier

REMOVAL & INSTALLATION

▶ **See Figures 216, 217, 218, 219, 220, 221, 222 and 223**

1. Drain the differential oil (see Section 1).

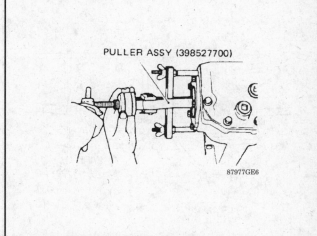

Fig. 215 Removing the differential side seal — Legacy shown

2. Raise the rear wheels and support the car on jackstands.

3. Remove the exhaust pipe and muffler as outlined in the Engine Removal portion of Section 3.

4. Remove the driveshaft and axle shafts.

5. Support the differential carrier with a transmission jack.

6. Remove the two nuts securing the differential to the rear mounting bracket.

7. Remove the two bolts securing the differential to the front mounting bracket.

8. Lower the jack and remove the differential.

9. To install, reverse Steps 1 through 8. Observe the following torque specifications:

• Rear mounting nuts: 53 ft. lbs. (72 Nm)
• Front mounting bolts: 53 ft. lbs. (72 Nm)

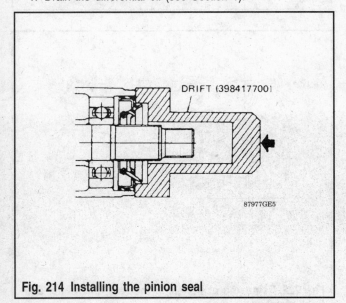

Fig. 214 Installing the pinion seal

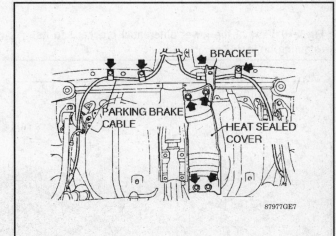

Fig. 216 The heat shield and parking brake cable brackets are retained by the indicated fasteners

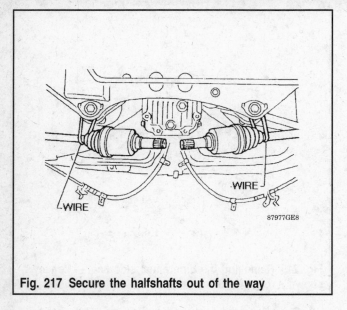

Fig. 217 Secure the halfshafts out of the way

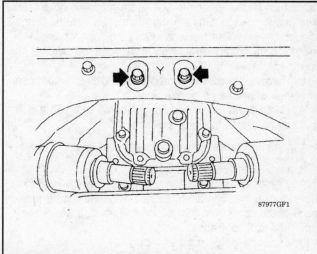

Fig. 220 View of the differential-to-crossmember retaining bolts

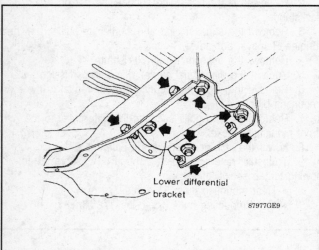

Fig. 218 View of the lower differential bracket and its retaining bolts

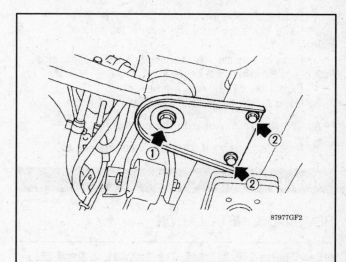

Fig. 221 View of the front member-to-body retaining bolts

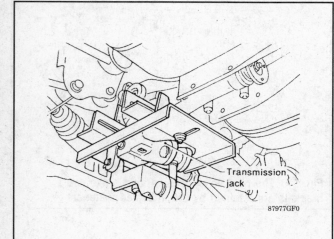

Fig. 219 Support the differential with a transmission jack

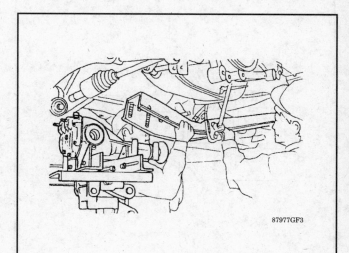

Fig. 222 Removing or installing the rear differential and front member

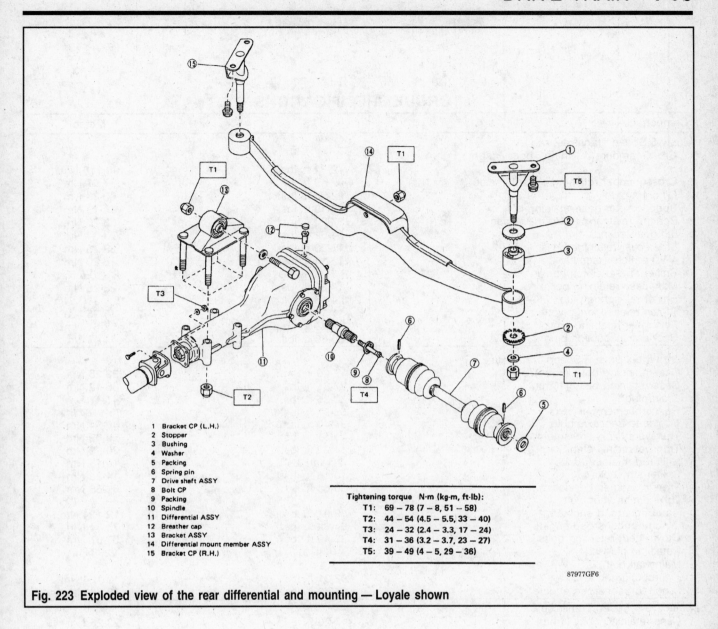

1 Bracket CP (L.H.)
2 Stopper
3 Bushing
4 Washer
5 Packing
6 Spring pin
7 Drive shaft ASSY
8 Bolt CP
9 Packing
10 Spindle
11 Differential ASSY
12 Breather cap
13 Bracket ASSY
14 Differential mount member ASSY
15 Bracket CP (R.H.)

Tightening torque N·m (kg-m, ft-lb):
T1: 69 – 78 (7 – 8, 51 – 58)
T2: 44 – 54 (4.5 – 5.5, 33 – 40)
T3: 24 – 32 (2.4 – 3.3, 17 – 24)
T4: 31 – 36 (3.2 – 3.7, 23 – 27)
T5: 39 – 49 (4 – 5, 29 – 36)

87977GF6

Fig. 223 Exploded view of the rear differential and mounting — Loyale shown

TORQUE SPECIFICATIONS

Component	U.S.	Metric
Justy 5 Speed Transaxle:		
Crossmember retaining bolts (right side)	72-87 ft. lbs.	98-118 Nm
Crossmember retaining bolts (left side)	27-49 ft. lbs.	37-67 Nm
Oil drain plug	22-28 ft. lbs.	30-38 Nm
Speedometer gear retaining bolt	10-13 ft. lbs.	14-18 Nm
Bearing retainer plate-to-main case	17-20 ft. lbs.	23-26 Nm
5th gear locknut	54-62 ft. lbs.	73-84 Nm
Side cover retaining bolts	17-20 ft. lbs.	23-26 Nm
4WD switch assembly	12-14 ft. lbs.	16-20 Nm
Shifter arm-to-clutch housing	6.7-7.8 ft. lbs.	9.1-10.6 Nm
Main case retaining bolts	17-20 ft. lbs.	23-26 Nm
Shifter rail spring plug	13.4-15.6 ft. lbs.	18.1-21.1 Nm
Clutch release fork pivot	11-18 ft. lbs.	15-25 Nm
Final gear retaining bolts	42-49 ft. lbs.	57-67 Nm
Backlash inspection plug	30-35 ft. lbs.	41-47 Nm
Front Wheel Drive 5 Speed Transaxle:		
Case retaining bolts (8mm)	17-20 ft. lbs.	23-26 Nm
Case retaining bolts (10mm)	27-31 ft. lbs.	36-42 Nm
Drain plug	30-35 ft. lbs.	41-47 Nm
Rear crossmember bolts	65-87 ft. lbs.①	88-118 Nm
Engine-to-transaxle bolts	34-40 ft. lbs.	46-54 Nm
Transverse link--crossmember	43-51 ft. lbs.	59-69 Nm
Transverse link--stabilizer	14-22 ft. lbs.	20-29 Nm
Shift rod retaining bolts	7-11 ft. lbs.	10-16 Nm
Shifter stay bolts	10-16 ft. lbs.	14-22 Nm
Front crossmember bolts	36-64 ft. lbs.	51-86 Nm
Drive pinion shaft bolt		
turbocharged engine	82-91 ft. lbs.	112-124 Nm
non-turbocharged engine	54-62 ft. lbs.	73-84 Nm
Crown gear retaining bolts	42-49 ft. lbs.	57-67 Nm
Retaining plugs	14 ft. lbs.	20 Nm
Mainshaft bolt		
turbocharged engine	82-91 ft. lbs.	112-124 Nm
non-turbocharged engine	54-62 ft. lbs.	73-84 Nm
Selective 5 Speed Transaxle:		
Case retaining bolts (8mm)	17-20 ft. lbs.	23-26 Nm
Case retaining bolts (10mm)	27-31 ft. lbs.	36-42 Nm
Drain plug	30-35 ft. lbs.	41-47 Nm
Transfer case bolts	14 ft. lbs.	20 Nm
Rear crossmember bolts	65-87 ft. lbs.	88-118 Nm
Engine-to-transaxle bolts	34-40 ft. lbs.	46-54 Nm
Transverse link--crossmember	43-51 ft. lbs.	59-69 Nm
Transverse link--stabilizer	14-22 ft. lbs.	20-29 Nm
Shift rod retaining bolts	7-11 ft. lbs.	10-16 Nm
Shifter stay bolts	10-16 ft. lbs.	14-22 Nm
Driveshaft retaining bolts	13-20 ft. lbs.	18-27 Nm
Center bearing bolts	25-33 ft. lbs.	34-44 Nm
Front crossmember bolts	36-64 ft. lbs.	51-86 Nm
4WD switch retaining bolts	13 ft. lbs.	18 Nm
Drive pinion shaft bolt	82-91 ft. lbs.	112-124 Nm
Crown gear retaining bolts	42-49 ft. lbs.	57-67 Nm
Retaining plugs	14 ft. lbs.	20 Nm
Input shaft holder retaining bolts	13-16 ft. lbs.	18-21 Nm

87977c01

TORQUE SPECIFICATIONS

Component	U.S.	Metric
Full-time 4WD transaxle:		
Case retaining bolts (8mm)	17-20 ft. lbs.	23-26 Nm
Case retaining bolts (10mm)	27-31 ft. lbs.	36-42 Nm
Drain plug	30-35 ft. lbs.	41-47 Nm
Transfer case bolts	14 ft. lbs.	20 Nm
Rear crossmember bolts	65-87 ft. lbs. ①	88-118 Nm
Engine-to-transaxle bolts	34-40 ft. lbs.	46-54 Nm
Transverse link--crossmember	43-51 ft. lbs.	59-69 Nm
Transverse link--stabilizer	14-22 ft. lbs.	20-29 Nm
Shift rod retaining bolts	7-11 ft. lbs.	10-16 Nm
Shifter stay bolts	10-16 ft. lbs.	14-22 Nm
Driveshaft retaining bolts	13-20 ft. lbs.	18-27 Nm
Center bearing bolts	25-33 ft. lbs.	34-44 Nm
Front crossmember bolts	36-64 ft. lbs.	51-86 Nm
4WD switch retaining bolts	13 ft. lbs.	18 Nm
Drive pinion shaft bolt	82-91 ft. lbs.	112-124 Nm
Crown gear retaining bolts	42-49 ft. lbs.	57-67 Nm
Retaining plugs	14 ft. lbs.	20 Nm
Input shaft holder retaining bolts	13-16 ft. lbs.	18-21 Nm
Clutch:		
Pressure plate bolts	12.7 ft. lbs.	17.2 Nm
Master cylinder mounting bolts	15 ft. lbs.	21 Nm
Slave cylinder and Damper	30 ft. lbs.	41 Nm
Clutch fluid lines	13 ft. lbs.	18 Nm
Automatic transaxle:		
Brake band adjusting bolt	18 ft. lbs.	25 Nm
XT:		
rear crossmember cushion bolts	20-35 ft. lbs.	27-37 Nm
rear crossmember front bolts	65-87 ft. lbs.	88-118 Nm
rear crossmember rear bolts	27-49 ft. lbs.	37-67 Nm
engine-to-transaxle bolts	34-40 ft. lbs.	46-54 Nm
transverse link bolt	43-51 ft. lbs.	59-69 Nm
stabilizer bolts	14-22 ft. lbs.	20-29 Nm
converter-to-driveplate	17-20 ft. lbs.	23-26 Nm
STD., Loyale and XT with 3 speed electronic transaxle:		
rear crossmember bolts	39-49 ft. lbs.	52-67 Nm
engine-to-transaxle bolts	34-40 ft. lbs.	46-54 Nm
driveshaft-to-pinion flange	13-20 ft. lbs	18-26 Nm
center bearing retaining bolts	25-33 ft. lbs.	34-44 Nm
transverse link bolt	43-51 ft. lbs.	59-69 Nm
stabilizer bolts	14-22 ft. lbs.	20-29 Nm
converter-to-driveplate	17-20 ft. lbs.	23-26 Nm
XT, Legacy and SVX with 4 speed electronic transaxle:		
rear crossmember bolts	39-49 ft. lbs. ②	52-67 Nm
engine-to-transaxle bolts	34-40 ft. lbs.	46-54 Nm
driveshaft-to-pinion flange	13-20 ft. lbs.	18-26 Nm
center bearing retaining bolts	25-33 ft. lbs.	34-44 Nm
transverse link bolt	43-51 ft. lbs.	59-69 Nm
stabilizer bolts	14-22 ft. lbs.	20-29 Nm
converter-to-driveplate	17-20 ft. lbs.	23-26 Nm

TORQUE SPECIFICATIONS

Component	U.S.	Metric
Driveshaft:		
Pinion flange bolts	17-24 ft. lbs.	24-32 Nm
Center bearing attaching bolts	25-33 ft. lbs.	34-44 Nm
Rear Axle:		
Pinion nut	123-145 ft. lbs.	167-196 Nm
Differential carrier:		
Rear mounting nuts	53 ft. lbs.	72 Nm
Front mounting bolts	53 ft. lbs.	72 Nm

① 1993-96 Impreza
T1: 17-27 ft. lbs. (23-36 Nm)
T2: 21-28 ft. lbs. (28-38 Nm)
T3: 20-35 ft. lbs. (27-47 Nm)
T4: 33-40 ft. lbs. (44-54 Nm)
T5: 35-49 ft. lbs. (47-67 Nm)
T6: 40-61 ft. lbs. (54-83 Nm)
1990-96 Legacy
T1: 35-49 ft. lbs. (47-67 Nm)
T2: 33-40 ft. lbs. (44-54 Nm)
T3: 21-28 ft. lbs. (28-38 Nm)
T4: 40-61 ft. lbs. (54-83 Nm)
T5: 20-35 ft. lbs. (27-47 Nm)
T6: 87-116 ft. lbs. (118-157 Nm)

② Impreza
T1: 9-17 ft. lbs. (13-23 Nm)
T2: 13-23 ft. lbs. (18-31 Nm)
T3: 33-40 ft. lbs. (44-54 Nm)
T4: 35-49 ft. lbs. (47-67 Nm)
T5: 40-61 ft. lbs. (54-83 Nm)
Legacy
T1: 35-49 ft. lbs. (47-67 Nm)
T2: 33-40 ft. lbs. (44-54 Nm)
T3: 13-23 ft. lbs. (18-31 Nm)
T4: 40-61 ft. lbs. (54-83 Nm)
T5: 9-17 ft. lbs. (13-23 Nm)

③ Impreza & Legacy
35-42 ft. lbs. (47-57 Nm)

④ SVX
T1: 40-61 ft. lbs. (54-83 Nm)
T2: 17-27 ft. lbs. (23-36 Nm)
T3: 20-35 ft. lbs. (27-47 Nm)

87977c03

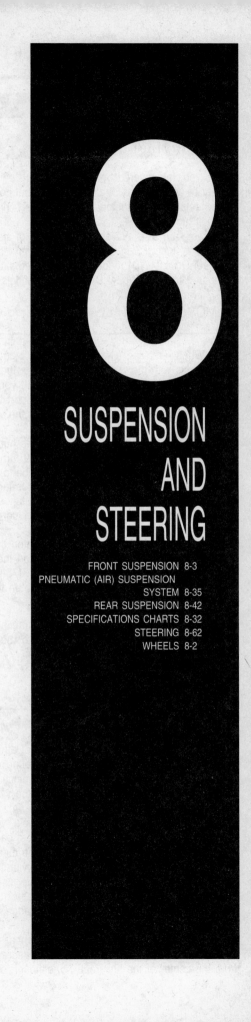

8

SUSPENSION
AND
STEERING

WHEELS

General Information

The vehicles covered by this manual are equipped with a variety of wheel styles of aluminum or steel construction. All the wheels from the factory are a one-piece rim design utilizing a 4 bolt lug pattern.

Wheels are also available in a variety of standard sizes from 14 in. high x 5 in. wide to 16 in. high x 7 in. wide. Most 4-Wheel Drive (4WD) models are equipped with larger rims as compared to the 2-Wheel Drive (2WD) models.

REMOVAL & INSTALLATION

1. When removing a wheel, loosen, but do not remove, all the lug nuts with the wheel on the ground, then raise and safely support the vehicle on jackstands. If you are working at home (not on a roadside emergency) support the vehicle safely using jackstand(s). Use the jack in the vehicle only for emergency.

2. If the wheel is stuck or rusted to the hub, turn all the lug nuts finger-tight, then back each one off 2 turns. Rest the vehicle back on the ground and rock it side-to-side. Have another person to help if necessary. This is far safer than hitting the wheel with the vehicle on jackstands.

3. When installing a wheel, tighten the lug nuts in a crisscross pattern.

4. Always use a torque wrench to tighten the lug nuts to avoid uneven tightening, which could distort the brake drum or disc. Tighten the lug nuts to 58-72 ft. lbs. (75-98 Nm) on all models except the SVX. On the SVX, tighten the lug nuts to 72-87 ft. lbs. (98-118 Nm).

➡**If installing aftermarket wheels, use the lug nuts provided with the wheels and tighten to the wheel manufacturer's specification.**

INSPECTION

▸ **See Figure 1**

Wheels can be distorted or bent and not affect dry road handling to a noticeable degree. Out of round wheels will show up as uneven tire wear, or will make it difficult to balance the tire. Wheel run-out can be checked with the wheel on or off the vehicle and with the tire on or off the rim. If measurement is to be made with the wheel off the vehicle, you will need an accurate mounting surface such as a wheel balancer.

Both lateral and radial run-out should be measured using a dial gauge. Lateral run-out is a sideways vibration causing a twist or wobble and is measured on a side surface. On a tire and wheel assembly, measure the sidewall of the tire, as close as possible to the tread shoulder design edge. On a rim, measure the run-out on the flange.

Radial run-out is the egg-shaped difference from a perfect circle. On a tire and wheel assembly, measure radial run-out from the center of the tire tread rib, although other tread ribs

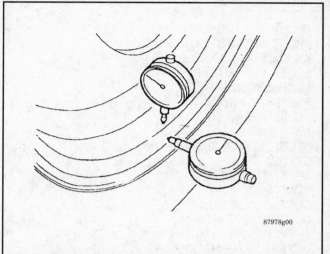

Fig. 1 Measuring the lateral and radial run-out on a wheel

can be measured, if necessary. The rim may be measured on either flange if the tire is removed.

1. Use a dial gauge to measure the run-out of the wheel or tire and wheel assembly, as applicable.

2. The lateral run-out limit is 0.059 in. (1.5mm) for steel wheels, 0.039 (1mm) for aluminum wheels. The radial run-out limit is 0.059 in. (1.5mm) for steel wheels, 0.039 in. (1mm) for aluminum wheels.

Wheel Lug Studs

REMOVAL & INSTALLATION

Disc Brake

➡**When replacing the front hub bolts on vehicles with anti-lock brakes, remove and replace only one wheel lug stud at a time to avoid misalignment the speed sensor exciter ring.**

1. Raise and support the front of the vehicle safely using jackstands, then remove the wheel.

2. Remove the brake pads and caliper. Support the caliper aside using wire or a coat hanger. For caliper removal and installation details, please refer to Section 9 of this manual.

3. Remove the outer wheel bearing and lift the rotor and hub off the axle. For wheel bearing removal, installation and adjustment steps, please refer to Section 1 of this manual.

4. Remove the retainer bolts securing the hub to the rotor hat, and separate the components.

5. Support the hub, then drive the stud out using a hammer or an arbor press or stud removal clamp.

To install:

6. Clean the stud hole with a wire brush and start the new stud with a hammer and drift pin. Do not use any lubricant or thread sealer.

7. If necessary, finish installing the stud using a press or stud installation clamp.

8. Install the hub to the rotor using new bolts.

9. Install the rotor on the vehicle, and adjust the wheel bearing.

10. Install the brake caliper and pads.

11. Install the tire, then remove the jackstands and carefully lower the vehicle.

Drum Brake

1. Raise and support the vehicle safely using jackstands, then remove the wheel.

2. Remove the brake drum. Refer to Section 9 for drum brake removal and installation steps.

✴✴WARNING

Do not hammer the wheel stud out to remove it. This will ruin the wheel bearing.

FRONT SUSPENSION

Coil Strut Suspension

▶ See Figures 2 and 3

All of the Subaru models covered in this manual use a strut type independent front suspension. The strut is surrounded by a coil spring. The top of the strut is mounted to the body through a rubber cushion to dampen vibration, and the lower end is mounted to the steering knuckle.

The transverse link has a permanently lubricated ball joint installed by nut at the outer end, and is fitted to the front cross member through a rubber cushion. The leading rod is bolted at the outer end to the transverse link and the inner end of the leading rod is connected to the leading rod bracket. The front cross member is bolted to the body through rubber cushions.

The stabilizer bar is connected to the front cross member, with the end connected to the transverse links. The overall

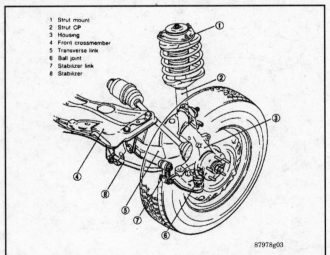

Fig. 2 Front suspension assembly — all models except SVX

3. Attach a stud removal clamp to the stud and press the stud out.

To install:

4. Clean the hole with a wire brush and start the new stud into the hole. Do not use any lubricant or thread sealer.

5. With the stud straight in the mounting hole, complete the installation using a stud installation clamp.

6. If a stud installation clamp is not available, stack 4 or 5 washers onto the stud and install the nut. Tighten the nut to draw the stud into place. It should be easy to feel when the stud is seated.

7. Install the brake drum.

8. Install the tire, then remove the jackstands and carefully lower the vehicle.

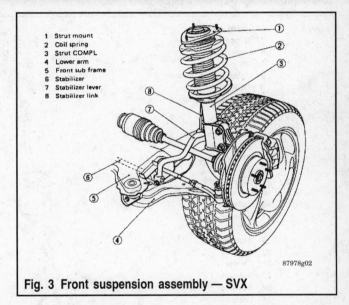

1 Strut mount
2 Coil spring
3 Strut COMPL
4 Lower arm
5 Front sub frame
6 Stabilizer
7 Stabilizer lever
8 Stabilizer link

Fig. 3 Front suspension assembly — SVX

design of the suspension reduces road vibration that is transmitted to the passenger compartment.

Pneumatic Strut Suspension

This air suspension system is used on all 4WD models except the Justy. The air suspension system is virtually identical to the standard strut type suspension, except that the coil springs are replaced by air springs. The addition of the air springs allows the vehicle ride to be adjusted by the operator, and it allows the suspension height to be maintained when the vehicle is loaded. Each of the air springs has a ride height sensor attached, that allows the height to be monitored individually at each wheel. A compressor distributes air to each of the air springs as it is needed.

A further description of the operation of, and repair of the pneumatic suspension can be found later in this section.

MacPherson Struts

REMOVAL & INSTALLATION

Justy

◗ **See Figure 4**

➡**Do not remove the large nut on top of the strut assembly unless the coil spring is properly compressed with a suitable spring compressor.**

1. Disconnect the negative battery cable.
2. Raise and safely support the vehicle on jackstands.
3. Remove the tire and wheel assembly.
4. Disconnect and cap the front brake hose at the strut mounting bracket.
5. Remove the bolt that secures the brake hose to the strut.
6. Remove the lower strut pinch bolt.
7. Using a suitable tool, slightly wedge open the lower strut mounting bracket, and slide the strut assembly out.
8. Lower the vehicle enough to open the hood.
9. Remove the upper strut plate mounting nuts.
10. Lower the strut assembly out of the vehicle.
To install:
11. Install the strut in the vehicle so the upper strut plate bolts pass through the strut tower bolt holes. Install the mounting nuts and tighten to 10 ft. lbs. (14 Nm).
12. Raise and safely support the vehicle.
13. Guide the lower end of the strut into the steering knuckle.
14. Install the pinch bolt and tighten to 32 ft. lbs. (44 Nm).
15. Install the bolt that secures the brake hose to the strut and tighten to 32 ft. lbs. (44 Nm).
16. Connect the brake hose at the strut mounting bracket.
17. Install the tire and wheel assembly.
18. Lower the vehicle.
19. Connect the negative battery cable.
20. Bleed the brake system.

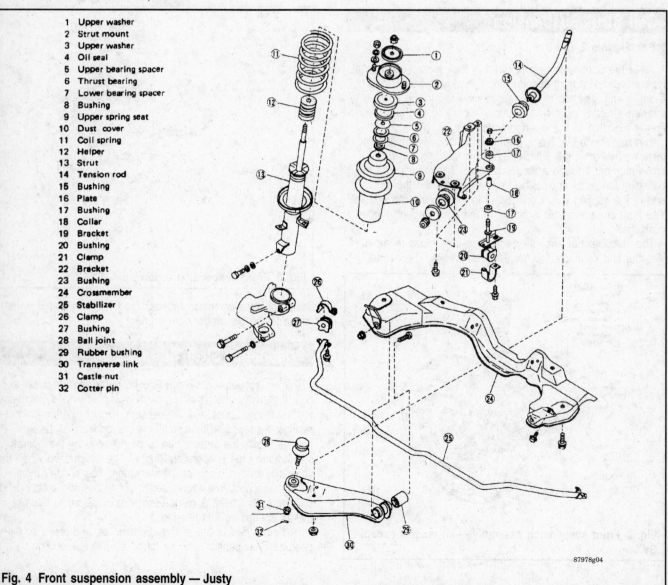

1 Upper washer
2 Strut mount
3 Upper washer
4 Oil seal
5 Upper bearing spacer
6 Thrust bearing
7 Lower bearing spacer
8 Bushing
9 Upper spring seat
10 Dust cover
11 Coil spring
12 Helper
13 Strut
14 Tension rod
15 Bushing
16 Plate
17 Bushing
18 Collar
19 Bracket
20 Bushing
21 Clamp
22 Bracket
23 Bushing
24 Crossmember
25 Stabilizer
26 Clamp
27 Bushing
28 Ball joint
29 Rubber bushing
30 Transverse link
31 Castle nut
32 Cotter pin

87978g04

Fig. 4 Front suspension assembly — Justy

21. Have the front end alignment checked by a qualified professional.

Sedan Coupe, Loyale, XT, Wagon and Brat

STANDARD STRUT

♦ See Figures 5, 6, 7 and 8

➡Do not remove the large nut on top of the strut assembly unless the coil spring is properly compressed with a suitable spring compressor.

1. Disconnect the negative battery cable.
2. Raise and safely support the vehicle safely on jackstands.
3. Remove the front wheel and tire assembly.
4. Disconnect and cap the front brake hose from the caliper.
5. Remove the brake hose securing clip from the strut bracket and remove the hose from the bracket.
6. Disconnect the parking brake cable from the caliper, if equipped.

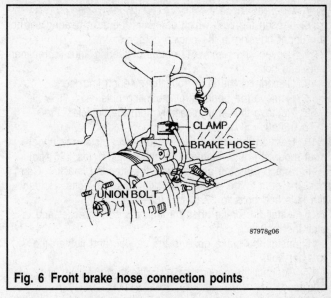

Fig. 6 Front brake hose connection points

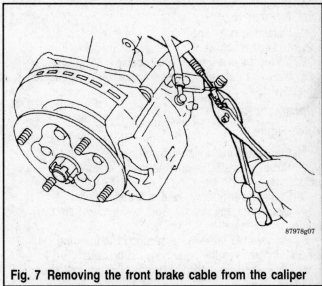

Fig. 7 Removing the front brake cable from the caliper

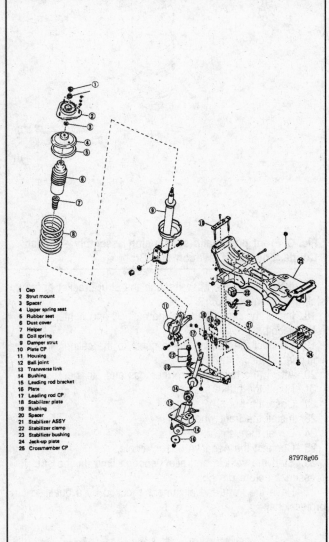

1 Cap
2 Strut mount
3 Spacer
4 Upper spring seat
5 Rubber seat
6 Dust cover
7 Helper
8 Coil spring
9 Damper strut
10 Plate CP
11 Housing
12 Ball joint
13 Transverse link
14 Bushing
15 Leading rod bracket
16 Plate
17 Leading rod CP
18 Stabilizer plate
19 Bushing
20 Spacer
21 Stabilizer ASSY
22 Stabilizer clamp
23 Stabilizer bushing
24 Jack-up plate
25 Crossmember CP

Fig. 5 Front standard suspension assembly — Sedan Coupe, Loyale, XT, Wagon and Brat

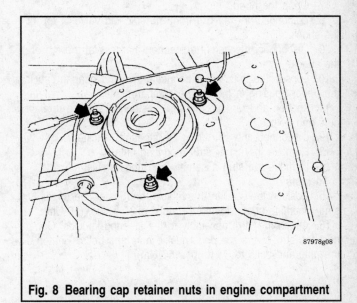

Fig. 8 Bearing cap retainer nuts in engine compartment

7. Open the hood.

8. Loosen the nuts which connects the strut bearing cap to the upper housing in the engine compartment.

9. Loosen and remove the strut-to-steering knuckle retainer nuts and bolts.

10. Disconnect the strut from the steering knuckle.

11. Remove the upper strut mounting nuts.

12. Remove the strut assembly from the vehicle.

To install:

13. Position the strut in the vehicle, and install the upper strut mounting nuts. Tighten the nuts to 27 ft. lbs. (36 Nm).

14. Attach the strut assembly to the steering knuckle. Connect the strut-to-the steering knuckle nuts and bolts. Tighten the nuts and bolts to 37 ft. lbs. (50 Nm).

15. Install the brake hose through the strut bracket and install the mounting clip.

16. Install the brake hose to the caliper, and tighten the retainer bolt.

17. Connect the parking brake cable to the caliper, if equipped.

18. Bleed the brake system.

19. Case the hood.

20. Install the front wheels.

21. Lower the vehicle.

22. Connect the negative battery cable.

23. Have the front end alignment checked by a qualified professional.

PNEUMATIC STRUT

▶ See Figure 9

1. Disconnect the negative battery cable.

2. Raise and safely support the vehicle safely on jackstands.

3. Remove the front wheel and tire assembly.

4. Disconnect and cap the front brake hose from the caliper.

5. Remove the brake hose securing clip from the strut bracket and remove the hose from the bracket.

6. Disconnect the parking brake cable from the caliper, if equipped.

7. Open the hood.

8. Disconnect the air line from the solenoid valve or top of the shock.

9. Disconnect the height adjustment harness at the top of the shock.

10. Loosen the nuts which connects the strut bearing cap to the upper housing in the engine compartment.

11. Loosen and remove the strut-to-steering knuckle retainer nuts and bolts.

12. Disconnect the strut from the steering knuckle.

13. Remove the upper strut mounting nuts.

14. Remove the strut assembly from the vehicle.

To install:

15. Position the strut in the vehicle, and install the upper strut mounting nuts. Tighten the nuts to 27 ft. lbs. (36 Nm).

16. Attach the strut assembly to the steering knuckle. Connect the strut-to-the steering knuckle nuts and bolts. Tighten the nuts and bolts to 37 ft. lbs. (50 Nm).

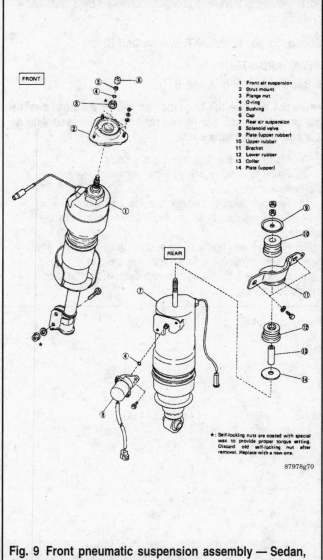

1 Front air suspension
2 Strut mount
3 Flange nut
4 O-ring
5 Bushing
6 Cap
7 Rear air suspension
8 Solenoid valve
9 Plate (upper rubber)
10 Upper rubber
11 Bracket
12 Lower rubber
13 Collar
14 Plate (upper)

★: Self-locking nuts are coated with special wax to provide proper torque setting. Discard old self-locking nut after removal. Replace with a new one.

87978g70

Fig. 9 Front pneumatic suspension assembly — Sedan, Coupe, Loyale, XT, Wagon and Brat

17. Install the brake hose through the strut bracket and install the mounting clip.

18. Install the brake hose to the caliper, and tighten the retainer bolt.

19. Connect the parking brake cable to the caliper, if equipped.

20. Attach the height control harness and air line.

21. Bleed the brake system.

22. Case the hood.

23. Install the front wheels.

24. Lower the vehicle.

25. Connect the negative battery cable.

26. Start the vehicle and allow enough time for the strut to pressurize before driving.

27. Have the front end alignment checked by a qualified professional.

Legacy and Impreza

STANDARD STRUT

◗ See Figures 10, 11, 12, 13, 14 and 15

➡Do not remove the large nut on top of the strut assembly unless the coil spring is properly compressed with a suitable spring compressor.

1. Disconnect the negative battery cable.
2. Raise and support the vehicle safely.
3. Remove the front wheel assembly.
4. Disconnect the ABS sensor, if equipped.
5. Remove the caliper, leaving the line connected and suspend it out of the way with a piece of wire or string.
6. Remove the clip attaching the brake line to the strut housing.
7. Matchmark the camber adjustment bolt to the strut housing as reference for installation.
8. If equipped with ABS, remove the bolt securing the sensor harness.

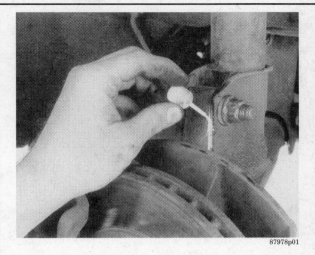

Fig. 11 Paint an alignment mark between the strut and steering knuckle assembly to ease realignment

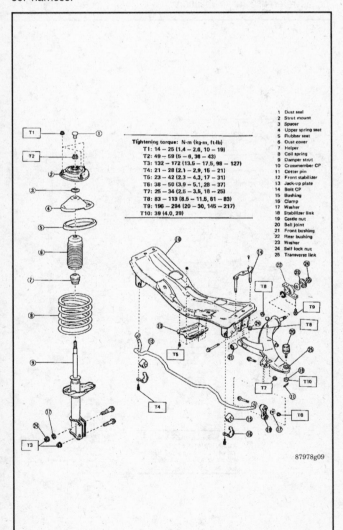

Fig. 10 Front suspension assembly — Legacy and Impreza

Tightening torque: N·m (kg-m, ft-lb)
T1: 14 — 25 (1.4 — 2.6, 10 — 19)
T2: 49 — 59 (5 — 6, 36 — 43)
T3: 132 — 172 (13.5 — 17.5, 98 — 127)
T4: 21 — 28 (2.1 — 2.9, 15 — 21)
T5: 23 — 42 (2.3 — 4.3, 17 — 31)
T6: 38 — 50 (3.9 — 5.1, 28 — 37)
T7: 25 — 34 (2.5 — 3.5, 18 — 25)
T8: 83 — 113 (8.5 — 11.5, 61 — 83)
T9: 196 — 294 (20 — 30, 145 — 217)
T10: 39 (4.0, 29)

1 Dust seal
2 Strut mount
3 Spacer
4 Upper spring seat
5 Rubber seat
6 Dust cover
7 Helper
8 Coil spring
9 Damper strut
10 Crossmember CP
11 Cotter pin
12 Front stabilizer
13 Jack-up plate
14 Bolt CP
15 Bushing
16 Clamp
17 Washer
18 Stabilizer link
19 Castle nut
20 Ball joint
21 Front bushing
22 Rear bushing
23 Washer
24 Self lock nut
25 Transverse link

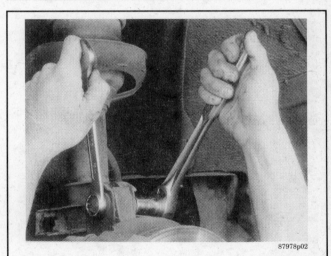

Fig. 12 Loosen the upper strut-to-steering knuckle retainer nut and bolt

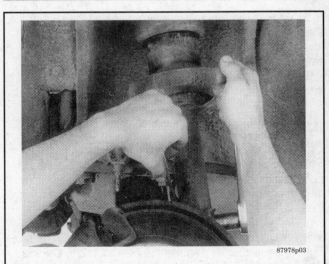

Fig. 13 Loosen the lower strut-to-steering knuckle nut and bolt

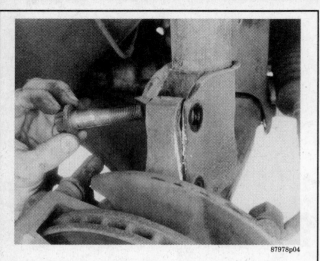

87978p04

Fig. 14 Remove the retainer bolts. The upper bolt's eccentric shaft allows camber adjustment

87978p05

Fig. 15 Lower the strut assembly out of the vehicle

9. Remove the two bolts and nuts securing the strut to the steering knuckle. Notice that the shaft of the top bolt is not round. This bolt is used for camber adjustment, and most always be installed in the top hole.

10. Remove the three nuts securing the strut to the body in the engine compartment.

11. Remove the strut and coil spring assembly from the vehicle.

To install:

12. Install the strut assembly into the vehicle.

13. Install the upper strut retainer nuts, and tighten the nuts to 15 ft. lbs. (20 Nm).

14. If equipped, install the ABS sensor harness, and tighten the bolt to 14 ft. lbs. (20 Nm).

15. Install the lower strut nuts and bolts. Make sure the alignment adjustment bolt is installed in the top mounting hole. Tighten the nuts, while securing the bolts to 112 ft. lbs. 152 Nm).

16. Install the caliper.

17. Attach the brake line to the strut and install the clip.

18. Install the front wheel.

19. Lower the vehicle to the floor.

20. Connect the negative battery cable.

21. Have the front wheel alignment checked by a qualified professional.

PNEUMATIC STRUT

▶ **See Figures 16, 17, 18, 19 and 20**

1. Disconnect the negative battery cable.

2. Raise and support the vehicle safely.

3. Remove the front wheel assembly.

4. From inside the engine compartment, disconnect the air line and height sensor harness from the strut assembly.

5. Disconnect the ABS sensor, if equipped.

6. Remove the caliper, leaving the line connected and suspend it out of the way with a piece of wire or string.

7. Remove the clip attaching the brake line to the strut housing.

8. Matchmark the camber adjustment bolt to the strut housing as reference for installation.

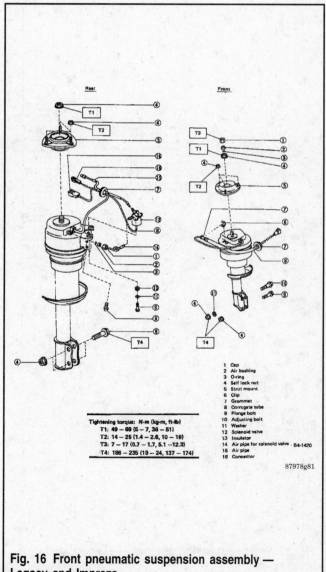

Tightening torque: N·m (kg-m, ft-lb)
T1: 49 – 69 (5 – 7, 36 – 51)
T2: 14 – 25 (1.4 – 2.6, 10 – 19)
T3: 7 – 17 (0.7 – 1.7, 5.1 – 12.3)
T4: 186 – 235 (19 – 24, 137 – 174)

1 Cap
2 Air bushing
3 O-ring
4 Self lock nut
5 Strut mount
6 Clip
7 Grommet
8 Corrugate tube
9 Flange bolt
10 Adjusting bolt
11 Washer
12 Solenoid valve
13 Insulator
14 Air pipe for solenoid valve · B4-1420
15 Air pipe
16 Connector

87978g81

Fig. 16 Front pneumatic suspension assembly — Legacy and Impreza

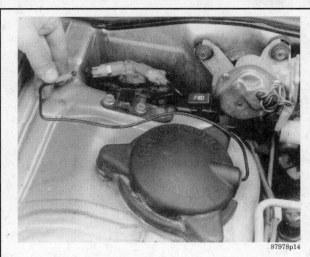

Fig. 17 Disconnect the air line from the solenoid valve — Legacy shown

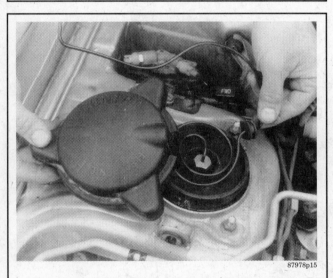

Fig. 18 Remove the plastic cover over the strut bearing

Fig. 19 Loosen the bearing cap retainer nuts

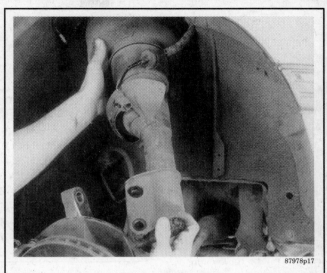

Fig. 20 Lower the strut assembly from the vehicle

9. If equipped with ABS, remove the bolt securing the sensor harness.

10. Remove the two bolts and nuts securing the strut to the steering knuckle. Notice that the shaft of the top bolt is not round. This bolt is used for camber adjustment, and most always be installed in the top hole.

11. Remove the three nuts securing the strut to the body in the engine compartment.

12. Remove the strut and coil spring assembly from the vehicle.

To install:

13. Install the strut assembly into the vehicle.

14. Install the upper strut retainer nuts, and tighten the nuts to 15 ft. lbs. (20 Nm).

15. If equipped, install the ABS sensor harness, and tighten the bolt to 14 ft. lbs. (20 Nm).

16. Install the lower strut nuts and bolts. Make sure the alignment adjustment bolt is installed in the top mounting hole. Tighten the nuts, while securing the bolts to 112 ft. lbs. 152 Nm).

17. Install the caliper.

18. Attach the brake line to the strut and install the clip.

19. Attach the height sensor harness and air line.

20. Install the front wheel.

21. Lower the vehicle to the floor.

22. Connect the negative battery cable.

23. Start the vehicle and allow enough time for the strut to pressurize before driving.

24. Have the front wheel alignment checked by a qualified professional.

SVX

▶ See Figure 21

➡Do not remove the large nut on top of the strut assembly unless the coil spring is properly compressed with a suitable spring compressor.

1. Disconnect the negative battery cable.
2. Raise and safely support the vehicle on jackstands.
3. Remove the tire and wheel assembly.
4. Disconnect the sway bar from the strut assembly.

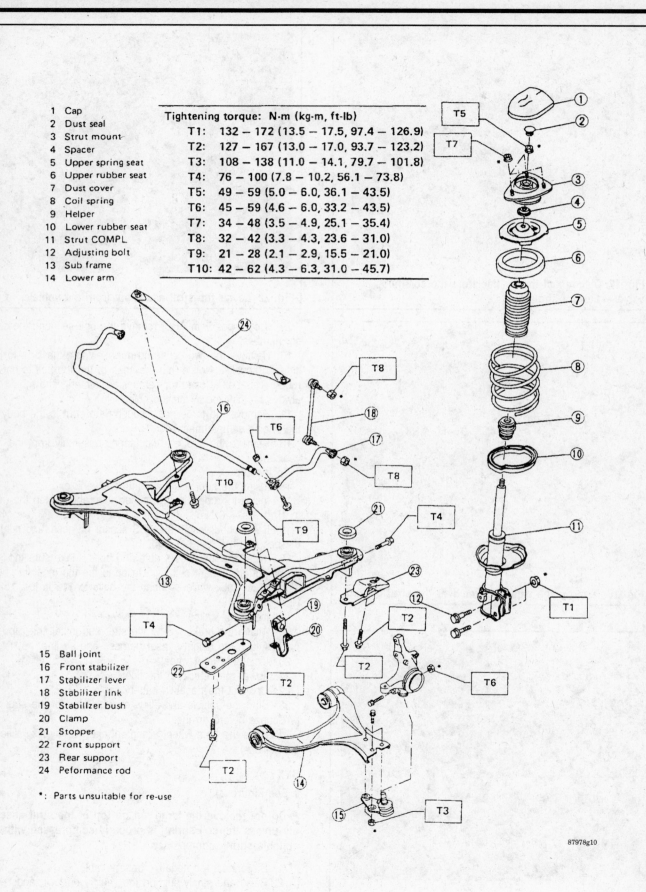

1 Cap
2 Dust seal
3 Strut mount
4 Spacer
5 Upper spring seat
6 Upper rubber seat
7 Dust cover
8 Coil spring
9 Helper
10 Lower rubber seat
11 Strut COMPL
12 Adjusting bolt
13 Sub frame
14 Lower arm

Tightening torque: N·m (kg-m, ft-lb)

T1: 132 — 172 (13.5 — 17.5, 97.4 — 126.9)
T2: 127 — 167 (13.0 — 17.0, 93.7 — 123.2)
T3: 108 — 138 (11.0 — 14.1, 79.7 — 101.8)
T4: 76 — 100 (7.8 — 10.2, 56.1 — 73.8)
T5: 49 — 59 (5.0 — 6.0, 36.1 — 43.5)
T6: 45 — 59 (4.6 — 6.0, 33.2 — 43.5)
T7: 34 — 48 (3.5 — 4.9, 25.1 — 35.4)
T8: 32 — 42 (3.3 — 4.3, 23.6 — 31.0)
T9: 21 — 28 (2.1 — 2.9, 15.5 — 21.0)
T10: 42 — 62 (4.3 — 6.3, 31.0 — 45.7)

15 Ball joint
16 Front stabilizer
17 Stabilizer lever
18 Stabilizer link
19 Stabilizer bush
20 Clamp
21 Stopper
22 Front support
23 Rear support
24 Peformance rod

*: Parts unsuitable for re-use

87978g10

Fig. 21 Front suspension assembly — SVX

5. Remove the bolt and bracket securing the ABS sensor wire to the strut assembly.

6. Remove the bolt and bracket securing the brake hose to the strut.

7. Scribe matchmarks on the camber adjusting bolt and the steering knuckle for installation purposes.

8. Remove the nuts from the lower strut mounting bolts. Remove the lower mounting bolt. The upper bolt **MUST** remain in place.

9. Support the lower control arm under the ball joint with a suitable jack.

10. Remove the strut mount cap in the engine compartment.

11. Remove the three strut plate mounting nuts.

12. Lower the jack about an inch and remove the strut-to-steering knuckle upper mounting bolt.

13. Remove the strut from the vehicle.

14. If the strut is to be replaced, remove the sway bar link.

To install:

15. Install the sway bar link on the strut and tighten the mounting nut to 28 ft. lbs. (37 Nm).

16. Install the strut assembly into the vehicle and install the upper mounting nuts and tighten to 30 ft. lbs. (41 Nm).

17. Install the strut mount cap.

18. Connect the strut to the steering knuckle and install the lower mounting through-bolts and loosely install the nuts.

19. Remove the jack.

20. Rotate the camber adjusting bolt so the matchmarks are in alignment. Tighten the mounting nuts to 112 ft. lbs. (152 Nm).

21. Install the brake hose bracket and bolt on the strut.

22. Install the ABS sensor bracket and bolt on the strut.

23. Connect the sway bar to the sway bar link and tighten the mounting nut to 28 ft. lbs. (37 Nm).

24. Install the tire and wheel assembly.

25. Lower the vehicle.

26. Connect the negative battery cable.

27. Check the front end alignment and adjust as necessary.

OVERHAUL

♦ **See Figures 22, 23, 24 and 25**

➡ Do not remove the large nut on top of the strut assembly unless the coil spring is properly compressed with a suitable spring compressor.

1. Remove the strut assembly from the vehicle.

❊❊WARNING

Remove the strut from the vehicle and install a spring compressor before removing the strut center nut.

2. Place the strut assembly in a vise with a holding tool and install a spring compressor.

3. Compress the spring slightly.

4. Loosen but do not remove the bearing cap locknut.

5. Compress the spring with the spring compressor then remove the locknut.

6. Remove the strut bearing cap, mounting insulator bracket and upper spring seat.

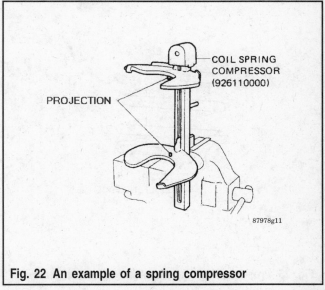

Fig. 22 An example of a spring compressor

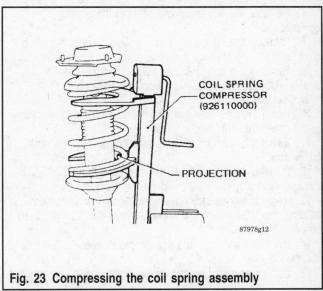

Fig. 23 Compressing the coil spring assembly

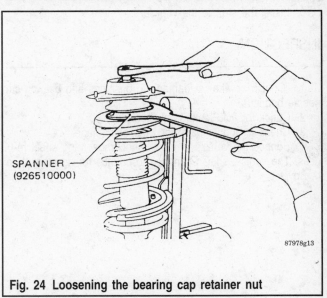

Fig. 24 Loosening the bearing cap retainer nut

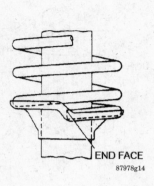

Fig. 25 Proper spring placement in lower strut plate

7. Remove the coil assembly, leaving the spring compressed.

8. Remove the strut boot and rebound bumper from the strut. Inspect and replace if worn.

9. Remove the strut retainer nut using a suitable wrench.Remove the strut insert from the assembly.

To install:

10. Install the strut into the chamber, and install the retainer nut. Tighten the nut snugly.

11. Install the rebound bumper and the boot to the strut piston rod.

12. Install the coil spring on the strut assembly. Make sure the spring is properly positioned on the lower bracket.

13. Install the upper spring seat, mounting insulator and bearing cap. Make sure the upper spring seat is facing the proper direction.

14. Install the locknut, and tighten the locknut to 36-43 ft. lbs. (47-56 Nm).

15. Loosen and remove the spring compressor from the coil spring.

16. Install the strut to the vehicle.

INSPECTION

1. Check for wear or damage to bushings and bearing cap needle bearings.

2. Check for fluid leaks from the struts.

3. Check all rubber parts for wear or damage.

4. Bounce the vehicle to check shock absorbing effectiveness. The vehicle should continue to bounce for no more than two cycles.

Ball Joint

REMOVAL & INSTALLATION

Justy

▶ See Figure 26

1. Disconnect the negative battery cable.

2. Raise and safely support the vehicle on jackstands.

3. Remove the tire and wheel assembly.

4. Remove the lower ball joint cotter pin and castle nut. Discard the cotter pin.

5. Separate the ball joint stud from the lower control arm assembly.

6. Remove the lower ball joint pinch bolt from the steering knuckle.

7. Spread the ears on the steering knuckle and disconnect the ball joint from the steering knuckle.

To install:

8. Install lower ball joint into the steering knuckle.

9. Install the ball joint pinch bolt and tighten to 33 ft. lbs. (44 Nm).

10. Guide the ball joint stud through the control arm.

11. Install the ball joint castle nut and tighten to 29 ft. lbs. (39 Nm).

12. Install the tire and wheel assembly.

13. Lower the vehicle.

14. Connect the negative battery cable.

Sedan Coupe, Loyale, XT, Wagon and Brat

▶ See Figures 27 and 28

1. Disconnect the negative battery cable.

2. Raise and safely support the vehicle on jackstands.

3. Remove the front wheel and tire assembly.

4. Remove the cotter pin from the lower ball joint castle nut, and discard.

5. Loosen and remove the castle nut.

6. Separate the ball joint stud from the lower control arm using a suitable tool.

7. Remove the lower ball joint to steering knuckle pinch bolt.

8. Using a suitable wedge, remove the lower ball joint from the steering knuckle.

To install:

9. Install the ball joint into the steering knuckle and install the pinch bolt. Tighten the bolt to 33 ft. lbs. (46 Nm).

10. Install the ball joint stud through the lower control arm and install the castle nut. Tighten the castle nut to 29 ft. lbs. (39 Nm).

11. Install a new cotter pin. If necessary to align the cotter pin tighten the nut. NEVER loosen the castle nut to align the cotter pin holes.

12. Install the wheel.

13. Lower the vehicle.

14. Connect the negative battery cable.

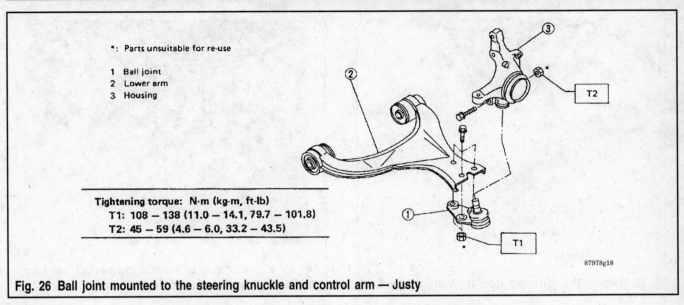

*: Parts unsuitable for re-use

1 Ball joint
2 Lower arm
3 Housing

Tightening torque: N·m (kg-m, ft-lb)
T1: 108 — 138 (11.0 — 14.1, 79.7 — 101.8)
T2: 45 — 59 (4.6 — 6.0, 33.2 — 43.5)

87978g18

Fig. 26 Ball joint mounted to the steering knuckle and control arm — Justy

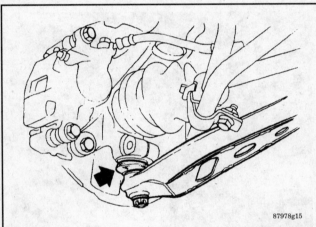

87978g15

Fig. 27 Ball joint mounted to the steering knuckle and control arm — Sedan, Coupe, Loyale, XT, Wagon and Brat

Legacy and Impreza
▶ See Figures 29, 30, 31, 32, 33, 34, 35, 36 and 37

1. Disconnect the negative battery cable.
2. Raise and support the vehicle safely on jackstands.
3. Remove the front wheel and tire assembly.
4. Remove the ball joint castle nut cotter pin. Discard the cotter pin.
5. Loosen and remove the castle nut.
6. Using a suitable puller or prytool, disconnect the ball joint from the lower control arm assembly.
7. Remove the bolt securing the ball joint to the steering knuckle. Use a suitable wedge to expand the steering knuckle connection point, and remove the ball joint.

To install:

8. Install the ball joint to the steering knuckle.
9. Install the bolt, and tighten the retaining bolt to 36 ft. lbs. (49 Nm).
10. Connect the ball joint to the lower control arm, and tighten the castle nut to 29 ft. lbs. (39 Nm). Then tighten the castle nut an additional 60° until the slot in the castle nut is

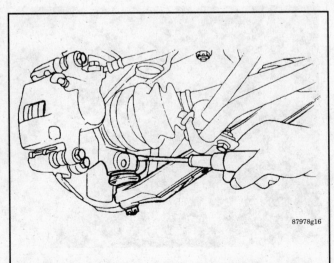

87978g16

Fig. 28 Prying the steering knuckle to remove the ball joint assembly

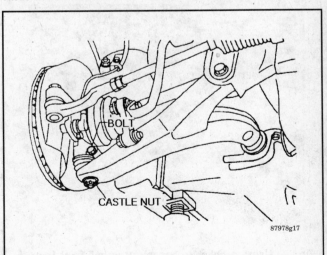

87978g17

Fig. 29 Ball joint mounted to the steering knuckle and control arm — Legacy and Impreza

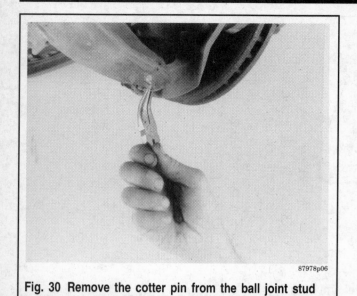

Fig. 30 Remove the cotter pin from the ball joint stud

Fig. 31 Loosen and remove the castle nut from the ball joint stud

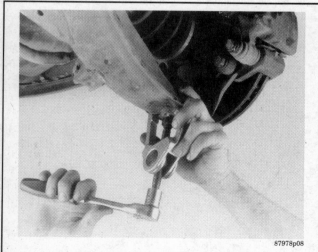

Fig. 32 Using a puller to separate the ball joint from the control arm

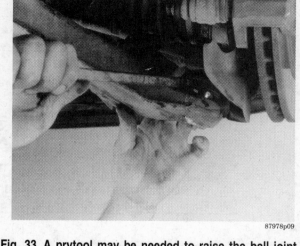

Fig. 33 A prytool may be needed to raise the ball joint stud enough to clear the control arm

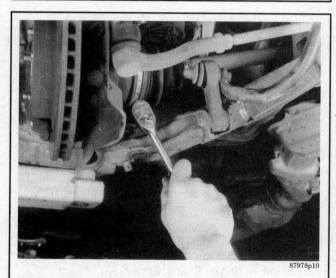

Fig. 34 Loosen the steering knuckle pinch bolt . . .

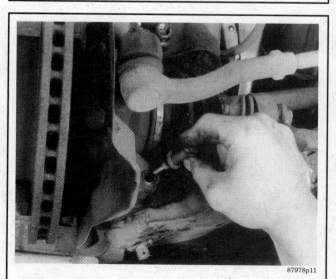

Fig. 35 . . . and remove from the mounting hole

87978p12

Fig. 36 Using a drift to wedge the steering knuckle mount enough . . .

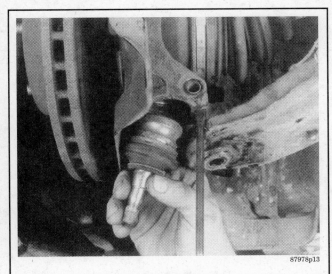

87978p13

Fig. 37 . . . to remove the ball joint

aligned with the cotter pin hole in the ball joint. Install a new cotter pin.

11. Install the wheel.
12. Lower the vehicle.
13. Connect the negative battery cable.

SVX

▶ See Figures 38 and 39

1. Raise and safely support the vehicle.
2. Remove the tire and wheel assembly.
3. Remove the ball joint-to-steering knuckle pinch bolt.
4. Separate the ball joint from the steering knuckle assembly.
5. Remove the three lower ball joint mounting nuts and remove the lower ball joint assembly.

To install:

6. Position the lower ball joint on the control arm and install the three mounting nuts. Tighten the mounting nuts to 91 ft. lbs. (123 Nm).

7. Guide the ball joint stud into the bottom of the steering knuckle until the notch in the stud is visible through the bolt hole in the steering knuckle. Install the pinch bolt and nut and tighten to 38 ft. lbs. (52 Nm).

8. Install the tire and wheel assembly.
9. Lower the vehicle.

INSPECTION

▶ See Figures 40 and 41

1. Raise and support the vehicle safely on jackstands.
2. Using a suitable prytool, position it under the wheel then pry upward on the wheel several times. If more than 0.012 in. (3mm) of movement is noticed at the ball joint it should be replaced.
3. Inspect the dust seal. If damaged or cracked, the ball joint should be replaced.

Sway Bar

REMOVAL & INSTALLATION

▶ See Figure 42

1. Disconnect the negative battery cable.
2. Raise and safely support the vehicle on jackstands.
3. Remove the sway bar bracket bolts from the outboard clamps at the tension rods.
4. Remove the sway bar to frame mounting bolts, then remove the frame brackets and bushings.
5. Remove the sway bar from the vehicle.

To install:

6. Position the sway bar on the vehicle.
7. Install the sway bar-to-frame bushings and brackets. Install and tighten the mounting bolts to 18 ft. lbs. (26 Nm).
8. Install the outboard clamps and mounting bolts on the tension rods and tighten to 18 ft. lbs. (26 Nm).
9. Lower the vehicle.
10. Connect the negative battery cable.

Sedan, Coupe, Loyale, XT, Wagon and Brat

▶ See Figure 43

1. Disconnect the negative battery cable.
2. Raise and safely support the vehicle on jackstands.
3. Remove the front tire and wheel assemblies.
4. Remove the sway bar link-to-lower control arm mounting nuts and bolts.
5. Remove the sway bar bracket-to-frame bolts and remove the sway bar from the vehicle.

To install:

6. Position the sway bar on the vehicle and loosely install the sway bar bracket to frame bolts.
7. Install the sway bar link-to-control arm mounting nuts and bolts and tighten to 22 ft. lbs. (29 Nm).
8. Tighten the sway bar bracket bolts to 21 ft. lbs. (28 Nm).
9. Install the tire and wheel assemblies.
10. Lower the vehicle.

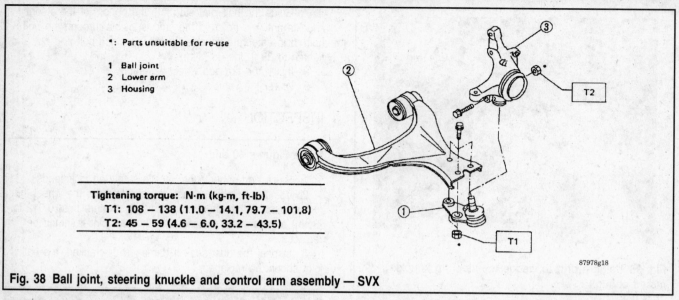

*: Parts unsuitable for re-use

1 Ball joint
2 Lower arm
3 Housing

Tightening torque: N·m (kg-m, ft-lb)
T1: 108 — 138 (11.0 — 14.1, 79.7 — 101.8)
T2: 45 — 59 (4.6 — 6.0, 33.2 — 43.5)

87978g18

Fig. 38 Ball joint, steering knuckle and control arm assembly — SVX

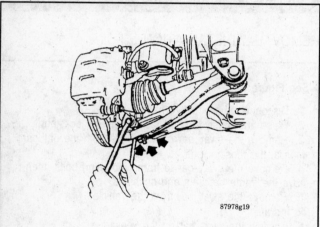

87978g19

Fig. 39 Loosening the steering knuckle pinch bolt. The arrows indicate the ball joint-to-control arm retaining nut locations

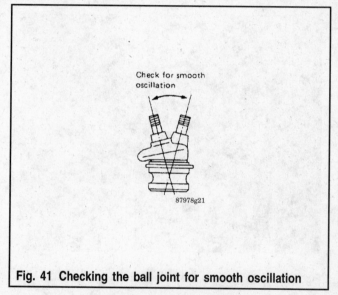

Check for smooth oscillation

87978g21

Fig. 41 Checking the ball joint for smooth oscillation

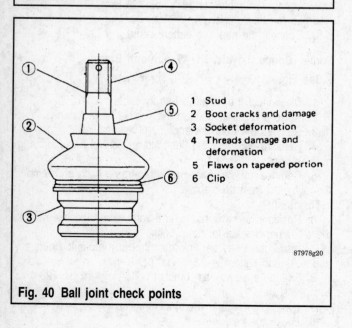

1 Stud
2 Boot cracks and damage
3 Socket deformation
4 Threads damage and deformation
5 Flaws on tapered portion
6 Clip

87978g20

Fig. 40 Ball joint check points

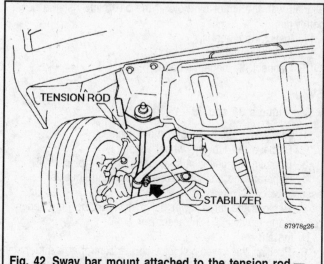

TENSION ROD

STABILIZER

87978g26

Fig. 42 Sway bar mount attached to the tension rod — Justy

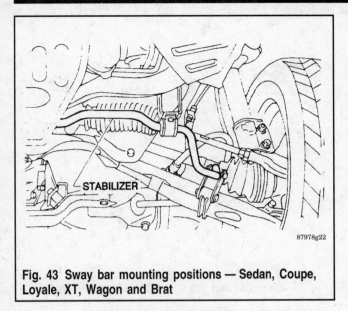

Fig. 43 Sway bar mounting positions — Sedan, Coupe, Loyale, XT, Wagon and Brat

11. Connect the negative battery cable.

Legacy and Impreza

▶ **See Figures 44, 45, 46, 47 and 48**

1. Raise and support the vehicle safely on jackstands.
2. Remove the crossmember-to-sway bar bolts.
3. Remove the sway bar-to-lower control arm bolts.
4. Remove the jack-up plate from the lower crossmember.
5. Remove the sway bar.

To install:

6. Install the sway bar and jack-up plate.
7. Align the bushings with the painted marks on the sway bar and temporarily tighten the mounting bolts.
8. Tighten the bolts to the following specifications:
   a. Jack-up plate-to-crossmember — 24 ft. lbs. (32 Nm)
   b. Sway bar link-to-lower control arm — 21 ft. lbs. (29 Nm)
   c. Sway bar-to-crossmember — 18 ft. lbs. (25 Nm)
9. Lower the vehicle.

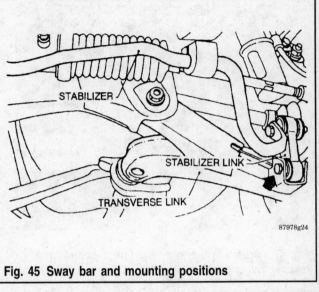

Fig. 45 Sway bar and mounting positions

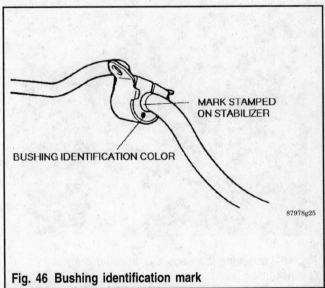

Fig. 46 Bushing identification mark

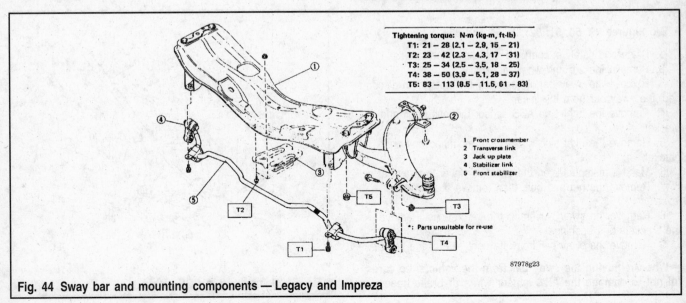

Tightening torque: N·m (kg-m, ft-lb)
T1: 21 — 28 (2.1 — 2.9, 15 — 21)
T2: 23 — 42 (2.3 — 4.3, 17 — 31)
T3: 25 — 34 (2.5 — 3.5, 18 — 25)
T4: 38 — 50 (3.9 — 5.1, 28 — 37)
T5: 83 — 113 (8.5 — 11.5, 61 — 83)

1 Front crossmember
2 Transverse link
3 Jack up plate
4 Stabilizer link
5 Front stabilizer

*: Parts unsuitable for re-use

Fig. 44 Sway bar and mounting components — Legacy and Impreza

Fig. 47 Loosening the sway bar link-to-control arm retainer nut and bolt

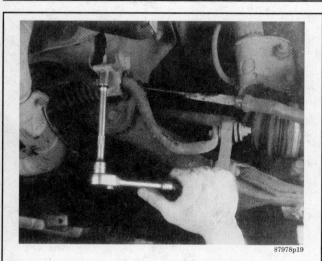

Fig. 48 Loosening the sway bay bushing bracket retainer bolt

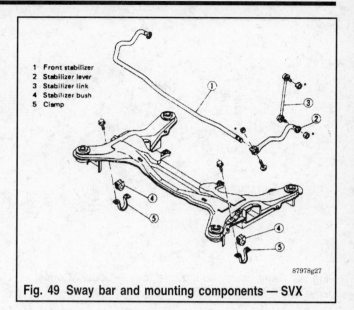

1 Front stabilizer
2 Stabilizer lever
3 Stabilizer link
4 Stabilizer bush
5 Clamp

Fig. 49 Sway bar and mounting components — SVX

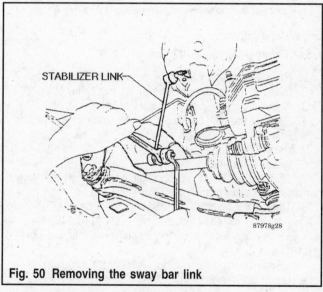

STABILIZER LINK

Fig. 50 Removing the sway bar link

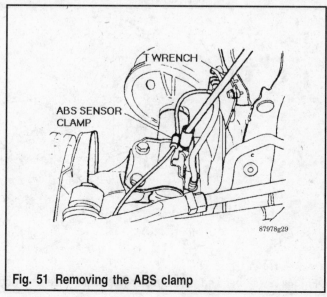

T WRENCH

ABS SENSOR
CLAMP

Fig. 51 Removing the ABS clamp

SVX

▶ **See Figures 49, 50, 51, 52, 53, 54 and 55**

1. Raise and safely support the vehicle on jackstands.
2. Remove the tire and wheel assembly.
3. Remove the sway bar link-to-sway bar nuts, then disconnect the sway bar from the links.
4. Remove the right side ABS sensor mounting bolt and bracket.
5. Remove the right side brake hose mounting bolt and bracket.
6. Make a matchmark on the sway bar lever-to-sway bar.
7. Remove the nut and bolt, then remove the sway bar lever.
8. Remove the sway bar bracket-to-frame bolts. Remove the brackets and bushings.
9. Remove the sway bar from the right side of the vehicle.

➡When removing the sway bar from the vehicle, be careful not to damage the ABS sensor wires or brake hoses.

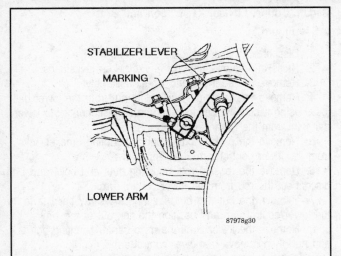

Fig. 52 Placing alignment marks on the sway bar and lever

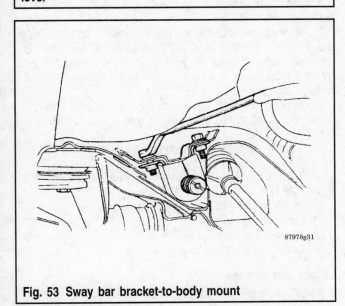

Fig. 53 Sway bar bracket-to-body mount

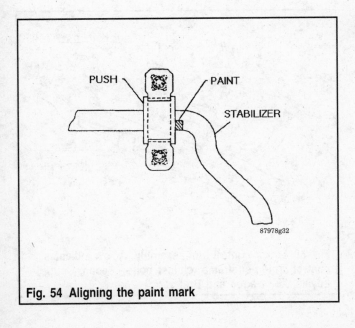

Fig. 54 Aligning the paint mark

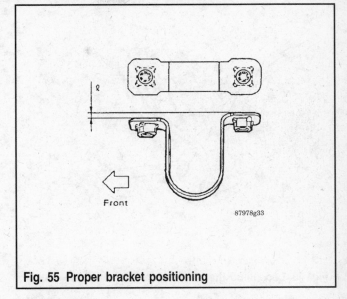

Fig. 55 Proper bracket positioning

To install:

10. Install the sway bar from the right side of the vehicle.
11. Install the sway bar bushings and brackets. Make sure paint marks on the sway bar align with the sway bar bushings.

➡ **When installing the sway bar brackets make sure they are positioned correctly. The front of the sway bar brackets are shorter than the rear.**

12. Install the mounting bolts loosely.
13. Install the sway bar lever with the matchmarks in alignment, and install the mounting nut and bolt, and tighten to 38 ft. lbs. (52 Nm).
14. Connect the sway bar to the sway bar links and install the mounting nuts. Tighten the mounting nuts to 38 ft. lbs. (52 Nm).
15. Tighten the sway bar-to frame mounting bolts to 18 ft. lbs. (26 Nm).
16. Install the brake hose bracket and bolt to the strut.
17. Install the ABS sensor bracket and bolt to the strut.
18. Install the tire and wheel assembly.
19. Lower the vehicle.

Lower Control Arm

REMOVAL & INSTALLATION

Justy

▶ **See Figures 56 and 57**

1. Disconnect the negative battery cable.
2. Raise and safely support the vehicle on jackstands.
3. Remove the tire and wheel assembly.
4. Remove the nuts that attach the tension rod to the control arm.
5. Remove the center undercover, if equipped.
6. Remove the tension rod bushing lock nut and remove the washer, bushing and tension rod.
7. Remove the control arm-to-crossmember mounting bolt.
8. Remove the lower ball joint pinch bolt from the steering knuckle.

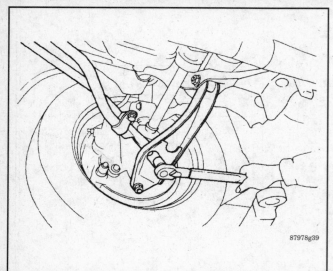

Fig. 56 Loosening the tension rod retainer nuts — Justy

Fig. 57 Removing the control arm-to-subframe retainer bolt

9. Spread the ears on the steering knuckle and disconnect the ball joint from the steering knuckle.

10. Remove the lower control arm.

To install:

11. Install the lower control arm on the vehicle, with the lower ball joint inserted into the steering knuckle.

12. Install the ball joint pinch bolt, and tighten to 33 ft. lbs. (44 Nm).

13. Install the tension rod through the frame bracket and install the bushing and washer, then tighten the nut to 47 ft. lbs. (64 Nm).

14. Connect the control arm to the crossmember and install the mounting bolt loosely.

15. Connect the tension rod to the control arm and tighten the nuts to 62 ft. lbs. (83 Nm).

16. Install the tire and wheel assembly.

17. Lower the vehicle.

18. Tighten the control arm-to-crossmember bolt to 50 ft. lbs. (69 Nm).

19. Connect the negative battery cable.

Sedan, Coupe, Loyale, XT, Wagon and Brat

♦ See Figure 58

1. Disconnect the negative battery cable.

2. Raise and safely support the vehicle on jackstands.

3. Remove the front tire and wheel assembly.

4. Remove the cotter pin and castle nut from the lower ball joint. Using a suitable ball joint separator, disconnect the lower ball joint from the lower control arm.

5. Remove the parking brake cable mounting bracket bolts from the lower control arm, if equipped.

6. Remove the tension rod mounting nuts and bolts and disconnect the rod from the lower control arm.

7. Remove the nut and bolt securing the sway bar link to the lower control arm and position the link out of the way.

8. Remove the lower control arm to-frame mounting bolt and nut, then remove the lower control arm.

To install:

9. Position the lower control arm in the vehicle and install the lower control arm-to-frame mounting nut and bolt. DO NOT tighten at this time.

10. Connect the strut rod to the lower control arm and install the mounting nuts and bolts. DO NOT tighten at this time.

11. Connect the lower ball joint to the lower control arm and install the castle nut and tighten to 22 ft. lbs. (29 Nm). Install a new cotter pin.

12. Connect the sway bar link to the lower control arm and install the mounting bolt and nut and tighten to 22 ft. lbs. (29 Nm).

13. Tighten the lower control arm-to-frame mounting bolt to 78 ft. lbs. (98 Nm).

14. Tighten the strut rod to control arm mounting bolts to 27 ft. lbs. (36 Nm).

15. Install the front tire and wheel assembly.

16. Lower the vehicle.

17. Connect the negative battery cable.

18. Check the front end alignment.

Legacy and Impreza

♦ See Figures 59, 60 and 61

1. Raise and support the vehicle safely on jackstands.

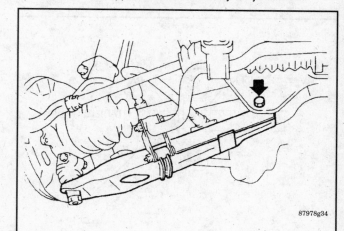

Fig. 58 Lower control arm assembly. Arrow indicates control arm-to-subframe retainer bolt — Sedan, Coupe, Loyale, XT, Wagon and Brat

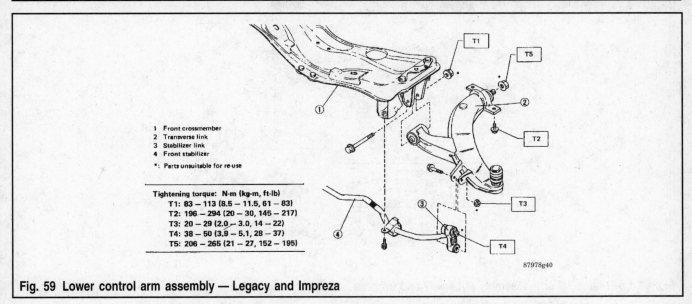

1 Front crossmember
2 Transverse link
3 Stabilizer link
4 Front stabilizer

*: Parts unsuitable for re-use

Tightening torque: N-m (kg-m, ft-lb)
T1: 83 — 113 (8.5 — 11.5, 61 — 83)
T2: 196 — 294 (20 — 30, 145 — 217)
T3: 20 — 29 (2.0 — 3.0, 14 — 22)
T4: 38 — 50 (3.9 — 5.1, 28 — 37)
T5: 206 — 265 (21 — 27, 152 — 195)

87978g40

Fig. 59 Lower control arm assembly — Legacy and Impreza

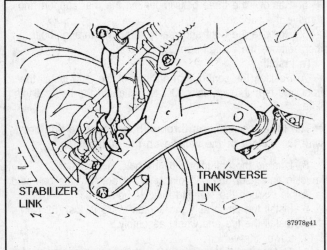

87978g41

Fig. 60 Remove the sway bar link attached to the control arm

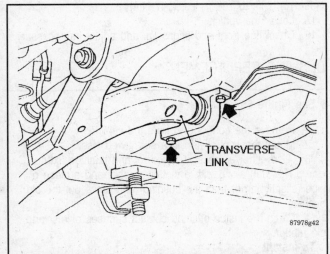

87978g42

Fig. 61 Remove the control arm-to-crossmember bolts and bracket

2. Remove the wheel and tire assembly.
3. Disconnect the sway bar from the lower control arm.
4. Remove the bolt securing the ball joint to the steering knuckle.
5. Remove the nuts (not bolts) securing the lower control arm to the crossmember.
6. Remove the bolts securing the bushing bracket of the lower control arm to body.
7. Remove the lower control arm-to-crossmember bolts, then remove the lower control arm.

To install:

8. Install the lower control arm and temporarily tighten the two bolts used to secure the rear bushing of the lower control arm to the body.

➡**These bolts should be tightened to such an extent that they can still move back and forth in the oblong shaped hole in the bracket which holds the busing.**

9. Install the bolts used to connect the lower control arm to the crossmember and temporarily tighten the nuts.
10. Insert the ball joint, and tighten the bolt.
11. Connect the sway bar link to the lower control arm and temporarily tighten the bolts.
12. Lower the vehicle and tighten the bolts to following specifications:
    a. Lower control arm-to-sway bar link; 21 ft. lbs. (27 Nm)
    b. Lower control arm-to-crossmember; 72 ft. lbs. (98 Nm)
    c. Lower control arm rear link bushing-to-body; 181 ft. lbs. (245 Nm)

➡**Move the rear bushing back and forth until the lower control arm link-to-rear bushing clearance is established before tightening the bolts.**

SVX

▶ **See Figures 62, 63 and 64**

1. Raise and safely support the vehicle on jackstands.
2. Remove the tire and wheel assembly.
3. Remove the lower ball joint-to-steering knuckle pinch bolt.
4. Separate the ball joint from the steering knuckle.

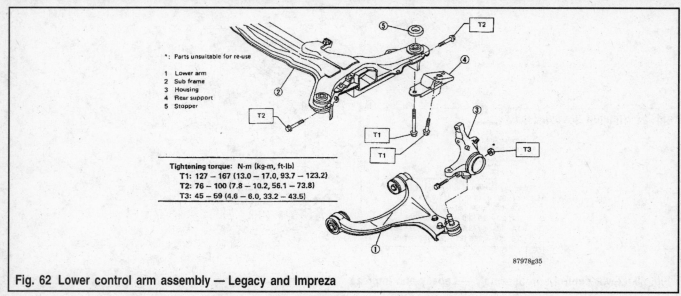

*: Parts unsuitable for re-use

1 Lower arm
2 Sub frame
3 Housing
4 Rear support
5 Stopper

Tightening torque: N·m (kg-m, ft-lb)
T1: 127 — 167 (13.0 — 17.0, 93.7 — 123.2)
T2: 76 — 100 (7.8 — 10.2, 56.1 — 73.8)
T3: 45 — 59 (4.6 — 6.0, 33.2 — 43.5)

87978g35

Fig. 62 Lower control arm assembly — Legacy and Impreza

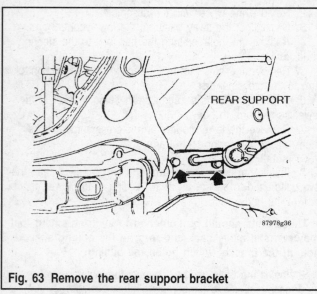

REAR SUPPORT

87978g36

Fig. 63 Remove the rear support bracket

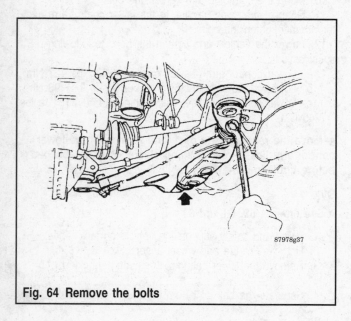

87978g37

Fig. 64 Remove the bolts

5. Remove the three bolts mounting the rear support and remove the support.

6. Remove the front and rear control arm through-bolts, then remove the control arm.

To install:

7. Position the control arm on the vehicle, and install the front and rear through-bolts. DO NOT tighten the bolts at this time.

➡**The lower control arm through-bolts must be tightened with the weight of the vehicle on the suspension.**

8. Line up the ball joint with the hole in the steering knuckle and insert the ball joint until the notch in the ball stud is visible through the steering knuckle hole.

9. Install the pinch bolt and tighten to 38 ft. lbs. (52 Nm).

10. Install the tire and wheel assembly.

11. Lower the vehicle.

12. Tighten the lower control arm through-bolts to 65 ft. lbs. (88 Nm).

13. Raise the vehicle.

14. Install the rear support and tighten the rear support mounting bolts to 108 ft. lbs. (147 Nm).

15. Lower the vehicle.

16. Check the front end alignment and adjust as necessary.

BUSHING REPLACEMENT

▶ **See Figure 65**

1. Remove the control arm from the vehicle.

2. Mount the control arm in a soft jawed vise.

3. Use either a press or a control arm bushing fixture (C-clamp like tool) along with a slotted washer and a piece of pipe (slightly larger than the bushing) and press out the old bushing.

4. Clean the inside bushing contact surfaces of rust and old rubber.

To install:

5. Apply a light coating of grease to both the replacement busing and bushing contact surfaces on the control arm.

6. Align the bushing according to the illustration.

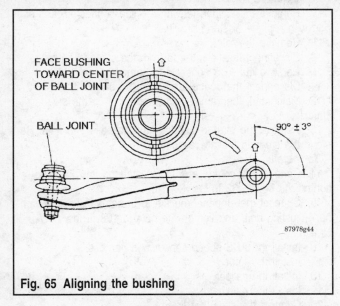

Fig. 65 Aligning the bushing

7. Install the bushing using the press tool. A bushing install clamp can also be used to compress the bushing into the control arm.

8. Install the control arm on the vehicle.

Knuckle and Spindle

REMOVAL & INSTALLATION

Justy

▶ See Figures 66, 67 and 68

1. Disconnect the negative battery cable.
2. Raise and support the vehicle safely on jackstands.
3. Remove the wheel and tire assembly.
4. Unstake and remove the axle nut.
5. Remove the halfshaft.
6. Remove the caliper, leaving the line connected and support with wire or string.
7. Remove the rotor.
8. Disconnect the tie rod end from the steering knuckle.
9. Disconnect the control arm from the ball joint.
10. Remove the strut-to-steering knuckle bolt and nut. Using a wedge, remove the steering knuckle assembly.

To install:

11. Connect the steering knuckle to the strut opening. Install the retainer nut and bolt, and tighten to 108 ft. lbs. (147 Nm).
12. Install the rotor.
13. Install the caliper.
14. Install the halfshaft.
15. Connect the tie rod to the steering knuckle.
16. Install a new axle hub nut. Tighten it to 137 ft. lbs. (186 Nm) and stake the nut.
17. Install the wheel.
18. Lower the vehicle.

Sedan, Coupe, Loyale, XT, Wagon and Brat

▶ See Figures 69 and 70

1. Disconnect the negative battery cable.

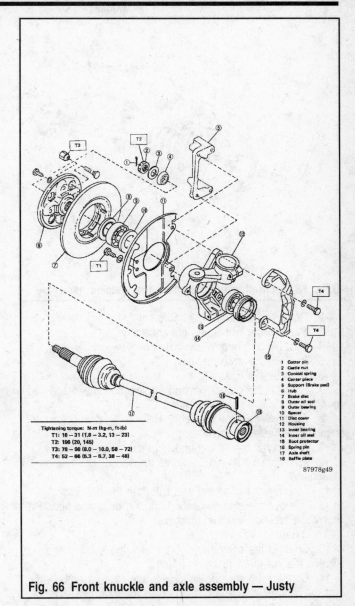

Tightening torque: N·m (kg-m, ft-lb)
T1: 18 — 31 (1.8 — 3.2, 13 — 23)
T2: 196 (20, 145)
T3: 78 — 98 (8.0 — 10.0, 58 — 72)
T4: 52 — 66 (5.3 — 6.7, 38 — 48)

1 Cotter pin
2 Castle nut
3 Conical spring
4 Center piece
5 Support (Brake pad)
6 Hub
7 Brake disc
8 Outer oil seal
9 Outer bearing
10 Spacer
11 Disc cover
12 Housing
13 Inner bearing
14 Inner oil seal
15 Boot protector
16 Spring pin
17 Axle shaft
18 Baffle plate

Fig. 66 Front knuckle and axle assembly — Justy

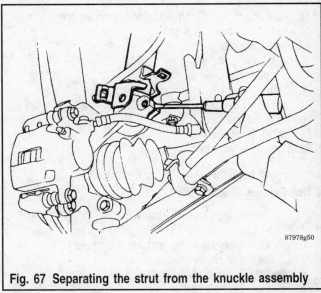

Fig. 67 Separating the strut from the knuckle assembly

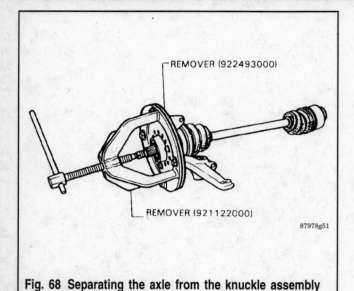

REMOVER (922493000)

REMOVER (921122000)

87978g51

Fig. 68 Separating the axle from the knuckle assembly

2. Raise and support the vehicle safely on jackstands.
3. Remove the wheel and tire assembly.
4. Unstake and remove the axle nut.
5. Remove the sway bar link.
6. Remove the halfshaft.
7. Remove the caliper, leaving the line connected and support using a piece of wire or string.
8. Remove the rotor assembly. Refer to Section 9 for rotor removal and installation steps.
9. Disconnect the tie rod end from the steering knuckle.
10. If equipped with ABS, remove the sensor and harness assembly.
11. Disconnect the control arm link from the ball joint.
12. Remove the strut-to-steering knuckle bolts and nuts. Remove the steering knuckle assembly.

To install:
13. Connect the control arm to the steering knuckle and tighten the nut to 32 ft. lbs. (44 Nm).
14. Connect the steering knuckle to the strut assembly, using the retainer nuts and bolts. Tighten the nuts to 108 ft. lbs. (147 Nm).
15. If equipped, install the ABS speed sensor and harness.
16. Install the rotor.
17. Install the caliper.
18. Install the halfshaft.
19. Connect the sway bar link.
20. Connect the tie rod to the steering knuckle.
21. Install a new axle hub nut. Tighten it to 137 ft. lbs. (186 Nm) and stake the nut.
22. Install the wheel.
23. Lower the vehicle.

Legacy and Impreza

▶ See Figures 71 and 72

1. Disconnect the negative battery cable.
2. Raise and support the vehicle safely on jackstands.
3. Remove the front wheel and tire assemblies.
4. Unstake and remove the axle nut.
5. Remove the sway bar link.
6. Remove the halfshaft.

7. Remove the caliper, leaving the line connected, and support with a piece of string or wire.
8. Remove the rotor.
9. Disconnect the tie rod end from the steering knuckle.
10. Remove the ABS sensor and harness assembly.
11. Disconnect the control arm from the ball joint.
12. Matchmark the camber adjustment bolt to the steering knuckle.
13. Remove the strut-to-steering knuckle bolts and nuts. Remove the steering knuckle assembly.

To install:
14. Connect the control arm to the steering knuckle, and tighten the bolt to 32 ft. lbs. (44 Nm).
15. Connect the steering knuckle to the strut, align the camber adjusting bolt, and tighten the nuts to 108 ft. lbs. (147 Nm).
16. Install the ABS speed sensor and harness.
17. Install the rotor.
18. Install the caliper.
19. Install the halfshaft.
20. Connect the sway bar link.
21. Connect the tie rod to the steering knuckle.
22. Install a new axle hub nut. Tighten the nut to 137 ft. lbs. (186 Nm) and stake the nut.
23. Install the wheel.
24. Lower the vehicle.
25. Check and adjust the front wheel alignment.

SVX

▶ See Figure 73

1. Disconnect the negative battery cable.
2. Raise and safely support the vehicle on jackstands.
3. Remove the tire and wheel assembly.
4. Unstake and remove the axle nut.
5. Remove the lower ball joint pinch bolt.
6. Disconnect the ABS sensor from the steering knuckle.
7. Remove the brake hose bracket bolt and bracket from the strut.
8. Matchmark the camber adjusting bolt on the strut and remove the mounting nuts and lower mounting bolt. DO NOT remove the upper bolt at this time.
9. Remove the caliper and caliper bracket as an assembly and support from the strut with string or wire. DO NOT allow the assembly to hang from the brake hose.
10. Separate the ball joint from the steering knuckle.
11. Remove the rotor.
12. Remove the cotter pin and castle nut from the tie rod end. Separate the tie rod end from the steering knuckle using a suitable puller.
13. Remove the upper strut mounting bolt and remove the steering knuckle.

To install:
14. Install the steering knuckle assembly onto the lower ball joint and loosely install the pinch bolt.
15. Line up the steering knuckle and strut and install the mounting bolts and nuts. Line up the matchmarks made during removal on the camber bolt and tighten the mounting nuts to 112 ft. lbs. (152 Nm).
16. Tighten the ball joint pinch bolt to 38 ft. lbs. (52 Nm).
17. Connect the tie rod end to the steering and tighten the castle nut to 29 ft. lbs. (39 Nm).

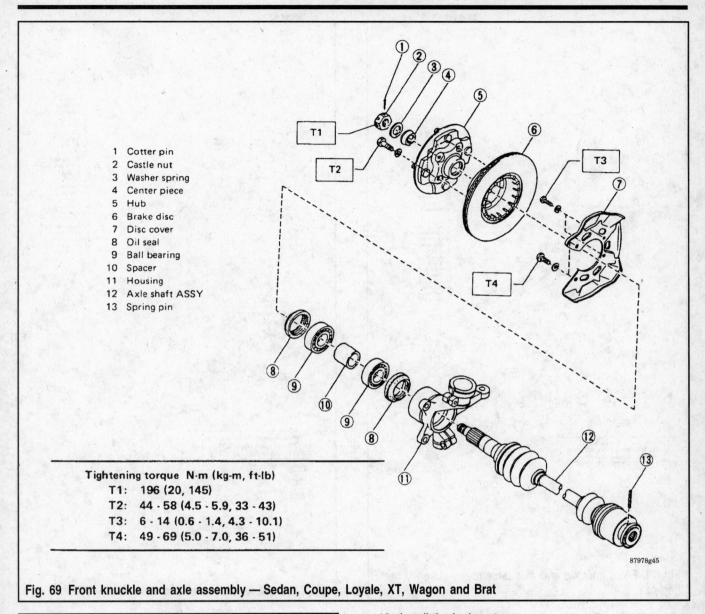

1 Cotter pin
2 Castle nut
3 Washer spring
4 Center piece
5 Hub
6 Brake disc
7 Disc cover
8 Oil seal
9 Ball bearing
10 Spacer
11 Housing
12 Axle shaft ASSY
13 Spring pin

Tightening torque N·m (kg-m, ft-lb)
T1:   196 (20, 145)
T2:   44 - 58 (4.5 - 5.9, 33 - 43)
T3:   6 - 14 (0.6 - 1.4, 4.3 - 10.1)
T4:   49 - 69 (5.0 - 7.0, 36 - 51)

87978g45

Fig. 69 Front knuckle and axle assembly — Sedan, Coupe, Loyale, XT, Wagon and Brat

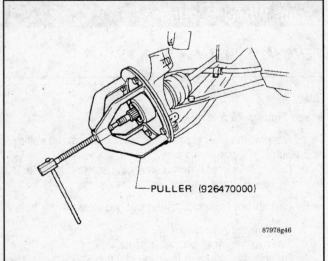

—PULLER (926470000)

87978g46

Fig. 70 Separating the axle from the knuckle assembly

18. Install the brake rotor.
19. Install the caliper and caliper mounting bracket. Tighten the caliper mounting bracket bolts to 58 ft. lbs. (78 Nm).
20. Connect the ABS sensor to the steering knuckle.
21. Connect the brake hose bracket to the strut and install the mounting bolt.
22. Install the axle nut and tighten to 137 ft. lbs. (187 Nm).
23. Install the dust cap.
24. Install the tire and wheel assembly.
25. Lower the vehicle.
26. Connect the negative battery cable.
27. Check the front end alignment and adjust as necessary.

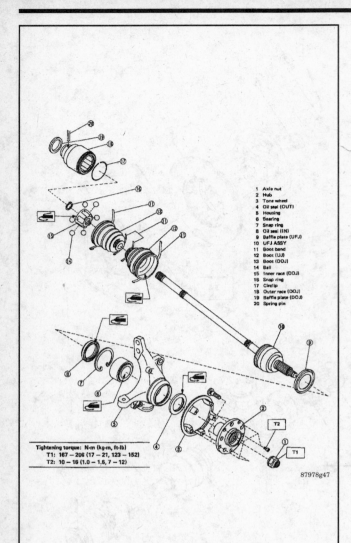

1 Axle nut
2 Hub
3 Tone wheel
4 Oil seal (OUT)
5 Housing
6 Bearing
7 Snap ring
8 Oil seal (IN)
9 Baffle plate (UFJ)
10 UFJ ASSY
11 Boot band
12 Boot (UJ)
13 Boot (DOJ)
14 Ball
15 Inner race (DOJ)
16 Snap ring
17 Circlip
18 Outer race (DOJ)
19 Baffle plate (DOJ)
20 Spring pin

Tightening torque: N·m (kg-m, ft-lb)
T1: 167 — 206 (17 — 21, 123 — 152)
T2: 10 — 16 (1.0 — 1.6, 7 — 12)

87978g47

Fig. 71 Front knuckle and axle assembly — Legacy and Impreza

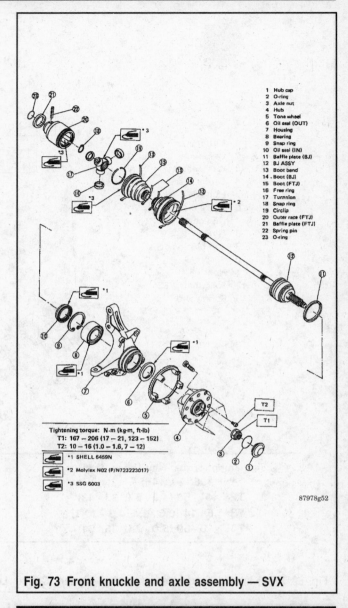

1 Hub cap
2 O-ring
3 Axle nut
4 Hub
5 Tone wheel
6 Oil seal (OUT)
7 Housing
8 Bearing
9 Snap ring (IN)
10 Oil seal (IN)
11 Baffle plate (BJ)
12 BJ ASSY
13 Boot band
14 Boot (BJ)
15 Boot (FTJ)
16 Free ring
17 Turnnion
18 Snap ring
19 Circlip
20 Outer race (FTJ)
21 Baffle plate (FTJ)
22 Spring pin
23 O-ring

Tightening torque: N·m (kg-m, ft-lb)
T1: 167 — 206 (17 — 21, 123 — 152)
T2: 10 — 16 (1.0 — 1.6, 7 — 12)

*1 SHELL 6459N
*2 Molylex N02 (P/N723223017)
*3 SSG 6003

87978g52

Fig. 73 Front knuckle and axle assembly — SVX

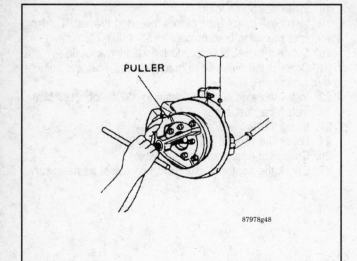

PULLER

87978g48

Fig. 72 Separating the axle from the knuckle assembly

Front Wheel Bearings

REMOVAL & INSTALLATION

Justy

▶ **See Figures 74 and 75**

1. Remove the steering knuckle assembly from the vehicle and place it in a soft-jawed vise.

2. Drive out or press the hub from the steering knuckle. If the inner bearing race remains in the hub, press it out.

➡**Be careful not to scratch the polished area of the hub.**

3. Remove the rotor shield.

4. Remove the inner and outer seals.

5. Remove the snapring from the steering knuckle.

6. Press the inner bearing race to remove the outer bearing.

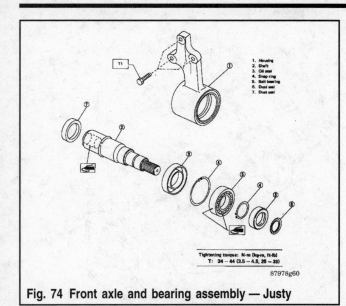

Fig. 74 Front axle and bearing assembly — Justy

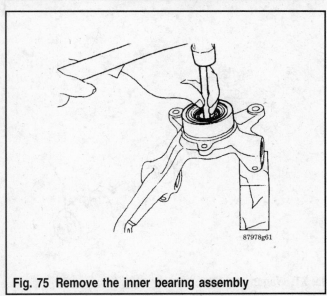

Fig. 75 Remove the inner bearing assembly

7. Press the wheel lugs from the hub.

➡️**To prevent deforming the hub, do not hammer the lugs out.**

To install:

8. Press new wheel lugs into the hub.

9. Clean the inside of the steering knuckle.

10. Remove the plastic lock from the inner race and press a new, greased bearing into the hub by pressing the outer race.

11. Install the snapring into its groove.

12. Press a new outer oil seal until it contacts the bottom of the housing.

13. Press a new inner oil seal until it contacts the circlip.

14. Apply grease to the oil seal lips.

15. Install the rotor shield and tighten the bolts to 10 ft. lbs. (14 Nm).

16. Attach the hub to the steering knuckle.

17. Press a new bearing into the hub by driving the inner race.

18. Install the steering knuckle.

Sedan, Coupe, Loyale, XT, Wagon and Brat

▶ **See Figures 76, 77 and 78**

1. Remove the steering knuckle assembly from the vehicle, and secure in a soft-jawed vise.

2. Drive out the hub from the steering knuckle. If the inner bearing race remains in the hub, press it out.

➡️**Be careful not to scratch the polished area of the hub.**

3. Remove the rotor shield.

4. Remove the inner and outer seals.

5. Remove the snapring from the steering knuckle.

6. Press the inner bearing race to remove the outer bearing.

7. If equipped with ABS, remove the tone ring.

8. Press the wheel lugs from the hub.

➡️**To prevent deforming the hub, do not hammer the lugs out.**

To install:

9. Press new wheel lugs into the hub.

10. If equipped, clean all foreign material from the hub and tone ring. Install the tone ring.

11. Clean the inside of the steering knuckle.

12. Remove the plastic lock from the inner race and press a new, greased bearing into the hub by pressing the outer race.

13. Install the snapring into its groove.

14. Press a new outer oil seal until it contacts the bottom of the housing.

15. Press a new inner oil seal until it contacts the circlip.

16. Apply grease to the oil seal lips.

17. Install the rotor shield and tighten the bolts to 10 ft. lbs. (14 Nm).

18. Attach the hub to the steering knuckle.

19. Press a new bearing into the hub by driving the inner race.

20. Install the steering knuckle.

Legacy and Impreza

▶ **See Figures 79, 80 and 81**

1. Remove the steering knuckle assembly from the vehicle.

2. Position the steering knuckle in a soft-jawed vise.

3. Press the hub from the steering knuckle. If the inner bearing race remains in the hub, press it out.

4. Remove the rotor shield.

5. Remove the inner and outer seals.

6. Remove the snapring from the steering knuckle.

7. Press the inner bearing race to remove the outer bearing.

8. If equipped with ABS, remove the tone ring.

9. Press the wheel lugs from the hub.

➡️**To prevent deforming the hub, do not hammer the lugs out.**

To install:

10. Press new wheel lugs into the hub.

11. If equipped, clean all foreign material from the hub and tone ring. Install the tone ring.

12. Clean the inside of the steering knuckle.

13. Remove the plastic lock from the inner race and press a new greased bearing into the hub by pressing the outer race.

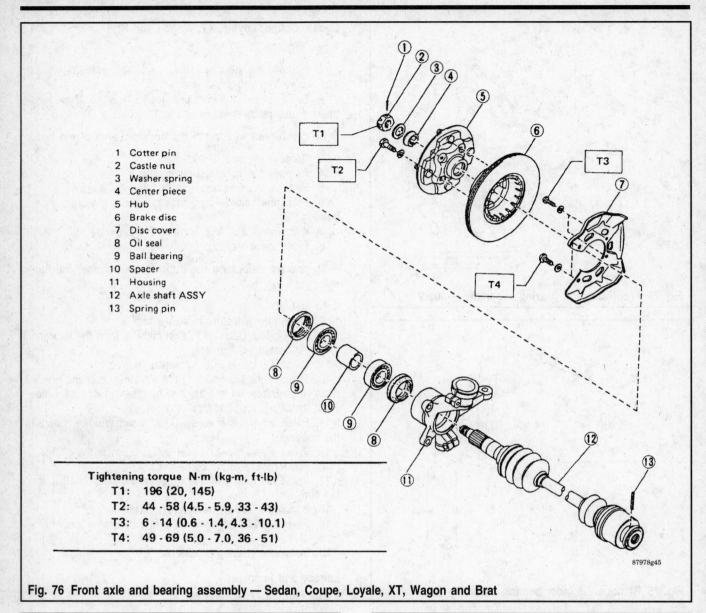

1 Cotter pin
2 Castle nut
3 Washer spring
4 Center piece
5 Hub
6 Brake disc
7 Disc cover
8 Oil seal
9 Ball bearing
10 Spacer
11 Housing
12 Axle shaft ASSY
13 Spring pin

Tightening torque N·m (kg-m, ft-lb)
T1:   196 (20, 145)
T2:   44 - 58 (4.5 - 5.9, 33 - 43)
T3:   6 - 14 (0.6 - 1.4, 4.3 - 10.1)
T4:   49 - 69 (5.0 - 7.0, 36 - 51)

87978g45

Fig. 76 Front axle and bearing assembly — Sedan, Coupe, Loyale, XT, Wagon and Brat

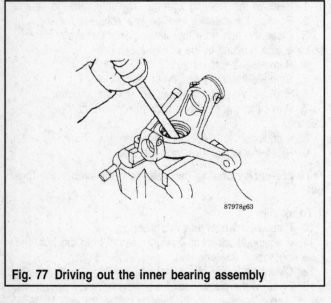

87978g63

Fig. 77 Driving out the inner bearing assembly

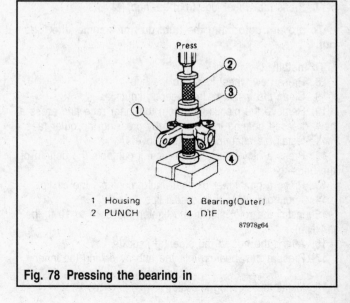

1 Housing   3 Bearing (Outer)
2 PUNCH   4 DIF

87978g64

Fig. 78 Pressing the bearing in

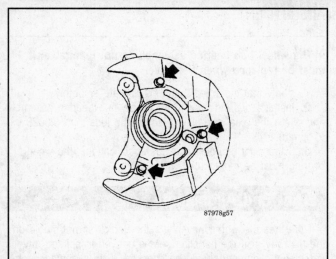

Fig. 79 Removing the brake backing plate — Legacy and Impreza

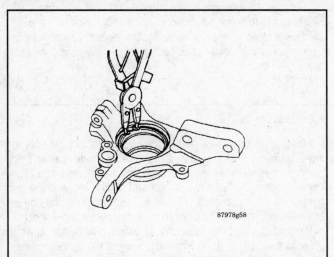

Fig. 80 Remove the snapring from inside the knuckle assembly

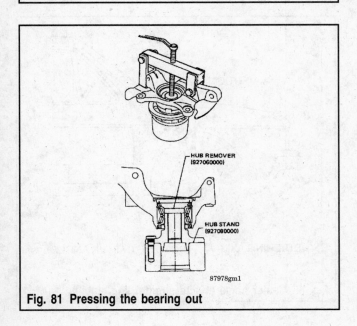

Fig. 81 Pressing the bearing out

14. Install the snapring into its groove.
15. Press a new outer oil seal until it contacts the bottom of the housing.
16. Press a new inner oil seal until it contacts the circlip.
17. Apply grease to the oil seal lips.
18. Install the rotor shield and tighten the bolts to 10 ft. lbs. (14 Nm).
19. Attach the hub to the steering knuckle.
20. Press a new bearing into the hub by driving the inner race.
21. Install the steering knuckle on the vehicle.

SVX

▶ **See Figures 82, 83, 84 and 85**

1. Remove the steering knuckle assembly from the vehicle.
2. Using a hub stand, 28099PA080 or equivalent, support the steering knuckle assembly.
3. Drive the hub out of the steering knuckle using tool 28099PA040, or equivalent hub remover.
4. Remove the backing plate from the steering knuckle.

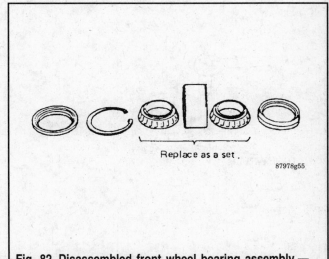

Fig. 82 Disassembled front wheel bearing assembly — SVX

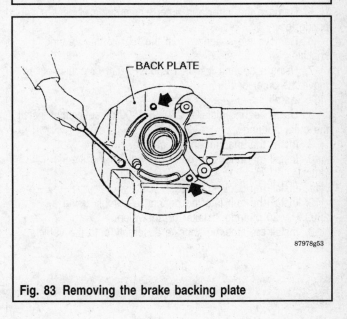

Fig. 83 Removing the brake backing plate

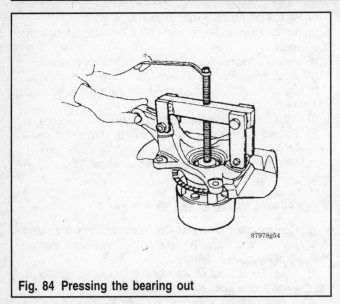

Fig. 84 Pressing the bearing out

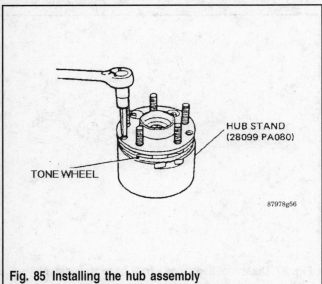

Fig. 85 Installing the hub assembly

5. Remove the inner and outer wheel seals using a suitable prying tool.

6. Remove the snapring from the rear of the steering knuckle.

7. Using a bearing installer, 28099PA000 or equivalent remove the outer bearing.

To install:

8. Using bearing installer 28099PA000 or equivalent install the outer bearing.

9. Install the snapring in the groove.

10. Install the inner and outer oil seals in the steering knuckle.

11. Install the backing plate.

12. Install the hub into the bearing assembly using a 28099PA020 bearing installer or equivalent.

13. Install the steering knuckle assembly onto the vehicle.

ADJUSTMENT

➡**The wheel hub bearing assembly is not repairable; it must be replaced when defective.**

1. Verify that the wheel bearings operate smoothly.

2. Install a dial indicator to the wheel hub bearing assembly and check the axial end-play; it should be less than 0.0020 in. (0.05mm).

3. If the axial end-play exceeds specifications, the wheel bearing must be replaced.

Front End Alignment

If the tires are worn unevenly, if the vehicle is not stable on the highway or if the handling seems uneven in spirited driving, wheel alignment should be checked. If an alignment problem is suspected, first check tire inflation and look for other possible causes such as worn suspension and steering components, accident damage or unmatched tires. Repairs may be necessary before the wheels can be properly aligned. Wheel alignment requires sophisticated equipment and can only be performed at a properly equipped shop.

CASTER

▶ **See Figure 86**

Wheel alignment is defined by three different adjustments in three planes. Looking at the vehicle from the side, caster angle describes the steering axis rather than a wheel angle. The steering knuckle is attached to the strut at the top and the control arm at the bottom. The wheel pivots around the line between these points to steer the vehicle. When the upper point is tilted back, this is described as positive caster. Having a positive caster tends to make the wheels self-centering, increasing directional stability. Excessive positive caster makes the wheels hard to steer, while an uneven caster will cause a pull to one side.

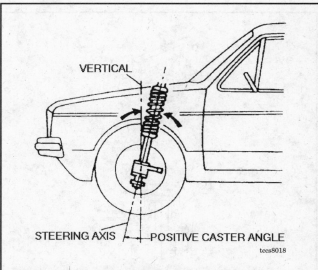

Fig. 86 Caster angle affects straight line stability

CAMBER

▶ **See Figures 87 and 88**

Looking at the wheels from the front of the vehicle, camber adjustment is the tilt of the wheel. When the wheel is tilted in at the top, this is negative camber. In a turn, a slight amount of negative camber helps maximize contact of the outside tire with the road. Too much negative camber makes the vehicle unstable in a straight line.

TOE-IN

▶ **See Figures 89 and 90**

Looking down at the wheels from above the vehicle, toe alignment is the distance between the front of the wheels relative to the distance between the back of the wheels. If the wheels are closer at the front, they are said to be toed-in or to have a negative toe. A small amount of negative toe enhances directional stability and provides a smoother ride on the highway. On most front wheel drive vehicles, standard toe adjustment is either zero or slightly positive. When power is applied to the front wheels, they tend to toe-in naturally.

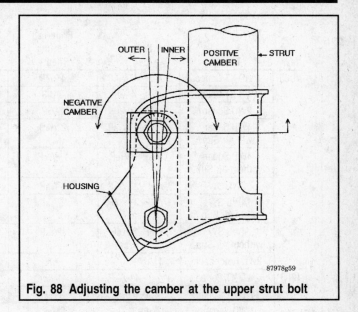

Fig. 88 Adjusting the camber at the upper strut bolt

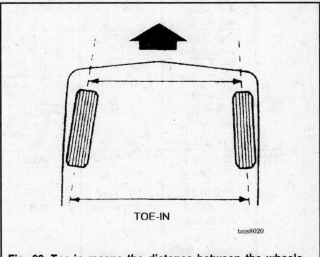

Fig. 89 Toe-in means the distance between the wheels is closer at the front than at the rear of the wheels

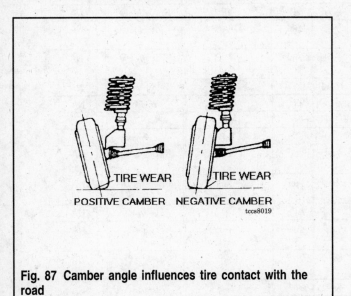

Fig. 87 Camber angle influences tire contact with the road

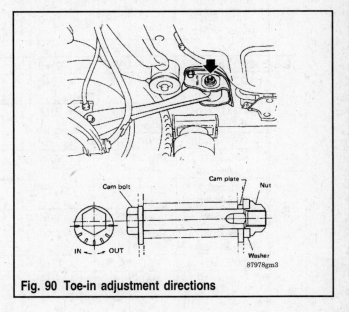

Fig. 90 Toe-in adjustment directions

Year	Model	Caster Range (deg.)	Caster Preferred Setting (deg.)	Camber Range (deg.)	Camber Preferred Setting (deg.)	Toe-in (in.)	Steering Axis Inclination (deg.)
1985	2WD XT Coupe	3⁵/₁₆P–4¹³/₁₆P	4¹/₁₆P	³/₄N–³/₄P	0	¹/₈–¹/₈	NA
	4WD XT Coupe	2⁵/₈P–4¹/₈P	3³/₈P	¹/₁₆N–1³/₈P	⁵/₈P	³/₆₄–¹/₈	NA
	2WD Sedan	1³/₄P–3¹/₄P	2¹/₂P	0–1¹/₂P	³/₄P	¹³/₆₄–³/₆₄	NA
	4WD Sedan with Air Sup.	1⁷/₁₆P–2¹⁵/₁₆P	2³/₁₆P	⁷/₁₆P–1¹⁵/₁₆P	1¹³/₁₆P	¹³/₆₄–³/₆₄A	NA
	4WD Sedan without Air Sup.	1¹/₁₆P–2⁹/₁₆P	1¹³/₁₆P	¹⁵/₁₆P–2⁷/₁₆P	1¹¹/₁₆P	¹³/₆₄–³/₆₄ ①	NA
	2WD SW	1⁵/₁₆P–2¹³/₁₆P	2¹/₁₆P	¹/₄P–1³/₄P	1P	¹³/₆₄–³/₆₄ ①	NA
	4WD SW with Air Sup.	1⁷/₁₆P–2¹⁵/₁₆P	2³/₁₆P	⁷/₁₆P–1¹⁵/₁₆P	1¹³/₁₆P	¹³/₆₄–³/₆₄ ①	NA
	4WD SW without Air Sup.	1³/₁₆P–2⁵/₁₆P	1⁹/₁₆P	¹⁵/₁₆P–2⁷/₁₆P	1³/₄P	¹³/₆₄–³/₆₄ ①	NA
	2WD Hatchback	1¹/₄N–¹/₄P	¹/₂N	1⁷/₁₆P–2¹⁵/₁₆P	2³/₁₆P	¹/₄–⁵/₃₂	NA
1986	2WD XT Coupe	3⁵/₁₆P–4¹³/₁₆P	4¹/₁₆P	³/₄N–³/₄P	0	¹/₈–¹/₈	NA
	4WD XT Coupe	2⁵/₈P–4¹/₈P	3³/₈P	¹/₁₆N–1³/₈P	⁵/₈P	³/₆₄–¹/₈	NA
	2WD Sedan	1³/₄P–3¹/₄P	2¹/₂P	0–1¹/₂P	³/₄P	¹³/₆₄–³/₆₄ ①	NA
	4WD Sedan with Air Sup.	1⁷/₁₆P–2¹⁵/₁₆P	2³/₁₆P	⁷/₁₆P–1¹⁵/₁₆P	1¹³/₁₆P	¹³/₆₄–³/₆₄ ①	NA
	4WD Sedan without Air Sup.	1¹/₁₆P–2⁹/₁₆P	1¹³/₁₆P	¹⁵/₁₆P–2⁷/₁₆P	1¹¹/₁₆P	¹³/₆₄–³/₆₄ ①	NA
	2WD SW	1⁵/₁₆P–2¹³/₁₆P	2¹/₁₆P	¹/₄P–1³/₄P	1P	¹³/₆₄–³/₆₄ ①	NA
	4WD SW with Air Sup.	1⁷/₁₆P–2¹⁵/₁₆P	2³/₁₆P	⁷/₁₆P–1¹⁵/₁₆P	1¹³/₁₆P	¹³/₆₄–³/₆₄ ①	NA
	4WD SW without Air Sup.	1³/₁₆P–2⁵/₁₆P	1⁹/₁₆P	¹⁵/₁₆P–2⁷/₁₆P	1³/₄P	¹³/₆₄–³/₆₄ ①	NA
	2WD Hatchback	1¹/₄N–¹/₄P	¹/₂N	1⁷/₁₆P–2¹⁵/₁₆P	2³/₁₆P	¹/₄–⁵/₃₂	NA
1987	2WD XT Coupe	3⁵/₁₆P–4¹³/₁₆P	4¹/₁₆P	³/₄N–³/₄P	0	¹/₈–¹/₈	NA
	4WD XT Coupe	2⁵/₈P–4¹/₈P	3³/₈P	¹/₁₆N–1³/₈P	⁵/₈P	³/₆₄–¹/₈	NA
	2WD Sedan	1³/₄P–3¹/₄P	2¹/₂P	0–1¹/₂P	³/₄P	¹³/₆₄–³/₆₄ ①	NA
	4WD Sedan with Air Sup.	1⁷/₁₆P–2¹⁵/₁₆P	2³/₁₆P	⁷/₁₆P–1¹⁵/₁₆P	1¹³/₁₆P	⁵/₆₄–⁵/₁₆ ①	NA
	4WD Sedan without Air Sup.	1¹/₁₆P–2⁹/₁₆P	1¹³/₁₆P	¹⁵/₁₆P–2⁷/₁₆P	1¹¹/₁₆P	⁵/₆₄–⁵/₁₆ ①	NA
	2WD SW	1⁵/₁₆P–2¹³/₁₆P	2¹/₁₆P	¹/₄P–1³/₄P	1 ⑧	¹³/₆₄–³/₆₄ ①	NA
	4WD SW with Air Sup.	1⁷/₁₆P–2¹⁵/₁₆P	2³/₁₆P	⁷/₁₆P–1¹⁵/₁₆P	1¹³/₁₆P	⁵/₆₄–⁵/₁₅ ①	NA
	4WD SW without Air Sup.	1³/₁₆P–2⁵/₁₆P	1⁹/₁₆P	¹⁵/₁₆P–2⁷/₁₆P	1³/₄P	⁵/₆₄–⁵/₁₆ ①	NA
	Justy	1¹/₂P–3¹/₂P	2¹/₂P	⁵/₁₆N–1¹¹/₁₆P	¹¹/₁₆P	³/₃₂–¹/₂ ①	NA
1988	2WD XT Coupe	3¹⁵/₁₆P–4¹³/₁₆P	4¹/₁₆P	³/₄N–³/₄P	0	¹/₈–¹/₈	NA
	4WD XT Coupe (4 cylinder)	2⁵/₈P–4¹/₈P	3³/₈P	¹/₁₆N–1³/₈P	⁵/₈P	³/₆₄–¹/₈	NA
	4WD XT Coupe (6 cylinder)	2³/₄P–4¹/₄P	3¹/₂P	¹/₁₆P–1⁹/₁₆P	1³/₁₆P	³/₆₄–¹³/₆₄	NA
	2WD Sedan	1³/₄P–3¹/₄P	2¹/₂P	0–1¹/₂P	³/₄P	¹³/₆₄–³/₆₄ ①	NA
	4WD Sedan with Air Susp.	1⁷/₁₆P–2¹⁵/₁₆P	2³/₁₆P	⁷/₁₆P–1¹⁵/₁₆P	1¹³/₁₆P	⁵/₆₄–⁵/₁₆ ①	NA
	4WD Sedan without Air Susp.	1¹/₁₆P–2⁹/₁₆P	1¹³/₁₆P	¹⁵/₁₆P–2⁷/₁₆P	1¹¹/₁₆P	⁵/₆₄–⁵/₁₆ ①	NA
	2WD SW	1⁵/₁₆P–2¹³/₁₆P	2¹/₁₆P	¹/₄P–1³/₄P	1P	¹³/₆₄–³/₆₄	NA
	4WD SW with Air Susp.	1⁷/₁₆P–2¹⁵/₁₆P	2³/₁₆P	⁷/₁₆P–1¹⁵/₁₆P	1¹³/₁₆P	⁵/₆₄–⁵/₁₅ ①	NA
	4WD SW	1³/₁₆P–2⁵/₁₆P	1⁹/₁₆P	¹⁵/₁₆P–2⁷/₁₆P	1³/₄P	⁵/₆₄–⁵/₁₆ ①	NA
	Justy	1¹/₂P–3¹/₂P	2¹/₂P	⁵/₁₆N–1¹¹/₁₆P	¹¹/₁₆P	³/₃₂–¹/₂ ①	NA

WHEEL ALIGNMENT

Year	Model	Caster Range (deg.)	Caster Preferred Setting (deg.)	Camber Range (deg.)	Camber Preferred Setting (deg.)	Toe-in (in.)	Steering Axis Inclination (deg.)
1989	2WD XT Coupe	$3\frac{15}{16}$P–$4\frac{13}{16}$P	$4\frac{1}{16}$P	$\frac{3}{4}$N–$\frac{3}{4}$P	0	$\frac{1}{8}$–$\frac{1}{8}$ [1]	NA
	4WD XT Coupe (4 cylinder)	$2\frac{5}{8}$P–$4\frac{1}{8}$P	$3\frac{3}{8}$P	$\frac{1}{16}$N–$1\frac{3}{8}$P	$\frac{5}{8}$P	$\frac{3}{8}$ [1]–$\frac{1}{8}$ [1]	NA
	4WD XT Coupe (6 cylinder)	$2\frac{3}{4}$P–$4\frac{1}{4}$P	$3\frac{1}{2}$P	$\frac{1}{16}$P–$1\frac{9}{16}$P	$\frac{13}{16}$P	$\frac{3}{8}$ [1]–$\frac{1}{8}$ [1]	NA
	2WD Sedan	$1\frac{3}{4}$P–$3\frac{1}{4}$P	$2\frac{1}{2}$P	0–$1\frac{1}{2}$P	$\frac{3}{4}$P	$\frac{1}{4}$–$\frac{1}{16}$ [1]	NA
	4WD Sedan with Air Susp.	$1\frac{7}{16}$P–$2\frac{15}{16}$P	$2\frac{3}{16}$P	$\frac{7}{16}$P–$1\frac{15}{16}$P	$1\frac{13}{16}$P	$\frac{1}{16}$ [1]–$\frac{3}{16}$ [1]	NA
	4WD Sedan without Air Susp.	$1\frac{1}{16}$P–$2\frac{9}{16}$P	$1\frac{13}{16}$P	$\frac{15}{16}$P–$2\frac{7}{16}$P	$1\frac{11}{16}$P	$\frac{1}{16}$ [1]–$\frac{3}{16}$ [1]	NA
	2WD SW	$1\frac{5}{16}$P–$2\frac{13}{16}$P	$2\frac{1}{16}$P	$\frac{1}{4}$P–$1\frac{3}{4}$P	1P	$\frac{1}{16}$ [1]–$\frac{3}{16}$ [1]	NA
	4WD SW with Air Susp.	$1\frac{7}{16}$P–$2\frac{15}{16}$P	$2\frac{3}{16}$P	$\frac{7}{16}$P–$1\frac{15}{16}$P	$1\frac{13}{16}$P	$\frac{1}{16}$ [1]–$\frac{3}{16}$ [1]	NA
	4WD SW	$\frac{13}{16}$P–$2\frac{5}{16}$P	$1\frac{9}{16}$P	$\frac{15}{16}$P–$2\frac{7}{16}$P	$1\frac{3}{4}$P	$\frac{1}{16}$ [1]–$\frac{3}{16}$ [1]	NA
	Justy	$1\frac{1}{2}$P–$3\frac{1}{2}$P	$2\frac{1}{2}$P	$\frac{5}{16}$N–$1\frac{11}{16}$P	$\frac{11}{16}$P	$\frac{5}{16}$–$\frac{1}{16}$ [1]	NA
	Legacy FWD Sedan [3]	$2\frac{1}{16}$P–$4\frac{1}{16}$P	$3\frac{1}{16}$P [4]	$\frac{3}{4}$N–$\frac{1}{4}$P	$\frac{1}{4}$N	$\frac{1}{16}$–$\frac{1}{16}$ [1]	NA
	Legacy 4WD Sedan [2]	2P–4P	3P	$\frac{1}{2}$N–$\frac{1}{2}$P	0	$\frac{1}{16}$–$\frac{1}{16}$ [1]	NA
1990	2WD XT Coupe	$3\frac{15}{16}$P–$4\frac{13}{16}$P	$4\frac{1}{16}$P	$\frac{3}{4}$N–$\frac{3}{4}$P	0	$\frac{1}{8}$–$\frac{1}{8}$ [1]	NA
	4WD XT Coupe (4 cylinder)	$2\frac{5}{8}$P–$4\frac{1}{8}$P	$3\frac{3}{8}$P	$\frac{1}{16}$N–$1\frac{3}{8}$P	$\frac{5}{8}$P	$\frac{3}{8}$ [1]–$\frac{1}{8}$ [1]	NA
	4WD XT Coupe (6 cylinder)	$2\frac{3}{4}$P–$4\frac{1}{4}$P	$3\frac{1}{2}$P	$\frac{1}{16}$P–$1\frac{9}{16}$P	$\frac{13}{16}$P	$\frac{3}{8}$ [1]–$\frac{1}{8}$ [1]	NA
	2WD Loyale Sedan	$1\frac{3}{4}$P–$3\frac{1}{4}$P	$2\frac{1}{2}$P	0–$1\frac{1}{2}$P	$\frac{3}{4}$P	$\frac{1}{4}$–$\frac{1}{16}$ [1]	NA
	4WD Loyale Sedan without Air Susp.	$1\frac{1}{16}$P–$2\frac{9}{16}$P	$1\frac{13}{16}$P	$\frac{15}{16}$P–$2\frac{7}{16}$P	$1\frac{11}{16}$P	$\frac{1}{16}$ [1]–$\frac{3}{16}$ [1]	NA
	2WD Loyale SW	$1\frac{5}{16}$P–$2\frac{13}{16}$P	$2\frac{1}{16}$P	$\frac{1}{4}$P–$1\frac{3}{4}$P	1P	$\frac{1}{16}$ [1]–$\frac{3}{16}$ [1]	NA
	4WD Loyale SW	$\frac{13}{16}$P–$2\frac{5}{16}$P	$1\frac{9}{16}$P	$\frac{15}{16}$P–$2\frac{7}{16}$P	$1\frac{3}{4}$P	$\frac{1}{16}$ [1]–$\frac{3}{16}$ [1]	NA
	Justy	$1\frac{1}{2}$P–$3\frac{1}{2}$P	$2\frac{1}{2}$P	$\frac{5}{16}$N–$1\frac{11}{16}$P	$\frac{11}{16}$P	$\frac{5}{16}$–$\frac{1}{16}$ [1]	NA
	Legacy FWD Sedan [3]	$2\frac{1}{16}$P–$4\frac{1}{16}$P	$3\frac{1}{16}$P [4]	$\frac{3}{4}$N–$\frac{1}{4}$P	$\frac{1}{4}$N	$\frac{1}{16}$–$\frac{1}{16}$ [1]	NA
	Legacy 4WD Sedan [2]	2P–4P	3P	$\frac{1}{2}$N–$\frac{1}{2}$P	0	$\frac{1}{16}$–$\frac{1}{16}$ [1]	NA
	Legacy 4WD Wagon	$1\frac{3}{4}$P–$3\frac{3}{4}$P	$2\frac{3}{4}$P	$\frac{1}{2}$N–$\frac{1}{2}$P	0	$\frac{1}{16}$–$\frac{1}{16}$ [1]	NA
1991	2WD XT Coupe	$3\frac{15}{16}$P–$4\frac{13}{16}$P	$4\frac{1}{16}$P	$\frac{3}{4}$N–$\frac{3}{4}$P	0	$\frac{1}{8}$–$\frac{1}{8}$ [1]	NA
	4WD XT Coupe (4 cylinder)	$2\frac{5}{8}$P–$4\frac{1}{8}$P	$3\frac{3}{8}$P	$\frac{1}{16}$N–$1\frac{3}{8}$P	$\frac{5}{8}$P	$\frac{3}{8}$ [1]–$\frac{1}{8}$ [1]	NA
	4WD XT Coupe (6 cylinder)	$2\frac{3}{4}$P–$4\frac{1}{4}$P	$3\frac{1}{2}$P	$\frac{1}{16}$P–$1\frac{9}{16}$P	$\frac{13}{16}$P	$\frac{3}{8}$ [1]–$\frac{1}{8}$ [1]	NA
	2WD Loyale Sedan	$1\frac{3}{4}$P–$3\frac{1}{4}$P	$2\frac{1}{2}$P	0–$1\frac{1}{2}$P	$\frac{3}{4}$P	$\frac{1}{4}$–$\frac{1}{16}$ [1]	NA
	4WD Loyale Sedan without Air Susp.	$1\frac{1}{16}$P–$2\frac{9}{16}$P	$1\frac{13}{16}$P	$\frac{15}{16}$P–$2\frac{7}{16}$P	$1\frac{11}{16}$P	$\frac{1}{16}$ [1]–$\frac{3}{16}$ [1]	NA
	2WD Loyale SW	$1\frac{5}{16}$P–$2\frac{13}{16}$P	$2\frac{1}{16}$P	$\frac{1}{4}$P–$1\frac{3}{4}$P	1P	$\frac{1}{16}$ [1]–$\frac{3}{16}$ [1]	NA
	4WD Loyale SW	$\frac{13}{16}$P–$2\frac{5}{16}$P	$1\frac{9}{16}$P	$\frac{15}{16}$P–$2\frac{7}{16}$P	$1\frac{3}{4}$P	$\frac{1}{16}$ [1]–$\frac{3}{16}$ [1]	NA
	Justy	$1\frac{1}{2}$P–$3\frac{1}{2}$P	$2\frac{1}{2}$P	$\frac{5}{16}$N–$1\frac{11}{16}$P	$\frac{11}{16}$P	$\frac{5}{16}$–$\frac{1}{16}$ [1]	NA
	Legacy FWD Sedan	$2\frac{1}{16}$P–$4\frac{1}{16}$P [3]	$3\frac{1}{16}$P [4]	$\frac{3}{4}$N–$\frac{1}{4}$P	$\frac{1}{4}$N	$\frac{1}{16}$–$\frac{1}{16}$ [1]	NA
	Legacy 4WD Sedan [2]	2P–4P	3P	$\frac{1}{2}$N–$\frac{1}{2}$P	0	$\frac{1}{16}$–$\frac{1}{16}$ [1]	NA
	Legacy 4WD Wagon	$1\frac{3}{4}$P–$3\frac{3}{4}$P	$2\frac{3}{4}$P	$\frac{1}{2}$N–$\frac{1}{2}$P	0	$\frac{1}{16}$–$\frac{1}{16}$ [1]	NA

87978c11

Year	Model	Caster Range (deg.)	Caster Preferred Setting (deg.)	Camber Range (deg.)	Camber Preferred Setting (deg.)	Toe-in (in.)	Steering Axis Inclination (deg.)
1992	2WD XT Coupe	$3^{15/16}$P–$4^{13/16}$P	$4^{1/16}$P	3/4 N–3/4 P	0	1/8–1/8 [1]	NA
	4WD XT Coupe (4 cylinder)	$2^{5/8}$P–$4^{1/8}$P	$3^{3/8}$P	1/16 N–$1^{3/8}$P	5/8 P	3/8 [1]–1/8 [1]	NA
	4WD XT Coupe (6 cylinder)	$2^{3/4}$P–$4^{1/4}$P	$3^{1/2}$P	1/16 P–$1^{9/16}$P	13/16 P	3/8 [1]–1/8 [1]	NA
	2WD Loyale Sedan	$1^{3/4}$P–$3^{1/4}$P	$2^{1/2}$P	0–$1^{1/2}$P	3/4 P	1/4–1/16 [1]	NA
	4WD Loyale Sedan without Air Susp.	$1^{1/16}$P–$2^{9/16}$P	$1^{13/16}$P	15/16 P–$2^{7/16}$P	$1^{11/16}$P	1/16 [1]–3/16 [1]	NA
	2WD Loyale SW	$1^{5/16}$P–$2^{13/16}$P	$2^{1/16}$P	1/4 P–$1^{3/4}$P	1 P	1/16 [1]–3/16 [1]	NA
	4WD Loyale SW	$1^{3/16}$P–$2^{5/16}$P	$1^{9/16}$P	15/16 P–$2^{7/16}$P	$1^{3/4}$P	1/16 [1]–3/16 [1]	NA
	Justy	$1^{1/2}$P–$3^{1/2}$P	$2^{1/2}$P	5/16 N–$1^{11/16}$P	11/16 P	5/16–1/16 [1]	NA
	Legacy FWD Sedan [3]	$2^{1/16}$P–$4^{1/16}$P	$3^{1/16}$P [4]	3/4 N–1/4 P	1/4 N	1/16–1/16 [1]	NA
1992	Legacy 4WD Sedan [2]	2P–4P	3P	1/2 N–1/2 P	0	1/16–1/16 [1]	NA
	Legacy 4WD Wagon	$1^{3/4}$P–$3^{3/4}$P	$2^{3/4}$P	1/2 N–1/2 P	0	1/16–1/16 [1]	NA
	SVX	$1^{3/4}$P–$3^{3/4}$P	$2^{3/4}$P	1/2 N–1/2 P	0	1/16–1/16 [1]	NA
1993	Justy	$1^{1/2}$ P–$3^{1/2}$P	$2^{1/2}$ P	5/16 N–$1^{11/16}$P	11/16 P	3/64 [1]–1/4	NA
	2WD Loyale Sedan	$1^{3/4}$P–$3^{1/4}$P	$2^{1/2}$P	0–1/2 P	3/4 P	3/64 [1]–13/64	NA
	4WD Loyale Sedan	$1^{1/16}$P–$2^{9/16}$P	$1^{13/16}$P	15/16 P–$2^{7/16}$P	$1^{11/16}$P	5/16 [1]–5/64 [1]	NA
	2WD Loyale SW	$1^{5/16}$P–$2^{13/16}$P	$2^{1/16}$P	1/4 P–$1^{3/4}$P	1P	3/64 [1]–13/64	NA
	4WD Loyale SW	$1^{3/16}$P–$2^{5/16}$P	$1^{9/16}$P	15/16 P–$2^{7/16}$P	$1^{3/4}$P	5/16 [1]–5/64 [1]	NA
	Impreza	2P–4P	3P	1/2 N–1/2 P	0	1/4–1/4	NA
	2WD Legacy Sedan	$2^{1/16}$ P–$4^{1/16}$P	$3^{1/16}$P	3/4 N–1/4 P	1/4 N	1/8 [1]–1/8	NA
	Legacy [5]	$1^{13/16}$ P–$3^{13/16}$ P	$2^{13/16}$P	3/4 N–1/4 P	1/4 N	1/8 [1]–1/8	NA
	Legacy [6]	2P–4P	3P	1/2 N–1/2 P	0	1/8 [1]–1/8	NA
	4WD Legacy SW without Air Susp.	$1^{3/4}$ P–$3^{3/4}$P	$2^{3/4}$P	1/2 N–1/2 P	0	1/8 [1]–1/8	NA
	SVX	$4^{1/6}$ P–$5^{9/16}$P	$4^{13/16}$P	13/16 N–5/16 P	7/16 N	1/8 [1]–1/8	NA
1994	Justy	$1^{1/2}$ P–$3^{1/2}$P	$2^{1/2}$P	5/16 N–$1^{11/16}$P	11/16 P	3/64 [1]–1/4	NA
	2WD Loyale Sedan	$1^{3/4}$ P–$3^{1/4}$P	$2^{1/2}$P	0–1/2 P	3/4 P	3/64 [1]–13/64	NA
	4WD Loyale Sedan	$1^{1/16}$ P–$2^{9/16}$P	$1^{13/16}$ P	15/16 P–$2^{7/16}$P	$1^{11/16}$P	5/16 [1]–5/64 [1]	NA
	2WD Loyale SW	$1^{5/16}$ P–$2^{13/16}$P	$2^{1/16}$P	1/4 P–$1^{3/4}$P	1P	3/64 [1]–13/64	NA
	4WD Loyale SW	$1^{3/16}$ P–$2^{5/16}$P	$1^{9/16}$P	15/16 P–$2^{7/16}$P	$1^{3/4}$P	5/16 [1]–5/64 [1]	NA
	Impreza	2P–4P	3P	1/2 N–1/2 P	0	1/4 [1]–1/4	NA
	2WD Legacy Sedan	$2^{1/16}$ P–$4^{1/16}$P	$3^{1/16}$P	3/4 N–1/4 P	1/4 N	1/8 [1]–1/8	NA
	Legacy [5]	$1^{13/16}$ P–$3^{13/16}$ P	$2^{13/16}$P	3/4 N–1/4 P	1/4 N	1/8 [1]–1/8	NA
	Legacy [6]	2P–4P	3P	1/2 N–1/2 P	0	1/8 [1]–1/8	NA
	4WD Legacy SW without Air Susp.	$1^{3/4}$ P–$3^{3/4}$P	$2^{3/4}$P	1/2 N–1/2 P	0	1/8 [1]–1/8	NA
	SVX	$4^{1/6}$ P–$5^{9/16}$P	$4^{13/16}$P	13/16 N–5/16 P	7/16 N	1/8 [1]–1/8	NA
1995	Impreza	2P–4P	3P	1/2 N–1/2 P	0	1/4 [1]–1/4	NA
	Legacy	$2^{1/16}$ P–$4^{1/16}$P	$3^{1/16}$P	9/16 N–7/16 P	1/16 N	1/8 [1]–1/8	$14^{1/4}$
	SVX	$4^{1/6}$ P–$5^{9/16}$P	$4^{13/16}$P	13/16 N–5/16 P	7/16 N	1/8 [1]–1/8	NA
1996	Impreza	2P–4P	3P	1/2 N–1/2 P	0	1/4 [1]–1/4	NA
	Legacy [7]	$2^{1/16}$ P–$4^{1/16}$P	$3^{1/16}$P	9/16 N–7/16 P	1/16 N	1/8 [1]–1/8	$14^{1/4}$
	Legacy [8]	$1^{13/16}$ P–$3^{13/16}$P	$2^{13/16}$P	3/16 N–13/16 P	5/16 P	1/8 [1]–1/8	$13^{1/2}$
	SVX	$4^{1/6}$ P–$5^{9/16}$P	$4^{13/16}$P	13/16 N–5/16 P	7/16 N	1/8 [1]–1/8	NA

Air Susp. - Air Suspension
SW - Station Wagon
N-Negative
P-Positive

[1] Toe out
[2] Same with air suspension
[3] Legacy FWD Wagon-1 13/16P-3 13/16P
[4] Legacy FWD Wagon-2 13/16P

[5] Applies to: FWD/4WD Turbo Sedans, FWD SW, 4WD Turbo SW without air suspension
[6] Applies to: 4WD Sedan, 4WD SW without air suspension
[7] Except Outback model
[8] Outback model

87978c12

PNEUMATIC (AIR) SUSPENSION SYSTEM

➥The basic mechanical components of the air suspension system is identical to those of the standard strut type suspension system. The only difference in the two systems are those directly related to the operation of the air suspension system itself. The servicing of the air suspension system components will be covered here, the rest of the components can be serviced by following the strut suspension service procedure found in this section.

General Information

The 4WD models are equipped with an air suspension and height control system to compensate for off road conditions and vehicle load. The system has two height control settings, NORMAL and High, which range from 1.0-1.5 in. (30-40mm) in height depending on the vehicle. To achieve the height changes, the air in each spring assembly is adjusted according to a vehicle height sensor located within the shock body.

System Components

▶ See Figures 91 and 92

The air suspension system uses a selector switch which changes the height to NORMAL or HIGH. A warning light indicates the vehicle height, and also illuminates in the event of system malfunction or failure.

There are vehicle height sensor built into each air suspension spring which detect proper vehicle height at each wheel.

The system include six solenoid valves and a control unit which open and close the valves in order. The control unit measures signals from each height adjuster, and signals one or more of the valves accordingly.

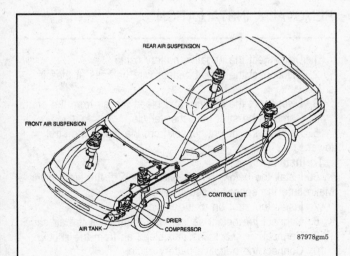

Fig. 91 Pneumatic suspension system components — 4WD Legacy and Impreza

Finally, an air tank and compressor are installed and are operated by a pressure switch. Because the air compressor can create condensation through its normal functioning, a drier is installed to dry the air from the air lines running to each shock assembly.

Diagnosis and Testing

▶ See Figure 93

The air suspension system incorporates a function which will display any malfunctions in the system by illuminating and blinking the height indicator lamp. If there is any abnormal conditions in the system, the height indicator will begin to blink, and the system should then be put into the self-diagnostic mode to determine the problem.

PROCEDURE

Sedan, Coupe, Loyale, XT, Wagon and Brat
▶ See Figure 94

1. Turn the ignition switch OFF, and the height selector switch to ON (HIGH).
2. Turn the ignition switch ON, then turn the ignition switch OFF.
3. Set the height selector switch to the OFF (NORMAL) position.
4. Turn the ignition switch ON, then turn the ignition switch OFF.
5. Set the height selector switch to the ON (HIGH) position and turn the ignition switch ON. The system is now in the self-diagnostic mode.
6. Determine the system malfunction code by observing the number of blinks of the vehicle height sensor lamp.
7. Check and correct any malfunctions.
8. To clear the memory and reset the system, turn the ignition switch OFF and disconnect the negative battery cable for at least 10 seconds.

Legacy and Impreza
▶ See Figures 94 and 95

1. Turn the ignition switch OFF.
2. Connect a jumper wire between terminal No. 1 and ground of the diagnostic connector under the driver side of the dash panel.
3. Turn the ignition switch ON.
4. The trouble codes will then be indicated by the blinking of the height indicator lamp.
5. Check and correct any system malfunctions.
6. To clear the memory and reset the system, turn the ignition switch OFF and disconnect the negative battery cable for at least 10 seconds.

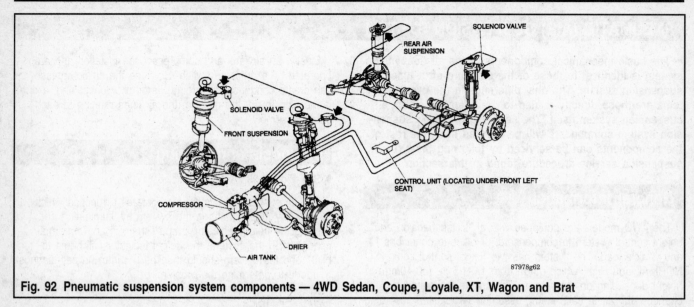

Fig. 92 Pneumatic suspension system components — 4WD Sedan, Coupe, Loyale, XT, Wagon and Brat

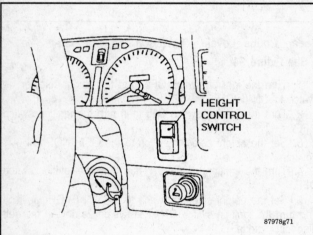

Fig. 93 Example of height control switch — Legacy and Impreza

Height Sensor

TESTING

Sedan, Coupe, Loyale, XT, Wagon and Brat

▶ See Figures 96 and 97

1. Disconnect the height sensor wire harness at the air shock.
2. Disconnect air shock line and bleed air from the shock.
3. Using an ohmmeter, check for continuity between the terminals of the height sensor side of the wire harness.
4. While using the ohmmeter, compress and extend the shock, and observe when there is continuity.

5. If not as specified replace or repair the height sensor.

Legacy and Impreza

▶ See Figures 98 and 99

1. Disconnect the air line from the solenoid valve.
2. Disconnect the height control wire harness.
3. With shock compressed, check that the resistance between terminal 2 and 4 is a minimum of 1 megohm.
4. With the shock expanded check that the resistance between terminal 2 and 4 is 0 ohms.
5. With the shock compressed, check that the resistance between terminal 2 and 3 is 0 ohms.
6. With the shock expanded, check that the resistance between terminal 2 and 3 is a minimum of 1 megohm.
7. If not as specified, replace the height sensor.

REMOVAL & INSTALLATION

1. Disconnect the negative battery cable.
2. Disconnect the height sensor wire harness at the air shock.
3. Disconnect the air line, and bleed the air from the strut.
4. Remove the strut from the vehicle.
5. Remove the height sensor from the top of the strut tower.

To install:

6. Install the height sensor into the top of the strut tower. Make sure the sensor is seated evenly.
7. Install the strut on to the vehicle.
8. Connect the height sensor wire harness at the air shock.
9. Connect air shock line and bleed air from the shock.
10. Connect the negative battery cable.
11. Start the vehicle, and allow the shock to build up air before driving.

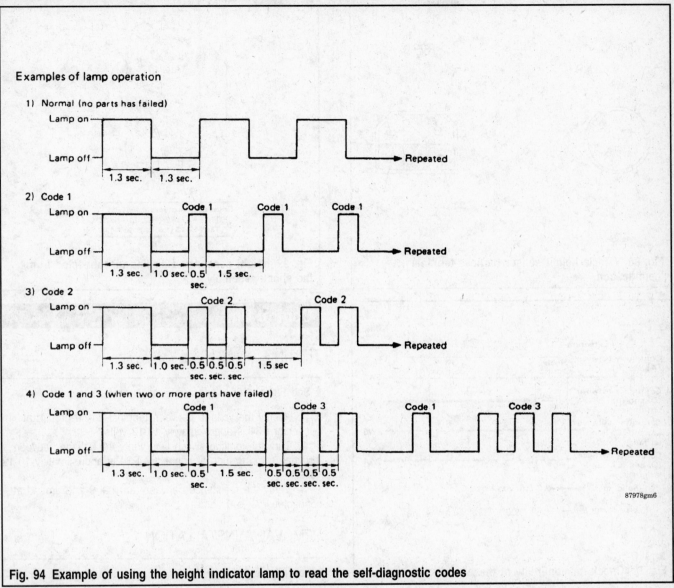

Fig. 94 Example of using the height indicator lamp to read the self-diagnostic codes

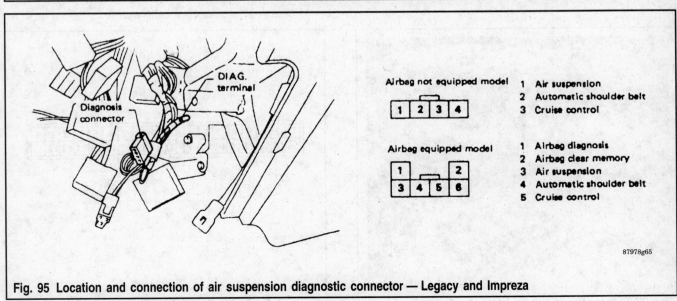

Fig. 95 Location and connection of air suspension diagnostic connector — Legacy and Impreza

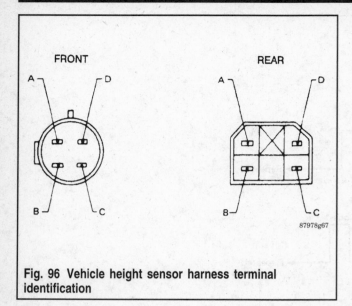

Fig. 96 Vehicle height sensor harness terminal identification

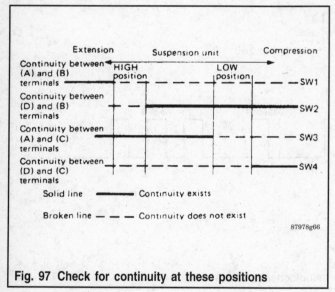

Fig. 97 Check for continuity at these positions

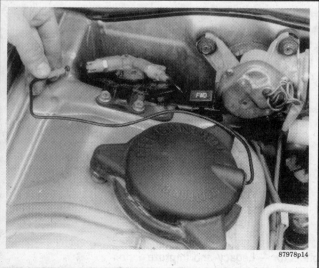

Fig. 98 Disconnecting the air line — front strut

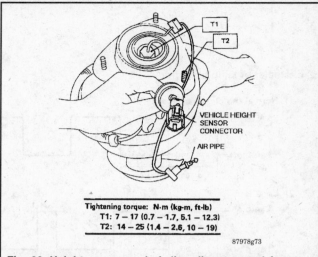

Tightening torque: N·m (kg-m, ft-lb)
T1: 7 – 17 (0.7 – 1.7, 5.1 – 12.3)
T2: 14 – 25 (1.4 – 2.6, 10 – 19)

Fig. 99 Height sensor and air line disconnected from the shock assembly

Control Unit

TESTING

▶ See Figure 100

1. Verify the voltage between terminal 2 and ground at connector P34 is approximately 10-12 volts.

2. Turn the ignition switch **ON**, verify the voltage between terminal 3 and ground at connector P34 is approximately 10-12 volts.

3. Verify the resistance between terminal 9 and ground at connector P34 is 0 ohms.

REMOVAL & INSTALLATION

▶ See Figure 101

1. Disconnect the negative battery cable.

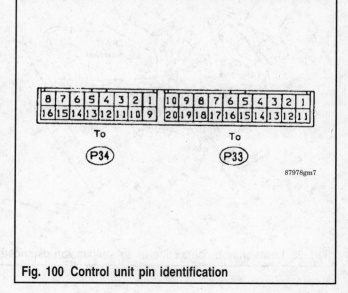

Fig. 100 Control unit pin identification

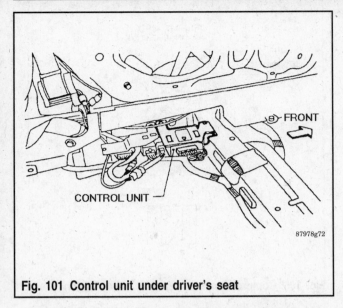

Fig. 101 Control unit under driver's seat

2. Remove the driver front seat assembly, and place aside.
3. Lift the carpet up, and unfasten the control unit retainer screws.
4. Unfasten the control unit wire harnesses.
To install:
5. Attach the wire harnesses to the control unit.
6. Position the control unit under the carpet, and secure in place with the retainer screws.
7. Install the driver front seat assembly
8. Connect the negative battery cable.
9. Confirm that the height control system functions correctly before driving the vehicle.

Solenoid Valve

TESTING

1. Disconnect the solenoid wire harness at the shock.
2. Apply 12 volts across each terminal of the solenoid valve.
3. Listen for sound of the solenoid functioning.
4. If no sound is heard, replace the solenoid valve.
5. Check for approximately 30 ohms of resistance between the terminals of the valve.
6. If not as specified, replace the solenoid valve.

REMOVAL & INSTALLATION

Front
▶ **See Figures 102 and 103**

1. Disconnect the negative battery cable.
2. Tag and disconnect the air lines attached to the solenoid valve.
3. Remove the bolts securing the solenoid valve to the bracket.
4. Disconnect the height sensor and compressor relay harnesses.

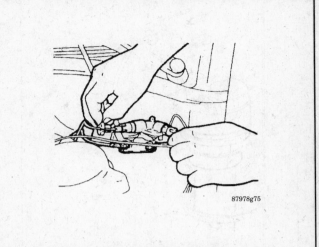

Fig. 102 Disconnecting the air lines from the left solenoid valve

Fig. 103 Right front solenoid valve behind the strut tower

5. Remove the solenoid valve.
To install:
6. Attach the compressor relay and height sensor wire harnesses.
7. Install the solenoid valve to the bracket, and secure in place with the retainer bolts. Tighten the bolts snugly.
8. Connect the air lines to the solenoid valve.
9. Connect the negative battery cable.
10. Start the vehicle, and allow enough time for air to fill the shock before driving.

Rear
▶ **See Figure 104**

1. Disconnect the negative battery cable.
2. Raise and safely support the rear of the vehicle on jackstands.
3. Remove the strut assembly from the vehicle.
4. Remove the solenoid valve protector.
5. Remove the solenoid from the strut assembly.

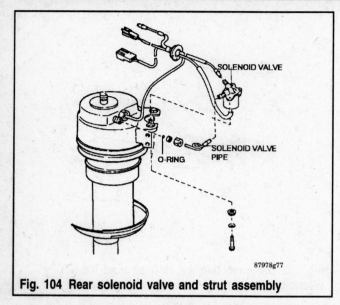

Fig. 104 Rear solenoid valve and strut assembly

6. Attach the solenoid to the strut. Tighten the retainer bolts snugly.

7. Disconnect the air lines from the solenoid valve.

To install:

8. Attach the air lines to the solenoid valve assembly.

9. Install the solenoid valve protector.

10. Install the strut assembly in the vehicle.

11. Lower the vehicle.

12. Connect the negative battery cable.

13. Start the vehicle, and allow enough time for air to fill the shock before driving.

Compressor Relay

TESTING

▶ **See Figure 105**

1. Remove the compressor relay from the fuse block in the engine compartment.

2. Verify that there is no continuity between terminals C and D using an ohmmeter.

3. Apply 12 volts across terminal B and ground terminal A. Then check that there is continuity between terminals C and D.

4. If not as specified, replace the relay.

REMOVAL & INSTALLATION

1. Locate the proper relay in the engine compartment fuse block for the air suspension compressor.

2. Disconnect the relay from the fuse block assembly.

To install:

3. Attach the relay to the terminal in the fuse panel.

4. Check and make sure the air suspension system functions correctly.

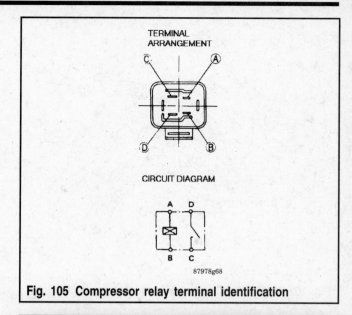

Fig. 105 Compressor relay terminal identification

Pressure Switch

TESTING

Sedan, Coupe, Loyale, XT, Wagon and Brat

1. Disconnect the pressure switch wire harness.

2. Connect an ohmmeter between the terminals of the pressure switch.

3. Verify that the pressure switch resistance is at least 1 megohm minimum when the compressor tank pressure is approximately 132-147 (910-1014 kPa).

4. Release the compressor tank pressure slowly, and verify that there is no resistance at the pressure switch terminals when the tank pressure reaches approximately 125 psi (862 kPa).

5. If not as specified, replace the pressure switch.

Legacy

1. Disconnect the pressure switch wire harness.

2. Connect an ohmmeter between the terminals of the pressure switch.

3. Verify the pressure switch resistance is at least 1 megohm when the compressor tank pressure is approximately 137 psi (945 kPa).

4. Release the compressor tank pressure slowly and verify that there is no resistance at the pressure switch terminals when the tank pressure reaches approximately 111 psi (765 kPa).

5. If not as specified, replace the pressure switch.

REMOVAL & INSTALLATION

1. Disconnect the negative battery cable.

2. Locate the air compressor assembly, and disconnect one air line from the compressor. The disconnected line will allow the compressor to pressure down slowly. Do not proceed until there is no more air escaping from the compressor assembly.

3. Loosen and remove the pressure switch from the compressor tank.

To install:

4. Install the pressure switch to the compressor tank, and tighten until snug.

5. Attach the air line to the compressor.

6. Connect the negative battery cable.

7. Start the engine, and allow enough time for the compressor to build up the proper amount of pressure before driving the vehicle.

Compressor

TESTING

Sedan, Coupe, Loyale, Wagon and Brat

1. Verify that there is approximately 12 volts at the compressor wire harness for the motor.

2. Ground the L wire (marked on the harness at the compressor) at the compressor and verify that the compressor motor operates.

3. If not as specified, replace the compressor.

XT

1. Verify that there is approximately 12 volts at the compressor wire harness for the motor.

2. Ground the LW wire (marked on the harness at the compressor) at the compressor and verify that the compressor motor operates.

3. If not as specified, replace the compressor.

Legacy

▶ See Figure 106

1. Disconnect the wire harness from the compressor.

2. Using an ohmmeter, verify that the resistance between terminals 1 and 3 is 2.5-3.5 ohms.

3. Apply 12 volts to terminals 1 and 3, and verify the compressor operates.

4. If not as specified, replace the compressor.

REMOVAL & INSTALLATION

▶ See Figures 107, 108 and 109

1. Disconnect the negative battery cable.
2. Raise and support the front of the vehicle on jackstands.
3. Remove the left front wheel.
4. Remove the front half portion of the mud guard.
5. Disconnect the air lines from the drier assembly. The lines do not have to be tagged, because the installation order is not important.
6. Disconnect the wire harness to the compressor.
7. Remove the compressor and drier mounting nuts and bolts.
8. Remove the compressor and drier as an assembly.

To install:

9. Position the compressor assembly on the bracket, and secure in place with the retainer nuts and bolts. Tighten the

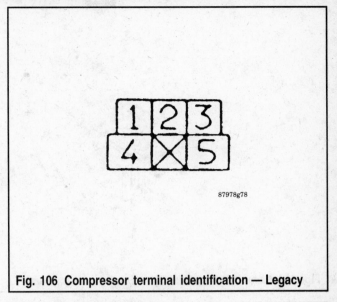
Fig. 106 Compressor terminal identification — Legacy

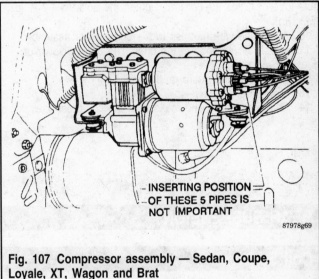
Fig. 107 Compressor assembly — Sedan, Coupe, Loyale, XT, Wagon and Brat

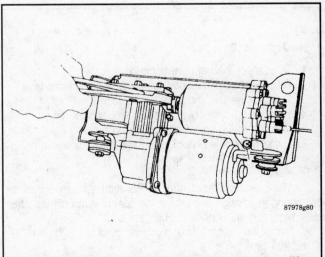
Fig. 108 To remove the tank, remove the clip, then lift out the tank

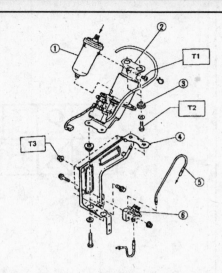

Tightening torque: N·m (kg-m, ft-lb)
T1: 1.5 — 3.9 (0.15 — 0.40, 1.1 — 2.9)
T2: 5.4 — 9.3 (0.55 — 0.95, 4.0 — 6.9)
T3: 10 — 18 (1.0 — 1.8, 7 — 13)

1 Drier
2 Compressor
3 Insulator
4 Compressor bracket
5 Compressor pipe
6 Manifold ASSY

87978g79

Fig. 109 Compressor assembly — Legacy and Impreza

nuts to 7-13 ft. lbs. (9-17 Nm). Tighten the bolts to 4-7 ft. lbs. (5-9 Nm).

10. Attach the wire harness to the compressor assembly.

11. Attach the air lines to the drier. The order or position does not matter.

12. Install the mud guard, and wheel.

13. Lower the vehicle.

14. Start the vehicle and make sure the compressor works.

REAR SUSPENSION

Coil Springs

REMOVAL & INSTALLATION

Justy

▶ See Figure 110

1. Disconnect the negative battery cable.
2. Raise and safely support the vehicle on jackstands.
3. Remove the tire and wheel assembly.
4. Remove the trim cover over the upper strut mount.
5. Remove the 2 upper strut mounting nuts.
6. Using a suitable prytool, push the lower control arm down, and remove the coil spring.

To install:

7. While pushing the control arm assembly down. install the coil spring in position, then raise the control arm until the strut plate mounting studs pass through the body.

8. Install the 2 upper strut mounting nuts and tighten to 47 ft. lbs. (64 Nm).

9. Install the trim cover over the upper strut plate.

10. Install the tire and wheel assembly.

Air Strut Assembly

REMOVAL & INSTALLATION

The air strut assembly is removed and installed in the same way as a standard strut assembly. Refer to the necessary procedure in this section for front or rear strut removal and installation.

When removing an air strut assembly, use care not to tear the struts rubber air chamber when removing and installing the assembly.

11. Lower the vehicle.

12. Connect the negative battery cable.

13. Check the front end alignment, and adjust as necessary.

MacPherson Struts

REMOVAL & INSTALLATION

Justy

▶ See Figures 111 and 112

1. Disconnect the negative battery cable.
2. Raise and safely support the vehicle on jackstands.
3. Remove the tire and wheel assembly.
4. Remove the trim cover over the upper strut mount.
5. Remove the 2 upper strut mounting nuts.
6. Using a suitable prytool, push the lower control arm down and remove the coil spring.
7. Remove the 2 lower strut mounting bolts and remove the strut from the vehicle.

To install:

8. Position the strut in the vehicle and install the lower mounting bolts and tighten to 57 ft. lbs. (79 Nm).

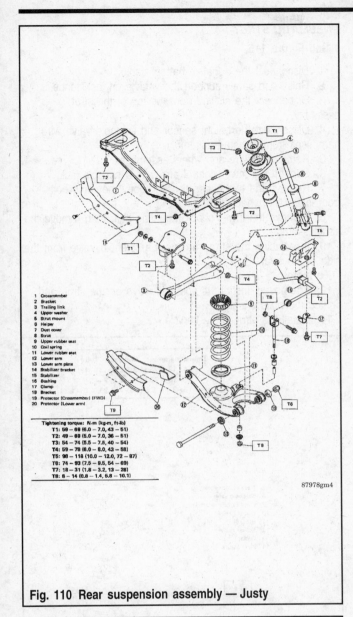

1 Crossmember
2 Bracket
3 Trailing link
4 Upper washer
5 Strut mount
6 Helper
7 Dust cover
8 Strut
9 Upper rubber seat
10 Coil spring
11 Lower rubber seat
12 Lower arm
13 Lower arm plate
14 Stabilizer bracket
15 Stabilizer
16 Bushing
17 Clamp
18 Bracket
19 Protector (Crossmember) (FWD)
20 Protector (Lower arm)

Tightening torque: N·m (kg-m, ft-lb)
T1: 59 — 69 (6.0 — 7.0, 43 — 51)
T2: 49 — 69 (5.0 — 7.0, 36 — 51)
T3: 54 — 74 (5.5 — 7.5, 40 — 54)
T4: 59 — 79 (6.0 — 8.0, 43 — 58)
T5: 98 — 118 (10.0 — 12.0, 72 — 87)
T6: 74 — 93 (7.5 — 9.5, 54 — 69)
T7: 18 — 31 (1.8 — 3.2, 13 — 28)
T8: 8 — 14 (0.8 — 1.4, 6.8 — 10.1)

87978gm4

Fig. 110 Rear suspension assembly — Justy

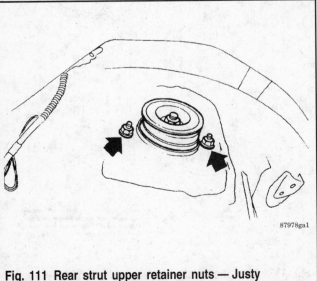

87978ga1

Fig. 111 Rear strut upper retainer nuts — Justy

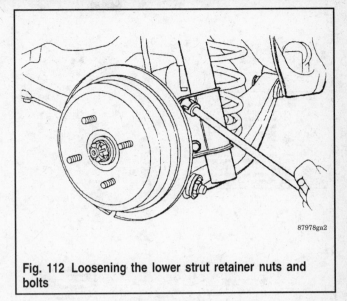

87978ga2

Fig. 112 Loosening the lower strut retainer nuts and bolts

9. Install the coil spring in position and raise the control arm until the strut plate mounting studs pass through the body.

10. Install the 2 upper strut mounting nuts and tighten to 47 ft. lbs. (64 Nm).

11. Install the trim cover over the upper strut plate.

12. Install the tire and wheel assembly.

13. Lower the vehicle.

14. Connect the negative battery cable.

15. Check the front end alignment and adjust as necessary.

Sedan, Coupe, Loyale, XT, Wagon and Brat

STANDARD STRUT

▶ **See Figures 113 and 114**

The rear coil spring on this vehicle is similar in design to the front struts. The coil spring is mounted on the strut, and requires a special procedure to remove.

✳✳CAUTION

DO NOT remove the center nut on the upper shock plate, or personal injury and/or component damage may result.

1. Raise and safely support the vehicle on jackstands.

2. Remove the tire and wheel assemblies.

3. Support the lower control arm with a suitable jack.

4. Remove the two upper shock-to-body mounting bolts from inside the wheel arch.

5. Remove the lower shock mounting bolt, then remove the strut assembly.

To install:

6. Install the strut in the vehicle.

7. Install the upper mounting bolts, and tighten to 27 ft. lbs. (36 Nm).

8. Connect the shock to the lower mount and tighten the mounting bolt to 87 ft. lbs. (118 ft. lbs).

9. Remove the support from under the control arm.

10. Install the tire and wheel assembly.

11. Lower the vehicle.

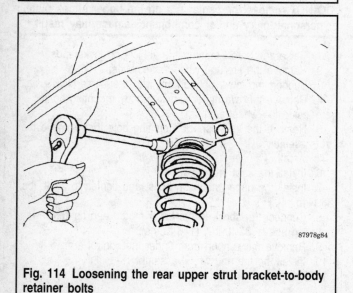

Tightening torque: N·m (kg·m, ft-lb)
T1: 18 — 25 (1.8 — 2.6, 13 — 19)
T2: 10 — 20 (1.0 — 2.0, 7.2 — 14.5)
T3: 88 — 127 (9.0 — 13.0, 65 — 94)
T4: 88 — 118 (9.0 — 12.0, 65 — 87)
T5: 18 — 22 (1.8 — 2.2, 13 — 16)
T6: 68 — 118 (7.0 — 12.0, 51 — 87)
T7: 88 — 103 (9.0 — 10.5, 65 — 76)
T8 (Bolt side): 69 — 88 (7.0 — 9.0, 51 — 65)
T9: 118 — 147 (12.0 — 15.0, 87 — 108)
T10: 127 — 147 (13.0 — 15.0, 94 — 108)
T11: 74 — 88 (7.5 — 9.0, 54 — 65)
T12: 27 — 47 (2.8 — 4.8, 20 — 35)

(FWD)
Station Wagon only
(4WD)

1 Upper rubber plate
2 Upper rubber
3 Bracket CP
4 Lower rubber
5 Collar
6 Spring seat plate
7 Upper spring seat
8 Rubber seat
9 Helper ASSY
10 Coil spring
11 Shock absorber CP
*12 Rear stabilizer
13 Helper (Station Wagon only)
14 Inner arm ASSY
15 Inner bushing
*16 Rear stabilizer bushing
*17 Rear stabilizer clamp
18 Rear bushing
19 Upper stopper
20 Front bushing
21 Crossmember CP
22 Bracket
23 Lower stopper
24 Outer bushing
25 Outer arm ASSY

*RX and air suspension vehicle only

★: Self-locking nuts are coated with special wax to provide proper torque setting. Discard old self-locking nut after removal. Replace with a new one.

87978g82

Fig. 113 Rear suspension assembly — Sedan, Coupe, Loyale, XT, Wagon and Brat

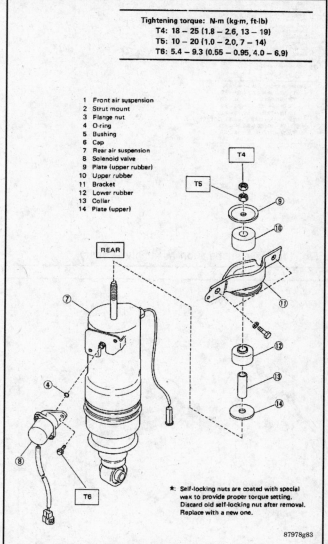

Fig. 114 Loosening the rear upper strut bracket-to-body retainer bolts

87978g84

PNEUMATIC STRUT

▶ **See Figure 115**

1. Disconnect the negative battery cable.
2. Raise and safely support the vehicle on jackstands.
3. Disconnect the air line from the top of the strut assembly.
4. Disconnect the height sensor and solenoid valve wire harnesses from the strut assembly.
5. Remove the tire and wheel assemblies.
6. Support the lower control arm with a suitable jack.
7. Remove the two upper shock-to-body mounting bolts from inside the wheel arch.
8. Remove the lower shock mounting bolt, then remove the strut assembly.
9. If replacing the strut. remove the solenoid valve from the side of the strut.

To install:

10. If removed, install the solenoid valve on the strut, and tighten the bolts snugly.
11. Install the strut in the vehicle.

Tightening torque: N·m (kg·m, ft-lb)
T4: 18 — 25 (1.8 — 2.6, 13 — 19)
T5: 10 — 20 (1.0 — 2.0, 7 — 14)
T6: 5.4 — 9.3 (0.55 — 0.95, 4.0 — 6.9)

1 Front air suspension
2 Strut mount
3 Flange nut
4 O-ring
5 Bushing
6 Cap
7 Rear air suspension
8 Solenoid valve
9 Plate (upper rubber)
10 Upper rubber
11 Bracket
12 Lower rubber
13 Collar
14 Plate (upper)

REAR

★: Self-locking nuts are coated with special wax to provide proper torque setting. Discard old self-locking nut after removal. Replace with a new one.

87978g83

Fig. 115 Rear pneumatic suspension assembly — Sedan, Coupe, Loyale, XT, Wagon and Brat

12. Install the upper mounting bolts, and tighten to 27 ft. lbs. (36 Nm).

13. Connect the shock to the lower mount and tighten the mounting bolt to 87 ft. lbs. (118 Nm).

14. Attach the height sensor, and solenoid valve wire harnesses to the strut.

15. Attach the air line to the top of the strut.

16. Remove the support from under the control arm.

17. Install the tire and wheel assembly.

18. Lower the vehicle.

19. Connect the negative battery cable.

20. Start the vehicle, and allow enough time for the shock to pressurize before driving the vehicle.

Legacy and Impreza

STANDARD STRUT

▶ See Figures 116, 117, 118, 119, 120, 121, 122 and 123

✳✳CAUTION

Do not remove the large nut on top of the strut assembly unless the coil spring is properly retained with a spring compressor.

1. On the Sedan, remove the rear seat assembly.

2. On the Wagon, remove the rear speaker grille and service hole cap.

3. Remove the strut mount cap.

4. Raise and support the vehicle safely on jackstands.

5. Remove the wheel and tire assembly.

6. Remove the brake hose clip.

7. Remove the union bolt from the brake caliper. Move the brake hose out of the way.

8. Remove the lower nuts and bolts securing the strut to the rear wheel housing.

9. From inside the vehicle, loosen and remove the retainer nuts securing the strut bearing cap to the strut tower.

10. Lower and remove the strut from the vehicle. **To install:**

11. Install the strut on to the vehicle, making sure to position the strut properly in the upper strut tower mounts. Refer to the

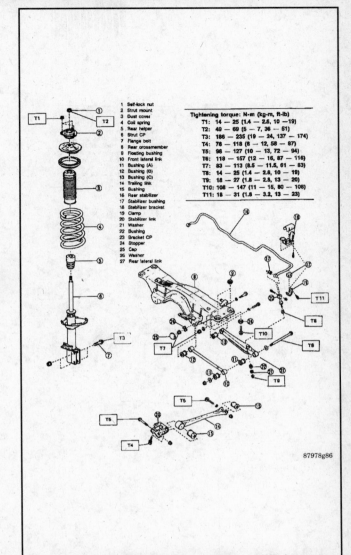

1	Self-lock nut	
2	Strut mount	
3	Dust cover	
4	Coil spring	
5	Rear helper	
6	Strut CP	
7	Flange bolt	
8	Rear crossmember	
9	Floating bushing	
10	Front lateral link	
11	Bushing (A)	
12	Bushing (B)	
13	Bushing (C)	
14	Trailing link	
15	Bushing	
16	Rear stabilizer	
17	Stabilizer bushing	
18	Stabilizer bracket	
19	Clamp	
20	Stabilizer link	
21	Washer	
22	Bushing	
23	Bracket CP	
24	Stopper	
25	Cap	
26	Washer	
27	Rear lateral link	

Tightening torque: N·m (kg-m, ft-lb)
T1: 14 — 25 (1.4 — 2.6, 10 — 19)
T2: 49 — 69 (5 — 7, 36 — 51)
T3: 186 — 235 (19 — 24, 137 — 174)
T4: 78 — 118 (8 — 12, 58 — 87)
T5: 98 — 127 (10 — 13, 72 — 94)
T6: 118 — 157 (12 — 16, 87 — 116)
T7: 83 — 113 (8.5 — 11.5, 61 — 83)
T8: 14 — 25 (1.4 — 2.6, 10 — 19)
T9: 18 — 27 (1.8 — 2.8, 13 — 20)
T10: 108 — 147 (11 — 15, 80 — 108)
T11: 18 — 31 (1.8 — 3.2, 13 — 23)

87978g86

Fig. 117 Rear standard strut assembly — AWD Legacy and Impreza

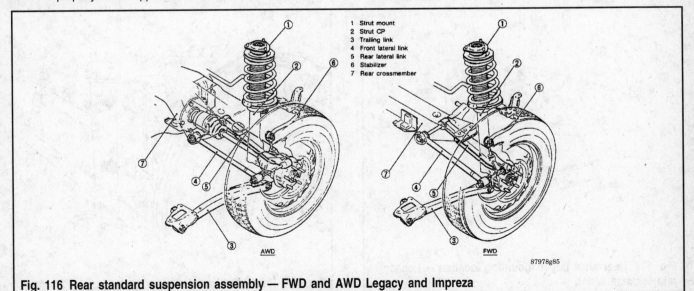

1 Strut mount
2 Strut CP
3 Trailing link
4 Front lateral link
5 Rear lateral link
6 Stabilizer
7 Rear crossmember

AWD   FWD

87978g85

Fig. 116 Rear standard suspension assembly — FWD and AWD Legacy and Impreza

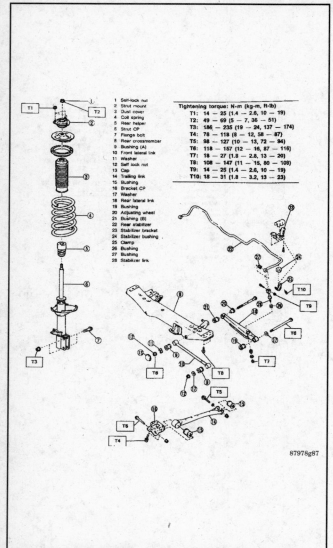

		Tightening torque: N·m (kg-m, ft-lb)
1	Self-lock nut	T1: 14 — 25 (1.4 — 2.6, 10 — 19)
2	Strut mount	T2: 49 — 69 (5 — 7, 36 — 51)
3	Dust cover	T3: 186 — 235 (19 — 24, 137 — 174)
4	Coil spring	T4: 76 — 118 (8 — 12, 58 — 87)
5	Rear helper	T5: 98 — 127 (10 — 13, 72 — 94)
6	Strut CP	T6: 118 — 157 (12 — 16, 87 — 116)
7	Flange bolt	T7: 18 — 27 (1.8 — 2.8, 13 — 20)
8	Rear crossmember	T8: 108 — 147 (11 — 15, 80 — 108)
9	Bushing (A)	T9: 14 — 25 (1.4 — 2.6, 10 — 19)
10	Front lateral link	T10: 18 — 31 (1.8 — 3.2, 13 — 23)
11	Washer	
12	Self lock nut	
13	Cap	
14	Trailing link	
15	Bushing	
16	Bracket CP	
17	Washer	
18	Rear lateral link	
19	Bushing	
20	Adjusting wheel	
21	Bushing (B)	
22	Rear stabilizer	
23	Stabilizer bracket	
24	Stabilizer bushing	
25	Clamp	
26	Bushing	
27	Bushing	
28	Stabilizer link	

87978g87

Fig. 118 Rear standard suspension assembly — FWD Legacy and Impreza

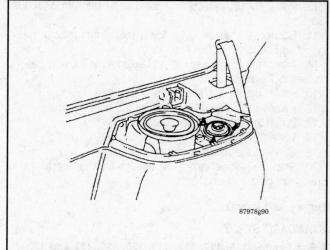

87978g90

Fig. 120 Rear strut upper mounting location — Legacy and Impreza wagon

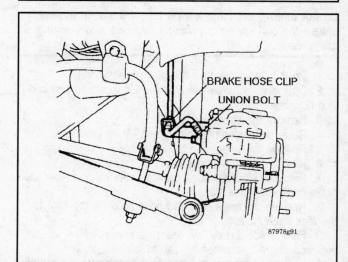

BRAKE HOSE CLIP

UNION BOLT

87978g91

Fig. 121 Brake hose retainer points on the strut assembly

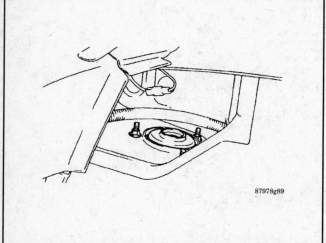

87978g89

Fig. 119 Rear strut upper mounting location — Legacy and Impreza sedan

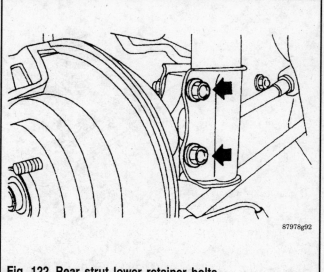

87978g92

Fig. 122 Rear strut lower retainer bolts

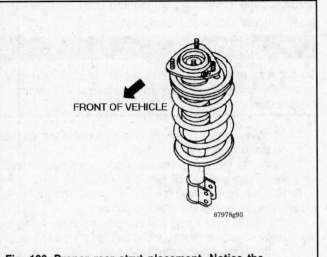

87978g93

Fig. 123 Proper rear strut placement. Notice the position of the coil

illustration if needed. Install the retainer nuts, and tighten to to 11 ft. lbs. (15 Nm).

12. Connect the strut to the rear wheel knuckle assembly, using the retainer nuts and bolts, and tighten the bolts to 145 ft. lbs. (196 Nm).

13. Install the brake union bolt, and tighten to 13 ft. lbs. (18 Nm).

14. Insert the brake hose clip.

15. Bleed the brakes.

16. Install the wheel.

17. Lower the vehicle.

18. Install the strut mount cap.

19. On Sedan, install the rear seat.

20. On Wagon, install the speaker grille.

PNEUMATIC STRUT

▶ See Figures 119, 120, 121, 122 and 124

1. Disconnect the negative battery cable.

2. On the Sedan, remove the rear seat assembly.

3. On the Wagon, remove the rear speaker grille and service hole cap.

4. Remove the strut mount cap.

5. Disconnect the air line from the top of the strut assembly.

6. Disconnect the height sensor and solenoid valve wire harnesses from the strut assembly.

7. Raise and support the vehicle safely on jackstands.

8. Remove the wheel and tire assembly.

9. Remove the brake hose clip.

10. Remove the union bolt from the brake caliper. Move the brake hose out of the way.

11. Remove the lower nuts and bolts securing the strut to the rear wheel housing.

12. From inside the vehicle, loosen and remove the retainer nuts securing the strut bearing cap to the strut tower.

13. Lower and remove the strut from the vehicle. **To install:**

14. Install the strut on to the vehicle, making sure to position the strut properly in the upper strut tower mounts. Refer to the

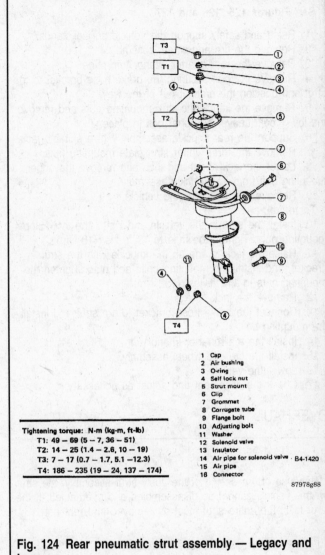

Tightening torque: N·m (kg-m, ft-lb)
T1: 49 — 69 (5 — 7, 36 — 51)
T2: 14 — 25 (1.4 — 2.6, 10 — 19)
T3: 7 — 17 (0.7 — 1.7, 5.1 —12.3)
T4: 186 — 235 (19 — 24, 137 — 174)

1	Cap
2	Air bushing
3	O-ring
4	Self lock nut
5	Strut mount
6	Clip
7	Grommet
8	Corrugate tube
9	Flange bolt
10	Adjusting bolt
11	Washer
12	Solenoid valve
13	Insulator
14	Air pipe for solenoid valve
15	Air pipe
16	Connector

B4-1420

87978g88

Fig. 124 Rear pneumatic strut assembly — Legacy and Impreza

illustration if needed. Install the retainer nuts, and tighten to to 11 ft. lbs. (15 Nm).

15. Connect the strut to the rear wheel knuckle assembly, using the retainer nuts and bolts, and tighten the bolts to 145 ft. lbs. (196 Nm).

16. Install the brake union bolt, and tighten to 13 ft. lbs. (18 Nm).

17. Insert the brake hose clip.

18. Bleed the brakes.

19. Install the wheel.

20. Lower the vehicle.

21. Attach the height sensor, and solenoid valve wire harnesses to the strut.

22. Attach the air line to the top of the strut.

23. Install the strut mount cap.

24. On Sedan, install the rear seat.

25. On Wagon. install the speaker grille.

26. Connect the negative battery cable.

27. Start the vehicle, and allow enough time for the shock to pressurize before driving the vehicle.

SVX

▶ **See Figures 125, 126 and 127**

1. Raise and safely support the vehicle on jackstands.
2. Remove the tire and wheel assembly.
3. Remove the rear quarter interior trim panel.
4. Remove the bolt securing the brake hose bracket to the strut and position the bracket out of the way.
5. Remove the knuckle-to-strut mounting nuts and remove the lower bolt. Leave the upper bolt in place.
6. Support the rear knuckle assembly with a suitable jack.
7. Remove the three upper strut plate mounting nuts.
8. Lower the jack about and inch and remove the upper mounting bolt from the knuckle assembly.
9. Remove the strut from the vehicle.

To install:

10. Install the strut in the vehicle and install the three upper mounting nuts. Tighten the nuts to 13 ft. lbs. (18 Nm).
11. Raise the jack to line up the knuckle with the strut bracket, and install the mounting bolts and nuts. Tighten the mounting nuts to 112 ft. lbs. (152 Nm).
12. Remove the jack.
13. Connect the brake hose bracket to the strut and install the mounting bolt.
14. Install the rear quarter interior trim.
15. Install the tire and wheel assembly.
16. Lower the vehicle.
17. Check the alignment and adjust as necessary.

OVERHAUL

Justy

Because of the design of the Justy strut assembly, the strut on this vehicle cannot be disassembled and overhauled. If the strut fails, the entire strut must be removed and replaced.

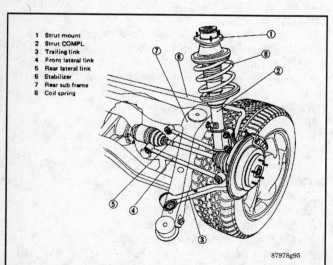

1 Strut mount
2 Strut COMPL
3 Trailing link
4 Front lateral link
5 Rear lateral link
6 Stabilizer
7 Rear sub frame
8 Coil spring

87978g95

Fig. 125 Rear strut and suspension assembly — SVX sedan

Sedan, Coupe, Loyale, XT, Wagon and Brat

▶ **See Figures 128, 129, 130 and 131**

> ✳✳**CAUTION**
>
> **Do not remove the large nut on top of the strut assembly unless the coil spring is properly retained with a spring compressor.**

1. Remove the strut assembly from the vehicle and secure in a soft jawed vise.
2. Compress the coil spring with a spring compressor until the upper spring seat can be turned by hand.
3. Remove the self locking nut on the top of the strut assembly, then remove the upper spring seat.
4. Remove the coil spring and compressor. If the spring is being replaced, slowly release the spring from the compressor and compress the new coil spring.

To install:

5. Place the proper end of the coil spring on the lower spring seat on the strut.
6. Install the insulator, upper spring seat and strut mount on the strut piston. Install a new self locking nut. Tighten the nut to 43 ft. lbs. (59 Nm).
7. Slowly release the spring compressor.
8. Install the strut on to the vehicle.

Legacy and Impreza

▶ **See Figure 132**

> ✳✳**CAUTION**
>
> **Do not remove the large nut on top of the strut assembly unless the coil spring is properly retained with a spring compressor.**

1. Remove the strut assembly from the vehicle and secure in a soft jawed vise.
2. Compress the coil spring with a spring compressor until the upper spring seat can be turned by hand.
3. Remove the self-locking nut on the top of the strut assembly, then remove the upper spring seat.
4. Remove the coil spring and compressor. If the spring is being replaced, slowly release the spring from the compressor and compress the new coil spring.

To install:

5. Place the proper end of the coil spring on the lower spring seat on the strut.
6. Install the insulator, upper spring seat and strut mount on the strut piston. Install a new self-locking nut. Tighten the nut to 43 ft. lbs. (59 Nm).
7. Slowly release the spring compressor.
8. Install the strut on to the vehicle.

SVX

▶ **See Figures 133, 134, 135 and 136**

> ✳✳**CAUTION**
>
> **Do not remove the large nut on top of the strut assembly unless the coil spring is properly retained with a spring compressor.**

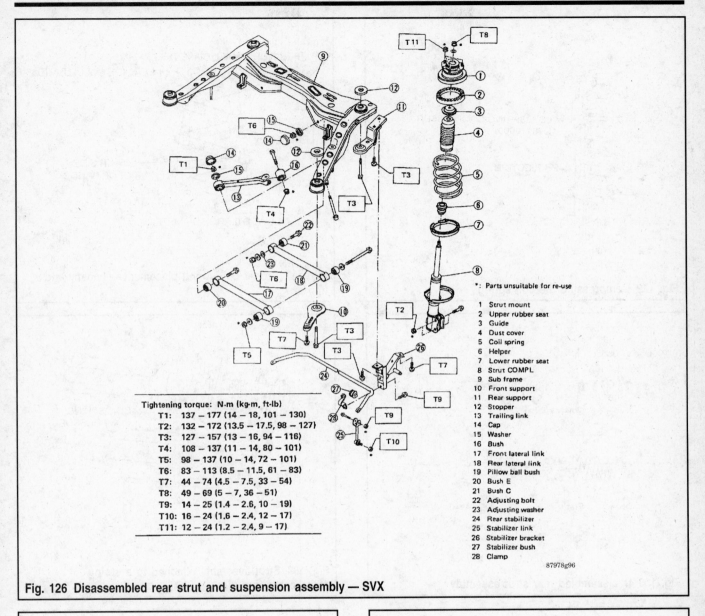

Tightening torque: N·m (kg-m, ft-lb)
T1: 137 − 177 (14 − 18, 101 − 130)
T2: 132 − 172 (13.5 − 17.5, 98 − 127)
T3: 127 − 157 (13 − 16, 94 − 116)
T4: 108 − 137 (11 − 14, 80 − 101)
T5: 98 − 137 (10 − 14, 72 − 101)
T6: 83 − 113 (8.5 − 11.5, 61 − 83)
T7: 44 − 74 (4.5 − 7.5, 33 − 54)
T8: 49 − 69 (5 − 7, 36 − 51)
T9: 14 − 25 (1.4 − 2.6, 10 − 19)
T10: 16 − 24 (1.6 − 2.4, 12 − 17)
T11: 12 − 24 (1.2 − 2.4, 9 − 17)

*: Parts unsuitable for re-use

1 Strut mount
2 Upper rubber seat
3 Guide
4 Dust cover
5 Coil spring
6 Helper
7 Lower rubber seat
8 Strut COMPL
9 Sub frame
10 Front support
11 Rear support
12 Stopper
13 Trailing link
14 Cap
15 Washer
16 Bush
17 Front lateral link
18 Rear lateral link
19 Pillow ball bush
20 Bush E
21 Bush C
22 Adjusting bolt
23 Adjusting washer
24 Rear stabilizer
25 Stabilizer link
26 Stabilizer bracket
27 Stabilizer bush
28 Clamp

87978g96

Fig. 126 Disassembled rear strut and suspension assembly — SVX

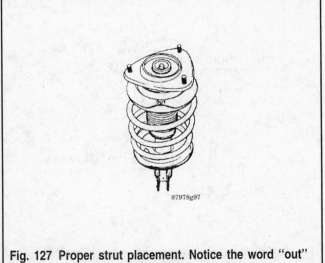

87978g97

Fig. 127 Proper strut placement. Notice the word "out" written on the upper spring plate

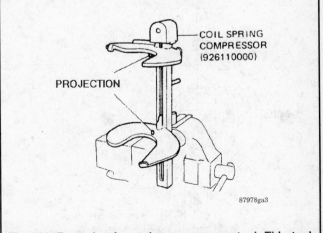

COIL SPRING COMPRESSOR (926110000)

PROJECTION

87978ga3

Fig. 128 Example of a spring compressor tool. This tool is secured in a vise, and the strut assembly is attached to it — Sedan, Coupe, Loyale, XT, Wagon and Brat

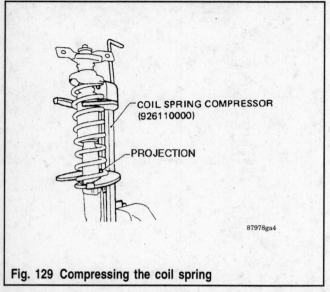

Fig. 129 Compressing the coil spring

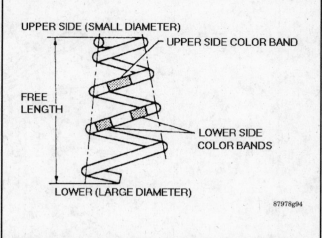

Fig. 132 Proper coil spring placement — Legacy and Impreza

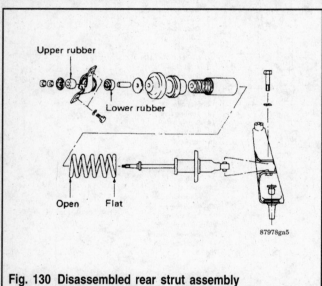

Fig. 130 Disassembled rear strut assembly

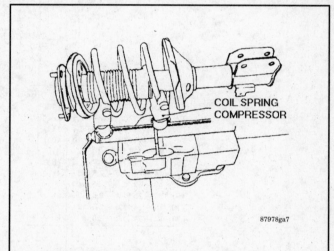

Fig. 133 Strut assembly attached to a spring compressor in a vise — SVX

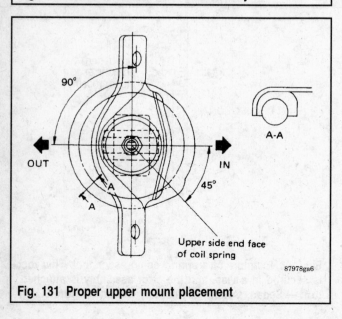

Fig. 131 Proper upper mount placement

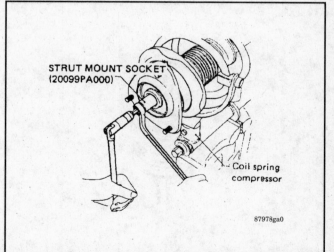

Fig. 134 With the spring compressed, remove the upper strut mounting nut

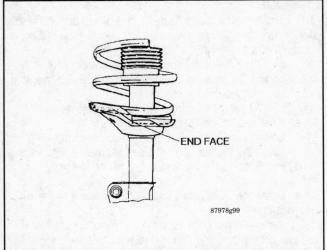

Fig. 135 Proper spring placement in the lower spring plate

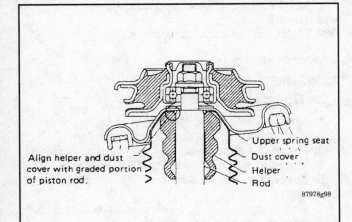

Fig. 136 Cutaway view of proper spring and mounting plate position

1. Remove the strut assembly from the vehicle and secure in a soft jawed vise.

2. Compress the coil spring with a spring compressor until the upper spring seat can be turned by hand.

3. Remove the self locking nut on the top of the strut assembly, then remove the upper spring seat.

4. Remove the coil spring and compressor. If the spring is being replaced, slowly release the spring from the compressor and compress the new coil spring.**To install:**

5. Place the proper end of the coil spring on the lower spring seat on the strut.

6. Install the insulator, upper spring seat and strut mount on the strut piston. Install a new self-locking nut. Tighten the nut to 43 ft. lbs. (59 Nm).

7. Slowly release the spring compressor.

8. Install the strut into the vehicle.

Control Arm

REMOVAL & INSTALLATION

Justy

▶ See Figure 137

1. Disconnect the negative battery cable.
2. Raise and safely support the vehicle on jackstands.
3. Remove the tire and wheel assembly.
4. Remove the trim cover over the upper strut mount.
5. Support the control arm with a suitable jack, and remove the long bolt that connects the knuckle to the outboard control arm.
6. Slowly lower the control arm to remove the coil spring.
7. Remove the inner control arm to frame nut and bolts, then remove the lower control arm.
   To install:
8. Position the control arm in the vehicle, and install the inner mounting bolt and nut. Tighten the bolt to 50 ft. lbs. (69 Nm).
9. Install the coil spring in position and raise the control arm until the outer control arm-to-knuckle bolt can be installed.
10. Install the long bolt and nut and tighten to 61 ft. lbs. (84 Nm).
11. Install the trim cover over the upper strut plate.
12. Remove the jack.
13. Install the tire and wheel assembly.
14. Lower the vehicle.
15. Connect the negative battery cable.
16. Check the front end alignment and adjust as necessary.

Sedan, Coupe, Loyale, XT, Wagon and Brat

▶ See Figure 138

OUTER CONTROL ARM

1. Raise and safely support the vehicle on jackstands.
2. Remove the tire and wheel assembly.
3. Support the control arm assembly with a suitable jack.

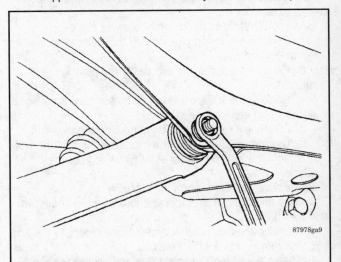

Fig. 137 Loosening the control arm-to-frame retainer nut and bolt — Justy

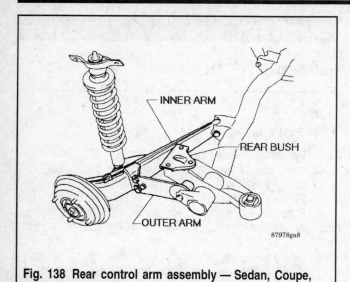

Fig. 138 Rear control arm assembly — Sedan, Coupe, Loyale, XT, Wagon and Brat

4. Remove the three bolts securing the inner and outer control arms together.

5. Remove the nut and bolt securing the outer control arm to the suspension assembly.

6. Remove the outer control arm.

To install:

7. Install the outer control arm, and install the bolt and nut securing the outer control arm to the suspension member. Tighten the bolt to 101 ft. lbs. (131 Nm).

8. Install the 3 outer control arm-to-inner control arm bolts, and tighten to 101 ft. lbs. (131 Nm).

9. Remove the control arm support.

10. Install the tire and wheel assembly.

11. Lower the vehicle.

12. Check and adjust the rear alignment.

INNER CONTROL ARM

1. Raise and safely support the vehicle on jackstands.

2. Remove the tire and wheel assembly.

3. Support the control arm assembly.

4. Remove the three bolts securing the inner and outer control arms together.

5. On 4WD vehicles perform the following steps.

a. Remove the spring pin securing the halfshaft to the carrier assembly.

b. Remove the cotter pin and castle nut from the rear halfshaft.

c. Remove the muffler and tail pipe assembly, if the right side is being serviced.

d. Disconnect the halfshaft from the differential carrier.

e. Using a suitable halfshaft removal tool, unseat the half-shaft from the hub and remove the halfshaft from the vehicle.

6. Remove the shock absorber assembly.

7. Cap and disconnect the brake hose at the rear suspension member.

8. Remove the inner control arm-to-frame mounting nut and bolt, and remove the control assembly.

9. With the assembly removed from the vehicle remove all necessary brake components.

To install:

10. Install the inner control arm in the vehicle and install the inner control arm mounting nut and bolt. Tighten the mounting bolt to 65 ft. lbs. (88 Nm).

11. Install the previously removed brake components.

12. Connect the brake hose at the rear suspension member.

13. Install the rear shock absorber.

14. On 4WD vehicles perform the following steps:

a. Insert the halfshaft into the hub.

b. Connect the halfshaft to the differential carrier.

c. Install the muffler and tail pipe assembly if removed.

d. Install the castle nut and cotter pin on the rear halfshaft.

e. Install the spring pin securing the halfshaft to the carrier assembly.

15. Install the three bolts securing the outer control arm to the inner control arm and tighten the bolts to 101 ft. lbs. (131 Nm).

16. Remove the control arm support.

17. Bleed the brake system.

18. Install the tire and wheel assembly.

19. Lower the vehicle.

20. Check and adjust the rear alignment.

Legacy and Impreza

FRONT WHEEL DRIVE

▶ **See Figures 139, 140 and 141**

1. Raise and support the vehicle safely on jackstands.

2. Remove the rear exhaust pipe and muffler.

3. Remove the stabilizer bar from the rear lateral link.

4. Matchmark the adjusting bolt to the crossmember.

5. Remove the bolts securing the lateral links to the crossmember.

6. Turn the lateral link cap counterclockwise until it contacts the stopper, then remove the cap.

7. Secure the lateral link adjusting bolt and loosen the self-locking nut.

8. If removing the right lateral links, remove the bolts securing the crossmember to the body.

9. Remove the adjustment bolt and links.

To install:

10. Install the lateral links, and insert the adjustment bolts.

11. If installing the right lateral links, install and tighten the crossmember-to-body bolts.

12. Secure the adjustment bolts and tighten the new nuts to 83 ft. lbs. (113 Nm).

13. Install the lateral link cap.

14. Install the bolts and new nuts securing the lateral links to the housing. Tighten the long bolt to 83 ft. lbs. (113 Nm) and short bolt to 33 ft. lbs. (44 Nm).

15. Install the stabilizer bar to the rear lateral link.

16. Install the exhaust and muffler assembly with new nuts and gaskets.

17. Install the wheel.

18. Check the rear wheel alignment.

ALL WHEEL DRIVE

▶ **See Figure 142**

1. Raise and support the vehicle safely on jackstands.

2. Remove the wheel.

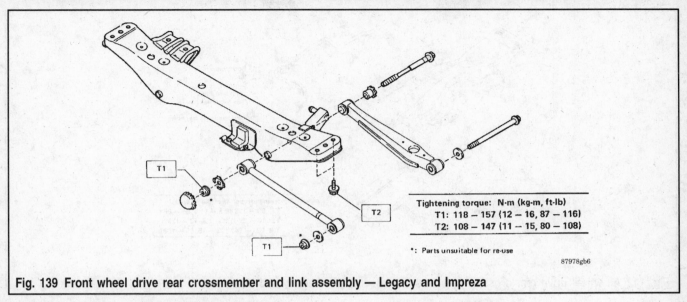

Tightening torque: N·m (kg-m, ft-lb)
T1: 118 — 157 (12 — 16, 87 — 116)
T2: 108 — 147 (11 — 15, 80 — 108)

*: Parts unsuitable for re-use

87978gb6

Fig. 139 Front wheel drive rear crossmember and link assembly — Legacy and Impreza

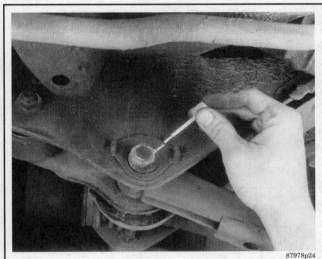

87978p24

Fig. 140 Matchmark the inside retainer/adjuster bolt . . .

87978p25

Fig. 141 . . . then loosen and remove the retainer/adjuster nut and bolt

3. Remove the stabilizers.

4. If equipped with ABS, disconnect the sensor harness from the trailing link.

5. Remove the bolt securing the trailing link to the housing.

6. Disconnect the inner CV-joint from the differential.

7. Matchmark the trailing link adjustment bolt to the crossmember.

8. Remove the outer lateral link on the housing side.

9. Secure the adjustment bolt and remove the nut.

10. Remove the bolts securing the lateral links to the crossmember and remove the links.

To install:

11. Install the lateral links and insert the bolts.

12. Install new nuts to the lateral link nuts and tighten them to 72 ft. lbs. (98 Nm).

13. Install the outer lateral link bolt on the housing side and tighten the new nut to 101 ft. lbs. (137 Nm).

14. Connect the CV-joint to the differential and insert a new roll pin.

15. Install the bolt securing the trailing link to the housing.

16. If equipped, connect the ABS harness to the trailing link.

17. Install the stabilizers.

18. Install the rear wheel.

19. Check the wheel alignment.

SVX

TRAILING LINK

▶ **See Figures 143, 144 and 145**

1. Raise and safely support the vehicle on jackstands.

2. Remove the tire and wheel assembly.

3. Disconnect the ABS sensor bracket and parking brake cable bracket from the trailing link.

4. Remove the cap from the front trailing link bushing.

5. Remove the front and rear through-bolts and nuts and remove the trailing link.

To install:

6. Install the trailing link and install the through-bolts and nuts. DO NOT tighten the nuts and bolts at this time.

7. Connect the ABS sensor bracket and parking brake cable to the trailing link.

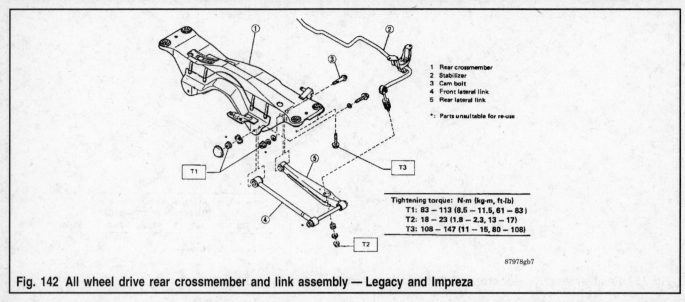

1 Rear crossmember
2 Stabilizer
3 Cam bolt
4 Front lateral link
5 Rear lateral link
*: Parts unsuitable for re-use

Tightening torque: N·m (kg-m, ft-lb)
T1: 83 — 113 (8.5 — 11.5, 61 — 83)
T2: 18 — 23 (1.8 — 2.3, 13 — 17)
T3: 108 — 147 (11 — 15, 80 — 108)

87978gb7

Fig. 142 All wheel drive rear crossmember and link assembly — Legacy and Impreza

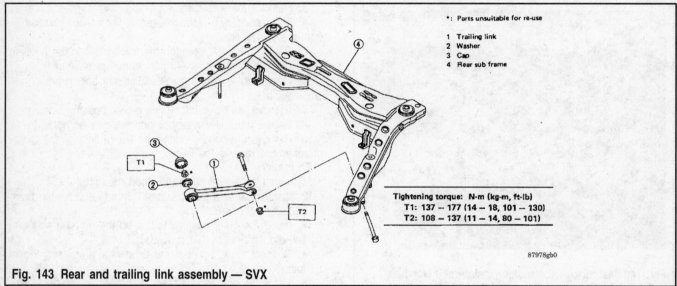

*: Parts unsuitable for re-use

1 Trailing link
2 Washer
3 Cap
4 Rear sub frame

Tightening torque: N·m (kg-m, ft-lb)
T1: 137 — 177 (14 — 18, 101 — 130)
T2: 108 — 137 (11 — 14, 80 — 101)

87978gb0

Fig. 143 Rear and trailing link assembly — SVX

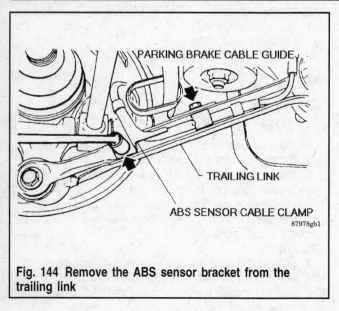

87978gb1

Fig. 144 Remove the ABS sensor bracket from the trailing link

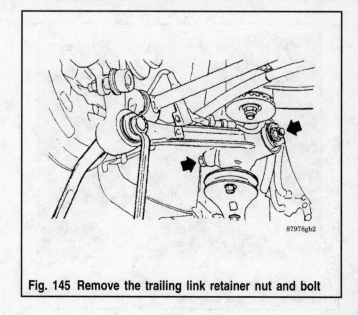

87978gb2

Fig. 145 Remove the trailing link retainer nut and bolt

8. Install the tire and wheel assembly.
9. Lower the vehicle.
10. Tighten the front trailing link through-bolt to 115 ft. lbs. (157 Nm) and install the cap.
11. Tighten the rear trailing link through-bolt to 90 ft. lbs. (123 Nm).

LATERAL LINK

▶ See Figures 146, 147 and 148

1. Raise and safely support the vehicle on jackstands.
2. Remove the tire and wheel assembly.
3. Remove the rear exhaust pipe.
4. Remove the rear sway bar link.
5. Remove the ABS sensor bracket and parking brake cable bracket from the trailing link.
6. Remove the bolt securing the parking brake cable bracket from the floor.
7. Disconnect the trailing link from the knuckle.
8. Remove the lateral link-to-knuckle through-bolt and nut.

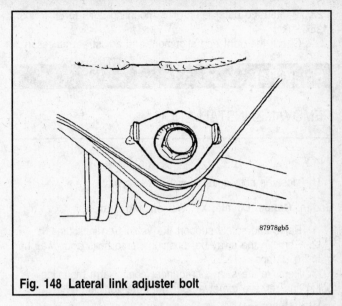

Fig. 148 Lateral link adjuster bolt

9. Separate the inboard CV-joint from the differential carrier.
10. Matchmark the alignment bolt on the lateral link for installation purposes.
11. Remove the mounting bolt and remove the lateral link.
To install:
12. Install the lateral link and install the adjusting bolt finger tight.
13. Connect the inboard CV-joint to the differential carrier.
14. Position the lateral links at the knuckle and install the through-bolt finger-tight.
15. Connect the trailing link to the knuckle and tighten the bolt to 90 ft. lbs. (123 Nm).
16. Install the parking brake cable bracket to the floor.
17. Connect the parking brake cable and ABS sensor brackets to the trailing link.
18. Install the rear sway bar link.
19. Install the rear exhaust pipe.
20. Install the tire and wheel assembly.
21. Lower the vehicle.
22. Tighten the inner lateral link mounting bolts to 72 ft. lbs. (98 Nm).

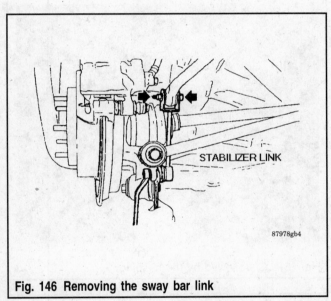

Fig. 146 Removing the sway bar link

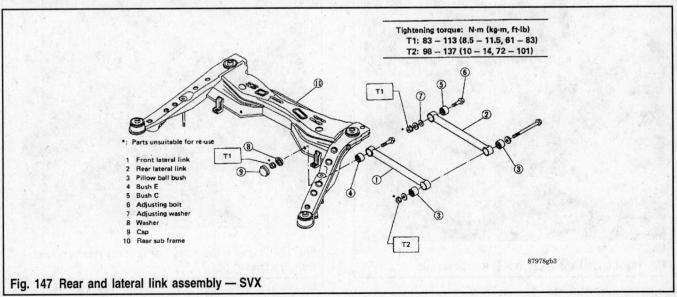

Fig. 147 Rear and lateral link assembly — SVX

23. Tighten the outer lateral link mounting bolts to 86 ft. lbs. (128 Nm).

24. Check the front end alignment and adjust as necessary.

Sway Bar

REMOVAL & INSTALLATION

Justy

The Justy is not equipped with a rear sway bar.

Sedan, Coupe, Loyale, XT, Wagon and Brat

1. Raise and safely support the vehicle on jackstands.
2. Remove the sway bar bushing clamp bolts and sway bar bushing clamps.
3. Remove the sway bar-to-inner control arm mounting bolts, and remove the sway bar from the vehicle.

To install:

4. Position the sway bar on the vehicle, and install the sway bar-to-inner control arm mounting bolts.
5. Install the sway bar bushing brackets and mounting bolts.
6. Lower the vehicle.

Legacy and Impreza

◆ **See Figures 149, 150, 151 and 152**

Sway bars are equipped on 4WD vehicles only.

1. Raise and safely support the vehicle on jackstands.
2. Remove the wheels.
3. Mark the location and direction of the stabilizer mounting clamps. This will ensure proper installation.
4. Remove the stabilizer-to-crossmember bolts.
5. Remove the bolts that secure the stabilizer to the control link.

To install:

6. Check all of the bushings for deformity or damage. Replace any bushing that shows signs of deterioration.

Fig. 150 . . . then remove the nut and washer . . .

Fig. 151 . . . followed by the bushing

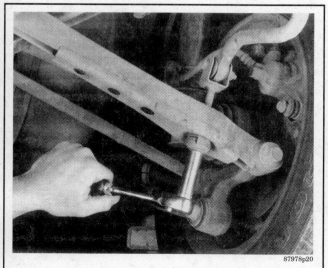

Fig. 149 Loosen the sway bar link retainer nut . . .

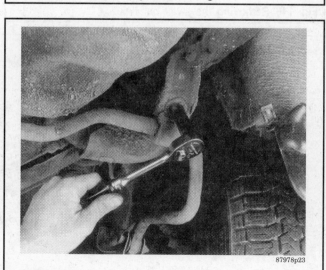

Fig. 152 Remove the sway bar bracket retainer bolts from the underbody

7. Install the bushings and clamps on the stabilizer, aligning any marks made during removal.

8. Install the stabilizer bar into position, and install the retaining bolts. Tighten bolts to the following amounts:
- Stabilizer link-to-control link — 13-17 ft. lbs. (18-23 Nm).
- Stabilizer-to-crossmember — 15-21 ft. lbs. (21-28 Nm).

9. Install the wheels and lower the vehicle.

SVX

▶ **See Figures 153, 154 and 155**

1. Raise and safely support the vehicle.
2. Remove the sway bar link-to-sway bar mounting nuts and bolts.

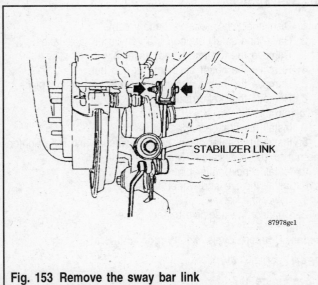

Fig. 153 Remove the sway bar link

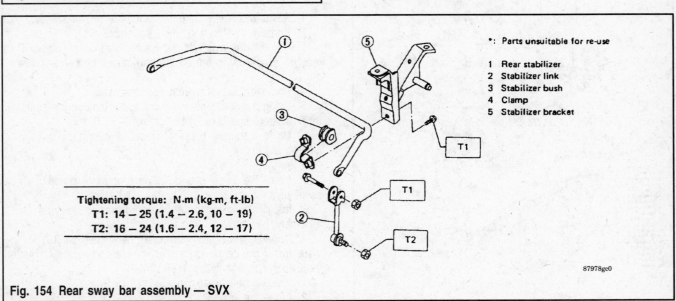

STABILIZER

87978gc2

Fig. 155 Remove the sway bar clamp

3. Remove the sway bar bracket mounting bolts, then remove the brackets from the frame.
4. Remove the sway bar.

To install:

5. Position the sway bar on the vehicle and install the sway bar brackets on the paint marks on the sway bar. Install the bolts and tighten to 15 ft. lbs. (20 Nm).

➡**When installing the sway bar brackets make sure the brackets are installed in the correct direction. The upper end of the bracket is shorter than the lower.**

6. Connect the sway bar to the sway bar links and tighten the mounting nuts and bolts to 15 ft. lbs. (20 Nm).
7. Lower the vehicle.

*: Parts unsuitable for re-use

1 Rear stabilizer
2 Stabilizer link
3 Stabilizer bush
4 Clamp
5 Stabilizer bracket

Tightening torque: N·m (kg-m, ft-lb)
T1: 14 — 25 (1.4 — 2.6, 10 — 19)
T2: 16 — 24 (1.6 — 2.4, 12 — 17)

87978gc0

Fig. 154 Rear sway bar assembly — SVX

Rear Wheel Bearings

REPLACEMENT

Justy

▶ See Figure 156

FRONT WHEEL DRIVE

1. Disconnect the negative battery cable.
2. Raise and safely support the vehicle on jackstands.
3. Remove the tire and wheel assembly.
4. Remove the dust cap from the brake drum.
5. Straighten the lock washer and remove the nut, lock washer and washer.
6. Pull the drum off the spindle using care not to drop the outer bearing.

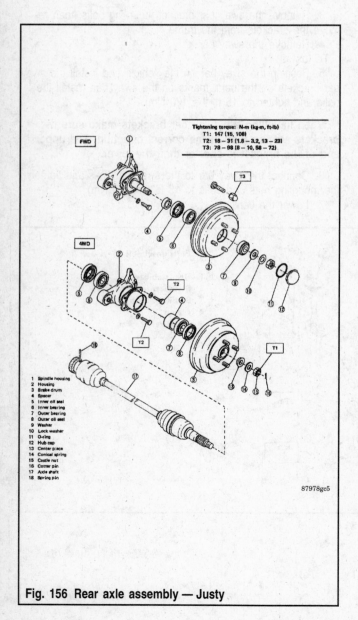

Tightening torque: N-m (kg-m, ft-lb)
T1: 147 (15, 108)
T2: 18 — 31 (1.8 — 3.2, 13 — 23)
T3: 78 — 98 (8 — 10, 58 — 72)

FWD
4WD

1 Spindle housing
2 Housing
3 Brake drum
4 Spacer
5 Inner oil seal
6 Inner bearing
7 Outer bearing
8 Outer oil seal
9 Washer
10 Lock washer
11 O-ring
12 Hub cap
13 Center piece
14 Conical spring
15 Castle nut
16 Cotter pin
17 Axle shaft
18 Spring pin

87978gc5

Fig. 156 Rear axle assembly — Justy

To install:

7. Install the drum on the spindle and install the outer bearing.
8. Install the washer, lock washer and nut. Tighten the nut as follows:
   a. Tighten the nut to 29 ft. lbs. (39 Nm).
   b. Rotate the drum several times in each direction.
   c. Loosen the nut until it is completely loose.
   d. Tighten the nut to 1 ft. lbs. (1 Nm).
9. Bend the lock washer to secure the nut.
10. Install the dust cap with a new oil seal.
11. Install the tire and wheel assembly.
12. Lower the vehicle.
13. Connect the negative battery cable.

ALL WHEEL DRIVE

1. Disconnect the negative battery cable.
2. Raise and safely support the vehicle on jackstands.
3. Remove the tire and wheel assembly.
4. Remove the cotter pin from the hub nut.
5. Remove the hub nut, conical washer and center piece.
6. Remove the brake drum.

To install:

7. Install the brake drum.
8. Install the center piece, conical; washer and nut. Tighten the nut to 108 ft. lbs. (147 Nm).
9. Install a new cotter pin.
10. Install the tire and wheel assembly.
11. Lower the vehicle.
12. Connect the negative battery cable.

Sedan, Coupe, Loyale, XT, Wagon and Brat

REAR DRUM — 4WD

▶ See Figure 157

1. Raise and safely support the vehicle on jackstands.
2. Remove the tire and wheel assembly.
3. Remove the axle nut, flat washer and center piece. It may be necessary to tap on the hub to get the center piece out.
4. Remove the brake drum from the axle.
5. Using a suitable seal removal tool, Remove the seals from the front and back of the drum.
6. Using a suitable press or clamp. drive out the drum bearing assembly.

To install:

7. Install the wheel bearing using a press or clamp assembly.
8. Install new seals to the front and rear of the drum assembly.
9. Carefully install the drum onto the splined shaft.
10. Install the center piece, flat washer and axle nut. Tighten the axle nut to 145 ft. lbs. (196 Nm).
11. Install a new cotter pin.
12. Install the wheel.
13. Adjust the rear brakes.
14. Lower the vehicle.

REAR DRUM — FRONT WHEEL DRIVE

▶ See Figure 158

1. Raise and safely support the vehicle on jackstands.

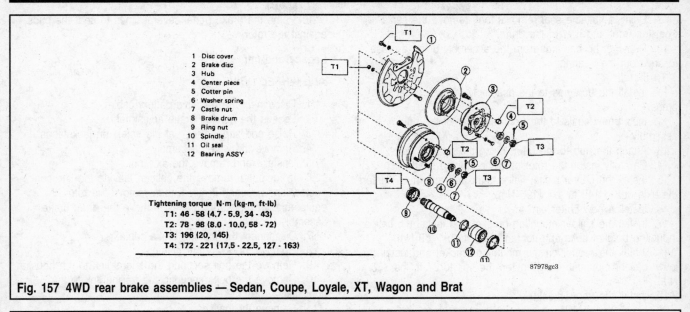

Fig. 157 4WD rear brake assemblies — Sedan, Coupe, Loyale, XT, Wagon and Brat

Key (Fig. 157):
1 Disc cover
2 Brake disc
3 Hub
4 Center piece
5 Cotter pin
6 Washer spring
7 Castle nut
8 Brake drum
9 Ring nut
10 Spindle
11 Oil seal
12 Bearing ASSY

Tightening torque N·m (kg-m, ft-lb)
T1: 46 - 58 (4.7 - 5.9, 34 - 43)
T2: 78 - 98 (8.0 - 10.0, 58 - 72)
T3: 196 (20, 145)
T4: 172 - 221 (17.5 - 22.5, 127 - 163)

87978gc3

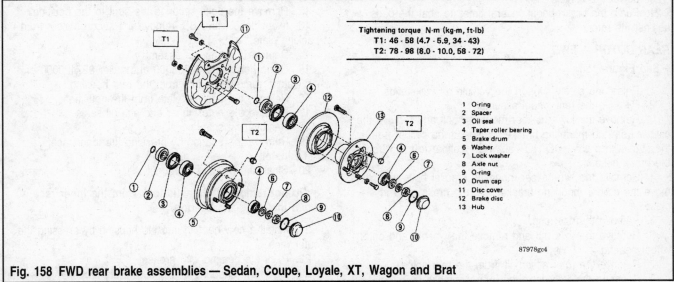

Fig. 158 FWD rear brake assemblies — Sedan, Coupe, Loyale, XT, Wagon and Brat

Tightening torque N·m (kg-m, ft-lb)
T1: 46 - 58 (4.7 - 5.9, 34 - 43)
T2: 78 - 98 (8.0 - 10.0, 58 - 72)

Key (Fig. 158):
1 O-ring
2 Spacer
3 Oil seal
4 Taper roller bearing
5 Brake drum
6 Washer
7 Lock washer
8 Axle nut
9 O-ring
10 Drum cap
11 Disc cover
12 Brake disc
13 Hub

87978gc4

2. Remove the rear wheel assembly.

3. Remove the dust cap.

4. Remove the axle nut and remove the washer and outer wheel bearing.

5. Remove the drum from the rear spindle.

6. Using a suitable seal removal tool, remove the seals from the front and rear of the drum.

7. Remove the wheel bearings by using a suitable press or clamp.

To install:

8. Install the wheel bearings into the drum using a press or clamp assembly.

9. Install new seals to the front and rear of the drum.

10. Install the rear drum assembly onto the spindle.

11. Install the outer wheel bearing and washer.

12. Install the axle nut.

13. Install the dust cap.

14. Install the wheel.

15. Adjust the rear brakes.

16. Lower the vehicle.

FRONT AND REAR ROTORS — 4WD

▶ See Figure 157

1. Raise and safely support the vehicle on jackstands.

2. Remove the tire and wheel assembly.

3. Remove the lower caliper mounting bolt and remove the caliper from the mounting bracket. Suspend the caliper from the strut with a wire. DO NOT allow the caliper to hang from the brake hose.

4. Remove the two caliper mounting bracket bolts and remove the caliper mounting bracket with the brake pads in place.

5. Remove the cotter pin from the axle nut.

6. Remove the axle nut, flat washer and center piece. It may be necessary to tap on the hub to get the center piece out.

7. Remove the brake rotor assembly from the axle.

8. Separate the rotor from the hub assembly, by removing the retainer bolts.

9. Using a suitable seal removal tool, remove the seals from the front and rear of the drum.

10. Remove the bearings from the assembly using a press to drive out the bearing.

To install:

11. Install the bearings to the assembly using a suitable press.

12. Install new seals to the front and rear of the hub assembly.

13. Attach the hub to the rotor, using the retainer bolts.

14. Carefully install the rotor onto the splined shaft.

15. Install the center piece, flat washer and axle nut. Tighten the axle nut to 145 ft. lbs. (196 Nm).

16. Install a new cotter pin.

17. Install the caliper mounting bracket and install the caliper mounting bracket bolts and tighten to 51 ft. lbs. (69 Nm).

18. Install the caliper on the mounting bracket and install the lower caliper mounting bolt. Tighten the bolt to 27 ft. lbs. (36 Nm).

19. Install the front wheel.

20. Lower the vehicle.

21. Pump the brake pedal several times to seat the pads against the rotor.

REAR ROTOR — FWD

▶ **See Figure 158**

1. Raise and safely support the vehicle on jackstands.

2. Remove the rear wheel assembly.

3. Remove the lower caliper mounting bolt and remove the caliper from the mounting bracket. Suspend the caliper from the strut with a wire. DO NOT allow the caliper to hang from the brake hose.

4. Remove the two caliper mounting bracket bolts and remove the caliper mounting bracket with the brake pads in place.

5. Remove the dust cap.

6. Remove the axle nut and remove the washer and outer wheel bearing.

7. Remove the rotor assembly from the rear spindle.

8. Separate the rotor from the hub assembly, by removing the retainer bolts.

9. Using a suitable seal removal tool, remove the seals from the front and rear of the drum.

10. Remove the bearings from the assembly using a press to drive out the bearing.

To install:

11. Install the bearings to the assembly using a suitable press.

12. Install new seals to the front and rear of the hub assembly.

13. Attach the hub to the rotor, using the retainer bolts.

14. Install the axle nut and washer.

15. Install the dust cap.

16. Install the caliper mounting bracket and install the caliper mounting bracket bolts and tighten to 43 ft. lbs. (52 Nm).

17. Install the caliper on the mounting bracket and install the lower caliper mounting bolt. Tighten the bolt to 27 ft. lbs. (36 Nm).

18. Install the front wheel.

19. Lower the vehicle.

20. Pump the brake pedal several times to seat the pads against the rotor.

Legacy and Impreza

ALL WHEEL DRIVE

1. Disconnect the negative battery cable.

2. Loosen the parking brake adjustment.

3. Raise and support the vehicle safely on jackstands.

4. Remove the wheel assembly.

5. Unstake and remove the axle nut.

6. If equipped, remove the caliper, leaving the line connected, and suspend it aside, then remove the rotor. If equipped with rear drum brakes, remove the drum brake assembly.

7. Disconnect the parking brake cable.

8. Remove the sway bar clamp.

9. Remove the bolt securing the lateral link to the housing.

10. Remove the bolts securing the trailing link to the housing.

11. Remove the halfshaft.

12. Remove the bolts securing the strut to the housing.

13. If equipped with ABS, remove the speed sensor from the backing plate.

14. Remove the housing assembly.

15. Using hub stand 92708000 and puller 927420000 or equivalent, remove the hub from the rear housing.

16. Remove the backing plate from the housing.

17. Remove the outer, inner and sub oil seals.

18. Remove the snapring.

19. Remove the bearing by pressing the inner race.

To install:

20. Clean the housing thoroughly.

➡ **Do not remove the plastic lock from the inner race when installing the bearing.**

21. Install a new bearing into the housing by pressing the outer race.

22. Pack the bearing with grease.

23. Install the snapring and ensure it fits properly.

24. Using installer 927460000 or equivalent, press in a new outer seal until it comes in contact with the snapring.

25. Using installer 927450000 or equivalent, press in a new inner seal until it contacts the bottom.

26. Install a new sub oil seal.

27. Apply grease to the oil seal lip.

28. Install the backing plate and tighten the bolts to 43 ft. lbs. (58 Nm).

29. Using installer 927450000 or equivalent, press in the hub into the housing.

30. Connect the housing to the strut and tighten the bolts to 119 ft. lbs. (162 Nm).

31. If equipped with ABS, install the speed sensor.

32. Install the halfshaft.

33. Connect the trailing link to the housing and tighten the bolt and new nut to 94 ft. lbs. (127 Nm).

34. Connect the lateral link to the housing and tighten the bolt and new nut to 116 ft. lbs. (157 Nm).

35. Install the sway bar clamp.

36. Connect the parking brake cable.

37. Install the rear brake assembly.

38. Install a new axle nut and tighten it to 152 ft. lbs. (206 Nm). Stake the nut.
39. Install the wheel.
40. Lower the vehicle.
41. Adjust the parking brake cable.
42. Connect the negative battery cable.

FRONT WHEEL DRIVE

1. Disconnect t he negative battery cable.
2. Loosen the parking brake adjustment.
3. Raise and support the vehicle safely on jackstands.
4. Remove the wheel assembly.
5. Unstake and remove the axle nut.
6. If equipped, remove the caliper, leaving the line connected and suspend it aside. Remove the rotor. Or if equipped with rear drum, remove the drum brake assembly.
7. Disconnect the parking brake cable.
8. Remove the bolt securing the lateral link to the spindle.
9. Remove the bolts securing the trailing link to the spindle.
10. Remove the bolts securing the strut to the spindle.
11. Remove the spindle assembly.
12. Remove the hub and bearing assembly from the spindle.

To install:

13. Pack the oil seal located and the rear of the hub with grease.
14. Install the hub on the spindle and temporarily tighten a new nut and washer to hold the hub in place.
15. Connect the spindle to the strut and tighten the bolts to 119 ft. lbs. (162 Nm).
16. Connect the trailing link to the spindle and tighten the bolt and new nut to 94 ft. lbs. (127 Nm).
17. Connect the lateral link to the spindle and tighten the bolt and new nut to 116 ft. lbs. (157 Nm).
18. Connect the parking brake cable.
19. Install the rear brake assembly.
20. Install a new axle nut and tighten it to 152 ft. lbs. (206 Nm). Stake the nut.
21. Install the wheel.
22. Lower the vehicle.
23. Adjust the parking brake cable.
24. Connect the negative battery cable.

SVX

1. Set the parking brake.
2. Raise and safely support the vehicle on jackstands.
3. Remove the rear wheel assembly.
4. Remove the dust cap and remove the axle nut.
5. Return the parking brake lever and remove the console box lid.
6. Loosen the parking brake adjuster nut.
7. Remove the stabilizer link.
8. Remove the ABS sensor and clamp.
9. Disconnect the parking brake cable clamp.
10. Disconnect the brake hose from the strut.
11. Loosen the caliper assembly securing bolts.
12. Disconnect the trailing link from the knuckle.
13. Remove the nut securing the lateral link to the knuckle.
14. Remove the two nuts securing the strut to the knuckle.
15. Remove the caliper assembly and fasten to the strut using wire.

16. Remove the rotor.
17. Remove the parking brake shoes and disconnect the cable from the shoe.
18. Remove the parking brake cable clamp and remove the cable from the back plate.
19. Separate the knuckle from the halfshaft.
20. Remove the mounting bolts and remove the knuckle.
21. Remove the bearings.

To install:

22. Install the bearings.
23. Install the knuckle and the mounting bolts.
24. Install the halfshaft into knuckle. Tighten the axle nut to 123-152 ft. lbs. (167-206 Nm).
25. Replace the parking brake cable to the back plate and install the cable clamp.
26. Connect the cable to the brake shoe and install the shoes.
27. Install the brake rotor and the caliper assembly.
28. Install the axle nut and the dust cap.
29. Install the nuts securing the strut to the knuckle. Tighten the nuts to 98-127 ft. lbs. (132-172 Nm).
30. Install the nut securing the lateral link to the knuckle.
31. Tighten the caliper assembly mounting bolts.
32. Connect the brake hose to the strut and connect the parking brake cable clamp.
33. Install the ABS sensor and clamp.
34. Install the stabilizer link.
35. Tighten the parking brake cable adjusting nut.
36. Install the console box lid.
37. Install the rear wheel.
38. Lower the vehicle.

Rear End Alignment

CASTER

Wheel alignment is defined by three different adjustments in three planes. Looking at the vehicle from the side, caster angle describes the steering axis rather than a wheel angle. The steering knuckle is attached to the strut at the top and the control arm at the bottom. The wheel pivots around the line between these points to steer the vehicle. When the upper point is tilted back, this is described as positive caster. Having a positive caster tends to make the wheels self-centering, increasing directional stability. Excessive positive caster makes the wheels hard to steer, while an uneven caster will cause a pull to one side.

CAMBER

Looking at the wheels from the front of the vehicle, camber adjustment is the tilt of the wheel. When the wheel is tilted in at the top, this is negative camber. In a turn, a slight amount of negative camber helps maximize contact of the outside tire with the road. Too much negative camber makes the vehicle unstable in a straight line.

TOE-IN

Looking down at the wheels from above the vehicle, toe alignment is the distance between the front of the wheels relative to the distance between the back of the wheels. If the wheels are closer at the front, they are said to be toed-in or to have a negative toe. A small amount of negative toe enhances directional stability and provides a smoother ride on the highway. On most front wheel drive vehicles, standard toe adjustment is either zero or slightly positive. When power is applied to the front wheels, they tend to toe-in naturally.

STEERING

Steering Wheel

REMOVAL & INSTALLATION

Justy

▶ See Figure 159

1. Disconnect the negative battery cable.

2. Remove the steering wheel horn cover, by carefully prying the cover off.
3. Disconnect the horn harness from the steering wheel.
4. Matchmark the steering wheel to the steering shaft and remove the shaft nut.
5. Using a steering wheel puller, remove the steering wheel.

To install:

6. Install the steering wheel on the steering shaft with the matchmarks in alignment.
7. Install the steering wheel mounting nut and tighten to 40 ft. lbs. (54 Nm).
8. Connect and install the horn pad on the wheel.
9. Install the steering wheel cover or ornament.
10. Connect the negative battery cable.

Sedan, Coupe, Loyale, Wagon, Brat and Legacy
▶ See Figures 160, 161, 162, 163 and 164

✳✳CAUTION

The air bag system must be disarmed before removing the steering wheel. Failure to do so may cause accidental deployment,

1. Disconnect the negative battery cable.

✳✳CAUTION

Wait at least 10 minutes after disarming the air bag to avoid accidental deployment.

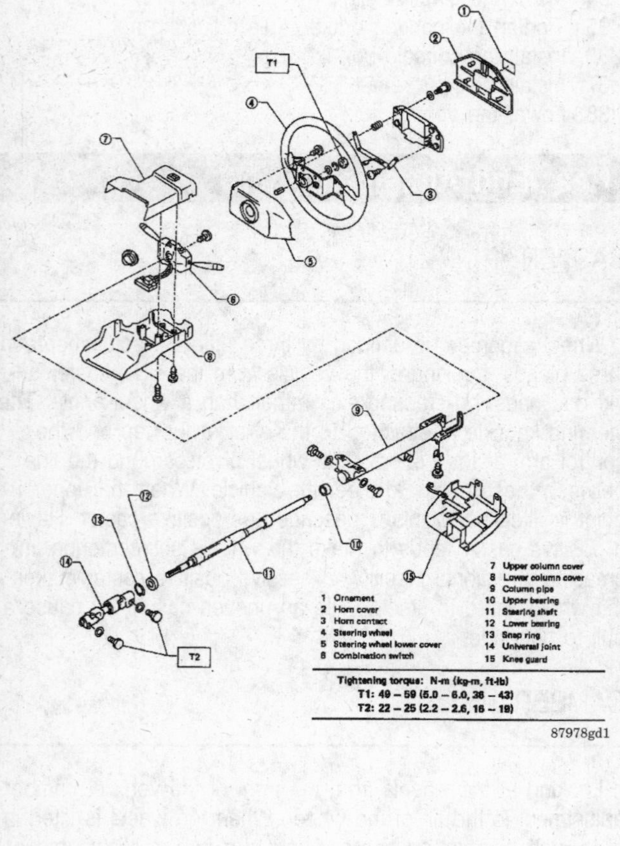

Fig. 159 Steering wheel and column components — Justy

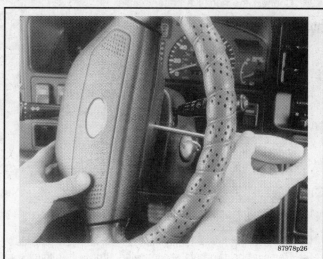

Fig. 160 Remove the center pad retainer screws — Legacy without an air bag

Fig. 161 Disconnect the horn harness from the steering wheel

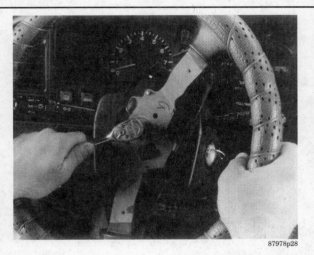
Fig. 162 Loosen and remove the steering wheel retainer nut

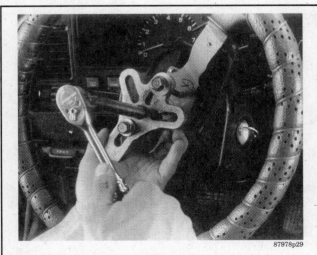
Fig. 163 Use a steering wheel puller to separate the steering wheel from the column shaft

Fig. 164 Lift the steering wheel off the shaft

2. Disconnect the horn lead from the wiring harness, located beneath the instrument panel.

3. On models without air bag, remove the horn pad by removing the retainer screws from the bottom of the wheel.

4. On models with an air bag, working behind the steering wheel, remove the steering column covers. Use a No. 30 Torx® bit and remove the air bag module retaining bolts.

❋❋CAUTION

Always carry an air bag assembly, with the bag and trim cover, away from your body. Store the assembly facing upward; never place the assembly face down on any surface.

5. Disconnect the air bag module connector and remove the module from the steering wheel. Place the module face up on a flat surface.

6. Matchmark the steering wheel and the column for installation.

7. Remove the steering wheel retaining nut. Using a steering wheel puller tool, remove the steering wheel from the column.

To install:

8. Install the steering wheel on the column aligning the marks made during removal. Tighten the center nut to 22-29 ft. lbs. (29-39 Nm).

➡Do not hammer on the steering wheel or the steering column, as damage to the collapsible column could result.

9. Install the horn pad or air bag assembly and the column covers.

10. Connect all electrical leads.

11. Connect the negative battery cable.

XT

◗ See Figure 165

1. Disconnect the negative battery cable.
2. Loosen the telescoping lever.
3. Remove the two screws from the rear of the steering wheel.

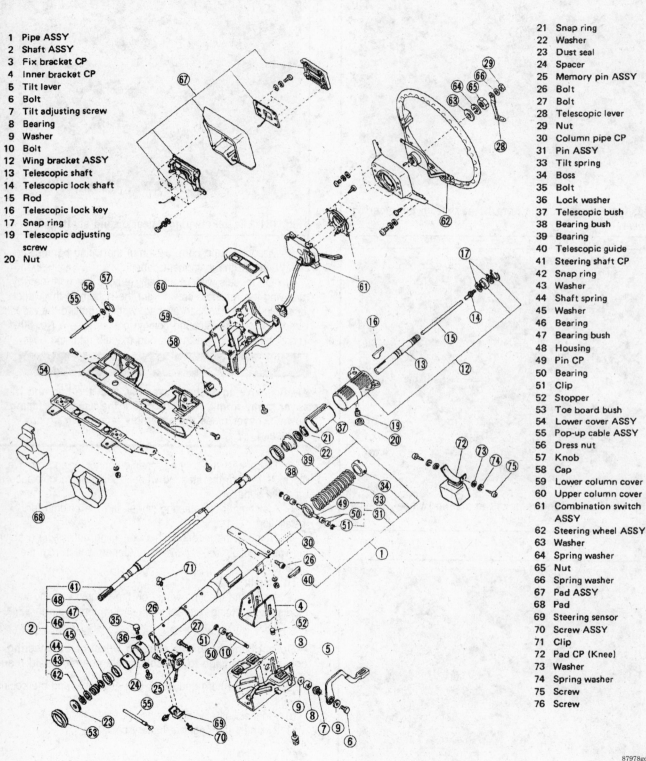

1 Pipe ASSY
2 Shaft ASSY
3 Fix bracket CP
4 Inner bracket CP
5 Tilt lever
6 Bolt
7 Tilt adjusting screw
8 Bearing
9 Washer
10 Bolt
12 Wing bracket ASSY
13 Telescopic shaft
14 Telescopic lock shaft
15 Rod
16 Telescopic lock key
17 Snap ring
19 Telescopic adjusting
   screw
20 Nut

21 Snap ring
22 Washer
23 Dust seal
24 Spacer
25 Memory pin ASSY
26 Bolt
27 Bolt
28 Telescopic lever
29 Nut
30 Column pipe CP
31 Pin ASSY
33 Tilt spring
34 Boss
35 Bolt
36 Lock washer
37 Telescopic bush
38 Bearing bush
39 Bearing
40 Telescopic guide
41 Steering shaft CP
42 Snap ring
43 Washer
44 Shaft spring
45 Washer
46 Bearing
47 Bearing bush
48 Housing
49 Pin CP
50 Bearing
51 Clip
52 Stopper
53 Toe board bush
54 Lower cover ASSY
55 Pop-up cable ASSY
56 Dress nut
57 Knob
58 Cap
59 Lower column cover
60 Upper column cover
61 Combination switch
   ASSY
62 Steering wheel ASSY
63 Washer
64 Spring washer
65 Nut
66 Spring washer
67 Pad ASSY
68 Pad
69 Steering sensor
70 Screw ASSY
71 Clip
72 Pad CP (Knee)
73 Washer
74 Spring washer
75 Screw
76 Screw

87978gd3

Fig. 165 Steering wheel and column components — XT

4. Remove the horn pad and harness.
5. Matchmark the steering wheel to the steering shaft.
6. Remove the steering wheel mounting nut and remove the telescoping lever.
7. Using a steering wheel puller, remove the steering wheel.

To install:

8. Install the steering wheel on the steering shaft with the matchmarks in alignment.
9. Install the telescoping lever and tighten the mounting nut to 25 ft. lbs. (34 Nm).
10. Install the horn pad, harness and horn pad mounting screws.
11. Connect the negative battery cable.

Impreza

▶ See Figure 166

✳✳CAUTION

The air bag system must be disarmed before removing the steering wheel. Failure to do so may cause accidental deployment, property damage or personal injury.

1. Turn the ignition switch **OFF**.
2. Disconnect the negative battery cable first and then the positive battery cable. Wait at least 20 seconds before proceeding.

➡**Failure to wait after disconnecting the negative battery cable can result in accidental deployment of the air bag resulting in personal injury and costly repairs.**

3. Remove the covers on both sides of the steering wheel and remove the four Torx® bolts.
4. Disconnect the air bag and horn electrical harnesses from the back of the air bag. Remove the air bag.

✳✳CAUTION

Always carry an air bag assembly, with the bag and trim cover, away from your body. Store the assembly facing upward; never place the assembly face down on any surface.

5. Matchmark the steering wheel to the splines.
6. Remove the steering wheel retaining nut.
7. Using a puller, remove the steering wheel.

To install:

8. Install the steering wheel with the matchmarks in alignment and tighten the nut to 25 ft. lbs. (34 Nm).
9. Connect the electrical connectors to the air bag.
10. Install the air bag and tighten the Torx® screws. Install the covers.
11. Connect the positive battery cable first and then the negative battery cable.

SVX

▶ See Figure 167

✳✳CAUTION

The air bag system must be disarmed before removing the steering wheel. Failure to do so may cause accidental deployment, property damage or personal injury.

1. Disconnect the negative and positive battery cables and let vehicle stand for ten minutes before continuing work.
2. Make sure the ignition switch is off, and has been off for thirty seconds before continuing.
3. Remove the left and right side steering wheel caps from the rear of the steering wheel.
4. Disconnect the air bag system connector at the harness spool.
5. Set the tires in a straight ahead position.

✳✳CAUTION

Always carry an air bag assembly, with the bag and trim cover, away from your body. Store the assembly facing upward; never place the assembly face down on any surface.

6. Remove the screws securing the air bag module assembly.
7. Disconnect the electrical connector from the rear of the module.
8. Disconnect the horn and cruise control wires.
9. Matchmark the steering wheel to the steering shaft.
10. Remove the steering wheel mounting nut.
11. Using a steering wheel puller, remove the steering wheel.

To install:

12. Align the matchmarks and install the steering wheel. Tighten the nut to 25 ft. lbs. (34 Nm)
13. Connect the electrical harnesses to the inflator module.
14. Install the inflator module on the steering wheel and install the mounting screws.
15. Connect the air bag system connector at the harness spool.
16. Install the steering wheel covers.
17. Connect the negative and positive battery cables.

Combination Switch

REMOVAL & INSTALLATION

Justy

1. Disconnect the negative battery cable.
2. Remove the steering wheel.
3. Remove the upper and lower steering column covers.
4. Remove the combination switch mounting screws.
5. Disconnect the electrical harness from the combination switch.
6. Remove the combination switch assembly.

To install:

7. Install the combination switch over the steering shaft.

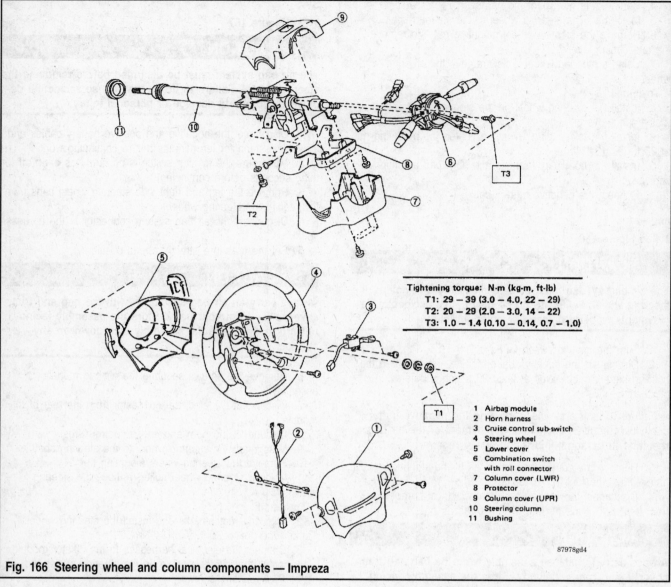

Tightening torque: N·m (kg-m, ft-lb)
T1: 29 — 39 (3.0 — 4.0, 22 — 29)
T2: 20 — 29 (2.0 — 3.0, 14 — 22)
T3: 1.0 — 1.4 (0.10 — 0.14, 0.7 — 1.0)

1 Airbag module
2 Horn harness
3 Cruise control sub-switch
4 Steering wheel
5 Lower cover
6 Combination switch
   with roll connector
7 Column cover (LWR)
8 Protector
9 Column cover (UPR)
10 Steering column
11 Bushing

87978gd4

Fig. 166 Steering wheel and column components — Impreza

8. Install the mounting screws.
9. Connect the electrical connector to the combination switch.
10. Install the upper and lower steering column covers.
11. Install the steering wheel.
12. Connect the negative battery cable.

Sedan, Coupe, Loyale, Wagon and Brat

1. Disconnect the negative battery cable.
2. Remove the steering wheel.
3. Remove the upper and lower steering column covers.
4. Disconnect the electrical harnesses from the combination switch.
5. Remove the three combination switch mounting screws.
6. Remove the combination switch from the steering column.

To install:
7. Install the combination switch on the steering column.
8. Position the switch and install the three mounting screws.
9. Connect the combination switch electrical harness.

10. Install the steering column covers.
11. Install the steering wheel.
12. Connect the negative battery cable.

XT

1. Disconnect the negative battery cable.
2. Remove the mounting screws and remove the lower cover.
3. Remove the screws securing the upper and lower cover together and remove the covers from the steering column.
4. Remove the steering wheel.
5. Remove the clip and band fitting the harness to the steering column and disconnect the combination switch electrical harnesses.
6. Remove the combination switch mounting screws and remove the switch from the control wing bracket.

To install:
7. Position the combination switch on the control wing bracket and install the mounting screws.
8. Connect the electrical connectors and install the clip securing the harness to the steering column.

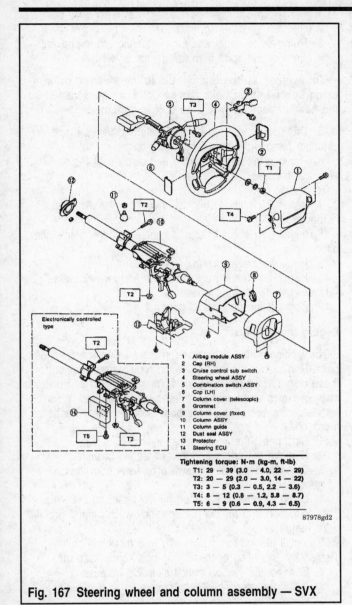

Fig. 167 Steering wheel and column assembly — SVX

1 Airbag module ASSY
2 Cap (RH)
3 Cruise control sub switch
4 Steering wheel ASSY
5 Combination switch ASSY
6 Cap (LH)
7 Column cover (telescopic)
8 Grommet
9 Column cover (fixed)
10 Column ASSY
11 Column guide
12 Dust seal ASSY
13 Protector
14 Steering ECU

Tightening torque: N·m (kg-m, ft-lb)
T1: 29 — 39 (3.0 — 4.0, 22 — 29)
T2: 20 — 29 (2.0 — 3.0, 14 — 22)
T3: 3 — 5 (0.3 — 0.5, 2.2 — 3.6)
T4: 8 — 12 (0.8 — 1.2, 5.8 — 8.7)
T5: 6 — 9 (0.6 — 0.9, 4.3 — 6.5)

87978gd2

9. Install the upper and lower steering column cover and install the connecting screws.
10. Install the lower cover under the steering column.
11. Connect the negative battery cable.

Legacy and Impreza

> **⁕⁕CAUTION**
>
> **The air bag system must be disarmed before removing the steering wheel. Failure to do so may cause accidental deployment, property damage or personal injury.**

WITH AIR BAG

1. Disconnect the negative battery cable.
2. Remove the lower instrument panel.

3. Remove the steering wheel.

> **⁕⁕CAUTION**
>
> **Always carry an air bag assembly, with the bag and trim cover, away from your body. Store the assembly facing upward; never place the assembly face down on any surface.**

4. Disconnect the combination switch electrical harnesses from the body harness connector.
5. Remove the steering column covers.
6. Remove the 2 retaining screws and combination switch.

To install:

7. Ensure the combination switches are OFF and the front wheels are in the straight ahead position.
8. Install the combination switch and tighten the screws.
9. Install the center roll connector.
10. Connect the electrical harnesses.
11. Install the steering column covers.
12. Install the steering wheel.
13. Connect the combination switch electrical connectors.
14. Connect the negative battery cable.

WITHOUT AIR BAG

1. Disconnect the negative battery cable.
2. Remove the steering column covers.
3. Remove the knee protector.
4. Disconnect the combination switch electrical harness and hold-down band.
5. Remove the 2 screws and combination switch.

To install:

6. Route the combination switch electrical harness around the steering system. Connect the electrical harness and install the hold-down.

➡**If equipped with an automatic transaxle, do not place the combination switch over the key interlock release knob.**

7. Position the combination switch and tighten the screws.
8. Install the knee protector and ensure the harness is not caught by adjacent parts.
9. Install the steering column covers.
10. Install the steering wheel.
11. Connect the negative battery cable.

SVX

> **⁕⁕CAUTION**
>
> **The air bag system must be disarmed before removing the steering wheel. Failure to do so may cause accidental deployment, property damage or personal injury.**

1. Disconnect the negative battery cable. If equipped with an air bag, wait at least 10 minutes before doing any work to allow the air bag time to disarm.

2. Remove the steering wheel.

✳✳CAUTION

Always carry an air bag assembly, with the bag and trim cover, away from your body. Store the assembly facing upward; never place the assembly face down on any surface.

3. Remove the upper steering column cover mounting screws and remove the upper and lower halves of the covers.

4. Disconnect the combination switch electrical harness.

5. Remove the switch mounting screws and remove the combination switch.

To install:

6. Position the switch on the steering column and install the mounting screws.

7. Connect the combination switch electrical harness.

8. Install the upper and lower steering column covers and the cover mounting screws.

9. Install the steering wheel. If equipped with an air bag, install the air bag module.

10. Connect the negative battery cable. Check the air bag warning light for proper operation.

Ignition Switch

REMOVAL & INSTALLATION

Justy

1. Disconnect the negative battery cable.
2. Remove the steering wheel.
3. Remove the upper and lower steering column covers.
4. Remove the knob from the hazard switch.

➡**The ignition switch is mounted to the steering column using special shear bolts. These bolts are constructed so the heads shear off when the bolt is tightened.**

5. Drill pilot holes in the shear bolts and using a screw extractor remove the switch mounting bolts.

6. Remove the ignition switch and disconnect the switch electrical harness.

To install:

7. Install the ignition switch and connect the electrical harness.

8. Install new shear bolts and tighten until the heads shear off.

9. Install the hazard knob.
10. Install the steering column upper and lower covers.
11. Install the steering wheel.
12. Connect the negative battery cable.

Sedan, Coupe, Loyale, XT, Wagon and Brat

1. Disconnect the negative battery cable.

2. Remove the steering wheel.
3. Remove the upper and lower steering column covers.
4. Remove the knob from the hazard switch.

➡**The ignition switch is mounted to the steering column using special shear bolts. These bolts are constructed so the heads shear off when the bolt is tightened.**

5. Drill pilot holes in the shear bolts and using a screw extractor remove the switch mounting bolts.

6. Remove the ignition switch and disconnect the switch electrical harness.

To install:

7. Install the ignition switch and connect the electrical harness.

8. Install new shear bolts and tighten until the heads shear off.

9. Install the hazard knob.
10. Install the steering column upper and lower covers.
11. Install the steering wheel.
12. Connect the negative battery cable.

Legacy and Impreza

The ignition switch is mounted in place using special shear bolts. Removal of the ignition switch requires replacement of these bolts. When removing the bolts it is easiest if you use a suitable punch and hammer to tap the bolts around. When installing new bolts tighten the bolts until the shear heads break off.

1. Disconnect the negative battery cable.
2. Remove the upper and lower steering column covers.
3. Disconnect the ignition switch harness from the body harness.

4. Using a drift and hammer, hit the heads of the shear bolts to loosen and remove the ignition switch mounting bolts.

To install:

5. Install the ignition switch with new mounting bolts. Tighten the mounting bolts until the bolt heads snap off.

6. Connect the ignition switch electrical harness.
7. Install the steering column covers.
8. Connect the negative battery cable.

SVX

1. Disconnect the negative battery cable.
2. Remove the upper steering column cover mounting screws and remove the upper and lower halves of the covers.

3. Disconnect the ignition switch electrical harness.

4. Remove the switch mounting screws and remove the ignition switch.

To install:

5. Position the switch on the steering column and install the mounting screws.

6. Connect the switch electrical connector.

7. Install the upper and lower steering column covers and the cover mounting screws.

8. Connect the negative battery cable.

Steering Column

REMOVAL & INSTALLATION

Justy

▶ **See Figures 168, 169, 170 and 171**

1. Disconnect the negative battery cable.
2. Remove the trim panel under the steering wheel.
3. Remove the universal joint cover.
4. Remove the universal joint.
5. Disconnect the electrical harnesses for the ignition switch and combination switch.
6. Remove the nuts securing the bracket under the steering column.
7. Disconnect the steering shaft from the rack and pinion assembly and remove the steering column assembly.

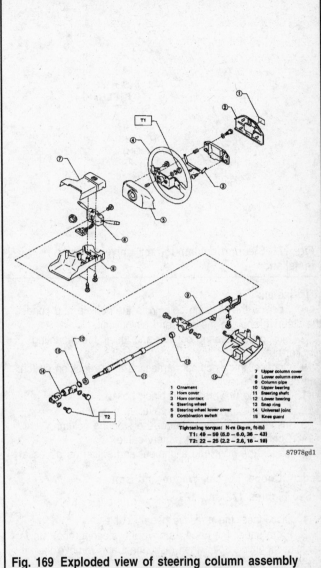

Fig. 169 Exploded view of steering column assembly

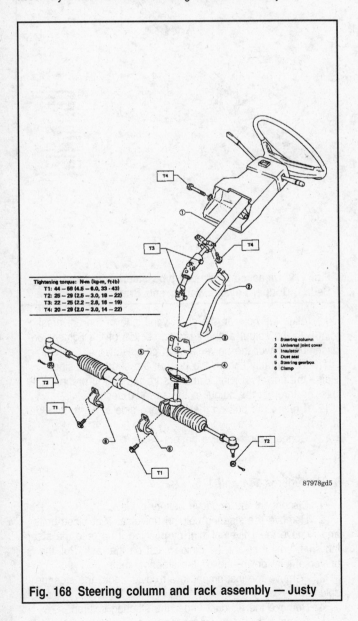

Fig. 168 Steering column and rack assembly — Justy

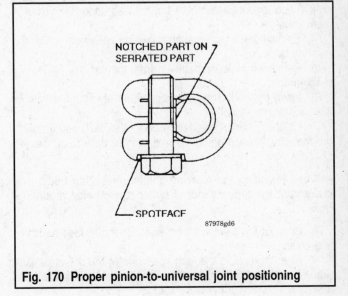

Fig. 170 Proper pinion-to-universal joint positioning

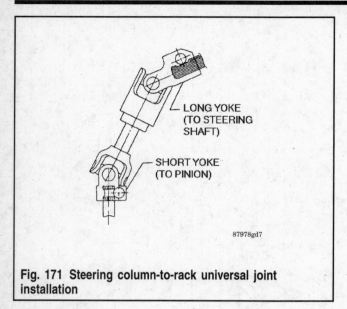

Fig. 171 Steering column-to-rack universal joint installation

To install:

8. Position the steering column in the vehicle and connect the steering shaft to the rack and pinion unit.

9. Lift up the steering column and install the mounting bracket nuts.

10. Connect the electrical harnesses to the ignition switch and combination switch.

11. Install the universal joint pinch bolts.

12. Install the universal joint cover.

13. Install the trim panel under the steering column.

14. Connect the negative battery cable.

15. Check the front end alignment and adjust as necessary.

Sedan, Coupe, Loyale, Wagon and Brat

▶ See Figures 172 and 173

1. Disconnect the negative battery cable.

2. From under the hood, remove the steering shaft universal joint mounting bolts, then disconnect and remove the universal joint from the steering shaft.

3. Disconnect the electrical harnesses from the combination switch, and ignition switch from the harness under the instrument panel.

4. Remove the steering shaft mounting bolts from under the steering column.

5. Remove the steering column from the vehicle.

To install:

6. Insert the end of the steering column through the hole in the floor pan grommet.

7. Lift the column into position under the dash and install the mounting bolts. Tighten the mounting bolts to 22 ft. lbs. (29 Nm).

➡**When installing the steering column mounting bolts, make sure the ground wire is under the left side mounting bolt.**

8. Connect the electrical harnesses for the ignition switch and combination switch.

9. Align the hole in the long yoke side of the universal joint with the cutout at the serrated section of the steering shaft assembly end, install the universal joint.

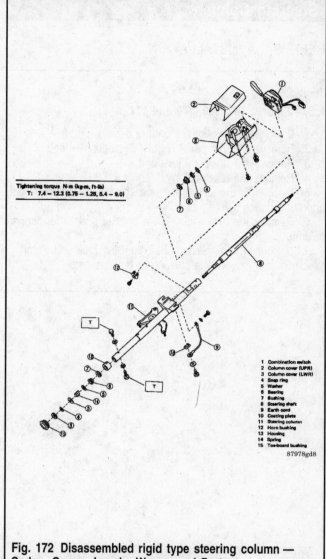

Fig. 172 Disassembled rigid type steering column — Sedan, Coupe, Loyale, Wagon and Brat

10. Align the hole on the short yoke side of the universal joint with the cutout at the serrated section of the tighten rod assembly. Lower the universal joint completely.

11. Temporarily tighten the bolt on the short yoke side. Raise the universal joint to make sure the bolt is properly passing through the cutout in the serrated section.

12. Tighten the bolt on the long yoke side to 17 ft. lbs. (24 ft. lbs).

13. Connect the negative battery cable.

XT

▶ See Figures 174 and 175

1. Disconnect the negative battery cable.

2. Remove the steering column universal joint pinch bolts and remove the universal joint by pushing it up onto the steering shaft until it clears the pinion shaft on the rack. Pull the universal joint down and off the steering shaft.

3. Remove the instrument lower cover under the steering column.

4. Remove the air duct under the steering column.

5. Remove the protector by removing the screw and clip.

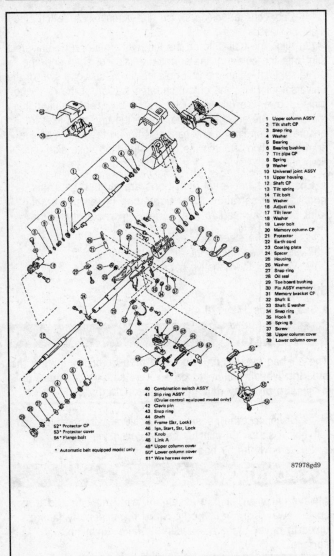

1	Upper column ASSY
2	Tilt shaft CP
3	Snap ring
4	Washer
5	Bearing
6	Bearing bushing
7	Tilt pipe CP
8	Spring
9	Washer
10	Universal joint ASSY
11	Upper housing
12	Shaft CP
13	Tilt spring
14	Tilt bolt
15	Washer
16	Adjust nut
17	Tilt lever
18	Lever bolt
19	Memory column CP
20	Protector
21	Earth cord
22	Coating plate
23	Spacer
24	Housing
25	Washer
26	Snap ring
27	Oil seal
28	Toe board bushing
29	Pin ASSY memory
30	Memory bracket CP
31	Shaft E
32	Shaft E washer
33	Snap ring
34	Hook 9
35	Spring B
36	Screw
37	Upper column cover
38	Lower column cover
40	Combination switch ASSY
41	Slip ring ASSY (Cruise control equipped model only)
42	Clevis pin
43	Snap ring
44	Shaft
45	Frame (Str, Lock)
46	Ign, Start, Str, Lock
47	Knob
48	Link A
49*	Upper column cover
50*	Lower column cover
51*	Wire harness cover
52*	Protector CP
53*	Protector cover
54*	Flange bolt
	* Automatic belt equipped model only

87978gd9

**Fig. 173 Disassembled tilt type steering column —
Sedan, Coupe, Loyale, Wagon, and Brat**

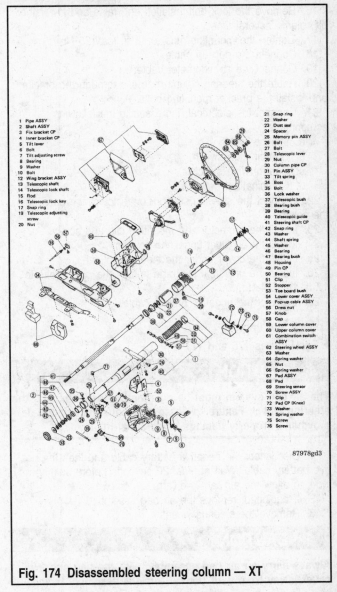

1	Pipe ASSY	21	Snap ring
2	Shaft ASSY	22	Washer
3	Fix bracket CP	23	Dust seal
4	Inner bracket CP	24	Spacer
5	Tilt lever	25	Memory pin ASSY
6	Bolt	26	Bolt
7	Tilt adjusting screw	27	Bolt
8	Bearing	28	Telescopic lever
9	Washer	29	Nut
10	Bolt	30	Column pipe CP
11	Wing bracket ASSY	31	Pin ASSY
12	Telescopic shaft	32	Tilt spring
13	Telescopic lock shaft	33	Boss
14	Rod	34	Bolt
15	Telescopic lock key	35	Lock washer
16	Snap ring	37	Telescopic bolt
17	Telescopic adjusting screw	38	Bearing bush
18		39	Bearing
19		40	Telescopic guide
20	Nut	41	Steering shaft CP
		42	Snap ring
		43	Washer
		44	Shaft spring
		45	Washer
		46	Bearing
		47	Bearing bush
		48	Housing
		49	Pin CP
		50	Bearing
		51	Clip
		52	Stopper
		53	Toe board bush
		54	Lower cover ASSY
		55	Pop-up cable ASSY
		56	Dress nut
		57	Knob
		58	Cap
		59	Lower column cover
		60	Upper column cover
		61	Combination switch ASSY
		62	Steering wheel ASSY
		63	Washer
		64	Spring washer
		65	Nut
		66	Spring washer
		67	Pad ASSY
		68	Pad
		69	Steering sensor
		70	Screw ASSY
		71	Clip
		72	Pad CP (Knee)
		73	Washer
		74	Spring washer
		75	Screw
		76	Screw

87978gd3

Fig. 174 Disassembled steering column — XT

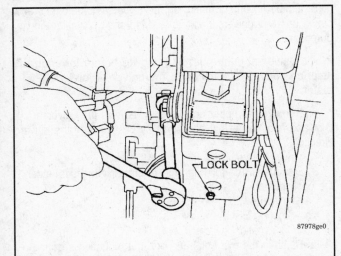

LOCK BOLT

87978ge0

**Fig. 175 Removing the steering column-to-dash panel
retainer bolts**

6. Disconnect the steering sensor wiring at the base of the column.

7. Disconnect the electrical harnesses from the following components:

   a. Ignition switch

   b. Combination switch

   c. Control wing switch

   d. Combination meter

8. Remove the screws securing the under column harness bracket.

9. Disconnect the speedometer cable.

10. Extend the steering column, remove the cable and compress the steering column and lock it there.

11. Install a lock bolt from below the steering column bracket.

12. Remove the steering column mounting bolts.

13. Remove the steering column from the vehicle.

To install:

14. Position the steering column in the vehicle with the end of the steering shaft through the opening in the floor.

15. Install, but DO NOT tighten the column mounting bolts.

16. Remove the lock bolt installed and raise and lower the tilt column several times.

17. Tighten the mounting nuts to 18 ft. lbs. (25 Nm).

18. Connect the pop up cable.

19. Connect the speedometer cable.

20. Route the steering column harness through the bracket and install the bracket mounting bolts.

21. Connect the electrical harnesses to the following components:
    a. Ignition switch
    b. Combination switch
    c. Control wing switch
    d. Combination meter

22. Connect the steering sensor connector at the base of the column.

23. Install the protector and mounting clip and screw.

24. Install the air duct under the column.

25. Install the cover under the steering column.

26. Install the universal joint and tighten the pinch bolts to 17 ft. lbs. (24 Nm).

27. Connect the negative battery cable.

Legacy and Impreza

▶ **See Figures 176 and 177**

✳✳CAUTION

The air bag system must be disarmed before removing the steering wheel. Failure to do so may cause accidental deployment, property damage or personal injury.

1. Disconnect the negative battery cable and then the positive battery cable. Wait at least 20 seconds before starting any work to allow the air bag to disarm.

2. If equipped, remove the air bag assembly.

3. Remove the steering wheel.

✳✳CAUTION

Always carry an air bag assembly, with the bag and trim cover, away from your body. Store the assembly facing upward; never place the assembly face down on any surface.

4. Raise and support the vehicle safely on jackstands.

5. Matchmark the universal joint to the splines for installation reference.

6. Remove the universal joint bolts and remove the universal joint.

7. Lower the vehicle.

8. Remove the lower drivers side instrument panel facing.

9. Disconnect the ignition switch and combination switch electrical harnesses from the main harness.

10. Remove the two steering column retaining bolts.

11. Pull the steering shaft assembly from the hole in the toe board.

To install:

12. Insert the steering shaft into the toe board grommet.

13. Install the steering column retaining bolts and tighten them to 18 ft. lbs. (25 Nm).

14. Connect the ignition switch and combination switch electrical harnesses.

15. Align the bolt hole on the long yoke side of the universal joint with the cutout at the serrated section of shaft end and universal joint. Align the bolt hole on the short yoke side of the universal joint with the cutout serrated section of the rack and pinion. Lower the universal joint completely. Temporarily tighten the bolt on the short yoke side. Raise the universal joint to ensure the bolt is properly passing through the cutout on the serrated section. Tighten the bolt on the long yoke side and then short yoke side to 17 ft. lbs. (24 Nm).

➡**Ensure the universal joint bolts are aligned with the notch in the serration. Over tightening of the universal joint bolts may lead to heavy steering wheel operation.**

16. Install the steering wheel.

17. If removed, install the air bag assembly.

18. Connect the negative battery cable.

SVX

▶ **See Figures 178, 179 and 180**

✳✳CAUTION

The air bag system must be disarmed before removing the steering wheel. Failure to do so may cause accidental deployment, property damage or personal injury.

1. Disconnect the negative and positive battery cables and let vehicle sit for ten minutes before continuing work.

2. Remove the air bag module.

✳✳CAUTION

Always carry an air bag assembly, with the bag and trim cover, away from your body. Store the assembly facing upward; never place the assembly face down on any surface.

3. Remove the steering wheel.

4. Raise and safely support the vehicle on jackstands.

5. Scribe alignment marks on the universal joint-to-rack and pinion unit and universal joint-to-steering shaft for installation purposes.

➡**The universal joint must be removed before lowering the steering column or damage to the universal joint will result.**

6. Remove the upper and lower bolts from the universal joint and remove the universal joint by pushing it in the upward direction.

7. Lower the vehicle.

8. Disconnect the following the electrical harnesses under the dash board:
    a. Ignition switch
    b. Steering ECU
    c. Combination switch

9. Remove the two bolts and one nut mounting securing the steering column to the instrument panel brace.

10. Lower the steering column slightly and pull the column out of the hole in the floor board.

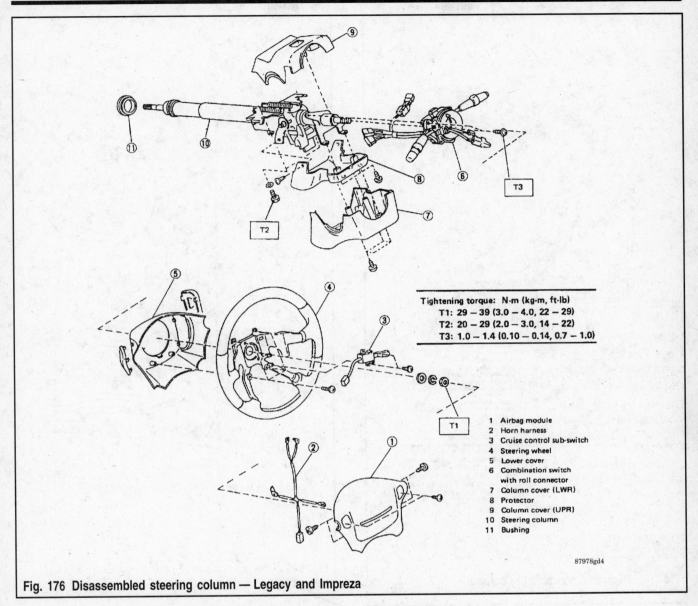

Tightening torque: N·m (kg-m, ft-lb)
T1: 29 — 39 (3.0 — 4.0, 22 — 29)
T2: 20 — 29 (2.0 — 3.0, 14 — 22)
T3: 1.0 — 1.4 (0.10 — 0.14, 0.7 — 1.0)

1 Airbag module
2 Horn harness
3 Cruise control sub-switch
4 Steering wheel
5 Lower cover
6 Combination switch
   with roll connector
7 Column cover (LWR)
8 Protector
9 Column cover (UPR)
10 Steering column
11 Bushing

87978gd4

Fig. 176 Disassembled steering column — Legacy and Impreza

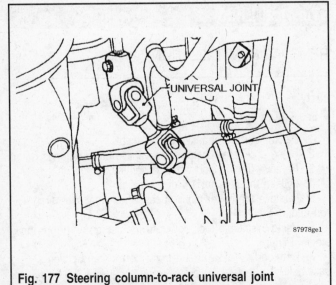

UNIVERSAL JOINT

87978ge1

Fig. 177 Steering column-to-rack universal joint

To install:

11. Install the steering column into the vehicle so the base of the steering shaft passes through the hole in the floor board.

12. Install the mounting bolts and nut and tighten to 18 ft. lbs. (25 Nm).

13. Connect the following the electrical harnesses under the dashboard:
    a. Ignition switch
    b. Steering ECU
    c. Combination switch

14. Raise and safely support the vehicle.

15. Install the universal joint with the matchmarks in alignment. Install it on the steering shaft then pulling it down onto the rack and pinion unit.

16. Install the universal joint pinch bolts and tighten to 18 ft. lbs. (25 Nm).

17. Lower the vehicle.

18. Install the steering wheel and the air bag module.

19. Connect the negative and positive battery cables.

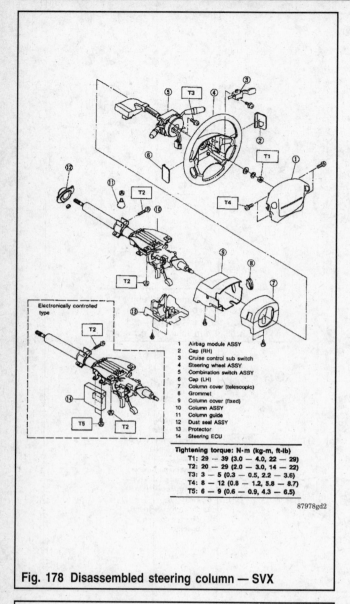

1	Airbag module ASSY
2	Cap (RH)
3	Cruise control sub switch
4	Steering wheel ASSY
5	Combination switch ASSY
6	Cap (LH)
7	Column cover (telescopic)
8	Grommet
9	Column cover (fixed)
10	Column ASSY
11	Column guide
12	Dust seal ASSY
13	Protector
14	Steering ECU

Tightening torque: N·m (kg-m, ft-lb)
T1: 29 — 39 (3.0 — 4.0, 22 — 29)
T2: 20 — 29 (2.0 — 3.0, 14 — 22)
T3: 3 — 5 (0.3 — 0.5, 2.2 — 3.6)
T4: 8 — 12 (0.8 — 1.2, 5.8 — 8.7)
T5: 6 — 9 (0.6 — 0.9, 4.3 — 6.5)

87978gd2

Fig. 178 Disassembled steering column — SVX

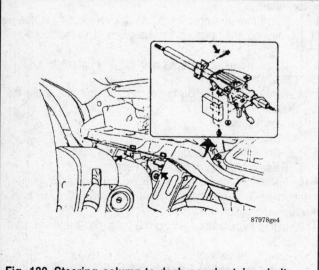

87978ge4

Fig. 180 Steering column-to-dash panel retainer bolts

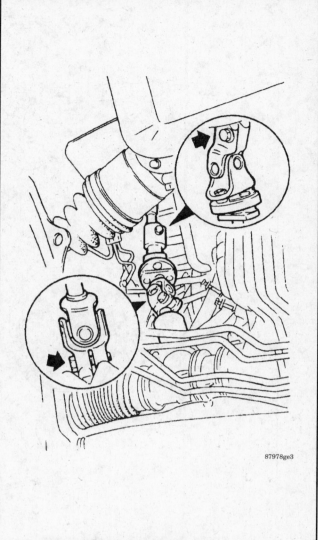

87978ge3

Fig. 179 Steering column-to-rack universal joint connection

Tie Rod Ends

REMOVAL & INSTALLATION

Justy

▶ See Figure 181

1. Disconnect the negative battery cable.
2. Raise and safely support the vehicle on jackstands.
3. Remove the tire and wheel assembly.
4. Loosen the jam nut 1/4 of a turn.
5. Remove the cotter pin and castle nut from the outer tie rod end.
6. Using a suitable tool, separate the tie rod end from the steering knuckle.
7. Unthread the tie rod end from the rack and pinion assembly.

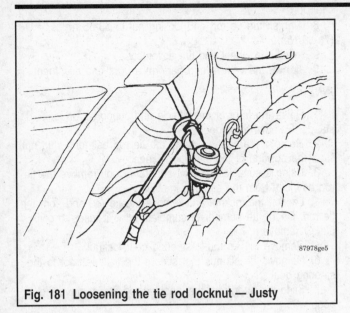

Fig. 181 Loosening the tie rod locknut — Justy

To install:

8. Thread the tie rod end onto the rack and pinion assembly until it is up against the jam nut.

9. Install the tie rod stud through the steering knuckle and install the castle nut. Tighten the castle nut to 20 ft. lbs. (27 Nm).

10. Install a new cotter pin.

11. Install the tire and wheel assembly.

12. Lower the vehicle.

13. Connect the negative battery cable.

14. Check the front end alignment and adjust as necessary.

Sedan, Coupe, Loyale, XT, Wagon and Brat

▶ **See Figure 182**

1. Disconnect the negative battery cable.

2. Raise and safely support the vehicle on jackstands.

3. Remove the front tire and wheel assembly.

4. Remove the cotter pin from the outer tire rod end.

5. Remove the castle nut.

6. Loosen the jam nut from the inner tie rod end to outer tie rod end. Only back the nut off about an 1/8 of a turn.

7. Separate the outer tie rod end from the steering knuckle using suitable tool.

8. Unthread the outer tie rod end from the inner tie rod. Leave the jam nut in place as a reference for installation.

To install:

9. Thread the tie rod end onto the inner tie rod until it contacts the jam nut.

10. Connect the outer tie rod end to the steering knuckle and install the castle nut.

11. Tighten the castle nut to 22 ft. lbs. (29 Nm). Install a new cotter pin.

12. Install the tire and wheel assembly.

13. Lower the vehicle.

14. Check and adjust the alignment. Tighten the jam nut to 22 ft. lbs. (29 Nm).

Legacy and Impreza

OUTER

▶ **See Figures 183, 184, 185 and 186**

1. Raise the front of the vehicle and support it on jackstands. Remove the wheel.

2. Remove the cotter pin and the tie rod ball joint stud nut. Note the position of the steering linkage.

3. Using a suitable ball joint separator tool, remove the tie rod ball joint from the steering knuckle.

4. Loosen the locknut and remove the tie rod end from the tie rod. Count the number of complete turns it takes to completely remove it.

To install:

5. Install the new tie rod end, turning it in exactly as many turns as it was to remove the old one. Make sure it is correctly positioned in relationship to the steering linkage.

6. Connect the outer tie rod end-to-steering knuckle and install the castle nut. Tighten the nut to 18-22 ft. lbs. (25-29 Nm.).

➡ **If the cotter pin holes do not line up never loosen the nut to install the pin. The nut can be tightened up to 60 degrees additional rotation to line up the cotter pin holes.**

7. Install a new cotter pin to the castle nut.

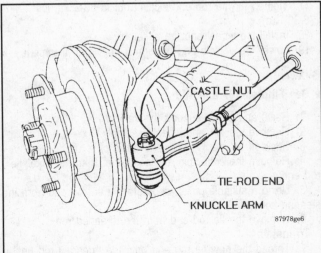

Fig. 182 Tie rod connected to the steering knuckle assembly — Sedan, Coupe, Loyale, XT, Wagon and Brat

Fig. 183 Loosen the tie rod locknut — Legacy

Fig. 184 Remove the cotter pin from the castle nut

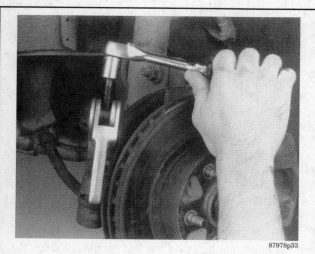

Fig. 185 Using a tie rod tool to separate the tie rod from the steering knuckle

Fig. 186 While counting the turns, remove the tie rod end

8. Tighten the tie rod end locking nut to 58-65 ft. lbs. (78-88 Nm).

9. Install the wheel and tire assembly.

10. Lower the vehicle and perform a front end alignment.

INNER

1. Raise the front of the vehicle and support it on jackstands. Remove the wheel.

2. Remove the cotter pin and the tie rod ball joint stud nut. Note the position of the steering linkage.

3. Using a suitable ball joint separator tool, remove the tie rod ball joint from the steering knuckle.

4. Loosen the locknut and remove the tie rod end from the tie rod. Count the number of complete turns it takes to completely remove it.

5. Remove the tie rod-to-steering gear locknut.

6. Remove the clamps that secure the flexible boot to the steering gear.

7. Slide the boot from the inner tie rod and remove the boot.

8. Bend the lock plate tabs from the inner tie rod end nut.

9. Loosen the inner tie rod end nut from the steering gear and remove the inner tie rod end.

To install:

10. Using a new lock plate, install the inner tie rod end and tighten the tie rod to 51-65 ft. lbs. (69-88 Nm).

11. Bend the tabs of the new lock plate to secure the inner tie rod end.

12. Slide the boot onto the steering gear and secure it with new clamps.

13. Install the outer tie rod-to-steering gear locknut.

14. Install the outer tie rod end, turning it in exactly as many turns as it was to remove the old one. Make sure it is correctly positioned in relationship to the steering linkage.

15. Connect the outer tie rod end-to-steering knuckle and install the castle nut. Tighten the nut to 18-22 ft. lbs. (25-29 Nm.).

➡ **If the cotter pin holes do not line up never loosen the nut to install the pin. The nut can be tightened up to 60 degrees additional rotation to line up the cotter pin holes.**

16. Install a new cotter pin to the castle nut.

17. Tighten the tie rod end locking nut to 58-65 ft. lbs. (78-88 Nm).

18. Install the wheel and tire assembly.

19. Lower the vehicle and perform a front end alignment.

SVX

▶ **See Figures 187 and 188**

1. Raise and safely support the vehicle.

2. Remove the tire and wheel assembly.

3. Back off the tie rod end jam nut ¼ of a turn.

4. Remove the cotter pin and castle nut from the outer tie rod end.

5. Using a suitable puller, separate the tie rod end from the steering knuckle.

6. Remove the tie rod end from the threaded rod.

To install:

7. Thread the new tie rod end onto the threaded rod until it contacts the jam nut.

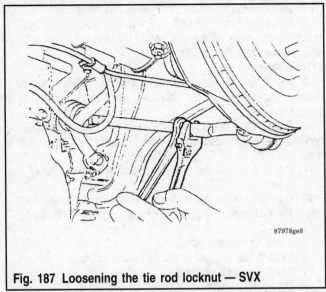

Fig. 187 Loosening the tie rod locknut — SVX

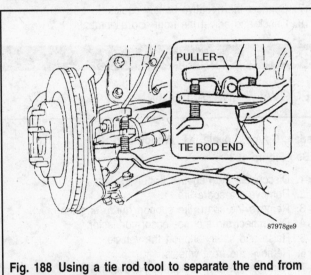

Fig. 188 Using a tie rod tool to separate the end from the steering knuckle

8. Insert the tie rod end ball stud into the steering knuckle and install the castle nut. Tighten the castle nut to 29 ft. lbs. (39 Nm). Install a new cotter pin.

9. Tighten the jam nut to 62 ft. lbs. (83 Nm).

10. Install the tire and wheel assembly.

11. Lower the vehicle.

12. Check the front end alignment and adjust as necessary.

Manual Steering Gear

REMOVAL & INSTALLATION

Justy

▶ **See Figures 189, 190 and 191**

1. Disconnect the negative battery cable.
2. Raise and safely support the vehicle.
3. Remove the tire and wheel assembly.

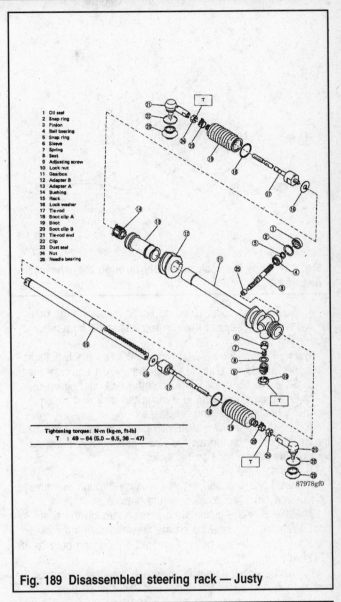

1 Oil seal
2 Snap ring
3 Pinion
4 Ball bearing
5 Snap ring
6 Sleeve
7 Spring
8 Seat
9 Adjusting screw
10 Lock nut
11 Gearbox
12 Adapter B
13 Adapter A
14 Bushing
15 Rack
16 Lock washer
17 Tie-rod
18 Boot clip A
19 Boot
20 Boot clip B
21 Tie-rod end
22 Clip
23 Dust seal
24 Nut
25 Needle bearing

Tightening torque: N·m (kg-m, ft-lb)
T : 49 — 64 (5.0 — 6.5, 36 — 47)

Fig. 189 Disassembled steering rack — Justy

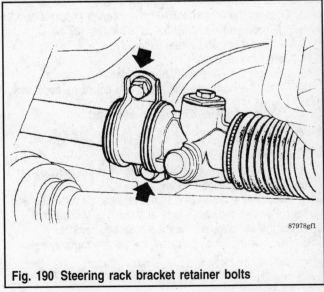

Fig. 190 Steering rack bracket retainer bolts

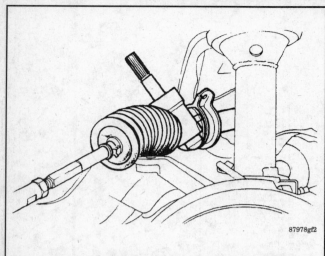

87978gf2

Fig. 191 Slide the rack assembly through the wheelwell opening

4. Remove the cotter pins and castle nuts from the outer tie rod ends and separate the tie rod ball studs from the steering knuckles.

5. From inside the vehicle, remove the two pinch bolts at the upper and lower ends of the steering shaft universal joints.

6. Slide the universal joint up off the rack and pinion unit.

7. From under the vehicle remove the rack and pinion mounting bracket bolts and brackets.

8. Pull the rack down slightly to clear the pinion shaft past the dust boot. Once the rack is clear, pull the assembly out through the drivers side tie rod hole.

To install:

9. Install the rack and pinion assembly through the driver's side tie rod hole and position on the firewall.

10. Make sure the pinion shaft passes through the dust boot. With the rack situated on the firewall install the rack mounting brackets and bolts. Tighten the mounting bolts to 48 ft. lbs. (67 Nm).

11. From inside the vehicle, slide the universal joint over the pinion shaft and install the upper and lower pinch bolts. Tighten the pinch bolts to 17 ft. lbs. (23 Nm).

12. Connect the tie rod ends to the steering knuckles and install the castle nuts and tighten to 20 ft. lbs. (27 Nm).

13. Install the tire and wheel assembly.

14. Lower the vehicle.

15. Connect the negative battery cable.

16. Check the front end alignment and adjust as necessary.

Sedan, Coupe, Loyale, XT, Wagon and Brat

▶ See Figure 192

1. Disconnect the negative battery cable.

2. Raise and safely support the vehicle on jackstands.

3. Remove the front wheels.

4. Remove the cotter pins from the outer tie rod ends and discard. Remove the castle nuts and using a suitable tool separate the tie rod ends from the steering knuckles.

5. Remove the pinch bolt from the tighten rod universal joint.

6. Loosen the exhaust manifold mounting nuts and lower the front exhaust pipe.

7. Remove the four rack and pinion mounting bolts.

8. Move the gear box toward the pinion side. When the pinion shaft comes off the rod, rotate the gearbox rearward and remove from the vehicle.

To install:

9. Install the rack and pinion unit from the drivers side and move it into position so the universal joint can be connected to the pinion shaft.

10. Position the rack and pinion unit on the crossmember and install the four mounting bolts and brackets. Tighten the mounting bolts to 44 ft. lbs. (59 Nm).

11. Install the universal joint pinch bolt and tighten to 17 ft. lbs. (24 Nm).

12. Connect the tie rod ends to the steering knuckles and install the castle nuts. Tighten the castle nuts to 20 ft. lbs. (27 Nm).

13. Install new cotter pins.

14. Tighten the exhaust manifold mounting bolts.

15. Install the front wheels.

16. Lower the vehicle.

17. Connect the negative battery cable.

18. Check and adjust the front end alignment.

Power Steering Gear

REMOVAL & INSTALLATION

Sedan, Coupe, Loyale, XT, Wagon and Brat

▶ See Figure 193

1. Disconnect the negative battery cable.

2. Remove the spare tire.

3. Remove the spare tire support (turbo engines only).

4. Disconnect the thermo-sensor connector.

5. Raise and safely support the vehicle.

6. Remove the front wheels.

7. Remove the front exhaust pipe assembly.

8. Remove the cotter pins and castle nuts from the outer tie rod ends. Using a suitable puller disconnect the tie rod ends from the steering knuckles.

9. Remove the jack up plate.

10. Disconnect the pipe joint at the center of the rack and connect a vinyl hose to the pipe and joint. Turn the wheel side to side to push the fluid out of the rack. Repeat the same procedure on the second line.

11. Remove the lower universal joint pinch bolt then remove the upper bolt and push the universal joint upward.

12. Remove the remaining two lines from the rack and pinion unit.

13. Remove the rack and pinion mounting bolts and remove the rack and pinion assembly.

To install:

14. Install the rack and pinion unit in the vehicle and position on the crossmember and install the mounting brackets and mounting bolts. Tighten the mounting bolts to 44 ft. lbs. (59 Nm).

15. Connect the power steering lines to the rack and pinion unit. tighten the fittings to 10 ft. lbs. (14 Nm).

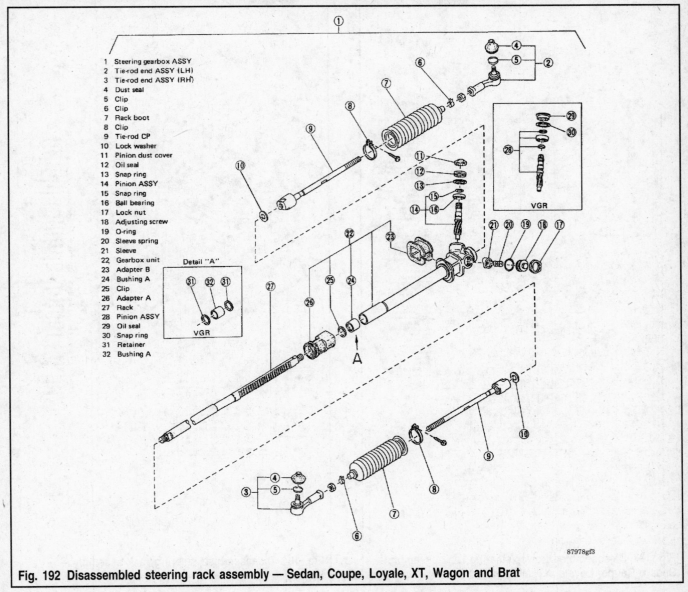

1 Steering gearbox ASSY
2 Tie-rod end ASSY (LH)
3 Tie-rod end ASSY (RH)
4 Dust seal
5 Clip
6 Clip
7 Rack boot
8 Clip
9 Tie-rod CP
10 Lock washer
11 Pinion dust cover
12 Oil seal
13 Snap ring
14 Pinion ASSY
15 Snap ring
16 Ball bearing
17 Lock nut
18 Adjusting screw
19 O-ring
20 Sleeve spring
21 Sleeve
22 Gearbox unit
23 Adapter B
24 Bushing A
25 Clip
26 Adapter A
27 Rack
28 Pinion ASSY
29 Oil seal
30 Snap ring
31 Retainer
32 Bushing A

Detail "A"

VGR

VGR

A

87978gf3

Fig. 192 Disassembled steering rack assembly — Sedan, Coupe, Loyale, XT, Wagon and Brat

16. Install the universal joint as follows:

a. Align the bolt hole of the long yoke with the notch in the serration the column assembly. Push the joint on completely.

b. Align the bolt hole of the short yoke with the notch in the input shaft serration of the gearbox. Lower the joint fully.

c. Install the bolt on the short yoke and raise the joint. Then check that the bolt is installed correctly in the serration notch.

d. Tighten the long yoke bolt to 17 ft. lbs. (24 Nm).

17. Connect the tie rod ends to the steering knuckles and install the castle nuts and tighten to 20 ft. lbs. (27 Nm).

18. Install new cotter pins.

19. Install the front exhaust pipe.

20. Install the front wheels.

21. Lower the vehicle.

22. Connect the thermo sensor connector.

23. Connect the negative battery cable.

24. Refill the power steering system and start the vehicle and check for leaks.

25. Raise the vehicle and install the jack up plate.

26. Lower the vehicle.

27. Install the spare tire bracket, if removed.

28. Install the spare tire.

29. Check the fluid and top off as necessary.

Legacy

▶ **See Figures 194, 195, 196, 197 and 198**

1. Disconnect the negative battery cable.

2. Raise and support the vehicle safely.

3. Remove the front tire and wheel assemblies.

4. Disconnect the electrical connector from the oxygen sensor. Remove the front exhaust pipe assembly.

5. Remove the tie rod end cotter pin and loosen the castle nut. Using a ball joint puller, separate the tie rod ends from the steering knuckle arm.

6. Remove the jack up plate and the front stabilizer bar.

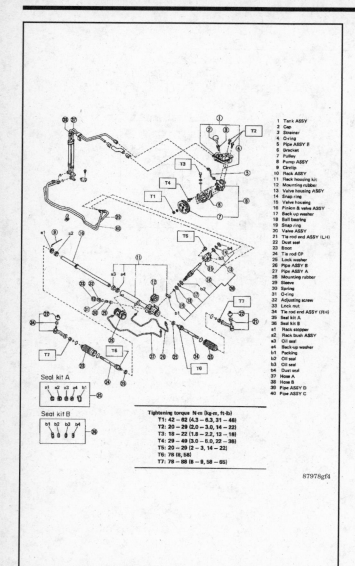

Tightening torque: N·m (kg·m, ft-lb)
T1: 42 – 62 (4.3 – 6.3, 31 – 46)
T2: 20 – 29 (2.0 – 3.0, 14 – 22)
T3: 18 – 22 (1.8 – 2.2, 13 – 18)
T4: 29 – 49 (3.0 – 5.0, 22 – 38)
T5: 20 – 29 (2 – 3, 14 – 22)
T6: 78 (8, 58)
T7: 78 – 88 (8 – 9, 58 – 65)

1 Tank ASSY
2 Cap
3 Strainer
4 O-ring
5 Pipe ASSY E
6 Bracket
7 Pulley
8 Pump ASSY
9 Circlip
10 Rack ASSY
11 Rack housing kit
12 Mounting rubber
13 Valve housing ASSY
14 Snap ring
15 Valve housing
16 Pinion & valve ASSY
17 Back up washer
18 Ball bearing
19 Snap ring
20 Valve ring
21 Tie rod end ASSY (LH)
22 Dust seal
23 Boot
24 Tie rod CP
25 Lock washer
26 Pipe ASSY B
27 Pipe ASSY A
28 Mounting rubber
29 Sleeve
30 Spring
31 O-ring
32 Adjusting screw
33 Lock nut
34 Tie rod end ASSY (RH)
35 Seal kit A
36 Seal kit B
a1 Rack stopper
a2 Rack bush ASSY
a3 Oil seal
a4 Back-up washer
b1 Packing
b2 Oil seal
b3 Oil seal
b4 Dust seal
37 Hose A
38 Hose B
39 Pipe ASSY D
40 Pipe ASSY C

87978gf4

Fig. 193 Disassembled power steering rack assembly — Sedan, Coupe, Loyale, XT, Wagon and Brat

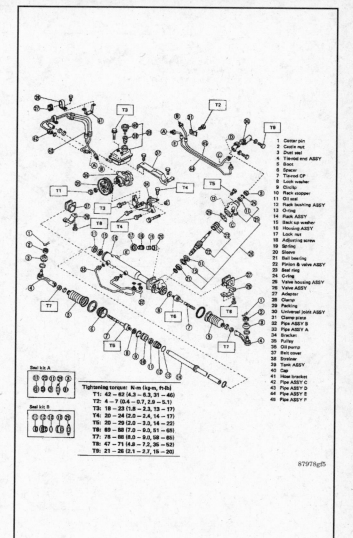

Tightening torque: N·m (kg·m, ft-lb)
T1: 42 – 62 (4.3 – 6.3, 31 – 46)
T2: 4 – 7 (0.4 – 0.7, 2.9 – 5.1)
T3: 18 – 23 (1.8 – 2.3, 13 – 17)
T4: 20 – 24 (2.0 – 2.4, 14 – 17)
T5: 20 – 29 (2.0 – 3.0, 14 – 22)
T6: 69 – 88 (7.0 – 9.0, 51 – 65)
T7: 78 – 88 (8.0 – 9.0, 58 – 65)
T8: 47 – 71 (4.8 – 7.2, 35 – 52)
T9: 21 – 26 (2.1 – 2.7, 15 – 20)

1 Cotter pin
2 Castle nut
3 Dust seal
4 Tie-rod end ASSY
5 Boot
6 Spacer
7 Tie-rod CP
8 Lock washer
9 Circlip
10 Rack stopper
11 Oil seal
12 Rack bushing ASSY
13 O-ring
14 Rack
15 Back up washer
16 Housing ASSY
17 Lock nut
18 Adjusting screw
19 Spring
20 Sleeve
21 Ball bearing
22 Pinion & valve ASSY
23 Seal ring
24 C-ring
25 Valve housing ASSY
26 Valve ASSY
27 Adapter
28 Clamp
29 Packing
30 Universal joint ASSY
31 Clamp plate
32 Pipe ASSY B
33 Pipe ASSY A
34 Bracket
35 Pulley
36 Oil pump
37 Belt cover
38 Strainer
39 Tank ASSY
40 Cap
41 Hose bracket
42 Pipe ASSY C
43 Pipe ASSY D
44 Pipe ASSY E
45 Pipe ASSY F

87978gf5

Fig. 194 Disassembled steering rack assembly — Legacy

87978p35

Fig. 195 Loosening the steering column-to-rack pinch bolt — Legacy

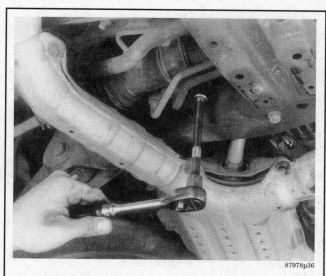

87978p36

Fig. 196 Removing the steering rack retainer bolts

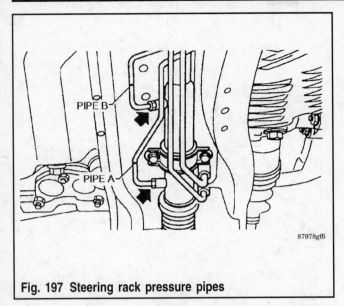

Fig. 197 Steering rack pressure pipes

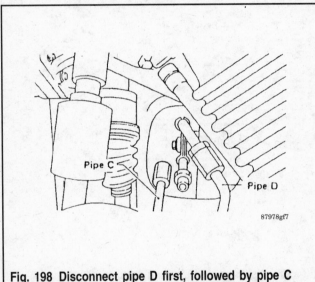

Fig. 198 Disconnect pipe D first, followed by pipe C

7. From the power steering rack, remove the center pressure pipe, connect a vinyl hose to the pipe and joint, then turn the steering wheel to discharge the fluid into a container.

➡**When discharging the power steering fluid (line A and B), turn the steering wheel fully, left and right. Be sure to disconnect the other pipe and drain the fluid in the same manner.**

8. From the control valve of the gearbox assembly, remove the power steering **C** and **D** pressure pipes. Remove pipe **D** first and pipe **C** second.

9. If not disconnected when draining the fluid from the control valve of the gearbox assembly, remove the power steering **A** and **B** pressure pipes. Remove pipe **A** first and pipe **B** second.

10. Remove the power steering gearbox to crossmember assembly bolts. Remove the gearbox assembly from the vehicle.

To install:

11. Install the power steering rack and tighten the rack to crossmember bolts to 35-52 ft. lbs. (47-70 Nm). When install-

ing the universal joint assembly, be sure to align the matchmarks.

12. Tighten the power steering pressure pipes 7-12 ft. lbs. (10-16 Nm), the universal joint assembly to power steering gearbox bolts 16-19 ft. lbs. (22-24 Nm) and the universal joint assembly to steering shaft bolts 16-19 ft. lbs. (22-24 Nm).

13. Tighten the tie rod end to steering knuckle nut 18-22 ft. lbs. (25-29 Nm). After torquing this nut, turn it up to 60 degrees further to align the cotter pin hole. Install a new cotter pin.

14. Install the tires and tighten the wheel lug nuts to specification.

15. Refill and bleed the power steering system.

16. Check and adjust the toe-in and the steering angle.

Impreza

1. Disconnect the negative battery cable.
2. Raise and support the vehicle safely.
3. Remove the front wheels.
4. Remove the front Y-pipe.
5. Remove the tie rod end cotter pin and nut. Using a puller, disconnect the tie rod ends from the steering knuckle.
6. Remove the jack-up plate and front sway bar.
7. Disconnect the fluid lines from the rack and pinion.
8. Matchmark the universal joint to the serration in the steering rack for installation reference.
9. Remove the universal joint bolts and lift the joint upward disconnecting it from the rack and pinion shaft.
10. Remove the clamps bolts securing the rack and pinion to the crossmember. Remove the rack and pinion.

To install:

11. Install the rack and pinion and tighten the clamp bolts to 43 ft. lbs. (59 Nm).

12. Align the steering rack to the universal joint. Push the long yoke of the joint all the way into the serrated position of the steering shaft, setting the bolt hole in the cut-out. Pull the short yoke all the way out of the serrated portion of the rack and pinion, setting the bolt hole in the cut-out. Insert the bolt through the short yoke. Pull the yoke and ensure the bolt is properly engaged in the cut-out. Fasten the short yoke side with the spring washer and bolt, then fasten the yoke side. Tighten the bolts to 17 ft. lbs. (24 Nm).

13. Connect the tie rod ends to the steering knuckle.
14. Install the sway bar and jack-up plate.
15. Install the Y-pipe with new gaskets and nuts.
16. Install the wheels.
17. Lower the vehicle.
18. Fill and bleed the steering system.

SVX

▶ **See Figures 199, 200 and 201**

1. Disconnect the negative battery cable.
2. Disconnect the O₂ sensor connector and the steering harness connector.
3. Raise and safely support the vehicle.
4. Remove the front under cover.
5. Disconnect the O₂ sensor harness from the clip.
6. Remove the collector cover and rear catalytic converter cover.
7. Disconnect the front exhaust pipe.

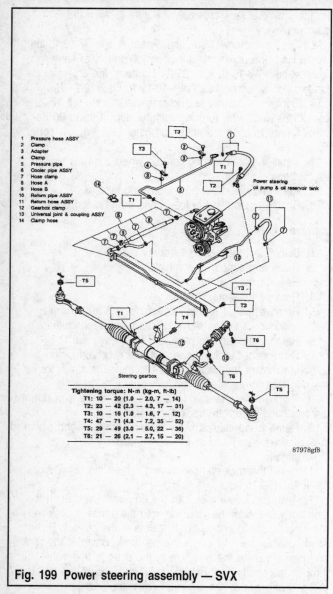

1 Pressure hose ASSY
2 Clamp
3 Adapter
4 Clamp
5 Pressure pipe
6 Cooler pipe ASSY
7 Hose clamp
8 Hose A
9 Hose B
10 Return pipe ASSY
11 Return hose ASSY
12 Gearbox clamp
13 Universal joint & coupling ASSY
14 Clamp hose

Power steering oil pump & oil reservoir tank

Steering gearbox

Tightening torque: N·m (kg-m, ft-lb)
T1: 10 — 20 (1.0 — 2.0, 7 — 14)
T2: 23 — 42 (2.3 — 4.3, 17 — 31)
T3: 10 — 16 (1.0 — 1.6, 7 — 12)
T4: 47 — 71 (4.8 — 7.2, 35 — 52)
T5: 29 — 49 (3.0 — 5.0, 22 — 36)
T6: 21 — 26 (2.1 — 2.7, 15 — 20)

87978gf8

Fig. 199 Power steering assembly — SVX

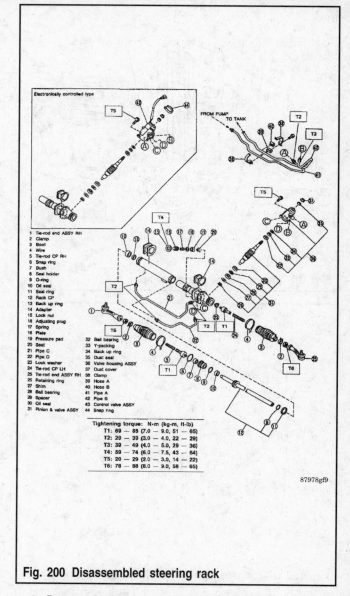

Electronically controlled type

FROM PUMP TO TANK

1 Tie-rod end ASSY RH
2 Clamp
3 Boot
4 Wire
5 Tie-rod CP RH
6 Snap ring
7 Bush
8 Seal holder
9 O-ring
10 Oil seal
11 Seal ring
12 Rack CP
13 Back up ring
14 Adapter
15 Lock nut
16 Adjusting plug
17 Spring
18 Plate
19 Pressure pad
20 Seat
21 Pipe C
22 Pipe D
23 Lock washer
24 Tie-rod CP LH
25 Tie-rod end ASSY RH
26 Retaining ring
27 Shim
28 Ball bearing
29 Spacer
30 Oil seal
31 Pinion & valve ASSY
32 Ball bearing
33 Y-packing
34 Back up ring
35 Dust seal
36 Valve housing ASSY
37 Dust cover
38 Clamp
39 Hose A
40 Hose B
41 Pipe A
42 Pipe B
43 Control valve ASSY
44 Snap ring

Tightening torque: N·m (kg-m, ft-lb)
T1: 69 — 88 (7.0 — 9.0, 51 — 65)
T2: 29 — 39 (3.0 — 4.0, 22 — 29)
T3: 39 — 49 (4.0 — 5.0, 29 — 36)
T4: 59 — 74 (6.0 — 7.5, 43 — 54)
T5: 20 — 29 (2.0 — 3.0, 14 — 22)
T6: 78 — 88 (8.0 — 9.0, 58 — 65)

87978gf9

Fig. 200 Disassembled steering rack

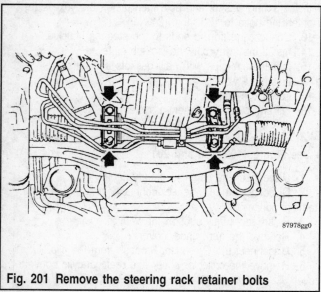

87978gg0

Fig. 201 Remove the steering rack retainer bolts

8. Remove the cotter pin and castle nut from the outer tie rod ends and separate the tie rods from the steering knuckles using a suitable puller.

9. Remove the spring pin securing the halfshaft to the transaxle.

10. Disconnect the halfshaft from the transaxle.

11. Disconnect the power steering lines one at a time. After disconnecting each allow the line to hang into a drain pan while you rotate the wheel lock to lock. This will purge the power steering fluid from the rack and pinion unit.

12. Disconnect and remove the performance rod.

13. Remove the lower ball joint pinch bolt on the right side. Separate the ball joint from the steering knuckle.

14. Matchmark the universal joint to the rack and pinion unit and the steering shaft.

15. Remove the upper and lower pinch bolts on the universal joint and push the joint up to remove it from the rack and pinion unit. Once it clears the rack pull it down and off the steering shaft.

16. Remove the bolts securing the rack and pinion unit to the vehicle underbody.

17. Remove the rack by performing the following:
   a. Turn the rack so the control valve faces the rear.
   b. Move the rack to the right so the left tie rod can be removed from the rack assembly.
   c. Remove the rack from the vehicle.

To install:
18. Install the rack and pinion unit into the vehicle.
19. Install the mounting bolts and tighten to 44 ft. lbs. (59 Nm).
20. Install the universal with the matchmarks in line onto the steering shaft first and then down over the rack pinion shaft. Install the pinch bolts and tighten them to 17 ft. lbs. (24 Nm)
21. Connect the ball joint to the steering knuckle and tighten the pinch bolt to 38 ft. lbs. (52 Nm).
22. Install the performance rod.
23. Connect the power steering lines to the rack and pinion unit.
24. Connect the halfshaft to the axle and install a new spring pin.
25. Connect the tie rod ends to the steering knuckles and tighten the castle nuts to 29 ft. lbs. (39 Nm).
26. Install the front exhaust pipe.
27. Install the exhaust covers removed.
28. Connect the O₂ sensor harness to the clip.
29. Install the front under cover.
30. Install the tire and wheel assembly.
31. Lower the vehicle.
32. Connect the steering harness connector and O₂ sensor connector.
33. Connect the negative battery cable.
34. Check the front end alignment and adjust as necessary.

Steering Pump

REMOVAL & INSTALLATION

Sedan, Coupe, Loyale, Wagon and Brat
▶ See Figures 202, 203, 204, 205 and 206

1. Disconnect the negative battery cable.
2. Siphon the fluid from the reservoir into a suitable container.
3. Loosen, but **DO NOT** remove the power steering pulley mounting nut.
4. Remove the power steering belt.
5. Remove the pulley mounting nut and the pulley.
6. Disconnect the power steering hoses from the power steering pump.
7. Remove the two bolts and remove the power steering reservoir from the power steering pump.
8. Remove the three power steering pump mounting pump mounting bolts.
9. Remove the power steering pump and bracket as an assembly.
10. Remove the two bolts and remove the bracket from the pump.

To install:
11. Install the bracket on the power steering pump and tighten the mounting bolts to 15 ft. lbs. (20 Nm).

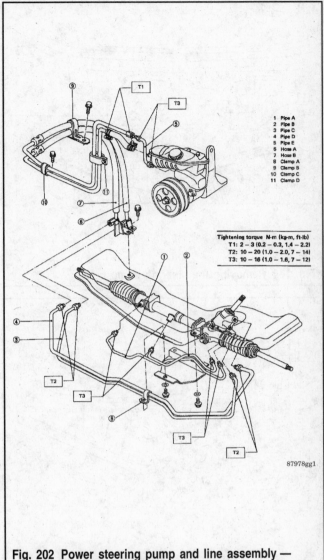

Fig. 202 Power steering pump and line assembly — Sedan, Coupe, Loyale, Wagon and Brat

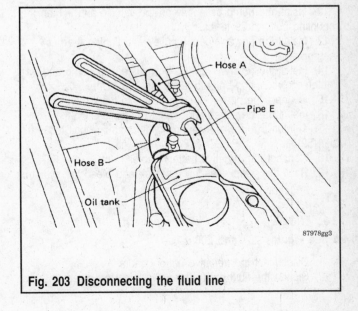

Fig. 203 Disconnecting the fluid line

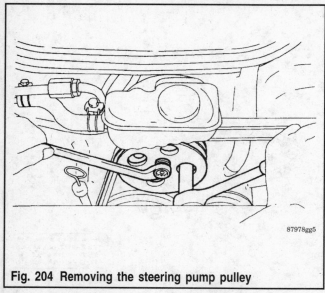

Fig. 204 Removing the steering pump pulley

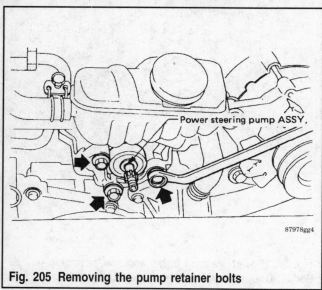

Power steering pump ASSY.

Fig. 205 Removing the pump retainer bolts

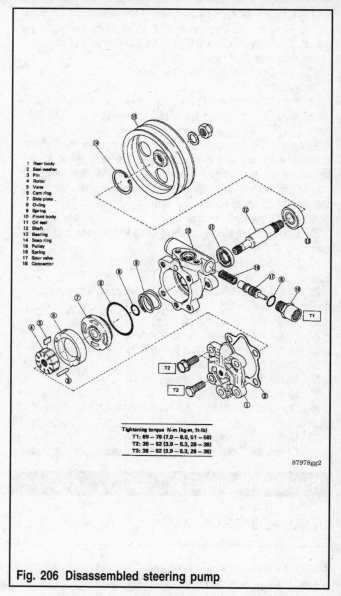

1 Rear body
2 Seal washer
3 Pin
4 Rotor
5 Vane
6 Cam ring
7 Side plate
8 O-ring
9 Spring
10 Front body
11 Oil seal
12 Shaft
13 Bearing
14 Snap ring
15 Pulley
16 Spring
17 Spur valve
18 Connector

Tightening torque N-m (kg-m, ft-lb)
T1: 69 — 78 (7.0 — 8.0, 51 — 58)
T2: 38 — 52 (3.9 — 5.3, 28 — 38)
T3: 38 — 52 (3.9 — 5.3, 28 — 38)

Fig. 206 Disassembled steering pump

12. Install the pump assembly on the vehicle and tighten the mounting bolts to 29 ft. lbs. (39 Nm).

13. Install the power steering pulley and tighten the nut temporarily.

14. Install the reservoir on the power steering pump and tighten the mounting bolts to 18 ft. lbs. (25 Nm).

15. Connect the power steering hoses to the pump.

16. Install the drive belt and adjust to specification.

17. Tighten the power steering pulley mounting bolt to 38 ft. lbs. (52 Nm).

18. Connect the negative battery cable.

19. Refill the power steering reservoir and bleed the system.

XT

1.8L ENGINE

▶ See Figures 207 and 208

1. Disconnect the negative battery cable.
2. Siphon the fluid out of the power steering reservoir.

3. Loosen but DO NOT remove the power steering pulley bolt.

4. Remove the power steering belt.

5. Remove the power steering pulley nut and remove the pulley.

6. Disconnect and cap the power steering lines from the pump and reservoir assembly.

7. Remove the clamp that secures the pressure line to the reservoir.

8. Remove the bolt that mounts the oil tank stay to the pump bracket.

9. Remove the two bolts on the top of the pump reservoir.

10. Remove the three steering pump mounting bolts from the front of the pump.

11. Remove the three bolts from the under side of the bracket and remove the power steering pump bracket.

12. Remove the two reservoir-to-pump bolts and remove the reservoir.

To install:

13. Install the power steering pump bracket on the engine and tighten the mounting bolts to 15 ft. lbs. (20 Nm).

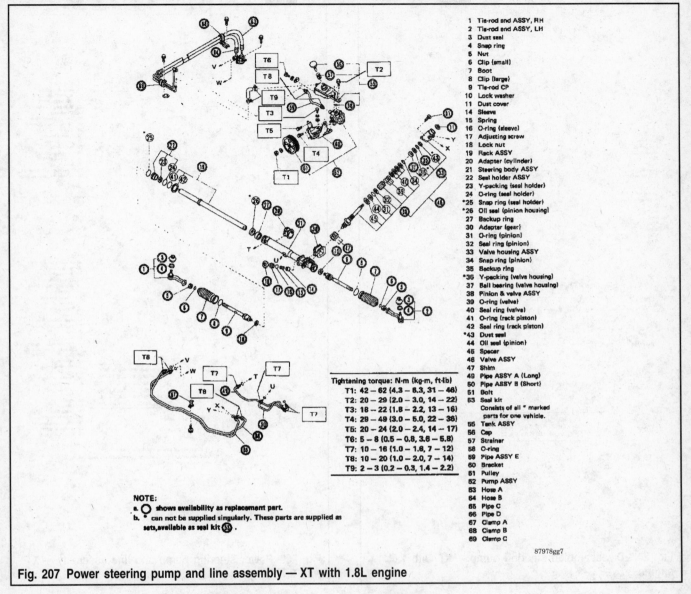

1	Tie-rod end ASSY, RH
2	Tie-rod end ASSY, LH
3	Dust seal
4	Snap ring
5	Nut
6	Clip (small)
7	Boot
8	Clip (large)
9	Tie-rod CP
10	Lock washer
11	Dust cover
14	Sleeve
15	Spring
16	O-ring (sleeve)
17	Adjusting screw
18	Lock nut
19	Rack ASSY
20	Adapter (cylinder)
21	Steering body ASSY
22	Seal holder ASSY
23	Y-packing (seal holder)
24	O-ring (seal holder)
*25	Snap ring (seal holder)
*26	Oil seal (pinion housing)
27	Backup ring
30	Adapter (gear)
31	O-ring (pinion)
32	Seal ring (pinion)
33	Valve housing ASSY
34	Snap ring (pinion)
35	Backup ring
*36	Y-packing (valve housing)
37	Ball bearing (valve housing)
38	Pinion & valve ASSY
39	O-ring (valve)
40	Seal ring (valve)
41	O-ring (rack piston)
42	Seal ring (rack piston)
*43	Dust seal
44	Oil seal (pinion)
45	Spacer
46	Valve ASSY
47	Shim
49	Pipe ASSY A (Long)
50	Pipe ASSY B (Short)
51	Bolt
53	Seal kit
	Consists of all * marked parts for one vehicle.
55	Tank ASSY
56	Cap
57	Strainer
58	O-ring
59	Pipe ASSY E
60	Bracket
61	Pulley
62	Pump ASSY
63	Hose A
64	Hose B
65	Pipe C
66	Pipe D
67	Clamp A
68	Clamp B
69	Clamp C

Tightening torque: N·m (kg-m, ft-lb)

T1: 42 — 62 (4.3 — 6.3, 31 — 46)
T2: 20 — 29 (2.0 — 3.0, 14 — 22)
T3: 18 — 22 (1.8 — 2.2, 13 — 16)
T4: 29 — 49 (3.0 — 5.0, 22 — 36)
T5: 20 — 24 (2.0 — 2.4, 14 — 17)
T6: 5 — 8 (0.5 — 0.8, 3.6 — 5.8)
T7: 10 — 16 (1.0 — 1.6, 7 — 12)
T8: 10 — 20 (1.0 — 2.0, 7 — 14)
T9: 2 — 3 (0.2 — 0.3, 1.4 — 2.2)

NOTE:
a. ◯ shows availability as replacement part.
b. • can not be supplied singularly. These parts are supplied as sets, available as seal kit ㊿ .

87978gg7

Fig. 207 Power steering pump and line assembly — XT with 1.8L engine

14. Install a new O-ring on the base of the reservoir port.

15. Install the reservoir on the pump and install the mounting bolts loosely.

16. Install the pump assembly onto the mounting bracket and tighten the mounting bolts to 29 ft. lbs. (39 Nm).

17. Secure the reservoir stay to the bracket and tighten the mounting bolt to 15 ft. lbs. (20 Nm).

18. Install the pulley on the pump and loosely install the mounting bolt.

19. Tighten the bolts on the top of the tank to 18 ft. lbs. (25 Nm).

20. Connect the power steering lines.

21. Install the power steering belt and tighten to specification.

22. Tighten the oil pump pulley mounting nut to 38 ft. lbs. (52 Nm).

23. Connect the negative battery cable.

24. Refill the power steering reservoir and bleed the steering system.

2.7L ENGINE

▶ See Figure 209

1. Disconnect the negative battery cable.

2. Disconnect the power controller connectors.

3. Remove the power controller mounting bolts and remove the controller.

4. Disconnect the harness and ground connectors from the pump motor.

5. Siphon the fluid from the reservoir.

6. Disconnect the power steering hoses from the pump assembly.

7. Remove the six pump mounting nuts and bolts.

8. Remove the pump assembly.

To install:

9. Install the pump assembly on the mounting bracket and tighten the mounting nuts and bolts to 24 ft. lbs. (32 Nm).

10. Connect the power steering lines to the pump assembly. Tighten the pressure line fitting to 10 ft. lbs. (15 Nm).

11. Connect the electrical connectors to the pump assembly.

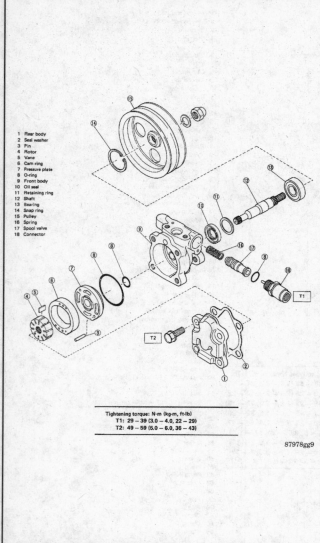

Fig. 208 Disassembled steering pump — XT with 1.8L engine

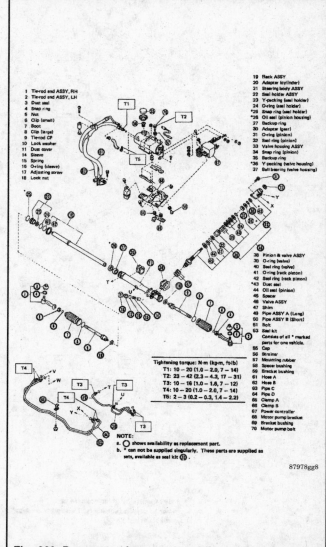

Fig. 209 Power steering pump and line assembly — XT with 2.7L engine

12. Install the power controller and tighten the mounting bolts to 4 ft. lbs. (6 Nm).

13. Connect the power controller and pump ground wires.

14. Connect the negative battery cable.

15. Refill and bleed the power steering system.

Legacy and Impreza

♦ See Figures 210, 211 and 212

1. Disconnect the negative battery cable.

2. Using a siphon, drain the power steering fluid from the reservoir.

3. Loosen, but do not remove the power steering pump pulley nut. Loosen the pulley drive belts.

4. Remove the power steering pump pulley nut and the pulley.

5. Disconnect and plug the **C** pressure hose from the oil pump. Disconnect the **D** pressure hose from the oil tank.

➡**To minimize the fluid loss from the reservoir, remove both bolts while the reservoir is pressed against the oil pump, then quickly remove the reservoir. It is a good idea to remove the pump and the reservoir as a unit, then separate the reservoir from the pump on a bench.**

6. Remove the power steering pump to bracket bolts. Remove the pump from the vehicle.

To install:

7. Install the power steering pump in the mounting bracket and install the mounting bolts loosely.

8. Connect the power steering hoses.

9. Install the power steering pump pulley and pulley mounting bolt loosely.

10. Install the drive belt over the pulley. DO NOT tighten the belt at this time.

11. Tighten the power steering pump to bracket bolts to 22-36 ft. lbs. (29-49 Nm).

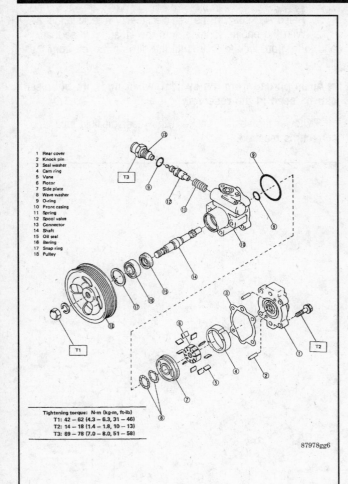

1 Rear cover
2 Knock pin
3 Seal washer
4 Cam ring
5 Vane
6 Rotor
7 Side plate
8 Wave washer
9 O-ring
10 Front casing
11 Spring
12 Spool valve
13 Connector
14 Shaft
15 Oil seal
16 Bering
17 Snap ring
18 Pulley

Tightening torque: N-m (kg-m, ft-lb)
T1: 42 — 62 (4.3 – 6.3, 31 – 46)
T2: 14 — 18 (1.4 – 1.8, 10 – 13)
T3: 69 — 78 (7.0 – 8.0, 51 – 58)

87978gg6

Fig. 210 Disassembled power steering pump — Legacy and Impreza

87978p37

Fig. 211 Using a suitable socket, remove the power steering pump retainer bolts

87978p38

Fig. 212 Lift the pump and reservoir assembly from the bracket — Legacy shown

12. Tighten the reservoir stay to bracket bolts to 14-17 ft. lbs. (20-24 Nm).

13. Tighten the reservoir to pump bolts to 14-22 ft. lbs. (20-29 Nm).

14. Tighten the pulley nut to pump nut to 31-46 ft. lbs. (42-62 Nm).

15. Adjust the power steering belt.

16. Refill the power steering reservoir. Bleed the power steering system.

SVX

▶ See Figures 213 and 214

1. Disconnect the negative battery cable.
2. Remove the drive belt cover.
3. Loosen the idler pulley mounting bolt. Loosen the slider bolt and remove the drive belt.
4. Remove the power steering pulley bolt and remove the power steering pulley.
5. Disconnect the electrical connector from the power steering pump.
6. Siphon the fluid out of the reservoir.
7. Disconnect and cap the oil return hose from the reservoir.
8. Disconnect and cap the power steering pressure hose from the pump assembly.
9. Remove the power steering pump bolts securing the pump to the bracket and the reservoir to the bracket.
10. Remove the power steering pump.

To install:

11. Install the power steering pump in the mounting bracket and install the mounting bolts. Tighten the mounting bolts to 15 ft. lbs. (20 Nm).
12. Connect the power steering pressure hose and tighten the fitting to 11 ft. lbs. (15 Nm).
13. Connect the return hose to the power steering reservoir.
14. Install the power steering pulley and tighten the mounting nut to 38 ft. lbs. (52 Nm).
15. Connect the electrical connector to the power steering pump.
16. Install the drive belt and tighten the slider bolt to achieve proper belt tension.

17. Tighten the idler pulley mounting bolts.
18. Install the belt cover.
19. Connect the negative battery cable.
20. Refill and bleed the power steering system.

1. Raise and support the vehicle safely on jackstands.
2. With the engine running, turn the steering wheel back and forth, from lock to lock, until the air is removed from the fluid.

➡**Air is purged from the system, when no more bubbles can be seen in the reservoir.**

3. Lower the vehicle, recheck the reservoir fluid level and correct, as required.

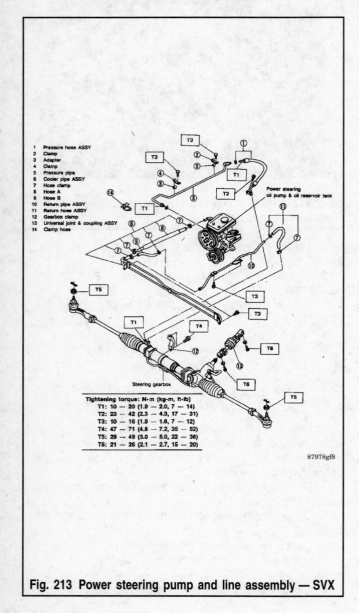

1 Pressure hose ASSY
2 Clamp
3 Adapter
4 Clamp
5 Pressure pipe
6 Cooler pipe ASSY
7 Hose clamp
8 Hose A
9 Hose B
10 Return pipe ASSY
11 Return hose ASSY
12 Gearbox clamp
13 Universal joint & coupling ASSY
14 Clamp hose

Power steering oil pump & oil reservoir tank

Steering gearbox

Tightening torque: N·m (kg-m, ft-lb)
T1: 10 — 20 (1.0 — 2.0, 7 — 14)
T2: 23 — 42 (2.3 — 4.3, 17 — 31)
T3: 10 — 16 (1.0 — 1.6, 7 — 12)
T4: 47 — 71 (4.8 — 7.2, 35 — 52)
T5: 29 — 49 (3.0 — 5.0, 22 — 36)
T6: 21 — 26 (2.1 — 2.7, 15 — 20)

87978gf8

Fig. 213 Power steering pump and line assembly — SVX

SYSTEM BLEEDING

➡ **Be sure the power steering reservoir is filled with fluid.**

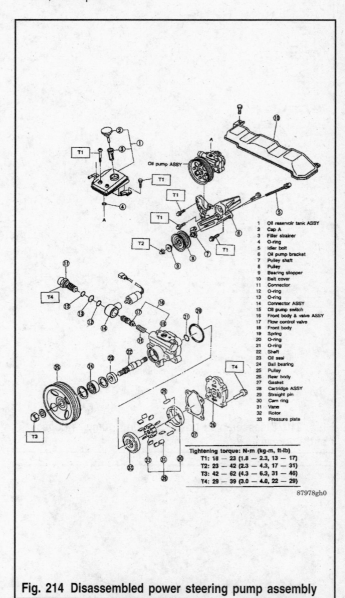

Oil pump ASSY

1 Oil reservoir tank ASSY
2 Cap A
3 Filler strainer
4 O-ring
5 Idler bolt
6 Oil pump bracket
7 Pulley shaft
8 Pulley
9 Bearing stopper
10 Belt cover
11 Connector
12 O-ring
13 O-ring
14 Connector ASSY
15 Oil pump switch
16 Front body & valve ASSY
17 Flow control valve
18 Front body
19 Spring
20 O-ring
21 O-ring
22 Shaft
23 Oil seal
24 Ball bearing
25 Pulley
26 Rear body
27 Gasket
28 Cartridge ASSY
29 Straight pin
30 Cam ring
31 Vane
32 Rotor
33 Pressure plate

Tightening torque: N·m (kg-m, ft-lb)
T1: 18 — 23 (1.8 — 2.3, 13 — 17)
T2: 23 — 42 (2.3 — 4.3, 17 — 31)
T3: 42 — 62 (4.3 — 6.3, 31 — 46)
T4: 29 — 39 (3.0 — 4.0, 22 — 29)

87978gh0

Fig. 214 Disassembled power steering pump assembly

TORQUE SPECIFICATIONS

Component	English	Metric
Lug nuts except SVX	58–72 ft. lbs.	78–98 Nm
Lug nuts SVX	72–87 ft. lbs.	98–118 Nm
Front Strut Assembly:		
Justy		
lower attaching bolts	25–40 ft. lbs.	34–54 Nm
upper attaching nuts	29–43 ft. lbs.	39–59 Nm
Except Justy		
attaching bolts	28–37 ft. lbs.	38–50 Nm
Strut upper plate retaining nut	22 ft. lbs	31 Nm
Ball Joint:		
Except SVX		
ball joint-to-housing bolt	28–37 ft. lbs.	38–50 Nm
ball joint-to-transverse link nut	29 ft. lbs.	39 Nm
SVX		
ball joint-to-control arm bolts	79.7–101.8 ft. lbs.	108–138 Nm
ball joint-to housing pinch bolt	33.2–43.5 ft. lbs.	45–59 Nm
Front Stabilizer:		
Except SVX		
jack-up plate-to-crossmember	17–31 ft. lbs.	2–42 Nm
stabilizer link-to-transverse link	18–25 ft. lbs.	25–34 Nm
stabilizer-to-crossmember	15–21 ft. lbs.	21–28 Nm
SVX		
stabilizer link-to-stabilizer lever	23–31 ft. lbs.	32–42 Nm
stabilizer bar-to-stabilizer lever	33–43 ft. lbs.	45–59 Nm
stabilizer bar-to-crossmember	15–21 ft. lbs.	21–28 Nm
Transverse Link:		
Justy		
transverse link-to-crossmember	43–58 ft. lbs.	59–78 Nm
tension rod-to-bracket bolt	40–54 ft. lbs.	54–74 Nm
tension rod-to-transverse link bolt	54–69 ft. lbs.	74–93 Nm
Loyale, STD. and XT		
transverse link bolt	43–51 ft. lbs.	59–69 Nm
stabilizer assembly bolts	14–22 ft. lbs.	20–29 Nm
Legacy		
transverse link-to-stabilizer	14–22 ft. lbs.	20–29 Nm
transverse link-to-crossmember	61–83 ft. lbs.	83–113 Nm
transverse link rear bushing-to-chassis	145–217 ft. lbs.	196–294 Nm
transverse link end bushing nut	152–195 ft. lbs.	206–265 Nm
SVX		
rear support-to-sub frame bolts	93–123 ft. lbs.	126–167 Nm
lower control arm retaining bolts	56–73 ft. lbs.	76–100 Nm

87978c08

TORQUE SPECIFICATIONS

Component	English	Metric
Rear Strut Assembly:		
Justy		
lower strut-to-housing bolts	72–87 ft. lbs.	98–118 Nm
upper strut mounting nuts	43–51 ft. lbs.	59–69 Nm
Loyale, STD. and XT		
lower strut attaching bolts	51–87 ft. lbs.	69–118 Nm
upper strut retaining bolts	65–94 ft. lbs.	88–127 Nm
Legacy		
lower strut mounting bolts	137–174 ft. lbs.	186–235 Nm
upper strut mounting nuts	36–51 ft. lbs.	49–69 Nm
SVX		
lower strut mounting bolts	98–127 ft. lbs.	132–172 Nm
upper strut mounting nuts	36–51 ft. lbs.	49–69 Nm
Rear Control Arms:		
Justy		
control arm-to-axle housing bolts	54–69 ft. lbs.	74–93 Nm
control arm-to-crossmember bolts	43–58 ft. lbs.	59–78 Nm
Loyale, STD. and XT		
inner arm-to-crossmember bolts	51–65 ft. lbs.	69–88 Nm
outer arm attaching bolts	94–108 ft. lbs.	127–147 Nm
Legacy		
trailing link mounting bolts	72–94 ft. lbs.	98–127 Nm
lateral link through bolts—		
FWD models	61–83 ft. lbs.	83–113 Nm
4WD models	87–116 ft. lbs.	118–157 Nm
SVX		
rear trailing link-to-housing bolt	80–101 ft. lbs.	137–177 Nm
front trailing link through bolt	101–130 ft. lbs.	137–177 Nm
front lateral link-to-sub frame through bolt		
(bolt without cap for the end)	72–101 ft. lbs.	98–137 Nm
rear lateral link-to-sub frame through bolt		
(bolt with cap, closest to the differential)	61–83 ft. lbs.	83–113 Nm
stabilizer link nut	12–17 ft. lbs.	16–14 Nm
Steering Wheel:		
retaining nut		
Justy	36–43 ft. lbs.	49–59 Nm
Loyale, STD. and XT	22–29 ft. lbs.	29–39 Nm
Legacy and SVX	22–29 ft. lbs.	29–39 Nm
Manual Steering Gear:		
Rack and pinion mounting bolts		
Justy and XT	33–43 ft. lbs.	44–59 Nm
Except Justy and XT	35–52 ft. lbs.	48–66 Nm

87978c09

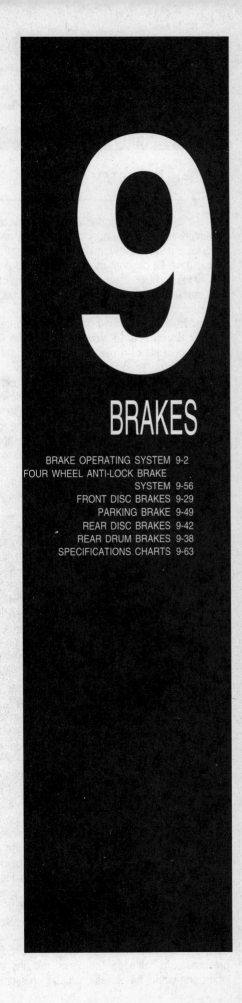

9

BRAKES

BRAKE OPERATING SYSTEM

Understanding the Brakes

HYDRAULIC SYSTEM

The brake pedal operates a hydraulic system that is used for 2 reasons. First, fluid under pressure can be carried to all parts of the vehicle by small hoses or metal lines without taking up a lot of room or causing routing problems. Second, the hydraulic fluid offers a great mechanical advantage; little foot pressure is required on the pedal, but a great deal of pressure is generated at the wheels.

The brake pedal is linked to a piston in the brake master cylinder, which is filled with hydraulic brake fluid. The master cylinder consists of a cylinder, containing a small piston and a fluid reservoir.

Modern master cylinders are actually 2 separate cylinders. The 2 cylinders are actually separated, allowing for emergency stopping power should one part of the system fail. The braking force is applied to one rear wheel and one front wheel in diagonal pattern. This system is known as the dual diagonal system.

The entire hydraulic system from the master cylinder to the wheels is full of hydraulic brake fluid. When the brake pedal is depressed, the pistons in the master cylinder are forced to move, exerting tremendous force on the fluid in the lines. The fluid has nowhere to go and forces the wheel cylinder piston (drum brakes) or caliper pistons (disc brakes) to exert pressure on the brake shoes or pads. The resulting friction between the brake shoe and wheel drum or the brake pad and disc slows the vehicle and eventually stops it.

Also attached to the brake pedal is a switch which lights the brake lights as the pedal is depressed. The lights stay **ON** until the brake pedal is released and returns to its normal position.

Each wheel cylinder in a drum brake system contains 2 pistons, one at either end, which push outward in opposite directions. In disc brake systems, the wheel cylinders are part of the caliper; there can be as many as 4 or as few as 1. Whether disc or drum type, all pistons use some type of rubber seal to prevent leakage around the piston and a rubber dust boot seals the outer ends of the wheel cylinders against dirt and moisture.

When the brake pedal is released, a spring pushes the master cylinder pistons back to their normal position. Check valves in the master cylinder piston allow fluid to flow toward the wheel cylinders or calipers as the piston returns. As the brake shoe return springs pull the brake shoes back to the released position, excess fluid returns to the master cylinder through compensating ports, which have been uncovered as the pistons move back. Any fluid that has leaked from the system will also be replaced through the compensating ports.

All brake systems use a switch to activate a light, warning of brake failure. The switch is located in a valve mounted near the master cylinder. A piston in the valve receives pressure on each end from the front and rear brake circuits. When the pressures are balanced, the piston remains stationary but when one circuit has a leak, greater pressure during the application of the brakes will force the piston to one side or the other, closing the switch and activating the warning light.

Disc brake systems also have a metering valve to prevent the front disc brakes from engaging before the rear brakes have contacted the drums. This ensures that the front brakes will not normally be used alone to stop the vehicle. A proportioning valve is also used to limit pressure to the rear brakes to prevent rear wheel lock-up during hard braking.

DRUM BRAKES

Drum brakes use two brake shoes mounted on a stationary backing plate. These shoes are positioned inside a circular cast iron drum which rotates with the wheel assembly. The shoes are held in place by springs; this allows them to slide toward the drums (when they are applied) while keeping the linings and drums in alignment. The shoes are actuated by a wheel cylinder which is usually mounted at the top of the backing plate. When the brakes are applied, hydraulic pressure forces the wheel cylinder's two actuating links outward. Since these links bear directly against the top of the brake shoes, the tops of the shoes are forced outward against the inner side of the drum. This action forces the bottoms of the two shoes to contact the brake drum by rotating the entire assembly slightly (known as servo action). When pressure within the wheel cylinder is relieved, return springs pull the shoes back away from the drum.

Most modern drum brakes are designed to self-adjust during application when the vehicle is moving in reverse. This motion causes both shoes to rotate very slightly with the drum, rocking an adjusting lever. The self-adjusters are only intended to compensate for normal wear. Although the adjustment is "automatic", there is a definite method to actuate the self-adjuster, which is done during normal driving. Driving the vehicle in reverse and applying the brakes usually activates the automatic adjusters. If the brake pedal was low, you should be able to feel an increase in the height of the brake pedal.

DISC BRAKES

Instead of the traditional expanding brakes that press outward against a circular drum, disc brake systems utilize a cast iron disc with brake pads positioned on either side of it. Braking effect is achieved in a manner similar to the way you would squeeze a spinning disc between your fingers. The disc (rotor) is a one-piece casting with cooling fins between the two braking surfaces. This enables air to circulate between the braking surfaces making them less sensitive to heat buildup and more resistant to fade. Dirt and water do not affect braking action since contaminants are thrown off by the centrifugal action of the rotor or scraped off by the pads. Also, the equal clamping action of the two brake pads tends to ensure uniform, straight-line stops. All disc brakes are inherently self-adjusting.There are three general types of disc brake:

1. A fixed caliper, 4-piston type.

2. A floating caliper, single piston type.

3. A sliding caliper, single piston type.

The fixed caliper design uses two pistons mounted on either side of the rotor (in each side of the caliper). The caliper is mounted rigidly and does not move.

The sliding and floating designs are quite similar and often considered as one. The pad on the inside of the rotor is moved into contact with the rotor by hydraulic force. The caliper, which is not held in a fixed position, moves slightly, bringing the outside pad into contact with the rotor. There are various methods of attaching floating calipers; some pivot at the bottom or top and some slide on mounting bolts.

POWER BRAKE BOOSTERS

A vacuum diaphragm is located behind the master cylinder and assists the driver in applying the brakes, reducing both the effort and travel he must put into moving the brake pedal.

The vacuum diaphragm housing is connected to the intake manifold by a vacuum hose. A check valve at the point where the hose enters the diaphragm housing ensures that during periods of low manifold vacuum brake assist vacuum will not be lost.

Depressing the brake pedal closes off the vacuum source and allows atmospheric pressure to enter on one side of the diaphragm. This causes the master cylinder pistons to move and apply the brakes. When the brake pedal is released, vacuum is applied to both sides of the diaphragm and return springs return the diaphragm and master cylinder pistons to the released position. If the vacuum fails, the brake pedal rod will butt against the end of the master cylinder actuating rod and direct mechanical application will occur as the pedal is depressed.

Subaru uses a dual hydraulic system, with the brakes connected diagonally. In other words, the right front and left rear brakes are on the same hydraulic line and the left front and right rear are on the other line. This has the added advantage of front disc emergency braking, should either of the hydraulic systems fail. The diagonal rear brake serves to counteract the sway from single front disc braking.

A leading/trailing drum brake is used for the rear brakes, with disc brakes for the front. All Subarus are equipped with a brake warning light, which is activated when a defect in the brake system occurs.

HYDRAULIC SYSTEM

The hydraulic system is composed of the master cylinder and brake booster, the brake lines, the brake pressure differential valve(s), the wheel cylinders (drum brakes) and calipers (disc brakes).

The master cylinder serves as a brake fluid reservoir and (along with the booster) as a hydraulic pump. Brake fluid is stored in the two sections of the master cylinder. Each section corresponds to each part of the dual braking system. This tandem master cylinder is required by Federal law as a safety device.

When the brake pedal is depressed, it moves a piston mounted in the bottom of the master cylinder. The movement of this piston creates hydraulic pressure in the master cylinder. This pressure is carried to the wheel cylinders or the calipers by brake lines, passing through the pressure differential or proportioning valve.

When the hydraulic pressure reaches the wheels, after the pedal has been depressed, it enters the wheel cylinders or calipers. Here it comes into contact with a piston(s). The hydraulic pressure causes the piston(s) to move, which moves the brake shoes or pads (disc brakes), causing them to contact the drums or rotors (disc brakes). Friction between the brake shoes and the drums causes the vehicle to slow. There is a relationship between the amount of pressure that is applied to the brake peal and the amount of force which moves the brake shoes against the drums. Therefore, the harder the brake pedal is depressed, the quicker the vehicle will stop.

Since the hydraulic system is one which operates on fluids, air is a natural enemy of the brake system. Air in the hydraulic system retards the passage of hydraulic pressure from the master cylinder to the wheels. Anytime a hydraulic component below the master cylinder is opened or removed, the system must be bled of air to ensure proper operation. Air trapped in the hydraulic system can also cause the brake warning light to turn **ON**, even though the system has not failed. This is especially true after repairs have been performed on the system.

HILL HOLDER SYSTEM

▶ **See Figure 1**

A feature unique to Subaru, the hill holder is a system designed to engage a single brake channel when a manual transaxle vehicle is stopped on an uphill. The system, in effect, holds the vehicle, to enable ease of starting on an uphill.

The system consists of the basic brake system components and the addition of the Pressure Hold Valve (PHV). The pressure hold valve is connected to one of the service brake pipes. When the clutch pedal is depressed on an uphill, the pushrod in the PHV is pushed in and/or pulled out by the camshaft that is interlinked with the clutch pedal to change the clearance between the PHV ball and the seal. This opens or closes the hydraulic system to the brakes.

The operation of the system is fairly simple; when the car is stopped on an uphill, and the clutch is pressed along with the brake pedal (as in any normal stop), the cam mechanism in the PHV moves the ball valve. This, in effect, applies one side of the brake system and your foot can be taken off of the brake pedal and moved to the gas pedal. As you begin to move the vehicle and release the clutch, the brake system is then also released and you can begin moving ahead. This all has the same effect as stopping on a hill and putting the parking brake on, to make taking off easier.

The hill holder feature is standard on all manual shift models of Subaru from 1985-92, except for the Justy.

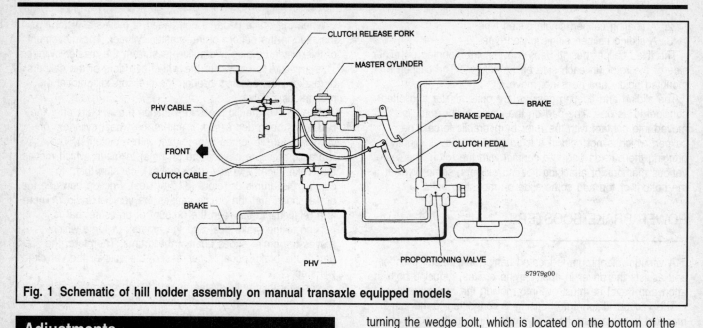

Fig. 1 Schematic of hill holder assembly on manual transaxle equipped models

Adjustments

FRONT DISC BRAKES

Disc brakes are not adjustable. They are, in effect, self-adjusting during normal operation.

REAR DRUM BRAKES

Coupe, Sedan, Wagon, Brat, Loyale and XT
▶ See Figure 2

Perform rear brake adjustment every 6 months/6,000 miles (9662 km), whichever occurs first. Adjust the rear brakes by

turning the wedge bolt, which is located on the bottom of the backing plate.
1. Raise and safely support the vehicle on jackstands.
2. Remove the rubber cap from the adjusting screw.
3. Tighten the adjuster until the wheel ceases to rotate.
4. Back off the adjuster 180°.
5. Verify that the wheel turns easily by hand.
6. Install the rubber cap on the adjuster screw.
7. Lower the vehicle.

Justy
▶ See Figure 3

The Justy rear drum brakes use a conventional style star wheel adjuster mechanism. To adjust the brakes, remove the rubber adjuster hole cover and, using a slightly curved small prybar inserted through the hole, turn the star wheel until the brake shoes begin to drag on the brake drum. The wheel should be hard to turn, then back off the adjuster slightly, until the wheel frees up.

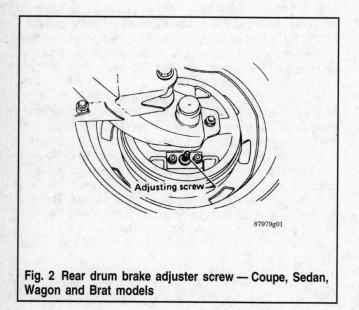

Fig. 2 Rear drum brake adjuster screw — Coupe, Sedan, Wagon and Brat models

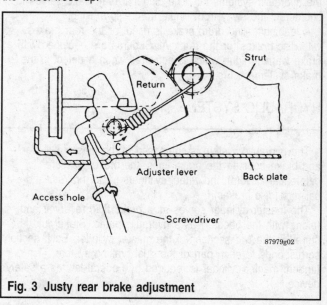

Fig. 3 Justy rear brake adjustment

BRAKE PEDAL

Justy

▶ See Figure 4

The brake pedal travel is the distance the pedal moves toward the floor from the fully released position.

1. Start the engine and allow it to reach normal operating temperature. Measure brake pedal height between the floor of the vehicle and the top of the pedal after the engine is revved several times. Ensure that the pedal is fully returned by the pedal return spring. Pedal height should be 3.54-3.74 in. (90-95mm).

2. Turn **OFF** the engine, and adjust the brake pedal as follows:

    a. Disconnect the stop light switch connector.

    b. Loosen the stop light switch locknut and back the switch away from brake pedal.

    c. Adjust the brake pedal to the specified height.

    d. Tighten the pushrod locknut to 4-7 ft. lbs. (5-9 Nm).

    e. Attach the switch connector.

✳✳CAUTION

Properly disarm the air bag on vehicles equipped with the SRS system. Failure to do so can cause serious injury. The procedure can be found in Section 6 of this manual under the heading "Supplemental Restraint System".

If the operation of the brake light switch is not smooth and/or the stroke is not within specified value, replace the switch with a new one.

Coupe, Sedan, Wagon, Loyale and Brat

▶ See Figure 5

The brake pedal travel is the distance the pedal moves toward the floor from the fully released position.

1. Start the engine and allow it to reach normal operating temperature. Measure brake pedal height between the floor of the vehicle and the top of the pedal after the engine is revved

several times. Ensure that the pedal is fully returned by the pedal return spring. Pedal height should be 6.22 in. (15.8cm).

2. Turn **OFF** the engine. Depress the brake pedal several times. Measure the pedal free-play. If the measured free-play is not within the specification of 0.020-0.098 in. (0.5-2.5mm), adjust the brake pedal as follows:

    a. Disconnect the stop light switch connector.

    b. Loosen the stop light switch locknut and back the switch away from brake pedal.

    c. Loosen the locknut on the pushrod and adjust the brake pedal to the specified height.

    d. Tighten the pushrod locknut to 4-7 ft. lbs. (5-9 Nm).

    e. Adjust the stop light switch to adjust the pedal free-play and attach the connector.

✳✳CAUTION

Properly disarm the air bag on vehicles equipped with the SRS system. Failure to do so can cause serious injury. The procedure can be found in Section 6 of this manual under the heading "Supplemental Restraint System".

If the operation of the brake light switch is not smooth and/or the stroke is not within specified value, replace the switch with a new one.

XT

▶ See Figure 6

The brake pedal travel is the distance the pedal moves toward the floor from the fully released position.

1. Start the engine and allow it to reach normal operating temperature. Measure brake pedal height between the floor of the vehicle and the top of the pedal after the engine is revved several times. Ensure that the pedal is fully returned by the pedal return spring. Pedal height should be 5.06-5.49 in. (12.8-14.0cm).

2. Turn **OFF** the engine. Depress the brake pedal several times. Measure the pedal free-play. If the measured free-play is not within the specification of 0.020-0.098 in. (0.5-2.5mm), adjust brake pedal as follows:

    a. Disconnect the stop light switch connector.

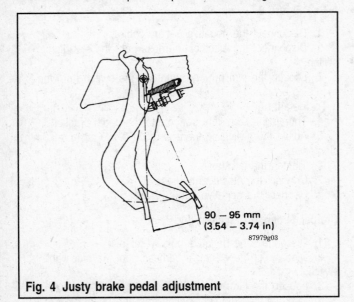

90 — 95 mm
(3.54 — 3.74 in)

87979g03

Fig. 4 Justy brake pedal adjustment

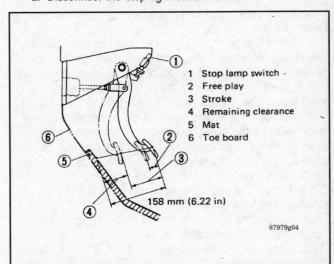

1 Stop lamp switch
2 Free play
3 Stroke
4 Remaining clearance
5 Mat
6 Toe board

158 mm (6.22 in)

87979g04

Fig. 5 Brake pedal adjustment — Coupe, Sedan, Wagon, Loyale and Brat

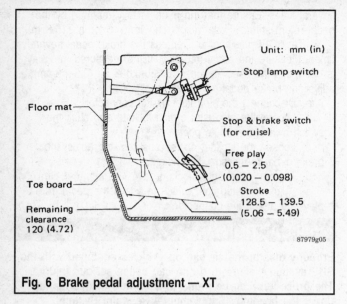

Fig. 6 Brake pedal adjustment — XT

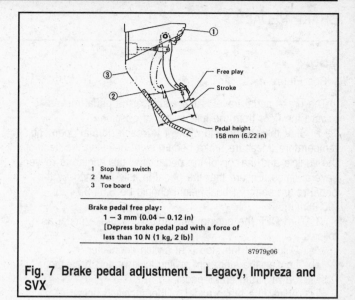

Fig. 7 Brake pedal adjustment — Legacy, Impreza and SVX

b. Loosen the stop light switch locknut and back the switch away from the brake pedal.

c. Loosen the locknut on the pushrod and adjust the brake pedal to the specified height.

d. Tighten the pushrod locknut to 4-7 ft. lbs. (5-9 Nm).

e. Adjust the stop light switch to adjust the pedal free-play and attach the connector.

❊❊CAUTION

Properly disarm the air bag on vehicles equipped with the SRS system. Failure to do so can cause serious injury. The procedure can be found in Section 6 of this manual under the heading "Supplemental Restraint System".

If the operation of the brake light switch is not smooth and/or the stroke is not within specified value, replace the switch with a new one.

Legacy, Impreza and SVX
▶ See Figure 7

The brake pedal travel is the distance the pedal moves toward the floor from the fully released position.

1. Start the engine and allow it to reach normal operating temperature. Measure brake pedal height between the floor of the vehicle and the top of the pedal after the engine is revved several times. Ensure that the pedal is fully returned by the pedal return spring. Pedal height should be 6.22 in. (15.8cm).

2. Turn **OFF** the engine. Depress the brake pedal several times. Measure the pedal free-play. If the measured free-play is not within the specification of 0.04-0.12 in. (1-3mm), adjust the brake pedal as follows:

a. Disconnect the stop light switch connector.

b. Loosen the stop light switch locknut and back the switch away from brake pedal.

c. Loosen the locknut on the pushrod and adjust the brake pedal to the specified height.

d. Tighten the pushrod locknut to 4-7 ft. lbs. (5-9 Nm).

e. Adjust the stop light switch to adjust the pedal free-play and attach connector.

❊❊CAUTION

Properly disarm the air bag on vehicles equipped with the SRS system. Failure to do so can cause serious injury. The procedure can be found in Section 6 of this manual under the heading "Supplemental Restraint System".

If the operation of the brake light switch is not smooth and/or the stroke is not within specified value, replace the switch with a new one.

Brake Light Switch

REMOVAL & INSTALLATION

Justy
▶ See Figure 8

1. Disconnect the negative battery cable.

2. Disconnect the electrical harness from the stop light switch.

3. Loosen the jam nut and unthread the switch from the mounting bracket.

To install:

4. Thread the stop light switch into the pedal bracket.

5. Adjust the switch so there is 0.071-0.130 in. (1.8-3.3mm) clearance.

6. Tighten the jam nut.

7. Connect the electrical harness.

8. Connect the negative battery cable.

Coupe, Sedan, XT, Wagon and Brat

1. Disconnect the negative battery cable.

2. Disconnect the electrical harness from the stop light switch.

3. Loosen the jam nut on the switch.

4. Remove the stop light switch from the pedal bracket.

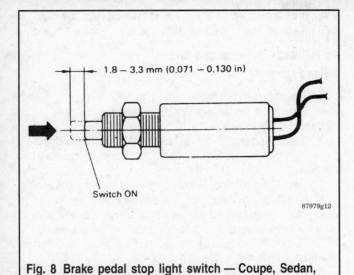

Fig. 8 Brake pedal stop light switch — Coupe, Sedan, Wagon, Justy, Loyale and Brat

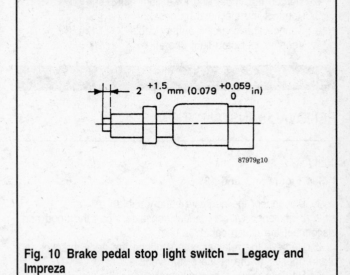

Fig. 10 Brake pedal stop light switch — Legacy and Impreza

To install:

5. Thread the stop light switch into the pedal bracket.

6. Adjust the switch so the plunger travel is 0.071-0.130 in. (1.8-3.3mm).

7. Tighten the jam nut.

8. Connect the stop light switch electrical connector.

9. Connect the negative battery cable.

10. Verify proper stop light operation and adjust the switch as necessary.

Legacy and Impreza
▶ See Figures 9 and 10

1. Disconnect the negative battery cable.

2. Disconnect the electrical harness from the stop light switch.

3. Remove the stop light switch locknut and remove the switch from the bracket.

To install:

4. Install the switch in the brake pedal bracket and adjust the switch using the two locknuts.

5. Adjust the switch so that 0.079 in. (2mm) of the plunger is exposed. Tighten the locknut after adjustment to 53-86 inch lbs. (6-10 Nm).

6. Connect the electrical harness to the switch.

7. Connect the negative battery cable.

8. Verify proper stop light operation.

SVX
▶ See Figure 11

1. Disconnect the negative battery cable.

2. Disconnect the electrical harness from the stop light switch.

3. Remove the lower jam nut from the stop light switch.

4. Back off the upper jam nut and unscrew the switch from the brake pedal bracket.

To install:

5. With the upper jam nut on the switch, thread the switch into the brake pedal bracket.

6. Install the lower jam nut on the switch.

7. Adjust the switch so there is 0.079-0.138 in. (2-3.5mm) of clearance.

Fig. 9 Brake pedal stop light switch below the steering column — Legacy

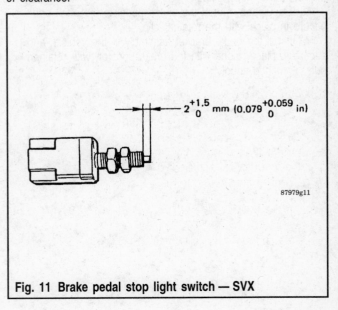

Fig. 11 Brake pedal stop light switch — SVX

8. Tighten the upper and lower jam nuts.
9. Connect the electrical harness.
10. Connect the negative battery cable.
11. Verify proper stop light operation.

Brake Pedal

REMOVAL & INSTALLATION

Justy

▶ **See Figures 12 and 13**

1. Disconnect the negative battery cable.
2. If equipped with a manual transaxle, open the hood and disconnect the clutch cable.
3. Remove the retainer nuts securing the pedal bracket and brake booster to the inside of the vehicle.
4. Remove the steering column-to-pedal bracket upper attaching bolt.
5. Remove the stop light switch and harness.
6. Detach the clutch cable from the clutch pedal assembly.
7. Separate the brake pedal from the booster pushrod.
8. Remove the pedal assembly from the vehicle.
9. If equipped with a manual transaxle, remove the clutch switch and bracket assembly.
10. Remove the circlip, then remove the clutch pedal.
11. Pull the shaft out and remove the brake pedal and bushings.
12. Remove the stop light switch.
   To install:
13. Temporarily install the stop light switch to the pedal bracket.
14. Mount the bushing in the clutch and brake pedal assemblies. Apply grease to the shaft, then insert it into the bracket and mount the brake pedal, washer (if equipped), bushing and return spring.
15. Pass the shaft through the bracket assembly so that the shaft end becomes visible from the opposite end. Align the shaft end with the hole in the attaching plate, and fully insert the shaft into the bracket.
16. If equipped, mount the clutch pedal to the shaft and secure in place with the retainer clip.
17. Install the pedal bracket assembly in the vehicle, and secure in place, along with the brake booster, with retainer nuts, tightened snugly.

18. If equipped with a manual transaxle, connect the clutch cable. Connect the negative battery cable.

Coupe, Sedan, Wagon and Brat

▶ **See Figure 14**

1. Disconnect the negative battery cable.
2. Disconnect the accelerator cable from the carburetor/throttle body assembly.
3. If equipped with a manual transaxle, detach the clutch cable from the release fork clamp on the transaxle case and toe board.
4. Detach the trim panel from below the steering column.
5. Detach the pushrod from the brake pedal.
6. Tag and disconnect the stop light switch and any other electrical harnesses attached to the pedal cluster assembly.
7. Remove the retainer nuts securing the pedal bracket and brake booster to the inside of the vehicle.
8. Remove the steering column-to-pedal bracket upper attaching bolt.
9. Detach the accelerator pedal return spring, then remove the accelerator pedal assembly.
10. Disconnect the brake pedal return spring.
11. Remove the circlip from the pedal shaft.
12. Pull the shaft out, then remove the brake pedal and, if equipped, the clutch pedal and bushings.
13. Remove the stop light switch.
   To install:
14. Install the stop light switch to the pedal bracket.
15. Mount the bushing in the clutch and brake pedal assemblies. Apply grease to the shaft, then insert it into the bracket and mount the brake pedal, washer (if equipped), bushing and return springs.
16. Apply grease to the accelerator pedal, and install onto the pedal bracket assembly.
17. Pass the shaft through the bracket assembly so that the shaft end becomes visible from the opposite end. Align the shaft end with the hole in the attaching plate, and fully insert the shaft into the bracket.
18. If equipped, mount the clutch pedal to the shaft and secure in place with the retainer clip.
19. Install the pedal bracket assembly in the vehicle, and secure in place, along with the brake booster, with retainer nuts, tightened snugly.
20. If equipped with a manual transaxle, connect the clutch cable. Connect the negative battery cable.

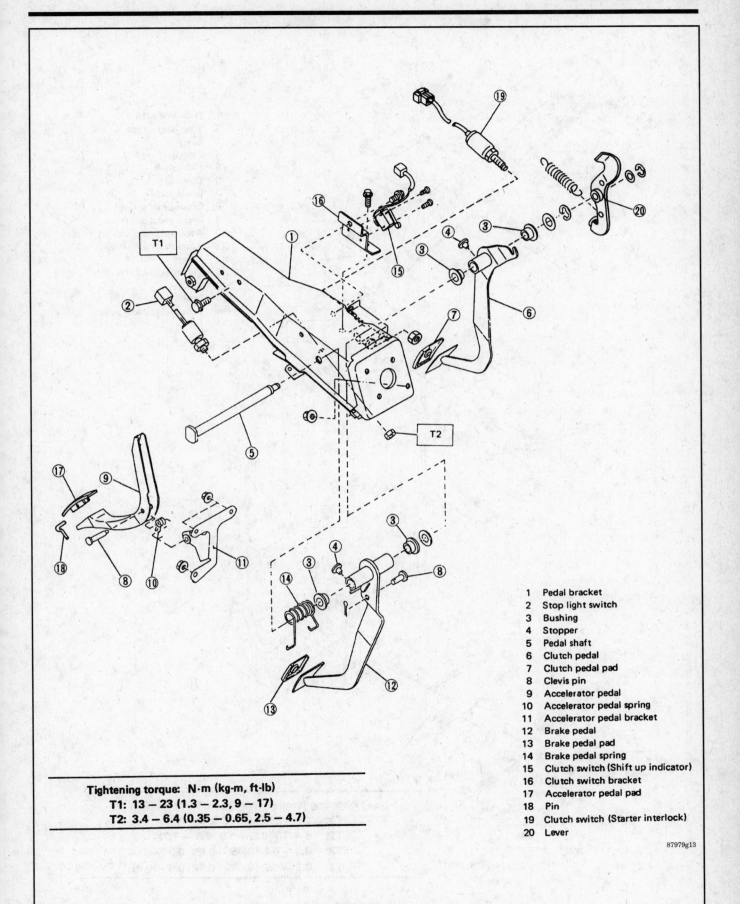

Tightening torque: N·m (kg-m, ft-lb)
  T1: 13 — 23 (1.3 — 2.3, 9 — 17)
  T2: 3.4 — 6.4 (0.35 — 0.65, 2.5 — 4.7)

1 Pedal bracket
2 Stop light switch
3 Bushing
4 Stopper
5 Pedal shaft
6 Clutch pedal
7 Clutch pedal pad
8 Clevis pin
9 Accelerator pedal
10 Accelerator pedal spring
11 Accelerator pedal bracket
12 Brake pedal
13 Brake pedal pad
14 Brake pedal spring
15 Clutch switch (Shift up indicator)
16 Clutch switch bracket
17 Accelerator pedal pad
18 Pin
19 Clutch switch (Starter interlock)
20 Lever

87979g13

Fig. 12 Brake pedal and bracket assembly — Justy with manual transaxle

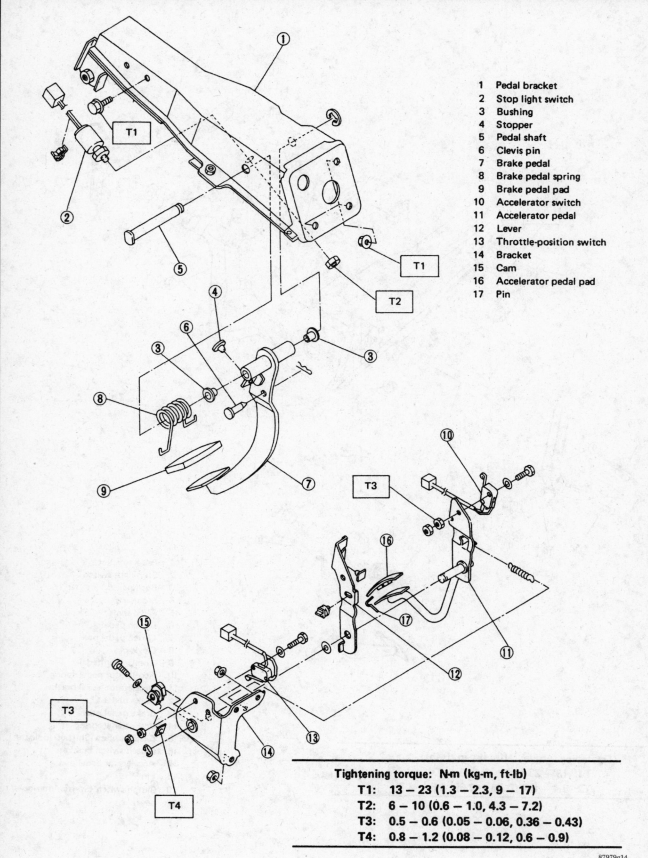

1 Pedal bracket
2 Stop light switch
3 Bushing
4 Stopper
5 Pedal shaft
6 Clevis pin
7 Brake pedal
8 Brake pedal spring
9 Brake pedal pad
10 Accelerator switch
11 Accelerator pedal
12 Lever
13 Throttle-position switch
14 Bracket
15 Cam
16 Accelerator pedal pad
17 Pin

Tightening torque: N·m (kg-m, ft-lb)	
T1:	13 — 23 (1.3 — 2.3, 9 — 17)
T2:	6 — 10 (0.6 — 1.0, 4.3 — 7.2)
T3:	0.5 — 0.6 (0.05 — 0.06, 0.36 — 0.43)
T4:	0.8 — 1.2 (0.08 — 0.12, 0.6 — 0.9)

87979g14

Fig. 13 Brake pedal and bracket assembly — Justy with ECV transaxle

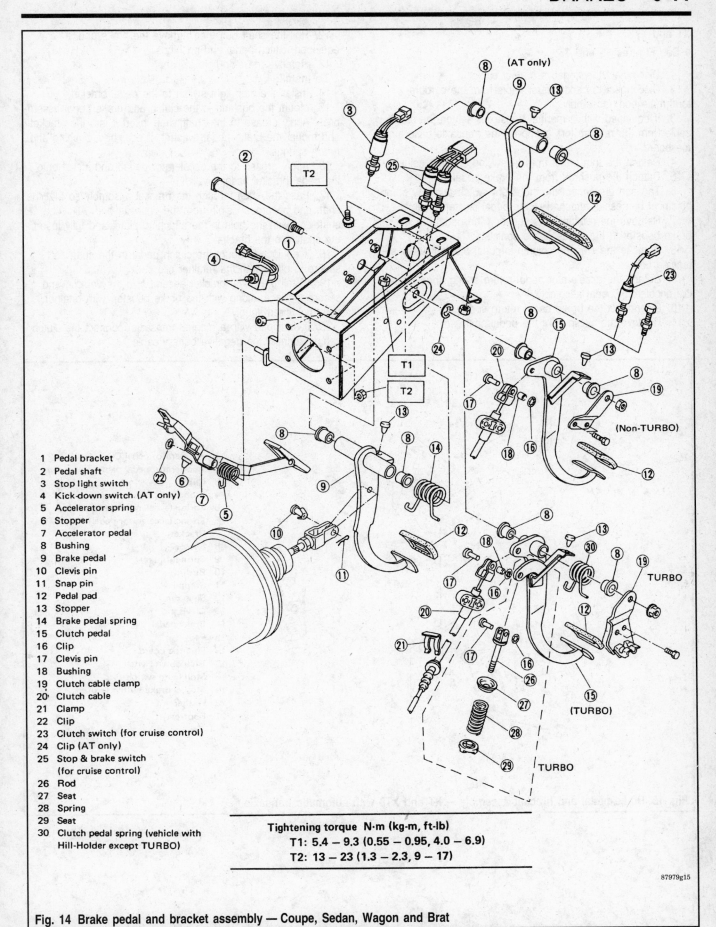

1 Pedal bracket
2 Pedal shaft
3 Stop light switch
4 Kick-down switch (AT only)
5 Accelerator spring
6 Stopper
7 Accelerator pedal
8 Bushing
9 Brake pedal
10 Clevis pin
11 Snap pin
12 Pedal pad
13 Stopper
14 Brake pedal spring
15 Clutch pedal
16 Clip
17 Clevis pin
18 Bushing
19 Clutch cable clamp
20 Clutch cable
21 Clamp
22 Clip
23 Clutch switch (for cruise control)
24 Clip (AT only)
25 Stop & brake switch
   (for cruise control)
26 Rod
27 Seat
28 Spring
29 Seat
30 Clutch pedal spring (vehicle with
   Hill-Holder except TURBO)

Tightening torque N·m (kg-m, ft-lb)
T1: 5.4 — 9.3 (0.55 — 0.95, 4.0 — 6.9)
T2: 13 — 23 (1.3 — 2.3, 9 — 17)

87979g15

Fig. 14 Brake pedal and bracket assembly — Coupe, Sedan, Wagon and Brat

XT and XT6

▶ **See Figures 15 and 16**

1. Disconnect the negative battery cable.
2. Disconnect the accelerator cable from the carburetor/throttle body assembly.
3. If equipped with a manual transaxle, detach the clutch cable from the release fork clamp on the transaxle case and toe board.
4. Detach the trim panel from below the steering column.
5. Detach the pushrod from the brake pedal.
6. Tag and disconnect the stop light switch and any other electrical harnesses attached to the pedal cluster assembly.
7. Remove the retainer nuts securing the pedal bracket and brake booster to the inside of the vehicle.
8. Remove the steering column-to-pedal bracket upper attaching bolt.
9. Detach the accelerator pedal return spring, then remove the accelerator pedal assembly.
10. Disconnect the brake pedal return spring.
11. Remove the circlip from the pedal shaft.

12. Pull the shaft out, then remove the brake and, if equipped, clutch pedal and bushings.
13. Remove the stop light switch.

To install:

14. Install the stop light switch to the pedal bracket.
15. Mount the bushing in the clutch and brake pedal assemblies. Apply grease to the shaft, then insert it into the bracket and mount the brake pedal, washer, if equipped, bushing and return springs.
16. Apply grease to the accelerator pedal, and install onto the pedal bracket assembly.
17. Pass the shaft through the bracket assembly so that the shaft end becomes visible from the opposite end. Align the shaft end with the hole in the attaching plate, and fully insert the shaft into the bracket.
18. If equipped, mount the clutch pedal to the shaft and secure in place with the retainer clip.
19. Install the pedal bracket assembly in the vehicle, and secure in place, along with the brake booster, with retainer nuts, tightened snugly.
20. If equipped with a manual transaxle, connect the clutch cable. Connect the negative battery cable.

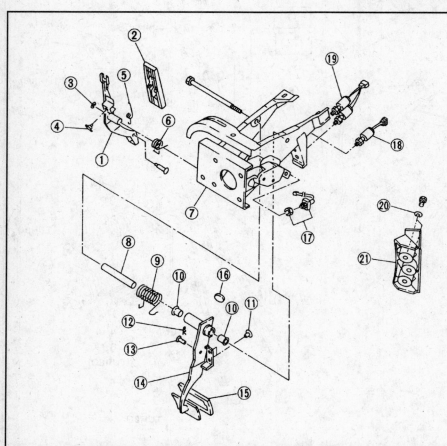

1	Accelerator pedal CP
2	Accelerator pedal pad
3	Clip
4	Stopper
5	Spring (accelerator pedal pad)
6	Spring (accelerator pedal)
7	Bracket
8	Spacer
9	Spring (brake)
10	Bushing
11	Stopper
12	Snap pin
13	Clevis pin
14	Brake pedal
15	Pad
16	Plug toe board
17	Kick down switch
18	Stop lamp switch
19	Stop & brake switch (cruise)
20	Washer
21	Footrest

87979g17

Fig. 15 Brake pedal and bracket assembly — XT and XT6 with automatic transaxle

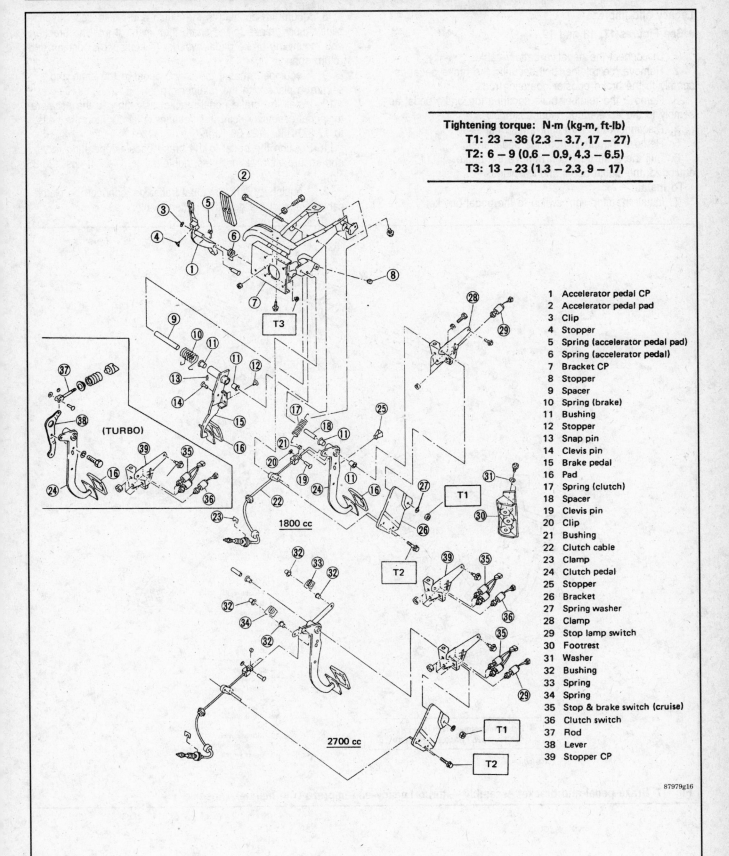

Tightening torque: N·m (kg-m, ft-lb)
T1: 23 — 36 (2.3 — 3.7, 17 — 27)
T2: 6 — 9 (0.6 — 0.9, 4.3 — 6.5)
T3: 13 — 23 (1.3 — 2.3, 9 — 17)

1   Accelerator pedal CP
2   Accelerator pedal pad
3   Clip
4   Stopper
5   Spring (accelerator pedal pad)
6   Spring (accelerator pedal)
7   Bracket CP
8   Stopper
9   Spacer
10 Spring (brake)
11 Bushing
12 Stopper
13 Snap pin
14 Clevis pin
15 Brake pedal
16 Pad
17 Spring (clutch)
18 Spacer
19 Clevis pin
20 Clip
21 Bushing
22 Clutch cable
23 Clamp
24 Clutch pedal
25 Stopper
26 Bracket
27 Spring washer
28 Clamp
29 Stop lamp switch
30 Footrest
31 Washer
32 Bushing
33 Spring
34 Spring
35 Stop & brake switch (cruise)
36 Clutch switch
37 Rod
38 Lever
39 Stopper CP

87979g16

Fig. 16 Brake pedal and bracket assembly — XT and XT6 with manual transaxle

Legacy and Impreza

▶ **See Figures 17, 18 and 19**

1. Disconnect the negative battery cable.

2. Remove the retainer bolt securing the brake pedal assembly to the brake booster operating rod.

3. Remove the retainer bolts securing the brake pedal assembly to the accelerator pedal assembly.

4. Disconnect the stop light switch harness.

5. Remove the circlip from the pedal shaft.

6. Pull the shaft out, then remove the brake and, if equipped, the clutch pedal and bushings.

To install:

7. Install the stop light switch to the pedal bracket.

8. Mount the bushing in the clutch and brake pedal assemblies. Apply grease to the shaft, then insert it into the bracket and mount the brake pedal, washer (if equipped), bushing and return springs.

9. If equipped, mount the clutch pedal to the shaft and secure in place with the retainer clip.

10. Install the brake pedal bracket assembly to the accelerator pedal assembly using the retainer bolts. Tighten the bolts to 17-27 ft. lbs. (23-36 Nm).

11. Position the pedal to the brake booster operating rod, and secure with retainer nuts, tightened to 17-27 ft. lbs. (23-36 Nm).

12. If equipped with a manual transaxle, connect the clutch cable. Connect the negative battery cable.

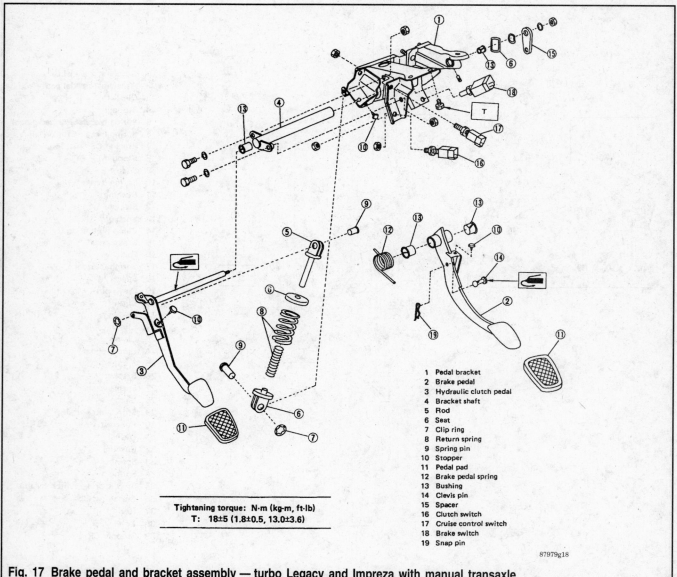

1	Pedal bracket
2	Brake pedal
3	Hydraulic clutch pedal
4	Bracket shaft
5	Rod
6	Seat
7	Clip ring
8	Return spring
9	Spring pin
10	Stopper
11	Pedal pad
12	Brake pedal spring
13	Bushing
14	Clevis pin
15	Spacer
16	Clutch switch
17	Cruise control switch
18	Brake switch
19	Snap pin

Tightening torque: N·m (kg-m, ft-lb)
T: 18±5 (1.8±0.5, 13.0±3.6)

87979g18

Fig. 17 Brake pedal and bracket assembly — turbo Legacy and Impreza with manual transaxle

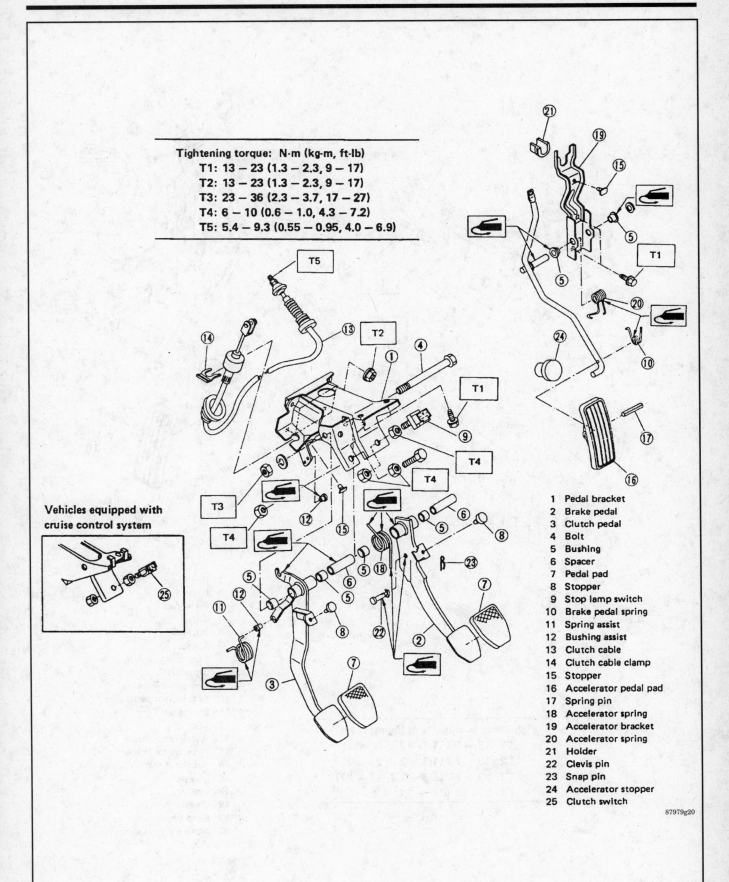

Tightening torque: N·m (kg-m, ft-lb)
T1: 13 — 23 (1.3 — 2.3, 9 — 17)
T2: 13 — 23 (1.3 — 2.3, 9 — 17)
T3: 23 — 36 (2.3 — 3.7, 17 — 27)
T4: 6 — 10 (0.6 — 1.0, 4.3 — 7.2)
T5: 5.4 — 9.3 (0.55 — 0.95, 4.0 — 6.9)

Vehicles equipped with
cruise control system

1 Pedal bracket
2 Brake pedal
3 Clutch pedal
4 Bolt
5 Bushing
6 Spacer
7 Pedal pad
8 Stopper
9 Stop lamp switch
10 Brake pedal spring
11 Spring assist
12 Bushing assist
13 Clutch cable
14 Clutch cable clamp
15 Stopper
16 Accelerator pedal pad
17 Spring pin
18 Accelerator spring
19 Accelerator bracket
20 Accelerator spring
21 Holder
22 Clevis pin
23 Snap pin
24 Accelerator stopper
25 Clutch switch

87979g20

Fig. 18 Brake pedal and bracket assembly — non-turbo Legacy and Impreza with manual transaxle

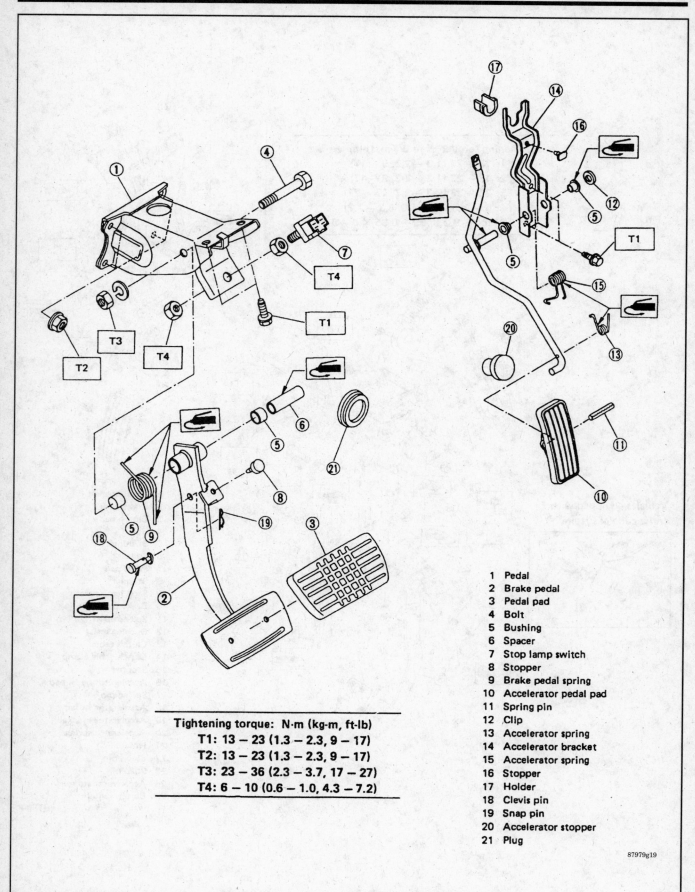

Tightening torque: N·m (kg-m, ft-lb)
T1: 13 — 23 (1.3 — 2.3, 9 — 17)
T2: 13 — 23 (1.3 — 2.3, 9 — 17)
T3: 23 — 36 (2.3 — 3.7, 17 — 27)
T4: 6 — 10 (0.6 — 1.0, 4.3 — 7.2)

1 Pedal
2 Brake pedal
3 Pedal pad
4 Bolt
5 Bushing
6 Spacer
7 Stop lamp switch
8 Stopper
9 Brake pedal spring
10 Accelerator pedal pad
11 Spring pin
12 Clip
13 Accelerator spring
14 Accelerator bracket
15 Accelerator spring
16 Stopper
17 Holder
18 Clevis pin
19 Snap pin
20 Accelerator stopper
21 Plug

87979g19

Fig. 19 Brake pedal and bracket assembly — Legacy and Impreza with automatic transaxle

SVX

▶ **See Figure 20**

1. Disconnect the negative battery cable.

2. Remove the steering wheel, followed by the steering shaft assembly. Refer to the procedure in Section 8 of this manual.

3. Remove the front driver seat from the vehicle. Refer to Section 10 for removal and installation steps.

4. Disconnect the stop light switch harness.

5. Remove the snap pin which connects the brake pedal and operating rod.

➡**The operating rod length is preset at the factory. Do not attempt to loosen the locknut.**

6. Remove the retainer bolts securing the pedal assembly in place. Remove the bracket and pedal assembly from the vehicle.

7. Remove the circlip from the pedal shaft.

8. Pull the shaft out, then remove the brake and, if equipped, the clutch pedal and bushings.

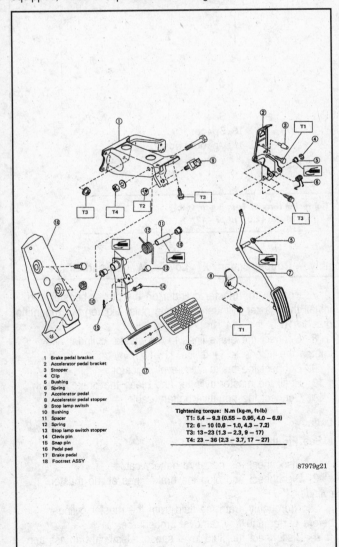

1	Brake pedal bracket
2	Accelerator pedal bracket
3	Stopper
4	Clip
5	Bushing
6	Spring
7	Accelerator pedal
8	Accelerator pedal stopper
9	Stop lamp switch
10	Bushing
11	Spacer
12	Spring
13	Stop lamp switch stopper
14	Clevis pin
15	Snap pin
16	Pedal pad
17	Brake pedal
18	Footrest ASSY

Tightening torque: N.m (kg-m, ft-lb)
T1: 5.4 — 9.3 (0.55 — 0.95, 4.0 — 6.9)
T2: 6 — 10 (0.6 — 1.0, 4.3 — 7.2)
T3: 13 — 23 (1.3 — 2.3, 9 — 17)
T4: 23 — 36 (2.3 — 3.7, 17 — 27)

87979g21

Fig. 20 Brake pedal and bracket assembly — SVX

To install:

9. Install the stop light switch to the pedal bracket.

10. Mount the bushing in the clutch and brake pedal assemblies. Apply grease to the shaft, then insert it into the bracket and mount the brake pedal, washer (if equipped), bushing and return springs.

11. Position the pedal assembly in the vehicle, and secure in place with the retainer bolts. Tighten the bolts to 9-17 ft. lbs. (12-22 Nm).

12. Attach the brake pedal to the operating rod using the snap pin to secure.

13. Install the driver seat, followed by the steering shaft and wheel.

14. Connect the negative battery cable.

Master Cylinder

REMOVAL & INSTALLATION

Justy and Impreza

1. Disconnect the negative battery cable.

2. Siphon the brake fluid out of the master cylinder reservoir.

3. Disconnect the electrical connector from the brake fluid warning light.

4. Disconnect and cap the brake pipes from the master cylinder.

5. Remove the two master cylinder mounting nuts.

6. Remove the master cylinder from the mounting studs.

To install:

7. If a new master cylinder is being installed, it must be bench bled first. Refer to the bleeding procedure later in this section.

8. Install the master cylinder on the mounting studs and tighten the mounting nuts to 10 ft. lbs. (13 Nm).

9. Connect the brake pipes to the master cylinder and tighten the fittings to 13 ft. lbs. (18 Nm).

10. Connect the electrical connector to the brake fluid warning switch.

11. Refill the master cylinder.

12. Connect the negative battery cable.

13. Bleed the brake system, as described later in this section.

Coupe, Sedan, XT, Loyale, Wagon and Brat

▶ **See Figures 21 and 22**

1. Disconnect the negative battery cable.

2. Siphon the brake fluid from the master cylinder.

3. Disconnect the brake fluid level indicator harness.

4. Disconnect and cap the brake lines from the master cylinder.

5. Remove the master cylinder mounting nuts and remove the master cylinder.

To install:

6. Before installing a new master cylinder, it must first be bench bled. Refer to the bleeding procedure later in this section.

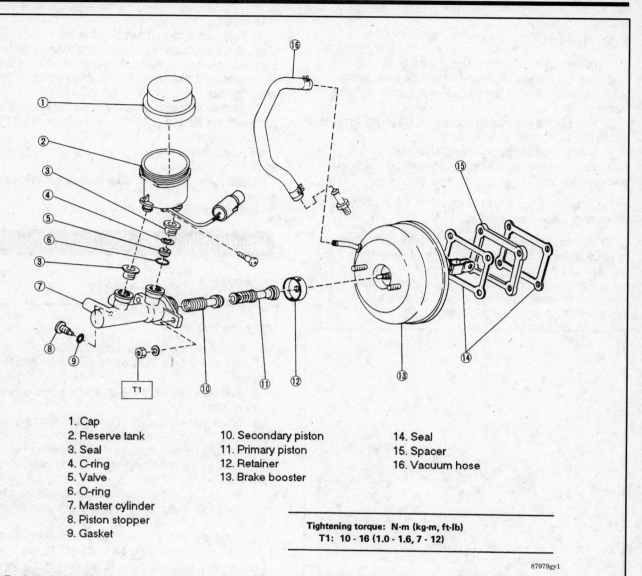

1. Cap
2. Reserve tank
3. Seal
4. C-ring
5. Valve
6. O-ring
7. Master cylinder
8. Piston stopper
9. Gasket
10. Secondary piston
11. Primary piston
12. Retainer
13. Brake booster
14. Seal
15. Spacer
16. Vacuum hose

Tightening torque: N·m (kg-m, ft-lb)
T1: 10 - 16 (1.0 - 1.6, 7 - 12)

87979gy1

Fig. 21 Exploded view of the master cylinder and booster assembly — Coupe, Sedan, XT, Loyale, Wagon and Brat

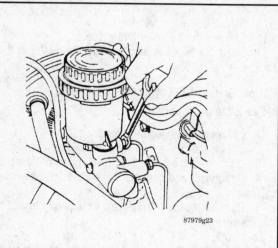

87979g23

Fig. 22 Use a flare-end wrench to disconnect the brake lines from the master cylinder

7. Position the master cylinder on the power booster and install the master cylinder mounting nuts. Tighten the mounting nuts to 10 ft. lbs. (14 Nm).

8. Connect the brake lines to the master cylinder and tighten the fittings to 11 ft. lbs. (15 Nm).

9. Connect the brake fluid level indicator.

10. Refill the master cylinder and bleed the brake system.

11. Connect the negative battery cable.

Legacy

▶ See Figures 23, 24 and 25

1. Disconnect the negative battery cable.

2. Disconnect and plug the brake lines at the master cylinder.

3. Thoroughly drain the fluid from the master cylinder before performing any removal procedures.

4. Disconnect the fluid level sensor electrical harness connector from the master cylinder.

5. Remove the master cylinder-to-power brake booster retaining nuts. Remove the master cylinder from its mounting.

Fig. 23 Siphon as much brake fluid out of the reservoir

Fig. 24 Unfasten the reservoir electrical harness

Fig. 25 Loosen the master cylinder retainer nuts

To install:

6. Bench bleed the master cylinder prior to installation. Refer to the bleeding procedure later in this section.

7. Install the master cylinder on the power booster and tighten the nuts to 7-13 ft. lbs. (10-18 Nm).

8. Connect the fluid level indicator.

9. Connect the brake lines and tighten the flarenut to 9-13 ft. lbs. (13-18 Nm).

10. Bleed the brake system as required.

SVX

1. Siphon the brake fluid out of the master cylinder reservoir.

2. Disconnect the electrical harness from the brake fluid sensor.

3. Cap and disconnect the brake lines from the master cylinder.

4. Remove the master cylinder mounting nuts.

5. Remove the master cylinder.

To install:

6. If installing a new master cylinder, bench bleed prior to installation. Refer to the bleeding procedure later in this section.

7. Install the master cylinder on the booster studs.

8. Install the master cylinder mounting nuts and tighten to 10 ft. lbs. (14 Nm).

9. Connect the brake lines to the master cylinder and tighten the fittings to 11 ft. lbs. (15 Nm).

10. Connect the electrical connector to the brake fluid sensor.

11. Refill the master cylinder with fluid.

12. Bleed the brake system.

Power Brake Booster

The power brake booster uses engine manifold vacuum against a diaphragm to assist in the application of the brakes. The vacuum is regulated to be proportional to the pressure placed on the pedal.

✲✲CAUTION

Properly disarm the air bag on vehicles equipped with the SRS system. Failure to do so can cause serious injury. The procedure can be found in Section 6 of this manual under the heading "Supplemental Restraint System".

If brake performance is questionable and the booster unit is suspect, conduct the following tests:

AIRTIGHTNESS TEST

1. Apply the hand brake and start the engine.

2. Run the engine for one or two minutes, then turn it **OFF**.

3. Apply the brakes several times using the same force as in normal braking. The pedal stroke should be greatest on the first application and become smaller with each additional stroke. If no change occurs in the pedal height while it is applied, the power brake unit could be faulty.

OPERATION CHECK

1. With the engine off, apply the brakes several times using normal pedal pressure. Make sure the pedal height does not vary on each stroke.
2. With the brakes applied, start the engine.
3. When the engine starts, the brake pedal should move slightly toward the floor. If no change in the pedal height occurs, the power brake unit could be faulty.

INSPECTION

Inspect the vacuum hose and check valve periodically, the hose for cracking or brittleness. The check valve (engine running and brakes applied) for air leaks. Replace the hose or valve if necessary. Sometimes a stuck check valve can act like a bad power booster. If this is suspected, replace the check valve.

Rebuilding a power brake booster or doing a complete pressure test requires special gauges and tools. It is just not practical for the car owner to attempt servicing the unit, except to remove and replace it.

REMOVAL & INSTALLATION

Justy

1. Disconnect the negative battery cable.
2. Remove the master cylinder.
3. Disconnect the vacuum line from the power booster.
4. From under the dashboard, remove the snapring from the booster pushrod.
5. Remove the pushrod clevis pin.
6. Remove the power booster mounting nuts.
7. Remove the power booster from under the hood.
To install:
8. Install the power booster on the firewall.
9. From under the dashboard, install the mounting nuts and tighten to 13 ft. lbs. (18 Nm).
10. Connect the pushrod to the brake pedal and install the clevis pin and snapring.
11. Install the master cylinder on the power booster.
12. Connect the vacuum line to the booster.
13. Bleed the brake system.
14. Connect the negative battery cable.

Coupe, Sedan, XT, Loyale, Wagon and Brat
▶ **See Figures 21 and 26**

1. Disconnect the negative battery cable.
2. From under the hood, perform the following:
   a. Disconnect the electrical harness from the fluid level indicator.
   b. Disconnect and cap the brake lines from the master cylinder.
   c. Remove the master cylinder mounting nuts.
   d. Disconnect the vacuum hose from the booster.

3. From under the dashboard, perform the following steps:
   a. Remove the snap pin and clevis pin securing the booster pushrod to the brake pedal.
   b. Remove the four power booster mounting nuts.
4. Remove the power booster from under the hood. When removing the booster be careful not to damage the brake lines.
To install:
5. Install the brake booster on the firewall.
6. From under the dashboard install the four mounting nuts and tighten to 13 ft. lbs. (18 Nm).
7. Connect the booster pushrod to the brake pedal, then install the clevis pin and snap pin.
8. Connect the vacuum line to the booster.
9. Install the master cylinder and tighten the mounting nuts to 10 ft. lbs. (14 Nm).
10. Connect the brake lines to the master cylinder and tighten the fittings to 11 ft. lbs. (16 Nm).
11. Connect the electrical connector to the brake fluid level sensor.
12. Bleed the brake system.

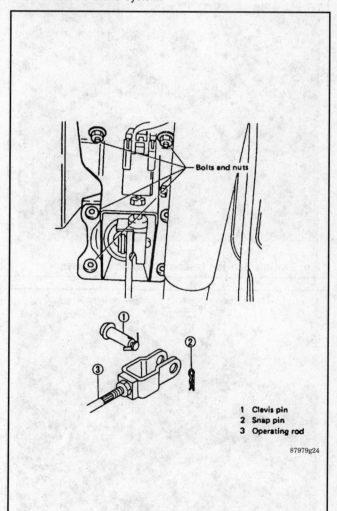

1 Clevis pin
2 Snap pin
3 Operating rod

87979g24

Fig. 26 Brake booster pushrod and connecting hardware

13. Connect the negative battery cable.

Impreza and Legacy

1. Remove the master cylinder.
2. Disconnect the vacuum hose from the brake booster.
3. Working under the instrument panel, remove the cotter pin and clevis pin from the operating rod bracket. Remove the brake booster mounting nuts.
4. Remove the brake booster from the engine compartment.

To install:

5. Position the power booster in the engine compartment.
6. Install the mounting nuts. Tighten the nuts to 9-17 ft. lbs. (13-23 Nm).
7. Install the clevis pin with a new cotter pin.
8. Adjust the brake booster operating rod.
9. Connect the vacuum line to the booster.
10. Install the master cylinder.

SVX

▶ **See Figures 27 and 28**

1. Disconnect the negative battery cable.
2. Raise and safely support the vehicle on jackstands.
3. Disconnect the sway bar from the frame.
4. Drain about 1.5 qts. (1.42 liters) of transmission fluid from the transaxle.
5. Remove the bolts securing the upper and lower sides of the transaxle dipstick tube.
6. Remove the cruise control actuator, if equipped.
7. Disconnect the positive battery cable from the starter.
8. Discharge the A/C system using an approved recycling/recovery machine.
9. Remove the low side A/C pipe.
10. Disconnect the vacuum line from the brake booster.
11. Remove the master cylinder from the power booster.
12. From under the dash, remove the snapring and clevis pin from the brake booster pushrod at the brake pedal.
13. Remove the four nuts mounting the power booster to the firewall.

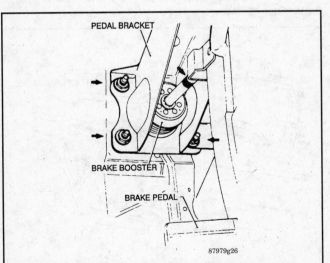

Fig. 27 Remove the brake booster retainer nuts from inside the vehicle

14. Remove the power booster.

To install:

15. Install the power booster on the firewall and install the four mounting nuts. Tighten the mounting nuts to 9-13 ft. lbs. (13-18 Nm).
16. Connect the power booster pushrod to the brake pedal and install the clevis pin and snapring.
17. Install the master cylinder on the power booster.
18. Connect the vacuum line to the power booster.
19. Install the low side A/C pipe.
20. Recharge the A/C system using an approved recycling/recovery machine.
21. Connect the positive battery cable to the starter.
22. Install the cruise control actuator.
23. Install the dipstick tube mounting bolts.
24. Top off the transmission fluid.
25. Connect the sway bar to the subframe.
26. Lower the vehicle.
27. Connect the negative battery cable.

ADJUSTMENT

Legacy and Impreza

1. Turn the engine **OFF**.
2. Disconnect the vacuum line from the brake booster.
3. Loosen the operating rod locknut and adjust the rod until there is 0.04-0.12 in. (1-3mm) of play in the brake pedal.
4. Tighten the locknut.

Proportioning Valve

REMOVAL & INSTALLATION

Justy

▶ **See Figure 29**

1. Disconnect the negative battery cable.
2. From under the hood, disconnect and cap the six brake pipes from the proportioning valve.
3. Remove the proportioning valve mounting bolts and remove the proportioning valve.

To install:

4. Install the proportioning valve on the strut tower, then install the mounting bolts and tighten to 4 ft. lbs. (6 Nm).
5. Connect the brake pipes to the proportioning valve and tighten the fittings to 12 ft. lbs. (17 Nm).
6. Connect the negative battery cable.
7. Bleed the brake system.

Coupe, Sedan, XT, Loyale, Wagon and Brat

▶ **See Figure 30**

1. Raise and safely support the vehicle on jackstands.
2. Disconnect and cap the four brake lines from the proportioning valve.
3. Unfasten the mounting bolt and remove the proportioning valve from the bracket.

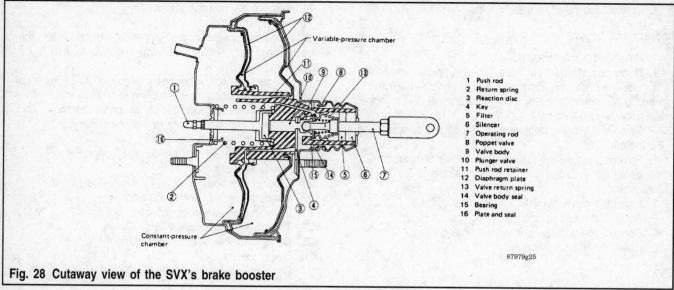

1	Push rod
2	Return spring
3	Reaction disc
4	Key
5	Filter
6	Silencer
7	Operating rod
8	Poppet valve
9	Valve body
10	Plunger valve
11	Push rod retainer
12	Diaphragm plate
13	Valve return spring
14	Valve body seal
15	Bearing
16	Plate and seal

Fig. 28 Cutaway view of the SVX's brake booster

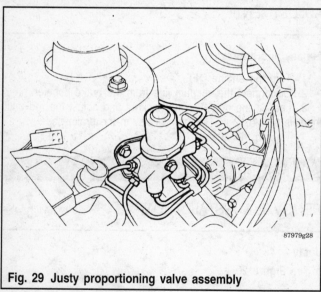

Fig. 29 Justy proportioning valve assembly

To install:

4. Position the proportioning valve on the bracket and install the mounting bolt. Tighten the mounting bolt to 18 ft. lbs. (25 Nm).

5. Connect the brake lines to the proportioning valve and tighten the fittings to 11 ft. lbs. (16 Nm).

6. Bleed the brake system.

7. Lower the vehicle.

8. Top off the master cylinder.

Legacy and Impreza

▶ See Figure 31

Do not disassemble the proportioning valve; the valve must be replaced as an assembly.

1. Remove the 4 lines from the proportioning valve. Cap each brake line to prevent debris from entering.

2. Remove the proportioning valve from the bracket.

To install:

3. Install the proportioning valve to the bracket, and tighten the retainer hardware snugly.

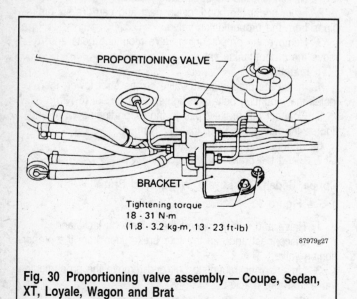

Fig. 30 Proportioning valve assembly — Coupe, Sedan, XT, Loyale, Wagon and Brat

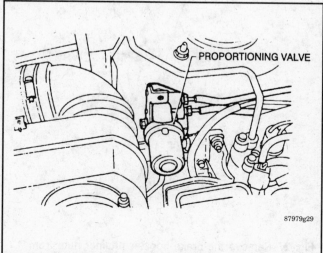

Fig. 31 Proportioning valve assembly — Legacy and Impreza

4. Connect the brake lines to the proportioning valve, and tighten the fittings to 11 ft. lbs. (15 Nm).

5. Bleed the hydraulic brake system and check the fittings for leaks.

SVX

▶ See Figure 32

1. Remove the washer cover.
2. Disconnect the electrical harness from the washer motor.
3. Disconnect the washer pipe from the body.
4. Remove the washer tank.
5. Disconnect and cap the brake pipes from the proportioning valve.
6. Remove the proportioning valve mounting bolts, then remove the proportioning valve.

To install:

7. Install the proportioning valve and mounting bolts. Tighten the mounting bolts to 11 ft. lbs. (16 Nm).
8. Connect the brake pipes to the proportioning valve. Tighten the fittings to 13 ft. lbs. (18 Nm).
9. Install the washer tank.
10. Connect the washer pipe to the body.
11. Connect the electrical harness to the washer motor.
12. Install the washer cover.
13. Bleed the brake system.

Brake Fluid Level Warning Indicator

The low brake fluid warning device (on cars so equipped) is contained in the reservoir of the master cylinder. If the brake fluid level falls about 0.71 in. (18mm) below the MAX line, a float closes an electrical circuit which causes the warning lamp on the dash panel to light.

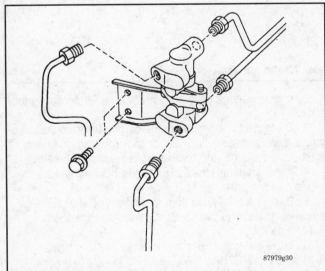

87979g30

Fig. 32 Proportioning valve assembly — SVX

Refilling the master cylinder will cause the warning lamp to go out. However, the entire brake system should be inspected for signs of leakage so the loss of brake fluid can be accounted for.

Pressure Hold Valve (PHV)

REMOVAL & INSTALLATION

▶ See Figures 33, 34 and 35

➡All manual transaxle equipped models covered by this manual, except Justy and SVX, are equipped with a Hill Holder assembly.

The pressure hold valve is the main component of the Hill Holder system. The valve is mounted in the engine compartment on the side frame rail closest to the master cylinder.

1. Drain the brake fluid from the master cylinder.
2. Remove the Hill Holder cable adjusting nut, clamp and cable mount from the clutch cable assembly in the engine compartment.
3. Detach the PHV cable from the mounting clips. Separate the connector bracket from the PHV support.
4. Disconnect the brake lines from the PHV. Use a flare wrench to prevent damage to the line nut.
5. Remove the PHV.

To install:

6. Position the PHV to the bracket, and secure in place using the retainer bolts. Tighten the bracket-to-PHV mounting bolts to 5-9 ft. lbs. (7-13 Nm).
7. Attach the brake lines to the PHV. Tighten the fitting to 9-13 ft. lbs. (13-18 Nm).
8. Attach the connector bracket to the PHV body, and secure with retainer bolts. Tighten to 5-9 ft. lbs. (7-13 Nm).
9. Attach the cable to the clutch cable assembly and clips.
10. Add brake fluid and bleed the brake system.
11. Adjust the hill holder cable.

ADJUSTMENT

1. Test the Hill Holder on a steep hill with NO traffic.
2. If the engine stalls when the clutch pedal/Hill Holder is released, loosen the adjusting nut gradually until smooth starting and no stalling is enabled.
3. If the vehicle slips backwards when the clutch pedal/Hill Holder is released, tighten the adjusting nut so that the Hill Holder is released after the clutch engages.

➡When adjusting the control cable nut, be sure to prevent the cable from turning.

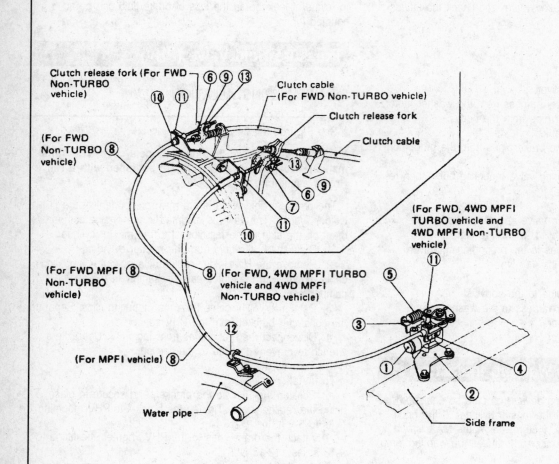

Clutch release fork (For FWD Non-TURBO vehicle)

Clutch cable (For FWD Non-TURBO vehicle)

Clutch release fork

Clutch cable

(For FWD Non-TURBO vehicle)

(For FWD MPFI Non-TURBO vehicle)

(For FWD, 4WD MPFI TURBO vehicle and 4WD MPFI Non-TURBO vehicle)

(For MPFI vehicle)

(For FWD, 4WD MPFI TURBO vehicle and 4WD MPFI Non-TURBO vehicle)

Water pipe

Side frame

1 PHV (Pressure hold valve)
2 Support
3 Hook (spring)
4 Stay (PHV)
5 Return spring
6 Pin
7 Snap pin
8 PHV cable
9 Adjusting nut
10 Bracket (cable)
11 Clamp
12 Clip
13 Lock nut

87979g31

Fig. 33 Pressure hold valve assembly — Coupe, Sedan, XT, Loyale, Wagon and Brat

Brake Hoses and Pipes

REMOVAL & INSTALLATION

✼✼WARNING

Clean, high quality brake fluid is essential to the safe and proper operation of the brake system. You should always buy the highest quality brake fluid that is available. If the brake fluid becomes contaminated, drain and flush the system, then refill the master cylinder with new fluid. Never reuse any brake fluid. Any brake fluid that is removed from the system should be discarded.

Brake Hose

▶ **See Figures 36, 37, 38 and 39**

1. Raise the end of the vehicle which contains the hose to be repaired, then support the vehicle safely using jackstands.

2. If necessary, remove the wheel for easier access to the hose.

3. Disconnect the hose from the caliper and plug the opening to avoid excessive fluid loss or contamination. If sealing washers are used at the connection, remove and discard.

4. If the line is attached to a support bracket, remove the clip to free the hose.

5. Disconnect the hose from the brake line and plug the openings to avoid excessive fluid loss or contamination.

To install:

6. Install the brake hose to the brake line and tighten to 9-13 ft. lbs. (12-17 Nm).

7. Install the brake hose to the caliper using NEW washers, if equipped, then tighten the retainer to 11-15 ft. lbs. (15-21 Nm) for front hoses, or 12-14 ft. lbs. (16-20 Nm) for rear hoses.

8. Attach the brake hose to the bracket, and secure in place with the retainer clip.

9. Remove the supports and lower the vehicle.

10. Properly bleed the brake system, then check the connections for leaks.

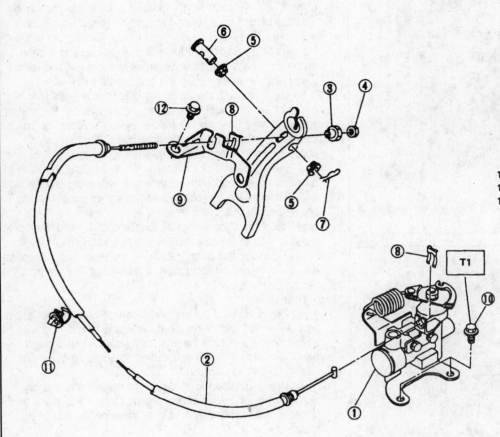

1 PHV (Pressure hold valve)
2 PHV cable ASSY
3 Adjusting nut
4 Nut
5 Bushing (PHV CABLE)
6 Pin (PHV CABLE)
7 Snap pin
8 Clamp
9 Bracket (PHV CABLE)
10 Flange bolt
11 Clip
12 Bolt

87979g32

Fig. 34 Pressure hold valve assembly — Legacy and Impreza

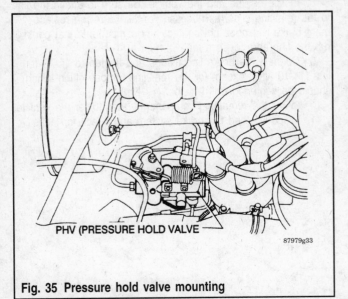

PHV (PRESSURE HOLD VALVE

87979g33

Fig. 35 Pressure hold valve mounting

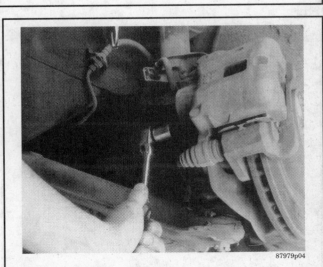

87979p04

Fig. 36 Loosen the brake hose retainer bolt at the rear of the caliper

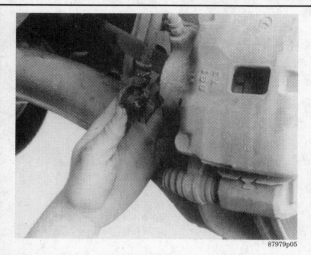

Fig. 37 Remove the retainer bolts and sealing washer, if equipped

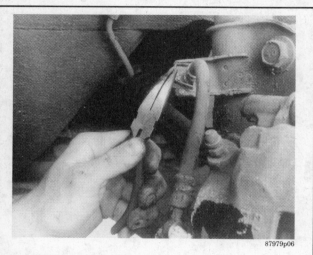

Fig. 38 If the brake hose is attached to a bracket, remove the retainer clip . . .

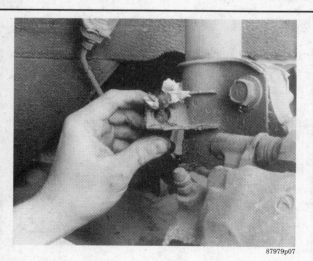

Fig. 39 . . . and slide the hose through the bracket. Notice that the hose end is protected

Brake Line

There are 2 options available when replacing a brake line. The first, and probably preferable, is to replace the entire line using a line of similar length which is already equipped with machined flared ends. Such lines are usually available from auto parts stores and usually require only a minimum of bending in order to properly fit them to the vehicle. The second option is to bend and flare the entire replacement line (or a repair section of line) using the appropriate tools.

Buying a line with machined flares is usually preferable because of the time and effort saved, not to mention the cost of special tools if they are not readily available. Also, machined flares are usually of a much higher quality than those produced by hand flaring tools or kits.

1. Raise the end of the vehicle which contains the hose to be repaired, then support the vehicle safely using jackstands.

2. Remove the components necessary for access to the brake line which is being replaced.

3. Disconnect the fittings at each end of the line, then plug the openings to prevent excessive fluid loss or contamination.

4. Trace the line from one end to the other and disconnect the line from any retaining clips, then remove the line from the vehicle.

To install:

5. Try to obtain a replacement line that is the same length as the line that was removed. If the line is longer, you will have to cut it and flare the end, or if you have decided to repair a portion of the line, see the procedure on brake line flaring, later in this section.

6. Use a suitable tubing bender to make the necessary bends in the line. Work slowly and carefully; try to make the bends look as close as possible to those on the line being replaced.

➡ When bending the brake line, be careful not to kink or crack the line. If the brake line becomes kinked or cracked, it must be replaced.

7. Before installing the brake line, flush it with brake cleaner to remove any dirt or foreign material.

8. Install the line into the vehicle. Be sure to attach the line to the retaining clips, as necessary. Make sure the replacement brake line does not contact any components that could rub the line and cause a leak.

9. Connect the brake line fittings and tighten to 11-15 ft. lbs. (14-19 Nm), except for the rear line-to-hose fitting which should be tightened to 14 ft. lbs. (19 Nm).

10. Install the remaining components, then lower the vehicle.

11. Properly bleed the brake system and check for leaks.

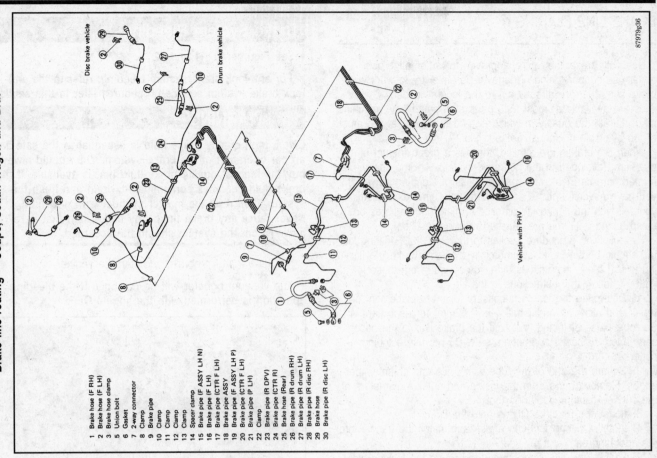

Brake line routing — Coupe, Sedan Wagon and Brat

1. Brake hose (F RH)
2. Brake hose (F LH)
3. Brake hose clamp
5. Union bolt
6. Gasket
7. 2-way connector
8. Clamp
9. Brake pipe
10. Clamp
11. Clamp
12. Clamp
13. Clamp
14. Clamp
15. Spacer clamp
16. Brake pipe (F ASSY LH N)
17. Brake pipe (F LH)
18. Brake pipe (CTR F LH)
19. Brake pipe ASSY
20. Brake pipe (F ASSY LH P)
21. Brake pipe (CTR F LH)
22. Brake pipe (P LH)
23. Clamp
24. Brake pipe (R DPV)
25. Brake pipe (CTR R)
26. Brake hose (Rear)
27. Brake pipe (R drum RH)
28. Brake pipe (R drum LH)
29. Brake pipe (R disc RH)
30. Brake hose (R disc LH)
31. Brake pipe (R disc LH)

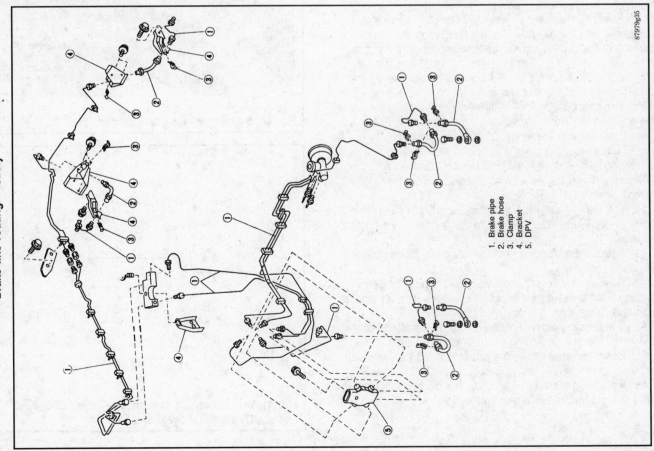

Brake line routing — Justy

1. Brake pipe
2. Brake hose
3. Clamp
4. Bracket
5. DPV

BRAKE LINE FLARING

Use only brake line tubing approved for automotive use; never use copper tubing. Whenever possible, try to work with brake lines that are already cut to the length needed. These lines are available at most auto parts stores and have machine made flares, the quality of which is hard to duplicate with most of the available inexpensive flaring kits.

When the brakes are applied, there is a great amount of pressure developed in the hydraulic system. An improperly formed flare can leak with resultant loss of stopping power. If you have never formed a double-flare, take time to familiarize yourself with the flaring kit; practice forming double-flares on scrap tubing until you are satisfied with the results.

The following procedure applies to the SA9193BR flaring kit, but should be similar to commercially available brake-line flaring kits. If these instructions differ in any way from those in your kit, follow the instructions in the kit.

1. Determine the length necessary for the replacement or repair and allow an additional 1/8 in. (3.2mm) for each flare. Select a piece of tubing, then cut the brake line to the necessary length using an appropriate saw. Do not use a tubing cutter.

2. Square the end of the tube with a file and chamfer the edges. Remove burrs from the inside and outside diameters of the cut line using a deburring tool.

3. Install the required fittings onto the line.

4. Install a flaring tool into a vise and install the handle into the operating cam.

5. Loosen the die clamp screw and rotate the locking plate to expose the die carrier opening.

6. Select the required die set (4.75mm DIN) and install in the carrier with the full side of either half facing the clamp screw and the counter bore of both halves facing the punch turret.

7. Insert the prepared line through the rear of the die and push forward until the line end is flush with the die face.

8. Make sure the rear of both halves of the die rest against the hexagon die stops, then rotate the locking plate to the fully closed position and clamp the die firmly by tightening the clamp screw.

9. Rotate the punch turret until the appropriate size (4.75mm DIN) points towards the open end of the line to be flared.

10. Pull the operating handle against the line resistance in order to create the flare, then return the handle to the original position.

11. Release the clamp screw and rotate the locking plate to the open position.

12. Remove the die set and line, then separate by gently tapping both halves on the bench. Inspect the flare for proper size and shape.

13. If necessary, repeat Steps 2-12 for the other end of the line or for the end of the line which is being repaired.

14. Bend the replacement line or section using a line bending tool.

15. If repairing the original line, join the old and new sections using a female union and tighten.

Brake System Bleeding

▶ See Figures 40, 41 and 42

➡ For anti-lock brake system bleeding, refer to the anti-lock brake system service procedures later in this section.

✳✳WARNING

Clean, high quality brake fluid is essential to the safe and proper operation of the brake system. You should always buy the highest quality brake fluid that is available. If the brake fluid becomes contaminated, drain and flush the system, then refill the master cylinder with new fluid. Never reuse any brake fluid. Any brake fluid that is removed from the system should be discarded.

1. Set the parking brake and start the engine.

➡ The vacuum booster will be damaged if the bleeding operation is performed with the engine OFF.

Fig. 40 Bleeding a rear brake caliper

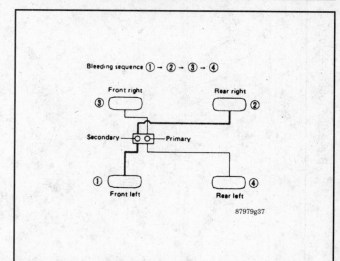

Fig. 41 Brake bleeding sequence — Justy, Coupe, Sedan, XT, Wagon, Loyale and Brat

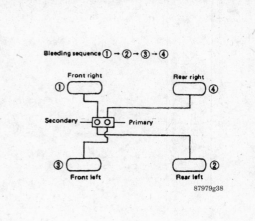

Bleeding sequence ① → ② → ③ → ④

Front right ①

Rear right ④

Secondary — Primary

③ Front left

② Rear left

87979g38

Fig. 42 Brake bleeding sequence — Legacy, Impreza and SVX

2. Remove the master cylinder reservoir cap and fill the reservoir with brake fluid. Keep the reservoir at least half full during the bleeding operation.

3. If the master cylinder is replaced or overhauled, first bleed the air from the master cylinder and then from each caliper or wheel cylinder. Bleed the master cylinder as follows:

   a. Disconnect the left front wheel brake line from the master cylinder.

   b. Have an assistant depress the brake pedal slowly once and hold it depressed.

   c. Seal the delivery port of the master cylinder where the line was disconnected with a finger, then release the brake pedal slowly.

   d. Release the finger from the delivery port when the brake pedal returns completely.

   e. Reconnect the brake line to the master cylinder.

   f. Have an assistant depress the brake pedal slowly once and hold it depressed.

   g. Loosen the left front wheel brake line at the master cylinder.

   h. Retighten the brake line, then release the brake pedal slowly.

   i. Repeat Steps 3g-h, until no air comes out from the port when the brake line is loosened.

   j. Bleed the air from the right front wheel brake line connection by repeating Steps 3a-i, but this time disconnect/loosen the right front wheel brake line.

4. Bleed the air from each wheel as follows:

   a. Place the proper size flare or box-end wrench over the bleeder screw.

   b. Cover the bleeder screw with a transparent tube and submerge the free end of the tube in a transparent container containing brake fluid.

   c. Have an assistant pump the brake pedal 3 times, then hold it depressed.

   d. Remove the air along with the brake fluid by loosening the bleeder screw.

   e. Retighten the bleeder screw, then release the brake pedal slowly.

   f. Repeat Steps 3c-e until the air is completely removed. It may be necessary to repeat the bleeding procedure 10 or more times for front wheels and 15 or more times for rear wheels.

   g. After the bleeding operation is completed on each individual wheel, check the level of brake fluid in the reservoir and replenish up to the **MAX** level, if necessary.

   h. Go to the next wheel in sequence after each wheel is bled.

5. Depress the brake pedal to check if sponginess is felt after the air has been removed from all wheel cylinders and calipers. If the pedal feels spongy, the entire bleeding procedure must be repeated.

6. Install the master cylinder reservoir cap.

FRONT DISC BRAKES

✳✳CAUTION

Brake pads may contain asbestos, which has been determined to be a cancer causing agent. Never clean the brake surfaces with compressed air! Avoid inhaling any dust from any brake surface! When cleaning brake surfaces, use a commercially available brake cleaning fluid.

Disc Brake Pads

REMOVAL & INSTALLATION

▶ See Figures 43, 44, 45, 46, 47, 48, 49 and 50

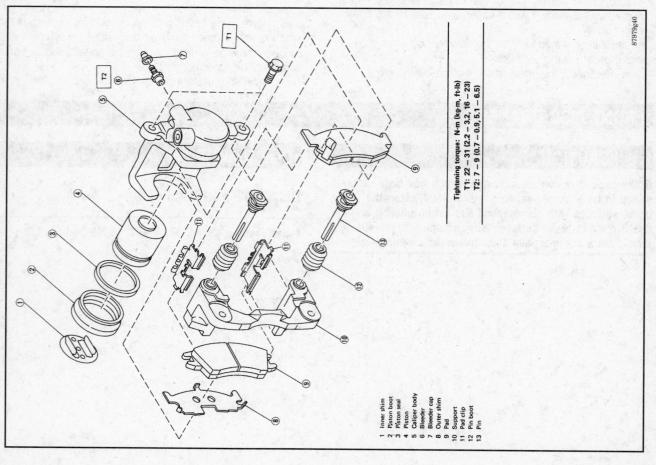

Front caliper and pad assembly — Justy with 13-inch wheel

87979g41

Tightening torque: N·m (kg-m, ft-lb)
T1: 22 – 31 (2.2 – 3.2, 16 – 23)
T2: 7 – 9 (0.7 – 0.9, 5.1 – 6.5)
T3: 34 – 44 (3.5 – 4.5, 25 – 33)

1 Inner shim
2 Piston boot
3 Piston seal
4 Piston
5 Caliper body
6 Bleeder
7 Bleeder cap
8 Outer shim
9 Pad
10 Support
11 Pad clip
12 Pin boot
13 Pin
14 Boot sleeve
15 Sleeve

Front caliper and pad assembly — Justy with 12-inch wheel

87979g40

Tightening torque: N·m (kg-m, ft-lb)
T1: 22 – 31 (2.2 – 3.2, 16 – 23)
T2: 7 – 9 (0.7 – 0.9, 5.1 – 6.5)

1 Inner shim
2 Piston boot
3 Piston seal
4 Piston
5 Caliper body
6 Bleeder
7 Bleeder cap
8 Outer shim
9 Pad
10 Support
11 Pad clip
12 Pin boot
13 Pin

Front caliper and pad assembly — non-turbo Legacy and Impreza

1 Support
2 Pad COMPL (Inside)
3 Pad COMPL (Outside)
4 Lock pin
5 Guide pin boot
6 Lock pin boot
7 Lock pin sleeve
8 Guide pin
9 Pad clip
10 Outer shim
11 Inner shim
12 Shim
13 Front brake disc
14 Front disc cover
15 Bolt
16 Washer
17 Air bleeder screw
18 Piston
19 Piston seal
20 Piston boot
21 Caliper body

Tightening torque: N-m (kg-m, ft-lb)
T1: 7 – 9 (0.7 – 0.9, 5.1 – 6.5)
T2: 34 – 44 (3.5 – 4.5, 25 – 33)
T3: 34 – 44 (3.5 – 4.5, 25 – 33)
T4: 69 – 88 (7 – 9, 51 – 65)
T5: 6 – 14 (0.6 – 1.4, 4.3 – 10.1)

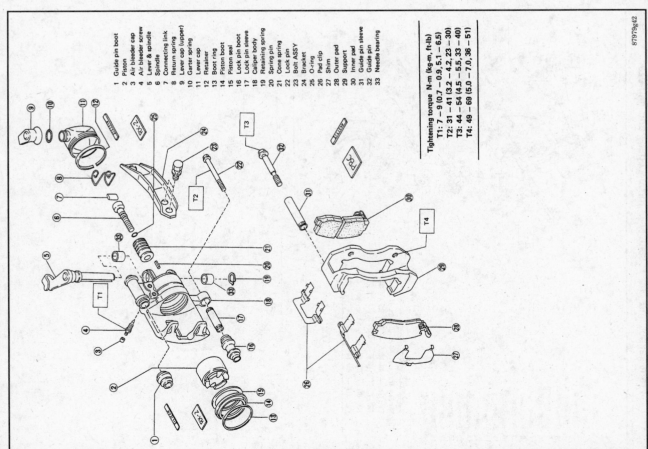

Front caliper and pad assembly — Coupe, Sedan, XT, Loyale, Wagon and Brat

1 Guide pin boot
2 Piston
3 Air bleeder cap
4 Air bleeder screw
5 Lever & spindle
6 Spindle
7 Connecting link
8 Return spring
9 Lever cap (upper)
10 Lever cap
11 Lever cap
12 Retainer
13 Boot ring
14 Piston boot
15 Piston seal
16 Lock pin boot
17 Lock pin sleeve
18 Caliper body
19 Retaining spring
20 Spring pin
21 Cone spring
22 Lock pin
23 Bolt ASSY
24 Bracket
25 O-ring
26 Pad clip
27 Shim
28 Outer pad
29 Support
30 Inner pad
31 Guide pin sleeve
32 Guide pin
33 Needle bearing

Tightening torque N-m (kg-m, ft-lb)
T1: 7 – 9 (0.7 – 0.9, 5.1 – 6.5)
T2: 31 – 41 (3.2 – 4.2, 23 – 30)
T3: 44 – 54 (4.5 – 5.5, 33 – 40)
T4: 49 – 69 (5.0 – 7.0, 36 – 51)

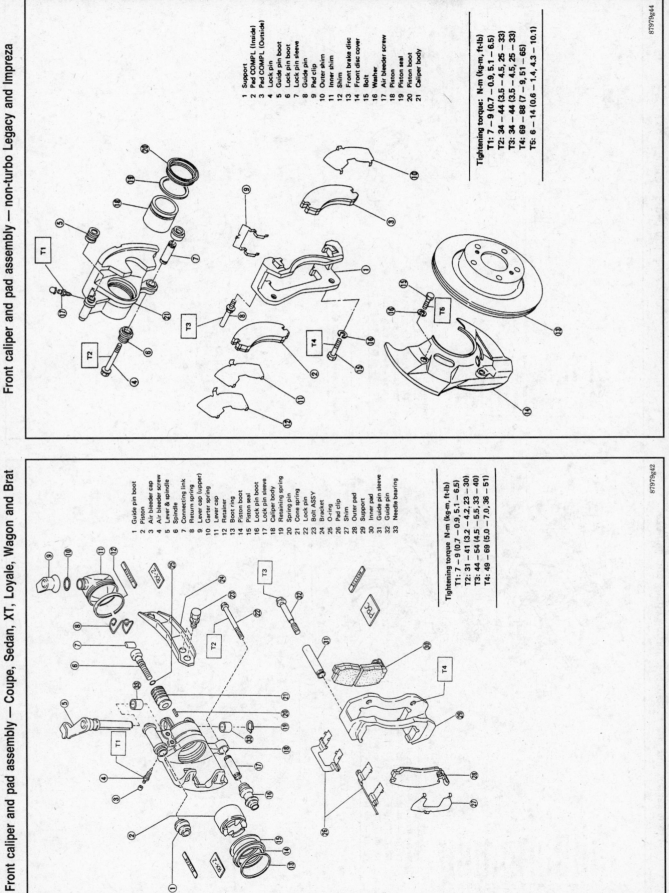

Front caliper and pad assembly — SVX

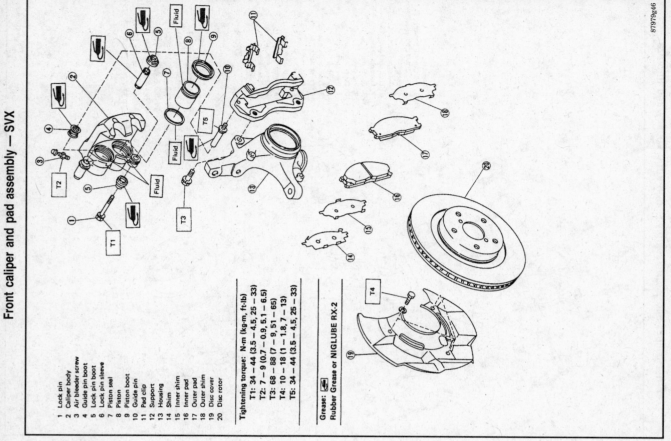

87979g46

Tightening torque: N·m (kg-m, ft-lb)
T1: 34 — 44 (3.5 — 4.5, 25 — 33)
T2: 7 — 9 (0.7 — 0.9, 5.1 — 6.5)
T3: 68 — 88 (7 — 9, 51 — 65)
T4: 10 — 18 (1 — 1.8, 7 — 13)
T5: 34 — 44 (3.5 — 4.5, 25 — 33)

Grease:
Rubber Grease or NIGLUBE RX-2

1 Lock pin
2 Caliper body
3 Air bleeder screw
4 Guide pin boot
5 Lock pin boot
6 Lock pin sleeve
7 Piston seal
8 Piston
9 Piston boot
10 Guide pin
11 Pad clip
12 Support
13 Housing
14 Shim
15 Inner shim
16 Inner pad
17 Outer pad
18 Outer shim
19 Disc cover
20 Disc rotor

Front caliper and pad assembly — turbo Legacy and Impreza

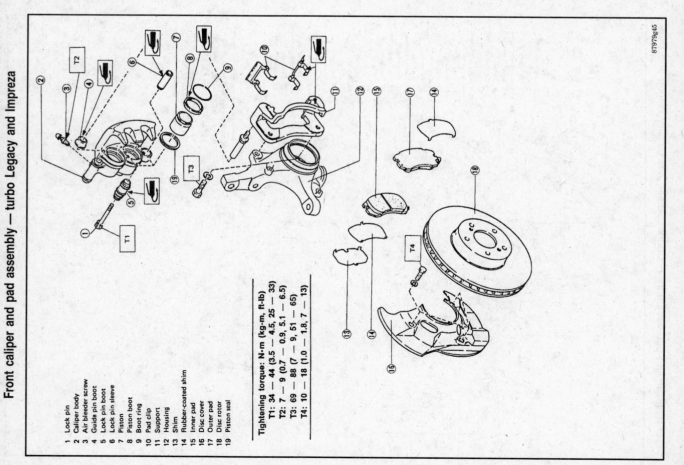

87979g45

Tightening torque: N·m (kg-m, ft-lb)
T1: 34 — 44 (3.5 — 4.5, 25 — 33)
T2: 7 — 9 (0.7 — 0.9, 5.1 — 6.5)
T3: 69 — 88 (7 — 9, 51 — 65)
T4: 10 — 18 (1.0 — 1.8, 7 — 13)

1 Lock pin
2 Caliper body
3 Air bleeder screw
4 Guide pin boot
5 Lock pin boot
6 Lock pin sleeve
7 Piston
8 Piston boot
9 Boot ring
10 Pad clip
11 Support
12 Housing
13 Shim
14 Rubber-coated shim
15 Inner pad
16 Disc cover
17 Outer pad
18 Disc rotor
19 Piston seal

✳✳WARNING

Before beginning the procedure, determine whether your vehicle is equipped with a front parking brake assembly. If equipped with front parking brakes, only compress the piston slightly, or the piston screw could be damaged.

1. Remove a small portion of brake fluid from the master cylinder reservoir.

2. Raise and support the vehicle safely on jackstands. Remove the wheel assemblies.

3. Use a C-clamp to compress the piston into the caliper bore.

➡If your vehicle is equipped with front parking brakes, compress the piston only slightly.

4. Release the parking brake and disconnect the cable from the caliper lever, if equipped.

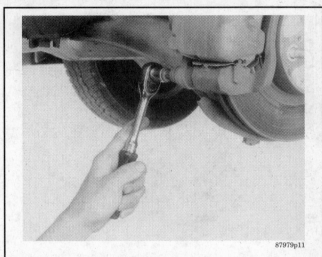

Fig. 45 Loosen and remove the caliper lower retainer bolt

Fig. 43 Front caliper assembly — Legacy

Fig. 46 Lift the caliper up to access the pads

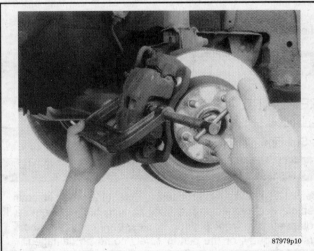

Fig. 44 Use a C-clamp to compress the piston into the caliper bore

Fig. 47 Slide the outer pad out . . .

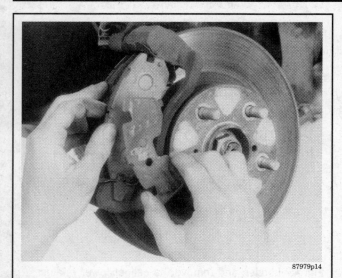
87979p14
Fig. 48 . . . and remove the backing plate

87979p15
Fig. 49 Slide the inner pad out

87979p16
Fig. 50 Remove the pad retainer clips from the bracket and inspect

5. Remove the lock pin bolts from the lower portion of the caliper.

6. Swing the caliper upward to access the pads.

7. Remove the disc brake pads, noting the position of the backing plates and retainer clips.

➡If equipped with a parking brake, use a suitable tool to rotate the piston back into the caliper bore.

To install:

8. Inspect the brake rotor, calipers and retaining components. Correct worn or damaged parts as necessary.

9. Install the new pads into the calipers, being sure all shims and clips are in their original positions.

10. Swing the calipers down into position and install the lock pin bolts. Tighten the lock pin bolts to the following specifications:

   a. Justy: 16-23 ft. lbs. (22-31 Nm).

   b. Coupe, Sedan, XT, Loyale, Wagon and Brat: 33-40 ft. lbs. (44-54 Nm).

   c. Legacy and Impreza: 25-33 ft. lbs. (34-44 Nm).

   d. SVX: 25-33 ft. lbs. (34-44 Nm).

11. Reconnect the parking brake cable, if equipped, and fill the master cylinder reservoir.

12. Install the wheel assembly. Bleed the brakes as required and lower the vehicle. Road test the vehicle.

INSPECTION

Brake pads should be inspected once a year or at 6,000 mile (9,662 km) intervals, whichever occurs first. Check both ends of the outboard pad, looking in at each end of the caliper; then check the lining thickness of the inboard pad, looking down through the inspection hole. On riveted pads, the lining should be more than $\frac{1}{32}$ in. (0.8mm) thick above the rivet (so that the lining is thicker than the metal backing in most cases), in order to prevent the rivet from scoring the rotor. On bonded brake pads, a minimum lining thickness of $\frac{1}{32}$ in. (0.8mm) above the backing plate should be used to determine necessary replacement intervals. Keep in mind that any applicable state inspection standards that are more stringent take precedence. All four front pads MUST be replaced as a set if one shows excessive wear.

Brake Caliper

REMOVAL & INSTALLATION

▶ **See Figures 51, 52, 53 and 54**

❊❊WARNING

Before beginning the procedure, determine whether your vehicle is equipped with a front parking brake assembly. If equipped with front parking brakes, only compress the piston slightly, or the piston screw could be damaged.

1. Remove as much brake fluid as possible from the master cylinder reservoir.

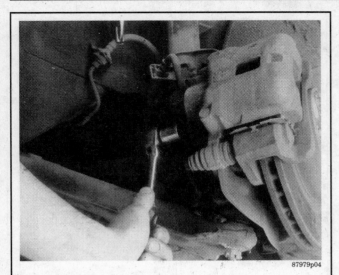

Fig. 51 Loosen the brake hose retainer bolt . . .

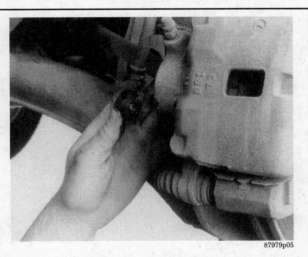

Fig. 52 . . . and remove the retainer bolt. Discard the sealing washers

Fig. 53 Loosen and remove the caliper bracket upper and lower retainer bolts

Fig. 54 Lift the caliper and bracket assembly off the rotor and spindle assembly

2. Raise and support the vehicle safely on jackstands. Remove the front wheels.

3. Use a C-clamp to compress the piston into the caliper bore.

➡If your vehicle is equipped with front parking brakes, compress the piston only slightly.

4. Release the parking brake and disconnect the cable from the caliper lever, if equipped.

5. Remove the brake hose from the caliper body and plug the hose to prevent the entrance of dirt or moisture.

6. Remove the caliper bracket retainer bolts.

7. Slide the caliper and bracket assembly off the spindle and rotor.

8. Remove the brake pads, backing plate and retainer clips.

9. Compress the piston assembly into the cylinder bore.

➡If equipped with a parking brake, use a suitable tool to rotate the piston back into the caliper bore.

To install:

10. Install the caliper bracket to the spindle assembly, and secure in place with the retainer bolts. Tighten the retainer bolts to 25-33 ft. lbs. (32-43 Nm).

11. Install the pad retainer clips, brake pads, backing plate and caliper.

12. Install the hand brake cable, if equipped.

13. Connect the brake hose using new sealing washers, and tighten the fitting to 11-15 ft. lbs. (15-21 Nm).

14. Bleed the brake system. Install the wheels and lower the vehicle. Check the fluid level in the master cylinder.

OVERHAUL

▶ See Figures 55, 56, 57, 58 and 59

1. Remove the brake caliper from the vehicle and place on a clean work surface.

2. Remove the inlet fitting from the brake caliper and drain all brake fluid.

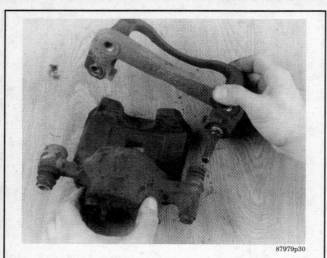

Fig. 55 Place the caliper assembly on a clean work surface and remove the bracket

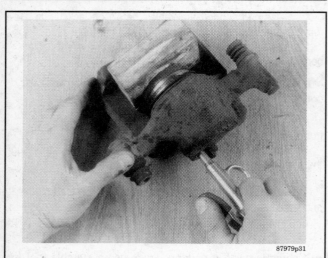

Fig. 56 Position a piece of wood as shown, then use low pressure compressed air to push out the piston

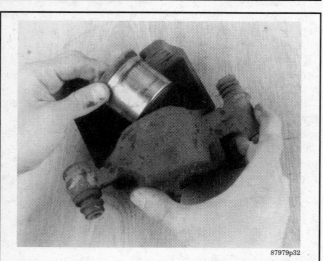

Fig. 57 Remove the piston from the caliper assembly and inspect

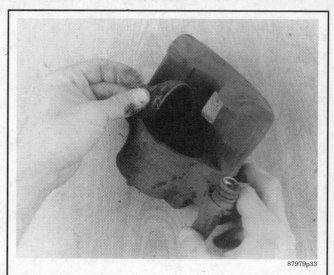

Fig. 58 Remove the piston boot from the caliper . . .

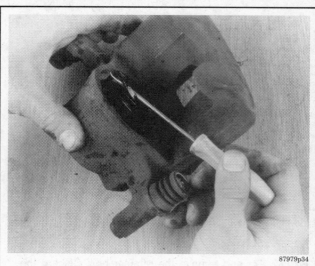

Fig. 59 . . . and the seal from inside the caliper bore

3. Place a piece of wood in the caliper opening. Use low pressure compressed air and force the piston from the bore.

✳✳CAUTION

DO NOT apply high pressure compressed air to the caliper bore. The piston may jump out, causing damage to the piston and/or the operator. Be ABSOLUTELY SURE to keep your fingers away from the piston while air is being applied.

4. Remove and discard the piston boot and seal. Be careful not to scratch the bore while removing the pieces. Use of a metal tool is NOT recommended.
5. Inspect the piston and the caliper bore for damage or corrosion. Replace the caliper and/or the piston if necessary.
6. Remove the bleeder screw and rubber cap if equipped.
7. Clean all of the parts with non-mineral based solvent and blow dry with compressed air. All rubber parts should be replaced.

8. Inspect the guide pins for corrosion, and replace if necessary. When installing the guide pins, coat them with a silicone lubricant.

To assemble:

9. Lubricate the piston, caliper and seal with clean brake fluid.

10. Install the seal into the caliper bore, making sure it is not twisted in the bore groove.

11. Install the boot onto the piston, then position the piston into the caliper bore.

12. If the caliper is equipped with a parking brake, then use a suitable tool to rotate the piston back into the caliper bore.

13. If not equipped with a parking brake, bottom the piston into the bore using your hand and a piece of wood to compress the piston.

14. Install the bleeder valve and tighten to 6-7 ft. lbs. (8-9 Nm).

15. Install the caliper to the vehicle and properly bleed the hydraulic brake system.

Brake Disc (Rotor)

REMOVAL & INSTALLATION

1985-86 Models

1. Raise the vehicle and support safely on jackstands.

2. Remove the front wheel, handbrake cable, caliper and caliper bracket. Support the caliper from a suspension part using a piece of wire. Make sure the brake hose is not distorted.

3. Remove the axle shaft nut and pull the disc off the axle shaft with a puller.

4. Remove the 4 bolts which hold the disc to the hub.

5. Separate the hub from the rotor.

To install:

6. Position the hub to the rotor, making sure the retainer bolt holes align.

7. Install the hub-to-rotor retainer bolts, and tighten to 36-51 ft. lbs. (48-69 Nm).

8. Install the hub/rotor assembly on the halfshaft. Tighten the nut to specification.

9. Install the caliper bracket, followed by the caliper and brake pads.

10. Install the wheel and tire assembly, and lower the vehicle.

1987-96 Models

▶ See Figures 60 and 61

1. Raise and safely support the vehicle on jackstands.

2. Remove the front wheel and tire assembly.

3. Remove the brake caliper and bracket assembly, and suspend out of the way with a piece of wire.

4. Remove the castle nut.

5. Remove the conical spring(s) around one or more of the lug studs.

6. Thread two suitably sized metric bolts into the holes in the rotor hat. Evenly tighten both bolts to separate the rotor from the hub assembly.

7. Pull the rotor from the hub and halfshaft.

Fig. 60 Thread two bolts into the holes in the rotor hat to separate the rotor from the hub assembly

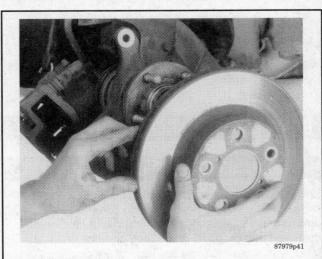

Fig. 61 When the rotor is freed from the hub, slide it off the studs

To install:

8. Install the hub and disc assembly on the axle shaft. Install the conical spring(s) and castle nut. Ensure that each conical spring is installed in the correct direction, then temporarily tighten the castle nut.

9. Install the caliper assembly and tighten the bolts to specification.

10. Tighten the castle nut and tighten to specification. Install the wheel(s) and lower the vehicle.

INSPECTION

▶ See Figure 62

Check the disc brake rotor for scoring, cracks or other damage. If rotor run-out is checked, this should be measured while the rotor is installed. Use a dial gauge to check rotor run-out.

1. Raise and support the rear of the vehicle safely using jackstands.

2. Remove the rear wheels.

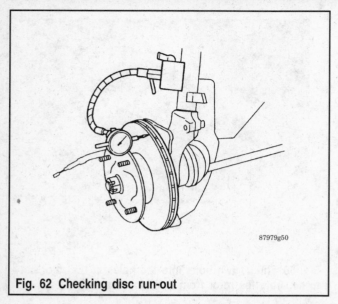

Fig. 62 Checking disc run-out

3. Visually inspect the rotor for cracks, excessive scoring or other damage. A light scoring of the surface is normal and should not be considered detrimental to brake operation.

➡Before attempting to check rotor run-out on all vehicles, the bearings must be in good condition and exhibit no excessive play.

REAR DRUM BRAKES

✳✳CAUTION

Brake shoes may contain asbestos, which has been determined to be a cancer causing agent. Never clean the brake surfaces with compressed air! Avoid inhaling any dust from any brake surface! When cleaning brake surfaces, use a commercially available brake cleaning fluid.

Brake Drums

REMOVAL & INSTALLATION

1. Raise and support the rear of the vehicle safely on jackstands.
2. Remove the rear tire and wheel assembly.
3. Matchmark the drum to the hub or hub studs for installation purposes.
4. Pry off the center cap, then remove the cotter pin, castle nut, and center retainer washer. Remove the center washer by inserting a screwdriver into the center slit and lightly tapping.
5. If the drum will not come off past the shoes, it will be necessary to retract the brake shoe adjusting screw. Remove the access hole cover from the backing plate and turn the adjuster to retract the linings away from the drum.
   To install:
6. Install the drum, aligning the matchmarks made during removal.

4. Check the disc for excessive run-out using a dial indicator:
   a. Position and secure a dial indicator so that the button contacts the disc about 0.20 in. (5mm) from the outer edge. Set the dial indicator to zero.
   b. Rotate the disc one complete revolution. The lateral run-out reading should not exceed 0.039 in. (0.10mm). If the reading is excessive, recondition or replace the disc.
5. Check the disc minimum thickness and the disc parallelism (thickness variation):
   a. Use a micrometer to check the disc thickness at 4 locations around the disc. Make sure the measuring point is at the same distance from the edge at all locations.
   b. The thickness should be greater than the minimum specification (which is normally cast onto the disc) and should not vary more than 0.0005 in. (0.013mm). If the variations are excessive, recondition or replace the disc. A disc which is smaller than the discard dimension MUST be replaced for safety.
   Refinishing of brake rotors can be handled at machine shops equipped for brake work.

7. Install the center retainer washer and castle nut. Tighten the castle nut to 108 ft. lbs. (147 Nm). Install a new cotter pin.
8. Install the center cap.
9. Adjust the brake shoes.
10. Install the rear tire and wheel assembly.
11. Repeat Steps 2-10 for the other rear wheel, if necessary.
12. Remove the jackstands and carefully lower the vehicle.

INSPECTION

Clean all grease, brake fluid, and other contaminants from the brake drum using a suitable brake cleaner. Visually check the drum for scoring, cracks, or other damage and replace, if necessary.

Check the drum inner diameter using a brake shoe clearance gauge. There are 2 important specifications when discussing rear drum diameters. The refinish diameter is the maximum diameter to which the drum may be machined. This diameter allows room for drum wear after it has been machined and returned to service. The discard diameter is the point at which the drum becomes unsafe to use and must be discarded. NEVER refinish a drum to the discard diameter. If after refinishing the drum the diameter is within 0.030 in. (0.76mm) of the discard diameter, the drum MUST be replaced.

After removing the brake drum, inspect the inner braking surface for excessive wear or damage. If it is unevenly worn, streaked, or cracked, have it resurfaced or replaced. The standard inside diameter of the brake drum is 7.087 in. (180mm). The maximum allowed diameter is 7.165 in. (182mm).

ADJUSTMENT

Bearing Preload
▶ See Figure 63

1. Tighten the castle nut to 36 ft. lbs. (47 Nm), while rotating the drum back and forth to seat the bearing. Loosen the nut about 0.25 in. (6mm).

2. Attach a spring scale to one of the wheel studs. Pull on the spring scale at a 90 degree angle to the diameter of the brake drum and measure the force required to start the drum turning. It should be 2.6-4.0 lbs. Loosen or tighten the nut slightly to get the correct rolling resistance.

3. When the rolling resistance is correct, bend the lockwasher over to hold the nut in place.

Brake Shoes

INSPECTION

Remove the drum and inspect the lining thickness of both brake shoes. The rear brake shoes should be replaced if the lining is less than 0.039 in. (1mm) thick above the rivet (so that the lining is thicker than the metal shoe backing in most cases), in order to prevent the rivet from scoring the drum. On bonded shoes, the thickness of the bonded lining should be 0.039 in. (1mm) above the metal shoe backing plate. As with all brake service, keep in mind that applicable local regulations, if more stringent, take precedence over these specifications.

Inspect the brake shoes for excessive or uneven wear, fluid contamination, bent and/or broken parts and cracks. If any of these conditions exist, replace the brake shoes.

➡Brake shoes should always be replaced in sets.

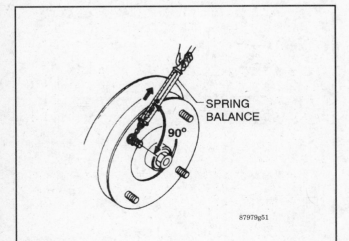

SPRING BALANCE

90°

87979g51

Fig. 63 Turn the rear drum while holding a spring scale 90° from the drum's diameter to measure starting force

REMOVAL & INSTALLATION

▶ See Figures 64, 65, 66, 67 and 68

➡Only service one brake assembly at a time. This will allow for visual comparison in the event of difficulty.

1. Raise the vehicle and safely support on jackstands. Remove the wheel and tire assembly.

2. Remove the brake drum.

3. Remove both return springs carefully with a pair of brake pliers or equivalent.

4. Remove both retaining clips by first turning them 90 degrees with a pair of pliers to line up the slot in the lip with the flat end of the pin, then pull them off the pins.

5. Disconnect the brake shoes from the adjuster side first, then the wheel cylinder side, and pull them off the backing plate.

6. If equipped with rear drum parking brakes, unfasten the parking brake cable from the parking lever on the rearward brake shoe.

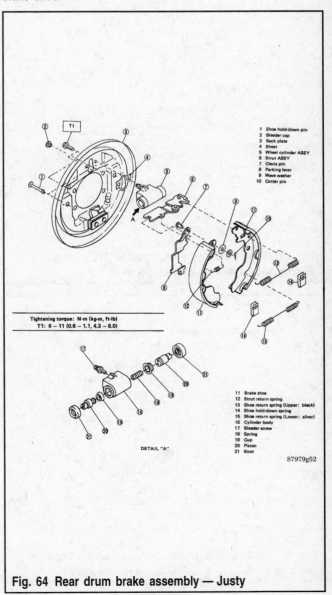

1 Shoe hold-down pin
2 Bleeder cap
3 Back plate
4 Sheet
5 Wheel cylinder ASSY
6 Strut ASSY
7 Clevis pin
8 Parking lever
9 Wave washer
10 Cotter pin

Tightening torque: N·m (kg-m, ft-lb)
T1: 6 — 11 (0.6 — 1.1, 4.3 — 8.0)

11 Brake shoe
12 Strut return spring
13 Shoe return spring (Upper: black)
14 Shoe hold-down spring
15 Shoe return spring (Lower: silver)
16 Cylinder body
17 Bleeder screw
18 Spring
19 Cup
20 Piston
21 Boot

DETAIL "A"

87979g52

Fig. 64 Rear drum brake assembly — Justy

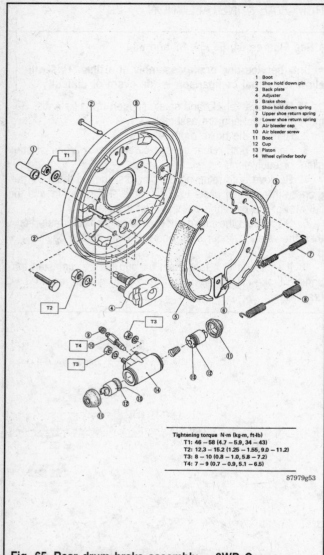

1 Boot
2 Shoe hold down pin
3 Back plate
4 Adjuster
5 Brake shoe
6 Shoe hold down spring
7 Upper shoe return spring
8 Lower shoe return spring
9 Air bleeder cap
10 Air bleeder screw
11 Boot
12 Cup
13 Piston
14 Wheel cylinder body

Tightening torque N·m (kg-m, ft-lb)
T1: 46 — 58 (4.7 — 5.9, 34 — 43)
T2: 12.3 — 15.2 (1.25 — 1.55, 9.0 — 11.2)
T3: 8 — 10 (0.8 — 1.0, 5.8 — 7.2)
T4: 7 — 9 (0.7 — 0.9, 5.1 — 6.5)

87979g53

Fig. 65 Rear drum brake assembly — 2WD Coupe, Sedan, XT, Loyale, Wagon and Brat

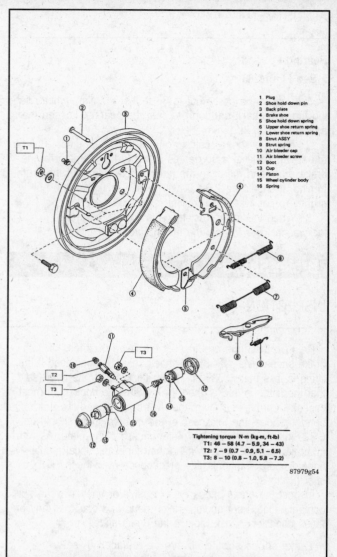

1 Plug
2 Shoe hold down pin
3 Back plate
4 Brake shoe
5 Shoe hold down spring
6 Upper shoe return spring
7 Lower shoe return spring
8 Strut ASSY
9 Strut spring
10 Air bleeder cap
11 Air bleeder screw
12 Boot
13 Cup
14 Piston
15 Wheel cylinder body
16 Spring

Tightening torque N·m (kg-m, ft-lb)
T1: 46 — 58 (4.7 — 5.9, 34 — 43)
T2: 7 — 9 (0.7 — 0.9, 5.1 — 6.5)
T3: 8 — 10 (0.8 — 1.0, 5.8 — 7.2)

87979g54

Fig. 66 Rear drum brake assembly — 4WD Coupe, Sedan, XT, Loyale, Wagon and Brat

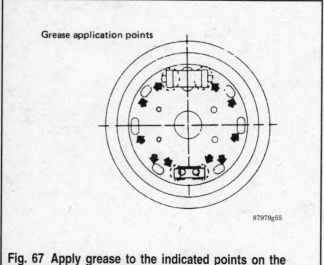

Grease application points

87979g55

Fig. 67 Apply grease to the indicated points on the backing plate before installing the brake shoes

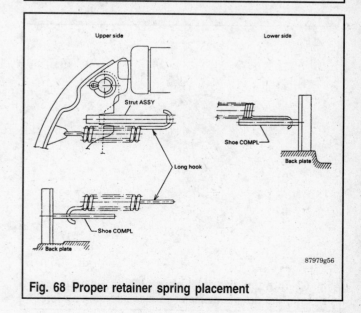

Upper side

Lower side

Strut ASSY

Long hook

Shoe COMPL

Shoe COMPL

Back plate

Back plate

87979g56

Fig. 68 Proper retainer spring placement

7. Inspect all the brake shoe installation hardware and replace any piece(s) which are worn or damaged.

To install:

8. Apply brake grease to the backing plate where the brake shoes contact it.

9. Install the brake shoes to the wheel cylinder, then to the adjuster. Secure in place with the two pins and retaining clips.

✳✳WARNING

Be careful to keep the grease off the linings. If grease gets on the linings, it could cause reduced braking performance.

10. Assemble the return springs. The upper spring is thinner.
11. Adjust the brake shoe diameter to 7 in. (180mm). Measure the diameter in at least 3 places around the shoes.
12. Install the drum and adjust the brake shoes.
13. Install the wheel and tire assembly, then lower the vehicle.

Wheel Cylinders

REMOVAL & INSTALLATION

▶ **See Figures 69 and 70**

1. Raise and safely support the rear of the vehicle on jackstands.
2. Remove the wheel and tire assembly.
3. Remove the brake shoes, as outlined earlier in this section.
4. Disconnect and plug the fluid line for the wheel cylinder at the backing plate.
5. Remove the wheel cylinder mounting bolt, then remove the wheel cylinder from the backing plate. Be careful not to lose the sheet shim that is behind the backing plate.

To install:

6. Install the wheel cylinder into position on the backing plate; be sure to place the sheet shim behind it.

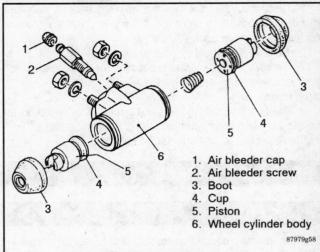

1. Air bleeder cap
2. Air bleeder screw
3. Boot
4. Cup
5. Piston
6. Wheel cylinder body

87979g58

Fig. 70 Rear wheel cylinder assembly — 2WD Coupe, Sedan, XT, Loyale, Wagon and Brat

7. Tighten the wheel cylinder mounting bolt to 8 ft. lbs. (11 Nm) on Justy and 5-7 ft. lbs. (8-10 Nm) on Loyale, STD. and XT.
8. Reconnect the fluid line to the wheel cylinder.
9. Install the brake system components. Install the wheel and tire assembly.
10. Lower the vehicle. Fill and bleed the brake system.

Brake Backing Plate

REMOVAL & INSTALLATION

1. Raise and support the rear of the vehicle safely on jackstands.
2. Remove the tire and wheel assembly.
3. Matchmark and remove the brake drum.
4. Remove the brake shoes, springs and other components, and place them on a flat surface. It is a good idea to organize the parts in a pattern to reflect their final installation.

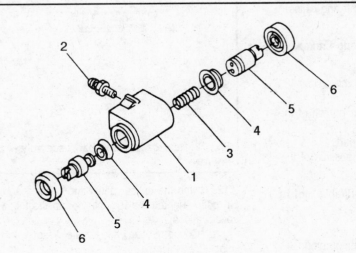

1. Cylinder body
2. Bleeder screw
3. Spring
4. Cup
5. Piston
6. Boot

87979g57

Fig. 69 Rear wheel cylinder assembly — Justy

5. Disconnect the inlet tube line from the back of the wheel cylinder. Immediately plug or cap the line to prevent system contamination or excessive fluid loss.

6. Remove the wheel cylinder assembly.

7. Remove the retainer bolts securing the backing plate to the rear trailing arm assembly.

To install:

8. Position the backing plate and gasket, if equipped, to the trailing arm, and secure in place using the retainer bolts. Tighten the bolts to 34-43 ft. lbs. (44-56 Nm).

REAR DISC BRAKES

✺✺CAUTION

Brake pads may contain asbestos, which has been determined to be a cancer causing agent. Never clean the brake surfaces with compressed air! Avoid inhaling any dust from any brake surface! When cleaning brake surfaces, use a commercially available brake cleaning fluid.

Brake Pads

REMOVAL & INSTALLATION

▶ See Figures 71, 72, 73, 74, 75, 76, 77, 78, 79 and 80

✺✺WARNING

Before beginning the procedure, determine whether your vehicle is equipped with a rear parking brake assembly. If equipped with rear parking brakes, only compress the piston slightly, or the piston screw could be damaged.

1. Make sure the parking brake is disengaged.

2. Remove a small portion of brake fluid from the master cylinder reservoir.

3. Raise and safely support the vehicle on jackstands.

4. Remove the wheel assembly.

5. Use a C-clamp to compress the piston into the caliper bore.

➡ **If your vehicle is equipped with rear parking brakes, compress the piston only slightly.**

6. Disconnect the parking brake cable from the caliper lever.

7. Remove the lock pin bolts from the lower portion of the caliper.

8. Swing the caliper upward to access the pads.

9. Remove the brake disc pads, noting the position of the backing plates and retainer clips.

➡ **If equipped with a parking brake, use a suitable tool to rotate the piston back into the caliper bore.**

To install:

10. Inspect the brake rotor, caliper and retaining components. Correct as necessary.

11. Install the new pads into the caliper, being sure all shims and clips are in their original positions.

9. Install the wheel cylinder and bolts along with the hydraulic line.

10. Position and secure the brake shoes and assorted springs and components.

11. Attach the brake drum.

12. Bleed the brake system.

13. Install the wheel and tire assembly. Lower the vehicle.

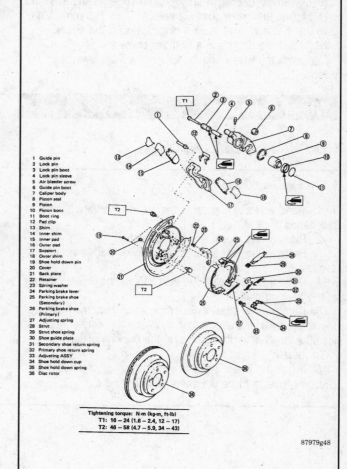

1	Guide pin
2	Lock pin
3	Lock pin boot
4	Lock pin sleeve
5	Air bleeder screw
6	Guide pin boot
7	Caliper body
8	Piston seal
9	Piston
10	Piston boot
11	Boot ring
12	Pad clip
13	Shim
14	Inner shim
15	Inner pad
16	Outer pad
17	Support
18	Outer shim
19	Shoe hold down pin
20	Cover
21	Back plate
22	Retainer
23	Spring washer
24	Parking brake lever
25	Parking brake shoe (Secondary)
26	Parking brake shoe (Primary)
27	Adjusting spring
28	Strut
29	Strut shoe spring
30	Shoe guide plate
31	Secondary shoe return spring
32	Primary shoe return spring
33	Adjusting ASSY
34	Shoe hold down cup
35	Shoe hold down spring
36	Disc rotor

Tightening torque: N·m (kg-m, ft-lb)
T1: 16 — 24 (1.6 — 2.4, 12 — 17)
T2: 46 — 58 (4.7 — 5.9, 34 — 43)

87979g48

Fig. 71 Rear caliper and pad assembly — Legacy and Impreza

12. Swing the caliper down into position and install the lock pin bolts. Tighten the lock pin bolt to the following specifications:

   a. Coupe, Sedan, XT, Loyale, Wagon and Brat: 16-23 ft. lbs. (22-31 Nm).

   b. Legacy and Impreza: 12-17 ft. lbs. (16-24 Nm).

   c. SVX: 12-17 ft. lbs. (16-24 Nm).

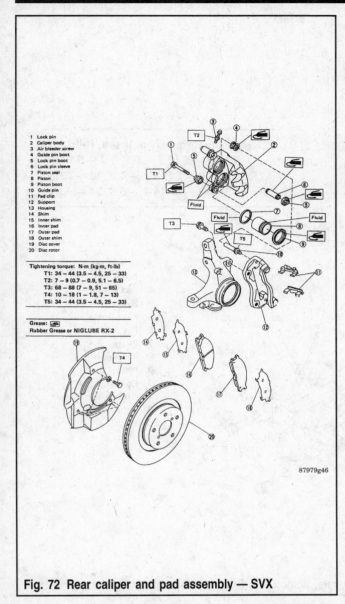

1 Lock pin
2 Caliper body
3 Air bleeder screw
4 Guide pin boot
5 Lock pin boot
6 Lock pin sleeve
7 Piston seal
8 Piston
9 Piston boot
10 Guide pin
11 Pad clip
12 Support
13 Housing
14 Shim
15 Inner shim
16 Inner pad
17 Outer pad
18 Outer shim
19 Disc cover
20 Disc rotor

Tightening torque: N·m (kg-m, ft-lb)
T1: 34 – 44 (3.5 – 4.5, 25 – 33)
T2: 7 – 9 (0.7 – 0.9, 5.1 – 6.5)
T3: 68 – 88 (7 – 9, 51 – 65)
T4: 10 – 18 (1 – 1.8, 7 – 13)
T5: 34 – 44 (3.5 – 4.5, 25 – 33)

Grease:
Rubber Grease or NIGLUBE RX-2

87979g46

Fig. 72 Rear caliper and pad assembly — SVX

13. Reconnect the parking brake cable, and install the wheel assembly.

14. Repeat Steps 4-13 for the other side of the vehicle.

15. Fill the master cylinder reservoir. Bleed the brakes as required and lower the vehicle. Road test the vehicle.

INSPECTION

Brake pads should be inspected once a year or at 6,000 mile (9,662 km) intervals, whichever occurs first. Check both ends of the outboard pad, looking in at each end of the caliper; then check the lining thickness of the inboard pad, looking down through the inspection hole. On riveted pads, the lining should be more than 1/32 in. (0.8mm) thick above the rivet (so that the lining is thicker than the metal backing in most cases), in order to prevent the rivet from scoring the rotor. On bonded brake pads, a minimum lining thickness of 1/32 in. (0.8mm) above the backing plate should be used to determine necessary replacement intervals. Keep in mind that any applicable state inspection standards that are more stringent take prece-

dence. All four rear pads MUST be replaced as a set if one shows excessive wear.

Brake Caliper

REMOVAL & INSTALLATION

▶ See Figures 81, 82, 83 and 84

✳✳WARNING

Before beginning the procedure, determine whether your vehicle is equipped with a rear parking brake assembly. If equipped with rear parking brakes, only compress the piston slightly, or the piston screw could be damaged.

1. Remove as much brake fluid as possible from the master cylinder reservoir.
2. Raise and support the vehicle safely on jackstands. Remove the rear wheels.
3. Use a C-clamp to compress the piston into the caliper bore.

➡**If your vehicle is equipped with rear parking brakes, compress the piston only slightly.**

4. Release the parking brake and disconnect the cable from the caliper lever, if equipped.
5. Remove the brake hose from the caliper body and plug the hose to prevent the entrance of dirt or moisture.
6. Remove the caliper bracket retainer bolts.
7. Slide the caliper and bracket assembly off the spindle and rotor.
8. Remove the brake pads, backing plate and retainer clips.
9. Compress the piston assembly into the cylinder bore.

➡**If equipped with a parking brake, use a suitable tool to rotate the piston back into the caliper bore.**

To install:
10. Install the caliper bracket to the spindle assembly, and secure in place with the retainer bolts. Tighten the retainer bolts to 16-23 ft. lbs. (22-31 Nm) for all models except Legacy, Impreza and SVX. For Legacy, Impreza and SVX, tighten the retainer bolts to 12-17 ft. lbs. (16-22 Nm).
11. Install the pad retainer clips, brake pads, backing plate and caliper.
12. Install the hand brake cable, if equipped.
13. Connect the brake hose using new sealing washers, and tighten the fitting to 12-14 ft. lbs. (16-20 Nm).
14. Repeat Steps 3-13 for the other side of the vehicle, if necessary.
15. Bleed the brake system. Install the wheels and lower the vehicle. Check the fluid level in the master cylinder.

OVERHAUL

▶ See Figures 85, 86, 87, 88 and 89

1. Remove the brake caliper from the vehicle and place on a clean work surface.

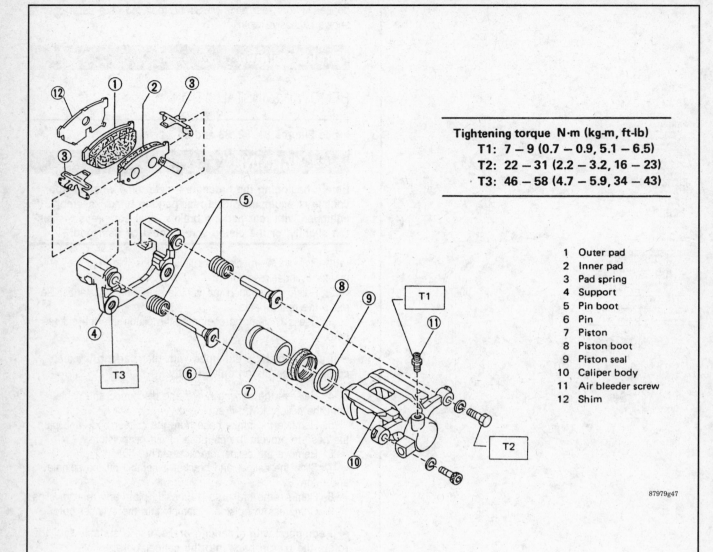

Tightening torque N·m (kg-m, ft-lb)
T1: 7 — 9 (0.7 — 0.9, 5.1 — 6.5)
T2: 22 — 31 (2.2 — 3.2, 16 — 23)
T3: 46 — 58 (4.7 — 5.9, 34 — 43)

1 Outer pad
2 Inner pad
3 Pad spring
4 Support
5 Pin boot
6 Pin
7 Piston
8 Piston boot
9 Piston seal
10 Caliper body
11 Air bleeder screw
12 Shim

87979g47

Fig. 73 Rear caliper and pad assembly — Coupe, Sedan, XT, Loyale, Wagon and Brat

87979p17

Fig. 74 Rear caliper assembly — Legacy

87979p18

Fig. 75 Use a C-clamp to compress the piston slightly into the caliper bore

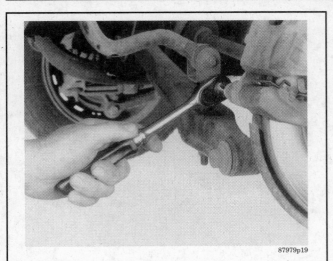

Fig. 76 Loosen and remove the caliper lower retainer bolt

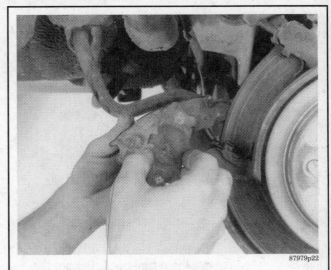

Fig. 79 . . . and remove the backing plate

Fig. 77 Lift the caliper up to access the pads

Fig. 80 Remove the pad retainer clips from the bracket and inspect

Fig. 78 Slide the outer pad out . . .

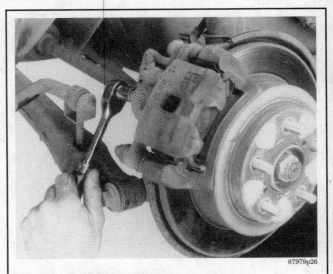

Fig. 81 Loosen the brake hose retainer bolt . . .

Fig. 82 . . . and remove the retainer bolt. Discard the sealing washers

Fig. 83 Loosen and remove the caliper bracket upper and lower retainer bolts

Fig. 84 Lift the caliper and bracket assembly off the rotor and spindle assembly

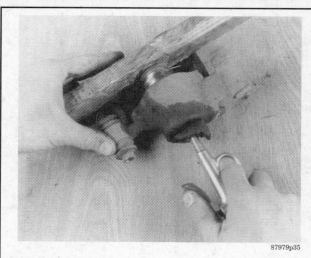

Fig. 85 Position a piece of wood as shown, then use low pressure compressed air to push out the piston

Fig. 86 Remove the piston from the caliper bore

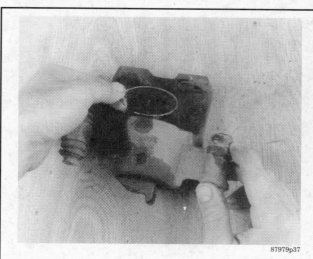

Fig. 87 If equipped, remove the piston boot retainer ring . . .

Fig. 88 . . . then remove the piston boot

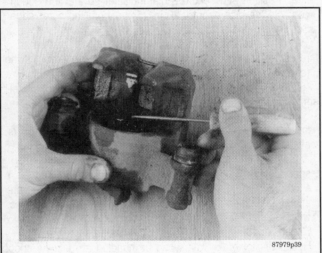

Fig. 89 Use a suitable pick tool to remove the piston seal

2. Remove the inlet fitting from the brake caliper and drain all brake fluid.

3. Place a piece of wood in the caliper opening. Use a small amount of compressed air and force the piston from the bore.

✳✳CAUTION

DO NOT apply too much air pressure to the caliper bore. The piston may jump out, causing damage to the piston and/or the operator. Be ABSOLUTELY SURE to keep your fingers away from the piston while air is being applied.

4. Remove the piston boot retainer ring, if equipped. Remove the piston boot and seal. A pick tool can be used to extract the seal from the caliper bore. Be careful not to scratch the bore while removing the pieces.

5. Inspect the piston and the caliper bore for damage or corrosion. Replace the caliper and/or the piston if necessary.

6. Remove the bleeder screw and rubber cap if equipped.

7. Clean all of the parts with non-mineral based solvent and blow dry with compressed air. All rubber parts should be replaced.

8. Inspect the guide pins for corrosion, and replace if necessary. When installing the guide pins, coat them with a silicone lubricant.

To assemble:

9. Lubricate the piston, caliper and seal with clean brake fluid.

10. Install the seal into the caliper bore, making sure it is not twisted in the bore groove.

11. Install the boot onto the piston, then position the piston into the caliper bore.

12. If the caliper is equipped with the parking brake, use a suitable tool to rotate the piston back into the caliper bore.

13. If not equipped with a parking brake, bottom the piston into the bore using your hand and a piece of wood to compress the piston.

14. Install the bleeder valve and tighten to 6-7 ft. lbs. (8-9 Nm).

15. Install the caliper to the vehicle and properly bleed the hydraulic brake system.

Brake Disc (Rotor)

REMOVAL & INSTALLATION

1985-86 Models

1. Raise the vehicle and support safely on jackstands.
2. Remove the front wheel, handbrake cable, caliper and caliper bracket. Support the caliper from a suspension part using a piece of wire. Make sure the brake hose is not distorted.
3. Remove the axle shaft nut and pull the disc off the axle shaft with a puller.
4. Remove the 4 bolts which hold the disc to the hub.
5. Separate the hub from the rotor.

To install:

6. Position the hub to the rotor, making sure the retainer bolt holes align.
7. Install the hub-to-rotor retainer bolts, and tighten to 36-51 ft. lbs. (48-69 Nm).
8. Install the hub/rotor assembly on the halfshaft. Tighten the nut to specification.
9. Install the caliper bracket, followed by the caliper and brake pads.
10. Install the wheel and tire assembly, and lower the vehicle.

1987-96 Models

▶ See Figures 90 and 91

1. Raise and safely support the vehicle on jackstands.
2. Remove the rear wheel and tire assembly.
3. Remove the brake caliper and bracket assembly, and suspend out of the way with a piece of wire.
4. Remove the castle nut.
5. Remove the conical spring(s) around one or more of the lug studs.

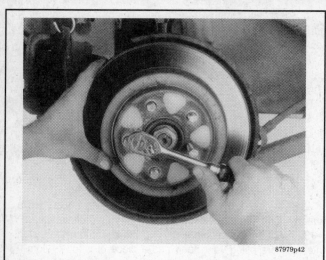

Fig. 90 To separate the rotor from the hub assembly, install and tighten two bolts into the rotor's holes

6. Thread two suitably sized metric bolts into the holes in the rotor hat. Evenly tighten both bolts to separate the rotor from the hub assembly.

7. Pull the rotor from the hub and halfshaft.

To install:

8. Install the hub and disc assembly on the axle shaft. Install the conical spring(s) and castle nut. Ensure that each conical spring is installed in the correct direction, then temporarily tighten the castle nut.

9. Install the caliper assembly and tighten the bolts to specification.

10. Tighten the castle nut to specification. Install the wheels and lower the vehicle.

Fig. 91 When the rotor is freed from the hub, slide it off the studs

INSPECTION

▶ See Figure 92

Check the disc brake rotor for scoring, cracks or other damage. If rotor run-out is checked, this should be measured while the rotor is installed. Use a dial gauge to check rotor run-out.

1. Raise and support the rear of the vehicle safely using jackstands.

2. Remove the rear wheels.

3. Visually inspect the rotor for cracks, excessive scoring or other damage. A light scoring of the surface is normal and should not be considered detrimental to brake operation.

➡Before attempting to check rotor run-out on all vehicles, the bearings must be in good condition and exhibit no excessive play.

4. Check the disc for excessive run-out using a dial indicator:

a. Position and secure a dial indicator so that the button contacts the disc about 0.20 in. (5mm) from the outer edge. Set the dial indicator to zero.

b. Rotate the disc one complete revolution. The lateral run-out reading should not exceed 0.039 in. (0.10mm). If the reading is excessive, recondition or replace the disc.

5. Check the disc minimum thickness and the disc parallelism (thickness variation):

a. Use a micrometer to check the disc thickness at 4 locations around the disc. Make sure the measuring point is at the same distance from the edge at all locations.

b. The thickness should be greater than the minimum specification (which is normally cast onto the disc) and should not vary more than 0.0005 in. (0.013mm). If the variations are excessive, recondition or replace the disc. A disc which is smaller than the discard dimension MUST be replaced for safety.

Refinishing of brake rotors can be handled at machine shops equipped for brake work.

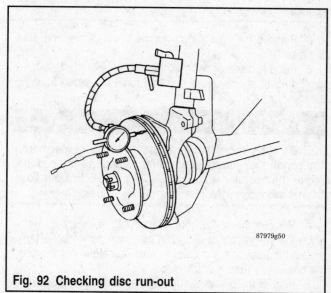

Fig. 92 Checking disc run-out

PARKING BRAKE

Cables

ADJUSTMENT

▶ See Figures 93, 94, 95, 96, 97 and 98

➡Before adjusting the cable, adjust the brake shoes, if so equipped.

1. Pull the parking brake lever up. Release it and repeat several times.

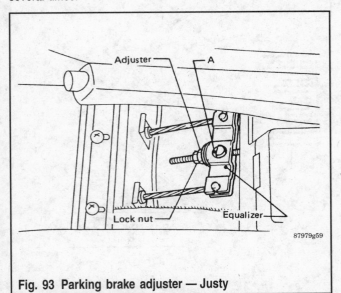

Fig. 93 Parking brake adjuster — Justy

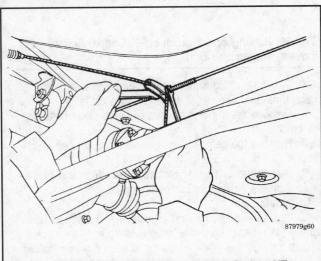

Fig. 94 Parking brake adjuster — Coupe, Sedan, XT, Loyale, Wagon and Brat

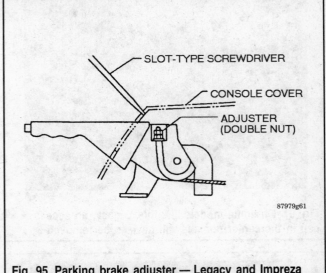

Fig. 95 Parking brake adjuster — Legacy and Impreza

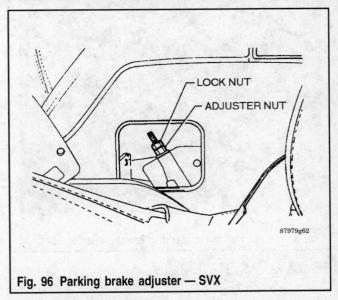

Fig. 96 Parking brake adjuster — SVX

2. It should take the specified number of notches to apply the parking brake.
- Justy: 8-9 notches
- Coupe, Sedan, XT, Loyale, Wagon and Brat: 3-4 notches
- Legacy and Impreza: 7-8 notches
- SVX: 6-7 notches

3. Loosen the locknut on the turnbuckle and adjust the length of the cable, so the parking brake is applied within specification.

4. Tighten the locknut and recheck operation of the parking brake lever.

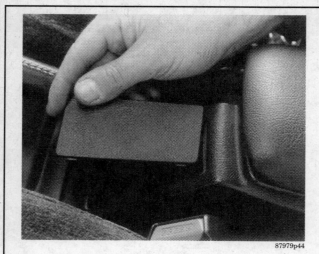

Fig. 97 On some models like this Legacy, an access cap in the center console will have to be removed . . .

Fig. 98 . . . to reach the parking brake adjuster nuts

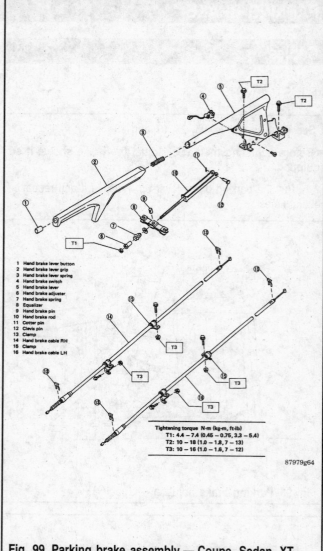

1 Hand brake lever button
2 Hand brake lever grip
3 Hand brake lever spring
4 Hand brake switch
5 Hand brake lever
6 Hand brake adjuster
7 Hand brake spring
8 Equalizer
9 Hand brake pin
10 Hand brake rod
11 Cotter pin
12 Clevis pin
13 Clamp
14 Hand brake cable RH
15 Clamp
16 Hand brake cable LH

Tightening torque N-m (kg-m, ft-lb)
T1: 4.4 — 7.4 (0.45 — 0.75, 3.3 — 5.4)
T2: 10 — 18 (1.0 — 1.8, 7 — 13)
T3: 10 — 16 (1.0 — 1.6, 7 — 12)

87979g64

Fig. 99 Parking brake assembly — Coupe, Sedan, XT, Loyale, Wagon and Brat

REMOVAL & INSTALLATION

➡The procedures given here are to be used as an outline. The position and number of clamps used to retain the parking brake cables may vary depending on vehicle year and time of production. Follow each of the cables from end to end, to be sure of routing and mounting.

Except Justy
▶ See Figures 99, 100 and 101

1. Raise and support the vehicle safely on jackstands. Remove the front wheels.
2. Remove the parking brake cover and loosen the locknut. Loosen the parking brake adjuster until the tension is released, then disconnect the inner cable ends from the equalizer.
3. Remove the clips that fasten the cable grommets in place where the cable passes through to the outside of the body.

4. Pull the parking brake cable clamp from the caliper or brake shoe and disconnect the end of the cable.
5. Remove the cable-to-transverse link bracket bolts and the bracket.
6. Remove the cable-to-crossmember bracket bolt and bracket.
7. Detach the cable rear crossmember guide and pull the cable from the passenger compartment.
   To install:
8. Install the cable through all guides and brackets, and tighten the retainer hardware snugly. Make sure the cable passes through the guide inside the driveshaft tunnel to the interior compartment. Install the cable onto the caliper end or brake shoe.
9. Install the cable to the parking brake lever. Adjust the brake shoes, if equipped, then the cable.
10. Ensure that the cable is not binding by applying and releasing the cable several times.
11. Lower the vehicle.

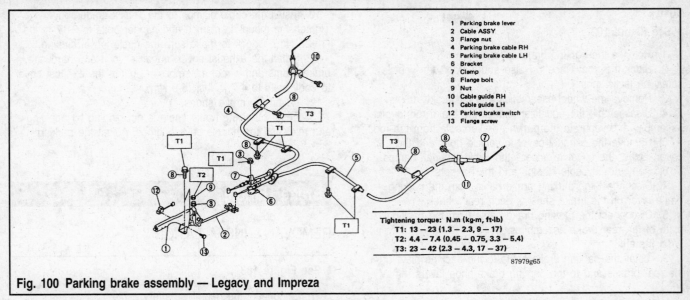

1 Parking brake lever
2 Cable ASSY
3 Flange nut
4 Parking brake cable RH
5 Parking brake cable LH
6 Bracket
7 Clamp
8 Flange bolt
9 Nut
10 Cable guide RH
11 Cable guide LH
12 Parking brake switch
13 Flange screw

Tightening torque: N·m (kg-m, ft-lb)
T1: 13 — 23 (1.3 — 2.3, 9 — 17)
T2: 4.4 — 7.4 (0.45 — 0.75, 3.3 — 5.4)
T3: 23 — 42 (2.3 — 4.3, 17 — 37)

87979g65

Fig. 100 Parking brake assembly — Legacy and Impreza

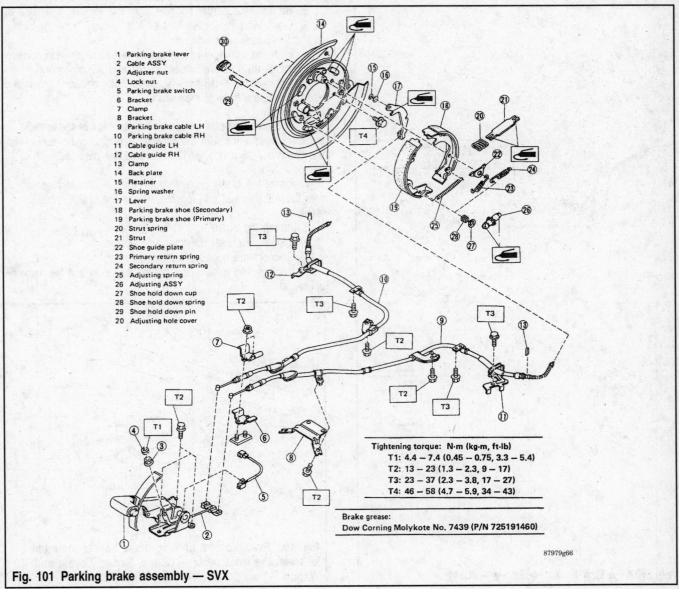

1 Parking brake lever
2 Cable ASSY
3 Adjuster nut
4 Lock nut
5 Parking brake switch
6 Bracket
7 Clamp
8 Bracket
9 Parking brake cable LH
10 Parking brake cable RH
11 Cable guide LH
12 Cable guide RH
13 Clamp
14 Back plate
15 Retainer
16 Spring washer
17 Lever
18 Parking brake shoe (Secondary)
19 Parking brake shoe (Primary)
20 Strut spring
21 Strut
22 Shoe guide plate
23 Primary return spring
24 Secondary return spring
25 Adjusting spring
26 Adjusting ASSY
27 Shoe hold down cup
28 Shoe hold down spring
29 Shoe hold down pin
20 Adjusting hole cover

Tightening torque: N·m (kg-m, ft-lb)
T1: 4.4 — 7.4 (0.45 — 0.75, 3.3 — 5.4)
T2: 13 — 23 (1.3 — 2.3, 9 — 17)
T3: 23 — 37 (2.3 — 3.8, 17 — 27)
T4: 46 — 58 (4.7 — 5.9, 34 — 43)

Brake grease:
Dow Corning Molykote No. 7439 (P/N 725191460)

87979g66

Fig. 101 Parking brake assembly — SVX

Justy

▶ **See Figure 102**

1. Release the parking brake lever.
2. Block the front wheels. Raise and support the vehicle safely on jackstands.
3. Remove the wheel assemblies and the brake drums.
4. Disassemble the equalizer joint at the brake rod-to-joint assembly, and separate the parking brake cable from the rod.
5. Remove the exhaust cover-to-vehicle bolts and the cover. Lower the cover to access the cable retainer clamps.
6. Remove the cable clamps and the hangers.
7. Disconnect the parking brake cable from the parking brake lever on the brake shoe at each rear wheel.
8. Disconnect the parking brake cable from the backing plate of the rear brake assemblies.

To install:

9. Install the parking brake cable to the backing plate of the rear brakes and to the parking brake shoe levers.

10. Install the cable clamps to the vehicle underbody. Tighten the mounting clamps and hanger bolts to 9-17 ft. lbs. (13-23 Nm). Check to make sure the cable is not binding.
11. Install the exhaust cover, equalizer joint and hardware, brake drums and wheel assemblies. Tighten the exhaust cover to body bolts to 4-7 ft. lbs. (5-9 Nm).
12. Adjust the brake shoes.
13. Ensure that the brake cable is not binding by applying and releasing the handle several times. Adjust the parking brake cable.
14. Lower the vehicle.

Brake Handle

REMOVAL & INSTALLATION

▶ **See Figure 103**

1. Disconnect the negative battery cable.
2. Remove the center console from the vehicle, if equipped.
3. Disconnect the brake light switch harness from the side of the lever assembly.
4. With the brake lever in the fully released position, loosen and remove the cable adjuster locknut and adjuster nut.
5. Remove the retainer nuts and/or bolts securing the brake assembly to the floor of the vehicle.

To install:

6. Position the brake assembly to the floor of the vehicle and secure in place with the retainer nuts and/or bolts. Tighten the bolts to 7-13 ft. lbs. (9-17 Nm), and the nuts to 36-60 ft. lbs. (4-7 Nm).
7. Install the brake cable through the bracket and secure with the adjuster nut and locknut. Adjust the brake cable tension.
8. Attach the brake light switch harness.
9. Install the center console, if equipped.
10. Connect the negative battery cable.
11. Engage and release the brake handle to test for smooth operation.

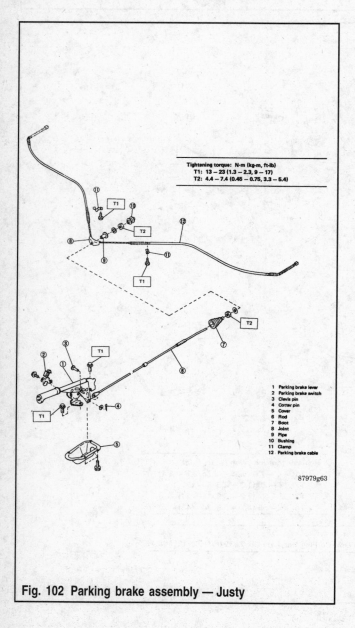

Tightening torque: N-m (kg-m, ft-lb)
T1: 13 – 23 (1.3 – 2.3, 9 – 17)
T2: 4.4 – 7.4 (0.45 – 0.75, 3.3 – 5.4)

1 Parking brake lever
2 Parking brake switch
3 Clevis pin
4 Cotter pin
5 Cover
6 Rod
7 Boot
8 Joint
9 Pipe
10 Bushing
11 Clamp
12 Parking brake cable

87979g63

Fig. 102 Parking brake assembly — Justy

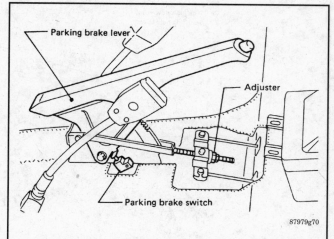

87979g70

Fig. 103 Example of a parking brake handle mounted between the front seats — Coupe, Sedan, Loyale and Wagon

Parking Brake Shoes

REMOVAL & INSTALLATION

▶ See Figures 101, 104, 105, 106, 107, 108, 109, 110, 111, 112, 113 and 114

Legacy, Impreza and SVX models equipped with rear disc brakes, incorporate a parking brake shoe assembly. This system uses the inside of the rear brake rotors as brake drums and has sets of brake shoes which act on the inner surface of the rotors to hold the vehicle. The mechanism that operates the parking brake shoes is the same as if it were a standard drum brake.

1. Raise and safely support the vehicle on jackstands. Remove the tire and wheel assemblies.

2. Remove the brake caliper and pad assemblies, as outlined earlier in this section. Do not disconnect the brake hose from the caliper. Support the caliper from the chassis with a piece of wire.

87979p46

Fig. 105 With the rotor removed, the parking brake shoe assembly is visible — Legacy

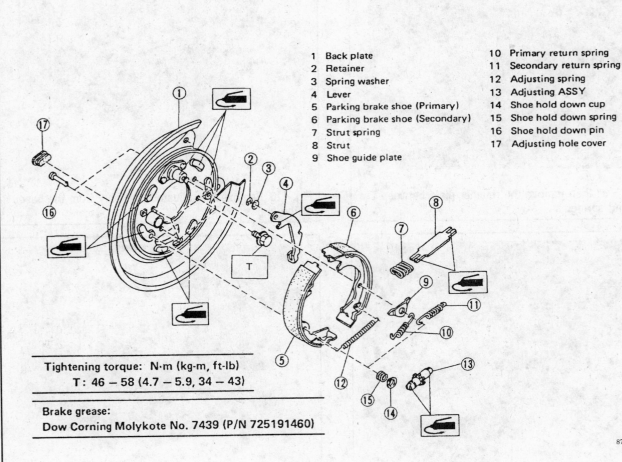

1 Back plate
2 Retainer
3 Spring washer
4 Lever
5 Parking brake shoe (Primary)
6 Parking brake shoe (Secondary)
7 Strut spring
8 Strut
9 Shoe guide plate
10 Primary return spring
11 Secondary return spring
12 Adjusting spring
13 Adjusting ASSY
14 Shoe hold down cup
15 Shoe hold down spring
16 Shoe hold down pin
17 Adjusting hole cover

Tightening torque: N·m (kg-m, ft-lb)
    T : 46 — 58 (4.7 — 5.9, 34 — 43)

Brake grease:
Dow Corning Molykote No. 7439 (P/N 725191460)

87979g67

Fig. 104 Parking brake shoe assembly — Legacy, Impreza and SVX

Fig. 106 Use a brake spring removal tool to remove the upper brake springs . . .

Fig. 107 . . . then remove the retainer plate between the shoes and springs

Fig. 108 Remove the hold-down clip . . .

Fig. 109 . . . followed by the hold-down pin

Fig. 110 Remove the adjuster assembly from the base of the shoes

Fig. 111 Detach the brake shoe from the lower retainer spring and strut

Fig. 112 Remove the other shoe from the strut and backing plate, and place aside

Fig. 113 Use pliers to pull the spring back, then detach the cable from the brake shoe lever

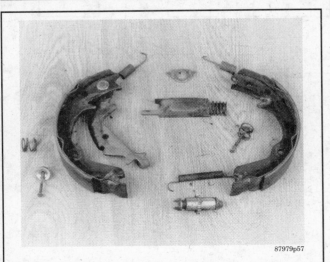

Fig. 114 Parking brake shoe components — Legacy, Impreza and SVX

3. Remove the brake disc assembly.

4. Remove the primary and secondary return springs from the brake shoes.

5. Remove the front hold-down spring and pin. Remove the brake shoe strut and strut spring.

6. Remove the adjuster assembly. Remove the brake shoes.

7. Remove the parking brake cable from the parking brake lever. Remove the parking brake lever from the brake shoe.

To install:

8. Apply a light coating of grease to the brake pad contact points. Install the parking brake lever onto the shoe.

9. Connect the parking brake cable to the lever. Install the adjusting screw spring to the trailing brake shoe.

10. Install the rear shoe hold-down spring and pin. Install the adjusting screw spring to the forward brake shoe.

11. Install the adjuster assembly in between the front and rear shoes. Install the strut assembly and the spring.

12. Install the shoe guide plate to the anchor pin and install the return springs.

13. Install the brake rotor, caliper and pad assemblies.

14. Repeat Steps 2-13 for the other side, if necessary.

15. Install the wheel and tire assemblies.

16. Adjust the parking brake shoes through the opening in the backing plate.

ADJUSTMENT

1. Raise and support the rear of the vehicle safely on jackstands.

2. Remove the rubber plug, if equipped, from the rear of the backing plate. The brake shoe adjuster wheel is accessed beneath this plug.

3. Insert a suitable brake adjustment tool into the backing plate slots and engage the lowest possible tooth on the star wheel. Move the end of the brake tool downward to move the star wheel upward and expand the adjusting screw. Repeat this operation until the brake shoes contact the rotor surface, then back off the adjuster 2 to 3 turns.

➡**The brake drag should be equal at both wheels.**

4. After the brakes are adjusted, install a rubber cover into each of the backing plate slots.

5. Remove the jackstands, and lower the vehicle.

➡**Pump the brake pedal to seat the brake shoes before moving the vehicle.**

FOUR WHEEL ANTI-LOCK BRAKE SYSTEM

General Description

▶ See Figures 115, 116 and 117

Anti-lock Braking Systems (ABS) are designed to prevent locked-wheel skidding during hard braking or during braking on slippery surfaces. The front wheels of a vehicle cannot apply steering force if they are locked and sliding; the vehicle will continue in its previous direction of travel. The four wheel anti-lock brake systems found on Subaru vehicles hold the wheels just below the point of locking, thereby allowing some steering response and preventing the rear of the vehicle from sliding sideways while braking.

There are conditions for which the ABS system provides no benefit. Hydroplaning is possible when the tires ride on a film of water, losing contact with the paved surface. This renders the vehicle totally uncontrollable until road contact is regained. Extreme steering maneuvers at high speed or cornering be-

yond the limits of tire adhesion can result in skidding which is independent of vehicle braking. For this reason, the system is named anti-lock rather than anti-skid.

Under normal braking conditions, the ABS system functions in the same manner as a standard brake system. The system is a combination of electrical and hydraulic components, working together to control the flow of brake fluid to the wheels when necessary.

The anti-lock brake system's Electronic Control Unit (ECU) is the electronic brain of the system, receiving and interpreting speed signals from the speed sensors. The ECU will enter anti-lock mode when it senses impending wheel lock at any wheel and immediately control the brake line pressure(s) to the affected wheel(s). The hydraulic actuator assembly is separate from the master cylinder and booster. It contains the wheel circuit valves used to control the brake fluid pressure to each wheel circuit. If the ABS becomes inoperative for any reason, the fail-safe system insures that the normal braking system is

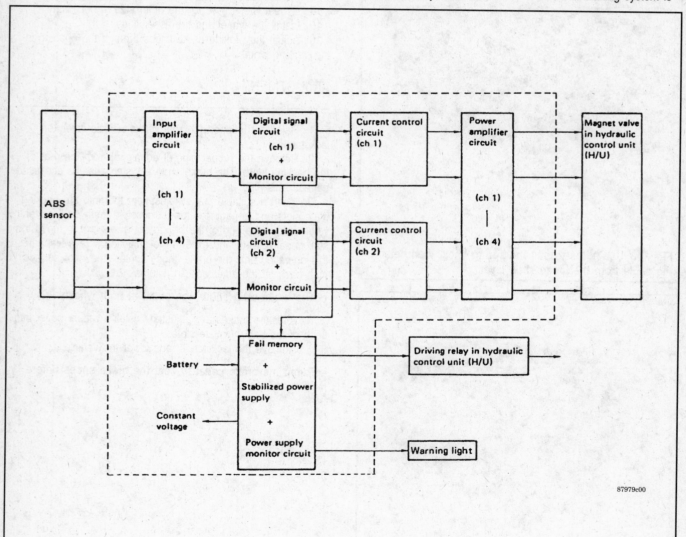

Fig. 115 ABS operational schematic

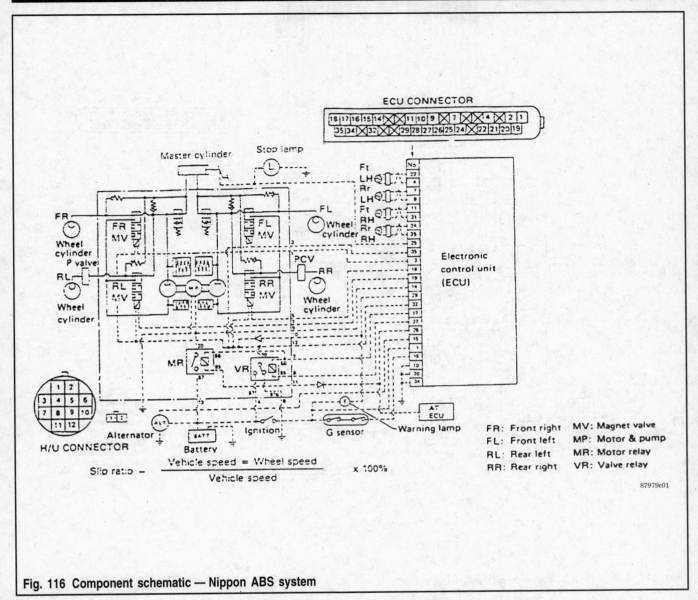

Fig. 116 Component schematic — Nippon ABS system

operative. The dashboard warning lamp is activated to show that the ABS is disabled.

SYSTEM OPERATION

The Subaru Legacy anti-lock brake system uses a 4-sensor, 4-channel system. A speed signal for each wheel is generated by a speed sensor at the wheel. The hydraulic actuator contains 4 control solenoids, one for each wheel brake line. The system is capable of controlling brake line fluid pressure to any or all of the wheels as the situation demands.

When the ECU receives signals showing one or more wheels about to lock, it sends an electrical signal to the solenoid valve(s) within the actuator to release the brake pressure in the line. The solenoid moves to a position which holds the present line pressure without allowing it to increase. If wheel deceleration is still outside the pre-programmed values, the solenoid is momentarily moved to a position which releases pressure from the line. As the wheel unlocks or rolls faster, the

ECU senses the increase and signals the solenoid to open, allowing the brake pedal to increase line pressure.

This cycling occurs several times per second when ABS is engaged. In this fashion, the wheels are kept just below the point of lock-up and control is maintained. When the hard braking ends, the ECU resets the solenoids to its normal or build mode. Brake line fluid pressures are then increased or modulated directly by pressure on the brake pedal. Fluid released to the ABS reservoirs is returned to the master cylinder by the pump and motor within the actuator.

The front and rear wheels are controlled individually, although the logic system in the ECU reacts only to the lowest rear wheel speed signal. This method is called Select Low and serves to prevent the rear wheels from getting greatly dissimilar signals which could upset directional stability.

The operator may hear a popping or clicking sound as the pump and/or control valves cycle on and off during normal operation. The sounds are due to normal operation and are not indicative of a system problem. Under most conditions, the sounds are only faintly audible. If ABS is engaged, the operator may notice some pulsation in the body of the vehicle dur-

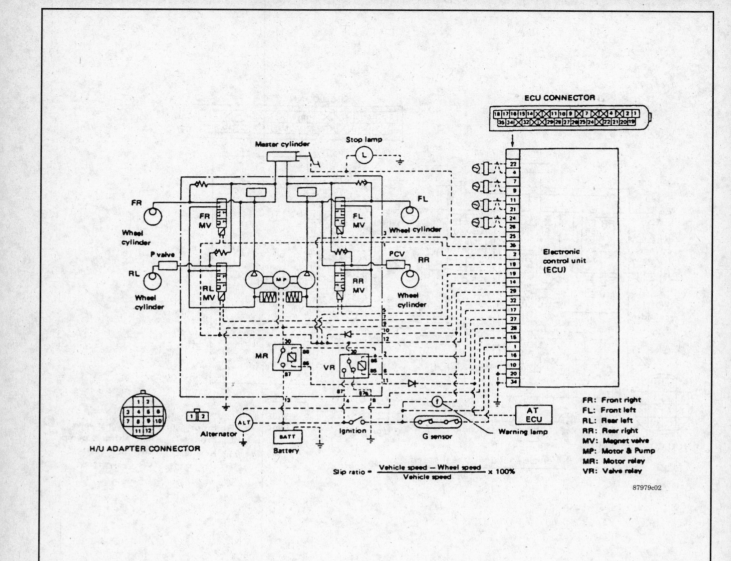

Fig. 117 Component schematic — Bosch ABS system

ing a hard stop; this is generally due to suspension shudder as the brake pressures are altered rapidly and the forces transfer to the vehicle.

Although the ABS system prevents wheel lock-up under hard braking, as brake pressure increases wheel slip is allowed to increase as well. This slip will result in some tire chirp during ABS operation. The sound should not be interpreted as lock-up, but rather than as an indication of the system holding the wheel(s) just outside the point of lock-up. Additionally, the final few feet of an ABS-engaged stop may be completed with the wheels locked; the electronic controls do not operate below about 3 mph (5 km/h).

SYSTEM COMPONENTS

▶ See Figures 118, 119 and 120

Wheel Speed Sensors

▶ See Figure 121

The speed of the front and rear wheels is monitored by the sensor. A toothed tone wheel rotates in front of the sensor, generating a small AC voltage which is transmitted to the ECU. The controller compares the signals and reacts to rapid loss of wheel speed at a particular wheel by engaging the ABS system. Each speed sensor is individually removable. In most cases, the toothed wheels may be replaced if damaged, but disassembly of other components such as hub and knuckle, constant velocity joints, or axles may be required.

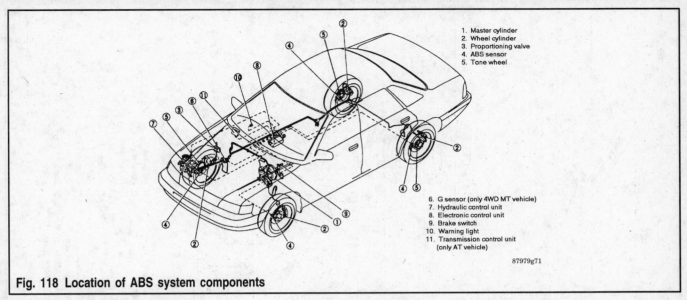

1. Master cylinder
2. Wheel cylinder
3. Proportioning valve
4. ABS sensor
5. Tone wheel

6. G sensor (only 4WD MT vehicle)
7. Hydraulic control unit
8. Electronic control unit
9. Brake switch
10. Warning light
11. Transmission control unit
    (only AT vehicle)

87979g71

Fig. 118 Location of ABS system components

ABS Electronic Control Unit (ECU)

▶ **See Figure 122**

The solid-state control unit computes the rotating speed of the wheels by the signal current sent from each sensor. When impending lock-up is detected, the ECU signals the actuator solenoids to move to predetermined positions to control brake fluid pressure to the wheels. The control unit also controls the on-off operation of the solenoid valve relay and the pump relay.

The ECU constantly monitors the function of components within the system. If any electrically detectable fault occurs, the control unit will illuminate the dashboard warning light to alert the operator. When the dash warning lamp is lit, the ABS system is disabled. The vehicle retains its normal braking capabilities without the benefit of anti-lock.

The ECU will assign and store a diagnostic or fault code. The code may be read and used for system diagnosis. If more than one fault occurs, the system will only display the first code noted. Repairs must be made based on the first code, after which the vehicle must be road tested to expose any subsequent faults.

The ECU is located under the right front seat.

ABS Hydraulic Unit

▶ **See Figure 123**

The actuator contains the solenoid control valves, pump and motor, reservoirs for temporary collection of brake fluid released from the lines as well as check and relief valves. The actuator is located at the right front of the engine compartment.

The relays and solenoids are controlled by the ECU. Under normal braking conditions, the solenoids are in the open or pressure-build position, allowing brake fluid to pass proportional to pedal pressure. During anti-lock function, the solenoids are commanded into positions to either hold or release brake fluid

line pressures as required. When anti-lock function is no longer needed, the solenoids reset to the normal position. Additionally, if the ECU detects a system fault, the solenoids are immediately set to the normal or default position.

The control relays for the pump motor and solenoid valves are located externally on the actuator case. These relays are the only components on or in the actuator which may be replaced. Any failure within the actuator requires the unit to be replaced.

ABS Warning Lamp

The ABS dashboard warning lamp is controlled by the ABS controller. The lamp will illuminate briefly when the ignition switch is turned **ON** as a bulb check. The lamp should then extinguish and remain out during vehicle operation. If only the ABS warning lamp illuminates while driving, the controller has noted a fault within the ABS system. ABS function is halted, but normal braking is maintained.

BRAKE Warning Lamp

The red BRAKE warning lamp on the dashboard functions in the usual manner, warning of a fault within the hydraulic system. It is possible that a hydraulic fault within the ABS system will also trigger the BRAKE lamp. If both the ANTI-LOCK and BRAKE warning lamps are illuminated, great care must be taken in operating the vehicle; the function of the conventional brake system may be impaired.

During diagnosis of apparent ABS problems, make certain that the problem is not rooted in the normal brake system.

G-Sensor

▶ **See Figure 124**

Found only on 4WD vehicles with manual transaxles, the G-sensor transmits a deceleration signal to the ECU. It is located on the right front wheelwell.

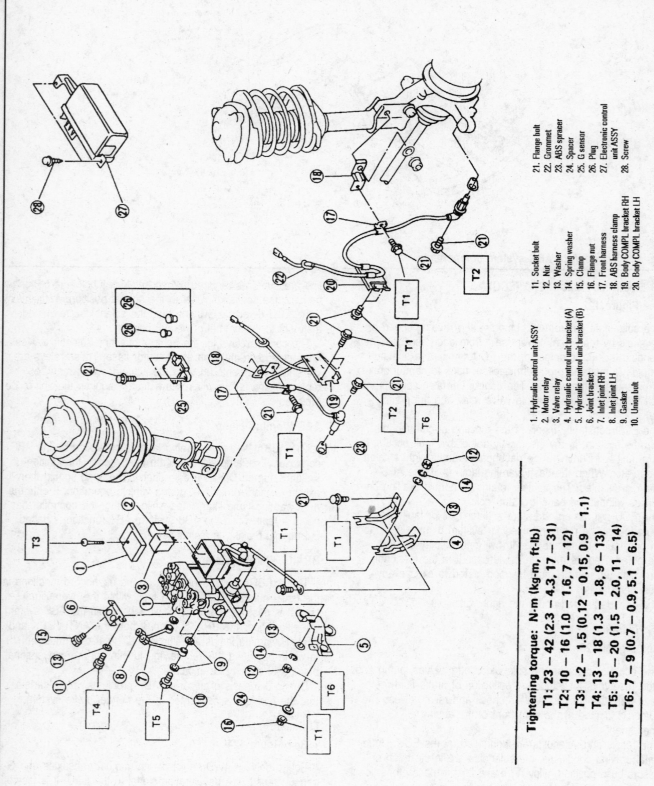

Tightening torque: N·m (kg-m, ft-lb)
T1: 23 — 42 (2.3 — 4.3, 17 — 31)
T2: 10 — 16 (1.0 — 1.6, 7 — 12)
T3: 1.2 — 1.5 (0.12 — 0.15, 0.9 — 1.1)
T4: 13 — 18 (1.3 — 1.8, 9 — 13)
T5: 15 — 20 (1.5 — 2.0, 11 — 14)
T6: 7 — 9 (0.7 — 0.9, 5.1 — 6.5)

1. Hydraulic control unit ASSY
2. Motor relay
3. Valve relay
4. Hydraulic control unit bracket (A)
5. Hydraulic control unit bracket (B)
6. Joint bracket
7. Inlet joint RH
8. Inlet joint LH
9. Gasket
10. Union bolt
11. Socket bolt
12. Nut
13. Washer
14. Spring washer
15. Clamp
16. Flange nut
17. Front harness
18. ABS harness clamp
19. Body COMPL bracket RH
20. Body COMPL bracket LH
21. Flange bolt
22. Grommet
23. ABS spacer
24. Spacer
25. G sensor
26. Plug
27. Electronic control unit ASSY
28. Screw

87979g87

Fig. 119 Front ABS components

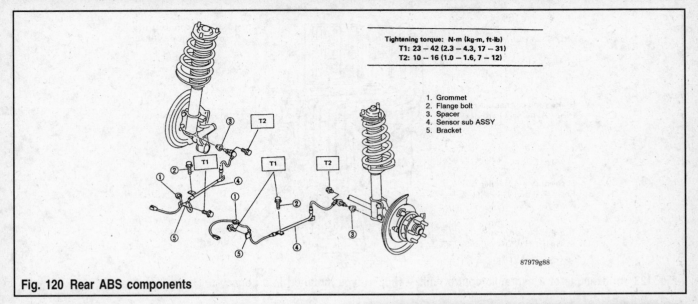

Tightening torque: N·m (kg-m, ft-lb)
T1: 23 — 42 (2.3 — 4.3, 17 — 31)
T2: 10 — 16 (1.0 — 1.6, 7 — 12)

1. Grommet
2. Flange bolt
3. Spacer
4. Sensor sub ASSY
5. Bracket

87979g88

Fig. 120 Rear ABS components

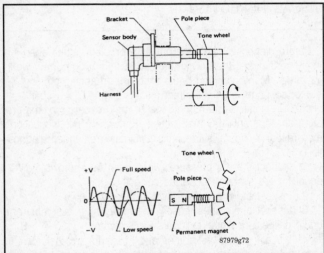

87979g72

Fig. 121 The mounted speed sensor's magnetic flux changes with variations in the tone wheel speed

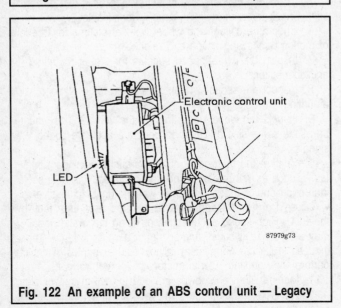

87979g73

Fig. 122 An example of an ABS control unit — Legacy

Diagnosis and Testing

SERVICE PRECAUTIONS

• If the vehicle is equipped with air bag or Supplemental Restraint Systems (SRS), always properly disable the system before working on or around system components.

• Always use a digital, high-impedance volt-ohmmeter (DVOM) for testing unless specified otherwise. Minimum impedance should be 10 kilo-ohms per volt.

• Certain components within the ABS system are not intended to be serviced or repaired individually. Only those components with removal and installation procedures should be serviced.

• Do not use rubber hoses or other parts not specifically specified for the ABS system. When using repair kits, replace all parts included in the kit. Partial or incorrect repair may lead to functional problems and require the replacement of components.

• Lubricate rubber parts with clean, fresh brake fluid to ease assembly. Do not use lubricated shop air to clean parts; damage to rubber components may result.

• Use only DOT 3 or 4 brake fluid from a sealed container.

• If any hydraulic component or line is removed or replaced, it may be necessary to bleed the entire system.

• A clean repair area is essential. Always clean the reservoir and cap thoroughly before removing the cap. The slightest amount of dirt in the fluid may plug an orifice and impair the system function. Perform repairs after components have been thoroughly cleaned. Do not allow ABS components to come into contact with any substance containing mineral oil; this includes used shop rags.

• The anti-lock brake control unit is a microprocessor similar to other computer units in the vehicle. Insure that the ignition switch is **OFF** and the negative battery cable disconnected before removing or installing controller harnesses. Avoid static electricity discharge at or near the controller.

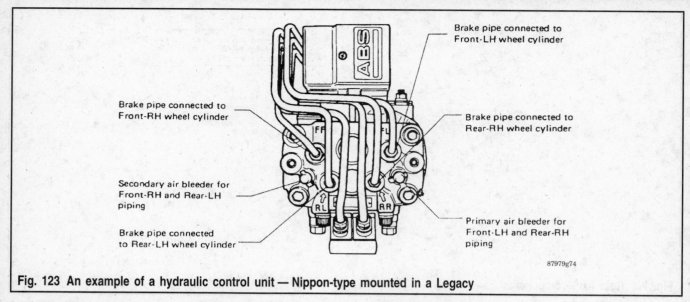

Brake pipe connected to
Front-RH wheel cylinder

Secondary air bleeder for
Front-RH and Rear-LH
piping

Brake pipe connected
to Rear-LH wheel cylinder

Brake pipe connected to
Front-LH wheel cylinder

Brake pipe connected to
Rear-RH wheel cylinder

Primary air bleeder for
Front-LH and Rear-RH
piping

87979g74

Fig. 123 An example of a hydraulic control unit — Nippon-type mounted in a Legacy

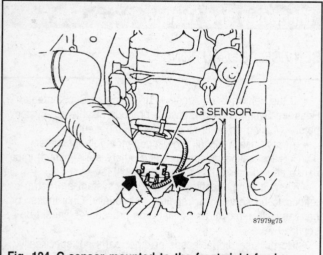

G SENSOR

87979g75

Fig. 124 G-sensor mounted to the front right fender apron

• If any arc welding is to be done on the vehicle, the ABS electronic controller should be disconnected before welding operations begin.

• If the vehicle is to be baked after paint repairs, disconnect and remove the ECU from the vehicle.

• Never disconnect any electrical connection with the ignition switch **ON** unless instructed to do so in a test.

• Avoid touching module connector pins.

• Leave new components and modules in the shipping package until ready to install them.

• Always touch a vehicle ground after sliding across a vehicle seat or walking across vinyl or carpeted floors to avoid static charge damage.

• Never allow welding cables to lie on, near or across any vehicle electrical wiring.

VISUAL INSPECTION

Before diagnosing an apparent ABS problem, make absolutely certain that the normal braking system is in correct working order. Many common brake problems (dragging parking brake, seepage, etc.) will affect the ABS system. A visual check of specific system components may reveal problems creating an apparent ABS malfunction. Performing this inspection may reveal a simple failure, thus eliminating extended diagnostic time.

1. Inspect the tire pressures; they must be approximately equal for the system to operate correctly.

2. Inspect the brake fluid level in the reservoir.

3. Inspect brake lines, hoses, master cylinder assembly and brake calipers or wheel cylinders for leakage.

4. Visually check brake lines and hoses for excessive wear, heat damage, punctures, contact with other parts, missing clips or holders, blockage or crimping.

5. Check the calipers and wheel cylinders for rust or corrosion. Check for proper sliding action if applicable.

6. Check the caliper and wheel cylinder pistons for freedom of motion during application and release.

7. Inspect the wheel speed sensors for proper mounting and connections.

8. Inspect the sensor wheels for broken teeth or poor mounting.

9. Inspect the wheels and tires on the vehicle. They must be of the same size and type to generate accurate speed signals.

10. Confirm the fault occurrence. Certain driver induced faults, such as not releasing the parking brake fully, will set a fault code and/or trigger the dash warning light. Excessive wheel spin on low-traction surfaces may be read as a fault by the ECU. High speed acceleration or riding the brake pedal may also set fault codes and/or trigger a warning lamp. These induced faults are not system failures, but examples of vehicle performance outside the parameters of the control unit.

11. Many system shutdowns are due to loss of sensor signals to or from the controller. The most common cause is not a failed sensor but a loose, corroded or dirty connector. Incor-

rect adjustment of the wheel speed sensor will cause a loss of wheel speed signal. Check harness and component connectors carefully.

TROUBLESHOOTING

Always begin with the visual inspection; many apparent ABS faults may be traced to the conventional brake system. After the visual inspection, put the vehicle into self-diagnostics and record any fault code displayed. Refer to the appropriate diagnostic chart for the code transmitted.

After repairs have been made based on the diagnostic code, again use self-diagnostics to check for additional codes.

If the ABS dash warning lamp is lit but no fault codes are present, refer to the General Troubleshooting charts for further guidance.

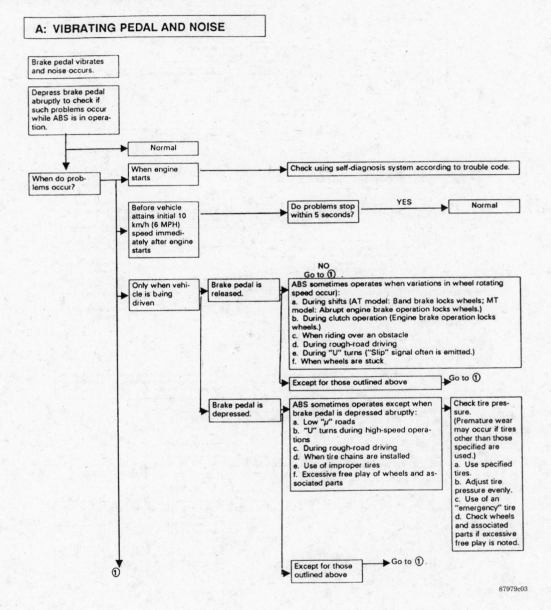

87979c03

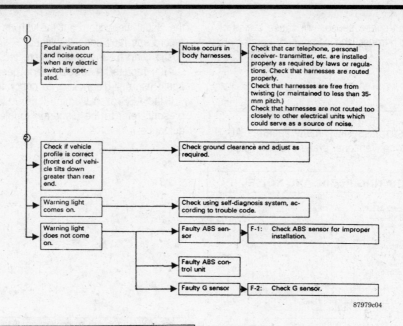

① Pedal vibration and noise occur when any electric switch is operated. → Noise occurs in body harnesses. → Check that car telephone, personal receiver- transmitter, etc. are installed properly as required by laws or regulations. Check that harnesses are routed properly.
Check that harnesses are free from twisting (or maintained to less than 35-mm pitch.)
Check that harnesses are not routed too closely to other electrical units which could serve as a source of noise.

② Check if vehicle profile is correct (front end of vehicle tilts down greater than rear end. → Check ground clearance and adjust as required.

Warning light comes on. → Check using self-diagnosis system, according to trouble code.

Warning light does not come on. → Faulty ABS sensor → F-1: Check ABS sensor for improper installation.
→ Faulty ABS control unit
→ Faulty G sensor → F-2: Check G sensor.

87979c04

B: EXCESSIVE STOPPING DISTANCE

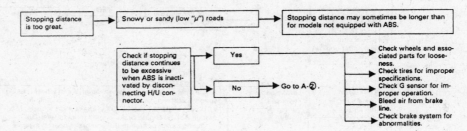

Stopping distance is too great. → Snowy or sandy (low "μ") roads → Stopping distance may sometimes be longer than for models not equipped with ABS.

Check if stopping distance continues to be excessive when ABS is inactivated by disconnecting H/U connector. → Yes → Check wheels and associated parts for looseness.
Check tires for improper specifications.
Check G sensor for improper operation.
Bleed air from brake line.
Check brake system for abnormalities.
→ No → Go to A-②.

C: IMPROPER PEDAL OPERATION

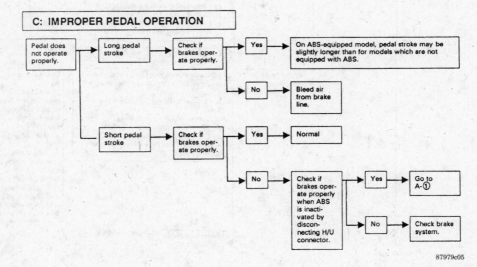

Pedal does not operate properly. → Long pedal stroke → Check if brakes operate properly. → Yes → On ABS-equipped model, pedal stroke may be slightly longer than for models which are not equipped with ABS.
→ No → Bleed air from brake line.

→ Short pedal stroke → Check if brakes operate properly. → Yes → Normal
→ No → Check if brakes operate properly when ABS is inactivated by disconnecting H/U connector. → Yes → Go to A-①
→ No → Check brake system.

87979c05

D: ABS INOPERATIVE

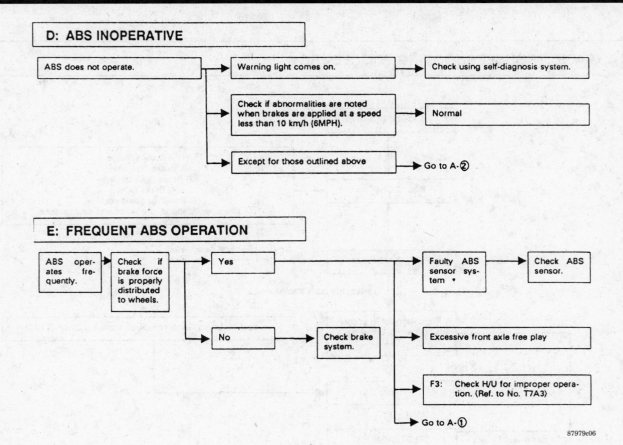

```
ABS does not operate. ──┬──▶ Warning light comes on. ──────────▶ Check using self-diagnosis system.

                        ├──▶ Check if abnormalities are noted  ──▶ Normal
                        │    when brakes are applied at a speed
                        │    less than 10 km/h (6MPH).

                        └──▶ Except for those outlined above  ──▶ Go to A-②
```

E: FREQUENT ABS OPERATION

```
ABS oper-    ──▶ Check if      ──┬──▶ Yes ────────────────▶ Faulty ABS    ──▶ Check ABS
ates  fre-       brake force   │                            sensor  sys-       sensor.
quently.         is properly   │                            tem •
                 distributed   │
                 to wheels.    │
                              └──▶ No  ──▶ Check brake  ──▶ Excessive front axle free play
                                          system.

                                                        ──▶ F3:   Check H/U for improper opera-
                                                                  tion. (Ref. to No. T7A3)

                                                        ──▶ Go to A-①
```

87979c06

A: BASIC TROUBLESHOOTING PROCEDURE

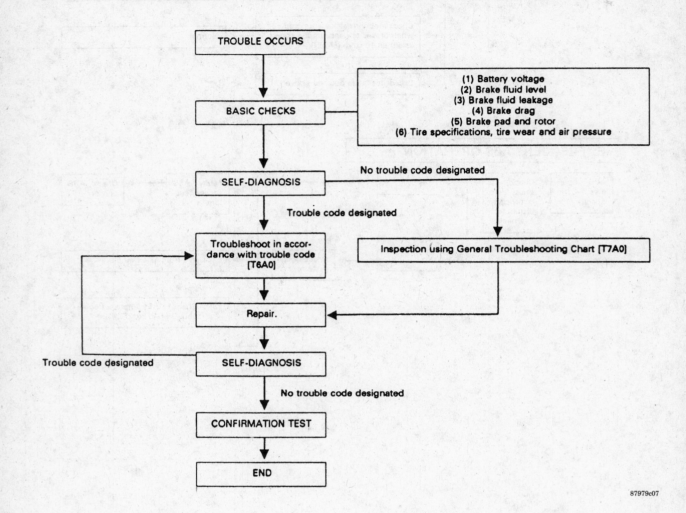

TROUBLE OCCURS

BASIC CHECKS

(1) Battery voltage
(2) Brake fluid level
(3) Brake fluid leakage
(4) Brake drag
(5) Brake pad and rotor
(6) Tire specifications, tire wear and air pressure

SELF-DIAGNOSIS — No trouble code designated

Trouble code designated

Troubleshoot in accordance with trouble code [T6A0]

Inspection using General Troubleshooting Chart [T7A0]

Repair.

Trouble code designated

SELF-DIAGNOSIS

No trouble code designated

CONFIRMATION TEST

END

87979c07

A: I/O SIGNAL VOLTAGE

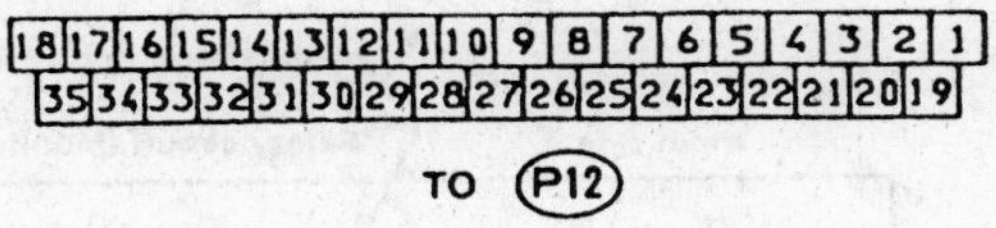

```
18 17 16 15 14 13 12 11 10 9 8 7 6 5 4 3 2 1
35 34 33 32 31 30 29 28 27 26 25 24 23 22 21 20 19
```

TO (P12)

Contents			Terminal No.	With engine idling	Input/output signals	
					Measured value	Measuring conditions
ABS sensor	Left front wheel		22, 5*	0V	200 — 300 mV (AC range)	• No. 22 or No. 5* — No. 4 • Vehicle speed 2.75 km/h (1.7 MPH)
	GND		4			
	Right front wheel		11	0V	200 — 300 mV (AC range)	• No. 11 — No. 21 • Vehicle speed 2.75 km/h (1.7 MPH)
	GND		21			
	Left rear wheel		7	0V	200 — 300 mV (AC range)	• No. 7 — No. 9 • Vehicle speed 2.75 km/h (1.7 MPH)
	GND		9			
	Right rear wheel		24	0V	200 — 300 mV (AC range)	• No. 24 — No. 26 • Vehicle speed 2.75 km/h (1.7 MPH)
	GND		26			
G sensor			16	13 — 14V	0V	
Stop light switch			25	0V	13 — 14V	When brake pedal is depressed.
Motor monitoring			14	0V	13 — 14V	When motor operates.
Valve power-supply monitoring			32	13 — 14V	13 — 14V	—
Hydraulic unit	Solenoid	Left front wheel	2	13 — 14V	0V	When solenoid is energized to produce output.
		Right front wheel	35	13 — 14V	0V	
		Left rear wheel	18	13 — 14V	0V	
		Right rear wheel	19	13 — 14V	0V	
	Valve relay coil		27	0V	0V	—
	Motor relay coil		28	13 — 14V	0V	When motor operates to produce output
Warning light			29	0V	13 — 14V	Ignition switch ON (Engine OFF)
Power supply	Alternator		15	13 — 14V	1.7V	Ignition switch ON (Engine OFF)
	Battery		1	13 — 14V	13 — 14V	—
	Relay coil (valve, motor, etc.)		17	13 — 14V	13 — 14V	—
Grounding line			10	0V	0V	—
			20	0V	0V	
			34	0V	0V	

*: FWD model

87979c10

B: I/O SIGNAL DIAGRAM

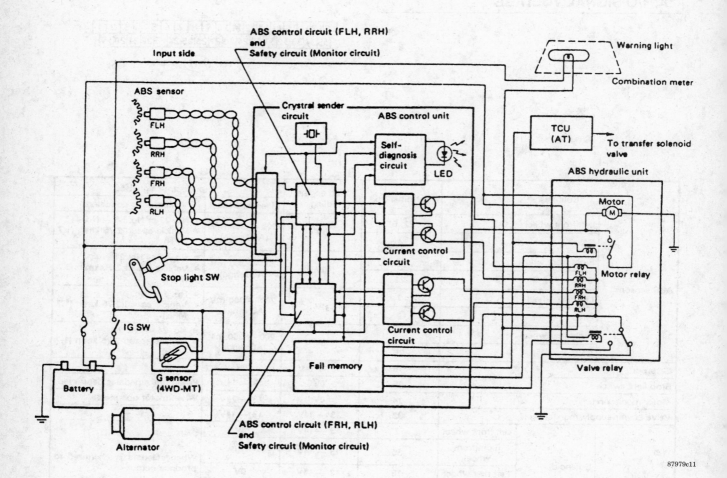

87979c11

Self-Diagnostics and Reading Codes
▶ See Figures 125 and 126

Drive the vehicle over 20 mph (32 km/h) for at least one minute. Stop the vehicle in a safe location with the engine running. If the self-diagnostic circuit detects a fault, the dash warning lamp will come on.

1. The fault code will be transmitted by the flashing of the LED display on the electronic control unit under the right passenger's seat.

2. The code will be transmitted automatically about 10-12 seconds after the ABS dashboard warning lamp comes on.

3. Read the number of short flashes as the number of the code; for example, 16 flashes represents Code 16. The flash pattern will repeat after a 5-13 second pause. Viewing the output several times is recommended for accuracy.

4. Both the LED and the dash warning lamp remain activated until the ignition key is switched OFF. When the ignition is switched OFF, the memory is erased and the code is lost. The vehicle must be re-driven and placed into self-diagnostics.

5. If the LED does not activate when the dash warning lamp is lit, the power supply may be inoperative.

Filling The System

The brake fluid reservoir is located on top of the master cylinder. Although no special procedures are needed to fill the fluid, the reservoir cap and surrounding area must be wiped clean of all dirt and debris before removing the cap. The slightest amount of dirt in the fluid can cause a system malfunction. Use only DOT 3 or 4 fluid from a sealed container. Use of old, polluted or non-approved fluid can seriously impair the function of the system.

The fluid level must be kept between the MAX and MIN lines at all times. Do not overfill beyond the MAX line; fluid spillage may result.

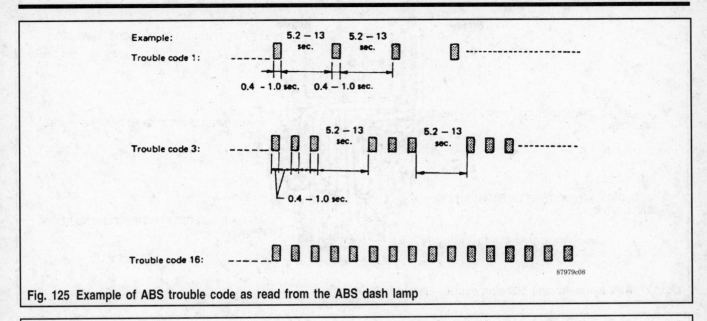

Fig. 125 Example of ABS trouble code as read from the ABS dash lamp

Trouble code	Contents of diagnosis	
0 [LED OFF]	Improper power line voltage or faulty harness	
1	Broken or shorted solenoid valve circuit(s) in hydraulic unit	Left front wheel control
2		Right front wheel control
3		Right rear wheel control
4		Left rear wheel control
5	Faulty ABS sensor	Left front wheel speed
6		Right front wheel speed
7		Right rear wheel speed
8		Left rear wheel speed
9	Faulty motor and/or motor relay or broken or shorted harness circuit	
10	Faulty valve relay or broken or shorted harness circuit Faulty valve relay or broken or shorted harness, or interrupted ABS (causing brakes to function as a conventional brake system)	
16	Faulty ABS control unit or G sensor or broken or shorted harness circuit Faulty ABS control unit or G sensor or broken or shorted harness, or malfunctioning system or line unidentified by vehicle speed sensor fail-safe function.	

Fig. 126 ABS trouble code list

Bleeding The ABS System

▶ **See Figures 127 and 128**

Bleeding the brake lines and components in the ABS system is performed using the common 2-person, manual bleeding method. A vinyl hose should be attached to each bleeder port, with the other end placed into a clear container partially filled with brake fluid.

If only one brake line, caliper or wheel cylinder has been loosened or replaced, then only that individual wheel needs bleeding. If any system component, such as master cylinder, proportioning valve or ABS hydraulic unit has been replaced, the entire system requires bleeding.

When bleeding the entire system, always begin with the wheels in the secondary brake circuit, then proceed to the primary circuit. The correct order is right front, left rear, left front and right rear. When bleeding, slowly depress the brake pedal and hold it down while the bleeder is opened for 1-2 seconds. Close the bleeder and release the pedal. Wait 3-4

seconds before the next pedal application. Rapid pedal pumping will actually complicate the bleeding and extend the procedure. When air bubbles are no longer seen in the escaping brake fluid, tighten the bleeder to 6 ft. lbs. (8 Nm).

If the hydraulic unit has been replaced or drained of fluid, it must be bled using specific procedures. This bleeding is not necessary under normal repair conditions not involving the hydraulic unit. To bleed the hydraulic unit:

1. Bleed the brake lines at all 4 wheels in the normal fashion.

2. Attach the vinyl hose to one of the bleeders on top of the hydraulic unit. Bleed this port in the same fashion as the wheels. Move the hose to the other bleeder port and repeat the bleeding. Both of these ports bleed the primary brake circuit in the actuator — front left and right rear.

3. Remove the cone screw from the secondary bleeder port and install a bleeder screw. Install the clear vinyl tube on the bleeder.

4. Open the bleeder and depress the brake pedal slowly; hold the pedal depressed.

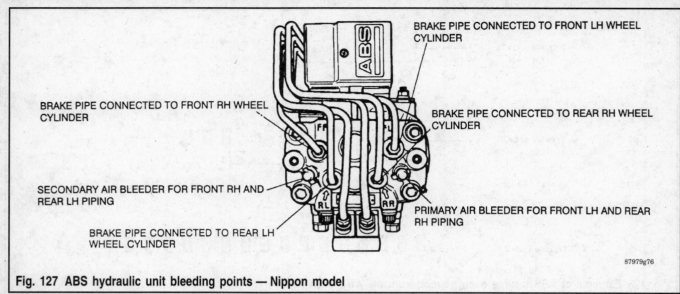

BRAKE PIPE CONNECTED TO FRONT LH WHEEL CYLINDER

BRAKE PIPE CONNECTED TO FRONT RH WHEEL CYLINDER

BRAKE PIPE CONNECTED TO REAR RH WHEEL CYLINDER

SECONDARY AIR BLEEDER FOR FRONT RH AND REAR LH PIPING

PRIMARY AIR BLEEDER FOR FRONT LH AND REAR RH PIPING

BRAKE PIPE CONNECTED TO REAR LH WHEEL CYLINDER

87979g76

Fig. 127 ABS hydraulic unit bleeding points — Nippon model

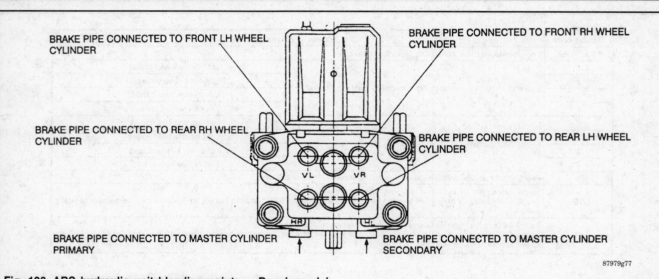

BRAKE PIPE CONNECTED TO FRONT LH WHEEL CYLINDER

BRAKE PIPE CONNECTED TO FRONT RH WHEEL CYLINDER

BRAKE PIPE CONNECTED TO REAR RH WHEEL CYLINDER

BRAKE PIPE CONNECTED TO REAR LH WHEEL CYLINDER

BRAKE PIPE CONNECTED TO MASTER CYLINDER PRIMARY

BRAKE PIPE CONNECTED TO MASTER CYLINDER SECONDARY

87979g77

Fig. 128 ABS hydraulic unit bleeding points — Bosch model

5. With the pedal depressed, intermittently apply the AV electrical signal to the solenoid valve. To apply the AV signal:

a. Disconnect both battery terminals.

b. Disconnect the 2-pin and 12-pin connectors at the hydraulic assembly.

c. At the 12-pin connector, connect terminals 1 and 3 to battery ground. Connect terminals 5 and 7 to the positive terminal of the battery. Take great care not to short terminals 5 and 7 to the grounded terminals nearby.

d. When the last connection is made, the AV signal is transmitted to the solenoids. Do not send this signal for more than 5 seconds. Break the connection at the positive terminal after 2-3 seconds.

6. When the brake pedal moves to the end of its stroke, close the bleeder and allow the pedal to return. If the AV

signal is not transmitted for any reason, the bleeder need not be closed before returning the pedal.

7. Repeat Steps 4, 5 and 6 until the fluid in the tube contains no air.

8. With the AV signal disconnected and the brake pedal released, remove the bleeder fitting and re-install the cone screw. Tighten the cone screw to 6 ft. lbs. (8 Nm).

9. Repeat the procedure from Step 3 for the other secondary bleeder port. Both secondary ports must be bled.

10. Carefully remove the jumper wires from the 12-pin connector. Do not allow the terminals to short to each other or to ground.

11. Connect the 2- and 12-pin connectors at the hydraulic unit. Connect the battery cables with the ignition **OFF**.

Electronic Control Unit (ECU)

REMOVAL & INSTALLATION

▶ See Figures 129 and 130

➡The control unit is located under the right front seat. On all models except the Legacy, the seat must be removed to gain access to the control unit. On the Legacy, the control unit can be reached by removing the door sill molding and pulling the carpet back.

1. Disconnect the negative battery cable. On all models except the Legacy, remove the right front seat. On the Legacy, remove the door sill molding and pull the carpet back.
2. Lift the carpet out of the way. Remove the 2 bolts holding the ECU to the body.
3. Lift the ECU away from the floor. Remove the small screws securing the connector to the control unit.

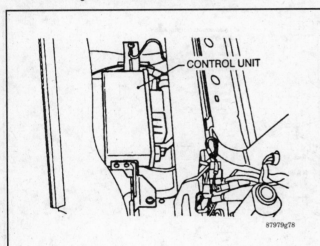

Fig. 129 ABS control unit mounted under the front passenger seat — Legacy

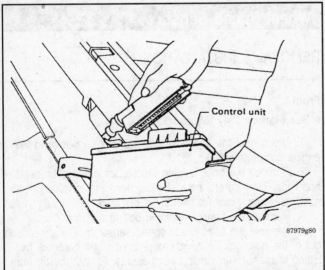

Fig. 130 Disconnecting the ABS control unit harness

4. Carefully disconnect the multi-pin harness connector from the ECU.
5. Reassemble in reverse order. Make certain the connector is firmly seated and not crooked. Always install the small connector retaining screws.

Hydraulic Actuator

REMOVAL & INSTALLATION

▶ See Figures 131, 132 and 133

1. Disconnect the harness connectors at the hydraulic unit.
2. Remove the emission canister from the engine compartment to allow access.
3. Disconnect the inlet and outlet lines from the top of the actuator. Label the lines before removal; exact reinstallation is required.
4. Immediately plug the lines and ports to prevent entry of dirt and debris into the system.
5. Remove the screw holding the ABS relay cover and remove the cover.
6. Remove the bolts holding the hydraulic unit bracket to the body. Note that one of these bolts has the pump motor ground lug attached.
7. Lift the actuator and bracket clear of the vehicle. Keep the unit upright at all times; do not drop or bump it.
8. The brackets and relays may be removed for transfer to a replacement unit.
9. Except for the 2 relays, the hydraulic unit contains no replaceable components. Never attempt to disassemble the unit or repair it.
   To install:
10. Install or transfer the relays and brackets. The nuts on the bushing bolts holding the hydraulic unit to the brackets should be tightened to 6 ft. lbs. (8 Nm).
11. Install the hydraulic unit and brackets into the engine compartment. The nuts and bolts holding the brackets to the body should be tightened to 25 ft. lbs. (34 Nm). Make certain

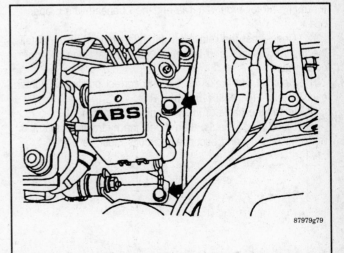

Fig. 131 ABS hydraulic assembly and mounting bolts in engine compartment

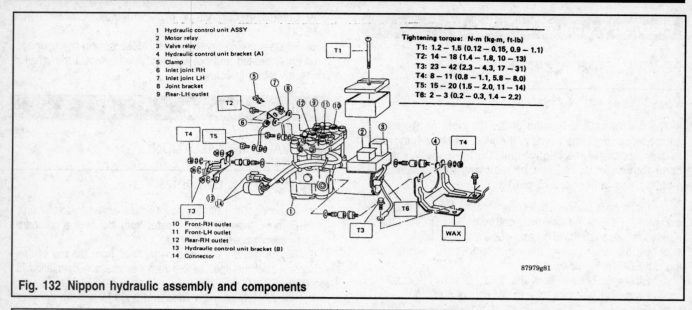

1 Hydraulic control unit ASSY
2 Motor relay
3 Valve relay
4 Hydraulic control unit bracket (A)
5 Clamp
6 Inlet joint RH
7 Inlet joint LH
8 Joint bracket
9 Rear-LH outlet

Tightening torque: N·m (kg-m, ft-lb)
T1: 1.2 – 1.5 (0.12 – 0.15, 0.9 – 1.1)
T2: 14 – 18 (1.4 – 1.8, 10 – 13)
T3: 23 – 42 (2.3 – 4.3, 17 – 31)
T4: 8 – 11 (0.8 – 1.1, 5.8 – 8.0)
T5: 15 – 20 (1.5 – 2.0, 11 – 14)
T6: 2 – 3 (0.2 – 0.3, 1.4 – 2.2)

10 Front-RH outlet
11 Front-LH outlet
12 Rear-RH outlet
13 Hydraulic control unit bracket (B)
14 Connector

Fig. 132 Nippon hydraulic assembly and components

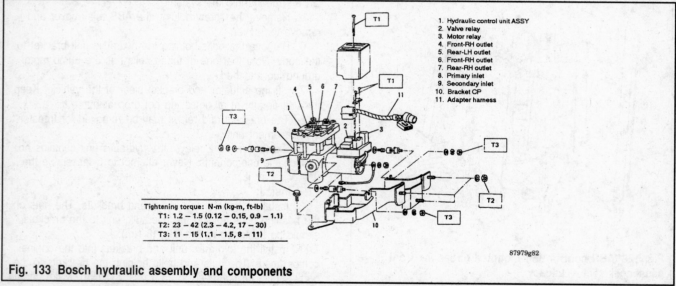

1. Hydraulic control unit ASSY
2. Valve relay
3. Motor relay
4. Front-RH outlet
5. Rear-LH outlet
6. Front-RH outlet
7. Rear-RH outlet
8. Primary inlet
9. Secondary inlet
10. Bracket CP
11. Adapter harness

Tightening torque: N·m (kg-m, ft-lb)
T1: 1.2 – 1.5 (0.12 – 0.15, 0.9 – 1.1)
T2: 23 – 42 (2.3 – 4.2, 17 – 30)
T3: 11 – 15 (1.1 – 1.5, 8 – 11)

Fig. 133 Bosch hydraulic assembly and components

the pump motor ground lug is engaged beneath the proper bolt.

12. Check that the relays are firmly seated in place. Install the relay cover box and tighten the screw just snug. Do not overtighten.

13. Connect the brake lines to the correct positions. Tighten each line to 11 ft. lbs. (15 Nm).

14. Install the canister in the engine compartment.

15. Bleed all 4 wheels, then bleed the hydraulic actuator. Both the primary and secondary circuits must be bled.

Wheel Speed Sensor

REMOVAL & INSTALLATION

Front

▶ **See Figures 134, 135 and 136**

1. Disconnect the speed sensor harness connector in the engine compartment.

2. Remove the bolts holding the sensor harness brackets and clips. Take careful note of placement and location of harness retainers; exact reassembly is required.

3. Remove the sensor retaining bolt at the front hub.

4. Remove the front wheel speed sensor by lifting it straight out of the housing. Do not damage the tip of the sensor by hitting it against surrounding components. Protect the tip from damage after it is removed. Inspect the sensor tip for any damage or accumulated debris. Clean or replace as necessary.

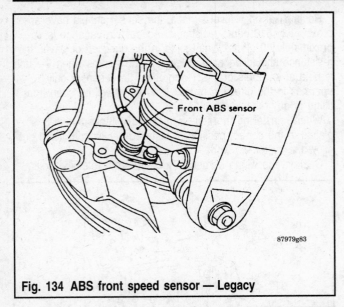

Fig. 134 ABS front speed sensor — Legacy

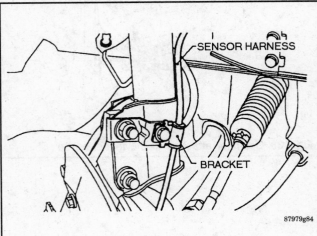

Fig. 135 Front ABS sensor harness and bracket attached to the strut assembly

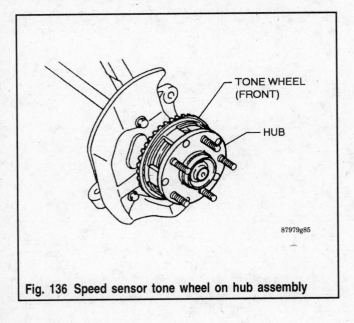

Fig. 136 Speed sensor tone wheel on hub assembly

To install:

5. Place the sensor into the mount without damaging or striking the tip.

6. Install the retaining bolt and tighten it to 10 ft. lbs. (14 Nm).

7. Remove the caliper and brake disc. Use a non-ferrous feeler gauge to check the clearance between the tip of the sensor and the tone wheel. Rotate the hub and check sensor-to-tone wheel clearance to the tone wheel at several locations. Standard clearance is 0.039-0.059 in. (1.0-1.5mm).

8. If the air gap to the tone wheel is too small, the sensor may be raised using special ABS sensor shims. Remove the sensor, install the shim and recheck. If clearance is too great, there is a problem with the tone wheel, the hub and/or the sensor.

9. Once the air gap is correct, reset the retaining bolt to the correct torque.

10. Working from the sensor end, install each harness clip and retainer, making sure the cable is routed exactly as before. Do not allow the cable to become twisted or kinked.

11. Connect the sensor to the ABS harness in the engine compartment.

Rear
▶ **See Figure 137**

1. Remove the rear seat. Disconnect the ABS harness connector.

2. Remove the rear sensor harness retaining bracket from the rear trailing link. Remove any other retainers or clips holding the harness. Take note of the cable routing and retainer placement; exact reassembly is required.

3. Remove the retaining bolt holding the sensor to the hub.

4. Remove the rear wheel speed sensor by lifting it straight out of the housing. Do not damage the tip of the sensor by hitting it against surrounding components. Protect the tip from damage after it is removed. Inspect the sensor tip for any damage or accumulated debris. Clean or replace as necessary.

To install:

5. Place the sensor into the mount without damaging or striking the tip.

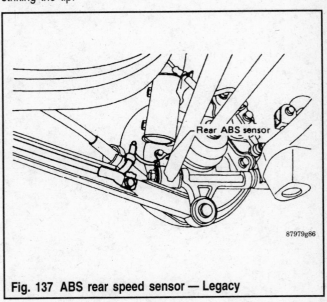

Fig. 137 ABS rear speed sensor — Legacy

6. Install the retaining bolt and tighten it to 10 ft. lbs. (14 Nm).

7. Remove the caliper and brake disc. Use a non-ferrous feeler gauge to check the clearance between the tip of the sensor and the tone wheel. Rotate the hub and check sensor-to-tone wheel clearance to the tone wheel at several locations. Standard clearance is 0.031-0.051 in. (0.8-1.3mm).

8. If the air gap to the tone wheel is too small, the sensor may be raised using special ABS sensor shims. Remove the sensor, install the shim and recheck. If clearance is too great, there is a problem with the tone wheel, the hub and/or the sensor.

9. Once the air gap is correct, again set the retaining bolt to the correct torque.

10. Working from the sensor end, install each harness clip and retainer, making sure the cable is routed exactly as before. Do not allow the cable to become twisted or kinked.

11. Connect the sensor to the ABS harness under the rear seat. Install the rear seat.

G-Sensor

REMOVAL & INSTALLATION

▶ See Figure 138

The G-sensor may be removed by unbolting it from the fender apron. Disconnect the wire harness and remove the unit. The G-sensor may be tested with an ohmmeter.

Resting flat on a level surface, the sensor should have approximately 610 ohms resistance. Acceptable variance is approximately 60 ohms. When tilted in the direction of travel, the resistance should become at least 100 kilo-ohms when the unit is held at an angle of 14-21 degrees. The G-sensor only operates in the direction of travel; no effect will be seen from tilting in any other direction.

When reinstalling the sensor, make absolutely certain it is placed in the correct position. If installed backwards, it will not allow the system to work.

Connect the wiring harness and secure the retaining bolts.

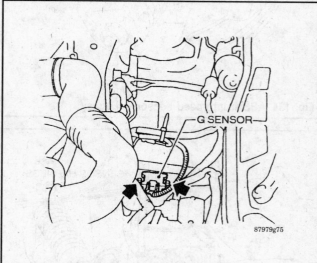

Fig. 138 G-sensor attached to the fender apron

BRAKE SPECIFICATIONS

All measurements in inches unless noted

Year	Model	Master Cylinder Bore	Brake Disc Original Thickness	Brake Disc Minimum Thickness	Maximum Runout	Brake Drum Diameter Original Inside Diameter	Brake Drum Diameter Max. Wear Limit	Brake Drum Diameter Maximum Machine Diameter	Minimum Lining Thickness Front	Minimum Lining Thickness Rear
1985	STD.	0.8125	0.710⑧	0.630①	0.0039	7.09	7.17	7.17	0.295	0.256②
	XT	0.8125	0.710⑧	0.630①	0.0039	7.09	7.17	7.17	0.295	0.256②
	Brat	0.8125	0.710	0.630	0.0039	7.09	7.17	7.17	0.295	0.059
1986	STD.	0.8125	0.710⑧	0.630①	0.0039	7.09	7.17	7.17	0.295	0.256②
	XT	0.8125	0.710⑧	0.630①	0.0039	7.09	7.17	7.17	0.295	0.256②
	Brat	0.8125	0.710	0.630	0.0039	7.09	7.17	7.17	0.295	0.059
1987	STD.	0.8125	0.710⑧	0.630①	0.0039	7.09	7.17	7.17	0.295	0.256②
	XT	0.8125	0.710⑧	0.630①	0.0039	7.09	7.17	7.17	0.295	0.256②
	Brat	0.8125	0.710	0.630	0.0039	7.09	7.17	7.17	0.295	0.059
	Justy	0.8125	0.709	0.610	0.0059	7.09	7.17	7.17	0.295③	0.067
1988	STD.	0.8125	0.710⑧	0.630①	0.0039	7.09	7.17	7.17	0.295	0.256②
	XT	0.8125	0.710⑧	0.630①	0.0039	7.09	7.17	7.17	0.295	0.256②
	XT6	0.9375	0.870⑧	0.787④	0.0039	—	—	—	0.295	0.315
	Justy	0.8125	0.709	0.610	0.0059	7.09	7.17	7.17	0.295③	0.067
1989	STD.	0.8125	0.710⑧	0.630①	0.0039	7.09	7.17	7.17	0.295	0.256②
	XT	0.8125	0.710⑧	0.630①	0.0039	7.09	7.17	7.17	0.295	0.256②
	XT6	0.9375	0.870⑧	0.787④	0.0039	—	—	—	0.295	0.315
	Justy	0.8125	0.709	0.610	0.0059	7.09	7.17	7.17	0.295③	0.067
1990	XT	0.8125	0.710⑧	0.630①	0.0039	7.09	7.17	7.17	0.295	0.256②
	XT6	0.9375	0.870⑧	0.787④	0.0039	—	—	—	0.295	0.315
	Justy	0.8125	0.709	0.610	0.0059	7.09	7.17	7.17	0.295③	0.067
	Loyale	0.8125	0.710⑧	0.630①	0.0039	7.09	7.17	7.17	0.295	0.256②
	Legacy	1.00⑤ ⑥	0.940⑧	0.870⑦	0.0039	—	—	—	0.295	0.256
1991	XT	0.8125	0.710⑧	0.630①	0.0039	7.09	7.17	7.17	0.295	0.256②
	XT6	0.9375	0.870⑧	0.787④	0.0039	—	—	—	0.295	0.315
	Justy	0.8125	0.709	0.610	0.0059	7.09	7.17	7.17	0.295③	0.067
	Loyale	0.8125	0.710⑧	0.630①	0.0039	7.09	7.17	7.17	0.295	0.256②
	Legacy	1.00⑤ ⑥	0.940⑧	0.870⑦	0.0039	—	—	—	0.295	0.256
1992	Justy	0.8125	0.709	0.610	0.0059	7.09	7.17	7.17	0.295③	0.067
	Loyale	0.8125	0.710⑧	0.630①	0.0039	7.09	7.17	7.17	0.295	0.256②
	Legacy	1.00⑤ ⑥	0.940⑧	0.870⑦	0.0039	—	—	—	0.295	0.256
	SVX	1.0625	1.100⑧	1.020①	0.0039	—	—	—	0.295	0.256

87979c25

BRAKE SPECIFICATIONS

All measurements in inches unless noted

Year	Model	Master Cylinder Bore	Original Thickness	Brake Disc Minimum Thickness	Maximum Runout	Brake Drum Diameter Original Inside Diameter	Max. Wear Limit	Maximum Machine Diameter	Minimum Lining Thickness Front	Rear
1993	Justy	0.8125	0.709	0.610	0.0059	7.09	7.17	7.17	0.295 ③	0.067
	Loyale	0.8125	0.710 ⑧	0.630 ①	0.0039	7.09	7.17	7.17	0.295	0.256 ②
	Impreza	0.9374 ⑫	0.710 ⑬	0.630 ⑭	0.0030 ⑮	9.00	9.08	9.08	0.295	0.256 ②
	Legacy	1.000 ⑨	0.940 ⑩	0.870 ⑪	0.0030	—	—	—	0.295	0.256
	SVX	1.0625	1.100 ⑧	1.020 ①	0.0039	—	—	—	0.295	0.256
1994	Justy	0.8125	0.709	0.610	0.0059	7.09	7.17	7.17	0.295 ③	0.067
	Loyale	0.8125	0.710 ⑧	0.630 ①	0.0039	7.09	7.17	7.17	0.295	0.256 ②
	Impreza	0.9374 ⑫	0.710 ⑬	0.630 ⑭	0.0030 ⑮	9.00	9.08	9.08	0.295	0.256 ②
	Legacy	1.000 ⑨	0.940 ⑩	0.870 ⑪	0.0030	—	—	—	0.295	0.256
	SVX	1.0625	1.100 ⑧	1.020 ①	0.0039	—	—	—	0.295	0.256
1995	Impreza	0.9374 ⑫	0.710 ⑬	0.630 ⑭	0.0030 ⑮	9.00	9.08	9.08	0.295	0.256 ②
	Legacy	0.9375 ⑥	0.940 ⑧	0.866 ①	0.0030 ⑮	9.00	9.08	9.08	0.295	0.256 ②
	SVX	1.0625	1.100 ⑧	1.020 ①	0.0039	—	—	—	0.295	0.256
1996	Impreza	0.9374 ⑯	0.710 ⑬	0.630 ⑭	0.0030 ⑮	9.00	9.08	9.08	0.295	0.256 ②
	Legacy	0.9375 ⑥	0.940 ⑧	0.866 ①	0.0030 ⑮	9.00	9.08	9.08	0.295	0.256 ②
	SVX	1.0625	1.100 ⑧	1.020 ①	0.0039	—	—	—	0.295	0.256

NOTE: STD. Includes 2 door, 3 door, 4 door and Wagon models
NA Not Available

① Rear disc: 0.335 in.
② With drum brakes: 0.059 in.
③ GL Models: 0.315 in.
④ Rear disc: 0.335 in.
⑤ LX model with 4WD: 1.0625 in.
⑥ With ABS, ABS/TCS, 2.5L or Outback step roof model: 1.0625 in.
⑦ Rear disc: 0.335 in.
⑧ Rear disc thickness: 0.390 in.
⑨ With Turbo or ABS: 1.059 in.

⑩ Rear disc: 0.390 - Non-Turbo; 0.710 - Turbo
⑪ Rear disc: 0.335 - Non Turbo; NA - Turbo
⑫ Except LS shown. LS: 1.00
⑬ Except w/14 in. wheels: 0.945
   Rear disc: 0.390
⑭ Except w/14 in. wheels: 0.866
   Rear disc: 0.335
⑮ Rear: 0.0039
⑯ Except LX and Outback: 1.00

87979c26

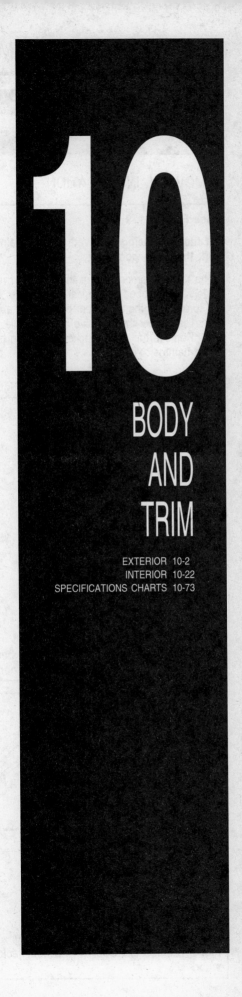

10

BODY AND TRIM

EXTERIOR

Doors

REMOVAL & INSTALLATION

▶ See Figures 1, 2 and 3

➡ If the door being removed is to be reinstalled, match-mark the hinge position.

The removal procedure for the front and rear doors (on models so equipped) is basically the same. The door hinge bolt torque and the alignment procedures are the same.

1. Disconnect the negative battery cable.
2. Remove the door checker spring pin by driving it upward with a hammer.

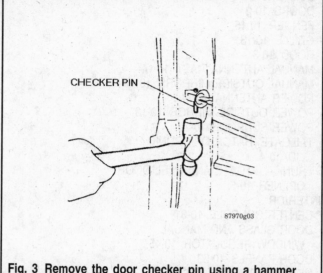

Fig. 3 Remove the door checker pin using a hammer

3. On models with power windows and/or locks, remove the lower A-pillar trim and disconnect the electrical leads.

4. Support the bottom of the door using a floor jack, with a block of wood on it to protect the door.

5. On Impreza, Justy, Legacy and SVX remove the hinge-to-door attaching bolts and remove the door from the vehicle. On Loyale, 1985-89 sedans, wagons, hatchbacks, and XT, remove the hinge-to-body bolts and remove the door.

6. Remove any needed trim components from the door.

To install:

7. Install the door on the floor jack and position it to the door hinges.

8. Install the door hinge bolts, making sure the alignment marks made during removal line up. Tighten the hinge bolts on Justy models to 14-19 ft. lbs. (20-25 Nm), on Impreza models to 20-27 ft. lbs. (27-37 Nm), on Loyale, 1985-89 sedans, wagons, hatchbacks, and XT to 18-25 ft. lbs. (25-34 Nm), and on Legacy and SVX to 14-22 ft. lbs. (20-29 Nm).

9. Remove the jack and check the door alignment around its perimeter, adjust it as needed by loosening the hinge bolts and moving it slightly.

ALIGNMENT

➡ The holes for the hinges are oversized to provide for latitude in alignment. Align the door hinges first, then the striker.

Hinges

1. If a door is being installed, first mount the door and tighten the hinge bolts lightly. If the door has not been removed, determine which hinge bolts must be loosed to effect alignment.

2. Loosen the necessary bolts just enough to allow the door to be moved with a padded prybar.

3. Move the door in small movements and check the fit after each movement. Be sure that there is no binding or

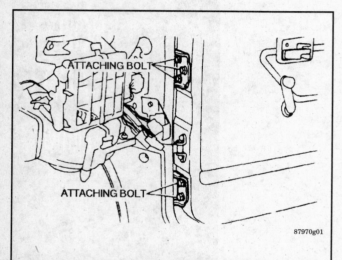

Fig. 1 Be sure the door is supported before removing either the hinge-to-body or hinge-to-door mounting bolts

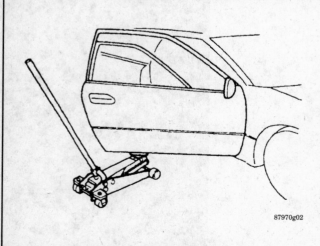

Fig. 2 Support the door with a floor jack and a block of wood

interference with adjacent panels. Keep repeating this procedure until the door is properly aligned. Tighten all the bolts. Shims may be either fabricated or purchased to install behind the hinges as an aid in alignment.

Striker Plate

➡The striker is attached to the pillar using oversized holes, providing latitude in movement.

Striker adjustment is made by loosening the bolts and moving the striker plate in the desired direction or adding or deleting shims behind the plate, or both. The striker is properly adjusted when the locking latch enters the striker without rubbing and the door closes fully and solidly, with no play when closed.

Hood

REMOVAL & INSTALLATION

▶ **See Figures 4, 5 and 6**

➡**You are going to need an assistant for this job.**

1. Open the hood and trace the outline of the hinges on the hood.

➡**On some models, the hood also has 2 struts that hold it open; these must be disconnected at the hood before it can be removed.**

2. While an assistant holds the hood, remove the hinge-to-hood bolts and lift the hood off.

3. Reverse the above process to install the hood. Align the outlines previously made. Tighten the hood retaining bolts to 9-17 ft. lbs. (13-23 Nm).

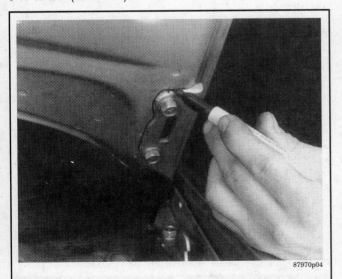

Fig. 4 Trace the outline of the hinges on the hood

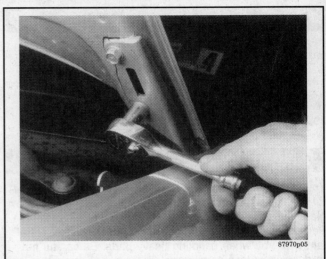

Fig. 5 While an assistant holds the hood, remove the hinge-to-hood bolts

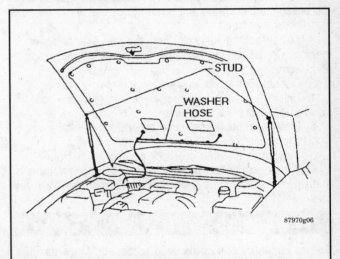

Fig. 6 On models so equipped, it will be necessary to remove the two support struts

4. Check that the hood closes properly. Adjust hood alignment, if necessary.

ALIGNMENT

Hood alignment can be adjusted front-to-rear or side-to-side by loosening the hood-to-hinge or hinge-to-body bolts. The front edge of the hood can be adjusted for closing height by adding or deleting shims under the hinges. The rear edge of the hood can be adjusted for closing height by raising or lowering the hood bumpers.

Tailgate, Hatch or Trunk Lid

REMOVAL & INSTALLATION

▶ See Figure 7

1985-89 Wagons, Impreza Wagon, Legacy Wagon, Loyale Wagon, and Justy

✳✳WARNING

You will need an assistant during this procedure. Be careful not to scratch coated surfaces of the body and window glass during removal. Place a cloth over the affected area. Be careful not to damage the trim panels. Have an assistant help you when handling heavy parts. Be careful not to damage or lose small parts.

1. Remove the clips from the trim panel using a trim panel clip puller and detach the trim panel. Be careful not to damage the clips or their holes.
2. Disconnect the connector from the rear gate defogger terminal. Do not pull the lead wire, but unlock the connector and disconnect.
3. Disconnect the wiper connector and rear washer hose.
4. Unlock connector and disconnect from rear gate door switch. Do not pull the lead wire.
5. Disconnect the license lamp connector and high mount stop lamp connector.
6. Disconnect the auto door lock actuator connector.
7. If the disconnected harness is reused, tie connector with a string and place on the upper side of the rear gate for ready use.

✳✳WARNING

Do not forcefully pull cords, lead wires, etc. since damage may result. Carefully extract them in a wavy motion while holding the connectors.

87970p07

Fig. 7 Remove the bolts which hold the gas stay to the rear gate

8. Remove the rear wiper arm, the cap and special nut. Then detach the trim panel, remove the bolt from the rear wiper and remove the wiper.
9. Completely open the rear gate. Then remove the bolts which hold the gas stay to the rear gate.

✳✳WARNING

Remove the bolts one at a time. Have a helper hold the rear gate while removing the bolts to prevent it from dropping. Be sure to place a folded cloth between the rear gate and body to prevent scratches.

10. Remove trim side rail, and remove roof trim clips as far as the center pillar.
11. Hang roof trim down to prevent it from bending. Then remove the nuts which hold the hinge with a ratchet wrench placed between the roof trim and the car body, and detach the hinge.
12. Remove the rear gate.
To install:
13. Position the rear gate onto the roof hinge.
14. Install the rear gate retaining nuts and tighten securely. Tighten the hinge mounting bolt-to-gate bolts to 14-22 ft. lbs. (20-29 Nm). Tighten the hinge mounting bolts-to-body to 14-22 ft. lbs. (20-29 Nm).
15. Position the roof trim and secure it using the retaining clips. Then install the trim side rails.
16. Install the gas stays to the rear gate and tighten the retaining bolt to 4-6 ft. lbs. (5-9 Nm) and the stud bolt to 7-13 ft. lbs. (10-18 Nm).
17. Close the rear gate and install the rear wiper, trim panel and wiper arm.
18. Connect the wiring harness to the rear wiper system.
19. Connect the auto door lock actuator connector.
20. Connect the license lamp connector and high mount stop lamp connector.
21. Connect the rear gate door switch.
22. Connect the wiper connector and rear washer hose.
23. Connect the connector to the rear gate defogger terminal.
24. Position the rear gate trim panel and install the retaining clips. Adjust the rear gate as needed.

Loyale and 1985-89 2-Door Hatchbacks

1. Fold left and right rear backrest forward.
2. Remove the shoulder anchors of the left and right front seat belts.
3. Remove the left and right tonneau cover levers.
4. Remove the left and right rear quarter upper trim.
5. Remove the rear skirt trim.
6. Remove the rear quarter rear trim panel.
7. Using a trim clip puller, remove the clips which secure the rear gate trim panel. Remove the trim panel.

✳✳WARNING

Be careful not to damage the clips and clip holes.

8. Disconnect the gas stay harness connector from the rear gate.

9. Remove the stud bolts which secure gas stay to rear gate.

✳✳WARNING

Remove the bolts one at a time. Have a helper hold the rear gate while removing the bolts to prevent it from dropping. Be sure to place a folded cloth between the rear gate and body to prevent scratches.

10. Remove the rear rail trim panel.
11. With a wrench inserted into the access hole, loosen the nuts which secure the hinge and remove the rear gate from the roof panel.
   To install:
12. Position the rear gate onto the hinges and tighten the retaining nuts to 14-21 ft. lbs. (20-30 Nm).
13. Install the rear trim panel.
14. Install the gas stays to the rear gate and tighten the stud bolts to 7-13 ft. lbs. (10-18 Nm).
15. Connect the gas stay harness to the rear gate.
16. Position the rear gate trim panel onto the rear gate and install the retainer clips.
17. Install the rear quarter, left and right upper and skirt trim.
18. Install the left and right tonneau cover levers.
19. Install the shoulder anchors of the left and right front seat belts.
20. Raise the left and right rear backrest.

Legacy Sedan, Loyale Sedan, Impreza, XT, SVX and 1985-89 Sedans
▶ See Figure 8

1. Open the trunk lid and mark the hinge to trunk lid position.
2. Remove the trunk lid mounting bolts and remove the trunk lid from the hinges.
3. Install the trunk lid into position, making sure to line up the marks made on the trunk lid during removal.
4. Tighten the trunk lid retaining bolts to 7-13 ft. lbs. (10-18 Nm) on Legacy, Loyale, 1985-89 Sedans, and XT, 9-17 ft. lbs. (13-23 Nm) on SVX.

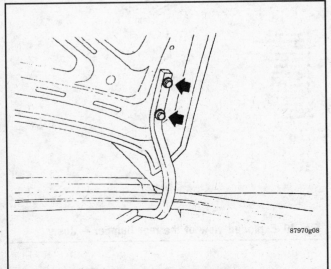

87970g08

Fig. 8 Trunk lid hinge-to-lid mounting bolts

ALIGNMENT

To align the tailgate or trunk lid, remove the glass stay, striker and buffer, and loosen bolts on hinges securing the tailgate to the body. Then adjust the clearance at the top of the end gate and the roof of the body 0.31-0.47 in. (8-10mm).
Side clearance should be 0-0.06 in. (0-1.5mm). Bottom of end gate to body clearance should be 0.15-0.27 in. (3.9-6.9mm). Replace the glass stay, striker and buffer and tighten the hinge bolts.

STRIKER ADJUSTMENT

Sideward, Fore-Aft and Vertical Adjustment

Loosen the striker mounting bolt, and adjust sideward alignment so that center of latch lines up with the center of striker. Be sure to adjust striker so that it engages latch in full lock position.
To vertically align latch and striker, adjust so that the tailgate or trunk lid and striker do not interfere with each other. Move the door up and down to make sure that it opens and closes properly.

Trunk, Liftgate and Fuel Door Opener

On some models a remote trunk, liftgate or fuel door opener system is used. A cable connected to a release handle alongside the drivers seat, goes to the rear of the car and is connected to the trunk/tailgate/fuel door latch assemblies. Each of the latch assemblies has an electrical switch that will illuminate if the lid or door is not closed properly.

REMOVAL & INSTALLATION

Opener Cables

1. Remove from the interior of the car the left side door sill moulding, and roll the carpet back to expose the cables.
2. Remove the left quarter trim panel and the left rear trim or trunk panel.
3. Remove the opener cover screws and the opener. Remove the release handles.
4. Remove the cables from their retaining clip.
5. Disconnect the cable at either the trunk/hatch release or the fuel door release.
6. Disconnect the cable at the release lever. Remove the cable from the vehicle.
   To install:
7. Install the new cable in position and connect it to the trunk/hatch or fuel door release. Connect the cable to the release handle.
8. Make sure the cable is seated in the retaining clips properly. Install the trim panels that were removed.
9. Connect the release lever handles and install the cover.

Bumpers

REMOVAL & INSTALLATION

Justy

FRONT

▶ See Figure 9

1. Disconnect the front bumper combination lamp wiring.
2. Remove the bumper attaching bolt in the wheel column. Then, move the bumper forward to disengage the clip connection at the side.
3. Remove the bumper.
4. Reverse the removal process to install the bumper. Tighten the bumper strut-to-body retaining bolts to 51-87 ft. lbs. (69-118 Nm), if removed. Tighten all bolts that retain plastic components to 4-6 ft. lbs. (5-9 Nm).

REAR

▶ See Figure 10

1. Remove the screws that connect the bumper side and rear quarter.
2. Open the rear gate and remove the bumper top connecting screws.
3. Remove the bumper bottom connecting screws.
4. Move the bumper slightly downward and remove it from the car.
5. Reverse the removal process to install the bumper. Tighten the bumper strut-to-body retaining bolts to 51-87 ft. lbs. (69-118 Nm), if removed. Tighten all bolts that retain plastic components to 4-6 ft. lbs. (5-9 Nm).

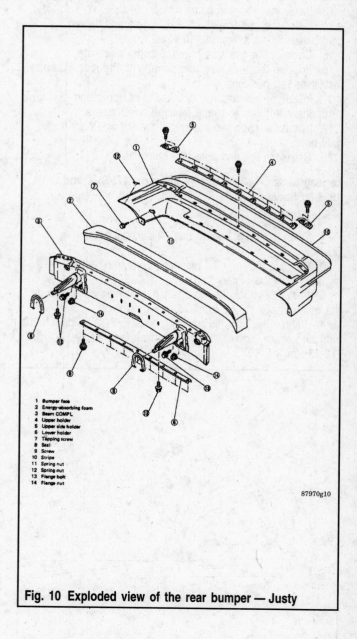

1	Bumper face
2	Energy-absorbing foam
3	Beam COMPL
4	Upper holder
5	Lower holder
6	Lower side holder
7	Side bracket
8	Nut
9	Flange bolt
10	Flange bolt
11	Bumper clip
12	Nut
13	License plate
14	Clip
15	Nut
16	Flange bolt
17	Screw
18	Bolt
19	Screw grommet
20	Bolt & washer ASSY
21	Stripe B
22	Stripe A

87970g09

Fig. 9 Exploded view of the front bumper — Justy

1	Bumper face
2	Energy-absorbing foam
3	Beam COMPL
4	Upper holder
5	Upper side holder
6	Lower holder
7	Tapping screw
8	Seal
9	Screw
10	Stripe
11	Spring nut
12	Spring nut
13	Flange bolt
14	Flange nut

87970g10

Fig. 10 Exploded view of the rear bumper — Justy

1985-89 Models Except XT; 1990-96 Loyale

FRONT

▶ See Figure 11

1. Disconnect the negative battery cable.
2. If not using a lift, remove the battery and canister.
3. If a lift is being used, remove the left and right undercovers.
4. Remove the left and right hold-down bands from the main harness and move the harness away from the bumper.
5. On models equipped with automatic transaxle, remove the clips that secure the automatic transaxle lines, and move the lines away from the front bumper.
6. On models with air conditioning, move the left transaxle line away from the bumper.
7. Insert rags between the front bumper and the car body to ensure sufficient clearance to insert a service tool to remove the bumper mounting bolts.
8. Disconnect the harness connectors from the left and right front turn signal lamps.
9. Place a container under the headlight washer unit to catch the fluid, and disconnect the headlight washer hoses.
10. Remove the bolts that secure the front bumper. With the help of an assistant, remove the bumper.

To install:

11. Install the front bumper in position and install the retaining bolts. Tighten the retaining bolts to 16 ft. lbs. (22 Nm).

12. Clearance between the bumper and upper skirt should be 0.25 in. (6mm) when viewed from the front of the car.
13. Reconnect the lighting assemblies and reposition all hoses.
14. Install the left and right undercovers.
15. Install the canister and the battery.

REAR — 4-DOOR SEDAN AND 2-DOOR HATCHBACK

▶ See Figure 12

1. Open the trunk lid. Remove the trunk trim panel clips and detach the trim.
2. Remove both the side and center trunk covers.
3. Disconnect the rear light harness connector.
4. Remove the 2 flange nuts.
5. Extract the rear bumper half way. Remove the grommet from the license plate harness, and remove the connector through the hole in the skirt section.
6. Remove the rear bumper horizontally.
7. Install the bumper in position and install all trim pieces removed.
8. Tighten the flange nuts to 22-31 ft. lbs. (29-42 Nm).

REAR — WAGON

▶ See Figure 13

1. Remove the 2 bolts that secure each lower end of the bumper to the body.
2. Remove the plug from the wall on each side of the center sub-trunk and remove the rear bumper retaining bolts.
3. Remove the bumper assembly from the vehicle.
4. Install the bumper assembly in position and tighten the retaining bolts to 52-73 ft. lbs. (66-100 Nm).

XT Coupe

FRONT

▶ See Figure 14

1. Position the vehicle on a lift.
2. Set the head lights to upper beam.
3. Remove the battery.
4. Raise the vehicle.
5. Remove the mud guards (inner plastic fender shields).

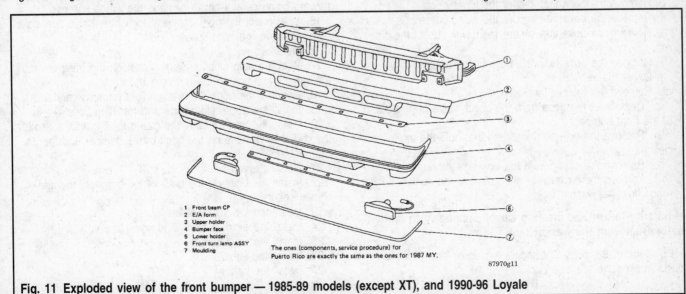

1 Front beam CP
2 E/A form
3 Upper holder
4 Bumper face
5 Lower holder
6 Front turn lamp ASSY
7 Moulding

The ones (components, service procedure) for Puerto Rico are exactly the same as the ones for 1987 MY.

87970g11

Fig. 11 Exploded view of the front bumper — 1985-89 models (except XT), and 1990-96 Loyale

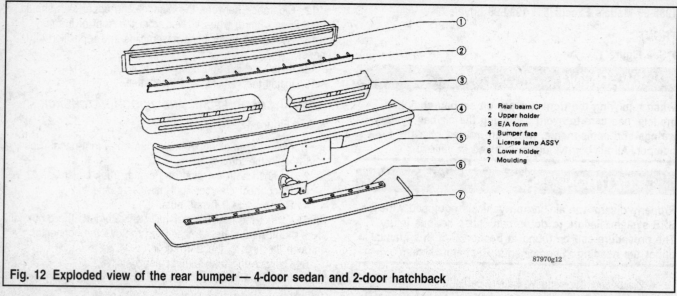

1 Rear beam CP
2 Upper holder
3 E/A form
4 Bumper face
5 License lamp ASSY
6 Lower holder
7 Moulding

87970g12

Fig. 12 Exploded view of the rear bumper — 4-door sedan and 2-door hatchback

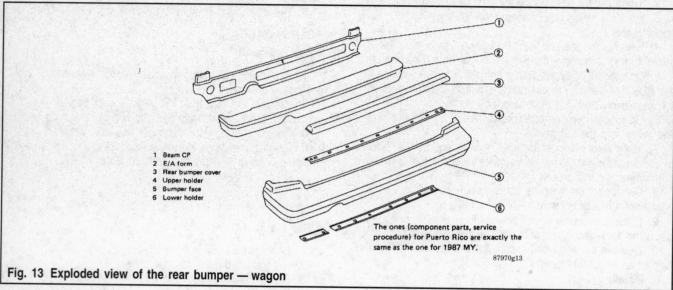

1 Beam CP
2 E/A form
3 Rear bumper cover
4 Upper holder
5 Bumper face
6 Lower holder

The ones (component parts, service procedure) for Puerto Rico are exactly the same as the one for 1987 MY.

87970g13

Fig. 13 Exploded view of the rear bumper — wagon

6. Remove the under cover and air dam skirts.
7. Remove the bolts that secure the lower ducts.
8. Remove the bolts that secure the side bumpers.
9. Remove the bolts that secure the lower side of the side ducts.
10. Remove the bolts from the back of the bumper stay.
11. Lower the vehicle.
12. Remove the washer tank:
   a. Disconnect the hose from the check valve on the back of the front bumper.
   b. Remove the bolts and washers that hold the air cleaner.
   c. Remove the clamp from the boot assembly.
   d. Remove the air cleaner, then remove the conical nuts which hold the washer tank.

➡**Be sure to turn the steering wheel completely to the left before removing the washer tank.**

13. Remove the bolts that secure the upper side of the side duct, and remove body side duct.

14. With the help of an assistant, slide the bumper slightly forward being careful not to damage the wiring harness.
15. Disconnect the front combination light harness connector.
16. Remove the front bumper.
To install:
17. With the help of an assistant, position the bumper onto the vehicle and tighten the retaining bolts.
18. Connect the front combination light harness connector.
19. Install the upper side ducts and retaining bolts.
20. Install the washer tank, the clamp for the boot assembly, the check valve hose on the back of the bumper and the air cleaner.
21. Raise the vehicle.
22. Install the bolts on the back of the bumper stay and tighten securely.
23. Install the lower side ducts.
24. Install the air dam skirts and under cover.
25. Install the mud guards.
26. Lower the vehicle.
27. Install the battery.

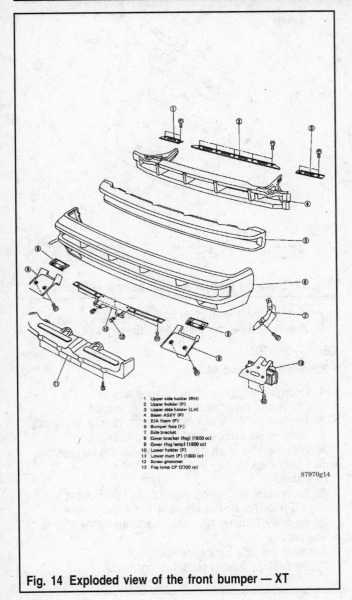

1 Upper side holder (RH)
2 Upper holder (F)
3 Upper side holder (LH)
4 Beam ASSY (F)
5 E/A foam (F)
6 Bumper face (F)
7 Side bracket
8 Cover bracket (fog) (1800 cc)
9 Cover (fog lamp) (1800 cc)
10 Lower holder (F)
11 Lower duct (F) (1800 cc)
12 Screw grommet
13 Fog lamp CP (2700 cc)

87970g14

Fig. 14 Exploded view of the front bumper — XT

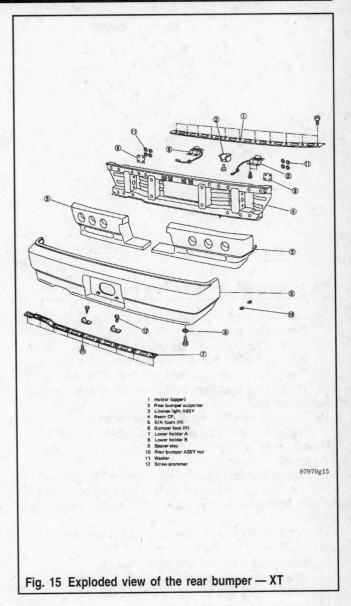

1 Holder (upper)
2 Rear bumper supporter
3 License light ASSY
4 Beam CP
5 E/A foam (R)
6 Bumper face (R)
7 Lower holder A
8 Lower holder B
9 Spacer stay
10 Rear bumper ASSY nut
11 Washer
12 Screw grommet

87970g15

Fig. 15 Exploded view of the rear bumper — XT

REAR

▶ See Figure 15

1. Open the trunk lid.
2. Remove the trunk lid trim.
3. Disconnect the license light harness connector, remove the grommet from the body and transfer the connector outside the trunk.
4. Remove the bolts that secure the sides of the rear bumper.
5. Remove the nuts that secure the bumper stays.
6. Remove the bumper.
7. Reverse the above process to install the bumper.
8. Adjust the clearance between the bumper and the rear combination light and between the bumper and the tail light to 0.31 in. (8mm).

Impreza

FRONT

▶ See Figure 16

✳✳WARNING

When removing the front bumper on these models, use care to avoid damaging the air bag system wirings and components, which are routed near the front bumper. All air bag wiring is wrapped in yellow.

✳✳CAUTION

Properly disarm the air bag on vehicles equipped with the SRS system. Failure to do so can cause serious injury. The procedure can be found in Section 6 of this manual under the heading "Supplemental Restraint System".

1. Disconnect the negative battery cable.
2. Remove the vapor canister.
3. Remove the front grille.

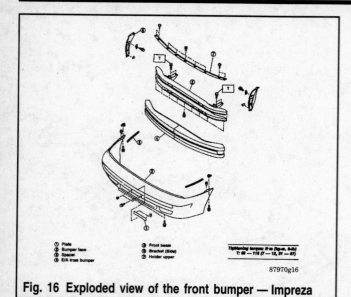

① Plate
② Bumper face
③ Spacer
④ E/A from bumper
⑤ Front beam
⑥ Bracket (Side)
⑦ Holder upper

Tightening torque: N·m (kg-m, ft-lb)
T: 90 — 115 (7 — 12, 51 — 87)

87970g16

Fig. 16 Exploded view of the front bumper — Impreza

4. Remove the left side parking light and headlight.
5. Remove the mud guard.
6. Remove the bolts from the side of the bumper.
7. Remove the bolt from the lower center of the bumper.
8. Remove the bolts from the lower side of the bumper.
9. Remove the bolts from the bumper stays on the engine compartment side.
10. Disconnect the turn signal light connector.
11. With the help of an assistant, remove the bumper assembly from the vehicle.

To install:
12. To facilitate installation, position the front bumper and attach the hook (located at the stay) to the body panel. Install the bolts from to the bumper stays on the engine compartment side.
13. Install the bolts to the lower side of the bumper.
14. Install the bolt to the lower center of the bumper.
15. Install the bolts to the side of the bumper.
16. Install the mud guard.
17. Install the left side parking light and headlight.
18. Connect the turn signal light connector.
19. Install the front grille.
20. Tighten all bolts securely.
21. Install the vapor canister and connect the negative battery cable.

REAR — SEDAN
▶ See Figure 17

1. Open the trunk lid and remove the rear trim panel and clips.
2. Disconnect the license plate light connector.
3. Remove the bolts and nuts from the side of the bumper.
4. Remove the bumper stay retaining bolts.
5. With the help of an assistant, remove the bumper assembly from the vehicle.

To install:
6. Install the bumper into position and install the stay retaining bolts.
7. Install the side bumper retaining bolts.

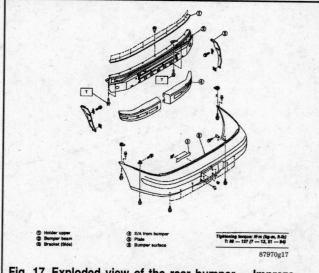

① Holder upper
② Bumper beam
③ Bracket (Side)
④ E/A from bumper
⑤ Plate
⑥ Bumper surface

Tightening torque: N·m (kg-m, ft-lb)
T: 90 — 127 (7 — 13, 51 — 94)

87970g17

Fig. 17 Exploded view of the rear bumper — Impreza

8. Connect the license plate light connector.
9. Install the rear trim panel and retaining clips.

REAR — WAGON
▶ See Figures 17 and 18

1. Open the tailgate and rear quarter trim lid.
2. Disconnect the license plate light connector.
3. Remove the bolts and nuts from the side of the bumper.
4. Remove the bumper stay retaining bolts.
5. With the help of an assistant, remove the bumper assembly from the vehicle.

To install:
6. To facilitate installation, position the rear bumper and attach the hook (located at the stay) to the body panel.
7. Install the bumper into position and install the stay retaining bolts.
8. Install the side bumper retaining bolts.
9. Connect the license plate light connector.

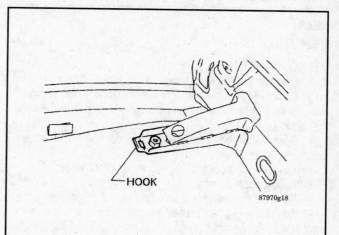

HOOK

87970g18

Fig. 18 To facilitate installation of the rear bumper, attach the hook (located at the stay) to the body panel — Impreza wagon

Legacy

FRONT

▶ See Figure 19

✳✳WARNING

When removing the front bumper on these models, use care to avoid damaging the air bag system wirings and components, which are routed near the front bumper. All air bag wiring is wrapped in yellow.

✳✳CAUTION

Properly disarm the air bag on vehicles equipped with the SRS system. Failure to do so can cause serious injury. The procedure can be found in Section 6 of this manual under the heading "Supplemental Restraint System".

1. Properly disarm the air bag system, on models equipped. Disconnect the negative battery cable.
2. Remove the vapor canister.

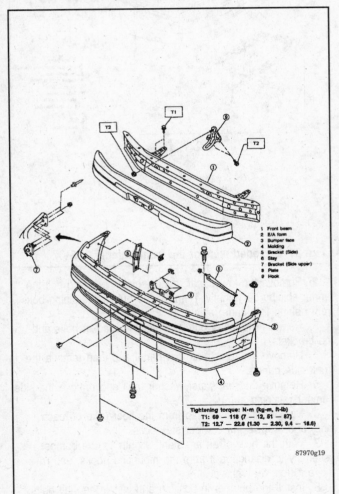

Tightening torque: N·m (kg-m, ft-lb)
T1: 69 — 118 (7 — 12, 51 — 87)
T2: 12.7 — 22.6 (1.30 — 2.30, 9.4 — 16.6)

87970g19

Fig. 19 Exploded view of the front bumper — Legacy sedan

3. Remove the inner fender shield.
4. Remove the bolts and nuts that retain the bumper at the side.
5. Remove the lower part of the bumper by releasing the clips.
6. From the engine compartment, remove the bumper stay retaining bolts.
7. With the help of an assistant, remove the bumper assembly from the vehicle.

To install:

8. Install the bumper into position and tighten the stay bolts to 51-87 ft. lbs. (69-118 Nm).
9. install the lower part of the bumper by pushing it firmly into place and engaging the clips.
10. Install the side bumper retaining nuts and bolts. Install the inner fender shield.
11. Install the vapor canister and connect the negative battery cable.

REAR

▶ See Figure 20

1. Open the trunk lid or tailgate and remove the rear trim panel and clips.
2. Remove the bolts and nuts from the side of the bumper.
3. Remove the bumper stay retaining bolts.
4. With the help of an assistant, remove the bumper assembly from the vehicle.
5. Install the bumper into position and install the stay retaining bolts. Tighten the bolts to 51-87 ft. lbs. (69-118 Nm).
6. Install the side bumper retaining bolts. Install the rear trim panel.

SVX

FRONT

▶ See Figure 21

✳✳WARNING

When removing the front bumper on these models, use care to avoid damaging the air bag system wirings and components, which are routed near the front bumper. All air bag wiring is wrapped in yellow.

✳✳CAUTION

Properly disarm the air bag on vehicles equipped with the SRS system. Failure to do so can·cause serious injury. The procedure can be found in Section 6 of this manual under the heading "Supplemental Restraint System".

1. Properly disarm the air bag system and disconnect the negative battery cable.
2. Raise and safely support the vehicle. Remove the engine under cover.
3. Detach the front side of the inner fender guards and remove the side bumper bolts.
4. Remove the bumper side stay from the bumper.
5. Remove the bolts securing the lower side of the bumper to the body.
6. Remove the front combination lamp assemblies and remove the bumper retaining bolt from behind the assemblies.

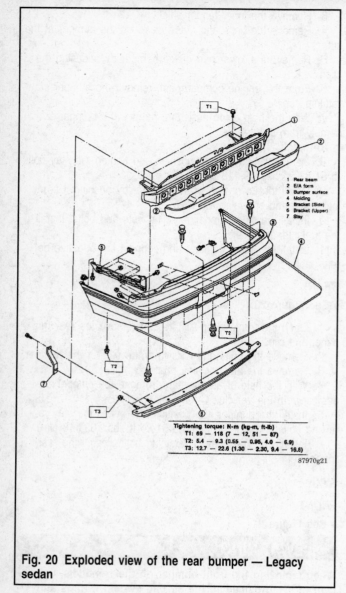

1 Rear beam
2 E/A form
3 Bumper surface
4 Molding
5 Bracket (Side)
6 Bracket (Upper)
7 Stay

Tightening torque: N·m (kg-m, ft-lb)
T1: 69 — 118 (7 — 12, 51 — 87)
T2: 5.4 — 9.3 (0.55 — 0.95, 4.0 — 6.9)
T3: 12.7 — 22.6 (1.30 — 2.30, 9.4 — 16.5)

87970g21

Fig. 20 Exploded view of the rear bumper — Legacy sedan

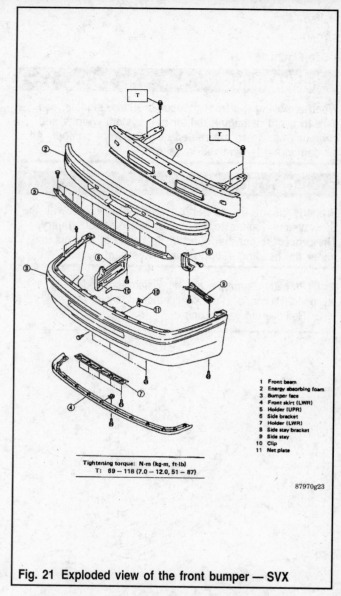

1 Front beam
2 Energy absorbing foam
3 Bumper face
4 Front skirt (LWR)
5 Holder (UPR)
6 Side bracket
7 Holder (LWR)
8 Side stay bracket
9 Side stay
10 Clip
11 Net plate

Tightening torque: N·m (kg-m, ft-lb)
T: 69 — 118 (7.0 — 12.0, 51 — 87)

87970g23

Fig. 21 Exploded view of the front bumper — SVX

7. Remove the vapor canister from its bracket.

8. In the engine compartment, remove the bumper stay retaining bolts. With the help of an assistant, remove the bumper assembly from the vehicle.

To install:

9. Install the bumper into position and install the bumper stay retaining bolts. Tighten the bolts to 51-87 ft. lbs. (69-118 Nm).

10. Install the vapor canister into position. Install the side bumper retaining bolts and the combination lamp assemblies.

11. Install the bumper side stays and the inner fender guard bolts.

12. Install the lower bumper-to-body bolts.

13. Install the engine undercover and lower the vehicle.

REAR

▶ See Figure 22

1. Raise and safely support the rear of the vehicle.

2. Remove the lower rear fender shield bolts and pull the fender shields out slightly. Remove the bumper retaining bolts from behind the fender shield.

3. Remove the lower bumper retaining bracket bolts and the brackets.

4. Remove the rear trunk trim panel and then remove the trunk side panels.

5. Remove the rear wiper washer tank and remove the side bumper retaining nut.

6. Remove the plastic cap from the floor (one on each side) and remove the bumper stay bolts.

7. With the help of an assistant, slightly lift the bumper assembly to disengage it from the mounting hooks, and remove it from the vehicle.

8. Install the bumper in position and install the stay bolts. Tighten the stay bolts to 51-87 ft. lbs. (69-118 Nm).

9. Install the remaining bumper bolts and install all removed trim panels.

10. Install the lower fender shield retaining bolts and lower the vehicle.

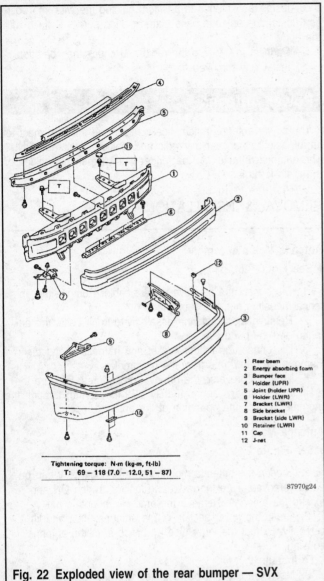

Fig. 22 Exploded view of the rear bumper — SVX

1 Rear beam
2 Energy absorbing foam
3 Bumper face
4 Holder (UPR)
5 Joint (holder UPR)
6 Holder (LWR)
7 Bracket (LWR)
8 Side bracket
9 Bracket (side LWR)
10 Retainer (LWR)
11 Cap
12 J-net

Tightening torque: N-m (kg-m, ft-lb)
T: 69 — 118 (7.0 — 12.0, 51 — 87)

87970g24

Grille

REMOVAL & INSTALLATION

▶ **See Figures 23 and 24**

To remove the grille on all Subaru models, simply unfasten the retaining screws and clips, then remove the grille from the vehicle. Use care not to break the grille when pulling it away from the vehicle body.

Manual Outside Mirrors

REMOVAL & INSTALLATION

1. Remove control knob handle.

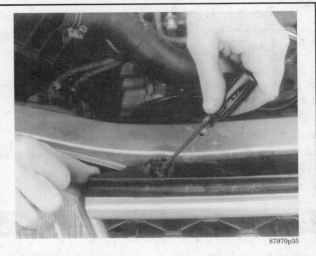

Fig. 23 While lightly pulling on the grille, carefully pry the clips from the body — 1991 Legacy shown

87970p35

Fig. 24 With the retaining clips released, the grille can be easily removed from the vehicle

87970p36

2. Remove door corner finisher panel.
3. Remove mirror body attaching screws, and then remove mirror body
4. Installation is in the reverse order of removal.

➡ **Apply sealer to the rear surface of door corner finisher panel during installation to prevent water leak.**

Power Outside Mirror

The mirrors are controlled by a single switch assembly, located on the instrument panel or the door panel. The motors that operate the mirrors are part of the mirror assembly and cannot be replaced separately.

The mirror switch consists of a left-right change over select knob and control knobs. The switch is ready to function only when the ignition switch is in the **ACC** or **ON** position. Movement of the mirror is accomplished by the motor, located in the mirror housing.

REMOVAL & INSTALLATION

▶ **See Figure 25**

1. Remove door corner finisher panel.
2. Remove mirror body attaching screws, and then remove mirror body
3. Disconnect the electrical connection.

➡**On SVX and Legacy models, it will be necessary to remove the door trim panel to gain access to the electrical connection.**

4. Installation is in the reverse order of removal.

Manual Antenna Mast

REMOVAL & INSTALLATION

1. Disconnect the negative battery cable.
2. Disconnect the antenna wire from the radio.
3. Push the antenna wire through the access hole under the instrument panel.

➡**To make installation easier, tie a string to the end of the antenna wire before removing it from the vehicle. Pull the string up with the antenna wire and allow one end to stay visible at the inside of the vehicle. When installing the antenna, tie the wire to the other end of the string and pull it through.**

4. On models with the antenna on the side of the windshield:
    a. Remove the A pillar trim.
    b. Loosen the antenna mounting nut located beneath the trim panel.
    c. Move the antenna upward slightly then pull it out of the pillar with the antenna lead.
5. On models with roof mounted antenna, remove the antenna base mounting screw and pull the antenna off of the roof, drawing the wire out of the opening.

6. Install the antenna in position, guiding the wire into position. Install the antenna base plate, making sure it is flush with the body.
7. Connect the wire to the radio and check the operation.
8. Install any removed trim.

Power Antenna

The power antenna automatically raises the antenna mast to its full height whenever the radio and ignition are turned **ON**. The antenna retracts into the fender when either the ignition or the radio is turned **OFF**.

REMOVAL & INSTALLATION

Antenna Motor Assembly
▶ **See Figure 26**

1. Disconnect the negative battery cable. Remove the antenna mounting nut and supporter.
2. Remove the 2 antenna assembly-to-trunk bolts, the antenna and the band clip.
3. Disconnect the feeder socket and harness connector. Remove the drain tube from the grommet.
4. To install, reverse the removal procedures. Be sure the drain tube protrudes approximately 0.79 in. (20mm) through the grommet. Check the operation of the antenna mast.

Antenna Mast
▶ **See Figure 27**

1. Loosen the antenna mounting nut enough so it can be easily removed. Turn the radio and ignition switch **ON** and extend the antenna. Remove the antenna mounting nut.
2. Grasp the lower section of the antenna mast and lift it vertically. Extract the inner pipe and rope from the antenna housing.

To install:
3. Insert the center pipe (supplied with the new antenna mast) into the antenna assembly tube until it bottoms.

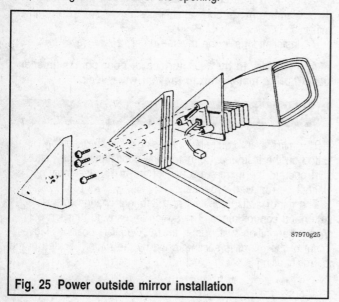

87970g25

Fig. 25 Power outside mirror installation

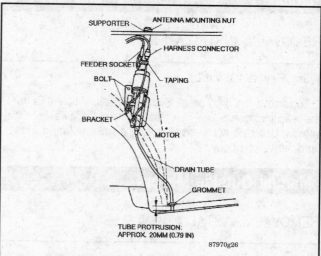

SUPPORTER — ANTENNA MOUNTING NUT
HARNESS CONNECTOR
FEEDER SOCKET
BOLT — TAPING
BRACKET
MOTOR
DRAIN TUBE
GROMMET

TUBE PROTRUSION:
APPROX. 20MM (0.79 IN)

87970g26

Fig. 26 Power antenna assembly mounting and components

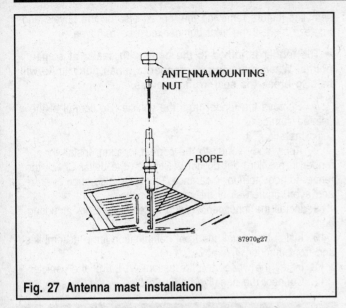

Fig. 27 Antenna mast installation

4. Insert the antenna rod rope into the antenna housing through the centering pipe with the rack facing outward; at the same time, turn the radio switch **OFF**.

5. Be sure the antenna mast is vertical to the antenna housing. This prevents the rack from sustaining damage and making it easier to insert the rope. Remove the centering pipe from the antenna housing and detach it from the rope.

6. Face the inner pipe spring toward the center of the vehicle and insert the inner pipe into the antenna housing. Temporarily tighten the antenna mounting nut.

7. Turn the radio switch **ON** and **OFF** to ensure the antenna rod extends and retracts properly. Tighten the antenna mounting nut.

Fender

REMOVAL & INSTALLATION

▶ See Figures 28, 29, 30, 31, 32 and 33

❊❊CAUTION

Properly disarm the air bag on vehicles equipped with the SRS system. Failure to do so can cause serious injury. The procedure can be found in Section 6 of this manual under the heading "Supplemental Restraint System".

1. On models equipped with an air bag, use caution when working on the front fenders, the air bag wiring and sensors are in this area.

2. Disconnect the negative battery cable.

3. Raise and support the front of the vehicle so that it is just off of the ground.

4. Remove the tire and wheel assembly.

5. Remove the inner fender skirt assembly bolts, clips and screws and remove it.

6. Remove the fender mounting bolts. On some models, it will be necessary to remove the front combination lamp as-

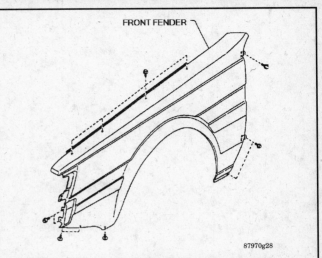

Fig. 28 Fender mounting bolt locations — Loyale and 1985-89 sedans, wagons, hatchbacks

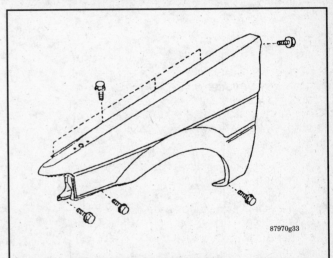

Fig. 29 Fender mounting bolt locations — Justy; SVX similar

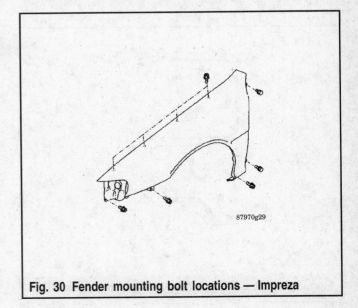

Fig. 30 Fender mounting bolt locations — Impreza

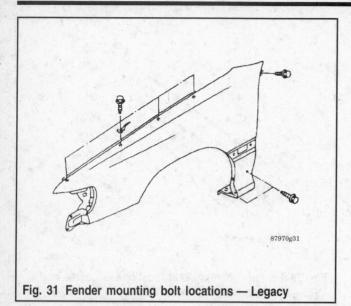

Fig. 31 Fender mounting bolt locations — Legacy

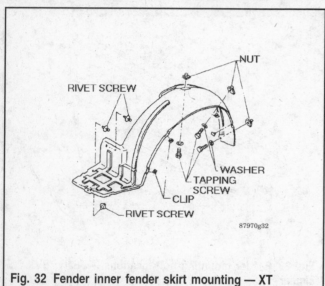

Fig. 32 Fender inner fender skirt mounting — XT

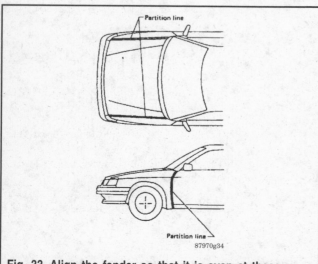

Fig. 33 Align the fender so that it is even at these points

semblies, before removing the fender, also on the Loyale and Impreza models the front bumper must be removed.

➡**The fender is joined to the body with sealer at some points. When removing the fender, a small putty knife will help to break the seal in these areas.**

7. Remove the fender from the vehicle. Be careful of the painted surfaces.

To install:

8. Apply body sealer to the correct location. Install the fender in position, but do not yet tighten the bolts. Check the fender-to-hood-to-door clearance. Once the clearance is correct and even, tighten all of the mounting bolts.

9. Install the inner fender skirt assembly and its mounting bolts.

10. Install the Install the front combination lamp assemblies and front bumper, if removed.

11. Install the wheel and tire assembly. Lower the vehicle.

12. Connect the negative battery cable.

Power Sunroof

▶ **See Figures 34 and 35**

➡**The sunroof assembly is equipped with water drain tubes. It is important to keep these drain tubes open. So it is recommended to blow compressed air through the drain tubes at regular intervals, in order to keep the drain tubes clear.**

REMOVAL & INSTALLATION

Except Impreza and SVX

SUNROOF LID ASSEMBLY

▶ **See Figure 36**

1. Completely close the sunroof glass. Completely open the sunshade. Remove the bracket cap and screws and detach the bracket cover.

2. Completely close the sunroof lid assembly and lift it up. Remove the 8 nuts, (6 nuts on 1995-96 Legacy) from the left and right ring bracket.

3. Working from inside the vehicle, slightly raise the sunroof lid assembly until it is disengaged from the link bracket. Hold both ends of the lid assembly and remove it at an angle.

SUNSHADE

1. Unhook the sunshade hooks. Move the sunroof lid assembly rearward.

2. Set the sunshade to the **FORWARD** position and remove the retaining nuts from both sides of the sunshade.

3. Installation is the reverse order of the removal procedure.

SUNROOF FRAME

▶ **See Figure 37**

1. Remove the sunroof trim. Disconnect the front and rear drain tubes.

2. On 1995-96 Legacy, remove the sunroof switch, and the center and rear room lamps.

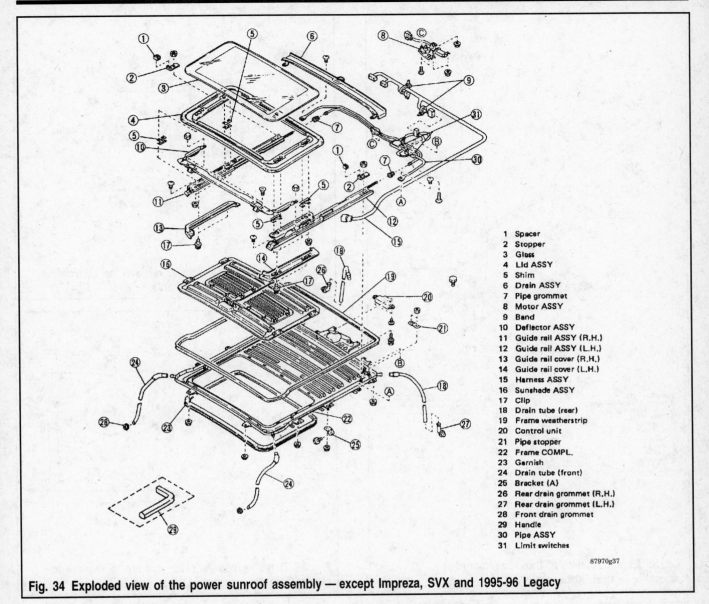

1 Spacer
2 Stopper
3 Glass
4 Lid ASSY
5 Shim
6 Drain ASSY
7 Pipe grommet
8 Motor ASSY
9 Band
10 Deflector ASSY
11 Guide rail ASSY (R.H.)
12 Guide rail ASSY (L.H.)
13 Guide rail cover (R.H.)
14 Guide rail cover (L.H.)
15 Harness ASSY
16 Sunshade ASSY
17 Clip
18 Drain tube (rear)
19 Frame weatherstrip
20 Control unit
21 Pipe stopper
22 Frame COMPL.
23 Garnish
24 Drain tube (front)
25 Bracket (A)
26 Rear drain grommet (R.H.)
27 Rear drain grommet (L.H.)
28 Front drain grommet
29 Handle
30 Pipe ASSY
31 Limit switches

87970g37

Fig. 34 Exploded view of the power sunroof assembly — except Impreza, SVX and 1995-96 Legacy

3. Remove the bolts which hold the sunroof frame and detach the sunroof frame.

4. Installation is the reverse order of the removal procedure.

SUNROOF MOTOR

▶ See Figure 38

1. Disconnect the negative battery cable. Remove the roof trim.

2. Remove the sunroof motor nut and harness coupler and remove the sunroof motor.

3. Installation of the motor is the reverse order of the removal procedure. The sunroof is operated by a switch, which is usually located in the headliner. The system is consists of the sunroof switch, motor drive cables and circuit breaker and a relay. The sunroof can be closed manually, (should it be necessary) by removing the headliner plug, insert the handle and turn the gear to close the sunroof.

Impreza and SVX

▶ See Figure 39

SUNROOF PANEL

▶ See Figures 39 and 40

1. Open the sunroof approximately 1/3 of the way.

2. Remove the clips attached to the front side of the sunroof trim by pulling the trim from the inside of the compartment.

3. Move the trim forward and detach the trim from the holder.

4. Close the sunroof, remove the sunroof panel retaining nuts and remove the sunroof from the vehicle.

5. Installation is the reverse order of the removal procedure. Make sure the sunroof is free from slack and noise when opened and closed. Adjust as necessary.

SUNROOF MOTOR AND RELAY

▶ See Figure 39

1. Disconnect the negative battery cable.

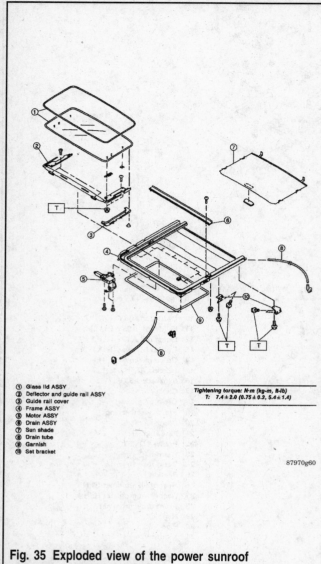

① Glass lid ASSY
② Deflector and guide rail ASSY
③ Guide rail cover
④ Frame ASSY
⑤ Motor ASSY
⑥ Drain ASSY
⑦ Sun shade
⑧ Drain tube
⑨ Garnish
⑩ Set bracket

Tightening torque: N·m (kg-m, ft-lb)
T: 7.4 ± 2.0 (0.75 ± 0.2, 5.4 ± 1.4)

87970g60

Fig. 35 Exploded view of the power sunroof assembly — 1995-96 Legacy

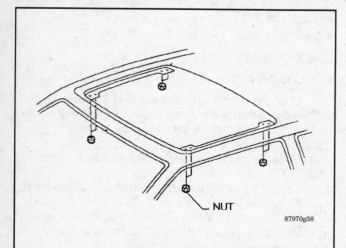

87970g38

Fig. 36 Remove these nuts to remove the sunroof lid — except Impreza and SVX

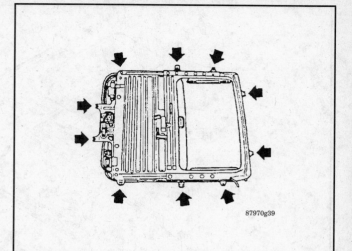

87970g39

Fig. 37 Remove these nuts to remove the sunroof frame — except Impreza and SVX

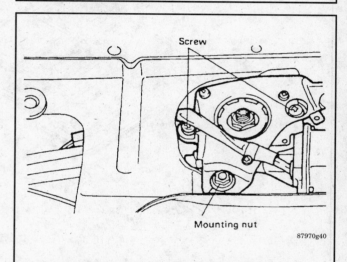

Screw

Mounting nut

87970g40

Fig. 38 Remove these screws and nut to remove the sunroof motor — except Impreza and SVX

2. Remove the rear quarter trim, pillar trim and roof trim
3. Disconnect the connector and remove the sunroof motor retaining screws. Pull out the motor and relay.
4. Installation is the reverse order of the removal procedure.

SUNROOF FRAME

▶ See Figures 39, 41, 42, 43, 44 and 45

1. Remove the rear quarter trim, pillar trim and roof trim.
2. Remove the sunroof panel as outlined in this section.
3. Disconnect the drain tubes.
4. Disconnect the connector between the body harness and the sunroof harness.
5. Loosen, but do not remove, the two mounting bolts near the motor.
6. Remove the two outside bolts, eight nuts and four adjusting nuts and remove the sunroof frame.
7. Loosen the set bracket mounting bolt.

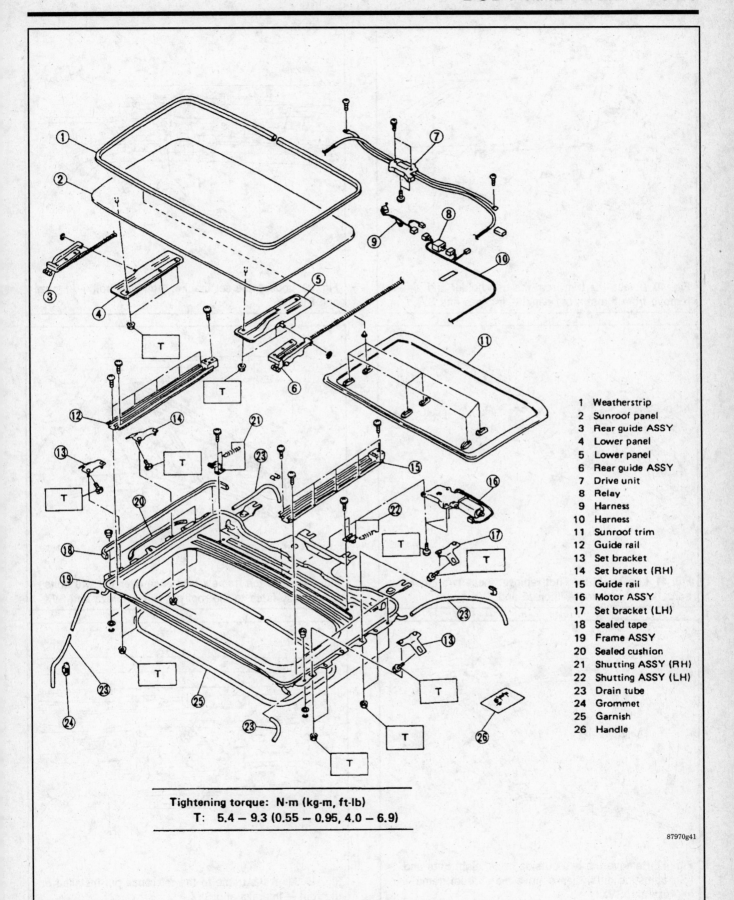

1   Weatherstrip
2   Sunroof panel
3   Rear guide ASSY
4   Lower panel
5   Lower panel
6   Rear guide ASSY
7   Drive unit
8   Relay
9   Harness
10 Harness
11 Sunroof trim
12 Guide rail
13 Set bracket
14 Set bracket (RH)
15 Guide rail
16 Motor ASSY
17 Set bracket (LH)
18 Sealed tape
19 Frame ASSY
20 Sealed cushion
21 Shutting ASSY (RH)
22 Shutting ASSY (LH)
23 Drain tube
24 Grommet
25 Garnish
26 Handle

Tightening torque: N·m (kg-m, ft-lb)
T: 5.4 — 9.3 (0.55 — 0.95, 4.0 — 6.9)

87970g41

Fig. 39 Exploded view of the power sunroof assembly — Impreza and SVX

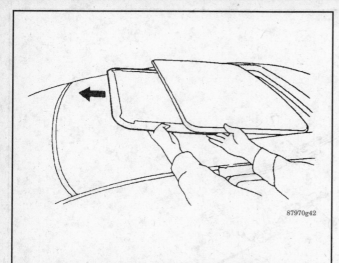

Fig. 40 Detach the trim from the trim holder and remove from the sunroof panel — Impreza and SVX

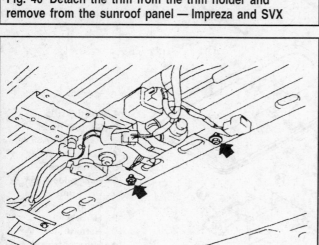

Fig. 41 Loosen, but do not remove, these two mounting bolts near the motor — Impreza and SVX

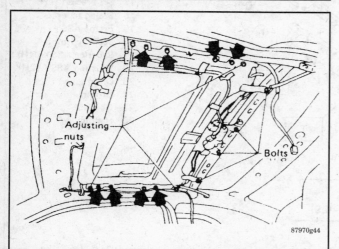

Fig. 42 Remove the two outside bolts, eight nuts and four adjusting nuts, then remove the sunroof frame — Impreza and SVX

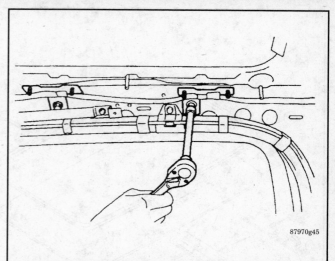

Fig. 43 Loosen the set bracket mounting bolt — Impreza and SVX

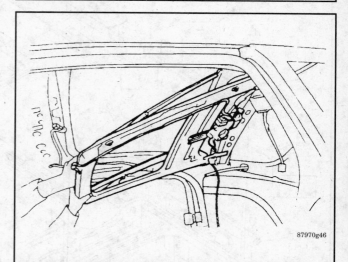

Fig. 44 Insert the frame's rear edge over the two bolts temporarily fitted to the roof brace — Impreza and SVX

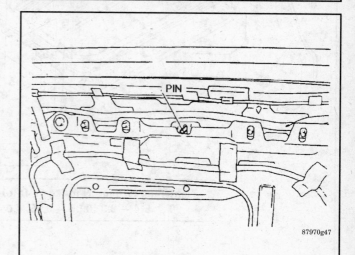

Fig. 45 Align the frame to the reference pin installed on the roof — Impreza and SVX

To install:

➡**The sunroof trim reference pin must be fitted in the holder notch.**

8. Insert the frame rear end slit to the two bolts temporary fitted to the roof brace.

9. Align the frame to the reference pin installed on the roof.

10. Tighten the adjusting nut to set the frame to its highest position. Temporarily tighten the nuts and bolts.

11. Install the sunroof panel as outlined in this section.

12. Adjust the height by turning the adjusting screw. The difference in height between the roof panel and the sunroof panel should be 0-0.039 in. (0 -1.0mm)

13. Adjust the front, rear, right and left side partitions. The partitions clearance should be 0.021-0.25 in. (5.4-6.4mm).

14. Tighten the set bracket mounting bolts.

15. Tighten the all remaining bolts and nuts.

16. Install the drain tubes securely.

17. Install the roof trim.

18. Install the garnish and place the garnish joint at the rear center of the body.

19. Install the sunroof trim, pillar trim and rear quarter trim.

20. After complete assembly, check the following:

- The garnish must be free of waves.
- There must be no clearance between the garnish and the sunroof trim when the sunroof is fully closed.
- The sunroof must be free from slack and noise when it is fully opened and closed.

ADJUSTMENTS

Except Impreza and SVX

HEIGHT ADJUSTMENT

▶ **See Figure 46**

1. Place shim(s) between the link bracket and the lid assembly to align the sunroof with the roof panel.

2. The difference in the height between the roof and the main seal should be adjusted to within the 0.028-0.059 in. (0.7-1.5mm) range.

HORIZONTAL ADJUSTMENT

1. Loosen the 8 nuts which hold the sunroof lid assembly.

2. Move the sunroof lid assembly to either side, along the oblong hole at the stay location, until proper adjustment is reached. Then tighten the nuts.

3. Check to see if the deflector is positioned at a proper height. The height of the deflector cannot be adjusted. Repair or replace the deflector if it is deformed or damaged.

SUNROOF CLOSING FORCE CHECK

▶ **See Figure 47**

1. After installing all removed parts, using a second person, have them hold the switch to close the sunroof while measuring the force required to stop the sunroof with a suitable spring scale.

2. Read the force on the scale as soon as the glass stops moving, then immediately release the switch and spring scale. The closing force should be 44-55 lbs. (20-25 kg).

3. If the force required to stop the sunroof is not within specifications, adjust it by turning the sunroof motor clutch adjusting nut. Turn the nut clockwise to increase the force or counterclockwise to decrease the force.

4. After proper adjustment has been made, install a new lockwasher and bend it against the flat of the adjusting nut.

Impreza and SVX

HEIGHT ADJUSTMENT

▶ **See Figure 48**

1. Adjust the height by turning the adjusting screw. The difference in height between the roof panel and the sunroof panel should be 0-0.039 in. (0-1.0mm)

HORIZONTAL ADJUSTMENT

▶ **See Figure 49**

1. Loosen the 8 nuts which hold the sunroof lid assembly.

2. Adjust the front, rear, right and left side partitions. The partitions clearance should be 0.021-0.25 in. (5.4-6.4mm).

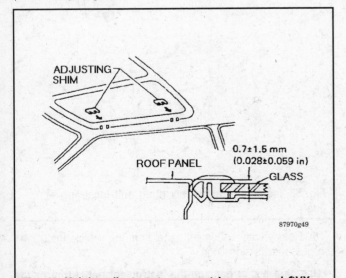

Fig. 46 Height adjustment — except Impreza and SVX

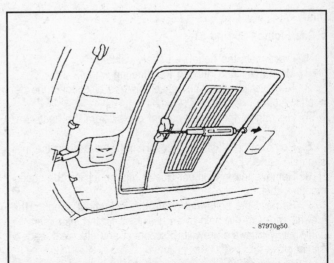

Fig. 47 Sunroof closing force check — except Impreza and SVX

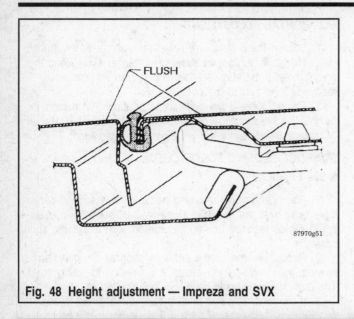

Fig. 48 Height adjustment — Impreza and SVX

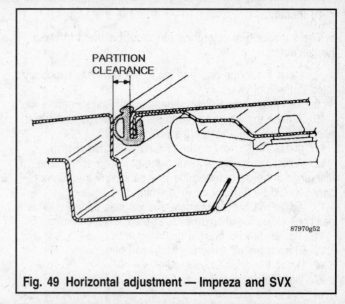

Fig. 49 Horizontal adjustment — Impreza and SVX

INTERIOR

Instrument Panel

✳✳CAUTION

Properly disarm the air bag on vehicles equipped with the SRS system. Failure to do so can cause serious injury. The procedure can be found in Section 6 of this manual under the heading "Supplemental Restraint System".

REMOVAL & INSTALLATION

➡While the instrument panel removal procedures here are specific for each vehicle, they should be used only as an outline. Manufacturers production changes and year-to-year trim level changes are not covered in these procedures.

Justy

▶ See Figures 50 and 51

1. Disconnect the negative battery cable.
2. Matchmark and remove the steering wheel.
3. Remove the glove box assembly and disconnect the defroster ducts.
4. Disconnect the heater control cables from the heater unit.
5. Remove the plastic bolt covers from the around the instrument panel.
6. Remove the instrument cluster, disconnecting the speedometer cable.
7. Remove the bolts that retain the instrument panel to the firewall and with the help of an assistant, lift the instrument panel away from the firewall. Disconnect any electrical leads at this point.

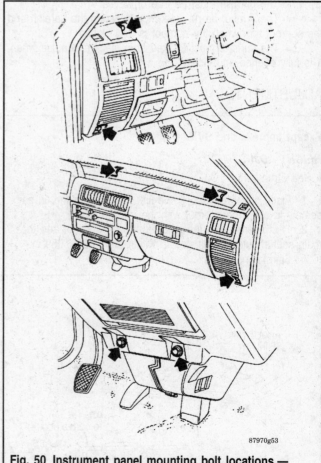

Fig. 50 Instrument panel mounting bolt locations — Justy

8. Remove the instrument panel from the vehicle through the passenger's side door.

➡Use care not to damage the instrument panel trim or the vehicle interior trim when removing the instrument panel.

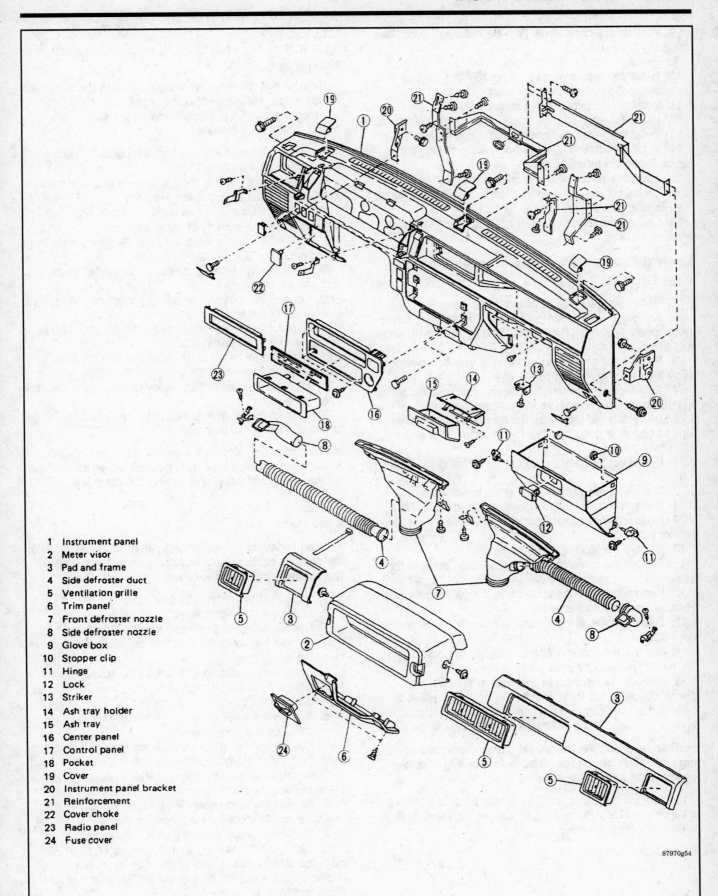

1   Instrument panel
2   Meter visor
3   Pad and frame
4   Side defroster duct
5   Ventilation grille
6   Trim panel
7   Front defroster nozzle
8   Side defroster nozzle
9   Glove box
10 Stopper clip
11 Hinge
12 Lock
13 Striker
14 Ash tray holder
15 Ash tray
16 Center panel
17 Control panel
18 Pocket
19 Cover
20 Instrument panel bracket
21 Reinforcement
22 Cover choke
23 Radio panel
24 Fuse cover

87970g54

Fig. 51 Exploded view of the instrument panel — Justy

9. Remove any components from the instrument panel that are going to be replaced.

To install:

10. Install the instrument panel in position with the help of an assistant. Connect all electrical leads.

11. Install the instrument panel retaining bolts.

12. Install the removed components on the instrument panel.

13. Install the heater duct and the glove box assembly.

14. Install the instrument cluster, connecting the speedometer cable and electrical leads.

15. Install any remaining components. Install the steering wheel on the column in the same position as removed. Tighten the center nut to 36-43 ft. lbs. (49-59 Nm).

16. Connect the negative battery cable. Check the operation of all accessories.

Loyale and 1985-89 Sedans, Wagons and Hatchbacks

▶ **See Figure 52**

1. Disconnect the negative battery cable.

2. Remove the lower trim panel on the driver's side (underneath steering column). The panel is held in place by 3 screws and trim clips.

3. Remove the bolts retaining the main fuse box assembly, allow the assembly to hang by the wires.

4. Remove the lower steering column cover and disconnect the ventilation duct from under the instrument panel.

5. Disconnect the cable from the air vent in the driver's side kick panel where it attaches to the control lever in the instrument panel.

6. Disconnect the temperature control cables at the heater unit.

7. Disconnect the vacuum lines at the heater case.

8. Disconnect the wiring harnesses on the driver's side.

9. Remove the instrument cluster an disconnect the speedometer cable.

10. Remove the steering wheel assembly.

11. Remove the center tray and console from between the seats.

12. Remove the lower trim panel from the passenger's side. Remove the glove box assembly.

13. Disconnect the wiring harness connectors on the passenger's side.

14. Remove the instrument panel retaining bolt covers from the panel. They can be pried gently upward.

15. Remove the instrument panel bolts in the following places; 2 bolts at the lower ends of the instrument panel, 2 bolts at the lower center of the panel, 2 bolts at the upper ends of the panel and 2 bolts at the upper center of the panel.

➡ **When removing the instrument panel, check that all wiring and cables are disconnected before pulling it completely away from the firewall.**

16. With the help of an assistant, lift the panel and remove it from the vehicle. Use care not to damage the panel or the interior trim when removing it.

To install:

17. With the help of an assistant, install the instrument panel into position at the firewall.

➡ **Be sure that no wires are caught between the panel and its mounting. Make sure that the panel is on top of the weatherstrip along the windshield and the strip is not folded along the windshield.**

18. Install the instrument panel retaining bolts. Install the bolt covers after tightening the bolts.

19. Connect the wiring at the passenger's side of the instrument panel. Install the glove box assembly.

20. Install the lower cover on the passenger's side. Install the center console and tray between the seats.

21. Install the steering wheel assembly. Tighten the steering wheel nut to 22-29 ft. lbs. (29-39 Nm).

22. Install the instrument cluster and connect the electrical wiring at the driver's side.

23. Connect the temperature control cables and the vacuum lines at the heater unit.

24. Connect the air vent cable at the driver's side air vent. Install the main fuse box in position.

25. Install the steering column lower trim and the lower instrument panel trim.

26. Install any remaining trim pieces and check the operation of all components.

27. Connect the negative battery cable and check the operation of all electrical components.

➡ **When checking electrical components, if any of the fuses should blow, check that there are no wires pinched by the instrument panel and correct it if there are.**

XT

▶ **See Figure 53**

➡ **When removing the instrument panel on the XT models, the steering shaft and column assembly are removed with the control wings as an assembly.**

1. Disconnect the negative battery cable.

2. Remove the steering wheel.

3. Remove the lower trim panel from the driver's side.

4. Remove the ventilation duct from the driver's side, it can be pulled out by hand.

5. Open the fuse box lid and remove the screws that retain the fuse box. Push the fuse box back and allow it to hang by the wires.

6. Remove the lower cover on the passenger's side. Remove the glove box door assembly.

7. Remove the trim panel from the top of the instrument panel by prying it gently at both ends and in the middle. You will have to pull it upward with your hands to release the clips, be careful not to bend or break it.

8. Remove the center console assembly. Be sure to remove the control knobs for the ventilation controls.

9. Remove the radio assembly.

10. Disconnect the steering shaft coupler at the floor. Remove the steering column covers. Remove the column-to-instrument panel support bolts and remove the column, control wings and shaft as an assembly.

11. Disconnect the wiring harnesses on the drivers and passenger's side.

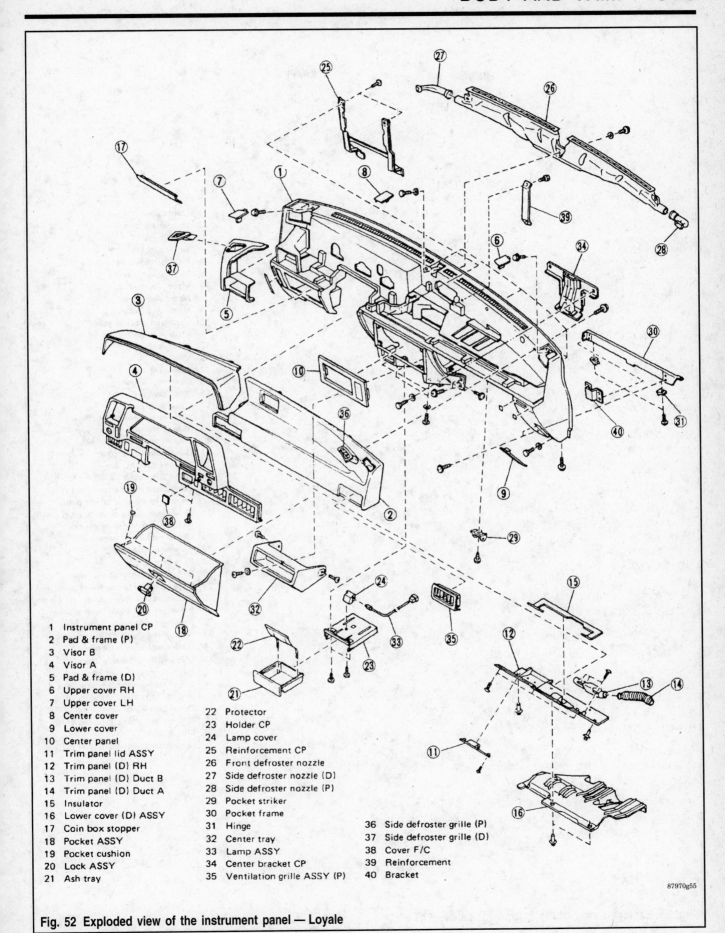

1 Instrument panel CP
2 Pad & frame (P)
3 Visor B
4 Visor A
5 Pad & frame (D)
6 Upper cover RH
7 Upper cover LH
8 Center cover
9 Lower cover
10 Center panel
11 Trim panel lid ASSY
12 Trim panel (D) RH
13 Trim panel (D) Duct B
14 Trim panel (D) Duct A
15 Insulator
16 Lower cover (D) ASSY
17 Coin box stopper
18 Pocket ASSY
19 Pocket cushion
20 Lock ASSY
21 Ash tray

22 Protector
23 Holder CP
24 Lamp cover
25 Reinforcement CP
26 Front defroster nozzle
27 Side defroster nozzle (D)
28 Side defroster nozzle (P)
29 Pocket striker
30 Pocket frame
31 Hinge
32 Center tray
33 Lamp ASSY
34 Center bracket CP
35 Ventilation grille ASSY (P)

36 Side defroster grille (P)
37 Side defroster grille (D)
38 Cover F/C
39 Reinforcement
40 Bracket

87970g55

Fig. 52 Exploded view of the instrument panel — Loyale

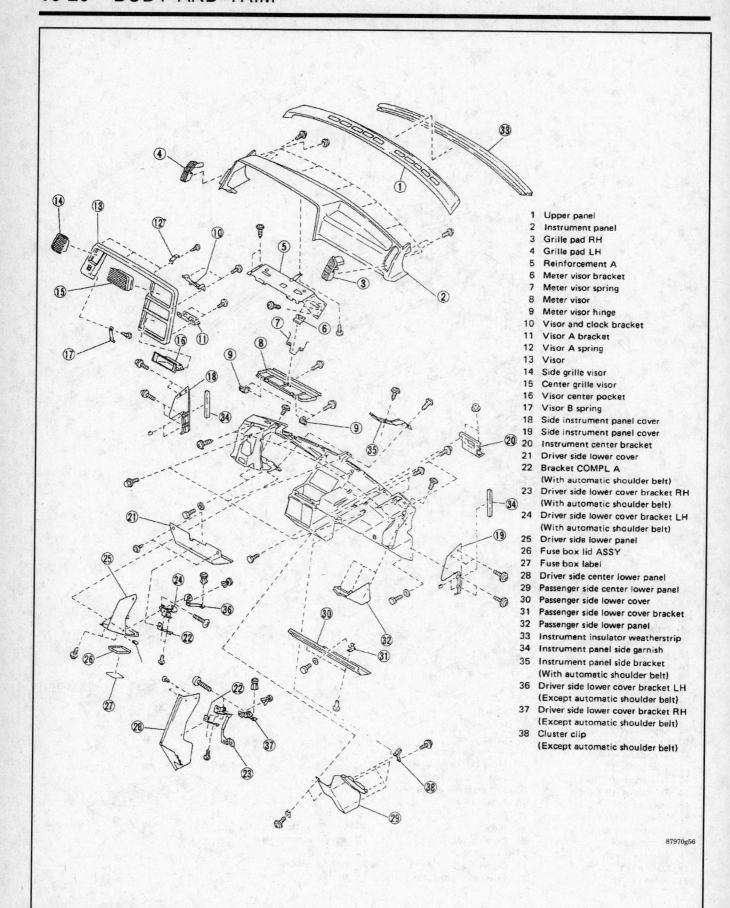

1 Upper panel
2 Instrument panel
3 Grille pad RH
4 Grille pad LH
5 Reinforcement A
6 Meter visor bracket
7 Meter visor spring
8 Meter visor
9 Meter visor hinge
10 Visor and clock bracket
11 Visor A bracket
12 Visor A spring
13 Visor
14 Side grille visor
15 Center grille visor
16 Visor center pocket
17 Visor B spring
18 Side instrument panel cover
19 Side instrument panel cover
20 Instrument center bracket
21 Driver side lower cover
22 Bracket COMPL A
   (With automatic shoulder belt)
23 Driver side lower cover bracket RH
   (With automatic shoulder belt)
24 Driver side lower cover bracket LH
   (With automatic shoulder belt)
25 Driver side lower panel
26 Fuse box lid ASSY
27 Fuse box label
28 Driver side center lower panel
29 Passenger side center lower panel
30 Passenger side lower cover
31 Passenger side lower cover bracket
32 Passenger side lower panel
33 Instrument insulator weatherstrip
34 Instrument panel side garnish
35 Instrument panel side bracket
   (With automatic shoulder belt)
36 Driver side lower cover bracket LH
   (Except automatic shoulder belt)
37 Driver side lower cover bracket RH
   (Except automatic shoulder belt)
38 Cluster clip
   (Except automatic shoulder belt)

87970g56

Fig. 53 Exploded view of the instrument panel — XT

12. Remove the 8 bolts that retain the instrument panel. With the help of an assistant, lift and remove the instrument panel.

➡ **When removing the instrument panel, check that all wiring and cables are disconnected before pulling it completely away from the firewall.**

13. With the help of an assistant, install the panel into position.

➡ **Be sure that no wires are caught between the panel and its mounting. Make sure that the panel is on top of the weatherstrip along the windshield and the strip is not folded along the windshield.**

14. Reconnect all electrical harnesses on the drivers and passenger's side of the vehicle.

15. Install the steering column assembly. See Section 8 of this manual for torque specifications and installation instructions.

16. Install the center console assembly. Install the glove box assembly.

17. Install the upper instrument panel trim.

18. Install the ventilation tube on the driver's side. Install the fuse box in position and install the lower driver's side trim panel.

19. Install the passenger's side lower trim panel. Install the radio and any other components removed.

20. Check the operation of all control levers and cables.

21. Connect the negative battery cable and check the operation of all electrical accessories.

➡ **When checking electrical components, if any of the fuses should blow, check that there are no wires pinched by the instrument panel and correct it if there are.**

Legacy

▶ **See Figures 54 and 55**

❊❊CAUTION

Properly disarm the air bag on vehicles equipped with the SRS system. Failure to do so can cause serious injury. The procedure can be found in Section 6 of this manual under the heading "Supplemental Restraint System".

1. Properly disarm the air bag system. Disconnect the negative battery cable.

2. Remove the center console retaining screws and remove the center console assembly.

3. Remove the instrument panel retaining bolt covers by prying them from the panel.

4. Remove the lower part of the front A pillar trim. Remove the instrument panel under covers from the drivers and passenger's sides.

5. Remove the hood release cable from the hood release lever.

6. Disconnect the wiring harness connectors under the instrument panel.

7. Remove the instrument cluster assembly. Remove the glove box assembly

8. Disconnect the ventilation control cables and electrical connectors at the heater unit. Disconnect the vacuum line at the blower housing.

9. Disconnect the radio antenna feeder wire. Disconnect the main harness connector at the fuse box.

10. Remove the lower steering column covers. Remove the steering column retaining bolts and allow the column to hang down.

11. Remove the instrument panel retaining bolts.

➡ **When removing the instrument panel, check that all wiring and cables are disconnected before pulling it completely away from the firewall.**

12. With the help of an assistant, lift and remove the instrument panel from the vehicle.

To install:

13. With the help of an assistant, install the instrument panel in position in the vehicle.

➡ **Be sure that no wires are caught between the panel and its mounting. Make sure that the panel is on top of the weatherstrip along the windshield and the strip is not folded along the windshield.**

14. Install the panel retaining bolts. Install the retaining bolt covers.

15. Raise the steering column into position. Install the steering column covers.

16. Connect all electrical connectors under the instrument panel. Connect the ventilation control cables and electrical leads.

17. Install the instrument cluster assembly. Install the glove box assembly.

18. Install the center console assembly.

19. Install and connect any remaining components. Install the undercovers.

20. Check the operation of all control cables and switches.

21. Connect the negative battery cable and check the operation of all electrical accessories.

➡ **When checking electrical components, if any of the fuses should blow, check that there are no wires pinched by the instrument panel and correct it if there are.**

SVX

▶ **See Figure 56**

❊❊CAUTION

Properly disarm the air bag on vehicles equipped with the SRS system. Failure to do so can cause serious injury. The procedure can be found in Section 6 of this manual under the heading "Supplemental Restraint System".

1. Properly disarm the air bag system. Disconnect the negative battery cable.

2. Remove the center console assembly retaining screws and remove the center console.

3. Remove the front A pillar upper trim pieces.

4. Remove the radio grounding wire, which is screwed to the floor just behind the shifter assembly.

5. Remove the power mirror switch and remove the bolt located behind it.

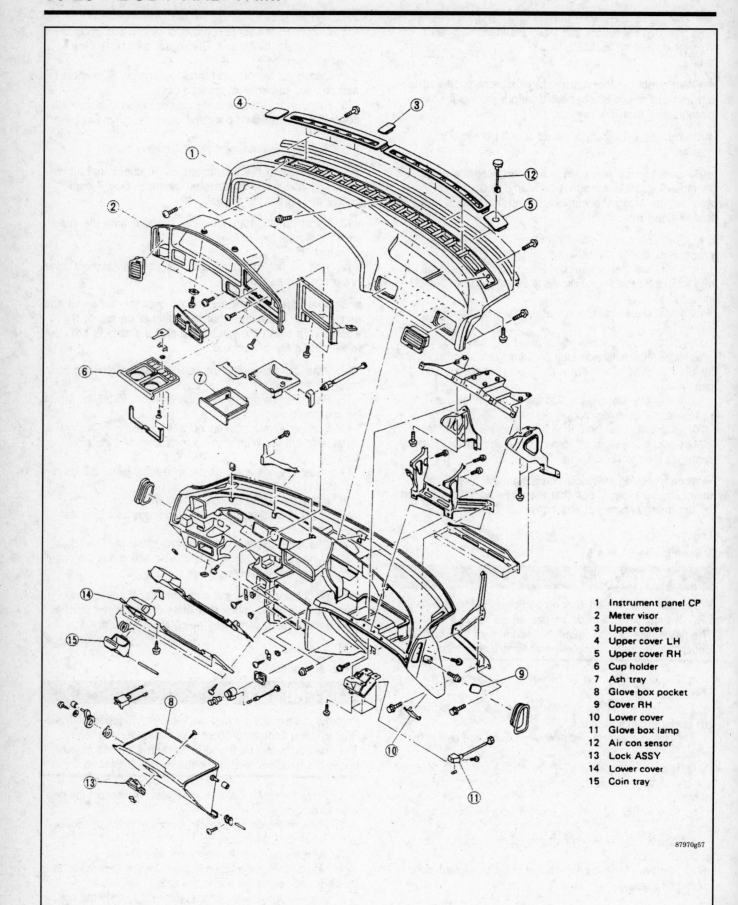

1 Instrument panel CP
2 Meter visor
3 Upper cover
4 Upper cover LH
5 Upper cover RH
6 Cup holder
7 Ash tray
8 Glove box pocket
9 Cover RH
10 Lower cover
11 Glove box lamp
12 Air con sensor
13 Lock ASSY
14 Lower cover
15 Coin tray

87970g57

Fig. 54 Exploded view of the instrument panel — 1990-94 Legacy

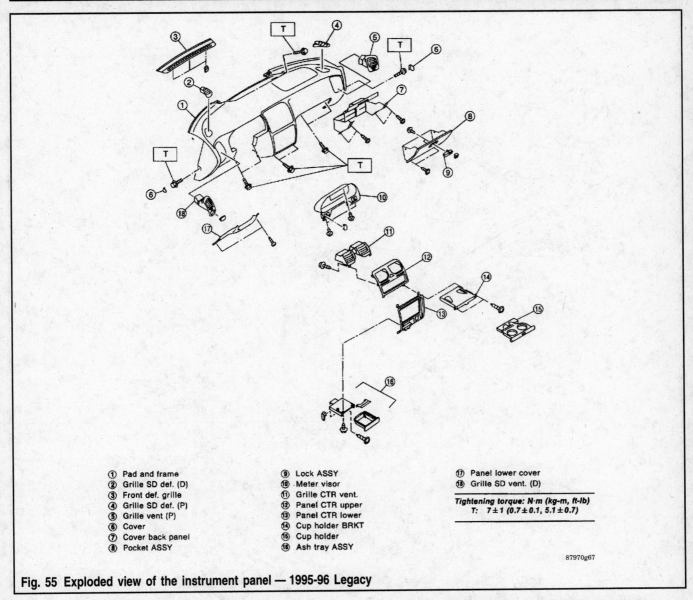

① Pad and frame	⑨ Lock ASSY	⑰ Panel lower cover
② Grille SD def. (D)	⑩ Meter visor	⑱ Grille SD vent. (D)
③ Front def. grille	⑪ Grille CTR vent.	
④ Grille SD def. (P)	⑫ Panel CTR upper	
⑤ Grille vent (P)	⑬ Panel CTR lower	
⑥ Cover	⑭ Cup holder BRKT	
⑦ Cover back panel	⑮ Cup holder	
⑧ Pocket ASSY	⑯ Ash tray ASSY	

Tightening torque: N·m (kg-m, ft-lb)
T: 7 ± 1 (0.7 ± 0.1, 5.1 ± 0.7)

87970g67

Fig. 55 Exploded view of the instrument panel — 1995-96 Legacy

6. Remove the lower driver's side instrument panel cover by removing the 6 clips and disconnecting the 3 connectors.

7. Remove the instrument cluster lower cover by removing the retaining bolts.

8. Disconnect the air bag assembly connector (YELLOW coated wires) at the bottom of the steering column.

9. Remove the lower steering column cover. Remove the steering column-to-bracket bolts and lower the column.

10. Remove the small bolt caps from both ends of the instrument panel and remove the bolts.

11. Remove the 2 sets of instrument panel switches by pulling them from their mountings. Disconnect the electrical leads from the switches.

12. Remove the instrument cluster visor assembly and remove the instrument cluster.

13. Remove the 4 bolts from behind where the instrument cluster was. Remove the 5 bolts from inside the glove box.

14. Disconnect the main harness connectors under the driver's side (6 connectors). Disconnect the 2 radio antenna leads.

➡ **When removing the instrument panel, check that all wiring and cables are disconnected before pulling it completely away from the firewall.**

15. With the help of an assistant, remove the instrument panel by pulling it sharply forward, this will release the retaining pins from the top of the panel. Remove the panel from the vehicle.

To install:

16. With the help of an assistant, install the panel into position in the vehicle. Align the pins at the top of the panel, with the grommets in the firewall and push the panel into position.

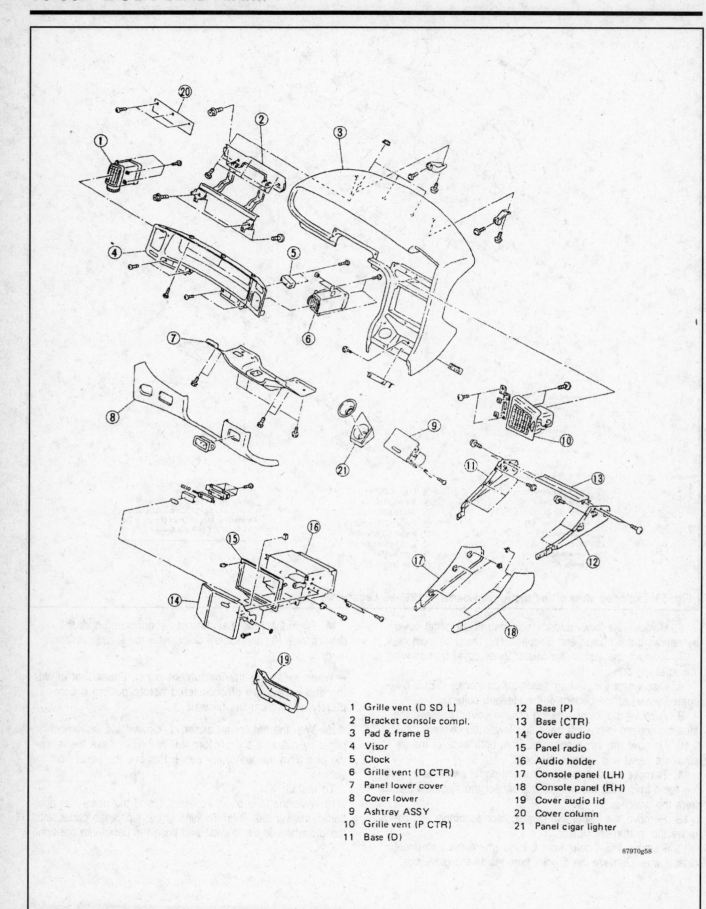

1 Grille vent (D SD L)
2 Bracket console compl.
3 Pad & frame B
4 Visor
5 Clock
6 Grille vent (D CTR)
7 Panel lower cover
8 Cover lower
9 Ashtray ASSY
10 Grille vent (P CTR)
11 Base (D)
12 Base (P)
13 Base (CTR)
14 Cover audio
15 Panel radio
16 Audio holder
17 Console panel (LH)
18 Console panel (RH)
19 Cover audio lid
20 Cover column
21 Panel cigar lighter

87970g58

Fig. 56 Exploded view of the instrument panel — 1992 SVX shown

Install the 4 screws in the instrument cluster opening and the 5 screws in the glove box opening.

➡**Be sure that no wires are caught between the panel and its mounting. Make sure that the panel is on top of the weatherstrip along the windshield and the strip is not folded along the windshield.**

17. Connect the main wiring harness connectors. Connect the antenna leads.

18. Install the instrument cluster assembly. Install the instrument panel switch assemblies.

19. Install the retaining bolts at the ends of the instrument panel and install the bolt caps.

20. Raise the steering column into position and install the retaining bolts.

21. Connect the air bag connectors. Install the instrument cluster lower cover.

22. Screw down the radio ground wire. Install the center console assembly. Install the lower instrument panel trim.

23. Install the bolt behind power mirror switch and install the switch.

24. Install any remaining components and trim pieces.

25. Check the operation of all cables and switches.

26. Connect the negative battery cable and check the operation of all electrical accessories.

➡**When checking electrical components, if any of the fuses should blow, check that there are no wires pinched by the instrument panel and correct it if there are.**

Impreza
◆ See Figure 57

✳✳WARNING

When removing the instrument panel on air bag equipped models, use care to avoid damaging the air bag system wirings harness, which is routed near the combination meter. All air bag wiring and connectors are colored yellow.

✳✳CAUTION

Properly disarm the air bag on vehicles equipped with the SRS system. Failure to do so can cause serious injury. The procedure can be found in Section 6 of this manual under the heading "Supplemental Restraint System".

1. Properly disarm the air bag systems and disconnect the negative battery cable.

2. Remove the rear console box.

3. Pull the cup holder.

4. Turn over the shift lever boot (manual transaxle models) or remove select lever cover (automatic transaxle models).

5. Remove the console cover.

6. Remove the audio assembly and disconnect the antenna cable and connectors.

7. Remove the lower cover and then disconnect the seat belt timer connector.

8. Remove the glove box.

9. Remove the instrument panel console.

10. Remove the two bolts and lower the steering column.

11. Remove the column cover.

12. Remove the hood opening lever.

13. Set the temperature control switch to MAX. COLD, and mode selector switch to the defroster position.

14. Disconnect both the temperature control cable and the mode selector cable from the link.

➡**Do not move the switch and link when installing.**

15. Tag or match mark the wiring connectors, then disconnect by holding the connectors and not the wiring.

16. Remove the six instrument panel retaining bolts and nuts.

17. Remove the front defroster grille and two bolts.

18. Carefully remove the instrument panel from the body and then disconnect the speedometer cable from the back of the combination meter.

To install:

19. With the help of an assistant, install the panel into position in the vehicle. Align the three pins at the top of the panel, with the grommets in the firewall and push the panel into position.

➡**Be sure that no wires are caught between the panel and its mounting.**

20. Install the front defroster grille and two bolts.

21. Install the six instrument panel retaining bolts and nuts.

22. Connect the wiring harness connectors.

23. Connect both the temperature control cable and the mode selector cable to the link.

➡**Do not move the switch and link when installing.**

24. Install the hood opening lever.

25. Install the column cover.

26. Install the two steering column retaining bolts.

27. Install the instrument panel console.

28. Install the glove box.

29. Connect the seat belt timer connector and Install the lower cover.

30. Install the audio assembly and connect the antenna cable and connectors.

31. Install the console cover.

32. Reposition the shift lever boot (manual transaxle models) or install the select lever cover (automatic transaxle models).

33. Install the cup holder.

34. Install the rear console box.

35. Connect the negative battery cable.

Center Console

REMOVAL & INSTALLATION

◆ See Figures 57, 58, 59, 60, 61, 62 and 63

✳✳CAUTION

Properly disarm the air bag on vehicles equipped with the SRS system. Failure to do so can cause serious injury. The procedure can be found in Section 6 of this manual under the heading "Supplemental Restraint System".

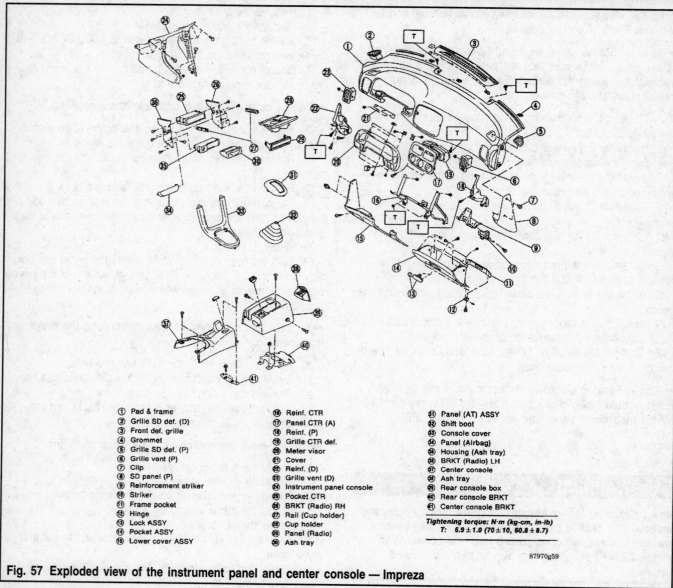

① Pad & frame	⑯ Reinf. CTR	㉛ Panel (AT) ASSY
② Grille SD def. (D)	⑰ Panel CTR (A)	㉜ Shift boot
③ Front def. grille	⑱ Reinf. (P)	㉝ Console cover
④ Grommet	⑲ Grille CTR def.	㉞ Panel (Airbag)
⑤ Grille SD def. (P)	⑳ Meter visor	㉟ Housing (Ash tray)
⑥ Grille vent (P)	㉑ Cover	㊱ BRKT (Radio) LH
⑦ Clip	㉒ Reinf. (D)	㊲ Center console
⑧ SD panel (P)	㉓ Grille vent (D)	㊳ Ash tray
⑨ Reinforcement striker	㉔ Instrument panel console	㊴ Rear console box
⑩ Striker	㉕ Pocket CTR	㊵ Rear console BRKT
⑪ Frame pocket	㉖ BRKT (Radio) RH	㊶ Center console BRKT
⑫ Hinge	㉗ Rail (Cup holder)	
⑬ Lock ASSY	㉘ Cup holder	**Tightening torque: N·m (kg-cm, in-lb)**
⑭ Pocket ASSY	㉙ Panel (Radio)	**T: 6.9 ± 1.0 (70 ± 10, 60.8 ± 8.7)**
⑮ Lower cover ASSY	㉚ Ash tray	

87970g59

Fig. 57 Exploded view of the instrument panel and center console — Impreza

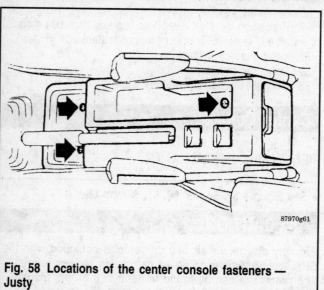

87970g61

Fig. 58 Locations of the center console fasteners — Justy

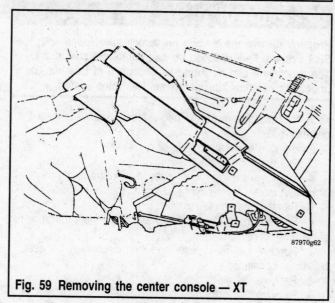

87970g62

Fig. 59 Removing the center console — XT

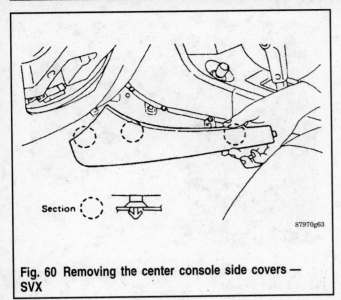

Fig. 60 Removing the center console side covers — SVX

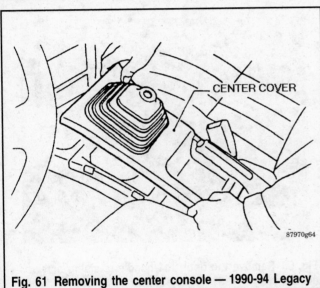

Fig. 61 Removing the center console — 1990-94 Legacy

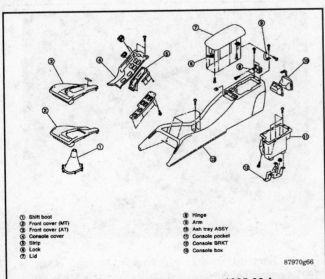

① Shift boot
② Front cover (MT)
③ Front cover (AT)
④ Console cover
⑤ Strip
⑥ Lock
⑦ Lid
⑧ Hinge
⑨ Arm
⑩ Ash tray ASSY
⑪ Console pocket
⑫ Console BRKT
⑬ Console box

87970g66

Fig. 62 Center console components — 1995-96 Legacy

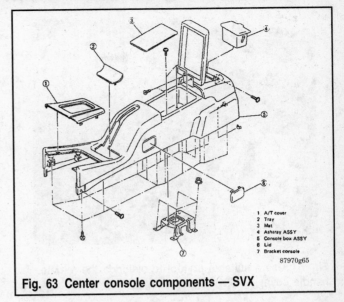

1 A/T cover
2 Tray
3 Mat
4 Ashtray ASSY
5 Console box ASSY
6 Lid
7 Bracket console

87970g65

Fig. 63 Center console components — SVX

1. Discharge the air bag system, on models equipped. Disconnect the negative battery cable.
2. On Loyale and 1985-89 sedans, wagons and hatchbacks, remove the tray from under the parking brake lever by prying it up.
3. Pull the parking brake up and remove the shifter knob (with manual transaxle).
4. Remove the console cover on XT and Impreza models and disconnect the cigarette lighter. Remove the ventilation control lever knobs. On XT models, remove the front seats.
5. On the SVX remove the side console panels by pulling them off (they are held in place by clips).
6. Remove any remaining console trays and covers.
7. Remove all console retaining screws and remove the console. On all models except the Legacy, the console comes out in one piece, on Legacy models the console comes out in 2 pieces.
   To install:
8. Install the console in position and install all retaining screws.
9. Install all console covers and boxes. Connect all electrical leads.
10. Install the seats on the XT models.
11. Connect the negative battery cable.
12. Check the console to make sure that shifting is not interfered with and that all pieces are positioned properly.

Door Panels

REMOVAL & INSTALLATION

Except SVX
▶ **See Figures 64, 65, 66, 67, 68, 69, 70 and 71**

1. Disconnect the negative battery cable.
2. On vehicles without power windows, remove the window handle by removing the retaining clip. Slide a flat bladed tool between the handle and the door panel and press inward on the retainer spring clip.

Fig. 64 Use a suitable prytool to dislodge the remote handle cover — 1991 Legacy shown

Fig. 67 Remove the gusset lower retaining screw — 1991 Legacy shown

Fig. 65 After prying the remote handle cover loose, remove it from the door panel — 1991 Legacy shown

Fig. 68 Remove the door pull handle retaining screw access plug — 1991 Legacy shown

Fig. 66 Remove the gusset lower retaining screw access cover — 1991 Legacy shown

Fig. 69 Remove the door pull handle retaining screw — 1991 Legacy shown

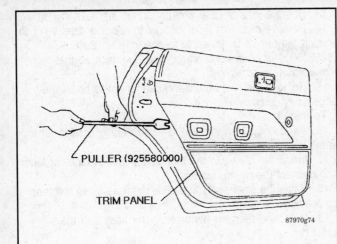

Fig. 70 Removing the door panel using a trim clip puller tool

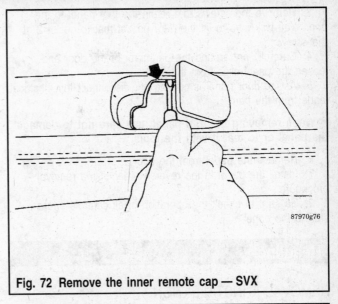

Fig. 72 Remove the inner remote cap — SVX

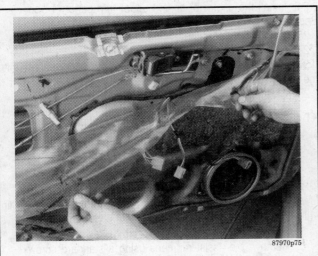

Fig. 71 Removing the door panel weather seal — 1991 Legacy shown; other models similar

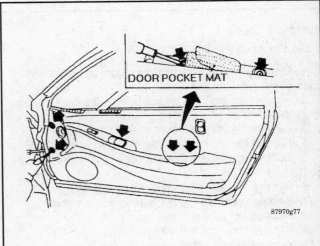

Fig. 73 Remove the door trim panel retaining screws — SVX

3. Use a suitable prying tool and remove the remote handle cover.

4. Remove screws which hold gusset cover, and detach cover.

5. Remove screws which hold pull handle and other screws located further inside. On models with power windows, the window switches come off with the door panels.

6. Remove the clip attached to trim panel using a trim clip puller tool. Then remove the trim panel. The plastic sealing cover can be removed from the door at this time, if needed.

➥When removing the trim panel, use care not to damage the panel or to tear it with the tools.

7. Install the trim panel in the reverse order of removal. Be sure that the panel is fully seated at all clips.

SVX

▶ See Figures 71, 72, 73 and 74

1. Disconnect the negative battery cable.
2. Remove the inner remote cap.

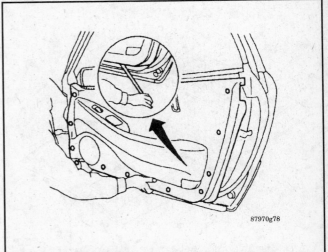

Fig. 74 Using a suitable tool, disengage the clips and remove the trim panel from the door — SVX

3. Remove the screws that retain the trim panel to the door. You will have to lift the door pocket mat to get at 2 of the screws.

4. Carefully pry around the perimeter of the door and loosen the panel clips from the door.

5. As the door panel is coming off, disconnect the electrical leads from the panel.

➡ When removing the trim panel, use care not to damage the panel or to tear it with the tools.

6. Remove the panel from the door.

7. Install the panel in the reverse order of the removal procedure.

8. Be sure to check the operation of all controls after installing the panel.

Headliner

REMOVAL & INSTALLATION

Except XT Coupe

▶ See Figure 75

1. Completely open front and rear doors and lower windows all the way.

2. Remove the seat belt anchor bolts at the upper section of the center pillar.

3. Remove the rear seat cushion and backrest.

4. Remove the front pillar and upper trim panel.

5. Remove the center pillar and upper trim panel (4-Door Sedan).

6. Remove the rear pillar upper trim panel (Wagon).

7. Remove upper side of rear quarter window garnish.

8. Remove roof side rear trim rail.

9. Remove front roof side trim rail.

10. Remove various assist rails.

11. Remove sunvisor, sunvisor hook and rearview mirror.

12. Move front seats all the way forward and fully fold left and right backrests.

13. Remove interior lamp and disconnect harness.

14. Remove clips that hold the roof trim, being careful not to scratch the trim. It is advisable to position Clip Puller (925580000 or equivalent) on roof trim's surface so that roof trim will not be scratched.

15. Remove the roof trim, being careful not to break the edges during removal.

To install:

16. Position the roof trim in the vehicle being careful not to break the edges.

17. Install the clips into the roof trim. Install the interior lamp and connect the wiring harness.

18. Raise the front seats and slide them as far to the rear as possible.

19. Install the rearview mirror, sunvisor hook and the sunvisor.

20. Install the various assist rails.

21. Install the front and rear roof side trim rail.

22. Install upper side of rear quarter window garnish.

23. Install the rear pillar upper trim panel (Wagon).

24. Install the center pillar and upper trim panel (4-Door Sedan).

25. Install the front pillar and upper trim panel.

26. Install the rear seat cushion and backrest.

27. Install the seat belt anchor bolts at the upper section of the center.

28. Close all doors and windows.

XT Coupe

▶ See Figures 76, 77 and 78

1. Completely open doors and windows all the way.

2. Fold the front seat backrest rearward.

3. Remove the sunroof escutcheon, (sunroof models).

4. Remove the clips which hold the rear trim rail, using Clip Puller (925580000 or equivalent).

5. Remove the rear quarter upper trim panel.

6. Remove the assist rail caps using a standard screwdriver, and remove the retaining screws.

7. Remove the front pillar upper trim panel.

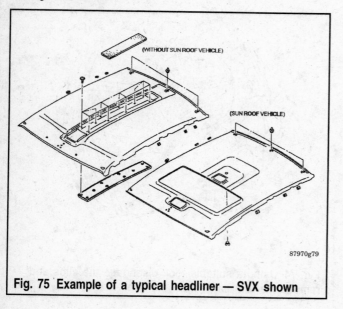

Fig. 75 Example of a typical headliner — SVX shown

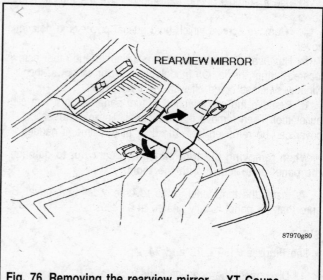

Fig. 76 Removing the rearview mirror — XT Coupe

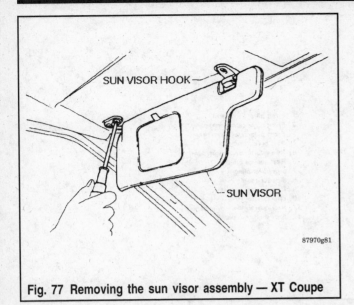

Fig. 77 Removing the sun visor assembly — XT Coupe

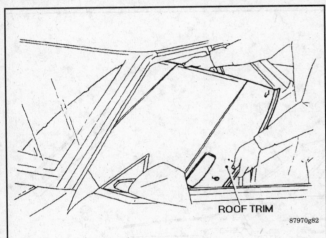

Fig. 78 Removing the headliner assembly through the driver's doorway — XT Coupe

8. Remove the rearview mirror cap.

➡**Straighten the tongues which engage with the rearview mirror stay in advance.**

9. Remove the spot and room lamp, and disconnect the harness connector.

10. Remove the rearview mirror.

11. Turn the roof clip on the passenger's side counterclockwise and remove.

12. Remove the coat hanger on the driver's side.

13. Remove the sun visor and hook.

14. Remove the clips which hold the trim to roof, using Clip Puller (925580000 or equivalent).

15. Remove the roof trim from the car body, being careful not to fold the edge section of the roof trim.

To install:

16. Work the panel into the vehicle through the door.

17. Install the roof trim to the car body, being careful not to fold edge section of roof trim.

18. Install the clips which hold trim to roof.

19. Install the hook and sun visor.

20. Install the coat hanger on the driver's side.

21. Install the roof clip on passenger's side and turn clockwise to install.

22. Install the rearview mirror.

23. Install the spot and room lamp, and connect the harness connector.

24. Install the rearview mirror cap.

25. Install the front pillar upper trim panel.

26. Install the assist rail caps and retaining screws.

27. Install the rear quarter upper trim panel.

28. Install the clips which hold rear trim rail.

29. Install the sunroof escutcheon, (sunroof models).

30. Raise the front seats and close the doors and windows.

Interior Trim

REMOVAL & INSTALLATION

◆ **See Figures 79, 80 and 81**

Removal of the interior trim panels is very simple if the time is taken to do it carefully. To remove any of the panels, all that is needed is a screwdriver and a trim removal tool.

Select the panel that you are going to remove and locate all of the retaining screws. Many of the screws are hidden behind plastic covers, so keep this in mind when looking. Once all of the screws are located, remove any interfering pieces, such as the removable panels in the XT or the Justy models. After removing the mounting screws, carefully pry the panel away from the body, releasing any retaining clips as needed. Be careful not to scratch or gouge the panels.

When installing the panels, make sure that they are aligned properly on all sides before tightening the screws. When tightening the screws, use an alternating pattern to tighten the panel evenly and prevent warpage.

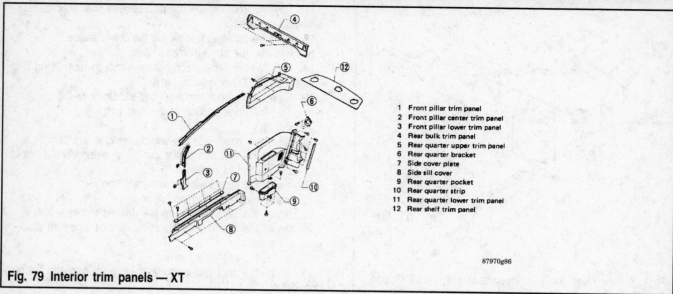

1 Front pillar trim panel
2 Front pillar center trim panel
3 Front pillar lower trim panel
4 Rear bulk trim panel
5 Rear quarter upper trim panel
6 Rear quarter bracket
7 Side cover plate
8 Side sill cover
9 Rear quarter pocket
10 Rear quarter strip
11 Rear quarter lower trim panel
12 Rear shelf trim panel

87970g86

Fig. 79 Interior trim panels — XT

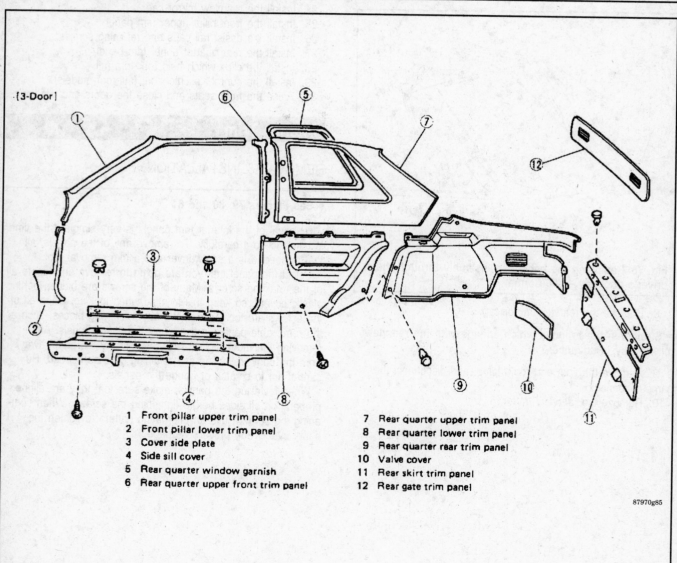

[3-Door]

1 Front pillar upper trim panel
2 Front pillar lower trim panel
3 Cover side plate
4 Side sill cover
5 Rear quarter window garnish
6 Rear quarter upper front trim panel

7 Rear quarter upper trim panel
8 Rear quarter lower trim panel
9 Rear quarter rear trim panel
10 Valve cover
11 Rear skirt trim panel
12 Rear gate trim panel

87970g85

Fig. 80 Interior trim panels — Loyale hatchback

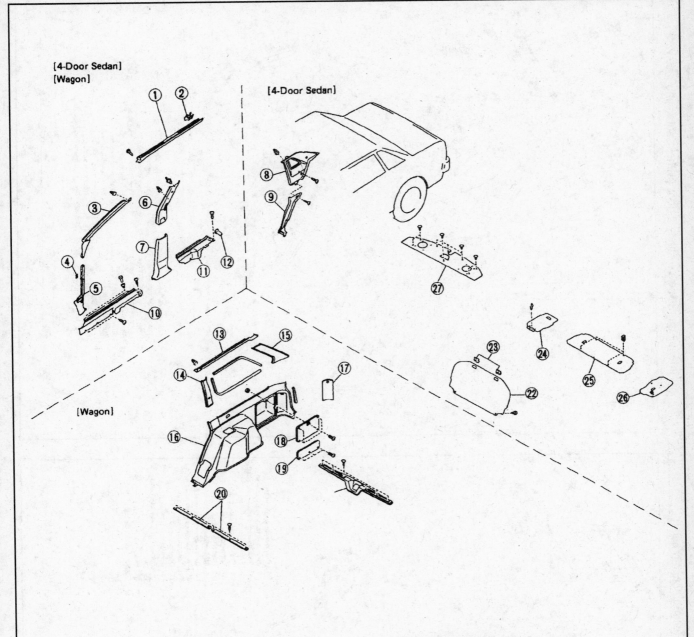

1 Front side trim rail	15 Rear pillar trim panel
2 Front trim rail clip	16 Rear quarter trim panel
3 Front pillar upper trim panel	17 Light cover
4 Front pillar lower clip	18 Pocket upper lid
5 Front pillar lower trim panel	19 Pocket lower lid
6 Center pillar upper trim panel	20 Front edge
7 Center pillar lower trim panel	21 Rear edge
8 Rear pillar upper trim panel	22 Trunk room front trim
9 Rear pillar lower trim panel	23 Clip
10 Front side sill cover	24 Trunk cover RH
11 Rear side sill cover	25 Trunk cover
12 Rear side sill strip	26 Trunk cover LH
13 Rear roof side trim rail	27 Rear shelf trim panel
14 Rear quarter pillar trim panel	

87970g84

Fig. 81 Interior trim panels — Loyale sedan and wagon

Interior trim panels — Justy 2-door (without automatic belts)

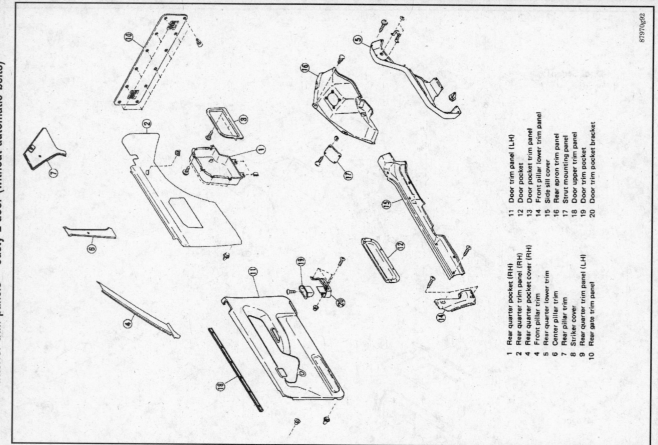

1 Rear quarter pocket (RH)
2 Rear quarter trim panel (RH)
3 Rear quarter pocket cover (RH)
4 Front pillar trim
5 Rear quarter lower trim
6 Center pillar trim
7 Rear pillar trim
8 Striker cover
9 Rear quarter trim panel (LH)
10 Rear gate trim panel
11 Door trim panel (LH)
12 Door pocket
13 Door pocket trim panel
14 Front pillar lower trim panel
15 Side sill cover
16 Rear apron trim panel
17 Strut mounting panel
18 Door upper trim panel
19 Door trim pocket
20 Door trim pocket bracket

Interior trim panels — Justy 2-door (with automatic belts)

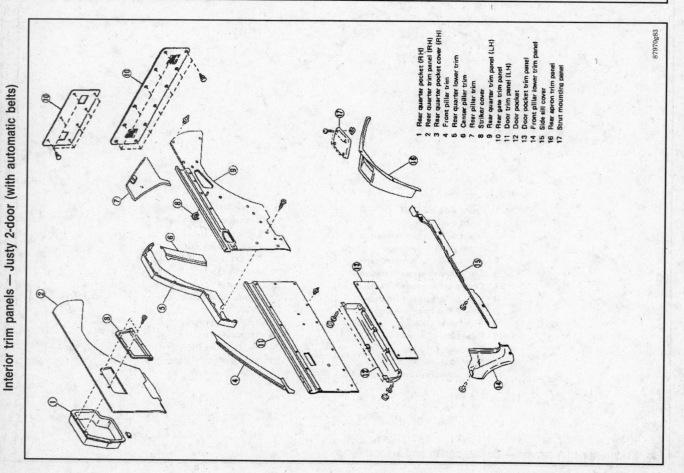

1 Rear quarter pocket (RH)
2 Rear quarter trim panel (RH)
3 Rear quarter pocket cover (RH)
4 Front pillar trim
5 Rear quarter lower trim
6 Center pillar trim
7 Rear pillar trim
8 Striker cover
9 Rear quarter trim panel (LH)
10 Rear gate trim panel
11 Door trim panel (LH)
12 Door pocket
13 Door pocket trim panel
14 Front pillar lower trim panel
15 Side sill cover
16 Rear apron trim panel
17 Strut mounting panel

Interior trim panels — Impreza

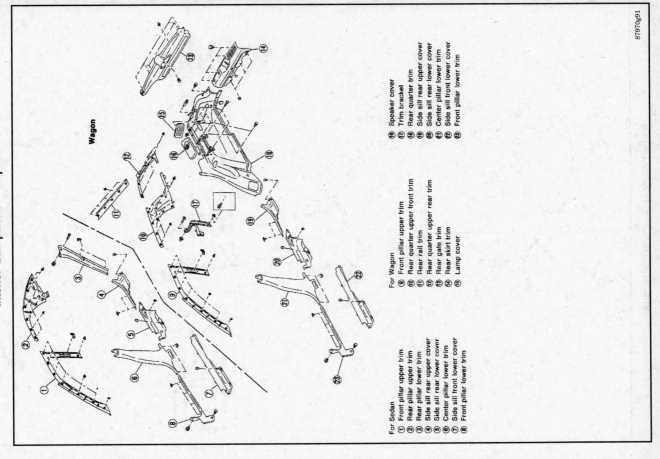

87970g91

Wagon

For Sedan
1 Front pillar upper trim
2 Rear pillar upper trim
3 Rear pillar lower trim
4 Side sill rear upper cover
5 Side sill rear lower cover
6 Center pillar lower trim
7 Side sill front lower cover
8 Front pillar lower trim

For Wagon
9 Front pillar upper trim
10 Rear quarter upper front trim
11 Rear rail trim
12 Rear quarter upper rear trim
13 Rear gate trim
14 Rear skirt trim
15 Lamp cover

16 Speaker cover
17 Trim bracket
18 Rear quarter trim
19 Side sill rear upper cover
20 Side sill rear lower cover
21 Center pillar lower trim
22 Side sill front lower cover
23 Front pillar lower trim

Interior trim panels — Justy 4-door

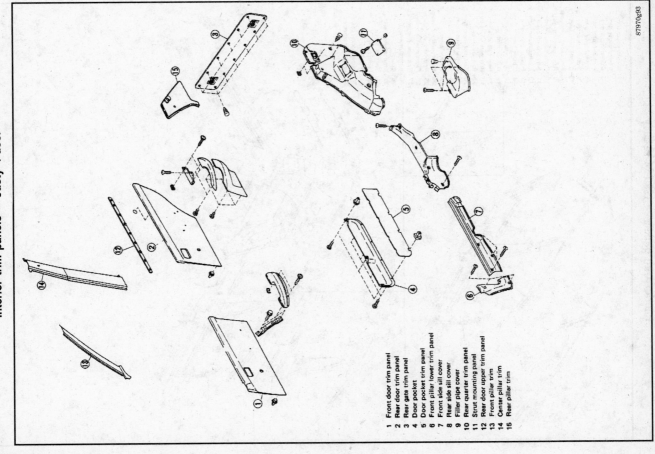

87970g93

1 Front door trim panel
2 Rear door trim panel
3 Rear gate trim panel
4 Door pocket
5 Door pocket trim panel
6 Front pillar lower trim panel
7 Front side sill cover
8 Rear side sill cover
9 Filler pipe cover
10 Rear quarter trim panel
11 Strut mounting panel
12 Rear door upper trim panel
13 Front pillar trim
14 Center pillar trim
15 Rear pillar trim

Interior trim panels — 1995-96 Legacy

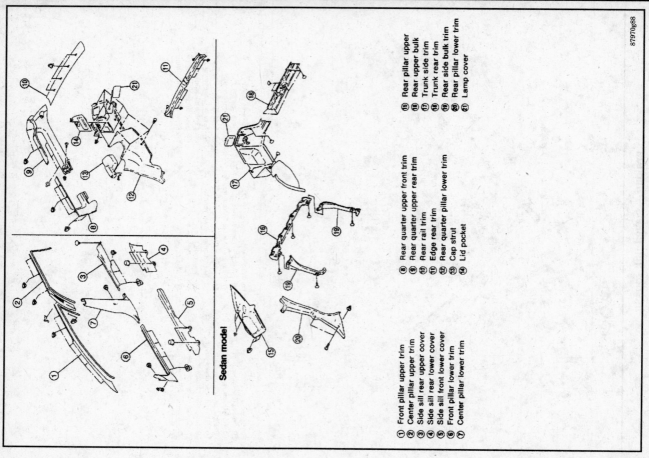

Sedan model

① Front pillar upper trim
② Center pillar upper trim
③ Side sill rear upper cover
④ Side sill rear lower cover
⑤ Side sill front lower cover
⑥ Front pillar lower trim
⑦ Center pillar lower trim

⑧ Rear quarter upper front trim
⑨ Rear quarter upper rear trim
⑩ Rear rail trim
⑪ Edge rear trim
⑫ Rear quarter pillar lower trim
⑬ Cap strut
⑭ Lid pocket

⑮ Rear pillar upper
⑯ Rear upper bulk
⑰ Trunk side trim
⑱ Trunk rear trim
⑲ Rear side bulk trim
⑳ Rear pillar lower trim
㉑ Lamp cover

Interior trim panels — 1990-94 Legacy

1 A pillar upper trim
2 B pillar upper trim
3 C pillar upper trim
4 A pillar center trim
5 A pillar lower trim
6 B pillar lower trim
7 C pillar lower trim
8 Front cover side plate
9 Rear cover side plate
10 Front side sill cover
11 Rear side sill cover
12 B pillar upper trim
13 B pillar upper trim
14 C pillar trim
15 Rear quarter rail trim
16 D pillar trim
17 Rear gate side trim
18 Rear gate upper trim
19 Rear rail trim
20 Rear gate lower trim
21 A pillar center trim
22 A pillar lower trim
23 B pillar lower trim
24 Front cover side plate
25 Rear cover side plate
26 Front side sill cover
27 Rear side sill cover
28 Rear quarter trim
29 Cover
30 Strut mount cover
31 Speaker grille
32 Lamp cover
33 Pocket
34 Upper pocket cover
35 Lower pocket cover

[Sedan]

[Wagon]

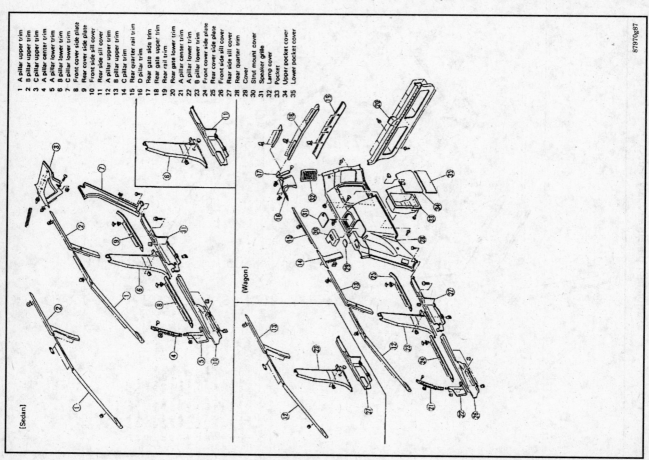

Interior trim panels (trunk area) — SVX

87970g90

1 Rear shelf trim
2 Cap
3 Speaker agrille
4 Trunk upper trim
5 Bulk side trim
6 Trunk side trim
7 Trunk rear panel trim
8 Garnish trunk
9 Trunk edge
10 R combi cover
11 Trunk mat

Interior trim panels — SVX

87970g89

1 Front pillar upper trim
2 Rear pillar upper trim
3 Rear quarter trim
4 Side sill lower cover
5 Front pillar lower trim
6 Side sill upper cover
7 Rear quarter BRKT
8 Pockt
9 Armrest
10 Garnish RQ
11 Garnish R PL UPR
12 Garnish R PL LWR

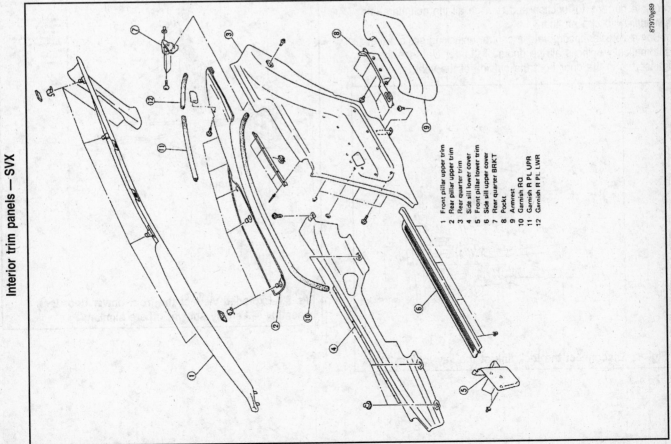

Manual Door Locks

REMOVAL & INSTALLATION

▶ See Figure 82

➡A key code is stamped on the lock cylinder to aid in replacing lost keys.

1. Remove the door trim panel.
2. Pull the weather sheet, gently, away from the door lock access holes.
3. Using a screwdriver, push the lock cylinder retaining clip upward, noting the position of the lock cylinder.
4. Remove the lock cylinder from the door.
5. Reverse Steps 1 through 4 to install the lock cylinder. It's a good idea to open the window before checking the lock operation, just in case it doesn't work properly.

Power Door Locks

SYSTEM DESCRIPTION

The power door locking system consists of switches, actuators and relays. Control switches are used to operate the system. Actuators are used to raise and lower the door lock buttons. These actuators are mounted inside the door assembly and are electrically operated once the switch is depressed. A control unit or functional relay is used to allow the system to regulate current, to function and to align all the actuators and switches with one another.

Some vehicles incorporate a central unlocking system that automatically unlocks all the doors of the vehicle once the key is inserted in the door from the outside of the vehicle.

Fig. 82 Disconnect the lock link at the key lock cylinder

REMOVAL & INSTALLATION

▶ See Figures 83 and 84

Door Lock Switch

1. Disconnect the negative battery cable.
2. Remove the door panel retaining screws.
3. Lift the door panel up and disconnect all the electrical connections required to separate the door panel from the door.
4. Remove the door panel from the vehicle. Remove the switch assembly from its mounting.
5. Installation is the reverse of the removal procedure.

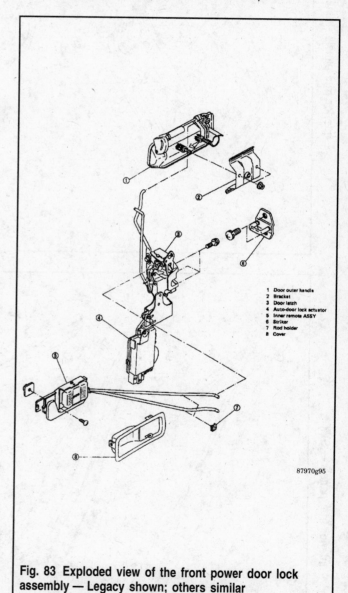

1 Door outer handle
2 Bracket
3 Door latch
4 Auto-door lock actuator
5 Inner remote ASSY
6 Striker
7 Rod holder
8 Cover

Fig. 83 Exploded view of the front power door lock assembly — Legacy shown; others similar

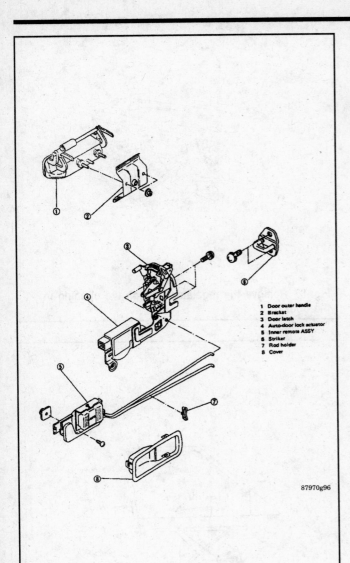

1 Door outer handle
2 Bracket
3 Door latch
4 Auto-door lock actuator
5 Inner remote ASSY
6 Striker
7 Rod holder
8 Cover

87970g96

Fig. 84 Exploded view of the rear power door lock assembly — Legacy shown; others similar

Door Lock Actuator

1. Disconnect the negative battery cable.
2. Remove the door panel.
3. Disconnect the actuator electrical connector. Disconnect the required linkage rods.

4. Remove the actuator assembly retaining screws. Remove the actuator assembly from the vehicle.
5. Installation is the reverse of the removal procedure.

Door Glass and Manual Window Regulator

REMOVAL & INSTALLATION

▶ **See Figures 85, 86, 87 and 88**

1. Remove the trim panel.
2. Remove the door handle assembly.
3. Remove the door panel sealing cover.
4. Remove the rear view mirror from the door.
5. Remove the outer weatherstrip.
6. Remove the inner stabilizer.
7. Loosen the upper stopper bolt from the front of door and glass stoppers, and move the door glass. Then, remove the upper stopper from the rear of the door. Remove the two bolts which hold the glass holder to the regulator slider.

➡ **When removing bolts on the regulator slider, move the glass to a position where the bolts can be seen through the service hole. Mark the position and tightening allowance of upper stopper bolts before removal. This will make adjustment after installation easy.**

8. Open the door, hold the door glass with both hands and pull it straight up from the door panel.
9. Remove the wire clip (manual type only).
10. Remove the regulator base plate and rail.
11. Remove the regulator assembly through the service hole in the underside of the door.

To install:

12. Replace any worn or broken parts. Lubricate all sliding parts and reinstall the regulator assembly.
13. Tighten the base plate mounting bolts 4-7 ft. lbs. (5-9 Nm) and the rail mounting nut 7-13 ft. lbs. (10-18 Nm).
14. Install the window glass in position in the regulator guide channel and tighten the bolts.
15. Adjust the window glass before putting the door back together.
16. Once the glass is adjusted properly, install the door panel and components.

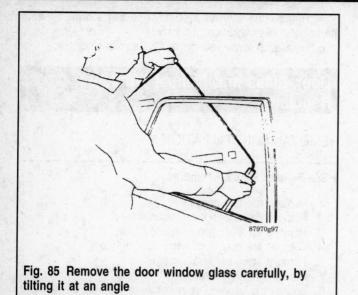

Fig. 85 Remove the door window glass carefully, by tilting it at an angle

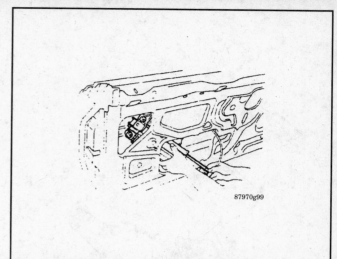

Fig. 87 Remove the regulator through the opening in the door

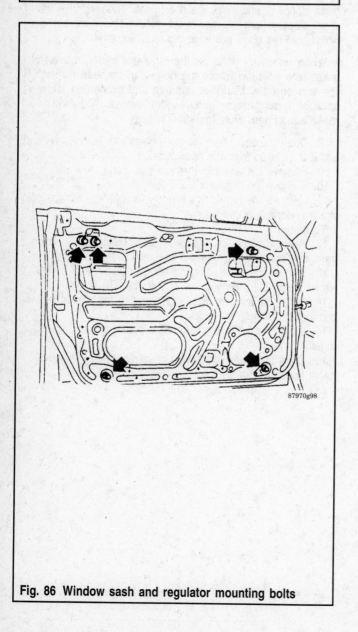

Fig. 86 Window sash and regulator mounting bolts

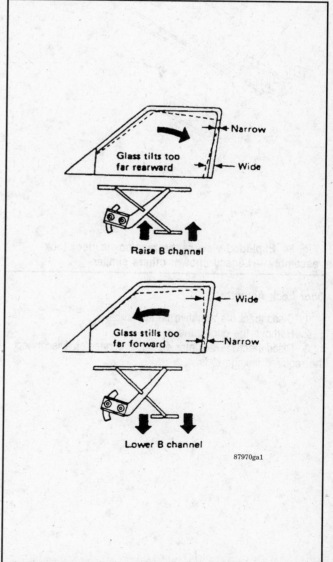

Fig. 88 Adjusting the position of the door window glass

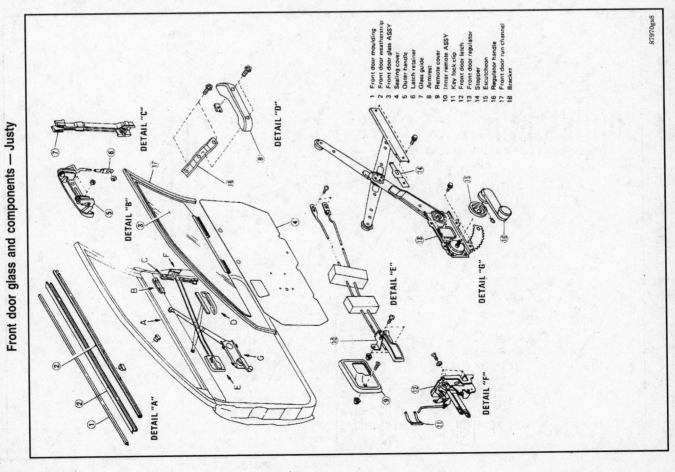

Rear door glass and components — Justy

87970ga9

1 Rear door moulding
2 Rear door weatherstrip
3 Rear door run channel
4 Rear door glass ASSY
5 Rear door partition weatherstrip
6 Rear door partition glass
7 Armrest
8 Rear door partition sash
9 Sealing cover
10 Remote cover
11 Inner remote ASSY
12 Rear door latch
13 Rear outer handle
14 Rear door regulator ASSY
15 Escutcheon
16 Regulator handle
17 Label (Child safety)

FREE LOCK
CHILD SAFETY

DETAIL "C"   DETAIL "G"
DETAIL "B"
DETAIL "D"
DETAIL "A"   DETAIL "E"   DETAIL "F"

Front door glass and components — Justy

87970ga8

1 Front door moulding
2 Front door weatherstrip
3 Front door glass ASSY
4 Sealing cover
5 Outer handle
6 Latch retainer
7 Glass guide
8 Armrest
9 Remote cover
10 Inner remote ASSY
11 Key lock clip
12 Front door latch
13 Front door regulator
14 Stopper
15 Escutcheon
16 Regulator handle
17 Front door run channel
18 Bracket

DETAIL "C"
DETAIL "D"
DETAIL "B"
DETAIL "A"   DETAIL "E"   DETAIL "G"   DETAIL "F"

Rear door glass and components — Loyale

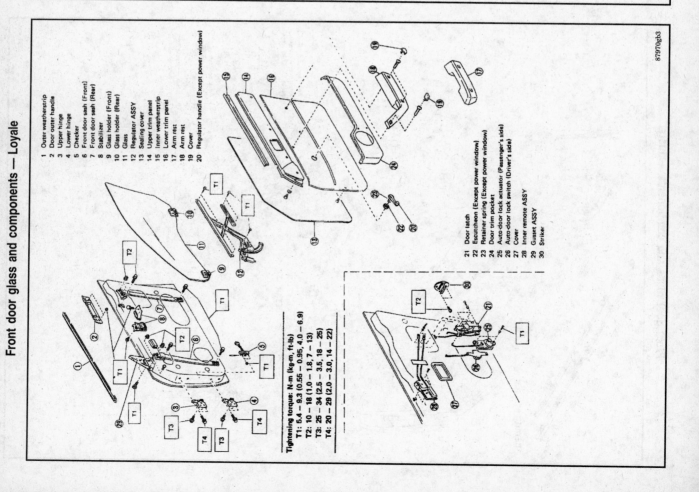

Tightening torque: N·m (kg-m, ft-lb)
T1: 5.4 — 9.3 (0.55 — 0.95, 4.0 — 6.9)
T2: 10 — 18 (1.0 — 1.8, 7 — 13)
T3: 25 — 34 (2.5 — 3.5, 18 — 25)
T4: 20 — 29 (2.0 — 3.0, 14 — 22)

1 Outer weatherstrip
2 Door outer handle
3 Upper hinge
4 Lower hinge
5 Checker
6 Front door sash (Front)
7 Front door sash (Rear)
8 Stabilizer
9 Glass holder (Front)
10 Glass holder (Rear)
11 Glass
12 Regulator ASSY
13 Sealing cover
14 Inner weatherstrip
15 Upper trim panel
16 Lower trim panel
17 Cover
18 Arm rest
19 Cap
20 Regulator handle (Except power window)
21 Escutcheon (Except power window)
22 Retainer spring (Except power window)
23 Door latch
24 Auto-door lock actuator
25 Cover
26 Inner remote ASSY
27 Striker

Front door glass and components — Loyale

1 Outer weatherstrip
2 Door outer handle
3 Upper hinge
4 Lower hinge
5 Checker
6 Front door sash (Front)
7 Front door sash (Rear)
8 Stabilizer
9 Glass holder (Front)
10 Glass holder (Rear)
11 Glass
12 Regulator ASSY
13 Sealing cover
14 Upper trim panel
15 Inner weatherstrip
16 Lower trim panel
17 Arm rest
18 Arm rest
19 Cover
20 Regulator handle (Except power window)
21 Door latch
22 Escutcheon (Except power window)
23 Retainer spring (Except power window)
24 Door trim pocket
25 Auto-door lock actuator (Passenger's side)
26 Auto-door lock switch (Driver's side)
27 Cover
28 Inner remote ASSY
29 Gusset ASSY
30 Striker

Tightening torque: N·m (kg-m, ft-lb)
T1: 5.4 — 9.3 (0.55 — 0.95, 4.0 — 6.9)
T2: 10 — 18 (1.0 — 1.8, 7 — 13)
T3: 25 — 34 (2.5 — 3.5, 18 — 25)
T4: 20 — 29 (2.0 — 3.0, 14 — 22)

87970gb4

87970gb3

Front door glass and regulator assemblies — SVX

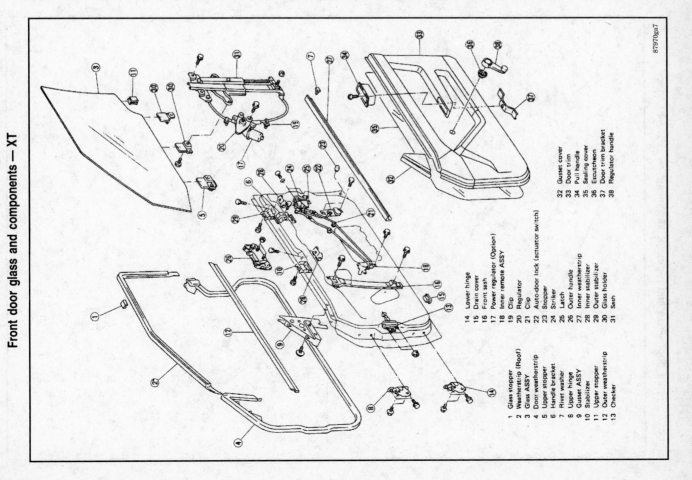

1 Door window upper glass ASSY
2 Fastener
3 Hole plug
4 Stopper
5 Protector
6 Checker
7 Checker pin
8 Outer weatherstrip
9 Outer stabilizer
10 Inner stabilizer
11 Door window lower glass ASSY
12 Lower sash ASSY
13 Regulator rail ASSY
14 Adjusting bolt
15 Regulator lock sleeve
16 Regulator wire ASSY
17 Regulator motor bracket
18 Regulator motor ASSY
19 Slider
20 Urethane pad

Tightening torque: N·m (kg-m, ft-lb)
T1: 5.4 — 9.3 (0.55 — 0.95, 4.0 — 6.9)
T2: 5.4 — 9.3 (0.55 — 0.95, 4.0 — 6.9)
T3: 10 — 18 (1.0 — 1.8, 7 — 13)

Front door glass and components — XT

1 Glass stopper
2 Weatherstrip (Roof)
3 Glass ASSY
4 Door weatherstrip
5 Upper stopper
6 Handle bracket
7 Rivet washer
8 Upper hinge
9 Gusset ASSY
10 Stabilizer
11 Upper stopper
12 Outer weatherstrip
13 Checker
14 Lower hinge
15 Drain cover
16 Front sash
17 Power regulator (Option)
18 Inner remote ASSY
19 Clip
20 Regulator
21 Clip
22 Auto-door lock (actuator switch)
23 Stopper
24 Striker
25 Latch
26 Outer handle
27 Inner weatherstrip
28 Inner stabilizer
29 Outer stabilizer
30 Glass holder
31 Sash
32 Gusset cover
33 Door trim
34 Pull handle
35 Sealing cover
36 Escutcheon
37 Door trim bracket
38 Regulator handle

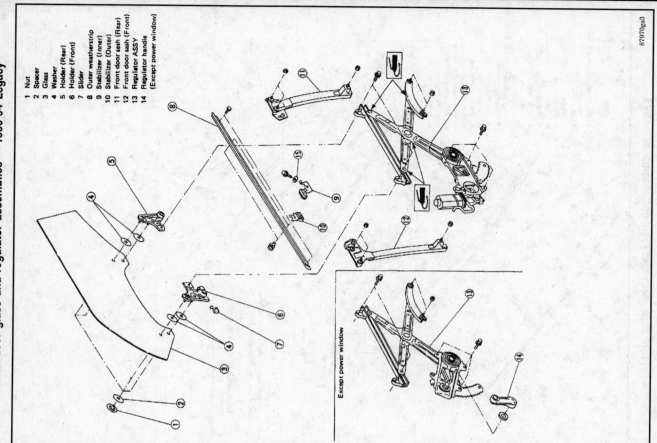

Rear door glass and regulator assemblies — 1990-94 Legacy

1 Nut
2 Spacer
3 Glass
4 Washer
5 Holder (Rear)
6 Holder (Front)
7 Slider
8 Outer weatherstrip
9 Stabilizer (Inner)
10 Stabilizer (Outer)
11 Front door sash (Rear)
12 Front door sash (Front)
13 Regulator ASSY
14 Regulator handle
(Except power window)

87970ga3

Except power window

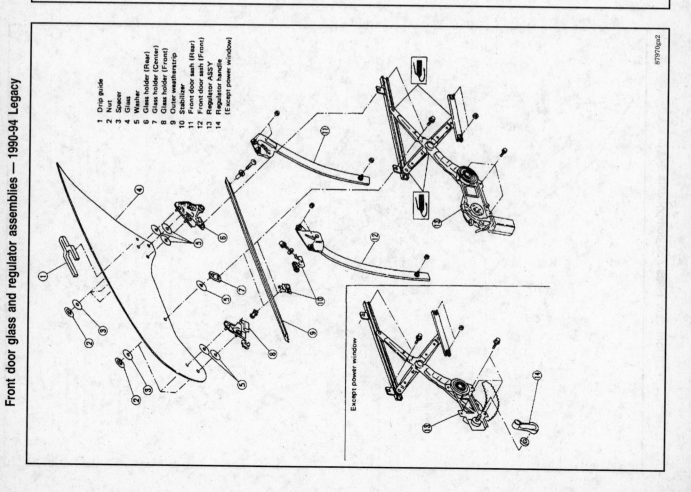

Front door glass and regulator assemblies — 1990-94 Legacy

1 Drip guide
2 Nut
3 Spacer
4 Glass
5 Washer
6 Glass holder (Rear)
7 Glass holder (Center)
8 Glass holder (Front)
9 Outer weatherstrip
10 Stabilizer
11 Front door sash (Rear)
12 Front door sash (Front)
13 Regulator ASSY
14 Regulator handle
(Except power window)

87970ga2

Except power window

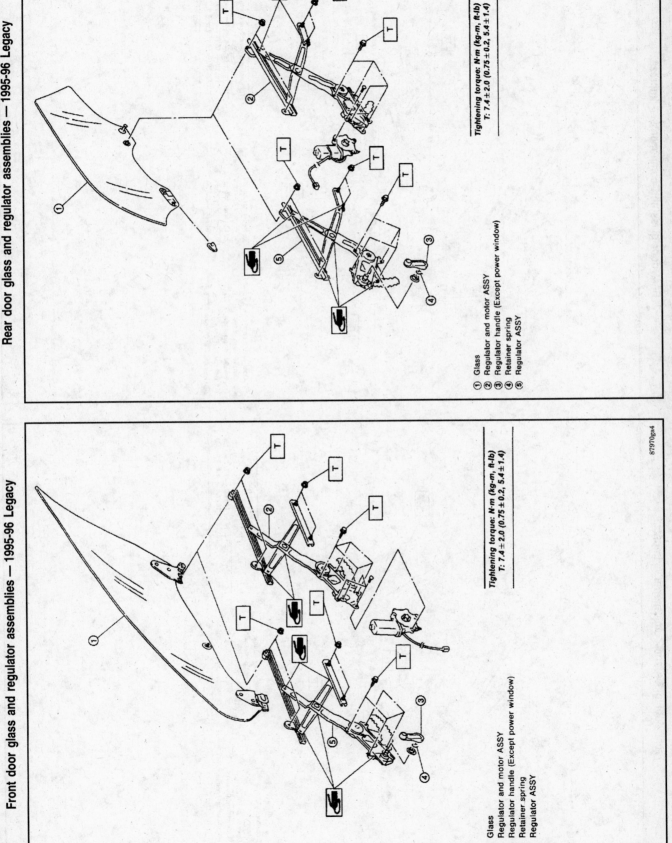

Rear door glass and regulator assemblies — 1995-96 Legacy

Tightening torque: N·m (kg-m, ft-lb)
T: 7.4 ± 2.0 (0.75 ± 0.2, 5.4 ± 1.4)

① Glass
② Regulator and motor ASSY
③ Regulator handle (Except power window)
④ Retainer spring
⑤ Regulator ASSY

87970ga5

Front door glass and regulator assemblies — 1995-96 Legacy

Tightening torque: N·m (kg-m, ft-lb)
T: 7.4 ± 2.0 (0.75 ± 0.2, 5.4 ± 1.4)

① Glass
② Regulator and motor ASSY
③ Regulator handle (Except power window)
④ Retainer spring
⑤ Regulator ASSY

87970ga4

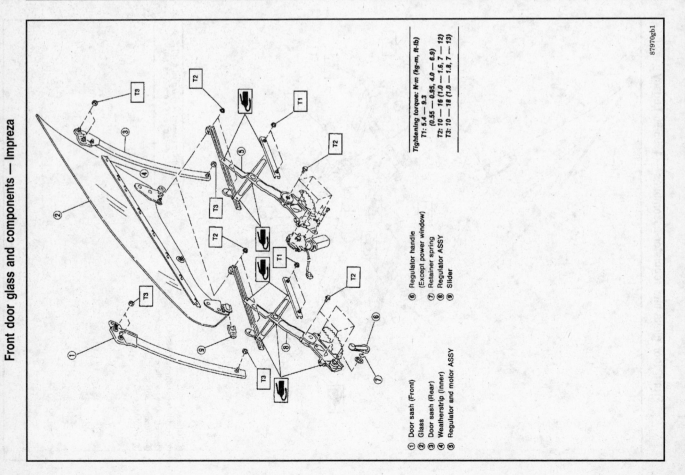

Rear door glass and components — Impreza

87970gb2

Tightening torque: N·m (kg-m, ft-lb)
T1: 5.4 — 9.3
(0.55 — 0.95, 4.0 — 6.9)
T2: 10 — 16 (1.0 — 1.6, 7 — 12)
T3: 10 — 18 (1.0 — 1.8, 7 — 13)

① Door sash (Front)
② Glass
③ Weatherstrip (Inner)
④ Door sash (Rear)
⑤ Regulator and motor ASSY
⑥ Regulator handle (Except power window)
⑦ Retainer spring
⑧ Regulator ASSY
⑨ Slider

Front door glass and components — Impreza

87970gb1

Tightening torque: N·m (kg-m, ft-lb)
T1: 5.4 — 9.3
(0.55 — 0.95, 4.0 — 6.9)
T2: 10 — 16 (1.0 — 1.6, 7 — 12)
T3: 10 — 18 (1.0 — 1.8, 7 — 13)

① Door sash (Front)
② Glass
③ Door sash (Rear)
④ Weatherstrip (Inner)
⑤ Regulator and motor ASSY
⑥ Regulator handle (Except power window)
⑦ Retainer spring
⑧ Regulator ASSY
⑨ Slider

Power Window System

The power windows can be operated only when the ignition switch is in the **ON** position. Operation of the windows is controlled by the main switch located in the master control panel, on the armrest of the driver's door. When the main switch is OFF, only the driver's door window can be opened and closed. When the main switch is ON, all door windows can be opened and closed by the driver, using the appropriate switch in the master control panel. The passenger windows can be opened by depressing the switch located on each passenger door panel.

REMOVAL & INSTALLATION

Regulator and Motor

▶ **See Figures 85, 86, 87, 88, 89, 90, 91 and 92**

1. Remove the trim panel.
2. Remove the remote assembly, if so equipped.
3. Remove the sealing cover.
4. Remove the rear view mirror from the door.
5. Remove the outer weatherstrip.
6. Remove the inner stabilizer.
7. Loosen the upper stopper bolt from the front of door and glass stoppers and move the door glass.
8. Remove the upper stopper from the rear of the door.
9. Remove the bolts which hold the glass holder to the regulator slider.

➡When removing bolts on the regulator slider, move the glass to a position where the bolts can be seen through the service hole. Make the position and tightening allowance of upper stopper bolts before removal. This will make adjustment after installation easy.

10. Open the door, hold the door glass with both hands and pull it straight up from the door panel.
11. Remove the wire clip (manual type only).
12. Remove the regulator base plate and rail.

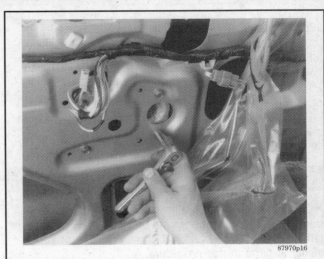

Fig. 90 Removing the power window motor retaining bolt — 1991 Legacy shown

Fig. 91 Removing the power window motor retaining screw — 1991 Legacy shown

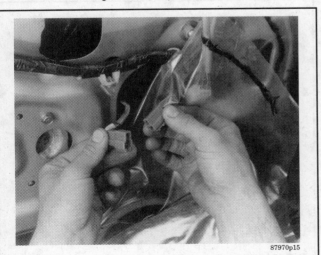

Fig. 89 Unfasten the power window motor's electrical connector — 1991 Legacy shown

Fig. 92 Remove the power window motor through the service hole — 1991 Legacy shown

13. Remove the regulator assembly through the service hole in the underside of the door.

14. Disconnect the electrical connectors to the window motor. Unbolt the motor and remove it through the lower service hole in the underside of the door.

15. Replace any worn or broken parts. Lubricate all sliding parts and reinstall.

16. Installation is the reverse of removal. Tighten the base plate mounting bolts 4-7 ft. lbs. (5-9 Nm) and the rail mounting nut 7-13 ft. lbs. (10-18 Nm).

Windshield and Rear Window Glass

➡ Bonded windshields require special tools and procedures. Due to this fact, removal and installation should be left to a qualified technician if you are unsure of your ability to perform this procedure.

✳✳CAUTION

The windshield knife cannot be used on the rear window of the sedan without damaging the surrounding grill. If the grill is not to be damaged, the rear window must be removed by using piano wire.

REMOVAL & INSTALLATION

▶ See Figures 93, 94, 95, 96, 97, 98, 99 and 100

➡ You'll need an assistant to complete this job.

1. Carefully remove the wiper arms and windshield molding.
2. Put protective tape on the body to prevent damage.
3. Apply soapy water to the surface of the adhesive agent so the knife blade slides smoothly.
4. Cut off excess adhesive agent.
5. Remove stoppers and spacers from glass.
6. Put the windshield knife into layer of adhesive.
7. Hold windshield knife in one hand and cut adhesive by pulling putty knife parallel to the glass while holding knife edge

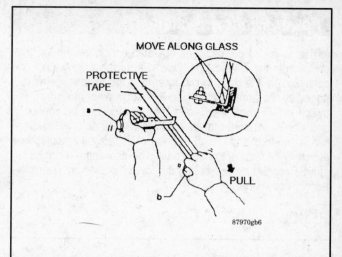

Fig. 94 Cut the adhesive by pulling the knife down with the extension handle

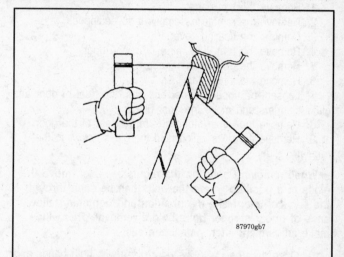

Fig. 95 The adhesive can also be cut by using a length of piano wire

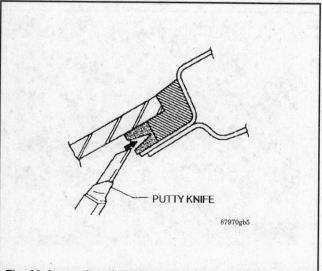

Fig. 93 Insert the windshield knife into the adhesive

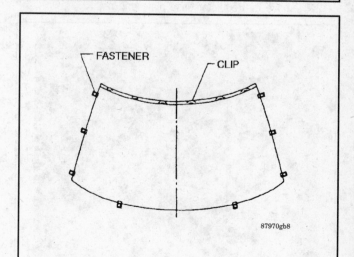

Fig. 96 Positioning of the fastener and clips — Legacy shown; other models similar

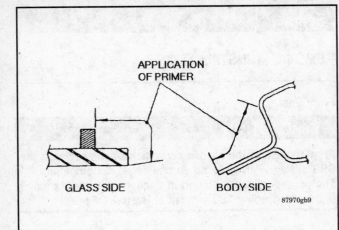

Fig. 97 Apply the sealant primer to these points around the windshield

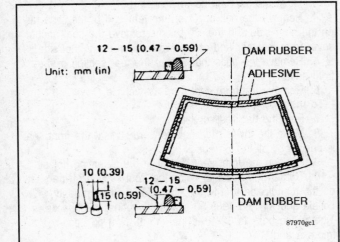

Fig. 98 Apply the rubber around these measurements

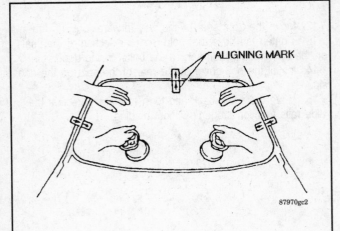

Fig. 99 Position the windshield carefully, aligning the marks made before applying the adhesive

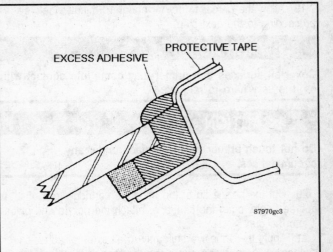

Fig. 100 Cut the excess adhesive until it is flush with the glass

at a right angle. Make sure that the knife stays along the surface of the glass.

➡When first putting knife into layer of adhesive, select a point with a wide gap between the body and glass.

8. Working from the inside of the car, apply even pressure to the windshield and push it outward, while an assistant removes it from the car.

To install:

9. After cutting layer of adhesive, remove the dam rubber left on the body.

10. Remove the remaining space stopper. At this time, also remove two-sided tape from spacer stopper completely.

11. Using a cutting knife, cut layer of adhesive sticking to the body and finish it into a smooth surface of about 2mm in thickness.

12. Thoroughly remove chips dirt and dust from the body surface.

13. Clean the body wall surface and the upper surface of the layer of adhesive with a solvent such as alcohol or white gasoline.

※※CAUTION

Never smoke or have any form of an open flame nearby when using alcohol or gasoline, as it is extremely flammable.

14. Place new spacer stoppers into positions from which the old ones where removed. Remove the tack paper from the back of the spacer stopper and stick it to the body firmly.

15. Place the windshield onto the body and adjust the position of the glass so that the gap between the body and glass is uniform on all sides.

16. Match mark the body and glass in several places.

17. Remove the glass from the body and clean the surface of glass to be adhered with alcohol or white gasoline.

18. Using a sponge, apply primer to the part of the glass and the part of the body to be adhered.

19. Allow the primer to dry for about 10 minutes before proceeding to the next step.

✳✳WARNING

Cover all surfaces that primer may come into contact with, as it is very hard to remove.

✳✳CAUTION

Do not touch primer coated surface under any circumstances.

20. Cut the nozzle tip of the adhesive cartridge to a 45 degree angle, open the cartridge, attach the nozzle and place it into the gun.

21. Apply the adhesive uniformly to all sides of adhesion surface while operating gun along the face of the glass edge. Adhesive build up should be 0.47-0.59 in. (12-15mm) from the glass surface.

22. With the help of an assistant, place the glass onto the body and align the match marks. Press the glass firmly into position, then add adhesive where needed.

23. Install the upper windshield molding and remove the excess adhesive with a spatula. Then clean with alcohol.

➡**After the molding has been installed, do not open the doors or move the car unless it is absolutely necessary. If the doors must be opened, lower the windows, and open and close the doors very gently. After one hour the car can be tested for water leakage.**

24. Install the front lower molding, front pillar cover, wiper wheel assembly and wiper arm assembly.

➡**When testing for water leakage, do not squirt a strong hose stream on the vehicle. If the vehicle must be moved, do so gently, sudden shock could cause the windshield to shift.**

25. After completing all operations, leave the vehicle alone for 24 hours. After 24 hours the vehicle may be driven, but should not be subjected to heavy shock for at least three days.

Seats

REMOVAL & INSTALLATION

Front Seat

✳✳CAUTION

Properly disarm the air bag on vehicles equipped with the SRS system. Failure to do so can cause serious injury. The procedure can be found in Section 6 of this manual under the heading "Supplemental Restraint System".

1. Properly disarm the air bag on models equipped. Disconnect the negative battery cable. Slide the front seat all the way back using the slide adjuster lever.

2. Remove the bolts that secure the front section of the seat.

3. Move the seat all the way forward.

4. Remove the bolt cover on the rear end of the slide rail on the door side. On the XT Coupe, remove the seat anchor cover from the rear end of the slide rail on the tunnel side.

5. Remove the bolts that secure the rear section of the front seat.

6. Remove the front seat from the vehicle.

   To install:

7. Fold the backrest forward.

8. Move the lower slide rails forward so that the front seat is positioned all the way back.

9. Position the front seat and align the mounting holes.

10. Tighten the bolt that holds the front section of the seat on the tunnel side to 14-29 ft. lbs. (20-39 Nm) on Justy, Loyale and XT and 1985-89 sedans, wagons, hatchbacks. Tighten the bolts to 32-46 ft. lbs. (43-63 Nm) on Legacy, Impreza and SVX.

11. Tighten the bolt that holds the front section of the seat on the door side to 14-29 ft. lbs. (20-39 Nm) on Justy, Loyale, XT, and 1985-89 sedans, wagons and hatchbacks. Tighten the bolts to 32-46 ft. lbs. (43-63 Nm) on Legacy, Impreza and SVX.

12. Move the front seat all the way forward.

13. Tighten the bolts that hold the rear section of the seat on the tunnel side, then tighten the bolts on the door side.

14. Install the bolt cover at the rear of the seat on the door side.

15. Move the seats back and forth to make sure that the slide rails function properly without binding.

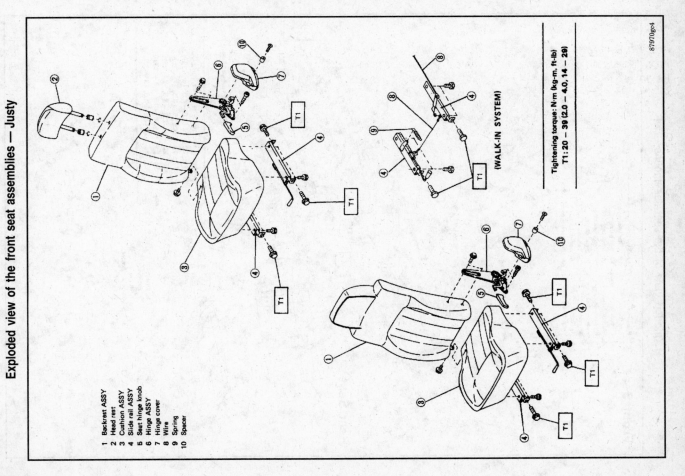

Exploded view of the front seat assemblies — Loyale

1 Hinge cover
2 Hinge ASSY
3 Reclining lever
4 Hinge cover
5 Headrest ASSY
6 Headrest cover
7 Bushing
8 Lock bushing
9 Backrest
10 Backrest frame
11 Ruck board
12 Cushion ASSY
13 Cushion frame
14 Bolt cover
15 Slide rail ASSY
16 Cable
17 Reclining hinge with pedal
18 Cushion frame
19 Bracket
20 Inner slide rail ASSY
21 Outer slide rail ASSY
22 Helper spring

Tightening torque: N·m (kg-m, ft-lb)
T: 20 — 39 (2.0 — 4.0, 14 — 29)

For "Walk-in System"

3-Door

87970gc5

Exploded view of the front seat assemblies — Justy

1 Backrest ASSY
2 Head rest
3 Cushion ASSY
4 Slide rail ASSY
5 Seat hinge knob
6 Hinge ASSY
7 Hinge cover
8 Wire
9 Spring
10 Spacer

(WALK-IN SYSTEM)

Tightening torque: N·m (kg-m, ft-lb)
T1: 20 — 39 (2.0 — 4.0, 14 — 29)

87970gc4

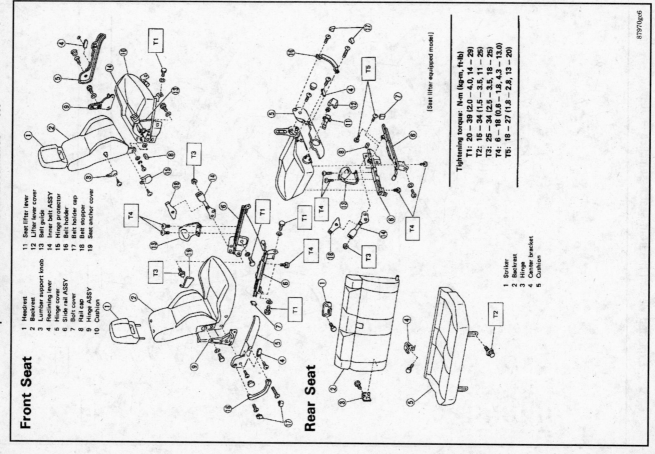

Exploded view of the front seat assembly — 1990-93 Legacy

87970gc7

1 Headrest
2 Backrest
3 Bushing
4 Lock bushing
5 Cushion ASSY
6 Hinge ASSY
7 Reclining lever
8 Hinge cover
9 Inner slide rail ASSY
10 Outer slide rail ASSY
11 Bolt cover
12 Cover

Tightening torque: N·m (kg·m, ft·lb)
T1: 42 — 62 (4.3 — 6.3, 31 — 46)
T2: 18 — 27 (1.8 — 2.8, 13 — 20)

Exploded view of the seat assemblies — XT

87970gc6

Front Seat

1 Headrest
2 Backrest
3 Lumbar support knob
4 Reclining lever
5 Hinge cover
6 Slide rail ASSY
7 Bolt cover
8 Rail cap
9 Hinge ASSY
10 Cushion

11 Seat lifter lever
12 Lifter lever cover
13 Belt guide
14 Inner belt ASSY
15 Hinge protector
16 Belt holder
17 Belt holder cap
18 Belt stopper
19 Seat anchor cover

[Seat lifter equipped model]

Tightening torque: N·m (kg·m, ft·lb)
T1: 20 — 39 (2.0 — 4.0, 14 — 29)
T2: 15 — 34 (1.5 — 3.5, 11 — 25)
T3: 25 — 34 (2.5 — 3.5, 18 — 25)
T4: 6 — 18 (0.6 — 1.8, 4.3 — 13.0)
T5: 18 — 27 (1.8 — 2.8, 13 — 20)

Rear Seat

1 Striker
2 Backrest
3 Hinge
4 Center bracket
5 Cushion

Exploded view of the front seat assembly — 1995-96 Legacy

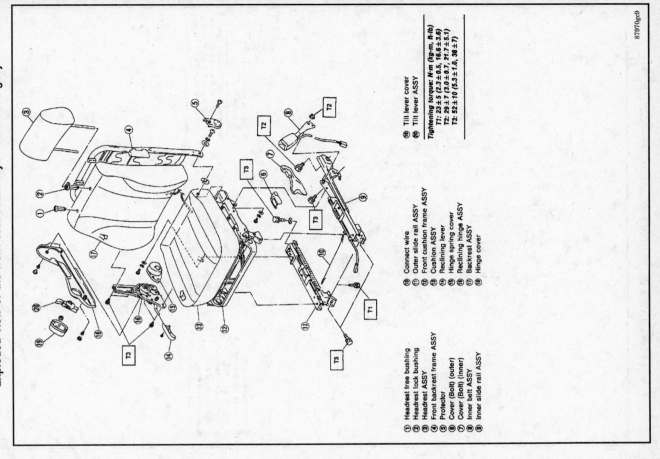

Tightening torque: N·m (kg-m, ft-lb)
T1: 23±5 (2.3±0.5, 16.6±3.6)
T2: 29±7 (3.0±0.7, 21.7±5.1)
T3: 52±10 (5.3±1.0, 38±7)

① Headrest free bushing
② Headrest lock bushing
③ Headrest ASSY
④ Front backrest frame ASSY
⑤ Protector
⑥ Cover (Bolt) (outer)
⑦ Cover (Bolt) (inner)
⑧ Inner belt ASSY
⑨ Inner slide rail ASSY
⑩ Connect wire
⑪ Outer slide rail ASSY
⑫ Front cushion frame ASSY
⑬ Cushion ASSY
⑭ Reclining lever
⑮ Hinge spring cover
⑯ Reclining hinge ASSY
⑰ Backrest ASSY
⑱ Hinge cover
⑲ Tilt lever cover
⑳ Tilt lever ASSY

Exploded view of the front seat assembly — 1994 Legacy (with heater)

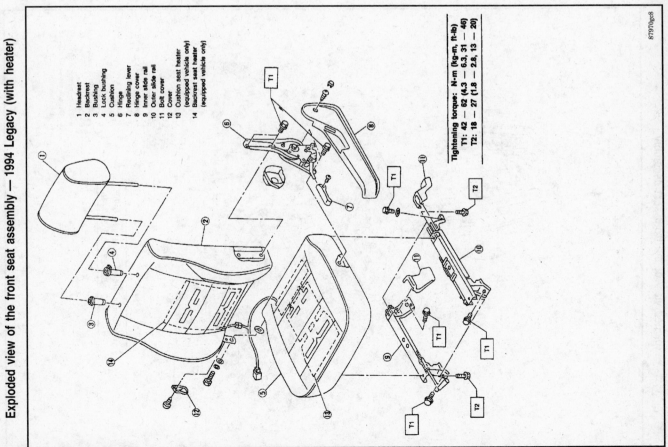

1 Headrest
2 Backrest
3 Bushing
4 Lock bushing
5 Cushion
6 Hinge
7 Reclining lever
8 Hinge cover
9 Inner side rail
10 Outer slide rail
11 Bolt cover
12 Cover
13 Cushion seat heater (equipped vehicle only)
14 Backrest seat heater (equipped vehicle only)

Tightening torque: N·m (kg-m, ft-lb)
T1: 42 — 62 (4.3 — 6.3, 31 — 46)
T2: 18 — 27 (1.8 — 2.8, 13 — 20)

Exploded view of the front seat assembly — Impreza

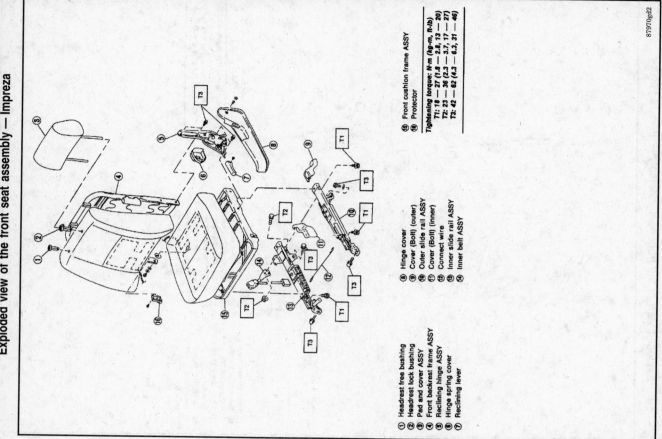

① Headrest free bushing
② Headrest lock bushing
③ Pad and cover ASSY
④ Front backrest frame ASSY
⑤ Reclining hinge ASSY
⑥ Hinge spring cover
⑦ Reclining lever
⑧ Hinge cover
⑨ Cover (Bolt) (outer)
⑩ Outer slide rail ASSY
⑪ Cover (Bolt) (inner)
⑫ Connect wire
⑬ Inner slide rail ASSY
⑭ Inner belt ASSY
⑮ Front cushion frame ASSY
⑯ Protector

Tightening torque: N·m (kg-m, ft-lb)
T1: 18 — 27 (1.8 — 2.8, 13 — 20)
T2: 23 — 36 (2.3 — 3.7, 17 — 27)
T3: 42 — 62 (4.3 — 6.3, 31 — 46)

Exploded view of the front seat assembly — SVX

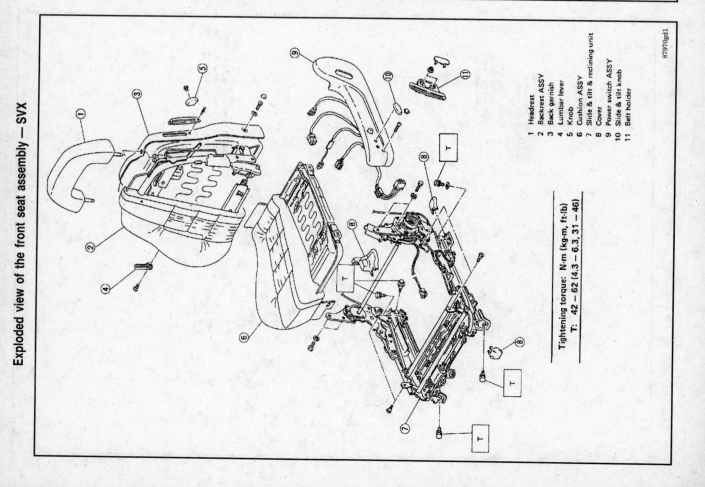

1 Headrest
2 Backrest ASSY
3 Back garnish
4 Lumbar lever
5 Knob
6 Cushion ASSY
7 Slide & tilt & reclining unit
8 Cover
9 Power switch ASSY
10 Slide & tilt knob
11 Belt holder

Tightening torque: N·m (kg-m, ft-lb)
T: 42 — 62 (4.3 — 6.3, 31 — 46)

Rear Seat

▶ **See Figure 101**

1. Remove the bolts that secure the front of the rear cushion to the floor. On the SVX the seat base is held in place by metal hooks. On some sedan models, the seat back is fastened by an attaching bolt at the bottom and metal hooks at the top.

2. Slightly raise the front side of the rear seat cushion and push the center of the rear section down. With the seat cushion held in that position, move it forward until it is unhooked.

3. Pass the rear seat belt through the slit in the rear section of the cushion.

4. Fold the rear seat backrest forward and remove the bolts which hold the hinge to the right side of the backrest. On the SVX, remove the bolts that retain the seatback.

5. Tilt the rear seat backrest approximately 15.75 in. (40cm) forward and slide it toward the right until it can be detached from the left bracket.

6. Remove the rear seat from the vehicle.

To install:

7. Install the seat back into position and install any retaining bolts.

8. Install the seat bottom cushion and tighten the retaining bolts to 3-5 ft. lbs. (4-7 Nm) on Justy, 11-25 ft. lbs. (15-34 Nm) on Loyale and XT, as well as 1985-89 sedans, wagons and hatchbacks, 13-23 ft. lbs. (18-31 Nm) on Legacy, Impreza and SVX.

9. Be sure that the seat belts are properly positioned and that the seat is securely mounted.

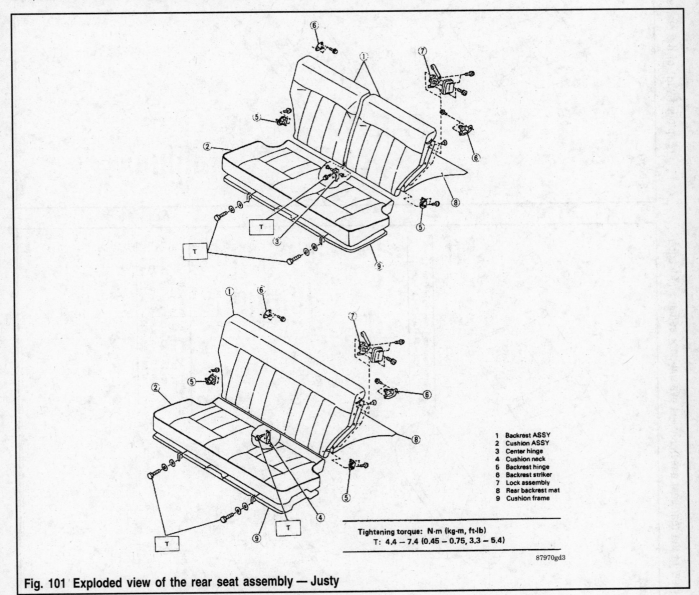

1 Backrest ASSY
2 Cushion ASSY
3 Center hinge
4 Cushion neck
5 Backrest hinge
6 Backrest striker
7 Lock assembly
8 Rear backrest mat
9 Cushion frame

Tightening torque: N·m (kg-m, ft-lb)
T: 4.4 – 7.4 (0.45 – 0.75, 3.3 – 5.4)

87970gd3

Fig. 101 Exploded view of the rear seat assembly — Justy

Exploded view of the rear seat assembly — Loyale hatchback

[3-Door]

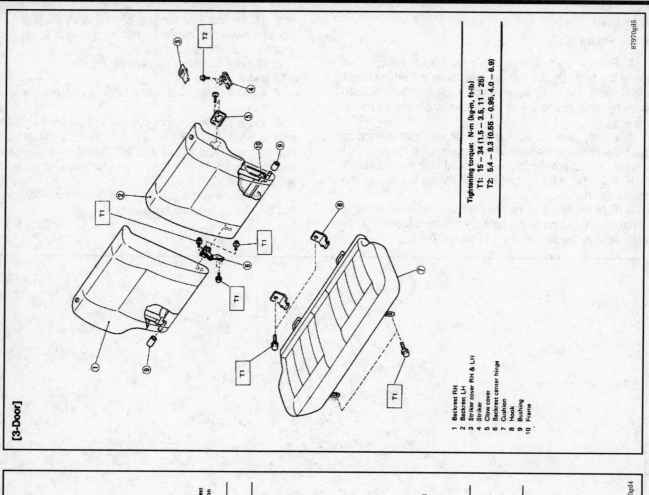

Tightening torque: N·m (kg-m, ft-lb)
T1: 15 − 34 (1.5 − 3.5, 11 − 25)
T2: 5.4 − 9.3 (0.55 − 0.95, 4.0 − 6.9)

1 Backrest RH
2 Backrest LH
3 Striker cover RH & LH
4 Striker
5 Claw cover
6 Backrest center hinge
7 Cushion
8 Hook
9 Bushing
10 Frame

Exploded view of the rear seat assembly — Loyale 4-door sedan and wagon

[4-Door Sedan]

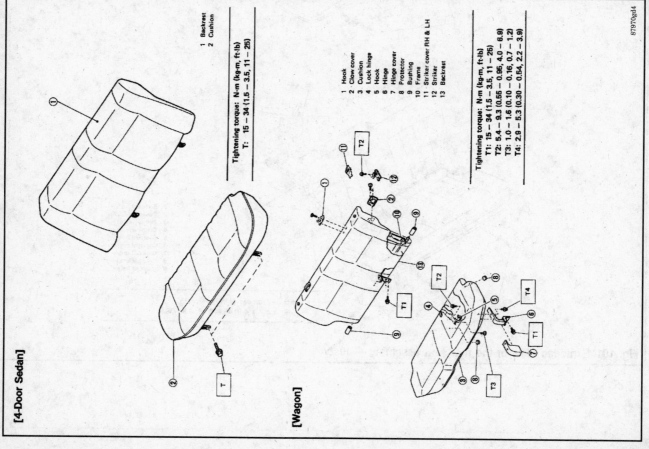

1 Backrest
2 Cushion

Tightening torque: N·m (kg-m, ft-lb)
T: 15 − 34 (1.5 − 3.5, 11 − 25)

[Wagon]

1 Hook
2 Claw cover
3 Cushion
4 Lock hinge
5 Hook
6 Hinge
7 Hinge cover
8 Protector
9 Bushing
10 Frame
11 Striker cover RH & LH
12 Striker
13 Backrest

Tightening torque: N·m (kg-m, ft-lb)
T1: 15 − 34 (1.5 − 3.5, 11 − 25)
T2: 5.4 − 9.3 (0.55 − 0.95, 4.0 − 6.9)
T3: 1.0 − 1.6 (0.10 − 0.16, 0.7 − 1.2)
T4: 2.9 − 5.3 (0.30 − 0.54, 2.2 − 3.9)

Exploded view of the rear seat assembly — Legacy wagon

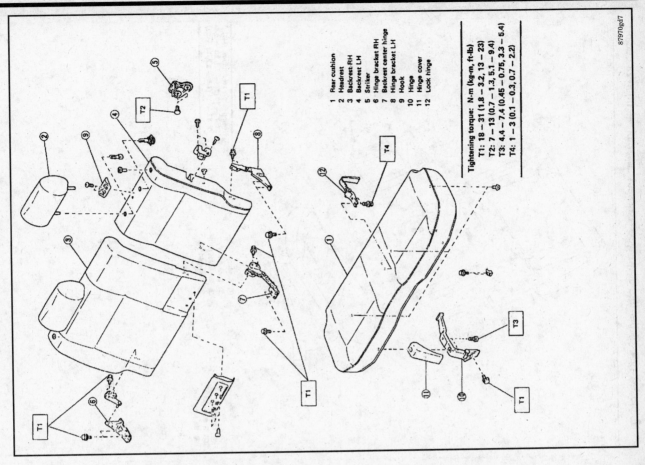

Tightening torque: N·m (kg-m, ft-lb)
T1: 18 — 31 (1.8 — 3.2, 13 — 23)
T2: 7 — 13 (0.7 — 1.3, 5.1 — 9.4)
T3: 4.4 — 7.4 (0.45 — 0.75, 3.3 — 5.4)
T4: 1 — 3 (0.1 — 0.3, 0.7 — 2.2)

1 Rear cushion
2 Headrest
3 Backrest RH
4 Backrest LH
5 Striker
6 Hinge bracket RH
7 Backrest center hinge
8 Hinge bracket LH
9 Hook
10 Hinge
11 Hinge cover
12 Lock hinge

87970gd7

Exploded view of the split fold-down type rear seat assembly — Legacy 4-door sedan

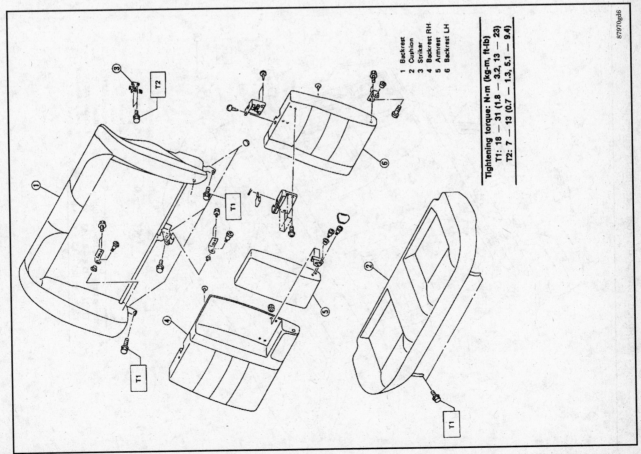

Tightening torque: N·m (kg-m, ft-lb)
T1: 18 — 31 (1.8 — 3.2, 13 — 23)
T2: 7 — 13 (0.7 — 1.3, 5.1 — 9.4)

1 Backrest
2 Cushion
3 Striker
4 Backrest RH
5 Armrest
6 Backrest LH

87970gd6

Exploded view of the fold-down type rear seat assembly — Impreza sedan

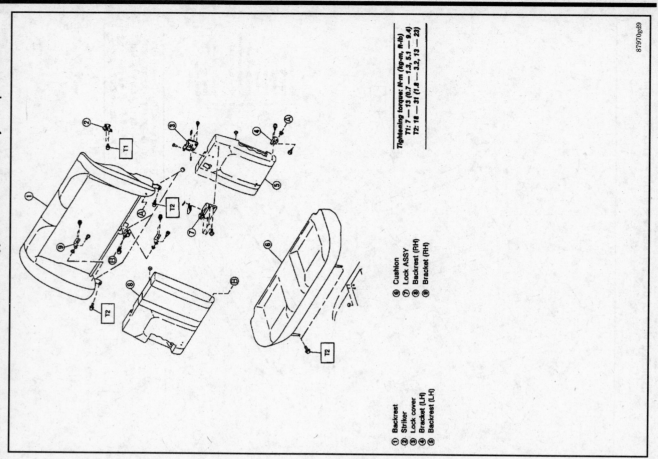

Tightening torque: N·m (kg-m, ft-lb)
T1: 7 — 13 (0.7 — 1.3, 5.1 — 9.4)
T2: 18 — 31 (1.8 — 3.2, 13 — 23)

① Backrest
② Striker
③ Lock cover
④ Bracket (LH)
⑤ Backrest (LH)
⑥ Cushion
⑦ Lock ASSY
⑧ Backrest (RH)
⑨ Bracket (RH)

Exploded view of the rear seat assembly — SVX

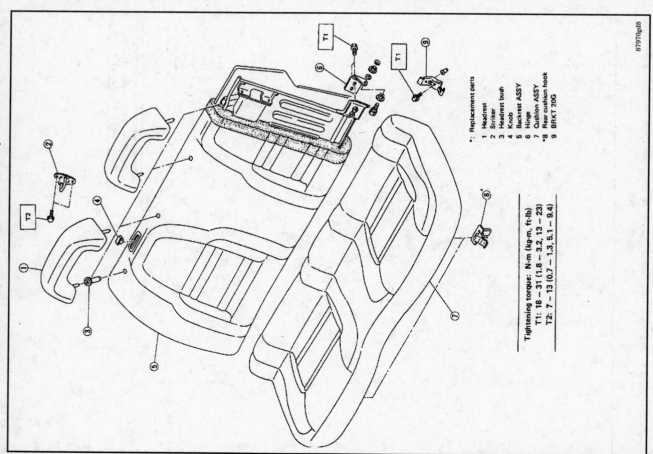

*: Replacement parts

1 Headrest
2 Striker
3 Headrest bush
4 Knob
5 Backrest ASSY
6 Hinge
7 Cushion ASSY
*8 Rear cushion hook
9 BRKT 20G

Tightening torque: N·m (kg-m, ft-lb)
T1: 18 — 31 (1.8 — 3.2, 13 — 23)
T2: 7 — 13 (0.7 — 1.3, 5.1 — 9.4)

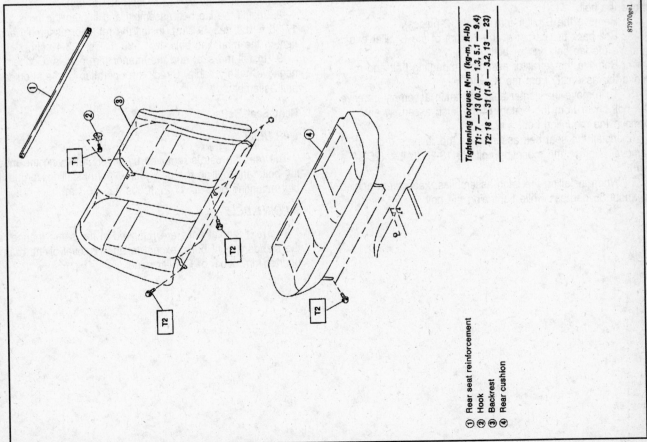

Exploded view of the rear seat assembly — Impreza wagon

Tightening torque: N·m (kg-m, ft-lb)
T1: 1 — 3 (0.1 — 0.3, 0.7 — 2.2)
T2: 4.4 — 7.4
(0.45 — 0.75, 3.3 — 5.4)
T3: 7 — 13 (0.7 — 1.3, 5.1 — 9.4)
T4: 18 — 31 (1.8 — 3.2, 13 — 23)

① Hinge bracket (RH)
② Backrest (RH)
③ Backrest (LH)
④ Striker
⑤ Hinge bracket (LH)
⑥ Lock hinge
⑦ Rear cushion
⑧ Hinge
⑨ Hinge cover
⑩ Backrest center hinge
⑪ Belt pocket
⑫ Pad ASSY pocket
⑬ Hook

Exploded view of the fixed type rear seat assembly — Impreza sedan

Tightening torque: N·m (kg-m, ft-lb)
T1: 7 — 13 (0.7 — 1.3, 5.1 — 9.4)
T2: 18 — 31 (1.8 — 3.2, 13 — 23)

① Rear seat reinforcement
② Hook
③ Backrest
④ Rear cushion

Seat Belt Systems

REMOVAL & INSTALLATION

◆ **See Figures 102 and 103**

All late model vehicles have 3-point front seat belts, some of the vehicles are equipped with automatic shoulder belts. Some models up to 1989 have standard lap belts in the back seat, while all later models have 3-point belts for rear seat passengers.

Front Standard 3-Point Belts

JUSTY

1. Disconnect the negative battery cable.
2. Remove the rear seat cushion and backrest.
3. Remove the rear quarter trim panel.
4. Remove the top screw and lower bolt on the retractor assembly.
5. Remove the cover at the top of the belt and remove the anchor bolt.
6. Remove the seat belt center latch by removing the parking brake cover and removing the mounting bolts.
7. Install the seat belt in the reverse order of removal. Tighten the mounting bolts to 18-25 ft. lbs. (25-34 Nm).

LEGACY, LOYALE, XT AND 1985-89 SEDANS, WAGONS, HATCHBACKS

1. Remove the top seat belt mounting bolt cover and remove the bolt.
2. Remove the B pillar trim panels (2 pieces).
3. Roll back the carpet at the bottom of the B pillar and remove the lap belt anchor bolt.
4. Remove the retractor assembly mounting bolt and remove the assembly from the vehicle.
5. To remove the center seat belt latch assembly, remove the bolt cover from the bottom of the latch assembly and remove the mounting bolt.
6. Install the seat belt assembly in the reverse order of removal. Tighten the mounting bolts to 18-25 ft. lbs. (25-34 Nm).
7. When installing the latch assemblies, keep them angled at about 55 degrees while tightening the bolt.

Front Automatic Shoulder Belt

The automatic shoulder belt assembly consists of a track that runs along the door frame, a motor and a belt anchor attached a moving metal tape in the rail assembly. This system uses a manual lap belt. The center mounting points for the automatic shoulder belts are retractor mechanisms that lock under sudden vehicle deceleration.

✳✳CAUTION

Properly disarm the air bag on vehicles equipped with the SRS system. Failure to do so can cause serious injury. The procedure can be found in Section 6 of this manual under the heading "Supplemental Restraint System".

EXCEPT JUSTY

1. Properly disarm the air bag on models equipped. Disconnect the negative battery cable.
2. Remove the center pillar trim and the front pillar trim.
3. Remove the shoulder belt track mounting bolts and remove the track.
4. Remove the drive unit mounting bolts and remove the drive unit.
5. Remove the lap belt assembly cover and remove the mounting bolts. Remove the lap belt assembly.
6. Remove the front seat assembly and remove the shoulder belt retractor assembly bolts and the retractor assembly.

To install:

7. Install the components in reverse order. Tighten the shoulder belt track bolts to 7-12 ft. lbs. (10-16 Nm). Tighten the drive unit bolts to 7-12 ft. lbs. (10-16 Nm).
8. Install the lap belt assembly and tighten the bolts to 17-36 ft. lbs. (23-49 Nm). Install the retractor assembly and tighten the mounting bolts to 17-36 ft. lbs. (23-49 Nm).
9. Install the seat and the interior trim panels. Connect the negative battery cable. Check the operation of the shoulder belt assembly.

Rear Seat Belts

LAP BELT

The rear lap belt is removed by simply removing the mounting bolts and pulling the belts out. When installing, torque the belt mounting bolts to 17-27 ft. lbs. (23-36 Nm).

3-POINT BELT

The rear 3-point belts are removed in the same manner as the standard front belts, except for the removal of the rear quarter trim panel or C pillar panel.

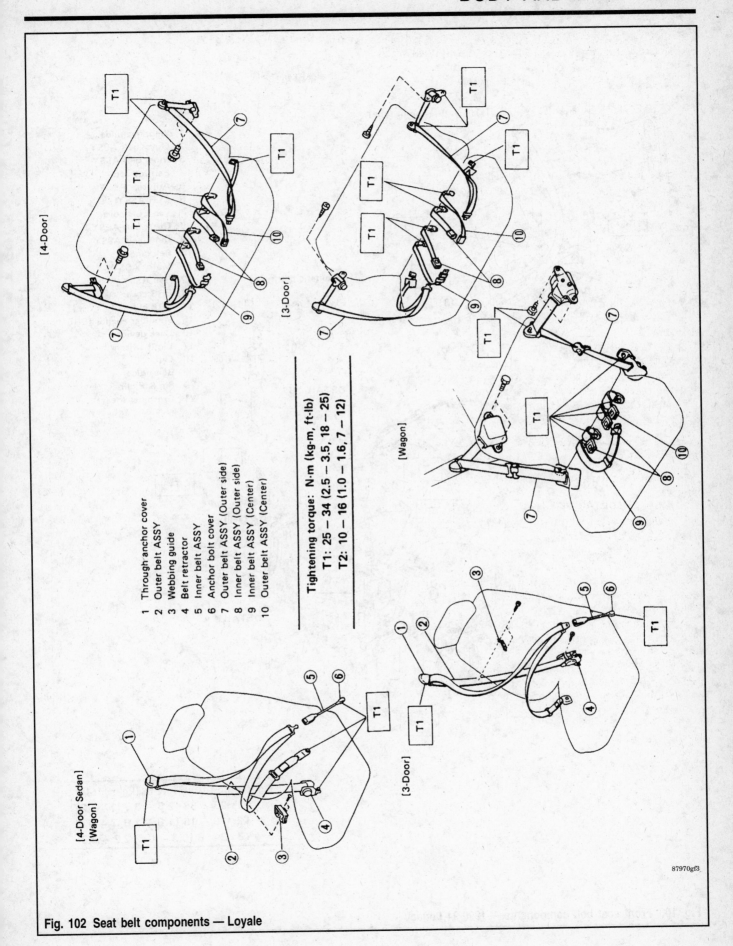

[4-Door]

[3-Door]

[Wagon]

Tightening torque: N·m (kg-m, ft-lb)
T1: 25 – 34 (2.5 – 3.5, 18 – 25)
T2: 10 – 16 (1.0 – 1.6, 7 – 12)

1   Through anchor cover
2   Outer belt ASSY
3   Webbing guide
4   Belt retractor
5   Inner belt ASSY
6   Anchor bolt cover
7   Outer belt ASSY (Outer side)
8   Inner belt ASSY (Outer side)
9   Inner belt ASSY (Center)
10 Outer belt ASSY (Center)

[4-Door Sedan]
[Wagon]

[3-Door]

Fig. 102 Seat belt components — Loyale

87970gf3

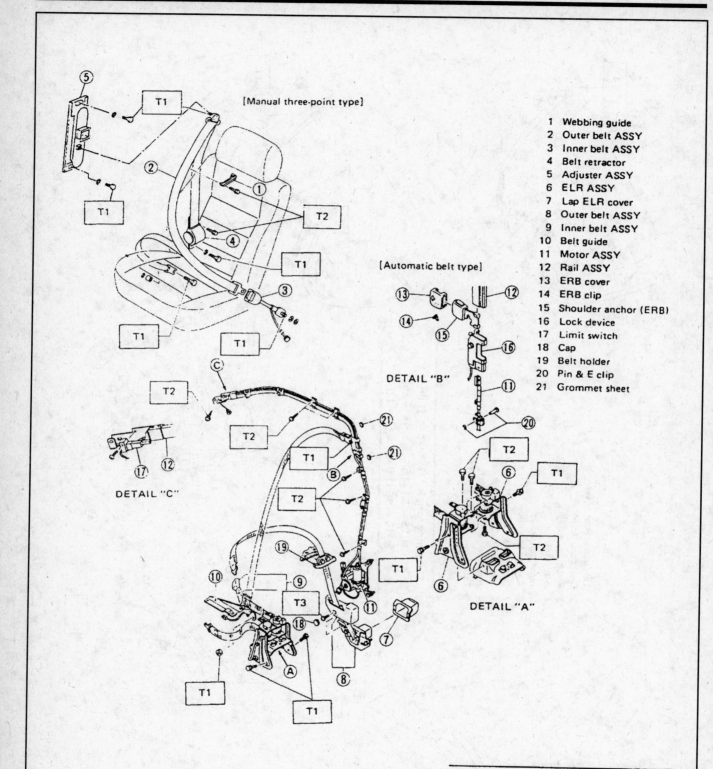

1 Webbing guide
2 Outer belt ASSY
3 Inner belt ASSY
4 Belt retractor
5 Adjuster ASSY
6 ELR ASSY
7 Lap ELR cover
8 Outer belt ASSY
9 Inner belt ASSY
10 Belt guide
11 Motor ASSY
12 Rail ASSY
13 ERB cover
14 ERB clip
15 Shoulder anchor (ERB)
16 Lock device
17 Limit switch
18 Cap
19 Belt holder
20 Pin & E clip
21 Grommet sheet

[Manual three-point type]

[Automatic belt type]

DETAIL "B"

DETAIL "C"

DETAIL "A"

Tightening torque: N·m (kg-m, ft-lb)
T1: 23 — 36 (2.3 — 3.7, 17 — 27)
T2: 10 — 16 (1.0 — 1.6, 7 — 12)
T3: 3 — 6 (0.3 — 0.6, 2.2 — 4.3)

87970ge8

Fig. 103 Front seat belt components — 1990-94 Legacy

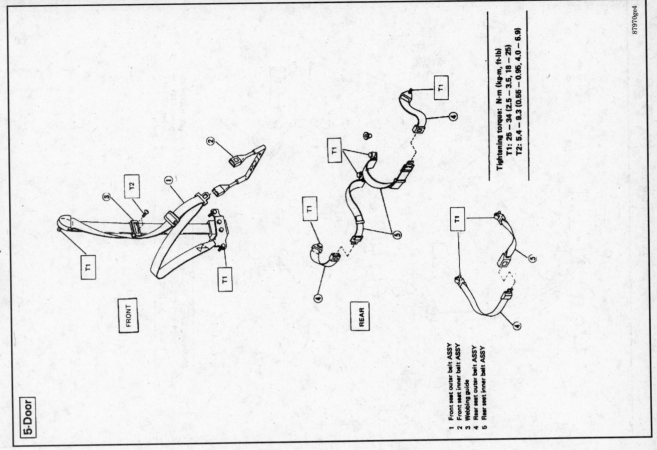

Seat belt components — Justy 4-door

5-Door

FRONT

REAR

Tightening torque: N·m (kg-m, ft-lb)
T1: 25 — 34 (2.5 — 3.5, 18 — 25)
T2: 5.4 — 8.3 (0.55 — 0.95, 4.0 — 6.9)

1 Front seat outer belt ASSY
2 Front seat inner belt ASSY
3 Webbing guide
4 Rear seat outer belt ASSY
5 Rear seat inner belt ASSY

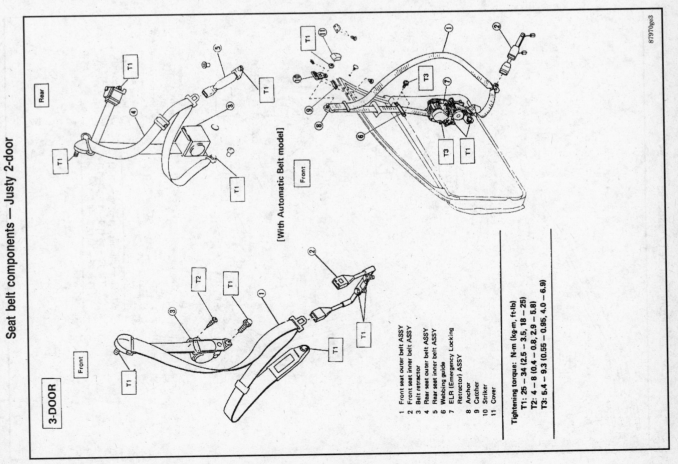

Seat belt components — Justy 2-door

3-DOOR

Front

Rear

[With Automatic Belt model]

Front

1 Front seat outer belt ASSY
2 Front seat inner belt ASSY
3 Belt retractor
4 Rear seat outer belt ASSY
5 Rear seat inner belt ASSY
6 Webbing guide
7 ELR (Emergency Locking
  Retractor) ASSY
8 Anchor
9 Catcher
10 Striker
11 Cover

Tightening torque: N·m (kg-m, ft-lb)
T1: 25 — 34 (2.5 — 3.5, 18 — 25)
T2: 4 — 8 (0.4 — 0.8, 2.9 — 5.8)
T3: 5.4 — 9.3 (0.55 — 0.95, 4.0 — 6.9)

Rear seat belt components — SVX

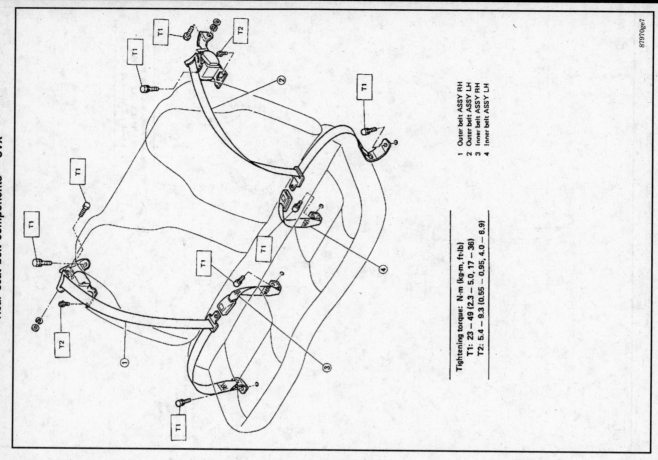

1 Outer belt ASSY RH
2 Outer belt ASSY LH
3 Inner belt ASSY RH
4 Inner belt ASSY LH

Tightening torque: N·m (kg-m, ft-lb)
T1: 23 ~ 49 (2.3 ~ 5.0, 17 ~ 36)
T2: 5.4 ~ 9.3 (0.55 ~ 0.95, 4.0 ~ 6.9)

87970ge7

Front seat belt components — SVX

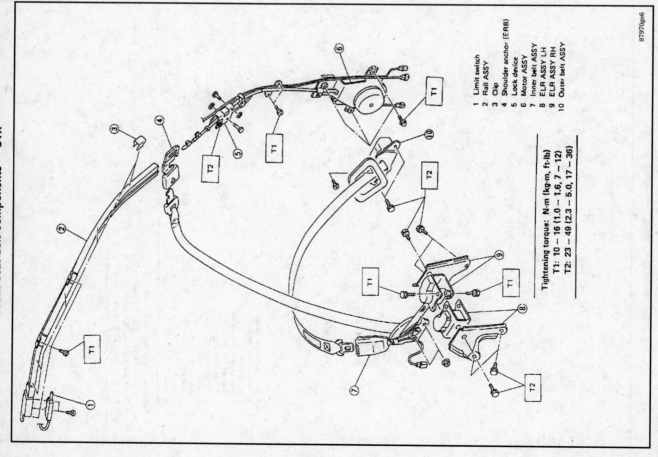

1 Limit switch
2 Rail ASSY
3 Clip
4 Shoulder anchor (ERB)
5 Lock device
6 Motor ASSY
7 Inner belt ASSY LH
8 ELR ASSY LH
9 ELR ASSY RH
10 Outer belt ASSY

Tightening torque: N·m (kg-m, ft-lb)
T1: 10 ~ 16 (1.0 ~ 1.6, 7 ~ 12)
T2: 23 ~ 49 (2.3 ~ 5.0, 17 ~ 36)

87970ge6

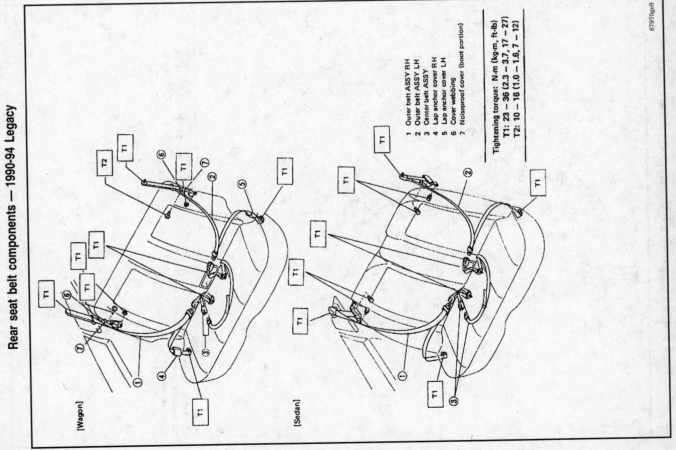

Rear seat belt components — Impreza

Wagon

Sedan

① Webbing cover (RH)
② Webbing cover (LH)
③ Outer seat belt (LH)
④ Center seat belt
⑤ Outer seat belt (RH)
⑥ Through cap (RH)
⑦ Through cap (LH)
⑧ Lap anchor cover (LH)
⑨ Lap anchor cover (RH)

Tightening torque: N·m (kg-m, ft-lb)
T1: 10 — 16 (1.0 — 1.6, 7 — 12)
T2: 23 — 49 (2.3 — 5.0, 17 — 36)

87970gf4

Rear seat belt components — 1990-94 Legacy

[Wagon]

[Sedan]

1 Outer belt ASSY RH
2 Outer belt ASSY LH
3 Center belt ASSY
4 Lap anchor cover RH
5 Lap anchor cover LH
6 Cover webbing
7 Noiseproof cover (boot portion)

Tightening torque: N·m (kg-m, ft-lb)
T1: 23 — 36 (2.3 — 3.7, 17 — 27)
T2: 10 — 16 (1.0 — 1.6, 7 — 12)

87970ge9

Rear seat belt components — 1995-96 Legacy

Wagon model

Sedan model

Tightening torque: N·m (kg-m, ft-lb)
T: 35 ± 13 (3.6 ± 1.3, 26 ± 9)

① Outer seat belt (LH)
② Center seat belt
③ Outer seat belt (RH)

④ Inner seat belt
⑤ Lap anchor cover (LH)
⑥ Lap anchor cover (RH)

87970gf2

Front seat belt components — Impreza and 1995-96 Legacy

Tightening torque: N·m (kg-m, ft-lb)
T1: 13 ± 3 (1.3 ± 0.3, 9.4 ± 2.2)
T2: 35 ± 13 (3.6 ± 1.3, 26 ± 9)

① Adjuster anchor ASSY
② Through anchor cover
③ Webbing guide
④ Inner belt ASSY
⑤ Outer belt ASSY

87970gf1

TORQUE SPECIFICATIONS

Component	U.S.	Metric
Bumper mounting bolts:		
Justy-front bumper support-to-body	51-87 ft. lbs.	69-118 Nm
Justy-rear bumper support-to-body	51-87 ft. lbs.	69-118 Nm
Loyale and 1985-89 except XT-front bumper bolts	16 ft. lbs.	22 Nm
Loyale and 1985-89 except XT-rear bumper bolts (except wagon)	22-31 ft. lbs.	29-42 Nm
Loyale and 1985-89 except XT, Wagon-rear bumper	52-73 ft. lbs.	66-100 Nm
Impreza, Legacy and SVX-front bumper	51-87 ft. lbs.	69-118 Nm
Impreza, Legacy and SVX-rear bumper	51-87 ft. lbs.	69-118 Nm
Door Hinge bolts:		
(Body Side)		
Justy	14-19 ft. lbs.	20-25 Nm
All except Justy, Legacy and SVX	18-25 ft. lbs.	25-34 Nm
Legacy and SVX	14-22 ft. lbs.	20-29 Nm
(Door Side)		
All except Impreza, Legacy, SVX	14-29 ft. lbs.	20-39 Nm
Legacy and SVX	32-46 ft. lbs.	43-63 Nm
Impreza	20-27 ft. lbs.	27-37 Nm
Front seat mounting bolts:		
Tunnel side		
All except Impreza, Legacy, SVX	14-29 ft. lbs.	20-39 Nm
Impreza, Legacy and SVX	32-46 ft. lbs.	43-63 Nm
Hood hinge bolts	9-17 ft. lbs.	13-23 Nm
Hood latch retaining bolts	7 ft. lbs.	10 Nm
Rear seat retaining bolts:		
Justy	3-5 ft. lbs.	4-7 Nm
All except Justy	11-25 ft. lbs.	15-34 Nm
Seat belt assembly mounting bolts:		
Standard 3-point belt		
All models	18-25 ft. lbs.	25-34 Nm
Power shoulder belt system		
Shoulder belt track bolts	7-12 ft. lbs.	10-16 Nm
Drive unit bolts	7-12 ft. lbs.	10-16 Nm
Lap belt assembly	17-36 ft. lbs.	23-49 Nm
Retractor assembly	17-36 ft. lbs.	23-49 Nm
Tailgate mounting bolts:		
Hinge-to-tailgate bolts	14-22 ft. lbs.	20-29 Nm
Hinge-to-body bolts	14-22 ft. lbs.	20-29 Nm
Gas strut-to-tailgate	4-6 ft. lbs.	5-9 Nm
Trunk lid bolts	9-17 ft. lbs.	13-23 Nm
Window track assembly:		
Base plate	4-7 ft. lbs.	5-9 Nm
Rail mounting nut	7-13 ft. lbs.	10-18 Nm

87970C01

GLOSSARY

AIR/FUEL RATIO: The ratio of air-to-gasoline by weight in the fuel mixture drawn into the engine.

AIR INJECTION: One method of reducing harmful exhaust emissions by injecting air into each of the exhaust ports of an engine. The fresh air entering the hot exhaust manifold causes any remaining fuel to be burned before it can exit the tailpipe.

ALTERNATOR: A device used for converting mechanical energy into electrical energy.

AMMETER: An instrument, calibrated in amperes, used to measure the flow of an electrical current in a circuit. Ammeters are always connected in series with the circuit being tested.

AMPERE: The rate of flow of electrical current present when one volt of electrical pressure is applied against one ohm of electrical resistance.

ANALOG COMPUTER: Any microprocessor that uses similar (analogous) electrical signals to make its calculations.

ARMATURE: A laminated, soft iron core wrapped by a wire that converts electrical energy to mechanical energy as in a motor or relay. When rotated in a magnetic field, it changes mechanical energy into electrical energy as in a generator.

ATMOSPHERIC PRESSURE: The pressure on the Earth's surface caused by the weight of the air in the atmosphere. At sea level, this pressure is 14.7 psi at 32°F (101 kPa at 0°C).

ATOMIZATION: The breaking down of a liquid into a fine mist that can be suspended in air.

AXIAL PLAY: Movement parallel to a shaft or bearing bore.

BACKFIRE: The sudden combustion of gases in the intake or exhaust system that results in a loud explosion.

BACKLASH: The clearance or play between two parts, such as meshed gears.

BACKPRESSURE: Restrictions in the exhaust system that slow the exit of exhaust gases from the combustion chamber.

BAKELITE: A heat resistant, plastic insulator material commonly used in printed circuit boards and transistorized components.

BALL BEARING: A bearing made up of hardened inner and outer races between which hardened steel balls roll.

BALLAST RESISTOR: A resistor in the primary ignition circuit that lowers voltage after the engine is started to reduce wear on ignition components.

BEARING: A friction reducing, supportive device usually located between a stationary part and a moving part.

BIMETAL TEMPERATURE SENSOR: Any sensor or switch made of two dissimilar types of metal that bend when heated or cooled due to the different expansion rates of the alloys. These types of sensors usually function as an on/off switch.

BLOWBY: Combustion gases, composed of water vapor and unburned fuel, that leak past the piston rings into the crankcase during normal engine operation. These gases are removed by the PCV system to prevent the buildup of harmful acids in the crankcase.

BRAKE PAD: A brake shoe and lining assembly used with disc brakes.

BRAKE SHOE: The backing for the brake lining. The term is, however, usually applied to the assembly of the brake backing and lining.

BUSHING: A liner, usually removable, for a bearing; an anti-friction liner used in place of a bearing.

CALIPER: A hydraulically activated device in a disc brake system, which is mounted straddling the brake rotor (disc). The caliper contains at least one piston and two brake pads. Hydraulic pressure on the piston(s) forces the pads against the rotor.

CAMSHAFT: A shaft in the engine on which are the lobes (cams) which operate the valves. The camshaft is driven by the crankshaft, via a belt, chain or gears, at one half the crankshaft speed.

CAPACITOR: A device which stores an electrical charge.

CARBON MONOXIDE (CO): A colorless, odorless gas given off as a normal byproduct of combustion. It is poisonous and extremely dangerous in confined areas, building up slowly to toxic levels without warning if adequate ventilation is not available.

CARBURETOR: A device, usually mounted on the intake manifold of an engine, which mixes the air and fuel in the proper proportion to allow even combustion.

CATALYTIC CONVERTER: A device installed in the exhaust system, like a muffler, that converts harmful byproducts of combustion into carbon dioxide and water vapor by means of a heat-producing chemical reaction.

CENTRIFUGAL ADVANCE: A mechanical method of advancing the spark timing by using flyweights in the distributor that react to centrifugal force generated by the distributor shaft rotation.

CHECK VALVE: Any one-way valve installed to permit the flow of air, fuel or vacuum in one direction only.

CHOKE: A device, usually a moveable valve, placed in the intake path of a carburetor to restrict the flow of air.

CIRCUIT: Any unbroken path through which an electrical current can flow. Also used to describe fuel flow in some instances.

CIRCUIT BREAKER: A switch which protects an electrical circuit from overload by opening the circuit when the current flow exceeds a predetermined level. Some circuit breakers must be reset manually, while most reset automatically.

COIL (IGNITION): A transformer in the ignition circuit which steps up the voltage provided to the spark plugs.

COMBINATION MANIFOLD: An assembly which includes both the intake and exhaust manifolds in one casting.

COMBINATION VALVE: A device used in some fuel systems that routes fuel vapors to a charcoal storage canister instead of venting them into the atmosphere. The valve relieves fuel tank pressure and allows fresh air into the tank as the fuel level drops to prevent a vapor lock situation.

COMPRESSION RATIO: The comparison of the total volume of the cylinder and combustion chamber with the piston at BDC and the piston at TDC.

CONDENSER: 1. An electrical device which acts to store an electrical charge, preventing voltage surges. 2. A radiator-like device in the air conditioning system in which refrigerant gas condenses into a liquid, giving off heat.

CONDUCTOR: Any material through which an electrical current can be transmitted easily.

CONTINUITY: Continuous or complete circuit. Can be checked with an ohmmeter.

COUNTERSHAFT: An intermediate shaft which is rotated by a mainshaft and transmits, in turn, that rotation to a working part.

CRANKCASE: The lower part of an engine in which the crankshaft and related parts operate.

CRANKSHAFT: The main driving shaft of an engine which receives reciprocating motion from the pistons and converts it to rotary motion.

CYLINDER: In an engine, the round hole in the engine block in which the piston(s) ride.

CYLINDER BLOCK: The main structural member of an engine in which is found the cylinders, crankshaft and other principal parts.

CYLINDER HEAD: The detachable portion of the engine, usually fastened to the top of the cylinder block and containing all or most of the combustion chambers. On overhead valve engines, it contains the valves and their operating parts. On overhead cam engines, it contains the camshaft as well.

DEAD CENTER: The extreme top or bottom of the piston stroke.

DETONATION: An unwanted explosion of the air/fuel mixture in the combustion chamber caused by excess heat and compression, advanced timing, or an overly lean mixture. Also referred to as "ping".

DIAPHRAGM: A thin, flexible wall separating two cavities, such as in a vacuum advance unit.

DIESELING: A condition in which hot spots in the combustion chamber cause the engine to run on after the key is turned off.

DIFFERENTIAL: A geared assembly which allows the transmission of motion between drive axles, giving one axle the ability to turn faster than the other.

DIODE: An electrical device that will allow current to flow in one direction only.

DISC BRAKE: A hydraulic braking assembly consisting of a brake disc, or rotor, mounted on an axle, and a caliper assembly containing, usually two brake pads which are activated by hydraulic pressure. The pads are forced against the sides of the disc, creating friction which slows the vehicle.

DISTRIBUTOR: A mechanically driven device on an engine which is responsible for electrically firing the spark plug at a predetermined point of the piston stroke.

DOWEL PIN: A pin, inserted in mating holes in two different parts allowing those parts to maintain a fixed relationship.

DRUM BRAKE: A braking system which consists of two brake shoes and one or two wheel cylinders, mounted on a fixed backing plate, and a brake drum, mounted on an axle, which revolves around the assembly.

DWELL: The rate, measured in degrees of shaft rotation, at which an electrical circuit cycles on and off.

ELECTRONIC CONTROL UNIT (ECU): Ignition module, module, amplifier or igniter. See Module for definition.

ELECTRONIC IGNITION: A system in which the timing and firing of the spark plugs is controlled by an electronic control unit, usually called a module. These systems have no points or condenser.

END-PLAY: The measured amount of axial movement in a shaft.

ENGINE: A device that converts heat into mechanical energy.

EXHAUST MANIFOLD: A set of cast passages or pipes which conduct exhaust gases from the engine.

FEELER GAUGE: A blade, usually metal, of precisely predetermined thickness, used to measure the clearance between two parts.

FIRING ORDER: The order in which combustion occurs in the cylinders of an engine. Also the order in which spark is distributed to the plugs by the distributor.

FLOODING: The presence of too much fuel in the intake manifold and combustion chamber which prevents the air/fuel mixture from firing, thereby causing a no-start situation.

FLYWHEEL: A disc shaped part bolted to the rear end of the crankshaft. Around the outer perimeter is affixed the ring gear. The starter drive engages the ring gear, turning the flywheel, which rotates the crankshaft, imparting the initial starting motion to the engine.

FOOT POUND (ft. lbs. or sometimes, ft.lb.): The amount of energy or work needed to raise an item weighing one pound, a distance of one foot.

FUSE: A protective device in a circuit which prevents circuit overload by breaking the circuit when a specific amperage is present. The device is constructed around a strip or wire of a lower amperage rating than the circuit it is designed to protect. When an amperage higher than that stamped on the fuse is present in the circuit, the strip or wire melts, opening the circuit.

GEAR RATIO: The ratio between the number of teeth on meshing gears.

GENERATOR: A device which converts mechanical energy into electrical energy.

HEAT RANGE: The measure of a spark plug's ability to dissipate heat from its firing end. The higher the heat range, the hotter the plug fires.

HUB: The center part of a wheel or gear.

HYDROCARBON (HC): Any chemical compound made up of hydrogen and carbon. A major pollutant formed by the engine as a byproduct of combustion.

HYDROMETER: An instrument used to measure the specific gravity of a solution.

INCH POUND (inch lbs.; sometimes in.lb. or in. lbs.): One twelfth of a foot pound.

INDUCTION: A means of transferring electrical energy in the form of a magnetic field. Principle used in the ignition coil to increase voltage.

INJECTOR: A device which receives metered fuel under relatively low pressure and is activated to inject the fuel into the engine under relatively high pressure at a predetermined time.

INPUT SHAFT: The shaft to which torque is applied, usually carrying the driving gear or gears.

INTAKE MANIFOLD: A casting of passages or pipes used to conduct air or a fuel/air mixture to the cylinders.

JOURNAL: The bearing surface within which a shaft operates.

KEY: A small block usually fitted in a notch between a shaft and a hub to prevent slippage of the two parts.

MANIFOLD: A casting of passages or set of pipes which connect the cylinders to an inlet or outlet source.

MANIFOLD VACUUM: Low pressure in an engine intake manifold formed just below the throttle plates. Manifold vacuum is highest at idle and drops under acceleration.

MASTER CYLINDER: The primary fluid pressurizing device in a hydraulic system. In automotive use, it is found in brake and hydraulic clutch systems and is pedal activated, either directly or, in a power brake system, through the power booster.

MODULE: Electronic control unit, amplifier or igniter of solid state or integrated design which controls the current flow in the ignition primary circuit based on input from the pick-up coil. When the module opens the primary circuit, high secondary voltage is induced in the coil.

NEEDLE BEARING: A bearing which consists of a number (usually a large number) of long, thin rollers.

OHM:(Ω) The unit used to measure the resistance of conductor-to-electrical flow. One ohm is the amount of resistance that limits current flow to one ampere in a circuit with one volt of pressure.

OHMMETER: An instrument used for measuring the resistance, in ohms, in an electrical circuit.

OUTPUT SHAFT: The shaft which transmits torque from a device, such as a transmission.

OVERDRIVE: A gear assembly which produces more shaft revolutions than that transmitted to it.

OVERHEAD CAMSHAFT (OHC): An engine configuration in which the camshaft is mounted on top of the cylinder head and operates the valve either directly or by means of rocker arms.

OVERHEAD VALVE (OHV): An engine configuration in which all of the valves are located in the cylinder head and the camshaft is located in the cylinder block. The camshaft operates the valves via lifters and pushrods.

OXIDES OF NITROGEN (NOx): Chemical compounds of nitrogen produced as a byproduct of combustion. They combine with hydrocarbons to produce smog.

OXYGEN SENSOR: Used with the feedback system to sense the presence of oxygen in the exhaust gas and signal the computer which can reference the voltage signal to an air/fuel ratio.

PINION: The smaller of two meshing gears.

PISTON RING: An open-ended ring which fits into a groove on the outer diameter of the piston. Its chief function is to form a seal between the piston and cylinder wall. Most automotive pistons have three rings: two for compression sealing; one for oil sealing.

PRELOAD: A predetermined load placed on a bearing during assembly or by adjustment.

PRIMARY CIRCUIT: The low voltage side of the ignition system which consists of the ignition switch, ballast resistor or resistance wire, bypass, coil, electronic control unit and pick-up coil as well as the connecting wires and harnesses.

PRESS FIT: The mating of two parts under pressure, due to the inner diameter of one being smaller than the outer diameter of the other, or vice versa; an interference fit.

RACE: The surface on the inner or outer ring of a bearing on which the balls, needles or rollers move.

REGULATOR: A device which maintains the amperage and/or voltage levels of a circuit at predetermined values.

RELAY: A switch which automatically opens and/or closes a circuit.

RESISTANCE: The opposition to the flow of current through a circuit or electrical device, and is measured in ohms. Resistance is equal to the voltage divided by the amperage.

RESISTOR: A device, usually made of wire, which offers a preset amount of resistance in an electrical circuit.

RING GEAR: The name given to a ring-shaped gear attached to a differential case, or affixed to a flywheel or as part of a planetary gear set.

ROLLER BEARING: A bearing made up of hardened inner and outer races between which hardened steel rollers move.

ROTOR: 1. The disc-shaped part of a disc brake assembly, upon which the brake pads bear; also called, brake disc. 2. The device mounted atop the distributor shaft, which passes current to the distributor cap tower contacts.

SECONDARY CIRCUIT: The high voltage side of the ignition system, usually above 20,000 volts. The secondary includes the ignition coil, coil wire, distributor cap and rotor, spark plug wires and spark plugs.

SENDING UNIT: A mechanical, electrical, hydraulic or electromagnetic device which transmits information to a gauge.

SENSOR: Any device designed to measure engine operating conditions or ambient pressures and temperatures. Usually electronic in nature and designed to send a voltage signal to an on-board computer, some sensors may operate as a simple on/off switch or they may provide a variable voltage signal (like a potentiometer) as conditions or measured parameters change.

SHIM: Spacers of precise, predetermined thickness used between parts to establish a proper working relationship.

SLAVE CYLINDER: In automotive use, a device in the hydraulic clutch system which is activated by hydraulic force, disengaging the clutch.

SOLENOID: A coil used to produce a magnetic field, the effect of which is to produce work.

SPARK PLUG: A device screwed into the combustion chamber of a spark ignition engine. The basic construction is a conductive core inside of a ceramic insulator, mounted in an outer conductive base. An electrical charge from the spark plug wire travels along the conductive core and jumps a preset air gap to a grounding point or points at the end of the conductive base. The resultant spark ignites the fuel/air mixture in the combustion chamber.

SPLINES: Ridges machined or cast onto the outer diameter of a shaft or inner diameter of a bore to enable parts to mate without rotation.

TACHOMETER: A device used to measure the rotary speed of an engine, shaft, gear, etc., usually in rotations per minute.

THERMOSTAT: A valve, located in the cooling system of an engine, which is closed when cold and opens gradually in response to engine heating, controlling the temperature of the coolant and rate of coolant flow.

TOP DEAD CENTER (TDC): The point at which the piston reaches the top of its travel on the compression stroke.

TORQUE: The twisting force applied to an object.

TORQUE CONVERTER: A turbine used to transmit power from a driving member to a driven member via hydraulic action, providing changes in drive ratio and torque. In automotive use, it links the driveplate at the rear of the engine to the automatic transmission.

TRANSDUCER: A device used to change a force into an electrical signal.

TRANSISTOR: A semi-conductor component which can be actuated by a small voltage to perform an electrical switching function.

TUNE-UP: A regular maintenance function, usually associated with the replacement and adjustment of parts and components in the electrical and fuel systems of a vehicle for the purpose of attaining optimum performance.

TURBOCHARGER: An exhaust driven pump which compresses intake air and forces it into the combustion chambers at higher than atmospheric pressures. The increased air pressure allows more fuel to be burned and results in increased horsepower being produced.

VACUUM ADVANCE: A device which advances the ignition timing in response to increased engine vacuum.

VACUUM GAUGE: An instrument used to measure the presence of vacuum in a chamber.

VALVE: A device which control the pressure, direction of flow or rate of flow of a liquid or gas.

VALVE CLEARANCE: The measured gap between the end of the valve stem and the rocker arm, cam lobe or follower that activates the valve.

VISCOSITY: The rating of a liquid's internal resistance to flow.

VOLTMETER: An instrument used for measuring electrical force in units called volts. Voltmeters are always connected parallel with the circuit being tested.

WHEEL CYLINDER: Found in the automotive drum brake assembly, it is a device, actuated by hydraulic pressure, which, through internal pistons, pushes the brake shoes outward against the drums.

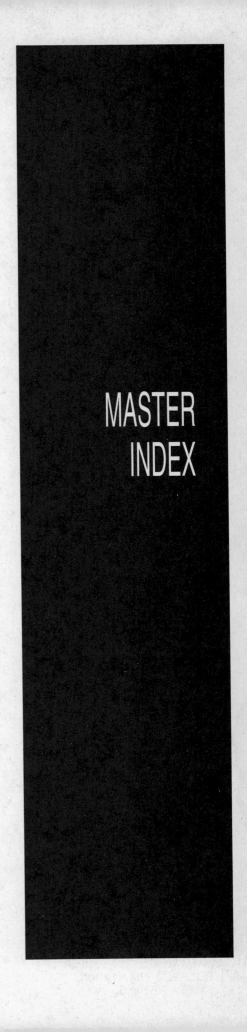

MASTER
INDEX